The New Handbook of
Organizational
Communication

To the memory of
W. Charles Redding,
friend, mentor, and colleague,
who planted and nurtured many of the seeds of the field of
organizational communication through his teaching and scholarship

◆ ◆ ◆

The New Handbook of

Organizational Communication

Advances in Theory, Research, and Methods

FREDRIC M. JABLIN
LINDA L. PUTNAM
Editors

Sage Publications, Inc.
International Educational and Professional Publisher
Thousand Oaks ▪ London ▪ New Delhi

For information:

Sage Publications, Inc.
2455 Teller Road
Thousand Oaks, California 91320
E-mail: order@sagepub.com

Sage Publications Ltd.
6 Bonhill Street
London EC2A 4PU
United Kingdom

Sage Publications India Pvt. Ltd.
M-32 Market
Greater Kailash I
New Delhi 110 048 India

Printed in the United States of America

Library of Congress Cataloging-in-Publication Data

Main entry under title:

The new handbook of organizational communication: Advances in theory, research, and methods / edited by Fredric M. Jablin and Linda L. Putnam.
    p. cm.
Includes bibliographical references and index.
  ISBN 0-8039-5503-0
  1. Communication in organizations. I. Jablin, Fredric M. II. Putnam, Linda.
  HD30.3.H3575   2000
    658.4′5—dc21   00-010051

This book is printed on acid-free paper.

01 02 03 04 05 10 9 8 7 6 5 4 3 2 1

Acquiring Editor:	Margaret H. Seawell
Editorial Assistant:	Heidi Van Middlesworth
Production Editor:	Astrid Virding
Editorial Assistant:	Victoria Cheng
Designer/Typesetter:	Janelle LeMaster
Cover Designer:	Ravi Balasuriya

Editorial Reviewers

Charles R. Bantz
Wayne State University

James R. Barker
U.S. Air Force Academy

George Cheney
University of Montana

Robin P. Clair
Purdue University

Steven R. Corman
Arizona State University

Stanley A. Deetz
University of Colorado at Boulder

Eric M. Eisenberg
University of South Florida

Maha El-Sinnawy
Texas A&M University

Gail T. Fairhurst
University of Cincinnati

Robert P. Gephart
University of Alberta. Canada

Robert Giacalone
University of North Carolina, Charlotte

Dennis Gioia
Pennsylvania State University

James E. Grunig
University of Maryland

Teresa M. Harrison
Rensselaer Polytechnic Institute

Robert L. Heath
University of Houston

George P. Huber
University of Texas at Austin

David Krackhardt
Carnegie Mellon University

Joanne Martin
Stanford University

Robert D. McPhee
Arizona State University

Michael J. Papa
Ohio University

Marshall Scott Poole
Texas A&M University

Patricia Riley
University of Southern California

David R. Seibold
University of California, Santa Barbara

Robert Shuter
Marquette University

Charles Steinfield
Michigan State University

Bryan C. Taylor
University of Colorado at Boulder

James R. Taylor
University of Montreal

Phillip K. Tompkins
University of Colorado at Boulder

Nick Trujillo
California State University, Sacramento

John Van Maanen
Massachusetts Institute of Technology

Joseph B. Walther
Rensselaer Polytechnic Institute

Steve Weiss
York University, Canada

Gary Yukl
State University of New York at Albany

Robert Zmud
University of Oklahoma

Theodore E. Zorn
University of Waikato, New Zealand

Contents

Part IV. Process: Communication Behavior in Organizations

Preface

During most of the planning and writing of this book, we referred to it as the "new" *Handbook of Organizational Communication*. There were several reasons for this. In particular, we felt that this volume was more than just a revision of the Jablin, Putnam, Roberts, and Porter *Handbook of Organizational Communication: An Interdisciplinary Perspective* published by Sage in 1987. In the years since the publication of the first handbook, new areas that had developed in the field called for a second edition that expanded the number of issues included in the original volume. Further, we knew that there were important topics not covered in chapters in the first handbook (because of space limitations) that needed to be addressed in any revision. At the same time, we felt that there were a number of chapters written for the first handbook that had "stood the test of time" and did not necessarily require revision. Finally, as the interests of the original editors changed it became apparent that we would not all be involved in the preparation of a follow-up to the original book. Thus, to a considerable extent we felt that this book was not a revision of the original handbook but rather a new volume.

There are some things that are "old" about the book as well. We have retained the same structure in organizing the chapters together in this new handbook as in the original one. Thus, the major parts of the book include discussions of theoretical and conceptual issues, context (internal and external environments), structure (patterns of organizational relationships), and processes (communication behavior in organizations). In addition, our goal in this volume is the same as in the first one: "to pull together many loose threads in the various strands of thinking and research about organizational communication and . . . to point toward new theory and empirical work that can further advance this [still fairly] young and energetic field." Consistent with the original handbook, this new book also maintains a multidisciplinary perspective to understanding organizational communication, explores issues (as relevant) at multiple levels of analysis, and includes numerous suggestions for future research and theory development.

So what exactly is new in this handbook? First, over half of the chapters explore topics that were not included in the original handbook. As a consequence, many new authors contributed to this book, while several of the authors or coauthors of chapters in the first handbook wrote chapters on new topics for this volume. Second, the first part of the book is focused not just on theoretical issues but on methodological ones as well, and chapters now present discussions of quantitative and qualitative research methods along with various forms of language/discourse analysis that are used in the study of organizational communication. Third, each chapter reviews and updates research in its respective area and also includes, wherever possible, discussions of relevant research and theory from around the world. Fourth, with the rapid diffusion since the 1990s of new information and communication technologies in organizations, we asked authors to develop the known and potential impacts of these technologies on communication phenomena. Finally, chapters in the book were not only reviewed by the editors but also by a distinguished board of outside readers, who provided suggestions for improving initial drafts of the essays.

The handbook now begins with a "prelude" that offers a brief, selective, historical overview of organizational communication as a discipline. Through reviewing and interpreting results of existing reviews of the field over the decades, Tompkins and Wanca-Thibault present a summary of the basic approaches, ideologies, and trends that have shaped the field's identity as it has matured. This discussion suggests that much of our future research will likely focus on developing new perspectives on old processes, relationships, problems, and issues, including the study of communication structures and networks, leader-follower communication, participation, feedback, information flow and the filtering of messages, the creation and interpretation of messages, and communication media and channels. At the same time a set of contemporary research metaphors—"discourse," "voice," and "performance"—that have emerged, guide much work in the field and are moving scholars to ask different kinds of questions and reconsider assumptions about traditional areas of study. These astute observations are clearly reflected in many of the chapters that follow in the handbook.

Part I of the book follows the prelude and explores a variety of issues related to working with and understanding organizational com-munication theories and research methods. The first two chapters focus on theoretical issues. The Deetz chapter explores conceptual foundations in organizational communication by examining how the concept "organizational communication" is used in the literature. This discussion is framed by consideration of the type of interaction favored by a conceptualization (local/emergent vs. elite/a priori) and the relation of the conceptualization to existing social orders (consensus seeking vs. dissensus seeking). Conrad and Haynes take a different turn in exploring theoretical issues by arguing that various forms of organizational communication theory and research share a common conceptual dilemma: a need to analyze the interconnections between social/organizational structures and symbolic action (the tension between action and structure). They illustrate this notion by identifying clusters of key concepts of organizational communication theory and how they have either tended to privilege one pole of the action-structure dualism over the other or integrate the two together.

The next three chapters in Part I explore methodological issues associated with the study of organizational communication. Putnam and Fairhurst begin by reviewing research and theory related to discourse analysis—the study of words and signifiers—in organizations. They classify approaches to analyzing language as a way of understanding organizational life into eight categories or perspectives: sociolinguistics, conversation analysis, cognitive linguistics, pragmatics, semiotics, literary and rhetorical language analysis, critical language studies, and postmodern language analysis. In the fourth chapter, Miller unpacks the assumptions, practices, and challenges facing quantitative organizational communication research. Among other things, she examines the quantitative elements of experimental, survey, and behavioral observation research methods, and she considers the challenges organizational communication scholars face in the design, collection, analysis and interpretation of quantitative data. The final chapter in this part provides an overview of the use of qualitative research methods in the study of organizational communication and the dilemmas faced by those using this approach. Specifically, Taylor and Trujillo consider the relationship between qualitative and quantitative research, criteria for evaluating qualitative research studies, and issues associated with "representation" and the role of critical theory in qualitative research. In brief, the chapters in this section review and critique existing conceptualizations and research methods associated with the study of organizational communication and suggest ways for improving future work in these areas.

Part II of the book focuses on the contexts of organizations, that is, on the role of internal and external environments in shaping communicative processes. Sutcliffe's chapter centers on organizational environments and organizational information processing, and in particular how organizations gather and interpret environmental information and how, in turn, they direct the flow of information to their environments to achieve organizational goals. Linkages between internal (e.g., employee relations, mission statements) and external (e.g., public relations, marketing) communication and the manner in which organizations attempt to manage issues and their identities are elaborated in Cheney and Christensen's chapter. More specifically, this essay discusses the increasing "fuzziness" of organizational boundaries and what this implies for conceptualizing and studying communication, organizational identity, and issue management. Consistent with many of the themes underlying other chapters in this section of the book, Finet develops a discourse-oriented approach to understanding the complex interactions between organizations and their sociopolitical environments (environmental clusters representing educational institutions, religious organizations, branches of government, charities, and the like). Building on the notions of "enacted environment" and conceptualizing of organizations as "conversations," Finet outlines the roles of two forms of organizational discourse—institutional rhetoric and everyday talk—in relations between organizations and their sociopolitical environments.

The final two chapters in Part II focus on issues related to communication and a particular domain of organizational environments: culture. Eisenberg and Riley begin by reviewing how the organizational culture metaphor has been used in communication research, and the basic assumptions on which a communicative view of culture is founded. A variety of frameworks with respect to the role of communication in the organizational culture literature are examined, including culture as symbolism and performance, text, identity, critique, cognition and as climate and effectiveness. Overall, culture is viewed as socially constructed in which organizational members enact, legitimize, and change their environments through their talk and its residue. Subsequently, Stohl examines communication and cultural variability in multinational organizations and the growth of globalization (here globalization refers to the increasingly interconnected global economy and the blurred spatial and temporal boundaries among nations and organizations). Two distinctive models (convergence, the pressures to become similar, and divergence, maintaining differences) to understanding communication, culture, and globalization are identified, and the dynamic tension between them is articulated. Taken together, these last two chapters in Part II suggest that the field of organizational communication is well positioned to lead the organization sciences generally in the study of culture in various organizational forms and at multiple levels of analysis.

The third part of the book considers one of the most traditional areas of study in organizational communication: how patterns of communication produce and are reproduced by organizational structure. In the first chapter in this section, Fairhurst explores hierarchical interdependencies between leaders and followers through an examination of basic dualisms and tensions that characterize the study of leadership communication. Three sets of dualisms (individual and system, cognitive outcomes and conversational practices, and transmission views and meaning-centered views of communication) and their interrelationships are described, and five particular research programs are analyzed to characterize the dualisms and tensions: the study of influence tactics, feedback, charisma and visionary leadership, leader-member exchange, and systems-interaction leadership research. After careful consideration of the issues, Fairhurst concludes that we have more to gain from embracing the complexities of the tensions that she has identified in the literature than in privileging particular poles of the dualisms. In the next chapter, Monge and Contractor review the theoretical mechanisms that have been used to understand the emergence, maintenance, and dissolution of intra- and interorganizational networks. This analysis, which explores ten major families of theories that have been used to explain various aspects of the evolution of networks, lead Monge and Contractor to a number of important conclusions. Among other things, they suggest that we have devoted more attention to studying the emergence of organizational networks than in trying to understand how networks are maintained or dissolved and that we need a more careful conception of communication issues associated with network linkages and the content of messages that produce and reproduce network structures.

In the third chapter in Part III, McPhee and Poole present an analysis of approaches that have been developed to understanding formal structure-communication relationships in organizations. In particular, they discuss relationships between communication and structure in terms of four viewpoints: the dimensional, configurational, multilevel, and "structure as communication" perspectives. As a result of their analysis of the literature, McPhee and Poole argue that future research in this area would benefit from exploring structure-communication relationships in terms of structural configurations and structure as a product of communication. Coincidentally,

the final chapter in this part examines relationships between computer-mediated communication and information systems (CISs) and organizational structuring. In particular, Rice and Gattiker present research related to three basic processes of CIS structuration—adoption/implementation, transformation, and institutionalization—and show how CISs and organizational structures may facilitate or constrain one another with respect to each process. In sum, the chapters in this section highlight the inherent interdependencies that exist between organizational structures and structuring and communication processes in and among organizations.

Part IV develops a number of processes within organizations that are closely associated with communication. These chapters tend to emphasize behavioral issues related to communicating and organizing and promote a dynamic as compared to static view of organizational communication. In the opening essay, Mumby explores relationships among what he considers to be three co-constructed and interdependent phenomena: power, communication, and organization. He also discusses implicit assumptions about communication in noncommunication theories of organizational power, postmodern conceptualizations of power and communication, and the ways in which feminist studies are enhancing our understanding of relations among power, communication, and organizing. Fulk and Jarvis-Collins follow with an analysis of one of the most common activities experienced in organizations: meetings. However, they explore research and theory related to what are becoming increasingly common forms of meetings, those that are mediated through communication technologies, including computer conferencing, teleconferencing, and group support systems. This presentation revolves around three theoretical perspectives on mediated meetings (media capacity theories, input-process-output models, and structuration) and a set of frequently studied communication phenomena in groups (participation, socioemotional expression, conflict and consensus, task efficiency, decision quality, and member satisfaction). Many of the issues discussed in the next chapter, contributed by Seibold and Shea, also concern communication processes in groups. More specifically, they focus attention on the communication characteristics of employee participation programs and the contexts in which they are often implemented, the communication processes through which they work, and the role of communication in moderating their effectiveness. The participation programs they analyze are quality circles, quality-of-work-life programs, employee stock ownership plans, self-directed work teams, and Scanlon gainsharing plans.

To some degree, each of the final three chapters in the book develops issues related to learning and communication in organizations. The essay by Weick and Ashford identifies links between organizational learning and communication and unpacks individual and interpersonal communication processes associated with learning. Although communication-related barriers to organizational learning are also described, suggestions are offered detailing how communication can help ameliorate some of the impediments to learning.

The next chapter is a discussion of communication, vocation, organizational anticipatory socialization, organizational entry and assimilation, and organizational disengagement/exit processes. Unlike the chapter in the first handbook, however, in this review and interpretation of research and theory Jablin discusses organizational entry and assimilation in term of assimilation-communication processes (orienting, socialization, training, mentoring, information seeking, information giving, relationship development, and role negotiation) rather than stages of organizational assimilation, and the chapter focuses on just one aspect of the voluntary turnover process: how leavers and stayers communicate through various stages of the organizational disengagement process.

In the concluding chapter, Jablin and Sias explore selected issues related to learning in their elaboration of research and theory on communication competence and in their developmental-ecological model of organizational communication competence. Potentially problematic assumptions and premises associated with the manner in which communication competence has been conceptualized and investigated in extant research are also outlined, and competence is considered in light of globalization, new information/communication technologies, various organizational forms and managerial philosophies, gender-related expectations and patterns of behavior, and shifts in the employment status (permanent or contingent) of workers. In sum, this last part of the book builds on and expands the set of communication-related organizing processes that was developed in the original handbook.

Although we thought we learned a lot from editing the first handbook that would facilitate preparation of this volume, it actually took longer to complete this book than the earlier one. In light of the delays associated with the completion of the book, we appreciate the patience of all those involved in this project, the many revisions of chapters, and the outstanding group of authors who contributed chapters to the book and with whom it has been a pleasure to work. We also would like to acknowledge the valuable assistance of our colleagues who served on the review board and provided valuable feedback, alternative perspectives, and advice to the contributing authors on early drafts of their essays. We are also indebted to Sophy Craze and Margaret Seawell, who worked with us in planning and preparing various stages of the handbook, and to the other professionals at Sage who assisted in the publication of the book. Without their encouragement and outstanding guidance this project would not have reached fruition. In addition, we would like to express appreciation to Kate Peterson, who worked on copy editing the book, and to Tom Kleiza and Angela Mims, who assisted in checking references and in helping to resolve questions associated with the book manuscript. Gratitude is also due to our respective colleagues at the University of

Richmond and Texas A&M University, whose support helped this book become a reality.

Finally, we would like to express special appreciation to our spouses and families for their support in the pursuit of this project; somehow handbooks seem to take on a life of their own, which results in numerous disruptions in the lives of those closest to the editors. As usual, we are in debt to our loved ones for their ability to endure, with a positive attitude, the projects we initiate. To conclude, we would also like to thank the many readers of the first version of the handbook for their kind comments about that book and their encouragement to prepare this new volume. We hope the final product of the long wait meets your expectations.

—*FREDRIC M. JABLIN*
—*LINDA L. PUTNAM*

Organizational Communication

Prelude and Prospects

PHILLIP K. TOMPKINS
University of Colorado at Boulder

MARYANNE WANCA-THIBAULT
University of Colorado at Colorado Springs

Organizational communication as a discipline grew tremendously over the latter part of the 20th century, but accompanying that growth was a struggle to establish a clear identity for the field. And even as we enter a new millennium, the ongoing evolution of complex organizations in an equally complex global environment has scholars continuing to define and redefine the focus, boundaries, and future of the field. This prelude to *The New Handbook of Organizational Communication: Advances in Theory, Research, and Methods* takes a historical approach to assessing where the field has been, as a way of surveying the directions the field is taking. The contributions we discuss here are by no means meant to include all of the paths the field has started down from time to time, nor does it propose to

outline all future areas of expansion and development. However, we do believe that the select perspectives we discuss here reflect major past and current approaches and research foci associated with the study of organizational communication.

We concentrate, then, on providing first a brief history of the rubrics, categories, and ideologies that have shaped the identity of the field. We do so by summarizing the findings of major reviews of the field that have been written over the years; in other words, we present a review of the conclusions of previous surveys of the field. Second, we note some trends in the study of organizational communication that we believe demonstrate a certain maturation of the field in that each moves the field in ways that question and deconstruct categories of the past while integrating domains and methods thought to be permanently at odds with each other. Old terministic screens give way to more inclusive ones. Division yields to merger. Mergers are subdivided. The field of organizational communication is enriched.

REVIEWING THE REVIEWS

Generally speaking, the "modern" study of organizational communication dates from the late 1930s and early 1940s (e.g., Heron, 1942; Jablin, 1990; Redding & Tompkins, 1988). The first major state-of-the-art summaries and theoretical frameworks associated with organizational communication began to appear in the mid-1960s (e.g., Guetzkow, 1965; Thayer, 1968; Tompkins, 1967). Among speech communication scholars, Tompkins's (1967) review represents the first summary of organizational communication research that focused on summarizing solely empirical research studies (about 100 in number). He used the categories of (1) formal and informal channels of communication and (2) superior-subordinate relations to integrate the many different problems and hypotheses pursued in the literature he assessed. As Burke (1966) noted in his famous essay "Terministic Screens," the nomenclature used to define a field not only serves to reflect and select reality, it also *deflects* reality; hence, the vocabulary/language of organizational communication draws attention to certain phenomena, and simultaneously draws it away from others. Thus, while Tompkins's review of the literature found that a downward, top-down management-focus shaped the majority of research about communication in organizations, including that conducted under the rubric of superior-subordinate communication, it is important to note that these labels and concerns deflected attention away from other topics and perspectives that would later be considered by a more mature field (e.g., upward communication, vertical feedback loops, and participation).

The next major summary-integration of organizational communication was published six years later by Redding (1972). This was a massive 538-page "book" in mimeograph form that was influential and highly valued among scholars and practitioners, although not widely available. Therefore, we give some attention to this very rare, out-of-print reference.

Redding's work, unlike Tompkins's much briefer, state-of-the-art paper, placed no empiricist restraints on itself, using even "how-to" literature as stuff for analysis. Redding suggested that while many of the categories Tompkins cited remain useful, "understanding of organizational communication will be enhanced if we go beyond the traditional categories and look at our subject in a frame of reference of basic theoretical concepts" (p. vii). Hence, Redding looked at the internal communication of organizations in terms of ten "postulates" and a set of related "corollaries or extensions" derived from human communication theory and interpreted in terms of the organizational setting. In addition, he discussed the concept of organizational climate and its relationship to effective communication.

The ten postulates presented a way to reframe the relevant research from an organizational communication perspective, and in doing so, to point to potential future areas of study. By discussing the research around these principles of human communication, Redding privileged the process and in some cases put a new spin on research findings (much of which were extrapolated from other social scientific fields). This, in turn, provided future leads or directions for communication researchers. Redding also extended Tompkins's discussion of the topics the field examined at the time: concepts such as feedback, redundancy, communication overload, and serial transmission effects.

Redding's first postulate positioned *meaning* in the interpretive processes of receivers

—not in the transmission (in contrast to the typical communication model of earlier eras). The failure to interpret messages correctly resulted in what Redding (1972) called the *content fallacy:*

> What happens all too often is that we keep tinkering with the content of the message-sender's message, rather than trying to find more ways of making sure that the message-receiver's responses are appropriate. This content fallacy leads us to believe that we are "getting through" to our audience, merely because we are getting through to ourselves. (p. 29)

Next, Redding claimed that in an organization "anything is a potential message" (p. ix). He proposed that the role of both verbal and nonverbal communication had yet to be sufficiently explored in organized settings. The third postulate he discussed was the importance of input/listening, suggesting that much of the "how to manage" literature was in reality targeting good listening skills. With a considerable amount of prescience, he noted that a key behavioral characteristic of a

> participative manager is his [*sic*] ability to listen to his associates, especially his subordinates. Moreover, such listening is generally described as "empathic"—which should be differentiated from other kinds of listening, e.g., listening in order to comprehend and retain information, listening in order to analyze logically, and listening in order to refute. (p. 34)

The fourth postulate proposed that the message received (versus the one sent or intended) is what a receiver will act upon. He used the psychological concept of selective perception to make the case that individuals in organizations will respond to messages based on their personal frames of reference. The fifth postulate supported the importance of feedback in organizations. He made an important distinction between *feedback receptiveness* (the extent to which managers are open to subordinate feedback) and *feedback responsiveness* (the extent to which managers give feedback to subordinates). In brief, he recognized that being an open, receptive receiver of feedback and being a responsive receiver, that is, appropriately responding to the feedback (doing something about the information provided by followers), are not the same things.

Redding's sixth postulate addressed the "cost factor," or efficiency, of communication interactions in organizations. Communication always entails the expenditure of energy. More communication is not necessarily better as he expressed in this simple formula: efficiency = effectiveness/cost. His seventh postulate suggested that the social need for *redundancy* must be balanced by the economic need of efficiency. Too much can evoke boredom; too little makes some messages incomprehensible, particularly if there is "noise" in the system. The eighth postulate, *communication overload,* described the problems associated with an individual's "channel capacity," or the individual's limits of message processing. Redding recommended the further investigation of such concepts as "uncertainty absorption" (how message senders and receivers absorb ambiguity and clarify and make sense of messages as they communicate them upward in the organization hierarchy; e.g., March & Simon, 1958) and the "exception principle" that organizations seemed to use in trying to cope with communication overload.

The ninth postulate dealt with the "serial transmission effect," or the changes of meaning—due to filtering and distortion—as messages are passed from individual to individual in a hierarchy or informal network. Redding again recommended research on this topic to gain a better understanding of the optimal number of "relays" in serial transmissions. And again, the emphasis is on the fidelity of reception—shared meanings. Finally, in the tenth postulate, Redding suggested that the organization's "climate" for communication was more important than communication skills and techniques. After summarizing the work of many researchers and theorists, Redding articulated a trend or a growing consensus; he called it the ideal managerial climate, the components of which are (1) supportiveness; (2) participative decision making; (3) trust, confidence, and credibility; (4) openness and candor; and (5) emphasis on high performance goals (pp. 139-416). The strength of the model was its comprehensive synthesis of research (representing work conducted in many fields).

In summary, Redding tried to connect his conception of communication theory to the study of organizations. This was necessary because many of the early studies were done in cognate disciplines with implicit and superficial notions about the communication process. Redding's communication theory in retrospect is interesting and penetrating in its own right, and also interesting for its degree of self-consciousness of the transition from the *transmission-orientation* of the speech field into a *reception-orientation* of the communication field. Postulate four—"message received in the only one that counts"—perfectly illustrates his awareness of the major changes then under way. In fact, the first five postulates all express in one way or another the new reception-orientation.

Postulate eight turned contemporary assumptions upside down by conceiving of organizations as devices that *restrict* the flow of information. Curiously, Redding felt the need to put the word *networks* in quotation marks to indicate that he was talking about serial communication systems rather than about the broadcasting variety that most people thought of when hearing the word at that time. Moreover, in his discussion of ten major research topics/extensions in the final section of the book, Redding concluded with an attempt to see the future via "the role of communication in an open-system, dynamic organization (a matrix of networks)," an expression that was prescient then and fresh today. Redding had linked the theoretical and empirical nomenclatures for the first time.

Building on and consistent with much of Redding's review, Jablin (1978) summarized

research conducted during the 1940s-1970s in terms of the predominant research questions associated with each era (see Table P.1). His analysis suggested that during each decade, scholars tended to explore many similar research topics and issues: characteristics of superior-subordinate communication, emergent communication networks and channels, and components and correlates of communication climates. As we shall see, many of these research questions continued as major foci of organizational communication research during the 1980s-1990s, although often packaged in terms of "new" research issues and problems associated with communicating and organizing. The late 1970s and early 1980s also saw several, more focused, reviews of research related to organizational communication, including summaries of studies in organizational/industrial psychology (Porter & Roberts, 1976), communication networks (Monge, Edwards, & Kirste, 1978), superior-subordinate communication (Jablin, 1979), organizational group communication (Jablin & Sussman, 1983), and feedback and task performance (Downs, Johnson, & Barge, 1984), among other topics. As Tompkins (1967) observed about the studies conducted in the 1960s, the study of organizational communication relied almost exclusively on "objective means of measuring the operation and consequences of an organizational communication system" (pp. 17-18). Thus, to a considerable degree, the field in its infancy and early adolescence was rather unquestioning about the nomenclature and assumptions of logical positivism (see also Redding & Tompkins, 1988).

Twelve years after Redding's review and 17 years after his first state-of-the-art paper, Tompkins (1984) again surveyed the field of organizational communication. In this analysis, he challenged what he described as the prevailing paradigm by arguing that the field was dominated by the "rational model," that the epistemological-methodological stance of most scholarship was positivistic, and that most research questions emanated from a managerial bias. He developed four overlap-

TABLE P.1   Past Priorities in Organizational Communication Research: 1940s-1970s

Era	Predominant Research Questions
1940s	- What effects do downward directed mass media communications have on employees? - Is an informed employee a productive employee?
1950s	- How do small-group communication networks affect organizational performance and member attitudes and behaviors? - How can emergent communication networks in organizations be measured? - What are the relationships between organizational members' attitudes and perceptions of their communication behavior (primarily upward and downward) and their on-the-job performance? - What is the relationship between the attitudes and performance of workers and the feedback they receive? - Is a well-informed employee a satisfied employee?
1960s	- What do organizational members perceive to be the communication correlates of "good" supervision? - To what degree is superior-subordinate semantic-information distance a problem in organizations? - What is the relationship between subordinates' job-related attitudes and productivity and the extent to which they perceive they participate in decision making? - In what ways do the actual and perceived communication behaviors of liaison and nonliaison roles within organizational communication networks differ?
1970s	- What are the components and correlates of superior-subordinate, work-group, and overall organizational communication climates? - What are the characteristics of work-group and organizational communication networks (and in particular, the distribution of "key" communication roles)?

SOURCE: Adapted from Jablin (1978).

ping challenges to the paradigm: action, power, levels, and process. Central to Tompkins's challenge or critique was the fallacy of reification, the idea that organizations are entities where communication is situated. Instead, Tompkins (1984) asserted that "communication *constitutes* organization" (p. 660, emphasis in the original), an idea inferred from Barnard (1938). From this standpoint, he suggested that organizations might be viewed as "systems of interacting individuals," who through communication are actively involved in the process of creating and re-creating their unique social order. In retrospect, we can say that this was a call for theoretical development

of the notion of communication as *both figure and ground* (see Putnam, Phillips, & Chapman, 1996).

Tompkins then surveyed the literature with the four challenges or critiques as terministic screens, developing four categories that supported the prevailing paradigm yet had potential for opening the field to other perspectives. Studies on the first two categories, formal and informal channels of communication, were characterized as "variable analysis" and as presenting merely a "slice of the organization." As a result, such an approach gave no account of how organizational systems are related to each other. Studies dealing with the third category, systems and holistic research, attempted to remedy that shortcoming by encouraging an understanding of communication-as-social-order. Finally, the fourth category moved beyond the intraorganizational communication issues and highlighted organizational environments and interorganizational research in expanding the domain of the discipline. Tompkins noted that much of the environment of an organization is other organizations, an idea first advanced again by Barnard (1938). As these interorganizational networks become more and more complex (and more and more global) and defined by technological change, organizational boundaries become less formal and rigid. Research in this area was said to have the potential for expanding the exploration of networks outside the defined boundaries of the organization, as well as "lining a profile of the organizational society itself" (p. 706).

In conclusion, Tompkins suggested that the then-current model or paradigm did not pay sufficient attention to the root metaphors of its concepts and approaches. Tompkins encouraged a shift from a mechanistic to an organic root metaphor, one that refuses to conceive organizational actors as cogs or nodes, and one that would have the advantage of framing organizations from an idiographic perspective rather than the ideal of the mechanistic root metaphor. And as such, this perspective had the potential to address the four critiques of the rational model by refocusing on (1) the importance of the actions of organizational members in creating and negotiating organizational reality; (2) power as an overarching force and organizational rhetoric as the system of persuasion; (3) the variability of levels or boundaries and the impact of interorganizational interaction on the system; and (4) process as the ongoing negotiation of organizational order, topics that have been sufficiently explored since then to warrant detailed attention in this handbook.

In 1983, an important "turn" came in the field with the publication of *Communication and Organizations: An Interpretive Approach*,[1] edited by Putnam and Pacanowsky, a volume that grew out of papers given at the First Conference on Interpretive Approaches to Organizational Communication at Alta, Utah, in 1981. The impact of the essays in this book was not so much in defining the boundaries, concepts, and research problems for the field—it was an anthology, not an integrative literature review—as it was in questioning what counted as knowledge in organizational communication. As explained in the introduction, the purposes of the book were (1) to explain the interpretive approach as it might apply to organizational communication, (2) to divide the interpretive approach into naturalistic and critical studies, and (3) to provide exemplar studies using the naturalistic and critical approaches. Thus, essays in the book suggested that the interpretive approach would enrich extant methodologies, which, as indicated above, were mainly "objective," quantitative in nature, and based on functionalist assumptions. In brief, the book reflected some new approaches to studying organizational communication by the use of a new terministic screen (albeit one based on the analytic framework of Burrell and Morgan, 1979, which was developed to explore sociological paradigms evident in organizational analysis generally; see Deetz, 1986, and Chapter 1, this volume).

A couple of years later, Putnam and Cheney (1985) took a slightly different approach by taking into account disciplinary roots of the field. They saw four general categories in previous analyses: channels, climate, network analysis, and superior-subordinate communication. In addition, they identified several trends or directions for future research, including information processing; political perspectives to communicating in organizations; organizational rhetoric, communication and organizational culture; the extension of Weick's (1979) work on enactment or meaning (cf. Redding's first postulate considered above); and research seeking to depict multiple perspectives on organization communication, not just that of management.

The most definitive *history* of the field of organizational communication was written by

Redding in 1985. This book chapter suggested a multitude of influences, both practical and academic, on the creation and development of the field and its emergence as a central area of study in the speech communication discipline. He gave three explanations to suggest why speech communication scholars assumed the organizational communication banner. The first was that other social scientists had abdicated responsibility, regarding communication problems as mere symptoms of deeper conditions. The second was that the speech field was well suited to fill this void because of its traditions, including the rhetorical perspective. The third explanation was given over to identifying persons in the speech field who had provided the leadership necessary to develop the new field (and characteristically, Redding modestly excluded himself from the group).

In 1988, Redding and Tompkins extended Redding's (1985) longitudinal perspective in commenting on the evolution of organizational communication theory, practice, and research methods. The period from 1900 to 1970 was divided into three approaches: *formulary-prescriptive, empirical-prescriptive,* and the *applied scientific.* The formulary-prescriptive position relied primarily on the development of sets of rules or commonsense prescriptions (based on traditional rhetorical theory) for effective business communication. This body of literature bore such titles as "business English," "business and professional speaking," and "winning friends and influencing people." The empirical-prescriptive phase was noted by a dependence on anecdotal and case study data, with a how-to perspective. The final position, applied scientific, was closely identified with traditional forms of scientific measurement used to explore organizational issues "objectively."

Redding and Tompkins (1988) divided the work done after 1970 as *modernistic, naturalistic,* and *critical,* spelling out in a matrix the main assumptions, methodologies, epistemologies, and ontologies used in each of the three. The modernistic (emerging postmodern perspectives at the time began to create a perspective on what it was assumed to be supplanting) approach assumed that organizations were natural, objective forms and, as such, subject to prediction and control. The modernists' mode is nomothetic, the discovery of lawlike regularities that can be applied across organizational contexts. The naturalistic orientation attempts an understanding and anticipation of communicative interactions through an ethnographic lens, a picture of "Gestalt-like knowledge of wholes, or a hermeneutic understanding of part-to-whole and vice versa" (p. 24). At the heart of this approach is the assumption that organizations are subjective forms that are socially constructed by their members. Finally, the critical approach is described by the authors as "a type of consciousness-raising, if not emancipation for, organizational members themselves" (p. 23). Today we could say that the critical theorists substituted for the previous identification with management—the management bias—an identification with other organizational stakeholders, often the lower-ranking members and workers. Redding and Tompkins articulated the primary goal of critical theorists as the critique and exposure of organizations and their practices in the hope of changing them from oppressive to empowering sites.

The publication in the late 1980s of two handbooks focused on compiling and interpreting organizational communication research and theory (Goldhaber & Barnett, 1988; Jablin, Putnam, Roberts, & Porter, 1987) represented a major milestone in the field's development. However, given that the editors of these two volumes did not join together to produce one handbook, the publication of two handbooks may suggest a lack of consensus among scholars with respect to the "stuff" of organizational communication, and as a consequence each of these efforts may reflect and deflect unique categories and approaches to defining the field.

The Jablin et al. (1987) volume clearly reflects a view of the study of organizational communication as (1) a phenomenon occurring at multiple, interrelated levels of analysis (dyadic, group, organizational, and extraorganizational); and (2) a multi-/interdisciplinary research enterprise, as evident in the volume's title, *Handbook of Organizational Communication: An Interdisciplinary Perspective,* as well as the various backgrounds of the editors and contributors to the book. As stated in the book's preface, the editors view organizational communication as a field "intersecting" many areas that had grown so rapidly in recent years that the problem in putting together a handbook was what to exclude versus what to include (a far cry from the task that faced Guetzkow, 1965, and Tompkins, 1967, in earlier reviews). In the end, they organized the book into four terministic "screens" or parts: (1) Theoretical Issues, (2) Context: Internal and External Environments, (3) Structure: Patterns of Organizational Relationships, and (4) Process: Communication Behavior in Organizations. Consistent with earlier reviews of the literature, the editors suggested that the last two parts of the book, *structure* (emergent communication networks, formal organization structure, superior-subordinate communication, and information technologies) and *process* (message exchange processes, power, politics and influence, conflict and negotiation, message flow and decision making, feedback, motivation and performance, and organizational entry, assimilation, and exit) "constitute what is ordinarily regarded as the central core of organizational communication" (Jablin et al., p. 8).

Goldhaber and Barnett (1988) parsed the field in a somewhat different manner. Their handbook is organized into three sections: (1) Theoretical Perspectives and Conceptual Advances in Organizational Communication, (2) Methodological Approaches, and (3) Organizational Communication in the Information Age. While these are merely section labels, and there is overlap in content among chapters included in Jablin et al. (1987) and Goldhaber and Barnett (1988), the lack of congruence in nomenclature between the two books in cate-

gorizing the field is noteworthy and indicative of distinct views on the centrality of various topics to the study of organizational communication. For example, Goldhaber and Barnett's book includes a section "Methodological Approaches," which draws attention to specific research methods the editors perceive as associated with the study of organizational communication. The methods discussed in this section (e.g., network analysis, gradient analysis) tend to focus on quantitative research methodologies associated with the study of communication and formal organizational structures. The methods section of the book does not include any chapters that specifically focus on qualitative, interpretive, or critical research methodologies, although in the foreword to the book the editors acknowledge that these approaches have grown in popularity among researchers (p. 2). Thus, while Jablin et al. (1987) deflect attention away from organizational communication research methods generally (perhaps because of the breadth of methodologies associated with a multi-/interdisciplinary perspective), Goldhaber and Barnett deflect attention away from interpretive methodologies in particular. In turn, whereas Jablin et al. draw attention to the information-communication contexts or environments of organizations by devoting a section of their book to these issues, Goldhaber and Barnett devote an entire section of their book to a more focused topic: organizational communication and new information technologies. Further, both volumes deflect attention away from ethical issues associated with the study and practice of organizational communication (e.g., Conrad, 1993; Redding, 1992), in that there are no chapters or even index entries related to this topic. While the above stances may reflect the preferences of the editors of the two books, they also may suggest that in the late 1980s the field was still in the process of conceptualizing its traditional domain and grappling with ways of approaching emerging areas of study.

Applying the Redding and Tompkins (1988) matrix to organizational communication articles published in 15 communication journals, Wert-Gray, Center, Brashers, and Meyers (1991) categorized research conducted in the field during the decade 1979-1989. They found that during that decade five topics accounted for over 65% of the research: (1) climate and culture; (2) superior-subordinate communication; (3) power, conflict, and politics; (4) information flow; and (5) public organizational communication. Methodologically, 57.8% of the research articles were modernistic (or positivistic) in orientation, 26% used a naturalistic approach, and only 2.1% manifested the critical approach. Although the sample of journals that Wert-Gray et al. included in their study is not inclusive of all the major outlets in which organizational communication research is published, their findings, along with the foci of chapter topics included in the two handbooks noted above, suggest that the so-called interpretive-critical revolution of the early 1980s was not quite as complete as many believed. Modernism was fairly well entrenched during the decade studied—even though the percentages may have changed in the years since the study was conducted.

In what the authors describe as a "reference index" of articles published in 61 journals, Allen, Gotcher, and Seibert (1993) identified the most heavily researched organizational communication topics from 1980 through 1991. Their typology (see Table P.2) emerged as a by-product of analyzing the articles, although the researchers suggest that the areas they used to categorize research are similar to those used in past reviews. According to their study, interpersonal relations, and in particular superior-subordinate communication, was the most researched topic, followed by communication skills, and organizational culture and symbolism. Deetz (1992) suggests that the review shows across topics significant growth in the "social construction of organizations and reality" (p. xiii) during the ten-year period reviewed. Although fairly comprehensive, this review has been criticized for what the researchers left out of their analysis

(e.g., handbooks, yearbook chapters, selected studies) and the manner in which they classified particular articles into topical areas, among other things (DeWine & Daniels, 1993).

The most recent major review and compilation of organizational communication research and theory was completed by Putnam et al. (1996). They approached the process of reviewing and interpreting the literature in a manner distinct from those discussed above: by identifying perspectives, in the form of metaphor clusters, that they believed characterize conceptualizations and approaches to the study of organizational communication. Each of the seven metaphor clusters they identified—conduit, lens, linkage, performance, symbol, voice, and discourse—can be considered a terministic screen/perspective, and as such "researchers can examine any organizational topic from one of these clusters" (Putnam et al., 1996, p. 394). However, it is important to note that since each metaphor varies in complexity and completeness with respect to the study of organizational communication (see Table P.3), it also reflects—as well as neglects—key elements of organizational communication phenomena.

For example, they illustrate the ways boundaries are part of organizational metaphors and how alternative ways of conceiving of organizations remove boundary as a central element. In addition, Putnam et al. (1996) suggest that "the criteria for choosing a particular metaphor are the researcher's goals, the ontological basis of both communication and organization, and the phenomenon that is most central to the organizing process" (p. 394).

In looking back at their analysis of the literature, Putnam et al. (1996) drew three conclusions about organizational communication research:

1. Despite limitations with respect to the completeness and complexity of the perspectives, "the conduit and the lens metaphors are the primary ways that organizational scholars treat communication" (p. 396).

TABLE P.2 Frequency of Publication of Organizational Communication Journal Articles by Topical Areas: 1980-1991

Frequency (total = 889)	Topic/Sample Subtopics
233	Interpersonal relations: includes superior-subordinate relations; interpersonal communication and conflict, stress, race and gender; and interviewing
120	Communication skills and strategies: includes persuasion, influence strategies, self-presentation, listening, feedback seeking and giving, supervisory communication skills, interviewing, and associations between skill proficiency and outcomes
99	Organizational culture and symbolism: includes rites and rituals, communication rules/norms, metaphors, organizational texts, stories, images, and myths
74	Information flow and channels: includes factors affecting information flow, information transmission, direction of communication, media preferences, and innovation
67	Power and influence: includes power and influence tactics, social construction of power, politics and games, language use, negotiation, bargaining, and argumentation
67	Positive outcomes associated with communication: includes studies that link communication outcomes such as commitment, performance, satisfaction, productivity, and burnout
67	Decision making and problem solving: includes participative decision making, factors influencing how decisions are made, and constraints on decision making
57	Communication networks: includes antecedents and outcomes associated with network membership, network measurement, network roles, and interorganizational networks
57	Cognitive, communication, and management styles: includes identification of styles and their relationships to outcomes, and relations between styles and behavior
53	Organization-environment communication interface: includes image-related communication, boundary spanning, information flows, and corporate discourse
45	Technology
42	Structure
41	Language and message content
41	Groups and organizational effectiveness
40	Uncertainty and information adequacy
28	Ethics
24	Cross-cultural
18	Climate

SOURCE: Adapted from a descriptive review of organizational communication articles published in 61 journals from 1980 to 1991 by Allen, Gotcher, and Seibert (1993). Articles may be included in more than one topical category.

TABLE P.3 Metaphors of Organizational Communication Research

Metaphor Cluster	*Orientation to Organization/ Communication Perspective/Examples of Research Foci*
Conduit	- Organization viewed as *containers* or channels of information flow - Communication equated with *transmission;* functions as a *tool* - Examples of research foci: formal and informal channels; comparisons among communication media; organizational structure and information overload, capacity, and adequacy
Lens	- Organization viewed as an *eye* that scans, sifts, and relays information - Communication equated with a *filtering* process, reception and perception processes - Examples of research foci: message distortion and ambiguity, information acquisition and decision making, gatekeeping, media richness
Linkage	- Organization viewed as *networks* of multiple, overlapping relationships - Communication equated with *connections* and interdependence - Examples of research foci: intra- and interorganizational network roles, patterns and structures, characteristics of ties/linkages
Performance	- Organization viewed as *coordinated actions* that enact their own rules, structures, and environment through social interaction - Communication equated with *social interaction,* dynamic processes of interlocking behaviors, reflexivity, collaboration, and sensemaking - Examples of research foci: enactment cycles, storytelling, symbolic convergence, jamming, co-constructing improvisations
Symbol	- Organization viewed as a *novel* or *literary text,* a symbolic milieu in which organizing is accomplished - Communication equated with *interpretation* and representation through the creation, maintenance, and transformation of meanings - Examples of research foci: narratives, organizational metaphors, rites, rituals, ceremonies, paradoxes and ironies, culture and language
Voice	- Organization viewed as a *chorus* of diverse voices - Communication equated with the *expression, suppression,* and *distortion* of the voices of organizational members - Examples of research foci: hegemony, power, ideology, marginalization of voices, empowerment, legitimation, unobtrusive control
Discourse	- Organization viewed as *texts,* ritualized patterns of interaction that transcend immediate conversations - Communication equated with *conversation,* as both process and structure/ context, intertwining both action and meaning - Examples of research foci: discourse as artifact/codes, structure and process, discursive practices, communication genres

SOURCE: Adapted from Putnam, Phillips, and Chapman (1996).

2. Examination of the metaphors provides strong support for the notion that "communication and organization are equivalent" (p. 396).

3. As evident in the growing popularity of metaphors of organizations as voice, texts, and discourse, it is possible that organizational communication "no longer mirrors or reflects reality, rather it is formative in that it creates and represents the process of organizing" (p. 396).

In other words, "figure and ground" are becoming more difficult to isolate in organizational communication research.

PROSPECTS AND CONCLUDING COMMENTS

In this section, we consider the implications of our review of reviews for future research and theory development in the field of organizational communication. Our conclusions are not meant to be comprehensive in nature, but reflect just a handful of themes we perceive are evident in our history and perhaps in the field's future.

First, examination of the topical reviews of literature suggests that a good part of our future research will continue to extend past research by developing "new" perspectives on "old" issues and problems associated with communication and organization. Thus, the field's traditional focus on leader-follower communication; communication networks and structures; the creation, sensing, and routing of information; information flow and participation in decision making; filtering and distortion of messages; communication channels; feedback processing; and the like will remain significant areas of study (see Tables P.1 and P.2). To a large extent, these topics tend to focus on the sorts of communication structures and processes that Jablin et al. (1987) suggested are frequently "regarded at the central core of organizational communication"

(p. 8). Thus, while the specific research questions will vary (e.g., the effects of a new communication technology on the processing of feedback, or communication patterns and roles in "new" organizational forms), much of our research will be expanding on topics that have a long history of study in organizational communication. However, since researchers who explored these topics in the past have tended to conceptualize and operationalize them in terms of the metaphors of "conduit," "lens," "linkages," and more recently "symbols" (Putnam et al., 1996), there is considerable room for advancement of knowledge through the investigation of these topics through (1) other appropriate metaphors and representations (ones that don't confound related assumptions about communication and organization), and (2) the chaining of "threads" of related metaphor clusters together to reveal interrelationships and possibly new metaphors.

Second, we see the emergence of research traditions founded on the metaphors of "voice," "discourse," and "performance" as part of a maturation of the field in that each moves the field in ways that question and deconstruct metaphors and categories of the past while integrating domains and methods thought to be permanently at odds with one another. For example, recent research exploring a construct central to the history of the field (see Redding, 1972)—participation—has enriched our understanding of this notion via consideration from a number of voice-based perspectives including concertive control (e.g., Barker, 1993; Tompkins & Cheney, 1985) and critical theory (e.g., Deetz, 1992), as well as in terms of "discourse" (e.g., Taylor, 1993, 1995) and network metaphors (e.g., Stohl, 1995). Another area of study that has been a focus of interest since the beginning of the field—communication networks—has also benefited from consideration via voice, discourse, and performance perspectives. For example, Taylor (1993) has suggested that networks themselves might be viewed as texts in that they represent relatively ritualized, structured patterns of interaction that "transcend" immediate conversations (see also recent research exploring "semantic" networks in organizations [e.g., Contractor, Eisenberg, & Monge, 1992] and recent studies of networks, meaning, and solidarity [e.g., Kiianmaa, 1997]). Reflective of the voice metaphor he adds that communication networks practically guarantee "that some influences remain unheard, and hence that some of the accounts which all organizations spontaneously develop are attended to regularly, and others are ignored" (p. 90). Alternatively, based on Tompkins and Cheney's (1985) work on control, Stohl (1995) posits that participation in networks can blur distinctions among individuals and groups in organizations and thereby "further an organization's ability to control unobtrusively individuals" (p. 147). These are important issues to consider and we believe demonstrate how traditional areas of organizational communication research can be enriched through analysis via the discourse, performance, and voice metaphors. They give us a richer nomenclature than we had in the past with which to select and reflect reality for analysis.

Finally, our analysis suggests that the field is now focusing more on communicational theorizing about organizing than in the recent past. In particular, Taylor's (1993, 1995; Taylor, Cooren, Giroux, & Robichard, 1996) work is noteworthy in that it attempts to "reconstruct" a communication-based theory of organization. In brief, he argues that conversations are the stuff of organizations, conversations lead to narratives or texts meaningful to the conversationalists, and organization is a communication system—"an ecology of conversation" (p. 244). Thus, he moves from a metaphor of communication as both the figure and ground, the paint and the canvas of an organization, to one of a "text produced by a set of authors, through conversation" (Taylor, 1993, p. 96). Recent contributions such as Taylor's as well as those of other scholars (e.g., Stohl's, 1995, effort to link relational theories of interpersonal communication with

network explanations of organizational functioning), like Redding's (1972) little-known attempt decades earlier, ground organizational studies in communication theory. Thus, they facilitate a view of organizations as communicational in nature, a perspective that we expect will be central to understanding the more fluid, fragmented, and chaotic forms of organizations and organizing that are expected in the future (e.g., Bergquist, 1993; McPhee & Poole, Chapter 13, this volume). In these contexts communication and organization are equivalent, discourse is organizing; it is the paint and the canvas, the figure and ground.

NOTE

1. Although Tompkins's summary chapter in the Arnold and Bowers handbook was published in 1984 and the Putnam and Pacanowsky book in 1983, we reverse the apparent chronological order because the Tompkins chapter was submitted in early 1980, some time before the Putnam-Pacanowsky book went to press. In fact, Putnam (1983) refers to the chapter as "(Tompkins, in press)" in her chapter on the interpretive perspective.

REFERENCES

Allen, M. W., Gotcher, J. M., & Seibert, J. H. (1993). A decade of organizational communication research: Journal articles 1980-1991. In S. A. Deetz (Ed.), *Communication yearbook 16* (pp. 252-330). Newbury Park, CA: Sage.

Barker, J. (1993). Tightening the iron cage: Concertive control in self-managing teams. *Administrative Science Quarterly, 38*, 408-437.

Barnard, C. (1938). *The functions of the executive.* Cambridge, MA: Harvard University Press.

Bergquist, W. (1993). *The postmodern organization: Mastering the art of irreversible change.* San Francisco: Jossey-Bass.

Burke, K. (1966). *Language as symbolic action.* Berkeley: University of California Press.

Burrell, G., & Morgan, G. (1979). *Sociological paradigms and organizational analysis.* London: Heinemann.

Conrad, C. (Ed.). (1993). *The ethical nexus.* Norwood, NJ: Ablex.

Contractor, N., Eisenberg, E., & Monge, P. (1992). *Antecedents and outcomes of interpretive diversity in or-*

ganizations*. Unpublished manuscript, University of Illinois, Urbana-Champaign.

Deetz, S. (1986). Describing differences in approaches to organization science: Rethinking Burrell and Morgan and their legacy. *Organization Science, 7*, 191-207.

Deetz, S. A. (1992). *Democracy in an age of corporate colonization*. Albany: State University of New York Press.

DeWine, S., & Daniels, T. (1993). Beyond the snapshot: Setting a research agenda in organizational communication. In S. A. Deetz (Ed.), *Communication yearbook 16* (pp. 331-346). Newbury Park, CA: Sage.

Downs, C. W., Johnson, K. M., & Barge, J. K. (1984). Communication feedback and task performance in organizations: A review of the literature. In H. H. Greenbaum, R. L. Falcione, S. A. Hellweg, & Associates (Eds.), *Organizational communication: Abstracts, analysis, and overview* (Vol. 9, pp. 13-48). Beverly Hills, CA: Sage.

Goldhaber, G. M., & Barnett, G. A. (Eds.). (1988). *Handbook of organizational communication*. Norwood, NJ: Ablex.

Guetzkow, H. (1965). Communication in organizations. In J. G. March (Ed.), *Handbook of organizations* (pp. 534-573). Chicago: Rand McNally.

Heron, A. R. (1942). *Sharing information with employees*. Palo Alto, CA: Stanford University Press.

Jablin, F. M. (1978, November). *Research priorities in organizational communication*. Paper presented at the annual meeting of the Speech Communication Association, Minneapolis.

Jablin, F. M. (1979). Superior-subordinate communication: The state-of-the-art. *Psychological Bulletin, 86*, 1201-1222.

Jablin, F. M. (1990). Organizational communication. In G. L. Dahnke & G. W. Clatterbuck (Eds.), *Human communication: Theory and research* (pp. 156-182). Belmont, CA: Wadsworth.

Jablin, F. M., Putnam, L. L., Roberts, K. H., & Porter, L. W. (Eds.). (1987). *Handbook of organizational communication: An interdisciplinary perspective*. Newbury Park, CA: Sage.

Jablin, F. M., & Sussman, L. (1983). Organizational group communication: A review of the literature and a model of the process. In H. H. Greenbaum, R. L. Falcione, S. A. Hellweg, & Associates (Eds.), *Organizational communication: Abstracts, analysis, and overview* (Vol. 8, pp. 11-50). Beverly Hills, CA: Sage.

Kiianmaa, A. (1997). *Moderni totemismi: Tutkimustyoelämästä, solidaarisuudesta ja sosiaalisista verkostoista keskiluokkaistuvassa Suomessa*. Helsinki, Finland: Jyvasklyla.

March, J. G., & Simon, H. A. (1958). *Organizations*. New York: John Wiley.

Monge, P. R., Edwards, J. A., & Kirste, K. K. (1978). The determinants of communication and structure in large organizations: A review of research. In B. D. Ruben (Ed.), *Communication yearbook 2* (pp. 311-331). New Brunswick, NJ: Transaction.

Porter, L. W., & Roberts, K. H. (1976). Communication in organizations. In M. D. Dunnette (Ed.), *Handbook of industrial and organizational psychology* (pp. 1553-1589). Chicago: Rand McNally.

Putnam, L. (1983). The interpretive perspective: An alternative to functionalism. In L. L. Putnam & M. E. Pacanowsky (Eds.), *Communication and organizations: An interpretive approach* (pp. 31-54). Beverly Hills, CA: Sage.

Putnam, L., & Cheney, G. (1985). Organizational communication: Historical developments and future directions. In T. Benson (Ed.), *Speech communication in the 20th century* (pp. 130-156). Carbondale: Southern Illinois University Press.

Putnam, L. L., & Pacanowsky, M. E. (Eds.). (1983). *Communication and organizations: An interpretive approach*. Beverly Hills, CA: Sage.

Putnam, L. L., Phillips, N., & Chapman, P. (1996). Metaphors of communication and organization. In S. R. Clegg, C. Hardy, & W. R. Nord (Eds.), *Handbook of organization studies* (pp. 375-408). Thousand Oaks, CA: Sage.

Redding, W. C. (1972). *Communication within the organization: An interpretive review of theory and research*. New York: Industrial Communication Council.

Redding, W. C. (1985). Stumbling toward an identity: The emergence of organizational communication as a field of study. In R. D. McPhee & P. K. Tompkins (Eds.), *Organizational communication: Traditional themes and new directions* (pp. 15-54). Newbury Park, CA: Sage.

Redding, W. C. (1992). *Ethics and the study of organizational communication: When will we wake up?* Paper presented at the Center for the Study of Ethics in Society, Western Michigan University, Kalamazoo.

Redding, W. C., & Tompkins, P. K. (1988). Organizational communication: Past and present tenses. In G. Goldhaber & G. Barnett (Eds.), *Handbook of organizational communication* (pp. 5-34). Norwood, NJ: Ablex.

Stohl, C. (1995). *Organizational communication: Connectedness in action*. Thousand Oaks, CA: Sage.

Taylor, J. (1993). *Rethinking the theory of organizational communication: How to read an organization*. Norwood, NJ: Ablex.

Taylor, J. (1995). Shifting from a heteronomous to an autonomous worldview of organizational communication: Communication theory on the cusp. *Communication Theory, 5*, 1-35.

Taylor, J., Cooren, F., Giroux, N., & Robichard, D. (1996). The communicational basis of organization: Between the conversation and the text. *Communication Theory, 6*, 1-39.

Thayer, L. (1968). *Communication and communication systems.* Homewood, IL: Irwin.

Tompkins, P. K. (1967). Organizational communication: A state-of-the-art review. In G. Richetto (Ed.), *Conference on organizational communication* (pp. 4-26). Huntsville, AL: National Aeronautics and Space Administration.

Tompkins, P. K. (1984). The functions of communication in organizations. In C. Arnold & J. Bowers (Eds.), *Handbook of rhetorical and communication theory* (pp. 659-719). New York: Allyn & Bacon.

Tompkins, P. K., & Cheney, G. (1985). Communication and unobtrusive control in contemporary organizations. In R. D. McPhee & P. K. Tompkins (Eds.), *Organizational communication: Traditional themes and new directions* (pp. 179-210). Newbury Park, CA: Sage.

Weick, K. E. (1979). *The social psychology of organizing* (2nd ed.). Reading, MA: Addison-Wesley.

Wert-Gray, S., Center, C., Brashers, D., & Meyers, R. (1991). Research topics and methodological orientations in organizational communication: A decade in review. *Communication Studies, 42,* 141-154.

PART I

Theoretical and Methodological Issues

1

Conceptual Foundations

❖ STANLEY DEETZ
University of Colorado at Boulder

For all of recorded history, people have studied and discussed communication processes within their dominant organizations. In many respects, these discussions differ little from those present during the past three decades of institutional organizational communication study. They have been concerned with the systematic manners by which communication practices can be used to help coordinate and control the activities of organizational members and relations with external constituencies. Our current situation is one of rapid social and organizational change putting great pressure on researchers today to continually develop useful concepts and studies to match the complex interactions characteristic of contemporary workplaces.

Organizational communication research is itself a rich communicative process. Researchers have developed and used their theories and research activities for many positive organizational outcomes. But their work also accomplishes a variety of intertwined life purposes, including the distinction of the researcher and the development and advancement of specific group interests. Fundamental assumptions about the nature of the world, methods of producing knowledge, and values are developed and advanced in the discourse of researchers. Such assumptions are necessary to produce any kind of understanding and knowledge and are usually most contested during periods of rapid change. While fundamental assumptions themselves are not open

3

to refutation, they are to exploration. Scholars rightfully ask of any research program, "To solve what problems?" "To what ends?" "Whose meanings?" "Whose knowledge?"

This essay hopes to foster useful discussions regarding how different scholars construct knowledge and justify practices about organizations, and also about the values, hopes, and groups' interest that they support. To that end, I begin with an overview of how the term *organizational communication* is used—what it delimits, organizes, or draws our attention to. Following this introduction, the central part of the chapter will develop a two-dimensional scheme for directing attention to similarities and differences among research programs. I will argue that the most interesting differences among social research programs can be displayed through looking at (1) the type of interaction particular researchers favor with other groups, characterized as *local/emergent* versus *elite/a priori* conceptions; and (2) the moves the research activity and report make toward closure or indeterminacy in that interaction, characterized as *consensus* seeking versus *dissensus* seeking. These two dimensions when put together provide a two by two matrix characterizing differences in research programs. I will discuss each of four "ideal type" research programs produced in this grid. Finally, I will conclude by looking at the researcher's choice processes in the contemporary context and looking at future research agenda.

ORGANIZATIONAL COMMUNICATION

What is organizational communication? The possibility of a shared answer to that question seems to be implied in producing a handbook of organizational communication or in detailing conceptual foundations for organizational communication studies. Clear and simple answers can be given. I could just provide a definition, compare it with alternative definitions, and get on with a review. Defini-

tions are nice; they set clear boundaries and justify my looking at the things I am interested in, and excluding the rest. But such definitions are inevitably arbitrary, usually provide political advantage for some group, and can as easily produce blinders as insight. Not only is debate possible over alternative definitions but also over the act of defining (Deetz, 1992, chap. 3; Smith, 1993; Taylor, 1993). Ultimately, the question "What is organizational communication?" is misleading. A more interesting question is, "What do we see or what are we able to do if we think of organizational communication in one way versus another?" Unlike a definition, the attempt here is not to get it right, but to understand our choices. Rather than killing the bird ("definition" definitio, to kill or make final) and getting on with the dissection, perhaps we should watch it fly for a while.

Three very different ways of conceptualizing "organizational communication" are available. Each of these provides different "attentions" and different boundaries regarding what should be covered in this volume and this chapter. Such conceptions guide research and teaching as well as provide an identity to a group of scholars. First, the focus could be on the development of organizational communication as a speciality in departments of communication and communication associations. Organizational communication study is whatever anyone does who is a member of these divisions or publishes in particular journals (see, e.g., Smeltzer, 1993). Like with other "sociologies of fields," time can be spent looking at the history of this development, what members of these divisions have studied and published, how many students major or achieve advanced degrees in this speciality, and how many jobs are available (see Redding, 1979). These are not unimportant concerns and such a conception either explicitly or implicitly has been used to determine what is or is not an organizational communication study in many if not most literature reviews (see Krone, Jablin, & Putnam, 1987; Meyers, Seibert, & Allen, 1993; Putnam & Cheney, 1985; Redding & Tompkins, 1988;

Richetto, 1977; Wert-Gray, Center, Brashers, & Meyers, 1991).[1] From these reviews we often gain more understanding of people, their relations, careers, and university politics than we do about the underlying conceptions of organizations and communication. Moving from reviews of studies to examining alternative theories in organizational communication studies and the social problems such studies address is often difficult. It is not surprising that these reviews often contain laments about the disunity of the field. This may well be an artifact of the organizing principle used.

A second approach to conceptualizing organizational communication focuses on communication as a phenomenon that exists in organizations. If such an object can be defined, then anyone who looks at or talks about that object is studying organizational communication. This is the logic behind many textbook definitions of organizational communication. Within this logic, any number of individuals from different academic units might study this phenomenon. In such a case, interdisciplinarity might be expected. With this focus one might ask what is "communication" in the organization and what is something else, what are the ways the phenomenon can be usefully subdivided, what are the variables that affect it or it affects, and what theories adequately explain it. Handbooks like this one usually work from this type of conception (see Krone et al., 1987). They assume that a unified phenomenon exists, and they form chapters based on subdivisions of the phenomenon or alternative sites where it appears. Introductory chapters like this one typically focus on the variety of ways that the same phenomenon has been examined.

Unfortunately for such a tack, many of the contemporary theories of organizations and communication deny that a unitary phenomenon exists out there. Thus, the phenomenon —organizational communication—is different for different theories. "Organizational communication" is not one phenomenon with many explanations; each form of explanation may conceptualize and explain a different phenomenon. Fixed subdivisions are always a kind of theoretical hegemony (where one theory's "organizational communication" is privileged over undiscussed others). When this happens, theory debate is reduced to methodological perspectivalism. When thought of as a distinct phenomenon, the conception of "organization" is often reduced to a "site" and the conception of "communication" often becomes narrow with social interaction conceptually reduced to empirical acts of information transfer, often the lowest common denominator (or dominator) in organizational communication (for discussion, see Axley, 1984; Putnam, Phillips, & Chapman, 1996; Smith, 1993; Taylor, 1993).

A third way to approach the issue is to think of communication as a way to describe and explain organizations. In the same way that psychology, sociology, or economics can be thought of as capable of explaining organizations' processes, communication might also be thought of as a distinct mode of explanation or way of thinking about organizations (see Deetz, 1994a; Pearce, 1989). Communication theory can be used to explain the production of social structures, psychological states, member categories, knowledge, and so forth rather than being conceptualized as simply one phenomenon among these others in organizations. The focus would be on the process of organizing through symbolic interaction rather than on "communication" within an "organization" (Hawes, 1974). From such a perspective the interest is not in theories of organizational communication but in producing a communication theory of organizations (Deetz, 1994a). Historically, few scholars in the academic units of organizational communication have approached the issue this way. Until recently, psychological or social-cultural explanations have been more often used in most studies. Gradually, since the early 1980s, scholars in communication departments as well as a large number of non-U.S. scholars and some scholars from other academic units have focused on organizations as complex discursive formations where discursive practices are both "in" organizations and productive of them. Because of the tendency to delimit organizational communication as a professional unit or a distinct phenomenon, until recently non-U.S. and non-communication scholars were often absent from reviews (e.g., the various works of Knights, Willmott, Hollway, Cooper, Burrell, Gergen, Power, Townley, and Alvesson).

In this review, I will accept this third way of thinking about organizational communication. The recursiveness of this position means that the production of the field as an academic unit and organizational communication as a distinct phenomenon are themselves discursive accomplishments. My analysis will thus work at a metalevel from which conceptions of organizations and processes in them by researchers and "organizational members" can themselves be seen "communicationally." This view allows a deeper analysis that can display how study results are produced rather than just providing here another review of results from different research programs. The duality of studying human interaction in a specific location and the assumption that human interaction is a core formative feature of world construction complicates analysis much but also greatly enriches it.

Largely I follow the instruction given by Bourdieu (1991):

> The social sciences deal with prenamed, preclassified realities which bear proper nouns and common nouns, titles, signs and acronyms. At the risk of unwittingly assuming responsibility for the acts of constitution of whose logic and necessity they are unaware, the social sciences must take as their object of study the social operations of *naming* and the rites of institution through which they are accomplished. (p. 106)

Attention can be drawn to how both they who study and they who participate "in" organizations produce phenomena in the world such as "organizations," "communication," "needs," "motivations," "information," "profits," and various personal and social divisions such as "men" and "women," "workers" and "management." Following this tack requires some understanding of a nonrepresentational or constitutive view of language that cannot be developed here at any length but ought to be familiar enough to most readers that a short development will suffice (see Deetz, 1992, chap. 5).

In line with modern discourse theory, conceptions are always contests for meaning (see Epstein, 1988; Weedon, 1987). Language does not name objects in the world; it is core to the process of constituting the indeterminant and ambiguous external world into specific objects. The appearance of labeling or categorizing existing objects is derived from this more fundamental act of object constitution through language. The world thus can be constituted in many ways depending on alternative systems of valuing. The most significant part of this contest for object constitution is the capacity to enact the lines of distinction producing some things as alike and others as different. Only secondarily is the contest over the positive or negative valance ascribed to the produced things. For example, feminist writers for years have shown how male dominance is maintained by the dominant group's ability to define the dimensions of difference and position themselves at the positive end of each dimension (see Treichler, 1989; Weedon, 1987). Marginalized groups, following this analysis, are defined as "the other" thus acquiring an identity and valued functions but only as given by the opposition pole in the dominant group's conceptual map (e.g., "emotionally supportive" rather than "rational" or "private" rather than "public"). They acquire a type of autonomy but only in a language/conceptual game not of their own choosing. In accepting the state of "other," they have little self-definition and the game is stacked (see Bourdieu, 1977, 1991).

From the communicative metaperspective taken here, the core process in understanding alternative research programs is to understand their discourse—how they perceive, think, and talk about organizational life. Understanding a discourse includes identification of the object distinctions they make, whose language is used in making those object distinctions, what and whose values and interests are carried with those distinctions, and how the conflicting descriptions of the world are handled as well as exploring their processes of self-justification and distinction from alternative research programs. Further, research programs differ in the extent to which they recognize and make explicit their own constitutive activities. Many researchers assume that they are merely discovering and naming real-world objects. To the extent that this is done much of the micropractice of research is missed.

MAPPING APPROACHES TO ORGANIZATIONAL COMMUNICATION STUDIES

Trying to produce any organizing scheme of these discourses accounting for different theoretical conceptions, methodological preferences, and value commitments is filled with difficulties. Each research program might well use different ways of comparing and contrasting itself with other programs. In fact a primary way that any research program establishes itself is in its means of distinction, both in the sense of producing a difference and giving itself the positive terms (see Bourdieu, 1991).

Many schemes have been proposed for organizing and thinking about alternative research programs. Most of these classify studies based on subdivisions of the organizational communication phenomenon or differences in research methods. For example, Wert-Gray et al. (1991) suggest three dominant areas of work: (1) information flow and channels, (2) climate, and (3) superior/subordinate. And Redding and Tompkins (1988) divide the work into (1) formal channels, (2) superior/subordinate communication, (3) informal channels, and (4) measuring and data collection. Putnam and Cheney (1985) suggest (1) channels, (2) communication climate, (3) superior/subordinate, (4) network analy-

sis, and (5) communication media with additional emerging perspectives. And in perhaps the most exhaustive study, Allen, Gotcher, and Seibert (1993) review 17 areas of work: (1) interpersonal relations, (2) communication skills, (3) culture and symbolism, (4) information flow and channels, (5) power and influence, (6) decision making and problem solving, (7) communication networks, (8) communication and management styles, (9) organization-environment interface, (10) technology, (11) language and messages, (12) structure, (13) uncertainty and information adequacy, (14) groups, (15) ethics, (16) cross-cultural, and (17) climate. These divisions and study counts are interesting and represent ways of thinking about the field that are fairly common. But such approaches tend to reify topical divisions that are the constructed outcomes of discursive processes thus treating them as natural rather than produced, hiding values and assumptions, and disowning the way these divisions preference particular studies of communication. Let us consider for a moment these preferences.

First, the topical orientation is itself not a neutral classification tool. It assumes and reproduces a particular view of communication and organizations. For example, it assumes an atomistic orientation to the world like the 19th-century natural science model and advantages studies that follow that model. Studies based in holistic assumptions, such as ethnographic approaches, may get put in a category like "culture" or "climate." This makes "culture" into one phenomenon among others in organizations that can be studied. Not only do cultural studies deny that culture is one thing among many *in* organizations, the classification buries the important things that ethnographic researchers said about organizations' structures and activities like channels and interpersonal relations. Only studies that explicitly study channels and interpersonal relations as isolated phenomena appear in those categories. Ethnographic researchers rarely study a topic, they study a particular site. What would we learn if we classified by site, the social problem considered, group allegiance, or the moral stance rather than topic? Topical divisions probably made sense when the vast majority of researchers believed that the elements of organizations were atomistic rather than holistic, that organizations were primarily a thing rather than a process, and that communication was a phenomenon among others rather than an approach one takes to organization studies. As these change so must our ways of accounting for similarities and differences in organization studies.

Second, the devices of data collection shape the review in further ways. In some of these reviews, the data pool is limited to *studies* published in *"communication" journals* and the manner of display is usually the *number* of essays. The classifying processes match assumptions of the natural science model thus both normalizing its preferred manner of report and overemphasizing its impact. The "field" looks different in reviews that consider scholarly book chapters, scholarly books, and/or unpublished research reports to companies instead of journal articles. Further, the concept of "studies" itself tends to get defined in terms of data collection, thus analytic and conceptual work, which often have great impact on the field and its practices, tend to be left out. And further yet, the concept of the "communication field" has often led to the omission of non-North American studies that organize "fields" differently and important "communication studies" on topics that are definitionally excluded. For example, the discursive studies in such journals as *Organization* or *Organization Studies,* communication-based studies in *Accounting, Organizations and Society,* and interaction studies in "sociology" are left out, and works by authors in management schools in such journals as *Management Communication Quarterly* are included. The tendency is to bias the counts toward studies from a psychological and managerial perspective. And finally, *quantity of studies* as a measure favors narrow quantitative analyses. What if we measured significance of impact, transformative

potential, or applicability to wider stakeholder interests? Each of these would provide different pictures of "our" studies and contribution and pressure the field's development in different ways.

I think we get further if we look at the practice of research and researcher commitments rather than looking at topics as if they could be freed from the researcher's orientation. As we become more diverse as a people and as researchers, a consideration of general research assumptions becomes more instructive. Reviewers looking at research assumptions and orientations have tended to focus more on methodological/epistemological differences than study topics. And rarely have they gone beyond methodological choices to a full consideration of the way theoretical and value commitments are carried with them.

Reviews that have considered research orientations have fairly high agreement in categories of classification. Putnam (1982; Putnam & Pacanowsky, 1983), for example, describes studies as functionalist, interpretive, and critical. Redding and Tompkins (1988) describe them in a parallel fashion as modernist, naturalistic, and critical (a scheme followed by Wert-Gray et al., 1991, in their methodological orientations). These authors would probably add "postmodernist" if they were writing these essays today. I suspect that these divisions are largely a result of the influence of Burrell and Morgan's (1979) popular discussion of sociological paradigms as functionalist, interpretive, radical humanist, and radical structuralist. Their paradigm descriptions have been very influential in management and communication studies, and the influence is well deserved. While I believe fundamentally flawed, their approach serves as a useful point of departure for further development (see Deetz, 1996).

Importantly, Burrell and Morgan's discussion of paradigmatic differences in the late 1970s gave legitimacy to fundamentally different research programs and enabled the development of different criteria for the evaluation of research. Their exhaustive review was not only valuable in itself, but they were able to provide an analysis that probed deeply into the assumptions on which different research programs were based. But harms were also created. I believe that there are reasons for this significant influence beyond the clarity of presentation and exhaustive compilation of literature. When the grid and discussion were published in 1979, those of us doing alternative work readily embraced the grid for it gave each of us a kind of asylum. While some of us were uncomfortable with the dimensions and philosophical analysis, we happily accepted the new-found capacity to present ourselves to mainstream critics as doing fundamentally different, but legitimate, kinds of research and began to work on concepts and evaluation criteria within our now produced as different and unitary communities. Many of those doing more mainstream work also found it appealing since, as I will argue, the conceptual distinctions Burrell and Morgan used to produce the grid were the same distinctions the mainstream tradition had used to discuss different research agendas. Thus, they reaffirm that tradition's conceptual map and provide a "safe" understanding of the developing alternatives. Further, the conception of paradigms as distinct schools of thought with their own problem statements and evaluative criteria could be used by the dominant "functionalists" to protect themselves from growing criticism (the isolationist strategy noted by Reed, 1985). They too would have a safe and separate place (see Rodríguez & Cai, 1994).

But as organization science and organizational communication research have continued to evolve, problems with the Burrell and Morgan grid and its adaptations have become more pressing. While not primarily a result of the original analysis, the four-paradigm solution has often led to quick categorizations and to debates around paradigm commensurability and appropriate use of the different paradigms (Hassard, 1991; Jackson & Carter, 1991; Parker & McHugh, 1991; Willmott, 1993). Some of these problems and debates arise from the tendency to reify concepts, es-

pecially in educational programs and materials. The Burrell and Morgan grid can easily produce four unitary paradigms, rather than provide two lines of differentiation that draw attention to important differences in research programs. Burrell and Morgan invite reification by claims of paradigmatic incommensurability, by staying at the level of theory and reconstructed science, and by accepting Kuhn's loose conception of paradigms. The dimensions of contrast can be used as a way of focusing attention to differences that make a difference rather than as a means of classification, but few writers and teachers have done so.

But my main concern is not paradigm commensurability or reification but rather the dimensions of contrast themselves. A deeper and more interesting understanding of contemporary research practices and debates is possible by focusing on other contrastive dimensions. The question is not: Are these the right categories or who fits in each? but: Are these differences that make a difference? Do these dimensions provide insight into genuine differences in research programs? I hope to aid rethinking the differences and similarities among different research approaches, with the aim of making our conflicts and discussions more productive rather than simply replacing four boxes with four different boxes. In many ways, the various adaptations of Burrell and Morgan have hampered the development of new research agenda and led to less than productive conceptions in the field.

Burrell and Morgan, and subsequently many organizational communication scholars, largely accepted the conceptual distinctions from sociological functionalism and its supporting philosophy of science. Burrell and Morgan performed a political intervention as they spoke on behalf of the oppositions, the negative terms, the "others" in "sociological functionalism's" conceptual map. For example, they accepted the traditional functionalist "subjective/objective" distinction but provided a careful development of "subjective" research. Thus, using the dominant conceptions, they merely asked, "Who is 'other'?" and "In what ways are they 'other'?" But they never questioned whether distinctions based on such conceptions as "subjective/objective" were useful at all (see Deetz, 1994a). In contrast to their analysis, each "other" (each marginalized paradigmatic group like "interpretivists" or "radical humanists") would have defined its difference from the dominant functionalist conceptions differently, that is, if they accepted their "groupness" at all (see Bernstein, 1983; Natter, Schatzki, & Jones, 1995). This positioning, as I have suggested, partly accounts for the rapid acceptance of the Burrell and Morgan's grid into the mainstream of management science and organizational communication discussions.

Further, this move protected functionalist researchers from the most damning critiques (and ones they would not understand, e.g., the "artifactual" quality of their "facts") in favor of their preferred battles (e.g., between their "objectivity" and others' "subjectivity"). At the same time, the most innovative of the new researchers found it now even more difficult to express what they did since they had to use a language in which their meanings did not fit (e.g., critical theorists and phenomenologists who did not accept "subject/object" dualism had to accept the classification as "subjective humanists" if they were to have a home at all). They had to choose between misrepresenting themselves clearly through Burrell and Morgan or representing themselves well but being considered obscure or bad writers. Thus, the effect was to normalize the emerging research paradigms favoring rather traditional directions even within them. For example, when Burrell and Morgan, and subsequently Putnam and others, provided "interpretive" work with the "subjective" ascription (even if now positively valued) they, perhaps unwittingly, tended to favor cultural studies that focused on member's meanings that were more subject to cultural management and managerial control. At the same time the "objective" ascription protected "functionalist" studies

from a thorough analysis of their hidden values and sources of subjectivity, as if they might be too objective—a preferred flaw—rather than too subjective—a flaw they would not understand. Similarly, the many critical theorists with strong suspicions of humanist philosophies suddenly found themselves either conceptualized as radical humanists or invisible (lost in some hole in paradigmatic space). The Frankfurt school's attack on the subjective domination in science all too often got lost in the radical humanist conception. My point is not that Burrell and Morgan and their followers were representationally wrong in the presentation of organization and organizational communication studies (for there are many representationally "right" schemes and surely the nearly 20 years since their work has led to many changes), but their conceptions continue to foster less interesting and productive conflicts and developments than are possible. The processes of differentiation in mainstream functionalist sociology must be abandoned before more challenging differentiations are possible and alternative research programs can be given a full complementary role.

By focusing on the constitutive moves of discourse in organizational research and organizational practice rather than in psychological, sociological, or economic theories of organizational behavior, more interesting differences can be displayed. In my development below, I will privilege programmatic differentiations rooted in what I will develop as a "dialogic" perspective. What Burrell and Morgan called "functionalist" research will thus be implicitly represented as an "other." In doing so, both the lines of division and the arguments that extend from this can be redrawn. "Functionalist" style work can be reclaimed as legitimate and useful (though neither cumulative or "true") in specifiable ways as reunderstood from dialogic conceptions. Nondialogic research programs will not be seen as alternative routes to truth, but as specific discourses that specify and provide answers to specific types of problems. By setting

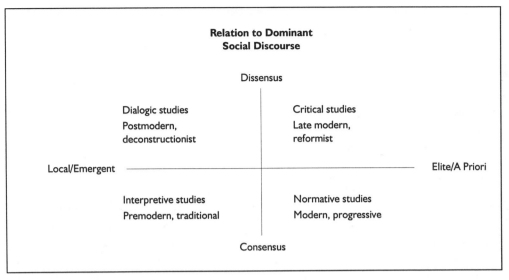

Figure 1.1. Contrasting Dimensions From the Metatheory of Representational Practices
SOURCE: Adapted from Deetz (1994d).

aside typical research claims of universality and/or certainty, different research traditions can provide productively complementary and conflictual insights into organizational life. The test of my suggested differentiations is not whether they provide a better map, but whether they provide an interesting (or what Rorty, 1989, developed as "edifying") way to talk about what is happening in research programs.

ALTERNATIVES FROM A COMMUNICATION PERSPECTIVE[2]

A more contemporary look at alternative communication research programs can be gained by locating research differences in what was conceptualized earlier as "discourses"—that is, the linguistic systems of distinction, the values enacted in those distinctions, the orientations to conflict and relations to other groups. Two dimensions of contrast will be developed here. Later in the essay, four prototypical discourses or research approaches—*normative, interpretive,*

critical, and *dialogic*—will be developed from these conceptions. See Figure 1.1.

First, differences among research orientations can be shown by contrasting "local/ emergent" research conceptions with "elite/a priori" ones. This dimension focuses on the origin of concepts and problem statements as part of the constitutive process in research.

Second, research orientations can be contrasted in the extent to which they work within a dominant set of structurings of knowledge, social relations, and identities (a reproductive practice), called here "consensus" discourse, and the extent to which they work to disrupt these structurings (a productive practice), called here "dissensus" discourse. This dimension focuses on the relation of research practices to the dominant social discourses within the organization studied, the research community, and/or wider community. I see these dimensions as analytic ideal types in Weber's sense mapping out two distinct continua. While categories of research programs are derivatively produced by the dimensions, the intent here is to aid attention to meaningful differences and similarities among different research activities rather than classification.

TABLE 1.1 Characterizations of the Local/Emergent–Elite/A Priori Dimension

Local/Emergent	Elite/A Priori
Comparative communities	Privileged community
Multiple language games	Fixed language game
Particularistic	Universalistic
Systematic philosophy as ethnocentric	Grounded in hoped for systematic philosophy
Atheoretical	Theory driven
Situationally or structural determinism	Methodological determinism
Nonfoundational	Foundational
Local narratives	Grand narrative of progress and emancipation
Sensuality and meaning as central concerns	Rationality and truth as central concerns
Situated, practical knowledge	Generalizable, theoretical knowledge
Tends to be feminine in attitude	Tends to be masculine in attitude
Sees the strange	Sees the familiar
Proceeds from the other	Proceeds from the self
Ontology of "otherness" over method	Epistemological and procedural issues rule over substantive assumptions

The Local/Emergent– Elite/A Priori Dimension

The key questions this dimension addresses are, where and how do research concepts arise, and thus, implicitly *whose* conceptions are used? In the two extremes, either concepts are developed in relation with organizational members and transformed in the research process or they are brought to the research "interaction" by the researcher and held static through the research process—concepts can be developed *with* or applied *to* the organizational members and activities being studied. This dimension can be characterized by a set of paired conceptions that flesh out contrasts embedded in the two poles. Table 1.1 presents an array of these contrasts. The choice of and stability of the language system are of central importance since the linguistic/conceptual system directs the statement of problems, the observational process itself in producing objects and highlighting and hiding potential experiences, the type of claims made, the report to external groups, and the

likely generalizations (whether appropriate or not) readers will make.

The local/emergent pole draws attention to researchers who work with an open language system and produce a form of knowledge characterized more by insight into empirical events than large-scale empirical generalizations. Central to their work is the situated nature of the research enterprise. Problem statements, the researcher's attention, and descriptions are worked out as a play between communities. The theoretical vocabulary carried into the research activity is often considered by the researcher as sensitizing or a guide to getting started constantly open to new meanings, translations, and redifferentiation based on interactions in the research process. Produced insights into organization processes may be particularistic regarding both time and place even though the emerging analytic frame is designed to aid in the deeper understanding of other particular settings. Cumulative understanding happens in providing stories or accounts that may provide insight into other sites rather than cumulative universal aspiring claims. The research attends to the feelings, intuitions, and multiple forms of rationality of both the researched and researcher rather than using a single logic of objectification or purified rationality. The study is guided more by concept formation than concept application. Distantiation and the "otherness" of the other (the way people and events exceed categories and classifications of them) are sought by the researcher to force reconception and linguistic change. This is considered more valuable than the identification and naming of preconceived traits, attributes, or groupings. Objectivity, to the extent that it is considered at all, arises out of the interplay and the constant ability of the researched to object and correct. The researcher is more a skilled collaborator in knowledge production than an expert observer.

The elite/a priori pole draws attention to the tendency in some types of research programs to privilege the particular language system of the researcher and the expertise of the research community as well as hold that language system constant throughout the research process. Such research tends to be heavily theory driven with careful attention to definitions prior to the research process. The experiences of the researched become coded into the researcher's language system. Demands of consistency and/or reliability require changes in the conceptual system to take place outside of rather than in the research process.

Whether intentional or not, the conceptual system of the researcher is considered better or more clearly represents what "really" is the case than that of everyday people and seeks generality beyond the various local systems of meaning. In privileging a language system, there is further a tendency to universalize and justify such moves by appeals to foundations or essentialist assumptions. Research claims, thus, are seen as freed from their local and temporal conditions of production. In most cases, these research approaches follow an enlightenment hope for producing rational knowledge not constrained by tradition or particular belief systems of the researcher or researched. The produced knowledge is treated as progressive or reformist in conception leading to increased capacities or well-being. The more "normative" versions openly proclaim "objectivity" and value neutrality based on the shared-language game and research methods, and tend to overlook the positions of their own community or alliances with other groups. The more "critical" versions quickly note the presence of values and distortions in normative work, and hold out the hope for a better, purer form of knowledge based in processes that include more interests and means of analysis in the work.

Focusing on the origin of concepts and problems using a dimension of "local/emergent–elite/a priori" allows three important gains. First, it acknowledges linguistic/social constructionism in all research positions and directs attention to whose concepts are used in object production and determination of what is problematic (see Deetz, 1973). Second, the focus on the origin of concepts helps distinguish fundamentally different kinds of knowledge. Elite/a priori conceptions lead more to the development of "theoretical codified" knowledge, a kind of "book" knowledge or "knowing about." Local/emergent conceptions lead more to the development of "practical" knowledge, a kind of "street wisdom" or a "knowing how." Third, this dimension helps us remember that both the application and discovery of concepts can demonstrate implicit or explicit political alliances with different groups in the organization or larger society. For example, to the extent that organizational researchers' concepts align with managerial conceptions and problem statements and are applied a priori in studies, the knowledge claims are intrinsically biased toward these interests as they are applied within the site community (Mumby, 1988). The knowledge claims become part of the same processes that are being studied, reproducing worldviews and personal identities and fostering particular interests within the organization (see Knights, 1992).

TABLE 1.2 Characterizations of the Consensus-Dissensus Dimension

Consensus	Dissensus
Trust	Suspicion
Hegemonic order as natural state	Conflicts over order as natural state
Naturalization of present	Present order is historicized and politicized
Integration and harmony are possible	Order indicates domination and suppressed conflicts
Research focuses on representation	Research focuses on challenge and reconsideration (representation)
Mirror (reflecting) dominant metaphor	Lens (seeing/reading as) dominant metaphor
Validity central concern	Insight and praxis central concern
Theory as abstraction	Theory as way of seeing
Unified science and triangulation	Positional complementarity
Science is neutral	Science is political
Life is discovery	Life is struggle and creation
Researcher anonymous and out of time and space	Researcher named and positioned
Autonomous/free agent	Historically/socially situated agent

The Consensus–Dissensus Dimension

The "consensus–dissensus" dimension draws attention to the relation of research to existing social orders. Consensus or dissensus should not be understood as agreement and disagreement but rather as presentation of unity or of difference, the continuation or disruption of any prevailing discourse. See Table 1.2 for conceptualization of this dimension. This dimension is similar to Burrell and Morgan's use of the traditional sociological distinction between an interest in "change" and "regulation," but enables some advantages. Rather than being class based, contemporary concerns with conflict and power focus on the ways predominant discourses (though often disorganized and disjunct) place limitations on people in general including managers and limit the successful functioning of organizations in meeting human needs. The focus is more on the suppression of diverse values and the presence of destructive control processes than on conflict among groups. The processes of domination today are less often seen as

macrosociological and more often seen as arising in normative or unobtrusive controls (see Barker, 1993; Etzioni, 1961; Tompkins & Cheney, 1985) and instantiated as routine micropractices in the work site itself (Ashcraft & Pacanowsky, 1996; Deetz, 1994b, 1994c, 1998; Knights & Willmott, 1989). The focus on discursive rather than group relations aids the understanding of domination and the various ways important organizational stakeholders are left out of discussions as well as the ways such forms of decisional skewing are reproduced.

The consensus pole draws attention to the way some research programs both seek order and treat order production as the dominant feature of natural and social systems. With such a conception, the primary goal of the research is to display a discovered order with a high degree of fidelity or verisimilitude. The descriptions hope to "mirror" entities and relations that exist out there in a relatively fixed state reflecting their "real" character. In the "normative" version this reality is treated like the natural world while in "interpretive" work it is a social world. Language is treated as a system of representations, to be neutralized and made transparent, used only to display the presumed shared world. Existing orders are largely treated as natural and unproblematic. To a large extent through the highlighting of ordering principles, such orders are perpetuated. Random events and deviance are downplayed in significance in looking at norms and the normal, and attention is usually to processes reducing deviance, uncertainty, and dissonance. In most cases where deviance is itself of attention, it tends to be normalized through looking at the production of deviant groups (i.e., other orders). Conflict and fragmentation are usually treated as system problems and attention is given to how orders deal with them in attempts at maintenance.

The dissensus pole draws attention to research programs that consider struggle, conflict, and tensions to be the natural state. Research itself is seen as inevitably a move in a conflictual site. The existing orders indicate the suppression of basic conflicts and along with that the domination of people and their full variety of interests. Research aims at challenging mechanisms of order maintenance to reclaim conflicts and tension. The nonnormative aspects of human conduct and extraordinary responses are emphasized along with the importance of largely random and chance events. Rather than language naming and describing, researcher conceptions are seen as striking a difference, de- and redifferentiating experience (Cooper, 1989; Cooper & Burrell, 1988; Deetz, 1992; Martin, 1990; Weedon, 1987). The "mirror" gives way to the "lens" as the dominant metaphor for language and theory noting the shifting analytic attempt to see what could not be seen before and showing the researcher as positioned and active (Deetz, 1992, chap. 3; Rorty, 1979). For dissensus style research, the generative capacity (the ability to challenge guiding assumptions, values, social practices, and routines) of an observation is more important than representational validity (see Gergen, 1978). The research is, in Knights's (1992) sense, "antipositive." Dissensus work does not deny

the significance of an ordered observed world, rather it takes it as a powerful (power filled) product and works to break reifications and objectifications to show fuller potential and variety than is immediately apparent. For example, consensus orientations in cultural studies seek to discover the organizational culture or cultures. Dissensus orientations show the fragmentation inherent in any claim of culture and the work required for site subjects to maintain coherence in the face of this as well as subjects' own forms of resistance (see Calás & Smircich, 1991; Holmer-Nadesan, 1996; Martin, 1990, 1992; Smircich & Calás, 1987; Trethewey, 1997). Consensus orientations apply role and identity classifications and relate them to other variables; dissensus orientations see identity as multiple, conflictual, and in process.

While these differences can be characterized clearly in abstraction, in continuous time every consensus arises out of and falls to dissensus, and every dissensus gives away to emerging (if temporary) consensus. The issue is not the ultimate outcome desired nor likely but rather which part of this flow through time is claimed in the research process. For example, while critical theorists clearly seek a social consensus that is more rational, their research tries to produce this through the creation of dissensus in place of dominant orders. For example, ideological critique in the critical theory conception of the negative dialectic is to reclaim conflict and destroy a false order rather than produce a new one. Thus, I place them on the dissensus end. Critical theories differ from many dialogic or "postmodern" positions in the production of dissensus. In critical theories, dissensus is produced by the use of elite understandings and procedures (as in Habermas, 1984, 1987; Kunda, 1992; Mumby, 1987; or several essays in Alvesson & Willmott, 1992). While in dialogic research, deconstructive processes are used to unmask elite conceptions thereby allowing organizational activities to be given new, multiple, and conflicting descriptions (Calás & Smircich, 1991; Kilduff, 1993; Laclau &

Mouffe, 1985; Linstead, 1993; Martin, 1990). The dialogic outcome requires a constant dedifferentiation and redifferentiation for the sake of demythologizing and enriching natural language and consequently opening to reconsideration the most basic and certain experiences of everyday work life.

PARADIGMS LOST, ORIENTATIONS STILL

The grid produced from these two dimensions provides a spatially and visually convenient, discursive four-space solution (hence we should always be easily reminded of its arbitrary and fictive character). I will describe these as different discourses to note a way of articulating arguments and engaging in research practices rather than a means of reconstructive self-naming. Each discourse provides an orientation to organizations, a way of constituting people and events in them, and a way of reporting on them. I hope that this also leads us to think about which discourse is being used or how it is joined with others rather than pigeonholing specific authors. Table 1.3 provides sketchy prototypical descriptions of each research orientation related to a dozen dimensions of interest shaping organizational communication research programs.

Calling these discourses "paradigms" would be a mistake for several reasons. First, each of these four discourses, which are provisionally held apart for viewing, is filled with internal conflict and strife—including theory debates, moments of incommensurability, dilettantes, and tyrants. Second, the edges are not demarcated. Most researchers and teachers do not cluster around a prototype of each, but gather at the crossroads, mix metaphors, and borrow lines from other discourses, dodging criticism by co-optation. Often practicing researchers happily move from one discourse to another without accounting for their own location. They operate like other organizational members borrowing on discourses that

suit their immediate purposes and the fashions of the moment (see Deetz, 1994b). There are certainly more and less serious plays across the lines, but the issue is not crossing but the seriousness of the play. Third, the discourses are not themselves sealed off from each other. They pose problems for each other and steal insights across the lines. For example, the philosophical fights between Habermas and Gadamer, Habermas and Lyotard, Habermas and Luhmann, and Foucault and everybody have left their traces in each one's work. From these struggles, the various organizational communication research programs based in these works have gained enriched conceptions of power, knowledge, agency, and political action (see, e.g., Mumby & Putnam, 1992).

Provisional ordering of discourses is not to police the lines, but to provide a view of the social resources from which researchers draw and an understanding of the stock arguments used in developing and justifying research activities and claims. The ideal types aid the understanding of differences that matter that are hard to see in the flow of research activity. Clarifying the tendencies in specific types of research positions helps clarify debates and the relation of different groups to them. For example, the interpretive, critical, and dialogic critiques of normative research are quite different. Normative researchers who are accustomed to making arguments against subjectivity and traditionalism simply miss the point of each of these critiques; they often reduce them to abstract and confused presentations of what they think "opponents" should be saying rather than concrete but different arguments from what they expected.

Further, while most researchers are not purists, their work carries assumptions and responsibilities that are central to understanding and evaluating their work, but are rarely explicit in study reports. For example, many feminists' writings carry a general sympathy with the conceptual and analytic power of *dialogic* research programs, while they still wish to have a political agenda that requires *critical* preconceptions that assume social di-

TABLE 1.3 Prototypical Discursive Features

Issue	Discourse			
	Normative	*Interpretive*	*Critical*	*Dialogic*
Basic goal	Lawlike relations among objects	Display unified culture	Unmask domination	Reclaim conflict
Method	Nomothetic science	Hermeneutics, ethnography	Cultural criticism, ideology critique	Deconstruction, genealogy
Hope	Progressive emancipation	Recovery of integrative values	Reformation of social order	Claim a space for lost voices
Metaphor of social relations	Economic	Social	Political	Mass
Organization metaphor	Marketplace	Community	Polity	Carnival
Problems addressed	Inefficiency, disorder	Meaninglessness, illegitimacy	Domination, consent	Marginalization, conflict suppression
Concern with communication	Fidelity, influence, information needs	Social acculturation, group affirmation	Misrecognition, systematic distortion	Discursive closure
Narrative style	Scientific/technical, strategic	Romantic, embracing	Therapeutic, directive	Ironic, ambivalent
Time identity	Modern	Premodern	Late modern	Postmodern
Organizational benefits	Control, expertise	Commitment, quality work life	Participation, expanded knowledge	Diversity, creativity
Mood	Optimistic	Friendly	Suspicious	Playful
Social fear	Disorder	Depersonalization	Authority	Totalization, normalization

visions and gender-based domination to be general (see Flax, 1990; Fraser & Nicholson, 1988; Mumby, 1996). Such works (e.g., Martin, 1990, 1992) can be classified as dialogic, but the ethical and political character of many of these studies cannot be justified easily with dialogic conceptions alone. The distinctions developed in this essay can help display the tensions and the resources from which such researchers draw to conduct and justify their work.

This can further be shown using my own work as an example. I often draw on conceptions from critical and dialogic writings. For me, critical theory conceptions of ideology and distorted communication provide useful sensitizing concepts and an analytic framework for looking for micropractices of unwarranted control, discursive closure, ideology, and skewed representation in organizational sites. But rarely are these conceptions closely tied to the full critical theory agenda. They require considerable reworking in specific sites, and the results of my studies aim more at finding and giving suppressed positions a means of expression than realizing an ideal speech situation or reaching a purer consensus (see Deetz, 1995b, 1998). What is important is not whether I am a late-modern critical theorist or a dialogic postmodernist, but rather the meaning and implications of concepts that I draw from these two competitive research orientations. My degree of consistency is of less interest than how I handle the tension and whether the two conceptual resources provide an interesting analysis or intervention. Some clarity and general understanding in alternative research orientations provide guidance and accountability or at least a common stock of material for building and evaluating new arguments in these cases. Further, exploring general orientations can help reveal assumptions hidden in one's own way of working since they remain unproblematic in one's own research community.

In an ideal research program, we might identify a complementary relation among research orientations with each asking different questions at different moments and each, at the appropriate moment, answering to the specific criteria of a particular orientation. This might operate in a rotation among incompatible orientations without any orientation being privileged or any orientation being reduced to a preliminary or supplementary role. For example, my work relies much on a conception of discursive closure, a conception that draws attention to places where cooperative decision making is hampered by arbitrary limits enacted in the discussion (see Deetz, 1992, pp. 187ff.). As a *critical* researcher I must show how these closures are intrusions of power relations usually based in or supporting social divisions that lead to distorted communication and a false consensus. My study appeals to reason, logical analyses, and a coherent demonstration. As a *dialogic* researcher I see these closures as the suppression of conflicts and see my own concerns with consensus and appeals to reason as simply different acts of privilege and potential closure. My analysis is now judged by the way indeterminacy is allowed to reemerge and the compelling quality of recovered claims and voices. But at another moment yet, I may well pose *normative* questions: Which means of closure are used most often? Who uses them? When are they used? Can people be taught to avoid them? A study designed to answer such questions now appeals to standards of definition, measurement, sampling, and quantitative data analysis. And further yet, there are *interpretive* concerns: What sense do these discursive moves have in a community? To what ends are they used? How are they self-understood and justified? What are their actual consequences in specific circumstances? Interpretive research standards are now relevant.

One can easily see how such a rotation through orientations might be constant and productive without losing the separation and tension among them. Such tensions could help enrich work from each orientation. Yet, to be honest, few research programs are treated this way and most researchers, like myself, follow their own lines of interest, commitments, and training, which either leads to an eclipse of questions and concerns from other orientations or at least leaves them for someone else who is interested in those problems. Taking seriously other works does not mean that we find other groups' issues and procedures as necessarily interesting or helpful nor should we naively believe that all of them are. But our claims and the relation between our claims and study procedures should be clear so that objections and conflicts can be on those grounds rather than on imposed traditional problem statements and methods. The point is for the researcher to be clear about what type of questions or claims drives the work at any particular time and how the work addresses the standards and criteria appropriate to it.

A basic understanding of alternative research orientations enables shorthand accounts and helps distinguish intentional and/or productive ambiguities from careless and/or unproductive ones. As a reviewer, I am often frustrated by nonreflective mixing of metaphors and conceptions in submitted essays. Often the claims made would require a different kind of study based on different assumptions and research activities. Partly, I think this arises from authors trying to anticipate reviewer needs for normative type generalizations while being committed to a nonnormative research orientation, but it also comes from inattention to what makes different kinds of research different. Clearly, a balance must be struck between (1) reifying research orientations through simplistic grids and subsequent overcharacterizations and rigid standards and (2) having each study try to be totally self-justifying and cut loose from any community. While I do not think there is any easy way out of this tension, having good dimensions of contrast and good characterizations helps. A very brief sketch of the four orientations aids further in highlighting differences and similarities in these community discourses along the suggested dimensions of difference.

The Discourse of Normative Studies

Normative research tends to accept organizations as naturally existing objects open to description, prediction, and control. Goals established by some specific group, usually upper management, are largely accepted as the goals of the organization and most often the research either implicitly or explicitly supports more efficient accomplishment of these goals. Because of this, commercial corporations are usually discussed in economic terms with issues discussed in relation to "rational" economic goals. The researchers producing this discourse have been described as functionalists, covering-law theorists, or simply practicing the variable analytic tradition. I describe this discourse as "normative" to emphasize the centrality of codification, the search for regularity and normalization, and the implied prescriptive claims (see Deetz, 1973; Hollway, 1984). This discourse is largely dominant in North America and in applied organizational research everywhere. Articles published by U.S. researchers employed by communication departments and published in "communication" journals have been mostly of this sort, though the mix is changing. Most textbooks are written in this discourse emphasizing topical divisions and research findings even when they review research established in other traditions.

The discourse is decisively modern in Gergen's (1992) sense and the knowledge is considered positive, cumulative, and progressive. A grand narrative of progressive emancipation from disease, disorder, and material deprivation is shaped by a commitment to make a better world through discovery of fundamental processes and increased production (Lyotard, 1984). While the organization is usually treated as an existing object produced for instrumental ends, usually making money, some conception of the invisible hand makes that goal well-integrated with other social goals of development and widespread availability of goods and services. Generally, the research is expressly apolitical and value neutral, but as already shown, values reside in elite conceptions, choice of problems to study, and relation to other groups.

Most of this work has implicitly supported an orderly, well-integrated world, with compliant members and regulated conflicts, and has accepted without examination existing organizational goals and member positions. They represent communication primarily in information and administration terms (see Beniger, 1986). Much of the discussion of communication in "information" terms assumes a control orientation and theories of persuasion and information transfer dominate much of the concern with most frequently studied topics such as supervisor/subordinate communication, compliance gaining, networks, power, and relations with the public. Normative works appear in three basic varieties each with distinct assumptions and goals of their own—covering laws, systems theory, and skill development.

Covering Laws

Research modeled on the search for lawlike generalizations in organizations until fairly recently has dominated organizational communication study. Research of this type was most explicitly defended in communication studies by Berger (1977) and reconstructed and well justified in Donaldson (1985; see also Barley & Kunda, 1992; DiMaggio, 1995; O'Keefe, 1976). The research practices mirror 19th-century conceptions of the natural sciences often involving the most recent advances in operationalization, hypothesization, statistical data reduction, and pattern "recognition" processes. Conceptions of operationalization, "objectivity," and lawlike relations are merely the most obvious form of practice. Conventional practices and methodological ("as if") determinism have in most cases replaced any strong allegiance to the positivist philosophy of science that grounds many of the methods and assumptions.

The "objects" constructed by the practices of this science are given qualities of constancy and permanence (universal across time and place), as if nature endowed them with specific attributes. The combination of a priori conceptions and the focus on consensus leads the artifacts of these research practices to be described as facts. This discourse typifies the development of many data retrieval systems and information technologies since information can be treated as fixed truth claims freed from the time, place, and procedures of production. Facts become commodities and communication can be reduced to a transmission/retrieval process (for discussion of consequences, see Boland, 1987; Coombs, Knights, & Willmott, 1992; Lyytinen & Hirschheim, 1988).

Theory and theory testing are central to the logic of the research and many of the statistical procedures of data reduction. Normative studies of this type are explicitly dependent on theory, though in practice the theoretical concerns may be reduced to a mere reference list of prior studies and theory testing to merely adding to a list of relations among variables of interest. One characteristic self-criticism is the lament over the lack of development or use of theory. Most of the studies work *as if* they were in a deductive theory testing mode even when their theoretical commitments are less than clear. Recently, Sutton and Staw (1995) demonstrated how references, data, variables, diagrams, and hypotheses are often used to cover up the lack of theory and actual theory testing.

This discourse is exemplified in studies of compliance gaining (e.g., Sullivan & Taylor, 1991), strategic message design and persuasion (e.g., Alexander, Penley, & Jernigan, 1991), supervision/subordinate interaction (Infante, Anderson, Martin, Herington, & Kim, 1993; Jablin, 1979; Sias & Jablin, 1995), and other places more completely described by Burrell and Morgan (1979) in their discussion of "functionalist." But it is also clearly present in those advocating the management of culture (e.g., Deal & Kennedy, 1982; Schein, 1992) through their conception of culture as an object to be strategically deployed (as Barley, Meyer, & Gash, 1988, have shown, this became very common in the 1980s). Most of the work on culture, climate, or varieties of total quality management (TQM) in organizational communication are more normative than interpretive owing to the way culture is treated as a variable or objective outcome within a larger strategic move of cultural management (see Shockley-Zalabak & Morley, 1994). Many of those working with new conceptions of organizations as "postmodern" (rather than post-modern approaches; Parker, 1992) have a discourse primarily structured in a normative fashion (e.g., Bergquist, 1993; Peters, 1987). Many Marxist studies, especially those done in contexts of Marxist domination of social discourse, use normative themes, but the elite group that gives rise to the concepts differs from those supporting most European and North American studies. Lenin's embracing of scientific management was in no way inconsistent. Strategic management in virtually every way is highly dependent on this discourse (Knights, 1992; Knights

& Morgan, 1991). Often team, quality, and participation programs are assessed using research procedures grounded in this perspective (e.g., Gordon, Infante, & Graham, 1988; Miller & Monge, 1985).

Studying communication in the organizational context poses some unique problems for this approach. The complexity and interdependence of organizational relationships challenge the rather atomistic and unidirectional models of both the theories and methods. And such relations are hard to duplicate in laboratory settings and control for numerous "extraneous" factors. Researchers have responded to this with much more sophisticated modeling and statistical analysis. Unfortunately, the outcomes of this are fairly abstract relations that lead to questions of validity and usefulness. Further, much of the research has turned to data collection from self-report interviews and survey questionnaires rather than direct observation (see Knapp, Putnam, & Davis, 1988). This has led to a preoccupation with measurement devices and with many studies that are more instrument than theory driven leaving the results difficult to understand or use in any systematic way.

Finally, most researchers conduct such studies primarily for generalization and use statistical significance tests, which allow generalization from the research sample to some population. But the question is often raised as to what is the appropriate "population" for the generalization. Many of the studies draw a sample from a single organization; presumably, this would indicate that this particular organization is the population about which the generalization is proposed. But most researchers want to generalize their findings to organizations in general. There the sample/population relation does not hold. Rarely has any program of work drawn a sample of enough organizations to warrant the type of generalizations made allowable within the assumptions of the studies themselves. Perhaps the Aston studies and the "communication audit" sponsored by the International Communi-

cation Association modeled after the Aston studies are partly used exceptions. The important point is that many normative style studies use the rhetorical power of the natural science model and principles of generalization and verification, but often cannot support their studies in organizations based on it. The discourse often conceals this (see Sutton & Staw, 1995). Many attempts have been made to summarize findings across studies, often using meta-analysis. Such studies are often contradictory and inconclusive and even further remove findings from theoretical commitments and specific site characteristics (see Baker, 1991; Miller & Monge, 1985; Wagner & Gooding, 1987; Wilkins & Anderson, 1991).

Systems Theory

During 1970s and 1980s, much theoretical attention was given to developing "systems" thinking in organizations, especially regarding the organization-environment relation spawned in part by the influence of Lawrence and Lorsch's (1967) work and the development of contingency theory (see Katz & Kahn, 1978; Monge, 1977, 1982; Monge, Farace, Eisenberg, Miller, & White, 1984). More recently, this work has become theoretically more sophisticated through conceptions of self-organizing systems and chaos theory (see Bellman & Roosta, 1987; Contractor, 1994; Senge, 1990; Weick, 1979).

While systems approaches continue the search for order and regularity and ultimately increased control by advantaged groups, they tend to emphasize holism over atomism and dynamic mutual causality over lawlike unidirectional causality. Rather than seeking surface-level, predictive variables the focus is on the deep processes of transformation that produce and interpret overt patterns of behavior—the processes of organizing rather than organizations. As Pettigrew (1990) described: "What is critical is not just events, but the underlying logics that give events meaning and significance . . . logics which may explain how and why these patterns occur in particular chronological sequence" (p. 273). In some cases, in Weick's work, for example, the focus is so strongly on emergent properties, the particular setting, and interpretive processes that the research begins to sound much like *interpretive* studies (see Daft & Weick, 1984). But still, the work is heavily guided by researcher conceptions, the search for regularities anticipated by the researcher, the interpretation of patterns in the researcher's logic, the view from the outside, the hope for enduring regularities, and the assumption of managerial goals. The assumptions and regularities sought differ, however, from those sought by covering laws and even early systems theories.

Contractor (1994) has done an excellent job of making these differences clear. Five conceptions are important.

1. Dynamic inferences: Covering-law theorists develop hypotheses that posit a direct or indirect casual link between variables. These can be tested using rather standard statistical packages (SPSS). Dynamic hypotheses, however, posit an underlying logic or relational mathematical rather than quantitative connection. Similar hypotheses developed by covering-law and systems theorists are the same only when one of two central covering-law assumptions are empirically present (or methodologically produced): (a) There is no change in the two variables over time, or (b) the change is exactly equal.

2. Mutual causality: While covering-law theories posit unidirectional causality, systems theory suggests that many variables exist in mutual or circular causal relations. In such cases, there can be no separation between independent and dependent variables since the casual relation between the variables runs both ways.

3. Historicity: Systems theory suggests that the relation between variables is often time dependent, hence universalizing claims or even generalizations cannot be assumed across time and place. Thus, variable relations (e.g., between trust and compliance) present early in the history of an organiza-

tion can become quite different as the organization ages. A generalization about organizational communication must always reference the time in the organization's history during which it was true.

4. Time irreversibility: Most covering-law models assume that social systems work like closed mechanical systems, hence if an increase in the quantity of a variable leads to an expected outcome then decreasing the quality of that variable will lead to less outcome. Rarely, however, are organizational relations simply transitive or stable like this.

5. Discontinuity: Covering-law theories assume that changes are usually quantitative and incremental. Systems theorists display the presence of sudden qualitative changes at certain thresholds.

Systems conceptions have clearly changed the way people and scholars think about organizations. Much theoretical writing is present. But generally, the empirical research has been more disappointing. Part of this arises from the dominance covering-law conceptions have had on defining the nature of "empirical" research. Frequently, process conceptions in systems theory are reduced to conceptions where covering-law data gathering and statistical analysis are applicable (see Everett, 1994; Monge, Cozzens, & Contractor, 1992). In many respects, systems conceptions are more productive in providing interesting and useful conceptions of complex organizational processes and interventions into them than they are in generating studies that result in journal publications (see Cecchin & Stratton, 1991). The conception of useful empirical work may well be biased in favor of covering-law style studies.

Communication Skills

The normative orientation not only guides much organizational communication research but also teaching and consulting activities. Arguably, much of the work going on under the title "organizational communication" is more skill development than research directed. Included is everything from interpersonal and basic management skills to public speaking and public relation skills. While it is not my intent to provide any review of this work, I think that it is important to show how textbooks as well as training and development programs have traditionally been connected with the normative approach to organization studies.

In most cases, the implied pedagogy in the writings has been didactic and reliant on the presumption of an expert body of knowledge. And most of the research on skills has used covering-law style assumptions to test hypotheses and measure effectiveness. Further, while there is a directive quality to this work, the skills and the knowledge base from which they are drawn are usually treated as value neutral and as equally available and valuable for different organizational members. In doing so, the influence and control orientation of this work are treated as natural and self-evident, and other human goals and communication purposes are rarely considered. Usually, upper management's goals for the organization are accepted as given and legitimate. Even when the skills are promoted primarily for self-interests, generally those interests are seen as well integrated with upper management's organizational goals. Recently, as teams, stakeholder participation, and organizational creativity and learning have become of greater concern there is increasingly critical attention to understanding skill needs culturally, to the power relations in teaching and textbooks, and to the needs and perspectives of alternative organizational stakeholders (Argyris, 1994; Eisenberg & Goodall, 1993; Grunig & Hunt, 1984; Sprague, 1992).

The Discourse of Interpretive Studies

The number and importance of interpretive studies grew rapidly during the 1980s. For most interpretive researchers, the organization is a social site, a special type of community that shares important characteristics with other types of communities. The emphasis is on a social rather than economic view of organizational activities. Traditional methods of studying communities are seen as especially useful. The expressed goal of many interpretive studies is to show how particular realities are socially produced and maintained through ordinary talk, stories, rites, rituals, and other daily activities. Most of the early attention for organizational communication researchers was derived from interest in the work of anthropologists such as Geertz (1973; see Pacanowsky & O'Donnell-Trujillo, 1982), phenomenological and symbolic interactionist-inspired work in sociology (Bantz, 1983; Bormann, 1983; Douglas, 1970; Strauss, 1978), and the growing interest in hermeneutics and qualitative research methods (Trujillo, 1987).

While theoretical tensions and competitive traditions have grown along with this work, like these sources, much of the writings have a clear preservationist, naturalistic tone. Allow me to start with the more "naturalistic" assumptions held by interpretive researchers in their studies of organizational culture before turning to some of the tensions that have developed. Like many of the more naturalistic anthropological studies, interpretive research often appears motivated to save or record a life form with its complexity and creativity before it is lost to modern, instrumental life. The concern with community is often connected with the maintenance of a traditional sense of shared values and common practices and the presumed simple harmonious inner life of people who lived in such communities. Gergen (1992) described the romantic sense of this discourse with its depth and connection to the inner life bordering on sentimentality at times. Because of this I refer to the time frame as premodern in Table 1.3. This suggests more a concern with those aspects of life that have not yet been systematized, instrumentalized, and brought under the control of modernism logics and sciences than a focus on the past.

Cultural studies in organizations are interpretive to the extent that they have not been captured by normative, modernist cooptations. Most interpretivists have taken culture to be an evocative metaphor for organizational life rather than a variable or thing that an organization has (Frost, Moore, Louis, Lundberg, & Martin, 1985, 1992; Smircich, 1983). Culture draws attention to what organizational members must know, believe, or be able to do in order to operate in a manner that is understandable and acceptable to other members and the means by which this knowledge, belief, and action routines are produced and reproduced. The interest in communication processes is far richer than that of meaning transmission present in normative work. Communication is considered to be a central means by which the meaning of organizational events is produced and sustained (Donnellon, Gray, & Bougon, 1986).

The basic function of interpretive work is "to translate the interests and concerns of one people into the interests and concerns of another" (Putnam, Bantz, Deetz, Mumby, & Van Maanen, 1993). The needs of translation require both a careful understanding of the other and an ability to present that understanding to one's own culture. A double hermeneutic (an interpretation of an interpreted world) and complex communicative process (metacommunication to the culturally different) is thus central to interpretive work and largely accounts for the situated and emergent nature of the understanding present in its texts (Barley, 1990).

The interpretive researcher often engages in some type of participant observation or other personal contact to collect material and work out understanding with the site community. Studies are usually done in the field and are based on a prolonged period of observation and/or depth interviewing. The interest is in the full person in the organization, thus social and life functions beyond the relation to the job are considered. The goals are much more open and emergent than in normative

work and much less connected to issues of efficiency and productivity. The workplace is seen as a site of human activity, one of those activities being "work" proper. The organization of the entire social community is of interest. While some writing might be somewhat impressionistic and focus on the surface feelings and meanings of either the cultural member or the researcher, generally, these would be considered weak and shallow studies. The point more often is to understand the social conditions of life giving rise to such feelings and meanings—the *deep* cultural read. Analytic attention is thus often directed to symbolism, metaphors, stories, jokes, advice and reason giving, narrative forms, rites and rituals, and the social functions of these activities (see, for examples and reviews, Brown, 1985; Browning, 1992; Goodall, 1990; Knuf, 1993; Smith & Eisenberg, 1987; Trujillo, 1987).

Interpretive studies accept much of the representational and consensual view of science seen in normative writings, but shift the relation between theoretical conceptions and the talk of the subjects under study. People are not considered to be objects like other objects, but are active sense makers like the researcher. Theory is given a far weaker role here. While theory may provide important sensitizing conceptions, it not a device of classification or tested in any simple and direct manner. The key conceptions and understandings must be worked out with the subjects under study. Research subjects can collaborate in displaying key features of their world. But like normative research, the pressure is to get it right, to display unified, consensual culture in the way that it "actually" exists. The report is to display convincingly a unified way of life with all its complexities and contradictions (Goodall, 1990; Pacanowsky & O'Donnell-Trujillo, 1982; Van Maanen, 1988). In DiMaggio's (1995) conceptions, theory in interpretive work is often a narrative account of social processes "with emphasis on empirical tests of the plausibility of the narrative as well as careful attention to the scope of the account" (p. 391).

One gets a sense in tracking this work over time that it is becoming less productive in itself and more treated as a supplement to other kinds of work. Barley et al. (1988) represented well how the early naturalistic and anthropological interest in organizational cultures gradually was eclipsed by a managerial interest in managing culture. Hence, much of the discussion of culture has been reduced to "cultural variables," and the studies became more normative and like the climate studies that preceded them. Data collection techniques and conceptions emergent in the field have been borrowed and then accepted a priori in coding and counting studies, for example, those correlating cultural characteristics with productivity measure or adaptation to change (e.g., Bastien, 1992; Fairhurst, 1993). And critical researchers often reinterpret interpretive studies adding critiques of meaning formations (Martin, 1992; Mumby, 1987). Still, interpretive work is an active and viable research orientation as it continues to evolve. A number of research approaches have been used to help sort out hidden meanings, often hidden as well from the site community participants owing to surface familiarity, and to organize the research process and the presentation of the study itself.

This essay will make no attempt to sort out the diverse ways that interpretive researchers have collected, analyzed, and reported the observations on which their work is based. Ethnography and similar conceptions of "naturalistic" inquiry already discussed remain the purest form of interpretive work. Specific site studies have been analyzed focusing on metaphors, symbols, and themes (Pacanowsky & O'Donnell-Trujillo, 1982; Smith & Eisenberg, 1987; Smith & Turner, 1995; Trujillo, 1987). Other studies have followed other traditions including dramaturgy (Goodall, 1990; Manning, 1992), negotiated order (Geist, 1995), structuration (Bastien, McPhee, & Bolton, 1995; Poole & McPhee, 1983), and rules theory (Schall, 1983). During the past 15 to 20 years, a rich array of studies has been completed. Together these have displayed how organizational cultures develop and change, how social groups conceive and han-

dle conflict, how institutional structures are challenged and/or reinstated, how cultures differ across national settings and management practices, and so forth (see Pepper, 1995).

Interpretive studies are also still evolving. Gradually, many researchers doing interpretive work have began to question the logic of displaying a consensual unified culture and have attended more to its fragmentation, tensions, and processes of conflict suppression (Frost et al., 1992; Marcus & Fischer, 1986; Martin, 1992). In this sense the work has become more dialogic in character. And works following structuration theory have become more critical than interpretive in character (Banks & Riley, 1993; Howard & Geist, 1995; Riley, 1983).

Since the mid-1980s, much of the self-reflection in interpretive work has focused on the relation of the research to the site community and the "voice" taken in the research report. Of importance are both the politics of representation and the role of the report author (Clifford & Marcus, 1986; Conquergood, 1991; Kauffman, 1992). Van Maanen (1988) summarized these relations as alternative tales. Further with greater attention to the relation to the community and action potential in research, interpretive work has become more participatory (Whyte, 1991). Reason (1994) described different types of participatory inquiry. These changes have continued to move much interpretative work to be more dialogic and critical in its account of itself and the type of work done.

The Discourse of Critical Studies

Critical researchers see organizations in general as social historical creations accomplished in conditions of struggle and power relations. Organizations are largely described as political sites, thus general social theories and especially theories of decision making in the public sphere are seen as appropriate.

While organizations could be positive social institutions providing forums for the articulation and resolution of important group conflicts over the use of natural resources, distribution of income, production of desirable goods and services, the development of personal qualities, and the direction of society, various forms of power and domination have led to skewed decision making and fostered social harms and significant waste and inefficiency. Either explicit or implicit in their presentation is a goal to demonstrate and critique forms of domination, asymmetry, and distorted communication through showing how reality can become obscured and misrecognized. Such insights help produce forums where the conflicts can be reclaimed, openly discussed, and resolved with fairness and justice.

Critical research aims at producing dissensus and providing forums for and models of discussion to aid in the building of more open consensus. Of special concern are forms of false consciousness, consent, systematically distorted communication, routines, and normalizations that produce partial interests and keep people' from genuinely understanding or acting on their own interests. Of the four orientations, critical studies have the most explicitly stated value commitments and the most explicit attention to moral and ethical issues. With this, much of the discourse has a suspicious and therapeutic tone, but also a theory of agency that provides an activist tone, a sense that people can and should act on these conditions and that improved understanding as well as access to communication forums is core to positive action. Theory development in critical theory often has an "enlightenment" quality, in DiMaggio's (1995) sense, whereby euphemisms are developed or exposed "clearing away conventional notions to make room for artful and exciting insights" (p. 391; see also Bourdieu, 1991, for the power of renaming).

The central goal of critical theory in organizational communication studies has been to create a society and workplaces that are free from domination and where all members can contribute equally to produce systems that meet human needs and lead to the progressive development of all. Studies have focused both on the relation of organizations to the wider society and their possible social effects of colonization (rationalization of society) and domination or destruction of the public sphere (Deetz, 1992; DuGay, 1997), and on internal processes in terms of the domination by instrumental reasoning, discursive closures, and consent processes (e.g., Alvesson, 1993; Clair, 1993a, 1993b; Forester, 1989; Mumby, 1987, 1988). As indicated they tend to enter their studies with a priori theoretical commitments, which aid them analytically to ferret out situations of domination and distortion. Critical studies include a large group of researchers who are different in theory and conception but who share important discursive features in their writing. They include Frankfurt school critical theorists (see Alvesson & Willmott, 1992, 1996; Czarniawska-Joerges, 1988; Mumby, 1988), conflict theorists (Benson, 1977; Dahrendorf, 1959), some structurationists (Banks & Riley, 1993; Giddens, 1984, 1991; Howard & Geist, 1995), some versions of feminist work (e.g., Allen, 1996, 1998; Benhabib, 1992; Ferguson, 1984, 1994), some Burkeans (Barker & Cheney, 1994; Tompkins & Cheney, 1985), and most doing labor process theory (Braverman, 1974; Burawoy, 1979, 1985; Knights & Willmott, 1990).

Critical theorists sometimes have a clear political agenda focused on the interests of specific identifiable groups such as women, workers, or people of color, but usually address general issues of goals, values, forms of consciousness, and communicative distortions within corporations. Their interest in ideologies considers disadvantaged groups difficulties in understanding their own political interest, but is usually addressed to people in general, challenging consumerism, careerism, and exclusive concern with economic growth (Allen, 1998; DuGay, 1997). Compared to Marxism, critical theory is not antimanagement per se, even though one tends to treat management as institutionalized and ideologies and practices of management as expressions of contemporary forms of domination. Two principal types of critical studies can be identified in organization studies: Ideological critique and communicative action.

Ideology Critique

Most of the critical work has focused on ideology critique. Analyses of ideologies show how specific interests fail to be realized because of people's inability to understand or act on their own interests. Some identified ideologies are group specific and others are held by people in technological-capitalist society in general. Ideological critique is guided by a priori researcher conceptions and aims at producing dissensus with the hope that the recovered conflicts and explicit concern with values will enable people to choose more clearly in their own interests.

The earliest ideological critiques of the workplace were offered by Marx. In his analyses of work processes, he focused primarily on practices of economic exploitation through direct coercion and structural differences in work relations between the owners of capital and the owners of their own labor. However, Marx also describes the manner in which the exploitative relation is disguised and made to appear legitimate. This is the origin of ideology critique. Clearly, the themes of domination and exploitation by owners and later by managers have been central to ideology critique of the workplace in this century (see works as varied as Braverman, 1974; Clegg & Dunkerley, 1980; Edwards, 1979). These later analyses became less concerned with class-based coercion and economic explanations through focusing on why coercion was so rarely necessary and on how systemic processes produce active consent (e.g., Burawoy, 1979, 1985; Czarniawska-Joerges, 1988; Deetz & Mumby, 1990; Gramsci, 1929-1935/

1971; Kunda, 1992; Vallas, 1993). Ideology produced in the workplace would supplement ideology present in the media and the growth of the consumer culture and the welfare state as accounting for workers' and other stakeholders' failure to act on their own interests.

Four themes recur in the numerous and varied writings about organizations working from such a perspective: (1) concern with reification, or the way a socially/historically constructed world would be treated as necessary, natural, and self-evident; (2) the suppression of conflicting interests and universalization of managerial interest; (3) the eclipse of reason and domination by instrumental reasoning processes; and (4) the evidence of consent.

In *reification,* a social formation is abstracted from the ongoing conflictual site of its origin and treated as a concrete, relatively fixed entity. The illusion that organizations and their processes are "natural" objects protects them from examination as produced under specific historical conditions (which are potentially passing) and out of specific power relations. Ideological critique is enabled by the elite-driven search for reifications in everyday life. The resultant critique demonstrates the arbitrary nature of "natural objects" and the power relations that result and sustain these forms for the sake of producing dissensus and discovering the remaining places of possible choice.

Lukács (1971), among many others (see Giddens, 1979), has shown that particular sectional interests are often *universalized* and treated as if they were everyone's interests, thus producing a false consensus. In contemporary corporate practices, managerial groups are privileged in decision making and research. *The* interests of the corporation are frequently equated with management's interests. For example, worker, supplier, or host community interests can be interpreted in terms of their effect on corporate—that is, universalized managerial—interests. As such they are exercised only occasionally and usually reactively and are often represented as simply economic commodities or "costs"— for example, the price the "corporation" must pay for labor, supplies, or environmental cleanup (Deetz, 1995b). Central to the universalization of managerial interest is the reduction of the multiple claims of ownership to financial ownership. In ideological critique, managerial advantages can be seen as produced historically and actively reproduced through ideological discursive practices in society and in corporations themselves (see Bullis & Tompkins, 1989; Deetz, 1992; Mumby, 1987). Critical theory joins other recent theories in arguing for the representation of the full variety of organizational stakeholders (see Carroll, 1989; Freeman & Liedtka, 1991).

Habermas (1971, 1984, 1987) has traced the social/historical emergence of *technical rationality* over competing forms of reason. Habermas described *technical reasoning* as instrumental, tending to be governed by the theoretical and hypothetical, and focusing on control through the development of means-ends chains. The natural opposite to this, Habermas conceptualizes as a *practical interest.* Practical reasoning focuses on the process of understanding and mutual determination of the ends to be sought rather than control and development of means of goal accomplishment. But in the contemporary social situation, the form and content of modern social science and the social constitution of expertise align with organizational structures to produce the domination of technical reasoning (see Alvesson, 1987a; Fischer, 1990; Mumby, 1988; Stablein & Nord, 1985). To the extent that technical reasoning dominates, it lays claim to the entire concept of rationality, and alternative forms of reason appear irrational. To a large extent, studies of the "human" side of organizations (climate, job enrichment, quality of work life, worker participation programs, and culture) have each been transformed from alternative ends into new means to be brought under technical control for extending the dominant group interests of the corporation (Alvesson, 1987a; Barker, 1993;

Wendt, 1994). The productive tension between the two becomes submerged to the efficient accomplishment of often unknown but surely "rational" and "legitimate" corporate goals (Carter & Jackson, 1987).

Early critical theorists focused primarily on bureaucracies and other forms of direct control and domination. As the work has developed and these forms have declined, more sophisticated conceptions of power have arisen. Various forms of indirect control have become of greater concern (see Edwards, 1979; Lukes, 1974). Many of the these forms of indirect control involve active "consent" of those controlled. *Consent* processes occur through the variety of situations and activities in which someone actively, though often unknowingly, accomplishes the interests of others in the faulty attempt to fulfill his or her own. People are oppressed but are also enticed into activities that create complicity in their own victimization (for examples, see Brunsson, 1989; Clair, 1993a; Pringle, 1989). As a result, rather than having open discussions, discussions are foreclosed or there appears to be no need for discussion. The interaction processes reproduce fixed identities, relations, and knowledge, and the variety of possible differences are lost. Thus, important discussions do not take place because there appears to be no reason for them. Consent often appears in direct forms as members actively subordinate themselves to obtain money, security, meaning, or identity; things that should result from the work process rather than subordination. In fact, both the subordination and requirement of it hamper the accomplishment of these work goals. Critical organizational communication research during the 1980s and 1990s includes a rather wide body of studies showing where culture and cultural engineering may be described as hegemonic (e.g., Alvesson, 1987b; Knights & Willmott, 1987; Mumby, 1988, 1997; Rosen, 1985). Other researchers have shown how normative, unobtrusive, or concertive control processes develop in organizations and subvert employee participation programs (see

Barker, 1993; Barker & Cheney, 1994; Barker, Melville, & Pacanowsky, 1993; Barley & Kunda, 1992; Bullis, 1991; Bullis & Tompkins, 1989; Etzioni, 1961; Kunda, 1992; Lazega, 1992; Schwartzman, 1989).

Several limitations of ideology critique have been demonstrated. Three criticisms appear most common. First, ideology critique appears ad hoc and reactive. It largely explains after the fact why something didn't happen. Second, the elitist is often criticized. Common concepts like false needs and false consciousness presume a basic weakness in insight and reasoning processes in the very same people it hopes to empower. The irony of an advocate of greater equality pronouncing what others should want or how they should perceive the world "better" is apparent to both dominant and dominated groups. Third, some accounts from ideology critique appear far too simplistic. These studies appear to claim a single dominant group that has intentionally worked out a system whereby domination through control of ideas could occur and its interest could be secured. Clearly, domination is not so simple. Certainly the power of ideology critique can be maintained without falling to these criticisms, and most studies today carefully avoid each problem. Largely this has been aided by the development of Habermas's theory of communicative action.

Communicative Action

While earlier critical studies focused on distortions of consciousness, thought, and meanings, Habermas's work since the late 1970s has concentrated on distortions in communication processes (Habermas, 1984, 1987). This project retains many of the features of ideology critique, including the ideal of sorting out constraining social ideas from those grounded in reason, but it envisages procedural ideals rather than substantive critique and thus becomes quite different from traditional ideology critique. It also introduces an affirmative agenda, not based on a utopia, but still on a hope of how we might reform institutions along the lines of morally driven discourse in situations approximating an "ideal speech situation" (see Mumby, 1988). Organizational communication scholars have developed these ideas to support more participatory communication and decision making in organizations and to display power-based limitations on organizational democratization (Cheney, 1995; Deetz, 1992, 1995b; Forester, 1989, 1993; Harrison, 1994). From a participation perspective, communication difficulties arise from communication practices that preclude value debate and conflict, that substitute images and imaginary relations for self-presentation and truth claims, that arbitrarily limit access to communication channels and forums, and that then lead to decisions based on arbitrary authority relations (see Deetz, 1992, for development).

Basically, Habermas argued that every speech act can function in communication by virtue of common presumptions made by speaker and listener. Even when these presumptions are not fulfilled in an actual situation, they serve as a base of appeal as failed conversation turns to argumentation regarding the disputed validity claims. The basic presumptions and validity claims arise out of four shared domains of reality: language, the external world, human relations, and the individual's internal world. The claims raised in each realm are, respectively: intelligibility, truth, correctness, and sincerity. Each competent, communicative act makes four types of claims: (1) presenting an available understandable expression, (2) asserting a knowledge proposition, (3) establishing legitimate social relations, and (4) disclosing the speaker's positioned experience. Any of these claims that cannot be brought to open dispute serves as the basis for systematically distorted communication. The ideal speech situation is to be recovered to avoid or overcome such distortions.

The ideal speech situation, thus, describes four basic guiding conditions as necessary for free and open participation in the resolution of conflicting claims. First, the attempt to reach understanding presupposes a symmetrical distribution of the chances to choose and apply speech acts that can be heard and understood. This would specify the minimal conditions of skills and opportunities for expression including access to meaningful forums, media, and channels of communication. Second, the understanding and representation of the external world needs to be freed from privileged preconceptions in the social development of "truth." Ideally, participants have the opportunity to express interpretations and explanations with conflicts resolved in reciprocal claims and counterclaims without privileging particular epistemologies or forms of data. The freedom from preconception implies an examination of any ideology that would privilege one form of discourse, disqualify certain possible participants, and universalize any particular sectional interest. Third, participants need to have the opportunity to establish legitimate social relations and norms for conduct and interaction. The rights and responsibilities of people are not given in advance by nature or by a privileged, universal value structure, but are negotiated through interaction. The reification of organizational structures and their maintenance without possible dispute and the presence of managerial prerogatives are examples of potential immorality in corporate discourse. Finally, interactants need to be able to express their own authentic interests, needs, and feelings. This would require freedom from various coercive and hegemonic processes by which the individual is unable to form experience openly, to develop and sustain competing identities, and to form expressions presenting them.

The most frequent objection to Habermas, and those who have followed this work, is that he has overemphasized reason and consensus and has only a negative view of power, which hampers both the conception of social change and seeing the possible positivity of power (see Benhabib, 1990; Lyotard, 1984). What Habermas does well is to give an arguable

standard for normative guidance to communication as a critique of domination, even if his position is distinctly Western, intellectual, and male (Fraser, 1987; see Benhabib, 1992, for a discussion of these problems and ways of recovering the critical thrust of his work). The participative conception of communication describes the possibility and conditions for mutual decision making and also provides a description of communication problems and inadequacies. In general, most strategic or instrumental communicative acts have the potential of asserting the speaker's opinion over the attempt to reach a more representative consensus. In such cases, an apparent agreement precludes the conflict that could lead to a new position of open mutual assent. In cases where the one-sidedness is apparent, usually the processes of assertion/counter-assertion and questions/answers reclaim a situation approximating participation.

Critical theorists have been very effective in showing the invisible constraints to mutual decision making in organizations. In many workplaces today, strategy and manipulation are disguised and control is exercised through manipulations of the natural, neutral, and self-evident. Critical work has both demonstrated the presence of ideological domination and processes of "discursive closure" and "systematically distorted communication" (see Deetz, 1992, chap. 7). While Habermas has been criticized for focusing too much on consensus at the expense of conflict and dissensus, implicit in his analyses is the recovery of conflict as an essential precursor to a new consensus and the perpetual critique of each new consensus as interaction continues.

The Discourse of Dialogic Studies

I have chosen the term *dialogic* rather than the more obvious *postmodernist* to organize this discourse because it attends to key features of this work and because of the growing commercial use of the term *postmodern*, resulting in increased difficulty in distinguishing realist assumptions about a changing world (a postmodern world) and a postmodern discourse, which denies realist claims about the world (Jones, 1992; Parker, 1992). The term also makes it easier to include older theorists such as Bakhtin for whom the term *postmodern* seems inappropriate (see Shotter, 1993). Dialogic perspectives are based in a recent set of philosophical writings originating most often in France. Of greatest interest are the writings emphasizing political issues and conceptions of fragmentation, textuality, and resistance. These philosophically based approaches to organization studies have emerged out of works of Bourdieu, Derrida, Lyotard, Kristiva, Foucault, Baudrillard, Deleuze and Guattari, and Laclau and Mouffe. Organizational researchers following the general themes of this work include Hawes (1991), Martin (1990), Calás and Smircich (1991), Mumby and Putnam (1992), Knights (1992), Burrell (1988), Bhabha (1990), Barker and Cheney (1994), Holmer-Nadesan (1997), Ashcraft (1998), and several of the essays in Hassard and Parker (1993). As with critical writings, this is a wide group of writers and positions with their own disputes, but their work shares features and moves that can be highlighted in treating them together.

Like critical studies, the concern is often with asymmetry and domination in organizational decision making, but unlike the critical studies' predefinition of groups and types of domination, dialogic studies focus more on micropolitical processes and the joined nature of power and resistance. Domination is seen as fluid, situational, and without place or origin. Even group and personal identities cannot be seen as fixed or unitary. The attention is to reclaim conflicts suppressed in everyday experiences, meaning systems, and self-conceptions. Rather than a reformation of the world, dialogic studies hope to show the partiality (the incompletion and one-sidedness) of reality and the hidden points of resistance and complexity. In place of an active political agenda and utopian ideals, attention centers on the space for a continually transforming world through recovery of marginalized and suppressed peoples and aspects of people.

Dialogic research emphasizes dissensus production and the local/situated nature of understanding. Many of the conceptions on which this is based are difficult and not terribly well known by organizational communication scholars. Owing to this I will provide some greater detail here. Seven themes will be highlighted: (1) *the centrality of discourse,* emphasizing language as systems of distinctions that are central to social construction processes; (2) *fragmented identities,* demonstrating the problem of an autonomous, self-determining individual as the origin of meaning; (3) *the critique of the philosophy of presence,* focusing on object indeterminacy and the constructed nature of people and reality; (4) *the loss of foundations and master narratives,* arguing against integrative meta-narratives and large-scale theoretical systems such as Marxism or functionalism; (5) *the knowledge/power connection,* examining the role of claims of expertise and truth in systems of domination; (6) *hyperreality,* emphasizing the fluid and hyperreal nature of the contemporary world and role of mass media and information technologies; and (7) *research as resistance and indeterminacy,* stressing research as important to change processes and providing voice to that which is lost or covered up in everyday life. Each of these has an impact on conceptions of quality communication, processes of decision making, and research directions.

The Centrality of Discourse

Most current dialogic studies grew out of French structuralism by taking seriously the "linguistic turn" in philosophy. In this sense, dialogic studies developed the French tradition by making the same move on structuralist thought that Habermas and others in critical studies did on ideological critique in the development of communicative action in the German tradition. Language replaces consciousness as central to experience. Textual/

discursive fields replaced the structure of the unconscious and/or cultural structures claimed as universal. Both critical and dialogic theorists used these to fight a two-front war; first, against normative researchers and other objectivists with their science aimed at controlling nature and people, and second, against interpretive researchers and other humanists with their privileging of individual experience, unique human rights, and naive versions of human freedom. As discussed later, the linguistic turn enabled a critique of normative research's claim of objectivity through examining the processes by which objects are socially constituted and the role of language in that process and simultaneously a critique of interpretive research through demonstrating the fragmentation of cultures and personal identities and removing the psychological subject from the center of experience. Focusing on language allowed a conception of social constructionism that denied the normative claim of certainty and objective truth and the interpretivists' reliance on experience and neutral cultural claims that led them to miss the social/linguistic politics of experience. Communication thus becomes a mode of explanation of organizations and activities associated with them rather than a phenomenon to be explained within them.

Many organizational researchers have used this insight to produce discursive, communication-centered analyses of organizations. Many of the more empirical dialogic studies, but not all, have followed Foucault's conception of discourse. For example, Knights and Willmott (1989) and Mills (1994) demonstrated the way being subjected led to particular forms of subjugation; Knights and Morgan (1991) used Foucault's discursive practices to show the construction of person and world in the discourse of strategy; Townley (1993) applied it to the discourse of human resource management; and I (Deetz, 1998) have shown how self-surveillance and self-subordination replace explicit control systems in knowledge-intensive companies. Works following other related philosophical perspectives on discourse have tended to be somewhat more theoretical (e.g., Burrell, 1988; Cooper, 1989; Deetz, 1994d; Hawes, 1991).

Fragmented Identities

The position on the person follows directly from the conception of discourse. Enlightenment thought centered knowledge and understanding in a conception of an autonomous and coherent subject. This conception leads to an emphasis on—what was developed in this essay as—a consensus discourse in science and society. Dialogic studies reject the notion of the autonomous, self-determining individual as the center of the social universe and in its place suggest the complex, conflictual subject with an emphasis on fundamental dissensus (see Garsten & Grey, 1997; Henriques, Hollway, Urwin, Venn, & Walkerdine, 1984; Mills, 1994; Nukala, 1996).

There are two versions of this critique of a secure unitary identity. The first suggests that the Western conception of *man* as a centered subject has always been a myth. Freud's work is used to show the growing awareness in Western thought of the difficulties with it. People have always been filled with conflicts. The conception of a unitary autonomous self was a fiction used to suppress those conflicts and privilege masculinity, rationality, vision, and control. To the extent that dominant discourses spoke the person, the person gained a secure identity but participated in the reproduction of domination marginalizing the other parts of the self and other groups. The sense of autonomy served to cover this subservience and to give conflict a negative connotation. The privileging of consensus and naturalization of a constructed world tended to hide basic conflicts and conceptualize the ones that did arise as based on misunderstandings, incomplete knowledge, or prejudice.

The other dialogic critique suggests that identity was relatively stable in homogeneous societies and their organizations with few available discourses. In contemporary, heterogeneous, global, teleconnected societies and globalization the available discourses expand greatly. Since identity is a discursive production, in this new situation the individual acquires so many simultaneous identities through different competing discourses that fragmentation is virtually inevitable (see Deetz, 1995b; Gergen, 1991). As society becomes more fragmented and/or virtual, the identity-stabilizing forces for organizations as well as people are lost. Such a position suggests the possibility of tremendous freedom and opportunity for marginalized groups and suppressed aspects of each person to be conceptualized and discussed in more heterogeneous societies and chaotic organizations. But the multiplicity of discourses can also lead to what Giddens (1991) called "ontological insecurities." Such insecurities regarding identity can lead to strategies that aim to secure a "normal" identity (see Knights & Morgan, 1991; Knights & Willmott, 1985, 1989). This loose self is open to manipulation (since the stable background of a dominant reproductive discourse is weakened) and can be "jerked" about in the system, leading to a sense of excitement and even "ecstasy" but also can be conversion prone and easily controlled by system forces (as in Baudrillard's conception of simulation, 1988; Deetz, 1994d).

The conception of a fluid conflictual identity, however, creates difficulties in developing political action. Flax (1990), for example, shows the awkward position it leaves women in. If gender is treated as a social construction, one can show that the dominant discourse in modern organizations has produced women and their experience as marginal and "other"—that is, taking all the negative terms in the linguistic system and discourse. Ridding society of strong gender ascriptions and gendered identities—making gender irrelevant to work—is a meaningful activity to provide opportunities for women. But to accomplish such a move in the contemporary situation requires women to organize and show that gender is an issue across nearly all social situations—that is, to fix a centered identity. The dilemma is heightened regarding their experience, for if women's experiences arise out of an essential difference, they cannot be denied as important and needing to be taken into account, but to make the essentialist argument of distinct female experiences denies social constructionism and can easily be used to further stigmatize women as "other" in a society where men have more resources. Ironically, however, this is the type of deep tension and inability to develop a single coherent position that, rather than weakening dialogic work, gives it its reason for being.

The Critique of the Philosophy of Presence

Normative social science, as well as most of us in everyday life, treats the presence of objects as unproblematic and believes that language is to represent (re-present) these things. When asked what something is, we try to define it and list its essential attributes. Dialogic studies find such a position to be illusionary. Rather, the "elements" of the world are fundamentally indeterminant and can become many different determinant "objects" through different ways of attending to or encountering them. Linguistic and nonlinguistic practices direct attention and means of encountering the "elements" of organizations, thus are central to "object" production. Since the "elements" of organizations may be constructed/expressed as many different "objects," limited only by human creativity and reconfiguration of past understandings, meaning can never be final; objects and meanings are always incomplete and open to redetermination. Many different, and fundamentally irresolvable, "objectivities" thus exist in organizational life and research. The appearance of completeness and closure leads us to overlook the politics in and of construction and the possibilities for understandings hidden behind the apparent and obvious, thus a particular objectivity may be privileged.

Language is central to the production of objects in that it provides the social/historical distinctions that provide unity and difference. Language does not mirror the reality "out there" or people's mental states, but rather is a way of attending to both the insiders and outsiders providing them shape and character (Shotter, 1993; Shotter & Gergen, 1994). Further, the systems of differences or distinctions historically held by language are not fixed but metaphorical, full of contradictions and inconsistencies (Brown, 1990; Cooper & Burrell, 1988). Meaning, thus, is not universal and fixed, but precarious, fragmented, and situated. Since the research community, like others, can only escape this situation through distortion and closures, the conceptual base of research must also be, also already suggested, local and emergent.

Organizational communication researchers have used these conceptions to deconstruct objects of organizational life including the bounded concept of an organization and organizational rationality itself (Mumby & Putnam, 1992). Perhaps among the most productive have been those studying accounting practices. The bottom line, profit and loss, expenses, and so forth have no reality without specific practices creating them (Miller & O'Leary, 1987; Power, 1994). Others have looked at knowledge and information (Boland, 1987; Coombs et al., 1992). And others yet report practices (Sless, 1988) and categories of people (Epstein, 1988). Each of these shows the conditions necessary for objects to exist in organizational life and opens these objects to redetermination through initiating discussions and negotiations of reality that were not possible as long as hidden dominance held sway.

The Loss of Foundations and Master Narratives

Traditionally, the power of any social position has been gathered from its grounding or foundation. This grounding could either be to a metaphysical foundation—such as an external world in empiricism, mental structures in rationalism, human nature in humanism, or God in religion—or a narrative, a story of history—such as Marxism's class struggle, social Darwinism's survival of the fittest, or market economy's invisible hand. Positions based on such foundations and narratives are made to seem secure and inevitable and not opportunistic or driven by advantage. Certainly, much normative organizational research has been based on appeals to an "object" world, human nature, or laws of conduct. Critical research has a different foundational appeal to qualities of speech communities in its morally guided communicative action. Dialogic researchers are distinctly non- or antifoundational.

Again, like in the case of identity, dialogic researchers take two different but compatible stances in their critique of groundings. First, some argue that foundations and legitimating narratives have always been a hoax. Appeals to foundations have been used (usually unknowingly) to support a dominant view of the world and its order. As feminists, for example, argue following this position, the historical narrative has always been *his*tory. Empiricists' appeal to the nature of the external world covered up the force of their own concepts (and those borrowed from elite groups), methods, instruments, activities, and reports in constructing that world (Harding, 1991). Second, dialogic researchers note the growing social incredulity toward narratives and foundational moves. Lyotard (1984) showed the decline of *grand* narratives of "spirit" and "emancipation." The proliferation of options and growing political cynicism (or astuteness) of the public leads to a suspicion of legitimating moves. In Lyotard's sense perhaps all that is left is *local* narratives—that is, ad hoc and situated attempts at justification without appealing to themes that organize the whole of life.

The concern with integrative narratives has led to sensitive treatments of how stories in organizations connect to grand narratives and how different ones have a more local, situational character (see Martin, 1990). Other researchers have used this opening to display the false certainty in the master narratives in management (Calás & Smircich, 1991; Ingersoll & Adams, 1986). Jehenson (1984), for example, showed how narratives of "effectiveness," "expertise," and "excellence" were used to legitimize managerial control systems. In one of my own studies (Deetz, 1998), I show how narratives of "consultancy" and "integrated solutions" enabled a dominant coalition to maintain control through a financial crisis in a professional service company.

Dialogic researchers do not see the decline of foundations as necessarily leading to positive outcomes. Certainly, the decline of foundations and grand narratives removes the primary prop of security and certainty that dominant groups trade for subordination. But the replacement is not necessarily freedom and political possibility for marginalized groups. Lyotard demonstrated the rise of "performativity," which while developed as a measure of means toward social ends becomes an end in itself. The performativity standard provides new forms of control not directed by a vision of society and social good but simply more production and consumption (see Carter & Jackson, 1987). Many "quality" programs evidence this. Certainly, the loss of grand integrative narratives has not been missed by management groups. One could easily say that the common conceptions of corporate "visions" and "cultures" are strategic local narrative constructions to provide the integration and motivation in a pluralistic society formerly provided by the wider social narratives that have passed away.

A difficulty in dialogic research with the loss of foundations, as in the concept of fragmented identities, is how to generate a political stance in regard to these developments. Women have confronted this most directly in debates over whether men and women have distinctly different experiences grounded in biological sex. Without a grounding, the basis for large-scale political action is lacking, and resistance to domination, even general domination, becomes local and situational. If one rejects an essentialist foundation and believes that more than local resistance is needed, criti-cal theory may well provide the best remaining option, but not without costs (see Fraser & Nicholson, 1988).

The Knowledge/Power Connection

Within dialogic writings, power is treated far differently from most other writings on organizations. Foucault (1977, 1980, 1988) has led many in suggesting that the "power" of interest is not that which one possesses or acquires (Clegg, 1989; Jermier, Knights, & Nord, 1994). Such power is an outcome of more fundamental power relations. Power resides in the discursive practices and formations themselves. For example, the discourse that produces a "worker" both empowers and disempowers the group of individuals produced through this representation. In particular historical discourses, "workers" and "managers" are produced out of the open "elements" of organizational life and simultaneously provided with solidarity and interests as well as conflicts, material and symbolic resources, and self-understandings. Power thus resides in the demarcations and the systems of discourse that produce and sustain such groupings. Unions and managers mutually sustain the other in their conflicts. It is not the relative power of each that is of interest but how the distinction is reproduced.

One of the most useful terms entering into organization studies from Foucault's work on the knowledge/power connection has been his concept of "discipline." The demarcations developed in discourse provide forms of normative behavior. The combination of training, routines, self-surveillance, and experts provides resources for normalization, then discipline (Deetz, 1998; Knights & Collinson, 1987; Townley, 1993). From such a conception, normative research and the expertise produced from it are considered to provide resources for normalization and a veneer of truth for arbitrary and advantaging discursive practices (Hollway, 1984, 1991). The emphasis on dissensus discourse in dialogic research is aimed at disrupting normalization and provides competing power relations (Holmer-Nadesan, 1997; Knights, 1992; Trethewey, 1997).

Hyperreality

In dialogic conceptions, linguistic and nonlinguistic practices are considered to open a relation to external elements (people and world) and produce these elements in specific ways. As discussed earlier, the referent ("elements" of the world) has no specific character; it is always determinable in more ways than all the determinations or objects that have been made of it through various historical practices. To the extent that this "indeterminacy" is known (the "otherness" of elements shows), the domination present in any system can be disrupted and objects de- and redifferentiated. To the extent that indeterminacy is recognized, the possibility of self-referentiality in a textual system is avoided. Otherwise, the determinant object produced by the practices is referenced by the practices and the system remains closed.

The presence of media and information systems increases the possibility of such closure and the lack of connection to the external indeterminacy. The referent can disappear as anything more than another sign—a produced object. Thus properly signs would only reference other signs; images would be images of images. The system then becomes purely self-referential or what Baudrillard calls a *simulation* (see Deetz, 1994d, for an example). In such a world, in Baudrillard's analysis, signs, rather than connecting us to the outside world and providing a temporary determination, reference only linguistically already determined objects—the "map" leads us only to earlier "maps" of the world. The "model" is seen as the thing and "model" behavior replaces responsive action. Signs reach the structural limit of representation by referencing only themselves with little relation to any outside or interior. In such a situation, a particular fiction is not produced by a subject

in opposition to reality, but positions an imaginary world and subject in place of any real; it has no opposite, no outside. Baudrillard (1983) used the example of the difference between feigning and simulating an illness to show the character of this dialogic representation: "Feigning or dissimulation leaves the reality principle intact; the difference is always clear, it is only masked; whereas simulation threatens the difference between 'true' and 'false,' between 'real' and 'imaginary.' Since the simulator produces 'true' symptoms, is he ill or not? He cannot be treated objectively either as ill, or not ill" (p. 5).

Hochschild (1983) provided an organizational example of this (though from a theoretically different position) in her description of the appropriateness of flight attendants' emotions. Our traditional conceptions allow a fairly simple distinction between "real" spontaneous emotions that arise in response to perceived situations and "acting" where an employee fakes the managerially desired emotion. Hochschild shows, however, that the presence of "deep acting" makes this distinction misleading. In deep acting, the flight attendants in her studies learn to perceive or attend to the situation in such a way that the managerially desired emotion spontaneously arises in the employee. Is it fake or not? In the concepts here, it is self-referential. The system appears open and environmentally adaptive but closes or manipulates the environment in ways that the system adapts to the system reproduced environment. This is not unlike normative research constructing the world using the concepts of the same theory it hopes to test.

Research as Resistance and Indeterminacy

The role of dialogic research is very different from more traditional roles assigned to social science in both its emphasis on dissensus production and the local forms of knowledge. It primarily serves to attempt to open up the indeterminacy that modern social science, everyday conceptions, routines, and practices have closed off. The result is a kind of antipositive (or positivist) knowledge that Knights (1992) described. The primary methods are deconstruction, resistance readings, and genealogy.

Deconstruction works primarily to critique the philosophy of presence by recalling the suppressed terms that have become devalued in dominant systems of distinction. When the suppressed term is given value, the dependency of the positive term on the negative is revealed and a third term is recovered that shows a way of thinking or attending to the world that is not dependent on the opposition of the first two (see Calás & Smircich, 1991; Martin, 1990; Mumby, 1996; Mumby & Putnam, 1992). The resistance reading demonstrates the construction activity and problematizes any fixed relationship. The positive and the polar constructions are both displayed as acts of domination. Conflicts that were suppressed by the positive are brought back to redecision (see Westenholz, 1991). The conflictual field out of which objects are formed is recovered for creative redetermination—constant dedifferentiation and redifferentiation. Given the power of common sense and organizational routines, such rereads require rigor and imagination. The rereadings are formed out of a keen sense of irony, a serious playfulness, and are often guided by the pleasure one has in being freed from the dull compulsions of a world made too easy and too constraining. The point of research in this sense is not to get it right but to challenge guiding assumptions, fixed meanings and relations, and reopen the formative capacity of human beings in relation to others and the world.

A LOOK TO THE FUTURE

In looking at different organizational communication research programs, clearly different programs have different goals and assumptions and provide different forms of evaluation. I hope to have displayed differences that give insights into the diverse discourses in organizational communication studies today, displaying some of the ways that they are alike and different. The relation among these alternatives is not addressed well in exclusionary, pluralistic, supplementary, or integrative terms. Each orientation creates a vision of social problems and tries to address them. Different orientations have specific ways of answering the types of questions they pose and do not work terribly well in answering the questions of others.

I, like many others, sometimes wish we were all multilingual, that we could move across orientations with grace and ease, but this type of Teflon-coated, multiperspectival cosmopolitan envisioned by Morgan (1986) or Hassard (1991) is both illusionary and weak (see Parker & McHugh, 1991). Good scholars have deep commitments. Multiperspectivalism often leads to shallow readings and invites unexamined basic assumptions. Some scholars are more multilingual than others, but doing good work within an orientation still must be prized first. Ideally, alternative research programs can complement each other. Consensus without dissensus is stifling and finally maladaptive. Elite/a priori concepts are necessary and probably inevitable, but we can make them more temporary and open to reconfiguration.

Without a doubt, most organizational communication scholars are becoming both more knowledgeable about alternatives and more appreciative of the differences. This development allows us to get beyond relatively unproductive theoretical and methodological arguments to more basic and serious questions. The choice of orientation, to the extent that it can be freed from training and department/discipline politics, can probably be reduced to alternative conceptions of social good and preferred ways of living. This acceptance grounds theory and method debate in a moral debate that has been neither terribly common nor explicit in organizational communication studies. I agree with Gergen (1992) that organizational research and theory need to be evaluated as much by a question of "how shall we live?" as by verisimilitude and methodological rigor. Studies need to be understood and evaluated on their own terms, but should also appeal to the larger social concerns in which both the needs and means of accomplishment are contested.

Discussions of responsibility and value are still relatively infrequent in organizational communication research, but present (see various essays in Conrad, 1993; Deetz, 1995a; Deetz, Cohen, & Edley, 1997). Certainly, we have lagged behind moral and ethical discussions of organization available other places (e.g., Frederick, 1986; Freeman, 1991; Freeman & Liedtka, 1991; Gergen, 1995; Jackell, 1988; MacIntyre, 1984; Mangham, 1995). The justification for much organizational communication research has been aimed at improving the functioning of organizations and management as if they were value-neutral tools without regarding how these tools are applied or whose values are advanced. With such a conception, our research has often focused on the perfectibility of the tool rather than the ends it is used to advance. To the extent that this conception has been useful, organization studies have enhanced the effective use of resources and fulfillment of certain human needs. But many researchers now question this "tool" version of organizations and research, claiming that researchers paid insufficient attention to alternative needs and goals, and the numerous social and political consequences of organizational activities (see Marsden, 1993). Until recently, most organizational communication researchers accepted a managerial bias in their conceptions of organizations and articulations of organizational goals.

The business environment has changed in fundamental ways in the past two decades. These changes require rethinking decision making in corporations: Who should make the decisions? How should they be made? What criteria should be used to evaluate them? If companies are to stay economically viable and their host societies healthy, corporate decisions must be more responsive to rapidly changing environments and human needs. Understanding new values and the rights and capacities of other organizational members is initiating reforms of organizational communication research that are as sweeping as many contemporary changes in organizational life. Certainly, this is seen to some extent in the growth of teams, other participation programs, customer focus, and increased discussion of environmental and social responsibility.

More important than these new programs, in my mind however, is a growing shift in the conception of organizations themselves. This shift offers the greatest challenge and opportunity for organizational communication researchers. Generally, the conceptual shift can be characterized as moving from an "owner/manager" model to a "stakeholder" model of organizations (see Carroll, 1989; Deetz, 1995b; Freeman & Gilbert, 1988; Grunig & Hunt, 1984; Osigweh, 1994). In this model, a variety of groups in addition to stockholders and managers are seen as having made an investment and thus having a stake in corporate decisions. Proponents of such a view argue that in a democratic society all those affected by the activities of corporations (all *stakeholders*) have some representation rights. But beyond the question of rights, direct decisional influence by both internal and external constituencies can lead to greater effectiveness in meeting the diverse social and economic goals. A stakeholder model recognizes multiple forms of ownership and enables widespread participation and thus helps initiate important value debates.

In traditional models of organizations, the core processes in organizations were conceived as economic. Communication aided economic accomplishment, but wherever possible stakeholder representation was limited to economic representation. If communication-based decision making could be reduced to an economic calculation, it was. In a stakeholder model, the core processes involve several simultaneous goals. The interaction among stakeholders can be conceived as a negotiative process aiding mutual goal accomplishment. Communication is the means by which such negotiation takes place. Conceptions of human interaction, negotiation, and rationality developed by communication theorists are uniquely suited to these new needs. To make a full contribution, organizational communication researchers would need to use communication conceptions aimed at increasing genuine participation rather than increased influence and control. This change is still incomplete.

Many organization managers understand the need to attend to stakeholders today but have not accepted a stakeholder model. New communication and decision-making conceptions are often used to increase the number of *forums* in which stakeholder representation and debate could occur, but few have increased stakeholder *voice* (Deetz, 1995b; Deetz et al., 1997; Gordon, 1988). Attention to stakeholders in these cases is a strategic attempt to increase loyalty and commitment and decrease resistance rather than seeking genuine decisional input. The lack of voice results from constrained decisional contexts, inadequate or distorted information, socialization and colonization activities, and the solicitation of "consent" where stakeholders "choose" to suppress their own needs and internal value conflicts. Gradually, we are learning that the problem with traditional organizations was not simply bureaucracy, but control systems in a variety of forms. To overcome these problems, new conceptions of interaction can improve collaborative decision making within corporations. The critical and dialogic scholars were somewhat earlier in fully appreciating these changes while managers and managerial-biased researchers have been more ambivalent—often both advocating new conceptions and programs and subverting their full implementation. But both normative and interpretive researchers can de-

sign studies that enhance the functioning of the organization as a site of stakeholder coordination rather than a site of control. Finding new ways of organizing becomes everyone's job.

Understanding our alternatives requires understanding both the relation of conceptions to the various social stakeholders and the relation of research discourse to dominant social theories. Thinking through these relations provides an opening for discussion. We are learning the positive effects of human diversity as organizational members—beyond "separate but equal" and integration—and organizational communication research can benefit from better conceptual discussions of research diversity. In doing so, the ultimate point is not in arguing it out to get it right, but to reclaim the suppressed tensions and conflicts among the many contemporary stakeholders to negotiate a life together based in appreciation of difference and responsive decision making.

NOTES

1. Citations are selective throughout this essay. Rather than try to be exhaustive and produce a cluttered text with hundreds of references, I will reference what I consider to be well illustrative or especially useful developments and will bias the selection toward authors who work in communication departments. This essay was completed in 1996. Citations to literature published after that time are more limited.

2. Much of this discussion is adapted from Deetz (1996).

REFERENCES

Alexander, E., III, Penley, L., & Jernigan, I. E. (1991). The effect of individual differences on manager media choice. *Management Communication Quarterly, 5,* 155-173.

Allen, B. J. (1996). Feminist standpoint theory: A black woman's (re)view of organizational socialization. *Communication Studies, 47,* 257-271.

Allen, B. J. (1998). Black womanhood and feminist standpoints. *Management Communication Quarterly, 11*, 575-586.

Allen, M. W., Gotcher, J. M., & Seibert, J. H. (1993). A decade of organizational communication research: Journal articles 1980-1991. In S. A. Deetz (Ed.), *Communication yearbook 16* (pp. 252-330). Newbury Park, CA: Sage.

Alvesson, M. (1987a). *Organizational theory and technocratic consciousness: Rationality, ideology, and quality of work.* New York: Aldine de Gruyter.

Alvesson, M. (1987b). Organizations, culture and ideology. *International Studies of Management and Organizations, 17*, 4-18.

Alvesson, M. (1993). Cultural-ideological modes of management control. In S. A. Deetz (Ed.), *Communication yearbook 16* (pp. 3-42). Newbury Park, CA: Sage.

Alvesson, M., & Willmott, H. (Eds.). (1992). *Critical management studies.* London: Sage.

Alvesson, M., & Willmott, H. (1996). *Making sense of management: A critical introduction.* London: Sage.

Argyris, C. (1994, July-August). Good communication that blocks learning. *Harvard Business Review, 72*, 77-85.

Ashcraft, K. L. (1998). "I wouldn't say I'm a feminist, but . . . ": Organizational micropractice and gender identity. *Management Communication Quarterly, 11*, 587-597.

Ashcraft, K. L., & Pacanowsky, M. E. (1996). "A woman's worst enemy": Reflections on a narrative of organizational life and female identity. *Journal of Applied Communication Research, 24*, 217-239.

Axley, S. (1984). Managerial and organizational communication in terms of the conduit metaphor. *Academy of Management Review, 9*, 428-437.

Baker, M. (1991). Gender and verbal communication in professional settings: A review of the literature. *Management Communication Quarterly, 5*, 36-63.

Banks, S., & Riley, P. (1993). Structuration theory as an ontology for communication research. In S. A. Deetz (Ed.), *Communication yearbook 16* (pp. 167-196). Newbury Park, CA: Sage.

Bantz, C. (1983). Naturalistic research traditions. In L. L. Putnam & M. E. Pacanowsky (Eds.), *Communication and organizations: An interpretive approach* (pp. 55-72). Beverly Hills, CA: Sage.

Barker, J. (1993). Tightening the iron cage—Concertive control in self-managing teams. *Administrative Science Quarterly, 38*, 408-437.

Barker, J., & Cheney, G. (1994). The concept and the practice of discipline in contemporary organizational life. *Communication Monographs, 61*, 19-43.

Barker, J., Melville, C., & Pacanowsky, M. (1993). Self-directed teams at XEL: Changes in communication practices during a program of cultural transformation. *Journal of Applied Communication Research, 21*, 297-312.

Barley, S. (1990). Images of imaging: Notes on doing longitudinal field work. *Organization Science, 1*, 220-247.

Barley, S., & Kunda, G. (1992). Design and devotion: Surges of rational and normative ideologies of control in managerial discourse. *Administrative Science Quarterly, 37*, 363-399.

Barley, S., Meyer, G., & Gash, D. (1988). Cultures of culture: Academics, practitioners and the pragmatics of normative control. *Administrative Science Quarterly, 33*, 24-60.

Bastien, D. (1992). Change in organizational culture: The use of linguistic methods in a corporate acquisition. *Management Communication Quarterly, 5*, 403-442.

Bastien, D., McPhee, R., & Bolton, K. (1995). A study and extended theory of the structuration of climate. *Communication Monographs, 62*, 87-109.

Baudrillard, J. (1983). *Simulations.* New York: Semiotext(e).

Baudrillard, J. (1988). Simulacra and simulations. In M. Poster (Ed.), *Jean Baudrillard: Selected writings* (pp. 166-184). Stanford, CA: Stanford University Press.

Bellman, R., & Roosta, R. (1987). On a class of self-organizing communication networks. In F. Yates (Ed.), *Self-organizing systems.* New York: Plenum.

Benhabib, S. (1990). Afterward: Communicative ethics and current controversies in practical philosophy. In S. Benhabib & F. Dallmayr (Eds.), *The communicative ethics controversy* (pp. 330-369). Cambridge, MA: MIT Press.

Benhabib, S. (1992). *Situating the self: Gender, community and postmodernism in contemporary ethics.* Cambridge, UK: Polity.

Beniger, J. (1986). *The control revolution.* Cambridge, MA: Harvard University Press.

Benson, K. (1977). Organizations: A dialectical view. *Administrative Science Quarterly, 22*, 1-21.

Berger, C. R. (1977). The covering law perspective as a theoretical basis for the study of human communication. *Communication Quarterly, 25*, 7-18.

Bergquist, W. (1993). *The postmodern organization: Mastering the art of irreversible change.* San Francisco: Jossey-Bass.

Bernstein, R. (1983). *Beyond objectivism and relativism.* Philadelphia: University of Pennsylvania Press.

Bhabha, H. (1990). The other question: Difference, discrimination and the discourse of colonialism. In R. Ferguson, M. Gever, & T. Minh-Ha, with C. West (Eds.), *Out there: Marginalization and contemporary culture.* Cambridge, MA: MIT Press.

Boland, R. (1987). The information of information systems. In R. Boland & R. Hirschheim (Eds.), *Critical issues in information systems research* (pp. 363-379). New York: John Wiley.

Bormann, E. (1983). Symbolic convergence: Organizational communication and culture. In L. L. Putnam &

M. E. Pacanowsky (Eds.), *Communication and organizations: An interpretive approach* (pp. 99-122). Beverly Hills, CA: Sage.

Bourdieu, P. (1977). *Outline of a theory of practice.* Cambridge, UK: Cambridge University Press.

Bourdieu, P. (1991). *Language and symbolic power.* Cambridge, UK: Polity.

Braverman, H. (1974). *Labor and monopoly capital.* New York: Monthly Review Press.

Brown, M. H. (1985). That reminds me of a story: Speech action in organizational socialization. *Western Journal of Speech Communication, 49,* 27-42.

Brown, R. H. (1990). Rhetoric, textuality, and the postmodern turn in sociological theory. *Sociological Theory, 8,* 188-197.

Browning, L. (1992). Lists and stories as organizational communication. *Communication Theory, 2,* 281-302.

Brunsson, N. (1989). *The organization of hypocrisy: Talk, decisions and action in organizations.* New York: John Wiley.

Bullis, C. (1991). Communication practices as unobtrusive control: An observational study. *Communication Studies, 42,* 254-271.

Bullis, C., & Tompkins, P. (1989). The forest ranger revisited: A study of control processes and identification. *Communication Monographs, 56,* 287-306.

Burawoy, M. (1979). *Manufacturing consent.* Chicago: University of Chicago Press.

Burawoy, M. (1985). *The politics of production: Factory regimes under capitalism and socialism.* London: Verso.

Burrell, G. (1988). Modernism, postmodernism and organisational analysis 2: The contribution of Michel Foucault. *Organisation Studies, 9,* 221-235.

Burrell, G., & Morgan, G. (1979). *Sociological paradigms and organizational analysis.* London: Heinemann.

Calás, M., & Smircich, L. (1991). Voicing seduction to silence leadership. *Organization Studies, 12,* 567-602.

Carroll, A. (1989). *Business and society: Ethics and stakeholder management.* Cincinnati, OH: South-Western.

Carter, P., & Jackson, N. (1987). Management, myth, and metatheory—From scarcity to post scarcity. *International Studies of Management and Organizations, 17,* 64-89.

Cecchin, G., & Stratton, P. (1991). Extending systemic consultation from families to management. *Human Systems: The Journal of Systemic Consultation and Management, 2,* 3-13.

Cheney, G. (1995). Democracy in the workplace: Theory and practice from the perspective of communication. *Journal of Applied Communication Research, 23,* 167-200.

Clair, R. (1993a). The bureaucratization, commodification, and privatization of sexual harassment through

institutional discourse. *Management Communication Quarterly, 7,* 123-157.

Clair, R. (1993b). The use of framing devices to sequester organizational narratives: Hegemony and harassment. *Communication Monographs, 60,* 113-136.

Clegg, S. (1989). *Frameworks of power.* Newbury Park, CA: Sage.

Clegg, S., & Dunkerley, D. (1980). *Organizations, class and control.* Boston: Routledge and Kegan Paul.

Clifford, J., & Marcus, G. E. (Eds.). (1986). *Writing culture.* Berkeley: University of California Press.

Conquergood, D. (1991). Rethinking ethnography: Toward a critical cultural politics. *Communication Monographs, 58,* 179-194.

Conrad, C. (Ed.). (1993). *Ethical nexus.* Norwood, NJ: Ablex.

Contractor, N. (1994). Self-organizing systems perspective in the study of organizational communication. In B. Kovacic (Ed.), *New approaches to organizational communication* (pp. 39-66). Albany: State University of New York Press.

Coombs, R., Knights, D., & Willmott, H. (1992). Culture, control, and competition: Towards a conceptual framework for the study of information technology in organizations. *Organization Studies, 13,* 51-72.

Cooper, R. (1989). Modernism, postmodernism and organisational analysis 3: The contribution of Jacques Derrida. *Organisation Studies, 10,* 479-502.

Cooper, R., & Burrell, G. (1988). Modernism, postmodernism and organisational analysis. *Organization Studies, 9,* 91-112.

Czarniawska-Joerges, B. (1988). *Ideological control in nonideological organizations.* New York: Praeger.

Daft, R., & Weick, K. (1984). Toward a model of organizations as interpretive systems. *Academy of Management Review, 9,* 284-295.

Dahrendorf, R. (1959). *Class and class conflict in industrial society.* Stanford, CA: Stanford University Press.

Deal, T., & Kennedy, A. (1982). *Corporate cultures.* Reading, MA: Addison-Wesley.

Deetz, S. (1973). An understanding of science and a hermeneutic science of understanding. *Journal of Communication, 23,* 139-159.

Deetz, S. (1992). *Democracy in the age of corporate colonization: Developments in communication and the politics of everyday life.* Albany: State University of New York Press.

Deetz, S. (1994a). The future of the discipline: The challenges, the research, and the social contribution. In S. A. Deetz (Ed.), *Communication yearbook 17* (pp. 565-600). Thousand Oaks, CA: Sage.

Deetz, S. (1994b). The micropolitics of identity formation in the workplace: The case of a knowledge intensive firm. *Human Studies, 17,* 1-22.

Deetz, S. (1994c). The new politics of the workplace: Ideology and other unobtrusive controls. In H. Simons & M. Billig (Eds.), *After postmodernism:*

Reconstructing ideology critique (pp. 172-199). Thousand Oaks, CA: Sage.

Deetz, S. (1994d). Representative practices and the political analysis of corporations. In B. Kovacic (Ed.), *Organizational communication: New perspectives* (pp. 209-242). Albany: State University of New York Press.

Deetz, S. (1995a). Character, corporate responsibility and the dialogic in the postmodern context. *Organization, 3,* 217-225.

Deetz, S. (1995b). *Transforming communication, transforming business: Building responsive and responsible workplaces.* Cresskill, NJ: Hampton.

Deetz, S. (1996). Describing differences in approaches to organizational science: Rethinking Burrell and Morgan and their legacy. *Organization Science, 7,* 191-207.

Deetz, S. (1998). Discursive formations, strategized subordination, and self-surveillance: An empirical case. In A. McKinlay & K. Starkey (Eds.), *Foucault, management and organization theory* (pp. 151-172). London: Sage.

Deetz, S., Cohen, D., & Edley, P. (1997). Toward a dialogic ethics in the context of international business organization. In F. Casmir (Ed.), *Ethics in intercultural and international communication* (pp. 183-226). Hillsdale, NJ: Lawrence Erlbaum.

Deetz, S., & Mumby, D. (1990). Power, discourse, and the workplace: Reclaiming the critical tradition in communication studies in organizations. In J. A. Anderson (Ed.), *Communication yearbook 13* (pp. 18-47). Newbury Park, CA: Sage.

DiMaggio, P. (1995). Comments on what theory is not. *Administrative Science Quarterly, 40,* 391-397.

Donaldson, L. (1985). *In defense of organizational theory: A reply to critics.* Cambridge, UK: Cambridge University Press.

Donnellon, A., Gray, B., & Bougon, M. (1986). Communication, meaning, and organized action. *Administrative Science Quarterly, 31,* 43-55.

Douglas, J. D. (Ed.). (1970). *Understanding everyday life.* Chicago: Aldine.

DuGay, P. (1997). *Production of culture, cultures of production.* London: Sage.

Edwards, R. (1979). *Contested terrain: The transformation of the workplace in the twentieth century.* New York: Basic Books.

Eisenberg, E., & Goodall, H. L., Jr. (1993). *Organizational communication: Balancing creativity and constraint.* New York: St. Martin's.

Epstein, C. (1988). *Deceptive distinctions.* New Haven, CT: Yale University Press.

Etzioni, A. (1961). *A comparative analysis of complex organizations.* New York: Free Press.

Everett, J. (1994). Communication and sociocultural evolution in organizations and organizational populations. *Communication Theory, 4,* 93-110.

Fairhurst, G. (1993). Echoes of the vision: When the rest of the organization talks quality. *Management Communication Quarterly, 6,* 331-371.

Ferguson, K. (1984). *The feminist case against bureaucracy.* Philadelphia: Temple University Press.

Ferguson, K. (1994). On bringing more theory, more voices and more politics to the study of organizations. *Organization, 1,* 81-100.

Fischer, F. (1990). *Technocracy and the politics of expertise.* Newbury Park, CA: Sage.

Flax, J. (1990). *Thinking fragments: Psychoanalysis, feminism and postmodernism in the contemporary west.* Berkeley: University of California Press.

Forester, J. (1989). *Planning in the face of power.* Berkeley: University of California Press.

Forester, J. (1993). *Critical theory, public policy, and planning practice.* Albany: State University of New York Press.

Foucault, M. (1977). *Discipline and punish: The birth of the prison* (A. Sheridan, Trans.). New York: Pantheon.

Foucault, M. (1980). *The history of sexuality* (R. Hurley, Trans.). New York: Pantheon.

Foucault, M. (1988). Technologies of the self. In L. Martin, H. Gutman, & P. Hutton (Eds.), *Technologies of the self* (pp. 16-49). Amherst: University of Massachusetts Press.

Fraser, N. (1987). What's critical about critical theory? The case of Habermas and gender. In S. Benhabib & D. Cornell (Eds.), *Feminism as critique* (pp. 31-55). Cambridge, UK: Polity.

Fraser, N., & Nicholson, L. (1988). Social criticism without philosophy: An encounter between feminism and postmodernism. *Theory, Culture, & Society, 5,* 373-394.

Frederick, W. C. (1986). Toward CSR3: Why ethical analysis is indispensable and unavoidable in corporate affairs. *California Management Review, 28,* 126-141.

Freeman, R. E. (Ed.). (1991). *Business ethics: The state of the art.* New York: Oxford University Press.

Freeman, R. E., & Gilbert, D. (1988). *Corporate strategy and the search for ethics.* Englewood Cliffs, NJ: Prentice Hall.

Freeman, R. E., & Liedtka, J. (1991). Corporate social responsibility: A critical approach. *Business Horizons, 34,* 92-101.

Frost, P., Moore, L., Louis, M., Lundberg, C., & Martin, J. (Eds.). (1985). *Organizational culture.* Beverly Hills, CA: Sage.

Frost, P., Moore, L., Louis, M., Lundberg, C., & Martin, J. (Eds.). (1992). *Rethinking culture.* Newbury Park, CA: Sage.

Garsten, C., & Grey, C. (1997). How to become oneself: Discourses of subjectivity in post-bureaucratic organizations. *Organization, 4,* 211-228.

Geertz, C. (1973). *The interpretation of cultures.* New York: Basic Books.

Geist, P. (1995). Negotiating whose order? Communicating to negotiate identities and revise organizational structures. In A. Nicotera (Ed.), *Conflict in organizations: Communicative processes*. Albany: State University of New York Press.

Gergen, K. (1978). Toward generative theory. *Journal of Personality and Social Psychology, 36,* 1344-1360.

Gergen, K. (1991). *The saturated self: Dilemmas of identity in contemporary life*. New York: Basic Books.

Gergen, K. (1992). Organizational theory in the postmodern era. In M. Reed & M. Hughes (Eds.), *Rethinking organization* (pp. 207-226). London: Sage.

Gergen, K. (1995). Global organization: From imperialism to ethical vision. *Organization, 2,* 519-532.

Giddens, A. (1979). *Control problems in social theory*. Berkeley: University of California Press.

Giddens, A. (1984). *The constitution of society*. Berkeley: University of California Press.

Giddens, A. (1991). *Modernity and self-identity: Self and society in the late modern age*. Stanford, CA: Stanford University Press.

Goodall, H. L. (1990). A theatre of motives and the "meaningful orders of persons and things." In J. A. Anderson (Ed.), *Communication yearbook 13* (pp. 69-94). Newbury Park, CA: Sage.

Gordon, W. (1988). Range of employee voice. *Employee Responsibilities and Rights Journal, 1,* 283-299.

Gordon, W., Infante, D., & Graham, E. (1988). Corporate conditions conductive to employee voice: A subordinate perspective. *Employee Responsibilities and Rights Journal, 1,* 101-110.

Gramsci, A. (1971). *Selections from the prison notebooks* (Q. Hoare & G. N. Smith, Trans.). New York: International. (Original work published 1929-1935)

Grunig, J., & Hunt, T. (1984). *Managing public relations*. New York: Holt, Rinehart & Winston.

Habermas, J. (1971). *Knowledge and human interests* (J. Shapiro, Trans.). Boston: Beacon.

Habermas, J. (1984). *The theory of communicative action: Vol. 1. Reason and the rationalization of society* (T. McCarthy, Trans.). Boston: Beacon.

Habermas, J. (1987). *The theory of communicative action: Vol. 2. Lifeworld and system* (T. McCarthy, Trans.). Boston: Beacon.

Harding, S. (1991). *Whose science? Whose knowledge?* Ithaca, NY: Cornell University Press.

Harrison, T. (1994). Communication and interdependence in democratic organizations. In S. A. Deetz (Ed.), *Communication yearbook 17* (pp. 247-274). Thousand Oaks, CA: Sage.

Hassard, J. (1991). Multiple paradigms and organizational analysis: A case study. *Organization Studies, 12,* 275-299.

Hassard, J., & Parker, M. (Eds.). (1993). *Postmodernism and organizations*. London: Sage.

Hawes, L. (1974). Social collectivities as communication: Perspectives on organizational behavior. *Quarterly Journal of Speech, 60,* 497-502.

Hawes, L. (1991). Organising narratives/codes/poetics. *Journal of Organizational Change Management, 4,* 45-51.

Henriques, J., Hollway, W., Urwin, C., Venn, C., & Walkerdine, V. (Eds.). (1984). *Changing the subject*. New York: Methuen.

Hochschild, A. (1983). *The managed heart*. Berkeley: University of California Press.

Hollway, W. (1984). Fitting work: Psychological assessment in organizations. In J. Henriques, W. Hollway, C. Urwin, C. Venn, & V. Walkerdine. (Eds.), *Changing the subject* (pp. 26-59). New York: Methuen.

Hollway, W. (1991). *Work psychology and organizational behavior*. London: Sage.

Holmer-Nadesan, M. (1996). Organizational identity and space of action. *Organization Studies, 17,* 49-81.

Holmer-Nadesan, M. (1997). Constructing paper dolls: The discourse of personality testing in organizational practices. *Communication Theory, 7,* 189-218.

Howard, L., & Geist, P. (1995). Ideological positioning in organizational change: The dialectic of control in a merging organization. *Communication Monographs, 62,* 110-131.

Infante, D., Anderson, C., Martin, M., Herington, A., & Kim, J. (1993). Subordinates' satisfaction and perceptions of superiors' compliance gaining tactics, argumentativeness, verbal aggressiveness, and style. *Management Communication Quarterly, 6,* 307-326.

Ingersoll, V., & Adams, G. (1986). Beyond organizational boundaries: Exploring the managerial myth. *Administration and Society, 18,* 360-381.

Jablin, F. M. (1979). Superior-subordinate communication: The state of the art. *Psychological Bulletin, 86,* 1201-1222.

Jackell, R. (1988). *Moral mazes: The world of corporate managers*. New York: Oxford University Press.

Jackson, N., & Carter, P. (1991). In defense of paradigm incommensurability. *Organization Studies, 12,* 109-127.

Jehenson, R. (1984). Effectiveness, expertise and excellence as ideological fictions: A contribution to a critical phenomenology of the formal organization. *Human Studies, 7,* 3-21.

Jermier, J., Knights, D., & Nord, W. (Eds.). (1994). *Resistance and power in organizations*. London: Routledge.

Jones, D. (1992). Postmodern perspectives on organisational communication. *Australian Journal of Communication, 19,* 30-37.

Katz, D., & Kahn, R. (1978). *The social psychology of organizations* (2nd ed.). New York: John Wiley.

Kauffman, B. (1992). Feminist facts: Interview strategies and political subjects in ethnography. *Communication Theory, 2,* 187-206.

Kilduff, M. (1993). Deconstructing organizations. *Academy of Management Review, 18,* 13-31.

Knapp, M., Putnam, L., & Davis, L. (1988). Measuring interpersonal conflict in organizations. *Management Communication Quarterly, 1,* 414-429.

Knights, D. (1992). Changing spaces: The disruptive impact of a new epistemological location for the study of management. *Academy of Management Review, 17,* 514-536.

Knights, D., & Collinson, D. (1987). Disciplining the shop floor: A comparison of the disciplinary effects of managerial psychology and financial accounting. *Accounting, Organizations and Society, 12,* 457-477.

Knights, D., & Morgan, G. (1991). Corporate strategy, organizations, and subjectivity: A critique. *Organization Studies, 12,* 251-273.

Knights, D., & Willmott, H. (1985). Power and identity in theory and practice. *Sociological Review, 33,* 22-46.

Knights, D., & Willmott, H. (1987). Organisational culture as management strategy. *International Studies of Management and Organization, 17,* 40-63.

Knights, D., & Willmott, H. (1989). Power and subjectivity at work: From degradation to subjugation in social relations. *Sociology, 23,* 535-558.

Knights, D., & Willmott, H. (Eds.). (1990). *Labour process theory.* London: Macmillan.

Knuf, J. (1993). "Ritual" in organizational culture theory: Some theoretical reflections and a plea for greater terminological rigor. In S. A. Deetz (Ed.), *Communication yearbook 16* (pp. 43-53). Newbury Park, CA: Sage.

Krone, K. J., Jablin, F. M., & Putnam, L. L. (1987). Communication theory and organizational communication: Multiple perspectives. In F. M. Jablin, L. L. Putnam, K. H. Roberts, & L. W. Porter (Eds.), *Handbook of organizational communication: An interdisciplinary perspective* (pp. 18-40). Newbury Park, CA: Sage.

Kunda, G. (1992). *Engineering culture: Control and commitment in a high-tech corporation.* Philadelphia: Temple University Press.

Laclau, E., & Mouffe, C. (1985). *Hegemony and socialist strategy* (W. Moore & P. Cammack, Trans.). London: Verso.

Lawrence, P., & Lorsch, J. (1967). Differentiation and integration in complex organizations. *Administrative Science Quarterly, 12,* 147.

Lazega, E. (1992). *Micropolitics of knowledge: Communication and indirect control in workgroups.* New York: Aldine de Gruyter.

Linstead, S. (1993). Deconstruction in the study of organizations. In J. Hassard & M. Parker (Eds.), *Postmodernism and organizations* (pp. 49-70). London: Sage.

Lukács, G. (1971). *History and class consciousness* (R. Livingstone, Trans.). London: Merlin.

Lukes, S. (1974). *Power: A radical view.* London: Macmillan.

Lyotard, J.-F. (1984). *The postmodern condition: A report on knowledge* (G. Bennington & B. Massumi, Trans.). Minneapolis: University of Minnesota Press.

Lyytinen, K., & Hirschheim, R. (1988). Information systems as rational discourse: An application of Habermas's theory of communicative action. *Scandinavian Journal of Management, 4,* 19-30.

MacIntyre, A. (1984). *After virtue: A study in moral theory* (2nd ed.). Notre Dame, IN: University of Notre Dame Press.

Mangham, I. (1995). MacIntyre and managers. *Organization, 3,* 181-204.

Manning, P. (1992). *Organizational communication.* New York: Aldine de Gruyter.

Marcus, G., & Fischer, M. (1986). *Anthropology as cultural critique.* Chicago: University of Chicago Press.

Marsden, R. (1993). The politics of organizational analysis. *Organization Studies, 14,* 93-124.

Martin, J. (1990). Deconstructing organizational taboos: The suppression of gender conflict in organizations. *Organization Science, 1,* 339-359.

Martin, J. (1992). *Cultures in organizations: Three perspectives.* New York: Oxford University Press.

Meyers, R., Seibert, J., & Allen, M. (1993). A decade of organizational communication research: Journal articles 1980-1991. In S. A. Deetz (Ed.), *Communication yearbook 16* (pp. 252-330). Newbury Park, CA: Sage.

Miller, K., & Monge, P. (1985). Participation, satisfaction, and productivity: A meta-analytic review. *Academy of Management Journal, 29,* 727-753.

Miller, P., & O'Leary, T. (1987). Accounting and the construction of the governable person. *Accounting, Organizations and Society, 12,* 235-265.

Mills, A. (1994). Man/aging subjectivity, silencing diversity. *Organization, 2,* 243-269.

Monge, P. (1977). The systems perspective as a theoretical basis for the study of human communication. *Communication Quarterly, 25,* 19-29.

Monge, P. (1982). Systems theory and research in the study of organizational communication: The correspondence problem. *Human Communication Research, 8,* 245-261.

Monge, P., Cozzens, J., & Contractor, N. (1992). Communication and motivation predictors of the dynamics of innovation. *Organization Science, 2,* 1-25.

Monge, P., Farace, E., Eisenberg, E., Miller, K., & White, K. (1984). The process of studying process in organizational communication. *Journal of Communication, 34,* 22-34.

Morgan, G. (1986). *Images of organization.* Beverly Hills, CA: Sage.

Mumby, D. (1987). The political function of narrative in organizations. *Communication Monographs, 54,* 113-127.

Mumby, D. (1988). *Communication and power in organizations: Discourse, ideology, and domination.* Norwood, NJ: Ablex.

Mumby, D., & Putnam, L. (1992). The politics of emotion: A feminist reading of bounded rationality. *Academy of Management Review, 17,* 465-486.

Mumby, D. K. (1996). Feminism, postmodernism, and organizational communication: A critical reading. *Management Communication Quarterly, 9,* 259-295.

Mumby, D. K. (1997). The problem of hegemony: Re-reading Gramsci for organizational communication studies. *Western Journal of Communication, 61,* 343-375.

Nukala, S. (1996). *The discursive construction of Asian-American employees.* Unpublished doctoral dissertation, Rutgers University, New Brunswick, NJ.

Natter, W., Schatzki, T., & Jones, J. P., III. (1995). *Objectivity and its other.* New York: Guilford.

O'Keefe, D. (1976). Logical empiricism and the study of human communication. *Speech Monographs, 42,* 169-183.

Osigweh, C. (1994). A stakeholder perspective of employee responsibilities and rights. *Employee Responsibilities and Rights Journal, 7,* 279-296.

Pacanowsky, M., & O'Donnell-Trujillo, N. (1982). Communication and organizational cultures. *Western Journal of Speech Communication, 46,* 115-130.

Parker, M. (1992). Postmodern organizations or postmodern organization theory? *Organization Studies, 13,* 1-17.

Parker, M., & McHugh, G. (1991). Five tests in search of an author: A response to John Hassard's "Multiple paradigms and organizational analysis." *Organization Studies, 12,* 451-456.

Pearce, W. B. (1989). *Communication and the human condition.* Carbondale: Southern Illinois University Press.

Pepper, S. (1995). *Communicating in organizations: A cultural approach.* New York: McGraw-Hill.

Peters, T. (1987). *Thriving on chaos.* New York: Knopf.

Pettigrew, A. (1973). *The politics of organizational decision making.* London: Tavistock.

Pettigrew, A. (1990). Longitudinal field research on change. *Organization Science, 1,* 267-292.

Poole, M. S., & McPhee, R. (1983). A structurational analysis of organizational climate. In L. L. Putnam & M. E. Pacanowsky (Eds.), *Communication and organizations: An interpretive approach* (pp. 195-220). Beverly Hills, CA: Sage.

Power, M. (1994). The audit society. In A. Hopwood & P. Miller (Eds.), *Accounting as social and institutional practice* (pp. 299-316). Cambridge, UK: Cambridge University Press.

Pringle, R. (1989). *Secretaries talk.* London: Verso.

Putnam, L. (1982). Paradigms for organizational communication research. *Western Journal of Speech Communication, 46,* 192-206.

Putnam, L., & Cheney, G. (1985). Organizational communication: Historical development and future directions. In T. Benson (Ed.), *Speech communication in the 20th century* (pp. 130-156). Carbondale: Southern Illinois University Press.

Putnam, L. L., & Pacanowsky, M. E. (Eds.). (1983). *Communication and organizations: An interpretive approach.* Beverly Hills, CA: Sage.

Putnam, L. L., Phillips, N., & Chapman, P. (1996). Metaphors of communication and organization. In S. R. Clegg, C. Hardy, & W. J. Nord (Eds.), *Handbook of organization studies* (pp. 375-408). London: Sage.

Putnam, L., Bantz, C., Deetz, S., Mumby, D., & Van Maanen, J. (1993). Ethnography versus critical theory: Debating organizational research. *Journal of Management Inquiry, 2,* 221-235.

Reason, P. (1994). Three approaches to participatory inquiry. In N. Denzin & Y. Lincoln (Eds.), *Handbook of qualitative research* (pp. 324-339). Thousand Oaks, CA: Sage.

Redding, W. C. (1979). Organizational communication theory and ideology: An overview. In D. Nimmo (Ed.), *Communication yearbook 3* (pp. 309-341). New Brunswick, NJ: Transaction.

Redding, C., & Tompkins, P. (1988). Organizational communication—Past and future tenses. In G. Goldhaber & G. Barnett (Eds.), *Handbook of organizational communication* (pp. 5-34). Norwood, NJ: Ablex.

Reed, M. (1985). *New directions in organizational analysis.* London: Tavistock.

Richetto, G. (1977). Organizational communication theory and research. In B. Ruben (Ed.), *Communication yearbook 1* (pp. 331-346). New Brunswick, NJ: Transaction.

Riley, P. (1983). A structurationist account of political cultures. *Administrative Science Quarterly, 28,* 414-438.

Rodríguez, J., & Cai, D. (1994). When your epistemology gets in the way. *Communication Education, 43,* 263-272.

Rorty, R. (1979). *Philosophy and the mirror of nature.* Princeton, NJ: Princeton University Press.

Rorty, R. (1989). *Contingency, irony and solidarity.* Cambridge, UK: Cambridge University Press.

Rosen, M. (1985). Breakfast at Spiro's: Dramaturgy and dominance. *Journal of Management, 11*(2), 31-48.

Schall, M. (1983). A communication-rules approach to organizational culture. *Administrative Science Quarterly, 28,* 557-581.

Schein, E. (1992). *Organizational culture and leadership* (2nd ed.). San Francisco: Jossey-Bass.

Schwartzman, H. B. (1989). *The meeting.* New York: Plenum.

Senge, P. (1990). *The fifth discipline: The art and practice of the learning organization.* New York: Doubleday.

Shockley-Zalabak, P., & Morley, D. (1994). Creating a culture: A longitudinal examination of the influence of management and employee values on communication rule stability and emergence. *Human Communication Research, 20,* 334-355.

Shotter, J. (1993). *Conversational realities: The construction of life through language.* Newbury Park, CA: Sage.

Shotter, J., & Gergen, K. (1994). Social construction: Knowledge, self, others, and continuing the conversation. In S. A. Deetz (Ed.), *Communication yearbook 17* (pp. 3-33). Thousand Oaks, CA: Sage.

Sias, P., & Jablin, F. (1995). Differential superior-subordinate relations, perceptions of fairness, and coworker communication. *Human Communication Research, 22,* 5-38.

Sless, D. (1988). Forms of control. *Australian Journal of Communication, 14,* 57-69.

Smeltzer, L. (1993). A de facto definition and focus of managerial communication. *Management Communication Quarterly, 6,* 428-440.

Smircich, L. (1983). Concepts of culture and organizational analysis. *Administrative Science Quarterly, 28,* 339-358.

Smircich, L., & Calás, M. B. (1987). Organizational culture: A critical assessment. In F. M. Jablin, L. L. Putnam, K. H. Roberts, & L. W. Porter (Eds.), *Handbook of organizational communication: An interdisciplinary perspective* (pp. 228-263). Newbury Park, CA: Sage.

Smith, R. (1993, May). *Images of organizational communication: Root-metaphors of the organization-communication relation.* Paper presented at the annual meeting of the International Communication Association, Washington, D.C.

Smith, R., & Eisenberg, E. (1987). Conflict at Disneyland: A root-metaphor analysis. *Communication Monographs, 54,* 367-380.

Smith, R., & Turner, P. (1995). A social constructionist reconfiguration of metaphor analysis: An application of "SCMA" to organizational socialization theorizing. *Communication Monographs, 62,* 152-181.

Sprague, J. (1992). Expanding the research agenda for instructional communication: Raising some unanswered questions. *Communication Education, 41,* 1-25.

Stablein, R., & Nord, W. (1985). Practical and emancipatory interests in organizational symbolism. *Journal of Management, 11*(2), 13-28.

Strauss, A. (1978). *Negotiations: Varieties, contexts, processes, and social order.* San Francisco: Jossey-Bass.

Sullivan, J., & Taylor, S. (1991). A cross-cultural test of compliance-gaining theory. *Management Communication Quarterly, 5,* 220-239.

Sutton, R., & Staw, B. (1995). What theory is not. *Administrative Science Quarterly, 40,* 371-384.

Taylor, J. (1993). *Rethinking the theory of organizational communication: How to read an organization.* Norwood, NJ: Ablex.

Tompkins, P., & Cheney, G. (1985). Communication and unobtrusive control in contemporary organizations. In R. McPhee & P. Tompkins (Eds.), *Organizational communication: Traditional themes and new directions* (pp. 179-210). Beverly Hills, CA: Sage.

Townley, B. (1993). Foucault, power/knowledge, and its relevance for human resource management. *Academy of Management Review, 18,* 518-545.

Treichler, P. (1989). What definitions do: Childbirth, cultural crisis, and the challenge to medical discourse. In B. Dervin, L. Grossberg, B. O'Keefe, & E. Wartella (Eds.), *Rethinking communication* (pp. 424-453). Newbury Park, CA: Sage.

Trethewey, A. (1997). Resistance, identity, and empowerment: A postmodern feminist analysis of clients in a human service organization. *Communication Monographs, 64,* 281-301.

Trujillo, N. (1987). Implication of interpretive approaches for organizational communication research and practice. In L. Thayer (Ed.), *Organization ↔ communication: Emerging perspectives II* (pp. 46-63). Norwood, NJ: Ablex.

Vallas, S. (1993). *Power in the workplace: The politics of production at AT&T.* Albany: State University of New York Press.

Van Maanen, J. (1988). *Tales from the field.* Chicago: University of Chicago Press.

Wagner, J., III, & Gooding, R. (1987). Effects of societal trends on participation research. *Administrative Science Quarterly, 32,* 241-262.

Weedon, C. (1987). *Feminist practice and poststructuralist theory.* Oxford, UK: Basil Blackwell.

Weick, K. E. (1979). *The social psychology of organizing* (2nd ed.). Reading, MA: Addison-Wesley.

Wendt, R. (1994). Learning to "walk the talk": A critical tale of the micropolitics at a total quality university. *Management Communication Quarterly, 8,* 5-45.

Wert-Gray, S., Center, C., Brashers, D., & Meyers, R. (1991). Research topics and methodological orientations in organizational communication: A decade in review. *Communication Studies, 42,* 141-154.

Westenholz, A. (1991). Democracy as "organizational divorce" and how postmodern democracy is stifled by unity and majority. *Economic and Industrial Democracy, 12,* 173-186.

Whyte, W. (Ed.). (1991). *Participatory action research.* Newbury Park, CA: Sage.

Willmott, H. (1993). Breaking the paradigm mentality. *Organization Studies, 14,* 681-719.

Wilkins, B., & Anderson, P. (1991). Gender differences and similarities in management communication. *Management Communication Quarterly, 5,* 6-35.

2

Development of Key Constructs

CHARLES CONRAD
Texas A&M University

JULIE HAYNES
Rowan University

Our goal in this chapter is to explore the key constructs of contemporary organizational communication theory. In doing so, we shall define the term *construct* quite literally, as a symbolic creation that enacts the worldview(s) of a language community. As such, constructs are the products of rhetorical processes through which groups of social actors—including groups of scholars—attribute meaning to actions and situations. Constructs come in at least three forms. Some constructs provide means of linking scholarly propositions to empirical observations. Others address conceptual problems that exist within theoretical frames. For instance, many of the key constructs of psychoanalytic theory are derived from and their character determined by problematic features of Freud's construction of unconscious motivation (Burke, 1941/1984). Still other constructs provide links among theoretical perspectives, just as the theory of relativity links chemistry and quantum mechanics. Of course, the notion that the humanities and the social sciences are rhetorical constructions is not new (Simons, 1989, 1990), but as far as we know it has not been used to examine the discourse of organizational communication.

Some commentators view organizational communication as an amalgam of disparate research traditions, each with its own core constructs, epistemological assumptions, and methodological commitments. These traditions are connected by a common subject matter (communication within or among organizations) and unified by a commitment to eclecticism (Goldhaber & Barnett, 1988b; Krone, Jablin, & Putnam, 1987; Leipzig & Moore, 1982). Definitional, conceptual, and methodological problems exist, but they are capable of being worked out within the research perspectives in which they arise. Since these disparate research orientations operate independently of one another, *problems* within one of them do not handicap the development of "normal science" within the others. Nor do these problems raise questions about the fundamental assumptions of different research orientations or threaten the notion of comfortable eclecticism.

We offer an alternative reading. On the one hand, we argue that the various threads of organizational communication research/theory are connected by a common conceptual problem—the need to analyze the interrelationship between symbolic action and social/organizational structures. Although each research orientation is defined by differing choices about how to deal with the action-structure problematic, they are unified by that common problem. Second, we suggest that the development of organizational communication and its component strains of research between 1985 and 1995 can informatively be read as an effort to grapple with problematic elements of a dualism between action and structure.[1]

ANALYZING
KEY CONSTRUCTS

The analytical process used in this essay is drawn from the work of Kenneth Burke (1941/1984, 1970). Throughout his work Burke argues that criticism must be empirical; that is, it must be grounded in the details of texts. He suggests that critics can "chart" the essential concepts present in a text and the interrelationships among those concepts (Berthold, 1976). Critics begin by isolating the key constructs in the text and represent

those concepts in a series of key terms. Some terms coalesce to form the unifying and central principles present in the text; some clusters represent competing principles. The relationships among these equated and contrasted clusters surface through structural configurations that lead critics from one construct to others. Then, through an iterative process, critics use that initial structural configuration to reexamine the text(s), searching for constructs that were not represented in their initial analysis (Conrad, 1984). The process continues until no significant residual constructs are left unaccounted for.

The critics' goal is to construct a *summation* of the core principles and their interrelationships, not to *summarize* every element of the text. This process does not mean that every construct in the text will emerge from the analysis. Indeed, many constructs are so closely interrelated that the principle underlying them can be represented by any one of them. Eventually, a hierarchy will emerge among the clusters of key terms, one that encapsulates the interrelationships among clusters of terms. This hierarchy will culminate in a central tension, an "agon" that "logically contains" (Burke, 1945/1969) the interrelationships among the clusters of terms.

Texts are not composed of seamless webs of associations. Indeed, they are made of constructs that are dialectically related to one another. Key constructs simultaneously reinforce and contradict one another—they merge and divide in complex webs of associations and contrasts. For example, Burke (1970) argues that the first three chapters of *Genesis* are defined by the constructs "God as author/creator" and "God as legislator/disciplinarian." These two senses of "authority" coalesce to define "God" as a multifaceted construct, and thereby articulate the tensions and contradictions implicit in Judeo-Christian notions of divinity. Each of the subordinate constructs in Judeo-Christian theology—guilt and catharsis, mortification and victimage, reward and retribution—are logically contained in this core tension.

Once critics extract a pattern of concepts and concept interrelationships from a text, they must articulate their interpretations of that pattern. Typically, critics will reverse the analytical process in their presentation of the outcome of the analysis, beginning with a discussion of the central construct/relationship and subsequently explaining how it is individuated in the component constructs and their interrelationships.

Our analysis of organizational communication research reveals six clusters of key constructs and construct interrelationships. No cluster is independent of the other clusters, although their interrelationships change as the decade progresses. No cluster is a seamless web of connections, and the conceptual tensions that exist within each construct system became articulated as they develop. Both the interrelationships among the clusters and the developmental processes of each cluster are understandable through an action-structure dialectic.

The Dialectic Between Action and Structure

It is not especially surprising that the "action-structure" pair emerges as the central tension in organizational communication research and theory. A number of commentators have argued that an action-structure dualism is the defining characteristic of modern Western social and organizational theory (see, e.g., Clegg, 1989, 1990; Dawe, 1970, 1978; Giddens, 1979, 1984; Reed, 1985). Historically, social theorists set forth two conflicting views of human action—one focusing on the myriad factors that determine human action and one concentrating on the processes through which social actors create and sustain social realities. These perspectives differ in their assumptions about the nature of human actors, the sources of action, and the key problematics faced by social theorists.

On the one hand is the doctrine of "social system" that focuses on structural configura-

tions and is articulated through a language of objectivity and externality (Dawe, 1978).[2] Although actors are viewed as choice-making beings, their choices are circumscribed by the characteristics of their "situations" (Dawe, 1978, p. 367). Through communicating with others in a society, individuals learn to accept the values and norms of their society and construct a self-identity that is appropriate to the roles they play. The result is a complex set of constraints that determines individuals' actions. Although the doctrine of social system does not necessarily exclude constructs like "choice" and "symbolic action," it severely restricts their scope and significance.

The central element of this doctrine is the "problem of order," the concern that individuals, "if left to their own devices, can and will create self-and-socially destructive anarchy and chaos" (Dawe, 1978, p. 370). Constraint is necessary for society to exist at all. Constraints exist outside of actors' immediate interpretations and choices. They are self-generating and self-maintaining (Dawe, 1970). The central challenge facing the doctrine of social system is maintaining a view of action as guided and constrained by "external" pressures while not slipping into situational determinism. "Constraint" is not the same thing as "determinism." The latter speaks of determination of individuals' thoughts and actions by forces that are exterior to them. The former speaks of the way social properties influence the choices and actions of members of social collectives (Giddens, 1984, pp. 96-107). But pressure to substitute determinism for constraint is inherent in the doctrine of social system, for the "problem of order" disappears in a determined social/organizational world.

On the other hand, a "doctrine of social action" focuses on subjective experience and voluntary/creative action (Dawe, 1978). Human beings are autonomous agents whose ongoing actions create and re-create both their own selves and their societies. The social world emerges through the actions and interactions of its members. This does not mean that social actors are not constrained by their societies. Indeed, actors create meaning systems that, in turn, constrain their actions. But constraint is not external to and superordinate over people. It is located in actors' actions and interactions, in humanly constructed and humanly reinforced structures of power and domination (Dawe, 1978).

The central element of the doctrine of social action is the "problem of control." In short, how can a view of humans as individual, choice-making beings account for similarities in patterns of action; in other words, how can actionist perspectives avoid slipping into the extreme of voluntarism/subjectivism? A doctrine of social action that omits or fails to explain social/cultural constraint is just as problematic as a doctrine of social system that denies or does not explain individual volition (Bhaskar, 1979). If actions are to be meaningful, people must act in accordance with the rules and resources available in their sociocultural situations. Even though rules and resources are created, re-created, or modified through social action, they are relatively stable within each episode of symbolic interaction. Thus, social/cultural rules and resources serve as guidelines and constraints on action.

However, how can actionist perspectives introduce a conception of constraint without sliding into determinism? According to actionist orientations, action and choice reside between the extremes of fate (determinism) and freedom (voluntarism). The challenge facing actionist perspectives is to remain between these two extremes. Eventually, advocates of the doctrine of social action attempted to solve this problem by constructing the concept of "internalization." External forces do not determine actors' choices, but they create ideas that social actors incorporate into their choices. For example, one's biological sex does not determine one's career choices, but the division of labor in a society leads to patterns of behavior that are codified in ideas (constructs) such as "gender roles" and "femininity/masculinity." Social actors still choose their gender identifications, but their choices (and thus their identifications and related behaviors) are patterned and predictable because

they have internalized social/cultural constraints. Different people internalize social "norms" to different degrees and in different ways, so variations in choices do occur—action is not determined by external factors. The concept of internalization allows actionist researchers to treat the structural guidelines and constraints present in a society as dimensions of social actors' perceptions and interpretations, rather than as external determinants of action. Through "internalization," actionist social theorists avoid both the problem of determinism and a slide toward pure voluntarism.

But "internalization" provides an illusory escape. Substituting internalization (or any of its relatives—"tacit knowledge," for example) for externality accepts the basic logic of the doctrine of social system. "Internalization" may expand the conception of how structural constraint is achieved and may broaden the range of options from which a social actor may "choose," but does not alter the locus of constraint itself—the conditions of action still are external to the actor (Dawe, 1970; Harris, 1980).

In addition, the "internalization" construct has three paradoxical effects. First, internalization elevates social norms to become *constitutive* of persons' identities, not just *regulative* of them. Societal constraint thus can be total—resistance is possible only when processes of internalization are flawed or incomplete. Thus, instead of moving social theory away from an oversocialized view of action (Granovetter, 1985), "internalization" expands and *reinforces* the notion of external constraint (Dawe, 1970, p. 209). Second, the internalization construct explains inaction much better than it explains action (Harris, 1980, p. 27). Any observed variability in social actors' choices within the same social context is explained in terms of the "degree" to which they have internalized cultural values and role definitions. Explaining positive choices in this way makes the whole concept of internalization/role circular (Harris, 1980, pp. 28-29). Actions still are either determined by social/cultural pressures or they are unintelligible (Dawe, 1978). Finally, "internalization" renders the concept of subjective meaning insignificant. If meaning is a function of a social self knowledgeably applying learned interpretive processes to learned definitions of situations, internalization is the only process that needs to be explained (Dawe, 1970, p. 209). Subjectivity/meaning is submerged in internalization and internalization reduces to socialization. Thus, with the addition of "internalization," the doctrine of social action "avoids" the problem of voluntarism/subjectivity by incorporating determinism-by-another- name.

The two doctrines are dialectically related to one another. Theorists working within the doctrine of social system will simultaneously be pulled toward determinism by a need to confront the problem of order and toward the doctrine of social action by the need to construct a human actor capable of choice and volition. Conversely, theorists working within the doctrine of social action will be pulled toward voluntarism by the need to avoid determinism, and toward concepts of social systems by the need to explain *patterns* of action (the problem of control). In the remainder of this essay, we suggest that the way in which the key constructs of organizational communication theory have developed can be understood in terms of this dialectical relationship between the doctrines of social system and social action.

Clusters That Privilege Structure Over Action

First, we examine three clusters of constructs that enact the two poles of the action-structure dualism. Two clusters, labeled "information exchange" and "superior-subordinate relationship," form the doctrine of social system, while a third, labeled "meaning creation," articulates an actionist doctrine. We then examine the development of three clusters of constructs that aim to integrate structure and action: structuration, identification/unobtrusive control, and critical theory.[3] Finally, we briefly examine construct systems that challenge the action-structure dialectic itself.

An Information Exchange Cluster

One primary cluster of constructs in organizational communication research included six key terms: *information, networks, uncertainty, message, load,* and especially later in the era, *technology*. The central term was *information*. In fact, communication was defined as the flow of information through networks of "conduits" (Axley, 1984; Monge & Miller, 1988; O'Connell, 1988; Wigand, 1988, p. 321). Information exists in "chunks" (Fulk & Mani, 1986; Krone et al., 1987; Roberts & O'Reilly, 1978) that often are called "messages." Information, in this mechanistic perspective, moves from one point in an organization to another; varies in quality; may be embedded in messages that are unclear or equivocal; influences the uncertainties that employees face; may be distorted by employees who are motivated to do so; may not arrive at the appropriate point(s) in organizational networks or may arrive at a time or in such a volume that it cannot be used efficiently. As the 1985-1995 era progressed, electronic technologies played an important part in conceptualizations of information flow. Different kinds of communication technologies produce different conduits that influence information flow in different ways, but the nature of *information* itself is constant, regardless of the kind of conduit or network involved.

In much information-exchange research, the concept of organizational "actors" is either absent or marginalized. When analyses include the concept, actors are defined as the users or processors of information, not as active agents involved in the cocreation of meanings and meaning systems (Huber & Daft, 1987). Typically, information-exchange research focuses on how employees' processes of searching for information lead them to process a flawed sample of the information that is theoretically available (Greenbaum, Hellweg, & Falcione, 1988; O'Connell, 1988, pp. 474-

475; O'Reilly, Chatman, & Anderson, 1987, pp. 604-618). Once information arrives (or is obtained, depending on the particular version of this term being used), it is processed—interpreted, integrated with other information, and remembered—processes that "distort" its "real" or "intended" meaning (O'Reilly et al., 1987, especially Figures 17.2, 17.3, and 17.4).[4]

Consistent with the doctrine of social systems, this research attempts to isolate the situational, task-oriented, and personality-related determinants of employees' attitudes, behaviors, or communicative acts, usually in complex, multivariable models. Topical summaries of this research are available in Allen, Gotcher, and Seibert (1993); Wert-Gray, Center, Brashers, and Meyers (1991); and Sutcliffe, Chapter 6, this volume.

Communication technology is treated as a determinant of information exchange, and technology use is seen as the outcome of various external determinants, for example, organizational design (Allen & Hauptman, 1990; Culnan & Markus, 1987; Huber, 1990); organizational structure, including centralization (Contractor & Eisenberg, 1991; Fulk & Dutton, 1985; Fulk, Schmitz, & Steinfield, 1991; Olson, 1982); information flow and "distortion" (Zmud, 1990); and processes of decision making and communication flow (O'Reilly et al., 1987; Sambamurthy & Poole, 1993).

In short, a "structure determines information exchange" construct system remains an important part of organizational communication research and theory, in spite of the extended critiques of functionalist research that emerged during the 1980s. Interrelationships among variables become more complex as the 1985-1995 era progresses, especially after advanced statistical techniques become available (Poole & McPhee, 1994), but the logic of the doctrine of social systems remains intact.

However, even as early as the mid-1980s a second strain of social-systems-oriented research emerges, one that introduces conceptions of social action into the orientation. The initial move comes through suggestions that information has a "symbolic" dimension that explains why people exchange different information than economic exchange models predict (see Eisenberg & Riley's, 1988, p. 136, summary of research by Feldman and March and by Larkey and Sproull). Information and processes of information exchange fulfill personal goals of organizational actors, regardless of the intentions of the individual who originally produced the information—goals like legitimating one's self, one's actions, or one's organization (see Eisenberg & Riley's, 1988, p. 136, summary of legitimation theory). Even behavioral decision theory (after Simon's pioneering work) defines messages as "things" that stimulate inferences, not transfer information (Euske & Roberts, 1987).

Efforts to incorporate actionist constructs into systems-oriented research also emerge in research on communication technology and communication networks. Some communication technology research begins to focus on the interrelationships between technology and meaning creation (e.g., Alexander, Penley, & Jernigan, 1991; Fulk et al., 1991; Keen, 1990; Trevino, Daft, & Lengel, 1990), and some studies employ "integrative" perspectives like structuration (DeSanctis & Poole, 1994; Poole & DeSanctis, 1990; Poole & Holmes, 1995). Reconceptualizations of communication networks, initiated at least as early as Monge and Eisenberg's (1987) and Danowski's (1988) analyses of emergent, meaning-centered networks, culminate in Stohl's (1995) conceptualization of networks as "connectedness in action." Networks extend beyond organizational "boundaries," now conceptualized as always permeable and never stable, to include the complex, multidimensional set of connections that each organizational member negotiates in her or his own life. In this expanded sense, "networks" not only "carry" meaning, they are composed of complex, constantly emerging systems of meaning and interpretation (Danowski, 1980). They "contain" organizational actors' relational histories and anticipations of future interactions (Putnam & Stohl, 1990) and "blur" traditional distinctions between "senders" and "receivers" of messages.

At first glance, these changes appear to constitute a major shift away from the doctrine of social system. The "symbolism" construct redefines "information" from a technical "measure of uncertainty" to more of an everyday notion of "symbols and other stimuli that affect our awareness" (Huber & Daft, 1987, p. 157, fn. 1). Organizational actors and their motives and needs move to a more central place in researchers' conceptualizations, creating more of a "receiver orientation" toward processes of information flow. Members of organizations play active roles in the communication process, and meaning is located in context-bound *uses* of information, not in information itself.

In important ways the shift to a receiver orientation inserts actionist constructs into structure-oriented research. However, these additions do not fundamentally change the definition of the information/uncertainty/message/load cluster of constructs. Information remains something that exists independent of perceivers, and is still some*thing* that social actors use and process, that is, obtain, interpret, distribute, and thus potentially distort. Information load still is defined in terms of the quantity of information received, the degree of uncertainty it contains (the extent to which the information can be interpreted differently by different actors), and its *variety*. The latter term is the composite of a number of factors that are external to organizational actors (diversity, independence of sources, turbulence, unpredictability, and instability). Thus, it is easily distorted by their processes of interpreting and exchanging it with others. It is contained in messages characterized by varying degrees of clarity/uncertainty that place different loads on receiver/interpreters. Information is the central construct embedded in a deeply articulated structural language of information exchange.

A Supervisor-Subordinate Relationship Cluster

Research on supervisor-subordinate relationships has been a central focus of organizational communication since the mid-1970s (see Jablin, 1979). This line of research continues to follow the doctrine of social system,

although, like information-exchange research, some moves have been made to incorporate actionist concepts. The key terms of this cluster are *supervisory communication, motivation, performance,* and *situation* (Cusella, 1987; Downs, Clampitt, & Pfeiffer, 1988). Communicating is something that supervisors do to accomplish something else—lead, motivate, influence, control (Thayer, 1988), evaluate, or direct (Cusella, 1987, p. 626). Although subordinates are tacit elements of supervisor-subordinate interactions, they typically are conceptualized as "passive information receptacles" (Cusella, 1987, p. 642). Research on organizational socialization casts subordinates in more active roles—as actors who make attributions about others' behaviors, negotiate role requirements, and influence their supervisors (Jablin, 1987b). Even in this context, supervisors are the "key communicators" because they possess the information that subordinates need to become socialized into their organizations (Falcione & Wilson, 1988).

The fourth key term in this cluster is *situation,* as in "situational determinants." A variety of personal and situational factors are cast as determinants of superior-subordinate communication. Frequently examined personal variables include gender, communicator style, and argumentativeness. Differences in supervisors' and subordinates' interpretive frames are said to create "semantic-informational distance," which contributes to distortion of information and to misunderstandings about what information really means (Dansereau & Markham, 1987). Inadequate organizational socialization increases these differences (Falcione & Wilson, 1988). Situational factors include many of the core constructs of the information exchange cluster (e.g., information flow, communication networks, and communication technology). These factors are cast as determinants of the effectiveness of superior-subordinate exchanges (Dansereau & Markham, 1987). This does not mean that researchers are conceptualizing superior-subordinate communication relationships as *embedded* in "the larger organizational context" (Dansereau & Markham, 1987), only that they construct a number of situational determinants of supervisor-subordinate communication (Cusella, 1987).

However, as the era progresses, a number of studies espouse a "receiver orientation" toward supervisor-subordinate communication. Subordinates are conceptualized as agents who actively seek out a variety of information, and who simultaneously process information from multiple, differing sources (Cusella, 1987; Falcione & Wilson, 1988). Employees' perceptions play a central role in research, as either dependent or independent variables (e.g., Chiles & Zorn, 1995; Eaves & Leathers, 1991; Husband, 1985; Marshall & Stohl, 1993; Sias & Jablin, 1995). Taking more of a receiver orientation in turn necessitates taking a process or "interactional" perspective on supervisor-subordinate exchanges (and vice versa). Jablin's "life-cycle" orientation toward processes of assimilation (Dansereau & Markham, 1987; Jablin, 1987b) and Fairhurst, Green, and Snavely's (1984a, 1984b) longitudinal studies of episodes in "chains" of control episodes are exemplars of this shift.

Discussions of organizational socialization and assimilation also introduce "internalization" as a core communicative process, and move the construct "control" to a central place in supervisor-subordinate research (Cusella, 1987). Some structure-oriented researchers respond to Stohl and Redding's (1987) call for message-centered research and outline factors that guide/constrain organizational actors' choices of communicative/message strategies (e.g., Gayle, 1991; Waldron, 1991). Others cast organizational actors in active "interpretive" roles, by examining the ways in which existing organizational meaning *systems* influence and/or constrain employees' interpretations of organizational actions (e.g., Bach, 1989; Morrill & Thomas, 1992; Stohl, 1993).

Each of these moves extends the systems doctrine by depicting organizational actors as active participants in organizational communication processes. They also lead to ways of substituting the construct "constraint" for situational "determinant." For example, Morrill and Thomas (1992) use longitudinal studies of superior-subordinate conflicts to examine processes of relational development. Their interpretations of a very rich data set focus on emergent contextual constraints rather than a priori situational determinants, but their foci remain on "*behavioral processes embedded in larger social systems*" (p. 400, emphasis in original).

In other cases, the merger of constraints and determinants surfaces in temporal terms, as recursive processes. Albrecht and Hall (1991a) call on structure-oriented researchers to recognize that employees' choices create and maintain communication networks while they focus on ways in which network type and centrality influence perceptions and commitments. Corman and Scott (1994) provide a detailed discussion of the recursive relationship between communicative action and network development. Similarly, Seibold and Contractor (1993) examine the recursive relationship that exists between the use of communication technologies and the creation and reproduction of organizational structures. By defining employees as receivers and interpreters of information, structure-oriented researchers incorporate actionist constructions. By substituting constraint for determinant, they reduce the likelihood that organizational communication research would slip into determinism. But neither shift changes the logic of the doctrine of organizational communication systems, and the continued publication of a sizable amount of research that does not incorporate these integrative constructs suggests that structure-oriented research continues to be a significant part of organizational communication.[5]

A Cluster That Privileges Action Over Structure

By the mid-1980s, a great deal of effort had been expended articulating the underlying assumptions of "interpretive" perspectives toward organizational communication. Although advocates often extolled the rich potential of these perspectives (Eisenberg & Riley, 1988; Putnam & Poole, 1987), organizational communication scholars produced relatively little actual interpretive, message-oriented, meaning-creation-centered research prior to 1985 (Deetz, 1992a; Huber & Daft, 1987; Stohl & Redding, 1987; Tompkins, 1987). But by the end of the 1980s, a rapidly growing body of action-oriented research had emerged. Initially, a number of scholars examined symbolic forms—stories, myths, rituals, and metaphors—as expressions or reflections of employees' taken-for-granted assumptions, or as strategies for maintaining organizational control (see Brown, 1990; Trice & Beyer, 1993, especially chaps. 3 and 5, for summaries). As the era progressed, relevant research often called for taking a performative perspective on organizational symbolism (Pacanowsky & O'Donnell-Trujillo, 1983), for examining story-*telling* as well as organizational stories, narrative *action* in addition to organizational narratives, the *enactment* of rituals as well as their meanings, and so on (Brown, 1990; Czarniawska-Joerges, 1994; Goodall, Wilson, & Waagen, 1986; Knuf, 1993).

The core constructs of this actionist cluster are *culture, meanings/messages, symbolism,* and *ambiguity.* Some applications of this cluster focus on the ways in which organizational communication practices and cultural artifacts articulate and reflect the shared meanings of a social collective (Cheney & Vibbert, 1987; Smircich & Calás, 1987; Triandis & Albert, 1987). Others examine the processes through which meanings become shared and cultures and subcultures are formed and sustained through symbolic action (Eisenberg & Riley, 1988; Huber & Daft, 1987; Krone et al., 1987; Tompkins, 1987). Still others examine the processes through which ambiguity is managed symbolically. Additional uses of this cluster linked the meaning-symbolism-ambiguity nexus to a number of other constructs—for example, power (Frost, 1987), communication rules (Cushman, Sanderson-King, & Smith, 1988; Monge & Eisenberg, 1987), socialization (Eisenberg & Riley, 1988; Falcione & Wilson, 1988; Jablin, 1987b), and rhetoric (Tompkins, 1987).[6]

The core problematic for actionist perspectives is a tendency to slide toward a subjectivist/actionist extreme. Actions are divorced from the societal and organizational contexts within which they occur. Organizational symbolism is "romanticized"; that is, its meaning is interpreted/constructed without a systematic analysis of the structural configurations surrounding its creation and enactment (Turner, 1992, p. 61; see also Burke, 1991; Deetz, 1994; Ebers, 1985). Organizational texts are treated as self-referential entities rather than as dynamic processes that emerge and develop within particular socioeconomic-organizational contexts through interactional, intersubjective processes. Voluntarist/subjectivist/romanticized analyses generate partial depictions of human symbolic action. For example, recognizing that a society or organization is constituted by a symbolic network does not in itself explain why a particular system of symbols was chosen, what these symbols convey or signify, or why and how the symbol system managed to become relatively autonomous (Ash, 1990; Baudrillard, 1988; Castoriadis, 1987; Turner, 1992). In short, "although institutions are unavoidably symbolic, they cannot be *reduced* to the symbolic" (Turner, 1992, p. 52) without a retreat into relativism; if resistance and transformation are to be possible, constraint cannot be reduced to ideation.

Actionist organizational communication researchers have avoided these subjectivist tendencies by incorporating some concept of situational "constraint" into their analysis, much as structure-oriented researchers avoided determinist extremes by incorporating actionist constructs. The operant "meaning systems" and dominant interpretive processes of organizational cultures/subcultures are depicted as strong influences on organizational action. As a result, the range of "choice" available to organizational actors in actionist research is limited; voluntarism/subjectivism is avoided. However, this adjustment also makes it difficult to maintain a distinction between external "determinants" and situational "constraints" (see Alvesson, 1987, for a critique of this type of "organizational culture" research). Of course, constraint is not the same thing as determinant. But once actionist researchers introduce pressures that are external to immediate communicative interactions into their research, it is difficult for them to avoid introducing other structure-oriented constructs.

Assessing the Development of the Key Constructs

In many ways, organizational communication evidences the developmental processes that Dawe and others have outlined for social theory in general. Two differing strains of research coexist, one focusing on systems and one concentrating on action. Both strains move toward incorporating key constructs of the other strain, thereby avoiding the extremes of voluntarism and determinism. However, the development of organizational communication construct systems has differed in two ways from the trajectory Dave described for social theory as a whole. First, a substantial amount of "pure" systems-oriented research continues to be produced, in spite of frequent critiques of functionalist research and in spite of efforts by some structure-oriented researchers to incorporate actionist constructs into the doctrine. Second, there has been little or no tendency for actionist-oriented organizational communication researchers to slide toward a voluntarist/subjectivist extreme. The early introduction of "constraint" into actionist research seems to have prevented any tendency to romanticize the symbolic, to divorce symbolic action from systemic pressures, although the pressures to do so continue to exist because they are inherent in the logic of the doctrine of social action.

Three Clusters That Strive to Integrate Action and Structure

The dialectical relationship between action and structure means that tensions will exist in any effort to explain social or organizational action. One way of managing these tensions is to introduce modifying constructs into each doctrine. Another is to construct perspectives that explicitly integrate action and structure within the same construct system. Paradoxi-

cally, the dialectical tensions between action and structure are especially visible, and especially complicated, in efforts to develop truly integrative perspectives. The challenge faced by integrative perspectives is to retain a balance in the dialectical relationship between action and structure. Only then is it possible to deal simultaneously with the problem of order and the problem of consent. Three differing integrative frameworks were proposed by organizational communication researchers between 1985 and 1995: structuration, identification/unobtrusive control, and critical theory. Each of these perspectives developed in ways that were influenced by the action-structure dialectic.

Structuration

Applying structuration theory to organizational communication generates a new cluster of key constructs, all linked to an overall construct labeled the "duality of structure." This is the notion that action both produces/reproduces/transforms structure and is possible only because of the existence of structural conditions—the interactional rules and the material and communicative resources that are available to members of a particular society at a particular place and time. Like structure, action also is multidimensional, with component constructs labeled "agency," "symbolic interaction," "subjectivity/ intersubjectivity," and "knowledgeability." These two clusters are linked together by a third cluster, composed of the constructs "power," "production/reproduction," and "resistance/ transformation."

Giddens's conception of the duality of structure is a particularly appropriate vehicle for dealing with the action-structure dialectic because it is grounded in both an extensive critique of the doctrine of social system and the doctrine of social action (see Giddens, 1976, 1979). Giddens rejects the determinism of the doctrine of social system, but also argues that actionist perspectives tend to collapse structural factors into attributes of action. Material conditions are reduced to ideation. The strength of structuration is its ability to avoid both sets of problems; the difficulty of applying structuration is to maintain this kind of balance. The probative force of structuration is lost if the perspective is reduced to either determinism or voluntarism. Structurationist organizational communication research has avoided the temptations of determinism; the attractions of voluntarism have been more difficult to resist.

Structurationist organizational communication originated during an era of extensive criticism of social-system-oriented organizational communication research. For example, Riley (1983) explicitly casts her use of structuration as a rejection of functionalism and an affirmation of interpretive studies of organizational cultures (pp. 414-415). Poole and McPhee's (1983) initial application of structuration to organizational climate begins with an extended critique of systems-oriented research. Monge and Eisenberg (1987) argue that Giddens's notions of "provinces of meaning" would provide a corrective for the problems facing systems-oriented network analysis (pp. 332-333). Eisenberg and Riley (1988) contend that structuration provides a potentially valuable perspective for studying organizational symbolism. Symbolic acts are central to the constitution of organizational "reality," a dynamic revealed in processes of socializing newcomers, legitimizing activities, creating and sustaining power relationships, and managing organizational change (pp. 136-142; see also Eisenberg & Riley, Chapter 9, this volume).[7] For each of these authors, structuration promises a communication-centered (or at least a language-centered), process-oriented perspective for analyzing social action in institutional and institutionalized settings. In particular, Giddens's duality of structure provides a process-oriented framework for scholars to explore the emergence, reproduction, and transformation of meaning systems and communicative interaction. In short, structuration includes constructs that integrate the key terms of the doctrine of social action and those of the doctrine of social system. The resulting perspective serves as a corrective to deterministic tendencies while not ignoring social structure or reducing it to ideation.

But structuration was introduced into organizational communication amid multiple calls for an "interpretive" turn. Because the central claim of this intellectual climate was an affirmation of actionist social science, the context made it difficult for researchers to maintain a balance between action and structure and resist pressures to reduce the perspective to a version of actionism. We suggest that as structurationist organizational communication research developed, two different "schools" emerged. In one, pressures to reduce this integrative perspective to actionism were more influential than in the other.

Actionist structuration. Actionist structuration focuses on how structure influences action while de-emphasizing the processes through which action influences structure. For example, Banks and Riley (1993) examine the ways in which tensions between two cultural assumptions—Americans' focus on individual advancement combined with American engineers' commitments to their profession, on the one hand, and Japanese managers' commitment to "community" combined with the practice of staying with the same firm throughout their career, on the other hand—are managed and reproduced through a language game of control. Banks and Riley effectively describe structural constraints on action—existing rules/resources, temporal and spatial contexts (p. 174), institutionalized practices (p. 177), and actors' ontological insecurities (p. 172) and reflexive self-monitoring (p. 171)—as does similar research by Fairhurst (1993), Fairhurst and Chandler (1989), Harrison (1994), and Shockley-Zalabak and Morley (1994). Each of these studies provides (1) sophisticated analyses of the ways in which situational constraints guide communicative acts, and (2) brief treatments of how action reproduces structural constraint, but (3) little systematic analysis of the origins or possible transformation of these structural constraints. Of course, there is nothing in the underlying assumptions of structuration that would preclude a focus on the construction or transformation of constraint. In fact, at least one actionist structuration study has done so (Keough & Lake, 1993). But our reading of this strain of structurationist research indicates that the tendency has been to move toward the actionist pole of the action-structure continuum and that reversing that tendency will require a reformulation of this interpretation of structuration.

Integrated structuration. A second "school" of structurationist organizational communication research was developed by Poole, McPhee, and their associates. This perspective differed from actionist structuration in two ways. First, although it initially evidenced an actionist bias, it eventually included an explicit critique of social actionism. Second, it developed an extended distinction between the concept of the duality of structure and a dualism between action and structure. In the initial articulation of this version of structuration, neither of these differentiating constructs was developed in any detail (Poole & McPhee, 1983). In addition, there were a number of internal tensions within their application of structuration to such topics as organizational climate. At times they discuss the action-structure problematic at a conceptual level, but subsequently reduced it to methodological/aggregational issues (see, e.g., p. 197). And like actionist structuration, their analysis sometimes slid into a social action perspective that de-emphasized structure (see, e.g., Poole and McPhee's, 1983, reinterpretation of Johnson's climate research, p. 101).

However, as this school of structuration developed, it moved toward an integrative version of structuration. This shift started in Poole's (1985) expanded critique of social-system-oriented perspectives on organizational climate and McPhee's (1985) discussion of formal organizational structure. Poole provides a structurationist interpretation of the ongoing debate about "objective" versus "subjective" measurement of the climate construct and offers an explicit critique of social

action views (p. 97). McPhee extends Giddens's concept of the duality of structure to argue that structure infuses communicative action in three ways: as an indirect constraint on communication, through its involvement in technical languages, and as a legitimizing process. Action cannot be wholly voluntary/subjective because structure (1) "binds" it to a particular place and time ("distanciation"), and (2) limits actors' strategic choices to options that are meaningful in their society ("reflexive monitoring"). But action is not *determined* by structure because some form of resistance always is possible. All actors retain some capacity to act and are knowledgeable about their capacities—they know how to "penetrate" social structures (the "dialectic of resistance and control"). Consequently, individual actions and interpretive frames are integrated with processes of producing/reproducing/transforming structure (pp. 168-171).

Poole, Seibold, and McPhee (1985) move even farther toward an integrative view of structuration by explicitly rejecting a dualism between social structure and social action (pp. 74-75, 81-82), by examining the problem of subjectivity in social action perspectives (p. 90), and by expanding their analysis of the situatedness of action (pp. 77-79) and the ways in which structure infuses action (pp. 79-80). Subsequently, they redefine traditional conceptions of "rules" to include structure (p. 98) and strategic choice-making (p. 90). Thus, like Giddens, they critique both social-structure-oriented research as the language of social action and perspectives that separate action and structure.

The advantages of this integrative model of structuration have become progressively more clear as this school developed. The most important advantage involves the ability to simultaneously examine the ways in which action is guided and constrained by structural processes and the ways in which action reproduces and/or transforms those guidelines and constraints. Some integrated structuration research has examined action-structure transformation in general (Laird-Brenton, 1993), some has examined the impact of action on (structural) rules and resources (Bastien, McPhee, & Bolton, 1995), while others have examined the dialectic between ideological positioning and changing organizational structures (Howard & Geist, 1995). These extensions of structuration focused increasing attention on the ways in which symbolic action reproduces, and potentially transforms, structural constraints. For example, Bastien et al. (1995) explain how municipal employees were able to draw on the protections of civil service systems as a basis for resisting changes being imposed by a newly elected administration, while employing discourse that reinterpreted upper management's penchant for secrecy about coming organizational changes. Consequently, their actions simultaneously reproduced/sedimented some elements of the structure they faced while creating new, and in many ways unintended, rules and resources that subsequently guided and constrained action.

When read together, these two versions of structuration (1) suggest a perspective through which the information, relationship, and meaning-creation clusters might be integrated, and (2) indicate how easily integrative perspectives might slide into an actionist extreme.

Unobtrusive Control and Identification

The constructs "unobtrusive control" and "identification" proposed by Tompkins, Cheney, and their associates provided a different approach to integrating action and structure. Subordinate constructs/terms include *power/control, internalization, meaning systems,* and *symbolic interaction.* Tompkins and Cheney (1983) contended that organizational life is inherently a decision-making (choice-making) process,

a means of tapping the mutual influences of people and organizations. As stated above, organizations (as well as the various units within

them) communicate decisional premises to their members; members, in turn, make decisions. The decisions themselves also communicate to the organization (i.e., the managers) and to other members something about decisional premises. Members, while engaged in decision-making activity, may echo the premises propounded by the organization, modify them, or communicate premises obtained from another source. The organization may then respond to these decisions as favorable or unfavorable in light of its interests. The decision-making process is thus continually being re-created by both the organization and its members. (p. 124)

Identification enters into the process of unobtrusive control in two ways. First, it enables organizational actors to cope with the multiple, overlapping, and often incongruent demands that make up organizational situations. Second, and conversely, identification opens actors up to persuasive communication from "the organization," making it easier to inculcate the decision premises embedded in the organization's dominant ideology. The former function allows employees to engage in action that is individually meaningful, including action that resists social/organizational control. But paradoxically, the second function restricts actors' freedom and volition by embedding processes of social/organizational control in processes of internalization, identification, and identity formation. Like structuration, the key contribution of the unobtrusive control/identification construct is its ability to simultaneously confront both the problem of control and the problem of consent. And like structuration, the key challenge facing researchers who use the construct system is to maintain a balance between the actionist and the structural dimensions of the construct.

Developing the identification/unobtrusive control construct. In subsequent essays, Cheney and Tompkins extend and refine their analysis of unobtrusive control and identification in two ways. One extension links the constructs more explicitly to processes of individual identity formation and transformation. The other extension situates the construct within the broader socioeconomic-political context of Western capitalist democracies.

Identification is an active process by which individuals define themselves in terms of their social/organizational scene (Cheney, 1983a, 1983b). Identification processes are ongoing and in flux because interpretations/evaluations of our experiences affirm or disconfirm our identifications with organizations (1983a). Identity is grounded in processes of negotiating a unique and constantly changing combination of partially conflicting corporate "we's" (1983a; Cheney & Christensen, Chapter 7, this volume).

Tompkins and Cheney provide a deeper analysis of the broader societal context surrounding processes of identification, identity formation, and unobtrusive control in a 1985 essay. They argue that traditional neo-positivist research is incapable of analyzing social/organizational "power" or acts of achieving control. They discuss the way in which imbalances of power favor institutional actors over individuals and examine changes in the way that power is exercised within Western organizations. By extending Karl Weick's (1979) work on "double interacts" to encompass control, they provide a way to analyze the *processes* through which social/organizational structures are "reproduced" through interaction.

The unobtrusive control/identification construct is important for two reasons. First, in their brief critique of the doctrine of social action, Cheney and Tompkins introduce concepts of structural constraint into a process-oriented perspective on power and control. As Dawe (1970, 1978) noted, the challenge faced by perspectives that attempt to integrate action and structure is to maintain a balanced, dialectical relationship between the two. Only then is it possible to avoid the problems of determinism and explain how ac-

tion can transform social and organizational structures.

Tompkins and Cheney avoid both sets of problems. First, they build an analysis of the historical-material constraints that have affected the development of modern organizations into the theory of unobtrusive control. Meanings and meaning systems are contextualized as historical constructions that develop and are sustained through action within social/organizational structures. Consequently, the problems of voluntarism and subjectivism that characterize traditional actionist perspectives are minimized.

Second, the focus on tensions among multiple identifications included in later versions of the perspective avoids some of the problems of the doctrine of social system. Tompkins and Cheney construct social/organizational actors as persons who constantly are involved in managing multiple, incongruent selves. This view of identification shifts the "internalization" construct away from an ideational version of determinism to become an aspect of the dynamic relationship between structure and action. Without the concept of multiple identifications, identification could easily be reduced to internalization, a construct that tends to totalize social and organizational control and explains inaction and consent but not action and resistance.

Managing tensions of/in unobtrusive control/identification. Unfortunately, some applications of Tompkins and Cheney's perspective do tend to reduce the concept of organizational "identification" to "internalization." In some studies, identification is treated as an outcome of being socialized to internalize new roles and role constraints (Barge & Musambria, 1992); in others, it entails internalizing organizational beliefs and values or becoming acculturated to mindlessly enact organizational practices (Bullis, 1993b; Czarniawska-Joerges, 1994; Ferraris, Carveth, & Parrish-Sprowl, 1993; Treadwell & Harrison, 1994).

Fortunately, other identification research has been able to maintain the probative force of the model by focusing on the processes through which tensions among actors' multiple identifications are managed. For example, Bullis and Tompkins (1989) examine the ways in which hiring employees with different kinds of occupational socialization has complicated unobtrusive control in the U.S. Forest Service (for additional examples, see Trice & Beyer, 1993, chap. 5). Baxter (1994) provides a rich analysis of the ways in which the tension between individuality and social control that characterizes Anglo-American culture is individuated in the discourse of two academic subcultures. She also examines the ways in which that discourse reproduces personal and cultural identities. Barker and Tompkins (1994) employ the concept of identification as the "management" of multiple, sometimes conflicting identities to examine the tensions that exist between identifying with one's work group (team) and identifying with one's organization. Different modes of managing multiple identities explain observed differences in the level of identification between organizational newcomers and seasoned veterans.

Scott (1996) examines the impact that a "structural" factor—the extent to which workers and work groups are geographically dispersed—has on identification processes. Four factors influence degree of organizational identification: the extent to which the identification pressures from different organizational "targets" (work group, regional office, state office, etc.) are congruent with one another, the extent to which employees have had similar occupational socialization experiences, tenure in the organization, and the "immediacy" (work group/team vs. other sources) of identification pressures. Barker, Melville, and Pacanowsky (1993) find that two sources of tension influence identification processes: the "stage" of a change from traditional forms of control to concertive/team/identification strategies, and the incongruities that are created

when management imposes an "antihierarchical" system on employees. The integrative potential of the unobtrusive control/identification construct system is illustrated most effectively in Barker's (1993) study of how bureaucratic structures were modified, transformed, and reproduced during an organization's shift to a "team" system. Bureaucratic practices guide and constrain actors' interpretations and strategic responses to teams. But those interpretations/responses also led to a number of unintended consequences, transformations of structure and action, and new forms of self-and-other surveillance and discipline.

Taken together, these studies enact the tensions implicit in the unobtrusive control/identification perspective. Many locate "constraint" in the ideas/selves/interpretive processes of organizational actors and illustrate the tendency to reduce the perspective to ideation/internalization. Others retain the concept of multiple identifications, and thus are able to construct identity formation as a contingent, complex, and fragile process. Ideational constraints constantly are being negotiated, but the negotiation is sustained by an integrated and constrained organizational self. By controlling reductionist tendencies, these applications illustrate the integrative potential of the identification/unobtrusive control construct system.[8]

Critical Theory

A final integrating framework emerges from applications of differing variations of *critical theory* (see, e.g., Alvesson, 1993; Clair, 1993b; Mumby, 1987, 1993a; Taylor, 1992, 1993; Taylor & Conrad, 1992; Wood, 1992).[9] Like other actionist perspectives, critical theory emerged as a response to structural determinism. While the target of traditional doctrines of social action was the determinism of neo-positivist social science, the target of critical theory was the determinism of orthodox (or "vulgar") Marxism (Held, 1980). If language and symbolic action were mere reflections of the material structure of industrial capitalism, as Marx and Engels seem to argue, how could symbolic action influence that structure (Aune, 1994; Coward & Ellis, 1977)? If "capitalism is indeed governed by lawful regularities that doom it to be supplanted by a new socialist society . . . why then stress that 'the point is to change it'? . . . . Why must persons be mobilized and exhorted to discipline themselves to behave in conformity with necessary laws by which, it would seem, they would in any event be bound?" (Gouldner, 1980, p. 32). In short, there is a fundamental contradiction within orthodox Marxism, an inherent tension between structure and struggle: How is struggle (action) even possible, and how can it possibly succeed if material conditions are determining?

Critical theorists confront this contradiction by rejecting the structural determinism of orthodox Marxism and foregrounding a theory of action/communication. They cannot abandon concepts of structural constraint, but seek to avoid determinism by integrating constraint into the beliefs/ideas/ideologies of social and organizational actors. It is through ideas that constraint is actualized, and through action that constraints are created and transformed. Of course, like the other frameworks discussed in this section, the challenge facing critical theorists is to integrate action and structure without merely substituting ideational determinism for structural determinism.

Two variants of critical organizational communication theory have accepted this challenge. The central construct of the first version is "ideology," and its constituent terms are *consent, agency,* and *interests.* The latter term differentiates the two versions of critical theory. An ideological view of interests argues that members of some sectors of a society/economic/culture use ideological communication to dominate the interests of other sectors. Communicative processes encourage members of a society to *reify* its key characteristics, to view existing arrangements as natural (inevitable) and normal (expected and morally correct) (Deetz, 1995; Therborn,

1980).[10] Abercrombie (1980) has labeled this perspective the "dominant ideology thesis." This perspective assumes that the interests of members of various sectors of an economy/society are knowable, both to researcher-theorists who study the society/economy and potentially to the groups of individuals who occupy each sector of it. Emancipation begins when all members of the society/economy are made aware of the communicative practices that privilege one set of interests over others (Papa, Arwal, & Singhal, 1995).

Of course, ideological definitions of interests are problematic in many ways. They fail to explain how the ideology of the dominant class became dominant in the first place or how oppositional ideas emerge or get heard at all. Consequently, they cannot explain either resistance or transformation except as the result of failed communication by the dominant class. In addition, they provide an overly simplistic, almost information-theory-oriented, view of messages as seamless, coherent, and univocal (Abercrombie, 1980; Elster, 1984).

An alternative version of critical theory focuses on "communicative action," a construct whose constituent terms include *participation/democracy* (Cheney, 1995; Harrison, 1994; Witten, 1993), *discursive closure* (processes through which the voices of some persons and groups are distorted or muted and some kinds of claims are trivialized or defined out of possibility) (Deetz, 1992b, 1995), *power* (Conrad & Ryan, 1985; Deetz & Mumby, 1990; Mumby, 1987, 1988), *meaning* (Mumby, 1989), *practices* (Howard & Geist, 1995; Huspek & Kendall, 1991), and *symbolism,* as well as *interests.* Unlike ideological definitions of interests, the communicative action cluster defines interests as processes through which all members of a society/economy are dominated by its modes of rationality. Interests, so defined, underlie a wide range of inequities that affect different groups of people in different ways (Alvesson, 1987; Habermas, 1979, 1984, 1987; Mumby, 1988).

"Symbolism" is an inherently power-laden process. Organizational stories (Ehrenhaus, 1993; Helmer, 1993), narratives (Mumby, 1993a; Witten, 1993), metaphors (McMillan

& Cheney, 1996; Salvador & Markham, 1995), and texts (Banks, 1994; Laird-Brenton, 1993) obscure differing interests, short-circuit participation/democracy by closing off legitimate communication, and reproduce existing patterns of power and domination. Symbolic action, and the modes of rationality created by it, are hegemonic, encouraging persons to consent to the circumstances of their domination (Alvesson, 1993; Clair, 1993a, 1993b; Condit, 1994; Conrad, 1988; Mumby, 1987, 1988). Neither researcher-theorists nor members of dominant groups are immune to the effects of these hegemonic processes (MacIntyre, 1981).

This perspective has been criticized on a number of grounds, one of which is particularly relevant to organizational communication research/theory. The "actor" that is constructed by and in communicative action with critical theory is a unified, rational, autonomous subject who is either alienated by patriarchal, capitalistic work organizations or is "ensnared in contemporary illusions" about them (Alvesson & Willmott, 1992). In extreme versions of the perspective, social/organizational actors are unaware of and incapable of critically analyzing the "totally administered" societies/organizations of which they are a part. Societies (and organizations) are so "dominated by the ideological apparatuses of the state or by omnipresent powers symbolized by Bentham's Panopticon" that "actors," as well as "agents" of change, disappear (Touraine, 1985, p. 767). As in some versions of internalization/identification, problems related to structural determinism are merely replaced by the problems of ideational determinism. In neither case is the action-structure problematic managed successfully.

Critical theorists, particularly those who focus on "communicative action," go to great lengths to avoid suggesting that socialization is totally effective, or that hegemonic domination is complete, but the logic of their position provides little alternative. The only kind of consciousness that is available to members of society/organizations is a false consciousness, an interpretation of "reality" that treats patterns of domination as natural and normal.

Resistance to domination leads only to increased alienation or further domination; the dialectical relationships between action and social structure that might provide grounds for transformation disappear. Because these tensions are central to critical theory, they also are present in critical-theory-oriented organizational communication research.

Assessing the Development of Integrative Perspectives

Integrative perspectives simultaneously confront the action-structure dialectic and illustrate its component pressures. The key problem facing integrative frameworks is to maintain a balance between structural and actional pressures. For all three of the perspectives surveyed in this chapter, the key threat is the tendency to reduce their construct systems to ideation/action. Structurationist research may focus so completely on the "taken for granted" assumptions of a culture/organization that structural rules, resources, and constraints are slighted or ignored. "Identification" can be so total that the opportunities for resistance embedded in broad sociocultural practices disappear. Critical theorists can become so concerned with avoiding structural determinism that they become trapped in doctrines of "false consciousness." In all three instances, ideational/ideological constraint is totalized. Social actors have no more freedom of choice and social structures have no more possibility for being transformed than they do in deterministic doctrines of social system.

CHALLENGING KEY CONSTRUCTS

A number of perspectives recently have emerged in organizational communication theory and research to challenge the construct system that developed during the 1980s and early 1990s. Some of these alternatives challenge by foregrounding concepts of resistance and transformation and de-emphasizing notions of constraint. Other alternatives launch a more fundamental challenge by rejecting the dualism between action and structure that underlies the entire construct system.

Creating Space for Resistance and Transformation

Perhaps the most important construct in contemporary organizational communication theory is "constraint." Incorporating it helps social systems researchers at least appear to avoid the excessive determinism of functionalist social science. Conversely, locating social and organizational constraint in the selves and ideas (beliefs, values, and frames of reference) of organizational members allows actionist researchers to at least appear to avoid sliding into pure voluntarism/subjectivism. However, as we suggest throughout this chapter, the construct "constraint" may not achieve either of these objectives. On the one hand, the distinction between determinant and constraint can easily be blurred, particularly through constructs like internalization or hegemony. On the other hand, "constraint" can be so de-emphasized that even integrative perspectives can be transformed into actionism, a move that is especially easy in an intellectual context suspicious of determinism.

Some organizational communication scholars have extended this critique, arguing that "constraint" must be fundamentally reconceptualized before organizational communication research and theory can fully represent the dynamic interplay between consent and resistance or explain how social/organizational constraints are transformed. One reformulation of "constraint" develops and highlights two additional constructs, the *knowledgeability* of organizational actors, and the *unintended consequences* of action (Giddens, 1984). Organizational actors understand the "material" conditions they face, indeed they can act meaningfully only because they are knowledgeable about the rules and resources that exist in particular situations (Bhaskar, 1979, p. 43). But being knowledgeable about

constraints and the likely effects of different courses of action does not imply that organizational members are able to control the effects of their actions. All acts, whether they seem to be compliant or resistant, have both intended and unintended consequences. It is through these unintended consequences that social and organizational structures are modified by actors whose knowledge is socially constrained (Bhaskar, 1979, pp. 44-45). Examples of research that foreground these constructs are Browning's (1992) discussion of the multivocality of organizational discourse, the progressiveness/historicity of story interpretations, and the difference between local and distant knowledge; Corman and Scott's (1994) and Banks and Riley's (1993) treatments of the unintended consequences of action; McPhee and Corman's (1995) analysis of the "hierarchicalization" of networking processes; and Clair's (1993a, 1993b, 1994) analyses of "reframing" and resistance.

Another reformulation of "constraint" has emerged via versions of critical theory that focus on communicative action (Carnegie, 1996; Scott, 1993). This work critiques views of constraint, identification, and identity formation that overestimate the power of socialization processes and underestimate organizational actors' abilities to engage in strategic resistance (Cheney & Christensen, 1994; see also Cheney & Christensen, Chapter 7, this volume). By doing so, they challenge traditional conceptions of constraint and provide conceptual space within which concepts of resistance and transformation can be developed. Examples include Huspek's (1993) critique/synthesis of the work of Bourdieu and Giddens, Mumby's (1988) extension of Habermas and Foucault, and recent reinterpretations of the "unobtrusive control" construct. Drawing heavily on Foucault, Barker and Cheney (1994) substitute "discipline" for "constraint," thereby foregrounding resistance, while Cheney and Stohl (1991) examine the recursive processes through which recent changes in European economic systems and communicative action are mutually transformative. This alternative conceptualization is important because it undermines the modifications made in both actionist and structure-oriented research to deal with the action-structure problematic. Without those modifications, tensions within the overall construct system are magnified once more, and the potential for sliding into determinist or actionist extremes reappears.

Postmodernist Challenges

A second challenge comes from perspectives that reject the action-structure dualism itself. Although a number of recently emerging perspectives do so, the most visible one among organizational communication theorists is *postmodernism*.[11] Of course, it is impossible to provide a comprehensive summary of the many versions of postmodernist thought (see Deetz, Chapter 1, and Mumby, Chapter 15, this volume). Instead we briefly sketch postmodernist social/organizational theory and discuss the implications that it holds for organizational communication theory.[12]

Postmodernity (the era) is characterized by a rejection of the modernist notion that it is possible to find rational solutions to social/organizational problems. The modern era is defined by faith in human beings' ability to discover broad explanations of all of human experience, to construct "grand narratives" that explain the sources, origins, perpetuation, and solutions to (or escapes from) social/organizational problems. Embedded in this project are efforts to describe *the* relationship between communicative action and social structure. Postmodernity is characterized by the "death" of all of these assumptions.[13] The postmodern world is simply too complex, too unstable, and too fragmented to be adequately explained by *any* grand narrative or totalizing theory. Consequently, postmodernist social/organizational theory abandons the central goal of modernist science—constructing universal conclusions through the accumulation of "data"—and the key distinctions of modern social science—between science and fiction, reality and unreality. The goal of postmodernist social science is to develop new questions, not to stipulate "answers" to old ones.

Insight comes through the *deconstruction* of texts, not through *constructing* social theories grounded in *reconstructions* of subjects' experiences.

In postmodernist approaches, symbolic action is merged with social/organizational structure. But the action-structure nexus is replete with fissures, tensions, and contradictions. Social/organizational life is a process of negotiating these tensions and contradictions in a particular configuration of time and space. It should be viewed as recurring, routinized "practices" that simultaneously are both symbolic action and social/organizational structure. "Identity" is a tenuous, emergent process. Social actors are enmeshed in multiple, conflicting identifications, where selves and relationships are fragmented, where the knowledge/meaning systems of modernism are meaningless. Organizations are sites where members subject themselves and one another to various practices, where discourse sustains mutually reinforcing patterns of power and powerlessness, and where language obscures the politics of organizational experience. "Power" resides in these discursive/linguistic practices, including the formation of organizational "knowledge" and claims about it.[14] Because power exists at the intersection of multiple, conflicting pressures, it is fluid and fragmented. It emerges as people continually define themselves through practices localized in particular time-space configurations.

Postmodernists argue that modernist constructions separate power/constraint from action/resistance by locating the former in social/organizational structures or internalized ideas and locating the latter in action. As a result, modernists find it difficult to explain how action/resistance might transform structure, power, or constraint. These difficulties are unnecessary because they result from modernists' arbitrary decision to separate action and structure (Clegg, 1989; Fielding, 1988). By refusing to separate structure/constraint/power from action/resistance, postmodernist theory avoids these difficulties. Every disciplinary practice has resistance embedded within it: "With every 'positive' move in disciplinary practices, there is an oppositional one" (Deetz, 1992a, p. 366, 1992b). For example, the symbols of traditional hierarchical organizations simultaneously accent differences in status and authority and draw attention to the arbitrary and political nature of organizational hierarchies, thus undermining the potency of those symbols (Kunda, 1991). Even covert, inactive, seemingly neutral practices such as absence can function as resistance (Barker & Cheney, 1994). As a result, transformation is an inherent part of ongoing practices. It can be explained without having to construct additional concepts to link action and structure (Baudrillard, 1983; Collinson, 1988; Deetz, Chapter 1, this volume; Gergen, 1992; Harris, 1980).

Of course, postmodernist assumptions have been widely criticized. Two criticisms are especially relevant to this chapter. First, some critics argue that postmodernist social/organizational theory neither *eliminates* nor *avoids* the action-structure problematic, it merely *elides* it by collapsing social structure into discursive/linguistic practices (Anderson, 1984; Eagleton, 1983; Rosenau, 1992).[15] However, this move creates its own problems. Language is not like other social/organizational structures—it is much slower to change than economic, political, or religious structures; it has no material constraints (e.g., no scarcity); and it is axiomatically linked to *individuals*. Thus, collapsing social/organizational structure into language/practices does not *integrate* structure into action, it merely defines it out of existence. With no concept of structure, action is no longer tied to material conditions or the practices of social *collectives*. In postmodernist theory,

> power loses any historical determination: there are no longer specific holders of power, nor any specific goals which its exercise serves. (Anderson, 1984, p. 51)

> The adoption of the language model as the "key to all mythologies," far from clarifying or decoding the relations between structure and subject, led from a rhetorical absolutism of the

first to a fragmented fetishism of the second, without ever advancing a theory of their *relations*. Such a theory, historically determinate and sectorally differentiated, could only be developed in a dialectical respect for their interdependence. (p. 55)

As a result, postmodernist social theory is unable to integrate its analysis of institutions (i.e., social collectives) with its treatment of the individual self (Best, 1994; Ritzer, 1997, p. 250).

A second and related criticism of most postmodernist social theory is that it lacks a theory of agency (Best, 1994; O'Neill, 1995; Ritzer, 1997, pp. 248-251). While deconstruction can *destroy* (Deleuze & Guattari, 1977/1983, p. 311), it cannot *create* a vision of what society/organizations ought to be like (Coles, 1991; Gitlin, 1988) nor does it provide a theory of praxis to influence societal/organizational change (Giddens, 1990; Habermas, 1981, 1986, 1991).[16]

However, postmodernist social/organizational theory does force organizational communication theorists to reconsider the dominant action-structure dualism, both as a representation of social/organizational life and as an explanation of organizational texts. And whether or not organizational communication theorists choose to embrace postmodernist theories, we must find ways to explain the multiplicity of organizational forms that are rapidly emerging in the world economy (Eisenberg & Goodall, 1997; Ritzer, 1997).

SUMMARY AND CONCLUSIONS

In this chapter, we have constructed "organizational communication research" as a rhetorical act, a set of symbolic strategies that forms and is informed by a particular discourse community. Our focus has been on processes of emergence and change in part because organizational communication is so diverse and has developed so rapidly during the past 15 years, and in part because understanding a language community always entails examining processes of symbolic transformation (Frye, 1957; Shils, 1968).

Some transformative pressures are intrinsic to language communities themselves—tensions and incongruities that must be managed communicatively if the community is to continue. The decade between 1985 and 1995 witnessed a marked increase in both the amount of organizational communication research being conducted and the diversity of theoretical frames employed in that research. On the one hand, structure-oriented research, dominant at the beginning of the era, has continued to play a significant role, although concepts of "perception" and "interpretation" are more visible in structure-oriented research and the deterministic assumptions underlying this perspective are "softened" by substituting "constraint" for "determinant." For the rest of organizational communication theory and research, the decade was characterized by substantial theoretical ferment. The two most important trends seemed to be the elevation of complex models of "constraint" and the articulation of a number of challenging perspectives. The resulting diversity of views, often based on conflicting or contradictory core assumptions, has been accompanied by the growth of an ideology of "comfortable eclecticism" (see Goldhaber & Barnett, 1988a, p. 2, for an early articulation of this ideology).

A doctrine of "eclecticism" has the advantage of allowing a discourse community to avoid fragmentation by encouraging the creation of multiple closed paradigms that coexist peacefully (Ackroyd, 1992). It may produce rapid (albeit "normal") scientific "progress," defined both in terms of the generation of substantial amounts of research and the progressive refinement and elaboration of each paradigm. But as Deetz (1992a) has noted, a rhetoric of eclecticism also precludes meaningful critique of fundamental assumptions and undermines the kinds of dialogue that facilitates further transformation (also see Feyerabend, 1975/1993; Gergen, 1982).

Other transformative pressures are extrinsic to language communities—changes in the surrounding intellectual climate and/or socioeconomic milieu (Cheney, 1995; Deetz, 1995; Finet, Chapter 8, this volume). Just as intrinsic pressures generated fundamental changes in organizational communication theory during the past decade, these extrinsic pressures promise to have a profound effect on what we do, how we think, and what kind of community we will become.

NOTES

1. We chose 1985 as a starting point because by that date the critical and interpretive turns in organizational communication scholarship that began in the late 1970s had solidified sufficiently to allow the publication of a number of coherent summary volumes (e.g., Goldhaber & Barnett, 1988b; Jablin, Putnam, Roberts, & Porter, 1987; McPhee & Tompkins, 1985). We then surveyed essays in the journals published by the Speech Communication Association and International Communication Association between 1985 and 1995 (focusing on *Communication Monographs, Human Communication Research, Quarterly Journal of Speech, Journal of Applied Communication Research, Communication Theory,* and the *Communication Yearbooks*), and added sources that were cited frequently by relevant articles in these publications (articles in *Communication Research* and *Management Communication Quarterly* were frequently added to the survey during this phase). Complete citations are included in the references.

2. Dawe prefers the term *doctrine* to the more common terms *paradigm* or *theory* because it is a way of viewing social action and social theory: "the judgments of value, a social philosophy as well as a system of concepts or of general propositions" (citing Aron, 1968, p. v; cited in Dawe, 1970, p. 208). Following Dawe, we will first present the two doctrines as more distinct and antithetical than they actually are, eventually arguing that attempts to mediate the different doctrines are the core of contemporary social theory.

3. We use the term *theory* (in both critical theory and systems theory) solely because the term is commonly used by organizational communication scholars. Our concern in this chapter is with broad conceptual frameworks, which are defined by a particular set of epistemic assumptions, each of which encompasses a variety of what often are called theories.

4. Our survey of recent organizational communication research identified many studies that operate within an information-exchange construct system. In addition to those cited in the text of this chapter, see Adams and

Parrott (1994); Albrecht and Hall (1991b); Franz and Jin (1995); Holowitz and Wilson (1993); Jablin (1987a); Johnson (1988); Kramer (1993); Miller, Johnstone, and Grau (1994); Plax, Beatty, and Feingold (1991); Poole and DeSanctis (1992); Ralston (1993); and Rogers (1988).

5. Additional related sources include Corman (1990); Cushman and Sanderson-King (1993); Drecksel (1991); Ellis and Miller (1993); Everett (1994); Fairhurst (1988); Fairhurst and Chandler (1989); Fairhurst, Rogers, and Sarr (1987); Falcione, Sussman, and Herden (1987); Fink and Chen (1995); Franz and Jin (1995); Gayle (1991); Hammer and Martin (1992); Hirokawa, Mickey, and Miura (1991); Miller and Monge (1987); Monge and Miller (1988); Monge, Cozzens, and Contractor (1992); Morrill and Thomas (1992); Peterson and Sorenson (1991); Putnam and Sorenson (1992); Richmond and Roach (1992); Stewart, Gudykunst, and Ting-Toomey (1982); Stohl (1986); and Waldron (1991).

6. Actionist organizational communication research not cited in this section includes Alvesson (1993); Banks and Banks (1991); Barge and Musambria (1992); Barker et al. (1993); Barker and Tompkins (1994); Bastien et al. (1995); Baxter (1994); Bingham and Burelson (1989); Bullis (1993a); Cheney and Christensen (1994); Coffman (1992); Cragan and Shields (1992); Ferraris et al. (1993); Goodall (1990); Hess (1993); Hogan (1989); Howard and Geist (1995); Huspek (1993); Jablonski (1988); Laird-Brenton (1993); Levitt and Nass (1994); McPhee (1993); Mumby (1987); Peterson and Sorenson (1991); Ralston and Kirkwood (1995); Shockley-Zalabak and Morely (1994); Smith and Turner (1995); Stohl (1993); Strine (1992); Sypher (1991); Taylor and Conrad (1992); Tracy and Baratz (1993); Treadwell and Harrison (1994); and Wood (1992).

7. Eisenberg and Riley's summary of issues facing organizational symbolism researchers—the extent to which meaning systems can be treated as shared by multiple organizational members, the degree to which symbolic action is conscious or unconscious, and the potential limitations of social constructionist views of organizations—are remarkably similar to existing critiques of the language of social action, particularly those presented in Giddens's (1976, 1979) early work. But they treated these issues as problems in the application of the doctrine of social action in organizational communication research rather than as problematic elements of the perspective itself.

8. Some identification/concertive control research takes a "postmodernist" perspective. It will be considered later in this chapter.

9. Because other chapters in this volume deal at great length with this strain of research (in particular, those chapters by Deetz, by Mumby, by Putnam and Fairhurst, and by Eisenberg and Riley), we will describe its key constructs only briefly. We also accept Deetz's and Mumby's decision to differentiate "critical theory" and "postmodernist/dissensus" perspectives. Interestingly, a very early precursor to the development of critical theories was introduced in Thayer's (1988) examination of "leadership" as a social construction. Thayer begins by asserting that organizational communication researchers have largely ignored leadership because of their excessively narrow definition of communication as a process of conveying information or ideas (for a similar analysis, see Deetz, 1992b, 1994). He subsequently argues that leadership is a distinctively Western construction, one that functions to create feelings of control over events, outcomes, and so on (1992b, pp. 233-234).

10. This construction separates "leadership" from organizational contexts and legitimizes the empirically questionable assumption that leaders cause organizational outcomes. Recent shifts in orientation from leadership "traits" and "styles" to leadership as adaptation to situational contingencies merely serve to insert researchers further into the dominant ideology (Thayer, 1988, p. 238).

11. Three other perspectives are relevant. Two approaches combine action and structure conceptually but separate them temporally or spatially. Temporally oriented models hold action constant during one time period and structure constant during another. One dimension (action or structure) may create or influence the conditions under which the other operates, or the two may influence one another mutually over time with "swings" from the dominance of one to the dominance of the other (Archer, 1982; Poole & Van de Ven, 1989). Temporal approaches include Tushman and Romanelli's (1985) punctuated equilibrium model in organizational theory and self-organizing systems theory in organizational communication (Baldwin-Leveque & Poole, 1996). Spatially oriented models focus on processes through which action and structure are intertwined across organizational levels, for example, linking action at the microlevel of analysis with structure at a macrolevel (Coleman, 1986; Poole & Van de Ven, 1989; Van de Ven & Poole, 1988). The key to this approach is treating both micro- and macrolevels simultaneously, as in Buckley's "morphogenesis" perspective (Archer, 1982). A third perspective that has explicitly rejected the action-structure dualism has been labeled "flexible structuration theory" (Barnett & Thayer, 1997; Poole, 1994; Seibold & Contractor, 1993).

Space limitations preclude our describing these perspectives in detail, and it is too early in their development to be able to predict the extent to which they will be accepted by organizational communication theorists or to assess the degree to which they actually do avoid the action-structure problematic. But each is a promising alternative to the dominant construct system.

12. More detailed treatments are provided in the chapters by Deetz, Mumby, Cheney and Christensen, Taylor and Trujillo, and Putnam and Fairhurst in this volume, and extended analyses of the implications of postmodernism to social/organizational theory and to social science are available in Boje, Gephart, and Thatchenkery (1996); Calás and Smircich (1991); Clegg (1994); Ritzer (1997); and Rosenau (1992). Examples of feminist postmodernist organizational communication

research include Bingham (1994); Blair, Brown, and Baxter (1994); Bullis (1993a); Buzzanell (1994); Calás and Smircich (1992); Clair (1993a, 1993b, 1994); Gregg (1993); Marshall (1993); Mumby (1993b, this volume); Mumby and Putnam (1992); Strine (1992); and West and Zimmerman (1987).

13. Postmodern theorists differ in their views of the relationship between the modern and postmodern eras. Some posit a dramatic rupture, an end to the modern era and a beginning of the postmodern one (e.g., Baudrillard and Virilio). Others see a continuity in which postmodernity has grown out of modernity (Jameson, Laclau and Mouffe, and some postmodern feminists such as Nancy Fraser and Donna Haraway). Others suggest that "we can see *modernity and postmodernity as engaged in a long-running relationship with one another,* with postmodernity continually pointing out the limitations of modernity (for example, Lyotard)" (Ritzer, 1997, p. 8).

14. Unlike critical theories that focus on revealing conflicting "interests," postmodernist perspectives focus on the ways in which discourse sustains mutually reinforcing patterns of power and powerlessness. Postmodernists argue that actionist perspectives privilege individual experience, linguistic action, integrated selves, and voluntarism. Doing so creates a set of discourse practices that obscure the politics of organizational experience (see Salaman, 1986, and Reed, 1985, for a more detailed explanation; see Deetz, Chapter 1, this volume).

15. Some postmodernists, notably Foucault and Laclau and Mouffe, confront this problem by including both material practices and language within their construction of "discourse." For example, the physical structure of a prison and the medical practices of treating insanity are nonlinguistic "discourse."

16. Ritzer (1997) argues that this is, ironically, most true of Marxian postmodernists like Jameson, and less so of Baudrillard. It is less true of Deleuze and Guattari, Laclau and Mouffe, and feminists such as Donna Haraway, all of whom offer theories of social change and views of "good" societies.

REFERENCES

Abercrombie, N. (1980). *The dominant ideology thesis.* London: Allen and Unwin.

Ackroyd, S. (1992). Paradigms lost: Paradise regained? In M. Reed & M. Hughes (Eds.), *Rethinking organization: New directions in organization theory and analysis* (pp. 102-119). London: Sage.

Adams, R., & Parrott, R. (1994). Pediatric nurses' communication of role expectations of parents to hospitalized children. *Journal of Applied Communication Research, 22,* 36-47.

Albrecht, T., & Hall, B. (1991a). Facilitating talk about new ideas: The role of personal relationships in organizational innovation. *Communication Monographs, 58,* 273-289.

Albrecht, T., & Hall, B. (1991b). Relationship and content differences between elites and outsiders in innovation networks. *Human Communication Research, 17,* 535-562.

Alexander, E., III, Penley, L., & Jernigan, I. E. (1991). The effects of individual differences on manager media choice. *Management Communication Quarterly, 5,* 155-173.

Allen, M., Gotcher, J. M., & Seibert, J. (1993). A decade of organizational communication research: 1980-1991. In S. A. Deetz (Ed.), *Communication yearbook 16* (pp. 252-330). Newbury Park, CA: Sage.

Allen, T. J., & Hauptman, O. (1990). The substitution of communication technologies for organizational structure in research and development. In J. Fulk & C. Steinfield (Eds.), *Organizations and communication technology* (pp. 237-274). Newbury Park, CA: Sage.

Alvesson, M. (1987). *Organizational theory and technocratic consciousness.* New York: Aldine de Gruyter.

Alvesson, M. (1993). Cultural-ideological modes of management control. In S. A. Deetz (Ed.), *Communication yearbook 16* (pp. 3-42). Newbury Park, CA: Sage.

Alvesson, M., & Willmott, H. (1992). On the idea of emancipation in management and organization studies. *Academy of Management Review, 17,* 432-464.

Anderson, P. (1984). *In the tracks of historical materialism.* Chicago: University of Chicago Press.

Archer, M. (1982). Morphogenesis versus structuration. *British Journal of Sociology, 33,* 455-483.

Aron, R. (1968). *Main currents in sociological thought* (Vol. 2). New York: Weidenfeld & Nicholson.

Ash, M. (1990). *Journey into the eye of a needle.* Devon, UK: Green.

Aune, J. (1994). *Rhetoric and Marxism.* Boulder, CO: Westview.

Axley, S. R. (1984). Managerial and organizational communication in terms of the conduit metaphor. *Academy of Management Review, 9,* 428-437.

Bach, B. W. (1989). The effect of multiplex relationships upon innovation adaptation. *Communication Monographs, 56,* 133-151.

Baldwin-Leveque, C., & Poole, M. S. (1996). Systems thinking in organizational communication inquiry. In P. Salem (Ed.), *Organizational communication and change.* Creskill, NJ: Hampton.

Banks, S. (1994). Performing flight announcements: The case of flight attendants' work discourse. *Text and Performance Quarterly, 14,* 253-267.

Banks, S., & Banks, A. (1991). Translation as problematic discourse in organizations. *Journal of Applied Communication Research, 19,* 223-241.

Banks, S., & Riley, P. (1993). Structuration theory as an ontology for communication research. In S. A. Deetz

(Ed.), *Communication yearbook 17* (pp. 167-196). Newbury Park: Sage.

Barge, K., & Musambria, G. (1992). Turning points in chair-faculty relations. *Journal of Applied Communication Research, 20,* 54-71.

Barker, J. R. (1993). Tightening the iron cage: Concertive control in self-managing teams. *Administrative Science Quarterly, 38,* 408-437.

Barker, J. R., & Cheney, G. (1994). The concept and practices of discipline in contemporary organizational life. *Communication Monographs, 61,* 20-43.

Barker, J. R., Melville, C. W., & Pacanowsky, M. E. (1993). Self-directed teams at Xel. *Journal of Applied Communication Research, 21,* 297-312.

Barker, J. R., & Tompkins, P. (1994). Identification in the self-managing organization. *Human Communication Research, 21,* 223-240.

Barnett, G. A., & Thayer, L. (Eds.). (1997). *Communication—Organization 6.* Norwood, NJ: Ablex.

Bastien, D. T., McPhee, R. D., & Bolton, K. A. (1995). A study and extended theory of the structuration of climate. *Communication Monographs, 62,* 87-109.

Baudrillard, J. (1983). *Simulations.* New York: Semiotext(e).

Baudrillard, J. (1988). *Selected writings* (M. Poster, Ed.). Cambridge, UK: Polity.

Baxter, L. (1994). "Talking things through" and "putting it in writing." *Journal of Applied Communication Research, 21,* 313-326.

Berthold, C. (1976). Kenneth Burke's cluster-agon method: Its development and an application. *Central States Speech Journal, 27,* 302-309.

Best, S. (1994). Foucault, postmodernism, and social theory. In D. R. Dickens & A. Fontana (Eds.), *Postmodernism and social inquiry* (pp. 25-52). New York: Guilford.

Bhaskar, R. (1979). *The possibility of naturalism.* Atlantic Highlands, NJ: Humanities Press.

Bingham, S. (Ed.). (1994). *Conceptualizing sexual harassment as discursive practice.* Westport, CT: Greenwood.

Bingham, S., & Burleson, B. R. (1989). Multiple effects of messages with multiple goals. *Human Communication Research, 16,* 184-216.

Blair, C., Brown, J. R., & Baxter, L. A. (1994). Disciplining the feminine. *Quarterly Journal of Speech, 80,* 383-409.

Boje, D., Gephart, R. P., & Thatchenkery, T. J. (1996). *Postmodern management and organizational theory.* Thousand Oaks, CA: Sage.

Brown, M. H. (1990). Defining stories in organizations: Characteristics and functions. In J. A. Anderson (Ed.), *Communication yearbook 13* (pp. 162-190). Newbury Park, CA: Sage.

Browning, L. D. (1992). Lists and stories as organizational communication. *Communication Theory, 2,* 281-302.

Bullis, C. (1993a). At least it's a start. In S. A. Deetz (Ed.), *Communication yearbook 16* (pp. 144-154). Newbury Park, CA: Sage.

Bullis, C. (1993b). Organizational socialization research. *Communication Monographs, 60,* 10-17.

Bullis, C., & Tompkins, P. (1989). The forest ranger revisited: A study of control practices and identification. *Communication Monographs, 56,* 287-306.

Burke, K. (1969). *A grammar of motives.* Berkeley: University of California Press. (Original work published 1945)

Burke, K. (1970). *Rhetoric of religion.* Berkeley: University of California Press.

Burke, K. (1984). *The philosophy of literary form* (3rd ed.). Berkeley: University of California Press. (Original work published 1941)

Burke, K. (1991). Auscultation, creation, and revision. In J. Chesebro (Ed.), *Extensions of the Burkeian system* (pp. 42-172). Tuscaloosa: University of Alabama Press.

Buzzanell, P. (1994). Gaining a voice: Feminist organizational communication theorizing. *Management Communication Quarterly, 7,* 339-383.

Calás, M., & Smircich, L. (1991). Voicing seduction to silence leadership. *Organization Studies, 12,* 567-602.

Calás, M., & Smircich, L. (1992). Rewriting gender into organizational theorizing: Directions from feminist perspectives. In M. Reed & M. Hughes (Eds.), *Rethinking organization: New directions in organizational theory and analysis* (pp. 227-253). London: Sage.

Carnegie, S. (1996). *The hidden emotions of tourism.* Unpublished master's thesis, Texas A&M University, College Station.

Castoriadis, C. (1987). *The imaginary institution of society* (K. Blamey, Trans.). Cambridge, UK: Polity.

Cheney, G. (1983a). On the various and changing meanings of organizational membership: A field study of organizational identification. *Communication Monographs, 50,* 343-363.

Cheney, G. (1983b). The rhetoric of identification and the study of organizational communication. *Quarterly Journal of Speech, 69,* 143-158.

Cheney, G. (1995). Democracy in the workplace. *Journal of Applied Communication Research, 23,* 167-200.

Cheney, G., & Christensen, L. T. (1994). Articulating identity in an organizational age. In S. A. Deetz (Ed.), *Communication yearbook 17* (pp. 222-235). Thousand Oaks, CA: Sage.

Cheney, G., & Stohl, C. (1991). European transformations and their communicative implications. *Journal of Applied Communication Research, 19,* 330-339.

Cheney, G., & Vibbert, S. L. (1987). Corporate discourse: Public relations and issue management. In F. M. Jablin, L. L. Putnam, K. H. Robert, & L. W. Porter (Eds.), *Handbook of organizational communica-*

tion: An interdisciplinary perspective (pp. 165-194). Newbury Park, CA: Sage.

Chiles, A. M., & Zorn, T. (1995). Empowerment in organizations: Employees' perceptions of the influences on empowerment. *Journal of Applied Communication Research, 23,* 1-25.

Clair, R. P. (1993a). The bureaucratization, commodification, and privatization of sexual harassment through institutional discourse. *Management Communication Quarterly, 7,* 123-157.

Clair, R. P. (1993b). The use of framing devises to sequester organizational narratives. *Communication Monographs, 60,* 113-136.

Clair, R. P. (1994). Hegemony and harassment: A discursive practice. In S. Bingham (Ed.), *Conceptualizing sexual harassment as discursive practice* (pp. 59-70). Westport, CT: Greenwood.

Clegg, S. (1989). *Frameworks of power.* Newbury Park, CA: Sage.

Clegg, S. (1990). *Modern organizations: Organizations in a postmodern world.* Newbury Park, CA: Sage.

Clegg, S. (1994). Power relations and the constitution of the resistant subject. In J. M. Jermier, D. Knights, & W. R. Nord (Eds.), *Resistance and power in organizations* (pp. 274-325). London: Routledge.

Coffman, S. L. (1992). Staff problems with geriatric care in two types of health care organizations. *Journal of Applied Communication Research, 20,* 292-307.

Coleman, J. S. (1986). Social theory, social research, and a theory of action. *American Journal of Sociology, 16,* 1309-1335.

Coles, R. (1991). Foucault's dialogical artistic ethos. *Theory, Culture and Society, 8,* 99-120.

Collinson, D. (1988). "Engineering humor": Masculinity, joking and conflict in shop-floor relations. *Organization Studies, 9,* 181-199.

Condit, C. (1994). Hegemony in mass mediated society. *Critical Studies in Mass Communication, 11,* 205-230.

Conrad, C. (1984). Phases, pentads, and dramatistic critical process. *Central States Speech Journal, 35,* 94-104.

Conrad, C. (1988). Work songs, hegemony, and illusions of self. *Critical Studies in Mass Communication, 5,* 179-194.

Conrad, C., & Ryan, M. (1985). Power, praxis, and self in organizational communication theory. In R. McPhee & P. Tompkins (Eds.), *Organizational communication: Traditional themes and new directions* (pp. 235-258). Beverly Hills, CA: Sage.

Contractor, N. S., & Eisenberg, E. (1991). Communication networks and new media in organizations. In J. Fulk & C. Steinfield (Eds.), *Organizations and communication technology* (pp. 145-174). Newbury Park, CA: Sage.

Corman, S. R. (1990). A model of perceived communication in collective networks. *Human Communication Research, 16,* 582-602.

Corman, S. R., & Scott, C. R. (1994). Perceived networks, activity foci, and observable communication in social collectives. *Communication Theory, 4,* 171-190.

Coward, R., & Ellis, J. (1977). *Language and materialism.* Boston: Routledge and Kegan Paul.

Cragan, J., & Shields, D. (1992). The use of symbolic convergence theory in corporate strategic planning. *Journal of Applied Communication Research, 20,* 199-218.

Culnan, M. J., & Markus, M. L. (1987). Information technologies. In F. M. Jablin, L. L. Putnam, K. H. Roberts, & L. W. Porter (Eds.), *Handbook of organizational communication: An interdisciplinary perspective* (pp. 420-444). Newbury Park, CA: Sage.

Cushman, D., & Sanderson-King, S. (1993). High-speed management. In S. A. Deetz (Ed.), *Communication yearbook 16* (pp. 209-236). Newbury Park, CA: Sage.

Cushman, D. P., Sanderson-King, S., & Smith, T., III. (1988). The rules perspective on organizational communication research. In G. Goldhaber & G. Barnett (Eds.), *Handbook of organizational communication* (pp. 55-94). Norwood, NJ: Ablex.

Cusella, L. P. (1987). Feedback, motivation, and performance. In F. M. Jablin, L. L. Putnam, K. H. Roberts, & L. W. Porter (Eds.), *Handbook of organizational communication: An interdisciplinary perspective* (pp. 624-678). Newbury Park, CA: Sage.

Czarniawska-Joerges, B. (1994). Narratives of individual and organizational identities. In S. A. Deetz (Ed.), *Communication yearbook 17* (pp. 190-210). Thousand Oaks, CA: Sage.

Danowski, J. A. (1980). Group attitude uniformity and connectivity of organizational communication networks for production, innovation, and maintenance content. *Human Communication Research, 6,* 299-308.

Danowski, J. A. (1988). Organizational infographics and automated auditing: Using computers to unobtrusively gather as well as analyze communication. In G. Goldhaber & G. Barnett (Eds.), *Handbook of organizational communication* (pp. 385-434). Norwood, NJ: Ablex.

Dansereau, F., & Markham, S. E. (1987). Superior-subordinate communication: Multiple levels of analysis. In F. M. Jablin, L. L. Putnam, K. H. Roberts, & L. W. Porter (Eds.), *Handbook of organizational communication: An interdisciplinary perspective* (pp. 343-388). Newbury Park, CA: Sage.

Dawe, A. (1970). The two sociologies. *British Journal of Sociology, 21,* 207-218.

Dawe, A. (1978). Theories of social action. In T. Bottomore & R. Nisbet (Eds.), *A history of sociological analysis* (pp. 362-417). New York: Basic Books.

Deetz, S. (1992a). *Democracy in an age of corporate colonization.* Albany: State University of New York Press.

Deetz, S. (1992b). Disciplinary power in the modern corporation, discursive practice and conflict suppression. In M. Alvesson & H. Willmott (Eds.), *Critical management studies* (pp. 106-142). London: Sage.

Deetz, S. (1994). Representative practices and the political analysis of corporations: Building a communication perspective in organization studies. In B. Kovacic (Ed.), *Organizational communication: New perspectives* (pp. 209-242). Albany: State University of New York Press.

Deetz, S. (1995). *Transforming communication, transforming business: Building responsive and responsible workplaces.* Cresskill, NJ: Hampton.

Deetz, S., & Mumby, D. K. (1990). Power, discourse, and the workplace: Reclaiming the critical tradition. In J. A. Anderson (Ed.), *Communication yearbook 13* (pp. 18-47). Newbury Park, CA: Sage.

Deleuze, G., & Guattari, F. (1983). *Anti-Oedipus: Capitalism and schizophrenia.* Minneapolis: University of Minnesota Press. (Original work published 1977)

DeSanctis, G., & Poole, M. S. (1994). Capturing the complexity in advanced technology use: Adaptive structuration theory. *Organization Science, 5,* 121-147.

Downs, C., Clampitt, P., & Pfeiffer, A. (1988). Communication and organizational outcomes. In G. Goldhaber & G. Barnett (Eds.), *Handbook of organizational communication* (pp. 171-212). Norwood, NJ: Ablex.

Drecksel, G. L. (1991). Leadership research: Some issues. In J. A. Anderson (Ed.), *Communication yearbook 14* (pp. 535-546). Newbury Park, CA: Sage.

Eagleton, T. (1983). *Literary theory: An introduction.* Minneapolis: University of Minnesota Press.

Eaves, M., & Leathers, D. (1991). Context as communication: McDonald's vs. Burger King. *Journal of Applied Communication Research, 19,* 263-289.

Ebers, M. (1985). Understanding organizations—The poetic mode. *Journal of Management, 7*(2), 51-62.

Ehrenhaus, P. (1993). Cultural narratives and the therapeutic motif: The political containment of Vietnam veterans. In D. Mumby (Ed.), *Narrative and social control* (pp. 77-96). Newbury Park, CA: Sage.

Eisenberg, E. M., & Goodall, H. L. (1997). *Organizational communication: Balancing creativity and constraint* (2nd ed.). New York: St. Martin's.

Eisenberg, E. M., & Riley, P. (1988). Organizational symbols and sense-making. In G. Goldhaber & G. Barnett (Eds.), *Handbook of organizational communication* (pp. 131-150). Norwood, NJ: Ablex.

Ellis, B. H., & Miller, K. (1993). The role of assertiveness, personal control, and participation in the prediction of nurse burnout. *Journal of Applied Communication Research, 21,* 327-335.

Elster, J. (1984). *Ulysses and the sirens.* Cambridge, UK: Cambridge University Press.

Euske, N. A., & Roberts, K. H. (1987). Evolving perspectives in organization theory: Communication implications. In F. M. Jablin, L. L. Putnam, K. H. Roberts, & L. W. Porter (Eds.), *Handbook of organizational communication: An interdisciplinary perspective* (pp. 41-69). Newbury Park, CA: Sage.

Everett, J. L. (1994). Communication and sociocultural evolution in organizations and organizational populations. *Communication Theory, 4,* 93-110.

Fairhurst, G. T. (1988). Male-female communication on the job: Literature review and commentary. In M. McLaughlin (Ed.), *Communication yearbook 11* (pp. 83-116). Newbury Park, CA: Sage.

Fairhurst, G. T. (1993). The leader-member exchange patterns of women leaders in industry. *Communication Monographs, 60,* 321-351.

Fairhurst, G. T., & Chandler, T. (1989). Social structure in leader-member interactions. *Communication Monographs, 56,* 215-239.

Fairhurst, G. T., Green, S., & Snavely, B. (1984a). Face support in controlling poor performance. *Human Communication Research, 11,* 272-295.

Fairhurst, G. T., Green, S., & Snavely, B. (1984b). Managerial control and discipline: Whips and chains. In R. N. Bostrom (Ed.), *Communication yearbook 8* (pp. 558-593). Beverly Hills, CA: Sage.

Fairhurst, G. T., Rogers, L. E., & Sarr, R. A. (1987). Manager-subordinate control patterns and judgments about the relationship. In M. McLaughlin (Ed.), *Communication yearbook 10* (pp. 395-415). Newbury Park, CA: Sage.

Falcione, R. L., Sussman, L., & Herden, R. P. (1987). Communication climate in organizations. In F. M. Jablin, L. L. Putnam, K. H. Roberts, & L. W. Porter (Eds.), *Handbook of organizational communication: An interdisciplinary perspective* (pp. 195-227). Newbury Park, CA: Sage.

Falcione, R. L., & Wilson, C. E. (1988). Socialization processes in organizations. In G. Goldhaber & G. Barnett (Eds.), *Handbook of organizational communication* (pp. 151-170). Norwood, NJ: Ablex.

Ferraris, C., Carveth, R., & Parrish-Sprowl, J. (1993). Interface precision benchworks: A case study in organizational identification. *Journal of Applied Communication Research, 21,* 336-357.

Feyerabend, P. K. (1993). *Against method* (3rd ed.). London: Verso. (Original work published 1975)

Fielding, N. (Ed.). (1988). *Actions and structure.* London: Sage.

Fink, E. L., & Chen, S. (1995). A Galileo analysis of organizational climate. *Human Communication Research, 21,* 484-521.

Franz, C., & Jin, K. G. (1995). The structure of group conflict in a collaborative work group during information systems development. *Journal of Applied Communication Research, 23,* 108-127.

Frost, P. J. (1987). Power, politics, and influence. In F. M. Jablin, L. L. Putnam, K. H. Roberts, & L. W. Porter (Eds.), *Handbook of organizational communica-*

tion: An interdisciplinary perspective (pp. 503-548). Newbury Park, CA: Sage.

Frye, N. (1957). *Anatomy of criticism.* Princeton, NJ: Princeton University Press.

Fulk, J., & Dutton, W. (1985). Videoconferencing as an organizational information system: Assessing the role of electronic meetings. *Systems, Objectives, Solutions, 4,* 105-118.

Fulk, J., & Mani, S. (1986). Distortion of communication in hierarchical relationships. In M. McLaughlin (Ed.), *Communication yearbook 9* (pp. 483-510). Beverly Hills, CA: Sage.

Fulk, J., Schmitz, J., & Steinfield, C. (1991). A social influence model of technology use. In J. Fulk & C. Steinfield (Eds.), *Organizations and communication technology* (pp. 117-140). Newbury Park, CA: Sage.

Gayle, B. M. (1991). Sex equity in workplace conflict management. *Journal of Applied Communication Research, 19,* 152-169.

Gergen, K. (1982). *Toward transformation in social knowledge.* New York: Springer-Verlag.

Gergen, K. (1992). Organization theory in the postmodern era. In M. Reed & M. Hughes (Eds.), *Rethinking organization: New directions in organization theory and analysis* (pp. 207-226). London: Sage.

Giddens, A. (1976). *New rules of sociological method.* New York: Basic Books.

Giddens, A. (1979). *Central problems in social theory.* Berkeley: University of California Press.

Giddens, A. (1984). *The constitution of society.* Berkeley: University of California Press.

Giddens, A. (1990). *The consequences of modernity.* Stanford, CA: Stanford University Press.

Gitlin, T. (1988, November 1). Hip-deep in postmodernism. *New York Times Book Review,* pp. 35-36.

Goldhaber, G. M., & Barnett, G. (1988a). Foreword. In G. Goldhaber & G. Barnett (Eds.), *Handbook of organizational communication* (pp. 1-4). Norwood, NJ: Ablex.

Goldhaber, G. M., & Barnett, G. (Eds.). (1988b). *Handbook of organizational communication.* Norwood, NJ: Ablex.

Goodall, H. L. (1990). Theatre of motives and the meaningful orders of persons and things. In J. A. Anderson (Ed.), *Communication yearbook 13* (pp. 69-94). Newbury Park, CA: Sage.

Goodall, H. L., Wilson, G., & Waagen, C. (1986). The performance appraisal interview. *Quarterly Journal of Speech, 72,* 74-87.

Gouldner, A. (1980). *The two Marxisms.* New York: Oxford University Press.

Granovetter, M. (1985). Economic action and social structure: The problem of embeddedness. *American Journal of Sociology, 91,* 481-510.

Greenbaum, H. H., Hellweg, S. A., & Falcione, R. L. (1988). Organizational communication evolution: An overview 1950-1981. In G. Goldhaber & G.

Barnett (Eds.), *Handbook of organizational communication* (pp. 275-318). Norwood, NJ: Ablex.

Gregg, N. (1993). Politics of identity/politics of location: Women workers organizing in a postmodern world. *Women's Studies in Communication, 16,* 1-33.

Habermas, J. (1979). *Communication and the evolution of society* (T. McCarthy, Trans.). Boston: Beacon.

Habermas, J. (1981). Modernity versus postmodernity. *New German Critique, 22,* 3-14.

Habermas, J. (1984). *The theory of communicative action* (Vol. 1). (T. McCarthy, Trans.). Boston: Beacon.

Habermas, J. (1986). The genealogical writing of history: On some aporias in Foucault's theory of power. *Canadian Journal of Political and Social Theory, 10,* 1-9.

Habermas, J. (1987). *The theory of communicative action* (Vol. 2). (T. McCarthy, Trans.). Boston: Beacon.

Habermas, J. (1991). A reply. In A. Honneth & H. Joas (Eds.), *Essays on Jürgen Habermas's* The Theory of Communicative Action (pp. 215-264). Cambridge, UK: Cambridge University Press.

Hammer, M. R., & Martin, J. N. (1992). The effects of cross-cultural training on American managers in a Japanese-American joint venture. *Journal of Applied Communication Research, 20,* 161-182.

Harris, C. C. (1980). *Fundamental concepts and the sociological enterprise.* London: Croom Helm.

Harrison, T. (1994). Communication and interdependence in democratic organizations. In S. A. Deetz (Ed.), *Communication yearbook 17* (pp. 247-274). Thousand Oaks, CA: Sage.

Held, D. (1980). *Introduction to critical theory.* Berkeley: University of California Press.

Helmer, J. (1993). Storytelling in the creation and maintenance of organizational tension and stratification. *Southern Communication Journal, 59,* 34-44.

Hess, J. A. (1993). Assimilating newcomers into the organization: A cultural perspective. *Journal of Applied Communication Research, 21,* 189-196.

Hirokawa, R. M., Mickey, J., & Miura, S. (1991). Effects of request legitimacy on the compliance-gaining tactics of male and female managers. *Communication Monographs, 58,* 421-436.

Hogan, J. M. (1989). Managing dissent in the Catholic Church. *Quarterly Journal of Speech, 75,* 400-415.

Holowitz, J., & Wilson, C. (1993). Structured interviewing in volunteer selection. *Journal of Applied Communication Research, 21,* 41-52.

Howard, L. A., & Geist, P. (1995). Ideological positioning in organizational change: The dialectic of control in a merging organization. *Communication Monographs, 62,* 110-131.

Huber, G. (1990). A theory of the effects of advanced information technologies on organizational design, intelligence, and decision making. In J. Fulk & C. Steinfield (Eds.), *Organizations and communication technology* (pp. 237-274). Newbury Park, CA: Sage.

Huber, G. P., & Daft, R. L. (1987). The information environments of organizations. In F. M. Jablin, L. L. Putnam, K. H. Roberts, & L. W. Porter (Eds.), *Handbook of organizational communication: An interdisciplinary perspective* (pp. 130-164). Newbury Park, CA: Sage.

Husband, R. (1985). Toward a grounded typology of organizational leadership behavior. *Quarterly Journal of Speech, 71,* 103-118.

Huspek, M. (1993). Dueling structures. *Communication Theory, 1,* 1-25.

Huspek, M., & Kendall, K. (1991). On withholding political voice: An analysis of the political vocabulary of a "nonpolitical" speech community. *Quarterly Journal of Speech, 77,* 1-19.

Jablin, F. M. (1979). Superior-subordinate communication. *Psychological Bulletin, 86,* 1201-1222.

Jablin, F. M. (1987a). Formal organization structure. In F. M. Jablin, L. L. Putnam, K. H. Roberts, & L. W. Porter (Eds.), *Handbook of organizational communication: An interdisciplinary perspective* (pp. 389-419). Newbury Park, CA: Sage.

Jablin, F. M. (1987b). Organizational entry, assimilation, and exit. In F. M. Jablin, L. L. Putnam, K. H. Roberts, & L. W. Porter (Eds.), *Handbook of organizational communication: An interdisciplinary perspective* (pp. 679-740). Newbury Park, CA: Sage.

Jablin, F. M., Putnam, L. L., Roberts, K. H., & Porter, L. W. (Eds.). (1987). *Handbook of organizational communication: An interdisciplinary perspective.* Newbury Park, CA: Sage.

Jablonski, C. (1988). Rhetoric, paradox and the movement for women's ordination in the Roman Catholic Church. *Quarterly Journal of Speech, 74,* 164-183.

Johnson, J. D. (1988). On the use of communication gradients. In G. Goldhaber & G. Barnett (Eds.), *Handbook of organizational communication* (pp. 361-384). Norwood, NJ: Ablex.

Keen, P. (1990). Telecommunications and organizational choice. In J. Fulk & C. Steinfield (Eds.), *Organizations and communication technology* (pp. 295-312). Newbury Park, CA: Sage.

Keough, C., & Lake, R. (1993). Values as structuring properties of contract negotiations. In C. Conrad (Ed.), *The ethical nexus* (pp. 171-192). Norwood, NJ: Ablex.

Krone, K. J., Jablin, F. M., & Putnam, L. L. (1987). Communication theory and organizational communication: Multiple perspectives. In F. M. Jablin, L. L. Putnam, K. H. Roberts, & L. W. Porter (Eds.), *Handbook of organizational communication: An interdisciplinary perspective* (pp. 18-40). Newbury Park, CA: Sage.

Knuf, J. (1993). "Ritual" in organizational culture theory. In S. A. Deetz (Ed.), *Communication yearbook 16* (pp. 61-103). Newbury Park, CA: Sage.

Kramer, M. (1993). Communication after job transfers: Social exchange processes. *Human Communication Research, 20,* 147-174.

Kunda, G. (1991). *Ritual and the management of corporate culture: A critical perspective.* Paper presented at the 8th International Conference on Organizational Symbolism, Copenhagen, Denmark.

Laird-Brenton, A. (1993). Demystifying the magic of language: A critical linguistic case analysis of legitimation of authority. *Journal of Applied Communication Research, 21,* 227-244.

Leipzig, J. S., & Moore, E. (1982). Organizational communication: A review and analysis of three current approaches to the field. *Journal of Business Communication, 19,* 77-92.

Levitt, B., & Nass, C. (1994). Organizational narratives and person/identity distinction. In S. A. Deetz (Ed.), *Communication yearbook 17* (pp. 236-246). Thousand Oaks, CA: Sage.

MacIntyre, A. (1981). *After virtue.* Notre Dame, IN: Notre Dame University Press.

Marshall, A., & Stohl, C. (1993). Participating as participation. *Communication Monographs, 60,* 137-157.

Marshall, J. (1993). Viewing organizational communication from a feminist perspective. In S. A. Deetz (Ed.), *Communication yearbook 16* (pp. 122-143). Newbury Park, CA: Sage.

McMillan, J., & Cheney, G. (1996). The student as consumer: The implications and limitations of a metaphor. *Communication Education, 45,* 1-15.

McPhee, R. (1985). Formal structure and organizational communication. In R. McPhee & P. Tompkins (Eds.), *Organizational communication: Traditional themes and new directions* (pp. 149-178). Beverly Hills, CA: Sage.

McPhee, R. D. (1993). Cultural-ideological modes of control: An examination of concept formation. In S. A. Deetz (Ed.), *Communication yearbook 16* (pp. 43-53). Newbury Park, CA: Sage.

McPhee, R. D., & Corman, S. R. (1995). An activity-based theory of communication networks in organizations, applied to the case of a local church. *Communication Monographs, 62,* 132-151.

McPhee, R., & Tompkins, P. (Eds.). (1985). *Organizational communication: Traditional themes and new directions.* Beverly Hills, CA: Sage.

Miller, K. I., & Monge, P. R. (1987). The development and test of a system of organizational participation and allocation. In M. McLaughlin (Ed.), *Communication yearbook 10* (pp. 431-455). Newbury Park, CA: Sage.

Miller, V. D., Johnstone, J. R., & Grau, J. (1994). Antecedents to willingness to participate in a planned organizational change. *Journal of Applied Communication Research, 22,* 59-80.

Monge, P. R., & Eisenberg, E. M. (1987). Emergent communication networks. In F. M. Jablin, L. L. Putnam, K. H. Roberts, & L. W. Porter (Eds.), *Hand-

book of organizational communication: An interdisciplinary perspective (pp. 304-342). Newbury Park, CA: Sage.

Monge, P. R., & Miller, K. I. (1988). Participative processes in organizations. In G. Goldhaber & G. Barnett (Eds.), *Handbook of organizational communication* (pp. 213-230). Norwood, NJ: Ablex.

Monge, P. R., Cozzens, J., & Contractor, N. (1992). Communication and motivation predictors of the dynamics of innovation. *Organization Science, 2,* 1-25.

Morrill, C., & Thomas, C. K. (1992). Organizational conflict management as disputing process. *Human Communication Research, 18,* 400-428.

Mumby, D. (1987). The political function of narrative in organizations. *Communication Monographs, 54,* 113-127.

Mumby, D. (1988). *Communication and power in organizations.* Norwood, NJ: Ablex.

Mumby, D. (1989). Ideology and the social construction of meaning: A communication perspective. *Communication Quarterly, 37,* 18-25.

Mumby, D. (1993a). Critical organizational communication studies. *Communication Monographs, 60,* 18-25.

Mumby, D. (1993b). Feminism and the critique of organizational communication. In S. A. Deetz (Ed.), *Communication yearbook 16* (pp. 155-166). Newbury Park, CA: Sage.

Mumby, D., & Putnam, L. (1992). The politics of emotion: A feminist reading of bounded rationality. *Academy of Management Review, 17,* 465-486.

O'Connell, S. E. (1988). Human communication in the high tech office. In G. Goldhaber & G. Barnett (Eds.), *Handbook of organizational communication* (pp. 473-482). Norwood, NJ: Ablex.

Olson, M. H. (1982). New information technology and organizational culture. *MIS Quarterly,* pp. 426-478.

O'Neill, J. (1995). The disciplinary society: From Weber to Foucault. *British Journal of Sociology, 37,* 42-60.

O'Reilly, C. A., Chatman, J. A., & Anderson, J. C. (1987). Message flow and decision making. In F. M. Jablin, L. L. Putnam, K. H. Roberts, & L. W. Porter (Eds.), *Handbook of organizational communication: An interdisciplinary perspective* (pp. 600-623). Newbury Park, CA: Sage.

Pacanowsky, M., & O'Donnell-Trujillo, N. (1983). Organizational communication as cultural performance. *Communication Monographs, 50,* 126-147.

Papa, M., Arwal, M. A., & Singhal, A. (1995). Dialectic of control and emancipation in organizing for change. *Communication Theory, 5,* 189-223.

Peterson, M. F., & Sorenson, R. L. (1991). Cognitive processes in leadership: Interpreting and handling events in an organizational context. In J. A. Anderson (Ed.), *Communication yearbook 14* (pp. 501-534). Newbury Park, CA: Sage.

Plax, T., Beatty, M., & Feingold, P. (1991). Predicting verbal plan complexity from decision rule orienta-

tion among business students and corporate executives. *Journal of Applied Communication Research, 19,* 242-262.

Poole, M. S. (1985). Communication and organizational climates: Review, critique, and a new perspective. In R. McPhee & P. Tompkins (Eds.), *Organizational communication: Traditional themes and new directions* (pp. 79-108). Beverly Hills, CA: Sage.

Poole, M. S. (1994). *A turn of the wheel: The case for a renewal of systems inquiry in organizational communication research.* Paper presented at the annual meeting of the Speech Communication Association, Atlanta, GA.

Poole, M. S., & DeSanctis, G. (1990). Understanding the use of group decision support systems: The theory of adaptive structuration. In J. Fulk & C. Steinfield (Eds.), *Organizations and communication technology* (pp. 173-193). Newbury Park, CA: Sage.

Poole, M. S., & DeSanctis, G. (1992). Microlevel structuration in computer-supported group decision-making. *Human Communication Research, 19,* 5-49.

Poole, M. S., & Holmes, M. (1995). Decision development in computer-assisted group decision making. *Human Communication Research, 22,* 90-127.

Poole, M. S., & McPhee, R. D. (1983). A structurational analysis of organizational climate. In L. L. Putnam & M. E. Pacanowsky (Eds.), *Communication and organizations: An interpretive approach* (pp. 195-220). Beverly Hills, CA: Sage.

Poole, M. S., & McPhee, R. D. (1994). Methodology in interpersonal communication research. In M. Knapp & G. R. Miller (Eds.), *Handbook of interpersonal communication* (2nd ed., pp. 42-100). Thousand Oaks, CA: Sage.

Poole, M. S., Seibold, D. R., & McPhee, R. D. (1985). Group decision-making as a structurational process. *Quarterly Journal of Speech, 71,* 74-102.

Poole, M. S., & Van de Ven, A. H. (1989). Using paradox to build management and organization theories. *Academy of Management Review, 14,* 562-578.

Putnam, L., & Sorenson, R. (1982). Equivocal messages in organizations. *Human Communication Research, 8,* 114-132.

Putnam, L., & Stohl, C. (1990). Bona fide groups: A reconceptualization of groups in context. *Communication Studies, 41,* 248-265.

Putnam, L. L., & Poole, M. S. (1987). Conflict and negotiation. In F. M. Jablin, L. L. Putnam, K. H. Roberts, & L. W. Porter (Eds.), *Handbook of organizational communication: An interdisciplinary perspective* (pp. 549-599). Newbury Park, CA: Sage.

Ralston, S. (1993). Applicant communication satisfaction, intent to accept second interview offers, and recruiter communication style. *Journal of Applied Communication Research, 21,* 53-65.

Ralston, S. M., & Kirkwood, W. G. (1995). Overcoming managerial bias in employment interviewing. *Journal of Applied Communication Research, 23,* 75-92.

Reed, M. (1985). *Redirections in organizational analysis.* London: Tavistock.

Richmond, V. P., & Roach, K. D. (1992). Willingness to communicate and employee success in U.S. organizations. *Journal of Applied Communication Research, 20,* 95-115.

Riley, P. (1983). A structurationist account of political cultures. *Administrative Science Quarterly, 28,* 414-438.

Ritzer, G. (1997). *Postmodern social theory.* New York: McGraw-Hill.

Roberts, K., & O'Reilly, C. (1978). Organizations as communication structures: An empirical approach. *Human Communication Research, 4,* 283-293.

Rogers, E. M. (1988). Information technologies: How organizations are changing. In G. Goldhaber & G. Barnett (Eds.), *Handbook of organizational communication* (pp. 437-452). Norwood, NJ: Ablex.

Rosenau, P. M. (1992). *Postmodernism and the social sciences.* Princeton, NJ: Princeton University Press.

Salaman, G. (1986). *Working.* London: Tavistock.

Salvador, M., & Markham, A. (1995). The rhetoric of self-directive management and the operation of organizational power. *Communication Reports, 8,* 45-53.

Sambamurthy, V., & Poole, M. S. (1993). The effects of variations in capabilities of GDSS designs on management of cognitive conflict in groups. *Information Systems Research, 3,* 224-251.

Scott, C. R. (1996, May). *Identification with multiple targets in a geographically dispersed organization.* Paper presented at the annual meeting of the International Communication Association, Chicago.

Scott, J. C. (1993). *Domination and the arts of resistance: Hidden transcripts.* New Haven, CT: Yale University Press.

Seibold, D. R., & Contractor, N. (1993). Issues for a theory of high-speed management. In S. A. Deetz (Ed.), *Communication yearbook 16* (pp. 237-246). Newbury Park, CA: Sage.

Shils, E. (1968). The concept and function of ideology. In D. Sills (Ed.), *The international encyclopedia of the social sciences* (Vol. 7, pp. 66-76). New York: Crowell, Collier and Macmillan.

Shockley-Zalabak, P., & Morley, D. D. (1994). Creating a culture. *Human Communication Research, 20,* 334-355.

Sias, P., & Jablin, F. M. (1995). Differential superior-subordinate relations, perceptions of fairness, and coworker communication. *Human Communication Research, 22,* 5-38.

Simons, H. (1989). *Rhetoric in the human sciences.* London: Sage.

Simons, H. (1990). *The rhetorical turn, invention and persuasion in the conduct of inquiry.* Chicago: University of Chicago Press.

Smircich, L., & Calás, M. B. (1987). Organizational culture: A critical assessment. In F. M. Jablin, L. L. Putnam, K. H. Roberts, & L. W. Porter (Eds.), *Handbook of organizational communication: An interdisciplinary perspective* (pp. 228-263). Newbury Park, CA: Sage.

Smith, R. C., & Turner, P. K. (1995). A social constructionist reconfiguration of metaphor analysis: An application of "SCMA" to organizational socialization theorizing. *Communication Monographs, 62,* 152-181.

Stewart, L. P., Gudykunst, W. B., & Ting-Toomey, S. (1986). The effects of decision-making style on openness and satisfaction within Japanese organizations. *Communication Monographs, 53,* 236-251.

Stohl, C. (1986). Bridging the parallel organization: A study of quality circle effectiveness. In J. Burgoon (Ed.), *Communication yearbook 10* (pp. 473-496). Beverly Hills, CA: Sage.

Stohl, C. (1993). European managers' interpretations of participation: A semantic network analysis. *Human Communication Research, 20,* 97-117.

Stohl, C. (1995). *Organizational communication: Connectedness in action.* Thousand Oaks, CA: Sage.

Stohl, C., & Redding, W. C. (1987). Messages and message exchange processes. In F. M. Jablin, L. L. Putnam, K. H. Roberts, & L. W. Porter (Eds.), *Handbook of organizational communication: An interdisciplinary perspective* (pp. 451-502). Newbury Park, CA: Sage.

Strine, M. S. (1992). Understanding "how things work": Sexual harassment and academic culture. *Journal of Applied Communication Research, 20,* 391-400.

Sypher, B. D. (1991). A message-centered approach to leadership. In J. A. Anderson (Ed.), *Communication yearbook 14* (pp. 547-559). Newbury Park, CA: Sage.

Taylor, B. (1992). The politics of the nuclear text. *Quarterly Journal of Speech, 78,* 429-449.

Taylor, B. (1993). Register of the repressed. *Quarterly Journal of Speech, 79,* 267-285.

Taylor, B., & Conrad, C. (1992). Narratives of sexual harassment: Organizational dimensions. *Journal of Applied Communication Research, 20,* 401-418.

Thayer, L. (1988). Leadership/communication: A critical review and a modest proposal. In G. Goldhaber & G. Barnett (Eds.), *Handbook of organizational communication* (pp. 231-264). Norwood, NJ: Ablex.

Therborn, G. (1980). *The ideology of power and the power of ideology.* London: Verso.

Tompkins, P. K. (1987). Translating organizational theory: Symbolism over substance. In F. M. Jablin, L. L. Putnam, K. H. Roberts, & L. W. Porter (Eds.), *Handbook of organizational communication: An interdisciplinary perspective* (pp. 70-96). Newbury Park, CA: Sage.

Tompkins, P. K., & Cheney, G. (1983). Account analysis of organizations: Decision making and identification. In L. L. Putnam & M. E. Pacanowsky (Eds.), *Communication and organizations: An interpretive approach* (pp. 123-146). Beverly Hills, CA: Sage.

Tompkins, P. K., & Cheney, G. (1985). Communication and unobtrusive control in contemporary organizations. In R. McPhee & P. Tompkins (Eds.), *Organizational communication: Traditional themes and new directions* (pp. 179-210). Beverly Hills, CA: Sage.

Touraine, A. (1985). An introduction to the study of social movements. *Social Research, 52,* 763-771.

Tracy, K., & Baratz, S. (1993). Intellectual discussion in the academy as situated discourse. *Communication Monographs, 60,* 300-320.

Treadwell, D. F., & Harrison, T. (1994). Conceptualizing and assessing organizational image. *Communication Monographs, 61,* 63-85.

Trevino, L. K., Daft, R. L., & Lengel, R. H. (1990). Understanding managers' media choices: A symbolic interactionist perspective. In J. Fulk & C. Steinfield (Eds.), *Organizations and communication technology* (pp. 71-94). Newbury Park, CA: Sage.

Triandis, H. C., & Albert, R. D. (1987). Cross-cultural perspectives. In F. M. Jablin, L. L. Putnam, K. H. Roberts, & L. W. Porter (Eds.), *Handbook of organizational communication: An interdisciplinary perspective* (pp. 264-296). Newbury Park, CA: Sage.

Trice, H., & Beyer, J. (1993). *The cultures of work organizations.* Englewood Cliffs, NJ: Prentice Hall.

Tushman, M. L., & Romanelli, E. (1985). Organizational evolution: A metamorphosis model of convergence and reorientation. In B. Staw & L. Cummings (Eds.), *Research in organizational behavior* (Vol. 7, pp. 171-222). Greenwich, CT: JAI.

Turner, B. (1992). The symbolic understanding of organizations. In M. Reed & M. Hughes (Eds.), *Re-thinking organization: New directions in organization theory and analysis* (pp. 46-66). London: Sage.

Van de Ven, A. H., & Poole, M. S. (1988). Paradoxical requirements for a theory of organizational change. In R. Quinn & K. Cameron (Eds.), *Paradox and transformation: Toward a theory of change in organizations and management* (pp. 19-63). Cambridge, MA: Ballinger.

Waldron, V. (1991). Achieving communication goals in superior-subordinate relationships. *Communication Monographs, 58,* 289-306.

Weick, K. E. (1979). *The social psychology of organizing* (2nd ed.). Reading, MA: Addison-Wesley.

Wert-Gray, S., Center, C., Brashers, D., & Meyers, R. (1991). Research topics and methodological orientations in organizational communication: A decade in review. *Communication Studies, 42,* 141-154.

West, C., & Zimmerman, D. (1987). Doing gender. *Gender & Society, 1,* 125-151.

Wigand, R. T. (1988). Communication network analysis: History and overview. In G. H. Goldhaber & G. A. Barnett (Eds.), *Handbook of organizational communication* (pp. 319-360). Norwood, NJ: Ablex.

Witten, M. (1993). Narrative and the culture of obedience at the workplace. In D. Mumby (Ed.), *Narrative and social control: Critical perspectives* (pp. 97-118). Newbury Park, CA: Sage.

Wood, J. T. (1992). Telling our stories: Narratives as a basis for theorizing sexual harassment. *Journal of Applied Communication Research, 20,* 349-362.

Zmud, R. (1990). Opportunities for strategic information manipulation through new information technology. In J. Fulk & C. Steinfield (Eds.), *Organizations and communication technology* (pp. 95-116). Newbury Park, CA: Sage.

3

Discourse Analysis in Organizations

Issues and Concerns

LINDA L. PUTNAM
Texas A&M University

GAIL T. FAIRHURST
University of Cincinnati

anguage analysis has moved into a prominent place in organizational studies. Once the domain of scholars of linguistics and sociology, language is more than just a specialized vernacular or a unique code system. Although language is vital for understanding organizational symbols, recent shifts in both organizational theory and discourse analysis suggest that language is more than elements of narrative structure and words that reflect themes, rules, and norms of behavior. Even though discourse analysis is clearly a type of methodology, language is more than an analytical tool used to gain insights about organizational constructs. Finally, although the study of language is an interdisciplinary pursuit in its own right, discourse patterns fuse with organiza-

tional processes in ways that make language and organizations a unique domain—one that differs from the study of linguistics in general and discourse analysis in other social settings. To begin the process of building theory in this area, this chapter reviews the literature on language and organization and delineates specific challenges in this research domain.

The interdisciplinary roots of language analysis date back to rhetorical and literary studies, particularly ones that originated with the philosophical treatises of the ancient Greeks more than 2,000 years ago (van Dijk, 1985). The rhetorical and literary perspectives drew from poetics and examine figures of speech such as metaphors, metonymy, synecdoche, and irony (Brown, 1977). Other approaches in the rhetorical tradition focused on persuasion, argumentation, and reasoning (Toulmin, 1958). These studies centered on language's strategic functions of making claims, supporting positions, and developing relationships between audiences and speakers/writers. The entry of anthropology and sociology into the study of words and grammatical forms marked the beginning of applying modern linguistics to social and historical texts. In the 1960s, the French structuralists broadened linguistic analyses by focusing on the context of utterances, genres of discourse, and social situations. Drawing from these views, theorists of social construction and phenomenology examined subjective and intersubjective meanings that emanated from language use, and critical theorists highlighted the way discourse aids in suppressing voice through hegemony, unobtrusive control, and ideology.

The rise of poststructuralism, with its emphasis on the science of signs, cast language as a structural system of relationships in which meanings and signification are constantly deferred (Huyssen, 1986; Saussure, 1916/1974). Poststructuralists contend that words and texts have no fixed or stable meanings. Object, ideas, and symbols are constituted through signifiers or referents linked to other referents. They purport that webs of practices embodied in discourses become logics of surveillance, disciplinary practices, and histories of texts (Foucault, 1979; Townley, 1993). Discourse is also a salient component of deconstruction, in which researchers disassemble texts by examining the privileging and concealing of words and antinomies (Derrida, 1982). Another postmodern approach that centers on discourse is actor-network theory in which scripts reflexively constitute networks of texts that become centered and decentered (Akrich & Latour, 1992; Latour, 1988, 1996b). Clearly, the study of language and discourse in the process of organizing has reached its maturity; consequently, it needs synthesis and critique as an ontological base for the study of organizations.

DEFINITIONS AND FRAMEWORK FOR THE CHAPTER

Discourse analysis, in this chapter, is defined as the study of words and signifiers, including the form or structure of these words, the use of language in context, and the meanings or interpretation of discursive practices (Fairhurst & Putnam, 1998). Language analyses encompass the study of verbal codes, utterances, conversations, interaction patterns, and signs. In this chapter, discourse is viewed as a way of knowing or a perspective for understanding organizational life. It is a lens or a point of entry for seeing, learning, and understanding ongoing events. As a lens, it provides a unique way to focus on the subtle aspects of organizing and to determine what is figure and ground in the framing of organizational events.

Even though language is intertwined with organizational symbols such as myths, rituals, and narratives, this review focuses directly on studies that make linguistic patterns the key to examining organizational life. Language is clearly central to the development of narrative text, but it is not identical to the structure of narratives as reflected in such elements as theme, plot, characterization, and scene. Hence, this chapter includes only those narrative studies of organizations that focus on the linguistics of storytelling. This essay includes studies on rhetorical analyses of organizations, particularly those that examine figures of speech such as troupes, irony, paradoxes, and dialogue.

Moreover, this chapter excludes essays that treat language and metaphors as metatheoretical perspectives for understanding the field (Boland & Greenberg, 1988; Morgan, 1980, 1997; Putnam, Phillips, & Chapman, 1996). Although these studies make valuable contributions, they represent a different body of literature, one that uses discourse to study the sociology of knowledge about organizational theory (Pinder & Bourgeois, 1982). In addition, this review mainly centers on studies that cross multiple organizational levels and units. Hence, investigations of doctor-patient interaction and clerk-customer exchanges that are primarily dyadic are not included in the purview of this chapter.

This essay undertakes a review and critique of the organizational discourse literature through unpacking the relationships among the constructs *language* and *organization.* Rather than presuming the existence of these constructs, this chapter seeks out the assumptions and their interconnections implicit in the use of these terms. This argument develops through a review, classification, and analysis of the organizational discourse literature.

To review and classify the literature, we employ a typology based on eight categories of language analysis: sociolinguistics, conversation analysis, cognitive linguistics, pragmatics, semiotics, literary and rhetorical language analysis, critical language studies, and postmodern language analysis. This classification scheme emanates from the literatures on discourse and organizations (Donnellon, 1986; Grant, Keenoy, & Oswick, 1998; Keenoy, Oswick, & Grant, 1997; Tulin, 1997) and represents a synthesis of the standard linguistic typologies (Haslett, 1987; van Dijk, 1985, 1997b). Even though these approaches differ in their emphases on discourse features, the categories are not "pure," nor are they mutually exclusive. Scholars often merge several approaches or borrow methodologies, foci, and constructs from different perspectives. What is critical in this chapter is an effort to reveal how language is defined and conceived in different studies, what features of discourse are privileged, and how discourse patterns relate to organizational processes and constructs.

These eight approaches draw from and highlight different features that become central in a particular discourse study. Discourse features refer to the characteristics or elements that comprise the language analysis. We contend that one or more features of language emerge as figure or become prominent in a study and the other elements remain in the background or are omitted from investigations. Eight interrelated features surface in this literature:

Codes: The features of naming, such as labels, jargon, vernacular, terminology, and signs

Structure: The patterns, order, syntax, sequence of words and phrases, and implicit/explicit rules for the use of discourse

Function: The purposes for language use and the links between discourse and organizational functions

Language user: The knowledge representations, expectations, scripts, frames, and cognition of users

Meaning: Interpretation, understandings, and reading of texts

Text: Sets of structured discourse patterns inscribed in organizations

Context: Organizational events, history, and parameters that shape interpretations of texts

Intertextuality: The interfaces between discourse, text, and institutional contexts

Although discourse analysts define these elements differently (e.g., shifting definitions of *texts* sometimes in the same studies), these elements frame the nature of studies and serve as a basis for analyzing language patterns. Determining which ones are privileged in a study and how these units are intertwined with organizational constructs and processes is the critical factor in organizational language analysis.

In addition, this review examines the way that discourse patterns relate to organizational processes and constructs. That is, researchers typically employ language as a tool for analyzing particular organizational constructs or processes. Hence, in many studies language analysis is a technique for conducting qualitative analysis. Researchers, then, are less interested in understanding discourse as a process of organizing and more concerned with particular constructs, for example, leadership, control/power, identity/image, conflict, or change. In other studies, language is treated as constitutive; therefore, organizational constructs grow out of the discourse, for example, identity or conflict. This chapter examines the language-organization relationship to see how discourse processes shape and are shaped by organizational constructs.

DISCOURSE TYPOLOGIES IN ORGANIZATIONAL STUDIES

In the organizational arena, language analysis has focused on both written and oral discourse, including the talk of administrators (Gronn, 1983; Gummer, 1984), analysis of the production of corporate documents (Keller-Cohen, 1987), and the links between writing and talking at work (Baxter, 1993; Hawes, 1976; Kaufer & Carley, 1993). These studies have embraced both the rhetorical and literary traditions and the traditional linguistic roots for studying discourse.

Early research on the study of language in organizations grew out of two major strands of work: professional talk and organizational culture. About a decade before organizational researchers became interested in discourse, language researchers began to focus on talk in institutional settings. Drawing from the work in conversation analysis and sociolinguistics, researchers examined the patterns of talk that characterized doctor-patient interaction (Fisher & Todd, 1983; Korsch & Negrete, 1972; Mishler, 1984), legal settings (Conley & O'Barr, 1990; Levi & Walker, 1990), therapist-counselor interviews (Labov & Fanshel, 1977; Turner, 1972), and classroom interactions (Gumperz & Herasimchuk, 1975; Mehan, 1979; Sinclair & Coulthard, 1975; Stubbs, 1976). In general, these studies centered on the form and structure of everyday talk framed by roles, identity, or occupational constraints. Hence, the process of organizing per se was not a central feature of these studies.

Culture was another strand of research that championed the critical role of discourse in organizational studies (see Eisenberg & Riley,

Chapter 9, this volume). Defined as a unique sense of place that each organization offers (Pacanowsky & O'Donnell-Trujillo, 1983), studies of organizational culture examine the use of slogans, creeds, jokes, and stories as a lens for understanding organizational life. Often referred to as "organizational symbolism" (Dandridge, Mitroff, & Joyce, 1980), studies of language use in organizations became fused with myths, rituals, and cultural artifacts (Ouchi & Wilkins, 1985; Schein, 1985).

These pioneers of language analysis in organizations developed typologies rooted in linguistics and literary forms. For example, in the late 1970s, Pettigrew (1979) defined organizations "as language systems" and Pondy (1978) treated leadership as a "language game" in which linguistic formations were connected to actions. The dominant typologies that surfaced in the early organizational culture literature adhered to symbolic views of language, for example, vocabularies, themes, tropes (Johnson, 1977), or to linguistic views of discourse analysis, for example, ethnomethodology and speech acts (Hawes, 1976). Drawing from the linguistic perspective, Donnellon (1986) set forth a typology for examining language as a system of cognitions. She posited six approaches: linguistics, psycholinguistics, sociolinguistics, ethnography of speaking, ethnomethodology, and interaction analysis and advocated focusing on conversation analysis to investigate how language displayed and enacted organizational cognitions. Tulin (1997) echoed this commitment to conversation analysis, but she employed structuration theory as a way of moving conversation analysis beyond its ethnomethodological roots. For Tulin, conversation was an accomplishment, a process that engendered social order and constituted organizational phenomena.

Other approaches to discourse studies include linguistics, rhetoric, philosophy, literature, and cognitive science (O'Connor, 1994). These approaches illustrate how language functions as a reflexive social act that represents cultural production. More recently,

Keenoy et al. (1997) and Grant et al. (1998) highlight the critical and postmodern perspectives to the study of language. Through focusing on text and intertexuality, they trace the conceptual roots of organizational discourse to speech acts, ethnomethodology, and semiology, but note that these origins infuse contemporary studies that center on organizational stories, metaphors, language games, and texts. They introduce an important distinction between monologic and dialogic views of discourse analysis. A monologic view centers on an uncontested singular interpretation or preferred reading of a text while a dialogic focus examines the multiple voices that contribute to pluralistic, contested, and paradoxical meanings that evolve from the interpenetration of texts among groups over time. Pragmatic approaches to discourse analysis also make this distinction between monologic and dialogic readings of texts (Haslett, 1987).

This review of literature integrates and draws from these summaries to present a typology of eight categories of language analysis in organizations: sociolinguistics, conversation analysis, cognitive linguistics, pragmatics and discourse analysis, semiotics, literary and rhetorical analyses, critical language studies, and postmodern language analysis (Fairhurst & Putnam, 1998; Haslett, 1987; Putnam, 1990a, 1994). These eight differ in the features of discourse that are privileged and the way discourse relates to organizational processes and constructs. Some approaches differ radically in the definitions and assumptions that underlie language analysis in organizations.

SOCIOLINGUISTICS

Sociolinguists treat language as an outgrowth of social categories. Researchers who embrace this perspective emphasize semantics or the lexicon that emanates from societal and structural differences, for example, socioeconomic class, education, or geographic location. Organizational studies on social class treat linguistic repertoires as housed within social systems. For example, Tompkins's (1962, 1965) study of communication within labor unions reveals semantic barriers and patterns of semantic information distance between hierarchical levels within the union. Tracing the roots of language to economic class, Tompkins also observes that union and corporate leaders share similar definitions of terminology while the rank and file differ from both groups in their perceptions of workplace vernacular. A study on language and the life-worlds of blue-collar and white-collar workers noted a similar pattern in that white-collar employees relied on bureaucratic language profiles while blue-collar workers draw from linguistic patterns rooted in technical production (Sands, 1981). To enhance their social and organizational positions, blue-collar women who have different ways of writing and talking pursue language education (Krol, 1991).

These class differences, however, become secondary to organizational variables in accounting for diversity in linguistic patterns. Basically, Tway (1975) reports no difference in lexical use between management and workers within the same department, but observes considerable variation across departments, especially when these units are geographically separated. Thus, departmental stratification and geographic separation account for distinct linguistic patterns among units.

Structural variables such as occupation, subculture groups, and hierarchical position also contribute to variations in linguistic repertoires. Specifically, scientists, especially biochemists, rely on technical and empirical talk in professional discourse but switch to contingency language in informal interactions about the field (Gilbert & Mulkay, 1984). These discourses produce contradictory positions when scientists engage in decision making about a pension fund (Cray, 1989).

For Barley (1983, 1986), differences between the vernacular of radiologists and technicians emanate from occupational training and organizational roles rather than from a universal scientific discourse. Occupations, then, functioned as speech communities that infuse organizations with specialized vocabularies (Coleman, 1985; Van Maanen & Barley, 1984). For example, bank tellers in a British financial institution emerge as a subculture through their routine avoidance of denominational words, such as *pound, note,* and *pence,* to shift attention away from the vast sums of money that flow through their hands (Taylor, 1987). In like manner, physicians employ highly specialized linguistic registers to produce medical reports. These registers incorporate abbreviations, use of technical terms, active verbs, length of utterances, and depersonalized pronouns (van Naerssen, 1985). Since doctors rarely receive formal training on how to write medical records, these patterns point to the existence of an occupationally based linguistic repertoire. Language also distinguishes occupational classification in the U.S. Navy with cadets using words like *spark, skivvy waver,* and *spook* to identify a radio operator, signal operator, and communication technician, respectively (Evered, 1983). Words, then, become markers for the class, occupation, and professional roles in organizations.

Linguistic repertoires also emerge from informal interactions among members of an organizational subculture. For instance, the nursing staff of a regional hospital uses a slang system to distinguish patients, referring to the more demanding ones as *crocks,* the members of stigmatized groups as *gomers,* and the physically unresponsive as *gorks* (Gordon, 1983). Although this language system seems dehumanizing and derogatory, it provides nurses with tension release that distances them from highly emotional situations. Drawing from the work of dialectical geographers and sociolinguists, Bastien (1992) examines different lexical systems in use within and between a parent company and an acquired company. In this study, individuals who either learn the language of the new company or hold onto their own lexical patterns are retained as employees in the new organization. Ironically, the groups that switch codes to adapt to both cultures either voluntarily resign or are downsized in the reorganization.

Finally, hierarchical position and organizational status are also structural features that differentiate lexical codes in organizations. Coleman (1985) links these different lexical systems to expertise and status in talking shop at work. Moreover, early organizational studies on the use of titles and forms of address reveal that this linguistic pattern is nonreciprocal and signifies status differences among employees (Brown & Ford, 1961; Slobin, Miller, & Porter, 1968, 1972). However, in organizations today, CEOs on down to the lower-ranked workers often exchange first names and refer to title and last name only in formal situations or in interactions with strangers (Morand, 1996). Morand hypothesizes that these changes evolve from an increase in lateral communication, organic forms of organizing, and informality in organizations over the past 30 years. Thus, in ambiguous or uncertain situations, name avoidance bridges power differences and enables subordinates to cope psychologically with the unfamiliar situations.

From a sociolinguistic perspective, language becomes a system or code in which organizational communities define their identities and relationships. Discourse indexes social structures; defines communication styles; and emanates from training, enculturation, and class systems that operate within and outside of the organization. In many ways, language as an artifact of organizations reflects occupation, department, and organizational role.

What is problematic in this approach is the treatment of organizational structures as social facts. Structures become fixtures or static forms rather than dynamic processes that emerge from organizational struggles. Meanings and interpretations of discourse are assumed rather than questioned; lexical codes surface as the central features of discourse.

Organizational constructs that this perspective privileges include structural units, roles, and levels. Issues of status and identity surface within the context variables of class, occupation, and position and emanate from organizational tasks and interaction settings (Drew & Heritage, 1992).

CONVERSATION ANALYSIS

Unlike sociolinguistics, conversation analysis (CA) focuses on the structure of language rather than its code. Order, syntax, and sequence of interaction occur within a dynamic rather than a static context. Conversations are accomplishments, ones produced, renewed, and transformed locally through interactions (Drew & Heritage, 1992). The term *accomplishment,* derived from ethnomethodology, refers to implicit rules that guide the syntax and structure of successive talk turns. Although traditional CA examines the way institutions constrain interactions (Drew & Heritage, 1992), the enactment of talk in organizations differs from the accomplishment of conversations in everyday interaction.

Organizational studies that employ CA cluster into five areas: (1) the opening and closing of interactions (McLaughlin, 1984; Pomerantz & Fehr, 1997); (2) turn taking, including hesitations, interruptions, silences, and talkovers (Boden, 1994; Sacks, Schegloff, & Jefferson, 1974); (3) adjacency pairs, such as question/answer (Boden, 1994; Levinson, 1983); (4) the initiation and management of topics (McLaughlin, 1984); and (5) patterns for handling conversational problems, such as disclaimers, alignments, accounts, and repairs (Hewitt & Stokes, 1975; Stokes & Hewitt, 1976).

Openings and Closings

Openings and closings of conversations played a critical role in shaping identities and managing impressions in institutional settings. For example, in a hospital setting, supervisory physicians must oversee the performance of internists without undermining the student's competency or authority as the "physician in charge" (Pomerantz, Fehr, & Ende, 1997). Hence, supervising physicians employ spatial positioning, ambiguous references, and such words as *working with, working together,* to equalize the role of intern and physician. In a job interview setting, recruiters manage impressions of their companies through using a sequence of summaries, positive statements, and continuity of interactions to close conversations with applicants (Ragan, 1983).

Turn Taking

Turn taking, the second area of conversational research in organizations, is aligned with power and control and the very concept of organizing. A turn refers to the utterances that mark a speaker's control of the floor. Coordinating conversations through turn taking focuses on the length of a turn, the rules for holding and allocating the floor, and the use of overlaps and interruptions to gain the floor (McLaughlin, 1984). Specifically, in market negotiations bargainers use hesitations, self-correction, and slow speech followed by increased volume and interruptions to gain control of the floor and signal agreement (Neu, 1988).

Other studies, particularly ones concerned with gender in organizations, focus on turn taking as manifestations of power (Tannen, 1994). In committee meetings, male supervisors talk longer and interrupt their colleagues more often than do female supervisors (James & Clarke, 1993; Woods, 1988; Zimmerman & West, 1975); their interruptions are aimed at clarifying issues, voicing agreements, and influencing the directions of conversations (Kennedy & Camden, 1983). However, in meetings in which both genders share the agenda, female committee members talk as long as their male counterparts do and joke, argue, and solicit responses more often than their male members do (Edelsky, 1981). Thus, opportunity to communicate and expectations mediate the use of talk turns and exert control in meetings. In a similar way, conversational sequences both tighten and loosen administrative reins in interactions between a school principal and his immediate subordinates (Gronn, 1983). Thus, turn taking in conversations functions both to empower and to control organizational meetings, depending on whether organizational members are involved in shaping agendas and meeting activities.

Leaving aside power issues, Boden (1994) emphasizes the organizing capacity of turn taking and turn-taking mechanisms such as adjacency pairs (e.g., question-answer, query-response). Because organizational action coheres as a sequence, the sequential pacing of talk is "deeply implicative of organizations themselves" (Boden, 1994, p. 206). She examines organizational agenda setting, report giving, decision making, and turn taking in interactional and sequential terms, thus highlighting what is organizing about discourse itself.

Adjacency Pairs

The third area of CA in organizations, the use of adjacency pairs or message sequences, is also linked to power and control. The term *adjacency pair* refers to a message/response sequence that occurs in a predictable manner, for example, question/answer, request/acceptance, demand/response. In job interview and training sessions, power relationships surface through the use of question-answer sequences. For example, answers to a job interviewer's question signal the applicant's comprehension or misunderstanding of the prior utterance. To keep the process controlled, interviewers rarely restate questions or correct the applicant. Rather, the applicant's ability to understand the interviewer's questions becomes a criterion for evaluating interviewee competence (Button, 1993). In job training programs, the use of marked speech and cryp-

tic answers disadvantage ethnic minorities in comparison with native speakers (Gumperz, 1992).

The use of adjacency pairs also reveals the way conversational patterns influence the design and management of communication systems. In an emergency dispatch setting, the management of call processing—the way that calls develop and are concluded—and the policies of particular organizations are oriented to the accomplishments of a request/response sequence (Whalen & Zimmerman, 1987; Zimmerman, 1992). Moreover, in a teachers' negotiation, use of a question-answer sequence is more effective than a demand-response sequence in eliciting information and concessions (Donohue & Diez, 1985).

Topic Shifts

Power and control also surface as dominant organizational features in the fourth area of CA: topic shifts. Topic shifts refer to changes in the themes or sequences of events from one utterance to the next. In one study, male physicians exert more control in decision making through introducing a higher frequency of topic shifts than women doctors do (Ainsworth-Vaughn, 1992). In a labor-management negotiation, bargainers, by using question-answer sequences, position their own side's proposals as salient in the discussion (Frances, 1986). Ironically, mediators of organizational disputes also use topic shifts to control the interactions of disputants, reduce emotional outbursts, and move disputants toward settlements (Frances, 1986; Greatbatch & Dingwall, 1994).

Disclaimers and Alignments

Differences between powerful and powerless speech are particularly salient in studies of the fifth area of CA in organizations: disclaimers and alignments (Haslett, 1987). Disclaimers are feedback strategies that aid in preventing conversational breakdowns, while alignments, accounts, and explanations are corrections used to repair conversational problems. Disclaimers qualify the force of utterances to avoid negative judgments through the use of metatalk, hedges, tag questions, and qualifiers. For example, statements like "I didn't mean it that way," "I'm not an authority on this issue," "This is your opinion, isn't it?" and "We *usually* take this course of action" exemplify the use of disclaimers.

Using disclaimers as indexes of speech, Fairhurst and Chandler (1989) illustrate the way subordinates display both powerful and powerless language to exert influence over their supervisors and preserve deference. Unlike in-group subordinates, out-group members use disclaimers and a verbatim report style to maintain social distance. In other studies, use of disclaimers reduces expert power, softens criticism, and facilitates group discussion (Dubois & Crouch, 1975; Holmes, 1984; Preisler, 1986). But in computer-mediated groups, use of disclaimers and powerless speech reduces credibility and the persuasiveness of group member messages (Adkins & Brashers, 1995). These studies indicate that disclaimers maintain role and status boundaries, foster efforts to include or empower subordinates, and influence judgments of credibility and persuasiveness among colleagues (Baker, 1991). Use of disclaimers in organizations, then, indicates that this language pattern is not necessarily a form of powerless speech. Mediating variables such as gender, expectations, and status influences both the use of and reaction to disclaimers.

Patterns of powerful and powerless speech surface in studies of alignments in organizational conversations. Alignments refer to the way that speakers use conversational devices to buffer or anticipate disruptions and misunderstandings (Stokes & Hewlitt, 1976). Through formulations, metatalk, accounts, and side sequences, alignments clarify meanings, convey intentions, and repair conversations. In employment situations, interviewers control conversational pacing through the use of summaries, formulations, and metatalk while applicants employ powerless forms of speech, such as qualifiers, speech fillers, and accounts (Ragan, 1983; Ragan & Hopper, 1981). But rather than suggesting powerlessness, the giving of accounts in selection interviews hinges on the interviewer's questions, the vulnerability of the job, and the applicant's recognition of his or her role (Morris, 1988). In selection interviews, accounts are regarded legitimate when they express doubts or interpretations of what the interviewer "is really asking." Account giving in conversations, then, underscores the relationship between interaction and social structure. That is, even when low-status participants offer accounts to gain access to the floor, these moves reflexively reaffirm the asymmetry and power differences between doctors and patients (Fisher & Groce, 1990) and between senators and witnesses in the Watergate hearings (Molotch & Boden, 1985).

CA highlights the structure of language through focusing on the syntax and coherence of interactions in organizations. Unlike the sociolinguistic perspective, both language and organizations are accomplishments; that is, power and control emanate from the way organizational members produce conversations and organizational roles influence the way that conversations are interactively structured. This perspective shows how conversations contribute to the production of organizational roles, for example, superiors-subordinates, labor-management, and interviewers-applicants; however, it presumes that organizations as entities exist prior to conversations. The focus of traditional CA, then, is primarily dyadic, centering on skilled activities and goal accomplishment of organizational members.

Within its ethnomethodological roots, moving CA to the macrolevel of analysis incurs inferential leaps. It is difficult to determine, even at the microlevel of meaning, that interruptions, silences, and sequencing of conversations reflect power or produce patterns of organizational control. That is, the structure of conversation itself is not necessarily reflective of the purposes, situations, and contextual history of participants (Haslett, 1987). Hence, differences in conversational patterns among men and women may reflect a number of organizational processes that are not apparent in the dyadic or group-level measures of interaction, for example, organizational culture, organizational identity, and even socialization patterns. However, work that explicitly combines ethnomethodology and conversation analysis, such as that by Boden (1994), has begun to address these issues.

In CA, producing, maintaining, and repairing conversations accomplish communication. Traditional conversation analysts rarely move away from a level of meaning or contextual understanding that is not embodied in the discourse. In like manner, language surfaces as conversational forms and structures that signify communication, for example, patterns of power and control in organizations. Although this perspective has a number of weaknesses, CA joins with speech act studies to form the foundation for discourse studies in organizations.

COGNITIVE LINGUISTICS

One spin-off of CA is cognitive linguistics, the study of discourse patterns that arise from mental processes, such as scripts, schemata, and frames (Schank & Abelson, 1977; Weick, 1995). Unlike CA, cognitive linguistics privileges the link between discourse forms and language users. Individuals as language users interpret or make sense of discourse through matching linguistic patterns with commonsense knowledge of events (Haslett, 1987). This knowledge stems from personal and vicarious experiences, prototypes for grammatical forms, expected sequences of events, and the framing of events.

In organizational studies, cognitive linguistics falls into the broad category of sensemaking, an interpretive perspective that focuses on assigning meaning to organizational activities and processes (Gioia, 1986; Weick, 1995).

Language contributes to sensemaking through identifying how cognitive texts are structured, how they are read, and how they break from routine conversational patterns (Louis & Sutton, 1991). The use of metaphors, speech acts, and sociolinguistics evokes particular schemata, ones rooted in cultural practices and organizational structures (Moch & Fields, 1985). Studies of cognitive linguistics also centers on message production and on the ways that the mind stores and retrieves linguistic texts (Lord & Kernan, 1987). Four areas of organizational research exemplify the cognitive linguistic perspective: scripts and schemata, cognitive mapping, semantic networks, and frames.

Scripts and Schemata

Scripts refer to mental representations or stereotypical sets of conversational events, for example, making a complaint, ordering a meal at a restaurant, conducting a job interview (Gioia & Poole, 1984). In the organizational literature, scholars employ language analysis to analyze scripts in performance appraisals (Gioia, Donnellon, & Sims, 1989), superior-subordinate relationships (Gioia & Sims, 1986), task coordination (Saferstein, 1992), and negotiations (Carroll & Payne, 1991). Interviewer use of positive expressions, subordinate use of acknowledgments early in the deliberations, and interviewer use of denials with low performers evolve from scripts that distinguish between low- and high-performing subordinates (Gioia et al., 1989). Other studies demonstrate that superiors' attributions of performance shift after they interact with their subordinates (Gioia & Sims, 1986).

In a negotiation setting, linguistic patterns reveal that novices share a common bargaining script, one that consists of incompatible interests, sequential issue settlement, impasse, and competitive behaviors (O'Connor & Adams, 1999). Many of these elements are linked to departures from rationality, such as faulty perceptions, encoding errors, and misinterpretation of information in negotiation situations (Carroll & Payne, 1991; Thompson & DeHarpport, 1994).

Schemata differ from scripts in referring to standards or general rules for moment-to-moment coordination (Weick, 1979). Language reflects organizational schemata, ones formed through hierarchical role and occupational expertise. Through schemata and semantic indirectness, discourse sedates targets and facilitates compliance with influence attempts (Drake & Moberg, 1986). Then, in interactions among members of a TV production team, individuals develop a common schema that translates into the script for a television drama (Saferstein, 1992).

Cognitive Mapping

Cognitive mapping differs from scripts and schemata through focusing on causal links among elements of organizing (Weick, 1979; Weick & Bougon, 1986). Language functions as nodes or codes in which meaning resides in the pattern among words rather than in any one concept. Linguistic phrases, then, constitute a coherent set of meanings in a cause map (Weick, 1979). Cause maps are collective structures in which shared explanations for events emerge from composites of individual mental models. For example, in Hall's (1984) study of the *Saturday Evening Post,* policy concepts fit into a tight-fitting cognitive map that reveals an imbalance in strategic thinking, leading to the organization's ultimate demise. In the Utrecht Jazz Orchestra, phrases linked to organizational actions intertwine in causal links to form an orderly social structure. This structure reflects different patterns of phrases arrayed on a continuum from left to right (Ford & Hegarty, 1984; Roos & Hall, 1980).

In addition to actions, underlying values form a key component of cognitive maps. For instance, Huff's (1988, 1990) analysis of goals, values, and chain relationships in superintendents' and school board members' speeches impinge on the context in which

strategic planning occurs. In negotiations, bargainers who treat utility as a subjective value reach more integrative agreements than dyads who regard it as an outgrowth of interpersonal relations (Simons, 1993).

Semantic Networks

Semantic networks, as a third arena of cognitive linguistics, also focus on patterns of meanings among organizational members (see Monge & Contractor, Chapter 12, this volume). The concept of *semantic networks* refers to the network patterns derived from linkages among individuals who have similar interpretations for the same words (Danowski, 1982; Monge & Eisenberg, 1987). Studies of semantic networks reveal differences between adopters and users of voice mail systems (Rice & Danowski, 1993), in annual reports prepared for U.S. and Japanese stockholders (Jang & Barnett, 1994), and in shared meanings for the concept *worker participation* within and between managers in five European countries (Stohl, 1993). Semantic networks, then, focus on the mapping or linkage of individuals who have similar meanings for words and phrases.

Framing

Framing, as the fourth area of cognitive linguistic studies, refers to worldviews, fields of vision, or perspectives for managing meaning (Fairhurst & Sarr, 1996; Putnam & Holmer, 1992). Theorists differ as to whether frames are primarily cognitive heuristics that shape human judgment (Neale & Bazerman, 1991) or whether they are processes developed through discourse and interaction patterns (Fairhurst & Sarr, 1996; Gray, 1997; Putnam & Holmer, 1992). Despite its origins, framing is both mental and social and linked to the labels members assign to situations. A frame encompasses figure-ground relationships, ties abstract words to concrete cues, and defines the parameters for what is included or excluded in an event.

Organizational studies on framing examine such constructs as leadership, new information technology, organizational memory, and conflict. Leaders frame organizational experiences through creating and communicating visions, confronting unanticipated events, and influencing others (Fairhurst, 1993a; Fairhurst & Sarr, 1996). The development of language tools through metaphor, jargon, contrast, spin, and catchphrases are ways that leaders enact and convey corporate visions. Fairhurst (1993a) highlights how managers use these linguistic devices to link actions to the new vision, to tie this vision to old norms, and to reduce ambiguity about change. Managers who use framing to personalize changes during this process are more effective than leaders who ignore framing when communicating this vision.

Executive frames also function as filters for shaping what is noticed, how it should be managed, and how events should be categorized (Starbuck & Milliken, 1988). Discourse about corporate strategy among middle managers frames the microdynamics of inclusion and exclusion within the corporate inner circle (Westley, 1990). The framing of technological innovations as either concrete or abstract is another arena in which mental models influence organizational experiences, particularly in the way employees first notice and label a new feature as novel or innovative (Orlikowski & Gash, 1994).

Research on cognitive linguistics also surfaces as collective remembering in organizations (Edwards & Middleton, 1986; Kaha, 1989; Middleton & Edwards, 1990). Specifically, conversations about the past reaffirm collective frames when members recall moments of socialization, precedents in decision making, and breaks from routines (Walsh & Ungson, 1991; Weick & Roberts, 1993). In effect, language is the way that organizational members coconstruct remembering and for-

getting (Shotter, 1990) and embody organizational memory (Yates, 1990). In the arena of conflict management, framing functions as a cognitive heuristic for decision making, as a representation of categories of experience, and as a means of redefining and transforming contract issues (Putnam & Holmer, 1992).

The cognitive approach privileges meaning rather than linguistic structures and codes. Meanings, however, are stored in cognitive systems of users; thus, language is a behavioral code to reveal cognitive interpretations (Donnellon, 1986) and to represent knowledge structures of a collective mind (Fairclough, 1989). Organizations, in this sense, resemble the human brain (Morgan, 1997). Studies of leadership, performance appraisals, and negotiation within this perspective privilege sensemaking as the fundamental approach to studying discourse and organization.

PRAGMATICS

Pragmatics is a broad term that refers to the study of language in context; hence, it is often treated as a generic category for a variety of discourse perspectives. Unlike cognitive linguistics and conversation analysis, pragmatics incorporates both the linguistic form and the communicative context of discourse; however, it privileges contextual features and focuses on discourse as action and symbolic interaction in speech communities. Although early studies examine isolated utterances, contemporary research centers on extended sequences of talk and the role of language in social contexts (Blum-Kulka, 1997). As with cognitive linguistics, meaning is a central feature of pragmatics, but action, context, and relationships contribute to the generative nature of meaning. In this perspective, individuals construct social actions through working out discrepancies between what is said and what is meant. This review of the pragmatic perspective highlights three schools: speech acts, ethnography of speaking, and interaction analysis. These schools of pragmatic studies, however, differ in the assumptions they make about language, the role of structure, and the way meaning enters into the organizing process.

Speech Acts

Speech act theory, drawn from the writings of Austin (1962) and Searle (1969), treats language as action. That is, by simply being uttered, words such as *promising, requesting, warning, asserting,* and *apologizing* perform actions through what is said. Speech acts, then, focus on functions and language texts rather than on code or linguistic structure. This approach assumes that a speaker's motives and intentions are embodied in what he or she says. Research on speech acts also addresses appropriate conventions of expression and ways to execute utterances effectively. The success of a speech act depends on the condition and rules necessary to execute actions embodied in the utterances. Searle (1979) sets forth five general types of speech acts, but only three of them, directives, politeness, and accounts, surface in the organizational literature.

Directives. Directives are speech acts that convey requests, invitations, instructions, orders, and/or commands. In the organizational arena, researchers study both the explicit and implicit use of directives. Comparing men and women in a volunteer task group, K. Jones (1992) finds no gender differences in the frequency, target, and types of directives in a group. Status variation and context intertwine to set the conditions for appropriate use of directives. Specifically, using expressions of solidarity in combination with speech acts overcomes the face-threatening potential of directive use. Similarly, in a formal contract negotiation, alignment of goals between teachers and administrators affect the appropriateness of directives (Donohue & Diez, 1985). Questions are more effective than imperative statements in eliciting information from the other side and in softening the blow of directives, particularly in the early stages of bargaining.

Another factor that affects the use of directives is expertise. In a study that compares different mediums of communication (e.g., e-mail, teleconferencing, face-to-face), Murray (1987) reports that project managers at IBM use promises to comply with requests or they reject them implicitly by invoking background knowledge and expertise. Moreover, novices lack detail in specifying their requests while experts overspecify their directives. Expertise also differentiates knowledge of radiologists and technologists, as evident in Barley's (1986) study of direction giving, countermands, and questions among new CT scanner users in an urban hospital.

As Murray's (1987) study illustrates, implicit use of directives functions as a form of politeness, particularly when subordinates communicate with superiors. Referred to as mitigators, implicit directives use words that soften the impact of requests and avoid triggering offense, such as *might, could, okay,* and *right.* In a study of Air Force crew members, Linde (1988) notes that the use of mitigators affects the interactional success of requests, which, in turn, influences safety and crew performance. Excessive use of indirect requests, particularly combined with topic change, however, may lead to ignoring requests and endangering the safety of the crew. Hence, excessive use of this type of directive may reduce compliance with a message.

Politeness and facework. Just as mitigators convey politeness, facework uses language to negotiate rights and obligations, to protect face, and to preserve autonomy. During bargaining, negotiators phrase demands ambiguously to defend face and to repair identity damaged through exchanging concessions. Politeness remarks simultaneously attack opponents through asserting a firm position and protect them through conceding on issues (Wilson, 1992). In a more relationally based negotiation, a cyclical pattern develops in which negotiators seek to restore a hostage taker's face while the hostage taker attacks the negotiator's face. Hostage situations are more likely to end in suicide if the perpetrator attacks his or her own face (Rogan & Hammer, 1994). However, status hierarchies may impinge on facework, as in a quality of work life program when managers engage in explicit face-threatening acts while employees respond with off-the-record and negative politeness strategies (O'Donnell, 1990). Thus, politeness remarks function as double-edged strategies for negotiating rights and preserving identity and autonomy.

Accounts and justifications. Accounts are linguistic patterns that function as explanations for unanticipated or untoward behavior (Scott & Lyman, 1968). As explanations, they address why something happened or why someone failed to do what was expected. Accounts encompass the use of excuses and justifications to address problematic actions. However, in using excuses the offending party admits that the behavior in question is wrong, but he or she denies responsibility for it; in using justifications a person admits personal responsibility for the untoward action but he or she denies the negative consequence of the action.

Analysis of accounts in organizations falls into the categories of superior-subordinate interaction, job interviews, conflict management, and decision making. In superior-subordinate interaction, managers give accounts in performance evaluations, budget request denials, announcements of layoffs, and justifications for unethical conduct (Bies & Sitkin, 1992). Research also focuses on the believability and effectiveness of subordinates' accounts when managers confront them about performance problems. In general, research suggests that use of accounts enhances subordinate perceptions of fairness in performance reviews and budget cuts (Bies & Shapiro, 1988; Bies, Shapiro, & Cummings, 1988; Greenberg, 1991), reduces a subordinate's feelings of anger (Baron, 1990), and enhances

adjustments and organizational commitment in layoff situations (Rousseau & Anton, 1988). Use of accounts in unethical situations reduces the negative effects of such actions as a boss taking credit for a subordinate's ideas (Bies & Shapiro, 1987), an employee disclosing information about errors to customers (Sitkin, Sutcliffe, & Reed, 1993), and a boss responding to charges of unethical company behavior (Garrett, Bradford, Meyers, & Becker, 1989). However, the prior history of the excuse-giver and the gender of the target influence the acceptability of accounts. That is, males and females evaluate excuses differently (Giacalone, 1988).

Employees also use social accounts to mitigate evaluations of poor performance. Even though these accounts reduce blame (Wood & Mitchell, 1981) and lead to more lenient disciplinary actions (Gioia & Sims, 1986), their plausibility depends on whether managers have experienced a similar situation, the employee has a good reputation, and the subordinate provides corroborating evidence (Morris & Coursey, 1989). Moreover, the use of apologies coupled with expressions of regret and promises to rectify the problem are more effective than the use of excuses (Braaten, Cody, & DeTienne, 1993).

Accounts enter into job interviews when applicants express doubts about their qualifications and when they interpret interviewers questions (Morris, 1988). Interviewers who provide excuses for rejecting job candidates receive higher ratings of fairness than do those who fail to give explanations (Bies & Moag, 1986; Bies & Shapiro, 1988). In other types of asymmetric interviews, such as a doctor-nurse interactions, subordinates give accounts through telling stories to display competence, to manage impressions, and to maintain institutional dominance (Fisher & Groce, 1990).

In addition to superior-subordinate interactions and job interviews, accounts aid in managing conflicts. Three types of accounts surface in conflict situations: provision of mitigating circumstances, exonerating explanations, and reframing (Sitkin & Bies, 1993).

Managers typically combine mitigating circumstances with control-oriented actions to handle confrontations. They typically avoid fault finding and seek explanations based on exonerating circumstances (Morris, Gaveras, Baker, & Coursey, 1990). In conflict situations, use of multiple explanations results in more effective outcomes than does providing only one account.

Accounts also function to buffer interactions against the potential for a conflict and to justify decisions (Bies, 1989; Schonbach, 1990). In commodity negotiations, accounts function as ways to identify and challenge relevant information and to secure agreements (Firth, 1994). They serve as premises for supporting and opposing proposals, for selecting targets of identification, and for developing decision premises (Geist & Chandler, 1984; Tompkins & Cheney, 1983). In effect, organizational accounts function proactively as strategies in conflict management and as creative ways to solve problems.

In addition to the study of accounts, speech acts serve as metaphors for understanding organizational change and business communication conventions. In this sense, organizational change emanates from discourses of initiating, understanding, performing, and closing— types of speech acts that invoke actions (Ford & Ford, 1995). Speech acts also provide a grammar for business failures through opting out, clashing, flouting, and violating rules (Ewald & Strine, 1983). These macrolevel approaches treat planned change and business failures as discursive practices composed of networks of speech acts rather than programs of strategic decisions.

Overall, the study of speech acts integrates language research with organizational action. In these studies, speech acts produce the process of organizing by simply being spoken. The shortcomings of this approach evolve from the speaker-listener relationship, the role of meaning in this perspective, and the link between discourse and action. Studies of speech acts often neglect the role of the listener in producing what is said; hence, meaning becomes removed from the dynamics of interaction. Similarly, the link between language and action in research on speech acts is too linear, sequential, literal, and direct to address complex relationships between communicating and organizing. Organization intentions are not neatly embodied in what is said, and the execution of utterances has political as well as contextual ramifications.

Ethnography of Speaking

Ethnography of speaking differs from speech acts in its focus on the immediate interactive context and the local accomplishments of organizing. Ethnography combines research on discourse, speech acts, and conversations to provide a basis for understanding expectations and typifications of actors (Spencer, 1994). In this perspective, discourse is more than talk— it is a way of encompassing the everyday routines of organizational members. Discourse and social meanings intertwine with immediate context to constitute the process of organizing and the nature of speech communities. Researchers within this perspective rely on naturalistic observations, field notes, and transcriptions to analyze how discourse is reflexively linked to organizational context. Studies of ethnography of speaking cluster into five categories: speech communities, communication rules, conversational performances, storytelling as performances, and symbolic interaction.

Speech communities. In this cluster of studies, speech situations provide a multilevel taxonomy for studying the appropriateness of language use in particular settings (Hymes, 1972). Speech communities coalesce around shared language use and schemata for interpreting linguistic codes. Studies that fall into this category typically highlight the lexical and semantic fields, cultural functions of language, and ways that language enacts community. Rather than being treated in isolation, communities shape the rules for and enact the meanings of speech acts such as joking, requesting, and demanding.

Research on language and speech communities contrast newcomers with veterans (Fletcher, 1990, 1991; Sigman, 1986; Van Maanen, 1973, 1978), note differences between professional and lay audiences in educational decision making (Mehan, 1983), and identify in-group and out-group members in leadership situations (Fairhurst, 1993b; Fortado, 1998; Morrill, 1991). Research on speaking culturally in organizations highlights the distinctiveness and functions of speech codes in Teamsterville (Philipsen, 1975, 1992), the language of veterans versus rookies at the police academy (Van Maanen 1973, 1978), and the native views of cultures and subcultures among Silicon Valley employees (Gregory, 1983). In the blue-collar, multiethnic working class of Teamsterville, language varies in levels of abstraction across occupational communities (Philipsen, 1992). In like manner, aphorisms, tag questions, denials, and indexical pronouns are guides to the underworld of cops. They paradoxically signal inclusion while they reaffirm that outsiders are excluded (Fletcher, 1991).

The accomplishment of task coordination and decision making also differentiates language use among organizational subgroups. For example, the activities of client selection and decision making about services emanate from different understandings of the term *battered woman* that surfaces in a women's clinic (Loseke, 1989). Labeling also influences expectations and behaviors of staff members who adjust to work at the women's shelter and to new residents in a nursing home. Terminology such as *Dr. Johnson's syndrome* and *auditions* characterizes residents who either refuse to accept their new home or are shunned by other residents. Labels, in this sense, indicate how similar or how different a new employee is from other individuals in his or her immediate area (Sigman, 1986).

The development of written documents involves task coordination rooted in negotiations between speech communities. Writing and talking, then, become forms of social interaction in which contrasting expectations of the function and audience of texts differentiate discourse communities (Pogner, 1999), shape who uses and has access to different modes of discourse (Hawes, 1976), and privilege speech community preferences for "talking things through" versus "putting them in writing" (Baxter, 1993). Use of imperative statements in technical communication becomes instances of task negotiation in which knowledge engineers and domain experts interpret ambiguity in standards and present diverse views of organizational accountability (Irons, 1998).

In like manner, educators responsible for making decisions about student enrollments in a special education program differentiate between the language of lay and professional advisers. In particular, phrases such as "the child has problems" locates the child's difficulties in internal and private causes rather than in institutional conditions. The mystique of this technical vocabulary privileges the judgment of professionals in these decisions (Mehan, 1983). Additional studies reveal that the laws governing public education, the amount of money allotted to school districts, and political considerations such as "out of district placement" also influence the pragmatics of what is said in decision-making meetings (Mehan, 1987).

Language also identifies informal speech communities in organizations. In conflicts among executives of CEO corporations, discourse that characterizes chivalry, warfare, and sports serves as a code of honor to distinguish the more from the less honorable employees. The culture of honor provides stability and predictability in uncertain and ambiguous times (Morrill, 1991, 1995). Use of nicknames in six different organizations also creates a speech community in which subordinates pit themselves against authorities to humanize the organizational process (Fortado, 1998).

The role of humor in organizations demonstrates how talk unites subcultures, relieves tension, and orders the social world. Ironically, the use of humor in the workforce also segments subcultures, creates stress, and highlights incongruencies. Self-deprecating jokes told by organizational newcomers create a bond to unite new and returning employees and to facilitate the accomplishment of work tasks (Vinton, 1989), but humor divides through separating high-authority figures from low-status personnel, as Coser (1959, 1960) observes in hospital administration meetings. In like manner, use of hyperboles and analogies in a university-based outpatient clinic segments physicians from residents and residents from nurses (Yoels & Clair, 1995). Humor unifies school staff members through embracing organizational values, but it also segments them through accenting belittling behaviors (Meyer, 1997). Joking lessens social distance between managers and workers (Duncan, 1983; Duncan & Feisal, 1989), but it maintains group boundaries through types of jokes told and behaviors deemed acceptable (Linstead, 1985; Sykes, 1966).

While humor releases tension and defuses nervousness, it also creates stress through increasing ambiguity and challenging the status quo. For example, lower-ranking police officers poke fun at shift sergeants and test the limits of permissible behaviors (Pogrebin & Poole, 1988). Poking fun aids in processing new information, reducing uncertainty (Ullian, 1976), and relieving boredom of meaningless work (Roy, 1960). However, it also demands a playfulness with language that highlights the incongruency of the absurd, irrational, and unexpected while helping participants establish order and consistency at work (Boland & Hoffman, 1986). Research on language in organizations, then, demonstrates how humor unites and divides, releases tension and creates stress, and reveals incongruencies while enabling employees to reaffirm multiple perspectives and develop a congruent social order.

Research on leadership also demonstrates how language aids in developing speech communities, particularly through enabling leaders to promote visions for change and to define in-group and out-group relationships. Leaders employ discourse to mobilize mean-

ing, to alter the prevailing wisdom, and to define what needs to be done. For example, in a case study of an insurance company president, Smircich and Morgan (1982) observe how the military phrase and imagery of "Operation June 30th" failed to incite action in getting employees to act with urgency and cooperation to reduce a backlog of claims.

Moreover, leaders and subordinates bond together in speech communities through using linguistic resources to constitute relational and group identities. Fairhurst (1993b) analyzes the work conversations of six leaders and 16 subordinates to identify discourse patterns that characterize high, medium, and low leader-member exchange (LMX). She reports that high LMX members are marked by the posing of broad questions, brainstorming, building common ground, and engaging in nonroutine problem solving, while low LMXs demonstrate more performance monitoring, face-threatening acts, and power games.

Communication rules. The study of rules that govern language use in particular settings extends the research on speech communities (Hymes, 1972). Communication rules are guidelines for appropriate actions; that is, rules are "followable, prescriptive, and contextual" (Haslett, 1987, p. 35) and account for the enactment of genres, roles, and rituals (Shimanoff, 1980). Through commonsense knowledge and past experiences, individuals share agreement on and an understanding of communication rules. Reactions to rule-governed behavior include compliance, noncompliance, ignorance, forgetfulness, and reflectiveness. In cases where misunderstandings occur and rules are violated, interactants may negotiate new rules for language use.

Organizational studies on communication rules examine how broadly defined rules emerge as narrowly defined procedures, for example, in the interactions within two narcotics enforcement units (Manning, 1977). Research also centers on rule invocation, simulation, and implementation in a health care group involved in potential layoffs (Sigman & Donnellon, 1989); on rules as a master contract (Harris & Cronen, 1979); and on insider-confirmed rules for exercising influence in two interfacing work groups (Schall, 1983). These studies affirm Manning's (1977) finding that participants invoke communication rules to influence interaction behaviors, bureaucratic procedures, and task activities in organizations.

Conversational performances. Within the broad rubric of ethnography of speaking, researchers also focus on the enactment of speech events rather than on the characteristics of speech communities or the rules for appropriate discourse in these settings. Hence, language not only symbolizes and manifests speech communities, it creates the performances of organizational life. Studies on conversational performances typically examine talk in the enactment of an event, a process, or an activity. Talk is the way conversation events are accomplished or the way discourse fuses with action to produce performances.

Just as leaders use language to manage meanings and negotiate in-group and out-group relationships, they also engage in conversational performances that are interactional, contextual, episodic, and improvisational (Pacanowsky & O'Donnell-Trujillo, 1983). Trujillo's (1983, 1985) study of Lou Polito, the owner of a car dealership, demonstrates how a leader invokes hierarchy, engages in playful episodes, accomplishes mutual recognition, and develops knowledge through conversational performances. Both Polito's selection of words and his sequences of discourse enact routines that illustrate how he leads. Leadership, in this sense, mobilizes resources and enacts organizing.

In a similar way, flight attendants engage in conversational performances. They perform highly patterned public announcements through engaging in increased loudness, use of pauses, elevation of pitch changes, and segmentation of phrases (Banks, 1994). These performances contribute to self-efficacy by controlling and regulating passenger safety while simultaneously attending to their com-fort. These stylized performances also aid in managing tensions between contradictory goals and loss of self-identity in the presence of social fragmentation.

Other studies examine conversation performances in informal meetings and within cross-functional teams. Namely, informal problem-solving sessions, as unplanned activities, occur in high-tech manufacturing firms against the backdrop of frequent formal meetings (Mangrum & Wieder, 1997). The use of short turns, frequent shifts in turn talk, and immediate feedback keeps participants on track and integrates contributions more effectively than do conversations in formal meetings. Cross-functional teams employ conversational performances to balance integration and differentiation across units (Donnellon, 1994, 1996). Use of imperative verbs, linguistic markers, and repeated pronoun references allow members to negotiate the contradictions that emerge from conflicting goals between units, the need for control, and the drive to both assimilate and distance team members from their functional units.

Conversational performances also enact major events such as the decision to strike or the enactment of a merger/acquisition. In a simulation of an organization, Donnellon, Gray, and Bougon (1986) examine the sequential and multilevel interactions among department members who use language to legitimate a decision to strike. Their reliance on linguistic indirection, argumentative appeals, and changes in affect result in a climate of confusion, which, in turn, supports the decision to strike. In a similar manner, the language of takeover in a merger situation facilitates diffusion and legitimation through sustaining order despite disruption. Stages and patterns that depict a hostile takeover vary over time, as reflected in the public discourse of courtship, warfare, and chivalry (Hirsch, 1986). In both instances, language legitimates decisions and shapes organizational actions.

Studies of conversational performances center on the way discourse and action intertwine to accomplish organizing and to enact speech communities. This approach to discourse analysis centers on the patterns or regularities that define speech episodes of leading, managing tensions, negotiating contradictory goals, and accomplishing organizational events.

Storytelling performances. In a similar manner, storytelling in organizations involves linguistic performances as well as narrative scripts. Studies of organizational narratives typically highlight the characters, scene, plots, and themes of narratives; they rarely center on the linguistic features of telling a story. Storytelling as performance occurs naturally in conversations through turn-by-turn situations (Jefferson, 1978), the joint construction, and the enactment of narratives (Boje, 1991). The dynamics of storytelling examine the way narratives are introduced in ongoing interactions, how listeners react and alter stories, and how stories affect subsequent dialogues. When stories become eclipsed, terse, or reduced to clichés and labels, language enacts these changes through narrative patterns and structures (Gabriel, 1998).

Research suggests that narrative performances differentiate among organizational subgroups, signal turbulence and organizational change, and aid in diagnosing problems. In particular, executives, venders, and salespeople use different mechanics such as filling in the blanks, glossing, and digressions to tell stories about organizational change (Boje, 1991). In times of turbulence and organizational change, members share terse and highly abbreviated narratives. As storytelling increases, the decision to proceed often weaves together multiple and ongoing narratives to enact themes for why and how changes are occurring (O'Connor, 1997). In many cases, storytelling emanates from organizational situations, such as repairing a broken copier, and it involves constructing identities between the past and present, socializing novices, and addressing problems in ambiguous situations. In these performances, storytelling moves from second to first person, from general to concise, and from descriptive

to didactic purposes (Orr, 1990). Moreover, each retelling of stories must incorporate different contexts, audience members, and historical circumstances. For example, Holt (1989) examines linguistic devices that constrain narrative characters and restrict performance features of storytelling in organizations. Transcriptions from six different organizations demonstrate how storytellers are bound by rules and yet free to act and how their reinterpretations of events emanate from codefinitions of self and organizations.

Symbolic interaction. The fifth type of research in ethnography of speaking privileges context and meaning rather than lexical codes, communication rules, or speech communities. Drawing from the work of G. H. Mead (1934) and Hubert Blumer (1969), symbolic interaction is a metatheory that includes a variety of schools of thought, particularly ones aligned with constructivist views of social reality. This perspective purports that human beings act toward other people based on meanings that are derived from social interactions and rooted in language and symbols. Symbolic interaction is situated directly in the world of social experience in which meanings are the keys to rich descriptions of self, social settings, and organizational actions (Schwandt, 1994).

Organizational structures and practices emerge through ongoing interactions and negotiations. Following Strauss's (1978) work, all social order is negotiated; hence, organizing is not possible without negotiation. Negotiations are patterned through lines of communication that establish, renew, revise, and reconstitute structural changes in organizing (Eisenberg & Riley, 1988; Fine, 1984). Most negotiated order studies focus on social actions and treat discourse as a taken-for-granted feature of organizations. However, Mellinger (1994) examines medical directives in radio calls between paramedics and emergency room nurses at a hospital. In this situation, the use of *if-then* language, mitigators, suggestions, and directive-response sequences function as directives to shape organizational reality. Paramedics and nurses are more likely to use directives to negotiate organizational order, if new information is provided, if actions need hospital coordination, and if paramedics are unable to fulfill an original suggestion. In like manner, Donohue and Roberto (1993) employ negotiated order to study the interaction patterns of ten FBI hostage negotiations. Disputants in this setting make, accept, and reject orders implicitly through using verbal immediacy to define the limits of their relationship.

Overall, ethnography of speaking centers on the way language accomplishes organizing through defining speech communities, adhering to communication rules, enacting conversational performances, producing storytelling, and negotiating orders. Ethnography of speaking combines semantic patterns of speech communities with linguistic structures to examine the social meanings of organizing. Studies center on the distinctiveness and functions of professional codes, accomplishments of task coordination and decision making, informal processes of conflict management, leader-member relationships, and organizational change. Sensemaking arises from the way that language typifies speech communities as well as from the meanings that organizational actors coconstruct through the process of organizing.

Interaction Analysis

Interaction analysis shifts the focus of pragmatics away from speech acts, codes, and communication rules to the functions and structures of talk. This approach uses standardized procedures for coding verbal behavior to examine categories and meanings embedded in structural patterns of talk (Poole, Folger, & Hewes, 1987). The literature in this area clusters into five different types of research: interaction process analysis, behaviorist studies, systems-interaction research, negotiation research, and adaptive structuration interpretive coding. Studies across the five

types differ in their observational modes (real-time observation, time sampling, or coding from tapes and transcripts); unit of analyses (speaking turn, thought unit, speech act; act, interact, double interact; act-to-act or phase); study designs (simulation vs. naturally occurring conversation); length of interactions studied (20 minutes or more); nature of the coding scheme (a priori or derived from the data); type of coding required (univocal or multifunctional); type of analyses (distributional or sequential); and theoretical base (e.g., reinforcement theory, systems theory, negotiation, structuration).

Interaction process analysis. Among the earliest interactional studies are those based on Bales's (1950) interaction process analysis (IPA), a coding scheme for analyzing the task/instrumental and socioemotional/expressive functions of group communication. Of the few organizational studies using IPA, Sargent and Miller's (1971) investigation of autocratic and democratic leaders is perhaps the best known. They report that democratic leaders use more questions and encouragement to increase participation, while autocratic leaders aim to enhance productivity by giving more orders and answering more questions. The SYMLOG (an acronym for systematic, multiple-level observation of groups) scheme, also based on Bales's pioneering work, is used to assess group interaction along three dimensions: dominance-submissiveness, friendly-unfriendly, and task orientation-emotional expressiveness (Bales & Cohen, 1979; for a review, see Keyton & Wall, 1989). Although Bales and Cohen (1979) present an interaction scoring method for observers, most organizational studies use retrospective rating methods for coding social interaction (e.g., Boethius, 1987; Cegala, Wall, & Rippey, 1987; Farrell, Schmitt, & Heinemann, 1988; Jesuino, 1985; Schantz, 1986).

Behaviorist studies. A second type of interactional analysis draws from reinforcement theory and the behaviorist tradition (Skinner, 1957, 1974). Based on the principles of operant conditioning, Komaki and colleagues employ the Operant Supervisory Taxonomy and Index (OSTI) to study the impact of leader monitoring on improved work unit performance (Komaki, Zlotnick, & Jensen, 1986). A comprehensive review of this research program can be found in Komaki (1998). Among the findings, Komaki (1986) reports that effective managers in a medical insurance firm spend more time in performance monitoring than do marginally effective managers. In a sailboat regatta where supervisory effectiveness is gauged by series standings, Komaki, Desselles, and Bowman (1989) observe that a skipper's racing success correlates significantly with the use of performance monitors and consequences. Finally, Komaki and Citera (1990) note that monitoring stimulates employees to talk about their own performance consequences, which encourages continued monitoring.

Based on work in leader reinforcement and punishment theory (Sims, 1977), goal setting theory (Locke, 1968), and social learning theory (Bandura, 1986), Sims and colleagues also address the relationship between employee performance and leader verbal behavior in their research on cognitive scripts. The organizational verbal behavior (OVB) categorization system codes for evaluation of employee performance and leader goal setting, task information, and attributions (Gioia et al., 1989; Gioia & Sims, 1986; Sims & Manz, 1984). Although this research is reviewed earlier in this chapter, it is worth noting that low-performing employees elicit several pronounced leader verbal behaviors, including frequent task-oriented statements, punitive statements and comparisons, and attribution requests (e.g., "Why haven't you finished this job?") (Gioia & Sims, 1986).

Systems-Interaction Research. Systems-interaction analysis, the third major type of research, is rooted in the application of systems theory to social interaction (e.g., Bateson,

1972; Fisher, 1978; Watzlawick, Beavin, & Jackson, 1967). This approach assumes that communicative acts in a social system constrain the options for future communicative behaviors in ways that develop unique and recognizable structured sequences. Redundancy or predictability of recurring communication patterns defines the structure of a system, while the nature and complexity of these patterns determine the system's function. The empirical focus of this research examines statistical patterning of acts and interacts to reveal how relational control arises from competing and dominating moves as opposed to neutral or leveling actions.

For example, Fairhurst and her colleagues use a relational control coding scheme developed by Rogers and Farace (1975) to examine control patterns in routine work interaction. Fairhurst, Rogers, and Sarr (1987) observe that manager dominance is linked to lower employee performance ratings, less understanding of employees, and lower employee desire for decision making. Courtright, Fairhurst, and Rogers (1989) examine control patterns in organic and mechanistic systems. They support Burns and Stalker's (1961) theory and observe more question-answer combinations in the organic system and more manager dominance and competitive patterns in the mechanistic system. Fairhurst, Green, and Courtright (1994) investigate the impact of plant history (organic from start-up or conversion to organic from mechanistic) and plant manager style (participative or autocratic) on manager-employee communication in five manufacturing plants. Conceptualized as sources of organizational inertia, a mechanistic history and an autocratic plant manager produce fewer challenges to managers' assertions and more employee approval seeking. When these inertial forces are absent, employees challenge manager assertions, initiate discussions, and experience less manager control than in mechanistic systems.

Other relational control studies include Watson (1982) and Watson-Dugan (1989), who employ Ellis's (1979) relational control coding scheme to study performance feedback and goal setting. Glauser and Tullar (1985) examine relational communication patterns of satisfying and dissatisfying officer-citizen telephone interactions and note that officers who engage in fewer competitive control struggles elicit more satisfying conversations than do ones who exert more control. Tullar's (1989) study of relational control patterns in the employment interview reveals that successful applicants are submissive when the interviewer is dominant and are dominant when the interviewer is submissive.

Negotiation research. Interactional analysis of negotiation forms the fourth category of organizational studies. Much of this literature draws from a systems-interaction approach or what Putnam (1990b) calls a process perspective. A process perspective is neither a variable nor a method, but an approach aimed at understanding the stages or phases of negotiations, message patterns or sequences of bargaining tactics, and the enactment of rules and norms in this context.

Several studies examine the effects of message functions on bargaining outcomes (Chatman, Putnam, & Sondak, 1991). For example, Theye and Seiler (1979) use Bales's (1950) IPA to code strategies and tactics in teacher-school board negotiations. Donohue (1981a, 1981b) tests a coding scheme based on the rules that govern attack, defend, and aggression tactics for distributive tasks. He reports that successful negotiators make more offers and stick to them, present fewer concessions, and deny others' arguments more often than do unsuccessful negotiators. Putnam and Wilson (1989) investigate four levels of outcomes in integrative bargaining (bridging, sharpening, trade-offs, and win-lose). Among their findings, exploratory problem solving and workability arguments are linked to bridging outcomes, while voicing preferences for positions and evaluating propositions result in win-lose settlements. Drawing from this investigation, Putnam, Wilson, and Turner (1990) compare early- and late-phase variations in a teacher-school board negotiation. Teachers and board members differ in their argumentation strategies at both early and late stages of the negotiations.

Weingart, Thompson, Bazerman, and Carroll (1990) examine negotiation behavior and individual-joint gains in a variable-sum buyer-seller negotiation task. They note that initial offers affect final outcomes differently across buyers and sellers, that negotiators reciprocate and balance both distributive and integrative tactics, and that information sharing has a positive effect on the efficiency of the arguments. Weingart, Bennett, and Brett (1993) report on two studies concerning the effect of motivation (cooperative, individualistic) and issue consideration (simultaneous, sequential) on negotiation process and outcome. Among the more notable findings, groups who exchange issues simultaneously share more information and have a greater understanding of the other sides' priorities than do those who discuss issues sequentially. Finally, Olekalns, Smith, and Walsh (1996) simulate an employment contract negotiation to test for cuing and response strategies across four types of distributive and integrative outcomes: stalemate, win-lose, suboptimum, and optimum.

While previous studies focus on the effects of communication on bargaining outcomes, other investigations center on the intervening effects of communication on outcomes. Using a modified version of Hopmann and Walcott's (1976) bargaining process analysis (BPAII), Putnam and Jones (1982) investigate the way frequency and sequence of bargaining talk mediates the effects of negotiated outcomes in a simulated grievance case study. In labor-management dyads that result in an agreement, an attack-defend cycle guards against conflict escalation. In impasse dyads, an act-react cycle, in which the parties match each other's offensive and defensive moves, produces an escalating pattern of one-upmanship.

Still other studies primarily describe bargaining tactics and language patterns rather than test for effects of communication on outcomes (e.g., Chatman et al., 1991; Donohue, Diez, & Hamilton, 1984). Bednar and Curington (1983), using the relational control coding scheme, examine the content and relationship aspects of negotiations in an oil company contract dispute. Holmes and Sykes (1993) and Holmes (1997) investigate phases in actual versus simulated hostage negotiations.

Adaptive structuration theory. The fifth type of interactional studies, adaptive structuration theory (AST), draws from structuration theory (Giddens, 1979, 1984; Poole, Seibold, & McPhee, 1985) and focuses on the mutual influence of technology and social processes on organizational change. DeSanctis and Poole (1994) call their analysis "interpretive coding" because, unlike most interaction analyses studies, they go beyond conventional meanings of message sequence and pattern to infer actor intentions (Poole & DeSanctis, 1992). Although some of their research is interpretive in character (DeSanctis, Poole, Dickson, & Jackson, 1993; Poole, DeSanctis, Kirsch, & Jackson, 1995), other studies employ a priori category schemes to focus on structural claims.

AST analysis centers on the way that groups incorporate a computerized decision support system (GDSS) into their processes (Watson, DeSanctis, & Poole, 1988). Interpretive coding uses AST to document the appropriation of structures as they arise from and occur within the discourse (e.g., direct use, relate to other structures, constrain the structure, or express judgments about the structure). This analysis, when combined with distinctions made between faithful and unfaithful appropriations and the attitudes that group members display toward the technology, demonstrates how AST coding extends beyond microlevel analyses to global (i.e., conversations, meetings, or documents as a whole) and institutional (e.g., longitudinal observation with the goal of identifying persistent patterns) levels. Two prominent studies include Poole and DeSanctis (1992) and DeSanctis and Poole (1994). Poole and DeSanctis (1992) report that consensus change and variations in the restrictiveness of the GDSS are related to differences in the structuration process.

DeSanctis and Poole (1994) illustrate how the same technology can be introduced to two difference groups, yet the effects of the technology differ according to each group's appropriation. Specifically, appropriations that are consistent with the intended use of the technology produce desirable decision processes and outcomes.

Other studies examine the impact of GDSSs on influence patterns in group interaction (Zigurs, Poole, & DeSanctis, 1988) and on conflict behavior (Poole, Holmes, & DeSanctis, 1991) in both laboratory and field contexts (e.g., DeSanctis, Poole, Lewis, & Desharnais, 1992). Finally, Contractor and Seibold (1993) use simulation data to show the AST deficiencies in explaining GDSSs appropriation over time. With the aim of advancing AST, they offer self-organizing systems theory as a solution to the problems with GDSS research.

Interaction analysis draws from studies of message functions and language structures to assess the frequency and types of verbal behaviors, the redundancy and predictability of talk in a communicative system, the sequences and stages of talk, and the links between structures of talk and interpretations of these patterns. As a form of pragmatics, interaction analysis is grounded in regularities and recurring patterns within a communication system. For the most part, with the exception of AST approaches, this research locates meaning in the unfolding process of the social system and treats language users as elements in the background of social systems. Communication, then, resides within the system of interaction patterns and meaning emanates from the functions and patterns of talk. Organizational constructs, such as leadership, managerial dominance, and strategies and tactics of negotiation, evolve from message patterns and communication systems rather than from semantics or conversational forms. Interaction analysis, as an approach for understanding linguistic systems, is criticized for its proliferation of category systems, its reliance on a priori categories, and the practice of specifying and categorizing meanings of utterances

(Firth, 1995). In effect, interaction analysis uses a static framework for analyzing a dynamic activity. In actuality, participants jointly constitute social meanings in ways that are more ephemeral, malleable, and negotiable than interaction analysis depicts.

Overall, pragmatics is a broad category of discourse, one that privileges the role of language in organizational context. Given the variation that exists among the three major clusters of discourse studies—speech acts, ethnography of speaking, and interaction analysis—pragmatics is not a uniform perspective, but rather an umbrella for studies that fit into subcategories of different relationships among discourse, meaning, action, and organizations. In research on speech acts, language is action that shapes organizing by being uttered. Both meaning and organizing are embodied in the utterances of what is said. In contrast, research on the ethnography of speaking centers on the way that language accomplishes organizing through developing speech communities, enacting performances, and negotiating orders. Accomplishments rather than utterances embody action and meaning as processes that actors coconstruct. Interaction analysis moves the study of language into systems of communication through focusing on the structure and regularities of message categories. Interaction systems depict such processes as leadership and negotiation by combining function and meaning into a priori forms. Thus, each of these schools privileges different features of discourse analysis and casts the link between language and organization differently.

SEMIOTICS

Semiotics, unlike the pragmatic perspective, centers on the way that interpretations evolve from signs or code systems. By examining a sign as anything that represents something else, semiotics broadens the focus of linguistic studies to include not only discourse but also nonverbal codes, images, actions, and objects. Semiotics emphasizes how language signifies, how it is related to an association among codes, and how it becomes a system of symbols (Stewart, 1986). Two different schools of semiotics surface in the organizational literature and serve as precursors to the postmodern approaches. The first approach, drawn from structuralism (Saussure, 1916/1974), casts language as a system of differences rooted in surface and deep levels of structure. The second approach, semiosis, treats language as a signifying process in which symbols become referents for objects and ideas (Peirce, 1931).

Structuralism

A structuralist perspective to the study of semiotics addresses the way deep structures give rise to surface forms. Deep structures underlie language system in which meaning develops through a system of logical opposites, narratives, or part-whole relationships. Even labels, metaphors, and platitudes function as symbol systems that signify deeper structures of organizational control (Czarniawska-Joerges & Joerges, 1988). Lexical variation and nonverbal behaviors of factory workers also function as semiotic code systems that reveal deep-level meanings of work and play (Tway, 1976). Semiotic analysis begins by identifying signs or signal units through searching for a set of codes, the rules that link these codes together, and the underlying values embedded in these codes (Fiol, 1989). In this analysis, semioticians uncover the hidden meanings or fundamental values that produce and organize sign systems through a set of constraints, rules, or choices. The deep structure, then, rests on central or universal principles that unify chains of signifiers. This unifying principle might be power/knowledge relationships, modes of production, or capitalist relations.

For example, Barley (1983) illustrates how a recurrent underlying value, the denial of death, permeates the culture of a funeral home and conveys the themes of naturalness and familiarity. By comparing the codes of a living sleeping person with those of a dead person, he illustrates how the signs that seem opposite are actually similar and how code rules at the deep level reinforce those at the surface level to form an interrelated semiotic system. With a similar focus on oppositional forms, Manning (1982a, 1982b, 1986, 1988) examines the underlying beliefs about crime in a study of emergency 911 or 999 telephone calls within two police departments. His analyses of caller times, sources, locations, and directions at the surface level reveal a system of codes in which action-inaction, complete-incomplete, and construction-reconstruction at the deep level produce loosely coupled webs of meanings for processing events. The occupational culture of police and the division of labor in the organization severely constrain interactions with callers and subvert representations of events.

Patterns of beliefs about the appropriate way to define internal and external relations characterize Fiol's (1989) semiotic narrative analysis of letters to shareholders in ten chemical companies, five of whom had engaged in joint ventures. Using the semiotic square to identify the underlying oppositions between strong-weak and internal-external, Fiol demonstrates how the belief systems of risky behaviors unify the semiotic codes of loss and gain in company images and justify the pursuit of joint ventures.

Structuralist approaches to semiotics lay the foundation for examining language as a system of codes, signs, and signifiers. However, this approach tends to reify structures, fixing form at surface and deep levels and treating meanings as unified and universal. By ignoring history and temporality, structuralists also fail to account for the production and reproduction of structures through language use.

Semiosis

A second type of semiotic analysis, known as semiosis, centers on the signifying process.

Developed by Peirce (1931), semiosis focuses on the relationship among the sign, the object or referent, and the interpretant. The sign stands for something or somebody, while the referent refers to the object or form in the material world. The interpretant is the mental image of the interpreter created or stimulated by the sign. In this perspective, signs are transparent in that they mirror the nature of being itself.

This approach to semiotics underlies research on organizational identity, corporate image, and marketing communication (Nöth, 1988). Organizational identity, as noted in Cheney and Christensen (Chapter 7, this volume), is what the company comes to represent or its formal profile, while corporate image is the impression created by a set of signs or the company's reputation (Christensen, 1995). In a semiotic analysis, corporate identity functions as sign, corporate image becomes the interpretant, and the organization is the referent or object. However, these elements are complex, interchangeable, and even contradictory in the dynamics of the signifying process. Such complexities include the way organizations become self-reflexive through processing data from marketing studies and image analyses (see Cheney & Christensen, this volume) and the way that corporate identities surface as referents behind the use of logos, names, merchandise, and ads (Balmer, 1995). Semiotics, then, demonstrates how the interplay between organizational identity and corporate image is a dynamic negotiation between sign and interpretant and one rooted in representations that are sociohistorical rather than based on fit with reality (Christensen & Askegaard, in press). This view of organizational identity and corporate image evolves through the interplay of texts and the relationships that exist among multiple signs (Eco, 1976).

In both of these perspectives, signs and symbols stand for something else; thus, language is representation in that it refers, substitutes, or interprets something else. Whether through a system of codes rooted in surface and deep structures or a set of meanings developed through a signifying process, this perspective treats discourse as a system of symbols that represents a nonlinguistic world of objects. By privileging codes and interpretants, semiotics treats organizing as developing chains of signifiers that represent belief systems and characterize corporate identity and images.

LITERARY AND RHETORICAL ANALYSES

Literary and rhetorical perspectives share an interest with semiotics in treating language as a signifying process. However, this approach centers on symbols rather than signs and highlights the meaning and contextual elements of language instead of the code and structural features. Rhetoric is often defined as using the available means of persuasion; hence, rhetorical approaches draw from classical methods of argumentation to examine corporate messages in crisis situations, organizational decision making, identification, and conflict management. Rhetorical and literary perspectives center on the text of discourse and the ways that meaning intertwines with function to shape messages and message responses.

Research on literary and rhetorical perspectives cluster into the following categories: rhetorical strategies in corporate advocacy, argument in organizational decision making and identification, and rhetorical and literary tropes. The last category includes literary approaches to organizations that conduct analyses on metaphors, metonymy, synecdoche, and irony.

Rhetorical Strategies in Corporate Advocacy

Research on corporate advocacy focuses on the management of public messages in promoting company positions, acknowledging events, and responding to organizational crises. Since this literature is reviewed extensively in Cheney and Vibbert (1987), this section synthesizes current studies on organizational crisis communication. The way that organizations respond to crisis situations parallels work on conversational repairs by focusing on how companies make excuses, provide explanations and justifications, and offer apologies and recompense (Barton, 1993; Benoit & Brinson, 1994; Hearit, 1994; Lukaszewski & Gmeiner, 1993). Often classified as rhetorical apologia, communication during corporate crises draws from research on facework, impression management, and persuasion (Allen & Caillouet, 1994; Benoit, 1992; Pinsdorf, 1987).

Most practitioners of corporate advocacy recommend candor in providing accounts for organizational disasters (Dougherty, 1992); however, given the legal constraints that corporations face, candor is typically couched in equivocal messages aimed at instilling labels or names for the event, promoting collective sensemaking, and persuading diverse audiences (Tyler, 1997). Selection of rhetorical strategies hinges on the goals of the organization, the type of crises, the prevailing attributions about the situation, and the primary target audience (Coombs, 1995).

Although maintaining a positive organizational image remains the dominant aim of these messages, the desire to shift blame, express mortification, and implement corrective action also guides the selection of strategies (Benoit & Brinson, 1994; Campbell, Follender, & Shane, 1998). To distance companies from a crisis event, corporations often label the crisis as an accident, a transgression, a faux pas, or sabotage, depending on whether the public sees the event as emanating from internal or external forces and from intentional or unintentional motives (Coombs, 1995). In an effort to shift blame, the company might separate the actions of culpable members from the corporate body (Brinson & Benoit, 1999; Gephart, 1993). To express mortification and ingratiation, a company might offset negative attributions with positive impressions or make promises for corrective action.

Corporations who fail to achieve these goals often select inappropriate strategies for particular audiences. Targets of corporate messages include victims, organizational members, shareholders, customers, clients, and the general public. Messages that are aimed at the financial, scientific, and legal communities may alienate victims and the general public, as occurred in Union Carbide's response to the Bhopal accident (Ice, 1991). In like manner, legal issues, as surfaced in the Exxon Valdez oil spill and the Dalkon Shield case, may influence corporations to target their messages to stockholders rather than to victims (Tyler, 1997). In contrast, the use of mortification and corrective action strategies, as exemplified in the Tylenol incident, seems appropriate to the external nature of the incident and the general public as an audience. In some situations, paradoxical messages emerge in which a company denies responsibility for a crisis while simultaneously being accountable for its actions or it may apologize for the crisis while disavowing any ownership of it (Tyler, 1997). In effect, in crisis situations the general public wants to hear ownership and apologies rather than excuses and justifications. Failure to acknowledge events, take ownership of the situation, or address particular stakeholders may lead to public rejection.

Although influenced by the work on speech acts and conversational repairs, rhetorical studies in crisis situations broaden discourse analysis to embrace both the content and context of communication. Rhetorical strategies in these situations not only invoke social action, but they also reveal ways that "speaking the right words" influences definitions of social reality and patterns of sensemaking in times of crisis. Public communication embodies persuasive appeals shaped by contextual constraints and aimed at particular audiences. Hence, meaning is intertwined with text and context, but messages are conceived in light of senders and receivers rather than through the way they are embedded in an interactive process.

Argument in Organizational Decision Making and Identification

Another persuasive strategy commonly used in organizations is argument. Defined as reason-giving aimed at supporting a claim, argument is linked to rationality or a coherent set of agreed-on rules and procedures (Weick & Browning, 1986). However, argument is more than a set of procedures, it is a form of discourse aimed at enhancing understanding. Reasoning, then, is a process of drawing inferences and making connections among events, motives, and actions. As Anderson (1983) demonstrates in his analysis of the Cuban missile crisis, organizational members come to understand a situation through novel arguments embedded in objections to a course of action rather than through presenting a prevailing position. Although a variety of perspectives on argument exist, the literature on organizational argument clusters into two areas: (1) decision premises and identification and (2) argument as policy deliberation.

Decision premises and organizational identification. Organizations are texts composed of connections among arguments (Tompkins, Tompkins, & Cheney, 1989). A text in this sense is not a written document, but a body of discourse produced through organizational actions and interactions. Tompkins and Cheney (1985) draw from Simon's (1976) notion of decision premises to show how organizations exert decision-making control through inculcating major premises in key words and topics. Thus, using the term *innovation* may signal that "innovation is desirable" through a process of reasoning known as the *enthymeme*. An enthymeme is an incomplete syllogism or a form of logic in which the major premise is implied and the audience draws the logical conclusion from linking the stated to the implied premises. For example, by stating the minor premise, "This product will make you look youthful," the audience completes the conclusion, "This product is desirable" through reasoning from a premise widely held in American society, "Looking youthful is desirable" (Tompkins et al., 1989).

Research in this area examines the way organizations inculcate decision premises as forms of identification and unobtrusive control. Drawn from Burke's (1950/1969b) theory of identification, Tompkins and Cheney (1985) note that the process of identification is necessary to cope with mystery and estrangement inherent in division of labor. Organizations aim to overcome the separation, estrangement, and mystery of hierarchy through creating and extending terminology (e.g., the naming of events) and through stretching old meanings into new "terministic screens" (Meyer, 1996; Tompkins, Fisher, Infante, & Tompkins, 1975).

Studies of organizational identification examine different written and oral texts to uncover decision premises. Using account analysis as a method, Tompkins and Cheney (1983) investigate the decision premises of teaching assistants who depart from a standardized course design. Their study reveals that accounts of deviation fit normative premises, reveal targets of identification, and are linked to zones of ambiguity in teaching assistant requirements. In a study of corporate periodicals, Cheney (1983) illustrates the way identification and decision premises arise in appeals to common ground, use of common enemies, and reference to the transcendent "we." DiSanza and Bullis (1999) extend this work by analyzing member responses to rhetorical appeals published in Forest Service newsletters. Their study reveals that organizational members recognize and complete decision premises, especially ones communicated through common ground appeals and "we" strategies in CEO policy statements. Quality circle manuals also promote identification

through subtle messages embedded in the rationale, criteria, and procedures that inculcate managerial concerns (Stohl & Coombs, 1988).

Other studies on decision premises demonstrate how the U.S. Catholic bishops recast their identity as a national unit through the use of enthymemes in peace initiatives (Cheney, 1991) and how organizations such as the U.S. Forest Service alter decision premises through changes in training of professionals (Bullis & Tompkins, 1989). Overall, decision premises embodied in organizational texts and inculcated through rhetorical strategies promote identification and underscore the pervasiveness of organizations as arguments.

Argument as policy deliberation. Persuasion and rhetorical strategies also underlie the research on policy deliberation and conflict management. Argument plays a critical role in this process because effective decisions often emerge from the interactive clash of opposing viewpoints (Anderson, 1983). These decisions emanate from shifts in language that define new themes and reformulate decision strategies (Huff, 1983). Research in this area clusters into two categories: arguments in bargaining and value-laden arguments.

Different perspectives guide the research on argumentation in bargaining and negotiation. Drawing from both simulated and actual negotiations, researchers examine arguments as persuasive tactics (Putnam & Jones, 1982; Roloff, Tutzauer, & Dailey, 1989), as invention (Bacharach & Lawler, 1981), and as issue development (Putnam et al., 1990). As persuasive tactics, arguments function as strategic maneuvers aimed at changing the opponents' attitudes and fostering concession making. As invention, arguments provide the rationale and justification for making claims about legitimacy and independence (Bacharach & Lawler, 1981; Keough & Lake, 1993). In issue definition, arguments center on the attack and defense of proposals, reason-giving through evidence and claims, case making, and stock issues (Putnam & Geist, 1985; Putnam & Wilson, 1989; Putnam, Wilson, Waltman, &

Turner, 1986; Schmidt, 1986). Bargainers often specialize in argument types in different stages of negotiation. In the early stages, they rely on harm and workability arguments to prepare their cases, but in the later stages they employ inherency and disadvantage arguments to weigh the costs of concessions and to rationalize a settlement (Putnam et al., 1990).

A second area of research on argumentation is value-laden appeals. Reasonableness and "good arguments" are not simply tightly reasoned cases. Rather, conflicting arguments produce and reproduce organizational values (Conrad, 1993; Smithin, 1987). In a study of boycotts against organizations, Meyers and Garrett (1993) investigate argument themes emanating from the corporate values of profitability and social responsibility. Using structuration theory, they note how contradictions serve as sites for incompatible values, how opposing values define communication differently for protest and target groups, and how organizations use competing arguments to reproduce their current structures. Conflicting and incompatible values also surface in studies on environmental innovation, as demonstrated in comparing UK and German companies (Steward & Conway, 1998). Documents on innovation from the UK corporations employ a limited environmental vocabulary, rooted in accountability and a knowledge/customer network. In contrast, German companies ground their arguments in an ethics of conviction, which privileges a broad environmental vocabulary and a regulator/supplier type of network.

Other studies demonstrate how multiple value hierarchies pervade organizational life, as Keough and Lake (1993) observe in their investigation of teaching assistants' bargaining. These hierarchies create different logics of action that link to core values of efficiency and growth evident in corporate annual reports (Cheney & Frenette, 1993). Discourse, then, is reconstituted in light of shifting constraints, as Hamilton (1997) illustrates in his study of rational and emotional appeals in the pay system of the National Health Service

Trust. Arguments reveal a shift from a public service ethos to an enterprise-culture logic through supporting or refuting wage issues.

In each of these approaches, argument is more than causal attributions (Bettman & Weitz, 1983) in which researchers focus on the amount or stability of reasoning; rather, argument is a means of persuasion rooted in controversy about the merits of issues. The content of the argument, the type of case making, and the joint interaction of participants play a critical role in organizational policy deliberations. In some ways, organizations are argument fields in which persuasive appeals are interwoven with praxis. Thus, the concept of "argument field" treats interaction at the microlevel as shaping and being influenced by arguments made at the macrolevel (Keough, 1987). In this sense, research on argument in organizational studies moves from emphasis on function and text to a focus on the relationship between text and context.

Rhetorical and Literary Tropes

Rhetoric is not just using language to persuade; it is also a means of human understanding and a process of constructing social reality (Watson, 1994). This perspective stands in opposition to the view that rhetoric is embellishment distinct from some other social reality (Bowles & Coates, 1993; Keenoy, 1990; Vaughn, 1994). In like manner, the use of literary tropes reveals both style and creation of text, but style is more than mere ornamentation. Literary tropes entail a variety of rhetorical forms, including alliteration, icons, euphemisms, and clichés. However, the four classic tropes, as presented by Burke (1945/1969a), Brown (1977), and Manning (1979), are metaphor, metonymy, synecdoche, and irony.

Metaphor. As the most basic of the master tropes, metaphor is a way of seeing things as if they were something else. By casting the unfamiliar in light of the known, metaphor bridges cognitive domains, legitimates actions, and guides behaviors (Lakoff & Johnson, 1980). Metaphor creates imagery that shifts figure-ground relationships by highlighting some features of language while suppressing others. As rich summaries of worldviews, metaphors subsume other metaphors, exist in clusters, and shift perspectives, often between surface and deep levels (Smith & Eisenberg, 1987; Smith & Turner, 1995).

Metaphor contributes to organizational analysis in three primary ways: creating and developing organizational theory, describing and understanding the discursive texture of organizations, and conducting organizational research (Cazal & Inns, 1998). Given the scope of literature in each of these areas, this review centers on metaphor analysis in two particular research domains: organizational change and conflict management (Grant & Oswick, 1996a). Other texts overview essays on metaphors as theory-building and methodological tools (see Alvesson, 1993; Brink, 1993; Grant & Oswick, 1996b; Morgan, 1980, 1997; Oswick & Grant, 1996b; Putnam et al., 1996; Tsoukas, 1991).

Through its generative quality, metaphor is an appealing approach for investigating organizational change, particularly in studies about information transfer in unfamiliar situations and in research on the organizational logic for change (Pondy, 1983; Sackmann, 1989). Metaphor facilitates new knowledge production (Morgan & Ramirez, 1984); introduces new perspectives and worldviews (Marshak, 1993, 1996); and contributes to transforming organizational processes and experiences through painting visions, arousing emotions, and inspiring commitment (Höpfl & Maddrell, 1996; Sackmann, 1989; Srivastva & Barrett, 1988; Vaughn, 1995). Although metaphors facilitate new knowledge and bridge the known with the unfamiliar (Barrett & Cooperrider, 1990), they also constrain learning and action through preserving ideologies (Tsoukas, 1993) and deepening organizational meanings and values (Broussine & Vince, 1996). Hence, within a symbol system, metaphor functions simultaneously to facilitate change and preserve stability.

Research on the role of root metaphors in conflict situations illustrates the way that metaphor functions at this dual level. For example, analysis of metaphors in the change management literature shows how downsizing becomes aligned with improving health and physical environment (e.g., "trim the fat," "bulging," "stormy seas of competition") as well as with violence and damaged bodies (e.g., "butchers," "frontal assault," "cutting muscle not just fat," "organizational anorexia") (Dunford & Palmer, 1996). Moreover, in a study of ownership of commodities, metaphors of the short-term logic of cost control run counter to images of long-term processes of human investment (Watson, 1994, 1995). Thus, the relationship between metaphors of change and the emergence of countermetaphors preserves continuity while promoting organizational changes. These contradictions often lead to conflict when efforts to alter root metaphors elicit overt struggles between competing ideologies (Dunn, 1990; Hirsch & Andrews, 1983; Smith & Eisenberg, 1987).

The way that metaphor reveals contradictions underscores the need to capture shifts in meaning and relationships among chains of images across organizational texts (Alvesson, 1993). Thus, metaphors do not represent inherent or stable meanings; rather, they function at the nexus of evolving symbols, text, and meaning. In this sense, organizations are living texts and metaphors are repertoires of meanings that point to the connections among terms in an evolving symbol system.

Metonymy, synecdoche, and irony. For the most part, the research on organizational metaphors overshadows organizational studies on metonymy, synecdoche, and irony. The broad concept of metaphor, however, subsumes and intertwines with the other three tropes (Manning, 1979; Oswick & Grant, 1996a). Whereas the term *metaphor* signifies diverse perspectives, the term *metonymy* refers to reduction. That is, metonymy is a figure of speech in which the whole stands for the parts, for example, the use of the word *heart* to stand for *emotions*. In particular, the term *culture* is often used as a metonymy for an organization's rites and rituals, myths, stories, and values. The whole of culture is represented through its different symbol systems. Through the process of reduction, an integrating term such as *culture* intertwines its parts into an associated pattern, one that is similar to using abbreviated phrases to refer to well-known jokes. In this sense, an organization, as an intangible unit, is likened to its visible and concrete parts (Burke, 1950/1969b).

Research on metonymy reveals how whole-part relationships develop alternative meanings and new patterns of association. In a study of police discourse, Manning (1979) illustrates how the concept of *drug use* becomes a crime through aligning this whole with parts of the criminal process, such as crime statistics, seizure data, and number of warrants. In Watson's (1995) study of a trade union talk, the National Health Service Trust employs metonymy to signify steps in a pendulum shift arbitration in which the parties agree to a no-strike policy. Drawing on a similar context, Putnam (1995) demonstrates how the terms *language* and *money* in a teachers' bargaining moves from referencing sections of the contract to signifying competing commodities that serve as a formula for a settlement.

Synecdoche reverses this process by using the part to signify the whole, for example, the term *crown* or *throne* to represent the king or queen. Synecdoche operates from the concept of representation. For example, some theorists use the terms *hierarchy* and *bureaucracy* to stand for organizations as reified entities. Manning (1979) points out how the concepts of *detective* and *case* in policing operate differently in drug investigations. Unlike regular policing, cases are not placed in central locations and delegated to drug investigators; rather, a case is a synecdoche that represents

storing information in an officer's head, developing key informant relationships, and processing files individually rather than as a unit.

Slogans, jargon, clichés, and credos also function as synecdoche to represent an organization's image. For instance, slogans about quality often function in a redundant and iconic way to proclaim standards of precision that, in turn, produce expectations for organizational action (Gorden & Nevins, 1987). However, a juxtaposition of jargon and themes from total quality management with those from high-commitment work systems reveals a critical gap in the concept of ownership, change, and organizational image of a manufacturing company (Fairhurst & Wendt, 1993).

Clichés also become persuasive by connecting taken-for-granted actions to corporate-wide mission statements, such as using the phrase "the bottom line" to represent big-budget firms and using the expression "work hard, play hard" to capture the glamour, long hours, and lucrative activity of modern accounting (Anderson-Gough, Grey, & Robson, 1998). In effect, the general and ubiquitous nature of clichés normalizes professional and organizational practices, functions as synecdoche to represent the corporation, and operates unobtrusively to exert managerial control.

When intended meanings in discourse contradict with conventional ones, irony becomes a way of producing unexpected outcomes (Brown, 1977; Westenholz, 1993). Irony parallels and closely relates to contradiction in its reliance on discourse to uncover tensions between what was said and what was meant. Ironies often lead to contradictions and paradoxes that contribute to theory building (Poole & Van de Ven, 1989) and to the conception of contradiction-centered organizations (Putnam, 1986; Trethewey, 1999). But as a rhetorical trope, irony arises from the context in which a speaker or researcher foregrounds a conventional meaning and then provides a twist or surprising reversal in interpretation (Weick & Browning, 1986). Contradictions arise in the text/subtext of a message and in the discursive practices of what an organization purports and what actually happens.

Irony opens new possibilities through uncovering perspectives on incongruity and exposing new meanings that challenge normative conventions and historical practices (Burke, 1950/1969b; Hatch & Ehrlich, 1993). As an example, Hatch's (1997) study of spontaneous humor reveals how managers coconstruct experiences about what is possible or impossible to change or what is valued and devalued in the organization. Managers interpret ironic remarks by invoking contextual knowledge; then, they reflexively construct their own identities as they reconstitute the organization.

Ironies also reveal contradictions, as noted in Manning's (1979) discovery of similarities between narcotic agents and drug users (e.g., meeting at strange hours, hanging out in bars, and dressing like criminals) and Filby and Willmott's (1988) finding that ironic humor produces trained incapacity through reifying self-image while exaggerating opposition to bureaucracy. Ironies facilitate engaging in paradoxical thinking to "deframe" meanings and establish new lines of communication (Westenholz, 1993). Employees who embrace the contradictions between solidarity and market orientation, internal and external, and ambiguous and unambiguous cut across frames of reference and argue for a new approach to organizational problems.

In summary, the rhetorical approach to discourse analysis in organizations centers on the interconnections among messages, functions, meanings, and contexts. Researchers intertwine these features in complex ways to examine rhetorical strategies that emanate from persuasion, argumentation, and literary tropes. Working with oral and written texts, researchers infer meanings through subtexts of discourse rooted in organizational circumstances and contexts. The immediacy of the rhetorical situation and the audience for a given message play a prominent role in interpreting meaning and constructing organizational reality. In many ways, literary and rhetorical studies of organizational texts provide the building blocks for discourse analysis in the critical and postmodern traditions.

CRITICAL LANGUAGE STUDIES

Unlike previous sections that examine language through particular methods of discourse analysis, critical and postmodern traditions focus on discourse and society (van Dijk, 1993, 1997a). Hence, these perspectives borrow from modes of discourse analysis previously discussed to achieve particular goals and uncover ways that language constitutes and reconstitutes social arrangements. Specifically, as Mumby notes in Chapter 15 in this volume, discourse analysis in critical theory centers on power and control, particularly the way different groups compete to serve their own interests and to control symbolic and discursive resources. In this perspective, discourse produces, maintains, and/or resists systems of power and inequality through ideology and hegemony (Mumby & Clair, 1997). Ideology is a system of beliefs and interpretive frames that mediates discourse and social structures, and hegemony is the way that subtle and often hidden forms of consent constitute power relationships (Mumby, 1988).

With the aim of exposing these relationships and suggesting alternative arrangements, critical theory examines the way hegemony shapes and is shaped by language use, the way powerful groups control language systems, and the way deep structures reveal power and ideology. For instance, Riley (1983) examines the deeply layered structures that sustain organizational cultures through the power embedded in political imagery and verbal symbols. Since other chapters in this handbook review literature on critical theory (see Deetz, Chapter 1; Conrad & Haynes, Chapter 2; Mumby, Chapter 15), this chapter centers on language as a particular feature of this research perspective. Specifically, it concentrates on four major features: narrative talk; rituals and texts; everyday talk; and ironies, contradictions, and paradoxes.

Narrative Talk

In this perspective, storytelling is not a neutral process; rather, stories function ideologically to represent the interests of dominant groups, instantiate values, reify structures, and reproduce power (Mumby, 1988). In Witten's (1993) view, narrative discourse is a mode of persuasion used to create and maintain a culture of obedience, to invent a credible history, and to exert covert control. For example, Mumby (1987) illustrates how reading narrative discourse through the lens of gender reproduces power relationships at IBM. In the classic story of Tom Watson, chair of the board, and the young female security officer who stopped Watson and asked him to put on his badge, use of the words such as *bride, ill-fitting uniform, white-shirted men,* and *trembling* reproduces power relationships through signifiers of class and gender. Even though the story argues for equality in following the rules, it reaffirms inequality through male and class dominance in the social order.

Similarly, in horse track racing, women grooms reproduce each other as marginalized members through telling stories about the "girls" who use their sexuality to gain success among the big trainers, while being alienated professionally from the legitimate grooms (Helmer, 1993). Through these oppositions, women participate in and provide consent for their exclusion from the structures of power and privilege. Finally, stories of sexual harassment, rooted in an ideology of denial and surprise, reveal the tensions between private and public arenas of organizational life (Strine, 1992; Taylor & Conrad, 1992; Wood, 1992). Victims of harassment often sequester their

stories by treating them as normal yet abnormal, inevitable yet immutable, and trivial but significant (Clair, 1993b). These oppositional tensions create doubt that often leads to responses of silence and inaction. Thus, through constructing, telling, and concealing stories, organizational members reproduce power relationships rooted in the institutional and societal structures.

Rituals and Texts

Rituals and rites. Discourse plays a critical role in enacting organizational rituals and rites, such as interviews, planning meetings, award ceremonies, and company parties. As routine events, rituals are patterned and repeated social activities and rites are scripted public ceremonies. Rituals and rites often consist of normative ways of speaking through situating control in routine practices. Performance interviews, as a genre of discourse, demonstrate how discourse reconstitutes power relationships. In an interview between the sales director and Japanese American employees of a large hotel chain, the sales director's use of indexical expressions and nonstandard speech enacts the linguistic pattern of "markedness," which, in turn, isolates minorities from the organizational mainstream (Banks, 1987). Power is also constituted in team meetings through juxtaposing seriousness and humor to create a cultural drama that melds occupational and personal frames into group objectives. For example, balancing seriousness and humor in the training workshops of a high-tech company elicits an ideology of strong organizational commitment (Kunda, 1992). Moreover, simultaneous use of humor and seriousness often results in a climate of ambiguity in which anecdotes and nuances of such terms as *wallop, slap, stunner* conceal gender and class and treat domestic violence as a normal activity (Saferstein, 1994).

Symbolic struggles also surface in business planning when alternative discourses replace original organizational expressions. In a reengineering team, business planning controls capital allocations through introducing new vocabularies to displace existing labels, as with the case of the Canadian government (Oakes, Townley, & Cooper, 1998). Thus, use of linguistic patterns, humor, and labeling construct and reaffirm power relationships through enacting collaborative processes that reflect dominant ideologies.

Even social rites such as award ceremonies and company parties enact power relationships through organizational dramas. At an annual awards breakfast, public orations that feature such words as *we are one, body of the church,* and *salary adjustment* reconstitute elite power in an advertising agency through enacting a ritual that unifies while separating, praises while criticizing, and rewards seniority while extolling performance (Rosen, 1985). Similarly, speeches at an annual Christmas party function to obscure and thus secure the economic foundation of the ad agency (Rosen, 1988). Organizational rites, then, are not simply social activities; they enact relations of domination and control, often embedded in the deep-level contradictory meanings that evolve from discursive practices.

Formal texts. Rituals as normative ways of speaking interface with written documents to instantiate ideology and power relationships. Critical analyses of these texts, including organizational policy statements, advertisements, budgets, and program documents, demonstrate how microlevel linguistic practices reflect back on and draw from social and institutional structures (Dent, 1991; Munro, 1995). For example, Clair's (1993a) study of policy statements on sexual harassment illustrates how bureaucracy treats sexuality in the workplace as a commodity. Use of such phrases as "just say no," "keep a record," and "report it" in conjunction with such strategies as minimizing the act, ambiguity, and joking fosters confessional and exclusionary discourses that, in turn, reify power relationships.

The rhetoric of commodity also surfaces in job advertisements and program materials (Fairclough & Wodak, 1997). Fairclough (1993) observes how universities, in their quest to be entrepreneurial, shift from a traditional academic mission to a goal of marketing educational services. Use of action verbs, managerial language, and self-promotion in these materials reflects how organizations enact commodity values that shift from an ideology of obligation. Organizations also sediment certain ideologies and themes (e.g., cost cutting, secrecy) in official documents, ones in which management and workers appropriate in different ways (Bastien, McPhee, & Bolton, 1995; Knights & Willmott, 1987). In effect, formal texts are genres in which organizations reproduce power relationships through constituting ideologies discursively.

Everyday Talk

Power relationships are also actively constructed through the work routines of everyday organizational life. These routines surface as members develop special vocabularies to depict organizational processes, to reflect political interests, and to resist managerial ideologies. That is, the labeling or naming of objects, people, and events exerts control over organizational processes. For instance, labeling the computer as *the smart machine, machine of the year,* and *the brain power* serves to legitimate information technology; defer decisions; blame machines; and root problems in professionalism, consumption, and technical power (Prasad, 1995).

In like manner, labeling or naming a discursive practice, such as sexual harassment, inscribes patterns of sensemaking that affect what people see, what gets silenced, and what is regarded as reasonable and acceptable (Wood, 1994). Even communication about such seemingly objective processes as pay scales are intertwined with language and power (Lang, 1986). In pay differentials, women and minorities are often isolated from the power relationships that control the definition and norms of equity (Clair & Thompson, 1996).

Language also becomes a source of power as speech communities vie to have their words and meanings accepted as legitimate. In particular, lumber workers' use of political vocabularies (e.g., "political hires," "shit talk," "gettin' down on workers") develops an ideology aimed at resisting the dominant group discourse but one that prohibits them from exerting organizational voice (Huspek & Kendall, 1991). Similar studies demonstrate how working-class males use humor to resist managerial control, conform to masculine norms, and influence fellow workers (Collinson, 1988, 1992). This form of resistance, however, rooted in an individualist ideology, proves to be ineffective in resisting managerial control.

Ironies, Contradictions, and Paradoxes

Everyday interactions also conceal contradictions in power relationships that reside at deep-structure levels. These contradictions surface through the way routine practices disclose the opposite of their intentions. Examples of these contradictions appear in reward structures and goal systems, when organizations expect performance while rewarding seniority and develop rules and regulations that act against the achievement of group goals (Kerr, 1975).

Contradictions also arise because ideologies shift over time revealing power struggles in primary and secondary contradictions. Using Giddens's structuration theory, Howard and Geist (1995) illustrate how the primary contradictions of autonomy and dependence in a utility company merger lead to secondary tensions of change versus stability, empowerment versus powerlessness, and identification versus estrangement. Employees assume positions of invincibility, diplomacy, defection, and betrayal through recognizing or ignoring

these contractions and through accepting or rejecting the new ideology. In a similar way, cynicism and ironic slogans conceal tensions between self and organizational identity, as noted in the contradictions between embracing and distancing organizational roles, affirming and denying identities, and blurring work and nonwork activities (Kunda, 1992).

Contradictions also lead to paradoxes in which mutually exclusive alternatives reflect back on and constrain organizational actions (Putnam, 1986). Contradictions that emanate from organizational documents and training programs underlie the paradoxes of participation and diversity training. Ironically, the most effective participation programs offer workers the least amount of input in decisions. In unpacking this irony, Stohl (1995) uncovers contradictions in the design, control, and compatibility of workplace participation that lead to paradoxes in commitment and cooperation. By ordering workers to participate voluntarily, employees often avoid conflicts, participate by not participating, and exert concertive control over team members (Barker, 1993; Stohl, 1995).

In a similar way, programs aimed at recruiting and promoting women and minorities develop ironies that result in paradoxical practices. For example, to avoid discrimination, companies isolate women and minorities and train them in special programs, and to reduce inequality in personnel actions, they develop separate criteria for hiring and promoting women (Wood & Conrad, 1983). These practices rooted in societal discourses on affirmative action invoke feelings of confusion and helplessness that, ironically, reconstitute women and minorities as powerless. Feelings of powerlessness in a small design company also emanate from paradoxes, particularly ones in which the exercise of control contradicts the ideology of autonomy (Markham, 1996). Through fusing the language of teamwork and strategic ambiguity with explosive negative feedback, organizational members enact a culture in which self-direction functions as a constraint rather than a freedom.

Organizational ironies and contradictions, then, reveal tensions and uncover ruptures in deep-seated meanings. In effect, the contradictions that surface in organizational discourse point out how language mystifies power relationships and identifies the fault lines for resistance against domination and control.

Studies that adopt a critical theory approach to discourse root language in ideology and power relationships. Thus, critical language studies privilege the context, function, and meaning to show how discourse enacts, reveals, and conceals the exercise of control. Empirical investigations highlight words and phrases, structures and patterns, and contextual meanings that link language to hegemonic processes and dominant ideologies. The use of semantics as a process of naming shapes ideologies that emanate from deep-structure understandings rather than from surface analysis of speech communities, texts, and organizational functions. Contradictions and ironies not only reveal the way that power operates in organizational discourse, but they also unearth the fault lines in which resistance can emerge.

POSTMODERN LANGUAGE ANALYSIS

Power and resistance are dominant themes in postmodern approaches to discourse analysis. But rather than being fixed within dominant coalitions, power is a contested concept, one instantiated in discourse through a dialectic of control. Power and resistance, then, develop from multiple and conflicting discourses linked to different knowledge regimes (Deetz, 1992, 1995). Hegemony is dialectical—subject to negotiation through competing meanings (Mumby & Stohl, 1991). For example, Murphy's (1998) study of flight attendants' "hidden transcripts" illustrates how discourse opens possibilities for resistance and change. Through the use of speech acts, euphemisms, and joking, flight attendants enact situations rooted in ambiguity that allow them to renegotiate their identities and modify localized practices. Thus, resistance arises from local rather than deep-seated meanings and power intertwines with knowledge to frame events within a historical and cultural context (Foucault, 1979; D. Jones, 1992).

Postmodern assumptions about power and local meanings have direct implications for discourse analysis. Specifically, postmodernism rejects grand narratives, challenges traditional notions of representation, and centers on the instability of meaning. Power and knowledge are produced, not in universal narratives, but in temporary language games and small stories located in space and time (Mauws & Phillips, 1995). Words and symbols do not represent or stand for a referent or idea, as the majority of linguistic approaches purport. Since no stable core or foundation exists on which to ground meaning, understanding emanates from inscribing value and creating signification within a particular process. Meanings, then, are often deferred from one linguistic symbol to another (Chia, 1996). In effect, postmodernism sets forth a crisis in representation. Since language functions as a system of difference, devoid of any stable and direct relationship with the natural world, texts are meaningful only as different people read and interpret them in multiple ways. Thus, texts slide into other texts as referents and meanings shift over time (Calás & Smircich, 1999).

Grounded in the work of Saussure (1916/1974), postmodernism privileges semiotics and rhetoric and treats language as a set of structured relations rather than a system of codes. However, these relations emanate from a system of difference, grounded in movement from presence to absence, metaphysics to irony, and text to intertexuality (Hassan, 1985). What is present in the text conceals what is absent or implied in this discourse. Difference makes the "the other term" visible through using presence and absence to show how language inscribes what it seeks to suppress and how it excludes the devalued other.

Postmodern approaches to language analysis privileges irony, metonymy, and rhetoric as discursive processes for reading and interpreting texts (Chia, 1996).

This review of discourse studies in the postmodern tradition clusters into three major categories: language as fragmentation and ambiguity, discourse as irony and paradox, and language as texts. The third category of language as texts subdivides into deconstructing texts, texts and conversations, and texts as dialogue.

Fragmentation and Ambiguity

Fragmentation and ambiguity are key constructs in a postmodern perspective. Both concepts stem from the way meaning shifts within the discursive terrain. Ambiguity refers to the absence of a clear interpretation or the presence of multiple plausible interpretations (Eisenberg, 1984; Weick, 1979). Fragmentation results from multiple voices and interpretations that separate rather than coalesce into a consensus (Martin, 1992; Meyerson, 1991). Multiple discourses contribute to fragmentation through the way different dynamics surface in the process of organizing. In particular, different discourses simultaneously infuse reflexive cycles and continuous changes in a global agency such as the Institute of Cultural Affairs (Thatchenkery & Upadhyaya, 1996). They also contribute to fragmentation through the use of localized meanings and situated discourses, such as phrases like "the bottom line" and "profit and loss" that have particular meanings across different accounting practices (Miller & O'Leary, 1987).

Ambiguities also open space to embrace multiple discourses through the contradictions and antagonisms that exist among organizational members. For example, supporters of a regional symphony use the terms *professionals, activists, volunteers,* and *business resources* in diverse ways to reflect the tensions among and sustain a multivocal culture (Rudd, 1995). Through ambiguity, the symphony becomes a place that is simultaneously creative and uncreative, passionate and pas-

sionless, realistic and unrealistic. In like manner, introducing novel discourse in a total quality management process (e.g., *cross-functional teams* and *empowerment*) juxtaposed with resistance language such as "beat it to death" and "not submit until we wave the white flag" creates ambiguity that simultaneously preserves and changes an organization (Barrett, Thomas, & Hocevar, 1995).

Ambiguity and fragmentation also characterize the interplay between acceptance and rejection of organizational identities. Phillips and Hardy (1997) demonstrate how the term *refugee* constructs the self as a product of the discursive struggles among four different governmental organizations. These agencies constitute refugees in fragmented ways as *bogus applicants, disguised economic migrants, clients, constituencies* and/or *dependents,* depending on the prevailing local practices of refugee determination.

Through analysis of a Working Together program, Holmer-Nadesan (1996) illustrates how responses to contradictory discourses in a large university provide space for service workers to shift among identification, counteridentification, and disidentification. "Bitching" as a form of discourse also serves as an ambivalent communication practice that constitutes organizational identities as both maintaining secretarial stereotypes and destabilizing clerical identities (Sotirin & Gottfried, 1999). For Pringle (1988), secretarial moments of bitching, gossiping, and joking enact a form of sexual power play that contributes not only to resistance but also to the tensions between rationality and emotionality in the workplace. In general, ambiguity and fragmentation arise from multiple discourses and the interplay of contradictions. These discourses, in turn, open up space for resistance and for shifting organizational power relations.

Irony and Paradox

Tensions between rationality and emotionality underlie postmodern views of irony and paradox. Unlike the rhetorical and critical perspectives, ironies and contradictions in this orientation stem from shifting meanings and fragmented practices rather than from deep-seated structures or rhetorical functions. In the postmodern perspective, irony aids in recognizing incongruity, holding incompatibilities together, and celebrating the contingencies of discourse. For instance, in her study of a women's social service organization, Trethewey (1999) demonstrates how an ironic stance both celebrates client resistance and "problematize[s] the distinctions between resistance and accommodation, between power and powerlessness, and between agency and subjection" (p. 161). Irony fosters contradictions that lead to paradoxes, such as promoting self-sufficiency by creating client dependency, empowering clients through controlling their behaviors, and developing trust through objectifying others (Trethewey, 1997).

Paradoxical discourse, as the simultaneous enactment of two mutually exclusive imperatives, surfaces in the postmodern perspective as chaotic, spontaneous, and nonrational. As with the rhetorical and critical perspectives, paradoxes are self-referential and often lead to vicious circles and double binds; hence, organizations typically want to eliminate, resolve, or transcend them (Smith & Berg, 1987). In the postmodern perspective, however, paradoxes, as illogical aspects of organizing, are empowering and beneficial. They provide counterintuitive insights, encourage nonrational thinking, and counterbalance organizations with Zen-like wisdom (Wendt, 1998).

In her analysis of organizational change, O'Connor (1995) illustrates how organizations learn from paradoxes. Applying narrative to an analysis of a high-tech manufacturing firm, O'Connor shows how involvement in organizational change entails coping with the paradoxes of absence/presence, inclusion/exclusion, retaining/losing jobs, and siding with/against champions of change. Organizations that embrace the *both-and* of these paradoxes engage in counterintuitive learning and feel empowered from the constant interplay of these contradictions. Overall, the study of irony and paradox in the postmodern perspective celebrates the contingencies of language through providing counterintuitive insights and promoting a self-referential process. Rather than creating paralysis, paradoxes open up discourse and embrace diversity.

Language as Texts

In addition to ironies and paradox, the concept of text takes on different nuances in the postmodern perspective. Linguistic and rhetorical scholars often treat *text* as written documents, reifications of experience, or social facts that represent coherent meanings or thematic unity (Cheney & Tompkins, 1988; Kets de Vries & Miller, 1987). Critical theorists, in turn, view texts as institutionalized forces or networks of intertextual relations that sustain power. In the postmodern perspective, *text* becomes a metaphor for organizing, the constellation of discursive practices, and the array of multiple fragmented meanings. Texts are temporal, self-reflexive, and grounded in both local experiences and historical meanings (Strine, 1988; Thatchenkery, 1992). Postmodernists also privilege intertextuality, as the way a given text embodies other texts within it. Studies of texts in the postmodern perspective cluster into these categories: deconstructing texts, texts and conversations, and dialogue as texts.

Deconstructing texts. In the postmodern perspective, language is inherently unstable. Its illusion of stability derives from a system of binary opposites in which one term of a pair is privileged over the other. Deconstruction is a literary method in which researchers disassemble a text through revealing the concealed and marginalized terms and opening the text for alternative interpretations (Derrida, 1976). A number of scholars have deconstructed classic texts to introduce multiple readings of organizational theory (see Calás & Smircich, 1999, for these citations). This review, however, centers on the analyses of empirical and practical texts aimed at exposing dualisms and providing alternative readings.

Four articles deconstruct the discourses of popular and practitioner textbooks on leadership, workforce diversity, constituent corporate directors, and stakeholders. Through juxtaposing leadership with seduction, Calás and Smircich (1991) demonstrate how the rhetoric of leadership parallels a seductive game and how leadership embodies multiple rather than unitary meanings. Similarly, Litvin's (1997) deconstruction of workforce diversity shows how society prescribes essentialistic categories and ignores the way that ongoing interaction accomplishes the presence of difference. In her analysis of recent texts, Bradshaw (1996) shows how oppositional pairs in the corporate boardroom discourse reaffirms the status quo and excludes women board members. Finally, Calton and Kurland (1996) recast organizational stakeholders as connected knowers in webs of relationships through deconstructing the oppositional pairs linked to autonomy, impartial reasoning, competition, and environmental control.

Empirical studies that deconstruct organizational texts focus on tensions between public and private and presence and absence in organizational life. In her analysis of a CEO memo, Martin (1990) examines the text and subtext of this message to illustrate how a high-ranking executive's pregnancy suppresses gender conflict, reifies existing structures, and challenges traditional dichotomies. The dialectic of presence/absence also characterizes worker accounts of quality management teams (Mumby & Stohl, 1991). Obligations to substitute for an absent team member leads employees to blame each other rather than management for an inadequate workforce. Thus, physical absence becomes a way of enacting the tensions between presence and absence at both the team and system levels.

The tensions between public and private and insider and outsider surface in Boje's (1995) deconstruction of the modernist and postmodernist readings of the Disney Corporation. Through examining the dualities embedded in documents and interviews, Boje observes how Disney struggles to maintain a grand narrative while marginalizing multiple voices and counterculture views. As a literary technique, deconstruction of organizational texts reveals the shadow-side of organizing and shows how power marginalizes certain discourses while privileging other voices.

Texts as dialogue. One way of fragmenting grand narratives into multiple local discourses is to privilege dialogue rather than monologue. Dialogue is a mode of communication that builds mutuality through the awareness of others, use of genuine or authentic discourse, and reliance on the unfolding interaction. Although viewed as a momentary accomplishment (Cissna & Anderson, 1998), the conditions for engaging in dialogue serve as the "praxis for mediating competing and contradictory discourses" (Hawes, 1999). Drawn from the work of Bakhtin (1981) and Buber (1923/1958), organizational studies of dialogue center on promoting learning through opening a "third space" for questioning, critiquing, reconfiguring interests, and affirming differences (Evered & Tannenbaum, 1992). Dialogue stresses balanced communication by providing parties with a chance to speak and be heard and to challenge the traditional positioning of authority (Eisenberg & Goodall, 1993).

Dialogue, then, is a genre of discourse that mediates the instabilities of difference through not only creating something new but also altering the identity of a system (Hawes, 1999). Thus, dialogue is closely linked to organizational learning (Isaacs, 1993, 1999) and the interplay of stability and change (Kristiansen & Bloch-Poulsen, 2000). Through developing a caring container, Kristiansen and Bloch-Poulsen illustrate how dialogic competencies and sequences of interaction enable managers and employees in a Danish industrial company to transcend a priori ways of relating, speak the unspoken across different organizational status positions, and become valid partners in producing new meanings. Similar approaches to understanding organizations surface in the work on appreciative inquiry (Barrett, 1995; Barrett & Cooperrider, 1990) and workplace relationships (Fletcher, 1999; McNamee, Gergen, & Associates, 1999). Although originating in modernism, dialogue as a postmodern discourse embraces fragmentation and ambiguity, privileges differences, and offers an alternative for parties to mediate contradictions and develop a third space.

Text and conversations. Playing off the tensions between text and conversation, Taylor and Cooren set forth a postmodern approach that embraces the duality between action and structure (Cooren, 1997, 1999, 2000; Cooren & Taylor, 1997, 1998; Groleau & Cooren, 1998; Taylor, 1995; Taylor & Cooren, 1997; Taylor, Cooren, Giroux, & Robichaud, 1996; Taylor & Van Every, 2000). They posit the discursive equivalent of the structure maxim—that structure is the medium and outcome of action. However, they substitute text for structure and treat text as the medium and outcome of conversation. Thus, the agency they ascribe to text, a non-human agent, fits the tenets of postmodern thinking and positions this approach within actor-network theory (Callon, 1986; Callon & Latour, 1981; Latour, 1993, 1994, 1996a), semiotics (Greimas, 1987), and activity theory (Engeström, 1987, 1990).

Taylor (1993) purports that language has inherent organizing properties similar to speech acts, sentence grammars, story grammars, argument structures, and lexicons. Cooren and Taylor (1997) also argue that the concept of interaction should be broadened to include the active role of non-human agents. This non-human agency is especially illustrated by the important role played by texts, machines, and architectural elements in organizational settings. These agents have struc-turing properties that are typically neglected in traditional organizational analyses.

Although the work in this area is primarily theoretical, recent articles test these ideas with empirical data. For example, Cooren and Fairhurst (in press) examine story grammars in an organizational downsizing to demonstrate the way "restorying" through workforce restructuring alters management policy. Groleau and Cooren (1998), Cooren and Taylor (1998), and Robichaud (1998) apply this approach to the implementation of organizational technology, the development of a parliamentary commission in a national assembly, and the way a municipality organizes a public discussion. Finally, Cooren and Taylor (2000) use this approach to analyze the organization of a coalition during an environmental controversy. Drawing from linguistic traditions, the interplay of text and conversation seeks to understand how the inherent properties of language ascribe organizing as texts. In this sense, text is both the medium and outcome of conversation.

Postmodern approaches privilege structural relations, texts, and intertexuality of meaning; however, meaning is unstable and often shifts among multiple and contradictory discourses. Power arises through a duality of control enacted in language games and local narratives. The self-referential and contradictory nature of meaning surfaces in paradoxes and ambiguities. As the embodiment of discursive practices and fragmented meanings, texts become the metaphors for organizing.

One particular problem that arises in both the postmodern and critical perspectives is a tendency to overlay a particular linguistic form onto an organizational phenomenon, without a careful inductive analysis of the underlying processes that influence this choice (Dunford & Palmer, 1996). Hence, the research functions deductively to label a pattern without noting the linguistic elements and discursive practices that comprise this form. That is, linguistic forms should not become templates to impose on organizational processes.

Linguistic analyses rooted in deconstruction typically avoid this pitfall. Deconstruction introduces alternative readings of texts by dismantling binary opposites, and dialogue mediates the tensions among disparate interpretations. Through focusing on the inherent properties of language, text and conversations in the postmodern perspective surface as isomorphic with organizing.

SUMMARY AND DISCUSSION

This chapter reviews the empirical literature on discourse and organizations in eight perspectives: sociolinguistics, conversation analysis, cognitive linguistics, pragmatics, semiotics, literary and rhetorical analysis, critical language studies, and postmodern language analysis. These approaches differ in definitions of language, salient linguistic features, and organizational processes. In the sociolinguistic perspective, language is a system of codes that indexes static organizational structures, occupational communities, and gender/class variables.

Conversation analysts focus on the syntax and coherence of talk, treating conversation as an accomplishment. Studies center on the opening and closings of talk in performance appraisals, turn taking and interruptions in organizational meetings, adjacency pairs in job interviews, topic shifts in decision making, and disclaimers in superior-subordinate interactions. Both sociolinguistics and conversation analysis treat organizations as institutional structures that exist prior to language use.

Cognitive linguistics shifts the focus of language to meanings that reside within language users; hence, organizing is a process of collective sensemaking triggered by discourse. Organizational studies focus on scripts and schemata, cognitive mapping, semantic networks, and frames. In the pragmatic perspective, discourse produces organizing through being uttered as a speech act, constituting speech communities, performing conversations, telling stories, negotiating orders, and enacting interaction sequences and patterns. Semiotics emphasizes sign systems and how language signifies through patterns of meaning in factory work, emergency call systems, and corporate images.

Literary and rhetorical perspectives highlight meaning, text, and context as the key features of language analysis. Studies in this area focus on rhetorical strategies in corporate advocacy, argument in decision making, and literary tropes in organizational change. Context plays a dominant role in critical language studies. Grounded in a concern about power and control, critical studies highlight narrative talk, rituals and texts, everyday talk, and contradictions in organizations. With an emphasis on text and intertexuality, postmodern language analysis treats discourse as a set of relations in which meaning shifts through fragmentation, ambiguity, and paradox. Studies on language as texts include deconstructions of popular and practitioner textbooks, dialogue as texts, and the links between text and conversations.

Whereas a decade ago there were relatively few studies on discourse processes in organizations, this review suggests that research is becoming prolific. Scholars from a wide range of backgrounds within the organizational sciences focus on an increasing number and variety of discursive forms that constitute organizational life. Analysis of this growing body of literature leads to several implications for future research.

First, analysis of the implicit relationship between language and communication supports a meaning-centered view of communication over a transmission model. Only interaction analysis and sociolinguistics depart from this general trend. The pendulum has also swung away from variable analytic models and the scientific method because they lose too many distinctive qualities of communication (Cronen, 1995). Correspondingly, scientific approaches to language analysis, which focus on the function, frequency, and regularity of organizational messages, appear less often than do interpretive methods, which focus on meaning, context, and structure. However, it is too soon to dismiss scientific methods because neither a focus on meaning nor frequency alone can answer the relevant questions about discourse and organizations.

Second, different approaches to language analysis share important conceptual distinctions that figure prominently in the debate about discourse and organization. In this debate, the relationships between discourse and organization emerge as reflective, constitutive, or equivalent (Cooren & Taylor, 1997; Smith, 1993). In the reflective relationship, language represents or reflects organizations as structures, occupational communities, levels of meanings, or systems of codes. In the constitutive relationship, discourse and organizations are active and dynamic and develop a relationship in which organizations produce language, language produces organizations, or the two coproduce each other. In the equivalency relationship, discourse and organizing are one in the same. That is, organizing is communicating through the intersection of conversation and text.

Fewer contemporary analyses of discourse and organization adopt a reflective relationship and a container view of organizations. This stance trivializes communication and language use, reifies the organization, and pays little attention to organizational change (Cooren & Taylor, 1997). Most perspectives included in this review embrace variations of social constructivism, which supports the production relationship of discourse and organization. These perspectives acknowledge the organizing potential of discourse while they maintain an assumption of organizational primacy (i.e., discourse and organization are inextricably bound but *separate* phenomena). By contrast, language analysis influenced by postmodernism is most compatible with an equivalency view, which casts organization and discourse as simultaneous achievements.

Fragmentation and decentering of the subject in postmodern perspectives parallels the way in which equivalency problematizes organization and discourse in each other's terms.

However, organizational discourse analysts in general are guilty of mixing their perspectives. Even within the same article, container-view descriptions, such as language as an *actualizing process* or discourse that *uncovers* or *reflects* the organization, are mixed with production-view descriptors, such as discourse that *accomplishes, defines,* or *produces* the organization. These references, in turn, are coupled with equivalency notions of discourse that are *simultaneously organizational.* As these perspectives become intertwined, either intentionally or inadvertently, the theoretical status of the discourse-organization relationship becomes unclear. In essence, organizational researchers need to be explicit in articulating their positions on the discourse-organization relationship.

Third, most of these perspectives struggle with the problem of context. These problems include (1) reifying context by treating the organization as static (e.g., sociolinguistics, ethnography of speaking), (2) focusing on conversational structures and failing to discern the broader organizational and societal issues (e.g., interaction analysis, conversation analysis), (3) analyzing excerpts of discourse out of context (e.g., discourse analysis, critical discourse analysis, postmodern analysis), and (4) failing to determine which aspects of organizational context contribute to particular language forms (e.g., ethnography of speaking).

Because context consists of any element that shapes the way people think and what they expect, its unwieldy nature creates a tendency to simplify levels of analysis and to treat context as a frame for social interaction rather than as an interactional achievement (Beach, 1995). But to fully understand the relationship between discourse and organization, language analysts need to complicate their views of context through "thick descriptions" of organizational processes that form a nexus of influences on discursive production.

Fourth, Mauws and Phillips (1999) recently note that the vast array of practices that constitute organizations not only requires identification, but also involves understanding patterns that emerge from these practices. This requirement raises a number of empirical questions about the relationship between discourse and organization, the sampling of discourse as a structured sets of texts, and differentiating between discursive and nondiscursive organizational practices.

Other empirical questions regarding the meaning of the term *organization* need to be raised. Like a Procrustean bed, different studies cast the organization in terms of its leadership; a set of team dynamics; a set of genres for communicating; or a response to an event, a controversy, or a change effort. Relatedly, examining the way individual linguistic forms contribute to a larger unit is not the same as examining how discourse and organization work in concert (i.e., the contingent basis on which they operate and take shape). The application of different linguistic perspectives complicates this issue (e.g., interaction analysis and ethnography). Finally, researchers need to investigate how linguistic patterns combine over time and how they contribute to larger and larger organizational units.

Boden's (1994) work is a case in point. Citing Giddens (1979, 1984) and drawing from Goffman's (1974) notion of the lamination of conversations, Boden argues that patterns take shape from multiple conversations on common topics and roles to knit together the organization as a whole. Even though she illustrates this process with a number of discursive forms (e.g., question-answer, turn taking, categorization devices), she never fully unpacks the lamination question. In essence, *how* do conversations layer to form patterns? Given that patterns form around common topics and roles, how do linguistic features combine to create an internal structure in this layering process, especially given the wide variety of linguistic patterns that contribute to this process? Moreover, how does one layered set of conversations connect to another set to construct larger organizational units? The lamination metaphor is a useful heuristic that most discourse analysts accept as a generating mechanism for structure, but the question of how the lamination process actually works remains unanswered.

Unfortunately, even if language analysts could resolve the lamination question, they must face a second dilemma; that is, discourse analysis primarily examines traces of conversation rather than conversations or texts per se. Even though texts have certain properties that conversations do not, including the capacity to transcend the local (Derrida, 1988), they are only partial. Inevitably, researches face a major sampling question because organizations produce an innumerable number and variety of texts from which to select. Conversations, briefings, meetings, e-mail messages, reports, and press releases are just a few of the discourses that organizations produce day after day, month after month, and year after year. How does a language analyst determine which texts to select? While some analysts argue that any text is part of the organization and thus worthy of study, ethnographic studies and event-related analyses often reveal that this assumption is risky. Not all texts have equal saliency in the process of organizing.

Finally, most of these studies, with the exception of semiotics and postmodernism, accept an artificial separation between discursive and nondiscursive practices, one that biases research toward discursive analyses. Even though conventional folk wisdom often demeans talk in favor of organizational action (Marshak, 1998), many language analysts continue to view talk and action as disjoint activities, even though they shift the emphasis to discourse. The problem is not their view of the relationship between talk and action; rather, it stems from their treatment of nondiscursive action as underrepresented in the analyses. More attention to context should address this concern.

However these issues get resolved, the study of discourse and organizations has come of age. Increasing numbers of organizational scholars recognize language and communication as fields of study that are intertwined, interdependent, and among the most promising in the search for knowledge about organizational life.

REFERENCES

Adkins, M., & Brashers, D. E. (1995). The power of language in computer-mediated groups. *Management Communication Quarterly, 8,* 289-322.

Ainsworth-Vaughn, N. (1992). Topic transitions in physician-patient interviews: Power, gender, and discourse change. *Language in Society, 21,* 409-426.

Akrich, M., & Latour, B. (1992). A summary of a convenient vocabulary for the semiotics of human and nonhuman assemblies. In W. Bijker & J. Law (Eds.), *Shaping technology, building society: Studies in sociotechnical change* (pp. 259-264). Cambridge, MA: MIT Press.

Allen, M. W., & Caillouet, R. H. (1994). Legitimate endeavors: Impression management strategies used by an organization in crisis. *Communication Monographs, 61,* 44-62.

Alvesson, M. (1993). The play of metaphors. In J. Hassard & M. Parker (Eds.), *Postmodernism and organizations* (pp. 114-131). London: Sage.

Anderson, P. A. (1983). Decision making by objection and the Cuban missile crisis. *Administrative Science Quarterly, 28,* 201-222.

Anderson-Gough, F., Grey, C., & Robson, K. (1998). "Work hard, play hard": An analysis of organizational cliché in two accountancy practices. *Organization, 5,* 565-592.

Austin, J. L. (1962). *How to do things with words.* Cambridge, MA: Harvard University Press.

Bacharach, S. B., & Lawler, E. J. (1981). *Bargaining: Power, tactics, and outcomes.* San Francisco: Jossey-Bass.

Baker, M. A. (1991). Gender and verbal communication in professional settings. *Management Communication Quarterly, 5,* 36-63.

Bakhtin, M. (1981). *The dialogic imagination* (C. Emerson & M. Holquist, Trans.). Austin: University of Texas Press.

Bales, R. F. (1950). *Interaction process analysis.* Cambridge, MA: Addison-Wesley.

Bales, R. F., & Cohen, S. P. (1979). *SYMLOG: A system for the multiple level observation of groups.* New York: Free Press.

Balmer, J. M. T. (1995). Corporate branding and connoisseurship. *Journal of General Management, 21*(1), 24-46.

Bandura, A. (1986). *Social foundations of thought and action.* Englewood Cliffs, NJ: Prentice Hall.

Banks, S. P. (1987). Achieving "unmarkedness" in organizational discourse: A praxis perspective on ethnolinguistic identity. *Journal of Language and Social Psychology, 6,* 171-189.

Banks, S. P. (1994). Performing public announcements: The case of flight attendants' work discourse. *Text and Performance Quarterly, 14,* 253-267.

Barker, J. (1993). Tightening the iron cage: Concertive control in self-managing teams. *Administrative Science Quarterly, 38,* 408-437.

Barley, S. R. (1983). Semiotics and the study of occupational and organizational culture. *Administrative Science Quarterly, 28,* 393-413.

Barley, S. R. (1986). Technology as an occasion for structuring: Evidence from observation of CT scanners and the social order of radiology departments. *Administrative Science Quarterly, 31,* 78-108.

Baron, R. A. (1990). Countering the effects of destructive criticism: The relative efficacy of four interventions. *Journal of Applied Psychology, 75,* 235-245.

Barrett, F. J. (1995). Creating appreciative learning cultures. *Organizational Dynamics, 24*(2), 36-49.

Barrett, F. J., & Cooperrider, D. L. (1990). Generative metaphor intervention: A new behavioral approach for working with systems divided by conflict and caught in defensive perception. *Journal of Applied Behavioral Science, 26*(2), 219-239.

Barrett, F. J., Thomas, G. F., Hocevar, S. P. (1995). The central role of discourse in large-scale change: A social construction perspective. *Journal of Applied Behavioral Science, 31,* 352-372.

Barton, L. (1993). *Crisis in organizations: Managing and communicating in the heat of chaos.* Cincinnati, OH: South-Western, College Division.

Bastien, D. T. (1992). Change in organizational culture: The use of linguistic methods in corporate acquisition. *Management Communication Quarterly, 5,* 403-442.

Bastien, D. T., McPhee, R. D., & Bolton, K. A. (1995). A study and extended theory of the structuration of climate. *Communication Monographs, 62,* 87-109.

Bateson, G. (1972). *Steps to an ecology of the mind.* New York: Ballantine.

Baxter, L. (1993). "Talking things through" and "putting it in writing": Two codes of communication in an academic institution. *Journal of Applied Communication Research, 21,* 313-326.

Beach, W. A. (1995). Conversation analysis: "Okay" as a clue for understanding consequentiality. In S. J. Sigman (Ed.), *The consequentiality of communication* (pp. 121-162). Hillsdale, NJ: Lawrence Erlbaum.

Bednar, D. A., & Curington, W. P. (1983). Interaction analysis: A tool for understanding negotiations. *Industrial and Labor Relations Review, 36,* 389-401.

Benoit, W. L. (1992, November). *Union Carbide and the Bhopal tragedy.* Paper presented at the annual meeting of the Speech Communication Association, Chicago.

Benoit, W. L., & Brinson, S. L. (1994). AT&T: "Apologies are not enough." *Communication Quarterly, 42,* 75-88.

Bettman, J. R., & Weitz, B. A. (1983). Attributions in the board room: Causal reasoning in corporate annual reports. *Administrative Science Quarterly, 28,* 165-183.

Bies, R. J. (1989). Managing conflict before it happens: The role of accounts. In M. A. Rahim (Ed.), *Managing conflict: An interdisciplinary approach* (pp. 83-91). New York: Praeger.

Bies, R. J., & Moag, J. S. (1986). Interactional justice: Communication criteria of fairness. In R. J. Lewicki, B. H. Sheppard, & M. H. Bazerman (Eds.), *Research on negotiation in organizations* (pp. 43-55). Greenwich, CT: JAI.

Bies, R. J., & Shapiro, D. L. (1987). Interactional fairness judgments: The influence of causal accounts. *Social Justice Research, 1,* 199-218.

Bies, R. J., & Shapiro, D. L. (1988). Voice and justification: The influence on procedural fairness judgements. *Academy of Management Journal, 31,* 676-685.

Bies, R. J., Shapiro, D. L., & Cummings, L. L. (1988). Causal accounts and managing organizational conflict: Is it enough to say it's not my fault? *Communication Research, 15,* 381-399.

Bies, R. J., & Sitkin, S. B. (1992). Excuse-making in organizations: Explanation as legitimation. In M. L. McLaughlin, M. J. Cody, & S. Read (Eds.), *Explaining one's self to others: Reason giving in a social context* (pp. 183-198). Hillsdale, NJ: Lawrence Erlbaum.

Blum-Kulka, S. (1997). Discourse pragmatics. In T. A. van Dijk (Ed.), *Discourse as social interaction* (Vol. 2, pp. 38-63). London: Sage.

Blumer, H. (1969). *Symbolic interactionism: Perspective and method.* Englewood Cliffs, NJ: Prentice Hall.

Boden, D. (1994). *The business of talk: Organizations in action.* Cambridge, UK: Polity.

Boethius, S. B. (1987). The view from the middle: Perceiving patterns of interaction in middle management groups. *International Journal of Small Group Research, 3,* 1-15.

Boje, D. M. (1991). The storytelling organization: A study of story performance in an office-supply firm. *Administrative Science Quarterly, 36,* 106-126.

Boje, D. M. (1995). Stories of the storytelling organization: A postmodern analysis of Disney as "Tamaraland." *Academy of Management Journal, 38,* 997-1035.

Boland, R. J., Jr., & Greenberg, R. H. (1988). Metaphorical structuring of organizational ambiguity. In L. R. Pondy, R. J. Boland, & H. Thomas (Eds.), *Managing ambiguity and change* (pp. 17-36). New York: John Wiley.

Boland, R. J., Jr., & Hoffman, R. (1986). Humor in a machine shop: An interpretation of symbolic action. In P. Frost, V. Mitchell, & W. Nord (Eds.), *Organization reality: Reports from the firing line* (pp. 371-376). Glenview, IL: Scott, Foresman.

Bowles, M. L., & Coates, G. (1993). Image and substance: The management of performance as rhetoric or reality? *Personnel Review, 22*(2), 3-21.

Braaten, D. O., Cody, M. J., & DeTienne, K. B. (1993). Account episodes in organizations: Remedial work and impression management. *Management Communication Quarterly, 6,* 219-250.

Bradshaw, P. (1996). Women as constituent directors: Re-reading current texts using a feminist-postmodernist approach. In D. M. Boje, R. P. Gephart, & T. J. Thatchenkery (Eds.), *Postmodern management and organization theory* (pp. 95-124). London: Sage.

Brink, T. L. (1993). Metaphor as data in the study of organizations. *Journal of Management Inquiry, 2,* 366-371.

Brinson, S. L., & Benoit, W. L. (1999). The tarnished star: Restoring Texaco's damaged public image. *Management Communication Quarterly, 12,* 483-510.

Broussine, M., & Vince, R. (1996). Working with metaphor towards organizational change. In C. Oswick & D. Grant (Eds.), *Organization development: Metaphorical explorations* (pp. 557-572). London: Pitman.

Brown, R., & Ford, M. (1961). Address in American English. *Journal of Abnormal and Social Psychology, 62,* 375-385.

Brown, R. H. (1977). *A poetic for sociology.* Cambridge, UK: Cambridge University Press.

Buber, M. (1958). *I and thou* (2nd ed., R. G. Smith, Trans.). New York: Scribner. (Original work published 1923)

Bullis, C., & Tompkins, P. K. (1989). The forest ranger revisited: A study of control practices and identification. *Communication Monographs, 56,* 287-306.

Burke, K. (1969a). *A grammar of motives.* Berkeley: University of California Press. (Original work published 1945)

Burke, K. (1969b). *A rhetoric of motives.* Berkeley: University of California Press. (Original work published 1950)

Burns, T., & Stalker, G. M. (1961). The management of innovation. London: Tavistock.

Button, G. (Ed.). (1993). *Technology in working order: Studies of work, interaction, and technology.* London: Routledge.

Calás, M. B., & Smircich, L. (1991). Voicing seduction to silence leadership. *Organization Studies, 12*(4), 567-602.

Calás, M. B., & Smircich, L. (1999). Past postmodernism? Reflections and tentative directions. *Academy of Management Review, 24*(4), 649-671.

Callon, M. (1986). Some elements of sociology of translation: The domestication of the scallops and the fishermen of St-Brieuc Bay. In J. Law (Ed.), *Power, action, belief* (pp. 196-233). London: Routledge and Kegan Paul.

Callon, M., & Latour, B. (1981). Unscrewing the big Leviathan: How actors macro-structure reality and how sociologists help them to do so. In A. Cicourel & K. Knorr-Cetina (Eds.), *Advances in social theory and methodology: Towards an integration of micro- and macro-sociologies* (pp. 277-303). Boston: Routledge and Kegan Paul.

Calton, J. M., & Kurland, N. B. (1996). A theory of stakeholder enabling: Giving voice to an emerging postmodern praxis of organizational discourse. In D. M. Boje, R. P. Gephart, & T. J. Thatchenkery (Eds.), *Postmodern management and organization theory* (pp. 154-177). London: Sage.

Campbell, K. S., Follender, S. I., & Shane, G. (1998). Preferred strategies for responding to hostile questions in environmental public meetings. *Management Communication Quarterly, 11,* 401-421.

Carroll, J. S., & Payne, J. W. (1991). An information processing approach to two party negotiations. In M. H. Bazerman, R. J. Lewicki, & B. H. Sheppard (Eds.), *Research on negotiation in organizations* (pp. 3-34). Greenwich, CT: JAI.

Cazal, D., & Inns, D. (1998). Metaphor, language, and meaning. In D. Grant, T. Keenoy, & C. Oswick (Eds.), *Discourse and organization* (pp. 177-192). London: Sage.

Cegala, D., Wall, V. D., & Rippey, G. (1987). An investigation of interaction involvement and the dimensions of SYMLOG: Perceived communication behaviors of persons in task-oriented groups. *Central States Speech Journal, 38,* 81-93.

Chatman, J. A., Putnam, L. L., & Sondak, H. (1991). Integrating communication and negotiation research. In M. H. Bazerman, R. J. Lewicki, & B. H. Sheppard (Eds.), *Research on negotiation in organizations* (pp. 139-164). Greenwich, CT: JAI.

Cheney, G. (1983). The rhetoric of identification and the study of organizational communication. *Quarterly Journal of Speech, 69,* 143-158.

Cheney, G. (1991). *Rhetoric in an organizational society: Managing multiple identities.* Columbia: University of South Carolina Press.

Cheney, G., & Frenette, G. (1993). Persuasion and organization: Values, logics, and accounts in contemporary corporate public discourse. In C. Conrad (Ed.), *Ethical nexus* (pp. 49-73). Norwood, NJ: Ablex.

Cheney, G., & Tompkins, P. K. (1988). On the facts of the text as the basis of human communication research. In J. A. Anderson (Ed.), *Communication yearbook 11* (pp. 455-481). Newbury Park, CA: Sage.

Cheney, G., & Vibbert, S. L. (1987). Corporate discourse: Public relations and issue management. In F. M. Jablin, L. L. Putnam, K. H. Roberts, & L. W. Porter (Eds.), *Handbook of organizational communication: An interdisciplinary perspective* (pp. 165-194). Newbury Park, CA: Sage.

Chia, R. (1996). *Organizational analysis as deconstructive practice.* New York: Walter de Gruyter.

Christensen, L. T. (1995). Buffering organisational identity in the marketing culture. *Organization Studies, 16,* 651-672.

Christensen, L. T., & Askegaard, S. (in press). Corporate identity and corporate image revisited: A semiotic perspective. *European Journal of Marketing.*

Cissna, K. N., & Anderson, R. (1998). Theorizing about dialogic moments: The Buber-Rogers position and postmodern themes. *Communication Theory, 8*(1), 63-104.

Clair, R. P. (1993a). The bureaucratization, commodification, and privatization of sexual harassment through institutional discourse. *Management Communication Quarterly, 7,* 123-157.

Clair, R. P. (1993b). The use of framing devices to sequester organizational narratives: Hegemony and harassment. *Communication Monographs, 60,* 113-136.

Clair, R. P., & Thompson, K. (1996). Pay discrimination as a discursive and material practice: A case concerning extended housework. *Journal of Applied Communication Research, 24,* 1-20.

Coleman, H. (1985). Talking shop: An overview of language and work. *International Journal of Sociology of Language, 51,* 105-129.

Collinson, D. (1988). Engineering humor: Masculinity, joking and conflict in shop-floor relations. *Organization Studies, 9,* 181-199.

Collinson, D. (1992). *Managing the shopfloor: Subjectivity, masculinity and workplace culture.* New York: Walter de Gruyter.

Conley, J. M., & O'Barr, W. M. (1990). *Rules versus relationships: The ethnography of legal discourse.* Chicago: University of Chicago Press.

Conrad, C. (1993). The ethical nexus: Conceptual grounding. In C. Conrad (Ed.), *Ethical nexus* (pp. 7-22). Norwood, NJ: Ablex.

Contractor, N. S., & Seibold, D. R. (1993). Theoretical frameworks for the study of structuring processes in group decision support systems: Adaptive structuration theory and self-organizing systems theory. *Human Communication Research, 19,* 528-563.

Coombs, W. T. (1995). Choosing the right words: The development of guidelines for the selection of the "appropriate" crisis-response strategies. *Management Communication Quarterly, 8,* 447-476.

Cooren, F. (1997). Actes de langage et semio-narrativite: Une analyse semiotique des indirections. *Semiotica, 116,* 339-273.

Cooren, F. (1999). Applying socio-semiotics to organizational communication: A new approach. *Management Communication Quarterly 13,* 294-304.

Cooren, F. (2000). *The organizing property of communication.* Amsterdam and Philadelphia: John Benjamins.

Cooren, F., & Fairhurst, G. T. (in press). The leader as a practical narrator: Leadership as the art of translating. In D. Holman & R. Thorpe (Eds.), *The manager as a practical author.* London: Sage.

Cooren, F., & Taylor, J. R. (1997). Organization as an effect of mediation: Redefining the link between organization and communication. *Communication Theory, 7,* 219-260.

Cooren, F., & Taylor, J. R. (1998). The procedural and rhetorical modes of the organizing dimension of communication: Discursive analysis of a parliamentary commission. *Communication Review, 3*(1-2), 65-101.

Cooren, F., & Taylor, J. R. (2000). Association and dissociation in an ecological controversy: The great whale case. In N. W. Coppola & B. Karis (Eds.), *Technical communication, deliberative rhetoric, and environmental discourse: Connections and directions* (pp. 171-190). Stamford, CT: Ablex.

Coser, R. L. (1959). Some social functions of laughter. *Human Relations, 12,* 171-182.

Coser, R. L. (1960). Laughter among colleagues. *Psychiatry, 23,* 81-95.

Courtright, J. A., Fairhurst, G. T., & Rogers, L. E. (1989). Interaction patterns in organic and mechanistic systems. *Academy of Management Journal, 32,* 773-802.

Cray, D. (1989). The use of symbols in multicriteria decision making. *Lecture Notes in Economics and Mathematical Systems, 335,* 100-111.

Cronen, V. E. (1995). Coordinated management of meaning: The consequentiality of communication and the recapturing of experience. In S. J. Sigman (Ed.), *The consequentiality of communication* (pp. 17-66). Hillsdale, NJ: Lawrence Erlbaum.

Czarniawska-Joerges, B., & Joerges, B. (1988). How to control things with words: Organizational talk and control. *Management Communication Quarterly, 2,* 170-193.

Dandridge, T. C., Mitroff, I., & Joyce, W. F. (1980). Organizational symbolism: A topic to expand organizational analysis. *Academy of Management Review, 5,* 77-82.

Danowski, J. A. (1982). A network-based content analysis methodology for computer-mediated communication: An illustration with a computer bulletin board. In R. Bostrum (Ed.), *Communication yearbook 6* (pp. 904-925). New Brunswick, NJ: Transaction Books.

Deetz, S. (1992). *Democracy in an age of corporate colonization.* Albany: State University of New York Press.

Deetz, S. (1995). *Transforming communication, transforming business: Building responsive and responsible workplaces.* Cresskill, NJ: Hampton.

Dent, J. (1991). Accounting and organizational cultures: A field study of the emergence of a new organizational reality. *Accounting, Organizations and Society, 18,* 705-732.

Derrida, J. (1976). *Of grammatology.* Baltimore: Johns Hopkins University Press.

Derrida, J. (1982). *Margins of philosophy.* Chicago: University of Chicago Press.

Derrida, J. (1988). *Limited Inc.* Chicago: Northwestern University Press.

DeSanctis, G., & Poole, M. S. (1994). Capturing the complexity in advanced technology use: Adaptive structuration theory. *Organizational Dynamics, 5,* 121-147.

DeSanctis, G., Poole, M. S., Dickson, G. W., & Jackson, B. M. (1993). Interpretive analysis of team use of group technologies. *Journal of Organizational Computing, 3,* 1-29.

DeSanctis, G., Poole, M. S., Lewis, H., & Desharnais, G. (1992). Using computing in quality team meetings: Initial observations from the IRS-Minnesota Project. *Journal of Management Information Systems, 8,* 7-26.

DiSanza, J. R., & Bullis, C. (1999). "Everybody identifies with Smokey the Bear": Employee responses to newsletter identification inducements at the U.S. Forest Service. *Management Communication Quarterly, 12,* 347-399.

Donnellon, A. (1986). Language and communication in organizations: Bridging cognition and behavior. In H. P. Sims, Jr. & D. A. Gioia (Eds.), *The thinking organization: Dynamics of organizational social cognition* (pp. 136-164). San Francisco: Jossey-Bass.

Donnellon, A. (1994). Team work: Linguistic models of negotiating differences. In R. J. Lewicki, B. H. Sheppard, & R. Bies (Eds.), *Research on negotiation in organizations* (Vol. 4, pp. 71-123). Greenwich, CT: JAI.

Donnellon, A. (1996). *Team talk: The power of language in team dynamics.* Boston: Harvard Business School Press.

Donnellon, A., Gray, B., & Bougon, M. G. (1986). Communication, meaning, and organized action. *Administrative Science Quarterly, 31,* 43-55.

Donohue, W. A. (1981a). Analyzing negotiation tactics: Development of a negotiation interact system. *Human Communication Research, 7,* 273-287.

Donohue, W. A. (1981b). Development of a model of rule use in negotiation interaction. *Communication Monographs, 48,* 106-120.

Donohue, W. A., & Diez, M. E. (1985). Directive use in negotiation interaction. *Communication Monographs, 52,* 305-318.

Donohue, W. A., Diez, M. E., & Hamilton, M. (1984). Coding naturalistic negotiation interaction. *Human Communication Research, 10,* 403-425.

Donohue, W. A., & Roberto, A. J. (1993). Relational development as negotiated order in hostage negotiation. *Human Communication Research, 20,* 175-198.

Dougherty, D. (1992). *Crisis communications: What every executive needs to know.* New York: Walker.

Drake, B. H., & Moberg, D. J. (1986). Communicating influence attempts in dyads: Linguistic sedatives and palliatives. *Administrative Science Quarterly, 11,* 567-584.

Drew, P., & Heritage, J. (Eds.). (1992). *Talk at work.* Cambridge, UK: Cambridge University Press.

Dubois, B. L., & Crouch, I. (1975). The question of tag questions in women's speech. *Language in Society, 4,* 289-294.

Duncan, W. J. (1983). The superiority theory of humor at work: Joking relationships as indicators of formal and informal status patterns in small, task-oriented groups. *Small Group Behavior, 16,* 556-564.

Duncan, W. J., & Feisal, J. P. (1989). No laughing matter: Patterns of humor in the work place. *Organizational Dynamics, 17,* 18-30.

Dunford, R., & Palmer, I. (1996). Metaphors in popular management discourse: The case of corporate restructuring. In D. Grant & C. Oswick (Eds.), *Metaphor and organizations* (pp. 95-109). Thousand Oaks, CA: Sage.

Dunn, S. (1990). Root metaphor in the old and new industrial relations. *British Journal of Industrial Relations, 28,* 1-31.

Eco, U. (1976). *A theory of semiotics.* Bloomington: University of Indiana Press.

Edelsky, C. (1981). Who's got the floor? *Language in Society, 10,* 383-421.

Edwards, D., & Middleton, D. (1986). Joint remembering: Constructing an account of shared experience through conversational discourse. *Discourse Processes, 9,* 423-459.

Eisenberg, E. M. (1984). Ambiguity as strategy in organizational communication. *Communication Monographs, 51,* 227-242.

Eisenberg, E. M., & Goodall, H. L., Jr. (1993). *Organizational communication: Balancing creativity and constraint.* New York: St. Martin's.

Eisenberg, E. M., & Riley, P. (1988). Organizational symbols and sense-making. In G. M. Goldhaber & G. A. Barnett (Eds.), *Handbook of organizational communication* (pp. 131-150). Norwood, NJ: Ablex.

Ellis, D. G. (1979). Relational control in two group systems. *Communication Monographs, 46,* 156-166.

Engeström, Y. (1987). *Learning by expanding: An activity-theoretical approach to developmental research.* Helsinki: Orienta-Konsultit Oy.

Engeström, Y. (1990). *Learning, working and imagining.* Helsinki: Orienta-Konsultit Oy.

Evered, R. (1983). The language of organizations: The case of the Navy. In L. R. Pondy, P. J. Frost, G. Morgan, & T. C. Dandridge (Eds.), *Organizational symbolism* (pp. 125-143). Greenwich, CT: JAI.

Evered, R., & Tannenbaum, R. (1992). A dialog on dialog. *Journal of Management Inquiry, 1,* 43-55.

Ewald, H. R., & Strine, D. (1983). Speech act theory and business communication conventions. *Journal of Business Communication, 20*(3), 13-25.

Fairclough, N. (1989). *Language and power.* New York: Longman.

Fairclough, N. (1993). Critical discourse analysis and the marketization of public discourse: The universities. *Discourse & Society, 4,* 133-168.

Fairclough, N., & Wodak, R. (1997). Critical discourse analysis. In T. A. van Dijk (Ed.), *Discourse as social interaction* (pp. 258-284). London: Sage.

Fairhurst, G. T. (1993a). Echoes of the vision: When the rest of the organization talks total quality. *Management Communication Quarterly, 6,* 331-371.

Fairhurst, G. T. (1993b). The leader-member exchange patterns of women leaders in industry: A discourse analysis. *Communication Monographs, 60,* 321-351.

Fairhurst, G. T., & Chandler, T. A. (1989). Social structure in leader-member interaction. *Communication Monographs, 56,* 215-239.

Fairhurst, G. T., Green, S. G., & Courtright, J. A. (1994). Inertial forces and the implementation of a socio-technical systems approach: A communication study. *Organization Science, 6,* 168-185.

Fairhurst, G. T., & Putnam, L. L. (1998). Reflections on the organization-communication equivalency question: The contributions of James Taylor and his colleagues. *Communication Review, 31,* 1-19.

Fairhurst, G. T., Rogers, L. E., & Sarr, R. A. (1987). Manager-subordinate control patterns and judgments about the relationship. In M. McLaughlin (Ed.), *Communication yearbook 10* (pp. 395-415). Newbury Park, CA: Sage.

Fairhurst, G. T., & Sarr, R. A. (1996). *The art of framing: Managing the language of leadership.* San Francisco: Jossey-Bass.

Fairhurst, G. T., & Wendt, R. F. (1993). The gap in total quality: A commentary. *Management Communication Quarterly, 6,* 441-451.

Farrell, M. P., Schmidt, M. H., & Heinemann, G. D. (1988). Organizational environments of health care teams: Impact on team development and implications for consultation. *International Journal of Small Group Research, 4,* 31-54.

Filby, I., & Willmott, H. (1988). Ideologies and contradictions in a public relations department: The seduction and impotence of a living myth. *Organization Studies, 9,* 335-349.

Fine, G. (1984). Negotiated orders and organizational cultures. *Annual Review of Sociology, 10,* 239-262.

Fiol, C. M. (1989). A semiotic analysis of corporate language: Organizational boundaries and joint venturing. *Administrative Science Quarterly, 34,* 277-303.

Firth, A. (1994). "Accounts" in negotiation discourse: A single-case analysis. *Journal of Pragmatics, 23,* 199-226.

Firth, A. (Ed.). (1995). *The discourse of negotiation: Studies of language in the workplace.* Oxford, UK: Pergamon.

Fisher, B. A. (1978). *Perspective on human communication.* New York: Macmillan.

Fisher, S., & Groce, S. B. (1990). Accounting practices in medical interviews. *Language in Society, 19,* 225-250.

Fisher, S., & Todd, D. D. (Eds.). (1983). *The social organization of doctor-patient communication.* Washington, DC: Center for Applied Linguistics.

Fletcher, C. (1990). *What cops know.* New York: Villard.

Fletcher, C. (1991). The police war story and the narrative of inequality. *Discourse & Society, 2,* 297-331.

Fletcher, J. K. (1999). *Disappearing acts: Gender, power, and relational practice at work.* Cambridge, MA: MIT Press.

Ford, J. D., & Ford, L. W. (1995). The role of conversations in producing intentional change in organizations. *Academy of Management Review, 20,* 541-570.

Ford, J. D., & Hegarty, W. H. (1984). Decision makers' beliefs about the causes and effects of structure: An exploratory study. *Academy of Management Journal, 27,* 271-291.

Fortado, B. (1998). Interpreting nicknames: A micropolitical portal. *Journal of Management Studies, 35,* 13-34.

Foucault, M. (1977). *Discipline and punish: The birth of the prison* (A. S. Smith, Trans.). New York: Random House.

Frances, D. W. (1986). Some structure of negotiation talk. *Language in Society, 15,* 53-79.

Gabriel, Y. (1998). Same old story or changing stories? In D. Grant, T. Keenoy, & C. Oswick (Eds.), *Discourse and organizations* (pp. 84-103). London: Sage.

Garrett, D. E., Bradford, J. L., Meyers, R. A., & Becker, J. (1989). Issues management and organizational accounts: An analysis of corporate responses to accusations of unethical business practices. *Journal of Business Ethics, 8,* 507-520.

Geist, P., & Chandler, T. (1984). Account analysis of influence in group decision-making. *Communication Monographs, 51,* 67-78.

Gephart, R. P., Jr. (1993). The textual approach: Risk and blame in disaster sense making. *Academy of Management Journal, 36,* 1465-1514.

Giacalone, R. A. (1988). The effect of administrative accounts and gender on the perception of leadership. *Group and Organization Studies, 13,* 195-207.

Giddens, A. (1979). *Central problems in social theory.* Berkeley: University of California Press.

Giddens, A. (1984). *The constitution of society.* Berkeley: University of California Press.

Gilbert, G. N., & Mulkay, M. (1984). *Opening Pandora's box: An analysis of scientists' discourse.* Cambridge, UK: Cambridge University Press.

Gioia, D. A. (1986). The state of the art in organizational social cognition. In H. P. Sims, Jr. & D. A. Gioia (Eds.), *The thinking organization* (pp. 336-356). San Francisco: Jossey-Bass.

Gioia, D. A., Donnellon, A., & Sims, H. P., Jr. (1989). Communication and cognition in appraisal: A tale of two paradigms. *Organization Studies, 10,* 503-530.

Gioia, D. A., & Poole, P. P. (1984). Scripts in organizational behavior. *Academy of Management Review, 9,* 449-459.

Gioia, D. A., & Sims, H. P., Jr. (1986). Cognition-behavior connections: Attribution and verbal behavior in leader-subordinate interactions. *Organizational Behavior and Human Decision Processes, 37,* 197-229.

Glauser, M. J., & Tullar, W. L. (1985). Citizen satisfaction with police officer-citizen interaction: Implications for changing the role of police organizations. *Journal of Applied Psychology, 70,* 514-527.

Goffman, E. (1974). *Frame analysis.* New York: Harper-Colophon.

Gorden, W. I., & Nevins, R. J. (1987). The language and rhetoric of quality: Made in the U.S.A. *Journal of Applied Communication Research, 15,* 19-34.

Gordon, D. P. (1983). Hospital slang for patients: Crocks, gomers, gorks, and others. *Language in Society, 12,* 173-185.

Grant, D., Keenoy, T., & Oswick, C. (1998). Organizational discourse: Of diversity, dichotomy and multi-disciplinarity. In D. Grant, T. Keenoy, & C. Oswick (Eds.), *Discourse and organization* (pp. 1-13). London: Sage.

Grant, D., & Oswick, C. (1996a). Introduction: Getting the measure of metaphors. In D. Grant & C. Oswick (Eds.), *Metaphor and organizations* (pp. 1-20). Thousand Oaks, CA: Sage.

Grant, D., & Oswick, C. (Eds.). (1996b). *Metaphor and organizations.* Thousand Oaks, CA: Sage.

Gray, B. (1997). Framing and reframing of intractable environmental disputes. In R. Lewicki, B. Sheppard, & B. Bies (Eds.), *Research on negotiation in organizations* (pp. 95-112). Greenwich, CT: JAI.

Greatbatch, D., & Dingwall, R. (1994). The interactive construction of interventions by divorce mediators. In J. P. Folger & T. S. Jones (Eds.), *New directions in mediation* (pp. 84-109). Thousand Oaks, CA: Sage.

Greenberg, J. (1991). Using explanations to manage impressions of performance appraisal fairness. *Employee Responsibilities and Rights Journal, 4,* 51-60.

Gregory, K. L. (1983). Native-view paradigms: Multiple cultures and culture conflicts in organizations. *Administrative Science Quarterly, 28,* 359-376.

Greimas, A. (1987). *On meaning: Selected writings in semiotic theory* (P. J. Perron & F. J. Collins, Trans.). Minneapolis: University of Minnesota Press.

Groleau, C., & Cooren, F. (1998). A socio-semiotic approach to computerization: Bridging the gap between ethnographers and system analysts. *Communication Review, 3*(1-2), 125-164.

Gronn, P. C. (1983). Talk as the work: The accomplishment of school administration. *Administrative Science Quarterly, 28,* 1-21.

Gummer, B. (1984). All we ever do is talk: Administrative talk as advice, influence and control. *Administration in Social Work, 8,* 113-123.

Gumperz, J. (1992). Contextualization and understanding. In A. Duranti & C. Goodwin (Eds.), *Rethinking context: Language as an interactive phenomenon* (pp. 229-252). Cambridge, UK: Cambridge University Press.

Gumperz, J., & Herasimchuk, E. (1975). The conversational analysis of social meaning: A study of classroom interaction. In B. Blount & M. M. Sanches (Eds.), *Sociocultural dimensions of language use* (pp. 81-115). New York: Academic Press.

Hall, R. I. (1984). The natural logic of management policy making: Its implications for the survival of an organization. *Management Science, 30,* 905-927.

Hamilton, P. M. (1997). Rhetorical discourse of local pay. *Organization, 4,* 229-254.

Harris, L., & Cronen, V. E. (1979). A rules-based model for the analysis and evaluation of organizational communication. *Communication Quarterly, 27,* 12-18.

Haslett, B. J. (1987). *Communication: Strategic action in context.* Hillsdale, NJ: Lawrence Erlbaum.

Hassan, I. (1985). The culture of postmodernism. *Theory, Culture and Society, 2*(3), 119-132.

Hatch, M. J. (1997). Irony and the social construction of contradiction in the humor of a management team. *Organization Science, 8,* 275-288.

Hatch, M. J., & Ehrlich, S. B. (1993). Spontaneous humor as an indicator of paradox and ambiguity in organizations. *Organization Studies, 14,* 505-526.

Hawes, L. C. (1976). How writing is used in talk: A study of communicative logic-in-use. *Quarterly Journal of Speech, 62,* 350-360.

Hawes, L. C. (1999). The dialogics of conversation: Power, control, and vulnerability. *Communication Theory, 9,* 229-264.

Hearit, K. M. (1994). Apologies and public relations crises at Chrysler, Toshiba, and Volvo. *Public Relations Review, 20,* 113-125.

Helmer, J. (1993). Storytelling in the creation and maintenance of organizational tension and stratification. *Southern Communication Journal, 59,* 34-44.

Hewitt, J. P., & Stokes, R. (1975). Aligning actions. *American Sociological Review, 41,* 838-849.

Hirsch, P. M. (1986). From ambushes to golden parachutes: Corporate takeovers as an instance of cultural framing and institutional integration. *American Journal of Sociology, 91,* 800-837.

Hirsch, P. M., & Andrews, J. A. Y. (1983). Ambushes, shootouts, and knights of the roundtable: The language of corporate takeovers. In L. R. Pondy, P. J. Frost, G. Morgan, & T. C. Dandridge (Eds.), *Organizational symbolism* (pp. 145-155). Greenwich, CT: JAI.

Holmer-Nadesan, M. (1996). Organizational identity and space of action. *Organization Studies, 17,* 49-81.

Holmes, J. (1984). Hedging your bets and sitting on the fence. *Te Reo, 27,* 47-62.

Holmes, M. E. (1997). Optimal matching analysis of negotiation phase sequences in simulated and authentic hostage negotiations. *Communication Reports, 10,* 1-9.

Holmes, M. E., & Sykes, R. E. (1993). A test of the fit of Gulliver's phase model to hostage negotiations. *Communication Studies, 44,* 38-55.

Holt, G. R. (1989). Talk about acting and constraint in stories about organizations. *Western Journal of Speech Communications, 53,* 374-397.

Höpfl, H., & Maddrell, J. (1996). Can you resist a dream? Evangelical metaphors and the appropriation of emotion. In D. Grant & C. Oswick (Eds.), *Metaphor and organizations* (pp. 200-212). Thousand Oaks, CA: Sage.

Hopmann, P. T., & Walcott, C. (1976). The impact of international conflict and debate on bargaining in arms control negotiations: An experimental analysis. *International Interactions, 2,* 189-206.

Howard, L. A., & Geist, P. (1995). Ideological positioning in organizational change: The dialectic of control in a merging organization. *Communication Monographs, 62,* 110-131.

Huff, A. S. (1983). A rhetorical examination of strategic change. In L. R. Pondy, P. J. Frost, G. Morgan, & T. C. Dandridge (Eds.), *Organizational symbolism* (pp. 167-183). Greenwich, CT: JAI.

Huff, A. S. (1988). Politics and argument as a means of coping with ambiguity and change. In L. R. Pondy, R. J. Boland, & H. Thomas (Eds.), *Managing ambiguity and change* (pp. 79-90). New York: John Wiley.

Huff, A. S. (Ed.). (1990). *Mapping strategic thought.* Chichester, UK: Wiley.

Huspek, M., & Kendall, K. (1991). On withholding political voice: An analysis of the political vocabulary of a "nonpolitical" speech community. *Quarterly Journal of Speech, 77,* 1-19.

Huyssen, A. (1986). *After the great divide.* Bloomington: Indiana University Press.

Hymes, D. (1972). Models for the interaction of language in social life. In J. J. Gumperz & D. Hymes (Eds.), *Directions in sociolinguistics: The ethnography of communication* (pp. 35-71). New York: Holt, Rinehart & Winston.

Ice, R. (1991). Corporate publics and rhetorical strategies: The case of Union Carbide's Bhopal crisis. *Management Communication Quarterly, 4*, 341-362.

Irons, L. R. (1998). Organizational and technical communication: Terminological ambiguity in representing work. *Management Communication Quarterly, 12*, 42-71.

Isaacs, W. (1999). *Dialogue and the art of thinking together.* New York: Doubleday.

Isaacs, W. N. (1993). Taking flight: Dialogue, collective thinking, and organizational learning. *Organizational Dynamics, 22*(2), 24-39.

James, D., & Clarke, S. (1993). Women, men and interruptions: A critical review. In D. Tannen (Ed.), *Gender and conversational interaction* (pp. 231-280). Oxford, UK: Oxford University Press.

Jang, H., & Barnett, G. A. (1994). Cultural differences in organizational communication: A semantic network analysis. *Bulletin de Methodologie Sociologique, 44*, 31-59.

Jefferson, G. (1978). Sequential aspects of story-telling in conversation. In J. Schenkein (Ed.), *Studies in the organization of conversational interaction* (pp. 219-248). New York: Academic Press.

Jesuino, J. C. (1985). Assessment of leaders by SYMLOG. *International Journal of Small Group Research, 1*, 887-888.

Johnson, B. (1977). *Communication: The process of organizing.* Boston: Allyn & Bacon.

Jones, D. (1992). Postmodern perspectives on organisational communication. *Australian Journal of Communication, 19*, 30-37.

Jones, K. (1992). A question of context: Directive use at a Morris team meeting. *Language in Society, 21*, 427-445.

Kaha, C. W. (1989). Memory as conversation. *Communication, 11*, 115-122.

Kaufer, D. S., & Carley, K. M. (1993). *Communication at a distance: The influence of print on sociocultural organization and change.* Hillsdale, NJ: Lawrence Erlbaum.

Keenoy, T. (1990). Human resource management: Rhetoric, reality and contradiction. *International Journal of Human Resource Management, 1*(3), 363-384.

Keenoy, T., Oswick, C., & Grant, D. (1997). Organizational discourses: Text and context. *Organization, 4*, 147-157.

Keller-Cohen, D. (1987). Literate practices in a modern credit union. *Language in Society, 16*, 7-23.

Kennedy, C. W., & Camden, C. T. (1983). A new look at interruptions. *Western Journal of Speech Communications, 47*, 45-58.

Keough, C. M. (1987). The nature and function of argument in organizational bargaining research. *Southern Speech Communication Journal, 53*, 1-17.

Keough, C. M., & Lake, R. A. (1993). Values as structuring properties of contract negotiation. In C. Conrad (Ed.), *Ethical nexus* (pp. 171-189). Norwood, NJ: Ablex.

Kerr, S. (1975). On the folly of rewarding A, while hoping for B. *Academy of Management Journal, 47*, 469-483.

Kets de Vries, M. F. R., & Miller, D. (1987). Interpreting organizational texts. *Journal of Management Studies, 24*(3), 233-247.

Keyton, J., & Wall, V. D. (1989). SYMLOG: Theory and method for measuring group and organizational communication. *Management Communication Quarterly, 2*, 544-567.

Knights, D., & Willmott, H. (1987). Organizational culture as management strategy: A critique and illustration from the financial service industry. *International Studies of Management and Organization, 17*, 40-63.

Komaki, J. L. (1986). Toward effective supervision: An operant analysis and comparison of managers at work. *Journal of Applied Psychology, 71*, 270-278.

Komaki, J. L. (1998). *Leadership from an operant perspective.* London: Routledge.

Komaki, J. L., & Citera, M. (1990). Beyond effective supervision: Identifying key interactions between superior and subordinate. *Leadership Quarterly, 1*, 91-106.

Komaki, J. L., Desselles, M. L., & Bowman, E. D. (1989). Definitely not a breeze: Extending an operant model of effective supervision to teams. *Journal of Applied Psychology, 74*, 522-529.

Komaki, J. L., Zlotnick, S., & Jensen, M. (1986). Development of an operant-based taxonomy and observational index of supervisory behavior. *Journal of Applied Psychology, 71*, 260-269.

Korsch, B. M., & Negrete, V. F. (1972). Doctor-patient communication. *Scientific American, 227*, 66-74.

Krol, T. F. (1991). Women talk about talk at work. *Discourse & Society, 2*, 461-476.

Kristiansen, M., & Bloch-Poulsen, J. (2000). The challenge of the unspoken in organizations: Caring container as a dialogic answer? *Southern Communication Journal, 65*(2-3), 176-190.

Kunda, G. (1992). *Engineering culture: Control and commitment in a high-tech corporation.* Philadelphia: Temple University Press.

Labov, W., & Fanshel, D. (1977). *Therapeutic discourse: Psychotherapy as conversation.* New York: Academic Press.

Lakoff, G., & Johnson, M. (1980). *Metaphors we live by.* Chicago: University of Chicago Press.

Lang, K. (1986). A language theory of discrimination. *Quarterly Journal of Economics, 51*, 363-382.

Latour, B. (1988). *The pasteurization of France.* Cambridge, MA: Harvard University Press.

Latour, B. (1993). *We have never been modern.* Cambridge, MA: Harvard University Press.

Latour, B. (1994). On technical mediation—Philosophy, sociology, and genealogy. *Common Knowledge, 3,* 29-64.

Latour, B. (1996a). *Aramis, or the love for technology.* Cambridge, MA: Harvard University Press.

Latour, B. (1996b). On interobjectivity. *Mind, Culture, and Activity, 3,* 228-245.

Levi, J., & Walker, A. G. (Eds.). (1990). *Language in the judicial process.* New York: Plenum.

Levinson, S. C. (1983). *Pragmatics.* Cambridge, UK: Cambridge University Press.

Linde, C. (1988). The quantitative study of communicative success: Politeness and accidents in aviation discourse. *Language in Society, 17,* 375-399.

Linstead, S. (1985). Jokers wild: The importance of humor and the maintenance of organizational culture. *Sociological Review, 33,* 741-767.

Litvin, D. R. (1997). The discourse of diversity: From biology to management. *Organization, 4,* 187-209.

Locke, E. A. (1968). Toward a theory of task motivation and incentives. *Organizational Behavior and Human Performance, 3,* 179-180.

Lord, R. G., & Kernan, M. C. (1987). Scripts as determinants of purposive behavior in organizations. *Academy of Management Review, 12,* 265-277.

Loseke, D. R. (1989). Creating clients: Social problems work in a shelter for battered women. In J. A. Holstein & G. Miller (Eds.), *Perspectives on social problems* (Vol. 1, pp. 173-193). Greenwich, CT: JAI.

Louis, M. R., & Sutton, R. I. (1991). Shifting cognitive gears: From habits of mind to active thinking. *Human Relations, 44,* 55-76.

Lukaszewski, J. E., & Gmeiner, J. (1993). The Exxon Valdez paradox. In J. A. Gottschalk (Ed.), *Crisis response: Inside stories on managing image under stress* (pp. 185-213). Detroit, MI: Visible Ink.

Mangrum, F. G., & Wieder, D. L. (1997, November). *Ad hoc gatherings for informal problem solving: Ordinary conversation with co-workers as labor for the company.* Paper presented at the annual conference of the National Communication Association, Chicago.

Manning, P. K. (1977). Rules in organizational context: Narcotics law enforcement in two settings. *Sociological Quarterly, 18,* 44-61.

Manning, P. K. (1979). Metaphors of the field: Varieties of organizational discourse. *Administrative Science Quarterly, 24,* 660-671.

Manning, P. K. (1982a). Organisational work: Enstructuration of the environment. *British Journal of Sociology, 2,* 118-139.

Manning, P. K. (1982b). Producing drama: Symbolic communication and the police. *Symbolic Interaction, 5,* 223-241.

Manning, P. K. (1986). Signwork. *Human Relations, 39,* 283-308.

Manning, P. K. (1988). *Symbolic communication: Signifying calls and the police response.* Cambridge, MA: MIT Press.

Markham, A. (1996). Designing discourse: A critical analysis of strategic ambiguity and workplace control. *Management Communication Quarterly, 9,* 389-421.

Marshak, R. J. (1993). Managing the metaphors of change. *Organizational Dynamics, 22,* 44-56.

Marshak, R. J. (1996). Metaphors, metaphoric fields and organizational change. In D. Grant & C. Oswick (Eds.), *Metaphor and organizations* (pp. 147-165). Thousand Oaks, CA: Sage.

Marshak, R. J. (1998). A discourse on discourse: Redeeming the meaning of talk. In D. Grant, T. Keenoy, & C. Oswick (Eds.), *Discourse and organization* (pp. 15-30). London: Sage.

Martin, J. (1990). Deconstructing organizational taboos: The suppression of gender conflicts in organizations. *Organization Science, 1,* 339-359.

Martin, J. (1992). *Cultures in organizations: Three perspectives.* New York: Oxford University Press.

Mauws, M. K., & Phillips, N. (1995). Understanding language games. *Organization Science, 6,* 322-334.

Mauws, M. K., & Phillips, N. (1999, May). *Beyond language games: Studying organizational change from a discourse analytic perspective.* Paper presented at the International Conference on Language in Organizational Change: What Makes a Difference, Ohio State University, Columbus.

McLaughlin, M. L. (1984). *How talk is organized.* Beverly Hills, CA: Sage.

Mead, G. (1934). *Mind, self, and society.* Chicago: University of Chicago Press.

Mehan, H. (1979). *Learning lessons: Social organization in the classroom.* Cambridge, MA: Harvard University Press.

Mehan, H. (1983). The role of language and the language of role in institutional decision making. *Language in Society, 12,* 187-211.

Mehan, H. (1987). Language and power in organizational process. *Discourse Processes, 10,* 291-301.

McNamee, S., Gergen, K. J., & Associates. (1999). *Relational responsibility: Resources for sustainable dialogue.* Thousand Oaks, CA: Sage.

Mellinger, W. M. (1994). Negotiated orders: The negotiation of directives in paramedic-nurse interaction. *Symbolic Interaction, 17,* 165-185.

Meyer, J. (1996). Seeking organizational unity: Building bridges in response to mystery. *Southern Communication Journal, 61,* 210-219.

Meyer, J. C. (1997). Humor in member narratives: Uniting and dividing at work. *Western Journal of Communication, 61,* 188-208.

Meyers, R. A., & Garrett, D. E. (1993). Contradictions, values, and organizational argument. In C. Conrad (Ed.), *Ethical nexus* (pp. 149-170). Norwood, NJ: Ablex.

Meyerson, D. E. (1991). Acknowledging and uncovering ambiguities in cultures. In P. J. Frost, L. F. Moore, M. R. Louis, C. C. Lundberg, & J. Martin (Eds.), *Reframing organizational culture* (pp. 254-270). Newbury Park, CA: Sage.

Middleton, D., & Edwards, D. (1990). Conversational remembering: A social psychological approach. In D. Middleton & D. Edwards (Eds.), *Collective remembering*. London: Sage.

Miller, P., & O'Leary, T. (1987). Accounting and the construction of the governable person. *Accounting, Organizations and Society, 12,* 235-265.

Mishler, E. (1984). *The discourse of medicine: Dialectics of medical interviews.* Norwood, NJ: Ablex.

Moch, M. K., & Fields, W. C. (1985). Developing a content analysis for interpreting language use in organizations. In S. B. Bacharach (Ed.), *Research in the sociology of organizations* (Vol. 4, pp. 81-126). Greenwich, CT: JAI.

Molotch, H. L., & Boden, D. (1985). Talking social structure: Discourse, domination, and the Watergate hearings. *American Sociological Review, 50,* 273-288.

Monge, P. R., & Eisenberg, E. M. (1987). Emergent communication networks. In F. M. Jablin, L. L. Putnam, K. H. Roberts, & L. W. Porter (Eds.), *Handbook of organizational communication: An interdisciplinary perspective* (pp. 304-342). Newbury Park, CA: Sage.

Morgan, G. (1980). Paradigms, metaphors, and puzzle solving in organization theory. *Administrative Science Quarterly, 24,* 605-622.

Morgan, G. (1997). *Images of organization* (2nd ed.). Thousand Oaks, CA: Sage.

Morgan, G., & Ramirez, R. (1984). Action learning: A holographic metaphor for guiding social change. *Human Relations, 37,* 1-28.

Morand, D. A. (1996). What's in a name? An exploration of the social dynamics of forms of address in organization. *Management Communication Quarterly, 9,* 422-451.

Morrill, C. (1991). Conflict management, honor and organizational change. *American Journal of Sociology, 97,* 585-621.

Morrill, C. (1995). *The executive way: Conflict management in corporations.* Chicago: University of Chicago Press.

Morris, G. H. (1988). Accounts in selection interviews. *Journal of Applied Communication Research, 15,* 82-98.

Morris, G. H., & Coursey, M. L. (1989). Negotiating the meaning of employees' conduct: How managers evaluate employees' accounts. *Southern Communication Journal, 54,* 185-205.

Morris, G. H., Gaveras, S. C., Baker, W. L., & Coursey, M. L. (1990). Aligning actions at work: How managers confront problems of employee performance. *Management Communication Quarterly, 3,* 303-333.

Mumby, D. K. (1987). The political function of narrative in organizations. *Communication Monographs, 54,* 113-127.

Mumby, D. K. (1988). *Communication and power in organizations: Discourse, ideology and domination.* Norwood, NJ: Ablex.

Mumby, D. K., & Clair, R. P. (1997). Organizational discourse. In T. A. van Dijk (Ed.), *Discourse as social interaction* (Vol. 2, pp. 181-205). London: Sage.

Mumby, D. K., & Stohl, C. (1991). Power and discourse in organizational studies: Absence and the dialectic of control. *Discourse & Society, 2,* 313-332.

Munro, R. (1995). Management by ambiguity: An archeology of the social in the absence of management accounting. *Critical Perspectives on Accounting, 6,* 433-482.

Murphy, A. G. (1998). Hidden transcripts of flight attendant resistance. *Management Communication Quarterly, 11,* 499-535.

Murray, D. E. (1987). Requests at work: Negotiating the conditions for conversation. *Management Communication Quarterly, 1,* 58-83.

Neale, M. A., & Bazerman, M. H. (1991). *Cognition and rationality in negotiation.* New York: Free Press.

Neu, J. (1988). Conversation structure: An explanation of bargaining behaviors in negotiations. *Management Communication Quarterly, 2,* 23-45.

Nöth, W. (1988). The language of commodities: Groundwork for a semiotics of consumer goods. *International Journal of Research in Marketing, 4,* 173-186.

Oakes, L. S., Townley, B., & Cooper, D. J. (1998). Business planning as pedagogy: Language and control in a changing institutional field. *Administrative Science Quarterly, 43,* 257-292.

O'Connor, E. S. (1994, August). *A modest proposal: The contribution of literacy theory and methods to organizational studies.* Paper presented at the Academy of Management meeting, Dallas, TX.

O'Connor, E. S. (1995). Paradoxes of participation: Textual analysis and organizational change. *Organization Studies, 16,* 769-803.

O'Connor, E. S. (1997). Telling decisions: The role of narrative in organizational decision making. In Z. Shapira (Ed.), *Organizational decision making* (pp. 304-323). New York: Cambridge University Press.

O'Connor, K. M., & Adams, A. A. (1999). What novices think about negotiation: A content analysis of scripts. *Negotiation Journal, 15*(2), 135-148.

O'Donnell, K. (1990). Difference and dominance: How labor and management talk conflict. In A. D. Grimshaw (Ed.), *Conflict talk* (pp. 210-240). Cambridge, UK: Cambridge University Press.

Olekalns, M., Smith, P. L., & Walsh, T. (1996). The process of negotiating: Strategies, timing, and outcomes. *Organizational Behavior and Human Decision Processes, 68,* 68-77.

Orlikowski, W. J., & Gash, D. C. (1994). Technological frames: Making sense of information technology in organizations. *ACM Transactions on Information Systems, 12,* 174-207.

Orr, J. E. (1990). Sharing knowledge, celebrating identity: Community memory in a service culture. In D. Middleton & D. Edwards (Eds.), *Collective remembering* (pp. 169-189). London: Sage.

Oswick, C., & Grant, D. (1996a). The organization of metaphors and the metaphors of organization: Where are we and where do we go from here? In D. Grant & C. Oswick (Eds.), *Metaphor and organizations* (pp. 213-226). Thousand Oaks, CA: Sage.

Oswick, C., & Grant, D. (Eds.). (1996b). *Organization development: Metaphorical explorations.* London: Pitman.

Ouchi, W. G., & Wilkins, A. L. (1985). Organizational culture. *Annual Review of Sociology, 11,* 457-483.

Pacanowsky, M. E., & O'Donnell-Trujillo, N. (1983). Organizational communication as cultural performance. *Communication Monographs, 50,* 126-147.

Peirce, C. S. (1931). *Collected papers.* Cambridge, MA: Harvard University Press.

Pettigrew, A. (1979). On studying organizational cultures. *Administrative Science Quarterly, 24,* 570-581.

Philipsen, G. (1975). Speaking "like a man" in Teamsterville: Cultural patterns of role-enactment in urban neighborhoods. *Quarterly Journal of Speech, 62,* 13-22.

Philipsen, G. (1992). *Speaking culturally: Explorations in social communication.* New York: State University of New York Press.

Phillips, N., & Hardy, C. (1997). Managing multiple identities: Discourse, legitimacy and resources in the UK refugee system. *Organization, 4,* 159-185.

Pinder, C. C., & Bourgeois, V. W. (1982). Controlling tropes in administrative science. *Administrative Science Quarterly, 27,* 641-652.

Pinsdorf, M. K. (1987). *Communicating when your company is under siege: Surviving public crisis.* Lexington, MA: D. C. Heath.

Pogner, K. (1999). Discourse community, culture and interaction: On writing by consulting engineers. In F. Bargiela-Chiappini & C. Nickerson (Eds.), *Writing business: Genres, media and discourse* (pp. 101-127). New York: Pearson Education Limited.

Pogrebin, M. R., & Poole, E. D. (1988). Humor in the briefing room: A study of the strategic uses of humor among police. *Journal of Contemporary Ethnography, 17,* 183-210.

Pomerantz, A., & Fehr, B. J. (1997). Conversation analysis: An approach to the study of social action as sense making practices. In T. A. van Dijk (Ed.), *Discourse as social interaction* (pp. 64-91). London: Sage.

Pomerantz, A., Fehr, B. J., & Ende, J. (1997). When supervising physicians see patients. *Human Communication Research, 23,* 589-615.

Pondy, L. R. (1978). Leadership is a language game. In M. W. McCall, Jr. & M. M. Lombardo (Eds.), *Leadership: Where else can we go?* (pp. 88-99). Durham, NC: Duke University Press.

Pondy, L. R. (1983). The role of metaphors and myths in organizations and in the facilitation of change. In L. R. Pondy, P. J. Frost, G. Morgan, & T. D. Dandridge (Eds.), *Organizational symbolism* (pp. 157-166). Greenwich, CT: JAI.

Poole, M. S., & DeSanctis, G. (1992). Microlevel structuration in computer-supported group decision-making. *Human Communication Research, 91,* 5-49.

Poole, M. S., DeSanctis, G., Kirsch, L., & Jackson, M. (1995). Group decision support systems as facilitators of quality team efforts. In L. R. Frey (Ed.), *Innovations in group facilitation techniques: Case studies of applications in naturalistic settings* (pp. 299-320). Creskill, NJ: Hampton.

Poole, M. S., Folger, J. P., & Hewes, D. (1987). Analyzing interpersonal interaction. In M. E. Roloff & G. R. Miller (Eds.), *Interpersonal processes: New directions in communication research* (pp. 220-256). Newbury Park, CA: Sage.

Poole, M. S., Holmes, M. E., & DeSanctis, G. (1991). Conflict management in a computer-supported meeting environment. *Management Science, 37,* 926-953.

Poole, M. S., Seibold, D. R., & McPhee, R. D. (1985). Group decision-making as a structurational process. *Quarterly Journal of Speech, 71,* 74-102.

Poole, M. S., & Van de Ven, A. H. (1989). Using paradox to build management and organization theories. *Academy of Management Review, 14,* 562-578.

Prasad, P. (1995). Working with the "smart" machine: Computerization and the discourse of anthropomorphism in organizations. *Studies in Cultures, Organizations and Societies, 1,* 253-265.

Preisler, B. (1986). *Linguistic sex roles in conversation.* Berlin: Mouton de Gruyter.

Pringle, R. (1988). *Secretaries talk: Sexuality, power, and work.* London: Verso.

Putnam, L. L. (1986). Contradictions and paradoxes in organizations. In L. Thayer (Ed.), *Organization–communication: Emerging perspectives I* (pp. 151-167). Norwood, NJ: Ablex.

Putnam, L. L. (1990a, August). *Language and meaning: Discourse approaches to the study of organizations.* Paper presented at the Academy of Management meeting, San Francisco.

Putnam, L. L. (1990b). Reframing integrative and distributive bargaining: A process perspective. In B. H. Sheppard, M. H. Bazerman, & R. J. Lewicki (Eds.), *Research on negotiation in organizations* (pp. 3-30). Greenwich, CT: JAI.

Putnam, L. L. (1994, August). *Language and meaning in organizations: A facilitator or a barrier?* Paper presented at the Academy of Management meeting, Dallas, TX.

Putnam, L. L. (1995). Formal negotiations: The productive side of organizational conflict. In A. M. Nicotera (Ed.), *Conflict and organizations: Communication processes* (pp. 183-200). Albany: State University of New York Press.

Putnam, L. L., & Geist, P. (1985). Argument in bargaining: An analysis of the reasoning process. *Southern Speech Communication Journal, 50,* 225-245.

Putnam, L. L., & Holmer, M. (1992). Framing, reframing, and issue development. In L. L. Putnam & M. E. Roloff (Eds.), *Communication and negotiation* (pp. 128-155). Newbury Park, CA: Sage.

Putnam, L. L., & Jones, T. S. (1982). Reciprocity in negotiations: An analysis of bargaining interaction. *Communication Monographs, 49,* 171-191.

Putnam, L. L., Phillips, N., & Chapman, P. (1996). Metaphors of communication and organization. In S. R. Clegg, C. Hardy, & W. R. Nord (Eds.), *Handbook of organization studies* (pp. 375-408). London: Sage.

Putnam, L. L., & Wilson, S. R. (1989). Argumentation and bargaining strategies as discriminators of integrative outcomes. In M. A. Rahim (Ed.), *Managing conflict: An interdisciplinary approach* (pp. 121-141). New York: Praeger.

Putnam, L. L., Wilson, S. R., & Turner, D. B. (1990). The evolution of policy arguments in teachers' negotiations. *Argumentation, 4,* 129-152.

Putnam, L. L., Wilson, S. R., Waltman, M. S., & Turner, D. (1986). The evolution of case arguments in teachers' bargaining. *Journal of the American Forensic Association, 23,* 63-81.

Ragan, S. L. (1983). A conversational analysis of alignment talk in job interviews. In R. Bostrum (Ed.), *Communication yearbook 7* (pp. 502-516). Beverly Hills, CA: Sage.

Ragan, S. L., & Hopper, R. (1981). Alignment talk in the job interview. *Journal of Applied Communication Research, 9,* 85-103.

Rice, R. E., & Danowski, J. A. (1993). Is it really just like a fancy answering machine? Comparing semantic networks of different types of voice mail users. *Journal of Business Communication, 30,* 369-397.

Riley, P. (1983). A structurationist account of political cultures. *Administrative Science Quarterly, 28,* 414-437.

Robichaud, D. (1998). Textualization and organizing: Illustrations from a public discussion process. *Communication Review, 3*(1-2), 103-124.

Rogan, R. G., & Hammer, M. R. (1994). Crisis negotiations: A preliminary investigation of facework in naturalistic conflict discourse. *Journal of Applied Communication Research, 22,* 216-231.

Rogers, L. E., & Farace, R. V. (1975). Relational communication analysis: New measurement procedures. *Human Communication Research, 1,* 222-239.

Roloff, M. E., Tutzauer, F. E., & Dailey, W. O. (1989). The role of argumentation in distributive and integrative bargaining contexts: Seeking relative advantage but at what cost? In M. A. Rahim (Ed.), *Managing conflict: An interdisciplinary approach* (pp. 109-119). New York: Praeger.

Roos, L. L., & Hall, R. I. (1980). Influence diagrams and organizational power. *Administrative Science Quarterly, 25,* 57-71.

Rosen, M. (1985). Breakfast at Spiro's: Dramaturgy and dominance. *Journal of Management, 11,* 31-48.

Rosen, M. (1988). You asked for it: Christmas at the bosses' expense. *Journal of Management Studies, 25,* 463-480.

Rousseau, D. M., & Anton, R. J. (1988). Fairness and implied contract obligations in job terminations: A policy-capturing study. *Human Performance, 1,* 273-289.

Roy, D. (1960). Banana time: Job satisfaction and informal interaction. *Human Organization, 18,* 156-168.

Rudd, G. (1995). The symbolic construction of organizational identities and community in a regional symphony. *Communication Studies, 46,* 201-221.

Sackmann, S. (1989). The role of metaphors in organization transformation. *Human Relations, 42,* 463-485.

Sacks, H., Schegloff, E. A., & Jefferson, G. (1974). A simplest systematics for the organization of turn-taking for conversation. *Language, 50,* 696-735.

Saferstein, B. (1992). Collective cognition and collaborative work: The effects of cognitive and communicative processes on the organization of television production. *Discourse & Society, 3,* 61-86.

Saferstein, B. (1994). Interaction and ideology at work: A case of constructing and constraining television violence. *Social Problems, 41,* 316-345.

Sands, R. (1981). Language and consciousness in industrial workers: Homeless minds? *International Journal of Sociology of Language, 32,* 55-64.

Sargent, J. F., & Miller, G. R. (1971). Some differences in certain communication behaviors of autocratic and democratic group leaders. *Journal of Communication, 21,* 233-252.

Saussure, F., de. (1974). *Course in general linguistics* (W. Baskin, Trans.). London: Fontana. (Original work published 1916)

Schall, M. S. (1983). A communication-rules approach to organizational culture. *Administrative Science Quarterly, 28,* 557-581.

Schank, R. C., & Abelson, R. P. (1977). *Scripts, plans, goals, and understanding.* Hillsdale, NJ: Lawrence Erlbaum.

Schantz, D. (1986). The use of SYMLOG as a diagnostic tool in drug-related problems on the job. *International Journal of Small Group Research, 2,* 219-224.

Schein, E. H. (1985). *Organizational culture and leadership*. San Francisco: Jossey-Bass.

Schmidt, D. P. (1986). Patterns of argument in business ethics. *Journal of Business Ethics, 5,* 501-509.

Schonbach, P. (1990). *Account episodes: The management of escalation of conflict*. Cambridge, UK: Cambridge University Press.

Schwandt, T. A. (1994). Constructivist, interpretivist approaches to human inquiry. In N. K. Denzin & Y. S. Lincoln (Eds.), *Handbook of qualitative research* (pp. 118-137). Thousand Oaks, CA: Sage.

Scott, M., & Lyman, S. (1968). Accounts. *American Sociological Review, 22,* 46-62.

Searle, J. R. (1969). *Speech acts: An essay in the philosophy of language*. London: Cambridge University Press.

Searle, J. R. (1979). *Expression and meaning: Studies in the theory of speech acts*. New York: Cambridge University Press.

Shimanoff, S. (1980). *Communication rules: Theory and research*. Beverly Hills, CA: Sage.

Shotter, J. (1990). The social construction of remembering and forgetting. In D. Middleton & D. Edwards (Eds.), *Collective remembering* (pp. 120-138). London: Sage.

Sigman, S. J. (1986). Adjustment to the nursing home as a social interaction accomplishment. *Journal of Applied Communication Research, 14,* 37-58.

Sigman, S. J., & Donnellon, A. (1989). Discourse rehearsal: Interaction simulating interaction. In D. Crookall & D. Saunders (Eds.), *Communication and simulation: From two fields to one theme* (pp. 69-81). London: Multilingual Matters.

Simon, H. A. (1976). *Administrative behavior* (3rd ed.). New York: Free Press.

Simons, T. (1993). Speech patterns and the concept of utility in cognitive maps: The case of integrative bargaining. *Academy of Management Journal, 36,* 139-156.

Sims, H. P., Jr. (1977). The leader as a manager of reinforcement contingencies: An empirical example and a model. In J. G. Hunt & L. L. Larson (Eds.), *Leadership: The cutting edge*. Carbondale: Southern Illinois University Press.

Sims, H. P., Jr., & Manz, C. C. (1984). Observing leader verbal behavior: Toward reciprocal determinism in leadership theory. *Journal of Applied Psychology, 69,* 222-232.

Sinclair, J. M., & Coulthard, M. (1975). *Towards an analysis of discourse: The English used by teachers and pupils*. Oxford, UK: Oxford University Press.

Sitkin, S., & Bies, R. J. (1993). Social accounts in conflict situations: Using explanations to manage conflict. *Human Relations, 46,* 349-370.

Sitkin, S. B., Sutcliffe, K. M., & Reed, L. (1993). Prescriptions for justice: Using social accounts to legitimate the exercise of professional control. *Social Justice Research, 6,* 87-111.

Skinner, B. F. (1957). *Verbal behavior*. Englewood Cliffs, NJ: Prentice Hall.

Skinner, B. F. (1974). *About behaviorism*. New York: Vintage.

Slobin, D., Miller, S., & Porter, L. (1968). Forms of address and social relations in a business organization. *Journal of Personality and Social Psychology, 8,* 289-293.

Slobin, D. I., Miller, S. H., & Porter, L. W. (1972). Forms of address and social relations in a business organization. In S. Moscovici (Ed.), *The psychosociology of language* (pp. 263-272). New York: Pergamon.

Smircich, L., & Morgan, G. (1982). Leadership: The management of meaning. *Journal of Applied Behavioral Studies, 18,* 257-273.

Smith, K. K., & Berg, D. N. (1987). *Paradoxes of group life*. San Francisco: Jossey-Bass.

Smith, R. C. (1993, May). *Images of organizational communication: Root metaphors of the organization-communication relation*. Paper presented at the annual conference of the International Communication Association, Washington, DC.

Smith, R. C., & Eisenberg, E. M. (1987). Conflict at Disneyland: A root-metaphor analysis. *Communication Monographs, 54,* 367-380.

Smith, R. C., & Turner, P. (1995). A social constructionist reconfiguration of metaphor analysis: An application of "SCMA" to organizational socialization theorizing. *Communication Monographs, 62,* 152-181.

Smithin, T. (1987). Argument in organizations. In C. L. Cooper & I. L. Mangham (Eds.), *Organizational analysis and development: A social construction of organizational behaviour* (pp. 61-80). Chichester, UK: Wiley.

Sotirin, P., & Gottfried, H. (1999). The ambivalent dynamics of secretarial "bitching": Control, resistance, and the construction of identity. *Organization, 6,* 57-80.

Spencer, J. W. (1994). Mutual relevance of ethnography and discourse. *Journal of Contemporary Ethnography, 23,* 267-279.

Srivastva, S., & Barrett, F. (1988). The transformation nature of metaphors in group development: A study in group theory. *Human Relations, 41,* 31-64.

Starbuck, W. H., & Milliken, F. J. (1988). Executives' perceptual filters: What they notice and how they make sense. In D. C. Hambrick (Ed.), *The executive effect: Concepts and methods for studying top managers* (pp. 35-65). Greenwich, CT: JAI.

Steward, F., & Conway, S. (1998). Situating discourse in environmental innovation networks. *Organization, 5,* 479-502.

Stewart, J. (1986). Speech and human being: A complement to semiotics. *Quarterly Journal of Speech, 72,* 55-73.

Stohl, C. (1993). European managers' interpretations of participation: A semantic network analysis. *Human Communication Research, 20,* 97-117.

Stohl, C. (1995). Paradoxes of participation. In R. Cesaria & P. Shockley-Zalabak (Eds.), *Organization means communication: Making the organizational communication concept relevant to practice* (pp. 199-215). Rome: Sipi Editore.

Stohl, C., & Coombs, W. T. (1988). Cooperation or co-optation: An analysis of quality circle training manuals. *Management Communication Quarterly, 2,* 63-89.

Stokes, R., & Hewitt, J. P. (1976). Disclaimers. *American Sociological Review, 40,* 1-11.

Strauss, A. (1978). *Negotiations: Varieties, contexts, processes, and social order.* San Francisco: Jossey-Bass.

Strine, M. S. (1988). Constructing "texts" and making inferences: Some reflections on textual reality in human communication research. In J. A. Anderson (Ed.), *Communication yearbook 11* (pp. 494-500). Newbury Park, CA: Sage.

Strine, M. S. (1992). Understanding "how things work": Sexual harassment and academic culture. *Journal of Applied Communication Research, 20,* 391-400.

Stubbs, M. (1976). *Language, schools and classrooms.* London: Methuen.

Sykes, A. J. M. (1966). Joking relationships in an industrial setting. *American Anthropologist, 68,* 188-193.

Tannen, D. (1994). *Talking from 9 to 5: Women and men in the workplace.* New York: Avon.

Taylor, B., & Conrad, C. R. (1992). Narratives of sexual harassment: Organizational dimensions. *Journal of Applied Communication Research, 20,* 401-418.

Taylor, J. R. (1993). *Rethinking the theory of organizational communication: How to read an organization.* Norwood, NJ: Ablex.

Taylor, J. R. (1995). Shifting from a heteronomous to an autonomous worldview of organizational communication: Communication theory on the cusp. *Communication Theory, 5,* 1-35.

Taylor, J. R., & Cooren, F. (1997). What makes communication "organizational"? How the many voices of a collectivity become the one voice of an organization. *Journal of Pragmatics, 27,* 409-438.

Taylor, J. R., Cooren, F., Giroux, N., & Robichaud, D. (1996). The communicational basis of organization: Between the conversation and the text. *Communication Theory, 6,* 1-39.

Taylor, J. R., & Van Every, E. (2000). *The emergent organization: Communication as its site and surface.* Mahwah, NJ: Lawrence Erlbaum.

Taylor, M. E. (1987). Functions of in-house language: Observations on data collected from some British financial institutions. *Language in Society, 16,* 1-7.

Thatchenkery, T. (1992). Organizations as "texts": Hermeneutics as a model for understanding organizational change. In W. A. Pasmore & R. W. Woodman (Eds.), *Research in organization development and change* (Vol. 6, pp. 197-233). Greenwich, CT: JAI.

Thatchenkery, T. J., & Upadhyaya, P. (1996). Organizations as a play of multiple and dynamic discourses: An example from a global social change organization. In D. M. Boje, R. P. Gephart, & T. J. Thatchenkery (Eds.), *Postmodern management and organization theory* (pp. 308-330). London: Sage.

Theye, L. D., & Seiler, W. J. (1979). Interaction analysis in collective bargaining: An alternative approach to the prediction of negotiated outcomes. In D. Nimmo (Ed.), *Communication yearbook 3* (pp. 375-392). New Brunswick, NJ: Transaction Books.

Thompson, L., & DeHarpport, T. (1994). Social judgment, feedback, and interpersonal learning in negotiation. *Organizational Behavior and Human Decision Processes, 58,* 327-345.

Tompkins, E. V. B., Tompkins, P. K., & Cheney, G. (1989). Organizations, texts, arguments, premises: Critical textualism and the study of organizational communication. *Journal of Management Systems, 1,* 35-48.

Tompkins, P. (1962). *An analysis of communication between headquarters and selected units of a national labor union.* Unpublished doctoral dissertation, Purdue University, West Lafayette, IN.

Tompkins, P. (1965). General semantics and "human relations." *Central States Speech Journal, 16,* 285-289.

Tompkins, P., Fisher, J., Infante, D., & Tompkins, E. (1975). Kenneth Burke and the inherent characteristics of formal organizations: A field study. *Speech Monographs, 42,* 135-142.

Tompkins, P. K., & Cheney, G. (1983). The uses of account analysis: A study of organization decision-making and identification. In L. L. Putnam & M. E. Pacanowsky (Eds.), *Communication and organizations: An interpretive approach* (pp. 123-146). Beverly Hills, CA: Sage.

Tompkins, P. K., & Cheney, G. (1985). Communication and unobtrusive control in contemporary organizations. In R. D. McPhee & P. K. Tompkins (Eds.), *Organizational communication: Traditional themes and new directions* (pp. 179-210). Beverly Hills, CA: Sage.

Toulmin, S. E. (1958). *The uses of argument.* Cambridge, UK: Cambridge University Press.

Townley, B. (1993). Foucault, power/knowledge, and its relevance for human resource management. *Academy of Management Review, 18,* 518-545.

Trethewey, A. (1997). Resistance, identity, and empowerment: A postmodern feminist analysis of clients in a human service organization. *Communication Monographs, 64,* 281-301.

Trethewey, A. (1999). Isn't it ironic: Using irony to explore the contradictions of organizational life. *Western Journal of Communication, 63,* 140-167.

Trujillo, N. (1983). "Performing" Mintzberg's roles: The nature of managerial communication. In L. L.

Putnam & M. E. Pacanowsky (Eds.), *Communication and organizations: An interpretive approach* (pp. 73-98). Beverly Hills, CA: Sage.

Trujillo, N. (1985). Organizational communication as cultural performance: Some managerial considerations. *Southern Speech Communication Journal, 50*, 201-224.

Tsoukas, H. (1991). The missing link: A transformational view of metaphors in organizational science. *Academy of Management Review, 16*, 566-585.

Tsoukas, H. (1993). Analogical reasoning and knowledge generation in organization theory. *Organization Studies, 14*, 323-346.

Tulin, M. F. (1997). Talking organization: Possibilities for conversation analysis in organizational behavior research. *Journal of Management Inquiry, 6*, 101-119.

Tullar, W. L. (1989). Relational control in the employment interview. *Journal of Applied Psychology, 74*, 971-977.

Turner, R. (1972). Some formal properties of therapy talk. In D. Sudnow (Ed.), *Studies in social interaction* (pp. 367-396). New York: Free Press.

Tway, P. (1975). Workplace isoglosses: Lexical variation and change in a factory setting. *Language in Society, 4*, 171-183.

Tway, P. (1976). Verbal and nonverbal communication of factory workers. *Semiotica, 16*, 29-44.

Tyler, L. (1997). Liability means never being able to say you're sorry: Corporate guilt, legal constraints, and defensiveness in corporate communication. *Management Communication Quarterly, 11*, 51-73.

Ullian, J. A. (1976). Joking at work. *Journal of Communication, 26*, 479-486.

van Dijk, T. A. (Ed.). (1985). *Handbook of discourse analysis*. New York: Academic Press.

van Dijk, T. A. (1993). Principles of critical discourse analysis. *Discourse & Society, 4*, 249-283.

van Dijk, T. A. (Ed.). (1997a). *Discourse as social interaction* (Vol. 1). London: Sage.

van Dijk, T. A. (1997b). The study of discourse. In T. A. van Dijk (Ed.), *Discourse as structure and process* (Vol. 1, pp. 1-34). London: Sage.

Van Maanen, J. (1973). Observations on the making of policemen. *Human Organization, 32*, 407-418.

Van Maanen, J. (1978). The asshole. In P. K. Manning & J. Van Maanen (Eds.), *Policing* (pp. 221-238). New York: Random House.

Van Maanen, J., & Barley, S. R. (1984). Occupational communities: Culture and control in organizations. In B. M. Staw & L. L. Cummings (Eds.), *Research in organizational behavior* (pp. 287-366). Greenwich, CT: JAI.

van Naerssen, M. M. (1985). Medical records: One variation of physicians' language. *International Journal of Sociology of Language, 51*, 43-73.

Vaughan, E. (1994). The trial between sense and sentiment: A reflection on the language of HRM. *Journal of General Management, 19*(3), 20-32.

Vaughn, M. A. (1995). Organization symbols: An analysis of their types and functions in a reborn organization. *Management Communication Quarterly, 9*, 219-250.

Vinton, K. L. (1989). Humor in the workplace: It is more than telling jokes. *Small Group Behavior, 20*, 151-166.

Walsh, J. P., & Ungson, G. R. (1991). Organizational memory. *Academy of Management Review, 16*, 57-91.

Watson, K. M. (1982). An analysis of communication patterns: A method for discriminating leader and subordinate roles. *Academy of Management Journal, 25*, 107-120.

Watson, R. T., DeSanctis, G., & Poole, M. S. (1988). Using a GDSS to facilitate group consensus: Some intended and unintended consequences. *MIS Quarterly, 12*, 463-478.

Watson, T. J. (1994). *In search of management: Culture, chaos and control in managerial work*. London: Routledge.

Watson, T. J. (1995). Rhetoric, discourse and argument in organizational sense making: A reflexive tale. *Organization Studies, 16*, 805-821.

Watson-Dugan, K. M. (1989). Ability and effort attributions: Do they affect how managers communicate performance feedback information? *Academy of Management Journal, 32*, 87-114.

Watzlawick, P., Beavin, J. H., & Jackson, D. D. (1967). *Pragmatics of human communication: A study of interactional patterns, pathologies, and paradoxes*. New York: Norton.

Weick, K. E. (1979). *The social psychology of organizing* (2nd ed.). Reading, MA: Addison-Wesley.

Weick, K. E. (1995). *Sensemaking in organizations*. Thousand Oaks, CA: Sage.

Weick, K. E., & Bougon, M. G. (1986). Organizations as cause maps. In H. P. Sims, Jr. & D. A. Gioia (Eds.), *Social cognition in organizations* (pp. 102-135). San Francisco: Jossey-Bass.

Weick, K. E., & Browning, L. D. (1986). Argument and narration in organizational communication. *Journal of Management, 12*, 243-260.

Weick, K. E., & Roberts, K. H. (1993). Collective mind in organizations: Heedful interrelating on flight decks. *Administrative Science Quarterly, 38*, 357-381.

Weingart, L. R., Bennett, R. J., & Brett, J. M. (1993). The impact of consideration of issues and motivational orientation on group negotiation process and outcome. *Journal of Applied Psychology, 78*, 504-517.

Weingart, L. R., Thompson, L. L., Bazerman, M. H., & Carroll, J. S. (1990). Tactical behavior and negotiation outcomes. *International Journal of Conflict Management, 1,* 7-31.

Wendt, R. F. (1998). The sound of one hand clapping: Counterintuitive lessons extracted from paradoxes and double binds in participative organizations. *Management Communication Quarterly, 11,* 323-371.

Westenholz, A. (1993). Paradoxical thinking and change in the frames of reference. *Organization Studies, 14,* 37-58.

Westley, F. R. (1990). Middle managers and strategy: Microdynamics of inclusion. *Strategic Management Journal, 11,* 337-351.

Whalen, M., & Zimmerman, D. H. (1987). Sequential and institutional contexts in calls for help. *Social Psychology Quarterly, 50,* 172-185.

Wilson, S. R. (1992). Face and facework in negotiation. In L. L. Putnam & M. E. Roloff (Eds.), *Communication and negotiation* (pp. 176-205). Newbury Park, CA: Sage.

Witten, M. (1993). Narrative and the culture of obedience at the workplace. In D. K. Mumby (Ed.), *Narrative and social control: Critical perspectives* (pp. 97-118). Newbury Park, CA: Sage.

Wood, J. T. (1992). Telling our stories: Narratives as a basis for theorizing sexual harassment. *Journal of Applied Communication Research, 20,* 349-362.

Wood, J. T. (1994). Saying it makes it so: The discursive construction of sexual harassment. In S. G. Bingham (Ed.), *Conceptualizing sexual harassment as discursive practice* (pp. 17-30). Westport, CT: Praeger.

Wood, J. T., & Conrad, C. (1983). Paradox in the experiences of professional women. *Western Journal of Communication, 47,* 305-322.

Wood, R. E., & Mitchell, T. R. (1981). Manager behavior in a social context: The impact of impression management on attributions and disciplinary action. *Organizational Behavior and Human Decision Processes, 28,* 356-378.

Woods, N. (1988). Talking shop: Sex and status as determinants of floor apportionment in a work setting. In J. Coates & D. Cameron (Eds.), *Women in their speech communities* (pp. 141-157). London: Longman.

Yates, J. (1990). For the record: The embodiment of organizational memory, 1850-1920. *Business and Economic History, 19,* 172-182.

Yoels, W. C., & Clair, J. M. (1995). Laughter in the clinic: Humor as social organization. *Symbolic Interaction, 18,* 39-58.

Zigurs, I., Poole, M. S., & DeSanctis, G. L. (1988). A study of influence in computer-mediated group decision making. *MIS Quarterly, 12,* 625-644.

Zimmerman, D. H. (1992). Achieving context: Openings in emergency calls. In G. Watson & R. Seiler (Eds.), *Text in context: Contributions in ethnomethodology* (pp. 35-71). Newbury Park, CA: Sage.

Zimmerman, D. H., & West, C. (1975). Sex roles, interruptions and silences in conversation. In B. Thorne & N. Henley (Eds.), *Language and sex: Differences and dominance* (pp. 105-129). Rowley, MA: Newbury House.

4

Quantitative Research Methods

❖ KATHERINE MILLER
Texas A&M University

During its history, the field of organizational communication has been marked by a variety of methodological traditions. Early lab experiments examining information flow were supplanted by survey research investigating perceptions of communication processes. In the 1970s, these methods were joined by sophisticated multivariate field and laboratory methodologies based largely on systems theory concepts. In the 1980s, the growing popularity of the culture metaphor and increasing dissatisfaction with scientific methods led many organizational communication scholars to embrace interpretive methods. And in the past ten years, more and more scholars are wedding those interpretive approaches with a critical theoretical stance.

As new methods have come onto the organizational communication scene, the old ones have not necessarily left quietly. Indeed, the "debates" and "conversations" in our literature (see, e.g., Hawes, Pacanowsky, & Faules, 1988; Putnam, Bantz, Deetz, Mumby, & Van Maanen, 1993) suggest that a variety of approaches still exist and that the proponents of these approaches are even willing to talk to each other and learn from each other. Thus, organizational communication scholarship today is marked by a healthy eclecticism in which a variety of research methods are accepted as legitimate.

In this chapter, I will consider quantitative approaches to organizational communication research by discussing their assumptive bases, typical practices, and emerging challenges. Before beginning this discussion, it is important to comment on the label used for the research methods considered in this chapter. The theoretical school that has spawned many of the methods discussed here has variously been referred to as functionalism (Burrell & Morgan, 1979; Putnam & Pacanowsky, 1983), postpositivism (Phillips, 1987), postempiricism (Manicas, 1987), normative (Deetz, 1994), and even naturalism (Bernstein, 1976). However, the research *methods* considered here share a value for understanding and explaining organizational communication process through some kind of quantification process (at widely varying levels of exactitude). Thus, because the concentration in this chapter is on *methodological* practices and challenges, the term *quantitative* will be used throughout.

BACKGROUND AND ASSUMPTIVE BASE

Quantitative approaches to research methodology within organizational communication have their roots in a logical positivist philosophy of science (e.g., Hempel, 1966). Though space does not permit a full exploration of these origins (see Suppe, 1977), logical positivism was marked by operationalism (the belief that all theoretical terms can and must be reduced to observable phenomena) and by the belief that a totally unbiased account of the world can be achieved through the careful application of the scientific method.[1] Logical positivists held that the physical and social worlds exist independent of our appreciation of them (realist ontology) and that an understanding of that world is found in a search for causal relationships and universal laws (positivist epistemology).

Allegiance to the logical positivist school of thought began waning soon after World War II, as philosophers of science began to question some of its main tenets, especially operationalism. New notions of "how science works" and "how science *should* work" became prominent on the scene (see, e.g., Feyerabend, 1975; Kuhn, 1962; Lakatos, 1970; Popper, 1962). Today, the classical form of logical positivism has been thoroughly debunked and is widely regarded as dead. However, allegiance to the principles of realism and objectivity has not died with it. Indeed, these assumptions are still viewed as highly viable by many organizational communication researchers, though in slightly altered form. The description of postpositivism presented by Phillips (1987, 1990) closely parallels the assumptive base of many quantitative researchers in organizational communication today. Thus, his work will be drawn on extensively in the following two sections.

Ontological Assumptions

Guba and Lincoln (1994) summarize the ontological position of postpositivists as "critical realism." Researchers in this tradition are realists in that they support "the view that entities exist independently of being perceived, or independently of our theories about them" (Phillips, 1987). However, this realism is tempered by the argument that humans cannot *fully* apprehend that reality and that the driving mechanisms in the social and physical world cannot be *fully* understood. As Smith (1990) states, "Realism is essential . . . because it poses 'at least in principle, a standard by which all human societies and their beliefs can be judged: they can all have beliefs about the world which turn out to be mistaken' (Trigg, 1985, p. 22)" (p. 171).

Phillips argues, however, that a realist ontology does not prohibit the advocacy of a "social construction of reality" (Berger & Luckmann, 1967). Rather, Phillips (1990) draws the distinction between *beliefs* about the reality and the objective reality (pp. 42-43). Making this distinction allows a quantitative researcher to appreciate (and investigate) multiple "realities" that are constructed by social collectives through communicative interaction. Quantitative researchers also argue that the social construction *process* is a regular one that can be studied through traditional social scientific methods. Wilson (1994) argues convincingly for this point regarding her own study of children's responses to the mass media:

> I believe that children's interpretations and responses are as richly individualistic as snowflakes. However, I also believe that there are common patterns that characterize a majority of young viewers and that those patterns are as predictable and explainable as the basic process by which all those unique snowflakes are formed from water. (p. 25)

Theorists advocating ontological positions clearly opposed to realism also see the usefulness of quantitative research methods in scholarship. For example, Deetz (1994), in arguing for an "emergent" ontology in communication studies, states that "in communication-based studies, quantitative analysis is a situated slice of the total research process arising out of and returning to constitutive processes" (p. 595). That is, quantitative researchers can contribute to the study of emergent processes by taking informative snapshots of those processes as they unfold.

Epistemological Assumptions

Quantitative researchers' assumptions about the grounds of social knowledge are also largely based on tenets originally developed by positivists in the physical sciences (Burrell & Morgan, 1979). These assumptions include the interlinked notions that (1) knowledge can best be gained through a search for regularities and causal relationships among components of the social world, (2) regularities and causal relationships can best be discovered if there is a complete separation between the investigator and the subject of the investigation, and (3) this separation can be guaranteed through the use of the scientific method. The scientific method is necessary because "scientists, like all men and women, are opinionated, dogmatic, ideological. . . . That is the very reason for insisting on procedural objectivity; to get the whole business outside of ourselves" (Kerlinger, 1979, p. 264).

Like ontological assumptions, however, most quantitative researchers in organizational communication have tempered these epistemological bases to what Guba (1990) has termed "modified objectivist." Quantitative scholars generally hold to the first assumption listed above. That is, the search for knowledge remains centered on causal explanations for regularities observed in the physical and social world. However, postpositivists have largely rejected the second assumption above, concluding that "the hope for a formal method, capable of being isolated from actual human judgment about the content of science (that is, about the nature of the world), and from human values seems to have evaporated" (Putnam, 1981, p. 192). Because this assumption of value-free inquiry is rejected, postpositivists have similarly rejected blind obedience to the scientific method. Instead, objectivity is seen as a "regulatory ideal." In other words, a quantitative researcher will use methods that strive to be as unbiased as possible and will attempt to be aware of any values that might compromise neutrality. However, because the possible fallibilities of the scientific method are recognized, the researcher will also rely on the critical scrutiny of a community of scholars to safeguard objectivity and maximize the growth of social scientific knowledge. As Bernstein (1976) argues, "The theorist must always be willing to submit his [*sic*] hypothetical claims to public discussion and testing, and ought to abandon any claims which have been refuted according to the canons of scientific research" (p. 44).

QUANTITATIVE METHODS: RESEARCH PRACTICES

In this section, I will consider several specific research methodologies widely used by quantitative organizational communication researchers: experimental methods, survey methods, and behavioral observation. For each methodology, I will briefly consider typical procedures for data collection and data analysis and cite exemplary studies from the organizational communication literature that have used the method being considered. The division of quantitative methods into these three categories is useful for the purpose of discussion, but it is also somewhat artificial. Experimental, survey, and behavioral observation techniques are not mutually exclusive, and a great many studies triangulate these techniques to gain a more complete and complex explanation of organizational communication phenomena (Albrecht & Ropp, 1982).

Experimental Research

Experimental research can be distinguished from all other types of research in that it involves the manipulation or control of the independent variable (Campbell & Stanley, 1963). Further, a true experiment can be distinguished from a quasi-experiment in that a true experiment involves the random assignment of participants to treatment conditions. The goal of an experimental study is to maximize the ability of a researcher to draw conclusions about the causal relationship between the independent variable and dependent variable. By controlling the independent variable, the researcher takes the first step in making these causal claims. The ability to infer causality is further enhanced if the researcher can rule out alternative explanations through randomization and other design and procedural choices (see classic texts by Campbell & Stanley, 1963, and Cook & Campbell, 1979, for detailed discussion).

Experimental studies can be undertaken in a variety of research settings. Because a true experiment involves the random assignment of participants to treatment groups as well as tight control over research procedures, such studies typically take place in laboratory settings. Though laboratory settings involve some sacrifice in terms of organizational realism (though see Locke, 1986, for an alternative view), they are often used to ferret out the specific mechanisms involved in organizational communication processes. Control over the independent variable can also be exercised in field experiments conducted in actual organizations. Such studies are typically quasi-experiments and may involve the manipulation of the independent variable through the use of scenarios or through organizational programs or subgroups that provide a "naturally occurring" field experiment. Quasi-experimental designs can also be employed to investigate organizational programs in which effects are evaluated over extended periods of time.

The data gathered in an experimental study are typically analyzed with statistical techniques that allow for the comparison of groups on the dependent variable(s) of interest. The procedures most typically used are from the family of techniques based on analysis of variance (ANOVA) (for complete discussion, see Keppel, 1982; Keppel & Zedeck, 1989). Variants of the basic ANOVA model allow for the analysis of multiple dependent variables (multivariate analysis of variance —MANOVA; for review, see Bochner & Fitzpatrick, 1980) or the analysis of additional variables that serve as covariates (analysis of covariance—ANCOVA). Some methodologists have also advocated the use of structural equation modeling in experimental research (Bagozzi, 1980) to allow the researcher to explicitly assess the impact of the manipulation on participant perceptions of the independent variable and to examine causal ordering among multiple dependent variables.

In organizational communication, several recent studies have used experimental methods. Papa and Pood (1988) studied the effect of coorientational accuracy on conflict resolution tactics in a field experiment. These researchers created dyads with either high or low coorientational accuracy regarding the organization's plan to use participative management, then analyzed the dependent variables of conflict resolution tactics and discussion satisfaction. Ellis (1992) investigated the impact of source credibility and uncertainty in the organizational change process by creating messages with varying types of social information about an upcoming departmental reorganization and measuring subsequent attitudes about the planned change. Both of these experimental designs are interesting in that they use naturally occurring organizational events (e.g., a plan to use participative management and a departmental reorganization) as a springboard for the manipulation of theoretically driven independent variables. The use of experimental techniques was particularly appropriate in that each researcher was attempting to delineate specific causal connections (e.g., between coorientation and tactic selection or between uncertainty and message acceptance) that would advance an established theoretical body of literature.

Survey and Interview Research

Researchers using survey and interview techniques within the quantitative tradition rely on the self-reports of research participants to make inferences about organizational communication processes (for more detail on survey research techniques, see Kerlinger, 1986; Warwick & Lininger, 1975). Researchers using these techniques generally base their work on the psychological perspective of organizational communication (Krone, Jablin, & Putnam, 1987), proposing that individual perceptions about communication processes have important theoretical and pragmatic implications. The self-reports of research participants are used to measure attitudes about communication events or relationships, to measure predispositions for particu-

lar communication behavior, or as a marker of other organizational communication behavior. Whether collecting data through written questionnaires, phone interviews, or face-to-face interviews, quantitative researchers typically use *structured* measurement instruments that include forced-choice items or structured open-ended questions.

In analyzing data from survey research, the investigator generally follows two sequential steps. First, the quality of the scales must be determined. Then, the theoretical relationships among the scales can be analyzed. At the simplest level, scale quality is assessed through face validity and a consideration of scale consistency such as Cronbach's alpha (Cronbach, 1951). In initial studies where scale development is the goal, exploratory factor analysis (EFA) might be used to uncover the dimensionality of the scales (Nunnally, 1978). However, many communication researchers have become disillusioned with this technique and have turned to confirmatory factor analysis (CFA) as a method for analyzing the quality of both newly developed and well-validated scales (for thorough discussions of CFA techniques, see Fink & Monge, 1985; Hunter & Gerbing, 1982; James, Mulaik, & Brett, 1982). The challenge of making choices regarding the assessment of measurement quality will be discussed later in this chapter.

After confirming the quality of the measurement instruments, the survey researcher then assesses the relationships among the constructs. At the simplest level, relationships are considered through techniques including correlation and multiple regression (for complete discussions, see Keppel & Zedeck, 1989; Pedhazur, 1982). However, because many organizational communication researchers are interested in more complex systems of relationships, in recent years scholars have turned to more sophisticated analytical techniques.[2] For example, many researchers now use path analytic techniques or structural equation modeling (for discussion, see Cappella, 1980; McPhee & Babrow, 1987) in their analysis of survey data in organizational communication. Again, choices among these more complex analytical techniques will be discussed later in this chapter.

Finally, if the self-report data collected are designed to be indicators of communicative activity in the organization, network analytic techniques are often employed. As Rice and Richards (1985) note, "The goal of network analysis is to obtain from low-level or raw relational data higher-level descriptions of the structure of the system" (p. 106). This higher-level description might be construed either in the form of "cohesion" (e.g., individuals are linked in the network if they talk to each other) or in the form of "structural equivalence" (e.g., individuals are linked in the network if they talk with a similar set of people) (Burt, 1978). These network constructs can then be used either as descriptions of organizational social systems or as antecedent or consequent conditions in higher-level explanations of organizational communication behavior (e.g., Eisenberg, Monge, & Miller, 1983; McPhee & Corman, 1995). For a more complete review of network analytic assumptions, techniques, and computer programs, see Wasserman and Faust (1994).

A wide range of recent organizational communication research has used survey research techniques (for a sampling of recent studies, see Barker & Tompkins, 1994; Fink & Chen, 1995; Kramer, 1993; Miller, Birkholt, Scott, & Stage, 1995; Treadwell & Harrison, 1994). I will briefly discuss three representative examples. Marshall and Stohl (1993) were interested in assessing the ways in which participation in communication networks and the empowerment derived from that participation led to valued organizational outcomes. Their survey design involved measures of network participation, perceived involvement, empowerment, and satisfaction. Performance appraisals were also obtained from members of the management team. Through correlational and regression techniques, Marshall and Stohl were able to explore the differential relationships among em-powerment, involvement, satisfaction, and performance.

A more complex analytical strategy was employed by Fulk (1993) in survey research taking a social constructivist approach to the investigation of communication technology in organizations. Using a survey of electronic mail users and structural equation modeling techniques (Joreskög & Sörbom, 1989), Fulk determined that social influences on technology-related attitudes and behaviors were consistently stronger when individuals reported a high level of attraction to their work groups.

A third recent study (Stohl, 1993) is useful in demonstrating the ways in which quantitative research methods can be applied to explain the processes through which organizational actors *interpret* their working worlds. Phillips (1990) argues that the "socially constructed realities" of actors can be objectively investigated with appropriate quantitative research methods. One method for doing this that has gained considerable favor in organizational communication is semantic network analysis (Monge & Eisenberg, 1987). This method allows the researcher to analyze the self-reported interpretations of research participants to create a map of the degree to which meanings for key organizational processes are shared. Stohl (1993) recently used this method to investigate the ways in which managers from varying national cultures differ in their interpretation of the participation construct.

Coding of Communication Behaviors and Archives

A third general research strategy used by quantitative organizational communication researchers involves the objective coding of communication behaviors or communication artifacts (see Bakeman & Gottman, 1986, for general discussion). Work in this genre is distinguished by its attempt to view the interaction or archives in an objective and reliable manner and by its search for systematic explanations of communication phenomena.

The first step for researchers in this tradition involves the collection of behavioral or archival data to be coded. The major concern at this point in the research is to assemble a data set that provides a valid representation of the communicative phenomenon under investigation. After the data set has been assembled, attention shifts to analysis. The first analytical step (often taken before or concomitantly with data collection) is the development of a coding scheme to be used in analyzing the data. Poole and McPhee (1995) discuss two routes for developing a coding system. First, an analytically complete coding system can be deduced through rules of formal logic (e.g., a logical choice tree). Second, and more typically, categories can be developed based on theoretical concerns and the text being studied. Poole and McPhee note a natural trade-off between these two techniques: "The second approach to designing classification systems is advantageous because it is more responsive to the particular nature of the discourse than the first, but it is correspondingly less 'clean' and its rules harder to apply consistently" (p. 62).

Application of the coding scheme typically involves having multiple independent coders both divide the data into the proper units to be coded and apply the coding scheme to those units. There are two assessments that can be made to support the validity of the classification system. The first of these, unitizing reliability (e.g., Guetzkow, 1950), involves the extent to which coders agree on the division of the text into analytical units. The second assessment to be made is classificatory reliability (e.g., Cohen, 1960; Holsti, 1969), and involves the extent to which coders agree on the classification of units into categories. For complete discussions of reliability assessment options and problems that often arise in the process of coding, see Folger, Hewes, and Poole (1984), Hewes (1985), and Zwick (1988).

After the data are coded, the researcher typically looks for patterns in the categorization. Because these data are usually coded at the nominal level, techniques such as ANOVA and regression are generally inappropriate as analytical choices. At the most basic level, then, coded interaction and archival data can be analyzed with nonparametric statistics such as chi-square. However, recent trends in organizational communication research point to the continuing importance of more advanced categorical data analysis techniques, particularly log-linear analysis (see, e.g., Bishop, Feinberg, & Holland, 1975) or, for the analysis of sequential categorical data, Markov modeling (see Hewes, 1975, 1979). Though these techniques are not without problems,[3] they allow for assessments of causality and the influence of time that are unavailable in more elementary procedures.

Several important examples of the use of behavioral observation and analysis are prominent in the organizational communication research literature. For example, Gail Fairhurst and her colleagues (see, e.g., Fairhurst, 1993; Fairhurst & Chandler, 1989; Fairhurst, Green, & Courtright, 1995; Fairhurst, Rogers, & Sarr, 1987) have used interaction analysis (along with discourse analysis) to investigate the relational control patterns used in supervisor-subordinate relationships. Research in decision making conducted by Scott Poole and his colleagues provides another example of behavioral coding in organizational communication research. In early work, Poole and Roth (1989) developed a typology of group decision paths and a procedure for coding types of interaction in decision-making groups. In subsequent work, these researchers have used the coding procedures to explore the nature of computer-mediated decision making, concentrating on conflict management (Poole, Holmes, & DeSanctis, 1991), microstructurational processes (Poole & DeSanctis, 1992), and the distinction between computer-mediated and face-to-face groups (Poole, Holmes, Watson, & DeSanctis, 1993). They have also extended the coding methodology in the development of a computer program for analyzing over-time decision sequences (Holmes & Poole, 1991).

CRITERIA FOR JUDGING QUANTITATIVE RESEARCH

The ontological and epistemological foundations that undergird quantitative scholarship suggest a clear direction for judging the quality of research efforts. That is, high-quality quantitative research in the postpositivist tradition provides an accurate and relatively unbiased account of the social world, provides well-supported explanations of relationships within that social world, and contributes to the advance of our knowledge about the social world. This suggests that such research can be judged in two ways. First, a piece of research can be compared with standards for how "proper" quantitative research should be conducted. As Smith (1990) notes, "The notion of the properly done study is central to postempiricists and they hold it is possible to distinguish unbiased, open, honest, and precise research from that which is not" (p. 172). Second, a piece of research can be judged in the context of the larger body of scholarship to which it is contributing.

The technical merits of functional research are typically assessed with standards of validity and reliability established in a wide array of social scientific disciplines (see, e.g., Kerlinger, 1986).[4] The standards of internal validity, external validity, measurement reliability, and measurement validity are summarized in Table 4.1.

Although these standards are well accepted among scholars using quantitative research methods, they are not without controversy. For example, several debates have centered around issues of external validity in organizational research, both in terms of generalizability of research participants and generalizability of research settings. This debate will be considered later in this chapter as one of the "challenges" facing quantitative researchers.

If a study is determined to be valid and reliable in the ways outlined in Table 4.1, the quantitative researcher would conclude that it provides a defensible explanation for the phenomenon under investigation. However, the technical quality of the study does not necessarily mean that it makes a meaningful contribution to our knowledge about organizational communication. As Wilson (1994) notes, "All of us have encountered empirical studies that are technically proficient and highly rigorous but which report findings that seem rather meaningless in light of current issues in communication" (p. 29).

Two general criteria can be offered regarding the contribution made by functionalist research. First, quantitative research should be grounded in established theory and research, or as Marshall (1990) states, the research should be tied to "the big picture" and be sensitive to "historical context" (pp. 194-195). Second, research in the postpositivist tradition should move beyond the extant literature and make an independent and significant contribution to that theoretical groundwork. The question of what constitutes a "significant" contribution is, of course, difficult to determine. Certainly, significance of contribution means more than deriving results that are statistically significant, and perhaps the significance of research can best be judged retrospectively. That is, if a piece of research stands the test of time by generating additional research questions, contributing to theoretical development, and motivating dialogue among scholars, it is truly significant scholarship.

QUANTITATIVE METHODS: RESEARCH CHALLENGES

Despite the entrenchment of quantitative methods in our scholarship, there are still a number of areas in which researchers using these approaches are confronted with challenges that are either inherent in quantitative methodology or have sprung from the typical conduct of quantitative research. These challenges are associated with all phases of the research process, from the conceptualization of the research program and design, to the

TABLE 4.1 Basic Criteria for Judging the Technical Merits of Quantitative Research

Criterion	Description	Methodological Strategies
Internal validity	The extent to which the researcher is sure that no confounding variables have influenced the relationship between the independent and dependent variables.	Use of random assignment to treatment groups and other design strategies that minimize alternative explanations for study results.
External validity	The extent to which the researcher can generalize study results to other actors, behaviors, and contexts.	Use of random sampling, representative organizational field sites, and realistic organizational activities.
Measurement reliability	The extent to which a measure is repeatable (over time) and consistent (with regard to multiple indicators or multiple coders).	Assess reliability through alpha, repeated measures, or interrater reliability coefficient. Enhance reliability through careful item construction, pretesting, and thorough training of coders.
Measurement validity	The extent to which a measure assesses the concept it is designed to assess. Includes content (face), construct, and pragmatic validity.	Assess through review of item content, comparison to relevant outcome variables, relationships within nomothetic network, consideration of multitrait-multimethod matrix.

collection of data, to statistical analysis, and to substantive interpretation. Although these portions of the research process are clearly interdependent, challenges associated with each of these areas will be considered separately in the remainder of this chapter.

Challenges of Research Design

Organizational communication scholars face the daunting task of investigating and understanding processes that are becoming increasingly complex. Organizations are messy sites—characterized by multiple layers of activity and constant change over time. Thus, an important challenge for quantitative scholars is to design research that is capable of captur-

ing the complexities of organizational life. Two aspects of this challenge are discussed below: Dealing with multiple levels of analysis in quantitative research, and incorporating time into our research designs.

Challenges Associated With Levels of Analysis

In some areas of communication scholarship, research interest is largely defined by the level of analysis. An example of such an area is small-group communication. Organizational communication, as well, could appear to the outsider to be a "single-level" phenomenon. However, systems theorists in communication have long recognized that multiple levels must be considered in an investigation of organizational phenomena (see, e.g., Farace,

Monge, & Russell, 1977). A look at our journals confirms this notion, as research investigations in organizational communication include the psychological processes of individuals, dyadic and group interaction, organizational culture and climate, and interorganizational transactions. Klein, Dansereau, and Hall (1994) suggest that levels issues should be considered in terms of (1) theory development, (2) data collection, and (3) data analysis.

Klein et al. (1994) first argue that an organizational theorist should carefully consider levels assumptions being made in theory. For example, a theory could specify the homogeneity of a group, the independence of individuals within a group, or a distinct patterning of individuals within a group. These distinctions are far from straightforward. For example, a debate has raged in the management literature regarding the status of the "climate" construct (see, e.g., Glick, 1988; James, Joyce, & Slocum, 1988). Is climate an individual-level variable that can be aggregated to the organizational level? Or is climate a property of the organization or subgroup apart from individual perceptions of climate? Further, many theories include attention to two or more levels. For example, leader-member exchange theory (see Graen & Scandura, 1987) includes constructs and effects on the individual, dyadic, and work group levels.

Once the level of theory is carefully considered and delineated, decisions about data collection and analysis must be addressed. Klein et al. (1994) argue that the researcher can either choose to collect data in a way that *conforms* to the level of the theory or to collect data in a way that will allow the researcher to *test* assumptions about the level of theory. For example, a theory of group decision making may propose that the *process* of decision making is substantively different from the process of individual decision making. The researcher could choose to either explore the process of group decision making further by collecting extensive data from groups or could test the assumptive base of the theory by contrasting data collected from individuals and groups. Klein et al. argue that "the ideal approach, however, is to employ multiple and varied measures of the constructs of a theory. When diverse measures of a construct demonstrate the variability predicted for the construct, researchers' confidence in the level of the construct is enhanced" (p. 211). As Klein et al. (1994) point out, similar dilemmas face the researcher in the analysis of data, and the picture becomes particularly complicated when the theory includes multiple levels:

> The development and testing of multiple-level theories magnifies these concerns. The strength of multiple-level theories is their complexity; they do not oversimplify organizational realities (Burstein, 1980). Specifying the level of each construct within a multiple-level theory aids theorists and researchers in managing such complexity. So, too, do efforts to align the assumptions of variability underlying the independent and dependent constructs. (p. 225)

A more specific proposal regarding the level-of-analysis challenge has recently been proposed by House, Rousseau, and Thomas-Hunt (1995). These scholars suggest that organizational research has traditionally been bifurcated into "micro" and "macro" camps and that fuller understanding of organizational phenomena will come only when we also look at the "meso" level. Mesotheory and research are defined as

> the simultaneous study of at least two levels of analysis wherein (a) one or more levels concern individual or group behavioral processes . . . , (b) one or more levels concern organizational processes . . . , and (c) the processes by which the levels of analysis are related are articulated in the form of bridging, or linking, propositions. (House et al., 1995, p. 73)

House et al. continue by proposing and discussing three ways in which micro- and macroprocesses can interact: isomorphisms (constituent components of a phenomenon are similar across levels of analysis), discontinuities (components manifest themselves differently at different levels of analysis), and interlevel relationships (bridging propositions are proposed to specify the process by which components at various levels of analysis affect each other). House et al.'s specific suggestions for dealing with interlevel relationships could be very useful for organizational communication scholars who routinely struggle with multiple-level research issues.

Consider, for example, the work of communication scholars investigating organizational groups. Though early scholars recognized the impact of individual members on small-group interaction, recent investigations have advocated adding another layer to our models of group functioning. Stohl began making this extension in organizational communication over ten years ago by considering quality circles as group structures "parallel" to the larger organizational structure (Stohl, 1986). More recently, Putnam and Stohl (1990) have advocated the study of "bona fide groups" in which organizational groups are characterized in terms of their stable yet permeable boundaries and their interdependence with the larger organizational context (see also Stohl, 1995). Lammers and Krikorian (1997) have demonstrated the complexity of research stemming from a bona fide group perspective in their study of hospital surgical teams. Lammers and Krikorian did not use the vocabulary of House et al. (1995) in their discussion of surgical teams, but their efforts to examine and operationalize some of the concepts proposed in Putnam and Stohl's original development of the bona fide group concept demonstrate some of the complex decisions that must be confronted in multilevel organizational communication research. For example, Lammers and Krikorian consider the complexity of using network analytic concepts such as connectedness across multiple levels of analysis. Though they note that connectedness scores could be computed at varying levels of analysis (e.g., perhaps

connectedness is an isomorphism), they further argue (Lammers & Krikorian, 1997, p. 23) that "it may be that the logics of connectedness vary across level" (e.g., perhaps connectedness is a discontinuity). Lammers and Krikorian's related discussions of tight and loose coupling, resource dependency, and internal and external authority systems demonstrate the challenging nature of cross-level organizational research.

Challenges Associated With Over-Time Processes

In addition to considering the complexity of multileveled organizational processes, communication researchers using quantitative methods must also deal with appropriate ways for incorporating the concept of process into their theorizing and research. The call for more attention to process in organizational communication has been most fully developed by Peter Monge and his colleagues (Monge, 1982, 1990; Monge, Farace, Eisenberg, White, & Miller, 1984) and has been echoed by scholars throughout disciplines of organization study. For example, two recent issues of *Organization Science* were devoted to issues of longitudinal design and analysis (see Huber & Van de Ven, 1995).

Scholars advocating longitudinal approaches argue that most of our theories of organizational communication are either explicitly or implicitly processual, but that our research methods have lagged behind these theories by considering cross-sectional data analyzed with regression or analysis of variance. To provide but one example, theories of organizational socialization are inherently processual. Yet it is the rare study (e.g., Kramer, 1993) that includes multiple data collection periods, let alone the observation and analytic procedures that would allow for a full mapping and understanding of the assimilation process. Thus, Monge and his colleagues urge organizational communication researchers to move beyond the strictures of cross-sectional research designs and analytical tools to consider methods that will allow a more complete assessment of organizational communication processes.

Monge's (1990) suggestions for moving ahead with processual research closely parallel Klein et al.'s suggestions regarding the issue of levels in research. Specifically, Monge recommends a careful conceptualization of the process notions inherent in our theories by considering each construct in terms of its continuity, magnitude of change, rate of change, trend, periodicity, and duration. After the processual qualities of theoretical constructs are carefully delineated, the researcher can follow up with appropriate longitudinal data collection procedures and appropriate analytical tools (e.g., Markov modeling, event history analysis, multivariate time series analysis).[5] However, Monge (1982) argues that progress with processual theorizing can be accomplished only by considering the correspondence among the nature of the theory, the nature of the data, and the analytical tools used. For explications of specific strategies useful in the design, conduct, and analysis of longitudinal research, the interested reader is referred to Van de Ven and Poole (1990), Glick, Huber, Miller, Doty, and Sutcliffe (1990), and Pettigrew (1990).

Consider, for example, the complications faced by scholars investigating the process of innovation adoption in organizations (e.g., Monge, Cozzens, & Contractor, 1992; Van de Ven & Poole, 1990). The study of innovation requires processual theories and methods because, as Van de Ven and Poole (1990) note, "although many studies have examined the antecedents to or consequences of innovation, very few have directly examined how and why innovations emerge, develop, grow, or terminate over time" (p. 313; see also Tornatsky et al., 1983). Van de Ven and Poole describe the procedures used to study the development of innovation in the Minnesota Innovation Research Program. Their multilayered and longitudinal approach involved the classification of innovation incidents, the coding of those

incidents, the transformation of incidents into a "bit-map event sequence," the analysis of sequence data with appropriate statistical techniques, and the identification of patterns among various sequences. This highly complex process yields important insights about the innovation process that would be unavailable through static techniques, but it also poses numerous land mines for the researcher. Each step of the process poses new and complex dilemmas regarding reliability, validity, appropriate statistical choice, and meaningful interpretation.

Challenges of Data Collection

The preceding section considered some of the challenges of designing research that considers the complexity of time and level in organizational research. Part of dealing with that complexity involved *collecting* data at multiple points in time and from multiple levels of these organization. But there are other challenges associated with data collection that must be considered by the quantitative researcher. Two of these challenges are considered in this section: challenges associated with the use of self-report data and challenges of gathering data that are representative of the people and processes under theoretical consideration.

Challenges Associated With Self-Report Data

Although the trend in communication research has been shifting toward an emphasis on interactional data, a great deal of organizational communication research remains grounded in the self-reports of research participants. This is not necessarily bad. When psychological variables or perceptions of communication processes constitute the phenomenon of interest, self-reports are the most appropriate means for collecting data. However, if the researcher is using the self-report as an indicator of actual communication behavior, there can be a great deal of slippage between the self-report and interaction. Further, there are other inherent challenges of using self-report data that must be considered by the quantitative researcher.

The first challenge associated with self-report data is the assessment of whether the self-report is a valid representation of the construct being considered. For example, there has been substantial debate regarding what is actually measured when researchers collect self-reports about conflict management style (see Knapp, Putnam, & Davis, 1988). Are these self-reports indicative of actual behavior, planned behavior, recalled behavior, or preferred behavior? Or are the self-reports totally unrelated to communicative interaction? This issue has been most thoroughly investigated with regard to communication network participation. A series of studies in the early 1980s (Bernard, Killworth, Kronnenfeld, & Sailer, 1984; Bernard, Killworth, & Sailer, 1982) demonstrated that perceptions of network participation are not valid indicators of observable communication behavior. Since then, communication scholars have been grappling with this issue (see Corman, 1990; Corman & Scott, 1994; Monge & Contractor, 1988; Monge & Eisenberg, 1987) by looking for better measurement techniques, assessing the importance of perceived communication apart from actual behavior, and considering theoretical models that could provide a vehicle for explaining and modeling these gaps between perception and behavior. The important development here is that self-reports are no longer seen as perfectly reliable stand-ins for behavioral assessment, and researchers are dealing with this lack of isomorphism both theoretically and methodologically.

Other challenges also come with the territory when using self-report data. One of these is the problem of social desirability (see Crowne & Marlowe, 1964). How can we know that respondents are giving us true reports of their perceptions and not simply telling us "what we want to hear" (or, just as dangerous, what management wants to hear)? Social desirability problems can be particularly vexing when assessing communicative behavior in which the goal is to assess *use* of the behavior rather than *appropriateness* of behavior. Social desirability problems have been argued to be present in measures of compliance-gaining techniques (Burleson et al., 1988; though see responses by Boster, 1988; Hunter, 1988; Seibold, 1988) and conflict management techniques (Wilson & Waltman, 1988). Within the confines of survey research, the problem of social desirability can probably best be curtailed by emphasizing the researcher's independent role, by assuring confidentiality or anonymity, and by convincing participants that their honesty and straightforwardness is truly valued. Wilson and Waltman (1988) also recommend eschewing "checklist" measures in favor of open-ended responses to hypothetical situations.

Finally, self-report data may lead to erroneous conclusions about the relationship between variables. When two or more constructs are measured using self-reports, those constructs might appear to be related simply because of the measurement techniques used (common method variance). For example, Wagner and Gooding (1987) conducted a meta-analysis of the participative decision-making literature and concluded that studies using self-reports of both participation and outcome variables yielded consistently stronger relationships than those in which alternative methods were used. Avoiding this problem requires a shifting from self-report to behavioral measures, or the careful development of self-report measures through multitrait/multimethod techniques (Althauser, 1974; Campbell & Fiske, 1959).

Challenges of Sample Representativeness

When considering organizational communication processes, quantitative scholars typically want to generalize the research to people, settings, and processes beyond the confines of the research project. This concern with external validity has most traditionally considered the generalizability of research participants and research settings. The debate regarding research participants typically considers the appropriateness of using college students in research investigating organizational processes. This issue is far from settled (see, e.g., Gordon, Slade, & Schmitt, 1986, 1987; Greenberg, 1987), but there does seem to be agreement on several issues. First, as Greenberg (1987) states, "student and nonstudent samples may be equally useful sources of information about the processes underlying organizational phenomena" (p. 158). However, this is the case only when care is taken to support the student sample as similar to the population being generalized to on relevant theoretical variables and when the student-based study is part of a larger research program justifying generalization to the organizational population of interest (see Gordon et al., 1986, 1987, for arguments; Walther, 1995, for organizational communication example). A similar debate has raged about the use of the laboratory setting in studies of organizational phenomena. This debate was thoroughly investigated in a volume edited by Edwin Locke (1986) in which meta-analytic techniques were used to compare laboratory and field-based investigation of critical organizational phenomena. The conclusion of these investigations was that "the data do not support the belief that lab studies produce different results than field studies" (Campbell, 1986, p. 276). This is not to suggest, though, that either setting is appropriate for any research question. Instead, choice of research participants and research site must be guided by the substantive issues of interest.

Drawing a generalizable sample of *people* is only part of the challenge for today's organizational communication researcher, however. With increasing reliance on text-based research, scholars must also consider the representativeness of the discourse or text under consideration. This debate has been most thoroughly explored in the area of discourse and interaction analysis in a consideration of what is to "count as evidence" in the study of texts and conversations. For example, Cappella (1990) vehemently argued against what he called "the method of proof by example" (p. 237) arguing that this method capitalizes on random occurrences in the text and is susceptible to selection bias. Jacobs (1990) disagrees, arguing that these biases are unlikely to occur, especially if there is "a community of analysts who actively set out to falsify the analysis of any particular study" (p. 247). No closure has been reached on this debate, but Fitch (1994) defends a middle road in which the researcher attempts to balance richness with precision. She argues for the criterion that "claims should be based on an adequate selection of the total corpus of data. In other words, claims should be saturated in data" (p. 36).

Analytical Challenges

In the previous sections on research design and data collection, it is clear that a challenge continually faced by quantitative researchers is dealing with the interdependence of the various phases of the research effort. Nowhere are the connections made more clear than in the process of analyzing quantitative data. Our care in designing research that captures the complexity of organizational communication processes will be of little use if we cannot analyze those data in a way that usefully informs us about those conceptual processes. Monge (1982) raised this issue over 15 years ago, arguing that although scholars in the systems theory tradition were proposing complex abstract insights about organizational communication behavior, those insights were of little use if they were not investigated through commensurably complex analytical tools. In this section, I will consider four specific quantitative analysis techniques that can be used to enhance the "match" between our theorizing and analysis at various phases of the research process. It should be noted, of course, that complex analytical tools are not always appropriate in organizational communication research. When asking simple questions, scholars should avoid the tendency to "kill gnats with a cannon" and use simple techniques capable of answering research questions in a straightforward and elegant manner. However, when required by complex theorizing, the following analytical strategies are useful components of the organizational communication researcher's arsenal.

First, as noted earlier, quantitative researchers are usually trying to contribute to an accumulation of knowledge about organizational communication processes, and thus try to build research attempts on past literature. Surprisingly, though, quantitative researchers rarely perform quantitative methods in the research review process. Instead, scholars typically rely on a narrative literature review, occasionally "counting" the number of significant and nonsignificant findings, in reaching conclusions about extant knowledge on a topic. However, a more comprehensive literature review strategy is available in the form of meta-analysis (Glass, McGaw, & Smith, 1981; Hunter, Schmidt, & Jackson, 1982). With meta-analytic techniques, a scholar is able to quantitatively cumulate findings over a variety of research projects, accounting for research artifacts such as sample size, measurement techniques, research context, and era of publication. Though meta- analyses are not without their problems (e.g., the "file drawer problem," incommensurability of measures and methods across studies, and problems of quantification from incomplete results), they provide an important avenue for organizing and summarizing the results of past research in an area (see, e.g., Miller & Monge, 1986).

A second area in which our analytical techniques should more appropriately mirror our theoretical sophistication is in the assessment of measurement instruments. We often have highly developed ideas about the constructs under investigation in our research, and we typically work hard to develop instruments designed to tap those constructs. However, we usually assess the quality of those instruments using overly simplistic methods such as test-retest reliability or coefficient alpha or using inherently underidentified methods such as exploratory factor analysis (EFA; see Fink & Monge, 1985). These techniques do not allow a thorough consideration of the strengths and flaws of our measurements, for they do not require the researcher to put theoretical assumptions about measurement to a specific test. A stronger alternative in many research situations is CFA. CFA requires the researcher to specify an a priori factor structure, then *confirm* that factor structure by statistically comparing the correlations created by the specified factor structure and the observed correlations. Model confirmation can involve either microanalytical tests of internal consistency and parallelism (see Hunter & Gerbing, 1982) or macroanalytic tests of goodness of fit (see Fink & Monge, 1985). CFA techniques are superior to EFA and simple tests of reliability both in terms of statistical rigor and theoretical grounding. As with most statistical procedures, the GIGO ("garbage in, garbage out") principle guides CFA operations. The strength of the final model confirmed through CFA is largely dependent on the quality of theorizing and on the quality of individual items created in the measurement development process.

Third, in investigating the relationship among variables, we often squander opportunities to gain insight about organizational communication processes because our analytical techniques do not match the complexity of our theorizing. For example, we might dichotomize or trichotomize an independent variable and analyze with ANOVA or MANOVA, rather than take advantage of the full range of our independent variable with regression techniques. Or if we use regression techniques, we might choose to investigate simple bivariate relationships or relationships with single dependent variables through the use of correlation and multiple regression. However, our theoretical frameworks, more often than not, propose more complex processes in which constructs are embedded in systems of relationships. Thus, a useful analytical alternative for investigating *relationships* among variables is structural equation modeling (Marcoulides & Schumacker, 1996; Schumacker & Lomax, 1996), sometimes known as path modeling or causal modeling. These techniques are generally based on the same mathematical model as regression and correlation but allow the investigation of systems with multiple causes and effects and complex feedback loops (see Monge, 1982). With some estimation procedures (e.g., full information maximum likelihood), the researcher is also able to assess the fit of the model to the data with tests of overidentifying restrictions.[6]

McPhee and Babrow (1987) argue convincingly that causal modeling is often underutilized in communication research. In their discussion of the "disuse" of causal modeling, they suggest a wide range of research situations in which causal modeling techniques are desirable (e.g., unreliable measurement, partial correlational analyses, extended systems of propositions). But McPhee and Babrow (1987) also point to a number of ways in which causal modeling is *mis*used in communication research in terms of theoretical standards, methodological standards, and presentational standards. Several issues seem particularly important to organizational communication researchers. First, causal modeling, like CFA, is a *confirmatory* technique and should be used only to test theoretically derived systems of relationships. Second, the power of the estimation procedures in causal modeling packages should be respected, especially when the researcher is attempting to simultaneously estimate measurement and causal models. Indeed, McPhee and Babrow (1987) recommend that "where there is substantial ambiguity about the causal structure of the measurement model" (p. 361) a least-squares technique should be used initially, followed by the maximum likelihood techniques of LISREL or a similar program.

A fourth area in which more sophisticated analytical strategies could be used to enhance

organizational communication research is in the actual theory development process. Theory development has often been construed as an "armchair" activity, in which insight is derived from past literature and extant theoretical frameworks. Theoretical insights created in the armchair are then taken to the field for testing. However, advances in computer technology can be used to make the theory *development* process a more exacting and exciting process. Specifically, through the use of computer simulations, various theoretical propositions can be "put to the test" with various starting values and taken to their logical conclusions. In this way, the theorist can explore the implications of a variety of theoretical assumptions and refine theory before taking the costly step of moving to the field for empirical testing. These procedures have been proposed as a means through which systems concepts can be rejuvenated in organizational communication theorizing (Poole, 1996) and have been demonstrated in recent work by Contractor and Seibold (1993). These researchers were looking for a theoretical system that would explain appropriation patterns for group decision support systems (GDSSs). Through the use of a computer simulation, Contractor and Seibold (1993) demonstrated that self-organizing systems theory has the potential to provide a dynamic and precise explanation of GDSS appropriation.

Interpretive Challenges

The quantitative researcher's job does not end with the computation of statistics and the assessment of significance. Indeed, it has often been noted that statistical significance should be evaluated separately from practical significance and that the import of results must be evaluated with reference to the larger corpus of knowledge about organizational communication processes. In the final section of this chapter, I will consider several challenges facing quantitative researchers as they attempt to make sense of their research findings.

The Art of Quantitative Interpretation

Qualitative research in organizational communication and throughout the social sciences has often been labeled "interpretive" (e.g., Putnam & Pacanowsky, 1983). Though the argument is rarely made explicitly, the implication of this labeling is that quantitative research does not involve the process of interpretation. This implicit argument has been taken to task in a recent article by Herbert M. Kritzler (1996) on interpretation in quantitative research. Kritzler makes a compelling case for the centrality of interpretation in quantitative research endeavors. Indeed, he argues:

> As one moves from previously existing texts of the type central to the humanities, through the textual materials of qualitative social science, to the quantitative data many of us use, the role of interpretation—which I broadly define as *the process of ascertaining the meaning(s) and implication(s) of a set of materials*—actually increases. . . . In quantitative social science, the analyst constructs both a first order text (in assembling the data) and a second order text (in the form of statistical results). With each additional step in the process, the role of interpretation increases, as do the technical elements that must be considered as part of the interpretive process. Thus, rather than being more divorced from the human process of interpretation, quantitative social science probably involves more levels of interpretation than does qualitative social science. (Kritzler, 1996, pp. 2-3, emphasis in original)

Kritzler goes on to detail the nature of interpretation in quantitative research. He first considers the multiple *levels* at which quantitative researchers must interpret results. At the first level, the results of statistical tools used in analysis must be understood. For example, how is one to interpret a significant canonical correlation? What does it mean to have a large "critical N" in a structural equation model? At the second level of interpretation, statistical results are used to identify anomalies and problems in the analysis. Is there restriction in range that must be considered? Have unreliable measurement instruments attenuated observed correlations? Has a small sample limited power to an untenable extent? These issues of interpretation are more complex than first-level interpretation and require an experienced analyst to fully appreciate. Finally, at the third level of interpretation, statistical patterns must be connected to broader theoretical concerns. Kritzler believes this level of analysis is "the most complex and the least understood" (p. 9) and suggests that third-level interpretation is accomplished both through reference to the context in which data were collected and theory was generated and to common "tropes" of quantitative analysis. He concludes by arguing that, as in qualitative analysis, the efficacy of an analyst's interpretation depends largely on the interaction between the researcher and the data. Even quantitative data "will speak only when they are properly questioned" (Bloch, 1953, p. 64).

Consider, for example, work in the area of participative decision making. There is little doubt from years of research that participation *can* have positive effects on employee satisfaction and productivity. Yet the questions of *how* and *why* with regard to participation in organizations are still up for some debate. Miller and Monge (1986) argued that theorists and researchers have variously advocated cognitive and affective channels through which participation could affect productivity and satisfaction. More recently, Barker and his colleagues (e.g., Barker, 1993; Barker & Tompkins, 1994) have proposed that concertive control processes are critical explanatory factors for understanding participative group effects. Clearly, these explanatory mechanisms cannot be sorted out without careful attention at all stages of the research process. The appropriate constructs must be measured (in ways commensurate with conceptualization), data must be collected at research sites and in a manner that will allow observation of critical processes, and data must be analyzed with tools that facilitate the assessment of various underlying causal structures.

Articulation With Qualitative Methods

In this chapter, I have reviewed quantitative approaches to organizational communication research. Obviously, these approaches are often seen as radically different from qualitative methods (see Taylor & Trujillo, Chapter 5, this volume). Quantitative approaches to research, based in the largely realist and objective assumptions of postpositivism, provide systematic means for generating and accumulating generalizable explanations about organizational communication processes. Research in this tradition is judged on the extent to which it meets classical standards of reliability and validity and contributes meaningfully to an accumulation of knowledge about organizational communication processes. Qualitative approaches to organizational communication research, in contrast, are based on a subjective or emergent (see Deetz, 1994) ontology and epistemology and view the research enterprise as one in which meaning and understanding are constructed through the interaction of knower and known.

Are these two general approaches to organizational communication research diametrically opposed and locked in a battle for supremacy in the field of organizational communication? Or can these approaches exist independently as alternative—but equally viable—approaches? Or is there a way that these approaches can be seen as interdependent parts of the greater research endeavor?

The contrasting ontological and epistemological assumptions of these two schools of thought would suggest that there are some points at which quantitative and qualitative researchers will *necessarily* diverge (though see Lee, 1991). That is, if a qualitative researcher denies the possibility of generalization and causal relationships, many quantitative practices must be rejected (e.g., significance testing, random sampling, experimental control). Similarly, if a quantitative researcher believes that it is desirable to achieve a detached and scientific explanation of organizational life, an ethnographic case study involving the active participation of the researcher will not be accepted as valid research. Further, it is unlikely that some "solutions" that have been proposed for this dilemma will be satisfactory to either camp. For example, the notion of using qualitative methods to "develop" research questions and quantitative methods to "test" those research questions (or vice versa) is probably distasteful to members of both schools of thought.

A more fruitful direction might be the one proposed by Gioia and his colleagues (Gioia & Pitre, 1990; Weaver & Gioia, 1994) in arguing for a multiparadigmatic approach to theory building. Gioia and Pitre (1990) examine the "transition zones" between various paradigms and suggest strategies for bridging these zones. Weaver and Gioia (1994) further the argument for the commensurability of paradigms, positing that various paradigms of inquiry serve to "selectively bracket" social phenomena. They maintain that structuration theory (Giddens, 1976, 1979, 1984) provides means for understanding this selective bracketing and a point of connection between assumptions of interpretivists and postpositivists. Weaver and Gioia (1994) explain:

> Structuration provides a basis for seeing how organizational scholars can invoke different assumptions, pursue different goals, ask different research questions, and use different approaches, but nonetheless be engaged in inquiry with commonalities despite such diversities. . . . Structuration theory shows just how the selective bracketing of social phenomena can occur. (pp. 577-578)

Weaver and Gioia (1994) then go on to argue that structuration theory's central construct of the "dualism" can serve to break down oppositional dichotomies and illuminate "positions, processes or entities whose various aspects may be temporarily bracketed" (p. 578). For example, in proposing the "duality of structure," Giddens (1976) argues that social structures "are both constituted 'by' human agency, and yet at the same time are the very 'medium' of this constitution" (p. 121). Thus, the structuration process, by considering both the *process* of social structure constitution and the *effects* those constitutions have on practices, provides a fertile ground for both postpositivist and interpretive theorists and for both quantitative and qualitative researchers. Qualitative methods are necessary for gaining a local understanding of how the interaction of organizational members creates rules and structures. Quantitative research methods can be used to investigate the more stable ways in which those reified structures constrain and enable organizational behavior and communication.

Interestingly, scholars within the field of organizational communication are poised to take a leading role in this theoretical bridging of the qualitative and quantitative camps. Organizational communication scholars have been vocal proponents of structuration theory for many years. For example, this framework has been used to enhance our understanding of the political nature of organizational cultures (Riley, 1983), formal organizational communication structures (McPhee, 1985), group decision making (Poole, Seibold, & McPhee, 1986), and communication network participation (Corman & Scott, 1994).

Two recent research programs are particularly illustrative of the power of this theoretical paradigm for understanding communication phenomena through both quantitative and qualitative lenses. Joanne Yates and Wanda Orlikowski (e.g., Orlikowski & Yates, 1994; Yates & Orlikowski, 1992) draw on structuration theory in examining the ways in which "communication genres" are enacted in organizations or organizational communities. In a second line of research, Gerardine DiSanctis and Marshall Scott Poole have advocated the use of adaptive structuration theory for understanding the complexity of communication technologies such as group decision support systems (see DeSanctis & Poole, 1994, for a recent and comprehensive discussion). These scholars advocate a multilevel and multimethod research approach that holds great promise for explaining the ways in which "technology and social structures mutually shape one another over time" (DeSanctis & Poole, 1994, p. 125). DeSanctis and Poole's (1994) discussion of the analytical research strategies necessary for a consideration of the appropriation process is notable in its inclusion of both quantitative and qualitative techniques (see pp. 138-139).

In conclusion, though quantitative and qualitative researchers advance very different research agendas and goals, structuration theory provides one possible framework that can allow both schools to work together in enhancing our knowledge of the creation, sustenance, and constraining effects of organizational communication processes. Because of these metatheoretical possibilities, and the tradition of healthy dialogue within the field of organizational communication, it seems likely that both quantitative and qualitative research programs will continue to thrive in our research.

NOTES

1. Watt and van den Berg (1995), in a recent explication of quantitative research methods for communication, note the following requirements that differentiate scientific methods from "naive science" (pp. 12-14): selection of abstract concepts to represent observable phenomena, defining concepts both conceptually and operationally, linking concepts through propositions, testing theories with observable evidence, controlling alternative explanations through study design, making definitions and procedures public for scrutiny by the scientific community, using unbiased evidence in making truth claims, and objective reconciliation of theory and observation.

2. Several multivariate techniques used by organizational communication researchers are discussed in this chapter. Others that cannot be discussed due to space limitations include multivariate multiple regression, canonical correlation, and discriminant analysis. For a discussion of the use of these, and other, multivariate techniques in human communication research, see Monge and Cappella (1980).

3. McPhee and Corman (1995) note problems with this family of techniques including the complexity and difficulty of interpretation and reliance on statistical tests that are overly sensitive to sample size.

4. Technical merits of the study can also be considered with regard to the appropriate choice and execution of statistical techniques. Because these issues vary substantially depending on the analytical choices made in a study, they will not be discussed in detail here. The interested reader is referred to relevant sources on specific statistical procedures referenced in the course of this chapter.

5. More complete information on analytical techniques and choices can be found in the following sources. For event history analysis, see Allison (1984). For Markov analysis, see Bartholomew (1976). For time series analysis, see Box and Jenkins (1976). For an overview of sequence methods, see Abbott (1990).

6. A variety of goodness-of-fit tests are available in statistical software packages such as LISREL (Jöreskog & Sörbom, 1989). Because these goodness-of-fit indexes (based on chi-square) are sensitive to sample size, Hoetler (1983) has suggested the use of the "critical N" statistic to account for sample size. The use of the chi-square to degrees of freedom ratio (Bentler & Bonett, 1980) for this correction is not recommended, however.

REFERENCES

Abbott, A. (1990). A primer on sequence methods. *Organization Science, 1,* 375-392.

Albrecht, T. L., & Ropp, V. A. (1982). The study of network structuring in organizations through the use of method triangulation. *Western Journal of Speech Communication, 46,* 162-178.

Allison, P. D. (1984). *Event history analysis.* Beverly Hills, CA: Sage.

Althauser, R. P. (1974). Inferring validity from the multitrait-multimethod matrix: Another assessment. In H. L. Costner (Ed.), *Sociological methodology 1974* (pp. 106-127). San Francisco: Jossey-Bass.

Bagozzi, R. M. (1980). *Causal models in marketing.* New York: John Wiley.

Bakeman, R., & Gottman, J. M. (1986). *Observing interaction.* Cambridge, UK: Cambridge University Press.

Barker, J. R. (1993). Tightening the iron cage: Concertive control in self-managing teams. *Administrative Science Quarterly, 38,* 408-437.

Barker, J. R., & Tompkins, P. K. (1994). Identification in the self-managing organization: Characteristics of target and tenure. *Human Communication Research, 21,* 223-240.

Bartholomew, D. J. (1976). *Stochastic models for social processes.* New York: John Wiley.

Bentler, P. M., & Bonett, D. G. (1980). Significance tests and goodness of fit in the analysis of covariance structures. *Psychological Bulletin, 88,* 588-606.

Berger, P., & Luckmann, T. (1967). *The social construction of reality.* London: Penguin.

Bernard, H. R., Killworth, P. D., Kronnenfeld, D., & Sailer, L. (1984). On the validity of retrospective data: The problem of informant accuracy. *Annual Review of Anthropology, 13,* 495-517.

Bernard, H. R., Killworth, P. D., & Sailer, L. (1982). Informant accuracy in social network data V: An experimental attempt to predict actual communication from recalled data. *Social Science Research, 11,* 30-66.

Bernstein, R. (1976). *The restructuring of social and political theory.* Philadelphia: University of Pennsylvania Press.

Bishop, Y. M. M., Feinberg, S. E., & Holland, P. W. (1975). *Discrete multivariate analysis: Theory and practice.* Cambridge, MA: MIT Press.

Bloch, M. (1953). *The historian's craft.* New York: Knopf.

Bochner, A. P., & Fitzpatrick, M. A. (1980). Multivariate analysis of variance: Techniques, models, and applications in communication research. In P. R. Monge & J. N. Cappella (Eds.), *Multivariate techniques in human communication research* (pp. 143-174). New York: Academic Press.

Boster, F. J. (1988). Comments on the utility of compliance-gaining message selection tasks. *Human Communication Research, 15,* 169-177.

Box, G. E. P., & Jenkins, G. M. (1976). *Time series analysis: Forecasting and control.* Oakland, CA: Holden-Day.

Burleson, B. R., Wilson, S. R., Waltman, M. S., Goering, E. M., Ely, T. K., & Whaley, B. B. (1988). Item desirability effects in compliance-gaining research: Seven studies documenting artifacts in the strategy selection procedure. *Human Communication Research, 14,* 429-486.

Burrell, G., & Morgan, G. (1979). *Sociological paradigms and organisational analysis.* London: Heinemann.

Burstein, L. (1980). The analysis of multilevel data in educational research and evaluation. In D. C. Berliner (Ed.), *Review of research in education* (Vol. 8, pp. 153-233). Washington, DC: American Educational Research Association.

Burt, R. S. (1978). Cohesion versus structural equivalence as a basis for network subgroups. *Sociological Methods and Research, 7,* 189-212.

Campbell, D. T., & Fiske, D. W. (1959). Convergent and discriminant validation by the multitrait-multimethod matrix. *Psychological Bulletin, 56,* 81-105.

Campbell, D. T., & Stanley, J. C. (1963). *Experimental and quasi-experimental designs for research.* Chicago: Rand-McNally.

Campbell, J. P. (1986). Labs, fields, and straw issues. In E. A. Locke (Ed.), *Generalizing from laboratory to field settings* (pp. 269-279). Lexington, MA: Lexington Books.

Cappella, J. N. (1980). Structural equation modeling: An introduction. In P. R. Monge & J. N. Cappella (Eds.), *Multivariate techniques in human communication research* (pp. 57-110). New York: Academic Press.

Cappella, J. N. (1990). The method of proof by example in interaction analysis. *Communication Monographs, 57,* 236-242.

Cohen, J. (1960). A coefficient of agreement for nominal scales. *Educational and Psychological Measurement, 20,* 37-46.

Contractor, N. S., & Seibold, D. R. (1993). Theoretical frameworks for the study of structuring processes in group decision support systems: Adaptive structuration theory and self-organizing systems theory. *Human Communication Research, 19,* 528-563.

Cook, T. D., & Campbell, D. T. (1979). *Quasi-experimentation: Design and analysis issues for field settings.* Chicago: Rand-McNally.

Corman, S. R. (1990). A model of perceived communication in collective networks. *Human Communication Research, 16,* 582-602.

Corman, S. R., & Scott, C. R. (1994). Perceived networks, activity foci, and observable communication in social collectives. *Communication Theory, 4,* 171-190.

Cronbach, L. (1951). Coefficient alpha and the internal structure of tests. *Psychometrika, 16,* 297-334.

Crowne, D. P., & Marlowe, D. (1964). *The approval motive: Studies in evaluative dependence.* New York: John Wiley.

Deetz, S. A. (1994). Future of the discipline: The challenges, the research, and the social contribution. In S. A. Deetz (Ed.), *Communication yearbook 17* (pp. 565-600). Thousand Oaks, CA: Sage.

DeSanctis, G., & Poole, M. S. (1994). Capturing the complexity in advanced technology use: Adaptive structuration theory. *Organization Science, 5,* 121-147.

Eisenberg, E. M., Monge, P. R., & Miller, K. I. (1983). Involvement in communication networks as a predictor of organizational commitment. *Human Communication Research, 10,* 179-201.

Ellis, B. H. (1992). The effects of uncertainty and source credibility on attitudes about organizational change. *Management Communication Quarterly, 6,* 34-57.

Fairhurst, G. T. (1993). The leader-member exchange patterns of women leaders in industry: A discourse analysis. *Communication Monographs, 60,* 321-351.

Fairhurst, G. T., & Chandler, T. A. (1989). Social structure in leader-member interaction. *Communication Monographs, 56,* 215-239.

Fairhurst, G. T., Green, S., & Courtright, J. (1995). Inertial forces and the implementation of a socio-technical systems approach: A communication study. *Organization Science, 6,* 168-185.

Fairhurst, G. T., Rogers, L. E., & Sarr, R. A. (1987). Manager-subordinate control patterns and judgments about the relationship. In M. McLaughlin (Ed.), *Communication yearbook 10* (pp. 395-415). Newbury Park, CA: Sage.

Farace, R. V., Monge, P. R., & Russell, H. M. (1977). *Communicating and organizing.* Reading, MA: Addison-Wesley.

Feyerabend, P. (1975). *Against method.* London: New Left Books.

Fink, E. M., & Chen, S.-S. (1995). A Galileo analysis of organizational climate. *Human Communication Research, 21,* 494-521.

Fink, E. M., & Monge, P. R. (1985). An exploration of confirmatory factor analysis. In B. Dervin & M. J. Voigt (Eds.), *Progress in communication sciences* (Vol. 5, pp. 167-197). Norwood, NJ: Ablex.

Fitch, K. L. (1994). Criteria for evidence in qualitative research. *Western Journal of Communication, 58,* 32-38.

Folger, J. P., Hewes, D., & Poole, M. S. (1984). Coding social interaction. In B. Dervin & M. J. Voigt (Eds.), *Progress in communication sciences* (Vol. 4, pp. 115-161). New York: Ablex.

Fulk, J. (1993). Social construction of communication technology. *Academy of Management Journal, 36,* 921-950.

Giddens, A. (1976). *New rules for sociological method.* New York: Basic Books.

Giddens, A. (1979). *Central problems in social theory.* Berkeley: University of California Press.

Giddens, A. (1984). *The constitution of society: Outline of the theory of structure.* Berkeley: University of California Press.

Gioia, D. A., & Pitre, E. (1990). Multiparadigm perspectives on theory building. *Academy of Management Review, 15,* 584-602.

Glass, G. V., McGaw, B., & Smith, M. L. (1981). *Meta-analysis in social research.* Beverly Hills, CA: Sage.

Glick, W. H. (1988). Response: Organizations are not central tendencies: Shadowboxing in the dark, round 2. *Academy of Management Review, 13,* 133-137.

Glick, W. H., Huber, G. P., Miller, C. C., Doty, D. H., & Sutcliffe, K. M. (1990). Studying changes in organizational design and effectiveness: Retrospective event histories and periodic assessments. *Organization Science, 1,* 293-312.

Gordon, M. E., Slade, L. A., & Schmitt, N. (1986). The "science of the sophomore" revisited: From conjecture to empiricism. *Academy of Management Review, 11,* 191-207.

Gordon, M. E., Slade, L. A., & Schmitt, N. (1987). Students as guinea pigs: Porcine predictors and particularistic phenomena. *Academy of Management Review, 12,* 160-163.

Graen, G. B., & Scandura, T. A. (1987). Toward a psychology of dyadic organizing. In B. Staw & L. L. Cummings (Eds.), *Research in organizational behavior* (Vol. 9, pp. 175-208). Greenwich, CT: JAI.

Greenberg, J. (1987). The college sophomore as guinea pig: Setting the record straight. *Academy of Management Review, 12,* 157-159.

Guba, E. G. (1990). The alternative paradigm dialog. In E. G. Guba (Ed.), *The paradigm dialog* (pp. 17-27). Newbury Park, CA: Sage.

Guba, E. G., & Lincoln, Y. S. (1994). Competing paradigms in qualitative research. In N. K. Denzin & Y. S. Lincoln (Eds.), *Handbook of qualitative research* (pp. 105-117). Thousand Oaks, CA: Sage.

Guetzkow, H. (1950). Unitizing and categorizing problems in coding qualitative data. *Journal of Clinical Psychology, 6,* 47-57.

Hawes, L., Pacanowsky, M., & Faules, D. (1988). Approaches to the study of organizational communication: A conversation among three schools of thought. In G. M. Goldhaber & G. A. Barnett (Eds.), *Handbook of organizational communication* (pp. 41-53). Norwood, NJ: Ablex.

Hempel, C. (1966). *Philosophy of natural science.* Englewood Cliffs, NJ: Prentice Hall.

Hewes, D. E. (1975). Finite stochastic modeling of communication processes. *Human Communication Research, 1,* 217-283.

Hewes, D. E. (1979). The sequential analysis of social interaction. *Quarterly Journal of Speech, 65,* 56-73.

Hewes, D. E. (1985). Systematic biases in coded social interaction data. *Human Communication Research, 11,* 554-574.

Hoetler, J. H. (1983). The analysis of covariance structures: Goodness-of-fit indices. *Sociological Methods and Research, 11,* 325-344.

Holmes, M., & Poole, M. S. (1991). The longitudinal analysis of interaction. In B. Montgomery & S. Duck (Eds.), *Studying interpersonal interaction* (pp. 286-302). New York: Guilford.

Holsti, O. R. (1969). *Content analysis for the social sciences and humanities.* Reading, MA: Addison-Wesley.

House, R., Rousseau, D. M., & Thomas-Hunt, M. (1995). The meso paradigm: A framework for the integration of micro and macro organizational behavior. *Research in Organizational Behavior, 17,* 71-114.

Huber, G. P., & Van de Ven, A. H. (Eds.). (1995). *Longitudinal field research methods: Studying processes of organizational change.* Thousand Oaks, CA: Sage.

Hunter, J. E. (1988). Failure of the social desirability response set hypothesis. *Human Communication Research, 15,* 162-168.

Hunter, J. E., & Gerbing, D. W. (1982). Unidimensional measurement, second order factor analysis, and causal models. *Research in Organizational Behavior, 4,* 267-320.

Hunter, J. E., Schmidt, F. L., & Jackson, G. B. (1982). *Meta-analysis: Cumulating research findings across studies.* Beverly Hills, CA: Sage.

Jacobs, S. (1990). On the especially nice fit between qualitative analysis and the known properties of conversation. *Communication Monographs, 57,* 243-249.

James, L. R., Joyce, W. F., & Slocum, J. W. (1988). Comment: Organizations do not cognize. *Academy of Management Review, 13,* 129-132.

James, L. R., Mulaik, S. A., & Brett, J. M. (1982). *Causal analysis: Assumptions, models, and data.* Beverly Hills, CA: Sage.

Jöreskog, K. G., & Sörbom, D. (1989). *LISREL 7 user's reference guide.* Mooresville, IN: Scientific Software.

Keppel, G. (1982). *Design and analysis: A researchers handbook.* Englewood Cliffs, NJ: Prentice Hall.

Keppel, G., & Zedeck, S. (1989). *Data analysis for research designs.* New York: Freeman.

Kerlinger, F. N. (1979). *Behavioral research: A conceptual approach.* New York: Holt, Rinehart & Winston.

Kerlinger, F. N. (1986). *Foundations of behavioral research.* New York: Holt, Rinehart & Winston.

Klein, K. J., Dansereau, F., & Hall, R. J. (1994). Levels issues in theory development, data collection, and analysis. *Academy of Management Review, 19,* 195-229.

Knapp, M. L., Putnam, L. L., & Davis, L. J. (1988). Measuring interpersonal conflict in organizations: Where do we go from here? *Management Communication Quarterly, 1,* 414-429.

Kramer, M. W. (1993). Communication after job transfers: Social exchange processes in learning new roles. *Human Communication Research, 20,* 147-174.

Kritzler, H. M. (1996). The data puzzle: The nature of interpretation in quantitative research. *American Journal of Political Science, 40,* 1-32.

Krone, K. J., Jablin, F. M., & Putnam, L. L. (1987). Communication theory and organizational communication: Multiple perspectives. In F. M. Jablin, L. L. Putnam, K. H. Roberts, & L. W. Porter (Eds.), *Handbook of organizational communication: An interdisciplinary perspective* (pp. 18-40). Newbury Park, CA: Sage.

Kuhn, T. S. (1962). *The structure of scientific revolutions.* Chicago: University of Chicago Press.

Lakatos, I. (1970). Falsification and the methodology of scientific research programmes. In I. Lakatos & A. Musgrave (Eds.), *Criticism and the growth of knowledge* (pp. 91-196). Cambridge, UK: Cambridge University Press.

Lammers, J. C., & Krikorian, D. (1997). Theoretical extension and operationalization of the bona fide group construct with an application to surgical teams. *Journal of Applied Communication Research, 25,* 17-38.

Lee, A. S. (1991). Integrating positivist and interpretive approaches to organizational research. *Organization Science, 2,* 342-365.

Locke, E. A. (Ed.). (1986). *Generalizing from laboratory to field settings.* Lexington, MA: Lexington Books.

Manicas, P. (1987). *A history and philosophy of the social sciences.* Oxford, UK: Basil Blackwell.

Marcoulides, G. A., & Schumacker, R. E. (1996). *Advanced structural equation modeling: Issues and techniques.* Mahwah, NJ: Lawrence Erlbaum.

Marshall, A. A., & Stohl, C. (1993). Participating as participation: A network approach. *Communication Monographs, 60,* 137-157.

Marshall, C. (1990). Goodness criteria: Are they objective or judgment calls? In E. G. Guba (Ed.), *The paradigm dialog* (pp. 188-197). Newbury Park, CA: Sage.

McPhee, R. D. (1985). Formal structure and organizational communication. In R. D. McPhee & P. K. Tompkins (Eds.), *Organizational communication: Traditional themes and new directions* (pp. 149-177). Beverly Hills, CA: Sage.

McPhee, R. D., & Babrow, A. (1987). Causal modeling in communication research: Use, disuse, and misuse. *Communication Monographs, 54,* 344-366.

McPhee, R. D., & Corman, S. R. (1995). An activity-based theory of communication networks in organizations, applied to the case of a local church. *Communication Monographs, 62,* 132-151.

Miller, K., Birkholt, M., Scott, C., & Stage, C. (1995). Empathy and burnout in human service work: An extension of a communication model. *Communication Research, 22,* 123-147.

Miller, K. I., & Monge, P. R. (1986). Participation, satisfaction, and productivity: A meta-analytic review. *Academy of Management Journal, 29,* 727-753.

Monge, P. R. (1982). Systems theory and research in the study of organizational communication: The correspondence problem. *Human Communication Research, 8,* 245-261.

Monge, P. R. (1990). Theoretical and analytical issues in studying organizational processes. *Organization Science, 1,* 406-430.

Monge, P. R., & Cappella, J. N. (Eds.). (1980). *Multivariate techniques in human communication research.* New York: Academic Press.

Monge, P. R., & Contractor, N. S. (1988). Communication networks: Measurement techniques. In C. H. Tardy (Ed.), *A handbook for the study of human communication: Methods and instruments for observing, measuring, and assessing communication processes* (pp. 107-138). Norwood, NJ: Ablex.

Monge, P. R., Cozzens, M. D., & Contractor, N. S. (1992). Communication and motivational predictors of the dynamics of organization innovation. *Organization Science, 3,* 250-274.

Monge, P. R., & Eisenberg, E. M. (1987). Emergent communication networks. In F. M. Jablin, L. L. Putnam, K. H. Roberts, & L. W. Porter (Eds.), *Handbook of organizational communication: An interdisciplinary perspective* (pp. 304-342). Newbury Park, CA: Sage.

Monge, P. R., Farace, R. V., Eisenberg, E. M., White, L., & Miller, K. I. (1984). The process of studying process in organizational communication. *Journal of Communication, 34,* 22-43.

Nunnally, J. (1978). *Psychometric theory.* New York: McGraw-Hill.

Orlikowski, W. J., & Yates, J. (1994). Genre repertoire: The structuring of communicative practices in organizations. *Administrative Science Quarterly, 39,* 541-574.

Papa, M. J., & Pood, E. A. (1988). Coorientational accuracy and organizational conflict: An examination of tactic selection and discussion satisfaction. *Communication Research, 15,* 3-28.

Pedhazur, E. J. (1982). *Multiple regression in behavioral research.* New York: Holt, Rinehart & Winston.

Pettigrew, A. M. (1990). Longitudinal field research on change: Theory and practice. *Organization Science, 1,* 267-292.

Phillips, D. C. (1987). *Philosophy, science, and social inquiry.* Oxford, UK: Pergamon.

Phillips, D. C. (1990). Postpositivistic science: Myths and realities. In E. G. Guba (Ed.), *The paradigm dialog* (pp. 31-45). Newbury Park, CA: Sage.

Poole, M. S. (1996, February). *Another turn of the wheel: A return to systems theory in organizational communication.* Paper presented at the Conference on Organizational Communication and Change, Austin, TX.

Poole, M. S., & DeSanctis, G. (1992). Microstructural processes in computer-supported group decision-making. *Human Communication Research, 19,* 5-49.

Poole, M. S., Holmes, M., & DeSanctis, G. (1991). Conflict management in a computer-supported meeting environment. *Management Science, 37,* 926-953.

Poole, M. S., Holmes, M., Watson, R., & DeSanctis, G. (1993). Group decision support systems and group communication: A comparison of decision making in computer-supported and nonsupported groups. *Communication Research, 20,* 176-213.

Poole, M. S., & McPhee, R. D. (1995). Methodology in interpersonal communication research. In M. L. Knapp & G. R. Miller (Eds.), *Handbook of interper-*

sonal communication (2nd ed., pp. 42-100). Thousand Oaks, CA: Sage.

Poole, M. S., & Roth, J. (1989). Decision development in small groups IV: A typology of group decision paths. *Human Communication Research, 15,* 323-356.

Poole, M. S., Seibold, D. R., & McPhee, R. D. (1986). A structurational approach to theory-building in group decision-making research. In R. Y. Hirokawa & M. S. Poole (Eds.), *Communication and group decision-making* (pp. 237-264). Beverly Hills, CA: Sage.

Popper, K. (1962). *Conjectures and refutations.* New York: Harper.

Putnam, H. (1981). *Reason, truth, and history.* Cambridge, UK: Cambridge University Press.

Putnam, L. L., Bantz, C., Deetz, S., Mumby, D., & Van Maanen, J. (1993). Ethnography versus critical theory: Debating organizational research. *Journal of Management Inquiry, 2,* 221-235.

Putnam, L. L., & Pacanowsky, M. E. (Eds.). (1983). *Communication and organizations: An interpretive approach.* Beverly Hills, CA: Sage.

Putnam, L. L., & Stohl, C. (1990). Bona fide groups: A reconceptualization of groups in context. *Communication Studies, 41,* 248-265.

Rice, R. E., & Richards, W. D. (1985). An overview of network analysis methods and programs. In B. Dervin & M. J. Voigt (Eds.), *Progress in communication sciences* (Vol. 6, pp. 105-165). Norwood, NJ: Ablex.

Riley, P. (1983). A structurationist account of political cultures. *Administrative Science Quarterly, 28,* 414-437.

Schumacker, R. E., & Lomax, R. G. (1996). *A beginner's guide to structural equation modeling.* Mahwah, NJ: Lawrence Erlbaum.

Seibold, D. R. (1988). A response to "Item desirability in compliance-gaining research." *Human Communication Research, 15,* 152-161.

Smith, J. K. (1990). Goodness criteria: Alternative research paradigms and the problem of criteria. In E. G. Guba (Ed.), *The paradigm dialog* (pp. 167-187). Newbury Park, CA: Sage.

Stohl, C. (1986). Bridging the parallel organization: A study of quality circle effectiveness. In M. McLaughlin (Ed.), *Communication yearbook 10* (pp. 473-496). Beverly Hills, CA: Sage.

Stohl, C. (1993). European managers' interpretations of participation: A semantic network analysis. *Human Communication Research, 20,* 97-117.

Stohl, C. (1995). *Organizational communication: Connectedness in action.* Thousand Oaks, CA: Sage.

Suppe, F. (Ed.). (1977). *The structure of scientific theories* (2nd ed.). Urbana: University of Illinois Press.

Tornatsky, L. G., Eveland, J. D., Boylan, M. G., Hetzner, W. A., Johnson, E. C., Roltman, D., & Schneider, J. (1983). *The process of technological innovation: Reviewing the literature.* Washington, DC: National Science Foundation.

Treadwell, D. F., & Harrison, T. M. (1994). Conceptualizing and assessing organizational image: Model images, commitment, and communication. *Communication Monographs, 61,* 63-85.

Trigg, R. (1985). *Understanding social science.* Oxford, UK: Basil Blackwell.

Van de Ven, A. H., & Poole, M. S. (1990). Methods for studying innovation development in the Minnesota Innovation Research Program. *Organization Science 1,* 313-335.

Wagner, J. A., III, & Gooding, R. Z. (1987). Effects of societal trends on participative research. *Administrative Science Quarterly, 32,* 241-262.

Walther, J. B. (1995). Relational aspects of computer-mediated communication: Experimental observations over time. *Organization Science, 6,* 186-203.

Warwick, D., & Lininger, C. (1975). *The sample survey: Theory and practice.* New York: McGraw-Hill.

Wasserman, S., & Faust, K. (1994). *Social network analysis: Methods and applications.* Cambridge, UK: Cambridge University Press.

Watt, J. H., & van den Berg, S. A. (1995). *Research methods for communication science.* Boston: Allyn & Bacon.

Weaver, G. R., & Gioia, D. A. (1994). Paradigms lost: Incommensurability vs. structurationist inquiry. *Organization Studies, 15,* 565-590.

Wilson, B. J. (1994). A challenge to communication empiricists: Let's be more forthcoming about what we do. *Western Journal of Communication, 58,* 25-31.

Wilson, S. R., & Waltman, M. S. (1988). Assessing the Putnam-Wilson Organizational Communication Conflict Instrument (OCCI). *Management Communication Quarterly, 1,* 367-388.

Yates, J., & Orlikowski, W. J. (1992). Genres of organizational communication: A structurational approach to studying communication and media. *Academy of Management Review, 17,* 299-326.

Zwick, R. (1988). Another look at interrater agreement. *Psychological Bulletin, 103,* 274-378.

5

Qualitative Research Methods

BRYAN C. TAYLOR
University of Colorado at Boulder

NICK TRUJILLO
California State University, Sacramento

In the past two decades, a growing number of researchers have used qualitative methods to study various aspects of organizational communication. Researchers have turned to qualitative methods for a variety of reasons, including the recognition of the limitations of positivist epistemology and quantitative methods, as well as the acceptance of multiple approaches to the study of organizations. The increased use of qualitative methods in organizational communication also has reflected (or, more often, has followed) the trend set by scholars in anthropology, sociology, management, and other disciplines (see Denzin & Lincoln, 1994, for a review).

We welcome—indeed, we celebrate—the widespread use of qualitative methods by contemporary organizational communication scholars. In this chapter, we consider some of the issues and challenges that continue to confront researchers using these methods. Specifically, we begin the chapter with a discussion of some trends in the evolution of qualitative research in organizational communication. We then focus the majority of the chapter on key methodological issues and challenges confronting qualitative researchers. We conclude with a discussion of future trends in qualitative research.

THE EVOLUTION OF QUALITATIVE RESEARCH IN ORGANIZATIONAL COMMUNICATION

Defining Qualitative Research

We believe it is futile to propose any single, comprehensive definition of qualitative research. Like the term *postmodernism, qualita-*

tive research defies complete resolution. For some, the term connotes a general paradigm, involving epistemological and theoretical assumptions. For others, the term denotes a specific methodology with guiding implications for data collection and analysis. Consider, for example, the following multiple-choice question:

Qualitative research . . .

(a) is "a field of inquiry in its own right" that "privileges no single methodology over any other" (Denzin & Lincoln, 1994, pp. 1, 3);

(b) is "drawn to a broad, interpretive, postmodern, feminist and critical sensibility" as well as to "more narrowly defined positivist, postpositivistic, humanistic, and naturalistic conceptions of human experience" (Nelson, Treichler, & Grossberg, 1992, p. 4);

(c) "emphasizes inductive, interpretive methods applied to the everyday world which is seen as subjective and socially created" (Anderson, 1987, p. 384);

(d) "examines the qualities . . . of communication phenomena" whereby "data tend to be continuous rather than discrete, and the emphasis is on description and explanation more than on measurement and prediction" (Fitch, 1994a, p. 32); or

(e) "encompasses a variety of methods variously referred to as interpretive, naturalistic, phenomenological, or ethnographic" (Kreps, Herndon, & Arneson, 1993, p. 1).

The correct answer is, of course, "all of the above." A trick question perhaps, but qualitative research is a tricky area to define with much precision, because it is so large and amorphous, and because it is growing and changing even as you read this chapter. As Van Maanen (1995) noted, "New journals, new theories, new problems, new topics, and new critiques of older works multiply with each passing year" (p. 27). In fact, a truly comprehensive survey of qualitative research in organizational communication would likely result in a handbook at least the size of this volume (see Denzin & Lincoln, 1994) because it would include reviews of conversation analysis (see Drew & Heritage,

1992), ethnomethodology (see Heritage, 1984), grounded theory (see Browning, 1978), ethnography (see Schwartzman, 1993), rhetorical criticism (see McMillan, 1987), semiotics (see Barley, 1983), critical theory (see Deetz, 1992), feminism (see Buzzanell, 1994; Marshall, 1993), postmodernism (see Alvesson & Deetz, 1996), and others. We take heart in our current task from Van Maanen's (1995) observation that no single scholar can keep up with the developments in all of these subfields and that some filtering is inevitable: "It seems the best we can do these days is to selectively pursue and cultivate an ever diminishing proportion of the relevant literature that comes our way and assume an attitude of benign neglect towards the rest" (p. 27).

Although we do not have the space to fully review these various areas, we do not fully neglect them either. However, because we were commissioned to discuss the *methodological* issues and challenges facing scholars who conduct qualitative research, we proceed with the following agenda. Specifically, we discuss two issues that have been long-standing concerns of qualitative researchers—the relationship between qualitative and quantitative methods, and the criteria used to evaluate qualitative research—and two issues that have been raised recently in light of the popularity of critical approaches—the role of critical theory in qualitative research, and the poetics and politics of representation. Before we address these issues, though, we briefly review the evolution of qualitative research in organizational communication.

Trends in the Evolution of Qualitative Research in Sociology and Anthropology

In the introduction to their own massive handbook, Denzin and Lincoln (1994) described what they called five "moments" in the evolution of qualitative research in sociology and anthropology, two disciplines that have a rich history of qualitative research. We briefly review their discussion here because the trends they discuss have influenced other disciplines as well, including organizational communication. Although they discussed five discrete moments or phases, their model does not report deterministic sequences of exhaustive or mutually exclusive stages. Rather, these phases overlap with one another, and researchers continue to conduct scholarship reflecting trends from each period.

Denzin and Lincoln described the first moment, which occurred roughly from the early 1900s until World War II, as a "traditional period," one characterized by researchers "who wrote 'objective,' colonizing accounts of field experiences that were reflective of the positivist scientific paradigm" (p. 7). They billed Malinowski (1916/1948) as the pioneer of the period and cited the classic anthropological ethnographies of Radcliffe-Brown, Margaret Mead, and Gregory Bateson and the classic sociological ethnographies of Robert Park and the "Chicago school" as defining exemplars. They had Rosaldo (1989) eulogize the phase, debunking the now-transparent objectivism, imperialism, monumentalism, and timelessness of this research.

The second moment they described was the "modernist phase," a period that extended through the post-World War II years into the 1970s. Qualitative researchers of this period attempted to "formalize qualitative methods" through "postpositivist discourse" in a conscious effort to demonstrate reliability and validity (p. 8). It was the "golden age of rigorous qualitative analysis" (p. 8), an age when sociologists such as Howard Becker (Becker, Geer, Hughes, & Strauss, 1961) and Glaser and Strauss (1967) produced important work and when theories of ethnomethodology, phenomenology, feminism, and critical theory started to receive attention.

Denzin and Lincoln described the third phase as "the moment of blurred genres," a period from the early 1970s through the mid-1980s, when qualitative researchers embraced the use of multiple perspectives. They cast anthropologist Clifford Geertz (1973), with his call for "thick description," as the hero of this phase. They also suggested that the "naturalistic, postpositivistic, and constructionist paradigms gained power in this

period" (p. 9) as new journals such as *Urban Life* (now *Journal of Contemporary Ethnography*), *Qualitative Sociology,* and *Symbolic Interaction* came onto the scene.

Denzin and Lincoln noted that the fourth phase was triggered by a "profound rupture" in the mid-1980s that resulted in two related "crises." First, a "crisis of legitimation" problematized and politicized issues such as reliability, validity, truth, and meaning that had been viewed as "settled" in earlier phases. This crisis has led qualitative researchers to further embrace critical theory, feminism, ethnic studies, poststructuralism, and postmodernism in an effort to de- and reconstruct the very nature of scholarship. Second, a "crisis in representation" was articulated in the writings of Marcus and Fischer (1986), Clifford and Marcus (1986), and others who "made research and writing more reflexive, and called into question the issues of gender, class, and race" (p. 10) as influences on the research process. This crisis of representation problematized the very nature of authorship and led qualitative researchers to confront the autobiographical and political dimensions of all scholarship.

Denzin and Lincoln described the fifth moment of qualitative research as one of "coping with the present" (p. 576). They suggested that we are coping with the crises of legitimation and representation from the fourth moment; with the ongoing challenges of critical theory, feminism, ethnic studies, and postmodernism to the status quo; with the introduction of new research technologies; and with the juxtaposition of the sacred and the scientific as influences on research.

Trends in the Evolution of Qualitative Research in Organizational Communication

Several of the trends described by Denzin and Lincoln (1994) also characterize trends in the evolution of qualitative research in organizational communication. However, as an area of study distinct from sociology and anthropology, organizational communication has its own unique history (see Redding, 1985) and its own unique trends in the use of qualitative research. Here we briefly review some of the trends in the evolution of qualitative research in organizational communication. Again, these trends do not reflect any sort of deterministic sequence, but are suggestive of the historical development of qualitative research in our discipline.

Unlike sociology and anthropology, the field of organizational communication never really experienced a "traditional period" of *qualitative* research. However, Tompkins and Redding (1988) noted that the period from 1900 to 1940—what they called the "era of preparation" (p. 7)—included several areas of study such as "business speech," "industrial journalism," "proto-human relations," and even Dale Carnegie courses, which shared a "speech" tradition and reflected a rhetorical—and, thus, a more or less qualitative—approach (see also Redding, 1985). In addition, certain seminal management books of this early period that influenced subsequent research in organizational communication were based on extensive case studies, such as Barnard's (1938) *Functions of the Executive,* Roethlisberger and Dickson's (1939) *Management and the Worker,* and Simon's (1945) *Administrative Behavior.*

"Modernist" trends in organizational communication began in the 1940s and dominated research well into the early 1970s as researchers struggled to define "organizational communication" as a distinct and legitimate field. Tompkins and Redding (1988) referred to the early modernist period as one of "identification and consolidation," noting that researchers tried to deal with "the identity problem" of our emerging field (p. 15). In fact, Redding (1985) nominated *1959* as "The Year of Crystallization," when "industrial communication" had become recognized as a distinct field of study, and *1967* as "The Year of Official Acceptance," when the landmark Conference on Organizational Communication occurred in Huntsville, Alabama where researchers offered state-of-the-art reviews of the *empirical research* in organizational communication.

Although most of the methodologies that characterize "modernist" research in organizational communication were—and still are—quantitative ones applied by proponents of mechanistic, psychological, and systems approaches, some scholars also developed more qualitatively oriented approaches. Early in this period, communication scholars—like scholars in other fields—grappled with the implications of the famous "Hawthorne Studies" and subsequent debates about "human relations" approaches to management. Numerous case studies of communication in organizations dominated the early years of this period—especially in the form of doctoral dissertations at universities such as Northwestern, Ohio State, and Purdue (see Redding, 1985, for a review). Case study approaches, however, became post-World War II casualties when scholars in communication and other disciplines advocated large-scale experiments and surveys to satisfy institutional goals of prediction and control. Later in this period, scholars such as Ernest Bormann (1972; Bormann, Pratt, & Putnam, 1978), Phil Tompkins (Tompkins, Fisher, Infante, & Tompkins, 1975), and others (e.g., Chesbro, Cragan, & McCullough, 1973; Cowell, 1972; Sharf, 1978) drew on the unique rhetorical roots of our discipline and applied rhetorical criticism to the study of organizational communication, setting the stage for subsequent rhetorical analyses of organizational communication and corporate discourse (see Cheney, 1991; Cheney & Vibbert, 1987; McMillan, 1987; Putnam, Van Hoeven, & Bullis, 1991; Tompkins, 1978). Finally, other researchers suggested that ethnomethodology (Garfinkel, 1967) could be a useful qualitative method for studying the interactional reproduction of social order, leading to the development of conversation analysis, which has since become a thriving area of study in communication and which has been used to study organizational discourse (see Banks, 1994; Beach, 1994, 1995; Drew & Heritage, 1992; Geist & Hardesty, 1990).

Like other disciplines, organizational communication also experienced a period characterized by the blurring of genres as described in Denzin and Lincoln's "third moment." This trend in our field was incited during the 1970s and 1980s by the "new" idea that the expressive and symbolic dimensions of organizations warranted their study as cultures (see Eisenberg & Riley, Chapter 9, this volume). Even though sociologists had treated organizations as cultures for decades in their ethnographic studies of urban settings, scholars (and popular writers and consultants) in management, followed closely by those in organizational communication, fervently embraced the cultural model. Our field initiated in 1981 what became the annual Conference on Interpretive Approaches to the Study of Organizational Communication in Alta, Utah.[1] Following that first conference, and the subsequent publications resulting from the conference (Pacanowsky & Putnam, 1982; Putnam & Pacanowsky, 1983), there was a groundswell of conferences, curriculum offerings, journal articles, and books on organizational culture and symbolism. Organizational communication scholars such as Pacanowsky and O'Donnell-Trujillo (1982, 1983), Riley (1983), Eisenberg (1984), Goodall (1989), and others followed the lead of management scholars such as Van Maanen (1979), Burrell and Morgan (1979), Deal and Kennedy (1982), Smircich (1983), and others, paving the way for a bountiful decade of research. In fact, Allen, Gotcher, and Seibert (1993) noted that "organizational culture and symbolism" was the third most frequent topic in organizational communication from 1980 to 1991, resulting in 99 of the 889 journal articles they surveyed, outdistanced only by "interpersonal relations in organizations" (233) and "communication skills and strategies" (120). Perhaps most important, scholars in organizational communication started to use "new" qualitative methods of field research (such as ethnography) that forced us to spend more time in organizations; these qualitative methods continue to be used by researchers today (see Brown, 1985; Carbaugh, 1988; Goodall, 1991; Muto, 1993; Neumann & Eason, 1990; Smith & Eisenberg, 1987; Trujillo, 1992).

The "crises of legitimation and representation" that defined Denzin and Lincoln's fourth phase of qualitative research have also stimulated much discussion and debate in organizational communication. Although scholars first identified these crises during the counter-cultural ferment of the 1960s, debates surrounding these crises reached fruition during the late 1980s and 1990s as scholars offered widespread critiques of rationality, consumer-capitalism, militarism, racism, imperialism, and sexism that have implicated the academy in structures of oppression (see Trice & Beyer, 1993, pp. 23-32). For example, scholars in organizational communication have experienced *crises of legitimation* as we alternately embrace and react against critical theories in the organizational communication literature. These theories address how power and control dominate virtually every aspect of organizational communication and of research about its phenomena. Communication scholars such as Deetz (1982), Conrad (1983), Tompkins and Cheney (1983), Mumby (1987), and others followed the lead of management scholars such as Clegg (1975), Giddens (1979), Burawoy (1979), and others in paving the way for various programs of critical research that have thrived in the 1990s (see Deetz, Chapter 1, and Mumby, Chapter 15, this volume).

In addition, organizational communication scholars have experienced *crises of representation* in our struggles to articulate and evaluate the choices available for writing qualitative reports, choices that now include fictional and autobiographical forms as well as traditional social science formulas (see Brown & McMillan, 1991; Goodall, 1989, 1991; Jones, 1996; Pacanowsky, 1983, 1988; Phillips, 1995). Further, some researchers are arguing for the legitimacy of *performing* one's qualitative research (see Conquergood, 1989, 1991; Jackson, 1993; Maguire & Mohtar, 1994; Paget, 1990).

And, so, we in organizational communication, just like scholars in other disciplines, have arrived at the present moment of "coping," as we try to address the challenges of critical theory, feminism, ethnic studies, and postmodernism in the context of modernist and naturalistic traditions of qualitative research in organizational communication. As Lindlof (1995) commented on qualitative communication research in general:

> There is a growing sense that disciplinewide agreement about the goals and epistemology of a communication science may not be achievable. Communication research now accommodates many different styles of inquiry, living side by side. Some accept this situation reluctantly, some welcome it, and some resist it. (p. 7)

Lindlof explained that this theoretical and methodological pluralism characteristic of our discipline (and of most other disciplines) has been fostered by long-standing and ongoing debates among proponents of various perspectives (see "Ferment in the Field," 1983; Hawes, Pacanowsky, & Faules, 1988; Putnam, Bantz, Deetz, Mumby, & Van Maanen, 1993). As Faules (in Hawes et al., 1988) noted, pluralism "recognizes that all of the positions . . . have strengths and weaknesses" (p. 45). Indeed, we believe that it is naive and narrow-minded to assume that one particular theoretical or methodological perspective can completely reveal the complexities of organizational communication. Thus, we welcome the adoption of different perspectives and styles of inquiry, and we find much comfort in the range of theoretical and methodological choices available to organizational communication scholars. However, we also recognize that the selection of any particular theoretical and methodological perspective is always a political one that must be defended at virtually every step in the research process and that will be contested by advocates of alternative perspectives. Accordingly, we find the present to be an exciting and disturbing time to be a qualitative researcher, filled with paradox and politics, and with clarity and confusion, as we express our own sense—and try to push the boundaries—of what constitutes qualitative research in organizational communication.

KEY ISSUES AND CHALLENGES FACING QUALITATIVE RESEARCHERS

Several issues and challenges have confronted researchers as their applications of qualitative methods have evolved over the past several years. In this section, we discuss some of these issues and challenges that face us as we continue to conduct this research. In particular, we examine the relationship between qualitative and quantitative research, the role of critique in qualitative studies, the poetics and politics of representation, and criteria for evaluating qualitative studies.

The Relationship Between Quantitative and Qualitative Methods

There are many possible relationships between qualitative and quantitative approaches, depending, of course, on who is defining the relationship. Some scholars have argued that the two approaches can work very well together and have advocated the use of triangulation—the use of qualitative and quantitative methods in the same study (e.g., Albrecht & Ropp, 1982; Faules, 1982; Flick, 1992). Others have suggested that the two approaches are based ultimately on incompatible, even contradictory, epistemological underpinnings such that they should never be used together (e.g., Anderson, 1987; Bostrom & Donohew, 1992).

We believe it is relatively pointless to debate the merits of each approach in a qualitative-versus-quantitative type of debate. We agree with Miles and Huberman (1994) that "the quantitative-qualitative argument is essentially unproductive" and that there is "no reason to tie the distinction to epistemological preferences" (p. 41). Like Miles and Huberman, we believe that "the question is not whether the two sorts of data and associated methods can be linked during study design, but whether it should be done, how it will be done, and for what purposes" (p. 41).

Miles and Huberman (1994) suggested that each approach can help the other approach during the design, data collection, and data analysis stages of research. They argued that a quantitative approach can help a qualitative study during *design* "by finding a representative sample and locating deviant cases"; during *data collection* "by supplying background data, getting overlooked information, and helping avoid 'elite bias'"; and during *data analysis* "by showing the generality of specific observations . . . and verifying or casting new light on qualitative findings" (p. 41). On the other hand, a qualitative approach can help a quantitative study during *design* "by aiding with conceptual development and instrumentation"; during *data collection* "by making access and data collection easier"; and during *data analysis* "by validating, interpreting, clarifying, and illustrating quantitative findings" (p. 41).

In general, we support the use of multiple methods, quantitative and/or qualitative, in organizational communication research. However, we do not believe that triangulation can be used to "validate" data or findings in a directly positivistic sense. We believe that different methods tap into different dimensions of organizational communication and that no one method has more privileged access to organizational "reality" than any other. As Deetz (1982) argued with respect to interview methods in the context of observational methods, "Asking organizational members what they mean generates more talk, not privileged insight" (p. 135). Thus, we agree with Denzin and Lincoln (1994), who argued that "triangulation is not a tool or a strategy of validation, but an alternative to validation" such that "the combination of multiple methods . . . in a single study is best understood, then, as a strategy that adds rigor, breadth, and depth to any investigation" (p. 2; see also Flick, 1992). Similarly, Richardson (1994) suggested "crystallization" as an analytic stance

that deconstructs the traditional idea of validity as capturing a single, comprehensive truth: "The central image for 'validity' for postmodern texts is not the triangle—a rigid, fixed, two-dimensional object. Rather, the central image is the crystal, which combines symmetry and substance with an infinite variety of shapes, substances, transmutations, multidimensionalities, and angles of approach" (p. 522).

Several organizational communication scholars have used multiple methods in various ways in their research. Virtually all ethnographers use interview and participant-observation methods to collect data in organizations, and some use document analysis, content analysis, and other methods (see Bantz, 1993; Carbaugh, 1988; Goodall, 1991; Neumann, 1992; Scheibel, 1992). Other organizational communication scholars have used a variety of methods in their research as well. For example, Burrell, Buzzanell, and McMillan (1992) used questionnaire and open-ended interviews to collect data, and metaphor-analysis and content-analysis to analyze data, in their study of images of conflict among women in government. Similarly, Finet (1993) used questionnaire and open-ended interviews in her study of boundary-spanning and conflict in a New York agency. Waldron and Krone (1991) used open-ended interviews and an a priori coding system to collect data, and content analysis and log-linear analysis to analyze data in their study of the experience and expression of emotion in a corrections organization. Clair (1993a) conducted interviews and analyzed organizational documents in her critical analysis of sexual harassment in Big Ten universities. Putnam (1994) used survey and ethnographic data in her analysis of conflict in two teacher-school board negotiations. Watkins and Caillouet (1994) used participant observation and content analysis in their examination of impression management strategies used by members of a recycling facility experiencing crisis.

In sum, we believe that debates regarding which approach is "better" have become tiresome. After all, the worth of any theory or method is demonstrated not in debate, however clever, but in its utility for various communities of scholars and practitioners. We believe there are many possible relationships between qualitative and quantitative approaches to organizational communication, and we encourage researchers to demonstrate the value of these relationships in actual studies.

The Role of Critical Theory in Qualitative Research

The various crises of legitimation and representation discussed above have led scholars to examine the political nature of organizational reality and organizational research. These crises have encouraged many to adopt "critical" approaches that encourage researchers to *critique* (i.e., judge, evaluate) the organizations they study. In this section, we examine issues and challenges related to critique in qualitative research, as suggested by those who adopt the (often-overlapping) discourses of critical theory, feminism, and postmodernism. We emphasize that while we treat these discourses discretely, they often overlap in specific research projects (see, e.g., Holmer-Nadesan, 1996).

Critical Theory

Critical theory has become a popular perspective for organizational communication research in the 1990s. The term *critical theory* designates a tradition of social inquiry derived from Hegelian and Marxist philosophies, as well as more contemporary, neo-Marxist and Frankfurt schools of thought (see Mumby's chapter for a review). Applied to the study of organizational communication, critical theory is generally concerned with revealing, interrupting, and transforming the oppressive dimensions of corporate capitalism. These dimensions include hegemonic "deep-structures" and identities (such as "technical ratio-

nality" and "individualism") that are reproduced through language and interaction (such as in performance reviews). These elements function to maximize the profit and power of elites, alienate workers from authentic experience of their desires, inhibit their achievement of human potential and solidarity, and distort the democratic expression of diverse interests in organizational routines (such as decision making). Critical theory is explicitly political, and it has as its ultimate goal the "emancipation" of organizational members—the development of new lines of thought and practice that may enable undistorted dialogue and resolve unjust power asymmetries. In this view, organizational reality is inherently *contested* as different groups conduct their institutionalized struggles through various means (such as lockouts and sabotage), with the most important being *discursive* attempts to control the meanings and consequences of "work." Browner and Kubarski (1991), for example, argued that the managerial rhetoric of "professionalism" works to secure the loyalty and productivity of even low-paid clerical employees.

With respect to research "methodology," critical theorists typically engage in some form of "deconstruction." Proponents of this approach diverge from the classical interpretive goal of describing presences to argue the significance of absences—of possibilities for meaning that are systematically prevented from materializing in the repetitions and compulsions of organized interaction. Critical theorists hold that it is not the practice of research per se (such as the gathering of empirical data) that distinguishes different paradigms of organizational research so much as the nature of the assumptions and values used in developing research problems, and especially in interpreting data (Melody & Mansell, 1983). Indeed, although early critical studies in organizational communication tended to be meta-analyses[2] of other studies (e.g., Mumby, 1987), recent critical theorists have used participant-observation, interviewing, and other qualitative methods for data collection (see

Barker & Cheney, 1994; Cheney, 1995; Clair, 1993b; Deetz, 1994). What clearly distinguishes critical theorists from others who use qualitative methods is how they approach the data that they—or someone else—produce. For critical theorists, the goals of "data analysis" are, by definition, "to expose and critique the process by which a particular organizational ideology produces and reproduces the corresponding structure of power within the organization" and to provide "social actors themselves with the means by which to both critique and change the extant meaning structures of an organization" (Mumby, 1988, pp. 146, 147).

This condition that researchers *must* analyze the power relations in organizations—and provide a means for changing them—has led to inevitable debates between critical theorists and other researchers. Not surprisingly, critical theorists have vigorously indicted positivistic researchers—quantitative or qualitative—because positivists often claim objectivity, neglect the historical and cultural contexts of organizational processes, and unreflectively promote management priorities (such as effectiveness and efficiency). Indeed, critical researchers wish to expose how organizational research is subsequently implicated in perpetuating repressive systems of labor discipline.

However, critical theorists have also indicted interpretive researchers on a number of counts (see Fiske, 1991; Putnam et al., 1993; Thomas, 1993). Critical theorists have argued that ethnographers often display a political naiveté and narrow insularity in their depictions of order in organizational culture (due perhaps to a historical bias in anthropology toward studying tribal, "integrationist" cultures). From this critical view, interpretivism is not a politically neutral stance, but is one that potentially serves dominant managerial rationality (seeking, e.g., to design and impose a "strong" culture). Critical researchers argue that superficial accounts of apparently shared meanings can miss the hegemonic organization of "false consciousness" that often

underlies expressions of consensus. Qualitative research can also encourage passive spectatorship by its audiences toward the "interesting" features of organizational culture, cultivating an aesthetic experience that does not disturb or radicalize its consumers. Such accounts create premature closure on the fracturing absurdity, cruelty, and paradox that pervade the experiences of organizational members. Finally, critical researchers argue that ethnographers often do not problematize the means by which power is produced in organizations and in the qualitative research process itself. The ways that research goals are developed, and that researchers and subjects interact in the field, often confirm that the power to manage and the power to represent the Other are complementary. As Mumby stated, "The failure of ethnography lies in its refusal to assume an evaluative position" (in Putnam et al., 1993, p. 225). Thus, qualitative research may perpetuate oppression if for no other reason than that it fails to conceptualize and oppose it (one controversy here involves the "correct" theory of organizational ideology; see Beyer, Dunbar, & Meyer, 1988; Fitch, 1994b; Lannamann, 1994; Neumann, 1994). In this view, the research imperatives of "expose" and "awaken" replace those of "describe" and "interpret" (Hawes, 1983), and irony—an orientation that acknowledges how ambiguity and contradiction suffuse the production of knowledge among organizational members and researchers—replaces realism.

These claims have generated strong reactions from ethnographers, including those who counter that critical theorists hold a distorted view of their practices and that critical theory is a flawed and inappropriate foundation for qualitative research. Hammersley (1992, chap. 6), for example, argued that critical theorists have failed to demonstrate that the ideal of emancipation is itself either undistorted or inevitable, and is therefore any different from the "irrational" ideologies that it opposes. He also suggested that a "brute" Marxist position oversimplifies how power operates in organizational practice (because oppression is overdetermined by extraorganizational forces, because power inevitably begets resistance, and because organizational members may simultaneously be powerful victimizers and powerless victims). An additional flashpoint involves the criteria by which ethnographers may claim examples of false consciousness and ideological distortion. Researchers in the "ethnography of communication" tradition (see Carbaugh, 1991) hold that claims regarding struggle and ideological influence must be supported by explicit treatment of those features in the discourse of organizational members. Ethnographers in this tradition also disdain the Marxist-political investment by critical theorists in the subjects and outcome of their research; as Carbaugh (1989-1990) put it: "One does not necessarily have to evaluate a system in order to describe and theorize about it" (p. 264; see also Alvesson & Deetz, 1996; Philipsen, 1989-1990; Van Maanen, in Putnam et al., 1993, p. 229). For its opponents, critical theory compels a biased imposition of ideological values onto the research process and thus violates the goals of discovery and description essential to interpretive research. The elements of *intellectualism* (favoring abstract concepts and elaborate processes), *essentialism* (presuming the desire for autonomy in all workers), *negativism* (continually attacking management activity without providing workable solutions), and *elitism* (invalidating employees' sensemaking as false) in critical theory have inhibited its acceptance among communication scholars, even those influenced by democratic and progressive ideologies.

Despite this tension, there have been recent signs of rapprochement between ethnographers and critical theorists. Ethnographers are increasingly drawing on critical-theoretical conceptualizations of power and discipline in their studies of communication (see, e.g., Communication Studies, 1997; Conquergood, 1989, 1991; Goodall, 1991; Scheibel, 1994; Taylor, 1990, 1993; Trujillo, 1993; West, 1993). Alternately, some critical theorists are drawing on ethnographic methods to produce careful, detailed, and empathic descriptions of everyday organizational phenomena (Alvesson & Willmott, 1992; Barker & Cheney, 1994; Deetz, 1994; Forester, 1992; Willis, 1977). These descriptions assist critical theorists in exploring the contradictions between intersubjective understandings and objective social conditions, in detailing the discursive (re)production of organizational subjectivities, and in developing appropriate programs for action and change. These trends indicate that the tensions between critical theory and ethnography will continue to be productive —if not resolvable—ones for the study of organizational communication.

In summary, critical theorists have challenged organizational communication scholars to use research methods that enable us to uncover the ways in which organizational members use and are used by power. This critical challenge works best not as a litmus test for the quality and depth of a given study, but as a reminder that power is a prevalent and naturalized phenomena that we should consider in organizational research. In addition, critical theorists have challenged us to actually emancipate those who are oppressed by organizations. This is a far greater challenge, and it requires very different forms of research than currently used (such as the participatory research suggested but not practiced by Mumby, 1994), and very different forms of public-a(c)tion than the traditional textual media of journal articles or books (such as political activism; see Andersen, 1993).

Feminism

Like critical theory, feminism has become a popular perspective. And, like critical theory, "feminism" is not one particular theory, but a highly charged field of competing narratives about gender and sexual identities. These narratives include *liberal feminism,* which is primarily concerned with the inclusion of women in the rights and benefits traditionally afforded to men; *ideological/Marxist feminism,* which links female oppression to the system of social organization under capitalism; *radical feminism,* which celebrates women as fundamentally different from and better than their male oppressors, and emphasizes sexual separatism; *standpoint feminism,* which argues that women's marginalized position as Other in culture provides a resource of difference useful in critiquing and transforming misogynist institutions; and *poststructuralist and postmodern feminism,* which analyzes discourse to understand how gender identities are constructed and deployed as political processes. This last perspective diverges from other feminisms in not presuming, a priori, inherent differences between the sexes (see Bullis, 1993; Buzzanell, 1994; Donovan, 1985; Fine, 1993; Marshall, 1993; Ollenburger & Moore, 1992; Tong, 1989).

Despite their differences, feminist researchers share a commitment to critiquing gender bias in organizations and in organizational theory and research. Feminists have established that patriarchal and misogynistic elements of organizational structure and culture guide members to systematically devalue, marginalize, and annihilate women (e.g., in excluding them from important networks of informal communication). Women's "different" needs (e.g., maternity leave), which expose the organizational normalization of masculine values, are often ignored or dismissed by authorities. Beyond the "normal" demands of work, women are often subjected to ubiquitous forms of domination ranging from mundane degradation to sexual harassment to violent assault (see Clair, 1993a, 1993b; Loy & Stewart, 1984; Taylor & Conrad, 1992; Wood, 1992a, 1992b).

Feminist scholars have also challenged an implicit, "androcentric" gender bias in organizational theory and research. They argue that in their uncritical depictions of impersonal and hierarchical control systems, of technical and professional expertise, and of aggressive competition among amoral "individuals" concerned with victory and profit, many organizational researchers have naturalized ele-

ments of male sexuality as the essence of organizations. In addition, feminists argue that organizational researchers have adopted binary thinking that oversimplifies and reifies gender differences. From a (particularly poststructuralist) feminist perspective, researchers should not simply document the perceptions and behaviors of organizational members varied by biological sex (such as "male" and "female" styles of leadership), but they also should investigate the practices by which organizations conceptualize gender, and then deploy its meanings in ways that alternately oppress and please members (Gutek, 1985; Hearn, Sheppard, Tancred-Sheriff, & Burrell, 1989). In this view, gender is not simply an individual variable (a noun), but is an epistemological and political construct that guides the processes of both organization and research (a verb; see Rakow, 1986). Organizational scholars have been complicit, feminists argue, in sustaining the very structures that oppress women and in blinding their constituents to alternative forms of thought and practice (Calás & Smircich, 1991; Martin, 1990; Mumby & Putnam, 1992).[3]

While feminists continue to critique the gender bias of organizations and theory, they also make several challenges with respect to methodology. Feminists have criticized several elements of the "traditional" (primarily quantitative) research format, including its elitist selection of research topics (of those advancing the interests of men); its ritualized reproduction (in exclusively required quantitative methods courses in graduate curriculums); its biased research designs (those primarily sampling male subjects); its hierarchical exploitation of subjects; its illusion of objectivity; its improper interpretation and overgeneralization of findings (of those derived from male samples to mixed-sex populations); and finally, its inadequate use of data (e.g., in maintaining sexist policies).

This suspicion of quantitative methods does not mean, however, that there is a simple or direct mapping between feminist interests and *qualitative* methods. Qualitative methods are neither a necessary nor sufficient condition for the production of feminist research; feminist goals may be situationally met through the unique contributions of experimental and survey research, or through crystallizations of quantitative and qualitative methods (see Jayaratne & Stewart, 1991). We agree instead with arguments that "truly" feminist research (a highly contested term) is established in the content of research questions posed, in the selection of subjects, in the relations established between and among researchers and subjects, in the assumptions guiding the interpretation of data, and in the political uses to which research findings are put. With these elements in mind, we turn to five issues in feminist methodology that intersect with qualitative methods and organizational communication research.

First, we can identify a concern with *diversity.* Reinharz (1992), for example, has argued that "feminist research strives to recognize diversity" (p. 252) and that "diversity has become a new criterion for feminist research excellence" (p. 253). This concern is based on the belief that gender interacts with related constructs of race and class and sexual preference in the overlapping cultural contexts of postcolonialism, late capitalism, and patriarchy. As a result, the oppression of women through sexism is not independent from their oppression through racism and classism. Thus, feminists challenge organizational researchers to study women (and men) across a wide range of demographic categories and contexts. Feminists are struggling in this process to overcome a bias against representing working-class women of color in the production of social theory (Ollenburger & Moore, 1992). Sadly, the literature in organizational communication has offered very little diversity in terms of studies of women in organizations. With a few notable exceptions (see Eastland, 1993; Ligtenberg, 1994; Lont, 1990), most of the women studied by organizational communication scholars have been white, heterosexual, middle class, and corporate-managerial. We agree with Reinharz that

we need to embrace a form of *scholarly* "affirmative action to alter research projects" (p. 253). Obvious candidates for research, thus, involve "alternative" organizational forms that are explicitly lesbian and feminist in their characteristic structures, cultures, norms for emotional expression, patterns of development, and modes of conflict (see Ferree & Martin, 1995; Weston & Rofel, 1984).

Second, we can identify a concern with *involvement* among researchers and subjects. Reinharz (1992) has suggested that the relationship between these two groups inherently "leaves the realm of research and enters the personal lives of the individuals involved" (p. 263). The traditional authority of the researcher to unilaterally define problems, to determine methods of inquiry, and to interpret findings is rejected by feminists to emphasize the relational, collaborative, and nonhierarchical development of research goals and procedures. These qualities ideally permeate relationships among research team members, and between researchers and subjects. Research should also directly meet the needs of women and reflect a valuing of women as authorities on their own experience (Bristow & Esper, 1984; Duffy, 1985; Gergen, 1988). As Foss and Foss (1994) pointed out, feminist scholars "continually remind themselves and participants that the research product is a joint construction of the participants' experiences and interpretations and researchers' presentational expertise," and they concluded that feminist scholarship "produces not only knowledge—information about others' lives—but understanding—a capacity for insight, empathy, and attentive caring—that emerges from interaction with participants" (p. 41). Thus, researchers should not just develop "rapport" with these participants; they should develop meaningful relationships that transcend the research project and play an important part in the lives of those participants. Not surprisingly, few studies in organizational communication have reached this ideal. One exception is Kauffman's (1992) study of women artists, in which she argues that ethnographic interviews are not simply a means to *produce* data (in the form of a transcript text) reflecting theoretical concerns. They are, instead, *in and of themselves data* of collaborative performances of evolving, politically inflected relationships between interviewers and interviewees. Such data, she argued, should not be stripped to be aggregated, or to typify abstract concepts.

Third, we can identify a feminist concern with *accountable investment* by researchers. Feminist qualitative researchers are decidedly *not* objective (Mies, 1981)—a state that is viewed as neither possible nor desirable. Alternately, feminist researchers are explicitly accountable about their investment in their work (e.g., as a function of their class positions, sexual orientations, and personal histories), and about its consequences for those studied. Reinharz (1992) expressed this image of holistic research when she stated that feminism encourages "the involvement of the researcher as a person" (p. 258). This process, however, is neither straightforward nor easy. Marshall (1993), for example, reported that some feminist researchers face a dilemma involved in "exposing" through publication the "secrets" of vulnerable, subordinate women (which may subsequently be used by male authorities against their interests). Foss and Foss (1994) suggested that feminist researchers should "constantly monitor their own perspectives in regard to the personal experiences they gather" (p. 41).

Fourth, we can identify a feminist concern with *achieving social change* through qualitative research. Like other critical theories, emancipation and liberation are fundamental goals of feminist research. As Foss and Foss (1994) put it: "Feminist research is conducted for the purpose of improving women's lives. It is done to empower women—to assist them in developing strategies to make sense of and make choices about the world in which they live" (p. 42). With respect to organizations, feminists seek to "call out" and "disentangle" elements of gender and sexuality that are commonly distorted and suppressed in organi-

zational communication, such as empathy, intuition, cooperation, and dialogue (Ferguson, 1984). In this view, these elements need to be reintegrated as ethical principles to guide managers and researchers in revising androcentric assumptions about the "typical" traits and performances of organizational members. Clair (1993a), for example, suggested that "emancipatory discourse"—"discourse that promotes dialogue rather than closure" (p. 148)—can help in this endeavor, but feminists challenge us in organizational communication to do far more to accomplish change. Like critical theorists, feminists who study organizational politics must ultimately engage in meaningful political action of their own (see Harding, 1986; West, 1993). After all, if we only change the nature of what is published in our journals without changing the lives of the people we study, the goals of critical theory and feminism will never be reached.

Finally, we can identify a feminist concern with the *gendered nature of the qualitative research experience* (Bell, 1993; Golde, 1986). Given that organizations are often sexist cultures, female researchers are confronted with fieldwork challenges that their male counterparts are not (or, more precisely, generic challenges that are inflected by the researcher's gender). These challenges include the real and perceived need for sponsors, patrons, and general "protection" in negotiating hostile cultures (both resistant subjects and "protectors" may, in different ways, inhibit the research process); pressures to conform to sexual stereotypes and even to have sexual relations during data gathering (a gendered manifestation of the dilemmas of mutual obligation and reciprocity between fieldworkers and subjects); and the ongoing negotiation of suspicion from patriarchal interests toward the doubled Otherness of "woman" and "researcher." These challenges suggest the need for reflective pedagogy in the training of ethnographers, and for ongoing discussions of gendered "tactics" in fieldwork.

In summary, feminist organizational theory has challenged organizational communication scholars to use research methods for particular ends, including the creation of preservationistic accounts of situated experience; the satisfaction of real needs of organizational women (both those "in" and also "invisible" to the organization, such as organizational wives; see Kanter, 1977); the revision of assumptions and practices in organizational research so that gender "differences" are reflexively considered at every stage of the research process; and finally, the reform of organizational authority and theory in the interests of sexual justice.

Postmodernism

Postmodernism is another critical perspective that gained prominence in the organizational literature in the 1990s. Postmodernism has been described as everything from a social mood and historical period to a theoretical perspective (see Alvesson, 1995; Featherstone, 1991; Thompson, 1993). As applied to the study of organizations, Alvesson and Deetz (1996) described postmodernism as a "philosophically based research perspective" providing several topics and agendas for scholarship, including *the centrality of discourse* (defined as the use of language in interaction, as well as linguistically constituted systems of thought); *the fragmentation of self* (the existence of multiple, decentered, linguistically constituted and often competing forms of consciousness as identity "subject positions"); *the critique of the philosophy of presence* (in favor of the linguistic construction of reality); *the loss of master narratives* (the rejection of unified and authoritative images of the world in favor of local, situated narratives of experience); *the power/ knowledge connection* (the construction and reproduction of power through authoritative knowledge claims); *hyperreality* (reality experienced as intensive, pervasive mediation and simulation of material phenomena); and *resistance* (the attempt to open up the indeterminacy that modern science closes in its quest

for certainty and progress). These concerns are addressed to communication in both "modern" industrial-corporate organizations (which embody hierarchical differentiation, control, performativity, and rationality) and in emerging, postindustrial organizational forms (which embody fragmentation, turbulence, ambiguity, and creative play). (See Deetz's chapter for a more detailed discussion of these issues.)

With respect to *methodology*, proponents of postmodernism have offered a wide, vague, and contradictory range of options. Some suggest that postmodernism is best achieved through meta-analyses of organizational texts, including published research on organizations, while others argue that postmodernism energizes field research methods, especially ethnography.

Reading postmodernism in the context of critical theory, Alvesson and Deetz (1996) suggested that organizational researchers who draw on postmodernism typically use one of three methods: deconstruction, resistance readings, and/or genealogy (p. 36). *Deconstruction* describes the process of uncovering the tensions, contradictions, absences, and paradoxes in texts. Meaning is held to be not *in* the form of the text, but in the relationships among its signs; between those signs and their social, political, and economic uses; between the text and all other texts from which it draws its form and content (i.e., its *intertextuality*); and between the text and its readers. Calás and Smircich (1991), for example, provide a dizzying deconstruction of conventional discourse about organizational leadership to demonstrate its suppressed homosocial dimension in which masculine values dominate as a strategy for "seducing" masculine-identified organizational subjects. As Kilduff (1993) concluded, "Deconstruction is used not to abolish truth, science, logic, and philosophy, but to question how these concepts are present in texts and how they are employed to systematically exclude certain categories of thought and communication" (p. 15; see also Martin, 1992, pp. 135-141).

Although postmodernist deconstruction tends to focus on how organizations fragment, confound, and control members, Goodall (1992) has also used deconstruction to illustrate how organizations can empower people by examining one particular organizational artifact: the Nordstrom's employee handbook. He showed that by producing a brief (one-page) and strategically ambiguous "handbook" containing a single rule ("use your good judgment in all situations") followed by the statement "there will be no more additional rules," Nordstrom employees are encouraged to accept responsibility and to value creativity and initiative. As he concluded: "From a postmodern vantage, organizational communication is dedicated to sharing power, accepting responsibility, recognizing interdependence, and embodying—through appropriate displays of attitude and style—the 'unique sense of place' as a consumable commodity within fluid, ambiguous contexts of everyday business life" (p. 29).

Resistance readings similarly deconstruct textual meaning, but they do so by problematizing the role of the organizational analyst as a privileged observer who possesses the expertise to construct an authoritative metanarrative of organizational reality. Such readings are typically meta-analyses that reread organizational research accounts not as direct reflections of the organizations themselves, but of the logics and procedures by which researchers represent those organizations. Examples include Gusterson's (1993) and Taylor's (1996) reflections on "dialogic" representation of conflicting voices in nuclear weapons organizations.

Finally, Foucault's *genealogy* emphasizes how apparently divergent discourses of knowledge are embedded within a modern "episteme" (the dominant ways of knowing and speaking that characterize a particular historical period). For Foucault, these discourses lead to a network of practices that—despite their assertions—do not so much reflect truth as accomplish discipline. Working from this perspective, researchers

employ a historical focus to describe how particular methods for understanding and managing organizational members achieve authority, and thus, bear particular consequences for those members. Frequently, this perspective focuses on how the body is a symbolic "site" through which discourses create "technologies of the self" that attempt to maintain labor's productivity and efficiency. Barker and Cheney's (1994) analysis of how ostensibly progressive team-based management forms that have succeeded Taylorism, Fordism, and human relations lead to increasingly coercive control is one example of this strategy. Another is Jacques's (1996) study of the circular and fragmented "evolution" of American management's images of workers as, alternately, spiritual pilgrims, federal citizens, labor professionals, and bureaucratic cases.

Some scholars worry that empirical research will suffer with the postmodern emphasis on conducting meta-analyses of organizational documents and of organizational research texts. Dorst (1989) suggested that one implication of the postmodern breakdown between the researcher and the subject is that "field techniques for gathering information, participant observation and informant interview, will be conceptually demoted" (p. 208). Similarly, Vidich and Lyman (1994) hinted that the postmodern research enterprise "may become one devoted to reading texts and writing critiques" and that "the 'field' may be located in one's library or one's study" (p. 42).

However, other researchers, especially ethnographers, have exhibited excitement about integrating postmodern ideas into their field research. Trujillo (1993), for example, examined the hyperreality and commodification of experience at Dealey Plaza on the 25th anniversary of the assassination of John F. Kennedy. Gottschalk (1995) examined Las Vegas—a perennial favorite of postmodern ethnographers—as a (dis-)organized mediascape. Vidich and Lyman (1994) proposed that we may take "the onset of the postmodern condition as the very occasion for presenting a new kind of ethnography," one that reflects "an ethnographic attitude of engagement with a world that is ontologically absurd but always meaningful to those who live in it" (p. 42). Increasingly, ethnographers adopting this perspective turn to—if not corporate organizations in the traditional sense—what Foucault discussed as the increasing organization of the world (Burrell, 1988): the pervasive commercialization and rationalization of both public life and private experience. Linstead (1993) put the challenge this way:

> Postmodern ethnography interrogates traditional practice, asking of every representation "is this fact?" and refusing to come to any final conclusions. . . . It throws into question its own authority as an account, and whether it introduces the device of co-authorship or multiple voices or not, it nevertheless points to the possibility of an infinitude of interpretations and accounts. (p. 66)

As West (1993) concluded, "The future of ethnography lies in the ability of researchers to understand how Others articulate their sensemaking of their lives, while at the same time having the perspicacity to reveal the relations of power in which these Others' sensemaking is articulated" (p. 214).

In summary, critical theory, feminism, and postmodernism challenge organizational communication researchers to confront issues of power at every step in the research process. They challenge us to critique how power relations influence the lives of organizational women and men, and the ways that we design, conduct, and report our research. We now consider this latter issue of reporting research results.

The Poetics and Politics of Representation

As noted earlier, researchers across disciplines have experienced a crisis of representation. This dis-ease with realistic forms of re-search reporting was initially articulated by sociologists and anthropologists (Brown, 1977; Clifford & Marcus, 1986; Geertz, 1988; Marcus & Fischer, 1986; Myerhoff & Ruby, 1982) and has been further developed by those embracing postmodernism. "The postmodern critique has engendered something of a crisis," wrote Vidich and Lyman (1994), one in which "a new self-and-other consciousness has come to the fore, and the imperatives of reflexivity have shifted attention onto the literary, political, and historical features" of research (p. 41).

As suggested by these and other scholars, there are related political and poetic dimensions to this crisis in representation. The political dimension suggests that power is now understood to influence the very research processes of gathering and analyzing data as well as writing about our findings. For example, Rosaldo (1989) pointed out that "the dominant idea of a detached observer using neutral language to explain 'raw' data has been displaced by an alternate project that attempts to understand human conduct as it unfolds through time and in relation to its meaning for the actors" (p. 37). Accordingly, researchers are now advised to articulate not only how relations of power influence the members of the organizations we study but also how they influence the research process itself. Indeed, researchers are now disclosing the role we ourselves play in constructing images of the subjects we study. As Denzin (1994) put it: "Representation . . . is always self-presentation" because "the Other's presence is directly connected to the writers' self-presence in the text" (p. 503).

The self-awareness generated during this crisis of representation has led to a new concern for the poetics of scholarship, a movement that can be found in calls for new perspectives for conducting research and for new forms of presenting our scholarship. Many qualitative researchers—including those in organizational communication—have turned to "performance-centered research." One benefit of this perspective is that it orients researchers to situated, improvisational, and collaborative enactments of cultural scripts (see Lindlof, 1995, pp. 13-18). It is also productive for critical and postmodern researchers, however, because it "privileges particular, participatory, dynamic, intimate, precarious, embodied experience grounded in historical process, contingency, and ideology," and because it focuses on the "preeminently rhetorical nature" of communicative processes such as "ceremony, celebration, festival, parade, pageant, feast, and so forth" (Conquergood, 1991, pp. 187, 188; see also Banks, 1994; Bell & Forbes, 1994; Goodall, 1991; Knight, 1990; Presnell, 1994; Rogers, 1994; Trujillo & Dionisopoulos, 1987). Reflecting this postmodern stance, several studies in special issues of *Text and Performance Quarterly* (Hawes, 1994) and the *Journal of Contemporary Ethnography* (Ellis & Bochner, 1996) depict organizational performers and researchers as fluid subjectivities that are coconstructed through evolving, collaborative enactments of cultural identities such as gender, class, race, and profession. Organizational performance emerges in these articles as the locus of productive tensions between cultural disciplining of the subject and the disorganizing impulses of individual and group desires. Some of these studies problematize their own narrative form to promote reflexivity about the process by which knowledge claims are produced. In this way, the researchers are not documentarians but are implicated as coperformers. Both the process and the product of their research, in this view, become "performances" that evoke the situated performances of organizational members.

Researchers have turned to new forms of representation as well, especially with respect to *writing*. In his primer on ethnographic writing, Van Maanen (1988) identified two forms of writing in particular that some contemporary researchers have adopted. After he described conventional social science reports (or "realist" tales[4]) Van Maanen discussed "confessional" and "impressionist" tales, two related forms of writing that are not mutually

exclusive or exhaustive, but are illustrative of the forms that qualitative researchers can use in their representation of claims and data.

According to Van Maanen, *confessional tales* are distinguished by their "highly personalized styles and their self-absorbed mandates" (p. 73), and they exhibit *personalized author(ity)*, whereby "the details that matter . . . are those that constitute the field experience of the author" (p. 76) and a focus on the *fieldworker's point of view,* revealing tensions as the author struggles "back and forth between an insider's passionate perspective and an outsider's dispassionate one" (p. 77). Richardson (1994) referred to confessional writing as "the narrative of the self," and she concluded that by "writing these frankly subjective narratives, [researchers] are somewhat relieved of the problems of speaking for the 'Other,' because they are the Other in their texts" (p. 521).

We believe that confessional writing is important because our writing does not "capture" the essential truth of the organizations we study. Rather, it reveals how we as writing actors are materially and symbolically involved with those organizations through a process of reflecting on and describing our relationships with them. Unfortunately, while there have been many calls for confessional writing, there remain very few exemplars, especially in organizational communication.

One of the most provocative examples can be found in the work of Bob Krizek (1992) in his ethnography of the closing of Chicago's Comiskey Park in 1990. In the course of the article, Krizek framed the emotions of the "mourners" who narrated their memories of the ballpark with his own emotions, as he recalled going to the same ballpark to watch baseball games as a child with his father, who had died the year before the park closed. Here is how Krizek told his tale:

> Research was secondary in my mind . . . as I instinctively negotiated the ramps and stairways to those sacred seats [where we used to sit]. . . . I paused, took a few deep breaths, and then

held one as I sank into the chair closest to the aisle. For one brief moment the confidence of adulthood drifted away, replaced by the feelings of a lost five- or six-year-old boy, and I began to cry.

This may have been the first time I truly missed my dad or genuinely mourned his passing. . . . Like a frightened child, I rocked up and back in my chair and reached for his hand. The pain was immense and I reached our to hold my father's hand. I believe I succeeded. (pp. 34-35, 41)

Krizek (p. 50) concluded the article by putting the study in the context of his life (and perhaps vice versa): "This project was both painful and cleansing for me. The relationship with my father that I 'never quite understood' has become a bit clearer. I only wish that the five- or six-year-old boy still within me had a place to visit with him. Goodbye Comiskey; goodbye Dad" (see also Trujillo & Krizek, 1994).

Other examples of confessional writing in organizational communication can be found in Crawford's (1996) "personal ethnography," Eastland's (1993) discussion of liminality in her study of a 12-step recovery program, Pacanowsky's (1988) "fictional" story about the angst that a professor experiences at academic conventions, Benson's (1981) account of politics on the campaign trail, Goodall's (1989, 1991) books on his identity as "consulting detective," team ethnographers' personal reflections on their experiences at a "postmodern bar" (Communication Studies, 1997), Taylor's (1997) examination of the dialectical relationship between "personal" and "professional" interests in the production of nuclear weapons, and the special issue on sexual harassment in the *Journal of Applied Communication Research,* edited by Wood (1992a). Examples from other disciplines include Ronai's personal accounts of fieldwork as a topless dancer (1992) and of child sexual abuse (1995), Zola's (1983) compelling portrait of living with a disability, and Ellis's (1993) "story of a sudden death."

Impressionist writing can be as provocative as confessional writing, for it focuses on the drama of conducting a qualitative study. Van Maanen (1988) argued that impressionist writing exhibits *textual identity,* such that "dramatic recall" is used to recreate the experience of fieldwork; *fragmented knowledge,* revealed in a "novelistic" form whereby the tale "unfolds event by event" (p. 104); *characterization,* whereby various figures are developed as unique individuals with "such poses as befuddlement, mixed emotions, moral anguish, heightened sensitivity, compassion, enchantment, skepticism," and other emotions (p. 104); and *dramatic control,* whereby the writer produces an evocative *story,* with a plot line that has "interest (does it attract?), coherence (does it hang together?), and fidelity (does it seem true?)" (p. 105).

Not surprisingly, there are few exemplars of impressionistic writing in the organizational communication literature. One example can be found in Goodall's (1991) book *Living in the Rock 'n Roll Mystery,* which may be read as a postmodern update of classical studies of organizational and community life. Here, he describes his feelings about people in the Deep South of Birmingham, Alabama:

I fear the mere possibility of human connections between me and them based on the joke of a life that rushes us all too quickly to nowhere, regardless of our birth, looks, language, or money, and that requires us all to pay taxes along the way, taxes that are taken from wages that are never enough, wages that take time away from a life that is never enough, when what waits for us is the great trapdoor at the bottom end of the twentieth century that should mark our common generational tombstones thusly:

This citizen was born, reared, and educated,
Got a job in order to consume,
Consumed like hell,
Was famous, locally, for it
Realized that no matter how much was consumed it was
Never Enough,
Then retired,
Then died. (p. 180)

Other examples in organizational communication include Pacanowsky's (1983) fictional story of a police officer, based on his fieldwork at a police station; Brown and McMillan's (1991) "synthetic" narrative of socialization in a nursing home; and Jones's (1996) "kaleidoscopic" tale of women musicians at a folk music club. Examples from other disciplines include Richardson's (1992) long poem based on her interviews with unmarried mothers, Freeman's (1992) feminist interpretation of her "perfect Valentine," Hayano's (1982) portrait of poker players, and a special issue of the *Journal of Contemporary Ethnography*, edited by Ellis and Bochner (1996).

There are several strengths of confessional, impressionist, and other unconventional forms of writing. First, they vividly and sensitively use lyricism, nonlinearity, and pastiche (combinations of different textual fragments) to subvert the positivist premises of detachment, monologic authority, and noncontingent Truth. This writing demonstrates the "politics of form" that qualitative researchers can use to disrupt patriarchal and other realist theories. They also demonstrate how, as opposed to the belief that researchers choose methods ("the fallacy of the present choice"; Frost, Moore, Louis, Lundberg, & Martin, 1991, p. 331), *qualitative methods seem to choose researchers*. We refer here to the sense of fulfillment experienced by many researchers as they discover in qualitative methods a resonant "permission" that enables them to work through in their research the contradictions and ambiguities created in their personal histories and professional socializations (Martin, 1989; Weil, 1989).

Second, unconventional forms of writing are—despite sneering from some traditionalists about "rigor" (discussed below)—more challenging to write well, and they are almost always more interesting to read. Indeed, when we receive our quarterly issues of the *Journal of Contemporary Ethnography*, we read them with the same interest and passion that we experience when reading our monthly issues of the *New Yorker* or *Atlantic Monthly*. We have the fond hope that someday in the 21st century, audiences will read our communication journals with the same impassioned responses.[5] Such a hope, however, will come to fruition only if authors and editors are willing to risk their own professional identities to push the traditional boundaries of academic scholarship.

There are, however, some potential pitfalls and challenges associated with these forms of writing. One potential danger is that we may narcissistically emphasize ourselves over the very people we interact with in the field. As Fitch (1994a) pointed out, "The extended attention and heavy emphasis directed toward the researcher's place and state of mind sometimes degenerate into a kind of self-indulgence that [is] unproductive at best" (p. 35). We believe that the best research narratives focus on the organizational others while, at the same time, revealing how we as researchers are transformed during the process of studying the organization. In addition, the use of unconventional writing formats does not guarantee by fiat that a qualitative report is a quality report. As Van Maanen noted in his review of the first draft of this chapter, it is inappropriate if "novel work [is] simply assumed to be worthy poetics," adding that "there are lousy poems too and an ethnography cast as a short story is not necessarily a good short story." We treat the issues raised by these challenges in our subsequent discussion of evaluative criteria for qualitative research.

Perhaps the greatest challenge associated with unconventional forms of writing is that they are far more difficult to publish than conventional forms. Confessional and impressionist writing is subject to the highly arbitrary and selective tastes of editors and reviewers, and it is also subject to the ideological apparatus of academic publishing. Our own personal experience with manuscript submissions to journals suggests that criteria among editors and reviewers for "innovative" writing are often wildly divergent, idiosyncratic, poorly articulated, and occasionally approach ineffability.[6] In fact, responding to the question "What is 'good' postmodern ethnography?" one journal editor (D. Loseke, personal communication with Bryan Taylor,

April 9, 1996) stated: "I think of it like I think of 'pornography': I can't define it but I know it when I see it." We now briefly examine some of the issues involved in the politics of poetic representation.

The Politics of Poetics

Clearly, there are more calls for creative writing in organizational communication than there are exemplars. We believe this void is by no means surprising or accidental; rather, it is quite predictable given the politics of academia. We socialize our graduate students to use conventional forms of writing, and we employ publishing practices that encourage conventional forms of writing. West (1993) pointed out that "ethnography is enmeshed within the ideological practices of the academy" that "establish standards that are in direct opposition to the concerns of ethnographers" (p. 216). Some of these practices include truncating manuscripts to fit journal slots preformatted for shorter, quantitative reports; demanding that ethnographies conform to traditional, linear protocols of social science reporting formats; and devaluing narratives of personal experience as "subjective." These practices are in turn related to other traditional academic conventions, such as funding priorities for "traditional" research topics and methods; institutionally required rituals such as the literature review (and increasingly, the meta-analysis of statistical findings in a particular research area) that "box" researchers within a sedimented encoding of deductive and often sexist theorizing and that constrain (as a narrative performed for professional authorities) the questions they may legitimately ask about topics (see Aldag & Stearns, 1988); and requirements for academic retention and promotion (such as high numbers of rapidly produced, "well-placed" journal articles) that encourage reproduction of the status quo in "established" lines of research. These conventions often discourage researchers from using time- and labor-intensive ethnographic methods (particularly as these qualities aggravate

women's competing responsibilities involving childbearing and -rearing; see Moore, 1991; Podsakoff & Dalton, 1987). West concluded that changing the current situation will require qualitative researchers in communication to engage in actions that include publishing outside our field, "becoming editors of existing communication journals, creating new journals with new formats, and becoming more active in the political battles for power in our discipline and its organizations" (p. 218).[7]

Of course, writing is but one form of representation. And given the challenges of feminism and postmodernism, it may not be the most powerful form. As Conquergood (1991) challenged:

> It is one thing to talk about performance as a model for cultural process . . . as long as that performance-sensitive talk eventually gets "written down." . . . The hegemony of inscribed texts is never challenged by fieldwork because, after all is said and done, the final word is on paper. . . . It is interesting to note that even the most radical deconstructions still take place on the page. (p. 190)

Conquergood offered as one alternative *performance* itself, a form of representation advocated by Victor Turner (1986) and treated by Conquergood (1991) "as a complement, alternative, supplement, and critique of inscribed texts" (p. 191). Conquergood is one of the few scholars in communication to pursue this form of representation (see Conquergood, Friesema, Hunter, & Mansbridge, 1990; see also Welker & Goodall, 1997), and he has coproduced at least two documentaries based on his fieldwork: "Between Two Worlds: The Hmong Shaman in America" (1985) and "The Heart Broken in Half" (1990). Similarly, Mara Adelman and Peter Shultz (1994) produced a video, titled "The Pilgrim Must Embark: Living in Community," about community among people living with the AIDS virus.

Another intriguing use of performance has been adopted by Bonnie Johnson, Eric

Dishman, and their colleagues at Interval Research Corporation in Palo Alto, California (Burns, Dishman, Johnson, & Verplank, 1995). These researchers have been conducting "informances" (informative performances) for corporate clients and design engineers that draw upon ethnographic observations of computer users, conversation analytic methods to interpret field data, scenario-based interactive design techniques such as storytelling and storyboarding, and performances that they call "bodystorming" and "repping" (reenacting everyday people's performances). These informances are designed by these researchers to help engineers understand how technologies are actually used and imagine potential future uses, and to present new designs and prototypes within grounded and imagined future contexts.

In summary, the crisis of representation has radically challenged our assumptions about what constitutes the appropriate conduct and representation of our research. In our view, this crisis has provided opportunities to adopt alternative forms of writing and other strategies of representation that were unavailable to previous generations of organizational communication scholars. However, it must be remembered that these opportunities are availble only in a highly politicized academic en -vironment. We need to take more chances with our research, but in doing so, we run the risk of not finishing our dissertations on time, of having our article submissions rejected, and of being denied tenure and promotion, all because our research does not meet traditional requirements for "quality" scholarship. We now turn our attention to the issues involved in defining criteria for assessing the quality of qualitative research.

Criteria for Evaluating Qualitative Research

Scholars across disciplines have a wide variety of ideas regarding the appropriate criteria for evaluating qualitative research. In this section, we briefly review some of the criteria proposed by various scholars, especially those for "validity" in qualitative research, and we discuss the politics of assessing qualitative research in organizational communication.

Until recently, the standards used to assess qualitative research were primarily defined through a positivistic framework. When judged by positivist standards, qualitative studies of organizational communication usually have been found wanting. Indeed, they have been dismissed using such stereotypes as "soft," "imprecise," "unverifiable," "unreliable," and "nongeneralizable" (Aldag & Stearns, 1988; Lindlof, 1995). Often, these judgments have been unreflective, asserting positivist epistemology as the sole, correct, and seemingly inevitable approach to studying organizational phenomena. They have assumed the necessity of exact "correspondence" between a singular, objective reality, its quantitative measurement, and the representation of measurement activities and outcomes in the research text. In positivism, validity is guaranteed through the rigorous adoption of protocols that control against "bias" and that lead inexorably to either falsification or confirmation of hypotheses. In this way, positivists have presumed to develop universal and lawlike explanations of causal relationships between organizational variables to enable their prediction and control. Deployed against qualitative research, such reasoning has led critics such as Staw (1985) to complain that "beyond the hand-waving and travelogue that characterize most articles devoted to symbolism, we are still waiting for the real contributions to organizational science" (pp. 117-180). Such comments imply that qualitative research may be interesting but that it is ultimately unfit for the "higher" purposes of organization studies. Other positivists concede a preliminary and heuristic role for qualitative research in discovering organizational variables that can then be studied through more rigorous experimental and survey methodologies.

Qualitative researchers and their supporters have been equally vigorous in defending the integrity of their work, and they have done so through a variety of strategies. These strategies reflect the eclectic and contested nature of "qualitative research" as an interdisciplinary enterprise that spans a variety of methodological positions. As a result, multiple sets of criteria have emerged for the evaluation of qualitative research. These criteria are applied differently by different "interpretive communities" (e.g., by ethnographers, rhetorical critics, organizational consultants) to particular research texts. Although some standards seem consistent across these audiences (e.g., the description of meanings and practices among organizational members), disagreement exists among and between audiences about which evaluative criteria should be applied, and how they should be applied. This disagreement confirms a controversial but important tenet of qualitative research: Validity is attributed by audiences through the researcher's rhetorical evocation and satisfaction of normative standards in the research text itself. Ultimately, the value and significance of qualitative research are the province of *readers* (such as journal editors and manuscript reviewers) applying standards that are themselves contested, fluid, and rapidly evolving (Strine & Pacanowsky, 1985). As a result, we cannot claim here to represent a definitive consensus on standards of validity in qualitative research. We can, however, identify the seams and overlaps of an ongoing debate on the topic.

In general, we find arguments in this debate reflecting a continuum of epistemological positions ranging from "quasi-positivism" to "intepretivism" to "critical postmodernism." It is important to note that these positions are less pure types than heuristic punctuations of epistemological differences. There is as much debate within as between these positions, and any particular research text may reflect the influence of more than one position.

At the *quasi-positivist* end of the continuum, researchers value the programmatic execution of predetermined research protocols (e.g., involving the initial definition and rationalization of research questions), the confirmation of reliability through multiple observers, the generalization of "representative" textual and case study findings to larger populations, and the relevance of findings for prior, deductively tested theory (see, for examples in rhetorical and discourse analysis, Tompkins, 1994; Waitzkin, 1993). Here, qualitative methods achieve legitimacy as valued adjuncts to survey, experimental and variable analytic methods by achieving greater precision and detail in the analysis of actual micropractices in organizations. These benefits form trade-offs, however, against decreased researcher control over the organizational variables studied, and decreased ability to effectively generalize from the setting(s) studied to larger populations.

Recently, some theorists and methodologists (Eisenhardt, 1989; Hammersley, 1992; Tsoukas, 1989) have attempted to recuperate qualitative research within the larger (and more direct) opportunities for validity presented by idiographic, case study research. Such research, the authors note, is not restricted only to qualitative methods, and may involve the collection of quantitative data to offset the vivid but misleading impressions occasionally created by "soft" and "sensational" qualitative data. These authors draw on Yin's (1984) distinction between "sampling" and "replication" logics to explore how, through careful planning and execution, case studies can successfully generate and test theories. They do so by adding to—if not statistical generalizations about the distribution of variables within the population—*theoretical* understanding of the *operations* of those variables within that population. This process requires researchers to establish in advance the larger, aggregate population within which they wish the case to be understood as an exemplar. After deciding which target aggregate is desired, researchers can use official, published data to maximize the similarity between the characteristics of the aggregate and of the case. They can collaborate with other researchers to combine case studies as a series of quasi-experiments that generate, confirm, and disconfirm hypotheses. Cases that confirm emergent hypotheses enhance confidence in their validity, while cases that disconfirm them often provide an opportunity to refine and extend theory (Eisenhardt, 1989, p. 544).

Voices positioned at the *interpretivist* point in this continuum of criteria celebrate the inductive and meaning-centered focus of ethnographic research (see Anderson, 1987; Bantz, 1983; Bryman, 1988; Conrad, 1985; Fitch, 1994a; Kirk & Miller, 1986; Rosen, 1991; Silverman, 1993). External validity (i.e., generalizability) is construed as irrelevant, since any specific organization is viewed as a unique site of meanings and practices, whose complexity is to be explored and evoked by the researcher (Hansen & Kahnweiler, 1993). Description, interpretation, narrative skill, and empathic understanding take precedence; analytic claims may relate indirectly to existing concepts, but must be "relevant"—a somewhat generous and ambiguous criteria.

To elaborate, this interpretivist position on qualitative research holds that although organizational reality may admit a variety of interpretations, not all of them are equal. A valid, useful, and significant account is generally held to be one that

1. *Provides evidence of an involved and committed study* (i.e., it specifies the length of time spent by the researcher in the field, the number of organizational members studied, the frequency and quality of contact with informants, the groups that have been "theoretically sampled," etc.).
2. *Uses emic and inductive analysis* to preserve the naturally occurring features and discourse of the organizational scene and to depict both consensual and contested meanings among organizational members (i.e., it provides historical and cultural context necessary to understand the significance of events for both organizational members and professional audiences).
3. *Provides sufficient types and amounts of evidence to warrant the analytic claims being made* (i.e., it "saturates" claims with support and achieves relevance and richness by grounding them in the ongoing concerns of professional audiences regarding the topic, method, and theory).
4. *Provides evidence of a continuous and reflexive movement between explanations and data* (i.e., it indicates that initial, interpretive categories have been revised through expanding contact with the organizational scene, and may include "confessional" discourse about elements in the nonlinear process of ethnographic discovery, including false starts, backtracking, good and bad luck, serendipity, epiphanies, effects of the researcher on the researched—and vice versa— regrets, obstacles to access and inclusion posed by funding bodies and gatekeepers, and unfinished business).
5. *Shows rhetorical skill in language use* (i.e., it creates a clear, vivid, plausible, provocative, and compelling story of organizational life—also known as *verisimilitude*—that enables the reader to imaginatively enter the organizational life-world at issue and to reflect on the adequacy of its potential explanations).
6. *Uses representative data drawn from a corpus that is publicly available for review* (e.g., from transcripts of public speeches to copies of fieldnotes that are edited for confidentiality).
7. *Employs triangulation of multiple researchers, data sources, and/or methods, in addition to member checks, debriefings, and/or negative-case analysis* (which serve to enhance the accuracy and consistency of observations).

Collectively, these criteria establish the general conditions for credible qualitative accounts of organizational communication. Such accounts, however, may be indirectly related to theory. Theory here is held in tension as a resource establishing the significance of the ethnographic argument, and as a powerful "hammer" that may potentially shatter its emic character. In this view, the goal of interpretivist research is to contribute to the disciplinary enterprise of theory without succumbing to positivist tendencies toward totalization and reductionism. To achieve this goal, researchers suspend the introduction of theory into analysis until they have developed a holistic understanding of the scene. The separate discourses of organizational members and of theory are then brought into contact by researchers in a tentative, reflective manner. Heuristic connections that preserve the integrity of the documented scene are strengthened in the research report through the use of exemplars: condensed scenes of interaction that demonstrate relevant patterns and themes of interaction. Because the relationship between theory and ethnographic argument is a site of tension between inductive and deductive processes, it can also be a source of ambiguity in ethnographic pedagogy.

Finally, at the other end of the continuum is qualitative research from critical perspectives. A quality critical study is one that (1) discusses the relevant historical and cultural struggles between class, gender, and ethnic groups under study; (2) analyzes multiple forms and practices of power, ranging from outright coercion and the active constraint of minority voices to the normalization of premises that inhibit the very imagination of alternatives (see Lukes, 1974); (3) analyzes the various "tactics" of the powerless as they alternately accommodate, appropriate, resist, and transform the "strategies" of the powerful (see De Certeau, 1984); and (4) reflects on the extent to which research potentially or actually leads to changes in oppressive power relations and the emancipation of the powerless (see Lincoln, 1990, for a discussion of "catalytic" and "tactical" authenticity). In many ways, this fourth criterion of emancipation is the most important to critical studies. Mumby (in Putnam et al., 1993), for example, argued that validity from a critical perspective should not be "tied to conditions of verifiability or verisimilitude," but to "social transformation" whereby members "engage in self-reflection

and hence re-evaluate their conditions of existence" (p. 225). Similarly, West (1993) argued that ethnography is meaningful only in "its ability as a potential counter-hegemonic force" (p. 218). It is important to note that this ideal is contingent on the successful collaboration between researchers and subjects in developing and applying criteria for defining and resolving "distortions." This is a process, Deetz (1982, p. 147) conceded, that requires patience and faith.

With respect to criteria for *postmodern* qualitative research, we should note Lather's (1993) provocative discussion of "validity after poststructrualism" in which she explores the "antifoundational possibilities outside the limits of the normative framings of validity in the human sciences" (p. 677). In developing a reflexive "validity of transgression," she identifies the following four types: (1) an *ironic validity* that proliferates possible explanations to foreground the insufficiency of language for capturing and exhausting truth; (2) a *neopragmatic validity* that preserves contradictions within and between discourses to inhibit their resolution through imposition of master narratives; (3) a *rhizomatic validity* that simultaneously asserts and undermines interpretations by deferring the authority of claims to a network of competing, interanimating explanations; and (4) a *situated validity* that privileges partial, disruptive, and excessive feminine discourse to clarify patriarchal framing of knowledge fields.

These evaluative positions of quasi-positivism, interpretivism, and critical postmodernism reflect a range of standards by which qualitative researchers legitimate their studies of organizational communication. It is important to remember that these "technologies of validation" are not equally desired by all qualitative research audiences; indeed, each will have its preferred standards. Interpretivist-oriented readers, for example, may reject the quasi-positivistic demand for researchers to predetermine the aggregate contexts of their sites as an obstacle to achieving inductive understanding. In this view, such a practice might influence researchers to "see" organizational phenomena as exemplars of larger trends, rather than as local, practical accomplishments. Alternately, quasi-positivists may see this criterion as necessary to standardize and focus succeeding generations of qualitative research. Ultimately, these disagreements indicate how qualitative researchers *socially construct* validity in their discourse, within particular sets of codes and contracts with readers. The validity of qualitative methods hinges, then, not on their accuracy per se, but on their utility for the various evolving projects of organizational communication study (such as teaching, theory building, consulting, and research). At present, it appears that the participants in those projects—either through tolerance or failure to reflect on their root assumptions (Stewart, 1994)—are willing to live with ambiguity and diversity in evaluative criteria. The process by which disciplines develop and apply evaluative criteria for organizational research, of course, merits its own study (Jacques, 1992).

FUTURE ISSUES AND CHALLENGES FOR QUALITATIVE RESEARCHERS

Several issues and challenges will confront qualitative researchers in organizational communication in the new millennium, two of which we will consider here. First, we are excited about the challenges and possibilities for organizational communication research created by the emerging phenomena of *virtuality* and *cyberspace* (see Davidow & Malone, 1992; King & Cushman, 1995; Markham, 1998; Pruitt & Barrett, 1991; Reid, 1995). These terms index large-scale economic, technological, and cultural forces currently transforming post-Fordist organizational reality that must be studied by communication scholars. For example, researchers will need to become more sensitive to how computer networks and virtual workspaces destabilize the presumably formal structures of organizations by facilitating the

bypassing of hierarchies and the development of fine, complex gradations of fluid memberships (staff, consultant, "temp," etc.) available to employees through these technologies. In addition, the increasing use of computer-mediated communication and virtual reality systems among members affords researchers new opportunities to study the remapping of communicative codes and conventions from face-to-face onto mediated cultural realms. Researchers who engage in text-based qualitative research will need to understand how multimedia and hypertext technologies complicate and destabilize the very notion of the organizational "text." Finally, researchers should investigate how virtual systems recode working bodies into organizational cyborgs, holograms, and tokens of desire (see Stone, 1991).

Second, we are intrigued by the challenges and opportunities created by the topic of organizational *spirituality* (see Goodall, 1996; Reason, 1993). We believe that spirituality offers powerful narratives of purpose that alternately complement and subvert "official" organizational culture and control practices. As a medium of communion with a "higher power," spirituality potentially relativizes organizational authority and forms a competing source of identification for organizational members. Of course, the relationship between spirituality and organization is not only oppositional, because spirituality also provides a reassuring and nurturing narrative that compensates for the transient, fragmented experience of organizational life. In addition, members of "minority" groups present alternative spiritualities (besides traditional Western European Judeo-Christianity) that circulate in organizational cultures and structures, with important consequences for the legitimation of power.[8] Organizational communication researchers, as a result, can study spirituality as a form of community and experience that alternately flows with, in opposition to, and parallel to existing organizational structures.

In the final analysis, we in organizational communication must find ways to make more meaningful changes in our organizations and our communication. If we are truly honest with ourselves, we must admit that, for the most part, we have not really made a difference in the lives of the men and women we have studied. Certainly, we will continue to publish our research in academic books and journals, but we must energize those publications with better and more provocative writing so they are read by more than the students and instructors in our classes (who often do so involuntarily). We should also continue to engage in cross-disciplinary research with scholars from other fields. We should develop more meaningful relationships with the men and women we study in organizations. And we should engage in activist research and political action to make organizations safe and humane places for the work of communication, and the communication of work.

NOTES

1. I (Trujillo) was a Ph.D. student at Utah in 1981, and I felt truly blessed to be a participant at the first Alta conference and what seemed to be a defining moment in the field. Although I had read many organizational ethnographies as an undergraduate sociology major in the 1970s, I experienced a powerful excitement as I realized that scholars in organizational communication were crying for alternatives to the functionalist tradition. Several graduate students from the University of Texas also attended the conference, and I believe, no doubt naively, that we added an enthusiasm to the gathering that can only come from young, happy, and ripening grad students. In fact, after the conference, grad students from Utah and Texas declared our universities to be "sister schools," and we even had T-shirts printed with our new logo: an armadillo skiing down a mountain slope.

I (Taylor) was a member of the graduate cohort that succeeded Trujillo at Utah between 1984 and 1990. While I did not attend an Alta conference until 1989, I was drawn inexorably to the phenomena (if not the traditional research practices) of organizational communication due to my interest in critical theory and interpretive methods. I consider myself to be a highly interested "poacher" whose interests in discourse, power, and institutions intersect with the evolving projects of organizational communication research. It is significant in the writing of this chapter that Trujillo is primarily an ethnographer who has made use of critical theory, while I am primarily a cultural critic who has made use of organizational ethnography.

2. We use the term *meta-analysis* in two ways in this chapter. In most cases—such as the use of the term here—we are referring to reflexive intellectual work that investigates the premises and processes of published research. Only once do we use the term in its specialized meaning as a research technology for resolving statistical variance in the cumulative findings of a particular research area. When we use the term in this latter sense, we refer explicitly to its objectivist function.

3. We would like to offer a personal caveat at this point. Although some of our scholarship has been conducted from an avowedly feminist perspective (see Taylor, 1993; Taylor & Conrad, 1992; Trujillo, 1991, 1995), one of us (Trujillo) considers himself to be a "feminist," while the other (Taylor) is more comfortable with the label "pro-feminist," believing that biology is to some extent both boundary and destiny. However, I (Trujillo) have tired of continuing to debate those who argue—often in convention hotel hallways—that men cannot be feminists. Recently, I was pressured to drop out of an online discussion group after a debate raged on for several weeks about whether or not men should be "allowed" to participate, since the group involved women telling very personal stories. Even though most in the group agreed that the men who were part of the group were sensitive to the issues discussed by the women (and that it was virtually impossible to tell whether someone was really a man or a woman from their e-mail address anyway), the consensus was that men would be allowed to read messages but could not post any replies. When I quit the group in protest and called myself a "feminist," I received several replies, some of which chastised me for using that label, since I "could not possibly know what it was like to experience life as a woman."

I (Taylor) offer a similar exchange in which a feminist scholar in our field disclosed her reluctance to read one of my articles (1993) because "you're, well . . . you know . . . " Generally, I concede my limits in embracing all feminisms equally, and I try to keep the conversation going as a means of personal and professional growth. We both agree that our field should support all men and women who take the difficult and self-implicating journey to promote feminist research in organizational communication.

4. According to Van Maanen (1988), *realist tales* are characterized by four conventions: (1) *experiential author(ity)*, "the almost complete absence of the author from most segments of the finished text" (p. 46) focusing solely on the members of the culture who were studied; (2) a *documentary style* of writing "focused on minute, sometimes precious, but thoroughly mundane details of everyday life among the people studied" (p. 48); (3) a focus on the *native's point of view* using "accounts and explanations by members of the culture of the events in their lives" (p. 49); and (4) *interpretive omnipotence* whereby the researcher implies or directly asserts that his or her interpretations are the plausible ones with few questions about "whether they got it right, or whether there might be yet another, equally useful way to study,

characterize, display, read, or otherwise understand the accumulated field materials" (p. 51).

5. In his review of the first draft of this chapter, John Van Maanen shared a story with us that was told to him by the former editors of the *Journal of Contemporary Ethnography*. The story described how typesetters and copyeditors at Sage (the press that publishes *JCE*) fight for their assignments to *JCE* issues, because the articles are far more interesting and fun to edit than articles from most other scholarly journals.

6. For example, one of the authors (Trujillo) submitted a team-written postmodern ethnography for the special issue on ethnography in *Communication Studies* edited by Anderson and Holmes (1995). Anderson returned our manuscript *unreviewed* because, as he wrote, it was "too avant-garde." We subsequently submitted the same manuscript to the *Journal of Contemporary Ethnography;* it received a "revise and resubmit" review and was subsequently accepted for publication (see Communication Studies, 1997).

7. The formation in 1998 of an Ethnography Division within the National Communication Association is a significant development in this regard. We also experienced the politics of poetics firsthand in writing this chapter. When we decided to write the chapter together, we were in constant contact with each other through e-mail. As we developed our ideas (and our relationship), we challenged each other to think of ways to represent some of the issues and challenges of the chapter in the *writing* (the form) of the chapter. We came up with the idea of writing the chapter as an e-mail conversation, revealing our own personal perspectives on the issues while reflexively positioning ourselves in the chapter. However, when we ran this idea past Jablin and Putnam, the editors of this handbook, they instructed us not to write it as a dialogue but to write it in a more traditional didactic style to conform to the other chapters in the book. We are not condemning this decision per se, since we respect the editors and their editorial judgment (and we did, after all, want our chapter to be included in their handbook), but we noted the irony nonetheless.

8. One author (Taylor) knows a woman who has been both the subject and object of *pagan hexes* in conflicts with her fellow employees, actions that certainly exceed the boundaries of traditional disciplinary procedures.

REFERENCES

Albrecht, T. L., & Ropp, V. A. (1982). The study of network structuring in organizations through the use of method triangulation. *Western Journal of Speech Communication, 46,* 162-178.

Aldag, R. J., & Stearns, T. M. (1988). Issues in research methodology. *Journal of Management, 14,* 253-276.

Allen, M. W., Gotcher, J. M., & Seibert, J. H. (1993). A decade of organizational communication research: Journal articles 1980-1991. In S. A. Deetz (Ed.), *Communication yearbook 16* (pp. 252-330). Newbury Park, CA: Sage.

Alvesson, M. (1995). The meaning and meaninglessness of postmodernism: Some ironic remarks. *Organization Studies, 15,* 1047-1075.

Alvesson, M., & Deetz, S. (1996). Critical theory and postmodernism approaches to organizational studies. In S. R. Clegg, C. Hardy, & W. R. Nord (Eds.), *Handbook of organization studies* (pp. 191-217). London: Sage.

Alvesson, M., & Willmott, H. (1992). *Critical management studies.* London: Sage.

Andersen, P. A. (1993). Beyond criticism: The activist turn in ideological debate. *Western Journal of Communication, 57,* 247-256.

Anderson, J. (1987). *Communication research: Issues and methods.* New York: McGraw-Hill.

Anderson, J. (Ed.), & Holmes, M. E. (Assoc. Ed.). (1995). Ethnography [Special issue]. *Communication Studies, 46.*

Banks, S. P. (1994). Performing flight announcements: The case of flight attendants' work discourse. *Text and Performance Quarterly, 14,* 253-267.

Bantz, C. R. (1983). Naturalistic research traditions. In L. L. Putnam & M. E. Pacanowsky (Eds.), *Communication and organizations: An interpretive approach* (pp. 55-72). Beverly Hills, CA: Sage.

Bantz, C. R. (1993). *Understanding organizations: Interpreting organizational communication cultures.* Columbia: University of South Carolina Press.

Barker, J. R., & Cheney, G. (1994). The concept and the practices of discipline in contemporary organizational life. *Communication Monographs, 61,* 19-43.

Barley, S. R. (1983). Semiotics and the study of occupational and organizational cultures. *Administrative Science Quarterly, 28,* 393-413.

Barnard, C. I. (1938). *The functions of the executive.* Cambridge, MA: Harvard University Press.

Beach, W. A. (1994). Orienting to the phenomenon. In F. L. Casmir (Ed.), *Building communication theories: A socio-cultural approach* (pp. 133-163). Hillsdale, NJ: Lawrence Erlbaum.

Beach, W. A. (1995). Preserving and constraining options: "Okays" and "official" priorities in medical interviews. In G. H. Morris & R. Cheneil (Eds.), *Talk of the clinic* (pp. 259-289). Hillsdale, NJ: Lawrence Erlbaum.

Becker, H. S., Geer, B., Hughes, E. C., & Strauss, A. L. (1961). *Boys in white: Student culture in medical school.* Chicago: University of Chicago Press.

Bell, D. (1993). Introduction 1: The context. In D. Bell, P. Caplan, & W. J. Karim (Eds.), *Gendered fields: Women, men and ethnography* (pp. 1-17). New York: Routledge.

Bell, E., & Forbes, L. C. (1994). Office folklore in the academic paperwork empire: The interstitial space of gendered (con)texts. *Text and Performance Quarterly, 14,* 181-196.

Benson, T. W. (1981). Another shooting in Cowtown. *Quarterly Journal of Speech, 67,* 347-406.

Beyer, J. M., Dunbar, R. L., & Meyer, A. D. (1988). *Academy of Management Review, 13,* 483-489.

Bormann, E. G. (1972). Fantasy and rhetorical vision: The rhetorical criticism of social reality. *Quarterly Journal of Speech, 58,* 396-407.

Bormann, E. G., Pratt, J., & Putnam, L. (1978). Power, authority, and sex: Male response to female leadership. *Communication Monographs, 45,* 119-155.

Bostrom, R., & Donohew, L. (1992). The case for empiricism: Clarifying fundamental issues in communication theory. *Communication Monographs, 59,* 109-129.

Brown, M. H. (1985). That reminds me of a story: Speech action in organizational socialization. *Western Journal of Speech Communication, 49,* 27-42.

Brown, M. H., & McMillan, J. (1991). Culture as text: The development of an organizational narrative. *Southern Communication Journal, 57,* 49-60.

Brown, R. H. (1977). *A poetic for sociology.* Cambridge, UK: Cambridge University Press.

Browner, C. H., & Kubarski, K. (1991). The paradoxical control of American clerks. *Organization Studies, 12,* 233-250.

Bristow, A. R., & Esper, J. A. (1984). A feminist research ethos. *Humanity and Society, 8,* 489-496.

Browning, L. D. (1978). A grounded organizational communication theory derived from qualitative data. *Communication Monographs, 45,* 93-109.

Bryman, A. (1988). Introduction: Inside accounts and social research in organizations. In A. Bryman (Ed.), *Doing research in organizations* (pp. 1-20). New York: Routledge.

Bullis, C. (1993). Organizational socialization research: Enabling, constraining, and shifting perspectives. *Communication Monographs, 60,* 10-17.

Burawoy, M. (1979). *Manufacturing consent: Changes in the labor process under monopoly capitalism.* Chicago: University of Chicago Press.

Burns, C., Dishman, E., Johnson, B., & Verplank, B. (1995, August 8). *"Informance": Min(d)ing future contexts for scenario-based interaction design.* Performance, Palo Alto, CA.

Burrell, G. (1988). Modernism, postmodernism and organizational analysis 2: The contribution of Michel Foucault. *Organization Studies, 9,* 221-275.

Burrell, G., & Morgan, G. (1979). *Sociological paradigms and organizational analysis.* London: Heinemann.

Burrell, N. A., Buzzanell, P. M., & McMillan, J. J. (1992). Feminine tensions in conflict situations as revealed by metaphoric analyses. *Management Communication Quarterly, 6,* 115-149.

Buzzanell, P. M. (1994). Gaining a voice: Feminist organizational communication theorizing. *Management Communication Quarterly, 7,* 339-383.

Calás, M. B., & Smircich, L. (1991). Voicing seduction to silence leadership. *Organization Studies, 12,* 567-601.

Carbaugh, D. (1988). Cultural terms and tensions in the speech at a television station. *Western Journal of Speech Communication, 52,* 216-237.

Carbaugh, D. (1989-1990). The critical voice in ethnography of communication research. *Research on Language and Social Interaction, 23,* 261-282.

Carbaugh, D. (1991). Communication and cultural interpretation. *Quarterly Journal of Speech, 77,* 336-342.

Cheney, G. (1991). *Rhetoric in an organizational society: Managing multiple identities.* Columbia: University of South Carolina Press.

Cheney, G. (1995). Democracy in the workplace: Theory and practice from the perspective of communication. *Journal of Applied Communication Research, 23,* 167-200.

Cheney, G., & Vibbert, S. L. (1987). Corporate discourse: Public relations and issue management. In F. M. Jablin, L. L. Putnam, K. H. Roberts, & L. W. Porter (Eds.), *Handbook of organizational communication: An interdisciplinary perspective* (pp. 165-194). Newbury Park, CA: Sage.

Chesbro, J. W., Cragan, J. F., & McCullough, P. (1973). The small group techniques of the radical revolutionary: A synthetic study of consciousness raising. *Speech Monographs, 40,* 136-146.

Clair, R. P. (1993a). The bureaucratization, commodification, and privatization of sexual harassment through institutional discourse: A study of the "Big Ten" universities. *Management Communication Quarterly, 7,* 123-157.

Clair, R. P. (1993b). The use of framing devices to sequester organizational narratives: Hegemony and harassment. *Communication Monographs, 60,* 113-136.

Clegg, S. R. (1975). *The theory of power and organization.* London: Routledge and Kegan Paul.

Clifford, J., & Marcus, G. E. (Eds.). (1986). *Writing culture: The poetics and politics of ethnography.* Berkeley: University of California Press.

Communication Studies 298 [California State University, Sacramento]. (1997). Fragments of self at the postmodern bar. *Journal of Contemporary Ethnography, 26,* 251-292.

Conquergood, D. (1989). Poetics, play, process, and power: The performative turn in anthropology. *Text and Performance Quarterly, 9,* 82-88.

Conquergood, D. (1991). Rethinking ethnography: Towards a critical cultural politics. *Communication Monographs, 58,* 179-187.

Conquergood, D., Friesema, P., Hunter, A., & Mansbridge, J. (1990). *Dispersed ethnicity and community integration: Newcomers and established residents in the Albany Park area of Chicago.* Evanston: Northwestern University, Center for Urban Affairs and Policy Research.

Conrad, C. (1983). Organizational power: Faces and symbolic forms. In L. L. Putnam & M. E. Pacanowsky (Eds.), *Communication and organizations: An interpretive approach* (pp. 173-194). Beverly Hills, CA: Sage.

Conrad, C. (1985). Chrysanthemums and swords: A reading of contemporary organizational communication theory and research. *Southern Speech Communication Journal, 50,* 189-200.

Cowell, C. (1972). Group process as metaphor. *Journal of Communication, 22,* 113-123.

Crawford, L. (1996). Personal ethnography. *Communication Monographs, 63,* 158-170.

Davidow, W. H., & Malone, M. S. (1992). *The virtual corporation: Structuring and revitalizing the corporation for the 21st century.* New York: Harper Collins.

Deal, T. E., & Kennedy, A. A. (1982). *Corporate cultures: The rites and rituals of corporate life.* Reading, MA: Addison-Wesley.

De Certeau, M. (1984). *The practice of everyday life.* Berkeley: University of California Press.

Deetz, S. (1982). Critical interpretive research in organizational communication. *Western Journal of Speech Communication, 46,* 131-149.

Deetz, S. (1992). *Democracy in the age of corporate colonization.* Albany: State University of New York Press.

Deetz, S. (1994). The micro-politics of identity formation in the workplace: The case of a knowledge intensive firm. *Human Studies, 17,* 23-44.

Denzin, N. K. (1994). The art and politics of interpretation. In N. K. Denzin & Y. S. Lincoln (Eds.), *Handbook of qualitative research* (pp. 500-515). Thousand Oaks, CA: Sage.

Denzin, N. K., & Lincoln, Y. S. (1994). Introduction: Entering the field of qualitative research. In N. K. Denzin & Y. S. Lincoln (Eds.), *Handbook of qualitative research* (pp. 1-17). Thousand Oaks, CA: Sage.

Donovan, J. (1985). *Feminist theory: The intellectual traditions of American feminism.* New York: Unger.

Dorst, J. (1989). *The written suburb: An American site, an ethnographic dilemma.* Philadelphia: University of Philadelphia Press.

Drew, P., & Heritage, J. (Eds.). (1992). *Talk at work: Interaction in institutional settings.* Cambridge, UK: Cambridge University Press.

Duffy, M. E. (1985). A critique of research: A feminist perspective. *Health Care for Women International, 6,* 341-352.

Eastland, L. S. (1993). The dialectical nature of ethnography: Liminality, reflexivity, and understanding. In S. L. Herndon & G. L. Kreps (Eds.), *Qualitative research: Applications in organizational communication* (pp. 121-138). Cresskill, NJ: Hampton.

Eisenberg, E. M. (1984). Ambiguity as strategy in organizational communication. *Communication Monographs, 51,* 227-242.

Eisenhardt, K. E. (1989). Building theories from case study research. *Academy of Management Review, 14,* 532-550.

Ellis, C. (1993). Telling a story of a sudden death. *Sociological Quarterly, 34,* 711-730.

Ellis, C., & Bochner, A. (Eds.). (1996). Taking ethnography into the twenty-first century [Special issue]. *Journal of Contemporary Ethnography, 25.*

Featherstone, M. (1991). *Consumer culture and postmodernism.* London: Sage.

Faules, D. (1982). The use of multi-methods in the organizational setting. *Western Journal of Speech Communication, 46,* 150-161.

Ferguson, K. E. (1984). *The feminist case against bureaucracy.* Philadelphia: Temple University Press.

Ferment in the field. (1983). *Journal of Communication, 33.*

Ferree, M. M., & Martin, P. Y. (1995). *Feminist organizations: Harvest of the new women's movement.* Philadelphia: Temple University Press.

Fine, M. G. (1993). New voices in organizational communication: A feminist commentary and critique. In S. P. Bowen & N. Wyatt (Eds.), *Transforming visions: Feminist critiques in communication studies* (pp. 125-166). Cresskill, NJ: Hampton.

Finet, D. (1993). Effects of boundary spanning communication on the sociopolitical delegitimation of an organization. *Management Communication Quarterly, 7,* 36-66.

Fiske, J. (1991). Writing ethnographies: Contributions to a dialogue. *Quarterly Journal of Speech, 77,* 330-335.

Fitch, K. L. (1994a). Criteria for evidence in qualitative research. *Western Journal of Communication, 58,* 32-38.

Fitch, K. L. (1994b). Culture, ideology and interpersonal communication research. In S. A. Deetz (Ed.), *Communication yearbook 17* (pp. 104-135). Thousand Oaks, CA: Sage.

Flick, U. (1992). Triangulation revisited: Strategy of validation or alternative? *Journal for the Theory of Social Behavior, 22,* 175-198.

Forester, J. (1992). Critical ethnography: On fieldwork in a Habermasian way. In M. Alvesson & H. Willmott (Eds.), *Critical management studies* (pp. 46-65). Newbury Park, CA: Sage.

Foss, K. A., & Foss, S. K. (1994). Personal experience as evidence in feminist scholarship. *Western Journal of Communication, 58,* 39-43.

Freeman, J. (1992). The perfect Valentine. *Journal of Contemporary Ethnography, 20,* 478-483.

Frost, P. J., Moore, L. F., Louis, M. R., Lundberg, C. C., & Martin, J. (1991). Contexts and choices in organizational research. In P. J. Frost, L. F. Moore, M. R. Louis, C. C. Lundberg, & J. Martin (Eds.), *Reframing organizational culture* (pp. 327-334). Newbury Park, CA: Sage.

Garfinkel, H. (1967). *Studies in ethnomethdology.* Englewood Cliffs, NJ: Prentice Hall.

Geertz, C. (1973). *The interpretation of cultures.* New York: Basic Books.

Geertz, C. (1988). *Works and lives: The anthropologist as author.* Stanford, CA: Stanford University Press.

Geist, P., & Hardesty, M. (1990). Ideological positioning in professionals' narratives of quality medical care. In N. K. Denzin (Ed.), *Studies in symbolic interaction* (Vol. 11, pp. 257-284). Greenwich, CT: JAI.

Gergen, M. M. (1988). Toward a feminist metatheory and methodology in the social sciences. In M. M. Gergen (Ed.), *Feminist thought and the structure of knowledge* (pp. 87-104). New York: New York University Press.

Giddens, A. (1979). *Central problems in social theory.* London: Macmillan.

Glaser, B. G., & Strauss, A. L. (1967). *The discovery of grounded theory: Strategies for qualitative research.* Chicago: Aldine.

Golde, P. (1986). *Women in the field: Anthropological experiences* (2nd ed.). Berkeley: University of California Press.

Goodall, H. L. (1989). *Casing a promised land: The autobiography of an organizational detective as cultural ethnographer.* Carbondale: Southern Illinois University Press.

Goodall, H. L. (1991), *Living in the rock 'n roll mystery: Reading context, self, and others as clues.* Carbondale: Southern Illinois University Press.

Goodall, H. L. (1992). Empowerment, culture, and postmodern organizing: Deconstructing the Nordstrom Employee Handbook. *Journal of Organizational Change Management, 5,* 25-30.

Goodall, H. L. (1996). *Divine signs: Connecting spirit to community.* Carbondale: Southern Illinois University Press.

Gottschalk, D. (1995). Ethnographic fragments in postmodern spaces. *Journal of Contemporary Ethnography, 24,* 195-228.

Gusterson, H. (1993). Exploding anthropology's canon in the world of the bomb. *Journal of Contemporary Ethnography, 22,* 59-79.

Gutek, B. A. (1985). *Sex in the workplace.* San Francisco: Jossey-Bass.

Hammersley, M. (1992). *What's wrong with ethnography? Methodological explorations.* London: Routledge.

Hansen, C. D., & Kahnweiler, W. M. (1993). Storytelling: An instrument for understanding the dynamics of corporate relationships. *Human Relations, 46,* 1391-1409.

Harding, S. (1986). *The science question in feminism.* Ithaca, NY: Cornell University Press.

Hawes, L. C. (1983). Epilogue. In L. L. Putnam & M. E. Pacanowsky (Eds.), *Communication and organizations: An interpretive approach* (pp. 257-259). Beverly Hills, CA: Sage.

Hawes, L. C. (Ed.). (1994). Performance, organization and culture [Special issue]. *Text and Performance Quarterly, 14.*

Hawes, L., Pacanowsky, M., & Faules, D. (1988). Approaches to the study of organizations: A conversation among three schools of thought. In G. M. Goldhaber & G. A. Barnett (Eds.), *Handbook of organizational communication* (pp. 41-54). Norwood, NJ: Ablex.

Hayano, D. M. (1982). *Poker faces.* Berkeley: University of California Press.

Hearn, J., Sheppard, D. L., Tancred-Sheriff, P., & Burrell, G. (Eds.). (1989). *The sexuality of organization.* London: Sage.

Heritage, J. (1984). *Garfinkel and ethnomethodology.* Cambridge, UK: Polity.

Holmer-Nadesan, M. (1996). Organizational identity and space of action. *Organization Studies, 7,* 49-81.

Jackson, S. (1993). Ethnography and the audition: Performance as ideological critique. *Text and Performance Quarterly, 13,* 21-43.

Jacques, R. (1992). Critique and theory building: Producing knowledge "from the kitchen." *Academy of Management Review, 17,* 582-606.

Jacques, R. (1996). *Manufacturing the employee: Management knowledge from the 19th to the 21st centuries.* Thousand Oaks, CA: Sage.

Jayaratne, T. E., & Stewart, A. J. (1991). Quantitative and qualitative methods in the social sciences. In M. M. Fonow & J. A. Cook (Eds.), *Beyond methodology: Feminist scholarship as lived research* (pp. 85-106). Bloomington: Indiana University Press.

Jones, S. H. (1996). *Kaleidoscope notes: An ethnography.* Master's thesis, California State University, Sacramento.

Kanter, R. M. (1977). *Men and women of the corporation.* New York: Basic Books.

Kauffman, B. J. (1992). Feminist facts: Interview strategies and political subjects in ethnography. *Communication Theory, 2,* 187-206.

Kilduff, M. (1993). Deconstructing organizations. *Academy of Management Review, 18,* 13-31.

King, S. S., & Cushman, D. P. (1995). The high-speed management of organizational communication: Cushman, King and associates. In D. P. Cushman & B. Kovacic (Eds.), *Watershed research traditions in human communication theory* (pp. 177-210). Albany: State University of New York Press.

Kirk, J., & Miller, M. L. (1986). *Reliability and validity in qualitative research.* Beverly Hills, CA: Sage.

Knight, J. P. (1990). Literature as equipment for killing: Performance as rhetoric in military training camps. *Text and Performance Quarterly, 10,* 157-168.

Kreps, G. L., Herndon, S. L., & Arneson, P. (1993). Introduction: The power of qualitative research to address organizational issues. In S. L. Herndon & G. L. Kreps (Eds.), *Qualitative research: Applications in organizational communication* (pp. 1-18). Cresskill, NJ: Hampton.

Krizek, B. (1992). Remembrances and expectations: The investment of identity in the changing of Comiskey. *Elysian Fields Quarterly, 11,* 30-51.

Lannamann, J. W. (1994). The problem with disempowering ideology. In S. A. Deetz (Ed.), *Communication yearbook 17* (pp. 136-147). Thousand Oaks, CA: Sage.

Lather, P. (1993). Fertile obsession: Validity after poststructuralism. *Sociological Quarterly, 35,* 673-693.

Ligtenberg, A. K. (1994). *A woman's place is in the organization: An analysis of women's metaphors and stories of organizational life.* Master's thesis, California State University, Sacramento.

Lincoln, Y. S. (1990). The making of a constructive: A remembrance of transformations past. In E. G. Guba (Ed.), *The paradigm dialog* (pp. 67-87). Newbury Park, CA: Sage.

Lindlof, T. R. (1995). *Qualitative communication research methods.* Thousand Oaks, CA: Sage.

Linstead, S. (1993). Deconstruction in the study of organizations. In J. Hassard & M. Parker (Eds.), *Postmodernism and organizations* (pp. 49-70). Newbury Park, CA: Sage.

Lont, C. M. (1990). Persistence of subcultural organizations: An analysis surrounding the process of subcultural change. *Communication Quarterly, 38,* 1-12.

Loy, P. H., & Stewart, L. P. (1984). The extent and effects of the sexual harassment of working women. *Sociological Focus, 17,* 31-43.

Lukes, S. (1974). *Power: A radical view.* London: Macmillan.

Maguire, M., & Mohtar, L. F. (1994). Performance and the celebration of a subaltern counterpublic. *Text and Performance Quarterly, 14,* 238-252.

Malinowski, B. (1948). *Magic, science, and religion, and other essays.* New York: Natural History Press. (Original work published 1916)

Marcus, G., & Fischer, M. (1986). *Anthropology as cultural critique: An experimental moment in the human sciences.* Chicago: University of Chicago Press.

Markham, A. (1998). *Life online: Researching real experiene in virtual space.* Walnut Creek, CA: Alta Mira Press.

Marshall, J. (1993). Viewing organizational communication from a feminist perspective: A critique and some offerings. In S. A. Deetz (Ed.), *Communication yearbook 16* (pp. 122-143). Newbury Park, CA: Sage.

Martin, P. Y. (1989). The moral politics of organizations: Reflections of an unlikely feminist. *Journal of Applied Behavioral Science, 25,* 451-470.

Martin, J. (1990). Re-reading Weber: A feminist analysis. In E. Freeman (Ed.), *Ruffin series in business ethics.* Oxford, UK: Oxford University Press.

Martin, J. (1992). *Cultures in organizations: Three perspectives.* New York: Oxford University Press.

McMillan, J. J. (1987). In search of the organizational persona: A rationale for studying organizations rhetorically. In L. Thayer (Ed.), *Organization–communication: Emerging perspectives II* (pp. 21-45). Norwood, NJ: Ablex.

Melody, W. H., & Mansell, R. E. (1983). The debate over critical vs. administrative research: Circularity or challenge? *Journal of Communication, 33,* 103-116.

Mies, M. (1981). Towards a methodology for feminist research. In G. Bowles & R. Duelli-Klein (Eds.), *Theories of women's studies* (Vol. 2, pp. 25-46). Berkeley: University of California, Women's Studies Department.

Miles, M. B., & Huberman, A. M. (1994). *Qualitative data analysis* (2nd ed.). Thousand Oaks, CA: Sage.

Moore, L. F. (1991). Inside Aunt Virginia's kitchen. In P. J. Frost, L. F. Moore, M. R. Louis, C. Lundberg, & J. Martin (Eds.), *Reframing organizational culture* (pp. 366-372). Newbury Park, CA: Sage.

Mumby, D. K. (1987). The political function of narrative in organizations. *Communication Monographs, 54,* 113-127.

Mumby, D. K. (1988). *Communication and power in organizations: Discourse, ideology, and domination.* Norwood, NJ: Ablex.

Mumby, D. K. (1994). Critical organizational communication studies: The next 10 years. *Communication Monographs, 60,* 18-25.

Mumby, D., & Putnam, L. L. (1992). The politics of emotion: A feminist reading of bounded rationality. *Academy of Management Review, 17,* 465-486.

Muto, J. (1993). "Who's that in my bed?" The strange bedfellows made by the politics of applied qualitative organizational research. In S. L. Herndon & G. L. Kreps (Eds.), *Qualitative research: Applications in organizational communication* (pp. 19-28). Cresskill, NJ: Hampton.

Myerhoff, B., & Ruby, J. (1982). Introduction. In J. Ruby (Ed.), *A crack in the mirror: Reflexive perspectives in anthropology.* Philadelphia: University of Pennsylvania Press.

Nelson, C., Treichler, P. A., & Grossberg, L. (1992). Cultural studies. In L. Grossberg, C. Nelson, & P. A. Treichler (Eds.), *Cultural studies* (pp. 1-6). New York: Routledge.

Neumann, M. (1992). The trail through experience: Finding self in the recollection of travel. In C. Ellis & M. G. Flaherty (Eds.), *Investigating subjectivity:*

Research on lived experience (pp. 176-204). Newbury Park, CA: Sage.

Neumann, M. (1994). The contested spaces of cultural dialogue. In S. A. Deetz (Ed.), *Communication yearbook 17* (pp. 148-158). Thousand Oaks, CA: Sage.

Neumann, M., & Eason, D. (1990). Casino world: Bringing it all back home. *Cultural Studies, 4,* 45-60.

Ollenburger, J. C., & Moore, H. A. (1992). *A sociology of women: The intersection of patriarchy, capitalism and colonization.* Englewood Cliffs, NJ: Prentice Hall.

Pacanowsky, M. E. (1983). A small-town cop: Communication in, out, and about a crisis. In L. L. Putnam & M. E. Pacanowsky (Eds.), *Communication and organizations: An interpretive approach* (pp. 261-282). Beverly Hills, CA: Sage.

Pacanowsky, M. E. (1988). Slouching towards Chicago. *Quarterly Journal of Speech, 74,* 453-467.

Pacanowsky, M. E., & O'Donnell-Trujillo, N. (1982). Communication and organizational cultures. *Western Journal of Speech Communication, 46,* 115-130.

Pacanowsky, M. E., & O'Donnell-Trujillo, N. (1983). Organizational communication as cultural performance. *Communication Monographs, 50,* 126-147.

Pacanowsky, M. E., & Putnam, L. L. (1982). Introduction. *Western Journal of Speech Communication, 46,* 114.

Paget, M. (1990). Performing the text. *Journal of Contemporary Ethnography, 19,* 136-155.

Philipsen, G. (1989-1990). Some initial thoughts on the perils of "critique" in the ethnographic study of communicative practices. *Research on Language and Social Interaction, 23,* 251-260.

Phillips, N. (1995). Telling organizational tales: On the role of narrative fiction in the study of organizations. *Organization Studies, 16,* 625-649.

Podsakoff, P. M., & Dalton, D. R. (1987). Research methodology in organizational studies. *Journal of Management, 13,* 419-441.

Presnell, M. (1994). Postmodern ethnography: From representing the other to co-producing a text. In K. Carter & M. Presnell (Eds.), *Interpretive approaches to interpersonal communication* (pp. 11-43). Albany: State University of New York Press.

Pruitt, S., & Barrett, T. (1991). Corporate virtual workspace. In M. Benedikt (Ed.), *Cyberspace: First steps* (pp. 383-409). Cambridge, MA: MIT Press.

Putnam, L. L. (1994). Productive conflict: Negotiation as implicit coordination. *International Journal of Conflict Management, 5,* 284-298.

Putnam, L. L., Bantz, C., Deetz, S., Mumby, D., & Van Maanen, J. (1993). Ethnography versus critical theory: Debating organizational research. *Journal of Management Inquiry, 2,* 221-235.

Putnam, L. L., & Pacanowsky, M. E. (Eds.). (1983). *Communication and organizations: An interpretive approach.* Beverly Hills, CA: Sage.

Putnam, L. L., Van Hoeven, S. A., & Bullis, C. A. (1991). The role of rituals and fantasy themes in teachers' bargaining. *Western Journal of Communication, 55,* 85-103.

Rakow, L. F. (1986). Rethinking gender research in communication. *Journal of Communication, 36,* 11-26.

Reason, P. (1993). Sacred experience and sacred science. *Journal of Management Inquiry, 2,* 10-27.

Redding, W. C. (1985). Stumbling toward identity: The emergence of organizational communication as a field of study. In R. D. McPhee & P. K. Tompkins (Eds.), *Organizational communication: Traditional themes and new directions* (pp. 15-54). Beverly Hills, CA: Sage.

Reid, E. (1995). Virtual worlds: Culture and imagination. In S. Jones (Ed.), *Cyberspace: Computer-mediated communication and community* (pp. 164-183). Thousand Oaks, CA: Sage.

Reinharz, S. (1992). *Feminist methods in social research.* New York: Oxford University Press.

Richardson, L. (1992). The consequences of poetic representation: Writing the other, rewriting the self. In C. Ellis & M. G. Flaherty (Eds.), *Investigating subjectivity: Research on lived experience* (pp. 125-140). Newbury Park, CA: Sage.

Richardson, L. (1994). Writing: A method of inquiry. In N. K. Denzin & Y. S. Lincoln (Eds.), *Handbook of qualitative research* (pp. 516-529). Thousand Oaks, CA: Sage.

Riley, P. (1983). A structurationist account of political culture. *Administrative Science Quarterly, 28,* 414-437.

Roethlisberger, F. J., & Dickson, W. (1939). *Management and the worker.* New York: John Wiley.

Rogers, R. A. (1994). Rhythm and the performance of organization. *Text and Performance Quarterly, 14,* 222-237.

Ronai, C. R. (1992). The reflexive self through narrative: A night in the life of an erotic dancer/researcher. In C. Ellis & M. G. Flaherty (Eds.), *Investigating subjectivity: Research on lived experience* (pp. 102-124). Newbury Park, CA: Sage.

Ronai, C. R. (1995). Multiple reflections of child sex abuse: An argument for a layered account. *Journal of Contemporary Ethnography, 18,* 271-298.

Rosaldo, R. (1989). *Culture and truth: The remaking of social analysis.* Boston: Beacon.

Rosen, M. (1991). Coming to terms with the field: Understanding and doing organizational ethnography. *Journal of Management Studies, 28,* 1-24.

Scheibel, D. (1992). Faking identity in Clubland: The communicative performance of "fake ID." *Text and Performance Quarterly, 12,* 160-175.

Scheibel, D. (1994). Graffiti and "film school" culture: Displaying alienation. *Communication Monographs, 61,* 1-18.

Schwartzman, H. B. (1993). *Ethnography in organizations.* Newbury Park, CA: Sage.

Sharf, B. F. (1978). A rhetorical analysis of leadership emergence in small groups. *Communication Monographs, 45,* 156-172.

Silverman, D. (1993). *Interpreting qualitative data: Methods for analyzing talk, text and interaction.* London: Sage.

Simon, H. A. (1945). *Administrative behavior.* New York: Free Press.

Smircich, L. (1983). Concepts of culture and organizational analysis. *Administrative Science Quarterly, 28,* 339-358.

Smith, R. C., & Eisenberg, E. M. (1987). Conflict at Disneyland: A root-metaphor analysis. *Communication Monographs, 54,* 367-379.

Staw, B. M. (1985). Spinning on symbolism: A brief note on the future of symbolism in organizational research. *Journal of Management, 11,* 117-118.

Stewart, J. (1994). An interpretive approach to validity in interpersonal communication research. In K. Carter & M. Presnell (Eds.), *Interpretive approaches to validity in interpersonal communication research* (pp. 45-81). Albany: State University of New York Press.

Stone, A. R. (1991). Will the real body please stand up? Boundary stories about virtual cultures. In M. Benedikt (Ed.), *Cyberspace: First steps* (pp. 81-118). Cambridge, MA: MIT Press.

Strine, M. S., & Pacanowsky, M. (1985). How to read interpretive accounts of organizational life: Narrative bases of textual authority. *Southern Speech Communication Journal, 50,* 283-297.

Taylor, B. (1990). *Reminiscences of Los Alamos:* Narrative, critical theory, and the organizational subject. *Western Journal of Speech Communication, 54,* 395-419.

Taylor, B. (1993). Register of the repressed: Women's voice and body in the nuclear weapons organization. *Quarterly Journal of Speech, 79,* 267-285.

Taylor, B. (1996). Make bomb, save world: Reflections on dialogic nuclear ethnography. *Journal of Contemporary Ethnography, 25,* 120-143.

Taylor, B. (1997). Home zero: Images of home and field in nuclear-cultural studies. *Western Journal of Communication, 61,* 209-234,

Taylor, B., & Conrad, C. (1992). Narratives of sexual harassment: Organizational dimensions. *Journal of Applied Communication Research, 20,* 401-418.

Thomas, J. (1993). *Doing critical ethnography.* Newbury Park, CA: Sage.

Thompson, P. (1993). Post-modernism: Fatal distraction. In J. Hassard & M. Parker (Eds.), *Postmodernism and organizations* (pp. 183-203). London: Sage.

Tompkins, P. K. (1978). Organizational metamorphosis in space research and development. *Communication Monographs, 45,* 110-118.

Tompkins, P. K. (1994). Principles of rigor for assessing evidence in "qualitative" communication research. *Western Journal of Communication, 58,* 44-50.

Tompkins, P. K., & Cheney, G. (1983). Account analysis of organizations: Decision making and identification. In L. L. Putnam & M. E. Pacanowsky (Eds.), *Communication and organizations: An interpretive approach* (pp. 123-146). Beverly Hills, CA: Sage.

Tompkins, P. K., Fisher, J. Y., Infante, D. A., & Tompkins, E. L. (1975). Kenneth Burke and the inherent characteristics of formal organizations: A field study. *Speech Monographs, 42,* 135-142.

Tompkins, P. K., & Redding, W. C. (1988). Organizational communication: Past and present tenses. In G. M. Goldhaber & G. A. Barnett (Eds.), *Handbook of organizational communication* (pp. 5-33). Norwood, NJ: Ablex.

Tong, T. (1989). *Feminist thought: A comprehensive introduction.* Boulder, CO: Westview.

Trice, H. M., & Beyer, J. M. (1993). *The cultures of work organizations.* Englewood Cliffs, NJ: Prentice Hall.

Trujillo, N. (1991). Hegemonic masculinity on the mound: Media representations of Nolan Ryan and American sports culture. *Critical Studies in Mass Communication, 8,* 290-308.

Trujillo, N. (1992). Interpreting (the work and the talk of) baseball: Perspectives on ballpark culture. *Western Journal of Communication, 56,* 350-371.

Trujillo, N. (1993). Interpreting November 22: A critical ethnography of an assassination site. *Quarterly Journal of Speech, 79,* 447-466.

Trujillo, N. (1995). Machines, missiles, and men: Images of the male body on ABC's "Monday Night Football." *Sociology of Sport Journal, 12,* 403-423.

Trujillo, N., & Dionisopoulos, G. (1987). Cop talk, police stories, and the social construction of organizational drama. *Central States Speech Journal, 38,* 196-209.

Trujillo, N., & Krizek, B. (1994). Emotionality in the stands and in the field: Expressing self through baseball. *Journal of Sport and Social Issues, 18,* 303-325.

Tsoukas, H. (1989). The validity of idiographic research explanations. *Academy of Management Review, 14,* 551-561.

Turner, V. (1986). *The anthropology of performance.* New York: PAJ.

Van Maanen, J. (1979). The fact of fiction in organizational ethnography. *Administrative Science Quarterly, 24,* 539-550.

Van Maanen, J. (1988). *Tales of the field: On writing ethnography.* Chicago: University of Chicago Press.

Van Maanen, J. (1995). An end to innocence: The ethnography of ethnography. In J. Van Maanen (Ed.), *Representation in ethnography* (pp. 1-35). Thousand Oaks, CA: Sage.

Vidich, A. J., & Lyman, S. M. (1994). Qualitative methods: Their history in sociology and anthropology. In N. K. Denzin & Y. S. Lincoln (Eds.), *Handbook of* qualitative research (pp. 23-59). Thousand Oaks, CA: Sage.

Waitzkin, H. (1993). Interpretive analysis of spoken discourse: Dealing with the limitations of quantitative and qualitative methods. *Southern Communication Journal, 58,* 128-146.

Waldron, V. R., & Krone, K. J. (1991). The experience and expression of emotion in the workplace: A study of a corrections organization. *Management Communication Quarterly, 4,* 287-309.

Watkins, M., & Caillouet, R. H. (1994). Legitimation endeavors: Impression management strategies used by an organization in crisis. *Communication Monographs, 61,* 44-62.

Weil, M. (1989). Research on vulnerable populations. *Journal of Applied Behavioral Science, 25,* 419-437.

Welker, L. L., & Goodall, H. L. (1997). Representation, interpretation, and performance: Opening the text of Casing a Promised Land. *Text and Performance Quarterly, 17,* 109-122.

West, J. T. (1993). Ethnography and ideology: The politics of cultural representation. *Western Journal of Communication, 57,* 209-220.

Weston, K. M., & Rofel, L. B. (1984). Sexuality, class and conflict in a lesbian workplace. *Signs, 9,* 623-646.

Willis, P. (1977). *Learning to labour: How working class kids get working class jobs.* Franborough, UK: Saxon House.

Wood, J. T. (Ed.). (1992a). "Telling our stories": Sexual harassment in the communication discipline [Special issue]. *Journal of Applied Communication Research, 20.*

Wood, J. T. (1992b). "Telling our stories": Narratives as a basis for theorizing sexual harassment. *Journal of Applied Communication Research, 20,* 349-362.

Yin, R. (1984). *Case study research: Design and methods.* Beverly Hills, CA: Sage.

Zola, I. K. (1983). *Missing pieces: A chronicle of living with a disability.* Philadelphia: Temple University Press.

PART II

Context: Internal and External Environments

6

Organizational Environments and Organizational Information Processing

KATHLEEN M. SUTCLIFFE
University of Michigan

Organizations survive by making sense of and giving sense to their environments. Organizations acquire, interpret, and control flows of environmental information in order not to be blindsided by threats, unprepared for opportunities, or ineffective in managing interdependencies with resource controllers and other important stakeholders. It is this essential role of information and its effective use that makes communication fundamental to the study of organizational behavior. Because coping with environments can be both reac-

tive, as organizations respond to pressing problems and issues, and proactive, as organizations create opportunities previously unforeseen, any information-oriented treatment of organization-environment relations must account for outward as well as inward information flows. This chapter does both.

This chapter is focused on organizational environments and organizational information processing and is concerned with cross-boundary information flows oriented toward minimizing threats and maximizing opportu-

AUTHOR'S NOTE: I am grateful to Dennis Gioia, James Grunig, Fred Jablin, Sim Sitkin, and Karl Weick for helpful comments on a previous version and to Daniel Koger for help in sharpening many ideas in this chapter.

nities. The environment and information processing are dominant concepts in organization studies because processing information about the external environment is a key organizational and managerial activity. It is critical for adaptation and long-term survival (Galbraith, 1973; Weick, 1979). In fact, some scholars argue that information-gathering and information-processing roles—such as the kind of information managers have to work with, and the handling of information prior to decisions—are more crucial to the success of the firm than strategic decision making itself (Pfeffer & Salancik, 1978; Starbuck & Milliken, 1988; Weick, 1974). Consequently, at the heart of this chapter is the assumption that environmental information flows—the gathering and interpretation of environmental information—are crucial inputs to many organizational decisions and as such represent important processes to scholars of organizational communication. Yet information flows from organizations to their environments are as critical for organizational success as flows of information from environments to organizations.

It has long been accepted that organizations enhance their effectiveness and long-term legitimacy by proactively using communication to manage environmental interdependencies and shape their identities (Pfeffer & Salancik, 1978), yet interest in this area is gaining renewed momentum and is of increasing importance to scholars and others interested in organizational legitimacy (Elsbach, 1994; Elsbach & Sutton, 1992; Suchman, 1995), issues management and risk communication (Chess, Saville, Tamuz, & Greenberg, 1992; Chess, Tamuz, Saville, & Greenberg, 1992; Heath, 1988, 1994; Elsbach & Kramer, 1996; Heath & Nelson, 1986; Marcus & Goodman, 1991), and public relations (Cheney & Dionisopoulos, 1989; Cheney & Vibbert, 1987; Grunig, 1992), and to strategic management practitioners as well (Lev, 1992). Therefore, a second key assumption is that outflows of information related to strategy formulation, implementation, and

consequent outcomes serve as inputs to change the environment (Pfeffer & Salancik, 1978; Weick, 1979); a changed environment may have important implications for organizational legitimacy, performance, and future organizational behaviors.

This chapter departs from other treatments of organizational environments and information processing such as the chapter co-authored by Huber and Daft in the first edition of this handbook in two fundamental ways. First, it considers both the processing of incoming environmental information and the outward flow of information across organizational boundaries. Previous research in the management and organizational communication literatures examining how organizations manage environmental information has often been focused either on the processing of incoming environmental information or on the processing of outgoing information to the environment. This chapter not only reviews and updates the traditional literature on environments and information processing, but it also draws together several disparate research streams to develop a framework to better understand how organizations make sense of their environments and how organizations direct or control the flow of information back to the environment, presumably to affect organizational outcomes and identities.

Second, the chapter is directed by concerns for how organizations process and manage something they call an environment to enhance organizational effectiveness. By focusing on environmental sensing and interpretation systems and how organizations strategically use environmental information to enhance organizational effectiveness, this chapter takes a more macro-oriented approach to managerial and organizational communication processes, which is in stark contrast to many previous treatments of these issues. For example, prior work has considered the more micro-information processes related to the transmission and distribution of information internally (see Huber, 1982, 1991), and the use of information in decision making including the derivation of alternative courses of action, their evaluation, and the implementation of alternatives (see Huber, 1991; Huber & McDaniel, 1986; O'Reilly, 1983; and a special issue of *Strategic Management Journal,* 1993, 14[S2]).

My discussion in this chapter unfolds as follows. The first section is devoted to a historical overview of key perspectives on organizational environments and organizational information processing and more fully elaborates important issues overlooked or underdeveloped in previous work. In the second section, I discuss the processes by which environmental information is noticed and interpreted. The third section is focused on a discussion of information flows across organizational boundaries intended to preempt anticipated problems or hedge against unanticipated ones. The fourth section develops a framework to link incoming and outgoing flows of environmental information. The final section is devoted to a discussion of implications and future research directions.

ORGANIZATIONAL ENVIRONMENTS AND ORGANIZATIONAL INFORMATION PROCESSING: A HISTORICAL OVERVIEW

Concern with the concept of organizational environment has drawn serious academic attention for over 40 years, dating roughly from about 1956 to the present. Still, to date, only a few key perspectives describing environments are reflected in the literature. The assumptions underlying these key perspectives differ dramatically and are important not only because they influence our understanding of organization-environment relations, but also because they affect a discussion of communication-related implications. Several key perspectives on the environment are reviewed in the next section followed by a more general discussion of organizational information-processing theory.

Key Perspectives on the Environment

Objectivist Perspective

Most generally, the environment has been portrayed as a source of resources or as a source of information. The resource dependence perspective as developed by some scholars (e.g., Aldrich, 1979; Aldrich & Pfeffer, 1976; Pfeffer & Salancik, 1978) treats the environment as consisting of scarce resources for which organizations compete. Organizational outcomes are a function of both the level of resources (including the importance of a resource to the organization and the number of sources from which the resource is available) and the extent to which these resources are made available to organizations (i.e., the number, variety, and relative power of organizations competing for the resource). The resource dependence perspective suggests that organizations attempt to avoid becoming dependent on other organizations and seek to make other organizations dependent on them (Aldrich, 1979). Scholars adopting the resource dependence approach pay little attention to the processes by which organizations either obtain information about the environment or communicate information about the environment; however, they pay close attention to characteristics or dimensions of task environments.

The range of dimensions or characteristics describing task environments is large. In the organizational theory literature, organizational environments have been characterized as a set of components (e.g., economic, regulatory, technical, social), stakeholders (e.g., customers, competitors, suppliers), or as a set of attributes (e.g., instability, munificence, complexity) (Aldrich, 1979; Bourgeois, 1980; Dess & Beard, 1984). Industrial economists (e.g., Caves, 1980; Khandwalla, 1981), on the other hand, have characterized environments more broadly in terms of industry characteristics such as concentration of market power, entry barriers, changes in demand, or changes in product characteristics (Yasai-Ardekani, 1986). Organization theorists generally agree that three dimensions—stability, munificence, and complexity—are key environmental dimensions affecting organizations (Dess & Beard, 1984). These three dimensions reflect the nature and distribution of resources in environments thereby reflecting the extent of dependence and typically have been assessed using archival industry data such as industry sales, net assets, or capital expenditures.

The characterization of the environment as components, stakeholders, or attributes is often referred to as the "objective environment." The notion of an objective environment presumes that organizations are embedded within external independent environments that "constitute some thing or some set of forces to be adapted to, coaligned with, controlled, or controlled by" (Smircich & Stubbart, 1985, p. 725). As Smircich and Stubbart (1985) and others (e.g., Weick, 1979) highlight, conceptualizing environments as objective, concrete, external, or tangible implies that attributes, events, and processes are hard, measurable, and determinant. The goal of strategic management in an objective environment is to initiate strategic actions that will meet the real constraints and demands that exist "out there" (Smircich & Stubbart, 1985, p. 726).

Perceptual and Interpretivist Perspectives

In contrast to the characterization of environments as stocks of resources, environments also have been portrayed as a source of data that serves as the raw material from which organizational members fabricate information and subsequent organizational responses (Dill, 1962; Tushman & Nadler, 1978; Weick, 1979). Scholars adopting this perspective—sometimes known as the information-processing perspective—are concerned with the conditions under which information is noticed and how it is communicated and interpreted. In fact, viewing the environment as flows of data and information highlights the importance of perceptions and interpretations. It is generally agreed that

variations in environmental data as filtered through members' perceptions and interpretive schemes are a major factor explaining organizational change (Weick, 1979).

Scholars adopting the information view traditionally have considered environmental uncertainty and the equivocality of information available to decision makers as critical variables affecting organizational actions and outcomes (Aldrich, 1979; Weick, 1979). Environmental complexity, and unpredictability in terms of the frequency and direction of change, supposedly generates uncertainties for organizations and their members, which complicates rational decision-making processes and ultimately affects organizational outcomes. A way of linking the information view of environments with the resource view is to focus on perceived uncertainty and how executives perceive their environment. Scholars adopting the resource perspective generally agree that decision makers' perceptions of uncertainty and other external constraints or demands play a part in determining an organization's response to the situation of dependence (Pfeffer & Salancik, 1978).

The perceptual perspective on environments is similar to the objectivist perspective in that it also assumes that there is a real, material, external environment out there to be perceived (Smircich & Stubbart, 1985). Thus, in essence, there is little difference between the conception of objective and perceived environments. The difference between perceived and objective environments lies in the extent to which decision makers are (or can be) accurate assessors of the supposed "real" environment.

Much of the previous research examining the adaptation of organizations to their environments has implicitly assumed that decision makers accurately perceive environmental changes and demands and subsequently develop adaptive strategies based on their accurate perceptions. Yet empirical evidence supporting the idea that executives are veridical assessors of their environments is scant, and recent research has advanced several important theories that help to account for the lack of significant associations between objective (archival) and perceived environments (see Boyd, Dess, & Rasheed, 1993; Sutcliffe, 1994; and Sutcliffe & Huber, 1998, for analyses of probable causes).

Enactment Perspective

The enactment perspective to environments poses an alternative to the concreteness implied in the previous conceptualizations. The enactment or social construction perspective suggests that the environment is not an objective given; it is not even perceived. Rather, it is made or enacted (Weick, 1979). The central premise of the enactment perspective is that organizations create the environments that subsequently impinge on them (Abolafia & Kilduff, 1988). Enacted environments are socially created rather than concrete or material in that the environment is the joint product of the actions of purposeful actors and accompanying efforts to make sense out of these actions (Abolafia & Kilduff, 1988). Enactment transpires through communication processes in that entities involved in interactive relationships read each other's behavior and make attributions to make sense of the situation.

Enacted environments are not synonymous with perceived environments although perception is involved: "An enactment model implies that an environment of which strategists can make sense has been put there by strategists' patterns of action—not by a process of perceiving the environment, but by a process of making the environment" (Smircich & Stubbart, 1985, p. 727). Enactment occurs through the processes of attention and action (Weick, 1988). From an enactment perspective, the world is an ambiguous field of experience devoid of threats and opportunities. Decision makers pay attention to certain aspects of their environments as a consequence of attentional processes. Once data or information in the environment become stimuli and

penetrate an organization's cognitive system, decision makers give meaning to the information so that it makes sense and subsequently act on their interpretations. The resulting actions and outcomes are informational inputs for other entities in the environment, who ascribe meaning to the acts and subsequently react. As Weick (1988) highlights:

> *An enacted environment* is the residuum of changes produced by enactment. The word "residuum" is preferred to the word "residue" because residuum emphasizes that what is left after a process cannot be ignored or left out of account because it has potential significance (*Webster's Dictionary of Synonyms,* 1951, p. 694). The product of enactment is not an accident, an afterthought, or a byproduct. Instead it is an orderly, material, social construction that is subject to multiple interpretations. Enacted environments contain real objects such as reactors, pipes, and valves. The existence of these objects is not questioned, but their significance, meaning, and content is. These objects are inconsequential until they are acted upon and then incorporated retrospectively into events, situations, and explanations. (p. 307)

Information Environments

As noted earlier, traditional views of the environment highlight that organizations exist within environments that are independently given—no matter whether objective or perceived. If environments are seen as external and concrete, then it is natural for researchers and managers to be concerned with the extent to which managers accurately discern their environments. In a concrete world, "a premium is placed on the ability to measure, predict, and influence the environment to ensure successful adaptation to the contingencies it presents" (Smircich, 1983, p. 227). An implication of this line of thinking is that environmental information is a thing "out there" to be discovered and is independent from the meanings ascribed by organizational members.

In the first edition of this handbook, Huber and Daft (1987, p. 130) developed the concept of the information environment. The information environment constitutes the "raw material of organizational communication and actions" and as such is the sensable environment. Huber and Daft (1987) argued that the information environment mediates between the objective environment and the environment that is sensed by organizational members. One way to think about the components of the information environment is as follows: (a) occurrences, anything happening or changing in the environment; (b) acts, specific behaviors (including specific communication behaviors) stemming from resource allocation actions and decisions of other entities in an organization's environment; and (c) messages, events resulting from the decisions of other environmental actors that have specific, predetermined targets (Vertzberger, 1984, pp. 12-13). In other words, the information environment can be viewed as the interactive communication behaviors between organizations and the entities in their environment, the cognitions and meanings that executives develop from this communication or other messages, or the cognitions or meanings that executives develop from directly perceiving and interpreting other environmental information (i.e., occurrences or acts) (Grunig, 1997).

The information perspective is similar to the traditional perspectives recounted earlier in that it supports the notion of environments as independent, external, and tangible. Yet the notion of an information environment may be potentially misleading from a communication standpoint because it implies that information is a thing "out there" to be discovered and fails to take into account that information in the environment is not inherently meaningful or predefined (Heath, 1994, p. 41). Information is a variable in the communication process; it becomes meaningful only as a consequence of the evaluative schema that are used to process and assess it. Organizational members, through the sharing of information, and

through interpretive and enactment processes, socially construct information filters through which information is selected and interpreted and subsequently enacted through communication (Heath, 1994). Shared information and its accompanying interpretations are what communication is about. In other words, communication results when what one entity does and says is meaningful to another (Heath, 1994). Because the goals and actions of organizational subgroups are not monolithic and are likely to vary, organizational subgroups are likely to come into contact with different aspects of an organization's environment, are likely to differentially focus their attention and therefore notice only certain aspects of their organization's environment, and are likely to have unique zones of meaning (Heath, 1994) through which they filter information. Thus, it may be more accurate to think of information "environments" rather than a single environment.

Before concluding the discussion of the key perspectives of the environment, it is important to highlight the issue of boundaries. In contrast to the enactment perspective that favors a socially created symbolic world and abandons the idea of concrete material organizations/environments, the objective, perceived, and interpreted environmental perspectives presume real, material environments whose boundaries are clearly distinct from the concrete material organizations located within them. What is inside and outside the firm is clearly differentiated in more traditional perspectives because of legal factors (i.e., ownership issues) or as a consequence of other factors such as varied senses of identity, culture, or strategic priorities. Although some theorists acknowledge that boundaries are not fixed (Aldrich, 1979), more often than not, traditional perspectives have assumed that organization-environment boundaries are relatively static and well defined. Recent foci on process and value-chain management and viewing organizations and their environments as "boundaryless" strengthen the view that the boundaries between organizations and their environments are fluid, dynamic, and constantly evolving.

To summarize, few researchers would say that environments are totally objective, but even fewer would say that environments are totally constructed (Weick, 1983). Still, nothing has really emerged to replace these extreme views in spite of over 40 years of work. One way to accommodate the differences between perspectives is to postulate, as Weick (1983, p. 18) suggests, that grains of preexisting reality are at the core of decision makers' representations. Small, objective details are enlarged into constructions by interdependent actions. Sales fall, sales skyrocket, new competitors enter tight markets. Representations do not materialize out of thin air; things do exist.

Organizational Information Processing

Organizational information processing is often treated as an organizing concept for understanding a broad and interrelated range of phenomena of significance in organizational decision making, strategy formulation, and strategy implementation. In essence, organizational information-processing theory attempts to explain organizational behaviors by examining information flows occurring in and around organizations (Knight & McDaniel, 1979), and traditional approaches to information processing have been grounded primarily in the objectivist or perceptual perspectives. An organization's information-processing system is thought to include

- The exposure to information, readiness to attend to various environmental elements, and the development of strategies and sensory systems for searching the environment (Dill, 1962, p. 97)
- Communication and storage of information (Galbraith, 1973; Thompson, 1967; Tush-

man & Nadler, 1978) and mechanisms for transmitting information
- Development of interpretations systems that influence the transformation of data into information (Daft & Weick, 1984)
- Routines for translating information into action or for using information in decision making, strategy formulation, and strategy implementation

Early research drawing on the organizational information-processing perspective focused on the idea that uncertainty arises from certain characteristics in the environment, and to cope with this uncertainty, effective organizations match their information-processing capabilities (i.e., their designs) to the information-processing demands of the environment (i.e., level of uncertainty) (Galbraith, 1973; Huber, 1982; Thompson, 1967; Tushman & Nadler, 1978). Also known as the logistical perspective of information processing, this perspective focused on the capacity of organizational structures and processes to enhance or impede the transfer and transformation of data or information and subsequent decision-making capabilities (Huber, 1982). Empirical studies reflecting this perspective have focused on the effects of structural variables on communication networks, channels, and amount of communication. Specifically, studies drawing on the logistical perspective have examined the intraorganizational and more microlevel aspects of information processing and found, for example:

- Effective decision-making units differentially structure themselves depending on perceived environmental uncertainty (Duncan, 1973).
- For high-performing units, the greater the task interdependence, the greater the frequency of communication (Tushman, 1979).
- The credibility of the information source rather than expertise determines the extent

to which information is believed and used in decision making (O'Reilly & Roberts, 1974).

To summarize, the logistical view has examined how information processing and communication are enhanced or impeded by organizational design characteristics. An implicit assumption underlying the logistical view is that information is something that flows or is conveyed from one entity to another. The logistical view fails to take into account the idea that information has no inherent meaning and that it is given meaning through interpretive processes (Heath, 1994).

In contrast to the logistical perspective, much of the more recent work on organizational information processing, grounded in the interpretive and enactment perspectives, has focused more heavily on cognition and construction, viewing organizations as sensemaking and learning systems (Daft & Weick, 1984; Dutton & Jackson, 1987; Milliken, 1990; Starbuck & Milliken, 1988; Thomas, Clark, & Gioia, 1993). Information processing is reflected in the individual or collective abilities of organizational members to scan and interpret environmental information in order to increase knowledge of action-outcome links between the organization and its environment (Corner, Kinicki, & Keats, 1994; Daft & Weick, 1984, p. 286), presumably to enhance organizational performance (Thomas et al., 1993). Empirical studies reflecting these perspectives have explored, for example, the effects of antecedent and contextual factors on decision makers' interpretations of strategic information (Milliken, 1990; Thomas, Shankster, & Mathieu, 1994), the role that managerial characteristics play in issue identification and interpretation processes (Walsh, 1988), and how heuristics and framing may affect managers' strategic decision-making processes (Bateman & Zeithaml, 1989; Schwenk, 1984). The focus of the interpretive view is primarily on how information processing, and in particular, the interpretation of information, is influenced by factors unique to

the context such as organizational structures, organizational processes (i.e., communication processes), and the psychological and social-psychological characteris- tics of organizational members.

While some scholars suggest that the logistical and interpretive information-processing perspectives noted above are contradictory, in fact, they are complementary—especially from an organizational communication perspective. Organizational information processing includes both the transfer of information and the inference of meaning, and as such can be thought of as a communication process (O'Reilly & Pondy, 1979). In analyzing organizational information processing of organizational environments and evaluating its outcomes, it is natural to be concerned with the factors that affect how organizations and their members single out information in the environment or how messages penetrate an organizational system; the factors that affect how environmental information is interpreted; and how organizational responses, in particular communication responses, subsequently reshape the environment.

Concern with how environmental information is noticed, the individual and organizational factors that influence the interpretation of environmental information and the development of a representation of the environment and how it changes over time, and how organizations and their members use information and communication subsequently to reshape the environment are considered more fully below.

HOW ENVIRONMENTS BECOME KNOWN

In the following sections, I review research grounded primarily in the perceptual, interpretive, and enactment perspectives related to how organizations and their members come to know and cope with their environments through the processes of attention, interpretation, and action. Noticing environmental data or information is one key step in coping with environments. However, noticing information is not the only process that is important. Information is not inherently meaningful. As Ford and Baucus (1987, p. 367) note, facts don't speak for themselves—data are generally interpreted before they are useful for strategy formulation. This means that even though two organizations may notice the same things, their interpretations may differ and subsequent responses may differ as a result. Disentangling the process of noticing environmental stimuli from the process of interpreting environmental stimuli is useful for better understanding organizational adaptation and responsiveness and for isolating the communication dynamics related to each of the processes (Daft & Weick, 1984; Kiesler & Sproull, 1982; Starbuck & Milliken, 1988).

Many scholars have used the term *scanning* to refer to the observation of stimuli; other scholars argue that *noticing* is a more accurate term since scanning implies proactivity, or a more stimulus-specific search. In this chapter, I use the term noticing to refer to an awareness of environmental stimuli. The process of noticing stimuli can be both formal and informal, as well as voluntary and involuntary. Interpreting refers to the process of making sense of what is noticed.

Noticing Environmental Information

Noticing may be dominated by strategy or tactics. Strategic information processing generally is concerned with the fundamental position of an organization with its environment and higher-level organizational goals, is focused on nonroutine—perhaps discontinuous—problems and situations, is broad in scope, has a longer time horizon, and generally involves the top managers of an organization (Knight & McDaniel, 1979). In contrast, tactical information processing deals with more routine day-to-day problems and situations, generally operating and administrative issues, and often involves the middle and lower levels of an organization. Notwithstanding these distinctions, tactics can be thought of as strategy in that once they are implemented, they generate strategy. Nonetheless, this chapter is focused on the processing of environmental information of importance to the whole organization more generally. Consequently, in the following section I highlight the clusters of influences that are likely to enhance or impede the detection of important environmental information by an organization's top decision makers.

With few exceptions (see Bourgeois, 1985), the limited research examining the determinants of executives' environmental perceptions has been focused on the perceptions of a single manager (or CEO). However, there is reason to focus on the perception of a team of executives rather than on single individuals. First, few decisions affecting the entire organization and its relationship with its environment are made unilaterally by any single person. The chief executive often shares tasks, and to some extent, power with other members of the top management team (Hambrick & Mason, 1984). Further, while a number of organizational members may be involved in boundary-spanning roles collecting environmental data and channeling the data into the organization, the information generally converges at the organization's top level (Daft & Weick, 1984) and it is the collective that affects organizational decisions and subsequent responses (Hinz, Tindale, & Vollrath, 1997; Klimoski & Mohammed, 1994; Walsh, Henderson, & Deighton, 1988).

Second, as Zucker (1983) argues, attitudes and behaviors in formal organizations are highly institutionalized or governed by "common understandings about what is appropriate and, fundamentally, meaningful behavior" (p. 5). Organizational settings have been characterized as strong situations that exert powerful influences on individual perceptions, attitudes, and behaviors (Mischel, 1977). Consequently, it is assumed that the environmental characteristics noticed by a team of top managers amount to something more than what individual team members' notice. This stems from the assumption that, through social interchange, decision makers create collectively shared or consensual reality (Daft & Weick, 1984; Klimoski & Mohammed, 1994). Therefore, although individual processes serve to filter and distort decision makers' perceptions of what is going on, and what should be done about it, individual perceptions are likely to be influenced significantly by social information processes.

Before proceeding with a discussion of noticing, two comments are in order. First, as is often the case with complex phenomena, previous research has tended to focus on selected relationships between variables hypothesized to affect the detection of environmental information rather than on developing an integrated conceptual framework. Nonetheless, in recent years, managerial variables such as top management group structure and beliefs and other social characteristics, as well as organizational variables such as characteristics of the organization's information system, structure, and strategy, are frequently cited as the key determinants that affect the detection and selection of information. In essence, these factors moderate the degree to which data, information, and messages in the environment penetrate an organization's cognitive system and are transmitted, analyzed, or otherwise taken into account in strategic decisions and actions. The list of antecedents of effective environmental information noticing is not meant to be exhaustive.

A second limitation of the current literature on noticing processes, and perhaps an even more important one, is that researchers who study noticing/scanning often treat information and communication as one and the same. In fact, in much of the work related to noticing or scanning, information transfer can be substituted for communication. This is unfortunate and unnecessarily restrictive because communication is a big part of noticing or

sensing aspects of the environment. Thus, my discussion in the next section reflects the current state of the art, and not an effort to treat information and communication synonymously.

Top Management Group Characteristics

Past research suggests that environmental perceptions may be influenced by individuals' psychological characteristics such as tolerance for ambiguity or cognitive complexity (Downey, Hellriegel, & Slocum, 1977; Downey & Slocum, 1975; Gifford, Bobbitt, & Slocum, 1979). Still, empirical findings are inconsistent (Boyd et al., 1993), and no strong conclusions have been drawn about the influence of these factors. More recently, researchers have focused on demographic characteristics related to the composition of the top management group, hypothesizing that these factors more strongly influence the information processing of the team as a whole and how organizations and their members attend and select among data, information, and messages in the information environment (Hambrick, 1994; Hambrick & Mason, 1984).

Studies examining demographic factors have largely focused on the diversity of a team's work history and length of team tenure. For example, the work of Dearborn and Simon (1958) suggests that individuals with similar functional backgrounds will have similar perceptions. Each member of the top management team develops a way of seeing the world based on his or her past or current experience in a particular functional area. If this holds true, a more functionally diverse top management team not only will notice different environmental events but also will notice different features of the same events. "If people look for different things, when their observations are pooled they collectively see more than any one of them alone would see" (Weick, 1987, p. 116). Still, it also may be true that too much diversity may hinder team interactions or in other ways hamper managers' abilities to communicate effectively (Glick, Miller, & Huber, 1993; O'Reilly, Caldwell, & Barnett, 1989), which will constrain the group's information-processing capabilities as a whole. Although this reasoning makes sense, Hambrick (1994) argues that top management groups will quickly develop norms of interaction that facilitate frequent and fluid communication. In one of the few empirical studies to shed light on this issue, Sutcliffe (1994) found a negative association between work history diversity and the accurate detection of information related to the level of resources available in an organization's environment. Her results suggest that team interactions or other communication processes are repressed in more highly diverse teams and this hinders the sharing of certain types of information among team members.

The length of team tenure may also affect the environmental information that is sensed. The amount of time the members of a group have been together is related strongly to the degree of interaction and communication among group members (O'Reilly et al., 1989) and is critical to the development of shared attitudes and perspectives. Although longevity may lead to a similarity of perspectives and, perhaps, diminished communication because members think they know what everyone else is thinking (Katz, 1982), shorter-tenured teams may not know what to look for. Shorter-tenured teams may lack well-defined organizational frameworks or cognitive schemas, which hinders the recognition of salient information.

Hambrick and D'Aveni (1992) provide empirical support for the idea that longer-tenured teams are better at detecting important environmental information. In a comparative study of bankrupt and surviving firms, they found that the average team tenure in bankrupt firms was significantly shorter than the average team tenure in matched survivors. In addition, the average tenure of bankrupt teams declined monotonically over the five-year pe-

riod prior to bankruptcy. They concluded that shorter-tenured teams fall victim to flawed perceptions, deficient information processing, and subsequent strategic errors based on bad detection systems (Hambrick & D'Aveni, 1992, p. 1447). More direct evidence about the importance of enduring teams is provided by Sutcliffe (1994), who found a positive association between team tenure and the extent to which teams accurately detected the level of resources in their environment. She concluded that longer-tenured teams have more effective team communication patterns and/or more effective external communication networks, which gives them better access to information about resources than shorter-tenured teams.

In addition to team background characteristics, executives' capacities to notice information may also be shaped by other factors such as managerial discretion (Hambrick & Finkelstein, 1987), managerial values (Beyer, 1981; Hambrick & Brandon, 1988), managerial ideologies (Meyer, 1982), and beliefs about efficacy (Wood & Bandura, 1989). Managerial discretion—the latitude for action—may act as a perceptual lens by influencing both the range and the intensity of stimuli to which managers attend. Management teams who have a greater latitude of action will be attentive to a wider range of environmental information and may be more likely to pick up weak variations in environmental stimuli as a consequence of wider attention processes. If managers think they can take lots of action, "they can afford to pay attention to a wider variety of inputs because, whatever they see, they will have some way to cope with it" (Weick, 1988, p. 311). Meyer (1982) found that hospital administrators with a high degree of perceived discretion more carefully attended to the environment and attended to a wider range of environmental sectors than administrators with a low degree of perceived discretion. Managerial and organizational values and ideologies and collective efficacy also may be important filters that affect the screening and selection of stimuli.

Organizational Characteristics

Factors related to an organization's processes, structure, and design will also affect the detection of important environmental information. In the following section, I examine organizational information acquisition processes including organizational scanning routines, performance-monitoring routines, and top executives' scanning routines as well as factors related to an organization's structure, strategy, and resources.

Organizational scanning refers to the acquisition of information about the environment by lower-level and middle-level boundary spanners or subunits dedicated to the task of intelligence gathering and the subsequent communication of this information to relevant parties. Organizational scanning systems vary in intensity, formalization, and complexity (Fahey & King, 1977; Huber, 1991). Organizations may be highly vigilant in their scanning, may routinely scan, may probe for specific information in response to actual or suspected problems or opportunities or whenever the need arises, or simply may be on the alert for "nonroutine" (but relevant) information (Huber, 1991, p. 97). Intensive scanning routines are generally considered to lead to a more "wide-ranging sensing of the environment" (Huber, 1991, p. 97). Fundamental to these perspectives is the idea that more frequent scanning (i.e., a greater amount) enhances the recognition of environmental changes, threats, or opportunities—an idea empirically validated by Sutcliffe (1994).

Organizational scanning provides information about the overall business environment critical for planning, strategy formulation, and decision making. In contrast to scanning, performance monitoring provides more specific information about an organization's specific business situation and its effectiveness in fulfilling goals and the requirements of stakeholders (Eisenhardt, 1989; Huber, 1991). Information about current competitors, existing technologies, and product markets in which a firm operates is useful for making operational and tactical decisions; is important for uncovering or discovering idiosyncratic threats,

problems, or trends; and leads to a more timely and accurate detection of problems and opportunities (Eisenhardt, 1989). Decision makers in firms where performance is monitored continually sense the environment more quickly and accurately because they have frequent, mandatory, intense, face-to-face operations meetings (not limited to discussions of internal operations) and frequently receive written reports detailing performance targets (Eisenhardt, 1989). This enables decision makers to initiate corrective actions before substantial problems materialize (Eisenhardt, 1989). In addition to its effect on sensing processes, performance monitoring may also lead to higher performance indirectly through its effect on trust. It is possible that frequent interactions enable executive teams to develop social routines and patterns of trust that permit quick and reliable responses when situations get tough.

Executives also acquire information directly through their own efforts. The frequency or intensity of managerial scanning indirectly reflects the amount of information top management team members obtain about the environment (Hambrick, 1982). For example, studies by Kefalas and Schoderbek (1973) and Daft, Sormunen, and Parks (1988) suggest that top managers gain experience in selecting stimuli to attend to by scanning more, and as a consequence, are more adept at building an accurate picture of the environment. Consequently, when managers' observations are pooled they collectively formulate a better representation of their environment. Related to scanning is the idea that the choice of communication media will affect the extent to which executives get a deeper—and perhaps more accurate—picture of their environment. For example, studies by Daft and his colleagues (Daft, Bettenhausen, & Tyler, 1993; Daft & Lengel, 1984) have shown that richer media not only may allow for the resolution of ambiguity and the enhancement of understanding but also may induce deeper processing of environmental information.

An organization's design and structural characteristics such as the organization's internal pattern of tasks, roles, and administrative mechanisms also will affect the detection and selection of information. Organizational structures not only affect decisions about what information to collect but also the transmission, analysis, and interpretation of environmental information.

Formalization and complexity, for example, affect the detection and selection of environmental information by circumscribing patterns of attention and information collection as well as constraining opportunities for interaction and communication between boundary spanners and upper managers. High levels of differentiation and formalization may contribute to a widening reality gap if top executives become increasingly detached from those more closely connected with the environment (Aldrich & Auster, 1986, pp. 169-170). Centralization may affect executives' noticing capacities more directly. Orton and Weick (1990) and Weick (1976) have argued that loosely coupled systems more accurately register their environments than tightly coupled systems. To the extent that decentralization implies diversity in the goals and preferences of decision makers, decentralized executive teams may form a more complete picture of an environment because they tend to focus their attention on more, and more varied, indicators. Consequently, when managers pool their observations, they collectively formulate a better picture of the current environmental trends, threats, and opportunities than managers in more centralized organizations—an idea recently validated by Sutcliffe (1994).

In addition to organization structure, an organization's strategic orientation, degree of inertia (Boyd et al., 1993), and the presence of slack (Hambrick, 1994; Tushman & Romanelli, 1985) also may be influential in affecting what information is noticed. A firm's strategic orientation is associated with differing assumptions regarding the external environment (Daft & Weick, 1984), and this may directly affect executives' attentional processes. The strong pursuit of a dominant single strategy may lead executives to overlook important environmental features (Hambrick & Snow, 1977) because it delimits the focus of their attentions. This highlights that noticing is a limiting process in that the noticing of one thing eliminates the simultaneous noticing of something else (Pfeffer & Salancik, 1978; Weick, 1979). For example, firms pursuing cost leadership strategies are likely to be concerned with efficiency and other issues related to streamlining internal processes, and this may prove to be problematic for survival. A recent study of failing firms and matched survivors showed that managers in failing firms appear to pay less attention to certain aspects of their environment than do managers in the survivors (D'Aveni & MacMillan, 1990). Executives in firms surviving external crises differed significantly from executives in failing firms in that they (1) paid more attention to the external rather than internal environment, and (2) paid increasing attention to the output side of their environment by focusing on customers and other general economic factors affecting demand. In addition to the effects of strategic orientation on noticing processes, organizational inertia may also affect attention and the selection of information because inertia often leads organizational members to focus internally as search and decision-making processes atrophy (Boyd et al., 1993). Finally, slack may affect the extent to which executives notice environmental information because it often promotes a complacency or a decreased vigilance in searching out information about environmental changes (Tushman & Romanelli, 1985).

Interpreting Environmental Information

In the previous section, I reviewed the major factors that affect the sensing or noticing of environmental data and information and various communication-related implications. I now turn to a discussion of the factors that affect sensemaking or the interpretation of data and information. Once organizations and their members become aware of environmental information, further processing occurs as executives make sense of it and formulate an interpretation that provides the basis for decisions and actions. The interpretation process has a number of distinct aspects including "comprehending, understanding, explaining, attributing, extrapolating, and predicting" (Starbuck & Milliken, 1988, p. 51). Communication is integral to this process as meanings are shaped through advocacy, persuasion, and other power and influence processes.

Fundamental to the interpretation process is the categorization of data or information, which involves placing stimuli into frameworks (or schemata) to make sense of the stimuli (Starbuck & Milliken, 1988). While numerous categories are possible, the literature in strategic management highlights "opportunity" and "threat" as two salient general categories used by decision makers when interpreting information in regard to environmental changes, events, trends, or developments (Dutton & Jackson, 1987; Fredrickson, 1985; Jackson & Dutton, 1988). These general labels capture top executives' beliefs about the potential effects of environmental events and trends on the organization more broadly, and may even determine those effects because the extent to which top decision makers interpret environmental conditions as opportunities or threats predisposes them to respond in predictable ways (Dutton & Jackson, 1987).

Prior studies of interpretation processes often have focused on the characteristics of environmental issues and events (magnitude, urgency, etc.) and how issue characteristics affect the likelihood that executives will label environmental events as "threats" or "opportunities" (Dutton, Walton, & Abrahamson, 1989; Jackson & Dutton, 1988). Less attention has been paid to examining how managerial and contextual characteristics affect decision makers' interpretations, although recent research suggests there are several potential sources of influence (see Dutton, 1993a; Gioia & Thomas, 1996; Thomas et al., 1994). Three particularly important factors that are likely to affect executives' interpretations include managerial ideologies and beliefs (Dutton, 1993b; Meyer, 1982; Starbuck & Milliken, 1988), an organization's recent per-

formance history (Milliken & Lant, 1991), and the changing nature of the context (Dutton, 1993a).

Interpretations are conditioned by decision makers' repertoire of shared beliefs, values, and ideologies—by habits, beliefs about what is, and beliefs about what ought to be (Starbuck & Milliken, 1988). Shared beliefs and assumptions about possible future events, alternative courses of action, and consequences attached to these alternatives (i.e., the extent that managers perceive they have the latitude to take action) have been found to be important influences on managerial interpretations (Child, 1972; Daft & Weick, 1984; Hambrick & Finkelstein, 1987).

Opportunities are more likely to be constructed in organizations where multiple courses of action are envisioned and favored (Dutton, 1993b), or where decision makers perceive they have more control. Managers with a higher degree of discretion are likely to envision many courses of action and to perceive that they have a higher degree of control, which means they will be more likely than their counterparts with a low degree of discretion to frame environmental variations or discontinuities as opportunities.

An organization's recent performance history is another potentially important factor that influences how executives make sense of their environment (McCabe & Dutton, 1993; Milliken, 1990; Milliken & Lant, 1991). The degree to which decision makers believe their organization is performing more or less successfully activates powerful psychological processes that influence the extent to which managers view their environment as more or less threatening and subsequently influences top decision makers' thinking about strategic change (Milliken & Lant, 1991). Milliken (1990), for example, found that managers in high-performing organizations were less likely to interpret a particular environmental change as threatening than managers in low-performing organizations. This suggests that managers are more likely to interpret environmental contingencies as opportunities and less as threats when they believe their organization is performing well.

Differences in contextual conditions also create different motivating conditions for decision makers to construct their environments in particular ways (Dutton et al., 1989). Change is often seen as threatening (Staw, Sandelands, & Dutton, 1981), which suggests that decision makers in contexts that are unstable and changing may be more likely to interpret these events and conditions as threatening than decision makers in more stable contexts. Similarly, decision makers in contexts where resources are constrained are more likely to interpret environmental contingencies as threatening than are decision makers in more munificent contexts.

Action as a Mechanism to Enhance the Plausibility of Interpretations

This chapter is guided by the assumption that information processing is purposeful behavior by which individuals, groups, or organizations become aware of, handle, make sense of, resolve, or control data and information about the environment. One outcome of environmental information processing is a representation of the environment—a schema reflecting important trends, threats, and opportunities that decision makers use as the basis for strategic action. However, because of bounded rationality, individuals and organizations are limited as information processors, which suggests that a certain level of misperception is inevitable in every information-processing system. This may not be a problem when competition is low, when resources are plentiful, or when organizations are loosely coupled to other organizations in their environment. However, it may be a problem in very competitive markets, when organizations are tightly coupled to other organizations in their environments, or in industries where resources are constrained or limited. Thus, as Vertzberger (1990) and Weick (1995, pp. 56-57) argue, better information processing may not so much be characterized by an ability to choose between accurate images and misperceptions, but rather the ability to enhance plausibility and choose between different potential misperceptions.

Recent empirical research has shown that executives in failing and surviving firms differ in the speed with which they update mental models (Barr, Stimpert, & Huff, 1992; Hambrick & D'Aveni, 1992). One promising explanation to account for the performance differences relates to the idea that surviving firms engage less in more formalized scanning, strategic planning, and competitor analysis, and more in trial-and-error action, which may enhance plausibility because it facilitates both learning and dramatic changes in mental models of a firm's environment (Lyles & Mitroff, 1980; Weick, 1990a).

Formal systems for learning about competitive environments bog down in detail, are slow to operate, and often represent the environment as it was, not as it is. In these systems, opportunities for interaction and communication are often circumscribed. Consequently, executives in organizations relying on more formalized strategic planning or information systems are less likely to be aware of current environmental information than their counterparts in organizations without such systems. Action taking may be a better mechanism for generating data and for instantiating opportunities for dialogue, bargaining, negotiation, and persuasion that are essential for developing a good sense of what is going on. Further, action and cognition are mutually reinforcing, and communication is critical to this process. Actions allow for the assessment of causal beliefs that subsequently lead to new actions undertaken to test the newly asserted relationships. Over time, as supporting evidence mounts, more significant changes in beliefs and actions evolve (Barr et al., 1992; Weick, 1990a).

Some researchers have gone so far as to suggest that accurate environmental maps may be less important than any map that brings some order to the world and prompts action (Weick, 1990a). Action is important in organizations because it facilitates learning (Sitkin, Sutcliffe, & Weick, 1998). The pursuit of action generates new information and increases opportunities for communication that helps executives modify erroneous understandings and allows them to update previously held inaccurate perceptions (Sutcliffe, 1997). Consequently, executives in more action-oriented organizations are likely to develop better representations of a current environment and to more quickly update existing environmental models than their counterparts in organizations that are less action oriented. Second, more action-oriented organizations are likely to be more adaptable to future, changing environments than less action-oriented organizations. As noted earlier, however, how executives make sense of environmental data may be a critical factor in influencing action. For example, upbeat interpretations of the environment—sometimes called positive illusions—may enable managers to overcome inertial tendencies by propelling them to pursue goals that might look unattainable in environments assessed in utter objectivity. If current environments aren't seen accurately but executives remain nonthreatened, managers may undertake potentially difficult courses of action with enthusiasm, effort, and self-confidence necessary to bring about success.

To summarize, environments become known through the processes of noticing and interpreting, and communication dynamics are critical to each. Taken together, the results of the research presented earlier suggest that the observation or detection of environmental stimuli is enhanced or impeded by executives' interaction patterns (both intraorganizational and interorganizational); their communication capabilities including their abilities (and willingness) to share, surface, and attend to unique information; their abilities to resolve conflicts; the media used in communication; and intense scanning and performance-monitoring routines that provide opportunities for interaction and communication. Communica-

tion is equally important in the interpretation process. Communication is critical to the construction of information filters through which information is interpreted and is an integral part of enacting those interpretations.

OUTWARD INFORMATION FLOWS: AN OVERVIEW

To this point, I have focused on incoming information flows, and more specifically, on the processing of environmental information oriented primarily at adapting or reacting to environmental demands, contingencies, or constraints. However, as noted earlier, organizations proactively and strategically manage the flow of information outward to the environment to preempt anticipated problems or hedge against unanticipated ones (Grunig, 1984; Vertzberger, 1990), to manage the real or potential consequences of risks and crises (Heath, 1988; Heath & Nelson, 1986), to alter dependencies by affecting the relationship of the organization relative to other entities in its environment (Pfeffer & Salancik, 1978), and to enhance legitimacy and create value for the firm (Elsbach, 1994; Lev, 1992; Suchman, 1995). Understanding the flow of information outward from an organization to its environment is the focus of the following section.

Organizational communication scholars have paid attention to information flows from organizations to their environments—particularly in the areas of mass communication, issues management, and risk communication. Notwithstanding this attention, however, to a large extent, scholarship in mainstream organizational communication has focused on intraorganizational information processing and interpersonal communication among organizational members. Much of the work examining how organizations manage the flow of information to their environments has been done by scholars in the public relations domain. However, the contributions of public relations scholars have not yet been deeply incorporated into mainstream organizational communication and organizational theory literatures.

Information flows from organizations to their environments have received fragmented attention in the organizational theory literature. Two major theoretical perspectives in organizational theory have made reference to how organizations use information to manage their environments and improve legitimacy: impression management theories and institutional theories. Drawing on impression management theories, recent work in organizational theory has focused on the use of justifications to improve an organization's image to enhance performance (Bettman & Weitz, 1983; Salancik & Meindl, 1984; Staw, McKechnie, & Puffer, 1983), and on identifying the form and content of effective organizational accounts (Elsbach, 1994; Marcus & Goodman, 1991). Institutional theorists have focused on how organizations attempt to project legitimacy by highlighting the adoption of widely used and accepted practices (DiMaggio & Powell, 1983; Elsbach & Sutton, 1992; Feldman & March, 1981). Although organizational scholars assume that "managing strategically" means to accomplish the organization's mission coincident with managing environmental relationships, there has been little effort by organizational theorists to consolidate research examining differences in how and why organizations choose to manage the flow of information to the environment, the information tactics used, or the factors and mechanisms that affect external communication behaviors.

Corporate communication, public relations, and information/communication management have been used interchangeably in the organizational communication, public relations, and organization theory literatures (and are used here) to mean the management of information or communication between an organization and its environment, or more specifically, between an organization and its publics or stakeholders (Cheney & Dionisopoulos, 1989; Grunig & Hunt, 1984, p. 6).

According to Grunig and Hunt (1984, p. 6), communication management (i.e., strategic public relations) includes a myriad of activities (i.e., planning, execution, evaluation) aimed at enhancing an organization's communication with the external and internal groups that affect its ability to meet its goals. The presumed goal of strategic public relations is to increase a firm's autonomy and limit or circumscribe its dependence.

In the following sections, to further our understanding of how organizations manage flows of information to their environments, I draw heavily on research and theory in public relations, issues management, and crisis communication and examine (1) typologies of organizational information management behaviors, (2) determinants of information management behaviors and the mechanisms that influence outward information flows, and (3) the effectiveness of particular communication strategies.

Classifying External Information Behaviors

Typologies of communication behaviors are grounded in Thayer's (1968) concepts of synchronic and diachronic communication. "The purpose of synchronic communication is to 'synchronize' the behavior of a public with that of the organization so that the organization can continue to behave in the way it wants without interference. The purpose of diachronic communication is to negotiate a state of affairs that benefits both the organization and the public" (Grunig & Grunig, 1992, p. 287). Grunig and Hunt (1984) expanded these ideas and developed a typology of public relations behaviors useful not only for categorizing the types of communication behaviors exhibited in organizations but also for thinking about how organizations manage communicative relationships with their environments. The four types—*press agentry/ publicity, public information, two-way asymmetric,* and *two-way symmetric*—are described more fully below.

The press agentry model describes communication behaviors aimed at seeking favorable publicity or media attention in almost any way possible, especially in the mass media. Organizations practicing the public information model, on the other hand, disseminate relatively objective information—mostly accurate and positive rather than negative—through mass media, and other controlled media such as newsletters, brochures, and direct mail (Grunig, 1990). Both the press agentry and public information models are considered one-way communication models because they try to manipulate stakeholders for the benefit of the organization through hype or by disseminating exclusively favorable information without conducting research or planning.[1] The two-way asymmetrical model describes organizations that conduct research to identify the types of messages that are likely to produce the support of important stakeholders without having to change the behavior of the organization. Finally, the two-way symmetrical model describes organizations that use dialogue, bargaining, negotiation, and conflict management strategies to improve understanding and build relationships between an organization and its stakeholders.

Research examining these four behavioral types has shown that few organizations practice two-way symmetrical communication even though it is hypothesized to enhance firm performance (Grunig & Grunig, 1992). More typical is one-way (or even two-way) asymmetrical communication in which organizations refuse to accept responsibility for negative controversies, withhold information in hopes of diminishing alarm, or put a positive spin on events to frame situations in a more favorable light (e.g., Elsbach, 1994; Marcus & Goodman, 1991).

*Determining External
Information Behaviors*

Early theories predicting communication management practices were contingency based and examined how the types of communication behaviors exhibited by organizations vary as a consequence of organization type, the nature of the environment, and organization structure. Grunig and Hunt (1984), for example, argued that communication behaviors would vary depending on an organization's fundamental mission and goals (e.g., the type of organization). They proposed that sports, theater, or consumer product organizations would be most likely to employ the press agent model; government agencies and nonprofit organizations such as universities would be most likely to use the public information model; competitive firms would practice the two-way asymmetrical model; and regulated businesses would practice the two-way symmetrical model. Findings from a number of studies appear to support this line of thinking (Grunig & Grunig, 1992) with much of the variation attributed to an organization's history and the institutionalization of routines. For example, Grunig and Grunig (1992, p. 307) explain that public information may be most common in government because of the institutionalized confinements placed on its practice there.

Another stream of research examining determinants of organizational communication practices is grounded in assumptions related to resource dependence, autonomy, and the idea that organizations naturally want to dominate their environments and reduce their dependence by managing interdependencies with entities in the environment that restrict their autonomy (Pfeffer & Salancik, 1978). Central to these studies is the idea that environmental constraints or dependence influence external communication behaviors. For example, Grunig (1976) and Schneider (1985) hypothesized that symmetrical communication will be more likely in organic organizations facing constraining, uncertain environments. They argued that organizations facing environmental constraints and uncertainty will be prompted to establish symmetrical information flows to achieve stable, predictable, and dependable relations with other actors in the environment. Thus, as the complexity and uncertainty of the environment increase, the complexity of communication practices increases because effective coping requires organizations to seek information from their environments and also to disseminate information to the environment to forecast or forestall uncertainty and achieve a more reliable pattern of resource exchanges. While intuitively appealing, the hypotheses were not supported (Grunig, 1976; Schneider, 1985). Other studies in public relations have failed to support these ideas as well (Grunig & Grunig, 1989).

Recently, researchers have abandoned their focus on contingency explanations and have adopted a power-control perspective to explain externally directed communication behaviors (Grunig, 1990). Results from a five-year study of public relations by Grunig and his colleagues (see Grunig, 1992) suggest that external communication practices are affected by

- Organizational power (i.e., the worldview held by the dominant coalition and whether the dominant coalition includes a senior public relations executive)
- Organizational culture (an organizational culture that is flexible and favors shared responsibility for problem solving, and a dominant coalition whose beliefs and values are consistent with information sharing)
- The expertise and knowledge of the top public relations executive (a relatively powerful and valued senior public relations executive that can advise organizations about ways to implement two-way symmetrical communication; Dozier, 1992)

In addition to the influence of political and normative pressures arising internally, communication behaviors may also be affected by normative external forces. In fact, the institutional environment may impose pressures on organizations to justify activities or outputs (DiMaggio & Powell, 1983; Elsbach, 1994; Meyer & Rowan, 1977), and

these legitimacy pressures may affect outward information flows and organizational information management strategies more generally. The flow of information for purposes of increasing legitimacy can originate when an organization is motivated to demonstrate or improve its reputation, image, prestige, or congruence with prevailing norms in its institutional environment. Thus, it is important to consider the more symbolic aspects of information management and the idea that corporate communication may help to shape identity and legitimize an organization and its actions (Feldman & March, 1981; Sitkin, Sutcliffe, & Barrios-Choplin, 1992).

Public relations theory advances the prescription that organizations engaging in two-way symmetrical communication will be more effective than organizations practicing asymmetrical communication. This line of thinking is based on the idea that organizations can enhance their autonomy and legitimacy by proactively managing their interdependencies through interactive communication with the publics that provide the greatest threats and opportunities for the organization. Two-way communication including bargaining, negotiating, and strategies to reduce conflict help to bring about "symbiotic changes in the ideas, attitudes, and behaviors of both the organization and its publics" (Grunig, 1992, p. 29). Yet it is not surprising to find that effective organizations often mix the two-way models (Grunig & Grunig, 1992).

Organizations have multiple and conflicting goals and multiple and conflicting stakeholders interested in and affected by a constantly shifting mix of issues or problems. To deal with the stream of goals, stakeholders, and issues, organizations must balance the necessity of persuading stakeholders or publics with the necessity of negotiating with them. Thus, organizations mixing the two-way asymmetrical and symmetrical models, in fact, may be "strategically" managing the flow of outward information in that "it is in the strategic interest of organizations to change their behavior when they provoke opposition from the environment as well as to try to change the behavior of environmental stakeholders" (Grunig & Repper, 1992, p. 123).

Strategically managing communication with the environment is inextricably tied to environmental information processing and, more specifically, to the processes of noticing and interpreting environmental information concerning stakeholders, publics, and issues. Researchers in public relations and issues management emphasize that organization-environment relationships can best be understood by thinking of the environment in terms of organizations, stakeholders, publics, and issues (Grunig, 1992) in dynamic competition. Stakeholders, individuals, groups, or other organizations that can affect or are affected by organizational decisions, actions, policies, or practices become publics when they recognize organizational decisions or actions, outcomes, or related consequences as a problem and organize to do something about the issue(s) recognized (Grunig & Repper, 1992). While these relations are portrayed as simple and linear in theory, in reality, organization-stakeholder relations are more complex, dynamic, and ambiguous since different focal organizations are competing with one another for the attention and support of the same stakeholders. Communication, in particular, persuasion and advocacy, is critical for influencing interpretations that will predominate.

One potential concern with defining the environment as a network of important stakeholders and active publics concerned with problems is that it implies that communication management behaviors are primarily reactive, aimed at minimizing the potential threats of active publics. Yet organizations do more than respond to their environments in a cybernetic way. Rather than merely adapting to them, organizations proactively attempt to shape their environments through communication. That is, through communication, many organizations try to impose their preferred definition of situations and issues on their environments. The processes of how information penetrates an organization's cognitive system and how it is interpreted are underde-

veloped and sometimes taken for granted in much of the public relations literature (see Heath, 1994, for an exception). Yet, as noted throughout this chapter, understanding the dynamics and antecedents that pertain to how key organizational decision makers attend to and make sense of environmental elements, how interpretations affect subsequent organizational actions (including communication acts), and how environmental entities subsequently make sense of organizational actions and communication is at the heart of environmental information processing.

Although issues don't come automatically labeled as threats or opportunities, the way an issue is labeled (i.e., interpreted) may predictably affect organizational communication behaviors. Evidence by Chess, Tamuz, et al. (1992) suggests that two-way communication is often initiated when organizational members perceive that stakeholders or issues pose a moderate degree of threat or uncontrollability (rather than high or low degree of threat). This implies two things. First, if stakeholders are perceived as entirely quiescent, distant, or disinterested there is no motivation for symmetrical communication. Second, if stakeholder scrutiny or hostility is perceived to be too great, an organization may choose to ignore the threat and wall itself off to protect itself (Chess, Tamuz, et al., 1992). This reconfirms the importance interpretations play in affecting organizational actions—in this case communication actions. Research examining strategic decision makers' interpretations about their environments, publics, or issues may provide important insights about these issues.

External Information Flows, Legitimacy, and Organizational Performance

So far, I have described typical information management behaviors and discussed the factors and mechanisms that relevant theory suggests may influence outward information flows more generally. In this section, I examine information tactics more specifically, and how they differentially affect organizational legitimacy and performance. In an increasingly turbulent world, outward communication is particularly relevant before, during, or after scandals, accidents, crises, or other situations that threaten an organization's legitimacy. I use specific examples from risk communication, organizational theory, and strategic management to illustrate the outward communication strategies organizations use in preparation for or in response to legitimacy threats and how these tactics are related to organizational outcomes (for examples, see Heath, 1988, 1994; Heath & Nelson, 1986; Rowland & Rademacher, 1990; Small, 1991; for a more extensive discussion of specific communication tactics). The examples cited are meant to be illustrative, and I have not been exhaustive in citing relevant work. Thus, the examples are not wholly representative of each of the literatures sampled.

Chess, Tamuz, et al. (1992) and Chess, Saville, et al.'s (1992) in-depth case study of Sybron Chemicals provides insights not only into how firms can respond to volatile publics but also into the internal mechanisms, structures, and processes that influence both the type of and effectiveness of external communication. As Chess and her colleagues note, research into external communication is particularly relevant and timely given that, in the past ten years, technological failures have eroded public confidence in organizations' capabilities to reduce the likelihood of such crises. After several small crises (see Chess, Saville, et al., 1992, p. 432), Sybron Chemicals Inc. determined that its survival depended on improving relations with the community and subsequently developed effective, ongoing, two-way symmetrical communication practices aimed at managing risk. The results of the Chess, Saville, et al. study suggest that five internal factors affect the propensity to establish effective risk communication practices. First, risk communication is inextricably linked with risk management and other goals to improve health and safety. Second, symmetrical communication is more likely when a firm perceives important stakeholders as threatening the company's profitability. Third, diffusion of communication responsibilities among multiple organizational members at varying hierarchical levels is likely to increase two-way symmetrical communication with stakeholders; however, the success of such practices depends on the effectiveness of internal communication.[2] Fourth, risk communication requires the sensing and amplification of bad news, which often depend on a high degree of trust and openness among organizational members at all levels in the hierarchy. Finally, effective two-way communication is more likely when there are mechanisms to institutionalize organizational learning.

The case of Sybron Chemicals (Chess, Saville, et al., 1992; Chess, Tamuz, et al., 1992) and Small's (1991) analysis of Exxon's handling of the Valdez oil spill highlight that two-way communication aimed at preempting anticipated problems and managing the real or potential consequences of risks and crises can enhance firm legitimacy and performance in the long run. Still, it is more often the case that organizations fail to communicate with stakeholders until after a scandal or crisis occurs. Recent studies by Marcus and Goodman (1991) and Elsbach (1994) demonstrate, more specifically, how organizations construct communication intended to deflect public criticism following a crisis and how these different communication efforts influence performance.

Marcus and Goodman (1991) examined public managerial announcements after scandals, accidents, and public safety violations to determine investor reactions to two types of statements: accommodative statements in which management admits to the problem, accepts responsibility, and is ready to take remedial actions, and defensive statements in which management denies problem existence, confirms the firm's ability to generate revenue, and suggests the rapid resumption of normal operations (Marcus & Goodman, 1991, p. 286). They found that following accidents investors reacted more positively to defensive statements rather than to accommodative statements and that following scandals investors reacted more positively to accommodative statements rather than to defensive statements. Thus, in the short term, defensive accounts were more effective in protecting an organization's legitimacy; however, as the authors note, it was not possible to determine the longer-term effects of such a defensive posture. Nonetheless, Marcus and Goodman's study holds a very important implication. If defensiveness is the predominant response after serious accidents or crises, paradoxically, two-way communication will be curtailed at the precise time it is most needed because diminished interactions between an organization and its environment may constrain opportunities to ferret out unique solutions and remedies for resolving or rectifying the calamity.

Marcus and Goodman's (1991) findings are contrary to results reported by Elsbach (1994). In a more finely grained study exploring the construction and effectiveness of organizational accounts, Elsbach found that accommodative accounts containing references to widely institutionalized characteristics (e.g., legitimate hierarchies and roles, legitimate rules and procedures, legitimate goals or outcomes) are the most effective in protecting organizational legitimacy following moderately negative controversies. Both studies provide insights (albeit contradictory) into the types of accounts that are most effective in enhancing or regaining organizational legitimacy and performance following untoward events. More work needs to be done in this area to link organizational accounts, external communication practices, and organizational outcomes more generally.

In summarizing the discussion on outward information flows, several conclusions can be drawn. First, in theory, organizations reactively, proactively, and interactively communicate with their environments to preempt or

hedge against problems, to alter dependencies, to enhance legitimacy, and to create value for the firm; in practice, there are many variations in the ways organizations communicate with entities in their environments. Second, current research suggests external communication practices are determined at least in part by power, culture, the roles played by senior public relations executives, and institutional requirements. Third, linking current research describing organizational communication strategies with research examining organizational sensing and interpretative mechanisms can provide useful insights into questions related to what determines outward communication, what affects the form and content of organizational communication, and how communication is linked with organizational performance.

TOWARD AN INTEGRATIVE FRAMEWORK: AN ENVIRONMENTAL SENSEMAKING AND SENSEGIVING MODEL

In this chapter, I have conceptually separated environmental information coming into an organization from information going out to the environment for ease in discussing the two processes. This is not to imply, however, that the processes are independent. In fact, the processes are inextricably linked. Organizations survive by making sense of environmental information, and in the process of making sense of their environment and to gain legitimacy organizations attempt to influence the opinions and interpretations of stakeholders and other environmental entities by communicating and asserting "themselves into the community around them" (Heath, 1994, p. 27). The process continues as stakeholders confirm or disconfirm an organization's proposed vision and attempt to influence its realized form. Borrowing from the work of Gioia and Chittipeddi (1991), the concepts of "sensemaking" and "sensegiving" provide a useful framework for better understanding the link between the two processes. The framework is discussed more fully below.

Once environmental data, information, or messages are selected, somehow penetrate, or flow into an organization's cognitive system, they are interpreted and given meaning and are often used as the basis on which organizational actions are built. Therefore, interpretations related to the information to which organizational members attend is a critical component of processing information about the external environment. The sensemaking label highlights this meaning construction by organizational participants and that environmental data and information are often ambiguous and do not come neatly packaged. In the process of developing a meaningful framework for understanding the nature of the environment, organizational members construct and reconstruct their interpretations (Gioia & Chittipeddi, 1991), and this is the essence of sensemaking.

The sensegiving label highlights the process by which organizations and their members communicate with entities in their environment. The sensegiving process is focused on influencing the "sensemaking and meaning construction of others toward a preferred redefinition of organizational reality" (Gioia & Chittipeddi, 1991, p. 442). By what they do and what they say, organizations attempt to attract attention, gain acceptance, and assert opinions. Because information is not inherently meaningful, organizations use symbols and symbolic action to give sense to their environments: to communicate their (i.e., the organization's) preferred interpretative scheme, and also to negotiate, build harmony, and resolve conflict.

Although I describe sensemaking and sensegiving in an orderly and linear way, these processes are nonlinear, reciprocal, iterative, and dynamic. Executives single out particular information in the environment as a consequence of a number of factors; develop a cognitive representation of contingencies; label or interpret perceived pressing demands, threats, or opportunities; refine their conception of the organization in relation to its environment; and subsequently create a guiding vision for the organization (sensemaking). Following this interpretive work, organizations communicate this vision to stakeholders and other constituencies (sensegiving). Stakeholders and constituencies engage in sensemaking processes as they try to figure out the meaning of the organization's communication and in the process revise their understanding of the organization and their relationship to it (sensemaking). Following this interpretive process, these entities engage in sensegiving efforts as they provide feedback and confirm or disconfirm the organization's vision. In this way, sensemaking and sensegiving cycles correspond to periods dominated by *understanding* and *influencing*. "Sensemaking phases are those that deal primarily with understanding processes and the sensegiving phases are those that concern attempts to influence the way that another party understands or makes sense" (Gioia & Chittipeddi, 1991, p. 443).

Organizational sensemaking and sensegiving processes are not random. Weick and Daft's (1983) description of organizational interpretation modes provides a platform for understanding how differences in interpretation modes systematically affect information gathering and interpreting behaviors and subsequent communication acts aimed toward affecting other actors in their environment. Differences in interpretation systems affect how active organizations are in collecting environmental information, the information to which they attend, the labels organizations apply to the information they collect, and the predominant type of organizational communication practices (i.e., asymmetrical vs. symmetrical). In addition, interpretation modes affect the general communication stance an organization takes in giving sense to its environment by affecting how strongly an organization tries to influence stakeholder perceptions toward itself (i.e., the assertiveness of organizational communication).

Daft and Weick (1984; Weick & Daft, 1983) argue that interpretation systems vary along two dimensions—the extent to which management believes the environment to be objectively given or analyzable, and the degree to which organizations actively penetrate their environments to gather information. Combined, these distinctions form the basis of a framework of four interpretive modes— enacting, discovering, undirected viewing, and conditioned viewing—that differentially affect organizational sensemaking and sensegiving behaviors.

Enacting organizations construct their own environments because they believe the environment to be unanalyzable. They experiment, test, stimulate, and ignore precedent. Enacting organizations are likely to be the most assertive in attempting to influence or shape stakeholder attitudes. In this way, enacting organizations are likely to "give the most sense to" their environments than the other types. Consequently, enacting organizations may be predisposed to two-way asymmetrical communication behaviors (Grunig, 1984). The discovering mode also represents an active organization, but discovering organizations assume the external environment is concrete. Discovering organizations actively gather attitudinal data from stakeholders, and these data are interpreted as perceived environmental requirements. The externally directed communication of discovering organizations is likely to be adaptive and responsive to stakeholder demands and less assertive in manipulating stakeholder attitudes toward themselves. Because discovering organizations are likely to engage in a dynamic process of negotiating with important environmental entities, they may be predisposed to two-way symmetrical communication (Grunig, 1984). Organizations characterized by undirected viewing are nonintrusive and assume the environment to be unanalyzable. An undirected-viewing organization will be assertive in shaping stakeholder opinions when the opportunity arises. Undirected-viewing organizations may be predisposed to engage in one-way public information behaviors (Grunig, 1984) and will use informal opportunities such as telephone contacts about questions or complaints or annual shareholder meetings to learn about stakeholder opinions and to shape and influence those opinions (Weick & Daft, 1983). Finally, the conditioned-viewing mode represents less active organizations that assume an the environment to be analyzable. Conditioned-viewing organizations rely on formal data collection, planning, and forecasting and develop traditional interpretations about "constraints" in the environment. Communication by these organizations is likely to be reactive and may reflect a more defensive stance than the other types. Thus, organizations in the conditioned-viewing mode may be predisposed to one-way press agentry type behaviors (Grunig, 1984).

Organizations attempt to do more than respond to their environments in a reactive or adaptive way. Organizations try to shape their environments as well as adapt to them. Sensemaking and sensegiving processes are inextricably and reciprocally tied as sensemaking guides sensegiving and sensegiving guides sensemaking. The sensemaking and sensegiving framework provides an integrative perspective for understanding the processing of environmental information in that it links incoming with outgoing informational processes. The sensemaking and sensegiving framework also highlights the dynamism involved in environmental information processing. Finally, a focus on sensemaking and sensegiving moves us away from thinking about information processing from an "information flows" perspective. Thinking about inward and outward information flows may be potentially misleading. Flow is the process of transmitting information, yet information is not inherently meaningful. Meanings are not transferred; individuals and organizations determine the meaning of information (i.e., communication acts) based on evaluative schemas in use. Consequently, sensemaking and sensegiving better reflect that meanings are constituted and reconstituted through the dynamic, reciprocal, and iterative processing of environmental information.

IMPLICATIONS
FOR RESEARCH

The purpose of this chapter was to explore organizational environments and organizational information processing with the intention of highlighting issues that have been underdeveloped, disregarded, or otherwise overlooked in previous examinations of these topics. In this chapter, I have focused on sensing and interpreting processes related to incoming information flows and have also examined the flow of information outward from organizations to their environments. Environmental information processing embodies exchanges of information and inferences of meaning at the heart of communication theory and consequently is important for scholars interested in organizational communication. This chapter points to a number of areas to extend and enhance current research in organizational and communication theory.

Implications for Extending Current Research

One avenue of future research concerns the construct of environment. As noted in the discussion of the environment, despite over 40 years of work and widespread dissatisfaction with both extreme views (i.e., objective vs. enactment), little has emerged to replace them. This would seem a rich area for research. Are current models meaningful to strategic managers and other organizational members who analyze their organization's environment? Are they meaningful to researchers trying to understand communication issues related to how organizational members make sense of and give sense to their environments? For example, characterizing the envi-

ronment in terms of its attributes such as volatility, munificence, and complexity may be too abstract for managers and for researchers as well. Although these conceptualizations may make environmental analysis more tractable in theory, it may be of little use in practice. Consequently, researchers must continue with their efforts to redefine and refine the concept of "environment," both in terms of perceptions and in terms of objectively measured attributes and how subjectivity and objectivity are blended (Weick, 1983). Richer methods and longitudinal designs are needed (see Fahey & Narayanan, 1989). For example, studies linking the cognitive maps of the dominant coalition over time with descriptive data on the environmental context coupled with descriptions of internal and external communication processes may provide fruitful insights into how managers operationally think of their environments; how environmental maps are developed, changed, and updated over time; and the consequences of shifts in perceived boundaries.

A related question is whether the construct of "environment" is still useful in a post-industrial world (Huber, 1984). Given the increasing plurality of organizations and environments; their overlapping, shifting, and permeable boundaries; and multiple and conflicting goals, stakeholders, and publics interested in and affected by a constantly shifting mix of issues or problems, it may be more useful, as public relations scholars suggest (Grunig, 1997), to think of environments as networks or hierarchies of stakeholders, publics, and issues. Conceptualizing environments in network terms may be important for understanding external communication behaviors and for understanding the reciprocal influence of organizations on environments and environments on organizations. For example, by focusing on what information means to different units or entities within and among networks as well as how information flows and is distributed within and among networks, future studies may shed light on the extent to which the interpretive systems used by members in interlocking networks are compatible, complementary, or contradictory (Heath, 1994). Insights into these "zones of meaning" (Heath, 1994) will enable researchers to better understand and predict interlocking interactions between organizations and their environments. Studies in this area may also provide insights about the accuracy of decision makers' views of their environment and how accuracy is achieved because executives in organizations in tightly coupled systems, by necessity, may develop more accurate views of the environment than their counterparts in loosely coupled systems.

More needs to be said about accuracy. Even if a more tractable model of assessing the environment is found (i.e., stakeholders, publics, issues), the issue of accuracy is still salient. The question of how well organizations and their members are able to sense important trends or elements still remains. Although some researchers argue that perceptual accuracy is not necessary (Starbuck & Milliken, 1988), the quality of certain types of important organizational decisions or actions may be determined in large part by the degree to which perceptions of environmental information adequately or accurately represent reality. Planes crash (i.e., Tenerife) because airline crews misinterpret environmental information (Weick, 1990b). Wars get started because one side misinterprets the actions of the other (Vertzberger, 1984). Intel gets in trouble when it misreads the extent to which people care about flawed Pentium chips and subsequently adopts a cavalier communication stance. External communication based on flawed perceptions may negatively affect a firm's legitimacy.

An assumption underlying this chapter is that information processing is purposeful behavior by which individuals, groups, or organizations become aware of, handle, manage, resolve, or control data and information about the environment. The outcome of information processing is manifest in a representation of the environmental landscape. The quality of the information-processing process can be evaluated against its product by determining the accuracy of perception, or in other words, the extent of misperception produced (i.e., the discrepancy between the real world and perceptual world). This view is admittedly embedded in rational, strategic choice assumptions. However, because of bounded rationality, individuals and organizations are limited as information processors, which suggests, as noted earlier, that a certain level of misperception is inevitable in every information-processing system. Thus, better information processing may not so much be characterized by an ability to choose between accurate images and misperceptions, but rather the ability to enhance plausibility and choose between different potential misperceptions.

Although it is often true that the dynamism and complexity of environments preclude totally accurate perceptions, accuracy matters sometimes about some things. From a communication management perspective, the distinction between global accuracy and circumscribed accuracy may be important (Swann, 1984; Weick, 1995). Global accuracy is concerned with the perception of widely generalizable beliefs. Circumscribed accuracy is a more limiting concept and is focused on specific predictions in a limited number of contexts for short periods (Swann, 1984; Weick, 1995). Not all information in the environment is likely to be relevant for organizational success, and research suggests that attention to particular kinds of information may be crucial for survival (D'Aveni & MacMillan, 1990). One important implication is that some things must be sensed and communicated more accurately than others. Even though little is known about this or the communication processes that affect these attention and selection processes, it may be useful to investigate the communication dynamics related to how organizational members single out and give meaning to particular components of the information environment. Research in this area may be especially important for understanding the dynamic features of competitive interactions.

Two areas of future research may be relevant. First, studies examining symmetrical information flows within organizations (i.e., with internal stakeholders) may shed light on how communication affects attention and selection. For example, research by Smith, Grimm, Gannon, and Chen (1991) shows that firms respond faster to their competitors' tactical actions than to strategic actions. Two conclusions can be drawn from this study: (1) tactical actions in some way are more salient than strategic actions and therefore get detected more quickly and more frequently, and (2) it is much more difficult to interpret the information contained in strategic actions than tactical actions. Symmetrical information systems in which employees are provided mechanisms for dialogue with each other, with supervisors, and with top managers may help employees more deeply understand their organization's goals, plans, and relationships with key actors in the environment. This not only will enhance coordination among subsystems but also will enhance the achievement of strategic objectives because lower-level employees may be better primed to recognize important environmental signals and this ultimately will affect the quality of sensing and sensemaking processes. Second, symmetrical information will help organizational members to make sense of their situation, may facilitate commitment to work and to the organization, and may enhance rather than constrain organizational members' sensemaking abilities (Gioia & Chittipeddi, 1991).

In addition to research on symmetrical information within organizations, research related to organizational interpretation systems is also needed. Interpretation modes are not random, and differences in how organizations interpret environmental information is likely to play a critical role in responsiveness to the environment (Daft & Weick, 1984; Gioia & Thomas, 1996). One rich source of ideas for organizational communication scholars relates to systematically validating organizational interpretation modes, their determinants, and their consequences. Interpretation modes may determine an organization's responsiveness to its environment by affecting what gets sensed, how information is interpreted, and how an organization responds (including the type of communication behaviors such as asymmetrical vs. symmetrical and also the form and content of particular messages). Although these ideas are powerful, there is little empirical work in this area.

Additional research focused on the information environment may also be useful for understanding why important information is rejected, considered irrelevant, or unimportant or why unimportant information (i.e., noise) is considered meaningful, relevant, and important (Vertzberger, 1984). Organizational communication studies in the areas of deception, secrecy, silence, or the nonexistence of information may also provide useful insights about the information environment and information-processing quality.

Another avenue for extending current research builds on the idea that even though misperceptions of environmental information are inevitable as environmental complexity and turbulence increase, it is important to understand how such distortions occur particularly because distortions or misperceptions are likely to affect external communication practices. Although a number of perceptual errors or incongruencies may occur, there are two major mismatches. Executives may notice more of an environmental attribute when there is less or none, or may fail to notice an environmental attribute that is present in the environment. It is likely that seeing more when there is less will have a different effect on an organization's responsiveness and performance than seeing less when there is more. For example, seeing more when there is less may result in reduced efficiency or profitability as firms waste resources on unnecessary scanning or information-monitoring activities thereby hindering firm performance (Boyd et al., 1993). However, seeing less when there is more—failing to detect changes or conditions—may have a far greater potential for bringing about negative consequences for an organization. If the environment is changing and a firm fails to notice changes and initiate appropriate adaptive responses, the firm's survival may be threatened. This suggests that the performance consequences of failing to detect environmental changes will be more serious than the performance consequences of perceiving conditions that are not there.

Promising Avenues for Future Research

Past work provides a foundation on which the study of organizational information processing and environmental information flows can build. However, there are several promising new avenues of research opportunity that have been largely neglected in past work.

First, as the trend of global competition becomes increasingly dominant, scholars are particularly interested in the transferability of theories developed in Western economies to other countries. There is some evidence to suggest that models describing environmental information-processing activities in developed countries fail to adequately explain and predict the information-processing activities in developing countries (Kiggundu, Jorgensen, & Hafsi, 1983; Sawyerr, 1993). For example, Sawyerr (1993) found that Nigerian executives differed in important ways from their American counterparts in their scanning behaviors (e.g., types of sources used) and in terms of the attributes of the environment they identified as most important in affecting the organization's behavior. There is also research suggesting major differences in environmental intelligence systems between the United States and other countries (Ghoshal & Kim, 1986) and also in interpretation systems (Triandis & Albert, 1987). An examination of differences and similarities in information-processing behaviors across nations coupled with studies focusing on intercultural communication related both to sensemaking and to sensegiving processes seem important avenues for future research. If

we assume that environmental information sensing and processing are major sources of competitive advantage among firms that are increasingly similar in terms of their technological and managerial competencies, these research avenues could provide many interesting insights into these issues.

To this point, I have focused primarily on extending research primarily in the sensemaking area related to the processing of incoming environmental information. However, there is more work to be done in examining how and why organizations differ in managing flows of information to their environments and in examining the processes that affect symmetrical communication between organizations and their environments. Three areas related to the outward flow of information are in need of attention.

First, more attention needs to be paid to incorporating the extensive body of work in the public relations domain examining organizational communication management behaviors into mainstream communication and organization theories. In particular, integrating ideas from organizational communication theory and ideas related to interpretation and its role in influencing communication behaviors with public relations theory could genuinely enhance our understanding of these issues.

Second, although research examining the development and consequences of communication norms across organizational boundaries is growing, more work needs to be done in assessing the antecedents of such communication practices (e.g., Chess, Saville, et al., 1992; Chess, Tamuz, et al., 1992; Elsbach, 1994; Marcus & Goodman, 1991). This seems particularly relevant with the increasing predominance of network organizations and increasing emphasis on quality and continuous learning. Organizations often develop standardized communication routines that match the expectations or requirements imposed by various environmental contingencies (Feldman & March, 1981; Sitkin et al., 1992). The adoption of particular methods acceptable to key external groups may contribute to a firm's legitimacy and may be essential for continued survival and success (Meyer & Rowan, 1977). Over time, information flows, interactions, or communication patterns may become routinized within an industry or organizational field such that no alternative methods are considered, even when alternatives may be more efficient and effective (Sitkin et al., 1992). Research drawing on the institutional theory perspective may provide important insights.

Finally, with increasing attention being paid to the issues of opportunism and trust between organizations, research investigating the development of collaborative versus competitive interorganizational relations also may provide useful insights about flows of information across organizational boundaries. While competitive opportunism by environmental actors has been largely taken for granted in much of the strategic management and organizational theory literature, it may be useful to question these assumptions regarding the behavior of economic actors. Perhaps trusting behavior between economic actors can be identified and may lead to better outcomes in an interdependent world. Research integrating ideas from the literatures on competitive strategies, conflict, collaboration, and risk communication may provide a rich mixture from which to formulate a more comprehensive framework to explain corporate communication behaviors.

CONCLUSION

Organizations are information-obtaining and information-processing systems. Yet to think of organizations solely as thinking entities that make cybernetic adjustments to environments based on objective data regarding goal achievement can be misleading. It fails to acknowledge the inherent complexities in sensing and interpreting environmental information. Further, an information-processing perspective alone fails to highlight that organizations are more than adaptive systems. Organizations proactively attempt to shape their

environments by influencing the opinions and interpretations of stakeholders and other important environmental entities. This chapter has broadened the conception of organizational information processing by articulating the idea that organizations not only make sense of their environments but also give sense to their environments.

NOTES

1. Early public relations theories were dominated by the presupposition that the purpose of public relations was to manipulate the behavior of publics for the benefit of the organization (Grunig, 1992) and assumed that one-way communication is manipulative or asymmetric and that two-way communication is informative or symmetric. Yet, as Grunig (1984) highlights, "many organizations, such as universities or government agencies, provide one-way communication that is truthful and informative and benefits publics as much as or more than it benefits the organization. Other organizations use two-way communication to manipulate rather than adapt to publics. Their public relations practitioners do research—seek information—to determine what publics like and dislike about the organizations and then give information to those publics that describes the organization as having attributes the public favors and ignores attributes the public does not favor" (p. 8).

2. The effectiveness of decentralized communication responsibilities depends, in part, on the effectiveness of an organization's internal communication. As Small (1991) highlights in his study of Exxon's response to the Valdez oil spill, decentralized communication responsibilities can be problematic if an organization's internal communication is weak. If there is good two-way internal communication among all levels in the hierarchy, there is likely to be enhanced coordination among subsystems and a deeper understanding of the organization's goals, plans, and relationships with key actors in the environment. However, Small also points out that decentralized communication structures may be ineffective during crises or other untoward events.

REFERENCES

Abolafia, M. Y., & Kilduff, M. (1988). Enacting market crisis: The social construction of a speculative bubble. *Administrative Science Quarterly, 33,* 177-193.

Aldrich, H. (1979). *Organizations and environments.* Englewood Cliffs, NJ: Prentice Hall.

Aldrich, H., & Auster, E. R. (1986). Even dwarfs started small. In B. M. Staw & L. L. Cummings (Eds.), *Research in organizational behavior* (Vol. 8, pp. 165-198). Greenwich, CT: JAI.

Aldrich, H., & Pfeffer, J. (1976). Environments of organizations. *Annual Review of Sociology, 2,* 79-105.

Barr, P., Stimpert, J., & Huff, A. (1992). Cognitive change, strategic action, and organizational renewal. *Strategic Management Journal, 13,* 15-36.

Bateman, T. S., & Zeithaml, C. P. (1989). The psychological context of strategic decisions: A model and convergent experimental findings. *Strategic Management Journal, 9,* 71-78.

Bettman, J., & Weitz, B. (1983). Attributions in the board room: Causal reasoning in corporate annual reports. *Administrative Science Quarterly, 28,* 165-183.

Beyer, J. M. (1981). Ideologies, values, and decision making in organizations. In P. Nystrom & W. Starbuck (Eds.), *Handbook of organizational design* (pp. 166-202). New York: Oxford University Press.

Bourgeois, L. J. (1980). Strategy and environment: A conceptual integration. *Academy of Management Review, 5,* 25-29.

Bourgeois, L. J. (1985). Strategic goals, perceived uncertainty, and economic performance in volatile environments. *Academy of Management Journal, 28,* 548-573.

Boyd, B. K., Dess, G. G., & Rasheed, A. M. (1993). Divergence between archival and perceptual measures of the environment: Causes and consequences. *Academy of Management Review, 18,* 204-226.

Caves, R. E. (1980). Industrial organization, corporate strategy, and structure. *Journal of Economic Literature, 28,* 64-92.

Cheney, G., & Dionisopoulos, G. N. (1989). Public relations? No, relations with publics: A rhetorical-organizational approach to contemporary corporate communications. In C. H. Botan & V. Hazleton, Jr. (Eds.), *Public relations theory* (pp. 135-157). Hillsdale, NJ: Lawrence Erlbaum.

Cheney, G., & Vibbert, S. L. (1987). Corporate discourse: Public relations and issue management. In F. M. Jablin, L. L. Putnam, K. H. Roberts, & L. W. Porter (Eds.), *Handbook of organizational communication: An interdisciplinary perspective* (pp. 165-194). Newbury Park, CA: Sage.

Chess, C., Saville, A., Tamuz, M., & Greenberg, M. (1992). The organizational links between risk communication and risk management: The case of Sybron Chemicals Inc. *Risk Analysis, 12,* 431-438.

Chess, C., Tamuz, M., Saville, A., & Greenberg, M. (1992). Reducing uncertainty and increasing credibility: The case of Sybron Chemicals Inc. *Industrial Crisis Quarterly, 6,* 55-70.

Child, J. (1972). Organizational structure, environment, and performance: The role of strategic choice. *Sociology, 6,* 2-22.

Corner, P. D., Kinicki, A. J., & Keats, B. W. (1994). Integrating organizational and individual information processing perspectives on choice. *Organization Science, 5,* 294-308.

Daft, R. L., Bettenhausen, K. R., & Tyler, B. B. (1993). Implications of top managers' communication choices for strategic decisions. In G. P. Huber & W. H. Glick (Eds.), *Organizational change and redesign: Ideas and insights for improving performance* (pp. 112-146). New York: Oxford University Press.

Daft, R. L., & Lengel, R. H. (1984). Information richness: A new approach to managerial behavior and organization design. In B. M. Staw & L. L. Cummings (Eds.), *Research in organizational behavior* (Vol. 6, pp. 193-233). Greenwich, CT: JAI.

Daft, R. L., Sormunen, J., & Parks, D. (1988). Chief executive scanning, environmental characteristics, and company performance: An empirical study. *Strategic Management Journal, 9,* 123-139.

Daft, R. L. & Weick, K. E. (1984). Toward a model of organizations as interpretation systems. *Academy of Management Review, 9,* 284-295.

D'Aveni, R. A., & MacMillan, I. C. (1990). Crisis and the content of managerial communications: A study of the focus of attention of top managers in surviving and failing firms. *Administrative Science Quarterly, 35,* 634-657.

Dearborn, D. C., & Simon, H. A. (1958). Selective perception: A note on the departmental identification of executives. *Sociometry, 21,* 140-144.

Dess, G. G., & Beard, D. W. (1984). Dimensions of organizational task environments. *Administrative Science Quarterly, 29,* 52-73.

Dill, W. R. (1962). The impact of environment on organizational development. In S. Malick & E. H. Van Ness (Eds.), *Concepts and issues in administrative behavior* (pp. 94-109). Englewood Cliffs, NJ: Prentice Hall.

DiMaggio, P. J., & Powell, W. W. (1983). The iron cage revisited: Institutional isomorphism and collective rationality in organizational fields. *American Sociological Review, 48,* 147-160.

Downey, H. K., Hellriegel, D., & Slocum, J. W. (1977). Individual characteristics as sources of perceived uncertainty variability. *Human Relations, 30,* 161-174.

Downey, H. K., & Slocum, J. W. (1975). Uncertainty: Measures, research, and sources of variation. *Academy of Management Journal, 18,* 562-578.

Dozier, D. M. (1992). The organizational roles of communication and public relations practitioners. In J. E. Grunig (Ed.), *Excellence in public relations and communication management* (pp. 327-356). Hillsdale, NJ: Lawrence Erlbaum.

Duncan, R. B. (1973). Multiple decision-making structures in adapting to environmental uncertainty: The impact on organizational effectiveness. *Human Relations, 26,* 273-291.

Dutton, J. E. (1993a). Interpretations on automatic: A different view of strategic issue diagnosis. *Journal of Management Studies, 30,* 339-357.

Dutton, J. E. (1993b). The making of organizational opportunities. In L. L. Cummings & B. M. Staw (Eds.), *Research in organizational behavior* (Vol. 15, pp. 195-226). Greenwich, CT: JAI.

Dutton, J. E., & Jackson, S. E. (1987). Categorizing strategic issues: Links to organizational action. *Academy of Management Review, 12,* 76-90.

Dutton, J. W., Walton, E. J., & Abrahamson, E. (1989). Important dimensions of strategic issues: Separating the wheat from the chaff. *Journal of Management Studies, 26,* 379-396.

Eisenhardt, K. M. (1989). Making fast strategic decisions in high-velocity environments. *Academy of Management Journal, 32,* 543-576.

Elsbach, K. D. (1994). Managing organizational legitimacy in the California cattle industry: The construction and effectiveness of verbal accounts. *Administrative Science Quarterly, 39,* 57-88.

Elsbach, K. D., & Kramer, R. M. (1996). Members' responses to organizational identity threats: Encountering and countering *Business Week* rankings. *Administrative Science Quarterly, 41,* 442-476.

Elsbach, K. D., & Sutton, R. I. (1992). Acquiring organizational legitimacy through illegitimate actions: A marriage of institutional and impression management theories. *Academy of Management Journal, 35,* 699-738.

Fahey, L., & King, W. R. (1977). Environmental scanning for corporate planning. *Business Horizons, 20*(4), 61-71.

Fahey, L., & Narayanan, V. K. (1989). Linking changes in revealed causal maps and environmental change: An empirical study. *Journal of Management Studies, 26,* 361-378.

Feldman, M. S., & March, J. G. (1981). Information in organizations as signal and symbol. *Administrative Science Quarterly, 26,* 171-186.

Ford, J. D., & Baucus, D. A. (1987). Organizational adaptation to performance downturns: An interpretation-based perspective. *Academy of Management Review, 12,* 366-380.

Fredrickson, J. W. (1985). Effects of decision motive and organizational performance level on strategic decision processes. *Academy of Management Journal, 28,* 821-843.

Galbraith, J. R. (1973). *Designing complex organizations.* Reading, MA: Addison-Wesley.

Ghoshal, S., & Kim, S. K. (1986). Building effective intelligence systems for competitive advantage. *Sloan Management Review, 28,* 49-58.

Gifford, W. E., Bobbitt, H. R., & Slocum, J. W. (1979). Message characteristics and perceptions of uncertainty by organizational decision makers. *Academy of Management Journal, 22,* 458-481.

Gioia, D. A., & Chittipeddi, K. (1991). Sensemaking and sensegiving in strategic change initiation. *Strategic Management Journal, 12,* 433-448.

Gioia, D. A., & Thomas, J. B. (1996). Identity, image, and issue interpretation: Sensemaking during strategic change in academia. *Administrative Science Quarterly, 41,* 370-403.

Glick, W. H., Miller, C. C., & Huber, G. P. (1993). Upper-echelon diversity in organizations: Demographic, structural, and cognitive influences on organizational performance. In G. P. Huber & W. H. Glick (Eds.), *Organizational change and redesign: Ideas and insights for improving performance* (pp. 176-214). New York: Oxford University Press.

Grunig, J. E. (1976). Organizations and public relations: Testing a communication theory. *Journalism Monographs, 46* (Serial No. 46).

Grunig, J. E. (1984, Winter). Organizations, environments, and models of public relations. *Public Relations Research and Education, 1,* 6-29.

Grunig, J. E. (1990). Theory and practice of interactive media relations. *Public Relations Quarterly, 35*(3), 18-23.

Grunig, J. E. (Ed.). (1992). *Excellence in public relations and communication management.* Hillsdale, NJ: Lawrence Erlbaum.

Grunig, J. E. (1997). Public relations management in government and business. In J. L. Garnett (Ed.), *Handbook of administrative communication.* New York: Marcel Dekker.

Grunig, J. E., & Grunig, L. A. (1989). Toward a theory of the public relations behavior of organizations: Review of a program of research. In J. E. Grunig & L. A. Grunig (Eds.), *Public relations research annual* (Vol. 1, pp. 27-63). Hillsdale, NJ: Lawrence Erlbaum.

Grunig, J. E., & Grunig, L. A. (1992). Models of public relations and communication. In J. E. Grunig (Ed.), *Excellence in public relations and communication management* (pp. 285-325). Hillsdale, NJ: Lawrence Erlbaum.

Grunig, J. E., & Hunt, T. (1984). *Managing public relations.* New York: Holt, Rinehart & Winston.

Grunig, J. E., & Repper, F. C. (1992). Strategic management, publics, and issues. In J. E. Grunig (Ed.), *Excellence in public relations and communication management* (pp. 117-157). Hillsdale, NJ: Lawrence Erlbaum.

Hambrick, D. C. (1982). Environmental scanning and organizational strategy. *Strategic Management Journal, 3,* 159-174.

Hambrick, D. C. (1994). Top management groups: A conceptual integration and reconsideration of the "team" label. In B. M. Staw & L. L. Cummings (Eds.), *Research in organizational behavior* (Vol. 16, pp. 171-214). Greenwich, CT: JAI.

Hambrick, D. C., & Brandon, G. L. (1988). Executive values. In D. Hambrick (Ed.), *The executive effect:*

Concepts and methods for studying top managers (pp. 3-34). Greenwich, CT: JAI.

Hambrick, D. C., & D'Aveni, R. A. (1992). Top team deterioration as part of the downward spiral of large corporate bankruptcies. *Management Science, 38,* 1445-1466.

Hambrick, D. C., & Finkelstein, S. (1987). Managerial discretion: A bridge between polar views of organizational outcomes. In B. M. Staw & L. L. Cummings (Eds.), *Research in organizational behavior* (Vol. 9, pp. 369-406). Greenwich, CT: JAI.

Hambrick, D. C., & Mason, P. A. (1984). Upper echelons: The organization as a reflection of its top managers. *Academy of Management Review, 9,* 193-206.

Hambrick, D. C., & Snow, C. C. (1977). A contextual model of strategic decision making in organizations. *Academy of Management Proceedings,* pp. 109-112.

Heath, R. L. (1988). *Strategic issues management.* San Francisco: Jossey-Bass.

Heath, R. L. (1994). *The management of corporate communication.* Hillsdale, NJ: Lawrence Erlbaum.

Heath, R. L., & Nelson, R. A. (1986). *Issues management.* Beverly Hills, CA: Sage.

Hinz, V. B., Tindale, R. S., & Vollrath, D. A. (1997). The emerging conceptualization of groups as information processors. *Psychological Bulletin, 121,* 43-64.

Huber, G. P. (1982). Organizational information systems: Determinants of their performance and behavior. *Management Science, 28,* 138-155.

Huber, G. P. (1984). The nature and design of post-industrial organizations. *Management Science, 30,* 928-951.

Huber, G. P. (1991). Organizational learning: The contributing processes and literatures. *Organization Science, 2,* 88-115.

Huber, G. P., & Daft, R. L. (1987). The information environments of organizations. In F. M. Jablin, L. L. Putnam, K. H. Roberts, & L. W. Porter (Eds.), *Handbook of organizational communication: An interdisciplinary perspective* (pp. 130-164). Newbury Park, CA: Sage.

Huber, G. P., & McDaniel, R. R. (1986). The decision-making paradigm of organizational design. *Management Science, 32,* 572-589.

Jackson, S. E., & Dutton, J. E. (1988). Discerning threats and opportunities. *Administrative Science Quarterly, 33,* 370-388.

Katz, R. (1982). Project communication and performance: An investigation into the effects of group longevity. *Administrative Science Quarterly, 27,* 81-104.

Kefalas, A., & Schoderbek, P. P. (1973). Scanning the business environment—Some empirical results. *Decision Science, 4,* 63-74.

Khandwalla, P. N. (1981). Properties of competing organizations. In P. Nystrom & W. Starbuck (Eds.), *Handbook of organizational design* (pp. 409-432). New York: Oxford University Press.

Kiesler, S., & Sproull, L. (1982). Managerial responses to changing environments: Perspectives on problem sensing from social cognition. *Administrative Science Quarterly, 27,* 548-570.

Kiggundu, M. N., Jorgensen, J. J., & Hafsi, T. (1983). Administrative theory and practice in developing countries: A synthesis. *Administrative Science Quarterly, 28,* 66-84.

Klimoski, R., & Mohammed, S. (1994). Team mental model: Construct or metaphor? *Journal of Management, 20,* 403-437.

Knight, K. E., & McDaniel, R. R. (1979). *Organizations: An information systems perspective.* Belmont, CA: Wadsworth.

Lev, B. (1992). Information disclosure strategy. *California Management Review, 34,* 9-32.

Lyles, M. A., & Mitroff, I. I. (1980). Organizational problem formulation: An empirical study. *Administrative Science Quarterly, 25,* 102-119.

Marcus, A., & Goodman, R. (1991). Victims and shareholders: The dilemmas of presenting corporate policy during a crisis. *Academy of Management Journal, 34,* 281-305.

McCabe, D. L., & Dutton, J. E. (1993). Making sense of the environment: The role of perceived effectiveness. *Human Relations, 46,* 623-643.

Meyer, A. D. (1982). Adapting to environmental jolts. *Administrative Science Quarterly, 27,* 515-537.

Meyer, J. W., & Rowan, B. (1977). Institutionalized organizations: Formal structure as myth and ceremony. *American Journal of Sociology, 83,* 340-363.

Milliken, F. J. (1990). Perceiving and interpreting environmental change: An examination of college administrators' interpretation of changing demographics. *Academy of Management Journal, 33,* 42-63.

Milliken, F. J., & Lant, T. K. (1991). The effect of an organization's recent performance history on strategic persistence and change: The role of managerial interpretations. *Advances in Strategic Management, 7,* 129-156.

Mischel, W. (1977). The interaction of person and situation. In D. Magnusson & N. S. Endler (Eds.), *Personality at the crossroads: Current issues in interactional psychology* (pp. 333-352). Hillsdale, NJ: Lawrence Erlbaum.

O'Reilly, C. A. (1983). The use of information in organizational decision making: A model and some propositions. In B. M. Staw & L. L. Cummings (Eds.), *Research in organizational behavior* (Vol. 5, pp. 103-139). Greenwich, CT: JAI.

O'Reilly, C. A., Caldwell, D. F., & Barnett, W. P. (1989). Work group demography, social integration, and turnover. *Administrative Science Quarterly, 34,* 21-37.

O'Reilly, C. A., & Pondy, L. R. (1979). Organizational communication. In S. Kerr (Ed.), *Organizational behavior* (pp. 119-150). Columbus, OH: Grid.

O'Reilly, C. A., & Roberts, K. (1974). Information filtration in organizations: Three experiments. *Organizational Behavior and Human Performance, 11,* 253-265.

Orton, D., & Weick, K. E. (1990). Loosely coupled systems: A reconceptualization. *Academy of Management Review, 15,* 203-223.

Pfeffer, J., & Salancik, G. R. (1978). *The external control of organizations: A resource dependence perspective.* New York: Harper & Row.

Rowland, R. C., & Rademacher, T. (1990). The passive style of rhetorical crisis management: A case study of the superfund controversy. *Communication Studies, 41,* 327-342.

Salancik, G., & Meindl, J. (1984). Corporate attributions as strategic illusions of control. *Administrative Science Quarterly, 29,* 238-254.

Sawyerr, O. O. (1993). Environmental uncertainty and environmental scanning activities of Nigerian manufacturing executives: A comparative analysis. *Strategic Management Journal, 14,* 287-299.

Schneider, L. A. (1985). *Organizational structure, environmental niches, and public relations: The Hage-Hull typology of organizations as predictor of communication behavior.* Unpublished doctoral dissertation, University of Maryland, College Park.

Schwenk, C. R. (1984). Cognitive simplification processes in strategic decision making. *Strategic Management Journal, 5,* 111-128.

Sitkin, S. B., Sutcliffe, K. M., & Barrios-Choplin, J. R. (1992). A dual-capacity model of communication media choice in organizations. *Human Communication Research, 18,* 563-598.

Sitkin, S. B., Sutcliffe, K. M., & Weick, K. E. (1998). Organizational learning. In R. Dorf (Ed.), *The technology management handbook* (pp. 70-76). Boca Raton, FL: CRC.

Small, W. J. (1991). Exxon Valdez: How to spend billions and still get a black eye. *Public Relations Review, 17*(1), 9-25.

Smircich, L. (1983). Implications for management theory. In L. L. Putnam & M. E. Pacanowsky (Eds.), *Communication and organizations: An interpretive approach* (pp. 221-242). Beverly Hills, CA: Sage.

Smircich, L., & Stubbart, C. (1985). Strategic management in an enacted world. *Academy of Management Review, 10,* 724-736.

Smith, K. G., Grimm, C. M., Gannon, M. J., & Chen, M. (1991). Organizational information processing, competitive responses, and performance in the U.S. domestic airline industry. *Academy of Management Journal, 34,* 60-85.

Starbuck, W. H., & Milliken, F. J. (1988). Executive's perceptual filters: What they notice and how they make sense. In D. Hambrick (Ed.), *The executive effect: Concepts and methods for studying top managers* (pp. 35-66). Greenwich, CT: JAI.

Staw, B., McKechnie, P., & Puffer, S. (1983). The justification of organizational performance. *Administrative Science Quarterly, 28,* 582-600.

Staw, B. M., Sandelands, L. E., & Dutton, J. E. (1981). Threat-rigidity effects in organizational behavior: A multilevel analysis. *Administrative Science Quarterly, 26,* 501-524.

Suchman, M. C. (1995). Managing legitimacy: Strategic and institutional approaches. *Academy of Management Review, 20,* 571-610.

Sutcliffe, K. M. (1994). What executives notice: Accurate perceptions in top management teams. *Academy of Management Journal, 37,* 1360-1369.

Sutcliffe, K. M. (1997). The nuances of learning. In J. Walsh & A. Huff (Eds.), *Advances in strategic management* (Vol. 14, pp. 331-336). Greenwich, CT: JAI.

Sutcliffe, K. M., & Huber, G. (1998). Firm and industry as determinants of executive perceptions of the environment. *Strategic Management Journal, 19,* 793-807.

Swann, W. B., Jr. (1984). Quest for accuracy in person perception: A matter of pragmatics. *Psychological Review, 91,* 457-477.

Thayer, L. (1968). *Communication and communication systems.* Homewood, IL: Irwin.

Thomas, J. B., Clark, S. M., & Gioia, D. A. (1993). Strategic sensemaking and organizational performance: Linkages among scanning, interpretation, action, and outcomes. *Academy of Management Journal, 36,* 239-270.

Thomas, J. B., Shankster, L. J., & Mathieu, J. E. (1994). Antecedents to organizational issue interpretation: The roles of single-level, cross-level, and content cues. *Academy of Management Journal, 37,* 1252-1284.

Thompson, J. (1967). *Organizations in action.* New York: McGraw-Hill.

Triandis, H. C., & Albert, R. D. (1987). Cross-cultural perspectives. In F. M. Jablin, L. L. Putnam, K. H. Roberts, & L. W. Porter (Eds.), *Handbook of organizational communication: An interdisciplinary perspective* (pp. 264-295). Newbury Park, CA: Sage.

Tushman, M. (1979). Work characteristics and subunit communication structure: A contingency analysis. *Administrative Science Quarterly, 24,* 82-98.

Tushman, M., & Nadler, D. A. (1978). An information processing approach to organizational design. *Academy of Management Review, 3,* 82-98.

Tushman, M. L., & Romanelli, E. (1985). Organizational evolution: A metamorphosis model of convergence and reorientation. In L. L. Cummings & B. M. Staw (Eds). *Research in organizational behavior* (Vol. 7, pp. 171-232). Greenwich, CT: JAI.

Vertzberger, Y. Y. (1984). *Misperceptions in foreign policymaking: The Sino-Indian conflict 1959-1962.* Boulder, CO: Westview.

Vertzberger, Y. Y. (1990). *The world in their minds.* Stanford, CA: Stanford University Press.

Walsh, J. P. (1988). Selectivity and selective perception: An investigation of managers' belief structures and information processing. *Academy of Management Journal, 31,* 873-896.

Walsh, J. P., Henderson, C. M., & Deighton, J. (1988). Negotiated belief structures and decision performance: An empirical investigation. *Organizational Behavior and Human Decision Processes, 42,* 194-216.

Webster's dictionary of synonyms. (1951). Springfield, MA: G & C Merriam.

Weick, K. E. (1974). Review of the book *The nature of managerial work. Administrative Science Quarterly, 18,* 111-118.

Weick, K. E. (1976). Educational organizations as loosely-coupled systems. *Administrative Science Quarterly, 21,* 1-19.

Weick, K. E. (1979). *The social psychology of organizing* (2nd ed.). Reading, MA: Addison-Wesley.

Weick, K. E. (1983). Organizational communication: Toward a research agenda. In L. L. Putnam & M. E. Pacanowsky (Eds.), *Communication and organizations: An interpretive approach* (pp. 13-29). Beverly Hills, CA: Sage.

Weick, K. E. (1987). Organizational culture as a source of high reliability. *California Management Review, 29,* 112-127.

Weick, K. E. (1988). Enacted sensemaking in crisis situations. *Journal of Management Studies, 25,* 305-317.

Weick, K. E. (1990a). Cartographic myths in organizations. In A. S. Huff (Ed.), *Mapping strategic thought* (pp. 1-10). New York: John Wiley.

Weick, K. E. (1990b). The vulnerable system: An analysis of the Tenerife air disaster. *Journal of Management, 16,* 571-593.

Weick, K. E. (1995). *Sensemaking in organizations.* Thousand Oaks, CA: Sage.

Weick, K. E., & Daft, R. L. (1983). Effectiveness of interpretation systems. In K. S. Cameron & D. A. Whetten (Eds.), *Organizational effectiveness: A comparison of multiple models* (pp. 71-93). New York: Academic Press.

Wood, R., & Bandura, A. (1989). Social cognitive theory in organizational management. *Academy of Management Review, 14,* 361-384.

Yasai-Ardekani, M. (1986). Structural adaptations to environments. *Academy of Management Review, 11,* 9-21.

Zucker, L. G. (1983). Organizations as institutions. In S. Bacharach (Ed.), *Research in the sociology of organizations* (Vol. 2, pp. 1-47). Greenwich, CT: JAI.

7

Organizational Identity

Linkages Between Internal and External Communication

GEORGE CHENEY
University of Montana

LARS THØGER CHRISTENSEN
Copenhagen Business School

As a man adjusts himself to a certain environment he becomes a different individual; but in becoming a different individual he has affected the community in which he lives. It may be a slight effect, but in so far as he has adjusted himself, the adjustments have changed the type of environments to which he can respond and the world is accordingly a different world.

—George Herbert Mead (1934, p. 215)

With few exceptions, the externally directed communications of organizations have been defined by organizational communication scholars as activities outside the province of their concerns. Because the study of organizational communication traditionally has been focused on acts of communication between senders and receivers within the "container" of the organization—that is, within clearly defined organizational borders—most communication aimed at *external* audiences, and markets in particular, has been

AUTHORS' NOTE: We wish to thank Craig Carroll, James E. Grunig, Robert L. Heath, Fredric M. Jablin, Linda L. Putnam, Juliet Roper, Phillip K. Tompkins, Sarah Tracy, and Ted Zorn for their helpful comments on earlier drafts of this chapter.

regarded as alien to the field. Such a division is neither fruitful nor justifiable any longer. The notion of organizational boundaries is becoming increasingly problematic (although, it seems, an inescapable point of reference), and "internal" and "external" communications no longer constitute separate fields in practice (Ashforth & Mael, 1996; Berg, 1986; Christensen, 1994a; see also Alvesson, 1990; Berg & Gagliardi, 1985; Cheney, 1991). Further, from an epistemological perspective, organizational communication researchers are beginning to recognize the implications and limitations of their own metaphors, seeking to reconfigure notions such as "open" versus "closed" systems, the organization-environment interface, and the idea of the organization itself (cf. Putnam, Phillips, & Chapman, 1996; Smith, 1993; Taylor, 1993).

To secure and maintain a legitimate and recognizable place in material and symbolic markets, many organizations of today pursue a variety of complex communication activities. Such activities are not neatly circumscribed and often involve both internal and external functions in ways that blur their presumed boundaries. Nowhere is this clearer than in the fields and practices of public relations and issue management where internal groups now comprise part of the general audience that the organization wishes to address and where externally directed messages, accordingly, become an integral part of the organization's operating discourse. Many organizations have begun to realize the difficulties of convincing an external audience about their deeds (e.g., their protection of the environment or defense of human rights) if the *internal* audience does not accept the message—and vice versa. Although the stated goals of public relations and issue management traditionally have had a strong external orientation—for example, building relational bonds with publics, facilitating effective policy making, developing favorable images in the media, managing strategic stakeholders, and making the organization more responsible to society—practitioners are becoming aware

that the pursuit of these goals directly affects the organization itself and its own members. Public relations and issue management, therefore, should be regarded in close connection with other forms of organizational communication.

Within such a perspective, the most interesting question may not be what distinguishes the various kinds of communication practices from one another (although we do recognize that such differences are relevant in some contexts), but rather how these endeavors are integrated for the organization to communicate at least somewhat consistently to its many different audiences. Without such consistency, the organization of today will have difficulties sustaining and confirming a coherent sense of "self" necessary to maintain credibility and legitimacy in and outside the organization. As a consequence, a growing proportion of professional communication activities becomes integrated around the same overall concern: *identity* (see, e.g., Christensen & Cheney, 1994; Czarniawska-Joerges, 1994; Hatch & Schultz, 1997). While the problem of identity is not the only concern of large organizations and often not an explicitly stated objective, we observe the surprising extent to which the question of what the organization "is" or "stands for" or "wants to be" cuts across and unifies many different goals and concerns. In the corporate world of today, identity-related concerns have, in other words, become organizational preoccupations, even when organizations are ostensibly talking about other matters.

The preoccupation with *identity as an issue* indicates at least two difficulties facing contemporary organizations and their communication: (1) a persistent problem for organizations in drawing lines between themselves and the outside world—a problem that requires a thorough rethinking of our long-held notions of institutions as discrete units (such as a university's being "contained" by a campus or a multinational firm's having a "base" or a "headquarters"); and (2) the growing problem of *being heard* in a communication environment saturated with corporate messages. Of course, both of these trends are intensified by the rise of new computer and communications technologies. In the contemporary activities of public relations, issue management, marketing, advertising, and the like—what we might, for purposes of terminological economy here call "external organizational communication"—the ongoing rhetorical struggle for organizations of most kinds is to establish a clearly distinctive identity and at the same time connect with more general concerns so as to be maximally persuasive and effective. Because organizational messages are often organized around more than one purpose and aimed at more than one audience, we need to think of internal and external organizational communication as being closely intertwined, recognizing that along with attempts to speak "for" an organization using a unitary voice there will almost inevitably be the expression (or suppression) of multiple voices, identities, cultures, images, and interests (see Cheney, 1991, 1999; cf. Bakhtin, 1991).

PURPOSE AND OUTLINE OF THE CHAPTER

In this essay, we discuss and illustrate the ways in which organizations attempt to manage both identifiable issues and their own identities, arguing that those efforts have become so interwoven as to make their analytical separation unproductive if not impossible except in a discussion that is largely divorced from the reality of contemporary corporate communications. To accomplish our purposes, the essay unfolds through a number of subthemes each discussed in relation to the overall question of managing issues and identities.

First, it is crucial to recognize central features of the communication environment if we are going to understand well how contemporary organizations are behaving today through their dazzling array of highly visible communication practices. One purpose of this essay, then, is to establish a clear connection between the (post)modern symbolic environment of today and the integration of so-called external (e.g., public relations, marketing, and issues management) and internal (e.g., employee relations, statements of mission and policy, and organizational development) forms of organizational communications. Following this line of thought, we will consider how the contests over identity are related to such things as a growing fuzziness of organizational boundaries and the self-referential and sometimes nearly autonomous nature of public corporate symbols.

A second purpose of this essay is to bring together trends in corporate communications in seemingly disparate areas and in areas typically seen as foreign to the rubric of organizational communication (as a subdiscipline) — for example, corporate issue management, marketing, issue advertising—by revealing and analyzing their underlying and common concerns. None of this is to say that these various domains of communication activity are identical or that the differences between them are insignificant, but rather that their common features can be productively examined from the perspectives of communication and rhetoric, especially through assessments of the powerful and puzzling ways in which persuasion takes place in the organizational world of today.

A third purpose of our essay is to extend Cheney and Vibbert's (1987) commentary on the fields of public relations and issue management (in the previous handbook). Their analysis included both a historical section and an analysis of contemporary public relations practice. Among other things, their interpretive historical survey showed how conceptions of the organization as rhetor (or persuader) vis-à-vis its audiences have shifted over a century's time from a "reactive" and sometimes accommodative stance toward external threats toward more aggressive attempts to shape the *grounds* for discussing social and political issues of the day. That is, while public relations began with attempts by the railroads and oil companies to fend off harsh criticisms in the late 1800s, today the activity is far more broadly conceived. Cheney and Vibbert's analysis of contemporary practices and related research was organized around three dimensions, arguing that the public relations activity of large organizations today is (1) *rhetorical* in its attempt to establish the general premises for later and more specific claims, (2) *identity related* in that each organization must work to establish its unique "self" while connecting its concerns to those of the "cultural crowd," and (3) *political* in that many large organizations today are trying to exert political influence while usually avoiding being labeled as political actors. Together these features imply, as Cheney and Vibbert noted, that strict divisions between "internal" and "external" aspects of the corporate discourse become problematic. This observation is even more relevant today than it was a few years ago: The communication environment has intensified in a number of significant ways (see, e.g., Baudrillard, 1981, 1988), and with that intensification comes the need to integrate more fully the communicative efforts directed to the various publics of the organization (see, e.g., Cheney & Frenette, 1993). In our discussion, we will comment on these trends while extending Cheney and Vibbert's analysis and interpreting an even wider range of organizational communication activities (including some aspects of marketing, advertising, and strategic management).

Our discussion is based on descriptions and interpretations of current trends as they are represented in the scholarly literature. Moreover, we will draw on current and illustrative examples from print media, television, and the Internet. The overall purpose is to stimulate the discussion in and outside the broad field of organizational communication by offering a nontraditional and communication-centered perspective on the numerous and diverse ways in which large organizations relate to and "see" themselves as relating to their environments today and in the future.

The remainder of this essay is therefore divided into five sections: (1) an introduction to the area of external organizational communication, including a brief overview of the field of corporate issue management; (2) a characterization of the communication environment within which contemporary organizations operate and to which they contribute; (3) a discussion of the fuzziness of organizational boundaries and its implications for organizational identity and communication; (4) a reconceptualization of issue management through a discussion of self-reference and paradox in communication management; and (5) a conclusion, including a discussion of the wider context of this essay presented as surprises, paradoxes, and ethical concerns to which future research needs to be directed.

CORPORATE ISSUE MANAGEMENT IN THE CONTEXT OF EXTERNAL ORGANIZATIONAL COMMUNICATION

Because scholars of organizational communication traditionally have regarded external communication as being outside their purview, there is only a vague idea of the nature of such activities within the field. And most often this idea confirms the self-image of organizational communication as a contained activity, confined within formal organizational boundaries. Today, this image makes little sense and actually tends to obscure important theoretical and practical questions (cf. Smith, 1993). If we define organizational communication in general terms as a set of processes through which organizations create, negotiate, and manage meanings (including those related to their own constitution), *external* organizational communication can be thought of as a subset of those processes specifically concerned with meaning construction by way of an "external" environment (Taylor, Flanagin, Cheney, & Seibold, in press). However, since this understanding implies assumptions about boundaries that our discussion later in the essay will work against, we will talk about external organizational communication as communication directed to and from audiences considered in everyday terms to be nonmembers of the organization.

Convergence in External Organizational Communication

To conceive of internal and external communication as interrelated dimensions of organizational sensemaking means to move our focus beyond the "container" metaphor and to embrace communication activities traditionally relegated to academics and professionals in communication functions such as advertising, marketing, and public relations.

Each of these domains of activity, professions, and disciplines has its own history, tone, mythology, and reasons for announcing its importance in society. Advertising, born in the mid-19th century, used to concern itself primarily with the direct "selling" of a product or a service (Dyer, 1990). Public relations arose in the late 19th century as a defense-based means of responding to public attacks on an organization (Cheney & Vibbert, 1987). And marketing, developed as a response to the growing number of consumer movements after World War II, established itself strongly in the 1960s as a strategic perspective for anticipating, detecting, and responding to desires, needs, or preferences of target audiences of consumers (Kotler, 1991).

Today, each of these areas has a far less certain and specific orientation than previously. Advertising, for example, has expanded its focus to include "social advertising" on important sociopolitical causes, such as the preservation of tropical rain forests or the cancellation of the Third World debt. Public relations now embraces within its reach highly proactive activities such as "issues

management" and "identity management." And as we shall discuss below, the marketing perspective has gradually become a prevailing norm in the reordering of many organizations as customer driven or consumer driven (see the *Journal of Market-Focused Management*). This is to say that the genres have become blurred and may, as a consequence, have more in common than has usually been acknowledged within the self-promoting discourse of each field. As each area or profession has sought to extend its influence and reassert its specific importance, sometimes in a rather imperialistic way, this blurring of disciplinary boundaries becomes even more evident. Among the major external communications functions, marketing has probably been the most expansive in recent years.

The Expansion of the Marketing Orientation

Since the consumer unrests of the 1960s made business aware of the potential power of the market, marketing has established itself as a dominant principle of organizing in institutions of many different types. Traditionally speaking, marketing has comprised organizational activities designed to detect, assess, and respond to consumers' needs, wants, and desires. In more general terms, marketing can be thought of as a managerial *orientation* concerned primarily with the *satisfaction* of target audiences. The mythos of the marketing field sees the discipline as being an important advancement over earlier mass-production and sales-oriented perspectives chiefly because marketing *respects and engages* the consumer and his or her preferences (e.g., Keith, 1960; Kotler, 1991); marketing thus asserts itself as participatory, responsive, and above all democratic.

Regarding publics as consumers or customers, the marketing orientation has gradually made its way into all sectors of society such that many organizations, public as well as private, now openly describe themselves as "customer driven" (see, e.g., Gay & Salaman, 1992). And even where such descriptions seem somewhat inappropriate (e.g., in health care), we still find marketing present as a managerial ethos committing the organization to monitor its environments to keep abreast of changes in the market.

The expansive tendencies of marketing have often been criticized by leading public relations thinkers eager to distinguish their discipline from that of marketing (e.g., Grunig & Grunig, 1991). Among the differences typically emphasized to justify such a distinction are orientations with respect to target groups and operational goals. Whereas marketing traditionally concentrates on building and maintaining mutually satisfactory relationships with *customers,* public relations often sees itself dealing with a much broader range of *publics* to attain not only satisfaction but "accord and positive behavior among social groupings" (Broom, Lauzen, & Tucker, 1991; see also Grunig, 1993).

While acknowledging the significance of such differences, we would point out that marketing and public relations today have more in common than is commonly believed. Since Kotler and Levy (1969) introduced their "broadened concept of marketing," the marketing discipline has widened its scope considerably to include activities traditionally thought of as belonging in the realm of public relations. In line with traditional public relation concerns, scholars and practitioners in marketing have gradually begun to realize the importance of creating and maintaining a hospitable environment by fostering goodwill among all relevant stakeholders. As a consequence, a growing number of marketers are broadening their notion of the "customer" to include families, friends, and sometimes even society. Moreover, marketing principles are no longer restricted to the realm of private business but are applied to an increasing extent in social change efforts, such as birth rate limitation programs, antismoking campaigns, and heart disease prevention programs (e.g.,

Fine, 1981; Fox & Kotler, 1980; Kotler & Andreasen, 1987; Kotler & Roberto, 1989; Lazer & Kelly, 1973; Zaltman, Kotler, & Kaufman, 1972).

Obviously, these tendencies are not without practical problems. Since marketers take their point of departure as the wish to satisfy the needs and wants of (more or less broadly defined) customers, they may typically, as Fennell (1987, p. 293) claims, "seek to participate in behavior that is underway" rather than work to change behavioral patterns as they find them. Although marketing as a principle has a democratic impulse (Bouchet, 1991; Laufer & Paradeise, 1990)—in seeking out public opinion and suitable responses—it may not be the most appropriate model for dealing with more complex social and political issues or for soliciting deeper forms of citizen participation (a problem we shall return to later in the essay).

Nevertheless, the ubiquity of the marketing orientation and its reflection in the discourse and practice of management (Christensen, 1995a; Gay & Salaman, 1992) deserve careful analysis in today's society where we commonly speak of the marketing of hospitals, churches, schools, and individuals and their careers (see, e.g., Coupland, 1996; Fairclough, 1993; McMillan & Cheney, 1996). In other words, although the specific influences from marketing are often odd or problematic we want to emphasize that marketing—as a way of seeing and responding to environmental changes and developments—has become deeply rooted in the institutions of contemporary society. In fact, so taken for granted is this orientation that in the United States the term *American consumers* has now largely replaced *American people* and *American citizens* in public discourse. The same is true in public discourse with reference to China and other nations (Cheney, 1999, in press).

Further, and even more interesting from the perspective of this essay, marketing and public relations often operate from similar perspectives concerning organizations, boundaries, and environments. Because both disciplines have historical reasons for seeing their audiences as external forces able to make potent and often expensive claims on a business corporation, they share an image of the organization as an open and externally influenced system. Moreover, confronted with challenging and sometimes hostile environments, both disciplines have realized the value of organizational flexibility and the importance of being responsive to changes in opinions and preferences of target audiences. Interestingly, the value of flexibility is often so pronounced that organizational identity—in terms of stability or essence—is ignored or downplayed as a central management issue (see Christensen, 1995a; Kaldor, 1971). Following these values and implicit prescriptions, public relations and marketing have come to conceive of their communication with the external world as an ongoing dialogue. Although PR and marketing have grown out of rather asymmetrical perspectives on the communication between organizations and their publics, they both emphasize today that communication is, or at least should be, a two-way process through which the voices of all relevant parties are heard (see, e.g., Cheney & Dionisopoulos, 1989; DeLozier, 1976; Grunig, 1992; Leitch & Neilson, in press; Nickels, 1976; Pearson, 1989; Shimp, 1990; Stidsen & Schutte, 1972). Consequently, most organizations influenced by public relations or marketing experts find themselves engaged in frequent and extensive scanning and information-gathering activities. The differences and similarities between marketing and public relations are summarized generally in Table 7.1.

Public relations and marketing conceive of their audiences with different global labels—as "publics" and as "consumers"—but the fields' notions of how the organization should conceive of its own role vis-à-vis these audiences have interesting points in common. While management practices often contradict these shared perspectives and ideals, these ideas are extremely relevant in terms of how

organizations of today see themselves handling their relations with their environments.

Corporate Issue Management

We now turn our attention to the areas of study and practice commonly known today as "issue management" or "corporate advocacy." Issue management has become visible since the late 1970s, largely as a broader and more systematic analysis of how organizations engage the larger society through strategic communication. Although growing out of public relations, especially in its more proactive form, issue management also bears a resemblance to some contemporary marketing practices and concepts. Further, issue management (as an area of study) has come to employ a range of rhetorical principles while also drawing on the social-scientific study of persuasion. Issue management thus provides an important forum for exploring many of the ideas and concerns of this essay.

Corporate issue management grew out of a rising managerial concern with the intensified critique since the 1960s of industrial products (e.g., Nader & Green, 1973; Nader, Green, & Seligman, 1976), seductive advertising (e.g., Packard, 1969), and lack of environmental concern. Adding to this the attacks on the oil and other industries in the United States during the early to mid-1970s and the low ebb for U.S. public opinion of big business (Chase, 1984), it is hardly surprising that organizations of many types, but especially those in the embattled industries of oil, chemicals, and tobacco, began to address simultaneously in public discourse their own identities and the sociopolitical issues of the day (see the overview in Cheney & Vibbert, 1987, for a more detailed account).

Initially, corporate issue management was thought of as a "fire fighting" function centered primarily around bottom-line concerns (e.g., Ewing, 1987; Wartick & Rude, 1986). Issue management, thus, has often been de-

TABLE 7.1 Differences and Similarities Between Marketing and Public Relations

	Marketing	Public Relations
Traditional differences		
Target group	Markets/customers/consumers	Politics/stakeholders
Principal goal	Attracting and satisfying customers through the exchange of goods and values	Establishing and maintaining positive and beneficial relations between various groups
Shared perspectives		
General image of organization	An open and externally influenced system	
Communication ideal	Communication as an ongoing dialogue with the external world	
Prescription for management	Organizational flexibility and responsiveness vis-à-vis external wishes and demands	

scribed as an "early warning system" that makes it possible for organizations to minimize surprises (e.g., Wartick & Rude, 1986) and to manage more effectively in a turbulent environment (see also Arrington & Sawaya, 1984). Since the early 1980s, issue management and the related terms *crisis management, issue diagnosis,* and (corporate) *advocacy advertising* have come to refer to a range of more intensive activities on the part of the modern organization to shape and manage its environment more directly (e.g., Chase, 1984). As Hainsworth and Meng (1988) found in their survey of 25 large U.S. corporations, issue management is now seen by managers as "an action-oriented management function" that helps the organization identify potential issues relevant for its business and to organize activities to influence the development of those issues "in an effort to mitigate their consequences for the organization" (p. 28). Thus, while the development of corporate issue management as a discipline had a defensive impetus, its primary focus has gradually become the question of how to maintain and expand corporate control. In the words of

Chase (1984), "History can be created, not just survived" (p. 7).

At the same time, we witness a growing interest in more *symmetrical* relations, meaning some form of real dialogue between organizations and their publics (Grunig, 1992, in press); however, issue management has typically been *asymmetrical* in terms of how the organization actually deals with its constituencies or publics. Asymmetrical tendencies are often downplayed or denied today by references to corporations' involvement and responsibility in public policy processes, but the idea that "issue management is about power [over]," as Ewing (1987, p. 1) puts it, is still quite prevalent. In this one-way view of the communication process, communication itself is seen largely as the transmission of information and the shaping of audiences' attitudes, beliefs, and perhaps actions.

Issue Management as Communication

In line with Ewing's (1987) observation —though recognizing that the exercises of power and persuasion involved are more complex and subtle (see, e.g., Cheney & Frenette, 1993)—we would like to offer a definition of issue management that highlights its rhetorical dimension. Implicit in this definition is the view that communication not only mediates the space between human beings and "reality out there" but also helps to create the reality to which we respond. In this perspective, the world becomes real to us in large part through the symbolic and rhetorical constructions that we, as social actors, employ. For example, consider the point at which the mainstream media decide to recognize a "social movement" by calling it just that. While this is not to suggest that our words or labels bring the whole world into being—like a reduction (or extension) of the argument into mere "nominalism" would imply—it helps us to remember the creative, evocative, even "magical" potency of language in use and thus be aware of the powerfully creative *and* restrictive dimensions to the terms and images by which we describe our world (cf. Burke, 1966; Douglas, 1986).

In prevailing thought, an *issue* is often thought of as an unresolved or contestable matter "ready for decision" (Chase, 1984, p. 38). Understood this way, issues represent a more advanced stage in terms of awareness than simply trends or problems. According to Crable and Vibbert (1985, p. 5), issues are created "when one or more human agents [attach] significance to a situation or perceived problem" and, we should add, decide to *articulate* this attention publicly (see also Heath, 1988). In fact, this articulation may significantly affect the way an issue is understood to the general public. Such is precisely why debates over "what to call" important events and groups—even those yet to be noticed—can have such a broad persuasive impact. Rhetorical disputes over the meaning of such hallowed terms as *democracy, freedom, efficiency,* and *progress* often take on such importance in the United States and in other industrialized nations, although any measure of control over meaning must be seen as un-

certain, tentative, and often only localized. And such terms often function *simultaneously* as repositories of many meanings and as clichés almost devoid of meaning (cf. Cheney, 1999; McGee, 1980; White, 1984).

In rhetorical terms, *issue management* means that the organization attempts to both "read" the premises and attitudes of its audience and work to shape them, often *in advance* of any specific crisis or well-defined debate (Heath, 1980). Understood this way, then, the *issue* becomes a universe of discourse designed, managed, and ultimately, shaped by organizational rhetors and strategists in an attempt to shape the attitudes the audience hold toward the organization or its concerns. From this perspective, the audience or public becomes something that is "pursued" with the goals of understanding, persuasion, and control (cf. Bryant's, 1953, conception of the function of rhetoric as the adjustment of ideas to people and people to ideas; see also Crable and Vibbert's, 1986, reformulation of that famous definition in terms of organizations and their environments; see in addition Kuhn's, 1997, treatment of issue management as a genre of communication).

Clearly, the rhetorical perspective suggested here conceives of communication in much broader terms than is usually the case in prevailing theories of issue management (cf. Sproull, 1988, 1990). Rather than distinguishing between the strategic and the communication-related aspects of the issue management process (e.g., Grunig, in press; see also Chase, 1984), we see communication as a meta-concept that refers broadly to constructions and deconstructions of meaning at many different levels, including not only explicit communication campaigns but also the strategic planning process, the process of monitoring and analyzing issues, and corporate efforts to comply with changing norms and standards of social responsibility (cf. Heath & Cousino, 1990). In all such situations, corporate actors deal significantly with symbols and interpretations. To see communication merely as an identifiable campaign *tool* that supplements whatever an organization *does* (its behavior) is to fail to grasp the significance of interpretation in a wide range of organizational processes. Further, such a perspective ignores the possibility that corporate rhetorical persuasion has become more complex and subtle in the communication environment of today in which an excess of messages is the order of the day. (On the other hand, of course, we must resist the temptation to say that "everything is communication.")

Only recently have scholars in the communication discipline identified the fundamental rhetorical and communication-related aspects of corporate issue management practices. And only recently have organizational communication studies (and we perceive a similar trend in the transdisciplinary study of organizations) begun to reclaim the broad sociological and political interests that shaped the early works on organizations by Marx, Weber, Durkheim, and Simmel. Such research efforts are necessary and potentially significant for at least two reasons:

1. By continuing to refer unreflectively to a division of "internal" versus "external" organizational communication, we fail to recognize dramatically new communication practices. These practices include, for example, the intended influences on multiple audiences with a single organizational message and, conversely, adaptations made for different audiences. Also, observe the ways in which the "container" metaphor for organization has become so problematic even as it is still desired as a pragmatic and comforting point of reference (Cheney, 1992).
2. Note the ways organizational communication must be situated within the context of larger social and cultural trends, for example, in terms of the "marketing culture" and its relentless but problematic pursuit of consumers' opinions (Christensen, 1995a; Laufer & Paradeise, 1990).

In the following section, we will present and highlight a number of sociohistorical trends relevant for our understanding of external organizational communication and its specific conditions in contemporary society.

SETTING THE SCENE: IDENTITY AND COMMUNICATION IN THE CORPORATE SOCIETY

A shipwrecked woman stranded on a remote island puts a message in a bottle. As she sets out to throw the bottle into the sea, she realizes that she cannot see the water. It is covered with messages in bottles. In a nutshell, this is the problem confronting corporate communications of today. At the beginning of the 21st century, any communicator is confronted with the fact that professional communications have taken on a previously unseen scope and intensity pervading almost all aspects of human life. "The space is so saturated," as Baudrillard (1988, pp. 24ff.) puts it, "the pressure of all which wants to be heard so strong that [we] are no longer capable of knowing what [we] want" or, perhaps more important, who we are. The "explosion" of communication that we are witnessing, in other words, goes hand in hand with the question of identity. "Standing out" with a distinct and recognizable identity in this cluttered environment is at once absolutely necessary and almost impossible. As an organizing problem, the issue of identity, however, has deeper sociohistorical roots.

The Issue of Identity

The social order instituted by modernity implied a weakening of the bonds of local community and authority through which people traditionally defined their roles and positions in society (e.g., Nisbet, 1970). With the image of traditional society as a body (corpus) that provides its members with stable identities, Mongin (1982) describes modernity as a process of "decorporation" that dissolves ancient relations of community and authority. Without these relations, the modern individual is left without "markers of certainty" (Lefort,

1988) to guide the search for meaning and identity. Although modernity has established new and quite resilient points of guidance (e.g., individuality, the nation-state, the market, rationality, and bureaucracy), its foundations are open to questioning and are thus basically fragile (Bouchet, 1991; see also Weigert, Teitge, & Teitge, 1986). As a result, the question of identity has become a standing and often pressing issue for individuals and institutions in many different contexts (see Giddens, 1991; Lasch, 1978, 1984). The "extraordinary availability of identities" (Weigert et al., 1986) also signals a lack of and quest for meaning.

Today, individuals and organizations are in hot pursuit of solid, favorable identities even as such identities become harder to capture and sustain. This is especially the case in situations when issues turn into crises. For Royal Dutch Shell—today the largest corporation in Europe—identity has often been a salient issue. Well known for its controversial business interests in apartheid South Africa, the Shell name has for many years been associated, in the views of its critics, with cynicism and unethical business activities. To many observers, this negative image was confirmed by its 1995 decision, approved by the British government, to dump the oil platform Brent Spar into the North Sea. Following the announcement of the decision, the Shell corporation faced a previously unseen rash of negative reactions from organizations, consumers, and politicians, especially in northern Europe. While Greenpeace occupied Brent Spar to force Shell to scrap the platform on land, consumers and business corporations started a boycott of Shell that finally made the organization give up its dumping plans (see, e.g. Wätzold, 1996).

From the perspective of this essay, it is interesting to note that this case—behind the negotiations and strategic choices of the different actors—was *about* identity: that of Shell (that had struggled for several years with a bad image), of Greenpeace (that gradually had lost legitimacy and feared falling into oblivion), and of the involved politicians always eager to trade politically on the whims of the public. In this game, the environmental issue (how to retire an oil platform most safely) was often pushed aside to the benefit of identities and power positions of influential actors. Obviously, Shell lost this battle, but that does not necessarily imply that the consumer, or the environment, *won*. In 1996, Brent Spar was "parked" in a fjord in Norway waiting to be scrapped on land: a solution far more harmful to the environment, according to many environmental experts, than a dumping at sea. Although later findings seem to support Shell's initial position on the issue, the organization has realized that negative connotations are still related to the name of Shell. And as the recent media attention to its activities in Nigeria and Turkey indicates, identity has indeed become a standing and very complex issue for the organization.

But even in less critical and problematic situations, the question of identity is quite evident. If we accept the idea that organizational communication is essentially a process through which meaning is created, negotiated, and managed, we should expect to find identity at issue in most organizing processes, especially in those explicitly concerned with addressing external audiences.

The Communication Environment of Today

In the corporate landscape of today, the issue of identity is closely tied up with the ways organizations organize their "world" in terms of communication. To begin with, the key communication elements of source, message, and receiver are all much more complicated and less easily distinguished than in prior periods. As many organizations have come to realize, the principal management problem in today's marketplace of goods and ideas is not so much to provide commodities and services or to take stands on the salient issues of the day, but to do these things with a certain distinctiveness that allows the organization to create and legitimize itself, its particular "profile," and its advantageous position. This quest for visibility has made disciplines such as public relations, issue management, marketing, and advertising chief architects of organizational identity. To help organizations stand out and "break through the clutter," practitioners within these fields are continuously operating on the edge of established strategies and perspectives, hoping to discover the idea that will provide the organization with a momentary relief from the pressures of intensified communication. Interestingly, however, such measures are creating a situation in which established communication is continuously challenged and the *conditions* for communication are in constant change (Christensen, 1995b). Many organizations today engage in ongoing efforts to (re)shape their images, ever seeking the support of both internal and external audiences (see, e.g., Allen & Caillouet, 1994; Alvesson, 1990; Treadwell & Harrison, 1994), even though there may be in any given case little real harmony among various constituencies and the images they hold of the organization.

This problem is clearly present in advertising for consumer goods, but it is observable in the marketing of services and issues as well. As an example of the former, the strategies chosen by various computer companies in their attempts to emulate IBM comes to mind. Trading, for example, on IBM's well-known slogan "Think," another computer company, ICL, chose to suggest "Think ICL" (Olins, 1989). By *leaning on,* or exploiting, more well-known images or positions, such messages hope to "*capture* the mystery of other organizations" (Gallagher, 1990, emphasis added) while emphasizing small, but in a way still, significant differences. For less well-known companies or products, such "positioning" strategies are often necessary to gain visibility in a crowded marketplace.

Similar principles are activated when organizations take stands on prominent social and political issues. Benetton Corporation, for example, is well known for displaying tragedies and human disasters in its ads and this way attracting attention to pressing social and political issues. One recent example is its 2000 ad campaign, which features death row inmates. However, because Benetton's ads are not explicitly taking stands on these issues—the situations are merely *exhibited*—more directly expressed positions on these issues are open for other corporations to take up. Following the launch of one of Benetton's widely disputed ads showing a man dying of AIDS surrounded by his family, Esprit, another clothing company, tried to exploit the situation by stating that it was in fact donating money to *fight* AIDS. Similar strategies have been employed by other clothing companies. Although these companies will have difficulties challenging Benetton's number-one position in terms of media attention and public interest, their positioning attempts have definitely had an impact on Benetton and its communications. In later ads showing an undressed Luciano Benetton saying, "Give me back my clothes," the corporation asks the public to donate their used clothes to Caritas, a relief organization supported by Benetton. As this example demonstrates, corporate identities are often intertwined with the issues that organizations seek to address. Further, the case indicates that the *way* issues are managed is strongly affected by the dynamics of the communication environment.

In this complex and volatile environment, crowded with symbols referencing each other, any discourse on issues tends to develop its own logic relatively independent of its referent. The symbolism surrounding an organization's identity *can,* in other words, become something of a world of its own, even though it may often rely on other symbols to express what the organization is or is not. This is precisely why many contemporary consulting firms can speak of "giving organizations identities" or "creating identity packages." Further, because positions within this environment are defined in terms of other positions, the identity aimed at by the corporate actor is potentially reduced to what Perniola (1980) and Baudrillard (1981) call a "simulacrum," that is, an "autonomized" image without reference to anything but other images.[1]

Organizations that wish to express their stances on social issues need to take these dynamics of the communication environment into serious consideration. While striving to make the position of the organization clear, the issue manager of today has to realize that the impact of symbols employed to define a situation or bolster an image is fragile and often more dependent on the significance of other corporate symbols than on the specific issue in question.

At a more global level, issue managers need to realize that communication is not an unproblematic solution to crises or queries over identity. In terms of the plethora of corporate messages and their often peculiar character, the communication environment of today is radically different in substantive respects from that of, say, 40 to 50 years ago. On the one hand, *more* communication appears as a necessary solution to the constant challenges to corporate identity and legitimacy. The fact of more communication requires more communication, from the standpoint of any organization that seeks to be heard. On the other hand, we have to realize that communication itself, even in its widest sense, is an integral part of the problem it sets out to handle. A deeper understanding of the still emergent communication environment requires that the growing access to "information" and the mountain of messages are viewed not only in terms of the meanings or effects of *specific* or isolable messages but in terms of effects of the expansion of the communication universe *as a whole.* What is, on the one hand, the intensity of modern communication seems, on the other hand, to be the dissolution of communication itself, at least as understood in any deep or understanding-oriented way (cf. Baudrillard, 1983; Dervin, 1994).

THE FUZZINESS OF ORGANIZATIONAL BOUNDARIES

At the same time that organizations have become preoccupied, even obsessed, with the communication of their identities, the problem of defining organizational boundaries has become more acute than ever. As a consequence, organizations find it increasingly difficult to maintain clear distinctions between their internal and external communication.

To be sure, the problem of defining organizational boundaries was recognized in the scholarly literature two decades ago (see, e.g., Starbuck, 1976; Weick, 1979), but its present manifestations are directly related to the marketing ethos. With its ideal of organizational flexibility and responsiveness vis-à-vis external demands, the marketing ethos and its related management practices not only defy established images of the organization but also question traditional notions of the organization-environment interface (Christensen, 1996). Because such notions are central for our understanding of how issues are perceived and managed, we will sketch out below some relevant trends that today challenge the traditional reliance on the "container" metaphor for understanding organizational life. We do not have the space to examine in detail all relevant trends, but we will mention a few powerful indicators of what we mean.

Organizing Beyond the Organizational Boundary

It is well known that *service organizations* have often had difficulties in maintaining a clearly defined "sense of self," in large part because their clients or service recipients straddle the boundary of the organization (see, e.g., Adams, 1976). Long-term service recipients, in particular, are difficult to define as being fully "outside" the organization (see, e.g., Cheney, Block, & Gordon, 1986; Starbuck, 1976). Students, regular clients of advertising agencies, users of various therapies, and clients of image and identity consultants often find themselves in this category. Seemingly pedantic exercises such as determining whether an individual or group is "inside" or "outside" the organization (as depicted, e.g., with Venn diagrams) thus have tremendous practical implications.

This is especially the case today where the marketing orientation is being copied and implemented by organizations in all sectors. In many institutions of higher education in North America, Europe, and Australasia, the student is increasingly being talked about as a "consumer" or "customer," meaning not only that the organization is seeking to adapt to its primary audience (the service recipients) but also that the activities of many universities take on more and more of a self-promotional quality (see Fairclough, 1993; McMillan & Cheney, 1996), where the objective is often adding commodifiable "value" to the self and by extension to the institution (Gay, 1996). In such arrangements, students can become shapers of services to a greater degree than they have been in the past, largely through immediate responses to courses and instructors and through the registering of their desires with quick changes in curricula and student services. Such forms of "participation" or "engagement" tend to be rather shallow, however, requiring only limited exchanges of "information" and ignoring possibilities for intersubjective understanding.

Today, the spread of the marketing attitude seems to reach its apotheosis in some production arrangements where integration and flexibility have become central managerial criteria (see Christensen, 1996). In auto manufacturing, for example, the customer can be almost incorporated into the design process by way of new computer technology. As Achrol (1991) reports, some Japanese automobile companies have developed a system "by which the customer designs his or her car (from available options) in the dealer showroom on a computer linked directly to the factory production line" (p. 79). Such production arrangements are not necessarily dependent on advanced technology, although the expansion of e-commerce does facilitate this kind of consumer involvement. With relatively simple measures, the production of bicycles, for example, has in many cases become adapted considerably to individual preferences. Management practices like these seriously challenge the organization's ability to distinguish between inside and outside and, accordingly, its sense of "self." Because the specific operationalizations of the marketing ethos—as "consumer influence," "custom-made products," and so forth—are blurring the boundaries between the organization and its environment, identity is a standing issue for organizations influenced by this organizing ideal.

In principle, this is true as well for "network forms of organization," such as long-term strategic alliances and flexible manufacturing networks. These can be found in industries as diverse as construction, publishing, and film. Such organizational creatures are, as Powell (1990) observes, difficult to classify: Neither markets nor firms, they exhibit greater predictability than the former but greater flexibility than the latter (see also Arndt, 1979; Webster, 1992). Simultaneously, electronic and computerized communication systems now permit some organizations to exist without any spatially located headquarters. As a consequence, many employees now find themselves with "virtual offices" (e.g., James, 1993). As one example: In mountainous and long Norway, the health care system is experimenting with methods of electronic diagnosis where data collected from a patient in one place are received and "read" simultaneously by physicians in other locations. Such arrangements can serve to challenge traditional notions of where and what the organization *is,* especially because some service providers (in this example, physicians assistants or nurses) may rarely or never experience copresence with the doctors with whom they must coordinate efforts. These, and other, hard-to-classify organizational types, offer still more challenges to the idea of the organization as, in Richardson's (1972) apt description, "islands of planned coordination in a sea of market relations" (see Chapter 12, this volume)

Under all the circumstances mentioned here, the identity of the organization becomes more problematic and more precious (Scott & Carroll, 1999). This observation, however, is not restricted to these examples but applies as well to the management of *issues*. As contemporary organizations face a growing demand to listen to relevant publics before they carry out their operations, systematic efforts to *integrate* these publics somehow into deliberations when taking stands on salient issues gradually becomes a more common phenomenon. While this kind of integration may sometimes be more superficial than profound, organizations that implement such efforts no doubt find it increasingly difficult to distinguish clearly between themselves and their environment. This problem has important implications for contemporary corporate communications. Thus, it is hardly surprising that many organizations are consolidating their internal and external communications in a single office or function.

Communicating Across Boundaries

To uphold a sense of "self" while being flexible or existing as part of a larger network, organizations of today seek to integrate internal and external dimensions of their activities with the overall purpose of communicating one identity, although they may indeed pursue variations on a central theme. And while changes in an organization's identity over time are necessary for the organization to be adaptable, they are also risky in potentially undermining employee or consumer identification with the organization (see, e.g., Carroll, 1995). People become accustomed to an organization's "look." Thus, changes in the Betty Crocker persona of General Mills are made incrementally and carefully in response to cultural shifts and the public's image of the "appropriate" woman for the label (now a composite, computer-generated figure). We find much corporate communication today organized around identity as the overarching concern. In the following, we shall illustrate how this concern tends to blur the differences between external and internal messages.

In advertising, the content of messages often reflects the fact that contemporary organizations feel the need to remind not only consumers but also their own employees that they are still part of the corporate landscape, that their actions are legitimate, and their business ventures sound. Besides its functions as a traditional external medium, advertising may have an important *self*-enhancing dimension. When the German corporation Bayer expresses its concern for the environment in large expensive ads, it simultaneously addresses the consumer *and* tells its employees and investors that they are part of a "competent and responsible" corporation. An advertisement from BP America has a similar dual focus. Showing a dirty worker with a pipe wrench in his hand, the ad says: "It takes energy to make energy. From our riggers and roughnecks. From our planners, our traders, our service station attendants. From 38,000 BP America employees in all. Their energy has made BP America the largest producer of American oil, producing 800,000 barrels of oil a day. To make the most of our country's energy resources, we're making the most of our human ones." By linking the issue of energy resources to the question of work and employment, BP America hopes to establish in the minds of its many audiences an image of an industrious caretaker concerned at once with its employees and the environment. Speaking even more broadly, eight oil producers (BP, Norol, Shell, Chevron, Statoil, Texaco, Q8, and Total) have issued a joint ad that almost presents their product as the life-blood of society and a Promethean gift to humanity (cf. Crable & Vibbert, 1983). Composed of a number of simple images—icons of an oil refinery, an oil tanker, and an airplane—connected by pipelines, the ad says, trading on Walt Disney's famous TV show, "To all of you from all of us."

In these and similar cases, the messages are communicating both externally and internally, hoping to influence both consumers and stakeholders and to confirm the sending organization's own merits or good intentions. This way, market-related communication seeks to link internal and external audiences around the same concern, identity. And as van Riel (1995) points out, a strong corporate identity can raise employee motivation while inspiring confidence among an organization's external target groups.

Other kinds of corporate communications may serve a similar function. Corporate identity programs (Olins, 1989), design and architecture (Berg & Kreiner, 1990), art collections (Joy, 1993), and autobiographies (Ramanantsoa & Battaglia, 1991) are all examples of communications that cut across traditional organizational boundaries and seek to unify different audiences. As Ramanantsoa and Battaglia (1991) note, organizational autobiographies, memoirs, and self-portraits are becoming increasingly important for firms that actively want to manage their identity: "At first invisible and silent, later object of a discourse and battle-field, companies have now become the subject of their own discourse in an effort to win coherent identities, legitimacy, and institutionalization" (p. 2). Autobiographies are, in other words, playing several important roles for contemporary organizations. Externally, the autobiography may supplement more traditional public relations or marketing functions. Internally, it enacts a mirror structure that makes it possible for the members of the organization to perceive themselves as part of a whole, autonomous, and anthropomorphic entity with a strong and original (yet not too eccentric) personality. This is clearly the case with Procter & Gamble's own story as it is told in *The House That Ivory Built: 50 Years of Successful Marketing* (1989). Here an effort to claim a specific and very "personal" identity internally is combined with the wish to market itself externally as a legitimate corporate actor.

Whether or not such communications convince the audience about their *specific* content is, of course, an empirical question. In fact,

formal, established, and public symbols of an organization—as seen in the logo, mission statement, and so on—may well have little connection in a particular case with how individual organizational members image their organization. A full treatment of the range of influences inside the organization is certainly beyond the scope of this essay. But we emphasize that, despite the apparent "autonomy" of many of the public symbols that come to (re)present the organization, there is much that transpires between organizational members (both powerful decision makers and others) to determine the course of an organization's rhetorical enterprise. So in no way do we wish to presume a monolithic organization that speaks univocally to the world (cf. Bakhtin, 1981; Cheney, 1992; Christensen, 1997; Motion & Leitch, 2000), nor are we suggesting that corporate symbols have a complete life of their own. Still, given our intention here to bring activities such as marketing, public relations, and some kinds of advertising within the purview of organizational communication, we are necessarily stressing the creation, positioning, and transformation of those symbols that come to represent the organization to a variety of stakeholders.

When externally directed communication becomes an integral part of an organization's operating discourse, the self-enhancing dimension of communication may turn out to be more important than the substantive messages themselves. In such cases, organizations are not merely engaging in communication, in the sense of sending or receiving messages, but also *auto*-communicating, that is, communicating with themselves. Auto-communication, according to Lotman (1977, 1991), is a process of organizing through which a communicator evokes and enhances its own values or codes (see also Broms & Gahmberg, 1983). As many anthropologists (e.g., Geertz, 1973) and sociologists (e.g., Parsons, 1949) have noted, all societies communicate with themselves in a self-reinforcing manner about their most salient values or concerns (see also Lotman, 1977, 1991). In this process, the role of the external audience becomes more complex than is usually acknowledged: besides acting as receiver of the corporate message, the external audience represents an ideal reference point in terms of which the sender evaluates itself. In this "looking-glass" (Cooley, 1983), the communicator (person or group) recognizes itself, chiefly in terms of how it wants to be seen by others.

In contemporary organizations, auto-communication is stimulated by the quest for identity and a growing need among organizational members for identification and belongingness (see, e.g., Cheney, 1983a, 1983b, 1991; Cheney & Tompkins, 1987; Scott, Corman, & Cheney, 1998; Tompkins & Cheney, 1983, 1985). Rapid change in the job market makes organizational loyalty problematic, yet it is still desired by individuals and organizations. Within many organizations of varying types, members are searching for a connection with something larger than the self. This is particularly observable in value-based organizations such as religious and voluntary associations, but it applies as well to a range of organizations in all sectors. Under growing economic pressure and internal drives toward centralization, the Mondragón Cooperative Corporation, one of the largest systems of worker-owned co-ops in the world, is working to fortify its fundamental values, such as social solidarity and democracy, while reconfiguring itself as a "customer-driven" multinational corporation. However, it is clear that for this organization of 42,000 worker-owner-members, located in the Basque Country in Spain, many presumably externally driven programs and messages are serving also to maintain a need to identify with one's place of work. However, that strategy is meeting receptivity in some quarters and resistance from others, as internal constituencies struggle over the true "essence" or the defining goals and values of the corporation. Some worker-member-owners are identifying strongly with the cooperatives' new competitive posture toward the European Union and the global market (e.g., "We must grow or die"), while others

are maintaining greater allegiance to what they see as the "soul" or "heart" of the cooperatives: individual unit (or co-op) autonomy, employee participation in policy making, relative equality of members, and regional grounding of cooperative groups (or sectors). As the first author has discovered through his interviews in the worker-cooperative complex, a great deal of self-persuasion (about "who we are") is going on, fueled both by individual need and by perceived economic and social necessity. Interesting, too, is the fact that the organization is consciously moving into public relations and marketing activities at the same time that it is trying to expand its market base, maintain and increase jobs, implement self-directed work teams, and foster renewed member commitment to the larger cooperative enterprise (Cheney, 1999).

As these different examples indicate, organizations often communicate with themselves when they address audiences outside the "container" of the organization. Our discussion of the linkages between internal and external organizational communication, however, would be incomplete if it did not simultaneously acknowledge the significant ways in which *internal* communication activities and campaigns can be used for external purposes. Indeed, the organizational world of today is rich with such examples, with some being more apparent than others. In the following paragraphs, we will mention briefly a number of internal-external relationships ranging from unintentional effects of internal communication on external environments to deliberate and planned efforts to communicate externally by way of the organization's own employees (see Christensen, 1997).

Today, many organizations have come to realize that so-called internal matters—their organization of production, their use of resources, their handling of waste, and their treatment of employees—potentially communicate a strong message to the external world. For example, when the largest bank in Denmark, Danske Bank, announced internally that it would henceforth depend more on younger employees than on older ones in terms of its personnel policies, this message was caught by the media and turned into a public case of corporate cynicism, a case that severely damaged the bank's image.

Realizing that affairs *inside* the organization have shaping implications for *outside* communications, a growing number of organizations have begun to think of their employees as customers who, in accordance with the marketing orientation, also need to be satisfied. The concern for employees is not only reflected in public celebrations of internal achievements such as those found in annual reports, in the well-known "employee of the month" plaques (as displayed prominently for visitors of the organization to see), and in public awards ceremonies (e.g., for the most "family-friendly" governmental or third-sector agency, as is now popular in many communities in the United States and elsewhere) but also in efforts to respond to the needs and wants of employees beyond their worklife. While some organizations build fitness and child care centers for employees and families, others offer education and psychological support to spouses and offspring. Because such efforts are often described enthusiastically by the media, they have the potential of becoming part the organization's public relations campaign. But, of course, they can undermine PR efforts if the organization is seen as not living up to its very public standards.

It is not unusual that an organization makes a policy of building its business by building relationships with clients and other constituencies and is explicit in its commentary about this. For example, at Arthur Andersen, a group of accounting and consulting firms, employees are regularly urged to get involved in community organizations as a central part of their business. By doing so, the representatives of the companies can achieve several things at once: tout the accomplishments of the firm, make part of the external environment of the organization part of the organization (by "bring the community in"), and expand their client base.

Among the more direct efforts to communicate externally by way of internal voices we find attempts to use organizational members or employees as advocates or "ambassadors" to outside constituencies. General Motors, for example, consciously developed this strategy in the early 1980s when it integrated internal employee communications and external advertising and public relations. More specifically, the corporation relied on employees—who would receive both internally distributed memos and televised commercials—to spread the word about GM's new emphasis on safety as a foremost concern (Paonessa, 1982). In the case of an enormous organization like this one, employees can, in other words, be seen as a large "PR force" in themselves. Similarly, Gulf States Utilities (an electric and gas utility of Louisiana and Texas that was bought out by Entergy in the mid-1990s) invested a great deal of time and financial resources in communicating with employees in the early 1980s about a controversial nuclear power plant project in the clear hope that they, in turn, would talk with wider audiences about the company's record of safety, efficiency, and good management. In the view of top management, the corporation had over 3,500 potential employee-ambassadors (T. Zorn, personal communication, March 1997).

Clearly, the primary concern behind such efforts is the desire for control, not only of employees but also of the organization's identity, that is, how the organization is commonly represented. And since many organizations have come to believe that the points of contact between its members and the outside world communicate much stronger than well-crafted advertisements, the interest in understanding and managing these points of contact has increased remarkably. In line with Jan Carlzon's (former CEO of Scandinavian Airlines System) notion that every contact with a potential customer represents a "moment of truth" (i.e., a point when the customer decides to continue or discontinue further business with the organization) (Carlzon, 1987), many organizations have begun to think of their employees as fragments of their overall market communication strategy (see also Olins, 1989). Although there is a big difference between the sports organization that tries to foster a sense of internal cohesion and enthusiasm (and hopes that these feelings will be contagious to outsiders and potential supporters of a team) and the organization that develops extensive rules for how its employees can conduct their lives away from work, the same concern is at issue: the organization's identity.

Of course, many efforts at communicating an organization's preferred self-image, such as enhanced "efficiency," are today contradicted by employees' reports to outside "others" of, for example, wasted resources, cases of lavish spending, or cuts in staff that do not include reduced layers of upper administration. This seems to be precisely one of the problems faced by many institutions of higher education in the United States and elsewhere. Added to this is the complication of the public visibility of a campus. If a university complains of drastically limited funding and yet proudly displays new elegant buildings, the public will be understandably skeptical.

While acknowledging such limitations to organizational control of the external communication process, we need to be aware of the many ways in which presumably internal organizational communications emerge as or come to be part of an organization's external communication. Along with the cases of auto-communication mentioned earlier, these examples demonstrate that a clear distinction between internal and external organizational communication is impossible to uphold. Moreover, since the question of identity is so prominent—cutting across different messages often in attempts to link different audiences—we should expect this question to be present in most organizing processes that relate the organization to its surroundings, to shape the organization's outlook, and to affect its way of handling upcoming issues. In the following section, we shall discuss how this self-centeredness may prevent the organiza-

tion from being as open and responsive toward its surroundings as the disciplines of public relations, marketing, and issue management envision and prescribe.

RETHINKING CORPORATE ISSUE MANAGEMENT: IDENTITY, SELF-REFERENCE, AND PARADOX

In contrast to traditional perspectives within issue management, public relations, and marketing, we offer in the next section of this essay a more detailed consideration of the possibility that internal perceptions (identities, expectations, and strategies) strongly affect what problems are "seen," what potential solutions are envisioned, and how the problems are ultimately addressed. The discussion will proceed from a rather straightforward example of how organizational identity affects the diagnosis of issues to notions of self-reference in organizational information management and then to the more complex question of how the organizational approach to the environment may define and shape the issue in question.

Identity as Point of Reference

In their interesting study of the Port Authority of New York and New Jersey, Dutton and Dukerich (1991) illustrate very well how identity is a salient issue closely related to the ways organizations define, diagnose, and respond to problems in their surroundings. Dutton and her colleagues in other studies (e.g., Dutton, 1993; Dutton & Duncan, 1987) defined the diagnosis of strategic issues as an "individual-level, cognitive process through which decision makers form interpretations about organizational events, developments, and trends" (Dutton, 1993, p. 339). However, their interpretation of the Port Authority case necessarily moved them to a larger, social level of analysis. Among other things, Dutton and Dukerich found that "the organization's identity served as an important reference point that members used for assessing the importance of the issue at hand" (p. 543). Specifically, their study showed how much the organization's response to the growing homelessness problem in the 1980s and the organization's internal communication activities at the time were tied up with how organizational members *deliberately imagined* that their organization was being seen by outsiders. Further, Dutton and Dukerich even found that organization members' treatments of homelessness to some degree reflected how they perceived outsiders to be judging their *individual* characters.

While the case analysis of the Port Authority is quite revealing of the extent to which, even over time, an organization's response to an issue may be framed by perceptions of a collective identity, it fails to specify clearly the role of the external audience in shaping and in part constituting the organization's identity. Defining organizational identity in line with Albert and Whetten (1985), Dutton and Dukerich interpreted it as "what organizational members believe to be its central, enduring, and distinctive character" (p. 520). This definition focuses attention on what the organization's members think about their organization and does not address explicitly how the organization *is represented* either in its presumably univocal "corporate voice" or by outsiders (cf. Cheney & Tompkins, 1987). Although Dutton and Dukerich (1991) recognize the importance of outsiders in the construction of an organization's image, their definitions lead them to focus exclusively on the "inside" of the organization. Thus, the "mirror image" in terms of which the Port Authority, according to Dutton and Dukerich, judged and evaluated the issue of homelessness is simply seen as a passive reflection of the perception of the organization's members, not as a product related to social norms and values. In the

self-referential perspective that we will introduce below the "external" audience, by contrast, assumes a more central role. Besides being an ideal reference point in terms of which the organization continuously evaluates its own actions (e.g., through opinion polls and market analyses), the "external" audience becomes a social construct, shaped by prevalent managerial discourses and proactive organizations and constantly appealed to in the rhetoric of corporate actors (cf. Black's, 1970, notion of "the second persona").

Information in the Context of Organizational Self-Reference

At the same time that organizations are preoccupied with the issue of identity, they display an almost compulsive concern about their publics: consumers, politicians, interest groups, and so on. This concern—fueled by increased environmental uncertainty and shaped by marketing-inspired management norms—implies that most organizations of today are involved in extensive information-gathering programs and in constant attempts to predict and manage their future (see also Sutcliffe, Chapter 6, this volume). For that reason, contemporary organizations appear more open and sensitive toward their environments than ever before. Ironically, this openness often coexists with organizing practices that tend to close the organization in on itself.

The continuous collection and analysis of information are regarded by both public relations and marketing experts as indispensable for organizations operating in turbulent environments; however, the attitude toward information is not unified or consistent. As Thompson and Wildavsky (1986, p. 275) argue, people and organizations often *do not want* more information (see also Fornell & Westbrook, 1984; Weick & Ashford, Chapter 18, this volume), and when they do, they tend to handle it automatically and rather reductively within established frames of knowledge (see also Manning, 1986, 1988). More specifically, Manning (1986) argues that organizations inevitably translate external data into "idiosyncratic semiotic worlds" that reduce the complexity of the environment to more or less predetermined codes. This way, internal aspects of organizational communication merge in with the dialogue that organizations carry on with their environments.

Often the culture of an organization constitutes a "terministic screen" through which the organization views and evaluates its environment (Burke, 1966; Heath, 1990). This is clearly the case for the successful and well-known toy producer LEGO. For three generations, the culture of the LEGO Corporation has been characterized by a remarkable stability—a stability reflected in explicit corporate values such as tradition, reliability, managed and steady growth, long-term planning, economic independence, and central coordination (Thygesen Poulsen, 1993). To bolster this stability, LEGO has defined itself as being outside more volatile "May-fly markets." Moreover, its product program is standardized to fit a global consumer. Rather than adapting to local differences, the LEGO Corporation is taking the position that LEGO is a product for "everybody" and that it should be available, in more or less the same form, all over the world. To back up this perspective, LEGO is involved in research into the themes of "play" and "creativity" in different cultures and is continuously conducting its own surveys and focus groups to test the universality of its own products. Still, most of these measures are organized to detect and confirm *similarities* across cultures (as found in the second author's field research). While LEGO managers *do* recognize differences between markets, their interests are primarily vested in the issue of "sameness." Information that challenges this position and points in the direction of more *adaptive* strategies in terms of segmentation and communication has often been encountered, both via external and internal sources,

but has usually been rejected on the basis of LEGO's standardized global philosophy.

The interesting point here is the way organizations, such as the LEGO Corporation, establish systems of communication that tend to enhance organizational self-perceptions by grounding their own worldview and strategies in external opinions and demands. As initial assumptions are backed up by market research and strategic long-term planning, the relation with the environment tends to form a tightly closed circuit in which the organization confirms the basic elements of its own culture. Obviously, this practice can be quite detrimental to an organization. In his discussion of the asbestos industry and its earlier attempt to present its product as vital to society, Heath (1990) shows how management can be trapped by its own rhetoric and thus become insensitive to certain kinds of information. And clearly, this tendency may be one of the reasons why the LEGO Corporation was less successful for some years—a development that finally made the corporation move into new areas, such as computer technology.

Another important aspect of organizational information handling is related to the fact, explained so well by Feldman and March (1981), that often *the gathering process itself is more important than the actual information collected.* The sheer accumulation of information, in other words, is done by many organizations not so much because they use *all* those bits of data but because the gathering process and the heap assembled make organizations feel comfortable and appear rational to the outside world (see also Meyer & Rowan, 1977; Pfeffer, 1981; Pondy, Frost, Morgan, & Dandridge, 1983; Weick, 1979). Here too, the ritual *is* the message. Interestingly, formalized systems designed to help organizations perceive, analyze, and respond better to strategic issues (SIM systems) may serve similar functions. According to Dutton and Ottensmeyer (1987), "The simple presence of a formal SIM system may convey a sense of organizational potency or potential mastery over [the] environment" that helps preserve an illusion of organizational control (p. 361). In such cases, the rationalistic ritual of information pursuit becomes not only necessary but also sacred.

Through the use of systematic analyses and opinion polls, contemporary organizations demonstrate their adherence to a culture shaped by the marketing ethos. Likewise, by constantly putting out reports, organizations are able to assert their rational participation in the public discourse of the day (e.g., Feldman, 1989). However, as the following quotation suggests, the quest for information has further implications:

> The image given by the opinion poll is the image of opinion. It reflects to the perception of the politician a symmetrical image of the political activity that shapes it. As a consumer seduced by the images of products in the economic world, the man whose opinion is polled is also a consumer of images in the political sphere, which he regurgitates in the form of answers to survey questions. (Laufer & Paradeise, 1990, pp. 87-88)

In line with Baudrillard's writings on the masses (e.g., 1983), Laufer and Paradeise's essay on our "marketing democracy" points out that the relentless pursuit of "public opinion" enshrined in politics, public relations, advertising, and front-page surveys—and we could easily substitute "the organization" for "the politician" in the above passage—has created a world of discourse with its own internal dynamics. The talk about opinion polls that measure everything from political preferences to fashion consciousness engages everyone today in the sense that all are now able to participate in that discursive world. Having been polled on nearly every conceivable issue or preference, "the masses," according to Laufer and Paradeise, know they should be ready to express opinions on cue. Further, since the polling institution, according to Baudrillard (1983), has become a simulation process characterized by mutual seduction, the idea of uncovering or controlling a true or deep "public opinion" becomes

rather elusive (see Christensen & Cheney, in press). By "communicating" systematically with selected audiences, organizations promote the elusive ideal of "public opinion" while presuming to identify and respond to it. In this process, the message or text gives way to a metatext that communicates to the corporate culture of today its most basic myths about democracy, communication, and identity.

As a consequence, the "dialogue" between organizations and their environments takes on ironic, new meanings. In line with developments within self-referential systems (e.g., Luhmann, 1990; see also Maturana & Varela, 1980), it can be argued that organizations communicate with their "environment" not only to exchange information but also, and quite significantly, to maintain themselves and confirm their identities. As Maturana and Varela (1980) contend, identity is the primary issue of all living systems, an issue handled through self-referential communication, that is, communication through which the system specifies its own environment and the information necessary to maintain itself. As we have indicated above, organizations often seem to collect and handle information in such a self-referential manner. Of course, in a social system this tendency toward self-referential closure is modified by the need for external legitimacy and accreditation (e.g., Berg & Gagliardi, 1985; see also Meyer & Rowan, 1977). But this does not ensure the kind of openness prescribed by prevailing theories within public relations, marketing, and issue management. Since the preoccupation with *external* data often reflects an adherence to a certain management *discourse* rather than a sincere interest in information, organizations may still function as self-referentially closed even within an apparently open communication structure (cf. Luhmann, 1990).

Much organizational communication thus can be described as self-referential communication or auto-communication. And organizations often imitate one another in their attempts to be "cutting edge." As the management of corporate communications becomes more strategic—that is, proactive, integrative, and oriented toward long-term goals—this tendency is accentuated further.

The Paradox of Proactivity

In the corporate world of today, issue management reaches far beyond the practice of collecting and responding to information. As Cheney and Vibbert (1987) explain with respect to transformations in public relations activity and research since the mid-1970s, this practice has become more aggressive, more forward looking, more proactive (see also Chase, 1984; Hainsworth & Meng, 1988; Heath, 1988).

In everyday managerial usage, *proactivity* has come to refer to a more or less unspecified set of nondefensive or nonreactive practices through which organizations handle their relations with the external world. Instead of waiting for threats and opportunities to become manifest imperatives, the proactive organization attempts to influence and shape external developments in ways considered favorable in terms of its own aspirations. Organizations are clearly displaying proactive behavior when they seek to avoid being "caught by surprise" by demands or pressures from the environment: for example, new rules of trade within the European Union, increasing regulation of industrial waste, rising quality standards, or changing demands by labor unions. While this idea of *non*reactivity certainly grasps an important aspect of the activities of contemporary organizations, the wide-ranging implications of proactive management actually necessitate a deeper understanding of the phenomenon.

Ironically, the proactive stance can be seen as a creative *re*action to the increasing turbulence and the related reduction of predictability experienced in the market since the late 1950s (see Heath & Cousino, 1990). Within the fields of marketing and strategic management, these developments gave birth to a more prescriptive theory-building effort simultaneously concerned with the consumer or the public and the possibilities of extending managerial control through strategy and long-term planning. Together these considerations constitute what we have described above as the "marketing ethos." With its ambiguous norm of seeking to serve market needs and wants *before* these are expressed and objectified, the marketing orientation *is* largely proactive. As one marketing manager told the second author in a personal interview, the best strategy is "being at the forefront of the development we expect."

Being proactive means being involved in the definition and construction (albeit not necessarily control) of reality. Proactivity, thus, is implicated by Weick's (1979) notion of enactment whereby an organization's actions to a significant extent define the environments to which it is able to attend (e.g., governmental economic statistics, consultants' forecasts, the norms of competitors). By projecting internal concerns, intentions, and strategies onto its surroundings, the organization creates or simulates its own "environment" and, this way, sets the stage for its own future acts and sensemaking. But, because organizations are not always realizing just how narrowly they circumscribe their environments, this process can often be rather unintentional. In other cases, the process is largely intended through strong, controlling efforts to define the situation in self-serving and self-referential terms.

The relation between enactment and proactivity, thus, needs to be specified further. In contrast to Daft and Weick's (1984) often-cited model of organizations as interpretation systems, we need to emphasize that also apparently passive or reactive behaviors fall within the frame of enactment (cf. Weick, 1979). Interestingly, routine and largely reactive actions, such as explaining corporate performance to stockholders in annual reports, show the power of *defining* the situation. The "competitive edge" of the organization can be credited when the organization is successful, yet "fierce competition" from others can be blamed for sagging profits during the next year (Conrad, 1993). Whether the organization takes on the role of the accidental viewer, the passive detective, the active discoverer, or the experimenting doer (Daft & Weick, 1984), its ways of relating to its surroundings will always influence the definition of the situation in question. That is to say, diverse sorts of organizational "intentions" can lead to similar results. The differences among these different "enactment postures," however, are not trivial. Through *proactive* programs, the enactment dimension of organizational behavior becomes explicit and intensified to the extent of making the very enactment of the "environment" *itself* the primary goal of the management process. And clearly, organizations *have* become very self-conscious about their stances vis-à-vis the larger environment and about the "world" they are helping to bring into being. For example, as Bostdorff and Vibbert (1994) explain, large corporations and other organizations now routinely try to promote certain values (e.g., particular interpretations of "freedom") that they can then use to ground future persuasive campaigns.

What is at stake in this strategic approach is the desire for control. And often much of this activity is designed to get citizens as well as consumers to identify with some level of the organization. Whether the strategy involved can be characterized as "catalytic" or "dynamic"—that is, more or less offensive and assertive (Crable & Vibbert, 1985; cf. Jones & Chase, 1979)—its aim is to determine not only strategic outcomes but also the very *conditions* for business, including those of communication and competition themselves. Although the proactive approach claims to take its point of departure in the market or the larger environment, its preoccupation with *internal* aspirations and considerations makes proactivity in fact a rather self-centered enterprise. As Crable and Vibbert (1985) point out, an organization that wants to influence the development of issues needs continuously to "assess what it is, what it wants to be, and how the environment could be altered to the advantage of the organization" (p. 10).

This is not to suggest that various publics (e.g., activist groups, stockholders, govern-ments, competitors, and communities) are insignificant in the process of shaping issues and images of major corporations. Such groups often make powerful claims on the corporate actor—claims that sometimes force organizations to reconsider fundamentally their activities (e.g., Heath, 1988). However, this is most often the case when organizations respond reactively to changes in their larger environments. The more proactively such changes are managed, the more the direct role of the public is circumscribed by the organization through determining, for example, which voices from the outside deserve a hearing or how different opinions should be prioritized. Further, as Sutcliffe (this volume) points out, simply knowing *what* issues publics or stakeholders are concerned with does not help us understand *how* these issues are perceived, defined, and managed by the organization. Although many issues originate and unfold in environments regarded as external to the organization, the process of managing such issues strategically brings the organization and its specific outlook into the process (see also Kaldor, 1971; Smircich & Stubbart, 1985).

Issue Management as Proactive Communication

Through the pursuit of understanding and managing within a complex and turbulent environment of issues, organizations often establish the symbolic systems to which they are able to respond (Weick, 1979). This is especially the case when organizations are managed proactively.

Vibbert and Bostdorff (1993) offer an excellent example of corporate proactivity, spanning the private and public sectors, in their analysis of the behavior of the U.S. insurance industry during the so-called lawsuit crisis of the mid-1980s. In that instance, the Insurance Information Institute (III), an industrywide lobbying organization, employed a series of visible ads to explain rising insurance costs largely in terms of a litigation-crazy society and the corporate need for protective insurance. As the authors observe, there had been only a vague sense expressed in public discourse about something like a lawsuit "crisis." Yet the III apparently succeeded in locating the problem within the institution of the legal system, thereby defining a complex situation in polarizing terms, and clearly placing blame outside its own institutional borders.

It may be argued, of course, that the organizational rhetor in the case analyzed by Vibbert and Bostdorff (1993) not only defined the problem but also *identified* the problem in the first place, a strategy that could not have worked, rhetorically speaking, had the organization not "tapped into" some sort of suspicion or resentment already held by a significant segment of the citizenry. Whether this was exactly the case or not, Vibbert and Bostdorff's (1993) study clearly points out the way in which "crises" often emerge through being declared, defined, and interpreted by proactive corporate actors. This, of course, can be seen in a variety of discursive domains: political, economic, and social (see also Bostdorff's, 1994, treatment of the rhetorical shaping of various crises by U.S. presidents). To succeed in proclaiming a situation as urgent and especially to identify blameworthy parties is to mobilize opinion and responses. Conversely, if the reaction of an organizational rhetor comes to be viewed as insufficient or as minimizing a generally acknowledged crisis, then organizational credibility is threatened. This was indeed the case for the Exxon Corporation, following the Valdez oil spill in Alaska in 1989, as the corporation tried to define the disaster as an individual rather than a policy-related problem, focusing blame on the ship's captain and diverting attention away from potential regulations for strengthening ships' hulls (cf. Benson, 1988, on the Tylenol case; Ice, 1991, on the Bhopal disaster; and Benoit, 1995, on the image-restoration strategies of Sears).

What Vibbert and Bostdorff's (1993) analysis fails to describe is the relationship between issues and identities and the growing interrelatedness of internal and external organizational communication. In the self-referential perspective laid out in this chapter, the rhetorical efforts of the III would be described not only in terms of its presumed effects on an external audience but also as an auto-communicative ritual that helps constitute the rhetor itself and its identity in an emergent environment. The self-referential view, however, would include another important dimension. While a proactive management of issues may allow organizations (large, powerful organizations in particular) to define rhetorically their own discursive domain, it makes it possible for such organizations to determine the appropriate responses to the issues in question. And clearly, the III did have its own solution ready: raising insurance premiums. When organizational responses come, as some issue management scholars recommend (e.g., Chase, 1984), *before* the opinions by key audiences are crystallized, the organization has a tendency to close itself off from the larger, extraorganizational environment and communicate mainly within its own symbolic universe.

In proactive management, organizational responses may, in other words, often precede environmental stimuli. Still, the notion of a "response" suggests that even the proactive organization is in *dialogue* with its stakeholders. This assumption, however, needs to be modified. When organizations operate within a discursive universe enacted, in large part, through proactive strategies, they are significantly talking to themselves. The fact that many issues are not controlled, or controllable, by the organization (e.g., Hainsworth & Meng, 1988) does not undermine the logic of this particular argument: that organizations, when responding to their own enactments of an issue, are often communicating basically with themselves about their own expectations and concerns. Self-referential communication should thus be seen as a compelling tendency of issue management. This is clearly the case in the following example, which illustrates all the central dimensions discussed above: proactivity, auto-communication, and accordingly, identity.

The medical corporation Novo Nordisk (based in Denmark but with offices, manufacturing facilities, and associated companies in numerous countries) has become well known for its proactive stance on the "green" issue. In the early 1990s, the corporation issued a 40-page report on this issue, including a detailed evaluation of its own contributions to pollution. To disarm possible criticism, Novo Nordisk furthermore chose to let a well-known environmentalist evaluate publicly the report and the corrective measures taken. Managers within Novo Nordisk explained the report with reference to the growing environmental consciousness among investors and customers since the 1980s. While this influence is highly significant in the corporate world of today, the step taken by Novo Nordisk was proactive and not a reaction to *specific* environmental demands. The proactive strategy of Novo Nordisk has several interesting dimensions that will be discussed below.

As long as relatively few organizations are issuing comprehensive evaluations of themselves, those that *do* appear more responsible, internally as well as externally. And indeed, Novo Nordisk is now being cited widely as a *responsible organization* concerned about its employees, the local community, and the environment in general: an image that instills a sense of pride and belongingness among its employees and attracts new qualified personnel. The fact that this image or reputation most often is reproduced by people who have *not* read the report tells us a great deal about the communication environment of today. When the social space is saturated with corporate communication asserting social righteousness, only the indirect or more unusual messages are able to stand out and attract attention. And the report issued by Novo Nordisk is indeed communication. Although the report does reflect real changes in the *behavior* of the organization, including a number of internal measures taken to reduce pollution, it is first of all an elaborate piece of communication: a metatext that tells, by its very existence, the general public including Novo Nordisk's own members that this organization is willing to let action follow words.

And the report *did* commit Novo Nordisk to a number of specific goals. With its "eco-productivity index"—a notion that divides the amount of sold goods with the amount of raw materials, energy, water, and packing used in the production process—the report prescribed quite specifically how pollution was to be reduced: as an ongoing increase in the eco-productivity index. This self-imposed prescription is not easy to fulfill and puts a heavy burden on all departments of the organization. Interestingly, the proactive introduction of this index allows Novo Nordisk to define itself the measures necessary to reduce its pollution. This has tremendous advantages for the organization. Instead of responding *reactively* to environmental issues as they "pop up" in its surroundings, Novo Nordisk defines and shapes proactively the issues that it addresses: a strategy that allows it to operate in a more familiar universe defined, in large part, by its own actions.

Such measures cannot stand alone but require careful follow-up advocacy (see, e.g., Arrington & Sawaya, 1984) in many different fora: in the local community, the European Union, international environmental organizations, and the media. In the present case, the first steps to make environmental reporting compulsory in the chemical industry have already been taken by an industrial association of which Novo Nordisk is a prominent member. Further, Novo Nordisk carefully cultivates its relations with different publics by hosting regular meetings with neighbors, journalists, investors, insurance companies, employees, environmental groups, and politicians. In line with Grunig's (1992, in press) notion of "symmetrical public relations," these efforts seem to demonstrate a sincere interest on the part of Novo Nordisk in establishing a two-way dialogue with affected and relevant publics. Without rejecting this interpretation, it should be added that these relations also serve the very important function of making sure that the change measures imposed proactively by Novo Nordisk on itself in fact become the *future standards* of social responsibility. Since the organization's relations with these mentioned groups are very close—several powerful environmental groups publicly express their admiration of Novo Nordisk—there is a great likelihood that

Novo Nordisk will be successful in its efforts to shape future discussions on and standards of social responsibility.

In such cases, it is tempting to suggest that the relations are symbiotic and that the communication involved tends to establish a relatively closed universe of mutual understanding, not easily accessible to other publics. At least, this is an interesting possibility that any critical perspective on public relations needs to consider seriously. When operating effectively within this network, the organization is able to communicate with itself and, this way, confirm its up-to-date outlook and its identity as a responsible organization ready to take substantial measures to protect the environment.

Similar communication systems are being developed these days by many different kinds of organizations. German-based Bayer Corporation, for example, has established a communication center, BayKomm, that "actively seeks frank and open dialogue with the public about problems and questions relating to the chemical industry" (brochure from Bayer AG, Leverkusen, Germany). In its promotional material, Bayer describes BayKomm as "an important interface between the company and society." In BayKomm, the brochure continues, "Bayer tries to place dialogue with the public on a broad footing. BayKomm is designed as a bridge between Bayer and the outside world, between the chemical industry and society." For most of the public, however, the "communication" with Bayer is restricted to guided tours of the impressive BayKomm center. The professional dialogues and discussion rounds that BayKomm initiates are usually organized around selected *strategic* publics. Also, the topics discussed in these communication fora are not open questions of general interest but topics delimited to issues of strategic relevance to Bayer, such as recycling and gene technology. While such issues are often important to the general public as well, their shaping by Bayer in this particular setting implies that the dialogue may not be as open and symmetrical as it first appears.

Communication scholars who study organizations and their interactions with the environment, thus, should be aware of the possible limitations to the ideals of dialogue and responsiveness advocated so strongly today within public relations, marketing, and issue management. Such awareness is crucial, especially when we note that the restrictions on dialogue and responsiveness are not always intentional on the part of the organization. While many organizations today clearly hope to control their environment better by being proactive and at the forefront of new trends, the tendencies for proactive organizations to develop closed circuits of auto-communication may well be unintended consequences.

CONCLUSION: PUBLIC DISCOURSE, ETHICS, AND DEMOCRACY

As this essay has argued, in an unstable symbolic world issue management becomes closely tied up with the question of organizational identity. Following our description of today's communication environment, we commented on the preoccupation with "identities" in the public discourse of contemporary organizations. Specifically, we observed how identity and image have become perhaps the central issue (or set of issues) for many organizations today as they "talk" about themselves in a variety of media and communication arenas.

A central and overarching theme of this essay concerns the blurring of domains of organizational communication. We have illustrated how so-called external communication activities of contemporary organizations must be seen as closely connected to those presumably inside the container of the organization. Moreover, we have presented theoretical, historical, and practical reasons for establishing such a linkage both more strongly and more clearly in the scholarship of organizational communication. Finally, we have demonstrated how this complex communication situation is structuring the way organizations of today perceive and manage issues *as* identities, and identities as issues. In the remaining part of this chapter, we will summarize major points of the essay in the form of paradoxes, indicate a number of ethical concerns, and finally, point out some implications for research and practice.

Summary

To illustrate the complexity of managing issues in today's corporate world, it is useful to think of the communication involved as being based on a set of interrelated paradoxes. Besides summarizing and synthesizing the major points in the essay, it is our hope that these paradoxes will point the reader beyond the present text and stimulate further thinking within the field.

1. Because internal and external aspects of organizing are closely intertwined, communication that seems to be directed toward others may actually be auto-communicative, that is, directed primarily toward the self.
2. As a consequence of the "explosion" of information and communication that we are witnessing—an explosion that, ironically, seems to imply an *implosion* among receivers (see Baudrillard, 1983)—any corporate identity becomes a fragile construction whose uniqueness is entirely dependent on *other* identities and whose persistence over time requires even more communication.
3. Because proactive management, as we have indicated, has a *reactive* basis in the consumer unrest of the 1960s and beyond, the environments enacted through proactive corporate measures are rhetorically described as something "out there" to which the organization needs to adapt. However, within the self-referential perspective laid out in this essay, it can be argued that what is adapted (to) is in fact "the public," operating largely in a discursive universe defined by large corporate actors.
4. The kind of openness displayed by contemporary marketing-oriented organizations in

their relentless pursuit of "the will of the market" may, in other words, represent a certain kind of organizational closedness. Indeed, as Luhmann (1990) has explained so well, identity—for an individual or for a group—rests on the tension between *openness* and *closedness* (cf. Morin, 1986). Too open a system has no identity at all, no possibility for being distinguished from the larger universe. Too closed a system, in contrast, has no possibility for adaptation, and in its extreme form, ceases to have any self-reference when it has no reference to the larger world. To the extent that these terms are still meaningful descriptors of organizational communication practices, openness and closedness should be seen in dialectical interdependence.

Ethical Concerns

Our discussion of organizational communication, of course, has much wider social and political implications than even these paradoxes indicate, especially when we consider transformations in public and private discourse in recent decades (see, e.g., Habermas, 1981; Sennett, 1978). Although such developments are highly relevant to organizational communication scholarship, we do not have the space in this chapter to elaborate on all of the implications of these transformations. Instead, we will focus attention on a number of ethical concerns related to the major points in this essay. In doing so, we wish to distance ourselves from both a purely instrumental view of corporate communications and a perspective based in a hopeless form of postmodernism that implicitly argues that "there's nothing to be done."

Ethical-moral issues arise on multiple levels with respect to "external" organizational messages; these include (1) the posited character or integrity of the source of the message, (2) the defensibility of a particular message, (3) the legitimacy of a pattern or campaign of messages, (4) the practical impact of a message or the cumulative effect of a series of messages, (5) the openness of the structure of communication between an organization and its publics/audiences, (6) the articulation/representation of genuine public interests, and (7) the question of shared responsibility. Below we will comment briefly on each of these ethical arenas and their implications for practice.

1. *Integrity of the source of the message.* Our Western legal systems have enormous difficulties in dealing with the morality of corporate persons, largely because of the emphasis on definable and provable *intention*. At the same time, however, we do tend to ascribe intention, personality, and character to organizations, judging organizations by their actions. When the organization offers a *stated* purpose, we can hold the organization to its own word (see, e.g., Crable & Vibbert, 1983). To sidestep the thorny question of organizational intentionality yet hold organizations responsible, one option is to focus on the established awareness of harms. As Gibson (1994) observes, under certain conditions we may consider an organization as having a *culture* that suggests a disposition toward harmful actions. Thus, we may try to make a plausible case that an organization's culture encourages misrepresentations, intentional omissions of fact, and lies. But even in this case, the question of how to engage productively an organization's communication system remains how to penetrate and perhaps alter the organizational culture.

2. *The defensibility of a particular message.* This becomes a relevant domain of ethical evaluation for a variety of reasons, including questions about truth, the representation of interests, and the effect to which a message can be labeled propaganda (in its aggressive one-sidedness). The revelation of underlying interests is especially important in an age when, for example, many wholly private lobbying groups disguise their basic orientations with names such as "*Council* on Energy Awareness" and "Insurance Information *In-*

stitute." Moreover, as we have argued, the closed nature of many communication systems means that "business as usual" is likely to prevail and that organizations in many cases will be unlikely to see beyond limited interests and concerns associated with their own survival and identity. Often, vigorous efforts are necessary to uncover "who" or "what" is behind a particular message. Organizations, like individuals, should be required to declare their interests and reveal the sources of messages.

3. *The legitimacy of a pattern or campaign of messages.* To look at a wider persuasive campaign by or for organizations requires the analysis of patterns in verbal and visual messages. From an ethical perspective, this affords the opportunity to examine such features as consistency, adaptation to multiple audiences, and openness in response to challenges from outsiders. In terms of communication and rhetorical studies, the central question about adaptation becomes: At what point does adjustment to different audiences become misrepresentation of what the organization "really *is*"? (see, e.g., Cheney & Dionisopoulos, 1989). Of course, this question requires at least passing consideration of the ontological-epistemological problem of the "essence" of the organization (Cooren, 2000). Conversely, as we have suggested with our analysis of auto-communication, one must ask: When does an organization's communication system become so closed that it is merely talking to itself? This question can be at least partially addressed through an assessment of an organization's relations with its various publics, with special attention to real opportunities for input into the organization's policy-making apparatus.

4. *The practical impact of a message or set of messages.* The analyst of ethical aspects of external organizational communication may also choose to emphasize the intended or un-

intended effects of messages. Obviously, there can often be a clash between the stated or actual intention and the actual consequences of a message or campaign, as when advertising for a particular product or service functions to "cultivate" an unrelated attitude or practice (cf. Gerbner, Gross, Morgan, & Signorielli, 1980). Importantly, the cumulative effect of a series of organizational messages perceived by some public to be untruthful or inauthentic can be a wide and deep breach of trust (just as occurs with reports of corporate and governmental scandals). Further, the interrelations of internal and external communication can become apparent. In a study by Finet (1994), an organization's attempt to limit the influence of one of its outspoken members who publicly criticized it were circumscribed by the organization's own public image. The critic who focuses on the practical consequences of messages, of course, does not have to consider intentionality at all if he or she chooses to evaluate organizational actions solely on the basis of their pragmatic effects. But the critic does need to explain and defend reasonably objective standards for judgment in the case of a "text"-centered or message-centered evaluation: that is, explaining clearly how inferences about the "nature" of the organization are being made from its messages. Even more difficult to evaluate than specific claims in corporate communication is the more general idea of organizational or corporate sincerity. Tracy (1995), for example, offers a probing meta-analysis of the marketing of social responsibility as a corporate strategy, drawing on cases such as the London-based Body Shop and Vermont's Ben and Jerry's Ice Cream. She urges consumers and critics to do their best to assess both intent (e.g., through looking at the scope of a social-responsibility program vis-à-vis its announced claims) and impact (i.e., considering what actual benefits accrue to society as a result of the program).

5. *The structure of communication between an organization and its publics.* In addition to a focus on messages (or in contrast to it),

the ethics analyst can focus attention on the *relationship* between an organization and its various publics or audiences, including employees, consumers/clients, competitors, governmental agencies, and the wider citizenry. This is precisely what Grunig (e.g., 1992) advocates by presenting a two-way symmetrical model of public relations. While recognizing that communication systems may often be dominated by the organization, Grunig promotes the idea of genuine dialogue between organizations and other actors in their environment. Grunig's model goes a long way toward addressing the alienated position of the individual or group that desires to have a real forum for addressing a "corporate audience" (cf. Coleman, 1974). Also, the model encourages organizational persuaders to engage their audiences in meaningful ways.

Of course, encouraging practices along these lines is often enormously difficult, not only in terms of political and resource-related obstacles but also because of the maddening nature of the communication environment itself. Moreover, the critic of corporate communications should be aware of the possibility indicated in this essay that so-called symmetrical communication fora established by responsive organizations to further a dialogue with relevant publics may turn out to be relatively closed universes of thought organized around the interests, expectations, and enactments of the organizations themselves (Cheney & Christensen, in press). This way, organizations may still be able to "auto-communicate" within a two-way symmetrical framework. In spite of these complex problems, it seems difficult in a Western democratic society to imagine better solutions to the management of issues than an ongoing two-way dialogue between organizations and their stakeholders—a dialogue in which questions of interests and representation are constantly negotiated.

6. *The articulation/representation of genuine public interests.* The question of authentic or genuine public interest is an extremely complex one that could take the analyst of

ethics into the domains of political representation, power, critical theories (see, e.g., Lukes, 1974), and perhaps, beyond. Clearly, when an organization professes to represent broad, public or societal interests, its claims merit careful scrutiny. However, in a time when public-private partnerships and quasi-governmental institutions in some countries and communities have become almost the rule rather than the exception, simply trying to say who or what is representing the broad public becomes very trying.

This is not to say that we are left with no place to stand in critiquing blatantly self-serving communication campaigns—such as continuing efforts by U.S. tobacco companies to proclaim a *freedom* to smoke in response to warnings about passive consumption—but to say that *locating* public and private interests along with their presumed constituencies is often not an easy task. Since organizations cannot respond equally to all public interests, they will often choose to establish closer relations to those stakeholders with the most power, influence, and/or media attention (Kingo, 1996), hoping perhaps that such groups do represent the interests of the general public. And in some situations, this may indeed be the case. Following our preceding discussion, however, the analyst interested in ethical and democratic issues should pay attention to the possibility that the communication systems that are being developed these days—though avowedly to satisfy the general public's demand for insight and participation—are too closed around organizations and their *active* and resource-rich publics and stakeholders, each monitoring the other and themselves. This pattern suggests the model of "corporatism" (cf. Held, 1996). What appear, to some observers, as symmetrical systems of communication may, in other words, turn out to be "corporatist" systems organized around specific issues with only limited access to the nonorganized (see also Christensen & Jones, 1996; Livesey, 1999). Such a pattern of communication by and among well-established and resource-rich entities can exacerbate the problem of dominance of the "free speech" arena by corporate and other large or-

ganization interests (Bailey, 1996). Again, although these challenges confront the question of the meaning of democracy in the context of organizational communication and urge scholars and practitioners to be sensitive to the possible limitations and problems of organized dialogues (cf. Pearson, 1989; Sutcliffe, this volume), they do not disqualify the two-way symmetrical model as an important communication ideal or beacon in today's society.

7. *Shared responsibility.* The question of public interests, however, has another important dimension. On the one hand, the consumer or citizen may not see himself or herself as sharing responsibility for the creation and development of the product, the service, or the ethical standard—for example, an automobile, an education, or a rule for dumping waste—even if he or she has been involved in the decision-making process. The fact that marketing has facilitated the consumption of ideas and social issues does not necessarily imply, as some social marketers seem to suggest (e.g., Fine, 1981), an increased attention to or participation in important societal questions. Since the consumption of ideas has become a trend, the opposite may sometimes be the case. Indeed, this problem represents the most serious drawback of the marketing ethos (cf. Hirschman, 1983). On the other hand, while marketing-oriented organizations have considerably improved their ability to respond to the wishes of specific audiences, their notion of *how* such wishes are related to the general well-being of society is still rather vague. Response-*ability,* in other words, does not necessarily entail responsibility. In contemporary, market-oriented society where corporations demonstrate social responsibility by being open and responsive to claims made by organized publics, the central question is still how such maneuvers correspond with the pursuit of "the overall good." This is especially true because some corporations are up front about using values merely for marketing advantage (see McDonald & Gandz, 1992).

In the writings of scholars who promote the idea of a symmetrical dialogue between organizations and their publics, one senses the implicit assumption that organizations are behaving in a socially responsible manner as long as they adapt to the will of the general public. Can we be sure, however, that active, vocal, or affected publics represent the "whole" and that *their* articulation of an issue reflects the necessary wider concerns (Davis & Blomstrom, 1971)? Clearly, such questions are of utmost importance in a society in which the "pulse" of the opinion has become a central indicator of economic and political vitality. Redefined from citizen to consumer, the modern man or woman is now being pursued by organizational rhetors, managers, and decision makers with all available means. His or her wants, or rather voice, have become the currency most prized and convertible in this phase of modernity. With this development in mind, it is not surprising that Laufer and Paradeise (1990) speak ironically and poignantly of "marketing democracy."

Together, these concerns represent important bases for ethically informed criticism of the communication that organizations carry on between themselves and their environment. The larger question of identifying a perspective from which to examine the (un)ethical nature of organizational communication remains. This question is vexing, especially in light of the popular view of ethics in business from an economic-utility standpoint (Cheney, in press). That is, arguments for ethical practice are most compelling in many sectors when it can be established clearly that ethical behavior will improve performance on the bottom line (see the results of a survey of U.S. business speeches by Finet & Bal, 1995). In other words, a view of worklife as essentially amoral persists in modern industrial society. To talk about the value of behaving ethically *in itself* is frequently not persuasive. A measurable, economic end product becomes the warrant for making a case for "good business." And "just business" becomes a shorthand justification for all sorts of questionable corporate practices.

Nevertheless, Thomas Donaldson (e.g., 1989) offers an informed, philosophically and practically sensitive model for large organizations, including multinational corporations. Among other principles, Donaldson advances the notion of a "micro-social contract," based on the idea that any organization enters into a social contract with the society or societies within which it operates. The parameters for the contract become "negotiated" through consideration of basic human rights (e.g., freedom from coercion), including the rights of organizations. While most of Donaldson's case examples do not feature issues of communication, we can make the case for application of his model to the parts of organizations that are most heavily engaged in the production of symbols (i.e., public relations, advertising, marketing, employee communications, and human resource management). Further, Donaldson's model can be usefully seen in conjunction with Deetz's (1995) multiple-stakeholder approach, with the latter offering as ideals genuine dialogue through overcoming unnecessary constraints in organizational communication patterns. Still, any apparently straightforward application of a model of ethical organizational practice to organizational communication systems becomes complicated by the aspects of the postmodern communication environment we have featured in this essay. As organizations become more conscious of their roles as cocreators of the "external" reality to which they claim to adjust, the organizational adjustments *themselves* become important loci of inquiry. Because many such adjustments change the environment to which organizations can respond, refined and penetrating ethical critiques of organizational communications and organizational understandings of the world become all the more urgent.

Implications for Theory and Practice

In closing, the concepts and principles discussed in this essay present enormous practical and ethical challenges for analysts and practitioners in the broad and diverse field of organizational communication. We do not mean to suggest, however, that "there's *no* way through" the ambiguities, paradoxes, and circularities characterizing communication practices today. Below we will sketch out some possible implications based on the major points of the essay.

First, it is important to realize that there is great practical value in being *aware* of the features of an expanding yet constraining universe of communication. Awareness of the set of issues described here does not liberate the organizational message maker or critic from that universe, but it does give him or her certain places to stand, however contingent or local they may be, in making sense of what's going on and in saying something meaningful and perhaps helpful about it. Within the communication context we depict, coping becomes a reasonably high-minded goal. This does not imply that there cease to be opportunities for real betterment in the organization's relations with individuals and with the larger society. Clearly, the modernist confidence in advancing the human condition must be tempered and modified by postmodern understandings of the limits of all of our rational pursuits but that does not negate our noblest goals (such as vibrant democracy) as points of reference that are occasionally approachable and that keep us from allowing society to become worse than it would be without such images of progress. We simply must remember that our very own creations, symbols, can play games with us, such that today's vision of democracy through marketing can become tomorrow's antidemocratic or pseudo-democratic institution.

Second, and more specifically, there are a number of important implications related to the observation that internal and external aspects of organizational communication are interrelated. If traditional, internal communication is relevant to external audiences—and this may often be the case in a world that expects organizations to be socially and environmentally responsible—scholars and practitio-ners need to understand much organizational communication as market-related communication, that is, as communication with the potential of shaping opinions and actions among consumers and other publics. If externally directed messages have the strongest impact on the organization and its members—and, as our discussion and examples suggest, this is often the case—we may need to think of marketing communications and public relations as an integral part of the organizational discourse. Whereas the former observation logically implies that organizational communications and relations should be evaluated not only as internal phenomena but also in terms of their impact on external audiences (an idea implicit in some approaches to public relations; see, e.g., Grunig, 1992, in press), the consequences of the latter observation are, as we shall indicate below, more complex.

As we have already pointed out, marketing, strategy, and issue management justify themselves primarily through their claimed sensitivity to symbols, trends, and developments in markets and other public arenas. To acknowledge fully their *internal* significance, these disciplines need to develop and widen their sensitivity to cover also an understanding of the organization and its own central symbols and values. This kind of sensitivity makes it possible to integrate external communications with such internal concerns as, for example, the need to mobilize human resources (Berg, 1986). Clearly, such integrative efforts are necessary for all kinds of organizations that wish to operate consistently with their goals. Moreover, since organizational symbols and values to a great extent determine what environments organizations are able to "see," this latter kind of sensitivity or *self-reflectivity* may sometimes be more important than collecting information about external trends. To know the environment better, organizations should, in other words, try to know themselves (cf. Weick & Ashford, this volume). This point is probably the most important practical implication of the self-referential perspective laid out in this chapter. Scholars

and practitioners within the field of what traditionally is thought of as external communication need to learn to communicate consciously with themselves and their organizations about their most central meanings.
These meanings include internal images and
perceptions of what the organization "is," key
symbols of pride and motivation, basic assumptions about relevant publics and environments, established procedures and routines involved in opinion polls and market analyses,
tacit norms for interpreting data, briefing procedures and information exchange between
departments, and more generally, perceptions
of external information throughout the organization (see Christensen, 1994b). Being self-
reflective and sensitive to such dimensions
thus means trying to be aware of one's own
auto-communicative predispositions. Only
through such exercise can organizations hope
to counter the self-referential tendencies described in this essay.

Third and finally, we are aware that our description of current communication and management practices can have negative consequences in the sense that some organizations,
for strategic reasons, may choose to develop
communication systems of a more closed and
self-referential nature. Organizations, for example, that wish to *appear* open and responsive may find inspiration in our discussion of
proactive organizing practices and the possibility of "integrating" stakeholders through
the use of focused strategic dialogues.
Although such *as-if dialogues* are not a new
phenomenon confined to the corporate world
but are part of our experience with politics,
their present forms do present a real danger to
our ideals of participation and democracy.
Still, such worries should not keep us from describing, discussing, and critiquing significant
tendencies in the corporate world—whether
they conform to our ideals or not.

The tendencies discussed in this chapter indicate a great potential for changing the scope
and outlook of a number of disciplines such as
organizational theory, communication, marketing, management strategy, and issue management. Clearly, the greatest challenge for
the organizational communication researcher

is to develop new and meaningful concepts
able to reflect the real complexity of contemporary organizational communication, that is,
concepts that are not confined within traditional dichotomies between "open" and
"closed," "internal" and "external," "formal"
and "informal," and so forth. Thus, we need to
ask more probing questions about the relationships between various audiences and
publics with organizations that would presume to speak to them. For example: How
much openness is there in corporate communications that are seemingly directed outward? How much democracy is there even in
debates and discussions that appear to include
divergent parties and stakeholders? And how
much concern is there on the part of people for
corporate identities and other messages that
organizations spend so much time, energy,
and money on (Cheney & Christensen, in
press; Christensen & Cheney, in press)? At the
same time, of course, each researcher must
make decisions about "where to stand" with
respect to these phenomena. What practi-
cal-epistemological position to take, whether
or not to seek social change, and what sort of
ethical principles to develop represent perhaps
the most crucial decisions.

NOTE

1. We would like to circumnavigate the "*This* is
postmodernity?" discussion by arguing simply that the
point is not to label contemporary society but rather to
understand it better. While we recognize the fact that
trends brought together under the rubric of postmodernism have influenced a whole range of academic disciplines from literature to physics and that debates continue to rage over what each discipline "looks like" from
a postmodernist perspective, the point of this essay is not
to take sides in this debate.

REFERENCES

Achrol, R. S. (1991, October). Evolution of the marketing organization: New forms for turbulent environments. *Journal of Marketing, 55,* 77-93.
Adams, J. S. (1976). The structure and dynamics of behavior in organizational boundary roles. In M. D.

Dunnette (Ed.), *Handbook of industrial and organizational psychology* (pp. 1175-1199). Chicago: Rand McNally.

Albert, S., & Whetten, D. A. (1985). Organizational identity. In B. M. Staw & L. L. Cummings (Eds.), *Research in organizational behavior* (Vol. 7, pp. 263-295). Greenwich, CT: JAI.

Allen, M. W., & Caillouet, R. H. (1994). Legitimation endeavours: Impression management strategies used by an organization in crisis. *Communication Monographs, 41,* 44-62.

Alvesson, M. (1990). Organization: From substance to image? *Organization Studies, 11*(3), 373-394.

Arndt, J. (1979). Toward a concept of domesticated markets. *Journal of Marketing, 43,* 69-75.

Arrington, C. B., & Sawaya, R. N. (1984). Managing public affairs: Issues management in an uncertain environment. *California Management Review, 26*(4), 148-160.

Ashforth, B. E., & Mael, F. A. (1996). Organizational identity and strategy as a context for the individual. *Advances in Strategic Management, 13,* 19-64.

Bailey, W. (1996). Corporate/commercial speech and the marketplace first amendment: Whose right was it anyway? *Southern Communication Journal, 61,* 122-138.

Bakhtin, M. (1981). *The dialogic imagination: Four essays* (C. Emerson & M. Holquist, Trans., M. Holquist, Ed.). Austin: University of Texas Press.

Baudrillard, J. (1981). *Simulacres et simulation.* Paris: Galilée.

Baudrillard, J. (1983). *In the shadow of the silent majorities.* New York City: Semiotext(e).

Baudrillard, J. (1988). *The ecstasy of communication.* New York: Semiotext(e).

Benoit, W. L. (1995). Sears' repair of its auto service image: Image restoration discourse in the corporate sector. *Communication Studies, 46,* 89-105.

Benson, J. A. (1988). Crisis revisited: An analysis of strategies used by Tylenol in the second tampering episode. *Central States Speech Journal, 39,* 28-36.

Berg, P. O. (1986). Symbolic management of human resources. *Human Resource Management, 25,* 557-579.

Berg, P. O., & Gagliardi, P. (1985). *Corporate images: A symbolic perspective of the organization-environment interface.* Paper presented at the SCOS Corporate Images conference, Antibes, France.

Berg, P. O., & Kreiner, K. (1990). Corporate architecture: Turning physical settings into symbolic resources. In P. Gagliardi (Ed.), *Symbols and artifacts: Views of the corporate landscape* (pp. 41-67). Berlin: Walter de Gruyter.

Black, E. (1970). The second persona. *Quarterly Journal of Speech, 56,* 109-119.

Bostdorff, D. M. (1994). *The presidency and rhetoric of foreign crisis.* Colombia: University of South Carolina Press.

Bostdorff, D. M., & Vibbert, S. L. (1994). Values advocacy: Enhancing organizational images, deflecting public criticism, and grounding future arguments. *Public Relations Review, 20,* 141-158.

Bouchet, D. (1991). Advertising as a specific form of communication. In H. H. Larsen, D. G. Mick, & C. Alsted (Eds.), *Marketing and semiotics* (pp. 31-51). Copenhagen, Denmark: Handelshøjskolens Forlag.

Broms, H., & Gahmberg, H. (1983). Communication to self in organizations and cultures. *Administrative Science Quarterly, 28,* 482-495.

Broom, G. M., Lauzen, M. M., & Tucker, K. (1991). Public relations and marketing: Dividing the conceptual domain and operational turf. *Public Relations Review, 17*(3), 219-225.

Bryant, D. (1953). Rhetoric: Its functions and its scope. *Quarterly Journal of Speech, 39,* 401-424.

Burke, K. (1966). *Language as symbolic action.* Berkeley: University of California Press.

Carlzon, J. (1987). *Moments of truth.* Cambridge, MA: Ballinger.

Carroll, C. (1995). Rearticulating organizational identity: Exploring corporate images and employee identification. *Management Learning, 26,* 467-486.

Chase, W. H. (1984). *Issue management: Origins of the future.* Stamford, CT: Issue Action.

Cheney, G. (1983a). On the various and changing meanings of organizational membership: A field study of organizational identification. *Communication Monographs, 50,* 343-363.

Cheney, G. (1983b). The rhetoric of identification and the study of organizational communication. *Quarterly Journal of Speech, 69,* 143-158.

Cheney, G. (1991). *Rhetoric in an organizational society: Managing multiple identities.* Columbia: University of South Carolina Press.

Cheney, G. (1992). The corporate person (re)presents itself. In E. L. Toth & R. L. Heath (Eds.), *Rhetorical and critical approaches to public relations* (pp. 165-184). Hillsdale, NJ: Lawrence Erlbaum.

Cheney, G. (1999). *Values at work: Employee participation meets market pressure at Mondragón.* Ithaca, NY: Cornell University Press.

Cheney, G. (in press). Arguing about the place of values and ethics in market-oriented discourses of today. In S. Goldzwig & P. Sullivan (Eds.), *New approaches to rhetoric for the 21st century.* East Lansing: Michigan State University Press.

Cheney, G., Block, B. L., & Gordon, B. S. (1986). Perceptions of innovativeness and communication about innovations: A study of three types of service organizations. *Communication Quarterly, 34,* 213-230.

Cheney, G., & Christensen, L. T. (in press). Public relations as contested terrain: A critical response. In R. L. Heath & G. Vazquez (Eds.), *Handbook of public relations.* Thousand Oaks, CA: Sage.

Cheney, G., & Dionisopoulos, G. (1989). Public relations? No, relations with publics: A rhetorical-organizational approach to contemporary corporate communications. In C. H. Botan & V. Hazleton, Jr. (Eds.), *Public relations theory* (pp. 135-158). Hillsdale, NJ: Lawrence Erlbaum.

Cheney, G., & Frenette, G. (1993). Persuasion and organization: Values, logics and accounts in contemporary corporate public discourse. In C. Conrad (Ed.), *The ethical nexus* (pp. 49-74). Norwood, NJ: Ablex.

Cheney, G., & Tompkins, P. K. (1987). Coming to terms with organizational identification and commitment. *Central States Speech Journal, 38,* 1-15.

Cheney, G., & Vibbert, S. L. (1987). Corporate discourse: Public relations and issue management. In F. M. Jablin, L. L. Putnam, K. H. Roberts, & L. H. Porter (Eds.), *Handbook of organizational communication: An interdisciplinary perspective* (pp. 165-194). Newbury Park, CA: Sage.

Christensen, L. T. (1994a). *Markedskommunikation som organiseringsmåde. En kulturteoretisk analyse.* Copenhagen, Denmark: Akademisk Forlag.

Christensen, L. T. (1994b, November). Talking to ourselves: Management through auto-communication. *MTC Kontakten* (Jubilæumstidsskrift), pp. 32-37.

Christensen, L. T. (1995a). Buffering organizational identity in the marketing culture. *Organization Studies, 16*(4), 651-672.

Christensen, L. T. (1995b). Fra kosmetisk markedsføring til integreret strategi. Reflektioner over den "grønne" kommunikation. In J. P. Ulhøi (Ed.), *Virksomhedens miljøhåndbog* (No. 5, pp. 1-10). Copenhagen, Denmark: Børsens Forlag.

Christensen, L. T. (1996, February). *Communicating flexibility: A critical investigation of the discourse of organizational change.* Paper presented at the Organizational Communication and Change: Challenges in the Next Century conference, Austin, Texas.

Christensen, L. T. (1997, May). Marketing as auto-communication. *Consumption, Markets & Culture, 3,* 197-227.

Christensen, L. T., & Cheney, G. (1994). Articulating identity in an organizational age. In S. A. Deetz (Ed.), *Communication yearbook 17* (pp. 222-235). Thousand Oaks, CA: Sage.

Christensen, L. T., & Cheney, G. (in press). Self-absorption and self-seduction in the corporate identity game. In M. Schultz, M. J. Hatch, & M. H. Larsen (Eds.), *The expressive corporation.* Oxford, UK: Oxford University Press.

Christensen, L. T., & Jones, R. (1996). En symmestrisk dialog om miljøspørgsmålet? En kritisk analyse af nye dialogformer mellem virksomheder og forbrugere. In J. P. Ulhøi & H. Madsen (Eds.), *Miljøledelse—Tanker, erfaringer og visioner* (pp. 151-167). Copenhagen, Denmark: Børsens Forlag.

Coleman, J. S. (1974). *Power and the structure of society.* New York: Norton.

Conrad, C. (Ed.). (1993). *The ethical nexus.* Norwood, NJ: Ablex.

Cooley, C. H. (1983). *Human nature and the social order.* New Brunswick, NJ: Transaction Books.

Cooren, F. (2000). *The organizing property of communication.* Amsterdam, the Netherlands: John Benjamins.

Coupland, J. (1996). Dating advertisements: Discourse of the commodified self. *Discourse & Society, 7,* 187-208.

Crable, R. E., & Vibbert, S. L. (1983). Mobil's epideictic advocacy: "Observations" of Prometheus-bound. *Communication Monographs, 50,* 380-394.

Crable, R. E., & Vibbert, S. L. (1985). Managing issues and influencing public policy. *Public Relations Review, 11,* 3-16.

Crable, R. E., & Vibbert, S. L. (1986). *Public relations as communication management.* Edina, MN: Bellweather.

Czarniawska-Joerges, B. (1994). Narratives of individual and organizational identities. In S. A. Deetz (Ed.), *Communication yearbook 17* (pp. 193-221). Thousand Oaks, CA: Sage.

Daft, R. L., & Weick, K. E. (1984). Toward a model of organizations as interpretation systems. *Academy of Management Review, 9,* 284-295.

Davis, K., & Blomstrom, R. L. (1971). *Business, society, and environment: Social power and social response* (2nd ed.). New York: McGraw-Hill.

Deetz, S. (1995). *Transforming communication, transforming business: Building responsive and responsible workplaces.* Cresskill, NJ: Hampton.

DeLozier, M. W. (1976). *The marketing communication process.* New York: McGraw-Hill.

Dervin, B. (1994). Information ↔ democracy. *Journal of the American Society of Information Science, 45,* 369-385.

Donaldson, T. (1989). *The ethics of international business.* New York: Oxford University Press.

Douglas, M. (1986). *How institutions think.* Syracuse, NY: Syracuse University Press.

Dutton, J. E. (1993). Interpretations on automatic: A different view of strategic issue diagnosis. *Journal of Management Studies, 30,* 339-357.

Dutton, J. E., & Dukerich, J. M. (1991). Keeping an eye on the mirror: Image and identity in organizational adaptation. *Academy of Management Journal, 34,* 517-554.

Dutton, J. E., & Duncan, R. (1987). The creation of momentum for change through the process of strategic issue diagnosis. *Strategic Management Journal, 8,* 279-295.

Dutton, J. E., & Ottensmeyer, E. (1987). Strategic issue management systems: Forms, functions, and contexts. *Academy of Management Review, 12, 2,* 355-365.

Dyer, G. (1990). *Advertising as communication.* London: Routledge.

Ewing, R. P. (1987). *Managing the new bottom-line: Issues management for senior executives.* Homewood, IL: Dow Jones-Irwin.

Fairclough, N. (1993). Critical discourse analysis and the marketization of public discourse: The universities. *Discourse & Society, 4,* 133-168.

Feldman, M. (1989). *Order without design: Information production and policy making.* Stanford, CA: Stanford University Press.

Feldman, M. S., & March, J. G. (1981). Information in organizations as signal and symbol. *Administrative Science Quarterly, 26,* 171-186.

Fennell, G. (1987). A radical agenda for marketing science: Represent the marketing concept! In A. F. Firat, N. Dholakia, & R. P. Bagozzi (Eds.), *Philosophical and radical thought in marketing* (pp. 289-306). Lexington, MA: D. C. Heath.

Fine, S. H. (1981). *The marketing of ideas and social issues.* New York: Praeger.

Finet, D. (1994). Sociopolitical consequences of organizational expression. *Journal of Communication, 44,* 114-131.

Finet, D., & Bal, V. (1995, May). *The rhetoric of ethics and economics in organizational discourse.* Paper presented at the annual meeting of the International Communication Association, Albuquerque, NM.

Fornell, C., & Westbrook, R. A. (1984). The vicious cycle of consumer complaints. *Journal of Marketing, 48,* 68-78.

Fox, K., & Kotler, P. (1980). The marketing of social causes: The first 10 years. *Journal of Marketing, 44,* 24-33.

Gallagher, V. J. (1990, November). *Symbolic action, culture, permanence and change: A critical addition to organizational studies.* Paper presented at the Speech Communication Association convention, Chicago.

Gay, P. du. (1996). *Consumption and identity at work.* London: Sage.

Gay, P. du, & Salaman, G. (1992). The cult[ure] of the customer. *Journal of Management Studies, 29*(5), 615-633.

Geertz, C. (1973). *The interpretation of cultures.* New York: Basic Books.

Gerbner, G., Gross, L., Morgan, M., & Signorielli, N. (1980). The "mainstreaming" of America: Violence profile No. 10. *Journal of Communication, 30,* 10-29.

Gibson, K. (1994). Fictitious persons and real responsibilities. *Journal of Business Ethics, 13,* 1-7.

Giddens, A. (1991). *Modernity and self-identity.* Palo Alto, CA: Stanford University Press.

Grunig, J. E. (1992). *Excellence in public relations and communication management.* Hillsdale, NJ: Lawrence Erlbaum.

Grunig, J. E. (1993, September). Forholdet mellem public relations og marketing. *Mediekultur, 20,* 6-14.

Grunig, J. E. (in press). Public relations management in government and business. In J. L. Garnett (Ed.), *Handbook of administrative communication.* New York: Marcel Dekker.

Grunig, J. E., & Grunig, L. A. (1991). Conceptual differences in public relations and marketing: The case of health-care organizations. *Public Relations Review, 17*(3), 257-278.

Habermas, J. (1981). Modernity versus postmodernity. *New German Critique, 22,* 3-22.

Hainsworth, B., & Meng, M. (1988). How corporations define issue management. *Public Relations Review, 14*(4), 18-30.

Hatch, M. J., & Schultz, M. (1997). Relations between organizational culture, identity and image. *European Journal of Marketing, 31,* 356-365.

Heath, R. L. (1980). Corporate advocacy: An application of speech communication perspectives and skills—and more. *Communication Education, 29,* 370-377.

Heath, R. L. (Ed.). (1988). *Strategic issues management: How organizations influence and respond to public interests and policies.* San Francisco: Jossey-Bass.

Heath, R. L. (1990). Effects of internal rhetoric on management response to external issues: How corporate culture failed the asbestos industry. *Journal of Applied Communication Research, 18,* 153-167.

Heath, R. L., & Cousino, K. R. (1990). Issues management: End of first decade progress report. *Public Relations Review, 16*(1), 5-18.

Held, D. (1996). *Models of democracy* (2nd ed.). Stanford, CA: Stanford University Press.

Hirschman, E. C. (1983). Aesthetics, ideologies and the limits of the marketing concept. *Journal of Marketing, 47,* 45-55.

Ice, R. (1991). Corporate publics and rhetorical strategies: The case of Union Carbide's Bhopal crisis. *Management Communication Quarterly, 4,* 341-362.

James, B. (1993, November 8). If only work could be virtual, too. *International Herald Tribune,* p. 1.

Joy, A. (1993). The modern Medicis: Corporations as consumers of art. *Research in Consumer Behavior, 6,* 29-54.

Jones, B. L., & Chase, W. H. (1979). Managing public policy issues. *Public Relations Review, 2,* 3-23.

Kaldor, A. G. (1971). Imbricative marketing. *Journal of Marketing, 35,* 19-25.

Keith, R. J. (1960). The marketing revolution. *Journal of Marketing, 24,* 35-38.

Kingo, L. (1996, March). *Stakeholder interaction—A future challenge.* Keynote paper presented at the 3rd Conference of the Nordic Business Environmental Management Network, Aarhus, Denmark.

Kotler, P. (1991). *Marketing management: Analysis, planning, implementation, and control* (7th ed.). Englewood Cliffs, NJ: Prentice Hall.

Kotler, P., & Andreasen, A. R. (1987). *Strategic marketing for non-profit organizations* (Vol. 1). Englewood Cliffs, NJ: Prentice Hall.

Kotler, P., & Levy, S. J. (1969). Broadening the concept of marketing. *Journal of Marketing, 33,* 10-15.

Kotler, P., & Roberto, E. L. (1989). *Social marketing: Strategies for changing public behavior.* New York: Free Press.

Kuhn, T. (1997). The discourse of issues management: A genre of organizational communication. *Communication Quarterly, 45,* 188-210.

Lasch, C. (1978). *The culture of narcissism.* New York: Norton.

Lasch, C. (1984). *The minimal self: Psychic survival in troubled times.* London: Picador.

Laufer, R., & Paradeise, C. (1990). *Marketing democracy: Public opinion and media formation in democratic societies.* New Brunswick, NJ: Transaction.

Lazer, W., & Kelly, E. J. (Eds.). (1973). *Social marketing: Perspectives and viewpoints.* Homewood, IL: Irwin.

Lefort, C. (1988). *Democracy and political theory.* Cambridge, UK: Polity.

Leitch, S., & Neilson, D. (in press). Public relations and a theory of publics. In R. L. Heath & G. Vazquez (Eds.), *Handbook of public relations.* Thousand Oaks, CA: Sage.

Livesey, S. (1999). McDonald's and the Environmental Defense Fund: A case study of a green alliance. *Journal of Business Communication, 36,* 5-39.

Lotman, J. M. (1977). Two models of communication. In D. P. Lucid (Ed.), *Soviet semiotics: An anthology* (pp. 99-101). London: Johns Hopkins.

Lotman, J. M. (1991). *Universe of the mind: A semiotic theory of culture.* London: I. B. Tauris.

Luhmann, N. (1990). *Essays on self-reference.* New York: Colombia University Press.

Lukes, S. (1974). *Power: A radical view.* New York: Macmillan.

Manning, P. K. (1986). Signwork. *Human Relations, 39*(4), 283-308.

Manning, P. K. (1988). *Symbolic communication: Signifying calls and the police response.* Cambridge, MA: MIT Press.

Maturana, H. R., & Varela, F. J. (1980). *Autopoiesis and cognition: The realization of the living.* Dordrecht, Holland: D. Reidel.

McDonald, P., & Gandz, J. (1992). Getting value from shared values. *Organizational Dynamics, 20*(3), 64-77.

McGee, M. C. (1980). The "ideograph": A link between rhetoric and ideology. *Quarterly Journal of Speech, 66,* 1-16.

McMillan, J., & Cheney, G. (1996). The student as consumer: Implications and limitations of a metaphor. *Communication Education, 45,* 1-15.

Mead, G. H. (1934). *Mind, self, & society* (Vol. 1). Chicago: University of Chicago Press.

Meyer, J. W., & Rowan, B. (1977). Institutionalized organizations: Formal structure as myth and ceremony. *American Journal of Sociology, 83,* 340-363.

Mongin, O. (1982, February). La democratie a corps perdu. *Esprit, 2,* 206-212.

Morin, E. (1986). *La méthode 3: La connaissance de la connaissance. Livre premier: Antropo logie de la connaissance.* Paris: Seuil.

Motion, J., & Leitch, S. (2000, March). *The technologies of corporate identity.* Working paper, University of Auckland and University of Waikato, Hamilton, New Zealand.

Nader, R., & Green, M. J. (1973). *Corporate power in America: Ralph Nader's conference on corporate accountability.* New York: Grossman.

Nader, R., Green, M. J., & Seligman, J. (1976). *Taming the giant corporation.* New York: Norton.

Nickels, W. G. (1976). *Marketing communication and promotion.* Columbus, OH: Grid.

Nisbet, R. (1970). *The sociological tradition.* London: Heinemann.

Olins, W. (1989). *Corporate identity: Making business strategy visible through design.* New York: Thames & Hudson.

Packard, V. (1969). *The hidden persuaders* (21st printing). New York: McKay.

Paonessa, K. A. (1982). *Corporate advocacy in General Motors Corporation.* Unpublished master's thesis, Purdue University, IN.

Parsons, T. (1949). *The structure of social action.* New York: Free Press.

Pearson, R. (1989). Business ethics as communication ethics: Public relations practice and the idea of dialogue. In C. H. Botan & V. Hazleton, Jr. (Eds.), *Public relations theory* (pp. 111-131). Hillsdale, NJ: Lawrence Erlbaum.

Perniola, M. (1980). *La societá dei simulacri.* Bologna, Italy: Capelli.

Pfeffer, J. (1981). Management as symbolic action: The creation and maintenance of organizational paradigms. In L. L. Cummings & B. M. Staw (Eds.), *Research in organizational behavior* (Vol. 3, pp. 1-52). Greenwich, CT: JAI.

Pondy, L. R., Frost, P. J., Morgan, G., & Dandridge, T. C. (Eds.). (1983). *Organizational symbolism.* Greenwich, CT: JAI.

Powell, W. M. (1990). Neither market nor hierarchy: Network forms of organization. In B. M. Staw & L. L. Cummings (Eds.), *Research in organizational behavior* (Vol. 12, pp. 295-336). Greenwich, CT: JAI Press.

Procter & Gamble. (1989). *The house that Ivory built: 150 years of successful marketing.* Lincolnwood, IL: NTC Business Books.

Putnam, L. L., Phillips, N., & Chapman, P. (1996). Metaphors of communication and organization. In S. R. Clegg, C. Hardy, & W. R. Nord (Eds.), *Handbook of organization studies* (pp. 375-408). London: Sage.

Ramanantsoa, B., & Battaglia, V. (1991, June). *The autobiography of the firm: A means of deconstruction of the traditional images.* Paper presented at the eighth International SCOS Conference, Copenhagen, Denmark.

Richardson, G. B. (1972). The organization of industry. *Economic Journal, 82,* 883-896.

Scott, C. R., & Carroll, C. E. (1999, November). *If not now, then when? Exploring situated identifications among members of a dispersed organization.* Paper presented at the annual conference of the National Communication Association, Chicago.

Scott, C. R., Corman, S. A., & Cheney, G. (1998). The development of a structurational theory of identification in the organization. *Communication Theory, 8,* 298-336.

Sennett, R. (1978). *The fall of public man: On the social psychology of capitalism.* New York: Vintage.

Shimp, T. A. (1990). *Promotion management and marketing communications* (2nd ed.). Chicago: Dryden.

Smircich, L., & Stubbart, C. (1985). Strategic management in an enacted world. *Academy of Management Review, 10,* 724-736.

Smith, R. (1993, May). *Images of organizational communication: Root-metaphors of the organization-communication relation.* Paper presented at the annual meeting of the International Communication Association, Washington, DC.

Sproull, J. M. (1988). The new managerial rhetoric and the old criticism. *Quarterly Journal of Speech, 74,* 468-486.

Sproull, J. M. (1990). Organizational rhetoric and the rational-democratic society. *Journal of Applied Communication Research, 74,* 192-240.

Starbuck, W. H. (1976). Organizations and their environments. In M. D. Dunnette (Ed.), *Handbook of industrial and organizational psychology* (pp. 1069-1123) Chicago: Rand McNally.

Stidsen, B., & Schutte, T. F. (1972). Marketing as a communication system: The marketing concept revisited. *Journal of Marketing, 36,* 22-27.

Taylor, J. R. (1993). *Rethinking the theory of organizational communication: How to read an organization.* Norwood, NJ: Ablex.

Taylor, J. R., Flanagin, A. J., Cheney, G., & Seibold, D. R. (in press). Organizational communication research: Key moments, central concerns, and future challenges. In W. B. Gudykunst (Ed.), *Communication yearbook 24.* Thousand Oaks, CA: Sage.

Thompson, M., & Wildavsky, A. (1986). A cultural theory of information bias in organizations. *Journal of Management Studies, 23*(3), 273-286.

Thygesen Poulsen, P. (1993). *LEGO—En virksomhed og dens sjæl.* Albertslund, Denmark: Schultz.

Tompkins, P. K., & Cheney, G. (1983). Account analysis of organizations: Decision making and identification. In L. L. Putnam & M. E. Pacanowsky (Eds.), *Communication and organizations: An interpretive approach* (pp. 123-147). Beverly Hills, CA: Sage.

Tompkins, P. K., & Cheney, G. (1985). Communication and unobtrusive control in contemporary organizations. In R. D. McPhee & P. K. Tompkins (Eds.), *Organizational communication: Traditional themes and new directions* (pp. 179-210). Beverly Hills, CA: Sage.

Tracy, S. (1995). *Can public relations about social responsibility be socially responsible?* Unpublished paper, University of Colorado at Boulder.

Treadwell, D. F., & Harrison, T. M. (1994). Conceptualizing and assessing organizational image: Model images, commitment, and communication. *Communication Monographs, 61,* 63-85.

van Riel, C. B. M. (1995). *Principles of corporate communication.* London: Prentice Hall.

Vibbert, S. L., & Bostdorff, D. M. (1993). Issue management in the "lawsuit crisis." In C. Conrad (Ed.), *The ethical nexus* (pp. 103-120). Norwood, NJ: Ablex.

Wartick, S. L., & Rude, R. E. (1986). Issues management: Corporate fad or corporate function. *California Management Review, 29*(1), 124-140.

Wätzold, F. (1996). When environmentalists have power: A case study of the Brent Spar. In J. P. Ulhøi & H. Madsen (Eds.), *Industry and the environment: Practical applications of environmental management approaches in business.* Aarhus, Denmark: Aarhus Business School.

Webster, F. E., Jr. (1992). The changing role of marketing in the corporation. *Journal of Marketing, 56,* 1-17.

Weick, K. E. (1979). *The social psychology of organizing* (2nd ed.). Reading, MA: Addison-Wesley.

Weigert, A. J., Teitge, J. S., & Teitge, D. W. (1986). *Society and identity: Toward a sociological psychology.* Cambridge, UK: Cambridge University Press.

White, J. B. (1984). *When words lose their meaning: Constitutions and reconstitutions of language, character, and community.* Chicago: University of Chicago Press.

Zaltman, G., Kotler, P., & Kaufman, I. (Eds.). (1972). *Creating social change.* New York: Holt, Rinehart & Winston.

8

Sociopolitical Environments and Issues

DAYNA FINET
Writer, Austin, Texas

Historically, the field of organizational communication has prioritized analysis of *intra*organizational interaction. This focus involves a potentially infinite number of interesting and important questions. But it should not imply that organizational communication transcending organizational boundaries is less important. Rather, an organizational analyst might view the embeddedness of organizations in complex and dynamic sociopolitical environments, and the reciprocal influences of each upon the other, as good reason for concentrating even more directly on organizational communication within sociopolitical environments.

A note at the end of this chapter provides citations to a number of recent studies that have explored relationships between organizations and sociopolitical environments.[1] Both the volume and scope of this research demonstrate the vitality of this topic. Most of this current work uses one, or a combination, of three dominant theoretical approaches: (a) population ecology (Aldrich, 1979; Hannan & Carroll, 1992; Hannan & Freeman, 1977), (b) resource dependency theory (Pfeffer & Salancik, 1978), and (c) institutional theory (DiMaggio & Powell, 1983; Meyer & Rowan, 1977; Meyer & Scott, 1983; Powell & DiMaggio, 1991; Scott, 1987; Zucker, 1988). In the previous version of this handbook, Euske and Roberts (1987) outlined the relevance of these three approaches in terms of organizational communication. Their effort represents a helpful step in the development of a communicative approach to the topic of interaction between organizations and environments. Yet like many other examples in the organizational communication literature, the Euske and Roberts chapter is unfortunately limited by the authors' strategy of pinning post hoc "communication implications" onto existing theories that never intended to make communication their primary concern. In this chapter, I attempt to build on the foundation provided by Euske and Roberts. I introduce a new model of sociopolitically oriented organizational communication where the organizational discourses of institutional rhetoric and everyday talk play essential roles.

The chapter is organized into two main parts. The first section elaborates the discourse-centered model of organizations and their relations with their sociopolitical environments. This model extends Karl Weick's (1979) notion of the "enacted" environment and Taylor's (1995) articulation of organizational communication as "conversation." The second part of the chapter applies this model, using as illustration current research on the sociopolitical topics of sexual harassment, and family-work conflict.

THE DISCURSIVE MODEL OF ORGANIZATIONS AND SOCIOPOLITICAL ENVIRONMENTS

Early work on organizational environments emphasized market and technological environments (Burns & Stalker, 1961; Emery & Trist, 1965; Lawrence & Lorsch, 1967; Thompson, 1967). Later, this literature concentrated on sociopolitical environments (Aldrich, 1979; Hannan & Carroll, 1992; Hannan & Freeman, 1977; Meyer & Rowan, 1977; Meyer & Scott, 1983; Pfeffer & Salancik, 1978; Powell & DiMaggio, 1991; Scott, 1987; Zucker, 1988). Whichever its

orientation, all this literature is important for the reason that it acknowledges the significance of organizations' across-boundary interaction. Following Euske and Roberts's example, it thus makes sense to use this existing work as the initial foundation for a discursively grounded approach to the analysis of organizations and their relations with sociopolitical environments. Most basically, this discourse-centered model departs from the existing body of organization/environment research over an issue that has long preoccupied investigators. Much of the existing research in the field has assumed that organizations and environments are conceptually and empirically distinct. As a result, much of this work has involved the problem of "boundary specification," which distinguishes the organization from the environment with which it interacts. Its different strategy for handling this question represents the most elemental way in which a discourse-centered perspective prioritizes communication in the analysis of organizations' sociopolitical relations.

As Sutcliffe discusses in Chapter 6 in this handbook, discussion of the boundary specification question has centered on a debate over the comparatively objective or subjective character of organizational environments (Boyd, Dess, & Rasheed, 1993). This distinction has been variously labeled as, for example, a divergence between nominalist (objective) and realist (subjective) environments (Laumann, Marsden, & Prensky, 1983) or between archival (objective) and perceptual (subjective) ones (Boyd et al., 1993). The literature has tended to treat objective and subjective approaches to boundary specification as competing strategies, and the difference between them is easy to comprehend. Objectivists propose to establish empirical criteria for inclusion in the organization; whatever (or whoever) does not meet such criteria for organizational membership by definition then belongs to the organization's environment. Subjectivists are guided by organization members' perceptions of relevant external entities as the appropriate strategy for defining the organizational environment.

The problem of boundary specification is not insignificant, and both objective and subjective solutions have analytical utility if appropriately applied. But from the perspective of the discursive model developed in this chapter, this handling of the boundary specification question has encouraged two undesirable tendencies. First, it has led researchers to exaggerate the fixedness of organizational boundaries. Second, limiting boundary specification to objective and subjective techniques has caused researchers also to overlook the role of social practice, specifically as discourse, in organization-environment relations. At least two authors have created alternative conceptualizations of organization-environment relations that address these problems of boundary specification. Weick's (1979) notion of the "enacted" environment and Taylor's (1995) articulation of organizational "conversation" each lends conceptual support to a discourse-centered perspective on organizational relations within sociopolitical environments.

Weick's concept of the enacted environment addresses the problem of overly concretizing the organization-environment boundary as well as the problem of overlooking discursive social practices in the dynamics of organization and environment relations. In Weick's description, the concept of the enacted environment represents organizational boundaries as neither distinct nor static, but instead, as fundamentally permeable and fluid. According to Weick (1979), "boundaries between organizations and environment are never quite as clear-cut or stable as many organizational theorists think. These boundaries shift, disappear, and are arbitrarily drawn" (p. 132). Further, Weick's conceptualization of the enacted environment emphasizes the active (if not always self-reflective) role of patterned social practices as organizations and their members comprehend their external environments. According to Weick, enactment is naturally bound up with ecological change. On the one hand, organization members notice environmental occurrences and bracket these for collective attention. On the other hand, collective actions produce ecological change, which lead to other changes, and so on. Thus, in Weick's (1979) terms, "meaningful environments are the outputs of organizing, not inputs to it" (p. 131).

In his elaboration of organizational communication as conversation, Taylor likewise addresses both the issue of boundary precision and the role of social interaction in organization and environment relations. He rejects the notion of the organization-environment boundary as unambiguous, assumedly fixed. While not denying a distinctiveness of organization and environment, Taylor (1995) describes this boundary relationship as "self-generated [by the organization]: a membrane created from within by the process of self-reproduction. . . . Such boundary-establishing membranes, since they are constructed out of material common to all, do not totally isolate the organism from the world outside" (p. 8). Further, Taylor elaborates even more explicitly than does Weick the basic importance of discursive practices in organizations' communication within their social environments. Manifesting through organizational discourse the autopoietic quality of self-organizing, "an organization is not a physical structure . . . joined by material channels of communication, but a construction made out of conversation" (Taylor, 1995, p. 22) that simultaneously reflects and reproduces the social reality lived in the interactions of organization members. "Conversations are reflexive and self-organizing: they are produced by communication but are in turn the frame, or envelope, of the communication that generated them, in the absence of which communication would be impossible" (Taylor, 1995, p. 1).

In their ontological innovations, Weick and Taylor accomplish two common outcomes. First, they reduce the conceptual priority of the taken-for-granted separation of organization and environment and identify discursive practice as the principal feature in relationships between organizations and their larger environmental contexts. Second, they encourage an approach to organization-environment relations rooted in discursive process and practice, which the sociopolitically relevant example of "diversity" illustrates.

In analyzing diversity, traditional approaches to organization-environment relations would view the sociopolitical environment as the origin of normative change. Normative evolution would emerge in the form of specific demands regarding diversity, imposed on specific organizations from outside their boundaries. To cope, organizations would need to appropriately respond to these external expectations.

By contrast, Weick's and Taylor's work suggests that changing norms regarding gender and race actually reflect an ongoing cultural discussion occurring simultaneously within organizations and in their larger sociopolitical environments. These overlapping across-boundary conversations sometimes complement and sometimes conflict with, but always reciprocally influence, each other.

Traditional literature on organization-environment relations would also view the implications of diversity, for relations between organizations and sociopolitical environments, as either material or perceptual. A materialist conceptualization might focus on the numbers of women or minority group members in particular organizational roles, for example. A perceptual frame might examine the extent to which organizational decision makers feel threatened by gender- or race-relevant regulation.

Weick and Taylor concentrate instead on the means by which organizational discourse creates, sustains, or disestablishes particular sociopolitical understandings. This discourse might adopt infinite form. It could emerge as rhetorical labeling, apparent in such terms as *affirmative action, reverse discrimination,* and indeed, the term *diversity* itself. It could appear in patterns of organizational interaction that segregate organization members into subgroups along lines of gender or race. Or this diversity-oriented discourse could show up in the form of specific recruitment and training practices that use interaction to help overcome the often vast perceptual and experiential gaps between members of these subgroups.

What Weick and Taylor do not yet accomplish is the more detailed articulation of discourse processes in organizational relations with sociopolitical environments. Remaining sections of this chapter attempt this, conceptualizing organizations' sociopolitically relevant interaction at the intersecting organizational discourses of "institutional rhetoric" and "everyday talk."

Conceptual Assumptions

Prior to a detailed presentation of the discursive model of organizational communication within sociopolitical environments, several preliminary conceptual assumptions warrant elaboration.

First, the relevant issues for understanding organizational communication within sociopolitical environments involves much more than just the ways in which social change affects (primarily internal) organizational communication "variables." Rather, the discursive practices of and within organizations also influence the larger sociopolitical context (Deetz, 1992), including the direction of social change. This means that organizations do not simply respond communicatively to societal changes that have occurred independent of these organizations' own discursive practices. Rather, organizational discourse contributes largely to the direction and nature of this societal transformation.

Second, to understand organizational discourse in the sociopolitical environment requires consideration of a multitude of diverse perspectives and voices both within and outside the organization. Certainly, organization members and those outside the organization's formal structure hold some common understandings based on their participation within a shared larger culture. Yet these people's experiences and meanings also vary by social location and personal history. The field of organizational communication has barely begun to explore such diversity of human experience. Such analysis is essential, though, to understand organizational discourse within a vastly complex and not necessarily coherent sociopolitical world.

Third, the analysis of sociopolitical issues and their importance for organizational discourse must emphasize politics. Social outcomes, good or bad, are not equally shared, and the preferences of some social interests, both within and outside organizations, are realized while the preferences of others are not. Thus, there will exist sometimes fierce conflict in the face of social change, and organizational discourse will both reflect and contribute to it. Because many of these issues are deeply affecting, they can involve exceptionally high-stakes conflict. To lose can cost dearly, often in the most essential human terms. Not surprisingly, then, politics are integral to the discussion of organizational discourse and sociopolitical environments.

The model presented in Figure 8.1 conceptualizes organizational interaction with sociopolitical environments as basically composed of the ongoing organizational discourses of institutional rhetoric and everyday talk. Organizational communication in the sociopolitical context includes both the externally directed corporate expression of relatively formal collective entities—"institutional rhetoric"—and the more diffuse but just as pervasive ongoing communication of the partially included individual members who people such collectives—"everyday talk." Adequate conceptualization of sociopolitically relevant organizational discourse must include both institutional rhetoric and everyday talk. Analysis of only one of these forms of discourse would significantly distort the representation of organizations' interaction in the sociopolitical context.

The corporate expression of interest advocacy inherent in practices of institutional rhetoric is relatively easy to recognize as sociopolitically relevant organizational discourse. However, the everyday interaction of individuals with multiple organizational affiliations also represents a significant means by which sociopolitically relevant communication across organizational boundaries is accomplished. Weick's (1979) concept of "partial inclusion" suggests why the discourse of individuals must also represent a primary aspect of the model of organizations' sociopolitical interaction. The idea of partial inclusion refers to the multiple, overlapping collective memberships of individuals. One person may simultaneously hold membership in the collective contexts of work organization, church, political organization, and family, for example. In effect, these individuals produce linkages across organizational boundaries in their everyday talk with different individuals from different organizational contexts. To concentrate analysis only on the institutional voice of formal organizations and neglect the everyday interaction of the individuals who make up organizations would consequently leave out a crucial element of any model of organizations and sociopolitical environments.

Institutional Rhetoric

Sociopolitically relevant organizational discourse in the form of institutional rhetoric involves collective expression intended to influence the larger social normative climate, with outcomes beneficial to the collective. Cheney's (1991) analysis of the rhetorical practices of the Roman Catholic Church in the United States exemplifies this form of discourse. Organizations engage in institutional rhetoric regarding social issues because these issues affect them, sometimes quite deeply. Institutional rhetoric promotes alternative interpretations of the meaning and significance of such changes, especially the degree to which they represent social problems and what policies and actions represent appropriate solutions. The primary role of institutional rhetoric in the discursive model of organizations' sociopolitical relations thus emphasizes the ways in which organizations strategically advocate their own perspectives, attempting to influence wider social meanings.

As a form of organizational discourse, institutional rhetoric demonstrates each of the

Sociopolitical Environments and Issues ◆ 275

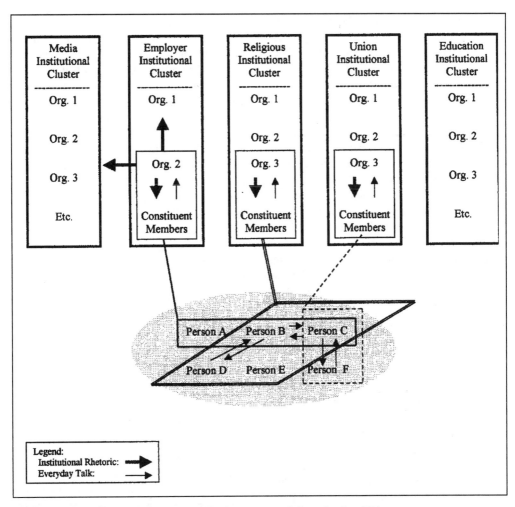

Figure 8.1. A Model of Sociopolitical Environments and Organizational Discourse

basic conceptual assumptions that underlies the discursive model of organizations' sociopolitical relations. Organizations that use institutional rhetoric to advocate their perspectives on sociopolitical issues may feel, and indeed, be deeply affected by, sociopolitical change. But they also influence, with varying degrees of conscious intent, the direction of this change. Certainly, the discursive practices of organizations from varied institutional contexts also reflect a multiplicity of social perspectives about which few common generalizations apply. And finally, the interaction among these various organizational viewpoints is clearly marked by often fierce competition for the sometimes zero-sum resource of societal legitimacy.

Discursive practices of institutional rhetoric are represented by the wide arrows in Figure 8.1. The model incorporates five exemplary institutional clusters—employing organizations, trade unions, media (journalism and popular culture), and educational institutions (primary, secondary, and higher education) and a cluster representing religious organizations—within which any number of specifically identifiable, relatively formal organizations might operate. Other institutional clusters are also possible (e.g., public interest groups, charitable organizations, policy institutions, branches of government).

Because the point of institutional rhetoric in the sociopolitical context is the strategic advocacy of organizational interests, the thick, solid lines represent rhetorical linkages established by the discursive engagement of organizations with other entities within the overall sociopolitical context to promote what are taken as these organizations' sociopolitical interests. Content of these rhetorical relations is infinitely variable, as is the variety of media used to convey its arguments. Depending on the target of its institutional rhetoric, the organization advocating its position on a given topic might employ a wide range of media, for example, employee handbooks, advocacy advertising, or lobbying communication.

To trace all possible linkages within the model would be confusing and, perhaps, incomprehensible, so the representation in Figure 8.1 illustrates as an example some of the discursive links that might be established by the institutional rhetoric of employing organizations. Organization members represent a common audience for sociopolitically relevant institutional rhetoric. In the example of an employing organization expressing its collective interest on a specific sociopolitically relevant topic, employees are (obviously) the organization members that the arguments of institutional rhetoric are designed to reach. Organizations also direct the discourse of institutional rhetoric to other organizations within the same or different institutional clusters to advocate their sociopolitical interests. Thus, the example in Figure 8.1 also includes a plausible, hypothetical institutionally rhetorical linkage from an employer to other organizations in its own cluster as well as the institutional cluster of media.

Everyday Talk

Obviously very different from organizational discourse in the form of institutional rhetoric, organizational discourse as talk focuses on the everyday conversations shared among organization members and between organization members and important other people, such as family members. These discussions affect the subjective and intersubjective understandings characteristic of individuals and the collective. The scholarly literature in the field of organizational communication contains plentiful examples of interpretive theory and research (Putnam & Pacanowsky, 1983) that explore this type of organizational discourse. People talk about sociopolitical issues because often these affect life on an important personal level every single day. As organizational discourse, this talk helps individuals to both define themselves and negotiate relations with others. Thus, the discursive model of organizations and sociopolitical environments emphasizes the ways in which organization members use such talk creatively, to sort out and deal with the complexities of meaning and implications for human action of sociopolitical change.

Like the discourse of institutional rhetoric, organizational discourse as talk illustrates each of the main conceptual aspects of organizational discourse in the sociopolitical context. Social changes can transform the kinds of topics people discuss in organizations, the kinds of people they interact with, the meanings they hold. Yet individuals also influence the emergence of these meanings through their own discursive involvement with other individuals. No single voice monopolizes the everyday talk surrounding issues of sociopolitical transformation. Rather, this conversation represents the various perspectives of a great number of parties variously interested in these changes. Finally, the conversation often becomes an argument as the voices, in their everyday talk, dispute over competing interpretations of the meaning and significance of sociopolitical change.

Though analytically distinct, the sociopolitically relevant discursive practices of everyday organizational talk are, in actuality, embedded within the larger context of institutional rhetoric. Thus, organizational discourse in the form of everyday talk appears along with the discursive practices of institutional rhetoric represented in Figure 8.1. Here the model employs thin arrows to symbolically represent individuals linked through talk to other people, in one or more organizations, in one or more of the institutional clusters contained in the model. The cluster of individuals (Persons A, B, C, etc. contained within the oval shape) below the institutional clusters represent the individuals who collectively comprise separate organizations within those clusters.

Organizational discourse as everyday talk functions primarily as individuals use this discourse to interpret and make sense of consequential sociopolitical change. Thus, in addition to the wide arrows that represent the context of institutional rhetoric within which individuals are embedded, thin solid arrows appearing in Figure 8.1 represent the interpersonal everyday talk that enables individual organization members to interpret the personal and collective meanings of transformation in the larger sociopolitical environment. The content of this talk, like the content of institutional rhetoric, is infinitely variable. The content of individuals' everyday talk about a given sociopolitical issue might involve, for instance, the simple expression of pleasure or frustration or perhaps instrumental talk, useful for problem solving and decision making. Specific patterns of within-and-across-organization conversational linkage, for any given person in any given temporal context, also can assume an infinite variety of forms. One employee's everyday talk about any number of sociopolitical topics might reflect, for example, that person's embeddedness in a social network based on church membership. In turn, the sociopolitically related everyday talk of another employee may occur within a context of that person's active involvement with other people in a civic or political group.

For purposes of clarity, Figure 8.1 illustrates one possible pattern of linkages based on the relations of everyday talk for a person with overlapping organizational identities as employee, trade union member, and church member. In this example, the individual with multiple organizational affiliations discursively spans the boundaries of these identifiably different organizational contexts, through the social practices of ordinary interpersonal interaction.

ORGANIZATIONAL DISCOURSE IN THE CONTEMPORARY SOCIOPOLITICAL ENVIRONMENT

A concern with topics of sociopolitical relevance has become increasingly apparent in recent organizational research, and a discourse-centered conceptualization of organization-environment relations in the sociopolitical context could productively inform much of this work. This section of the chapter applies the discursive model to two of these topics: sexual harassment and family-work conflict.

The number of specific topics that might be selected from the contemporary literature on sociopolitical issues and environments is large and wide ranging, and it would be impossible within the scope of a single chapter to provide an exhaustive survey of all the existing organizational research with sociopolitical relevance. The recent literature on the two topics examined here demonstrates especially clearly researchers' growing recognition of the mutuality of influence and effect between organizations, on the one hand, and the complex and often turbulent transformations taking place in the larger society, on the other. In other words, research on these topics demonstrates researchers' recognition that our society is in transition and organizations must deal with this while, at the same time, these organizations influence the directions such transitions take. But more important to its role exemplifying the discursive approach to organizations' sociopolitical relations, research on the topics of sexual harassment and family-work conflict (directly and indirectly) reflects both types of organizational discourse represented in the discursive model. Thus, these two issues have a special capacity to illustrate well how organizations' interaction within sociopolitical contexts can be more fruitfully understood from a perspective that makes organizational discourse analytically central.

Sexual Harassment

Scholars have recognized the important consequences of sexual harassment at least since Catherine MacKinnon's (1979) influential analysis of the legal and public policy debates centered around this issue. But concern over sexual harassment has grown dramatically since the early 1990s when, during his confirmation hearings, attorney Anita Hill accused Supreme Court nominee Clarence Thomas of sexual harassment (Morrison, 1992; Ragan, 1996; Siegel, 1996). The body of research literature on the topic has now become substantial (Axelrod, 1993; Berryman-Fink, 1993; Braun, 1993; Brown, 1993; Clair, 1993a, 1993b, 1994; Clair, McGoun, & Spirek, 1993; Foegen, 1992; Galvin, 1993; Gutek, Cohen, & Konrad, 1990; Kreps, 1993; Strine, 1992; Taylor & Conrad, 1992; Terpstra & Baker, 1988, 1992; Wells & Kracher, 1993; Witteman, 1993). More specifically, organizational communication researchers have shown more interest in this topic than in most other sociopolitical issues, so the discursive model of organizations' sociopolitical communication processes readily applies to the topic of sexual harassment.

Research on Sexual Harassment: Evidence of Institutional Rhetoric

Organizational discourse as institutional rhetoric involves the strategic collective advocacy of what organizations take to represent their sociopolitical interests. Organizations direct their institutional rhetoric at other organizations, within the same or different institutional clusters, and also toward their own individual members. Examples of institutional rhetoric in the context of sexual harassment include policy statements on harassment contained in company handbooks and training programs, press and popular cultural narratives from people who have experienced harassment, and legal definitions of harassment as articulated in court decisions.

Some existing research on the topic of harassment has specifically investigated organizational communication phenomena, which this chapter would label as institutional rhetoric. This work can be organized into three primary categories: (a) studies that describe organizations' efforts to use institutional rhetoric for positioning themselves, normatively, on the topic of sexual harassment; (b) work that has concerned the institutional rhetoric of media organizations on the topic of sexual harassment; and (c) research that has incorporated institutional rhetoric as an explanatory variable predictive of harassment-relevant organizational outcomes.

The first cluster of research on the topic of sexual harassment has focused on the rhetoric of organizational responses to societal concerns about harassment. These discursive efforts represent institutional rhetoric as they serve to strategically position organizational actors within the context of normative opinion on this controversial topic. Clair's (1993a) study provides an example of research within this cluster (see also Gutek, 1996). Her research examined official communication on the topic of harassment among the Big 10 universities. As institutional rhetoric, this discourse was intended to publicly situate the universities sympathetically within the context of a serious social problem. Ironically, Clair found this institutional rhetoric instead functioned to commodify, bureaucratize, and privatize the practice of harassment within the organizations.

Institutional rhetoric may also strategically situate employers with regard to their employees through policy statements and training programs that concentrate on the topic of harassment (Berryman-Fink, 1993; Blakely, Blakely, & Moorman, 1998; Galvin, 1993; Hulin, Fitzgerald, & Drasgow, 1996). Berryman-Fink describes organization-sponsored workshops and training programs in terms that the discursive model would call institutional rhetoric: collective statements of the normative positions that (a) harassment is not good, and (b) organizations bear some responsibility for reducing it. Berryman-Fink's research suggests that organizations can meet their obligations to discourage the undesirable practice of sexual harassment by promoting androgynous, "gender-flexible" communication among organization members. From a somewhat different perspective, Galvin's (1993) work explores the responsibility of academic organizations to clarify harassing statements and behavior for their faculties. Her research describes the discourse of institutional rhetoric in the sense that individual faculty members are not permitted to individually negotiate what statements and behaviors are considered to reflect sexual harassment. Rather, the institution determines which of these practices constitute harassment and then communicates these definitions to faculty members.

In the discursive model described in this chapter, media organizations represent a significant source of institutional rhetoric on practically any given sociopolitical topic, including sexual harassment. Institutional rhetoric functioning in this sense not only strategically positions media organizations in terms of their stance on a sociopolitical topic such as harassment but also contributes to the larger societal context of conversation and interpretation regarding such questions. Accordingly, a second group of studies has examined the harassment-related messages of mass media organizations. These messages represent institutional rhetoric in two ways. First, they strategically locate media organizations' own normative positions on the topic of harassment. Second, these messages also help to influence shifting interpretations of harassment within the larger normative culture. As an example of research along these lines, Axelrod (1993) studied representations of organizational sexuality in film, focusing on the ways in which institutional rhetoric embedded in films can influence broader societal norms about harassment. Axelrod concluded that film treatments that present harassment as amusing, or as an acceptable means for women to achieve organizational influence, in effect persuade the audiences to adopt these normative positions too. Braun's (1993) case study of an advertising agency's costly response to charges of sexism in its campaigns also provides an example of research that has examined the institutional rhetoric of mass media discourse about sexual harassment. In this study, institutional rhetoric took one form in the offensive content of campaigns developed for agency clients, which seemed to advocate greater tolerance of harassing behaviors. Institutional rhetoric also appeared in the agency's defensive and hostile response to complaints about these campaigns. Scornfully counterattacking its critics rather than listening and thoughtfully responding to them, the agency communicated its normative position on harassment in a misguided use of institutional rhetoric that angered agency critics and cost the agency both clients and income.

A third group of studies has implicitly identified institutional rhetoric as an explanation for the outcomes of harassment-related decision-making processes. For example, Wells and Kracher (1993) consider organizations' moral duty to define *hostile environment* not from an organizational point of view, but from the perspective of its (usually female) targets. These authors argue that if organizations can adopt in their own institutional rhetoric the voice of the women who most frequently experience sexual harassment, they can thereby better accomplish the overriding moral purpose of meeting the needs of those who have been harassed. Terpstra and Baker's (1988, 1992) research also demonstrates how institutional rhetoric may influence decision making in the context of sexual harassment. These studies examined the grounds associated with legal decisions favorable to harassment claimants. In this instance, institutional rhetoric is represented by the courts' articulation of criteria for determining that sexual harassment has occurred. Terpstra and Baker identified some of these criteria, including the severity of the harassing behavior, the presence of witnesses and documents, the notification of employers by harassment targets, and the remedial actions taken by companies in response to internal complaints. Outcomes affected by these criteria are tangible and significant. They include the determination itself that harassment has occurred, as well as decisions regarding the compensation awarded to its targets and the punishment dealt to its perpetrators.

Research on Sexual Harassment: Evidence of Everyday Talk

As the discursive model suggests, sociopolitical organizational discourse in the form of everyday talk is analytically distinct, but actually embedded within a context of institutional rhetoric. Everyday talk does not focus on the advocacy of strategic collective interests. Instead, people use everyday talk in a much more personal way, creatively employing this form of discourse to help sort out and deal with the everyday human complexities that sociopolitical controversy and change imply. Everyday talk occurs among the members of a single organization, and also involves personal relationships that cross organizational boundaries. The private, personal stories of harassment told to friends, family members, therapists, lawyers, support groups, and other potential helpers provide an example of sociopolitical discourse as everyday talk. A very different type of everyday talk about sexual harassment occurred during the Hill-Thomas hearings, when innumerable intraorganizational conversations sparked by the proceedings helped organization members to make sense of this controversial subject.

Research on the topic of sexual harassment has frequently focused on organizational discourse as everyday talk. This literature is represented by two clusters: (a) a group of studies that has examined everyday talk about sexual harassment as it has occurred in the form of personal harassment narratives, and (b) research that has focused on everyday talk in the form of ordinary interpersonal interaction among organization members.

Research analyzing personal narratives of harassment represents one cluster of studies examining everyday talk on the subject of sexual harassment. These narratives represent everyday talk in the sense that they are personal forms of expression, used both to recount and make sense of experiences that might represent sexual harassment. These narratives reflect everyday talk both influenced by the larger discursive context of institutional rhetoric about sexual harassment and also potentially capable of influencing it.

Among the number of studies that have examined sexual harassment from the perspective of personal narrative, Strine (1992) analyzed a series of personal harassment stories from a critical poststructuralist perspective. In this case, the everyday talk contained in her informants' narratives allowed Strine to detect means by which the individual, organizational, and social meanings of harassment are discursively constructed through everyday talk in organizations. In effect, everyday organizational talk privileges harassers' views of the severity and significance of their behavior and preserves a dominant patriarchal organizational order. Taylor and Conrad (1992) analyzed the same collection of harassment narratives. Like Strine, they identified the essentially political ways in which everyday talk about harassment respectively privileges and marginalizes organization members on gender grounds. Taylor and Conrad maintain that everyday talk about harassment systematically favors the interpretations given by perpetrators, usually men, and thereby reinforces existing patterns of male domination in the organizational setting. Brown (1993) used a somewhat different approach to explore the consequences of everyday talk, as personal narrative, for the construction of organizational meanings on the subject of sexual harassment. Based on actual interviews, Brown's "creative narrative" depicted a fictional conversation among female conference attendees. By relating their personal experiences with sexual harassment, these women were able to make sense of such incidents and discover creative means for dealing with them. Finally, Clair's (1993b) research also analyzed personal narrative to explore the role of women's everyday talk that reinforces more pervasive organizational understandings concerning harassment. Participants in Clair's research recounted incidents of harassment. These narrative accounts occasionally showed evidence of resistance by the women. More commonly, though, the narratives reflected the women's use of rhetorical framing devices to make sense of harassment in ways primarily unchallenging to dominant organizational ideology.

A second group of studies has examined interpersonal communication, which, as taken-for-granted, commonplace interaction among members of organizations, represents the discourse of everyday talk. For example, Clair et al. (1993) developed a typology of women's interpersonal responses to harassment. Forms of response in this typology range from the most passive, such as avoidance, to such aggressive responses as direct confrontation. As varieties of interpersonal interaction, these communicated responses to harassment represent the discursive domain of everyday talk. Witteman (1993) analyzed interactional characteristics common to the phenomena of sexual harassment and organizational romance, respectively, as well as the features of interaction that distinguish them. In this sense, Witteman's research explores interpersonal interaction as everyday discourse. Witteman considers such everyday talk as complimentary comments and looks to represent communication behaviors common to both sexual harassment and organizational romance. Analyses showed that nonreciprocated self-disclosure illustrates everyday talk more likely to be interpreted as harassment than as normal relational discourse. Similarly, Solomon and Williams (1997) have distinguished the communication characteristics of harassment as opposed to flirtation behavior. Gutek et al.'s (1990) research also features everyday talk as it influences collective meanings relevant to the topic of sexual harassment. These researchers found that greater sexualization of the workplace produced a higher level of harassing behavior. Significantly for the pur-poses of this chapter, the researchers employed a discursive measure of workplace sexualization, operationalized as the degree of ongoing everyday communication between women and men. More simply put, the greater the level of everyday between-sex talk, the greater the incidence of workplace sexual harassment. Finally, Foegen (1992) also concentrated on interpersonal communication as a reflection of everyday organizational talk about sexual harassment. In Foegen's research, everyday talk emerged in the form of organizational discussions specifically on the topic of sexual harassment. These discussions eventually resulted in greater discomfort and interpersonal conflict in subsequent interactions among organization members.

Interpenetration of Institutional Rhetoric and Everyday Talk

Organizational discourse at the levels of institutional rhetoric and everyday talk each has unique significance. Yet, and more important, these discourses interact with and mutually influence each other. For the sociopolitical example of sexual harassment, such discursive interpenetration might work in the following ways.

Though always subject to contestation and negotiation, the social practices of institutional rhetoric generate a societal context of meaning around sociopolitical questions such as sexual harassment (e.g., Mumby & Clair, 1997). This context represents the rhetorical voices of diverse collective interests with differing views on these issues. For example, positions advocated by institutional rhetoric might center on the very definition of harassment and whether it includes such behaviors as complimenting coworkers' appearance. In this example, social discourse, as institutional rhetoric, establishes what behaviors and communicative practices constitute harassment, whether these definitions represent widely consensual understandings, aggressively contested ones, or something in between. Thus, institutional rhetoric may contribute to the normative understanding that all commentary on the appearance of coworkers is inappropriate and, therefore, represents harassment.

Another example of the institutional rhetoric of sexual harassment might focus on responsibility for it. Assignment of responsibility might label perpetrators as wrongdoers, or on the other hand, just victims of confusion over changing social standards. In this sense, institutional rhetoric contributes to normative understandings about who should get the blame when harassment occurs. Thus, the discourse of institutional rhetoric might help to create a climate of sociopolitical meaning in which behaviors that offend other people are excused. In such a climate, people whose joking focuses on sexual topics or who use diminutive terms in communication with coworkers evade sanction because they "meant no harm."

Within the context of meaning generated through institutional rhetoric, individuals use everyday discourse to comprehend and interpret sociopolitical questions such as sexual harassment. These individuals generate meanings that may be complicit with or oppose certain positions expressed through institutional rhetoric. Two examples illustrate how discursive practices of everyday talk might play out within the contexts of institutional rhetoric about what constitutes harassment and whose responsibility it is.

In the first example, institutional rhetoric establishes a social context for defining what types of behaviors constitute harassment. Embedded in this normative context, discourse as everyday talk reflects and responds to these definitions. Thus, within a discursively influenced normative climate that classifies comments on personal appearance as inappropriate or offensive, a group of female coworkers discussing the supervisor's compliments may interpret these not as innocent pleasantries but instead as sexual harassment.

In the second example, institutional rhetoric establishes sociopolitical expectations regarding the question of responsibility for sexual harassment. Again, sociopolitically relevant organizational discourse in the form of everyday talk takes place within this context of normative meaning. Thus, when an organization's normative atmosphere dictates that responsibility for harassment is based not on the content of a message but on its (harmful) intent, older male employees may interpret their own communication as politeness rather than harassment. These men might accordingly continue to address young female employees using diminutive labels such as "honey" or "missy" or "sweetie." In turn, the women might employ everyday talk to express their objections to these terms.

Clair's (1994) study represents a rare example of research that has explored the intersecting discourses of institutional rhetoric and everyday talk. In this research, the target of a well-publicized harassment incident simulates the discourse of everyday talk in the form of interviews with the researcher, during which the research respondent interprets newspaper accounts—defined by the discursive model as institutional rhetoric—of the incident.

Family-Work Conflict

Ongoing redefinition of American families has come to represent a topic of increasing societal concern. Accordingly, the interest of organizational researchers in the subject of family-work conflict has also grown (Adams, 1993; Bandow, 1991; Covin & Brush, 1993; Crosby, 1991; Falkenberg & Monachello, 1990; Frone, Russell, & Cooper, 1992; Goodstein, 1994; Karambayya & Reilly, 1992; Lilly, Pitt-Catsouphes, & Googins, 1997; Lobel, 1991; Lobel & St. Clair, 1992; Mele, 1989; Miller, Stead, & Pereira, 1991; Pitt-Catsouphes & Googins, 1999; Schneer & Reitman, 1993; Williams & Alliger, 1994). Communication research specifically has not shown as much interest in this topic as in the question of sexual harassment. Nevertheless, the existing research on family-work conflict indirectly reflects concern with discursive variables and processes.

Research on Family-Work Conflict: Evidence of Institutional Rhetoric

Institutional rhetoric reflects the perspective of organizations, advocating their interests within the larger sociopolitical environment. One example of institutional rhetoric on the topic of family-work conflict might involve the promotion by organizations of their family-oriented benefits. Organizations' public arguments addressing legislation relevant to workers with families represent another illustration of the institutional rhetoric of family and work.

The literature on family-work conflict demonstrates extensive evidence of a concern with organizational features that resemble institutional rhetoric. This literature has included research concentrating on three primary themes: (a) specific arguments for and against progressive family and work policies, as these have been articulated through institutional rhetoric; (b) the identification of institutional rhetoric as a primary explanatory variable predicting organizations' responsiveness to their employees' family-related needs and expectations; and (c) the consequences, for individuals and families, of the emergent "mommy-track" and "daddy-track" phenomena, widely recognized contemporary terms largely constructed through the discursive processes of institutional rhetoric.

The public articulation of organizations' support of and opposition to progressive family and work policies reflects an important expression of institutional rhetoric that scholars have explored. Several investigators have examined the arguments used in the institutional rhetoric of the advocates of these progressive programs. In one such essay, Adams (1993) articulates common arguments made by organizations that employ institutional rhetoric strategically to position themselves as advocates for families. One such argument suggests that the morale benefits of these policies outweigh their costs. Another makes the point that supporting families is crucial to the long-term well-being of the whole society, business organizations included. Similarly, Mele (1989) analyzed the normative argument, expressed through institutional rhetoric, that organizations bear an ethical obligation to support the marital and parental responsibilities of their employees.

Scholars have also explored the logic evident in the institutional rhetoric of organizations that oppose progressive family-and-work policies. Adams (1993) identifies several of these arguments, which suggest that progressive family policies violate employee privacy, create perceptions of unfairness among employees (e.g., Young, 1999), unreasonably raise employee expectations, and pose excessive costs of regulatory compliance and liability. Bandow (1991) also examined the logic of opposition to progressive family policies as this has been articulated through institutional rhetoric. One such discursive theme maintains that more generous family benefits promote an economically detrimental ethic of entitlement among employees. Bandow also describes the rhetorically expressed logic that progressive family policies actually discriminate against married women and women with families, who earn less due to their family commitments.

Institutional rhetoric explains the responsiveness of organizations to their employees' family-related needs in a second category of research on the institutional rhetoric of family-work conflict. Consistent with this framework, Goodstein (1994) found that individual organizations respond strategically to external institutional pressures for their greater involvement in work and family issues (Witkowski, 1999), as these are communicated through institutional rhetoric. Organizations that experience more outside pressure to accommodate workers' family obligations do so. Organizations not facing such rhetorically expressed external expectations do little to assist with their employees' family obligations.

Institutional rhetoric has contributed to the discursive construction of meaning through its creation of such terms as the *mommy track* and its more contemporary parallel, the *daddy track*. These terms refer to the career patterns of women and men, respectively, who voluntarily choose to give their families priority over their work. Institutional rhetoric in this case has been articulated most obviously by media organizations, which have speculated on the practical consequences of these terms for the employees described by them. Findings from research have produced inconsistent conclusions about these effects. On the one hand, Lobel and St. Clair (1992) found that mommy-track and daddy-track workers with significant family commitments jeopardize their own compensation and opportunities for advancement. On the other hand, Schneer and Reitman (1993) discovered no apparent negative consequences for these workers, finding the earnings of men and women from "nontraditional" mommy-track and daddy-track families similar to those of their counterparts in "traditional" ones.

Research on Family-Work Conflict: Evidence of Everyday Talk

In addition to institutional rhetoric, the discursive model includes sociopolitically relevant organizational discourse in the form of everyday talk. Researchers of family-work conflict have not yet investigated questions that might be translated directly into the terminology of the discursive model. But these researchers have explored topics that indirectly suggest a potentially important explanatory role for sociopolitically relevant organizational discourse in the form of everyday talk. This literature includes three clusters: (a) studies that have described differing perceptions regarding family-work conflict among members of various organizational classes, which might reflect their different patterns of everyday talk; (b) research that has examined the significance of family-work conflict for patterns of everyday interaction among family members; and (c) research that has explored the constructive uses of everyday talk as people

adapt creatively to the tensions sometimes produced when family and work demands collide.

A first group of studies has investigated differing perceptions regarding the nature and extent of family-work tension among various organizational subgroups. This research has not concentrated directly on discourse, or indeed, on any type of communication at all. Yet although these studies simply group respondents according to demographic or organizational role, the discursive model would suggest that these different categories actually imply diverse discursive experience, which could explain different views of family-work conflict. In other words, the overall everyday discursive pattern for workers with responsibility for children will naturally include some people and topics that childless workers would not ordinarily discuss. In turn, these variant discursive patterns could result in differing interpretations of the significance of family-work conflict. For example, Covin and Brush (1993) found significant differences between students and human resource professionals in their perceptions of issues such as support for child care, parental responsibility, work commitment, and the impact of children on achievement motivation. Covin and Brush did not directly examine the communication patterns of their respondents. Nevertheless, the discursive model would propose that the typically dissimilar everyday discursive experience of these two groups merits investigation as a factor influencing their diverse perceptions of family-work conflict. Falkenberg and Monachello (1990) proposed the presence of subgroups among dual-earner households, based on such factors as the spouses' individual reasons for working, the responsibilities assumed by spouses in the home, and the spouses' sex, which significantly affect the nature of problems experienced by families. The discursive model suggests that membership in these subgroups implies different patterns of everyday talk. These diverse discursive patterns in turn affect the variety of family and work problems that Falkenberg and Monachello observed. A final study (Miller et al., 1991) within this cluster of research explored different perceptions of top managers and employees, respectively, concerning employees' dependent care obligations. These researchers found two significant perceptual divergences between members of these two organizational subgroups. First, while employees considered family obligations to affect job performance, top managers did not. Second, while employees considered employers to have some responsibility to assist their employees in their family care obligations, top managers did not. Again, the discursive model would explore these differences in terms of the varied discursive experiences of everyday talk that underlie them.

A discourse-based strategy would also reinterpret a second group of recent studies that has focused on consequences of family-work conflict outside the workplace. The discourse-based model incorporates everyday talk across organizational boundaries. Accordingly, research in this group suggests that everyday talk at home, as well as everyday talk at work, plays an important role in the social dynamics of family-work conflict. One study within this cluster of research (Karambayya & Reilly, 1992) discovered that women's role repertoire has expanded disproportionately compared with men's as a result of family-work conflicts. Further, the study found that women restructure their time more often than men do to meet family commitments. In discursive terms, these findings suggest that family-work conflict may have created a more expansive pattern of women's everyday talk in comparison to men's because women's lives appear still to demand greater social role flexibility than do men's. In contrast, Williams and Alliger (1994) found the discursive consequences of family-work conflict similar for women and men. However, their research reports pervasive feelings of tension and negative "mood spillover" between family and work, and vice versa, regardless of sex. A discursive perspective would logically extend the examination of these feelings by concentrating on the ways in which women's and men's everyday talk both reflects and contributes to it. Everyday talk about family-work conflict also affected both men and women in Frone et al.'s (1992) study.

Both male and female respondents reported greater intrusion of work-related demands into family life than of family-related obligations into work. The discursive implications of such findings might indicate that the nature of everyday talk at home will be more disrupted when work-related expectations increase. By comparison, patterns of everyday talk at work might be predictably less affected by family demands.

A final development in research on families and work has relevance in the context of the discursive perspective. This work has begun to explore the constructive outcomes people experience as they use everyday talk to help themselves adapt to the tensions of competition between these two contexts. Crosby (1991), a primary exemplar of research within this group, suggests that people who juggle work and family responsibilities may experience stress and difficulty but also the immense satisfaction of a more complex and satisfying, competent personal identity. Investigation of the creative uses of everyday talk both to accomplish and reveal personally productive outcomes represents a relevant application of the discursive model. Another study, by Karambayya and Reilly (1992), surveyed both partners in a set of dual-earner couples. Despite pressures of role expansion and work restructuring, couples with greater family involvement reported higher marital satisfaction and lower stress. In discursive terms, these findings may imply the positive potential of a more complex discursive environment that includes everyday talk in both work and family contexts. Finally, Lobel (1991) focused on individuals' relative investment in work and family roles. Lobel maintained that the typical assumption of negative role conflict obscures the more significant capacity of individuals to enact a self-identity in which work and family roles both represent important elements. Like those of other researchers reviewed in this section, Lobel's perspective also has discursive implications. In this instance, everyday talk reflects not an inevitable tension between work and family. Rather, everyday talk serves as the constructive means by which individuals find personal and social meaning as they discursively negotiate their family and work involvement.

Interpenetration of Institutional Rhetoric and Everyday Talk

Organizational discourse on the issue of family-work conflict demonstrates the discursive interpenetration of institutional rhetoric and everyday talk. Some examples illustrate how these processes of mutual influence might occur.

As for other sociopolitical issues, institutional rhetoric on the topic of family-work conflict serves to construct a societal context of meaning, composed of a variety of often competing rhetorical positions. For example, in the case of family-work conflict, the positions advocated by institutional rhetoric might focus on fairness in the development of solutions to the tension of competing family and work obligations. One such rhetorical view of fairness might suggest that organizations should more generously accommodate their employees' family commitments to compensate them for the societally significant responsibilities of childrearing and caretaking of the elderly. Yet, while such a normative inclination might prevail at any given time, the discourse of institutional rhetoric will also articulate competing logics of fairness as well. Such an alternative norm for fairness might argue, for example, that individuals who choose commitments to both work and family should take personal responsibility for the resulting extra strain on personal resources. In an alternative normative view, fairness might demand equality of treatment among employees regardless of differences in their personal lives.

The institutional rhetoric of family-work conflict might center on another normative question, the welfare of children. One position on this issue might argue that young children are permanently damaged when their mothers work outside the home. A competing view might emphasize the cognitive, emotional, and social benefits of a quality day care experience. Again, the discursive model predicts that one of these positions, expressed as insti-

tutional rhetoric, may dominate sociopolitical understanding at some times. At others, there may exist little consensus, and perhaps great social division, over which argument is "right."

Everyday discourse concerning the question of family-work conflict occurs within this larger societal context of meaning constructed largely through institutional rhetoric. In other words, institutional rhetoric establishes the positions in the larger sociopolitical discussion that various interests hold. Individuals variously attend to the arguments advanced through these rhetorical expressions, discuss them, interpret their significance, and act and speak in ways that either sustain or contradict certain positions articulated by this institutional rhetoric.

Examples suggest possible ways in which the discourse of everyday talk interacts with institutional rhetoric on the topic of family-work conflict, specifically the rhetoric that addresses questions of fairness and the welfare of children. In the first example, institutional rhetoric sets up the normative context for defining fairness relative to the sociopolitical issue of family-work conflict. In this example, a hypothetically dominant, rhetorically articulated normative perspective suggests that fairness is best served when employers make allowances for their employees' family obligations. Within this normative environment occur the discursive processes of everyday talk. Such everyday talk might challenge rather than accept norm-based accommodation of employees' family commitments. Thus, a group of single, childless employees may complain of the unfairness inherent when employees with families enjoy what others see as special, non-merit-based consideration. In the second example, institutional rhetoric about family-work conflict focused on the welfare of children. This discourse might argue that good day care programs actively benefit children. Within this rhetorically generated discursive field, individuals' everyday talk communicates a parallel concern with the well-being of children. Thus, parents who can visit their children at an on-site corporate day care facility enjoy a still rare (but increasingly common) form of everyday talk in their interaction with their children during the workday. More confident of their children's well-being through this proximity, the parents may also find everyday talk with their coworkers more satisfying and productive.

SUMMARY

This chapter dealt with a topic relatively novel in organizational communication analysis, focusing on the interactions of organizations in the context of their sociopolitical environments. The thinking presented here was inspired by Weick's notion of the "enacted environment" and Taylor's conceptualization of organizational "conversation" within an environmental context. Based on these ideas, the chapter proposed a model of organizational communication with sociopolitical environments in terms of the intersecting organizational discourses of institutional rhetoric and everyday talk. The chapter illustrated this model using the contemporary sociopolitical issues of sexual harassment and family-work conflict.

A concern with sociopolitical questions equally involves both the consequences of sociopolitical transformation for organizations and the implications of organizational practices for the larger culture. Such a focus is far from established within the field of organizational communication. But its continued development offers many exciting possibilities for organizational communication analysts compelled by the purpose of better understanding the larger societal significance of organizational discourse.

NOTE

1. In recent years, researchers have shown demonstrable enthusiasm for the three primary theoretical approaches to organization-environment relations, including studies based on *population ecology* (Barnett, 1990; Boeker, 1991, 1997; Castrogiovanni, 1991; Gimeno, Folta, Cooper, & Woo, 1997; Greve, 1999; Swaminathan & Delacroix, 1991; Tucker, Singh, & Meinhard, 1990;

Wholey & Sanchez, 1991), *resource dependence* (Baker, 1990; Boeker & Goodstein, 1991; Davis, 1991; Galaskiewicz & Wasserman, 1989; Goodstein & Boeker, 1991; Kraatz, 1998; Lang & Lockhart, 1990; Mizruchi, 1989, 1992; Mizruchi & Galaskiewicz, 1993; Mizruchi & Stearns, 1988; Oliver, 1991; Perrucci & Lewis, 1989; Singh & Harianto, 1989; Wade, O'Reilly, & Chandratat, 1990); and *institutional* (Abrahamson & Fairchild, 1999; Abrahamson & Rosenkopf, 1993; Baum & Oliver, 1991; D'Annuo, Sutton, & Price, 1991; DiMaggio, 1988; DiMaggio & Powell, 1983; Elsbach & Sutton, 1992; Finet, 1993, 1994a, 1994b; Gioia, Schultz, & Corley, 2000; Judge & Zeithaml, 1992; Leblebici, Salancik, & Copay, 1991; Mezias, 1990; Oliver, 1991; Tucker et al., 1990) perspectives.

REFERENCES

Abrahamson, E., & Fairchild, G. (1999). Management fashion: Lifecycles, triggers, and collective learning processes. *Administrative Science Quarterly, 44,* 708-740.

Abrahamson, E., & Rosenkopf, L. (1993). Institutional and competitive bandwagons: Using mathematical modeling as a tool to explore innovation diffusion. *Academy of Management Review, 18,* 487-517.

Adams, J. (1993). Juggling job and family. *Vital Speeches of the Day, 60,* 125-128.

Aldrich, H. (1979). *Organizations and environments.* Englewood Cliffs, NJ: Prentice Hall.

Axelrod, J. (1993). Sexual harassment in the movies and its effect on the audience. In G. Kreps (Ed.), *Sexual harassment: Communication implications* (pp. 107-117). Cresskill, NJ: Hampton.

Baker, W. (1990). Market networks and corporate behavior. *American Journal of Sociology, 96,* 589-625.

Bandow, D. (1991). Should Congress play with family leave? *Business and Society Review, 77,* 41-45.

Barnett, W. (1990). The organizational ecology of a technological system. *Administrative Science Quarterly, 35,* 31-60.

Baum, J., & Oliver, C. (1991). Institutional linkages and organizational mortality. *Administrative Science Quarterly, 36,* 187-218.

Berryman-Fink, C. (1993). Preventing sexual harassment through male-female communication training. In G. Kreps (Ed.), *Sexual harassment: Communication implications* (pp. 267-280). Cresskill, NJ: Hampton.

Blakely, G. L., Blakely, E. H., & Moorman, R. H. (1998). The effects of training on perceptions of sexual harassment allegations. *Journal of Applied Social Psychology, 8*(1), 71-83.

Boeker, W. (1991). Organizational strategy: An ecological perspective. *Academy of Management Journal, 34,* 613-635.

Boeker, W. (1997). Strategic change: The influence of managerial characteristics and organizational growth. *Academy of Management Journal, 40,* 152-170.

Boeker, W., & Goodstein, J. (1991). Organizational performance and adaptation: Effects of environment and performance on changes in board composition. *Academy of Management Journal, 34,* 805-826.

Boyd, B., Dess, G., & Rasheed, A. (1993). Divergence between archival and perceptual measures of the environment: Causes and consequences. *Academy of Management Review, 18,* 204-226.

Braun, M. (1993). Fallongate: The ad agency, the feminist, and the $10 million case of sexual harassment. In G. Kreps (Ed.), *Sexual harassment: Communication implications* (pp. 90-106). Cresskill, NJ: Hampton.

Brown, M. H. (1993). Sex and the workplace: "Watch your behind or they'll watch it for you." In G. Kreps (Ed.), *Sexual harassment: Communication implications* (pp. 118-130). Cresskill, NJ: Hampton.

Burns, T., & Stalker, G. (1961). *The management of innovation.* London: Tavistock.

Castrogiovanni, G. (1991). Environmental munificence: A theoretical assessment. *Academy of Management Review, 16,* 542-565.

Cheney, G. (1991). *Rhetoric in an organizational society: Managing multiple identities.* Columbia: University of South Carolina Press.

Clair, R. (1993a). The bureaucratization, commodification, and privatization of sexual harassment through institutional discourses: A study of the Big 10 universities. *Management Communication Quarterly, 7,* 123-157.

Clair, R. (1993b). The use of framing devices to sequester organizational narratives: Hegemony and harassment. *Communication Monographs, 60,* 113-136.

Clair, R. (1994). Resistance and oppression as a self-contained opposite: An organizational communication analysis of one man's story of sexual harassment. *Western Journal of Communication, 58,* 235-262.

Clair, R., McGoun, M., & Spirek, M. (1993). Sexual harassment responses of working women: An assessment of current communication-oriented typologies and perceived effectiveness and response. In G. Kreps (Ed.), *Sexual harassment: Communication implications* (pp. 209-233). Cresskill, NJ: Hampton.

Covin, T., & Brush, C. (1993). A comparison of student and human resource professional attitudes toward work and family issues. *Group & Organization Management, 18,* 29-49.

Crosby, F. (1991). *Juggling: The unexpected advantages of balancing career and home for women and their families.* New York: Free Press.

D'Aunno, T., Sutton, R., & Price, R. (1991). Isomorphism and external support in conflicting institutional environments: A study of drug abuse treatment units. *Academy of Management Journal, 34,* 636-661.

Davis, G. (1991). Agents without principles? The spread of the poison pill through the intercorporate network. *Administrative Science Quarterly, 36,* 583-613.

Deetz, S. (1992). *Democracy in an age of corporate colonization.* Albany: State University of New York Press.

DiMaggio, P. (1988). Interest and agency in institutional theory. In L. Zucker (Ed.), *Institutional patterns and organizations: Culture and environment* (pp. 3-21). Cambridge, MA: Ballinger.

DiMaggio, P., & Powell, W. (1983). The iron cage revisited: Institutional isomorphism and collective rationality in organizational fields. *American Sociological Review, 48,* 147-160.

Elsbach, K., & Sutton, R. (1992). Acquiring organizational legitimacy through illegitimate actions: A marriage of institutional and impression management theories. *Academy of Management Journal, 35,* 699-738.

Emery, F., & Trist, E. (1965). The causal texture of organizational environments. *Human Relations, 18,* 21-32.

Euske, N. A., & Roberts, K. H. (1987). Evolving perspectives in organization theory: Communication implications. In F. M. Jablin, L. L. Putnam, K. H. Roberts, & L. W. Porter (Eds.), *Handbook of organizational communication: An interdisciplinary perspective* (pp. 41-69). Newbury Park, CA: Sage.

Falkenberg, L., & Monachello, M. (1990). Dual-career and dual-income families: Do they have different needs? *Journal of Business Ethics, 9,* 339-351.

Finet, D. (1993). Effects of boundary spanning communication on the sociopolitical delegitimation of an organization. *Management Communication Quarterly, 7,* 36-66.

Finet, D. (1994a). Interest advocacy and the transformation in organizational communication. In B. Kovacic (Ed.), *New approaches to organizational communication* (pp. 169-190). Albany: State University of New York Press.

Finet, D. (1994b). Sociopolitical consequences of organizational expression. *Journal of Communication, 44*(4), 114-131.

Foegen, J. (1992). The double jeopardy of sexual harassment. *Business and Society Review, 82,* 31-35.

Frone, M., Russell, M., & Cooper, M. (1992). Prevalence of work-family conflict: Are work and family boundaries asymmetrically permeable? *Journal of Organizational Behavior, 13,* 723-729.

Galaskiewicz, J., & Wasserman, S. (1989). Mimetic processes within an interorganizational field: An empirical test. *Administrative Science Quarterly, 34,* 454-479.

Galvin, K. (1993). Preventing the problem: Preparing faculty members for the issues of sexual harassment. In G. Kreps (Ed.), *Sexual harassment: Communica-*

tion implications (pp. 257-266). Cresskill, NJ: Hampton.

Gimeno, J., Folta, T., Cooper, A., & Woo, C. (1997). Survival of the fittest? Entrepreneurial human capital and the persistence of underperforming firms. *Administrative Science Quarterly, 42,* 750-783.

Gioia, D. A., Schultz, M., & Corley, K. G. (2000). Organizational identity, image, and adaptive instability. *Academy of Management Review, 25,* 63-81.

Goodstein, J. (1994). Institutional pressures and strategic responsiveness: Employer involvement in work-family issues. *Academy of Management Journal, 37,* 350-382.

Goodstein, J., & Boeker, W. (1991). Turbulence at the top: A new perspective on governance structure changes and strategic change. *Academy of Management Journal, 34,* 306-330.

Greve, H. R. (1999). The effect of core change on performance inertia and regression toward the mean. *Administrative Science Quarterly, 44,* 590-614.

Gutek, B. (1996). Sexual harassment at work: When an organization fails to respond. In M. Stockdale (Ed.), *Sexual harassment in the workplace: Perspectives, frontiers, and response strategies* (pp. 272-290). Thousand Oaks, CA: Sage.

Gutek, B., Cohen, A., & Konrad, A. (1990). Predicting social-sexual behavior at work: A contact hypothesis. *Academy of Management Journal, 33,* 560-577.

Hannan, M., & Carroll, G. (1992). *Dynamics of organizational populations: Density, legitimation and competition.* New York: Oxford University Press.

Hannan, M., & Freeman, J. (1977). The population ecology of organizations. *American Journal of Sociology, 82,* 929-964.

Hulin, C. L., Fitzgerald, L. F., & Drasgow, F. (1996). Organizational influences on sexual harassment. In M. Stockdale (Ed.), *Sexual harassment in the workplace: Perspectives, frontiers, and response strategies* (pp. 127-150). Thousand Oaks, CA: Sage.

Judge, W., & Zeithaml, C. (1992). Institutional and strategic choice perspectives on board involvement in the strategic decision process. *Academy of Management Journal, 35,* 766-794.

Karambayya, R., & Reilly, A. (1992). Dual earner couples: Attitudes and actions in restructuring work for family. *Journal of Organizational Behavior, 13,* 585-601.

Kraatz, M. S. (1998). Learning by association? Interorganizational networks and adaptation to environmental change. *Academy of Management Journal, 41,* 621-643.

Kreps, G. (Ed.). (1993). *Sexual harassment: Communication implications.* Cresskill, NJ: Hampton.

Lang, J., & Lockhart, D. (1990). Increased environmental uncertainty and changes in board linkage patterns. *Academy of Management Journal, 33,* 106-128.

Laumann, E., Marsden, P., & Prensky, D. (1983). The boundary specification problem in network analysis. In R. Burt & M. Minor (Eds.), *Applied network analysis: A methodological introduction* (pp. 18-34). Beverly Hills, CA: Sage.

Lawrence, P., & Lorsch, J. (1967). Differentiation and integration in complex organizations. *Administrative Science Quarterly, 12,* 1-47.

Leblebici, H., Salancik, G., & Copay, A. (1991). Institutional change and the transformation of interorganizational fields: An organizational history of the U.S. radio broadcasting industry. *Administrative Science Quarterly, 36,* 333-363.

Lilly, T. A., Pitt-Catsouphes, M., & Googins, B. (1997). *Work-family research: An annotated bibliography.* Westport, CT: Greenwood.

Lobel, S. (1991). Allocation of investment in work and family roles: Alternative theories and implications for research. *Academy of Management Review, 16,* 507-521.

Lobel, S., & St. Clair, L. (1992). Effect of family responsibilities, gender, and career identity salience on performance outcomes. *Academy of Management Journal, 35,* 1057-1069.

MacKinnon, C. (1979). *Sexual harassment of working women: A case of sex discrimination.* New Haven, CT: Yale University Press.

Mele, D. (1989). Organization of work in the company and family rights of employees. *Journal of Business Ethics, 8,* 647-655.

Meyer, J., & Rowan, B. (1977). Institutionalized organizations: Formal structure as myth and ceremony. *American Journal of Sociology, 83,* 340-363.

Meyer, J., & Scott, W. (1983). *Organizational environments: Ritual and rationality.* Beverly Hills, CA: Sage.

Mezias, S. (1990). An institutional model of organizational practice: Financial reporting at the *Fortune* 500. *Administrative Science Quarterly, 35,* 431-457.

Miller, J., Stead, B., & Pereira, A. (1991). Dependent care and the workplace: An analysis of management and employee perceptions. *Journal of Business Ethics, 10,* 863-869.

Mizruchi, M. (1989). Similarity of political behavior among large American corporations. *American Journal of Sociology, 95,* 401-424.

Mizruchi, M. (1992). *The structure of corporate political action: Interfirm relations and their consequences.* Cambridge, MA: Harvard University Press.

Mizruchi, M., & Galaskiewicz, J. (1993). Networks of interorganizational relations. *Sociological Methods & Research, 22,* 46-70.

Mizruchi, M., & Stearns, L. (1988). A longitudinal study of the formation of interlocking directorates. *Administrative Science Quarterly, 33,* 194-210.

Morrison, T. (1992). *Race-ing justice, en-gendering power: Essays on Anita Hill, Clarence Thomas, and the construction of social reality.* New York: Pantheon.

Mumby, D. K., & Clair, R. P. (1997). Organizational discourse. In T. A. van Dijk (Ed.), *Discourse as social interaction* (pp. 181-206). London: Sage.

Oliver, C. (1991). Strategic responses to institutional processes. *Academy of Management Review, 16,* 145-179.

Perrucci, R., & Lewis, B. (1989). Interorganizational relations and community influence structure: A replication and extension. *Sociological Quarterly, 30,* 205-223.

Pfeffer, J., & Salancik, G. (1978). *The external control of organizations: A resource dependence perspective.* New York: Harper & Row.

Pitt-Catsouphes, M., & Googins, B. K. (1999). Preface. *Annals of the American Academy of Political and Social Science, 562,* 8-15.

Powell, W., & DiMaggio, P. (1991). *The new institutionalism in organizational analysis.* Chicago: University of Chicago Press.

Putnam, L. L., & Pacanowsky, M. E. (Eds.). (1983). *Communication and organizations: An interpretive approach.* Beverly Hills, CA: Sage.

Ragan, S. (1996). *The lynching of language: Gender, politics, and power in the Hill-Thomas hearings.* Urbana: University of Illinois Press.

Schneer, J., & Reitman, F. (1993). Effects of alternate family structures on managerial career paths. *Academy of Management Journal, 36,* 830-843.

Scott, R. (1987). The adolescence of institutional theory. *Administrative Science Quarterly, 32,* 413-511.

Siegel, P. (1996). *Outsiders looking in: A communication perspective on the Hill/Thomas hearings.* Cresskill, NJ: Hampton.

Singh, H., & Harianto, F. (1989). Management-board relationships, takeover risk, and the adoption of golden parachutes. *Academy of Management Journal, 32,* 7-24.

Solomon, D. H., & Williams, M. L. M. (1997). Perceptions of social-sexual communication at work: The effects of message, situation, and observer characteristics on judgments of sexual harassment. *Journal of Applied Communication Research, 25,* 196-216.

Strine, M. (1992). Understanding "how things work": Sexual harassment and academic culture. *Journal of Applied Communication Research, 20,* 391-400.

Swaminathan, A., & Delacroix, J. (1991). Differentiation within an organizational population: Additional evidence from the wine industry. *Academy of Management Journal, 34,* 679-692.

Taylor, B., & Conrad, C. (1992). Narratives of sexual harassment: Organizational dimensions. *Journal of Applied Communication Research, 20,* 401-418.

Taylor, J. (1995). Shifting from a heteronomous to an autonomous worldview of organizational communication: Communication theory on the cusp. *Communication Theory, 5,* 1-35.

Terpstra, D., & Baker, D. (1988). Outcomes of sexual harassment charges. *Academy of Management Journal, 31,* 185-194.

Terpstra, D., & Baker, D. (1992). Outcomes of federal court decision on sexual harassment. *Academy of Management Journal, 35,* 181-190.

Thompson, J. (1967). *Organizations in action.* New York: McGraw-Hill.

Tucker, D., Singh, J., & Meinhard, A. (1990). Organizational form, population dynamics, and institutional change: The founding patterns of voluntary organizations. *Academy of Management Journal, 33,* 151-178.

Wade, J., O'Reilly, C., & Chandratat, I. (1990). Golden parachutes: CEOs and the exercise of social influence. *Administrative Science Quarterly, 35,* 587-603.

Weick, K. E. (1979). *The social psychology of organizing* (2nd ed.). Reading, MA: Addison-Wesley.

Wells, D., & Kracher, B. (1993). Justice, sexual harassment, and the reasonable victim standard. *Journal of Business Ethics, 12,* 423-431.

Wholey, D., & Sanchez, S. (1991). The effects of regulatory tools on organizational populations. *Academy of Management Review, 16,* 743-767.

Williams, K., & Alliger, G. (1994). Role stressors, mood spillover, and perceptions of work-family conflict in employed parents. *Academy of Management Journal, 37,* 837-868.

Witkowski, K. (1999). Becoming family-friendly: Work-family program innovation among the largest U.S. corporations. *Research in the Sociology of Work, 7,* 203-232.

Witteman, H. (1993). The interface between sexual harassment and organizational romance. In G. Kreps (Ed.), *Sexual harassment: Communication implications* (pp. 27-62). Cresskill, NJ: Hampton.

Young, M. (1999). Work-family backlash: Begging the question, what's fair? *Annals of the American Academy of Political and Social Science, 562,* 32-46.

Zucker, L. (Ed.). (1988). *Institutional patterns and organizations: Culture and environment.* Cambridge, MA: Ballinger.

9

Organizational Culture

ERIC M. EISENBERG
University of South Florida

PATRICIA RILEY
University of Southern California

In the latter part of the 20th century, numerous scholars of organizational communication became entranced with the idea that understanding companies, churches, universities, government agencies, student clubs, or indeed any form of institution or organization could be enhanced through a cultural analysis or critique. The speed with which "organizational culture" emerged as a significant lens for communication scholars and other academics to examine or otherwise engage with organizations and institutions was astounding. The now ubiquitous nature of organizational culture as an academic concept likely began with its metaphorical success—it produced compelling narratives and insights that resonated with researchers who had previously lived in a world bounded by instruments, scales, networks, and central tendencies. The rather startling shift in organizational communication discourse and practice into this new arena of ethnographies, performances, tales, and texts will be examined in this chapter.

What may be most intriguing about the organizational culture concept, however, was the rapidity with which it became part of the folk taxa of everyday life. As the topic spread through the business press and everyday con-

AUTHORS' NOTE: We would like to thank Linda Putnam, Fred Jablin, Joanne Martin, and Nick Trujillo for their helpful comments on earlier drafts of this chapter.

versations, organizational discourse was soon peppered with such statements as "The culture here won't allow us to . . . " or "Our culture is very intense—we work hard and play harder." In our highly mediated and reflexive society, researchers and scholars often play a major role in the production and reproduction of ideas and practices that dramatically and recursively change the landscape of our existence (obvious examples would be communication campaigns designed to change dietary, smoking, or exercise patterns). Organizational culture was one of those interesting topics that quickly generated changes in both the community of scholars and the communities being studied. This chapter is thus an examination of organizational culture as well as the communication scholars who have been, and likely will continue to be, a part of one of the more visceral and enticing areas of organization studies.

This chapter differs from other reviews of organizational culture by setting forth a distinctively communicative view of the concept. It begins with a short "history" of organizational culture as a metaphor and its background in organizational communication. Next, we describe the basic assumptions that guide this communicative view of culture, and finally we review the significant contributions to the organizational culture literature. A subsequent section on future research is not only a list of what needs to be done but also a call for research that can continue to inform, illuminate, and excite organizational scholars.

CONTEXTUALIZING THE ORGANIZATIONAL CULTURE METAPHOR

It is critical to begin this story with the premise that the culture metaphor itself displays our biases: a concern about relations to others, a need to understand the contexts of communication, and a desire to identify fairly stable or at least recognizable categories of institutional and organizational habits and practices. Put differently, the organizational culture concept, as it is typically invoked, is itself a kind of cultural artifact that speaks loudly about our need for closure and our discomfort with ambiguity. There is little consensus on a definition of culture because the concept is so rich—welcoming newcomers, alternative angles, and varied connotations. Like many other *grande idées* of our time (e.g., leadership, economics, communication), the beauty of the culture metaphor lies more in its heuristic value than in any determinant authority.

Any attempt to create a "history" of a metaphor is problematic—especially a concise one. Clearly, not all perspectives can be covered, or even known, and ultimately the positions and ideas that are included take on privileged status. While the issues surrounding the emergence of organizational culture are certainly more complicated than portrayed here, newcomers to this area of study might find a generally linear, broad-strokes description of the culture conversation beneficial.

The origin of the term *organizational culture* is unknown, but the notion that factories, schools, and other institutions have cultures has existed for at least a half century (e.g., Jaques, 1951). In the 1960s, it was not unusual to describe culture as the best way to get a handle on organizational development. Bennis (1969) explained that organizational culture was of the utmost importance because "the only viable way to change organizations is to change their 'culture,' that is, to change the systems within which people work and live" (p. v). By the next decade, the term *culture* had become increasingly commonplace in the organizational development literature as both work groups and organizations were viewed as having cultures (e.g., Katz & Kahn, 1978). For example, French and Bell (1973) defined organizational development as "a long range effort to improve an organization's problem-solving and renewal processes, particularly through a more effective and collaborative management of organization culture

—with special emphasis on the culture of formal work teams" (p. 15).

Other organization theorists soon began using the concept, if not always using the term: For example, Pondy and Mitroff (1979) argued that a cultural metaphor should replace the systems metaphor in organization theory; Weick's influential book *The Social Psychology of Organizing* (1979) attempted to bridge the gap between systems theory and sensemaking by identifying systems of interpretation (i.e., cause maps); and Pettigrew (1979) used symbols, ritual, ideology, language, and myth to take a detailed look at the creation and transformation of an organization's culture. New methodologies were appropriated, such as Whyte's (1943) formulation of "participant observation," along with ample borrowing of the ethnographic approach from anthropology (see Clifford, 1983; Clifford & Marcus, 1986; Van Maanen, 1988).

For scholars in organizational communication, the interest shown by anthropologists, sociologists, and management theorists was fortuitous but only a small part of the story. At least three other trends emerged. First, communication theorists with a background in rhetoric and symbolic interaction examined organizational issues through a variety of interpretive and symbolic analyses and mentored students and colleagues who were taking similar approaches (e.g., Ernest Bormann, Phil Tompkins). Second, the particular appropriation to systems theory that was being elucidated in organizational communication studies had relocated communication as the central process in organizations and equated communicating with organizing (e.g., Farace, Monge, & Russell, 1977; Johnson, 1977). Third, the focus on interpretive approaches led organizational communication scholars to theories and research in anthropology (e.g., Geertz, Turner), sociology (e.g., Goffman, Whyte), and increasingly to European scholars (e.g., Foucault, Giddens, Habermas, Lyotard) who fueled hermeneutic, critical, and later postmodern organizational studies.

This "interpretive turn" in organizational communication studies, however, was seen by many as either returning to or simply building on the rich intellectual roots of rhetorical theory and criticism, which has long been concerned with issues of meaning, identification, and persuasion in social and institutional contexts (e.g., Tompkins, 1987).

Unlike scholars in other areas of organization studies that did not initially grasp the power of the metaphor, communication researchers displayed an instinctive appreciation for organizations as social entities that were constituted in interaction. From the early 1980s forward, communication processes were recast as the way organizations were constructed, maintained, and transformed. Thus, communication's constitutive role in creating organizational culture was identified and elucidated.

Additionally, a pivotal role was played by conferences on interpretive approaches to organizational communication (cf. Putnam & Pacanowsky, 1983) where the contributions of communication scholars to the academic literature on organizational culture were refined and made available to those outside the communication discipline. For researchers in a discipline that had come to recognize, although in some cases reluctantly, both humanistic and scientific scholarship, this was not a very radical or oppositional mode of scholarship. The communicative study of "organizational cultures" was instead an intriguing amalgam of ideas that drew together people who were already studying organizational symbols, narratives, metaphors, identity, and politics.

Few academic concepts have received the public recognition that has been accorded to organizational culture. In the early 1980s, the organizational culture concept exploded in the media through stories in *Business Week* and *Fortune* magazines, as well as in the enormously popular business books *In Search of Excellence* (Peters & Waterman, 1982) and *Corporate Cultures* (Deal & Kennedy, 1982). Then in 1983, *Administrative Science Quar-*

terly (Jelinek, Smircich, & Hirsch, 1983) published a special issue devoted to academic studies of organizational culture, and *Organizational Dynamics* created its own special issue, which was also accessible to practitioners. With genuine excitement and a lot of hype, organizational culture became both a part of the language of the business world and a flourishing stream of academic research.

There is no single story that accounts for the rapid growth in popularity of cultural perspectives across related but distinct organizational literatures. One crucial factor was critiques of the value and status of science, rationality, and technology, along with other dominant institutions of society. As a result, there was a movement to give voice to those who were marginalized under the current system (e.g., women, minorities, subordinates, inhabitants of the so-called third world countries). Alvesson (1993b) purported that a constellation of issues was responsible for the emergence of the culture approach in organizational studies. His list included a disaffection with the methods and results of traditional organizational research; an increased emphasis on the lived experience of organizational members and an awareness of global societal issues; a call for alternatives to authoritarian leadership; the productivity problems of Western societies, and in particular the United States (as compared to Japanese management); the emergence of new organizational forms in which behaviors are controlled more through identification and loyalty than through direct supervision; and the marketing of the culture concept by consulting firms such as McKinsey, which sponsored popular business books in the early 1980s.

For some or all of these reasons, the culture concept encouraged a group of otherwise conservative researchers to explore aspects of organizational life under a new theoretical umbrella that legitimated alternative research methodologies. For others, it helped craft a larger community of scholars with whom they could share research and ideas. A number of theorists, particularly management scholars,

however, soon declared that organizational culture was a "dead" academic endeavor because it had been so quickly and uncritically appropriated by functionalist researchers and practitioners (Smircich & Calás, 1987). Although problems of managerial bias can be identified in the administrative literature, we were not persuaded that the organizational metaphor was significantly corrupted. First, the use of the term by change agents such as organizational development specialists and other practitioners was clearly not new, merely inflated by academic and media attention. Second, these instrumental approaches served different audiences, and they could not silence interpretive, critical, or postmodern voices in the arena of organizational culture scholarship unless one of two key situations arose: (1) the topic became "tainted" in the eyes of current or prospective non-managerially oriented researchers, who then left the research arena; or (2) it became difficult to publish stimulating, nonutilitarian work of high quality (Riley, 1993). We have not uncovered significant evidence of either scenario, and especially not in organizational communication literature. Instead we found a variety of fascinating research projects in the literature to review and discuss. The diversity of perspectives was illuminating and welcomed. In this chapter, we have attempted to examine each alternative theme or paradigm of culture research from the standpoint of its own goals and practices.

A COMMUNICATIVE PERSPECTIVE ON ORGANIZATIONAL CULTURE

As previously mentioned, a communicative view of organizational culture sees communication as constitutive of culture. The process that we wish to label organizational culture consists solely of patterns of human action and its recursive behaviors (including talk and its symbolic residues) and meaning.

Our view of organizational culture is mediated by five assumptions that guide the typology we have developed for this review (for other typologies, see Bantz, 1993; Goodall, 1989, 1991; Pacanowsky & O'Donnell-Trujillo, 1983; Putnam, Phillips, & Chapman, 1996).

First, a communication perspective does not limit its interest to overt constructions with "extra meaning" such as central metaphors or key stories. It acknowledges the symbolic character of ordinary language and the ways in which cultural meanings are coconstructed in everyday conversation, textual evidence of patterns, and also the entire nonverbal, semiotic field, from the structure of parking lots (Goodall, 1989) to the structure of work processes (Alvesson, 1993a; Barley, 1983). Further, these fields are not simply observed but can also be cast in a physical, sensual way (Conquergood, 1991; Stoller, 1989).

Second, this vantage point offers a commentary on the tension between cognitive and behavioral approaches to human action, through a focus on communicative praxis. Of all human activities, human communication is the one in which interpretation and action most clearly coexist. Even though some explanations of human behavior may give weight to the constraining aspects of social and organizational structures, while others emphasize what is possible through individual agency, communication can be seen as an "interactive prism" through which all potentially enabling and constraining forces must pass (Mohan, 1993; Wentworth, 1980). Conceptualized this way, each instance of communication is a kind of crucible for culture, with the historical weight of language and past practices on the one hand, and the potential for innovation and novelty on the other. As power circulates within and between organizations, points of domination and of leverage for change coexist in the interactive moment.

Third, this approach takes into account broader patterns of communication in society and examines how they appear and interact at the organizational nexus. For example, studies of ethnicity, family systems, and media images of work may relate to an expanded notion of organizational culture, inasmuch as they act as constraints on behavior and serve as identity resources for members.

Fourth, a communication orientation takes full advantage of the various new options available for positioning the researcher. For example, Jackson's (1989) "radical empiricism" breaks down the perceived barriers between the researcher "self" and the organizational "other." Research on organizational culture can be either a tale told at a distance or something more impressionistic and confessional (Van Maanen, 1988).

Fifth, and perhaps most controversial, a communication perspective acknowledges the legitimacy of all motives for the study of culture, including the practical interests of organizational members seeking to enhance their effectiveness. An increased opportunity for dialogue about organizational culture, identity, and the change process (common topics in and around many companies and institutions) can potentially inform and empower organizational members. Workers (or managers) who are concerned about culture often acknowledge the interests and voices of multiple stakeholders and have used this information to reshape existing organizations and to launch new companies that seek alternatives to hierarchy and traditional, top-down models of organization. For example, a culturally "empowering" organization such as W. L. Gore (Pacanowsky, 1988) was described as a positive workplace that continuously improved itself in many arenas. And Cheney's (1995) article on a workers' cooperative in Spain (Mondragón) uncovered the organizational members' concern for effectiveness as the dialectic between an internal culture of workplace democracy and the exigencies of the global economic environment required an ongoing balancing act to maintain the cooperative's viability. This perspective does not, of course, condone attempts to engineer employee emotions or other manipulative uses of cultural knowledge that disadvantage workers.

THEMES IN STUDYING
ORGANIZATIONAL CULTURE

In the first version of this handbook, Smircich and Calás (1987) arrayed the organizational culture literature along three dimensions: paradigms, interests, and themes. The five cultural "themes" ranged from those that treat culture as a variable, something an organization has (e.g., comparative management and corporate culture), to those that treat culture as a root metaphor, something an organization is (organizational cognition, organizational symbolism, and unconscious processes). This category scheme is well known, often cited, and critiqued, but because it failed to capture a communicative perspective we developed an alternative schema for this chapter.

This chapter reviews the role of communication in the culture literature through the following thematic framework: culture as symbolism and performance, culture as text, culture as critique, culture as identity, culture as cognition, and culture as climate and effectiveness. This thematic display identified research that was rooted in a communicative process (symbolism and performance, text, critique, identity, and cognition) and in communicative goals (effectiveness and climate).

Culture as Symbolism
and Performance

It may at first appear that an "organizational symbolism" approach would be of greatest interest to—and perhaps even isomorphic with—an organizational communication perspective. But underneath this label was a host of divergent definitions and approaches—some in which communication played a central role, and others where communication was secondary, if not removed from the study.

The early studies of organizational symbolism, often characterized as the "management of meaning" perspective (e.g., Pfeffer, 1981), treated symbols similarly to the analysis of literary devices in basic English classes—as special expressions, artifacts, or events that occurred in organizations and were imbued with "extra" meaning. From this perspective, ordinary conversation and the arrangement of furniture would not constitute "symbolic action," but the dramatic choice of a metaphor in a speech to stockholders would. Taken this way, symbolic action was rare and significant, and such events were to be contrasted with the less "meaningful" substance of daily life.

To the communication scholar, this is a highly limited view of the symbolic, one that treats communication as a variable and places it "inside" of organizations. It ignored the symbolic nature of language and the semiotic significance of nonverbal communication. Some writers (e.g., Tompkins, 1987) rejected the distinction between "symbolism" and "substance" and assert that any substance that has meaning in organizations must also be symbolic. Partly in response to these critiques, an expanded view of organizational symbolism was developed by management theorists (cf. Frost, Moore, Louis, Lundberg, & Martin, 1991). The organizational symbolism perspective that they championed reflected a broad range of definitions and approaches to organizational culture, including "specialists" (Martin, 1992) who focus on vocabulary (e.g., Boland & Hoffman, 1983), narratives and stories (Brown, 1990a, 1990b; Mumby, 1988), ritual (Knuf, 1993), and hallway talk (Gronn, 1983) and "generalists" who attempt to develop a comprehensive view of all types of communication in creating, maintaining, and transforming organizational reality (e.g., Barley, 1990; Bormann, 1983; Van Maanen, 1991; Weick, 1991).

Several examples of such specialist work in organizational communication focused on the processual nature of culture. For instance, an early example in the communication literature was Conrad's (1983) work on power, which, borrowing from Giddens and Clegg, examined metaphors, myths, and rituals for their deep structuring patterns and implications in organizational conflict. Similarly, Smith and Eisenberg's (1987) examination of Disneyland used a root metaphor analysis to examine why this particularly "strong" culture was incapable of managing conflict and the tension between the practices the corporation engaged in during an economic downturn. What was unique about this particular incarnation of a "family" metaphor was its utopian nature—this conflict-free, paternalistic culture did not know how to engage in conflict and thus experienced traumatic results. A study by Putnam, Van Hoeven, and Bullis (1991) focused on the role of rituals and fantasy themes in teachers' bargaining. Their study located rites and ceremonies as mediators between public presentations of vision and the narratives generated in small-group interaction—an interesting cultural "mechanism." Another example was Trujillo's (1992) interpretation of the talk of baseball park culture for the reader to see both the interplay between talk and work and to the multivocal nature of the baseball environment.

Bantz (1993) attempted a comprehensive, generalist approach to the study of organizational culture. In his book, Bantz developed an integrated communication-based technique called organizational communication culture (OCC), which analyzed messages and their interpretations. Although the OCC method sometimes collapsed complex issues to provide an integrated approach, the technique demystified discourse on organizational culture and cleared the way for more field studies and less abstract debate. The OCC provided a fundamentally structurationist view of communication, in which all interactions are treated as inherently resource or constraint in pursuit of the maintenance or transformation of organizational reality.

Bantz was not alone in his application of structurationist approaches to the study of organizational culture. In an investigation of two professional firms' cultural politics, Riley's (1983) analysis of legitimation, domination, and signification processes uncovered several subgroups with cultural norms different from those articulated by the public spokespersons of the larger organizations and that were amazingly distinct from each other. These "subcultures" often borrowed rules from their relationships with client organizations and enacted them in ways that protected their interests by symbolizing alternative power structures. In a study of a television station, Carbaugh (1988) focused on Giddens's notion of discursive consciousness and interpreted codes of communication as a way of analyzing cultural systems of communication. He delineated three types of symbols: symbols as persons, symbols of speaking, and epitomizing symbols. He argued that a cultural analysis is not about symbols or a set of symbols, but a system of symbols that when taken together with all their tensions, complexity, and contradictions enlightens our understanding of the situated use of work speech.

Witmer (1997) used a structurationist approach to culture to analyze an unusual Alcoholics Anonymous organization—1,000 to 1,200 attended weekly—and its strong, charismatic founder (a self-described "low-bottom drunk"). She found that powerful rituals bound participants together in the discourses of recovery and spirituality and that organizational practices were clearly codified and well articulated. The power imbalance between the founder and other organizational members generated a personal dependency on him and embedded the participants' personal identities within the discursive structuring of the group.

Although it is not an avowedly "cultural" study, Howard and Geist (1995) used structuration to help identify ideological positioning as one sensemaking mechanism used by organizational members as they work their way through the turbulent change of a merger. They found that the discourse of invincibility created the impression that some members were "bulletproof" and free from the detrimental effects of the merger; the discourse of diplomacy allowed other members to preserve a role for themselves in the merged organization. The last positioning device, betrayal, distanced organizational members from the dehumanized environment of the merger and prevented them from becoming another "cog in the machine" (p. 129).

In the management and organization studies literature, early symbolic analysis research was critiqued for its singular focus on "pure" symbols (e.g., stories, jokes, rituals) as well as for being disconnected from the organization and the work (ignoring tasks, jobs, and core work processes) (e.g., Alvesson, 1993b). Barley (1983) was one of the first to make this case, illustrating a semiotic approach to the significance of seemingly mundane actions, such as how the placement of furniture and standard operating procedures for jobs revealed deeper levels of interpretation that constituted work culture.

Kunda (1992) attended to these critiques and captured the high art of symbolic analysis in his book *Engineering Culture*. Written after a one-year stay in a high-technology organization, the study set out to learn about the way an organization attempts to create and maintain a strong culture specifically because the management executives believe that normative control is a better ideology than bureaucratic control. Kunda also focused on the performance of ritual as a framing device where members acting as agents of the corporate interest attempted to establish shared definitions through the use of slogans and metaphors (e.g., "We are like a football team," p. 154). Challenges to these ritual frames, which Kunda called mini-dramas, served to suppress dissent at Tech and distance those who disagreed with the corporate ideology. Kunda noted that "Tech management takes the implications of its own rhetoric seriously and invests considerable energy in attempting to embed the rules, prescriptions, and admonitions of the culture in the fabric of everyday life in the company" (p. 218). He concluded that "Tech's engineered culture appears to be a pervasive, comprehensive, and demanding system of normative control based on the use of symbolic power" (p. 219). His research

pointed to the paradoxes associated with complex and ambiguous circumstances and the self-reflexivity of organizational members —"Members evaluate each other on their ability to express both embracement and distancing and to know when to stop" (p. 158).

Kunda, however, was not the first to examine cultures as performance. Communication scholars Pacanowsky and O'Donnell-Trujillo (1983) earlier argued that organizational communication researchers should look at "performances" in their quest to understand cultural processes. They noted that "it is easy enough to answer that cultural structures come into being through processes of communication. The problem with this assertion is not that it is wrong (because it is not), but that it is not helpful" (p. 129). In their attempt to isolate a locus of interpretation, Pacanowsky and O'Donnell-Trujillo described two connotations of performance that should form the basis of research: First is Goffman's (1959) notion of theatricality, and the second is Turner's (1980) sense of "accomplishing" or "bringing to completion" of order in social life. They then described five cultural performances in organizations that have been examined in the literature: ritual, passion, sociality, politics, and acculturation. One vivid example of this sense of performance as theatricality was captured in Trujillo and Dionisopoulos's (1987) investigation of police talk and organization, where the performative nature of work was displayed and critiqued. In this study, police talk and actions were examined to focus attention on membership, difference, and discursive practices that established normative understanding of policing through their cultural enactments of masculinity.

A related perspective was offered by Conquergood (1991), who stated that the modes of "discussion" in cultures were "not always and exclusively verbal: Issues and attitudes are expressed and contested in dance, music, gesture, food, ritual, artifact, symbol, action, as well as words" (p. 189). Conquergood suggested that fieldwork itself was a collaborative performance and that consideration should be given to the "rhetorical problematics of performance as an alternative form of 'publishing' research" (p. 190).

Recent scholarship in organizational communication responded to these requests. For example, Rogers's (1994) study on the narrative of "rhythm" and the performance of organization was an investigation/argument that viewed rhythm as an organization's enactment of order—the "culture's means of identifying, differentiation, and relating objects, sensations, events, and processes in the world" (p. 223). Of particular interest was the link between a Foucauldian sense of discipline and the rhythm of production (e.g., the mass distribution of uniform, commodified music and factory or assembly line rhythm). In a related vein, Knight (1990) described military "Jody" performances (e.g., "I got a wife and she is keen, Traded her for my M-16") as a co-opted communication form that dehumanized women and exemplified "literature as equipment for killing" (p. 166).

As these studies indicate, culture as performance moved far beyond early notions of significant "symbols" and artifacts and began to embrace a multivocal, eclectic, contradictory, and celebratory sense of organizational culture.

Culture as Text

A growing number of scholars situate themselves within a textual approach to organizational culture. Within this larger rubric, three rather distinct but loosely related approaches were uncovered. One approach focused on actual written texts in organizations such as newsletters, mission statements, and other documents written by organizational members. Another perspective expanded the textual metaphor to include the examination of spoken discourse. These studies analyzed the symbols, language, and practices produced in organizations as texts using literary theories and tools. Finally, a third enterprise conceived of the writing of organizational cul-

ture narratives (sometimes by scholars and sometimes the product of organizational members) as texts. Each of these perspectives is covered in turn.

The first of the three approaches—treatment of written organizational texts—was influenced by Ricoeur's (1971) notion of the "hermeneutics of suspicion," which helped shape the interpretive turn in literary theory and the humanities. For many organizational communication scholars, particularly those interested in rhetorical analysis, Ricoeur's specific focus on those signs that were "fixed by writing" (p. 529) renewed scholarly interest in organizational documents, interviews, and other textual manifestations of organizational life. One of the more interesting examples of written texts was Scheibel's (1994) reading of film school culture where he discovered that alienation was a key feature of the culture. Scheibel built his analysis around an important aspect of film school culture: its graffiti. He argued that cinema students romanticized their late nights of lonely editing by creating analogies between their isolation and the imagined experiences of great film directors. The students enacted their alienation through some plaintive and much humorous writing on the walls of the editing booths—for example, "those who can, direct; those who can't, edit" (p. 7) and "my film has turned against me" (p. 10).

The second perspective, which views spoken language as texts, has produced a number of interesting studies. Communication scholars Tompkins, Tompkins, and Cheney (1989) used "text" as a metaphor to analyze what we do and say in organizational life. In this sense, to see organizations as texts was to focus on the language and arguments of the organization (Tompkins & Cheney, 1988). The text metaphor legitimated the use of hermeneutic methods to unravel the symbolic document of a structured life-world by focusing on the modes of its production and interpretation.

A wonderful example of this approach is found in Taylor's (1990) analysis of personal narratives from the Manhattan Project (the production of the first atomic bomb at the Los Alamos Laboratory). This study was an example of a critical reading that aimed to reconstruct the organizational milieu. His reading suggested an organizational structure that authorized a "rational" subject for the first nuclear weapons organization. This rational culture allowed members to create a technical identity for themselves and for their work that sustained the hegemonic imperatives of nationalism and technological innovation.

Although it is not about a specific culture, Mumby and Putnam's (1992) rereading of the concept of bounded rationality has a similar flavor in that it is a critical reading of the discursive practices and the gendered identities that are a result of generic (read: masculine) organizational culture. Van Maanen and Kunda (1989) gave examples of these practices in their description of organizational cultures that act to emotionally control their members. Mumby and Putnam's reinterpretation of organizational practices as bounded emotionality had significant implications for researchers who are so used to their own vocabulary that they are unable "to recognize the cultural, historical, and political situatedness" of their analysis (p. 481).

The third and most common approach to texts focuses primarily on the written accounts of organizational culture. Following Geertz, many scholars have viewed organizational culture narratives as texts or as a kind of writing. In one of the better examples, Van Maanen (1988) categorized organizational ethnography into three basic types of "tales": realist, confessional, and impressionist, plus a cursory description of literary, formal, critical, and jointly told tales. Realist tales such as Whyte's (1943) *Street Corner Society,* a participant-observation of an Italian gang in the American Northeast, were easily recognized as traditional "objective" cultural descriptions from a somewhat detached observer (see Riley, 1991, for an alternative reading of "Cornerville" that used a narrative paradigm). Both latter types of ethnography—confessional and impressionist—implicate the re-

searcher and his or her biases and interactions as critical to the type of account that gets constructed. Impressionist tales, for example, are often tied to the chronological experiences of the ethnographer in the field, with the culture being inextricably bound to his or her particular encounters with it. Confessional tales are further distanced from traditional descriptive ethnography, in that they largely focus on the subjective experience of the researcher in the field. Confessional tales are closely paralleled by a movement in the social sciences toward autobiographical approaches to scholarship. For those who are familiar with Hunter Thompson and gonzo journalism, there was a close connection—in reading this work we learn more about the author than we do about the setting. Van Maanen's (1988) own studies of police work include examples of all three types of tales.

Martin (1992; see also Martin & Myerson, 1988) offered an alternative taxonomy of organizational culture research that, at a meta-level, treated organizational culture research as texts. She divided culture texts into three categories: integration, differentiation, and fragmentation. The integration text sought to define culture as everything that people in an organization "share" and was often closely associated with the themes of comparative management and corporate culture (although others investigating cognition and symbolism adopted this approach). The differentiation perspective, on the other hand, explicitly acknowledged the existence of different values, practices, and subcultures in organizations and highlighted the political struggles that were constantly a factor in achieving a negotiated order. This perspective is thus a close cousin of critical analysis, with its emphasis on power, conflict, and negotiation. Finally, the fragmentation perspective contended that so-called organizational cultures were characterized by ambiguity and that individuals and organizations had fluctuating boundaries and identities. These studies were most concerned with showing the practical and personal struggles involved in coping with wide-scale confusion and ambiguity. Consensus was seen as short-lived and issue specific (e.g., Kreiner & Schultz, 1993). This work captured the essence of postmodernism as applied to organizational cultures, in which "decentered" individuals constantly reconstructed their identities.

Martin's three-perspective system, when taken as a metatheory, implied that any culture, at any point in time, had some aspects congruent with all three perspectives. Further, if any of these points of view were excluded, then the potential power of cultural analysis was diminished (Martin, 1992). This is not dissimilar to Mumby and Putnam's (1992) request for scholars to draw on both the emotional and rational domains of experience. Such requests ask theorists to abandon efforts at constructing "final" organizational vocabularies but to, instead, maintain an ironic stance (Rorty, 1989).

An example of Martin's three-perspective system of cultural analysis is found in Eisenberg, Murphy, and Andrews (1998). This study of a university's search for a provost in a state that has a "sunshine law" (the search process is open to the public) uses narratives of integration, differentiation, and fragmentation as different "faces" from which to present the event and understand the multivocal nature of culture. In their analysis of the "nexus" of these three views—where a variety of cultural influences come together within a "[permeable and arbitrary] boundary" (p. 17)—they found that the varying perspectives appeared to be chosen for rhetorical reasons. Similar to a stucturationist study, Eisenberg et al. claimed that these perspectives could be drawn on as "resources that organizational actors use to communicate with multiple audiences" (p. 18).

In their postmodern questioning of the initial and common urge among culture researchers to seek integration and synthesis, Smircich and Calás (1987) have pushed scholars to think differently about their commonsense notions of culture. They posited that each "text" was an alternative "fiction" (in the sense of *fictive,* or something "made") and that the truth or falsity of a written account of culture was a meaningless question—what was salient were the rhetorical, political, and practical consequences of selecting one interpretation over another. They urged scholars to speak "culturally" in a multitude of voices and to transform the "organizational culture literature" into a "cultured organizational literature" (p. 257) in which all claims of knowledge about culture were open to investigation, and none would gain the status of permanent or totalizing truth.

Brown and McMillan (1991) also argued that unlike the move to focus on workplace documents or practices "as symbolic," postmodern scholars needed to redefine the terms *text* and *work* to distance "the work of an author from the 'work' of the receivers that might take the form of a response, and experience, a critique" (p. 50). Brown and McMillan reminded us of the authorial nature of all analytical descriptions. Whether it is the voice of the researcher or the voices of organizational members that is ultimately written down and "heard," Rabinow and Sullivan (1979) remarked that culture is "always multivocal and overdetermined, and both the observer and the observed are always enmeshed in it. . . . There is no privileged position, no absolute perspective, no final recounting" (p. 6).

Culture as Critique

Critical cultural studies and the associated area of postmodern resistance characterized much communication research on culture in the 1980s and 1990s. We will first cover critical scholarship and then discuss the postmodern strains in organizational culture research. Early critical cultural studies of organizations (e.g., Deetz & Kersten, 1983) primarily emphasized power (see Mumby, Chapter 15, this volume). Many scholars in communication consider the cultural manifestations of concepts such as "resistance to domination" evident in "hidden transcripts" and in the discourse and practices of corporate colonization (Deetz, 1992). Drawing on the work of Habermas, Foucault, and other critical and postmodern theorists, Deetz (1992) recounted the growing spread of corporate control in a global society. His approach to both the structural and linguistic manifestations of organizations has allowed communication researchers (and others) to focus on the intersection of societal and local organizational practices at both philosophical and pragmatic levels. The enormous amount of time most everyone spends in organizations, as well as the powerful inscription of organizational routines in our everyday lives (e.g., standardized work hours, day care centers, insurance-driven medical care), forces us to look at cultural praxis in a more enduring way (Deetz, 1992). Deetz and Kersten (1983) noted, "In such cases of domination, communication is systematically distorted" (p. 165).

Critical approaches emphasize that any representation of culture always comes from a particular perspective, with particular interests, and encourages researchers to be more reflexive about what these interests and biases might be (Jermier, 1991). Central to this approach in the organizational context has been a shift away from notions of productivity and organizational effectiveness to a concern for employees' quality of life (Aktouf, 1992). Strains of this "culture as critique" theme have been articulated within some of the previously reviewed literature. Much of the structurationist culture literature—with its attention focused on dominant patterns of control—provides clear examples. Heavily grounded in Foucault's concern with power in organizations, Ferguson's (1984) classic feminist "case against bureaucracy" critiqued the whole of organization science literature as embedded in an overly rational, paternalistic, dominating conception of organizing. Scholarship such as Brown and McMillan's (1991) that problematizes author/authority is another example.

An excellent case study of culture as critique was included in Barker and Cheney's (1994) examination of the ways that discipline "works" discursively in organizations. In a company they call Tech USA, one of the authors observed the organization's conversion to self-managing teams (following the lead of Peters & Waterman, 1982). They found that the teams began to identify with and apply these values to each other's activities (e.g., Mumby & Stohl, 1991). Tech USA's management had "crafted a vision statement that articulated a set of core values, which all employees were to use to guide their daily actions" (Barker & Cheney, 1994, p. 33). In this organization, the teams created sets of disciplinary discourses that acted as a cultural system of control. In one example, an employee complained that "the whole team is watching what I do" (p. 35). Barker and Cheney posit an interesting paradox: As organizations work to become more ethical, achieve higher values, and allow members greater autonomy, the organization becomes more "concertive" in its influence and individual control is diminished.

In a more postmodern vein, Goodall (1989, 1991) approached ethnography with the ideas of the "plural present" and of "mystery" (borrowed from Kenneth Burke). Acknowledging the plural present means that in any organization, in any culture, there are always multiple voices telling multiple versions of what is "really" going on. This is not, however, necessarily a problem. Cultures, according to Goodall, are not problems to be solved, but mysteries to be experienced again and again, each time with new insight but without any final resolution other than the continual rediscovery of self (Rorty, 1989).

Conquergood's (1991) notion of postmodern cultural study, and specifically ethnography, required a radical rethinking in light of the "double fall of scientism and imperialism" (p. 179). As the image of an objective, detached observer who used neutral language to describe or represent a unitary culture has increasingly come under fire (e.g., Jackson, 1989; Marcus & Fischer, 1986; Van Maanen, 1988), various types of cultural analysis have emerged. These newer conceptions all situate the researcher deep in the cultural context, complete with personal biases and practical agendas. Conquergood asked that we consider a number of issues, but key among them are the return of the body and rhetorical reflexivity.

Return of the body referred to the importance of active, physical immersion in the organization whose culture one wishes to describe. Cultural study from this perspective was an embodied practice, and while there were costs to be paid for getting "close," there were also significant benefits. Bodily immersion opened the ethnographer to senses other than the visual (cf. Stoller, 1989) and to explicit consideration of issues such as investigating the connections between sexuality and power and specifically sexual harassment. For instance, Clair (1993) provided a feminist critique of harassment in a way that is easily aligned with organizational culture. In Clair's view, what was most interesting were the personal narratives of harassment and how they acted as frames for either challenging or reproducing the dominant ideology. That certain organizational cultures encouraged different ways of speaking and acting with regard to this subject was clear (e.g., Rogers, 1994).

By invoking rhetorical reflexivity, Conquergood (1991) suggested that cultural study is increasingly seen reflexively—meaning that there can be no final, authoritative account of a culture (Geertz, 1988). Instead, ethnographies invariably reflect the writer/researchers' biases and ways of life as much as they do those under study—the construction of a culture that is "strange" or "foreign" only serves to underscore the supposed "normalness" of the writer's home perspective. What flows from this insight is a recognition of the need to understand the kinds of "descriptions" of culture that are seen as "appropriate for publication," and the sorts of knowledge that are seen as legitimate within the institutional structures of academia and society.

As if she were responding directly to Conquergood, Martin's (1992) final chapter critiqued the "imperialism" of her own metatheory, her assertions that studies might fall into one category or another, and in the presumption of "truth" that the taxonomy makes. Similarly, she questioned her ability to present the voices of the employees she interviewed as part of her studies and admitted that as author she edited conversations and selected quotes to make her chosen arguments as best as she could. Finally, she speculated about ways of making the whole enterprise more open-ended and dialogic.

There are, obviously, ways in which "culture" and "postmodernism" have always coexisted uneasily since culture has traditionally been the study of common meanings, integration, community, and values (the language of unification), and postmodernism is about difference, suspicion, fragmentation, and the rejection of epistemology (the language of polysemy). And postmodernism is not without its critics, for several fairly obvious reasons. First, the language used is often accessible only to the initiated or the very patient, often replete with jargon, words in quotes, and phrases in a variety of languages. Second, some believe the focus on deconstructing texts, rather than on taking action to improve the lives of organizational members, makes postmodernism seem like "an elitist language game played by intellectual initiates while Rome (or Los Angeles) burns—a diversion or excuse for action paralysis and social nihilism" (see Martin & Frost, 1996, for a detailed discussion). But postmodernism is now a cultural phenomenon of its own, pressing researchers to rethink their values, methods, and goals.

In their review of such concerns, Linstead and Grafton-Small (1992) argued that we need to approach culture as a discursive complex and appreciate the importance of the other and the seductive process of forming culture and image. They stressed the detailed articulation and analysis of everyday practices as a means of exploring the marginal creativity of culture consumers, particularly with respect to their socioeconomic and historical contexts. It is in the articulation of everyday communication practices that so much work remains to be done.

Culture as Identity

The concept of identity is a particularly important theme in the organizational culture literature, in part because of the postmodern "condition" of academic thought goaded by the rapidly changing face of our human geography. Many of the early conceptions of identity focused on national or ethnic identity, often under the rubric of comparative management, and delved into the ways organizations from different nations embodied characteristics or practices inherent in their cultural background. More recently, scholars have problematized the concept of identity in postmodern society. To explore the organizational culture research on identity, we have divided the review into subthemes: comparative management and self-identity.

Comparative Management

The comparative management perspective treats culture as though it was imported into organizations through the national, regional, and ethnic affiliations of employees (see Stohl, Chapter 10 in this volume, for greater detail). This approach stresses the significance of nationality over the power of any individual organization to influence member behavior (Hofstede, 1991). Most studies of this kind treat culture as an external variable and employ a traditional, functionalist approach. Perhaps the best-known, and one of the most exhaustive, studies of cross-national differences in cultural orientation was conducted by Hofstede (1983). He studied matched populations of IBM employees across 64 countries. In general, differences in national value systems were found along four (and later, five) largely independent dimensions but Hofstede agreed that they said little that is specific about IBM's culture.

Similarly, Erez and Earley (1993) saw culture as a set of mental programs that con-trolled behavior, and they argued that these mental sets varied from country to country. Their logic was that different national cultures produced people with different mental sets, who in turn both expected different behaviors of others and behaved differently themselves. In another well-known study, Shweder and LeVine (1984) contrasted Western egocentric cultures with Eastern sociocentric cultures and found them to have very different mental maps and behavioral expectations.

The simplistic nature of such research is called into question by research in organizational communication. Banks and Riley (1993) employed a structurationist lens to investigate the disembedding of rules and systems from other organizations or institutions in a Japanese subsidiary located in the United States. They found evidence of national identity and practices but also found disruptive contradictions, language confusion, and culturally based power systems that were interpreted differently by members of the various subcultures. In these days of permeable boundaries, joint ventures, and virtual teams, this type of analysis may provide further insight into the reproduction and transformation of polyvocal cultural understandings.

It is important to note that Wilkins and Ouchi (1983) and Hofstede, Neuijen, Ohayv, and Sanders (1990) believed that national cultures and organizational cultures are constituted differently and that terminological care is needed when speaking of "culture" in this research genre. Hofstede et al.'s position was that culture is a different phenomenon at the national level than it is at the organizational level and that shared perceptions of daily practices were the core of an organization's culture, not shared values as other authors working off a national or ethnic model have maintained.

Self-Identity

The idea of the self as a consistent integrated "thing" that confronts others in the world has been critiqued and the alternative argument advanced that what counts for "who you are" at any moment in time is constructed from those images that are currently available in the culture. Gergen (1991), for example, has been on the forefront in articulating a view of the self as fragmented. In postmodern conceptions of identity, the idea of a "bounded, interiorized self is a narrative convention" (Kondo, 1990, p. 25). Although his theorizing about self and identity differs somewhat, Giddens (1991) contended that self-identity is not a distinctive trait or even a collection of traits but is the "self as reflexively understood by the person in terms of her or his biography" (p. 53). In this sense, a person's identity is not found in behavior, or in the reactions of others (although this is part of the picture), but in the capacity to keep a particular narrative going (Giddens, 1991, p. 54). The "content" of self-identity varies much the ways stories do, in form and style, and socially and culturally. A key feature of this conceptualization is that the very core of identity—of choices we make about not only how to act but whom to be—is heavily influenced by our work and the choices available or not available to us.

Communication research has indicated that the choices for constructing identity in organizations are fraught with difficulties due to the myriad of situations that occur in organizational life (Cheney, 1991). By investigating the multiple roles and exigencies of members' lives in organizations, Cheney creatively explored both the constitutive role of communication in the managing of identity and varied responses to self-identity requirements in the cultural context of organizations. The problematizing of identity has included taking on fake or temporary identities (Scheibel, 1992). In his study of the communicative performances in "clubland" (the conventional communication practices of underage females and male gatekeepers in nightclubs), Scheibel finds faking an identity for entrance to an organization a challenging but commonly accomplished cultural performance. Although the larger implications for the reproduction of gendered organizations are clear, what is left

unexplored is the impact on individual narratives.

Whether identity is considered a feature of historical geography—still important to those individuals not able or unwilling to join either the great diaspora or the tourist class—or a process of working on one's self as a mosaic of organizational, familial, and societal roles, the concept is a metaphor for our time, a struggle for coherence amid multiple discourses and optional organizational forms.

Organizational Cognition

The discussion of self-identity reveals an interest in understanding the relationship between the social construction of the organization and the self-construction of individuals. One of the most commonly articulated views in the organizational culture literature is that this process is primarily cognitive. In other words, to understand the relationship between individuals and their organization one must investigate the cognitive frame that facilitates coordinated action. This approach to organizational culture is sometimes called the "ideational" perspective, and it defines culture as a pattern of shared assumptions, shared frame of reference, or a shared set of values and norms. While cognitive anthropologists have been the strongest proponents of this view (e.g., D'Andrade, 1984), this approach is evident in the literature on shared rules and cognitive patterns (see Barnett, 1988), in organization and management studies as shared values (Chatman & Jehn, 1994), and in studies of cognitive frames that dictate appropriate behavior (Thompson & Luthans, 1990).

When researchers analyze why organizational members behave as they do, they focus on what people say and take the response to be the reason for their behavior. Some scholars, such as Schein (1985), disagree:

> Yet, the underlying reasons for their behavior remain concealed or unconscious. To really understand a culture and to ascertain more completely the group's values and overt behavior, it

is imperative to delve into the underlying assumptions, which are typically unconscious
but which actually determine how group members perceive, think, and feel. (p. 3)

Similarly, Barnett (1988) maintained that
"culture consists of the habits and tendencies
to act in certain ways, but *not* the actions
themselves" (p. 102, emphasis ours). And
D'Andrade (1984) believed that the most
fruitful way to study culture is not through the
examination of messages but rather with the
study of individual "meaning systems."

In a study advancing the cognitive perspective, Shockley- Zalabak and Morley (1994)
combined an emphasis on shared values with
Schall's (1983) concerns about shared communication rules. They found that "management values during the formative years of an
organization were closely related to the values
of the employees initially hired into the organization. Additionally, management values
were related over time to both management
and employee perceptions of organizational
rules" (p. 352).[1]

Mohan (1993) adopted a cognitive approach in her discussion of cultural vision,
and in particular in her consideration of psychological, sociological, and historical "penetration." She centered on the degree to which a
culture was shared in the organization as a
cognitive conception. For example, psychological penetration was defined as the degree
of consistency of shared meanings, sociological penetration surfaced as the pervasiveness
of cultural assumptions, and historical penetration was the stability of cultural schemata
(cognitive frames) over time. In a study of semantic networks in organizations, Contractor,
Eisenberg, and Monge (1994) examined six
organizations to determine both the degree
and importance of consensus among employees on the meaning of the organization's vision, a key notion in organizational culture.
They found that interpretations varied widely.

Other scholars in communication and organizational behavior have argued for a cognitive approach to culture. Sackmann (1991) as-

serted that "what makes a collection of people
a cultural grouping is the fact that the people
hold the same cognitions in common" (p. 40).
Her fine-grained analysis divided cognitions
into three types of knowledge: descriptive, or
"dictionary" knowledge; causal-analytical, or
"directory" knowledge; and causal normative,
or "recipe" knowledge. All three are combined in cognitive maps that overlap to constitute an organization's culture. James, James,
and Ashe (1990), in a work admittedly more
directed at climate than culture, attacked social constructionism in claiming that no
meaning ever resides even partially outside of
individual cognitive systems. This is in sharp
contrast to the views of Mead (1934) or
Bakhtin (1981), both of whom have maintained that the meaning of any utterance is
never the sole possession of an individual—that the meaning of any word always belongs, in part, to someone else (Holquist,
1990).

Other writers also take a cognitive approach to culture, only to describe their approaches in ways that display subtle yet important differences. For example, Louis
(1990) came closest to "popular" understanding of culture when she stated that a common
culture means that people recognize the same
meanings for things, but do not necessarily
agree on them. Myerson (1991) presented social work culture more problematically when
she described it as a kind of "shared orientation" within which can exist multiple interpretations of specific concepts and behaviors.
Hofstede (1991) maintained that it is the
shared perceptions of daily work practices
(and not shared values or beliefs per se) that
are key to an organization's culture. Still others (e.g., Krackhardt & Kilduff, 1990) argued
that effective coordinated action depends
more on the quality of dyadic interpersonal relationships than on group or organization-
wide consensus on interpretations. McCollom's (1993) definition blended a cognitively
focused approach with the behavioral: "Culture is defined as the set of conscious and unconscious beliefs and values, *and* the patterns

of behavior (including language and symbol use) that provide identity and form a framework of meaning for a group of people" (p. 84, emphasis ours).

In summary, one of the "black holes" of the culture conversation has been the locus of the meanings that constitute culture, mostly played out between proponents of the ideational and behavioral schools. At the same time, many have staked their definitions somewhere in the fuzzy middle, viewing culture as "redundancies of interpretation and practice" (Barley, 1983) or "configurations of interpretations, *and* the ways they are enacted" (Martin, 1992, emphasis ours). D'Andrade (1984) made the point that prior to 1957, culture was seen mainly in terms of observable behaviors, actions, and customs and that the movement from this position to an increased interest in cognition was to be celebrated. Yet Geertz reminds us that a countermovement took place at the same time, one whose purpose was to critique the twin myths of "inner reality" and private language. The key point of this countermovement (with which Geertz is sympathetic) was to define culture as a conceptual structure that is separate from individual psychology—that is, to assert that meaning is both public and social (Bakhtin, 1981; Gergen, 1991; Vygotsky, 1962). In an attempt at arbitration, Shweder (1991) suggested that the question of where meaning (or culture) resides may be irrelevant, like asking whether "redness" resides in a color chip or in a perceptual system.

Clearly, part of this debate is also methodological—the quantitative instrumentation developed to uncover individualistic perceptions are often static and unconnected with the generative mechanisms that produce them. It is clear to us that organizations are first and foremost action systems (Pilotta, Widman, & Jasco, 1988) and that little is gained in trying to separate enactment from interpretation. For this reason, the organizational cognition approach, to the extent that it is characterized by a mostly private view of language and an individualistic bias, will fall short. This is not to say that cognitions are unimportant, only that their importance depends entirely on their relationship to action and behavior and to ongoing conduct within a public conversation (Mead, 1934).

Culture as Climate

There has always been a family resemblance between the culture as cognition research and climate studies in organizations, since much of the climate literature has been cognitively based. Those resemblances, however, have grown stronger during the past decade with an emphasis on the "acculturation" of climate. Perhaps no other research area has been so transfigured by the organizational culture metaphor as the umbrella concept of organizational climate.

The climate notion, adroitly described as an "attractive nuisance" (Bastien, McPhee, & Bolton, 1995), was a mélange of distinct research programs with competing theoretical orientations, different units of analysis, and nonequivalent measurement instruments loosely connected by the metaphor of the organization's atmosphere. Previous reviews on organizational climate (such as the one by Falcione, Sussman, & Herden, 1987, in the first edition of this handbook), written during or near the end when climate was an academic boom industry, typically divided the studies into three categories:

1. Climate as a set of attributes possessed by the organization—like an organizational personality—that was relatively enduring over time and persisted despite changes in individual members (e.g., Zohar, 1980)

2. Subgroup climates (e.g., Johnston, 1976)

3. The cognitive or psychological approach, which centered on individual summary perceptions (or the summary perceptions of subsystems) of the work environment rather than on organizational attributes (Hellriegel & Slocum, 1974; James & Jones, 1974)

Although a number of widely differing questionnaires and instruments were developed to measure climate, many used similar dimensions of autonomy, consideration, and reward orientation (Falcione et al., 1987).

The communication-related dimensions—such as supportiveness, trust, openness, participative decision making—most interested the organizational communication scholars and led to the concept of communication climate (e.g., Downs, 1979; Redding, 1972). Later, Poole and McPhee (1983) developed the argument that climate was actually intersubjective, related to specific organizational practices, and better understood as an ongoing process of structuration. This position was extended through Poole's (1985) notion of "kernel" climates that can be identified in an organization but are interpreted differently across subgroups and can change across time. Bastien et al. (1995) explicated how kernel themes were transformed into surface climates "in the course of reproducing the organization's culture and beliefs" (p. 87). Although their approach was not a culture study, it is indicative of the "regrounding" of much of the recent climate literature within the larger cultural metaphor.

With article titles such as "The Cultural Approach to the Formation of Organizational Climate" (Moran & Volkwein, 1992), "Climate and Culture Interaction and Qualitative Differences in Organizational Meanings" (Rentsch, 1990), and "Creating the Climate and Culture of Success" (Schneider, Gunnarson, & Niles-Jolly, 1994) and a book called *Organizational Climate and Culture* (Schneider, 1990), the shift in emphasis is quite apparent. Recent climate articles also display many practical concerns but little if any consideration of communication, for example, R&D project team climate (Youngbae & Lee, 1995), R&D marketing and interfunctional climates (Moenaert, Souder, Meyer, & DeSchoolmeester, 1994), sales-manager-salesperson solidarity (Strutton & Pelton, 1994), the relationship between climate and perceptions of personnel management practices (Toulson & Smith, 1994), looking for conducive climates (Turnipseed & Turnipseed, 1992), concern for customers and employees (Burke, Borucki, & Hurley, 1992), customer service (Schneider, Wheeler, & Cox, 1992), and the effects of climate on individual behavior and attitudes in organizations (Ostroff, 1993).

The growing fascination with culture management has also reconfigured, if not dominated, the research programs of organizational climate researchers. Early climate research was often descriptive in nature—calculating aggregate employee perceptions about such issues as goals and policies, supportive versus defensive atmosphere, and communication (Falcione & Kaplan, 1984). Although the number of climate studies undertaken has dropped significantly, most recent work positioned organizational climate in relation to culture and effectiveness (e.g., Schneider et al., 1994). The result is that most conceptions of organizational climate are best viewed as phenomena caused, changed, or managed by the organization's culture.

What promise does this acculturated form of climate hold for organizational communication? Perhaps if we refocus the research agenda and develop a core group of scholars to conduct research and provide critique its value could be significantly enhanced. While traditional communication climate studies are on the wane,[2] a revival of dynamic, intersubjective approaches to climate could bring alternative but complementary insights that would be superior to the more traditional attitude surveys that are so popular in large corporations today. These studies might explain how people feel about their organizations, and why, in ways that could engender ongoing dialogue between managers and employees—a precious activity in an era of massive restructurings, acquisitions and re-engineering.

Culture as Effectiveness

The practical focus in the acculturated climate research is understandable when read alongside the large body of instrumental organizational culture research. The "effectiveness" or "corporate culture" perspective is perhaps best known in the management literature and the popular press. This approach treats culture as values or practices that account for an organization's success and that can be managed to produce better business outcomes. Ouchi and Wilkins (1985) observed that "the contemporary student of organizational culture often takes the organization not as a natural solution to deep and universal forces but as a rational instrument designed by top management to shape the behavior of the employees in purposive ways" (p. 462). Alvesson (1993b) restated this tendency, through the eyes of a critical theorist, as the dominance of instrumental values in service of the technical cognitive interest.

The corporate culture perspective clusters into three interrelated areas of study: (1) the influence of founders and leaders on the creation and maintenance and transformation of cultures, (2) the work on "strong" cultures and their values, and (3) organizational change and the management of cultures.

Founders and Leaders

The corporate culture literature takes an activist stance toward the culture concept—culture is something to be created, shaped, and purposively transformed—and the studies that focus on founders and leaders are archetypal of this position. Primarily conducted by management and organizational studies researchers, these studies are not a mainstay of the communication discipline and as such, communication is not always the focus although it is clearly not ignored.

In Pettigrew's (1979) well-known essay on symbolic approaches to organizational cultures, using the founding and transformation of a British boarding school as its touchstone, his primary interest was in "how purpose, commitment, and order are generated in an or-

ganization both through the feelings and actions of its founder . . . man as a creator and manager of meaning" (p. 572). Attempting to redefine the prevailing organizational behavior interests away from the personality characteristics of leaders, Pettigrew stated that "the essential problem of entrepreneurship is the translation of individual drive into collective purpose and commitment. With this viewpoint the focus is not what makes the entrepreneur but rather what does the entrepreneur make" (p. 573). From this perspective, employee commitment is a requirement for a successful organization and this commitment must be earned by the founder or leader through vision, energy, sacrifice, and investment. Schein (1985) claimed that founders "teach" others through their actions and in this manner cultures are developed, learned, and embedded.

In one of the most vivid descriptions of the power of a founder to imagine an organization, McDonald (1991) described President Peter Ueberroth of the Los Angeles Olympic Organizing Committee. In her examination of such devices as the "Peter" test on Olympic knowledge, administered to all new employees by the president himself, the salience of the founder is codified. But it is in the description of the large staff gatherings—true rhetorical masterpieces with speakers like Jesse Jackson—where management's use of formal communication devices to create an organizational identity is clearly apparent. These devices are not without their dark side; McDonald also critiques their coercive nature. Smith and Eisenberg's (1987) exploration of Walt Disney's immortalization through "Disney University" and the "Disney philosophy" displayed a similar concern for the power of the formal communication devices and language surrounding the founder. And Siehl's (1985) examination of cultural influences "after the founder" looked for clues to the ongoing cultural routines in the residue of the founder's legacy in a variety of organizational enactments including language use and structured patterns of behavior.

Strong Cultures

Many companies, such as the ones mentioned above, are famous for their self-conscious focus on corporate culture (e.g., McDonald's, Disney, Hyatt, Pepsi), and founders spend a great deal of time engaged in aligning values, systems, personalities, communication, and practices through ongoing socialization and monitoring. Moreover, some research reports claim to reveal a connection between corporate culture and organizational effectiveness/performance. Interestingly, all of the research that finds positive results operationalizes culture in terms of shared values. One example is Kotter and Heskett's (1992) study of 200 companies. Using a simple measure of corporate culture (perceived degree of value consensus), they observed that so-called strong cultures that exhibit a high degree of value consensus do not necessarily result in excellent performance and can even be destructive unless included among their norms and values is a focus on adaptation to a changing environment. Moreover, when "performance-enhancing" cultures emerge, they tended to exhibit two critical elements: (1) the presence of an entrepreneur with an adaptive business philosophy; and (2) an effective business strategy that succeeds and consequently adds credibility to the entrepreneur's position, as he or she engages in a constant dialogue that encourages challenges to received wisdom and invites ongoing adaptation and change. Chatman and Jehn (1994) took a similar approach in examining the relationships among industry norms, organizational culture (values), and individual employee fit using a measure of organizational culture called the OCP (O'Reilly, Chatman, & Caldwell, 1991). In applying this measurement tool to different organizations within and across industries, Chatman and Jehn noted significant differences in values across industries, as well as differences among organizations, even those within relatively homogeneous industries.

Other researchers are skeptical of the entire culture-effectiveness project. Siehl and Martin (1990) believed that studies like Kotter and Heskett's (1992) are methodologically flawed since attitudes and values seldom reliably predict behavior. In their critique, Siehl and Martin maintained that this research is also on the "wrong track" and deflects energy from more useful avenues of research that might focus on symbolism, ethics, diversity, and the uneven distribution of power at work. Saffold (1988) is even more specific in his critique and argues that overly simplistic studies of culture that employ monolithic, superficial conceptions and measurements of culture are unlikely to reveal clear culture-performance links. His proposal is to investigate issues of cultural dispersion, potency, and complex interactions that may exist between aspects of culture and organizational performance.

Organizational Change and Managing Culture

The literature on organizational change and development acknowledges the role of culture in promoting, managing, or impeding change. The question, then, is whether managers or change agents can move cultures in specific directions to achieve certain organizational goals—for example, related to financial performance or issues like increased diversity. There is considerable debate about this subject, both with regard to techniques and to likelihood of success. In their attempt to enact planned culture change, many executives or leaders have found themselves in the awkward position of pushing an ideological stance that is at odds with the already established local culture. This dilemma has led to the conclusion that culture cannot be "managed" per se —although certain patterns of behavior can be encouraged and cultivated. Here we note a connection to the prior section on penetration. As long as organizational culture is approached cognitively in terms of shared meanings and assumptions, one is invariably tempted to try to alter these cognitions directly in a change effort and to be met with predictably high levels of resistance. Managers and consultants alike recognize that most improvement efforts of these kinds fail because they are "unnatural acts," incompatible with the local culture.

An alternative approach that treats "values" and "assumptions" as epiphenomena and aims instead to reshape practices—including communication practices—is less likely to be resisted, and paradoxically more likely to shape interpretations over time. Consequently, strategic change efforts are increasingly analyzing culture to maximize the chances of implementing new ways of doing business such as total quality management (TQM), self-managing work groups, and reengineering. With culture defined as present practices, many researchers argued that large-scale change efforts are impossible without, and as a result may constitute, widespread cultural change (e.g., Sashkin & Kiser, 1993; Spencer, 1994).

Alvesson (1993b) saw the instrumental view of culture—and the accompanying arguments about "good," "strong," or "ideal" cultures—as pervasive in the works of management theorists Schein (1985), Wilkins and Dyer (1988), and others (e.g., Baker, 1980; Trice & Beyer, 1984). He criticized these approaches as overly narrow and unlikely to reveal much about important, unplanned, organic changes initiated by employees, or by gradual changes in society. What passes for corporate culture, he maintained, is better referred to as management ideology: the norms and values that serve as ideals for a group. Corporate culture is bigger, less homogeneous, and more complex. Trying to extract a common set of values from an organization that employs a wide range of people, he argued, seems likely only to yield a superficial set of norms and values that may promote cohesiveness but have little impact on work behavior. Alvesson (1993b) also argued that in their attempts to identify culture as a "cause" of organizational performance, writers have systematically set up either an impoverished view of culture or a tautological theory. In other words, a broad view of culture, similar

to most anthropological definitions of the term, would include the process and outcomes of job performance as part of the corporate culture. When one author argued that a common culture promotes cohesion and communication, these positive "outcomes" seem part of the common culture. This suggests that the production of culture is a complex activity within which such concepts as cohesion and performance appear throughout the ongoing process of structuration.

Not all studies about organizational change, however, are conducted with a "management bias" or an impoverished view of culture, especially in the communication discipline. Howard and Geist's (1995) structurationist examination of organizational transformation is a prime example. Their examination of a merger was not undertaken to improve the results of the organizational change, nor do they underestimate the complexity of the situation. In fact, their study problematized the changes taking place and brought more voices into the discourse surrounding the changes. And not all descriptions of managing culture are solely designed to serve management's interests. For example, in his passionate account of life at W. L. Gore & Associates, Pacanowsky (1988) described the attitudes and practices of an "empowering" organization in which open, radically decentralized communication is the key feature of the culture. As a participant in the organization, Pacanowsky does not provide a detached account; rather, he offers an emotional argument for organizations that respect people, recognize maturity, and reward it. It serves as an argument for how this particular strong culture and its associated practices could be recreated elsewhere.

The motivations behind management's attempts to manipulate culture are well intentioned but are often naive. Usually, management begins with the hope of improving corporate performance by substituting a common vision and values for close supervision and autocratic management. While some scholars have argued that this practice is worse than overt domination (cf. Pilotta et al., 1988), many employees apparently see value-driven organizations as better places to work. Alvesson and Willmott (1992), however, argue that while it is easy to point out the forces of domination at work, life could be worse, and some emancipation from the abuses of power is better than none at all.

The corporate culture view engenders valuable conversations, particularly in the workplace, in that it encourages managers and employees to talk about their history, critique their activities, think in terms of processes, notice their interdependence, and take seriously human interaction. Its shortcomings stem from a monolithic view of culture, a superficial emphasis on norms and values, and a failure to consider the alternative cultures and countercultures that deserve attention and can also serve as sources of innovation and perhaps increased effectiveness.

This review of organizational culture themes has focused on the diversity of approaches and highlighted the difficulties and the vast terrain of this literature. This thematic display of culture as symbolism and performance and the approaches to texts, critique, identity, cognition, effectiveness, and climate force us to assess the congruences and disjunctures in this vast literature. As culture becomes the metaphor for all of our organizational lives, what seems salient in this work is its rapidly changing face, both as an academic concept and as a description of lived experiences. In the next section, we cover three issues that are grounds for future research investigations.

FUTURE RESEARCH ON ORGANIZATIONAL CULTURE

The following discussion of self and community, diversity, globalization, and technology is driven by a communication orientation but is also shaped by the material conditions of our environment and the belief that those conditions need to be problematized and reflexively analyzed. This perspective does not rule out alternative approaches—indeed, we welcome poetry, fiction, film documentaries, and many other alternative windows into, or canvases over, performances of the concept we gingerly call organizational culture. These alternative approaches are not purely the domain of academics, since corporations such as Honeywell use plays and art to engage members in discussions about their culture. Our sense of the critical issues that need investigation are evoked by our experiences and our reading of the organizational culture metaphor.

Self, Community, and Organizational Culture

Cultural practices—by any name—are inseparable from the stream of human life. The biological hallmark of our species, notably the presence of reflexive consciousness along with our comparatively low levels of instinct, requires the development of an elaborate social culture to guide human behavior (Geertz, 1973). The relationship between humans and their cultures, then, is a seamless and symbiotic one—human being and culture arise in relationship to one another, and cannot be separated in any meaningful way. "Being human" can thus make sense only in the context of culture(s), and the existence of any culture relies heavily on the thoughts and behavior of humans. As far as we know, humans are alone in their ability to say "I," and in so doing conceive of a "self" that is separate from an "other" or the "world." The self-other separation made possible by language and rationality is constantly under repair, as we seek identities that are simultaneously distinctive and aligned with social groups and organizations. Communication scholars thus need to investigate further the relationship between cultural phenomena in organizations such as gendered practices of team formation, the identity implications when families have multiple members employed in the same organization, or the continued strain on working parents trying to maintain positive identities in a mach-speed working world that does not leave enough time for the family.

If culture, then, provides generic cues to guide human behavior, then local cultures—organized along ethnic, gender, geographic, or organizational lines—serve as identity resources and exert powerful forces on human behavior. Academics in particular seem to want a renewed quest for community, to discover, resurrect, or invent places that seem like real places and can perhaps provide an enhanced sense of identification and support. In addition, much of this argument has to do with focusing less on the rights of individuals and more on their responsibilities to the local group (Etzioni, 1993). Deetz (e.g., 1985, 1992) has been one of the most articulate spokespersons for the importance of the relationship between organizational culture and communities. He argues that our dehumanizing, hierarchical, gendered discursive practices in organizations are indicative of a breakdown in community. As these practices are reproduced elsewhere in our lives, we need to recognize their wider power in society. Communication is at the forefront of this discussion because of its integral role in the structuring of both organizations and community. This is a call for communication scholars to focus on the "migration" of corporate practices into the community and family. For example, what values are at risk when educational institutions become "customer driven" or classrooms adopt TQM techniques? As faith in governments and political systems wanes, we also need to look toward new arenas of decision making such as immigrant support organizations, large networks of organizations like MADD (Mothers Against Drunk Driving), and activist groups like gay and lesbian legal action funds. We need to ask how the communicative practices of community organizations differ from more traditional/hierarchical organizations, if they do. For example, we know quite a bit about the culture-building activities of large-company

founders, but we know much less about those who started community-based organizations and what happened after they left.

These local cultures are the symbolic milieux, the "webs of significance" made famous by Weber and Geertz. But webs both provide easy travel and catch flies—culture always appears both as agency and constraint. At a theoretical level, understanding the role of culture as agency in both the production of self-identity and organizational change would be particularly illuminating. So, for example, can organizations that use concertive control also develop a reflexive dialogue about control? Research that examines the relationship between institutions and local organizations—for example, school boards, parents' groups, religious organizations—would be particularly salient. What do we really know about local community "power structures" (e.g., concerns about health or family) as they relate to disembedded practices brought directly from work? We need to investigate whether the decision-making practices are more open or participative, less gendered, or more moral.

Globalization and Organizational Culture

Globalization is causing widespread changes in multiple constructions of culture both in and outside of organizations. The reality of a global marketplace is leading to homogenization of products and services worldwide and the increasing presence and influence of corporations in public and private life (Deetz, 1992). And the rise of a global economy has meant a rapid destabilization of the labor force, such that companies demonstrate no allegiance to place and seek the best value for their labor dollars worldwide (Barnet & Cavanaugh, 1994). In an even broader sense, our present situation might be characterized as reflecting a crisis of loyalty or identification. The actions of global corporations serve to undermine the relied-on allegiances and commitments made between workers and employees in every company worldwide. Even in Japan, which has for decades relied on lifetime employment, the system is eroding. Business deals that formerly relied on trust and relationships are increasingly going to the lowest bidder in a hypercompetitive worldwide labor market. The result is a widespread feeling among workers of fear, instability, and the absence of loyalty. Culture researchers need to observe how this "new social contract" with employees is enacted and how workers express alienation (graffiti on the walls?) or fear. Are organizations finding spaces for alternative voices, or have they developed cultural panopticons that silence deviants? Another question is, How will employees establish alternative loyalties to the firm? This phenomenon is similar to what Barnet and Cavanaugh (1994) call "globalization from below," which they say is on the rise—emergent networks of people at the grassroots level taking responsibility for developing meaningful relationships in the face of (and often in direct response to) corporate colonization and homogenization.

There are issues that tie questions of self and community to globalization. Giddens's (1993) analysis makes it clear that the issue is not just whether or not we invest ourselves in a job or company that could disappear tomorrow, or one that might continue to exist without us, but the role these work experiences play in the trajectory and transformation of self and identity. This is essentially an issue of the reflexive construction of self as organized in concert with the economic, moral, and practical features of organizational culture(s). Restated, how are we changing and how are organizational cultures changing simultaneously within this environment of persistent organizational reinvention (Eisenberg, in press)?

The rise of multinational, "imperial" corporations has many implications for researchers of organizational culture (Barnet & Cavanaugh, 1994; Eisenberg & Goodall, 2000). Globalization has made organizations pay at-

tention to the contextual differences involved in doing business with consumers and employees originating in different cultures. More important, global capitalism and the accompanying decline of the political nation-state has led societies worldwide to be permeated by the substance of corporate culture, even in places where local or national cultures might better serve the interests of the people involved (Barnet & Cavanaugh, 1994). Scholars need to investigate the new relationships among employee groups of foreign national organizations and the adaptation, or diminution, of practices as corporate cultures intertwine with different national cultures. What are the implications for work effectiveness, solidarity, or decision making as "cultural enclaves" emerge within multiethnic organizations?

And the migratory nature of cultures is especially relevant given the close connection between large migrations, what Kotkin (1994) calls "diaspora by design," and the organizations that constitute the empire of these global tribes. For example, future organizational culture research might compare Taiwanese research and development organizations in the United States, which tend to be run by American-educated Chinese who are fluent in English, with Japanese research and development firms located in the States that are largely outposts manned by a rotating cadre of foreign executives. What are the local implications of that warning from the 1980s that "Chernobyl is everywhere"? In other words, how might we discuss the rising belief that there are no longer "others" only "us"? Since much of the focus concerning globalization is either on the media or the economy, we need to have a better understanding of the dominant cultural practices of those industries and institutions as well as the key organizations and leaders and a better understanding of the subcultures of professional groups such as economists and the fragmented lives of ex-patriots. A critical issue is our knowledge of the degree to which organizational culture is a mediated phenomenon. This is the question: What does culture mean in global organizations? Is it the constant structuring of local knowledge and practices within larger corporate systems?

Issues surrounding the mobility of the workforce have always been a societal concern, but they have not been a major feature of the organizational culture literature. Globalization is one of the drivers of growing workforce diversity in almost every industry, raising critical questions about ways of coordinating people of markedly different backgrounds to promote organizational and personal goals. Much of this challenge is communicative, but it is not just at the level of language translation. Key questions surround sensemaking in these environments; for example, are particular rhetorical forms developing that promote a sense of unity amid a diversity of interpretations? Training programs that deal with diversity or multicultural differences ought to be studied to determine the degree to which they are vehicles for personal growth and learning and/or hegemonic devices that attempt to impose cultural homogeneity in large organizations. This also suggests that we need to examine our related constructs culturally; for example, we would not be surprised to discover that our connotations of conflict resolution are overly parochial and that they may need expanding to explicate the tensions that arise from multiethnic cliques in the workplace. It appears that if we are to have a "cultured" organizational communication literature, then the cultural biases of our constructs and frameworks need to be more clearly articulated.

Technology

Technology is changing the nature of work in organizations, as well as the nature of jobs. As the saying goes, technology applies only to things that were not around when you were young. To many children born since the late 1970s, for example, computers are not a technology, but a taken-for-granted part of the social fabric. This is true even for children who have never seen a computer, because the language of information networks and virtual reality and their underlying principles form the basis of children's television shows and toys (e.g., Power Rangers, "transformers," virtual reality games). Some research has occurred in this increasingly important area—for example, Barley (1986), who studied the adoption of CT scanners; Prasad (1993), who took a "symbolic interactionist" approach to work computerization in an HMO setting; and Aydin (1989), who showed that organizational culture and professional subcultures (e.g., doctors vs. nurses vs. pharmacists vs. social workers) have a strong impact on the ways in which technology is implemented. But the larger work of theorizing about the role of technology in creating and changing culture across different locales remains relatively unexplored.

We can expect the new technologies of today (groupware and other computer-mediated communication, virtual reality, biotechnology, multimedia, and the Internet) to have as powerful an impact on work cultures as their predecessors (telephones, e-mail, and voice mail). For example, electronic mail has made an enormous difference in the way many companies look with regard to paper flow, hallway talk, closeness of supervision, perceptions of privacy, speed of expected turnaround of work, and politeness norms. The reason it is so important for organizational culture researchers to pay attention to technology is that technology plays a key role in the structuring of behavior—of space, time, and interaction patterns. For instance, in the era of online newspapers, an organizational credo like "all the news fit to print" becomes almost quaint. In addition, the future of many organizations—and this will likely be the case across most industries and parts of the world—will thus be largely characterized by flexible learning through instantaneous communication. We ought to investigate the cultural practices that will be critical not just for organizational effectiveness but also the individual management of identity. What sources of resistance will appear in response to this pace, these expectations, and the associated reward structure, and how will they be interpreted?

Just as the idea of "job" is falling under scrutiny today, the idea of an organization as a place bounded in space and time is already problematic. This trend began with telecommuting and various forms of strategic alliances that linked "coworkers" electronically. In some cases, electronic communication augments other media, but in an increasing number of situations, employees' sole sources of contact are virtual; hence the idea of a virtual office or virtual team in which people report being "here," at work, when they are in effect connected via network in cyberspace. Even when there is a physical workplace, employers are beginning to replace stationary offices with "portable" ones. At the advertising firm Chiat Day, for example, employees check in when they arrive at work and are issued a computer and a cellular phone, then are encouraged to work anywhere in the company (depending on the specific needs of the project). These new patterns of work have implications for our theorizing about what it means to be "local." Our understanding of power and authority in organizations needs to change so that we can distinguish status even when no one is "home" or when the lines between work and home are so blurred that they become difficult to see. The question for cultural scholars may be less whether these events are good or bad but how are they interpreted and what moral lens is being used to discuss them. We need to be able to identify the communicative construction as well as the communication skill and components of these newly flexible jobs. We need to be sensitive to issues of ageism in firms where the oldest vice president is 27. We need to ask what are the cultural implications of leaving many people out of the information revolution as the technology gap grows ever wider.

CONCLUSION

At one time, we considered titling this chapter "The Myth of Organizational Culture,"

suggesting that what passes for organizational culture is less distinctive and more reflective of larger societal groupings than most of us researchers would like to admit. In fact, the emphasis on benchmarking in business—evaluating oneself against other excellent companies—and the total quality movement led countless organizations to adopt eerily similar practices both within and outside of their industries (e.g., high-involvement management, shop floor control, capacity planning, future searches, strategic planning, reengineering, process improvement teams, learning organizations, knowledge management consultants, and training programs). None of this should be all that surprising, since the most significant information exchange among organizations has always occurred through personnel flows, where Company A hires a manager from Company B, or when workers in an industry (e.g., computers) move among companies following major developments and in pursuit of work. Nevertheless, the widespread acceleration of "cultural traffic" (Alvesson, 1993b) has led overall to reduced distinctiveness among companies and greater influence on the part of larger social groupings, such as gender, profession, class, and ethnicity, on organizational cultures. Arguably the most original contribution of Martin's (1992) book is her conceptualization of each organizational culture as a "nexus," a site at which cultural forces (practices, assumptions, values, interpretations) interact. The implication for communication research is that we must widen our lens in studying organizational culture and not assume that the reasons for organizational behavior are best found in or even near the organization. On the contrary, just as Geertz (1973) remarked that anthropologists "don't study villages, they study in villages," so too do organizational ethnographers study in organizations. As boundaries or organizations become less definite, it will make sense to worry less about "organizations" and more about the organizing and structuring of communicative relationships and our discursively produced environments. We need to push our conceptual development and the sophistication of our investigations. We need the resources to study large, networked organizations and the skills to delve into multiethnic cliques. We must adapt our theoretical frameworks so that we can use such concepts as complexity theory to investigate the myriad of cultural forces made manifest at an organizational nexus. We need to understand that our work becomes part of the cultural phenomena that we are studying and that we are, in part, reflexively creating the future of organizations.

NOTES

1. It is important to note that Schall's (1993) conception of culture as shared communicative rules is not a strictly cognitive approach since the rules operate on behaviors and do not regulate thoughts and cognitions.

2. We uncovered several unpublished dissertations from the early 1990s conducted by education researchers interested in communication climates in schools.

REFERENCES

Aktouf, 0. (1992). Management and theories of organizations in the 1990s: Toward a radical humanism. *Academy of Management Review, 17,* 407-432.

Alvesson, M. (1993a). Cultural-ideological modes of management control: A theory and a case study of a professional service company. In S. A. Deetz (Ed.), *Communication yearbook 16* (pp. 3-42). Newbury Park, CA: Sage.

Alvesson, M. (1993b). *Cultural perspectives on organizations.* New York: Cambridge University Press.

Alvesson, M., & Willmott, H. (1992). On the idea of emancipation in management and organizational studies. *Academy of Management Review, 17,* 432-465.

Aydin, C. (1989). Occupational adaptation to computerized medical information systems. *Journal of Health and Social Behavior, 30,* 163-179.

Baker, E. L. (1980). Managing organizational culture. *Management Review, 69,* 8-13.

Bakhtin, M. (1981). *The dialogic-imagination: Four essays by M. M. Bakhtin* (C. Emerson & M. Holquist, Trans.). Austin: University of Texas Press.

Banks, S., & Riley, P. (1993). Structuration theory as an ontology for communication research. In S. A. Deetz (Ed.), *Communication yearbook 16* (pp. 167-196). Newbury Park, CA: Sage.

Bantz, C. R. (1993). *Understanding organizations: Interpreting organizational communication cultures.* Columbia: University of South Carolina Press.

Barker, J. R., & Cheney, G. (1994). The concept and the practices of discipline in contemporary organizational life. *Communication Monographs, 61,* 19-43.

Barley, S. (1983). Semiotics and the study of occupational and organizational cultures. *Administrative Science Quarterly, 28,* 393-413.

Barley, S. (1986). Technology as an occasion for structuring: Evidence from observations of CT scanners and the social order of radiology departments. *Administrative Science Quarterly, 33,* 24-61.

Barley, S. (1990). The alignment of technology and structure through roles and networks. *Administrative Science Quarterly, 35,* 61-103.

Barnet, R. J., & Cavanaugh, J. (1994). Creating a level playing field. *Technology Review, 97,* 46-48.

Barnett, G. A. (1988). Communication and organizational culture. In G. M. Goldhaber & G. A. Barnett (Eds.), *Handbook of organizational communication* (pp. 101-130). Norwood, NJ: Ablex.

Bastien, D., McPhee, R. D., & Bolton, K. (1995). A study and extended theory of the structuration of climate. *Communication Monographs, 62,* 87-109.

Bennis, W. (1969). *Organizational development: Its nature, origins, and prospects.* Reading, MA: Addison-Wesley.

Boland, R., & Hoffman, R. (1983). Humor in a machine shop. In L. Pondy, P. Frost, G. Morgan, & T. Dandridge (Eds.), *Organizational symbolism* (pp. 187-198). Greenwich, CT: JAI.

Bormann, E. G. (1983). Symbolic convergence: Organizational communication and culture. In L. L. Putnam & M. E. Pacanowsky (Eds.), *Communication and organizations: An interpretive approach* (pp. 99-122). Beverly Hills, CA: Sage.

Brown, M. H. (1990a). Defining stories in organizations: Characteristics and functions. In J. A. Anderson (Ed.), *Communication yearbook 13* (pp. 162-190). Newbury Park, CA: Sage.

Brown, M. H. (1990b). "Reading" an organization's culture: An examination of stories in nursing homes. *Journal of Applied Communication Research, 18,* 64-75.

Brown, M. H., & McMillan, J. (1991). Culture as text: The development of an organizational narrative. *Southern Communication Journal, 49,* 27-42.

Burke, M. J., Borucki, C. C., & Hurley, A. (1992). Reconceptualizing psychological climate in a retail service environment: A multiple stakeholder perspective. *Journal of Applied Psychology, 7,* 717-730.

Carbaugh, D. (1988). Cultural terms and tensions in the speech at a television station. *Western Journal of Speech Communication, 52,* 216-237.

Chatman, J. A., & Jehn, K. A. (1994). Assessing the relationship between industry characteristics and organizational culture: How different can you be? *Academy of Management Journal, 37,* 522-553.

Cheney, G. (1991). *Rhetoric in organizational society: Managing multiple identities.* Columbia: University of South Carolina Press.

Cheney, G. (1995). Democracy in the workplace: Theory and practice from the communication perspective. *Journal of Applied Communication Research, 23,* 167-200.

Clair, R. (1993). The use of framing devices to sequester organizational narratives: Hegemony and harassment. *Communication Monographs, 60,* 113-136.

Clifford, J. (1983). On ethnographic authority. *Representations, 1,* 118-146.

Clifford, J., & Marcus, G. E. (1986). *Writing culture: The poetics and politics of ethnography.* Berkeley: University of California Press.

Conquergood, S. (1991). Rethinking ethnography: Towards a critical cultural politics. *Communication Monographs, 58,* 179-194.

Conrad, C. (1983). Organizational power: Faces and symbolic forms. In L. L. Putnam & M. E. Pacanowsky (Eds.), *Communication and organizations: An interpretive approach* (pp. 173-194). Beverly Hills, CA: Sage.

Contractor, N., Eisenberg, E. M., & Monge, P. (1994). Antecedents and outcomes of interpretive diversity in organizations. Paper presented at the annual meeting of the International Communication Association, May, Chicago.

D'Andrade, R. G. (1984). Cultural meaning systems. In R. A. Shweder & R. A. LeVine (Eds.), *Culture theory: Essays on mind, self, and emotion* (pp. 88-121). Cambridge, UK: Cambridge University Press.

Deal, T. E., & Kennedy, A. A. (1982). *Corporate cultures: The rites and rituals of corporate life.* Reading, MA: Addison-Wesley.

Deetz, S. A. (1985). Ethical considerations in cultural research in organizations. In P. J. Frost, L. F. Moore, M. R. Louis, C. C. Lundberg, & J. Martin (Eds.), *Organizational culture* (pp. 253-270). Beverly Hills, CA: Sage.

Deetz, S. A. (1992). *Democracy in an age of corporate colonization: Developments in communication and the politics of everyday life.* Albany: State University of New York Press.

Deetz, S. A., & Kersten, A. (1983). Critical models of interpretive research. In L. L. Putnam & M. E. Pacanowsky (Eds.), *Communication and organizations: An interpretive approach* (pp. 147-172). Beverly Hills, CA: Sage.

Downs, C. (1979). The relationship between communication and job satisfaction. In R. Houseman, C. Logue, & D. Freshley (Eds.). *Readings in interpersonal and organizational communication* (pp. 363-376). Boston: Allyn & Bacon.

Eisenberg, E. (In press). Building a mystery: Toward a new theory of communication and identity. *Journal of Communication.*

Eisenberg, E., & Goodall, H. L., Jr. (2000). *Organizational communication* (3rd ed.). New York: St. Martin's.

Eisenberg, E. M., Murphy, A., & Andrews, L. (1998). Openness and decision making in the search for a university provost. *Communication Monographs, 65,* 1-23.

Erez, M., & Earley, P. C. (1993). *Culture, self-identity, and work.* New York: Oxford University Press.

Etzioni, A. (1993). *The spirit of community: Rights, responsibilities, and the communitarian agenda.* New York: Crown.

Falcione, R. L., & Kaplan, E. A. (1984). Organizational climate, communication, and culture. In R. Bostrom (Ed.), *Communication yearbook 8* (pp. 285-309). Beverly Hills, CA: Sage.

Falcione, R. L., Sussman, L., & Herden, R. P. (1987). Communication climate in organizations. In F. M. Jablin, L. L. Putnam, K. H. Roberts, & L. W. Porter (Eds.), *Handbook of organizational communication: An interdisciplinary perspective* (pp. 195-227). Newbury Park, CA: Sage.

Farace, R. V., Monge, P. R., & Russell, H. M. (1977). *Communicating and organizing.* Reading, MA: Addison-Wesley.

Ferguson, K. (1984). *The feminist case against bureaucracy.* Philadelphia: Temple University Press.

French, W. L., & Bell, C. (1973). *Organizational development.* Englewood Cliffs, NJ: Prentice Hall.

Frost, P. J., Moore, L. F., Louis, M. R., Lundberg, C. C., & Martin, J. (Eds.). (1991). *Reframing organizational culture.* Newbury Park, CA: Sage.

Geertz, C. (1973). *The interpretation of cultures.* New York: Basic Books.

Geertz, C. (1988). *Works and lives: The anthropologist as author.* Stanford, CA: Stanford University Press.

Gergen, K. (1991). *The saturated self: Dilemmas of identity in contemporary life.* New York: Basic Books.

Giddens, A. (1991). *Modernity and self-identity: Self and society in the late modern age.* Stanford, CA: Stanford University Press.

Giddens, A. (1993). *New rules of sociological method* (2nd ed.). Stanford, CA: Stanford University Press.

Goffman, E. (1959). *The presentation of self in everyday life.* Garden City, NY: Anchor Doubleday.

Goodall, H. L. (1989). *Casing a promised land.* Carbondale: Southern Illinois University Press.

Goodall, H. L. (1991). *Living in the rock 'n roll mystery: Reading context, self, and others as clues.* Carbondale: Southern Illinois University Press.

Gronn, P. (1983). Talk as the work: The accomplishment of school administration. *Administrative Science Quarterly, 28,* 1-21.

Hellriegel, D., & Slocum, J. (1974). Organizational climate: Measures, research, and contingencies. *Academy of Management Journal, 17,* 255-280.

Hofstede, G. H. (1983). National cultures in four dimensions. *International Studies of Management and Organization, 13,* 46-74.

Hofstede, G. H. (1991). *Culture and organizations: Software of the mind.* New York: McGraw-Hill.

Hofstede, G. H., Neuijen, B., Ohayv, D. D., & Sanders, G. (1990). Measuring organizational cultures: A qualitative and quantitative study across twenty cases. *Administrative Science Quarterly, 35,* 286-316.

Holquist, M. (1990). *Dialogism: Bakhtin and his world.* London: Routledge.

Howard, L. A., & Geist, P. (1995). Ideological positioning in organizational change. *Communication Monographs, 62,* 110-131.

Jackson, M. (1989). *Paths toward a clearing.* Bloomington: Indiana University Press.

James, L. R., James, L. A., & Ashe, D. K. (1990). The meaning of organizations: The role of cognition and values. In B. Schneider (Ed.), *Organizational climate and culture* (pp. 40-84). San Francisco: Jossey-Bass.

James, L. R., & Jones, A. P. (1974). Organizational climate: A review of theory and research. *Psychological Bulletin, 16,* 74-113.

Jaques, E. (1951). *The changing culture of a factory: A study of authority and participation in an industrial setting.* London: Tavistock.

Jelinek, M., Smircich, L., & Hirsch, P. (Eds.). (1983). Organizational culture [Special issue]. *Administrative Science Quarterly, 28*(3).

Jermier, J. M. (1991). Critical epistemology and the study of organizational culture: Reflections on "Street Corner Society." In P. J. Frost, L. F. Moore, M. R. Louis, C. C. Lundberg, & J. Martin (Eds.), *Reframing organizational culture* (pp. 223-233). Newbury Park, CA: Sage.

Johnson, B. M. (1977). *Communication: The process of organizing.* Boston: Allyn & Bacon (Reprinted American Press, 1981)

Johnston, H. R., Jr. (1976). A new conceptualization of source of organizational climate. *Administrative Science Quarterly, 21,* 95-103.

Katz, D., & Kahn, R. L. (1978). *The social psychology of organizations* (2nd ed.). New York: John Wiley.

Knight, J. P. (1990). Literature as equipment for killing: Performance as rhetoric in military training camps. *Text and Performance Quarterly, 10,* 157-168.

Knuf, J. (1993). "Ritual" in organizational culture theory: Some theoretical reflections and a plea for terminological rigor. In S. A. Deetz (Ed.), *Communication yearbook 16* (pp. 112-121). Newbury Park, CA: Sage.

Kondo, D. (1990). *Crafting selves: Power, gender, and discourses of identity in a Japanese workplace.* Chicago: University of Chicago Press.

Kotkin, J. (1994). *Tribes: How race, religion, and identity determine success in the new global economy.* New York: Random House.

Kotter, J. P., & Heskett, J. L. (1992). *Corporate culture and performance.* New York: Free Press.

Krackhardt, D., & Kilduff, M. (1990). Friendship patterns and culture: The control of organizational diversity. *American Anthropologist, 91,* 142-155.

Kreiner, K., & Schultz, M. (1993). Informal collaboration in R&D: The formation of networks across organizations. *Organization Studies, 14,* 189-209.

Kunda, G. (1992). *Engineering culture: Control and commitment in a high-tech corporation.* Philadelphia: Temple University Press.

Linstead, S., & Grafton-Small, R. (1992). On reading organizational culture. *Organization Studies, 13,* 331-355.

Louis, M. R. (1990). Acculturation in the workplace: Newcomers as lay ethnographers. In B. Schneider (Ed.), *Organizational climate and culture* (pp. 85-129). San Francisco: Jossey-Bass.

Marcus, G. E., & Fischer, M. J. (Eds.). (1986). *Anthropology as cultural critique: An experimental moment in the human sciences.* Chicago: University of Chicago Press.

Martin, J. (1992). *Cultures in organizations: Three perspectives.* New York: Oxford University Press.

Martin, J., & Meyerson, D. (1988). Organizational culture and the denial, channeling and acknowledgement of ambiguity. In L. Pondy, R. Boland, Jr., & H. Thomas (Eds.), *Managing ambiguity and change* (pp. 93-125). New York: John Wiley.

McCollom, M. (1994). The cultures of work organizations. *Academy of Management Review, 19,* 836-839.

McDonald, P. (1991). The Los Angeles Olympic Organizing Committee: Developing organizational culture in the short run. In P. J. Frost, L. F. Moore, M. R. Louis, C. C. Lundberg, & J. Martin (Eds.), *Reframing organizational culture* (pp. 26-38). Newbury Park, CA: Sage.

Mead, G. H. (1934). *Mind, self and society.* Chicago: University of Chicago Press.

Moenaert, R., Souder, W. E., Meyer, A. D., & DeSchoolmeester, D. (1994). R and D marketing integration mechanisms, communication flows, and innovation success. *Journal of Product and Innovation Management, 7,* 31-46.

Mohan, M. (1993). *Organizational communication and cultural vision: Approaches for analysis.* Albany: State University of New York Press.

Moran, T., & Volkwein, J. F. (1992). The cultural approach to the formation of organizational climate. *Human Relations, 45,* 19-48.

Mumby, D. (1988). *Communication and power in organizations: Discourse, ideology and domination.* Norwood, NJ: Ablex.

Mumby, D. K., & Putnam, L. L. (1992). The politics of emotion: A feminist reading of bounded rationality. *Academy of Management Review, 17,* 465-486.

Mumby, D. K., & Stohl, C. (1991). Power and discourse in organization studies: Absence and the dialectic of control. *Discourse & Society, 2,* 313-332.

Myerson, D. (1991). Normal ambiguity? A glimpse of an occupational culture. In P. J. Frost, L. F. Moore, M. R. Louis, C. C. Lundberg, & J. Martin (Eds.), *Reframing organizational culture* (pp. 131-144). Newbury Park, CA: Sage.

O'Reilly, C., Chatman, J., & Caldwell, D. (1991). People and organizational culture: A Q-sort approach to assessing person-organization fit. *Academy of Management Journal, 34,* 487-516.

Ostroff, C. (1993). The effects of climate and personal influences on individual behavior and attitudes in organizations. *Organizational Behavior and Human Decision Processes, 56,* 56-91.

Ouchi, W., & Wilkins, A. (1985). Organizational culture. *Annual Review of Sociology, 11,* 457-483.

Pacanowsky, M. E. (1988). Communication and the empowering organization. In J. A. Anderson (Ed.), *Communication yearbook 11* (pp. 356-379). Newbury Park, CA: Sage.

Pacanowsky, M. E., & O'Donnell-Trujillo, N. (1983). Organizational communication as cultural performance. *Communication Monographs, 50,* 126-147.

Peters, T. J., & Waterman, R. J. (1982). *In search of excellence.* New York: Harper & Row.

Pettigrew, A. M. (1979). On studying organizational cultures. *Administrative Science Quarterly, 24,* 570-581.

Pfeffer, J. (1981). Management as symbolic action: The creation and maintenance of organization paradigms. In B. Staw & L. Cummings (Eds.), *Research in organizational behavior* (Vol. 3, pp. 1-52). Greenwich, CT: JAI.

Pilotta, J. J., Widman, T., & Jasco, S. A. (1988). Meaning and action in the organizational setting: An interpretive approach. In J. A. Anderson (Ed.), *Communication yearbook 11* (pp. 310-334). Newbury Park, CA: Sage.

Pondy, L. R., & Mitroff, I. (1979). Beyond open systems models of organizations. In B. M. Staw (Ed.), *Research in organizational behavior* (Vol. 1, pp. 3-39). Greenwich, CT: JAI.

Poole, M. S. (1985). Communication and organizational climates: Review, critique, and a new perspective. In R. McPhee & P. Tompkins (Eds.), *Organizational communication: Traditional themes and new directions* (pp. 79-108). Beverly Hills, CA: Sage.

Poole, M. S., & McPhee, R. D. (1983). A structurational analysis of organizational climate. In L. L. Putnam & M. E. Pacanowsky (Eds.), *Communication and organizations: An interpretive approach* (pp. 195-220). Beverly Hills, CA: Sage.

Prasad, P. (1993). Symbolic processes in the implementation of technological change: A symbolic interactionist study of work computerization. *Academy of Management Journal, 36,* 1400-1429.

Putnam, L. L., & Pacanowsky, M. E. (Eds.). (1983). *Communication and organizations: An interpretive approach.* Beverly Hills, CA: Sage.

Putnam, L. L., Phillips, N., & Chapman, P. (1996). Metaphors of communication and organization. In S. R. Clegg, C. Hardy, & W. R. Nord (Eds.), *Handbook of organization studies* (pp. 375-408). London: Sage.

Putnam, L. L., Van Hoeven, S. A., & Bullis, C. A. (1991). The role of rituals and fantasy themes in teachers' bargaining. *Western Journal of Speech Communication, 55,* 85-103.

Rabinow, P., & Sullivan, W. M. (1979). *Interpretive social science: A reader.* Berkeley: University of California Press.

Redding, C. (1972). *Communication within the organization: An interpretive review of theory and research.* New York: Industrial Communication Council.

Rentsch, J. R. (1990). Climate and culture interaction and qualitative differences in organizational meanings. *Journal of Applied Psychology, 75,* 668-682.

Ricoeur, P. (1971). The model of the text: Meaningful action considered as a text. *Social Research, 38,* 529-562.

Riley, P. (1983). A structurationist account of political cultures. *Administrative Science Quarterly, 28,* 414-437.

Riley, P. (1991). Cornerville as narration. In P. J. Frost, L. F. Moore, M. R. Louis, C. C. Lundberg, & J. Martin (Eds.), *Reframing organizational culture* (pp. 215-223). Newbury Park, CA: Sage.

Riley, P. (1993). Arguing for "ritualistic" pluralism: The tension between privilege and the mundane. In S. A. Deetz (Ed.), *Communication yearbook 16* (pp. 112-121). Newbury Park, CA: Sage.

Rogers, R. A. (1994). Rhythm and the performance of organization. *Text and Performance Quarterly, 14,* 222-237.

Rorty, R. (1989). *Contingency, irony, and solidarity.* Cambridge, UK: Cambridge University Press.

Sackmann, S. (1991). *Cultural knowledge in organizations.* Newbury Park, CA: Sage.

Saffold, G. (1988). Culture traits, strength, and organizational performance: Moving beyond strong culture. *Academy of Management Review, 13,* 546-559.

Sashkin, M., & Kiser, K. (1993). *Putting total quality management to work.* San Francisco: Berrett-Koehler.

Schall, M. S. (1983). A communication rules approach to organizational culture. *Administrative Science Quarterly, 28,* 557-587.

Scheibel, D. (1992). Faking identity in clubland: The communicative performance of "fake ID." *Text and Performance Quarterly, 12,* 160-175.

Scheibel, D. (1994). Graffiti and "film school" culture: Displaying alienation. *Communication Monographs, 61,* 1-18.

Schein, E. (1985). *Organizational culture and leadership.* San Francisco: Jossey-Bass.

Schneider, B. (Ed.). (1990). *Organizational climate and culture* (Frontiers of industrial and organizational psychology). San Francisco: Jossey-Bass.

Schneider, B., Gunnarson, S., & Niles-Jolly, K. (1994). Creating the climate and culture of success. *Organizational Dynamics, 23,* 17-30.

Schneider, B., Wheeler, J., & Cox, J. (1992). A passion for service: Using content analysis to explicate service climate themes. *Journal of Applied Psychology, 77,* 705-717.

Shockley-Zalabak, P., & Morley, D. D. (1994). Creating a culture: A longitudinal examination of the influence of management and employee values on communication rule stability and emergence. *Human Communication Research, 20,* 334-355.

Shweder, R. A. (1991). *Thinking through cultures: Expeditions in cultural psychology.* Cambridge, MA: Harvard University Press.

Shweder, R. A., & LeVine, R. A. (Eds.). (1984). *Cultural theory: Essays on mind, self, and emotion.* New York: Cambridge University Press.

Siehl, C. (1985). After the founder: An opportunity to manage culture. In P. J. Frost, L. F. Moore, M. R. Louis, C. C. Lundberg, & J. Martin (Eds.), *Organizational culture* (pp. 125-140). Beverly Hills, CA: Sage.

Siehl, C., & Martin, J. (1990). Organizational culture: A key to financial performance? In B. Schneider (Ed.), *Organizational climate and culture* (pp. 241-281). San Francisco: Jossey-Bass.

Smircich, L., & Calás, M. B. (1987). Organizational culture: A critical assessment. In F. M. Jablin, L. L. Putnam, K. H. Roberts, & L. W. Porter (Eds.), *Handbook of organizational communication: An interdisciplinary perspective* (pp. 228-263). Newbury Park, CA: Sage.

Smith, R. C., & Eisenberg, E. (1987). Conflict at Disneyland: A root-metaphor analysis. *Communication Monographs, 54,* 367-380.

Spencer, B. A. (1994). Models of organization and total quality management: A comparison and critical evaluation. *Academy of Management Review, 19,* 446-471.

Stoller, P. (1989). *The taste of ethnographic things.* Philadelphia: University of Pennsylvania Press.

Strutton, D., & Pelton, L. (1994). The relationship between psychological climate in sales organizations and sales manager-salesperson solidarity. *Mid-Atlantic Journal of Business, 30,* 153-175.

Taylor, B. C. (1990). Reminiscences of Los Alamos: Narrative, critical theory and the organizational subject. *Western Journal of Speech Communication, 54,* 395-419.

Taylor, B. C. (1993). Register of the repressed: Women's voice and body in the nuclear weapons organization. *Quarterly Journal of Speech, 79,* 267-285.

Thompson, K. R., & Luthans, F. (1990). Organizational culture: A behavioral perspective. In B. Schneider (Ed.), *Organizational climate and culture* (pp. 319-344). San Francisco: Jossey-Bass.

Tompkins, E. V. B., Tompkins, P. K., & Cheney, G. (1989). Organizations as arguments: Discovering, expressing, and analyzing the premises for decisions. *Journal of Management Systems, 1,* 35-48.

Tompkins, P. K. (1987). Translating organizational theory: Symbolism over substance. In F. M. Jablin, L. L. Putnam, K. H. Roberts, & L. W. Porter (Eds.), *Handbook of organizational communication: An interdisciplinary perspective* (pp. 70-96). Newbury Park, CA: Sage.

Tompkins, P. K., & Cheney, G. (1988). On the facts of the text as the basis of human communication research. In J. A. Anderson (Ed.), *Communication yearbook 11* (pp. 455-481). Newbury Park, CA: Sage.

Toulson, P., & Smith, M. (1994). The relationship between climate and employee perceptions of personnel management practices. *Public Personnel Management, 23,* 453-469.

Trice, H. M., & Beyer, J. M. (1984). Studying organizational cultures through rites and ceremonials. *Academy of Management Review, 9,* 653-669.

Trujillo, N. (1992). Interpreting (the work and talk of) baseball: Perspectives on baseball park culture. *Western Journal of Communication, 56,* 350-371.

Trujillo, N., & Dionisopoulos, G. (1987). Cop talk, police stories, and the social construction of organizational drama. *Central States Speech Journal, 38,* 196-209.

Turner, V. (1980). Social dramas and stories about them. *Critical Inquiry, 7,* 141-168.

Turnipseed, D., & Turnipseed, P. (1992). Assessing organizational climate: Exploratory results with a new diagnostic model. *Leadership and Organizational Development Journal, 13,* 7-15.

Van Maanen, J. (1988). *Tales of the field: On writing ethnography.* Chicago: University of Chicago Press.

Van Maanen, J. (1991). The smile factory: Work at Disneyland. In P. J. Frost, L. F. Moore, M. R. Louis, C. C. Lundberg, & J. Martin (Eds.), *Reframing organizational culture* (pp. 58-76). Newbury Park, CA: Sage.

Van Maanen, J., & Kunda, G. (1989). "Real feelings": Emotional expression and organizational culture. In L. L. Cummings & B. M. Staw (Eds.), *Research in organizational behavior* (Vol. 11, pp. 43-104). Greenwich, CT: JAI.

Vygotsky, L. S. (1962). Thought and language (E. Hanfmann & G. Vakar, Eds. and Trans.). Cambridge, MA: MIT Press.

Weick, K. E. (1979). *The social psychology of organizing* (2nd ed.). Reading, MA: Addison-Wesley.

Weick, K. E. (1991). The vulnerable system: An analysis of the Tenerife air disaster. In P. J. Frost, L. F. Moore, M. R. Louis, C. C. Lundberg, & J. Martin (Eds.), *Reframing organizational culture* (pp. 117-130). Newbury Park, CA: Sage.

Wentworth, W. (1980). *Context and understanding.* New York: Elsevier.

Whyte, W. F. (1943). *Street corner society.* Chicago: University of Chicago Press.

Wilkins, A., & Dyer, W. G. (1988). Toward culturally sensitive theories of culture change. *Academy of Management Review, 13,* 522-533.

Wilkins, A., & Ouchi, W. A. (1983). Efficient cultures: Exploring the relationship between culture and organizational performance. *Administrative Science Quarterly, 28,* 468-481.

Witmer, D. F. (1997). Communication and recovery: Structuration as an ontological approach to organizational culture. *Communication Monographs, 64,* 324-349.

Youngbae, K., & Lee, B. (1995). R and D project team climate and team performance in Korea: A multidimensional approach. *R&D Management, 25,* 179-197.

Zohar, D. (1980). Safety climate in industrial organizations: Theoretical and applied implications. *Journal of Applied Psychology, 65,* 96-102.

10

Globalizing Organizational Communication

CYNTHIA STOHL
Purdue University

My grandfather was local, my father was national, and I have become European. . . .
It is no longer true that you can stay local and survive.

—Antoine Ribald, chairman of the French manufacturer B.S.N.,
quoted in Magee (1989).

Just being a European company would constrain us.
Like Socrates, we are citizens of the world, we converse with all.

—Per Blanker, director of a large Danish can manufacturing plant,
personal interview, April 1989

In today's global business community, there is no single best approach . . . each culture has
its own way of building relationships, motivating employees, negotiating, and working.

—Fons Trompenaars (1994, p. 3)

On my office door at Purdue University there is a state map of Indiana showing the locations of over 315 organizations with significant international involvement.[1] Among the national flags scattered across the state we find a total of 95 Japanese-owned companies including Subaru-Isuzu Automotive; a corn-processing plant owned by the English company Lyle Stuart; a large German Health Diagnostics Corporation, Boerhinger-Mannein; the famous Irish paper company, Jefferson Smurfit; and literally hundreds of other companies with strong links in over 80 countries across five continents. And this map doesn't even feature the large number of voluntary/nonprofit organizations such as the YWCA, Amnesty International, and Greenpeace, which are part of a network of more than 18,000 international nongovernmental organizations that link individuals, families, and communities across the globe (Boulding, 1990). Nor does it include educational institutions such as Purdue University, which employs over 1,000 international faculty and scholars, enrolls over 4,100 international students, has faculty collaboration and exchange with more than 140 international institutions, and sends hundreds of students to study abroad every year (Office of International Programs, 1999).

Clearly, internationalization is ubiquitous. By the end of the 1980s, over two thirds of the American workforce was employed in organizations with international connections (Feld & Jordan, 1988). International business travel has become a burgeoning multibillion-dollar business, and every year hundreds of thousands of employees worldwide become "expatriates," moving around the globe, spending six weeks, six months, six years, or even longer on overseas assignments. Indeed, it is now virtually impossible to conceive of a completely domestic, unicultural organization or organizational communication practices that do not have intercultural dimensions. The Hudson report, *Workforce 2000*, highlights the increasing racial, gender, ethnic, cultural, lifestyle, and age mix of American organizations (Johnson & Packard, 1987); the open

borders of the European Union have diversified their workforces ("One to Us," 1994); the political upheavals across Europe, Asia, and Africa have increased immigration as well as global investments (Naik, 1993); and advances in transportation and communication technologies have minimized the saliency of geographic boundaries and national borders (Stohl, 1993).

Yet despite these trends, organizational communication scholarship has rarely addressed multinational and global organizing. Even in the extensive review chapter on cross-cultural perspectives in the *Handbook of Organizational Communication* published in 1987, only 15 of the 99 citations referenced articles in communication publications and 7 of those were in one volume edited by Gudykunst, Stewart, and Ting-Toomey (1985). Indeed, as late as 1994, when researchers in other fields had turned their attention to the importance of macrocultural issues in organizational studies (as evidenced, e.g., by special issues focusing on globalization in many of the major organizational journals[2]) communication scholars were still lamenting the lack of attention to communication issues in the multinational organization (MNO).

Because the bulk of research on MNOs has been conducted by business scholars and social psychologists, it is not surprising that the literature on both organizational universals and national cultural influences infrequently focuses on communication issues. (Shuter & Wiseman, 1994, p. 7)

But now, driven by contemporary sociopolitical events, the increasing power of multinationals, pragmatic questions of how to manage a multicultural workplace, the internationalization of the labor movement, and our own professional and personal international experiences, there is growing recognition that organizational communication processes can no longer be viewed as bounded within a unicultural framework. For example, communication journals are beginning to publish a greater number of research articles on intercultural communication in multinational organizations (e.g., Lindsley, 1999; Stage, 1999) and globalization processes (e.g., DeSanctis & Monge, 1998), and the latest books on globalization written by scholars outside our field identify the centrality of organizational communication processes (e.g., Held, McGrew, Goldblatt, & Perraton, 1999; Scholte, 2000; Waters, 1995).[3] In terms of pedagogy, the same trend can be found. Graduate and undergraduate courses on global organizations and communicating in the global workplace are being developed across the discipline (see, e.g., the Web sites of courses jointly developed by Contractor, Monge, and Stohl: http://www. Spcomm. uiuc.edu:1000/global/index.html).

Concomitantly, recent theoretical and methodological challenges to the dominant epistemology and traditional social-scientific paradigm have made our discipline less parochial and more cognizant of, open to, and interested in alternative voices and interpretations (Mumby & Stohl, 1996). Moreover, because these "meaning-centered" perspectives focus on the constitutive role of communication in shaping organizational reality they have raised questions about the bounded nature, objectivity, generalizability, and universality of our constructs and theories, questions and tensions that resonate with the pressures inherent in and the study of transnational organizing. Multinational organizations are at the intersection of diverse communicative, cultural, and social practices. By definition they transcend the narrow perspective that treats organizations as isolated from the wider cultural patterns characterizing society.

This chapter examines organizational literature that addresses communicative processes associated with increasing globalization and cultural variability in multinational organizations. In this context, globalization refers to the interconnected nature of the global economy, the interpenetration of global and domestic organizations, and communication technologies that blur temporal and spatial boundaries (see Rice & Gattiker, Chapter 14 in this volume, and Fulk & Collins-Jarvis, Chapter 16, for further discussions of the relationship between technology and globalization). Cultural variability entails the attitudes, values, beliefs, and ways of knowing and doing that are associated with different cultural identities that may influence organizational and communicative systems.

Two distinct research trends characterize the research on globalization and cultural variability: *convergence* and *divergence*[4] (cf. Inkeles, 1998). The convergence literature refers to a set of imperatives embedded in the global economy that results in similar organizational structuring across nations. Historically rooted in contingency theory, this literature assumes that specific features of the global environment determine organizational form and concomitant communication practices. Thus, even when cultural differences are recognized, the research minimizes these differences and emphasizes the similarity of structural adaptation. The convergence literature addresses changing patterns of organizational communication as they relate to the demands of a global system that requires flexibility, responsiveness, speed, knowledge production, and knowledge dissemination. Convergence research operates within a framework of technical/instrumental rationality concerned predominantly with issues of organizational effectiveness. Communication is viewed as a conduit for the acquisition of resources, capital, information, and expertise, and structure is seen as a complex web of relationships designed to meet the survival needs of an organization. Rather than exploring organizational differences, this approach examines the mechanisms by which globalization produces alternative yet converging organizational forms.

In contrast, the divergence literature focuses primarily on issues of cultural difference. Despite similar environmental pressures on organizations throughout the world, research in this area highlights the communicative diversity found in organizations across the globe. Grounded in issues of practical rationality (Habermas, 1984), the focus is on human interpretation and experience of the world as meaningful and intersubjectively constructed.

The divergence perspective has its roots in two disciplinary traditions: social psychology and anthropology. Research from a social-psychological position sees culture as shaping organizational behavior and influencing communication because culture structures individuals' perceptions and ideas of the world. Work grounded in the anthropological tradition sees organizations as sites of sensemaking and interpretive activity strongly influenced by cultural affiliations. Communication is the essence of culture, inextricably and reciprocally bound together, and effectiveness is rooted in the ability of people from different cultures to work together. Whereas the convergence perspective assumes that similar actions, messages, and processes function in similar ways across cultures, the divergence perspective assumes that similar communicative actions may arise from differing interpretations and visions. Collective action is not necessarily predicated on shared meaning or shared goals but rather on interlocking behaviors (Erez & Earley, 1993; Weick, 1969). Sorge (1983) sums up this perspective succinctly: "There is no culture free context of organization" (p. 136).

Taken together, these approaches capture the dialectical tensions inherent in the globalization of organizational experience (what Barber, 1992, identifies in the political sphere as the forces of Jihad vs. McWorld). The environmental and technological pressures on contemporary organizations to become more and more similar clash with the proprietary pull of cultural identifications, traditional values, and conventional practices of social life. The position taken here is that neither the convergence nor divergence perspective alone can adequately account for the complex organizational processes of globalization. Communication is simultaneously a tool, a resource, a rational selection mode that facilitates or inhibits organizational survival and an interpre-

tive symbolic process that plays a constitutive role in shaping organizational reality.

Within the global workplace, communication embodies the dynamic unfolding of relations between actors and organizations embedded in a set of social and cultural constraints and opportunities that transforms individual and group action into organizational consequences. Because organizational communication scholarship generally (1) focuses on structure, process, and interpretation; (2) is sensitive to the interplay of micro- and macrolevel processes; and (3) acknowledges the permeable and socially constructed boundaries of organizations; it is centrally positioned to explicate the means by which organizations adhere to dominant cultural patterns while adapting those patterns and structures to accommodate differences in and pressures of the global system. As this chapter indicates, however, our contributions to this burgeoning field of global experience and scholarship are in its infancy.

The following section addresses the convergence perspective, exploring how communication functions as a primary mechanism for the production, reproduction, and transformation of organizational forms. First, the communicative imperatives embedded in the technologies of globalization are identified. Second, organizational transformations from domestic to global forms of organizing are described through a brief analysis of the various typologies found in the literature. These typologies are important insofar as they describe the incremental and systematic convergence of communicative processes and structures in the global environment. Third, there is a discussion of the mechanisms of convergence, focusing directly on the communicative activities associated with the increased isomorphism that undergirds the convergence approach.

Challenges to and limitations of the convergence perspective are then examined. Assumptions of generalizability, the culturally neutral character of organizations, and the culture-free nature of theoretical perspectives are questioned. It is argued that the dynamic structuring of globalization is a culturally saturated process that can be better understood by focusing not only on the constraints and demands of the global environment but also on the meanings, interpretations, and sense-making activities that constitute multinational organizing.

The third section reviews the divergence literature and is organized around five interrelated themes: culture as a cerebral, aesthetic, or artifactual phenomenon; as a complex social pattern; or as communicative practice. Each theme represents a particular conceptualization of the relationship between culture and organizational communication. At the end of the section, several ironies that pervade the divergence literature are identified. Although the very foundation of the divergence perspective is grounded in the far-reaching importance of cultural difference, theoretical principles and the relationships among variables have typically been expected to be stable across cultural and national contexts. By ignoring the embedded nature of organizations, this approach also limits our ability to address the dialectic pressures inherent in the global environment.

The fourth section contains a detailed discussion of theoretical, methodological, and practical parochialisms that pervade both the convergence and divergence approaches to globalization. This discussion is designed to stimulate the development of creative and interdisciplinary research agendas that reflect the dynamic communicative processes of globalization and multiculturalism.

The final section of this chapter summarizes the ways in which organizational communication scholars are in a powerful position to explore globalization, not merely as a neutral phenomenon, but rather as a process fraught with ethical implications. Globalization has been conceived as both a threat to and the salvation of humanity. Economic integration, it has been argued, promotes prosperous stability and discordant stratification. Organizational convergence and divergence may help people to live their lives in more fruitful, peaceful, and satisfying ways or result in

forms of cultural/organizational imperialism that dwarf the powers of the state. The study of organizational communication can help us further understand the potential power, problems, and promise of globalization.

THE CONVERGENCE APPROACH

Whether the culture is Asian or European or North American, a large organization with many employees improves efficiency by specializing its activities but also by increasing and coordinating specialties. (Hickson, Hinings, MacMillan, & Schwitter, 1974, p. 64)

The universal, deterministic, and rational assumptions embedded in the convergence perspective are exemplified in a series of classic cross-national studies that were part of the influential Aston program in Britain in the 1970s. Operating within a contingency/systems perspective, Hickson and his colleagues (Hickson et al., 1974; Hickson, MacMillan, Azumi, & Horvath, 1979) argued that there is a transnational and stable relation between variables of organizational "context" especially size, technology, and dependence on other organizations, on the one hand, and the structural/communicative characteristics of work organizations, such as specialization and decentralization, on the other. This work further assumed that all organizations will pass through similar stages of structural development as they grow and that strategic commitments will necessarily shape the structures of the organizations, which in turn mold and strongly constrain communication processes.

Factors Influencing Convergence

Communicative Imperatives in the Global Environment

Despite critiques leveled at contingency theory in general, many contemporary scholars also suggest there are a set of imperatives embedded in the emerging communication technologies and the global economy that will result in the convergence of organizational structures and communicative practices across nations. "Common markets demand a common language, as well as a common currency, and they produce common behaviors . . . culture and nationality can seem only marginal elements in a working identity" (Barber, 1992, p. 54). Theorists argue that as the socioeconomic bases of societies become the same, new communication technologies become readily available, international labor markets are opened, global competition expands, and environmental turbulence and uncertainty increase, social arrangements will converge and replace culturally specific structures (e.g., Clifford, 1988; Tichy, 1990). Across cultures, global organizations are expected to move from "centrally coordinated, multi-level hierarchies toward a variety of more flexible structures that closely resemble networks rather than traditional pyramids" (Miles & Snow, 1992, p. 53). The new arrangements or "global forms" necessary for organizational survival include radical decentralization, intensified interdependence, high-density connections, demanding expectations, transparent performance standards, dispersed leadership, alliance building, and interorganizational reciprocity (Hastings, 1993; Jarvenpaa & Leidner, 1998; Miles & Snow, 1986; Monge & Fulk, 1999; Nohria & Barkley, 1994).

Typologies of Organizational Transformation

The transformation and convergence of domestic to global forms of organizing have been described in several ways. Typologies focus on the degree of internationalization of business and marketing functions (Ball & McCulloch, 1993); the primary orientation, strategy, managerial assumptions, and cultural sensitivity of the organization (Adler, 1991); the structural and communicative integration of business units across geographic boundaries (Varner & Beamer, 1995); the cultural mindset and orientation of upper management (Heenan & Perlmutter, 1979); the configuration of assets, capabilities, and operations; the role of overseas operations; and development and diffusion of knowledge (Bartlett & Ghoshal, 1986). Even the terms *multinational, international,* and *global* are used in different ways. For example, Bartlett and Ghoshal (1989) order the terms *multinational, global, international,* and *transnational* to describe the degree to which strategies, core competencies, and control are developed and maintained at centralized headquarters. Adler and Ghadar (1990), on the other hand, order the terms *domestic, international, multinational,* and *global* to describe the degree to which the organizing activities (both strategic and structural) incorporate a global perspective.

Despite these differences, however, each typology is based on similar responses to similar environmental constraints and contingencies. Table 10.1 presents a composite description/profile of each of five types of organizations typically described in the literature: domestic, multicultural, multinational, international, and global. These descriptions are based on the predominance of a single national/cultural identity, the perceived importance of an international orientation and perspective, the legitimacy of multiple voices and authority, the type of structure, the "ideal" management model, and the interconnected nature of interactions across a diversity of cultural groups.

Clearly, the convergence approach has within it an element of environmental determinism; that is, all organizations wish to survive and to do so they must adapt certain structures to the global environment. Moreover, communicative adaptation/convergence is considered a positive feature of organizations regardless of cultural differences and levels of economic development. Thus, the exploitative potential of certain global production practices regarding employment, displacement, factory development, outsourcing, and lean production tend to be ignored.

TABLE 10.1 Typology of Organizations

	Domestic	Multicultural	Multinational	International	Global
Predominant national orientation	Identification with one country and dominant culture; management recognition of only one culture within the work-place; internal and external linkages are perceived to be homogeneous	Identification with one country; some recognition by management of culturally diverse workforce; internal and external linkages, usually composed of subcultures within the dominant culture (e.g., African Americans, women)	Identification with one nationality while doing business in several countries; recognition by management of a multinational workforce, management, clientele, and environment; organization represents one national interest	Identification with two or more countries each of which has distinct cultural attributes; workforce, management, clients, suppliers, etc. are recognized to represent diverse national interests	Identification with the global system; transcend national borders; boundaryless organizations; within the workplace organizational membership takes precedence over national orientation; stateless corporation
Perceived importance of international orientation	None	Very little importance	Important	Extremely important	Dominant
Orientation toward subsidiaries and/or other cultural units	*Parochial:* There is no authoritative voice other than dominant culture	*Ethnocentric:* Authority is located with dominant cultural group, any accommodation to other cultures is at the micro/interpersonal level	*Polycentric:* Authority is vested in local nationals holding key positions in subsidiaries; managed from central headquarters, little communication between subsidiaries, communication with national headquarters	*Regiocentric:* Regional geographic basis for authority, personnel, and staffing development, interdependence across regions	*Geocentric:* Dispersed, interdependent, and specialized, differentiated contributions integrated into worldwide operations, development and sharing of knowledge worldwide; multinational flexibility and worldwide learning capability

(continued)

329

Table 10.1 Continued

	Domestic	Multicultural	Multinational	International	Global
Structure	Hierarchical, traditional bureaucratic and matrix structures; one centrally located headquarters	Teamwork, flattening of hierarchy; one centrally located headquarters	Managed from a central location in an essentially hierarchical manner; national subsidiaries, miniature replicas teamwork employed; centralized and globally scaled, overseas operations implement parent company strategies, develop and maintain knowledge at headquarters level	Joint hierarchy; international divisions that integrate global activities, joint ventures; teamwork within subsidiaries but not across; some decentralized decision making	Decentralization of decision making and sharing of responsibilities; heterarchy; headquarters and subsidiaries see themselves as part of an organic worldwide entity; global strategy, dominant, global alliances; multicentric
Management models	Monocultural: Cultural differences are ignored, not recognized	Cultural dominance: Differences are expected to be accommodated through assimilation with dominant culture	Cultural compromise: Differences are recognized and somewhat accepted but dominant culture is typically enacted in task domain	Cultural synergy: Work together to try to build a third culture	Cultural integration: Recognition of diverse cultures and business conditions, cultural adaptation in the task realm, cultural integrity in the expressive realm
Level of international interaction	Import/export: Possibly send representatives abroad	Import/export: Possibly send representatives abroad; intercultural communication among workforce	Intercultural communication among workforce, management, clients, customers, government officials, international communication technology	Loosely coupled; inter-cultural communication among workforce, management, clients, customers, government officials, international communication technology	Global networks, integrative, tightly coupled; intercultural communication among workforce, management, clients, customers, government officials; international communication technology

Unlike traditional contingency theory, however, where the organizational environment is conceived as a delineated set of contingencies emanating from the social, legal, political, economic, technological, and physical domains, the new convergence literature blurs the boundaries between an organization and the various sectors within the environment. Contemporary convergence literature transforms the view of organizations as bounded entities, separated in time and space from other parts of the environment to a position of permeability and flux, where there is no longer a clear distinction between the organization and its environment. Interorganizational networks are conceived as overlapping yet diffuse webs of interaction composed of suppliers, customers, unions, special interest groups, and competitors, as well as legal (e.g., rules, regulations, and obligations), political (treaties such as GATT), institutional (e.g., the International Monetary Fund), and cultural (e.g., ethnicity, religious affiliation) linkages that transcend what has typically been conceived of as relevant actors (Hatch, 1997). Communication is the means for bridging and bringing together the resources and contingencies that facilitate organizational transformation and survival in the global environment. The major question this literature addresses is, How do organizations adapt to the global environment?

Mechanisms of Convergence

In a provocative article on the "new institutionalism," DiMaggio and Powell (1983) ask, "Why is there such startling homogeneity of organizational forms and practices?" (p. 148). They distinguish between *competitive isomorphism,* which assumes a rationality that emphasizes market competition, niche change, and fitness, and *institutional isomorphism,* change that occurs through three communicative mechanisms. The first mechanism of institutional isomorphism, *coercive,* stems from political influence and legitimacy. The pressures to conform may be felt as force, as persuasion, or as invitations to join in collusion. The second process, *mimetic,* results from standard responses to uncertainty. When environments and organizational technologies are ambiguous, volatile, and poorly understood, organizations model themselves on other organizations. The third mechanism of isomorphism, *normative,* is associated with professionalization. They claim that the similarity of the formal education of the managerial class across cultures and the development of an interconnected matrix of information flows and personnel movement across organizations result not only in what Kanter (1977) refers to as the "homosocial reproduction of management" but to the development of similar organizational structures across organizational fields. Although DiMaggio and Powell (1991) go on to say that "the ubiquity of certain kinds of structural arrangements can more likely be credited to the universality of mimetic processes rather than to any concrete evidence that the adopted models enhance efficiency" (p. 70), mimesis as a response to environmental uncertainty is rooted in rational efforts to enhance survival in the global arena.

Communicative Convergence

Throughout this literature, the move toward global convergence is rooted in fundamental changes in organizational communication practices. If organizations are to flourish in the volatile global environment and meet the challenges of geographic dispersion, temporal asynchronicity, and cultural diversity (Monge, 1995), it is assumed that they must become more knowledge intensive, innovative, adaptive, flexible, efficient, and responsive to rapid change (Cushman & King, 1993; Kozminski & Cushman, 1993; Monge & Fulk, 1995, 1999; Taylor & Van Every, 1993). Cushman and King (1993) have developed "a new theory of organizational communication:

high-speed management" to address the "series of revolutions [that] have taken place within the global economy, transforming the theoretical basis for organizational coalignment, and thus all information and communication processes" (p. 209). They provide examples of how four dynamic communication processes—negotiated linking, New England town meetings, cross-functional teamwork, and best practices case studies—can enable organizations to improve effectiveness and gain competitive advantage. Negotiated linking, for example, is aimed at mobilizing external resources, and town meetings bring workers, suppliers, and customers together for intense discussions related to productivity, quality, and response time.

Likewise, at a University of Michigan symposium designed to set a global research and teaching agenda for American and European business schools in the 1990s (see Tichy, 1990), scholars and senior executives stressed communication issues related to coordination, integration, alliance building, network development, international team building, global leadership skills, and the development of a global managerial mindset. Weick and Van Orden (1990), for example, posit that the global organization will be an "organization without location" composed of fields of activities and systems of decision making rather than a single, static hierarchical entity. The new organizational form will "resemble temporary systems, federations, and project teams held together somewhat in the manner of the linking pins" (p. 56) and have a low degree of formalization, continual redefinition of task, low centralization, and ad hoc centers of authority located at critical but evolving locations. At the interpersonal level, they believe the global organization will encourage more complex and flexible strategies, greater participation and risk taking, and more open communication style and will experience more open management of conflict and more task orientation in the networks that emerge as a result of the conflict.

Overall, increasing experience with the processes of globalization has resulted in practitioners and scholars alike arguing for the inappropriateness of traditional hierarchical structuring and thinking and the development of alternative forms of organizing.

> Hierarchies do not contain the complexity in which society has to deal. . . . Neither a hierarchical organization nor a hierarchy of concepts can handle a network of environmental problems, for example, without leaving many dangerous gaps through which unforeseen problems may emerge and be uncontainable. (Lipnack & Stamps, 1986, pp. 162-163)

Empirically, the most dramatic changes can be seen in the Coca Cola Company, which in a move to make the company "more nimble" completely eliminated the very concepts of domestic and international. In a restructuring of business units on a regional but equal basis, the company eliminated the privileges and higher status of any one unit (Collins, 1996, p. 19). There are many other examples as well. The practitioner literature is filled with case studies of new organizational forms (e.g., Cusumano & Selby, 1995; Nonaka & Takeuchi, 1995), and scholars have begun addressing the theoretical implications of these new forms (e.g., Miles & Snow, 1986; Park & Ungson, 1997; Swan & Ettlie, 1997). Guterl (1989) documents how IBM, Corning, Apple Computer, and Philips, N.V. have moved from matrix hierarchical structures to less formal, "network" type organizations that will allow them to respond faster and more creatively in globally dispersed markets. Nonaka and Takeuchi (1995) illustrate how the highly successful "global organizational knowledge-creating" companies, such as Honda, Canon, Matsushita, and Nissan, have neither top-down nor bottom-up management systems but rather develop what they call "middle-up-down" management processes that "rely more on two-way communications such as dialogue, camp sessions, and drinking sessions" (p. 151).

Consider also the three components of "global network organizations" identified by Monge and Fulk (1995) "as a newly emerging organizational form" (p. 2) that transcends national boundaries and readily adapts to the volatile environment. Global network organizations,[5] which many view as the quintessential organizational form of the postindustrial global information society (see, e.g., Hastings, 1993; Miles & Snow, 1992; Mulgan, 1991), are

1. Built on flexible emergent communication networks, rather than traditional hierarchies
2. Develop highly flexible linkages that connect them to a changing, dynamic network of other organizations, transcending their local country-bound networks
3. Contain a highly sophisticated information technology structure that supports flexible emergent systems of communication

In their view, the global organization reflects communication relationships that transcend organizational levels and boundaries and "flexibility implies that these relationships wax and wane" (Monge & Fulk, 1995, p. 1).

Notwithstanding the technical and rational logic of this move toward the convergence of macrolevel/structural variables such as flattening hierarchies (Cleveland, 1985), global networking (Monge & Fulk, 1995), negotiated linking (Cushman & King, 1993), decentralization (Mitroff, 1987) and the increasing similarity of what Wiio (1989) refers to as hardware variables, that is, information sources, channels and their uses, number of messages, code systems, and communication networks, several limitations to these approaches have been identified. Some scholars suggest that "despite their contemporary framing," theories such as high-speed management still embody traditional managerial assumptions about linearity, continuity, and responsivity that are no longer appropriate (Seibold & Contractor, 1993). Poole (1993) further proposes that there are many alternatives to the demands, constraints, and opportunities of the global economy that are not considered in a theory such as high-speed management. Other scholars (e.g., Adler, Doktor, & Redding, 1986; Ady, 1994) argue

that despite what may seem to be convergence at the macrolevel, communication and sense-making activities are remaining culturally distinct and often undergoing increasing divergence. In this next section, we will address some of the challenges to the convergence perspective, paying particular attention to very recent developments in the organizational communication literature.

Challenging the Assumptions of Universality and Organizational Convergence

Intuitively, people have always assumed that bureaucratic structures and patterns of action differ in the different countries of the Western world and even more markedly between East and West. Men [*sic*] of action know it and never fail to take it into account. But contemporary social scientists . . . have not been concerned with such comparisons. (Crozier, 1964, p. 210)

More than 30 years ago, Michel Crozier, a French sociologist, highlighted the need to incorporate cultural variability into organizational research. His observations challenge three implicit assumptions, traditionally embedded in most organizational communication literature, and that still appear in most convergence literature: (1) research findings are generalizable across national contexts, (2) theories are culture free, and (3) organizations are culturally neutral.

Issues of Generalizability

Even a cursory look at our journals reveals that most articles rarely include a discussion of the cultural/national identifications of the employee/managerial sample unless the study is focusing specifically on issues of cultural variability. Nor do we often find a caveat pertaining to the limited scope of the conclusions or our theories in terms of the national/cultural generalizability. For example, the management and communication principles elaborated by the classical organizational theorists and elucidated in our texts and handbooks (e.g., Daniels & Spiker, 1994; Krone, Jablin, & Putnam, 1987; Miller, 1995; Tompkins, 1984) are usually presented as culture-free theories with universal applicability. Yet these theories may be as culturally bounded as the actual processes of organizing and managing (Boyacigiller & Adler, 1991). Consider the congruence between German Max Weber's emphasis on impersonal relations and the importance of written communication in a bureaucracy and cultural descriptions of Germany as a low-context culture in which information is vested in explicit codes rather than in relationships and the context surrounding the messages (Hall, 1976). There is also great consistency between Henri Fayol's, France's first management theorist, emphasis on centralization and unity of command and the French culture's high degree of uncertainty avoidance and power distance (Hofstede, 1984). We can further contrast Fayol's views with Scandinavians' tolerance for ambiguity and low status differentiation, the cultural background of many of the sociotechnical theorists who emphasized the importance of semiautonomous work groups (Emery, Thorsrud, & Trist, 1969). Indeed, it is hard not to conclude that these theorists' conceptions of organizing were, in some large part, a product of their cultural heritage. Asante (1987) makes the point directly:

> The preponderant Eurocentric myths of universalism, objectivity, and classical traditions retain a provincial European cast. . . . The problem with this is that cultural analysis takes a back seat to galloping ethnocentric interpretations of phenomena. (p. 9)

A noteworthy exception to this charge can be found in a provocative paper by Mayer (1996). In a communicative analysis of Deming's early and later writings on the principles of quality control and management (1943-1986), Mayer persuasively illustrates how the evolution of his work can, in large part, be attributed to the waning influence of American's short-term, linear, detailed, and analytic mode of thinking and the increasing influence of Japanese culture and philosophy including synthetic, long-term, holistic, and configural thinking. For example, in the early stages Deming stressed complexity, variation, and the use of scientific method for learning and improvement, whereas in the later stages his approach became more holistic, including emphasis on leadership, cooperation, and trust. Interestingly, Mayer points out that after many years of immersion in Japanese culture, Deming (1986) identifies performance evaluation and annual merit reviews as incompatible with a company's effectiveness because these processes orient workers toward quick fixes and stress their replaceability. In Japanese thinking, no part of the whole can be replaced without damage to the whole (Yoshida, 1989).

Cultural Differences

As the title of the following *New York Times* article, "It Takes More Than a Visa to Do Business in Mexico," suggests, understanding cultural differences is crucial for communicating and working in today's global environment. An excerpt from this article illustrates the types of cultural differences that are perceived to make a difference:

> In the Corning venture, the Mexicans sometimes saw the Americans as too direct, while the Vitro managers, in their dogged pursuit of politeness, sometimes seemed to the Americans unwilling to acknowledge problems and faults. . . . Another difference quite obvious from the beginning was the manner of making decisions. . . . The Mexicans sometimes thought Corning moved too fast; the Americans felt Vitro was too slow. (DePalma, 1994, pp. A16-A17)

The point is that, notwithstanding the increasing homogenization of organizational structures and technology discussed above, most empirical studies find that "cultural differences among nations do make a difference—often a substantial difference—in the way managers and workers behave in organizational settings" (Steers, Bischoff, & Higgins, 1992, p. 322). In a series of studies comparing Japanese and American managers' communication patterns, for example, although there were only minimal differences between the amount and direction of communication, there was a significant relationship between managers' national culture and the quality and the nature of the communication (Pascale & Athos, 1981). Inzerilli and Laurent (1983), comparing Western European cultures, also found communicative similarities with important differences. French managers had a more difficult time accepting subordinate roles than did English managers, even though hierarchy was perceived as necessary and appropriate under the same conditions by both cultural groups.

Thus, we can see that despite increased convergence of organizational structures at the macrolevel, the significance and meanings given to many of these features continues to diverge across cultural contexts. Fons Trompenaars (1994), one of the foremost proponents of the need for managers and scholars to develop a culturally based understanding of organizing, makes the point pragmatically. In addressing the technological and economic imperatives built into traditional organizational theory, he states:

But the wrong questions have been asked. The issue is not whether a hierarchy in the Netherlands has six levels, as does a similar company in Singapore, but what hierarchy and those levels mean to the Dutch and Singaporeans. Where the meaning is totally different, for example a chain of command rather than a family, then human resource policies developed to implement the first will seriously miscommunicate in the latter context. (Trompenaars, 1994, p. 7)

Embedded within Trompenaars's argument are two critical issues for the study of organizational communication in the global system that are not addressed by the convergence theorists. First, there is a comparative question (i.e., are there systematic differences in sensemaking activities among employees in different cultures?). Second, he raises questions related to intercultural interactions (i.e., what happens when people from various cultures interact with one another in an organizational setting?). In both cases, the answers can be found only in the study of communication.

Indeed, the focus on questions of meaning, interpretation, sensemaking, and interaction highlights further the contributions communication scholars can make to the study of multinational/multicultural organizing. Communication is the substance of global organizing in the sense that through everyday communication practices, organizational members collectively engage in the construction of a complex system of meanings that are intersubjectively shared and commonly misunderstood. This construction is strongly influenced by the cultural connections individuals bring into the system that transcend organizational boundaries (Stohl, 1995). Moreover, as organizations simultaneously become more integrated yet geographically dispersed, diverse, and homogenized, increasingly participative while heavily reliant on sophisticated information technologies, intercultural communication is no longer an "extranormal aspect of organizing nor a distinct kind of face-to-face communication that can be distinguished from other 'types' of communication. . . . Intercultural communication constitutes organizing processes that permeates all levels of activity and interpretation" (Stohl, 1993, p. 381).

Overall, then, communication scholarship can contribute to the understanding of global organizing at two levels: (1) the dynamic structuring of globalization, and (2) the culturally saturated processes of organizing and sensemaking. However, before examining the relationship among culture, communication, and organization it is first necessary to understand what is meant by culture and how it is associated with organizational divergence.

THE DIVERGENCE APPROACH

Japanese and American management practices are 95% the same and differ in all important respects. (Takeo Fujisawa, cited in Adler et al., 1986, p. 295)

Fujisawa, cofounder of Honda Motor Company, is clearly suggesting there are important differences between the American and Japanese cultures that influence the processes of organizing in significant and systematic ways. His observations make a strong case for the divergence perspective, but he does not help us tackle one of the thorniest issues in social science: What do we mean by culture, and how is it related to collective action?

Definitions and Themes of Culture

Indeed, Raymond Williams (1976) suggests that "culture is one of the two or three most complicated words in the English language" (p. 4). Geertz (1973) notes that in a 27-page chapter of *Mirror for Man,* Kluckhohn (1949) defined culture in at least 11 distinct ways ranging from "the total way of life" to culture as a map, a sieve, and a matrix. By the mid-1950s, Kroeber and Kluckhohn (1954) had already collected over 300 definitions of culture. And just as there is a plethora of definitions of culture, scholars have identified literally dozens of dimensions of cultural variability, that is, societal patterns of beliefs,

values, and practices that distinguish one group from another (Triandis, 1983).

Table 10.2 synthesizes this work and presents an overview of 12 dimensions of cultural variability that have been associated with important differences in organizational communication practices. These dimensions describe cultural orientations related to qualities of individuals, their relationships to nature, relationships with others, primary types of activities, and orientations toward time and space.[6]

But if we argue that pressures toward divergence are coterminous with a drive toward convergence, that is, even under similar global constraints and opportunities, the culturally saturated processes of communication and interpretation will likely result in different ways of organizing, we must have a sense not only of cultural dimensions but more specifically of how culture is conceptualized. Based on an exhaustive review of the meanings of culture in philosophy, critical aesthetics, literary criticism, anthropology, and sociology, Jenks (1993) develops a typology of cultural themes or categories that is quite useful (in an adapted form) for understanding the ways in which the relationship between culture and organizational communication practices has been studied. These adapted themes are labeled "culture as cerebral," "culture as aesthetic," "culture as artifact," "culture as a complex social pattern," and "culture as communicative practice."

Each theme provides a complementary pathway for exploring how, despite similar market and environmental pressures, cultural differences result in divergent forms of organizing activities. Within each set of literature, the focal features of culture, the topics most frequently studied, the role of communication, the dominant theoretical perspective, and the types of research and methods found across the literature are identified. Table 10.3 summarizes these conclusions. For example, when culture is viewed as a cerebral phenomenon, divergent meanings and structures are seen as a direct result of the different cognitions and values cultural groups have

TABLE 10.2 Dimensions of Cultural Variability

Dimension	Constructs	Illustrative Impacts on Organizational Communication Practices
Orientation to nature	Control over/harmony with/ subjugation to (Triandis, 1983)	Degree of comfort and use of technology
Orientation to human nature	People are basically good/bad/ mixture (McGregor, 1960)	Degree of emphasis on control and surveillance
	Quality (social connections determine evaluation/performance; actions determine evaluation) (Parsons & Shils, 1951)	Degree of mobility, the importance of achievements (what person does) vs. ascribed status (who person is)
	Sex differences are innate/learned	Degree of integration of women into the workforce
Orientation to time	Monochronic/polychronic (Hall, 1976)	Degree to which schedules are adhered to; degree to which tasks are completed linearly
	Past/present/future (Kluckhohn & Strodtbeck, 1961)	Attitudes toward change and innovation; type of planning
Orientation to action	Being/being in becoming/doing (Kluckhohn & Strodtbeck, 1961)	Degree to which stress is placed on improvements and accomplishments; importance of job satisfaction
	Affectivity/affectivity neutral (Parsons & Shils, 1951)	Need for immediate gratification
Orientation to communication	Low context/high context (Hall, 1976)	Different emphasis on verbal or nonverbal messages; degree of communication directness; relative importance of relational networks
	Associative/abstractive (Glenn, 1981)	Context-dependent meanings; specific definitional requirements; type of information formally presented; types of arguments that are persuasive— emotionally based vs. data driven
Orientation to space	Private/public (Hall, 1966)	Requirements for personal space; office layout; private office vs. open office
Orientation to authority	High power distance (hierarchical)/ low power distance (equality) (Hofstede, 1984)	Levels of hierarchy; adherence to the chain of command; respect for titles and status; degree of worker participation
Orientation to community	Individualism/collectivism (Hofstede, 1984)	Motivational incentives; degree to which task is valued over relationships; basis of hiring and promotion; type of socialization practices; degree to which shame or guilt drives employees and managers

(continued)

TABLE 10.2 Continued

Dimension	Constructs	Illustrative Impacts on Organizational Communication Practices
	Familialism (Redding, 1990)	Hiring practices; influence strategies
Orientation to goals	Instrumental (competitive)/ expressive (cooperative)	Degree of stress placed on quality of work life vs. attainment of materialistic goals; degree of gender differentiation; degree of assertiveness and nurturing value of specific motivators
	Masculine/feminine (Hofstede, 1984)	
	Process/goals (Glenn, 1981)	Emphasis on here and now
Orientation to structure	Simple/complex (Murdock & Provost, 1973)	Degree of hierarchical differentiation
	High uncertainty avoidance/ low uncertainty avoidance (Hofstede, 1984)	Degree of need for predictability and rules, both written and unwritten
	Tight/loose (Witkin & Berry, 1975)	Degree of pressure to conform to role definitions
	In-group/out-group (Triandis, 1983)	
Orientation to formality	Formal/informal	Adherence to traditions; attitudes toward change; importance of protocol; preponderance of rituals; emphasis on verbal and nonverbal appropriateness
Orientation to needs	Materialist/postmaterialist (Inglehart, 1977)	Degree to which employees focus on meeting physiological needs such as safety and sustenance as compared to meeting social and self-actualization needs such as belonging and self esteem

about the way the world operates, issues of cause and effect, human nature, and so on. Rooted in the social psychological tradition, communication is portrayed as an outcome of the composite values and cognitions associated with a particular culture. There is a strong focus on training and the development of intercultural communicative competence, culture shock and assimilation, authority relations, and conflict and negotiation. Research tends to be managerially focused, quantitative, and comparative.

In contrast, when culture is viewed as an embodied and collective category that refers to the aesthetic pursuits of a group of people,

organizational arrangements are seen as extensions of societal principles of beauty and design. Communication is a way of knowing, a dynamic display of aesthetic qualities. This research tends to be more macro oriented and philosophically grounded, less focused on managerial prerogatives, and more concerned with the role of organizations in the larger society. Rooted in issues of practical rationality, each approach focuses on human interpretation and experience of the world as meaningful and intersubjectively constructed.

Clearly, these approaches are not mutually exclusive. To begin, culture enters organizations artfully, unself-consciously, and piece-

TABLE 10.3 Typology of Culture and Its Relation With Organizational Communication

	Culture as				
	Cerebral	*Aesthetic*	*Artifact*	*A Complex Social Pattern*	*Communicative Practice*
Focus	Values, cognitions	Principles of beauty and design	Artifacts	Normative and routine patterns	Everyday interactions
Role of communication	An outcome	A way of knowing	A thing, a sedimented symbol	A transmitter	A constitutive element
	Communication is shaped by one's perceptions and ideas of the world	Communication reflects societal sense of beauty and balance	Communication is a manifestation and elaboration of culture	Communication is the enactment and reinforcement of cultural conditioning	Communication is quintessentially culture, an interpretive sensemaking process
Frequently studied topics	Communicative competence, culture shock; training and development; manager-worker relations; power, conflict; compliance gaining; and negotiation	Role of organization in society; organizational structure and design	Business letters, annual reports; handbooks; newsletters; business cards; gifts; logos	Gender and racial relations; class structure; power; role of economic/occupational institutions; identification of culture-specific constructs; communication ethics	Organizational identity; nonverbal communication; organizational messages; language issues; worker participation; organizational democracy
Dominant perspective	Microindividual and dyadic	Macrosocial	Micro-object	Macrosocietal	Interconnectedness between micro- and macrolevels of analysis
	Managerial	Societal	Managerial	Microinterpersonal	Worker and managerial
	Social-psychological tradition	Philosophical tradition	Social-psychological tradition	Anthropological tradition	Anthropological tradition
Types of research	Etic, empirical and theoretical, comparative, quantitative methods	Emic, theoretical, case studies	Etic/emic, empirical, discourse analytic techniques, semantic networks, quantitative methods	Etic/emic, empirical and theoretical, comparative case studies, ethnographies; interpretive, qualitative and quantitative methods	Emic, empirical and theoretical; interpretive, qualitative and quantitative methods

meal through several avenues simultaneously (Sorge, 1983). Culture has been hypothesized to affect organizations through (1) political/ legal prescriptions and prohibitions, legal requirements, and regulations; (2) constraints and opportunities of the institutional environment; (3) preferences (values) and premises about what organizations can and should be; (4) rites, rituals, and other communicative practices; (5) the ways in which individuals perform their roles and relate to one another; (6) the mindsets of occupational communities; (7) the manner by which problems are solved; and (8) the instantiations of spatio/ temporal boundaries.

Second, across categories, definitions of culture share several assumptions. These include (1) culture is not innate, it is learned and passed on from one generation to another; (2) culture may change but transformation is slow; (3) individual aspects of culture are interrelated; (4) culture is shared and defines the boundaries of social groups; and (5) culture is simultaneously overt and covert, public and private, explicit and implicit, known and unknown.

Third, both culture-general and culture-specific approaches to communication are found across categories. In culture-specific research, scholars develop in-depth analyses of communication practices in a particular culture and may generalize about organizational communication practices in that specific cultural environment. In contrast, a culture-general approach identifies dimensions or ways in which cultures may vary across cultural contexts, using illustrations from particular cultures as examples of the more general concept (Victor, 1992).

Fourth, an important limitation has been noted by Child (1981):

> Although it is an oversimplification, the boundaries of culture are conventionally assumed to coincide with the boundaries of the nation-states. Culture is regarded as an expression of the values, norms, and habits which are deep rooted with the nation. (p. 304)

Indeed, across all these approaches we find that *nation* has been used as a proxy for *culture* for several reasons: (1) most theories of cultural variability use such a unit; (2) nationality has symbolic value—our identities are derived, in large part, by our affiliation to a nation-state; (3) nationality evokes a set of attributes, values, and stereotypes that becomes more conspicuous in a multinational environment; (4) organizational identity has traditionally been defined within national borders; and (5) globalization is conceptualized as a form of transcendence of the nation-state. Nonetheless, not everyone from a given country has the same culture. Ethnicity, race, age, gender, religion, sexual preference, region, and so forth comprise significant, often overlapping, cultural identifications. Every cultural context encompasses a multitude of individual patterns or modal types. Further, individuals do not necessarily conform to scripts written for them by a particular intersection of cultural identifications. But research has shown that national differences do exist in the variable distribution of individual types and in the social dynamics among these types. Within each macroculture, different patterns are reinforced, encouraged, and accepted, while others are ignored, marginalized, suppressed, or even punished (Maruyama, 1982). A serious challenge for both researchers and readers, then, is to maintain sensitivity to the potential dangers of stereotyping and remain cautious against minimizing or ignoring within-nation differences while simultaneously recognizing the value of the generalizations that are an inevitable consequence of cultural research.

Fifth, the relationship between national culture and organizational culture is neither simple nor straightforward. Most scholars agree that they are "phenomena of different orders; using the term 'culture' for both is . . . somewhat misleading" (Hofstede, Neuijen, Ohayr, & Sanders, 1990, p. 313). Even when two organizations are dominated by the same national-cultural affiliation, this does not necessarily mean the daily practices will be similar. Founder's values (Ashcraft & Pacanow-sky, 1995), type of industry (Maurice, Sorge, & Malcolm, 1981), and occupational communities (Van Maanen & Barley, 1984) are just a few of the features that contribute to the local culture of an organization (see Eisenberg & Riley, Chapter 9 in this volume, for an explication of organizational culture). Further, organizations are not simply passive recipients of culture. Organizational cultures simultaneously influence and are influenced by the larger cultures of which they are a part.

In summary, each cultural theme discussed below—culture as cerebral, culture as aesthetic, culture as artifact, culture as a complex social pattern, and culture as communicative practice—does not represent a mutually exclusive or inclusive representation of culture. Rather, the five themes are interrelated; each represents a specific conceptualization of the relationships among culture, communication, and organization. When taken together, this classification system provides a comprehensive guide for mapping the communicative dimensions of organizational divergence.

Cultural Themes as a Typology for the Study of Organizational Communication

> My purpose here is to present . . . readers with a map of our existing territory, and a guide to that map in the form of a classification, or a morphology, of the central concepts and ideas in terms of their meanings, origins, and overlaps . . . if this work succeeds . . . it will also have shown this classification is itself a cultural practice involving critical reading, judgment, and discernment, and adherence to an intellectual discipline (a symbolic culture). (Jenks, 1993, p. 3)

Culture as Cerebral

This approach to culture identifies it as a general state of mind, a cognitive phenomenon. Culture shapes behavior and influences communication because it structures one's perceptions and ideas of the world. Of central interest are systematic differences in (1) cognitive frames and (2) the strong association between cognition and values. The dimensions of cultural variability identified in Table 10.2 encapsulate the cultural "differences that make a difference" in communication studies. Friday (1989), for example, identifies specific differences between American and German managers' expectations regarding business relationships, personal needs, orientation to cooperation, status, confrontation, and common social intercourse and then predicts how these cognitive differences are manifest in contrasting styles of business discussions.

Cognitive frames. Triandis and Albert (1987) in the first edition of this handbook posit that culture reflects shared meanings, norms, and values and argue that the most important aspect of culture that affects organizational communication is "the cognitive frames societies provide their members for processing information that has been perceived" (p. 267). These cognitive frames reflect (1) the differing ways that cultures emphasize people, ideas, or actions; (2) the emphasis put on processes or goals; (3) differences in values; and (4) patterns of information processing and influence. Triandis (1983) illustrates how the classic management functions of defining goals, planning, and selecting, training, controlling, and motivating employees are facilitated and inhibited by the cognitive frames people bring to an organization.

The cognitive approach to culture undergirds most of the research on intercultural communicative competence in the workplace, intercultural training of managers and employees, and the experiences of culture shock and assimilation of expatriate employees. Models of culture shock are premised on the cognitive conflict, confusion, unpredictability, and frustration of uninterpretable cues that are created by the incongruence between what is expected from a particular cultural mindset and what actually happens in another culture (Storti, 1990; Tung, 1987). Cognitive differences are causally linked to cultural differences in decision making, negotiation, conflict, and management styles as well as organizational structures and authority relations (Cai & Drake, 1998; Hofstede, 1984; Laurent, 1983). Issues of selective perception, attributions, expectations, stereotyping, prejudice, ethnocentrism, and parochialism have all been explored as cognitive/cultural barriers to effective communication in the global workplace and the development of cultural synergy (see Adler, 1991; Brislin, 1989; Gudykunst, 1991; Harris & Moran, 1996; Moran & Harris, 1982).

Synergy, according to Moran and Harris (1982), is tied directly to organizational members' cognitions and is limited to immediate bounded interactions, neither transcending the particular nor generating systemic change. Cultural synergy "exists only in relation to a practical set of circumstances, and it occurs by necessity when two or possibly more culturally different groups come together" (p. 83). Cultural synergism creates groups that transcend any single culture, producing new and different systems of interaction. To enhance the synergistic potential of multinational groups, members are exhorted to recognize, empathize with, understand, and address cultural differences; develop a shared vision or superordinate goal; and develop mutual respect and provide feedback in culturally sensitive ways (Adler, 1991; Amir, 1969; Brislin, 1989). Success, always rooted in the dual processes of synthesis and accommodation, is determined by the dominant organizational interests.

Organizational training programs focused on the expatriate experience are also most often designed to sensitize individuals to their own cultural blinders and to increase awareness of cultural differences. Significantly, although some competency in the "other's" language is recognized as a significant contributor to the effective management of culture shock and successful interaction in the multinational workplace (Victor, 1992) the cognitively based research ignores, for the most part, language and/or translation issues in cross-cultural organizing. People are be-

lieved to become more open to cultural differences as they learn how their own culture influences perceptions, attitudes, values, and communication (Albert, 1983; Brislin, 1989; Gudykunst, 1991). In a study of managerial international competence, for example, Ratiu (1983) found that although the managers who were perceived as most international by their peers denied that "internationals" existed, they exhibited a different set of cognitive strategies for managing in a multicultural organization. International managers used a "blue loop strategy" (a microstrategy based on description, impression, private stereotypes, and modification) as compared to the less effective multicultural managers who used a "red loop strategy" (a macrostrategy rooted in explanation, theory, public stereotypes, and confirmation).

Culture conceived as a cerebral phenomenon that directly affects communication practices can also be seen in a set of studies conducted by Laurent and his colleagues (Inzerilli & Laurent, 1983; Laurent, 1983, 1986). Comparing the "implicit theories of management" of managers from ten European nations and the United States they concluded that the managers' sets of mental representations and preferences, and hence performance, were culturally determined. Managerial views of "proper management" and conceptions of structure as either instrumental (e.g., roles and positions are defined in terms of tasks and/or functions) or social (e.g., roles and positions are defined in terms of social status and authority) were associated with national origin. Significantly, Laurent (1986) found that cultural differences were not reduced when managers worked in the same multinational firm. "If anything there was slightly more divergence between the national groups within this multinational company than originally found in the INSEAD [an elite French business school] multinational study [i.e., where the international managerial sample came from different companies]."

Cognitions and values. Hofstede (1984), the most influential scholar in the area of culture and organizations today, defines culture as "the collective programming of the mind which distinguishes the members of one human group from another" (p. 210). Highlighting the information-processing aspects of organizations, he refers to the mental programs of employees as the "software of the mind" (Hofstede, 1991). Cultural values are of special significance in this approach. "The main cultural differences among nations lie in values" (Hofstede, 1991, p. 236) and nearly all our mental programs are affected by values that are reflected in our behavior. Basing his work on responses to questionnaires about work-related values of over 116,000 IBM employees in 50 countries, Hofstede (1984) originally identified four dimensions of cultural variability (power distance, uncertainty avoidance, masculinity, and individualism). In 1988, Hofstede and Bond added a fifth dimension, Confucian dynamism. The values associated with this dimension are rooted in Confucianism and the principles of stability, status, thrift, and shame.

Each of these dimensions reflects the differing values given to issues of equality, ambiguity, instrumentalism, and community in a particular country and are strongly associated with the ways in which individuals across the world perform roles and relate to one another. Chen and Chung (1994), for example, provide several examples of the ways in which four values of Confucianism, hierarchy, the family system, *jen* (benevolence), and the emphasis on education influence organizational communication processes such as the development of explicit rules, socialization activities, the elevated importance of socioemotional communication in the workplace, team development, and nonconfrontation conflict resolution. Stewart, Gudykunst, Ting-Toomey, and Nishida (1986) developed a questionnaire also based on Hofstede's (1984) decision-making style questionnaire and the ICA audit (Goldhaber & Rogers, 1979) to explore the influence of Japanese managerial decision-making style on Japanese employees' perceptions of communication openness and satisfaction.

Indeed, the communicative implications of Hofstede's dimensions are rich and provocative (see Teboul, Chen, & Fritz's [1994] set of speculative hypotheses based on these dimensions relating to formal organizational structure, informal networks, organizational assimilation, and new communication technologies). The individualism/collectivism dimension, for example, has been hypothesized to affect group dynamics such as social loafing (Earley, 1989) and decision shifts (Hong, 1978) both within unicultural groups (e.g., comparing Chinese managers interacting together with American managers interacting together) and multicultural settings (observing employees from different cultures as they interact together).

At times, we also find that Hofstede's work explicitly links values and communication. He argues, for example, that in high power distance countries such as Singapore, the Philippines, France, India, Venezuela, and Portugal, employers and employees are more likely to consider violating the chain of command as constituting serious insubordination. Low power distance countries such as Denmark, New Zealand, and Israel expect people to work around hierarchical chains and do not see hierarchy as an essential part of organizational life. When working in or with high power distance countries, Hofstede suggests, it is important to respect the authority structure and show deference to the formal hierarchy. In low power distance countries, organizations tend to be less formal and have more open communication across the social system (Hofstede, 1984).

Driskill (1995) substantiated these conclusions in a study of Euro-American and Asian Indian engineers. American and Indian coworkers identified situations involving authority, role duties, and supervision as the most salient contexts for the emergence of strong cultural differences. Asian Indians felt that competent supervisors should provide daily and direct surveillance, were very comfortable with an authoritarian decision-making style, and were accustomed to strict adherence to job descriptions and titles. In contrast,

Euro-American workers placed less emphasis on titles and were more comfortable with collaborative decision making and less direct supervision. The results of semantic network analyses also indicate that managerial interpretations of the term *participation* by Danish, Dutch, English, French, and German middle managers were systematically associated with the nationality of the manager and that these differences were consistent with country scores on Hofstede's dimensions of power distance, uncertainty avoidance, and masculinity (Stohl, 1993).

All five of Hofstede's dimensions have also been studied in relation to conflict and negotiation styles (Lee & Rogan, 1991; Ohbuchi & Takahashi, 1994; Ting-Toomey et al., 1991), compliance-gaining and influence strategies (Sanborn, 1993; Smith & Peterson, 1988), managerial decision making (Vitell, Nwachuku, & Barnes, 1993), job and communication satisfaction (Bochner & Hesketh, 1994), and leadership (Smith & Tayeb, 1988). Most of the work in this area supports comparative predictions based on cultural identification (e.g., managers from collectivist cultures are more likely to move toward a single effective leadership style whereas managers from individualistic cultures adapt their styles to situational demands; Smith & Tayeb, 1988): Chinese managers (collectivist culture) have highest performance under group conditions of shared responsibility, American managers perform best when individually responsible for the task (Earley, 1989), managers from collectivist cultures are less likely to use influence strategies based on ingratiation and more likely to use strategies rooted in a collective sharing of responsibility (Smith & Peterson, 1988). Despite this evidence, however, there are a number of studies where the hypotheses are not supported.

In a comprehensive review of the international business negotiation literature, Wilson, Cai, Campbell, Donohue, and Drake (1994) identify several studies whose findings do not fit this model. Lee and Rogan (1991) predicted that managers from collectivist cultures

would "place more emphasis on maintaining interpersonal harmony than accomplishing tasks" and therefore would prefer nonconfrontational conflict styles, but their data indicate American managers were more likely to use nonconfrontational styles than their Korean counterparts. In a detailed analysis of bargaining, Graham and his colleagues (Graham, 1985; Graham, Evenko, & Rajan, 1992) did not find significant differences among Brazilian, Japanese, Russian, and U.S. managers' bargaining techniques, although they did find substantial differences in the nonverbal and discourse features of negotiation interaction. Belieav, Muller, and Punnett (1985), however, did find American managers' influence styles more individualistic, impatient, and time conscious than Soviet managers' styles.

Wilson et al. (1994) persuasively argue that these discrepancies are rooted in the far too simple and direct causal relationship that is posited in this literature between culture and communication. Individuals' cultural values and cognitions affect their interactions but only in conjunction and at times in conflict with other personal, situational, structural, and contextual factors. The issue, they suggest, is not whether cultural differences are associated with divergent forms of communicating but rather that the relationship among culture, communication, and organization is more complex than the culture-as-cerebral literature suggests. Specifically, the cognitive approach tends to isolate individuals from the social fabric within which organizations are embedded. However, the processes studied by these scholars, such as negotiating, compliance gaining, adhering to chains of command, and decision making, take place within intricately interwoven cultural tapestries that transcend individuals.

Culture as Aesthetic

In contrast to the atomistic and microanalytic cognitive approach to culture, culture as aesthetic references the macroprocesses that constitute society. In this sense, culture invokes a state of intellectual and moral development in society and refers to the aesthetic, artistic, literary, musical, and intellectual pursuits of a group of people. Culture is associated with civilization, enlightenment, refinement, and polish (Jenks, 1993). Within this theme there are two major foci: (1) cultural principles of beauty and design and (2) communication activities and aesthetics. In general, this literature argues that organizational communication is a dynamic display of aesthetic qualities. Divergent communication processes and structures reflect and reproduce a collective aesthetic. Communication is a way of knowing. Communication activities and organizational forms are elaborated not as utilitarian responses to the challenges of a volatile global environment but rather as a form of knowledge and action that comprises a culture's pattern of sensibility to and appreciation of the value and beauty of forms (Kuhn, 1996).

Cultural principles of beauty and design. Although few scholars in communication have approached the study of organizational divergence from an aesthetic perspective, there are a few noteworthy exceptions in the organizational literature (see Clair & Kunkel, 1998). In one of the earliest references to aesthetics in global organizations, Mitroff (1987) examines the aesthetic principles embodied in a Japanese garden (e.g., nature is not conceived as an orderly precise machine, everything superfluous to the total effect of the garden is discarded, the gardener is concerned with the interaction of every part —shapes, colors, slopes, sounds). Mitroff argues that these represent the deepest expression of Japanese culture which can help us understand the success of Japanese organizational structures such as "just in time" inventory, the communication systems associated with decision making and quality control, and societal institutions such as the Ministry of International Trade and Industry. It is important to note that Mitroff is not claiming that the Japanese have explicitly or deliber-

ately used the concept of a garden in the design of their factories, compensation systems, treatment of employees, or the communication environment. "But," he writes, "there is an uncanny parallel. . . . Is it really any surprise to find a preoccupation with quality in a society that places such emphasis on the value of individual stones?" (p. 179).

More recently, in a series of essays on aesthetics and organizations (Calás & Smircich, 1996) several scholars take the position that (1) aesthetics is an important way of knowing the processual and everyday aspects of organizations (Kuhn, 1996; Ottensmeyer, 1996; White, 1996), and (2) theories of aesthetics help us understand the human artistry of organizational experience in the global marketplace (Buie, 1996). By involving scholars from several countries and disciplines, this special issue explicitly "sought to gain greater understanding of the relationships of cultural and social factors to aesthetics" (Ottensmeyer, 1996, p. 192) and thereby better describe, comprehend, and contend with the complexities of global organizations.

Communication activities and aesthetics. When culture is seen as aesthetic, the focus is not so much on organizational artifacts (for a fascinating exception, see Strati's [1996] discussion of chairs and the aesthetic dimension of organizations) but rather on communicative activity and the manner in which organizational life is approached and understood. Kuhn (1996), for example, forcefully argues that aesthetics are reflected in the processual/communicative aspects of organizations:

> The aesthetics of organizations will be displayed dynamically, since they are more akin to those of performing/conducting/directing/producing music, plays, dance, preaching, song, instruction, spectacles, sports, parades, ceremonies, dinners—even life itself. (p. 220)

Despite this resonance with a communicative perspective, few scholars have used aesthetics as a basis for exploring organizational divergence. Yet as the plethora of recent titles suggests (e.g., *Artful Work,* Richards, 1997; "Zen and the Art of Teamwork," Lieber, 1995; *Aesthetics and Economics,* Mossetto, 1993; "Aesthetic Components of Management Ethics," Brady, 1986), cultural principles and philosophies of aesthetics are beginning to infiltrate our understanding of organizational experience. At this time, however, artifacts are most often studied as a concrete embodiment of culture rather than as an interactive and dynamic process of aesthetic sensibility.

Culture as Concrete Artifact

According to Jenks (1993), culture is often "viewed as the collective body of arts and intellectual work within one society. It includes a firmly established notion of culture as the realm of the produced and sedimented symbolism" (pp. 11-12). In this approach to culture, the emphasis is on the artifacts produced by human interaction. Communication is studied as a "thing" to be analyzed that physically embodies cultural differences. Two types of artifacts are distinguished: (1) communication artifacts (productions such as employee newsletters and corporate handbooks), and (2) objects intended for other uses (such as desks or gifts). All organizational artifacts are seen as communicative manifestations of culture.

Communication artifacts. Corporate handbooks, manuals, annual reports, and business letters are just some of the artifacts that may be examined as material manifestations of culture (Anderson & Imperia, 1992; Danowski & Huang, 1994; DeVries, 1994; Fiol, 1989; Varner, 1988a, 1988b). Jang and Barnett (1994) examined the impact of national culture on organizational culture by analyzing the full texts of 35 chief operating officers' letters from the annual reports of 18 American and 17 Japanese companies. The clusters derived from semantic network analysis indicated that the companies' businesses were not reflected in the texts but attributes

of national culture were strongly linked to the artifact. Varner's (1988a, 1988b) studies of German, American, and French business correspondence and DeVries's (1994) assessment of written artifacts throughout the world provide striking examples of the ways in which business cards, business letter format, stationery, and specific linguistic elements of the business letter such as salutations, closes, and forms of address organizationally reproduce and reinforce cultural preferences, values, and attitudes. Studies indicate, for example, that cultural ideas of directness and indirectness are firmly established in the business plans, reports, and other written documents of organizations. Varner and Beamer (1995) argue that the contrasts between direct and indirect interactive strategies often result in employees from each culture finding the others' messages tedious, equivocal, unfocused, inappropriate, incompetent, and at times, intentionally frustrating.

Artifacts as cultural communication. Reardon's (1981) study of gift giving provides an intriguing look at the way in which artifacts embody culture. Her interviews with multinational managers indicate that gift giving is a prevalent and important aspect of international business communication. Not only does the gift itself embody cultural meaning, but colors, shapes, and numbers are further instantiations of cultural standards of appropriateness. Goering (1991), in an eight-nation study of voluntary organizations related to a specific health problem, Rett syndrome, examined another type of artifact: organizational logos. Although all country groups used hands in their logos (a basic characteristic of Rett syndrome is compulsive hand gestures), she found systematic differences in the degree of intensity/gentleness and individualism/supportiveness portrayed in the logos that were consistent with country scores on Hofstede's dimensions of cultural variability.

Overall in this approach, researchers "find" culture in the empirical artifact and the object itself is endowed with cultural traces. The microanalytic focus provides compelling examples of how divergence "looks" in the workplace, but does little to help us understand the links between culture, communication, and organization. The next two approaches have a stronger focus on collective sensemaking activities and interpretative processes.

Culture as a Complex Social Pattern

In this approach, culture is "regarded as the whole way of life of a people" (Jenks, 1993, p. 12). This perspective is the most general and pervasive. Rather than focusing on the ideational system, the focus is on culture as an adaptive system (Child & Tayeb, 1983). Culture is conceived as the "normative glue that holds a system together" (Smircich, 1983) and is composed of the "standards for deciding what is, what can be done, how one feels about 'it,' and how one goes about doing 'it' " (Goodenough, 1970). Organizations are seen as sociocultural entities placed in a particular society within a particular historical context; communicative processes are always grounded in the historical, political, institutional, and economic interstices of society (see, e.g., Kozminski & Obloj, 1993, and Gorski, 1993, for communicative analyses of organizing in the developing market economy in Eastern Europe). Communication transmits what is meaningful within a particular sociocultural context, enacting and reinforcing the distinctive patterns of a given culture. Research within this tradition highlights the ways in which organizations are positioned within society and the ways particular patterns, such as class, gender, and race, are enacted within the organization and identifies specific communicative constructs and concepts that have meaning only within a particular cultural pattern.

Papa, Auwal, and Singhal's (1995) study of the Grameen Bank's successful organizational mobilization and socioeconomic improvement of poor and landless Bangladeshi women serves as an exemplar of the way in which reciprocal relationships among the dominant organizations in society, subcultures of gender and class, and the structural/interactional features of organizations are embedded within this approach. Invoking coorientation theory, the theory of concertive control, and critical feminist theories, Papa et al. include a study of the broad social context of Bangladesh as well as a close analysis of the micropractices of daily organizing.

Their work illuminates how women and men relate to the means of production in an undeveloped economy and explores the ways in which organizational communication becomes the transmitter for empowering women (both in the organization and society) while simultaneously preserving male dominance. For example, because Bangladeshi women are confined to their homes, either in accordance with cultural practices or child care demands, the organization income-generating schemes (contrary to women's traditional role in the culture) were designed to allow women to stay close to home. The educational programs of the Grameen Bank challenged the men who wished to control the economic and social activities of women but were delivered to the women in a paternalistic manner. "Most of the women members are fed information that is intended to serve as a guide for their lives, rather than developing that guide for themselves" (Papa et al., 1995, p. 215). Organizational policies enabled women to relate equally to the means of production by giving them equal access to credit (further undermining the oppressive force of the traditional moneylenders) while coincidentally limiting the income-earning potential because they are restricted from selling their products themselves.

The position of organizations in society. When culture is seen as a complex social pattern, the position of economic/occupational institutions within the matrix becomes a fulcrum for understanding organizational communication. For example, some scholars put great significance on the fact that (1) the role of a Japanese business organization is not solely to gain wealth or to display strength but also to contribute to the progress of the community and the nation (see Mitroff, 1987); (2) German economic organizations are seen as a means toward the creation of social stability (Powell, 1995); (3) several cultures (including the United States) operate with efficiency and maximization of profit as the sine qua non of organizations (Thurow, 1983); and (4) in companies such as IRI in Italy, Unilever in Britain, and Belgium's Société Generale de Belgique, widespread societal employment is a primary function of the organization and efficiency is a secondary or tertiary goal (Victor, 1992). As a consequence, they suggest, "what is acceptable or prudent management practice in the United States is often seen as impractical —or even immoral—in other regions of the world" (Steers et al., 1992, p. 321).

These cultural patterns provide an interesting arena for communication research that has been relatively unexplored. For example, the differential manner in which General Motors and Honda faced production cuts in 1993 (GM laid off workers whereas Honda added training to their responsibilities, cut the hours of production per workers, and kept the workforce stable; Sanger, 1993) and AT&T's rationale and decision to lay off 40,000 workers even though the company was making a profit (Andrews, 1992) can help us understand the ways in which organizations rhetorically and instrumentally enact the cultural role of economic institutions.

This approach to culture and organizational communication is most evident in the myriad studies and books that examine distinguishing characteristics of Japanese practices based on political/economic history and institutions to understand their success in the global economy (e.g., Lincoln & Kalleberg, 1990; Mitroff, 1987; Ouchi, 1981; Van Wolferen, 1989). For example, Cole's (1989) insightful book *Strategies for Learning: Small Group Activities in American, Japanese, and Swedish Industry* identifies cultural conditions that strongly influenced how particular organizational strategies related to teamwork were enacted in organizations across three countries. In particular, he notes that the private sector consultants associated with the implementation of quality circle programs in the United States were nonexistent in either Japanese or Swedish cultures and shows how the trajectory of quality circle implementations was affected by the different types of interactions, linkages, and organizational/institutional environments associated with each culture.

Victor (1992) further identifies nine types of cultural patterns that strongly influence organization communication processes across societies: kinship and family structure, educational systems and ties, class systems and economic stratification, gender roles, religion, occupational institutions, political and judicial systems, mobility and geographic attachment, and recreational institutions. His review links the cultural importance of family and kinship ties to hiring practices, investment opportunities, promotion, and organizational identification processes. Although institutional affiliations, such as where one attended college, are important in most societies, they have been shown to play a more critical role in the acquisition of knowledge, resources, and network linkages associated with power and control in some cultures than others (Wysocki, 1988; Zeldin, 1984). Religious and theological influences can be seen in anticipatory socialization practices, attitudes toward work, organizational rituals, and the role of women in organizations (Boulding, 1990).

Class, gender, and racial issues. The cultural patterns most often linked to multinational communication processes include class structure, economic stratification, gender roles, and racial identities. Feminist and critical organizational scholars commonly argue that gender relations, similar to class relations, are embedded within the larger culture and create an intraorganizational "relation of power which must be continually maintained, extended, and interactively recreated in the face of changing social conditions" (Walker, 1985, p. 72). Moody's (1997) comprehensive study of contemporary global labor relations and Ryder's (1997) plea that globalization must include social justice for all workers articulate today's concerns with multinational management strategies, international organizations such as the International Monetary Fund, and the ongoing transformation of global capitalism.

Several studies, based on community and organizational ethnographies (see Bossen, 1984), oral histories and interviews (Beneria & Roldan, 1987; Williams, 1990), network analyses (Rosen, 1982), participant observations (Rothstein, 1982), demographic analyses of work group distributions and occupational structure (Faulkner & Lawson, 1991), comparative analyses of the reorganization of production across neo-Fordist states (Gottfried, 1995), and data from UN publications, country-based data, and newsletters from women's organizations (Moghadam, 1999), have examined how changing global and economic conditions in Latin American, Indian, African, and Asian cultural contexts have affected issues of empowerment and employment for both men and women. Fuentes and Ehrenreich (1983), in a book-length study titled *Women in the Global Factory,* argue that multinational corporations in both Latin and Asian cultures exploit female workers by appealing to workers' "feminine sex roles through such organizational activities as beauty pageants and cooking classes; while on the other hand, these corporations resist unionization and repress collective protest" (p. 162). Fernandez-Kelly (1983) studies how working in the export-processing multinational plants in Mexico (*maquiladoras*) affects Mexican families and concludes that women enter factories not as autonomous individuals but as members of highly interconnected and dependent networks that contribute to women's continued structural and interpersonal oppression. Not surprisingly, research also shows that cultural inequities in gender roles permeate the communication ac-

tivities and policies of international unions (Cockburn, 1991) and global attempts at organizing workers (Lubin & Winslow, 1990).

Managerially oriented research has also looked at the communicative implications of cultural patterns of gender and race. Adler (1987) argues that although many of the constraints women face are similar across cultures, there are two distinct models of gender that are culturally based and influence the availability of jobs, strategies for organizational change, reward systems, and so on. One model, typically American, is the equity model, based on assumed similarity. The complementary model is based on assumed difference and is found in Scandinavian, Latin European, African, and Asian cultures. In the equity model, Adler argues, the primary change variables include legal prescriptions to open jobs to women and the training of women in management skills. Change strategies in the complementary model revolve around the creation of enabling conditions for both male and female contributions to be rewarded and combined.

Several books and articles have also explored issues of gender and race as they apply to cultural adjustment within a multinational environment. The difficulties and barriers international businesswomen face around the world have been well documented (e.g., Adler & Izraeli, 1988; Rossman, 1990), and studies are beginning to address the ethical dimensions of expatriate placement in relation to issues of gender and race (Adler, 1991). Although little communication research has yet addressed the pragmatic implications of cultural differences in what actions (if any) legally or experientially constitute sexual or racial harassment, the increasing number of women and minorities who work in multinational environments makes this an important area for future research (see Eyraud, 1993). Moreover, empirical data from international business surveys indicate that spousal involvement in the decision to relocate as well as his or her positive adjustment to the foreign country is critical to the expatriate employee's successful assimilation and work performance

(Berge, 1987; Thornburg, 1990), and research has begun to address the communicative dimensions of cultural adjustment for both the employee and the employee's family (see Stohl, 1995).

Cultural constructs. As suggested above, the focus on how distinctive patterns are transmitted through communication leads scholars to identify specific constructs or concepts that have meaning only within the patterned context. These concepts are believed to embody that particular social world and provide an avenue into understanding organizational phenomena. This research operates within an emic viewpoint; that is, the units of analysis are developed from within the culture and may not be comparable across cultures. Steers et al. (1992), for example, discuss the implications for equity theory and worker motivation of the African tradition of *ubuntu,* in which clan obligations make it natural for individuals routinely to share available resources and rewards regardless of who worked to obtain them. DeMente (1981) explicates the sociohistorical context of three Japanese terms, *wa,* which may be roughly translated as peace and harmony; *tatemae,* which implies face or facade; and *honne,* defined as honest voice, to illustrate the ethical principles that underlie Japanese organizational communication practices including what may seem to Western sensibilities their penchant for not being true to their word.[7]

Cultural constructs have also been identified as a way to understand the differences in communication ethics. What may be considered bribery, begging, or blackmail in Western culture, for example, may be *chai* or *zawadi* in eastern Africa, Swahili terms associated with gift giving, relational development, and traditional courtesy (Fadiman, 1986). Indeed, a great deal of research indicates that in many cultures, relational development, based on specific instrumental goals, is not only accepted but seen as a legitimate and appropriate way to do business and attain desirable resources. Hu and Grove (1991) explicate how the development of obligation networks called

Guanxi or *kuan-hsi* is central to influence and compliance-gaining attempts in Chinese organizations and Chinese society in general. These exchanges are not used in a cold or calculating manner, but are seen as the "grease" that makes daily life run smooth. In these cultures, those who do not grant special feeling or treatment to those who attempt to establish such instrumental connections may be blamed for "lacking human feeling" (Chang & Holt, 1991, p. 260).

Archer and Fitch (1994) similarly describe the Colombian concept of *palanca* (literally a lever, interpersonally, a connection) as the most purely instrumental form or aspect of an interpersonal relationship. "To move a palanca" or "to shake out a palanca" is to use a relationship like a tool to obtain some objective including getting a job or obtaining scarce resources, service, information, cooperation, or authorizations. They demonstrate how palanca involves transcending rules or scarcity and is inherently a hierarchical action. This ethnographic work is an excellent example of how basic beliefs about persons and relationships pervasive in a culture's interpersonal ideology may be present in organizational communication practices.

Clearly, ethnographic methods are especially appropriate in the study of divergence because "ethnography provides a system of analysis that allows its user to overcome stereotyping by understanding the logic of the way people communicate as a function of their culture" (Victor, 1992, p. 4). The assumptions embedded within an ethnographic approach are closely associated with the conceptualization of culture as communicative practice. These include

1. "Culture extends beyond the walls of organizations and involves in-depth examinations of cultural institutions such as schools, family, voluntary organization, and where possible successful native businesses."
2. "Language and culture are inextricably interwoven."
3. There are "systemic connections between cultural beliefs and the varied behaviors

they generate" (Archer & Fitch, 1994, pp. 88-89).

A distinguishing characteristic between conceptualizing culture as a complex social pattern and as communicative practice, however, is the latter's focus on the active, constitutive role of communication, language, and messages in the social construction of organizations. Within this last theme, communication does not represent culture; rather, discourse articulates identity and communication constitutes culture.

Culture as Communicative Practice

When scholars approach culture as communicative practice, they are generally concerned with the constitutive role of communication in shaping organizational experience and action. Culture is grounded materially in day-to-day communication activity that cannot be separated from the organization. This perspective rejects the notion that organizations are reified structures; rather, organizations are ongoing products of communication practices that influence and are influenced by connections individuals bring into the system that transcend organizational boundaries. Organizations emerge from the collective, interactive processes of generating and interpreting messages and creating networks of understanding through a matrix of coordinated activities and the ongoing relationships among the subjective and emotional experiences of its members (Krone, Chen, Sloan, & Gallant, 1995; Stohl, 1995). Cultural identification thereby permeates, constrains, and facilitates organizational communication; organizations are the "nexus" of various, communicative, cultural, and social practices (Martin, 1992).

In this approach, communication and culture are inextricably and reciprocally bound. Culture becomes public in the meanings people construct in collective/communicative activity. Hall (1959), for example, "treats culture in its entirety as a form of communication" (p. 28) and goes so far to claim that "culture is

communication and communication is culture" (Hall, 1976, p. 169). Hall's framework distinguishes four communicative/cultural domains that help organize this disparate literature: (1) time (a "silent language" that "speaks more plainly than words"; Hall, 1959, p. 1); (2) context (the information that surrounds the interpretation of an event); (3) space (a "hidden dimension" that results in people of different cultures inhabiting different sensory worlds); and (4) message flow (how messages are constructed and communicated among individuals). Two other foci are (5) language (issues related to multilingualism and the possible choice of one working language) and (6) communication effectiveness (a construct isomorphic with cultural survival).

Time. Hall (1976; Hall & Hall, 1987, 1990) uses the terms *monochronic* and *polychronic* to capture the ways in which tempo, rhythm, synchrony, scheduling, lead time, and the rate of information flow become organizational instantiations of culture. In monochronic cultures, time is conceived as material, linear, and substantial, and hence organizations within these cultures (e.g., German, British) tend to compartmentalize functions and people, focus on punctuality and deadlines, and schedule the workday so that people deal with one thing at a time. In polychronic cultures (such as found in the Latin countries), time is nonlinear and insubstantial. Organizational schedules are not nearly as important nor rigidly adhered to, businesspeople do not sequence meetings or activities in a linear fashion, and people are involved with many things at once. In a series of interviews with Asian Indian and Euro-American coworkers, Driskill (1995) found that different perceptions and enactment of time were perceived to be a salient cultural difference during intercultural interactions. Both sets of employees discussed the influence of culture in relation to the perceived pressures associated with deadlines (flexible vs. rigid deadlines) and expectations for task completion (understanding vs. not understanding the time required for task accomplishment). Culture, we see, is embedded in the sensemaking activities of the organization.

Context. According to Hall (1976), "contexting" reflects the types of messages employees create, desire, and understand. Some cultures are distinguished by highly interconnected and extensive communication networks and operate as high-context-message producers where information spreads rapidly and is fairly uncontrolled. A high-context communication or message is one in which most of the information is already in the person and the relationship while very little is in the coded, explicit part of the message. As a result, for most transactions within high-context organizations, people do not require nor do they expect much more background—the context is already very rich with information in which to carry on the transaction. However, when business associates do not know one another, a great deal of time must first be spent establishing the relationship and developing an elaborated context. Then, and only then, can business be conducted. Cultures with segmented networks are low-context-message producers; information is highly focused, compartmentalized, and controlled. Low-context cultures tend to separate personal relationships from work relationships; the mass of the information is vested in the explicit code not in the relationships. Consequently, each time people interact with others they expect and need detailed information.

Space. Space, as a hidden dimension of communication, instantiates the structure of experience as it is molded by culture. From this perspective, the spatial and social aspects of a phenomenon are inseparable; space is not just occupied, it is lived and imbued with meaning (Dear & Wolch, 1989; Harvey, 1989; Massey, 1984). For example, several discussions of the Chinese earth force *feng shui* capture the sense of culture as communicative practice (Adler, 1991; DeMente, 1989). Space with "bad feng shui" is believed to prevent an employee from being in har-

mony with nature and will bring failure to its occupants. Feng shui permeates Chinese business practices insofar as communication reproduces and reinforces activities affected by the layout, design, spatial arrangement, and orientation of worksites and houses. Culture is embedded in the communicative activities surrounding the assignment, choice, creation, design, and use of work space.

Hall's groundbreaking cross-cultural work on proxemics, including research on fixed-feature space (buildings, office layouts, functional/spatial segregation), semi-fixed-feature space (furniture arrangements, positions of material objects), and the use and definition of informal space, as basic ways of organizing the activities of people and groups, foreshadows the recent work of many critical, feminist, and postmodern theorists (e.g., Harvey, 1989; Soja, 1989; Spain, 1992). Although many of these scholars are not part of the organizational communication community, they take a meaning-centered approach focusing attention on how space is not only constructed and represented but how it reproduces meanings and power relations within organizations across cultural contexts. For these scholars, communication is not representational, it constitutes knowledge and truth; discourse articulates identity, communication constitutes culture.

Spain (1992), working within a feminist perspective, explores the social construction of domestic and organizational space across cultures ranging from nonindustrial cultures in Mongolia, South America, the Philippines, and the South Pacific to institutional and organizational arrangements in Indian, Algerian, and American societies. She hypothesizes that initial status differences between women and men create certain types of "gendered spaces" and that institutionalized gender segregation then reinforces prevailing cultural male advantage. Tracing workplace designs from the Panopticon through the home office, Spain reveals the common thread of reinforcement of cultural stratification systems through spatial arrangements.

Message flow. Studies that conceptualize culture as communicative practice not only compare and contrast the differences among the structural and interactional features of organizing as cultural production but also explore the significance and meaning organizational members attribute to the features of organizations. In this sense, the approach is quite similar to what Geertz (1973) describes as a "semiotic concept of culture" in which the focus is on meanings, interpretive frames, and action as public document or text. Organizational forms are culture's substance; organizations are viewed as symbolic activity.

Several studies indicate that managerial and employee interpretations of what is interpersonally appropriate are embodied in the communicative/cultural practices in the workplace. "Built right into the social arrangements of an organization . . . is a thoroughly embracing conception of the member and not merely a conception of him qua member, but, behind this is a conception of him qua human being" (Goffman, 1959, cited in Deetz, 1992, p. 45). For example, studies show that organizational face-saving practices reproduce and reinforce either high- or low-context cultures. Employees from high-context cultures pay much closer attention to the relationship, avoiding direct confrontation and negative interactions, enabling the maintenance and continued development of highly connected multiplex networks (Kras, 1988). In Japan, face-saving is so critical that managers and employees will use a "politeness strategy" composed of indirection and ambiguity so as to ensure that a person does not unintentionally lose face (Barnlund, 1989).

Language. Clearly, as the above examples illustrate, culture as communicative practice transcends issues of language differences in the workplace. Nonetheless, linguistic diversity in the workplace is a critical issue. Surveys of corporate leaders, for example, indicate the "new global aspirations and modern developments in management structures and styles depend even more heavily on good linguistic communication between all members of staff" (Lester, 1984, p. 42). In a series of interviews with corporate workers in several multinational corporations, American, German, and Japanese employees reported that the most serious source of difficulties in their everyday interactions was language (see http://webct.cc.purdue.edu/COM224 for the texts of these interviews). Hilton (1992) reports that although American employees were very critical of their international colleagues' misunderstanding of terminology, poor pronunciation, and inadequate grammar and believed language issues affected productivity, they made no attempt to learn even the most simple foreign phrases. Bantz (1993) notes that although cross-national research teams usually agree on a working language, differences in language competence, comfort in working in a nonnative tongue, and nontransferability of some abstract concepts sometimes minimized the contributions members could make to the team and strongly affected conflict management and the emergence of norms.

Studies outside the field of organizational communication indicate increasing dominance of English as the language of business (Berns, 1992; Grabe, 1988). English has even been adopted as the official company language in multinationals such as the Italian firm Olivetti, Dutch-owned Phillips Corporation, and the Japanese company Komatsu (Varner & Beamer, 1995). Rationales for a "one language" policy include arguments based on instrumental efficiency and interpersonal effectiveness. Having one official language, it is suggested, eliminates the need for costly and time-consuming translation in both written and oral communication, saves money on training and technology, and minimizes cycle time and awkwardness of interaction (Altman, 1989). The predominance of one language, it is argued, also builds social cohesion and trust, allows people to do their jobs better, and makes the work environment safer (Chan, 1995).

When culture is viewed as communicative practice, however, the importance of language choice in the workplace goes far beyond issues of productivity and effectiveness. "The meanings of culture are carried chiefly in symbolic conveyances, language being the most general and pervasive of symbolic system" (Nash, 1990). As communication scholars have so often demonstrated, language not only directs what we say but influences how we shape and frame experience, mediates the meanings we assign to action, helps define members of in- and out-groups, and confers status distinctions (e.g., Giles, 1977; Hymes, 1974; Milroy & Margraine, 1980; Whorf, 1952). When people are asked to comment on other languages, they most often comment on their perceptions of the other cultures (Flaitz, 1988).

Language and cultural identity are inextricably bound together, thus the linguistic context of organizational practices has meaning that transcends instrumentality. Studies show, for example, that in international governmental organizations such as the United Nations and the various commissions associated with the European Union, ministers and officials who are quite competent in English, French, or German, and will speak these languages during informal interactions, still insist on conducting business in their own language regardless of the time or immense cost involved in providing simultaneous translation (Tugendhat, 1988). "It is in our manner of communicating that we display our cultural uniqueness" (Barnlund, 1989, p. 33). Thus, we can see that from the perspective of culture as communicative practice, the pragmatic choice of an official organizational language not only has instrumental effects but enacts who and what is respected, validates certain types of knowledge claims, and creates expertise and privilege (Berns, 1992; Flaitz, 1988).

The French, of course, provide the best known examples of virulent opposition to the hegemony of the English language, but from many quarters there is concern that the increasing use of English as the common business language will lead to an erosion of national identity, the privileging of native English speakers within the workforce, and the encroachment of American values (Berns, 1992). Grabe (1988) writes:

> The English language users of information represent an information cartel: there is no reason to expect that a system which bestows such power upon its controllers would be altered or adapted by these controllers to allow a more democratic system of information management. (p. 68)

In the United States, where the number of employees who speak Tagalog, Spanish, Eastern European, and Asian languages has increased dramatically in the past ten years, several organizations, such as the Walt Disney Corporation, meat packing systems, insurance companies, and medical centers, have developed "English only" policies. Many of these policies have been shown to violate Title VII of the Civil Rights Act of 1964 insofar as they discriminate against specific classes of workers. The legal opinion thus far is that if English-only policies are initiated it must be a legitimate "business necessity" including productivity, quality, and safety; applied only during working hours, not lunch or breaks; and applied to all bilingual employees in the same manner (Chan, 1995). But the issues go much further than Chan's (1995) recommendation that there needs to be a balance among employees' right to communicate in ways in which they are most comfortable, the need for protection from harassment, and the organization's desire to promote a harmonious, cohesive, and safe work environment. Issues of identity, power, and control are tied to language.

One recent approach to the study of multilingualism or "overcoming Babel" in the workplace relates to the processes of translation as organizational practice (see Kölmel & Payne, 1989).[8] Scholars have addressed issues related to translation and the preservation of coherence in meaning (Kirk, 1986), the challenges of different argumentation styles (Hatim, 1989), barriers to effective translation (Brislin, 1989), and the cultural role of the interpreter within various contexts such as conferences, meetings, and negotiations (Altman, 1989). For example,

> in Anglo-Saxon negotiations, the translator is supposed to be neutral, like a black box through which words in one language enter and words in another language exit. The translator in more collectivist cultures will usually serve the national group, engaging them in lengthy asides and attempting to mediate misunderstandings arising from culture as well as language. Very often he or she may be the top negotiator in the group and an interpreter rather than a translator. (Trompenaars, 1994, p. 93)

Banks and Banks (1991), in one of the few organizational communication studies to address directly issues of language diversity in the workplace, demonstrate how the process of translation as mediation (Neubert, 1989), creation (Steiner, 1975), and domination (Glassgold, 1987) pose several other types of interactive problematics. The first type of translation is concerned only with the mechanisms of transferring meaning "accurately" from one language system to another. In the second formulation, translation is "conceived as a cultural transformation of texts," and the translator is viewed as an author/speaker whose sociocultural context, rather than the original sociocultural context, becomes central to the meanings generated by the process. The third process, translation as domination, addresses the political and ideological dimensions of discourse. Banks and Banks suggest that translators constrain meanings by their acts and hence "power relations are both encoded in and partially constituted in the discourse." Their discourse analysis of both the English and Spanish versions of a meeting between the general manager of a hotel and 75 workers whose dominant language is Spanish indicates that the three problems involving translation in the workplace—inaccuracies, losses of common sociocultural contexts, and changes to power relationships—were all present. They argue that

> translation has the potential to degrade coincident meanings so that worker task accomplishment, productivity, commitment to programs and institution, and compliance are all vulnerable to erosion. The key practical issue is what can be done to mitigate the negative effects of translation. Although research is just beginning there appear to be two classes of remedies that can help the situation—procedural actions and attitudinal changes. . . . Long-term organizational ends will be fostered by an attitude of appreciation for language diversity while recognizing the impracticality of treating all languages identically or equally. (Banks & Banks, 1991, pp. 235-236)

Communication effectiveness. Taken together, the studies of linguistic diversity in an organizational setting establish how working together intensifies and highlights cultural differences. As suggested earlier, work on "cultural synergy" (Adler, 1980; Moran & Harris, 1982) and "third-culture building" (Casmir, 1993) also identifies the interactional features and competencies that best maximize the organizational advantages and minimize the disadvantages associated with cultural diversity. The strong managerial and cognitive perspective found in the synergy literature, however, is countered by researchers who view culture as communicative practice. While interested in global accommodation and organizational change, these communication scholars challenge notions of whose interests constitute and should provide measures of effectiveness. They problematize the very ground on which intercultural effectiveness is based.

Shuter (1993), for example, champions the practice of "culturalism" as an option to synergy, third-culture building, and multiculturalism. Like synergy, third-culture building

(Casmir, 1993) entails the commingling of cultural backgrounds to produce a new and different, blended culture, while multiculturalism is an enactment and celebration of cultural, racial, and ethnic differences. Shuter argues that in the contemporary workplace the retention and preservation of cultural identity is as important as the development of pragmatic and instrumental interdependence privileged in the synergy literature. Culturalism emphasizes interdependence, compromise, consensus, cultural adaptation, and development only in the task domain, that is, the performance of activities and behaviors by culturally diverse individuals for mutual gain; cultural integrity is maintained in the expressive realm. By viewing culture as communicative practice, Shuter gives voice to what is called for in multiculturalism (the retention of cultural identity and attitudinal, value, and behavioral differences) in the socioemotional domain while providing for the development of a new voice through communicative practices at the pragmatic level of task completion.

In a series of ethnographies that explore Japanese transplants in the United States, a set of industrial anthropologists goes even further and challenges the notion that multicultural interaction reflects a process of developing, generating, and perpetuating consensus. Rather, they address the processes by which intercultural organizational practices can fragment, mutilate, shrink, deform, and hollow out culture (Hamada & Yaguchi, 1994; Kleinburg, 1994; White & Rackerby, 1994). Hamada and Yaguchi, for example, explore how a corporate ideology, rooted in the paternalistic principles of the traditional Japanese household, begins to dissipate as a schism develops between the principles manifested in symbols (e.g., corporate manuals, ambiguous job descriptions) and the original logic (corporate familialism) of the practices. As Japanese management becomes sensitive to local conditions in the American Midwest, management tries to enhance and strengthen the "family" metaphor but the practices become incongruent with the intent. The culture loses interactive substance through "(1) the process

of growing dissonance between perceived social reality and underlying cultural assumptions, and (2) the process of growing dissonance between manifested symbols and their original meanings" (Hamada & Yaguchi, 1994, p. 194).

Recent studies of the communicative practices associated with worker participation and democracy also address the tensions that arise among individual and group identities, cultural integrity and accommodation, and the maintenance and enactment of traditional values and competitive performance in the global workplace (Alvesson, 1987; Cheney, 1995; Deetz, 1992; Giroux, 1992; Giroux & Fenocchi, 1995; Stohl, 1995). Studying the transition from local to global organizing in one of the oldest employee-owned cooperatives in the world, Mondragón, in the Basque region of Spain, Cheney (1995, 1999) looks at what it means to approach democracy, participation, and culture as self-critical, self-regenerating, and self-correcting communication processes. Giroux (1992) examines four decision-making cases in the Movement Desjardins in Quebec and addresses the ways in which "relations based on shared meaning" allow the cooperatives to maintain its sociocultural project, "relations based on use" form the economic project, and "relations based on property" give control over execution of the cooperative projects. In these studies, cultural values such as solidarity and equality are realized to a great extent through talk. Cheney finds participation and democracy are continually contested terms, and Stohl (1995) specifies the paradox of compatibility to describe the interactive pressures that evolve when cultural practices are incompatible with prescribed participative acts. Giroux's (1992) longitudinal study of participation of women in two cultural sector cooperatives in Quebec concludes that notwithstanding the democratic discourse maintained in cooperatives, actual practice by no means reflected gender equality in these organizations.

Overall, culture as communicative practice unveils the emergent and often contradictory relationships among the subjective experiences, multiple languages, behavioral patterns, and volatile structures inherent in multinational organizations. The consistent coupling of culture and communication puts meaning-centered interpretive processes at the center of the study of global organizing.

Ironies Found in the Divergence Literature

In summary, across all conceptualizations of culture, the divergence literature provides strong evidence that the dynamic structures of contemporary organizations are produced and reproduced through the culturally saturated processes of organizing. Although some scholars suggest that culture is less significant to the web of rules and organizational structuring the further a country is along the road toward industrialization (Knudsen, 1995), cultural differences are blatantly obvious in organizational communication processes across both highly industrialized and less industrialized capitalistic nations. Systematic structural, processual, and interpretive distinctions are found across cultures despite environmental pressures toward organizational convergence. Culture enters organizations artfully, unself-consciously, and piecemeal through several avenues simultaneously. People create, enter, and leave organizations not as autonomous individuals but as members of highly interconnected and interdependent cultural networks.

However, what is not clear in this literature is the association between the mechanisms and processes of communicative convergence and divergence. That is, as provocative as the relationships among culture, communication, and organizing may be there is still little information about the conditions under which convergence or divergence takes precedence or explorations and explanations of the dynamic interplay among the two. Yet it is the continual management of these opposing forces that constitutes contemporary organizational experience. The imperatives of the global market, the availability of international resources,

the fluidity of a worldwide workforce, and the development and use of new communication/information technologies are making unprecedented demands on today's organizations while simultaneously people's cultural identities are becoming more salient both in and outside the workplace.

There are several ironies that pervade the divergence literature that contribute to this lack of coherence and integration across perspectives. To begin, much of the divergence literature is atheoretical, treating culture as a residual category or independent variable presumed to account for variations in organizing but with little explanation for how this happens. Tayeb (1992) cautions:

> Evoking national and cultural explanations for the existence of similarities or differences enables researchers to better understand their research only if the similarities and differences are an integrated aspect of their theoretical frameworks. (p. 133)

Second, despite the fundamental assumption that cultural differences significantly affect social practices, the theoretical principles and the relationships among variables are expected to be stable and unchanging across differing cultural milieux. Ironically, the presumption that relationships among constructs will be the same across cultures magnifies the possibility that researchers will interpret communication differences as meaningful when in fact the differences may be more apparent than real. By minimizing the possibility of finding evidence of convergence, the divergence literature possibly exaggerates the effects of culture and masks the synchronous homogenizing effects of globalization.

Third, a great deal of the divergence literature simply extends traditional topics into the global arena, conceptualizing questions, organizations, and communication in the same ways they have always been conceived. Without a radical reconfiguration of what constitutes relevant organizational boundaries, a decentering of organizational activities, and a reconsideration of communicative practices as the cause, medium, and outcome of fragmented organizational structures, the divergence research enacts "business as usual." We may continue to learn more about how organizations differ across cultures, yet the macro- and microlevel implications of the embedded nature of contemporary organizational communication will remain obscure.

In the next section, the implications of the theoretical, methodological, and practical parochialisms that imbue both the convergence and the divergence literature are further detailed. As we shall see, our typical ways of doing both types of research are challenged by the unsettled systems of cultured relations that permeate disciplinary practices.

THEORETICAL, METHODOLOGICAL, AND PRACTICAL ISSUES IN GLOBALIZING ORGANIZATIONAL COMMUNICATION

Some prominent scholars in the field argue, in essence, that the academic establishment impedes or constrains the conduct and dissemination of international or cross-national efforts. This is done presumably through the use of parochial and culture-bound theories of management, through the insistence on traditional research methods as the criteria for journal acceptance, and through the downplaying of cross-cultural studies in our doctoral programs. (Steers et al., 1992, p. 322)

At first glance, the issues raised by Steers et al., writing about the management discipline, either do not seem to apply to the field of organizational communication or at most represent only a small fragment of our field. After all, we often self-consciously distinguish ourselves by the widely disparate methods, epistemologies, and theoretical assumptions that bind us together (e.g., Smith, 1993), and we collectively celebrate the plurality of voices in our field that give expres-

sion to various forms of knowledge, relations, and ways of organizing (Mumby & Stohl, 1996).

Nonetheless, Steers and his colleagues raise three important issues for our consideration. Each of these concerns, specified here as *theoretical, methodological,* and *pragmatic* parochialism, addresses issues of conception and praxis for the study of globalization and communication in multinational organizations. As suggested earlier, several of the theories they identified as "culture bound" have had a strong and continuing influence on organizational communication research. Yet rarely have we been concerned with the cross-cultural applicability of the theories we employ. Moreover, even though contemporary communication theories seem well suited to address the dynamic tensions embedded in the interpersonal, organizational, and community interfaces of global systems, these multilevel, interdependent, constraining, and enabling alignments are rarely studied together. Second, despite our field's acceptance of both interpretive and social-scientific methods, important methodological issues have not been resolved. Methodological parochialism refers to issues of transferability of research protocols, approaches to establishing construct validity and interpretive reliability, statistical appropriateness, and language into a culturally diverse, multilingual research environment.

Pragmatic parochialism encompasses the third concern. Although there has been recognition that it is counterproductive for our discipline to maintain a Maginot Line of scientific and scholarly isolationism (Jamieson & Cappella, 1996; Stohl, 1993), the subdivisions in our field and academic departments often resemble national borders in their capacity to limit knowledge, restrict cooperation, and impede collaboration. Arbitrary disciplinary boundaries not only create barriers for learning but also limit the types of questions researchers ask, the conceptualization of relevant constructs, the types of organizations we study, the ways we search for the answers, and the ethical stances we take. The issues faced by communication scholars as we try to understand, map, and reconcile the processes of divergence and convergence are paralleled in the debates contesting the efficacy of comparative politics and international relations scholars, and more generally, the relative value of area studies specialists and global experts. They too are struggling to find ways to study and "understand how the broad currents of social change are shaped, altered, and redefined as they come into contact with a variety of local circumstances" (Heginbotham, 1994, p. A68).

Most assuredly, issues of generalizability, interpretive reliability, methodological appropriateness, and disciplinary isolationism are not unique to global and multicultural organizational communication research. The relative newness and rapid burgeoning of this area of study, however, coupled with the increasing globalization of the production of knowledge, make these concerns particularly salient in this context. Each of these issues is designed to challenge and stimulate scholars to reconsider past practices and develop creative and collaborative solutions that reflect the dynamic and complex environment of contemporary organizations. (See Table 10.4 for a summary of the issues and strategies.)

Theoretical Parochialism

A major premise of this chapter is that organizational communication takes place at the intersection of contexts, actors, relations, and activities that cannot be disassociated from one another. Theories therefore need to encompass the ways in which economic/organizational action is embedded in ongoing and overlapping systems of social relations constituting and reproducing trust/mistrust, power/control, and order/chaos in the global system. Yet despite the potential utility of structuration, postmodern, critical, chaos, and network/systems theories to address the multilevel and opposing forces of convergence and divergence, very little of our research has focused on communication efforts to organize

global transformation within a local system. Moreover, little consideration has been accorded the cultural biases of the theoretical perspectives we have used to study organizational convergence or divergence.

Cross-Cultural Applicability

Several scholars have identified cultural biases embedded in the social-scientific and interpretive theories that have influenced organizational studies of convergence and divergence. From motivation, attribution, equity, and contingency theories to critical theory, postmodernism, and feminism, the Eurocentric foundations of these theories belie their universality and cross-cultural applicability (Asante, 1987; Boyacigiller & Adler, 1991; Hofstede, 1984; Sanborn, 1993).

Lee and Jablin (1992), in one of the few communication studies to address directly the issue of theoretical universalism (see Sullivan & Taylor's [1991] empirical test of compliance-gaining theory in international settings for another exception), found the transferability of Hirschman's (1970) theory of exit, voice, loyalty, and neglect to the East Asian cultural context was not straightforward. Their study, based on surveys and written responses to hypothetical scenarios, compared the communicative responses of Korean, Japanese, and American students to dissatisfying work conditions. The results supported the generalizability of Hirschman's model to Korean culture but the comparisons between cultures were quite provocative. Specifically, although they found that Korean and Japanese respondents were significantly more loyal in their communicative responses to dissatisfying work conditions than were the American respondents, a close examination of the probabilities, patterns, and meanings of the communicative responses underscored the importance of specific differences (in this case values of the family and individual competitiveness) even among workers from different

TABLE 10.4 Suggestions for Future Research

Issue	Strategy
Theoretical parochialism	
Overgeneralized theoretical applications	Explicitly address the constraints and influence of our own cultural values on how we conceptualize organizational phenomena
	Study non-U.S. and non-Western organizations from both etic and emic perspectives
	Develop thick descriptions of organizational communication and the contexts in which organizations are embedded
Interpretive reliability and construct validity	Establish the equivalency of constructs and operationalizations prior to the interpretation of comparative results
Implicit universalism	Explication of the cultural and geographic domain of theory and research project
	Indicate the national and cultural aspects of the research sample
Methodological parochialism	
Method transferability	Triangulation of social-scientific and interpretive methods
	Integration of qualitative and quantitative approaches
Statistical appropriateness	Pretest measures on matching cultural sample
	Develop alternative procedures
	Use nonparametric statistics
Assumptions of homogeneity	Specify relevant subcultural identifications of sample
Language choice	Back translations
	Translation by mediation teams
	Multilingual research team
Practical parochialism	
Insularity of researchers	Create multinational, multicultural, interdisciplinary research teams
Limited models	Expand the organizational domain of our research (i.e., nonprofit, alternative organizations, governmental organizations, nongovernmental organizations)
Limited topics	Explore issues such as the impact of communication technologies, ethics from both convergence and divergence perspectives

countries who share a common sociocultural heritage.

Relationships Among Theoretical Concepts

Other studies that have looked at the cross-cultural applicability of communication constructs also suggest that posited theoretical relationships supported in one cultural context may not exist in the same form in another context. For example, Kleinburg's (1994) ethnography of a Japanese transplant notes markedly different interpretations of, and strong concern or lack of concern for, ambiguity expressed by American and Japanese employees in the same company. She concludes that the definition of organizational ambiguity itself is culturally constructed. Morley, Shockley-Zalabak, and Cesaria (1997), using a rule-based approach, found that the relationships among organizational rules, culture themes, founder values, hierarchical position, communication activities, and perceptions of a variety of organizational outcomes were similar in Italian and American high-technology companies although there was far less agreement on what constitutes value rules within the Italian companies. Ticehurst (1992) found that the communication satisfaction questionnaire tapped different functions of communication satisfaction for Australians as compared to Americans.

Clearly, issues of theoretical parochialism are complex, and there is a great need for more sophisticated and programmatic ethnographies, case studies, and comparative research that are consistent with the multivocal, equivocal, and embedded activities that comprise organizing. Increased awareness of the constraints and the efficacy of our theories, however, must also be coupled with a reconsideration of our own research agendas in light of our own "cultural baggage." That is, organizational communication scholars need to address explicitly the constraints and influence of our own cultured practices on how we conceptualize and study organizational phenomena. For example, even the idea of searching for generalizable and universal theory is culture specific. Engaging in self-reflection and expanding our organizational horizons will not only help communication researchers learn more about the limits and the strengths of current theory, but it will enable us to develop new theory and insights into the processes of organizing. The disjunctures provide an opportunity to reexamine the assumptions underlying our theories and the posited relationships among theoretical concepts; the convergences enable us to build a strong foundation on which to address contemporary issues in the global workplace.

Moreover, concerns related to the transferability and comprehensiveness of theory in case and comparative studies must not only extend to theoretical foundations but also to the appropriateness of the statistical and methodological assumptions underlying the procedures and instruments developed to explore or test theory. Boyacigiller and Adler (1991) argue that "even when the applicability of these theories to other cultures is tested, researchers usually select methods that are most acceptable according to American norms, thereby rendering results that are culturally conditioned" (p. 272).

Methodological Parochialism

Within the field of organizational communication, a number of widely used survey instruments such as the ICA audit, the Organizational Commitment Questionnaire, job satisfaction indexes, managerial style questionnaires, upward influence surveys, and participatory decision-making scales, developed in the United States and Western Europe, have been employed in cross-cultural comparative studies, and traditional univariate and multivariate statistical analyses have been undertaken (e.g., Barnett & Lee, 1995; Downs et al.,

1995; Hirokowa & Miyahara, 1986; Sanborn, 1993; Page & Wiseman, 1993; Stewart et al., 1986). Although each of these studies uses surveys that have been shown to be reliable and valid in the past, the heavy reliance on American and British workers to develop these questions, scales, and procedures raises questions about the appropriateness of the methods across cultural contexts.

Equivalence of Measures

Lincoln and Kalleberg (1990) found that when confronted with Likert type questions to which there were no socially correct answers, American employees tended to respond with relatively extreme measures whereas the Japanese counterparts tended to respond more toward the middle of the scale. Barnett and Lee (1995), on the other hand, found that when Americans are asked to estimate the dissimilarity among pairs of symbols, they tend to use far smaller scales than their Japanese or Taiwanese counterparts. Adler, Campbell, and Laurent (1989) found that Chinese managers from the People's Republic of China produced bimodal distribution of responses to several questions on the Laurent Management Questionnaire, which had a normal distribution when given to managers from nine European countries and the United States. Thus, traditional techniques, such as rescaling mean values for purposes of statistical comparison, may mask the most important differences to be found in a cross-cultural study.

These examples raise the strong possibility that not only does culture influence how we feel, what we value, what things mean, how we organize, and how we communicate but also affects the ways in which people respond to research protocols. We must, then, remain skeptical of studies such as that of Downs et al. (1995), who conclude that communication with supervisors, top management, and colleagues as well as communication climate were consistent predictors of commitment across the United States, Australia, and Guatemala when they used the standard items on the Communication Satisfaction Questionnaire (Downs & Hazen, 1977) and Organizational Commitment Inventory (Cook & Wall, 1980). Items such as "I sometimes feel like leaving this organization for good" and "Even if the firm were not doing well financially, I would be reluctant to change to another employer" may not be scaled in the same manner nor tap the American-based construct "organizational loyalty" for respondents in countries like Guatemala where for 40 years (until late 1996) thousands of citizens had been killed annually by a series of military governments aligned with leading industrialists and the economic elite.

Indeed, similar results may have very different causal explanations. Universal responses to the same set of constraints and the similarity of responses and structures may be affirming the rapid rate of cultural diffusion and imitation that is indicative of the interpenetration of global communications, management training, and popular culture (Dogan & Pelassy, 1984). Or as Adler et al. (1989) found, differential reasoning may be associated with the same responses. For example, although over 66% of Italian and Japanese managers agreed with the statement "It is important for managers to have precise answers to most of the questions his [sic] subordinates may raise about their work" (only 10% of the Swedish managers agreed) the reasons they gave were quite different. Italians explained that managers should be experts, whereas Japanese respondents believed, "A Japanese would never ask his boss a question he could not answer" (p. 70).

Riordan and Vandenberg (1994), using covariance structure analytic procedures, ask the central question: "Do employees of different cultures interpret work-related measures in an equivalent manner?" (p. 643). Looking at three measures strongly associated with organizational communication processes (i.e., the Organizational Commitment Questionnaire, Mowday, Steers, & Porter, 1979; the Organization-Based Self-Esteem instrument, Pierce, Gardner, Cummings, & Dunham,

1989; and the Satisfaction With My Supervisor scale, Vandenberg & Scarpello, 1992), the answer is a resounding no. Clearly, then, there is a need to establish the equivalency of constructs and measures prior to interpreting differences on self-report variables between culturally diverse groups. A priori, we cannot know that the same conceptual frame of reference will be evoked across cultures, that interview questions will be interpreted similarly, that network linkages are comparable, or that diverse groups will calibrate the scores of an instrument in the same manner.

Appropriateness of Methods

But it is not only the use of surveys and statistics alone that are of concern for researchers in a multicultural environment. The procedures and methods designed to collect both qualitative and quantitative data may be culturally inappropriate. For example, the use of hypothetical scenarios may not be a suitable methodology for cultures that typically engage in holistic thinking and circular patterns of thought and discourse, whereas they are quite useful in cultures characterized by linear, step-by-step cognitive patterns (Adler et al., 1989). Requests for certain types of organizational access may violate cultural norms, participatory observations may transgress cultural expectations, and interviewing techniques may compromise employees. Issues such as organizational entry, confidentiality, trust, social desirability, and informed consent are culturally constructed. Thus, regardless of whether we conduct ethnographies, interviews, participant observations, surveys, network analysis, or experiments, when researchers enter the global arena, cultural awareness, knowledge of others, and sensitivity are mandatory.

The sensibility that is needed is complicated by another potential form of methodological parochialism, the assumption of sample homogeneity. It is ironic that at a time when organizations and researchers are increasingly aware of, and sensitive to, issues of

diversity in the American workplace (Cox, 1993; Fine, 1991) so much of the research assumes that organizations within other countries are composed of monocultural workforces. For example, despite what we know of the linguistic and regional diversity within Chinese society, studies of Chinese managers often treat them as one unicultural sample, middle-level managers from Hong Kong are often collapsed into one cultural unit for analysis, members of British and American corporate boards of directors are assumed to represent the national characteristics of the corporation's national origin, and workers in a Mexican company are often all labeled "Mexican" (e.g., Chen & Chung, 1994; Kras, 1988; Krone, Garrett, & Chen, 1992). This homogenization is especially troublesome when the basic goal of the research is to do some form of cultural description or comparison among groups. Just as it has become standard to describe demographic characteristics such as gender, age, and race, researchers need to investigate, adapt to, and if relevant, report the national, regional, and linguistic diversity within their sample groups. Cultural identity embodies a difference that makes a difference.

Language and Translation

The interconnected nature of language and cultural identity also highlights the methodological significance of language choice in studies that cross national boundaries. We are faced with our own linguistic limitations in an environment in which the use of a particular language creates a system of relations that may be affirming or disconfirming, engaging or alienating participants in the research endeavor. Communication is, by its very nature, characterized by linguistic difference. Often there are no easy equivalents for terms or phrases (e.g., *manager* cannot be directly translated into either French or Italian, the English translation of the German term *papierkrieg* to red tape neutralizes a term that literally means paper war; see Victor, 1992), connotations and denotations are difficult for nonnative speakers to assess, the use of one language minimizes the diversity of the sampling frame and the comfort of the participants, and translation and interpretation are costly in terms of effort, time, and money. Nonetheless, with over 2,500 languages spoken around the world (Bryson, 1990) it is highly likely that research in contemporary organizations will take place in a multilingual environment.

Most cross-cultural researchers identify back translation as the most effective strategy for addressing issues of language diversity and equivalence (Varner & Beamer, 1995; Victor, 1992). Back translation is a two-step process. First, one translator (preferably a native speaker of one of the languages) puts the survey, interview questions, documents, and so forth into a second language, then the messages are translated back into the original language by a second translator. In this manner, blatant mistranslations as well as nuanced distortions can be identified. Adler et al. (1989), for example, express their dismay when they found that the item "Most conflicts in a company can be productive" on the Laurent management questionnaire became "Much physical violence in a company can be productive." on the Mandarin language questionnaire.

Wright, Lane, and Beamish (1988), however, identify several potential problems with back translations based on translators who (1) are unfamiliar with the technical vocabulary, (2) use a particular dialect that is inappropriate in the particular setting, and (3) are insensitive to political nuances and organizational constraints. Further, they indicate that there are often as many errors in back translations as there are in the original translations. In a comparative study of Thai and British organizations, Wright (1984) developed an alternative. She had a panel of four or five native speakers work through interview schedules and surveys (with the primary investigator providing input and explanation along the way), had another native speaker put their translations into graceful language, and then brought the translations back to the panel for a final evaluation.

Another approach designed to alleviate language problems and build on the strength embedded in linguistic diversity is to develop a multilingual research team who conceptualizes, develops, and collaboratively carries out the research project. Being able to move back and forth among relevant language groups enables scholars with multilingual skills to develop unique perspectives and insights at both the theoretical and praxis levels. Bantz (1993) provides a detailed look at his own experiences on a multilingual research team and as discussed earlier, gives many pragmatic suggestions for balancing issues of creativity and cohesiveness, effectiveness and efficiency, ethical responsibility and mutual respect within such groups. He describes the various tactics used to minimize the limitations of working in one language (English), including the legitimization and normalization of fast-spaced language switching during group discussion, which facilitated understanding, vigorous debate, and linguistic sensitivity.

Pragmatic Parochialism

According to the "law of requisite variety" (Weick, 1969), organizations, to survive, must develop complexity equivalent to the diversity of their interactive environments. And in today's volatile and increasingly complex and interconnected global system, organizations are diffusing functions, diversifying structures, integrating units, and creating greater degrees of flexibility. Likewise, researchers who work in and study these complex and evolving systems require diverse sets of skills and expertise.

Multidisciplinary and Multicultural Research

Organizational communication scholarship in the global environment requires at least an understanding of past and present economic, sociocultural, political, and business practices. It is no longer productive to isolate ourselves individually or wrap ourselves up collectively in the parochial cloth of our academic specialties. Multidisciplinary research teams can help facilitate requisite variety. Interdisciplinary research, however, without a multicultural component will not fully address the limiting consequences of traditional individualistic research programs. We need to develop more international collaborations, bringing together cultural insiders and outsiders, melding etic and emic perspectives. Just as the advantages of diverse work groups are well documented, anthropologists have long recognized that similarity, familiarity, and presumption (derived from a "native" perspective) may be impediments to analyses and descriptions that are not culture bound and trivial (Hamada & Yaguchi, 1994).

Pragmatic parochialism may also insinuate itself into the very fabric of our research in the most mundane manner yet have significant influence on our work. When choosing where to conduct our research, for example, "vacation empiricism," that is, choosing research sites based on availability and desirability of location, can severely limit the potential theoretical contributions of our work. Steers et al. (1992) urge that organizational researchers focus on "theory-based sampling, not sampling-based theory" (p. 328).

Diversifying Organizational Types

To address the demands of this new research agenda, we also need to be less parochial in the types of organizations we study. As this review indicates, most of the research on cultural variability and organizational communication is concentrated in the profit-making, multinational sector. International labor unions, nonprofit organizations, worker collectives, international governmental agencies, and transnational voluntary associations are just a few of the types of organizations markedly absent from the organizational communication literature. By sheer numbers alone they should be included in our typologies and studies (there are over 18,000 such organiza-

tions reported in the *Yearbook of International Organizations*), but their importance goes far beyond their ubiquitous presence.

At a time when we are looking for solutions to our social and global problems in new partnerships among business and industry, education, government, and citizen groups, who, how, and what we study have powerful ethical implications. The old social contract has been broken and the community-organizational-individual relationship has been transformed. Globalization does not serve all interests equally. Looking at different types of organizations can provide us with alternative models, metaphors, ways of organizing and coming together that may be better suited for dealing with the complex, volatile, multicultural issues facing us today. The parochial view of what constitutes an organization worthy of study severely limits what we can learn about, who we can learn from, and who we will learn with.

CONCLUSIONS

This is a world of complex connections. Joint ventures between McDonald's Restaurants of Canada and the Moscow city council (Vikhanski & Puffer, 1993) seem commonplace. Managerial decisions in a small savings and loan company in Ohio are tightly coupled with the value of British oil stocks (Boulding, 1990). Insensitivity to intercultural relationship formation by just a few members in an international work group can stymie years of sensitive negotiations and financial commitments to develop a cooperative joint venture (Seelye & Seelye-James, 1995). Power, influence, and financial resources of multinational corporations are far greater than those of many nations (Feld & Jordan, 1988). Employees can work closely together for the same company for years while remaining 12,000 miles and 12 time zones apart.

Thus, it is not surprising that in the years between the publication of the first and second editions of the *Handbook of Organizational Communication* the number of studies addressing communication processes and multinational organizing has dramatically increased. An essential part of contemporary organizational experience is communicating in a context of global interdependence and multiculturalism. Culture is not a thing that can be managed, controlled, or contained but rather a constitutive feature of organizing.

Certainly, the heightened interest in the dynamic tension between communication, culture, and organization invigorates traditional topics of study, giving them greater currency as well as opening up new sets of questions, issues, and concerns. A primary conclusion of this chapter is that organizations and individuals are simultaneously managing environmental, technological, and social pressures to become more similar while maintaining cultural differences. Influence attempts, compliance gaining, feedback, performance appraisals, and decision making take on greater complexity when individuals are trying to manage multiple and often conflicting identities in the global workplace. Organizational identification, team commitment, communication satisfaction, and communicative competence develop new meanings and new relations that transcend traditional organizational boundaries. Intercultural training, the involvement of the family in expatriate selection and adjustment, the role of organizations in community development, the introduction of new communication technologies, cultural conceptions of employee rights, and differing interpretations of harassment problematize concerns about communication ethics and definitions of responsible communication.

In other words, to understand and reconcile the processes of divergence and convergence, we need to continue to ask questions that focus on their interplay across cultural contexts. For example, uncertainty and ambiguity are constitutive features of the global environment. Does the management of ambiguity (as evidenced in mission statements, organizational symbols, and employee publications) allow organizations to manage the tensions between processes of convergence and divergence? Do organizations use distinctive communication strategies to manage ambiguity as they move from domestic to global forms of organizing? How do organizational socialization experiences and programs reinforce the concurrent strengthening/weakening of organizational/cultural identifications? What sorts of framing devices are used in leader-member communication to enact global changes while maintaining the integrity of individual affiliations?

These sorts of questions resonate with the practical tensions that exist between processes of convergence and divergence in a multicultural environment. Not circumscribed by traditional organizational or disciplinary boundaries, the field of organizational communication is ideally suited to address the interpenetration of multiple spheres and interpretations of communicative activity. Explorations of the properties of emergent networks that help or hinder organizations and individuals to compensate for the cultural tensions inherent in the global workplace; explications of how communication outside the workplace (at the international, national, local, and interpersonal levels) reflects, reinforces, or retracts efforts toward cultural/organizational convergence; and identification of what and how specific communicative structures, processes, and message characteristics enable individuals and organizations to transcend, manage, or eliminate potential clashes between local and global practices will contribute greatly to our understanding of the substance and process of global organizing.

In summary, organizational communication scholars are well positioned to study the dynamic structuring of globalization and the culturally saturated processes of organizing and sensemaking. As a field, we are sensitized to the central problematics of voice and pluralistic understandings of what counts as rational, unified by a fundamental concern with messages, interpretations, symbols, and discourse, and grounded by an integrative communication orientation that at its most basic level recognizes meaning as internally experienced, subjective, embedded within larger systems, and socially constructed. Our participation and contributions to the scholarly discourse of globalization are just beginning.

NOTES

1. The map is distributed by Public Service Indiana (PSI Energy, 1994).

2. See, for example, the introductions to special issues including those by Calás (1994), Earley and Singh (1995), and Tichy (1990).

3. Given the delay of the publication of this handbook, however, the majority of citations in this text are to articles published prior to 1997. Nonetheless, the conclusions drawn from this review are still representative. Organizational communication scholars continue to grapple with issues related to finding appropriate theoretical and methodological positions to enable us to participate fully and find our voice in the scholarly discourse of globalization.

4. Unlike communication adaptation theory where convergence is defined as the adjustment and accommodation of one's interpersonal communication style to match one's partner and divergence is narrowly construed as the adherence to cultural communication patterns in the face of difference (see Larkey, 1996, for a review of this literature), convergence here refers to the similar and mutual accommodation of organizational communication practices to external conditions. Divergence refers to the structural, processual, and interpretive distinctions within organizations that are a direct result of cultural differences that remain despite similar environmental pressures.

5. See the Monge and Contractor chapter in this volume for a discussion of global network organizations.

6. It is important to note that these dimensions do not refer to the values, behaviors, or communication of all people within any given culture; rather, they are generalized normative descriptions or stereotypes of large collectivities (Adler, 1991). Thus, these dimensions do not negate the existence of subcultures or individual differences. Indeed, throughout this literature scholars caution that knowledge of a person's culture cannot predict a particular individual's behavior (see Hofstede, 1984, pp. 24-25, for a discussion of the difference between ecological [between-culture] and within-society correlations).

7. See Goldman (1994) for a detailed review of another indigenous cultural precept, *ningensei*, that helps us understand Japanese organizational communication.

8. Another suggestion has been the use of an artificial or constructed language (Bryson, 1990). Indeed, over the past century several languages have been constructed, including Esperanto, Volapuk, Logolan, Frater, Anglic, and Sea speak, to neutralize linguistic difficulties and promote international understanding across contexts (Bryson, 1990). But despite the fervent arguments that "the unequal distribution of power between languages is a recipe for permanent language insecurity, or outright language oppression, for a large part of the world's population" (the 1996 Prague manifesto of the Movement for the International Language Esperanto; see www.esperanto.se), the practical, ideological, and social ramifications of this approach have doomed these efforts.

REFERENCES

Adler, N. (1980). *Cultural synergy: The management of cross-cultural organizations.* San Diego, CA: University Associates.

Adler, N. (1987). Women in management worldwide. *International Studies of Management and Organization, 16*(3-4), 3-32.

Adler, N. (1991). *International dimensions of organizational behavior* (2nd ed.). Boston: PWS-Kent.

Adler, N., Campbell, N., & Laurent, A. (1989, Spring). In search of appropriate methodology: From outside the People's Republic of China looking in. *Journal of International Business Studies, 20,* 61-74.

Adler, N., Doktor, R., & Redding, S. (1986). From the Atlantic to the Pacific century: Cross-cultural management reviewed. *Journal of Management, 12,* 295-318.

Adler, N., & Ghadar, L. (1990). International strategy from the perspective of people and culture. In A. Rugman (Ed.), *Research in global strategic management* (pp. 179-205). Greenwich, CT: JAI.

Adler, N., & Izraeli, D. (1988). *Women in management worldwide.* Armonk, NY: M. E. Sharpe.

Ady, J. (1994). *Minimizing threats to the validity of cross-cultural organizational research.* Thousand Oaks, CA: Sage.

Albert, R. (1983). The intercultural sensitizer or culture assimilator: A cognitive approach. In D. Landis & R. Brislin (Eds.), *Handbook of intercultural training: Issues in training methodology* (Vol. 2, pp. 186-217). New York: Pergamon.

Altman, J. (1989). Overcoming Babel: The role of the conference interpreter in the communication process. In R. Kölmel & J. Payne (Eds.), *Babel: The cultural and linguistic barriers between nations* (pp. 73-86). Aberdeen, Scotland: Aberdeen University Press.

Alvesson, M. (1987). Organization, culture, and ideology. *International Studies of Management and Organization, 17*, 4-18.

Amir, Y. (1969). Contact hypothesis in ethnic relations. *Psychological Bulletin, 71*, 319-341.

Anderson, C., & Imperia, G. (1992). The corporate annual report: A photo analysis of male and female portrayals. *Journal of Business Communication, 29*, 113-128.

Andrews, E. (1992, December 4). Job cuts at AT&T will total 40,000, 13% of its staff. *New York Times*, p. A1.

Archer, L., & Fitch, K. (1994). Communication in Latin American multinational organizations. In R. Wiseman & R. Shuter (Eds.), *Communicating in multinational organizations* (pp. 75-93). Thousand Oaks, CA: Sage.

Asante, M. (1987). *Afrocentric idea*. Philadelphia: Temple University Press.

Ashcraft, K., & Pacanowsky, M. (1995). *Beyond baby boom: An office dialogue of control*. Paper presented at the Top Three Panel, Organizational Communication Division, Speech Communication Association, San Antonio, TX.

Ball, D., & McCulloch, W. (1993). *International business: Introduction and essentials*. Plano, TX: Business Publications.

Banks, S., & Banks, A. (1991, November). Translation as problematic discourse in organizations. *Journal of Applied Communication Research*, 223-241.

Bantz, C. (1993). Cultural diversity and group cross-cultural team research. *Journal of Applied Communication Research, 20*, 1-19.

Barber, B. (1992, March). Jihad vs. McWorld. *Atlantic Monthly*, pp. 53-63.

Barnett, G., & Lee, M. (1995, May). *A symbols and meaning approach to organizational cultures of banks in the U.S., Japan and Taiwan*. Paper presented at the annual convention of the International Communication Association, Organizational Communication Division, Albuquerque, NM.

Barnlund, D. (1989, March-April). Public and private self in communicating in Japan. *Business Horizons*, pp. 32-40.

Bartlett, C., & Ghoshal, S. (1986, November-December). Tap your subsidiaries for global reach. *Harvard Business Review, 64*, 87-94.

Bartlett, C., & Ghoshal, S. (1989). *Managing across borders: The transnational solution*. Boston: Harvard Business School Press.

Belieav, E., Muller, T., & Punnett, B. (1985). Understanding the cultural environment: U.S. & USSR trade negotiations. *California Management Review, 27*, 100-112.

Beneria, L., & Roldan, M. (1987). *The crossroads of class and gender: Industrial homework, sub-contracting, and household dynamics in Mexico*. Chicago: University of Chicago Press.

Berge, M. (1987, July-August). Building bridges over the cultural rivers. *International Management, 42*, 61-62.

Berns, M. (1992). Sociolinguistics and the teaching of English in Europe beyond the 1990's. *World Englishes, 11*(1), 3-14.

Bochner, S., & Hesketh, B. (1994). Power distance, individualism, and job-related attitudes in a culturally diverse work group. *Journal of Cross-Cultural Psychology, 25*, 42-57.

Bossen, L. (1984). *The redivision of labor: Women and economic choice in four Guatemalan communities*. Albany: State University of New York Press.

Boulding, E. (1990). *Building a global-civic culture*. New York: Teachers College Press.

Boyacigiller, N., & Adler, N. (1991). The parochial dinosaur: Organizational science in a global context. *Academy of Management Review, 16*, 262-290.

Brady, F. (1986). Aesthetic components of management ethics. *Academy of Management Review, 11*, 337-344.

Brislin, R. (1989). Intercultural communication training. In M. K. Asante & W. Gudykunst (Eds.), *Handbook of international and intercultural communication* (pp. 441-457). Newbury Park, CA: Sage.

Bryson, B. (1990). *The mother tongue*. New York: William Morrow.

Buie, S. (1996). Market as Mandala: The erotic space of commerce. *Organization, 3*, 225-232.

Cai, D. & Drake, L. (1998). The business of business negotiation: Intercultural perspectives. In M. Roloff (Ed.), *Communication yearbook 21* (pp. 153-189). Thousand Oaks, CA: Sage.

Calás, M. (1994). Minerva's owl? *Organization, 1*, 243-248.

Calás, M., & Smircich, L. (Eds.). (1996). Essays on aesthetics and organization [Special section]. *Organization, 3*(2), 189-248.

Casmir, F. (1993). Third-culture building: A paradigm shift for international intercultural communication. In S. A. Deetz (Ed.), *Communication yearbook 16* (pp. 407-428). Newbury Park, CA: Sage.

Chan, B. (1995, Winter). Whose language is right? *The Diversity Factor*, pp. 28-30.

Chang, H., & Holt, G. (1991). More than relationship: Chinese interaction and the principle of kuan-hsi. *Communication Quarterly, 39*, 251-271.

Chen, G., & Chung, J. (1994). The impact of Confucianism on organizational communication. *Communication Quarterly, 42*(2), 93-105.

Cheney, G. (1995). Democracy in the workplace: Theory and practice from the perspective of communication. *Journal of Applied Communication Research, 23*, 1-34.

Cheney, G. (1999). *Values at work*. Ithaca, NY: Cornell University Press.

Child, J. (1981). Culture, contingency and capitalism in the cross-national study of organizations. In B. Shaw

& L. Cummings (Eds.), *Research in organizational behavior* (Vol. 3, pp. 303-356). Greenwich, CT: JAI.

Child, J., & Tayeb, M. (1983). Theoretical perspectives in cross-national organizational research. *International Studies of Management and Organization, 12,* 23-70.

Clair, R., & Kunkel, A. (1998). An organizational communication analysis of "unrealistic realities": Child abuse and the aesthetic resolution. *Communication Monographs, 65,* 24-46.

Cleveland, H. (1985). The twilight of hierarchy: Speculations on the global information society. *Public Administration Review, 45*(1), 185-195.

Clifford, J. (1988). *The predicament of culture.* Cambridge, MA: Harvard University Press.

Cockburn, D. (1991). *In the way of women: Men's resistance to sex equality in organizations.* Ithaca, NY: ILR.

Cole, R. (1989). *Strategies for learning: Small group activities in American, Japanese, and Swedish industry.* Berkeley: University of California Press.

Collins, G. (1996, January 13). Coke drops "domestic" and goes one world. *New York Times,* pp. 17, 19.

Cook, J., & Wall, T. (1980). New work attitude measures of trust, organizational commitment and personal need non-fulfillment. *Journal of Occupational Psychology, 53,* 39-52.

Cox, T. (1993). *Cultural diversity in organizations: Theory, research and practice.* San Francisco: Berrett-Koehler.

Crozier, M. (1964). *The bureaucratic phenomenon.* London: Tavistock.

Cushman, D., & King, S. (1993). High-speed management: A revolution in organizational communication in the 1990s. In S. A. Deetz (Ed.), *Communication yearbook 16* (pp. 209-236). Newbury Park, CA: Sage.

Cusumano, M., & Selby, W. (1995). *Microsoft secrets.* New York: Free Press.

Daniels, T., & Spiker, B. (1994). *Perspectives on organizational communication.* Dubuque, IA: William C. Brown.

Danowski, J., & Huang, H. (1994). *Organizational restructuring and changes in semantic networks in messages directed to external audiences.* Paper presented at the Organizational Communication Division of the International Communication Association, Sydney, Australia.

Dear, M., & Wolch, J. (1989). How territory shapes life. In J. Wolch & M. Dear (Eds.), *The power of geography* (pp. 3-18). Boston: Unwin Hyman.

Deetz, S. (1992). *Democracy in an age of corporate colonization.* Albany: State University of New York Press.

DeMente, B. (1981). *The Japanese way of doing business: The psychology of management in Japan.* Englewood Cliffs, NJ: Prentice Hall.

DeMente, B. (1989). *China's etiquette and ethics in business.* Lincolnwood, IL: NTC Business Books.

Deming, E. (1986). *Out of the crisis.* Cambridge, MA: MIT Press.

DePalma, A. (1994, June 26). It takes more than a visa to do business in Mexico. *New York Times,* pp. A16-A17.

DeSanctis, G., & Monge, P. (1998). Communication processes for virtual organizations. *Journal of Computer-Mediated Communication, 3*(4) (Introduction to special joint issue with *Organization Science:* Virtual Organizations, G. DeSanctis & P. Monge, Eds.) [Online]. Available: http://www.spcomm.uiuc.edu:1000/global/index/html.

DeVries, M. (1994). *Internationally yours: Writing and communicating successfully in today's global marketplace.* Boston: Houghton Mifflin.

DiMaggio, P., & Powell, W. (1983). The iron cage revisited: Institutional isomorphism and collective rationality in organizational fields. *American Sociological Review, 48,* 147-160.

DiMaggio, P., & Powell, W. (1991). *The new institutionalism in organizational analysis.* Chicago: University of Chicago Press.

Dogan, M., & Pelassy, D. (1990). *How to compare nations: Strategies in comparative politics.* Chatham, NJ: Chatham House.

Donaldson, T. (1989). *The ethics of international business.* New York: Oxford University Press.

Downs, C., & Hazen, M. (1977). A factor analytic study of communication satisfaction. *Journal of Business Communication, 14,* 63-74.

Downs, C., Downs, A., Potvin, T., Varona, F., Gribas, J., & Ticehurst, W. (1995, May). *A cross-cultural comparison of relationships between organizational commitment and organizational communication.* Paper presented at the annual convention of the International Communication Association, Organizational Communication Division, Albuquerque, NM.

Driskill, G. (1995). Managing cultural differences: A rules analysis in a bicultural organization. *Howard Journal of Communications, 5*(4), 353-372.

Earley, P. (1989). Social loafing and collectivism: A comparison of the United States and the People's Republic of China. *Administrative Science Quarterly, 34,* 565-581.

Earley, P. C., & Singh, H. (1995). International and intercultural management research: What's next? *Academy of Management Journal, 38,* 327-341.

Emery, F., Thorsrud, E., & Trist, E. (1969). *Form and content in industrial democracy.* London: Tavistock.

Erez, M., & Earley, P. C. (1995). *Culture, self-identity, and work.* Oxford, UK: Oxford University Press.

Eyraud, F. (1993). Equal pay and the value of work in industrialized countries. *International Labour Review, 1,* 33-48.

Fadiman, J. (1986). A traveler's guide to gifts and bribes. *Harvard Business Review, 64,* 122-136.

Faulkner, A., & Lawson, V. (1991). Employment versus empowerment: A case study of the nature of women's work in Ecuador. *Journal of Development Studies, 27*(4), 16-47.

Feld, W., & Jordan, R. (1988). *International organization: A comparative approach.* New York: Praeger.

Fernandez-Kelly, M. (1983). *For we are sold, I and my people: Women and industry in Mexico's frontier.* Albany: State University of New York Press.

Fine, M. (1991). New voices in the workplace: Research directions in multicultural communication. *Journal of Business Communication, 28,* 259-275.

Fiol, C. (1989). A semiotic analysis of corporate language: Organizational boundaries and joint venturing. *Administrative Science Quarterly, 34,* 277-303.

Flaitz, J. (1988). *The ideology of English: French perceptions of English as a world language.* Berlin, Germany: Mouton de Gruyter.

Friday, R. (1989). Contrasts in discussion behaviors of German and American managers. *International Journal of Intercultural Relations, 13,* 429-446.

Fuentes, A., & Ehrenreich, B. (1983). *Women in the global factory.* Boston: South End.

Gattiker, U. (1990). *Technology management in organizations.* London: Sage.

Geertz, C. (1973). *The interpretation of cultures.* New York: Basic Books.

Giles, H. (1977). *Language, ethnicity, and intergroup relations.* London: Academic Press.

Giroux, N. (1992). Participation and strategic decision-making in a cooperative. *Annals of Public and Cooperative Economics, 63*(1), 5-24.

Giroux, N., & Fenocchi, V. (1995). *Women and cooperatives: Ten years later.* Paper presented at the Society for Co-operative Studies, Stockholm, Sweden.

Glassgold, P. (1987). Translation: Culture's driving wedge. *Translation Review, 23,* 18-21.

Glenn, E. (1981). *Man and mankind: Conflict and communication between cultures.* Norwood, NJ: Ablex.

Goering, E. (1991). *Hands in need: Cultural variability and institutionalization in Rett syndrome organizations in the United States and Europe.* Ph.D. dissertation, Purdue University, West Lafayette, IN.

Goldhaber, G. M., & Rogers, D. P. (1979). *Auditing organizational communication systems: The ICA communication audit.* Dubuque, IA: Kendall/Hunt.

Goldman, A. (1994). Communication in Japanese multinational organizations. In R. Wiseman & R. Shuter (Eds.), *Communicating in multinational organizations* (pp. 45-74). Thousand Oaks, CA: Sage.

Goodenough, W. (1970). *Description and comparison in cultural anthropology.* Chicago: Aldine.

Gorski, M. (1993). Hyperinflation and stabilization in Poland. In A. Kozminski & D. Cushman (Eds.), *Organizational communication and management: A global perspective* (pp. 168-182). Albany: State University of New York Press.

Gottfried, H. (1995). Developing neo-Fordism: A comparative perspective. *Critical Sociology, 21*(3), 39-70.

Grabe, W. (1988). English; information access, and technology transfer: A rationale for English as an international language. *World Englishes, 7,* 63-72.

Graham, J. L. (1985). The influence of culture on the process of business negotiations: An exploratory study. *Journal of International Business Studies, 16,* 79-94.

Graham, J., Evenko, L., & Rajan, M. (1992). An empirical comparison of Soviet and American business negotiations. *Journal of International Business Studies, 23,* 387-415.

Gudykunst, W. (1991). *Bridging differences: Effective intergroup communication.* Newbury Park, CA: Sage.

Gudykunst, W., Stewart, L., & Ting-Toomey, S. (1985). *Communication, culture, and organizational processes.* Beverly Hills, CA: Sage.

Guterl, F. (1989, February). Goodbye, old matrix. *Dun's Business Month,* pp. 32-38.

Habermas, J. (1984). *Theory of communicative action.* Boston: Beacon.

Hall, E. (1959). *The silent language.* New York: Doubleday.

Hall, E. (1966). *The hidden dimension.* New York: Doubleday.

Hall, E. (1976). *Beyond culture.* Garden City, NY: Doubleday.

Hall, E., & Hall, M. (1987). *Hidden differences: Doing business with the Japanese.* New York: Doubleday Anchor.

Hall, E., & Hall, M. (1990). *Understanding cultural differences.* Yarmouth, ME: Intercultural Press.

Hamada, T., & Yaguchi, Y. (1994). Hollowing of industrial ideology: Japanese corporate families in America. In T. Hamada & W. Sibley (Eds.), *Anthropological perspectives on organizational culture* (pp. 193-218). Lanham, MD: University Press of America.

Harris, P., & Moran, R. (1996). *Managing cultural differences.* Houston, TX: Gulf.

Hatch, M. (1996). *Organization theory: Modern, symbolic-interpretive and postmodern perspectives.* Oxford, UK: Oxford University Press.

Harvey, D. (1989). *The urban experience.* Oxford, UK: Oxford University Press.

Hastings, C. (1993). *The new organization: Growing the culture of organizational networking.* London: McGraw-Hill.

Hatim, B. (1989). Argumentative styles across cultures: Linguistic form as the realization of rhetorical function. In R. Kölmel & J. Payne (Eds.), *Babel: The cultural and linguistic barriers between nations* (pp. 25-32). Aberdeen, Scotland: Aberdeen University Press.

Heenan, D., & Perlmutter, H. (1979). *Management in the industrial world.* New York: McGraw-Hill.

Heginbotham, S. (1994, October 19). Shifting the focus of international programs. *Chronicle of Higher Education,* p. A68.

Held, D., McGrew, A., Goldblatt, D., & Perraton, J, (1999). *Global transformations: Politics, economics and culture.* Stanford, CA: Stanford University Press.

Hickson, D., Hinings, C., MacMillan, C., & Schwitter, J. (1974). The culture-free context of organisation structure: A tri-national comparison. *Sociology, 8,* 59-80.

Hickson, D., MacMillan, C., Azumi, K., & Horvath, D. (1979). The grounds for comparative organization theory. In C. Lammers & D. Hickson (Eds.), *Organizations alike and unalike* (pp. 153-189). London: Routledge and Kegan Paul.

Hilton, C. (1992). International business communication: The place of English. *Journal of Business Communication, 29*(3), 253-265.

Hirokawa, R., & Miyahara, A. (1986). A comparison of influence strategies utilized by managers in American and Japanese organizations. *Communication Quarterly, 34,* 250-265.

Hirschman, A. (1970). *Exit, voice and loyalty responses to decline in firms, organizations and states.* Cambridge, MA: Harvard University Press.

Hofstede, G. (1984). *Culture's consequences: International differences in work-related values.* Beverly Hills, CA: Sage.

Hofstede, G. (1991). *Cultures and organizations: Software of the mind.* London: McGraw-Hill.

Hofstede, G., & Bond, M. H. (1988). The Confucius connection: From cultural roots to economic growth. *Organizational Dynamics, 16*(4), 4-21.

Hofstede, G., Neuijen, B., Ohayr, D., & Sanders, G. (1990). Measuring organizational culture: A qualitative and quantitative study across twenty cases. *Administrative Science Quarterly, 35,* 286-316.

Hong, L. (1978). Risky shift and cautious shift: Some direct evidence on the culture-value theory. *Social Psychology, 41,* 342-346.

Hu, W., & Grove, C. (1991). *Encountering the Chinese: A guide for Americans.* Yarmouth, ME: Intercultural Press.

Hymes, D. (1974). *Foundations in sociolinguistics: An ethnographic approach.* Philadelphia: University of Pennsylvania Press.

Inglehart, R. (1977). *The silent revolution changing values and political styles among Western publics.* Princeton, NJ: Princeton University Press.

Inkeles, A. (1998). *One world emerging? Convergence and divergence in industrial societies.* Boulder, CO: Westview.

Inzerilli, G., & Laurent, A. (1983). Managerial views of organization structure in France and the USA. *International Studies of Management and Organization, 13*(1-2), 97-118.

Jamieson, K., & Cappella, J. (1996). Bridging the disciplinary divide. *Political Science and Politics, 29,* 13-16.

Jang, H., & Barnett, G. (1994). Cultural differences in organizational communication: A semantic network analysis. *Bulletin de Methodologic Sociologique, 4,* 31-59.

Jarvenpaa, S. L., & Leidner, D. E. (1998). Communication and trust in global virtual teams. *Journal of Computer-Mediated Communication, 3*(4) (Special joint issue with *Organization Science:* Virtual Organizations, G. DeSanctis & P. Monge, Eds.) [Online]. Available: http://www.spcomm.uiuc.edu:1000/global/index/html.

Jenks, C. (1993). *Culture.* London: Routledge and Kegan Paul.

Johnson, W., & Packard, A. (1987). *Workforce 2000: Work and workers for the 21st century.* Indianapolis, IN: Hudson Institute.

Kanter, R. M. (1977). *Men and women of the corporation.* New York: Basic Books.

Kirk, R. (1986). *Translation determined.* Oxford, UK: Clarendon.

Kleinburg, J. (1994). Working here is like walking blindly into a dense forest. In T. Hamada & W. Sibley (Eds.), *Anthropological perspectives on organizational culture* (pp. 153-192). Lanham, MD: University Press of America.

Kluckhohn, C. (1949). *Mirror for man: A survey of human behavior and social attitudes.* Greenwich, CT: Fawcett.

Kluckhohn, F., & Strodtbeck, F. L. (1961). *Variations in value orientations.* Westport, CT: Greenwood.

Knudsen, H. (1995). *Employee participation in Europe.* London: Sage.

Kölmel, R., & Payne, J. (Eds.). (1989). *Babel: The cultural and linguistic barriers between nations.* Aberdeen, Scotland: Aberdeen University Press.

Kozminski, A., & Cushman, D. (1993). The rise of global communication and global management: An overview. In A. Kozminski & D. Cushman (Eds.), *Organizational communication and management: A global perspective* (pp. 3-5). Albany: State University of New York Press.

Kozminski, A., & Obloj, K. (1993). A framework for understanding Eastern Europe's problems in integrating into the global economy. In A. Kozminski & D. Cushman (Eds.), *Organizational communication and management: A global perspective* (pp. 55-68). Albany: State University of New York Press.

Kras, E. (1988). *Management in two cultures: Bridging the gap between U.S. and Mexican managers.* Yarmouth, ME: Intercultural Press.

Kroeber, A., & Kluckhohn, C. (1954). *Culture: A critical review of concepts and definitions.* New York: Random House.

Krone, K., Chen, L., Sloan, D., & Gallant, L. (1995, May). *Managerial emotionality in Chinese factories.*

Paper presented at the annual convention of the International Communication Association, Organizational Communication Division, Albuquerque, NM.

Krone, K., Garrett, M., & Chen, L. (1992). Managerial practices in Chinese factories: A preliminary investigation. *Journal of Business Communication, 29*(3), 229-252.

Krone, K. J., Jablin, F. M., & Putnam, L. L. (1987). Communication theory and organizational communication: Multiple perspectives. In F. M. Jablin, L. L. Putnam, K. H. Roberts, & L. W. Porter (Eds.), *Handbook of organizational communication: An interdisciplinary perspective* (pp. 18-40). Newbury Park, CA: Sage.

Kuhn, J. W. (1996). The misfit between organizational theory and processual art: A comment on White and Strati. *Organization, 3,* 219-224.

Larkey, L. (1996). Toward a theory of communicative interaction in culturally diverse work groups. *Academy of Management Review, 21,* 463-491.

Laurent, A. (1983). The cultural diversity of Western conceptions of management. *International Studies of Management and Organizations, 13*(1-2), 79-96.

Laurent, A. (1986). The cross-cultural puzzle of international human resource management. *Human Resource Management, 25*(1), 91-102.

Lee, H., & Rogan, R. (1991). A cross-cultural comparison of organizational conflict management behavior. *International Journal of Conflict Management, 2,* 181-199.

Lee, J., & Jablin, F. (1992). A cross-cultural investigation of exit, voice, loyalty and neglect as responses to dissatisfying work conditions. *Journal of Business Communication, 29*(3), 203-228.

Lester, T. (1984, July-August). Pulling down the language barrier. *International Management,* pp. 42-44.

Lieber, R. (1995, December 25). Zen and the art of teamwork. *Fortune, 132,* 218.

Lincoln, J., & Kalleberg, A. (1990). *Culture, control and commitment: A study of work organizations in the United States and Japan.* Cambridge, MA: University of Cambridge Press.

Lindsley, S. (1999). A layered model of problematic intercultural communication in U.S.-owned maquiladoras in Mexico. *Communication Monographs, 33,* 145-167.

Lipnack, J., & Stamps, J. (1986). *The networking book: People connecting with people.* London: Routledge and Kegan Paul.

Lubin, C., & Winslow, A. (1990). *Social justice for women.* London: Duke University Press.

Magee, J. (1989). 1992: Moves Americans must make. *Harvard Business Review, 3,* 78-89.

Martin, M. (1992). *Culture in organizations: Three perspectives.* New York: Oxford University Press.

Maruyama, M. (1982). New mindscapes for future business policy and management. *Technology, Forecasting, and Social Change, 21,* 53-76.

Massey, D. (1984). *Spatial division of labor: Social structures and the geography of production.* London: Macmillan.

Maurice, M., Sorge, A., & Malcolm, R. (1981). Societal differences in organizing manufacturing units: A comparison of France, West Germany, and Great Britain. *International Studies of Management and Organization, 10*(4), 74-100.

Mayer, A. M. (1996). *The evolution of total quality: Japan's cultural influence on the teachings of Dr. W. Edwards Deming.* Paper presented at the Central States Speech Association Convention, St. Paul, MN.

McGregor, D. (1960). *The human side of enterprise.* New York: McGraw-Hill,

Miles, R., & Snow, C. (1986). Organizations: New concepts for new forms. *California Management Review, 28*(3), 62-73.

Miles, R., & Snow, C. (1992). Causes of failure in network organizations. *California Management Review, 32,* 53-72

Miller, K. (1995). *Organizational communication: Approaches and processes.* Belmont, NY: Wadsworth.

Milroy, L., & Margraine, S. (1980). Vernacular language loyalty and social networks, *Language and Society, 9*(1), 43-70.

Mitroff, I. (1987). *Business* not *as usual: Rethinking our individual, corporate, and industrial strategies for global competition.* San Francisco: Jossey-Bass.

Moghadam, V. (1999). Gender and globalization: Female labor and women's mobilization. *Journal of World-Systems Research, 5*(2), 367-390. (Special issue: Globalization, S. Manning, Ed.).

Monge, P. (1995). Global network organizations. In R. Cesaria & P. Shockley-Zalabak (Eds.), *Organization means communication: Making the organizational communication concept relevant to practice* (pp. 135-151). Rome: Servizio Italiano Pubblicazioni Internationali Srl.

Monge, P., & Fulk, J. (1995, May). *Global network organizations.* Paper presented at the annual convention of the International Communication Association, Albuquerque, NM.

Monge, P., & Fulk, J. (1999). Communication technologies for global network organizations. In G. DeSanctis & J. Fulk (Eds.), *Communication technologies and organizational form* (pp. 71-100). Thousand Oaks, CA: Sage.

Moody, K. (1997). *Workers in a lean world.* London: Verso.

Moran, R., & Harris, P. (1982). *Managing cultural synergy.* Houston, TX: Gulf.

Morley, D., Shockley-Zalabak, P., & Cesaria, R. (1997). Organizational communication and culture: A study of 10 Italian high-technology companies. *Journal of Business Communication, 34,* 253-268.

Mossetto, G. (1993). *Aesthetics and economics.* Dordrecht, Netherlands: Kluwer Academic.

Mowday, R., Steers, R., & Porter, L. (1979). The measurement of organizational communication. *Journal of Vocational Behavior, 14,* 224-247.

Mulgan, G. (1991). *Communication and control: Networks and the new economies of communication.* New York: Guilford.

Mumby, D., & Stohl, C. (1996). Disciplining organizational communication studies. *Management Communication Quarterly, 10*(1), 50-72.

Murdock, G., & Provost, C. (1973). Measurement of cultural complexity, *Ethnology, 12,* 379-392.

Naik, G. (1993, October 4). Western investment in Eastern Europe grew sharply during the recent period. *Wall Street Journal,* p. A7.

Nash, C. (1990). *Narrative in culture: The uses of storytelling in the sciences, philosophy, and literature.* London and New York: Routledge.

Neubert, A. (1989). Translation as mediation. In R. Kölmel & J. Payne (Eds.), *Babel: The cultural and linguistic barriers between nations* (pp. 5-12). Aberdeen, Scotland: Aberdeen University Press.

Nohria, N., & Barkley, J. (1994). The virtual organization: Bureaucracy, technology and the implosion of control. In C. Heckscher & A. Donnellon (Eds.), *The post-bureaucratic organization: New perspectives on organizational change* (pp. 108-128). Thousand Oaks, CA: Sage.

Nonaka, I., & Takeuchi, H. (1995). *The knowledge-creating company.* New York: Oxford University Press.

Office of International Programs [Online]. (1999). West Lafayette, IN: Purdue University. Available: http://www.ippu.purdue.edu/index.html-ssi.

Ohbuchi, K., & Takahashi, Y. (1994). Cultural styles of conflict management in Japanese and Americans: Pass, correctness and effectiveness of strategies. *Journal of Applied Social Psychology, 55,* 49-67.

One to us, closed to them. (1994). *The Economist,* pp. 43-45.

Ottensmeyer, E. (1996). Too strong to stop, too sweet to lose: Aesthetics as a way to know organizations. *Organization, 3,* 189-194.

Ouchi, W. (1981). *Theory Z: How American business can meet the Japanese challenge.* Reading, MA: Addison-Wesley.

Page, N., & Wiseman, R. (1993). Supervisory behavior and worker satisfaction in the United States, Mexico, and Spain. *Journal of Business Communication, 30,* 161-179.

Papa, M., Auwal, M., & Singhal, A. (1995). Dialectic of control and emancipation in organizing for social change: A multitheoretic study of the Grameen Bank in Bangladesh. *Communication Theory, 5,* 189-223.

Park, S. H., & Ungson, G. R. (1997). The effect of national culture, organizational complementarity, and economic motivation on joint venture dissolution. *Academy of Management Journal, 40,* 279-307.

Parsons, T., & Shils, E. (1951). *Toward a general theory of action.* Cambridge, MA: Harvard University Press.

Pascale, R., & Athos, A. (1981). *The art of Japanese management: Applications for American executives.* New York: Warner.

Pierce, J., Gardner, D., Cummings, L., & Dunham, R. (1989). Organization-based self-esteem. *Academy of Management Journal, 32,* 622-648.

Poole, M. S. (1993). On the joys and sorrows of predicting the future of organizational communication. In S. A. Deetz (Ed.), *Communication yearbook 16* (pp. 247-251). Newbury Park, CA: Sage.

Powell, B. (1995, November). Keep your profits. *Newsweek,* p. 98.

PSI Enegy. (1984). *International companies in Indiana map.* Indianapolis, IN: Author.

Ratiu, I. (1983). Thinking internationally: A comparison of how international executives learn. *International Studies of Management and Organization, 13,* 139-153.

Reardon, K. (1981). *International gift customs: A guide for American executives.* Janesville, WI: Parker Pen Company.

Redding, S. (1990). *The spirit of Chinese capitalism.* Berlin: Walter de Gruyter.

Richards, D. (1997). *Artful work.* New York: Berkley.

Riordan, C., & Vandenberg, R. (1994). A central question in cross-cultural research: Do employees of different cultures interpret work-related measures in an equivalent manner? *Journal of Management, 20,* 643-671.

Rosen, B. (1982). *The industrial connection: Achievement and the family in developing societies.* New York: Aldine.

Rossman, M. (1990). *The international businesswoman of the 1990s.* New York: Praeger.

Rothstein, F. (1982). *Three different worlds: Women, men and children in an industrializing community.* Westport, CT: Greenwood.

Ryder, G. (1997, July). Globalization must include social justice for all workers. *World of Work: The Magazine of the ILO, 20,* 15.

Sanborn, G. (1993). *Understanding cultural diversity: The relationship of differences in communication styles with career outcomes among white and Asian Americans.* Unpublished doctoral dissertation, Purdue University, West Lafayette, IN.

Sanger, D. (1993, March 21). Facing production cuts in two automotive plants. *New York Times,* p. C1.

Scholte, J. (2000). *Globalization: A critical introduction.* London: Macmillan.

Seelye, H., & Seelye-James, A. (1995). *Culture clash: Managing in a multicultural world.* Lincolnwood, IL: NTC Business Books.

Seibold, D., & Contractor, N. (1993). Issues for a theory of high-speed management. In S. A. Deetz (Ed.),

Communication yearbook 16 (pp. 237-246). Newbury Park, CA: Sage.

Shuter, R. (1993). On third-culture building. In S. A. Deetz (Ed.), *Communication yearbook 16* (pp. 429-438). Newbury Park, CA: Sage.

Shuter, R., & Wiseman, R. L. (1994). Communication in multinational organizations: Conceptual, theoretical, and practical issues. In R. Wiseman & R. Shuter (Eds.), *Communicating in multinational organizations* (pp. 3-12). Thousand Oaks, CA: Sage.

Smircich, L. (1983). Concepts of culture and organizational analysis. *Administrative Science Quarterly, 28,* 339-358.

Smith, A., & Tayeb, M. (1988). Organizational structures and processes. In M. Bond (Ed.), *The cross-cultural challenge to social psychology* (pp. 116-127). Newbury Park, CA: Sage.

Smith, P., & Peterson, M. (1988). *Leadership, organizations and culture.* London: Sage.

Smith, R. (1993). *Organizational communication theorizing: Root-metaphors of the organization-communication relation.* Unpublished manuscript, Purdue University, West Lafayette, IN.

Soja, E. (1989). *Postmodern geographies: The reassertion of space in critical social theory.* London: Verso.

Sorge, A. (1983). Cultured organization. *International Studies of Management and Organization, 13,* 106-138.

Spain, D. (1992). *Gendered spaces.* Chapel Hill: University of North Carolina Press.

Stage, C. (1999). Negotiating organizational communication cultures in American subsidiaries doing business in Thailand. *Management Communication Quarterly, 13,* 245-280.

Steers, R., Bischoff, S., & Higgins, L. (1992). Cross-cultural management research: The fish and the fisherman. *Journal of Management Inquiry, 1,* 321-330.

Steiner, G. (1975). *After Babel: Aspects of language and translation.* London: Oxford University Press.

Stewart, L., Gudykunst, W., Ting-Toomey, S., & Nishida, T. (1986). The effects of decision making style on openness and satisfaction within Japanese organizations. *Communication Monographs, 53,* 236-251.

Stohl, C. (1993). International organizing and organizational communication. *Journal of Applied Communication Research, 21*(4), 377-390.

Stohl, C. (1995). *Organizational communication: Connectedness in action.* Thousand Oaks, CA: Sage.

Storti, C. (1990). *The art of crossing cultures.* Yarmouth, ME: Intercultural Press.

Strati, A. (1996). Organizations viewed through the lens of aesthetics. *Organization, 3,* 209-218.

Sullivan, J., & Taylor, S. (1991). A cross-cultural test of compliance gaining theory. *Management Communication Quarterly, 5,* 220-239.

Swan, P. F., & Ettlie, J. E. (1997). U.S.-Japanese manufacturing equity relationships. *Academy of Management Journal, 40,* 452-479.

Tayeb, M. (1992). *The global business environment: An introduction.* London: Sage.

Taylor, J., & Van Every, E. (1993). *The vulnerable fortress: Bureaucratic organization and management in the information age.* Toronto, Canada: University of Toronto Press.

Teboul, J., Chen, L., & Fritz, L. (1994). Communication in multinational organizations in the United States and Western Europe. In R. Wiseman & R. Shuter (Eds.), *Communicating in multinational organizations* (pp. 12-29). Thousand Oaks, CA: Sage.

Thornburg, L. (1990, September). Transfers need not mean dislocation. *Human Resources Magazine, 35,* 46-48.

Thurow, L. (1983). *Dangerous currents: The state of economics.* New York: Random House.

Tichy, N. (1990). The global challenge for business schools. *Human Resource Management, 29,* 1-4.

Ticehurst, W. (1992). *Organizational commitment in Australia, Japan and the United States.* Paper presented at the conference of the Australian and New Zealand Academy of Management, Sydney, Australia.

Ting-Toomey, S., Gao, G., Trubisky, P., Yang, Z., Kim, H., Lin, S., & Nishida, T. (1991). Culture, face maintenance, and styles of handling interpersonal conflict: A study of five cultures. *International Journal of Conflict Management, 2,* 275-292.

Tompkins, P. (1984). The functions of human communication in organization. In C. Arnold & J. Bowers (Eds.), *Handbook of rhetoric and communication theory* (pp. 659-713). Boston: Allyn & Bacon.

Triandis, H. (1983). Dimensions of cultural variation as parameters of organizational theories. *International Studies of Management and Organization, 12,* 139-169.

Triandis, H. C., & Albert, R. D. (1987). Cross-cultural perspectives. In F. M. Jablin, L. L. Putnam, K. H. Roberts, & L. W. Porter (Eds.), *Handbook of organizational communication: An interdisciplinary perspective* (pp. 264-296). Newbury Park, CA: Sage.

Trompenaars, F. (1994). *Riding the waves of culture: Understanding diversity in global business.* Chicago: Irwin.

Tugendhat, C. (1988). *Making sense of Europe.* New York: Columbia University Press.

Tung, R. (1987). Expatriate assignments: Enhancing success and minimizing failure. *Academy of Management Executive, 1,* 117-126.

Vandenberg, R., & Scarpello, V. (1992). A multitrait-multimethod assessment of the Satisfaction With My Supervisor scale. *Educational and Psychological Measurement, 52,* 203-212.

Van Maanen, J., & Barley, S. (1984). Occupational communities: Culture and control in organizations. In B.

Shaw & L. Cummings (Eds.), *Research in organizational behavior* (Vol. 6, pp. 287-365). Lanham, MD: University Press of America.

Van Wolferen, K. (1989). *The enigma of Japanese power: People and politics in a stateless nation.* New York: Knopf.

Varner, I. (1988a). A comparison of American and French business correspondence. *Journal of Business Communication 25*(4), 5-16.

Varner, I. (1988b). Cultural aspects of German and American business letters. *Journal of Language for International Business, 3*(1), 1-11.

Varner, I., & Beamer, L. (1995). *Intercultural communication: The global workplace.* Chicago: Irwin.

Victor, D. (1992). *International business communication.* New York: HarperCollins.

Vikhanski, O., & Puffer, S. (1993). Management evaluation and employee training at Moscow McDonald's. *European Management Journal, 11,* 102-107.

Vitell, S., Nwachuku, S., & Barnes, J. (1993). The effects of culture on ethical decision making: An application of Hofstede's typology. *Journal of Business Ethics, 12,* 753-760.

Walker, R. (1985). Class, division of labor, and employment in space. In D. Gregory & J. Ury (Eds.), *Social relations and spatial structures* (pp. 164-189). London: Macmillan.

Waters, M. (1995). *Globalization.* London: Routledge.

Weick, K. (1969). *The social psychology of organizing.* Reading, MA: Addison-Wesley.

Weick, K., & Van Orden, P. (1990). Organizing on a global scale: A research and teaching agenda. *Human Resource Management, 29,* 49-61.

White, D., & Rackerby, F. (1994). A regional perspective on the transfer of Japanese management practices to the United States. In T. Hamada & W. Sibley (Eds.), *Anthropological perspectives on organizational culture* (pp. 133-152). Lanham, MD: University Press of America.

White, D. (1996). It's working beautifully! Philosophical reflections on aesthetics and organizational theory. *Organization, 3,* 195-208.

Whorf, B. (1952). *Collected papers on metalinguistics.* Washington, DC: Department of State, Foreign Service Institute.

Wiio, O. (1989). *Intercultural and international issues and variables in comparative studies in organizational communication.* Paper presented at the meeting of the International Communication Association, San Francisco.

Williams, R. (1976). *Keywords.* London: Fontana.

Williams, W. (1990). Women and work in the third world: Indonesian women's oral histories. *Journal of Women's History, 2,* 183-189.

Wilson, S., Cai, D., Campbell, D., Donohue, W., & Drake, L. (1994). Cultural and communication processes in international business negotiations. In A. Nicotera (Ed.), *Conflict in organizations: Communicative processes* (pp. 169-188). Albany: State University of New York Press.

Witkin, H., & Berry, J. (1975). Psychological differences in cross-cultural perspectives. *Journal of Cross-Cultural Psychology, 6,* 4-87.

Wright, L. (1984). *Cross-cultural project negotiations in the service sector.* Unpublished doctoral dissertation, University of Western Ontario, London, Ontario, Canada.

Wright, L., Lane, N., & Beamish, P. (1988). International management research: Lessons from the field. *International Studies of Management and Organization, 18,* 55-71.

Wysocki, B. (1988). In Japan they even have cram schools for cram schools. *Wall Street Journal, 13,* pp. 1-16.

Yoshida, N. (1989). Deming management philosophy: Does it work in the U.S. as well as Japan? *Columbia Journal of World Business, 27,* 10-17.

Zeldin, T. (1984). *The French.* New York: Vintage.

PART III

Structure: Patterns of Organizational Interdependence

11

Dualisms in
Leadership Research

GAIL T. FAIRHURST
University of Cincinnati

There is evidence of several types of dualisms within the leadership communication literature. For example, in conceptualizing leadership researchers have been fond of contrasting leadership with managership (Bennis & Nanus, 1985; Zaleznik, 1977), transformational with transactional leaders (Bass, 1985; Burns, 1978), self-management with external or super-leadership (Manz & Sims, 1987, 1989), organic with mechanistic forms of authority (Burns & Stalker, 1961; Weick, 1987), consideration with initiating structure (Fleishman, 1953; Hemphill & Coons, 1957), participative with autocratic leadership styles (Bass, 1981; Tannenbaum & Schmidt, 1958), and formal with informal leaders (Levine, 1949) just to name a few. One of the most central dualisms in the leadership literature is the individual versus the collective. The history of leadership research has been very leader focused (Meindl, 1990), although interest in the collective is clearly growing. There also have been dual approaches to conceptualizing communication,

AUTHOR'S NOTE: I would like to thank Linda Putnam and Fred Jablin for their insightful editorial assistance. I am also indebted to Francois Cooren, George Graen, Steve Green, Bob Liden, Teresa Sabourin, Gary Yukl, and Ted Zorn for their helpful comments on earlier drafts of this chapter.

one approach focusing heavily on transmission and the other focusing on the formation of meaning (Putnam, 1983; Putnam, Phillips, & Chapman, 1996). Dualism is also apparent in the way leadership communication is studied. Some research focuses on what leaders and constituents see and experience in social interaction (e.g., Kipnis & Schmidt, 1988; Yukl & Tracey, 1992), while other research focuses on the accomplishment of mutually adjusting behaviors (e.g., Fairhurst, Green, & Courtright, 1995; Komaki & Citera, 1990). Finally, even social science inquiry itself forms a dual contrast between the "why" and "how do you know" questions of positivism versus the "how" and "why do you talk that way" questions of social constructionism (Putnam, 1983; Shotter, 1993).

Dualisms[1] are experienced as choice points within the research process; they are implicitly embedded in what and how we study. For example, extant theory usually favors one view of organizations, work, relationships, and truth over others. Like a camera angle, research methodologies offer a view of our subjects that inevitably precludes other angles and views. In both theory and methods, the buy-in process by researchers over time produces dominant versus marginal perspectives, mainstream versus emerging research, the *au couránt* versus the *passé*. Forced to choose among alternative views, the trade-offs of decision making often create dilemmas over the best way to proceed. For example, to focus on the exchange between leaders and constituents leaves questions about the role of vision, charisma, and language use in calculation of the exchange. To study surface structure power dynamics via influence tactics leaves unanswered questions about the deep structure linguistic influences that might prefigure the influence attempt. What communication scientists observe interactionally is accompanied by questions about what is experienced and vice versa. These dilemmas are constantly evolving as researchers come to grips with unanswered questions while discovering new ones.

The nature of the dualisms that leadership communication researchers confront ranges from the oppositional to the seemingly oppositional. For example, the individual versus the collective reflects a dualism between contradictory opposites (i.e., a dialectic). Too much focus on what leaders do bypasses the dynamics of the collective. Yet too much focus on the collective overlooks the individual's basis of action. A dualism can also reflect choices that are not necessarily mutually exclusive, but rely on conceptualizations that effectively set alternative views in opposition. Positivist versus critical-interpretive views of communication inquiry provide one such example. Finally, some dualisms reflect choices that are little more than rhetorical straw men. Difference turns into opposition only to highlight the features or relative advantages of one path over another (e.g., what is observed vs. experienced interactionally).

Dialectical theories of meaning suggest a reason why these various dualisms fuel our thinking about theory and research in leadership communication. Opposition is a bonding agent in our thought because we think by looking to the relation between things. We can know what something is by focusing on what it is not, although any number of "what it is not" ideas may be usefully contrasted with "what it is" (Rychlak, 1977). Derrida's (1976) *différance* attaches a similar fluidity to oppositional thinking.[2]

Since camps have been known to form around a given theory or research approach, dualisms may polarize researchers because of the tensions they create between alternate forms of research. However, on balance these tensions are healthy and energizing for a research community because of the debate they foster and the creative ideas they spawn (Pfeffer, 1981). This is a compelling reason, especially in a review essay, to refrain from choosing sides in these dualisms (assuming that no one approach garners the corner on truth) when each can provide a pragmatic means of understanding. In this respect, dualistic thinking is reminiscent of dialectical inquiry, which holds that both opposing poles of a dialectic are important regardless of how visible or dominant either pole might be. However, dialectical inquiry achieves its distinctive nature by going beyond the duality of a phenomenon to focus on the dynamic tension between unified opposites in a system and the possibility of resolution (Werner & Baxter, 1994).

Although important differences remain between a dualism and a dialectic (Baxter & Montgomery, 1996), a framework loosely modeled on a dialectical approach was selected to help make sense of this literature.[3] Although the dualisms marking leadership communication research are both oppositional and seemingly oppositional, their interplay over time is the subject of this chapter. With that in mind, four questions guide this effort. First, what are the dualisms and resulting tensions and dilemmas that characterize leadership communication research? Second, how do these dualisms currently intersect to form choice points in the literature? Third, how do these dualisms mark the evolution of leadership communication research in the past several years? To answer this question, I selected five fairly well-developed programs of research in leadership communication to document the dualisms that have surfaced in the past and present literature. Finally, how can these dualisms shape future leadership communication research? Following Kolb and Putnam's (1992) strategy, this chapter places particular emphasis on the understudied areas and choice points within the literature to suggest new directions for research.

The five research programs that are to be explored include the study of influence tactics, feedback, charisma and visionary leadership, leader-member exchange, and systems-interactional leadership research. While other important issues in leadership communication have been studied (e.g., gender, social support, empowerment, competence), the five programs reviewed have enough research to characterize the extant dualisms sufficiently and span the continuum of individual-

istic and systemic approaches. With some exceptions, most restrict their study of leadership to individuals who perform dyadically linked roles[4] in hierarchical organizations and who manifest relatively stable skills, styles, motives, expectancies, behaviors, and/or personalities in the performance of those roles.[5]

THE DUALISMS OF LEADERSHIP COMMUNICATION

As Figure 11.1 reveals, this chapter poses three sets of dualisms that characterize the literature on leadership communication.[6] The first, the individual and the system, is the primary dualism because of its influence on the existence and development of the two secondary dualisms: cognitive outcomes and conversational practices, and transmission and meaning-centered views of communication. The primary versus secondary nature of these dualisms is explained further after each dualism is defined.

Primary and Secondary Dualisms

Primary Dualism: The Individual and the System

One of the strongest pulls in leadership research is that between the individual and the collective or system. The term *individual* refers to leaders or constituents by themselves. However, the term *system* refers to a dyad, group, culture or subculture, organization, industry, or any way a collective can be configured. This primary dualism is bipolar and oppositional, essentially dialectical in nature. It is similar to the centrality accorded to the individual-system dialectic in the therapy literature (Bopp & Weeks, 1984; Weeks, 1986), the individual-collective dialectic in cultural studies (Hofstede, 1981), and the independence-connection dialectic in the literature on personal relationships (Baxter, 1990; Rawlins, 1992).

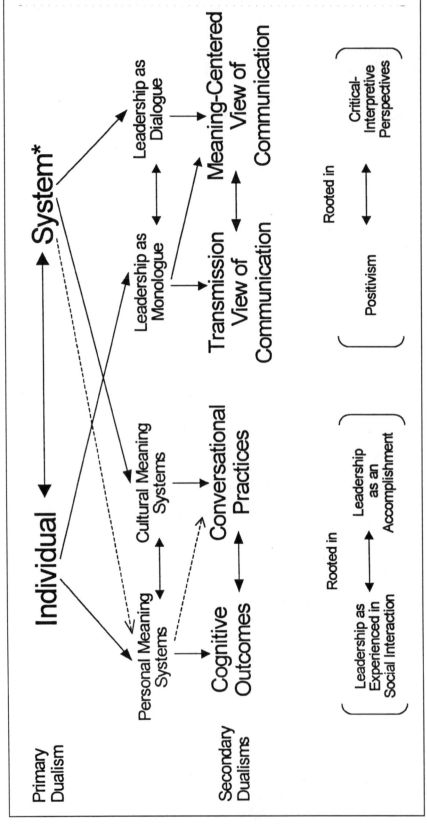

Figure 11.1. The Dualisms of Leadership Communication Research

*The arrow with the broken line indicates the combined influence of personal and cultural meaning systems on conversational practices.

There are definite patterns in the way researchers have managed the individual-system dualism in the leadership communication literature. Historically, dominant views of leadership have been shaped by a traditional psychological view of the world where in a figure-ground arrangement the individual is figure, the system is background, and communication is incidental or, at best, intervening. Over the past few decades, most of the ferment in leadership research occurred when the study of leadership traits gave way to the study of cognitions, acts, and meaning constructions (vs. coconstructions), all cut from the cloth of individualism. One implication of such an individualistic focus has been to romanticize and enhance the perceived role of the leader in effecting organizational outcomes (Meindl, Ehrlich, & Dukerich, 1985).

However, there are an increasing number of countervailing forces with a systems orientation. The literature within communication, leadership, and organizational development all illustrate this basic tendency. In communication research, Fisher (1985, 1986) reconceptualized leadership as an emergent property of group interaction. The locus of leadership is not the individual, but in the patterned sequential behavior of leaders and constituents who form an interactional system. A "systems-interactional" approach to leadership, to be discussed later, draws from general systems theory in emphasizing the properties of wholeness and interdependence and from information theory in emphasizing the redundancies in leader-constituent behavior.

A few years ago, the editor of *Leadership Quarterly* asked several leadership theorists to recast their theories at multiple levels of analysis. The upshot of this decision was to take many established theories beyond a focus on individuals and dyads to groups and organizations (Dansereau, 1995a, 1995b). Historically, leader-member exchange (LMX) has been one of the few leadership approaches to maintain an explicitly relationship focus almost from the outset. Interest in LMX research continues to be strong particularly in communication, LMX development, network applications, and intercultural studies.

In organizational development, relational concepts such as followership, empowerment, reciprocality, and leader accessibility are increasingly entering into the dialogue about leadership (Conger, 1989; Kouzes & Posner, 1993, 1995; Wheatley, 1992). Also in the organizational development literature, those who espouse such principles as systems theory (Senge, 1990), dialogue (Isaacs, 1993, 1999), and new science (Wheatley, 1992) are likewise eschewing an individualistic focus in favor of a systemic one. Senge and his colleagues now write about leadership communities where the leadership function is by necessity distributed to bring about organizational transformation (Senge et al., 1999). Thus, although an individualistic orientation has been the heavy favorite in leadership research, pressures are building to consider wider systems dynamics.

Finally, pressures are also building to treat individual-system tensions as problematic by focusing on how the tensions themselves are managed. The metaphors of leadership as jamming (Eisenberg, 1990) or jazz (DePree, 1993) are usually invoked in this regard because they simultaneously capture leadership's "improvisational nature and the need to mesh the competing voices of an ensemble into a coherent piece of music" (Barge, 1994b, p. 102).

Related to the individual-system dualism are two secondary dualisms that are not dialectical in nature. Before describing their interrelationships, each secondary dualism must first be defined.

Secondary Dualism: Cognitive Outcomes and Conversational Practices

A secondary dualism in leadership communication research focuses on cognitive outcomes and conversational practices (Drecksel,

1991; Sypher, 1991). Cognitive outcomes are the thoughts and feelings experienced before, during, or after social interaction, but always as a response to it. As Figure 11.1 reveals, they are rooted in the experience of social interaction—the internal, psychological processes that individuals use in interpreting and producing messages and other social behavior. For example, social cognitive approaches capture individual experience through a focus on the differences in cognitive structures that lead to different message interpretations or plans of action (Hewes & Planalp, 1987). Observable behavior is never studied in isolation of ongoing interpretive and production processes. The emphasis is always on subjective reactions to so-called objective messages (Hewes & Planalp, 1987).

Cognitive models of leadership, especially those with a concern for communication, deal with such issues as perception and attention, schemata, attributions, salience processes, and motivated, programmed, and script-driven choice processes (e.g., Peterson & Sorenson, 1991; Smith & Peterson, 1988). These models suggest that the leader-constituent relationship is a context for communication.

As Figure 11.1 suggests, the study of conversational practices is rooted in the view that leadership is an accomplishment—interactionally constructed in the reciprocal behaviors of people who must continually adjust to one another (Fisher, 1986). Relational communication research and discourse analysis, two approaches that focus on the conversational practices of leadership, suggest that how leaders and constituents act in relation to one another constitutes the relationship. The relationship is synonymous with communication because redundancies in patterns of communicating define the form of the relationship (Bateson, 1972; Rogers, Millar, & Bavelas, 1985). As Drecksel (1991) observed, "Leadership is located, observed, and interpreted as a communicative process comprising externalized and directly observable behaviors" (p. 538).

The basis of cognitive outcomes, experience, and the roots of conversational practices, accomplishments, are also interdependent. While leaders and constituents bring to the organization unique purposes, personalities, past experiences, expectations, and opinions, the specific nature of their relationship at a given time is a product of their social interaction. Simultaneously, the relationship gives to leaders and constituents certain characteristics that would not exist otherwise. Thus, the context of any leadership encounter engenders a disposition of professionalism and role behavior in leaders and an expectation of resources, understanding, and/or direction in constituents.[7] Therefore, both experience and accomplishment form an interdependence; without accomplishment, there is nothing to experience and without experience, there is no ability to respond.

Those who see leadership as experience study it by collecting cognitive outcomes in the form of self-report data. Communication researchers in this area often study frequent, anticipated, or imagined interactions between leaders and constituents. The ease with which these studies can be designed typically leads to large samples. But as Knapp, Miller, and Fudge (1994) point out, many communication researchers have questioned the adequacy of their knowledge of communication when it is based solely on self-report data (e.g., Barge & Schleuter, 1991; Corman & Krizek, 1993; Rogers et al., 1985):

> Can people accurately recall or predict some aspects of their interpersonal communication behavior . . . ? Have we developed a body of knowledge that is limited to what people think they would do? Isn't there a need to supplement or seek validation of self-reports with observations of actual interaction behavior? Is it enough to know attitudes, opinions, and perceptions of one interaction partner often removed from any interaction context? How will the preferences expressed on the questionnaire manifest themselves in the presence of another person or persons governed by situational constraints? (p. 10)

Other leadership communication researchers answer these questions by focusing on conversational practices and naturally occurring talk. While subjective views of reality may answer questions about the self-conscious basis of social action, scholars argue that research practices should include the study of actual communication because that which is relational is social and between people. Montgomery (1992) noted that "social phenomena are defined by the relations among their characteristics—be they people, places, goals, or behaviors—not by the characteristics themselves" (p. 480); hence, the instantiation of relationships in communication. As Bateson (1972) observed, communication *is* the relationship.

Because of the difficulty of obtaining and transcribing actual organizational talk, most leadership communication research is based on a conception of messages that fails to take into account the actual interactive practices associated with message production. Nowhere will this be more evident than in the voluminous literature concerning leader and constituent influence tactics. However, Knapp et al. (1994) are quite correct in noting the inadequacy of overt behavior by itself:

> Even though we still have much to learn from the study of overt behavior, it is already clear that, first, what transpires during interpersonal transactions is more than mere responses to manifest signals. Communicator expectations, fantasies, plans, and the like may provide the basis for response; behaviors not shown by the interaction partner may provide the basis for response; behaviors shown in previous interactions (with and not with the current partner) may guide and direct reactions. (p. 10)

Cognitive outcomes and conversational practices specify different, but interdependent units of analysis. Cognitive outcomes is the study of "what people mean," while conversational practices study "how behavior means" (Scheflen, 1974). Without people, there is no meaning. Without messages, there can be no communication.

Secondary Dualism: Transmission Views and Meaning-Centered Views of Communication

At the basis of the secondary dualism concerning transmission views and meaning-centered views of communication is the most basic tension facing social orders. As Figure 11.1 reveals, that tension lies between the constructed social world and the ongoing process of social construction (Benson, 1977). The reification of reality as a determinate influence on behavior forms a tension with reality in the making or its ongoing social construction. The interdependence between constructed and determinist views of reality surfaces from the knowledge that we make our own history, but not always under conditions of our choosing.

This fundamental tension is at the heart of social science inquiry. Positivist or determinist views of reality are associated with empirical and rational thought where reality is separate from the knower waiting to be discovered. In critical-interpretive views of reality, the individual takes an active, constructive role in creating knowledge through language and communication. Individuals are neither passive nor reactive, but intentional and reflexively self-aware. Taken to extremes, the upshot of the difference between the two views is that a determinist view essentially strips the individual of choice, while a socially constructed view may marginalize material constraints on behavior.

A transmission view of communication follows directly from the stance where reality is to be found or read (Morgan, 1986). The messages sent and received are assumed to have an objective reality about them. They exist independently of sender or receiver. By reifying messages in this way, communication becomes a tangible substance that flows through the organization conceived as a container. Putting content and meaning aside, the essence of a transmission view of communication lies more in transmission and channel effects: message directionality, frequency, and fidelity, blockages that inhibit transmission, and perceptual filters that hinder message reception (Fisher, 1978; Putnam, 1983).

In contrast to a transmission model, a meaning-centered view casts leaders and constituents as practical authors and coauthors. Practical authors exert choice over unchosen conditions whenever one linguistic formulation is chosen over possible others. According to Shotter (1993), an appropriate formulation of unchosen conditions creates

> (a) a "landscape" of enabling-constraints (Giddens, 1979) relevant for a range of next possible actions; (b) a network of "moral positions" or "commitments" (understood in terms of the rights and duties of the "players" on that landscape); and (c) [those who] are able to argue persuasively and authoritatively for this "landscape" amongst those who must work within it. (p. 149)

Authorship is contingent on understanding the formative power of language, which is the ability to create reality based on what may only be vaguely sensed intuitions or tendencies. An authorial view does not legitimate an "anything goes" view of authorship (Shotter, 1993), but neither does it place particular emphasis on the constraints on authorship. Thus, transmission and authorial views of communication appear to emphasize different, but complementary aspects of the communication process.

Relationships Among Dualisms

In considering how these dualisms intersect with one another, I have argued that the individual-system dualism is primary because of its influence on both of the secondary dualisms. The dominance of the individual-system dualism can be seen in pronounced tendencies to emphasize different sides of the secondary dualisms. These are only pronounced tendencies and not absolutes as examples can certainly be found to the contrary. Nevertheless, they are strong enough to propose an overarching framework as described in Figure 11.1. I will first consider the

influence of the individual-system dualism on cognitive outcomes and conversational practices followed by its influence on transmission views and meaning-centered views of communication.

Links to Cognitive Outcomes and Conversational Practices

Based on the tendencies within the literature, an individualistic focus leads one to favor cognitive outcomes while a systemic focus tends to favor conversational practices.[8] However, Figure 11.1 reveals the personal versus cultural basis of meaning that links the individual-system and the cognitive outcomes-conversational practices dualisms together. An individualistic orientation often focuses on cognitive outcomes through the study of personal meaning systems. A systemic orientation leads to a focus on conversational practices through the study of cultural meaning systems or the interpenetration of cultural and personal meaning systems.

An individualistic focus places a heavy emphasis on the individual's idiosyncratic view of the world, a view shaped by the accumulation of unique life experiences. As the integration of one's experiences schematize, these schemas yield the dimensions along which aspects of new situations will be measured and assigned meaning (Fiske & Taylor, 1991). The meaning assigned is considered personal and idiosyncratic because no two individuals or life journeys are ever the same. Cognitive outcomes as measured through self-reports are the usual data of choice.

However, self-reports have a tendency to perpetuate the myth that meaning construction is mostly private and personal rather than subject to historical and sociocultural influences (Lannamann, 1991).[9] A focus on system functioning leads one to favor the study of conversational practices, which makes it apparent that meaning is not solely private. Meaning is also cultural because there must be some means by which members of a language community communicate with one another. For example, symbolic interactionists call the process whereby private meanings are transformed into collective, enduring, taken-for-granted realities the "sedimentation of meanings" (Berger & Luckmann, 1966; Fine, 1992; Prasad, 1993). Sedimented or conventionalized meanings yield a repertoire of strategies and linguistic resources that "are accessible by members of the speech community for sensemaking and useable as currency to signal to one's partner the state of affect, respect, intimacy, or power at that moment" (Fairhurst, 1993b, p. 323). In this way, conventional meaning assignments in a language community often precede and prefigure more personal and idiosyncratic meaning construction (Sigman, 1987, 1992).

Personal and cultural sources of meaning are often cast as oppositional forms (Berger & Luckmann, 1966; Leont'ev, 1978; Ricoeur, 1971). Huspek and Kendall (1991) argue that personal meanings grow out of a set of practices that "belong uniquely to the individual . . . to make sense of the inner life and its relation to the external world" (p. 1). In contrast, cultural meanings grow out of a set of social practices beyond any individual experience providing socially validated ways of seeing and representing the world. Thus, an individualistic orientation leads one to favor cognitive outcomes through personal meaning systems. A systems orientation leads one to favor conversational practices through the study of the cultural or the interpenetration of the cultural with personal meaning systems.

Links to Transmission Views Versus Meaning-Centered Views of Communication

Figure 11.1 also reveals that leadership as a monologue versus leadership as a dialogue links the individual-system and the transmission-meaning dualisms together. Leadership as a monologue has its roots in two places. First, it hearkens back to transmission models of communication where the transfer of information goes from source to receiver where audiences are often undifferentiated masses. This view prohibits treating meaning as contested or problematic. Second, a monologue approach also draws from the symbolic views of leadership as proposed by Pfeffer (1981), Pondy (1978), and Bennis and Nanus (1985). The blending of symbolic leadership with a transmission model casts leaders as the primary architects of meaning through such vehicles as an organizational vision, mission, and statement of values (e.g., Shamir, Arthur, & House, 1994). Bennis and Nanus (1985) write in this regard, "An essential factor in leadership is the capacity to influence and *organize meaning* for the members of the organization" (p. 39, emphasis in the original).

A monologic approach conceives of members as largely surrendering their right to make meanings by virtue of their employment contract within a hierarchical organization. Smircich and Morgan (1982) reflect this view when they state, "Leadership involves a dependency relationship in which individuals surrender their power to interpret and define reality to others" (p. 258). As such, meanings are created by the leader and remain largely uncontested by constituents. As will be shown, the study of charisma benefits from such a view.

Dialogic views of leadership merge interactional models of communication that stress feedback and mutual effects with transactional models that focus on holism and sharing (Littlejohn, 1983). Dialogic views tend toward a social constructionist orientation where emphasis is given to the coconstruction of meaning (Cooperrider, Barrett, & Srivastva, 1995; Gergen, 1985). Coconstruction presumes that talk is essentially contested where contestation is not just about what exists, but includes competing perspectives, future possibilities, and prescriptions for action (Shotter, 1993). For example, the literature on organizational visions increasingly reflects the view that shared visions require contestation, not a monologic transfer of vision from one person to the next. According to Senge (1990):

Visions that are truly shared take time to emerge. They grow as a by-product of interactions of individual visions. Experience suggests that visions that are genuinely shared require ongoing conversation where individuals not only feel free to express their dreams, but learn how to listen to each other's dreams. Out of this listening, new insights into what is possible gradually emerge. (pp. 217-218)

In the organizational development literature, a dialogic focus also tends to minimize hierarchical distinctions while simultaneously promoting the notion of community (Kouzes & Posner, 1993). Note the absence of hierarchical framing in the Senge quote. There is no leader or constituent, only individuals engaged in a dialogue of conversing and listening.

In summary, the dualism between leadership as monologue and dialogue ties the individual-system and the transmission-meaning dualisms together. An individualistic focus produces the tendency to see the leader's communication in monologic and transmission terms. A systems focus emphasizes meaning as a social construction through leader-constituent dialogue.

Implications

The choice points or research dilemmas formed by these intersecting dualisms have enormous heuristic value. First, we can observe something of the nature of the conflict between scientists from different disciplines and theoretical orientations. For example, the pull away from the individual toward the system and its functioning for leadership researchers trained in psychology or a social cognitive orientation is often internal and, thus, nonantagonistic. The historical tendency to perceive communication as being incidental is counteracted by the observed effects of social interaction. These effects cannot be explained through the additive contribution of individuals and their perceptions.

However, communication scientists and others espousing a systems philosophy are much more likely to reject outright the individual as the exclusive orientation to leadership. Courtright, Fairhurst, and Rogers (1989) voice this position, "To understand social structure, however, knowing what people do individually is not sufficient. Rather, researchers must know what they do in conjunction with or in relationship to the other participants in an interaction" (p. 777); hence, their focus on the interact, two contiguous acts, as the minimally acceptable unit of analysis for leader-constituent communication.

In addition to providing an organizing framework for making sense of opposing views, a second heuristic associated with intersecting dualisms is that it opens up new directions for research. The reason for this is quite simple; most research programs manage the alternatives by favoring one approach over another for a given period of time (Werner & Baxter, 1994). Not all research programs favor the same approach, and the results can be used to pose questions from the understudied areas. In this way, future research may achieve a more complex view of the dualisms explored within this chapter.

To begin, we must characterize some specific points of departure. As previously indicated, I have selected five programs of leadership communication research where there has been enough study to characterize the dualisms and their resulting tensions. Their order of presentation corresponds to their orientation to the individual-system dualism. The study of influence tactics is the most individualistic of the programs because the influence process is largely conceived of as one-way. The study of feedback follows because organizational feedback research concentrates heavily on the individual's view of giving, seeking, or receiving feedback. Although the study of charisma historically has had strong individualistic leanings, individual-system tensions are increasingly articulated within this literature. By contrast, the study of visionary leadership is often more systemic than individual. Leader-member exchange, the fourth program of research, is more systemic than individual because it focuses on the leader-constituent relationship although typically from a social cognitive perspective. Finally, systems-interactional research is the most systemic of the approaches because of its emphasis on actual system functioning. As will become apparent, the systems approaches are as much in need of a counter-balancing individualistic focus as the individualistic approaches require attention to systemic concerns.

For each body of literature, I begin by characterizing some of the developments within the literature in the past several years in terms of the dualisms. I then use the understudied sides of the dualisms to identify new research directions.

INFLUENCE TACTICS

The study of interpersonal influence between leaders and constituents takes many forms. While some research focuses on defensive strategies where influence is exerted to protect and manage an identity in the offering of an account for some type of failure event (Bies & Sitkin, 1992; Braaten, Cody, & DeTienne, 1993; Schonbach, 1990), most of the research focuses on more proactive means to goal achievement (Arkin & Sheppard, 1990; Schlenker, 1980; Tedeschi, 1990). The most dominant body of research in this regard is the study of compliance gaining or influence tactics. Dualisms and tensions exist within this voluminous body of literature.

The Individual-System Dualism and Other Tensions

Although tensions around the individual-system dualism exist, the dominance of the individual has been significant. One person essentially asks another to do something with little or unspecified argument from the other; there is no parallel consideration of strategies for resisting another's influence attempts. Individuals have relational concerns (e.g., the relative status and power of the target, others' perceptions of interactional justice), but issues of relationship surface only as a context for the study of individual compliance-gaining behavior. Wider systems concerns are not of interest.

Most studies operate from a social cognitive perspective where cognitive outcomes are favored over conversational practices. The most popular measures are checklists that record global summary judgments recalled across all interactions. This method tends to obscure how strategy choice may combine with other strategies, may vary across situations, or may function within a sequence of reciprocal influence moves. Under this approach, the model of communication is "transmissional," and the social construction of meaning is taken for granted. Communication is strictly a medium for the self-conscious exercise of power based on some resource imbalance or dependency relationship.

The tendencies toward favoring the individual, cognitive outcomes, and a transmission view of communication reveal themselves in three questions dominating this type of research: (1) How can influence best be described? (2) What factors influence the production of tactics? and (3) What outcomes do the tactics produce? Table 11.1 summarizes a representative set of findings.

Describing Influence

The most widely used influence tactic scheme is the one developed by Kipnis and his colleagues (Kipnis & Schmidt, 1988; Kipnis, Schmidt, & Wilkinson, 1980; Schriesheim & Hinkin, 1990), who inductively derived a set of tactics for upward, downward, and lateral communication. Each tactic (assertiveness, ingratiation, rationality, exchange of benefits,

TABLE 11.1 Influence Tactic Research

Description of tactics	
Influence message analysis	Case, Dosier, Murkison, & Keys, 1988; Dosier, Case, & Keys, 1988; Mainiero, 1986; Tjosvold, 1985
Kipnis scheme	Kipnis & Schmidt, 1988; Kipnis, Schmidt, & Wilkinson, 1980; Schriesheim & Hinkin, 1990
Rational, soft, and hard	Farmer, Maslyn, Fedor, & Goodman, 1997; Kipnis & Schmidt, 1985; Deluga, 1991a, 1991b
Yukl scheme	Falbe & Yukl, 1992; Yukl, Falbe, & Youn, 1993; Yukl, Guinan, & Sottolano, 1995; Yukl, Kim, & Chavez, 1999; Yukl & Tracey, 1992
Influences on tactic use	
Agent versus target perspectives	Erez, Rim, & Keider, 1986; Xin & Tsui, 1996
Attractiveness of constituents	Garko, 1992
Authoritarian vs. participative leaders	Ansari & Kapoor, 1987
Consideration and initiating structure	Chacko, 1990; Cheng, 1983
Cross-cultural tactic use	Hirokawa & Miyahara, 1986; Sullivan & Taylor, 1991; Xin & Tsui, 1996
Directional differences	Erez, Rim, & Keider, 1986; Kipnis et al., 1980; Xin & Tsui, 1996; Yukl & Falbe, 1990; Yukl, Falbe, & Youn, 1993; Yukl & Tracey, 1992
Education	Farmer et al., 1997
Expectations for success	Kipnis et al., 1984
Expectations of constituent resistance	Sullivan, Albrecht, & Taylor, 1990

upward appeal, and coalition) has its own multi-item scale that is designed to assess retrospectively the frequency of tactic use for initial compliance gaining and then for follow-up attempts when resistance (unspecified) is encountered. In other research, tactics have been grouped into an alternative set of categories: rational (reason, exchange), soft (friendliness), and hard (assertiveness, higher authority, coalition) (e.g., Deluga, 1991a, 1991b; Farmer, Maslyn, Fedor, & Goodman, 1997; Kipnis & Schmidt, 1985).

While Kipnis and his colleagues used the agent's perspective to generate their influence tactics, Yukl and his colleagues (Falbe & Yukl, 1992; Yukl & Falbe, 1990; Yukl, Falbe, & Youn, 1993; Yukl, Guinan, & Sottolano, 1995; Yukl & Tracey, 1992) also focus on the target's perspective. Several of Kipnis's tactics overlap the Yukl scheme. However, the latter adds the tactics "inspirational appeal to values and emotion" and "consultation" (Yukl & Falbe, 1990) and different forms of rational persuasion (Yukl, Kim, & Chavez, 1999).

Finally, other studies have chosen not to supply subjects with a preformulated checklist of strategies. Instead, these studies ask subjects to construct messages whose features are then coded for influence form. Using a critical incident or hypothetical scenario methodology, incidents are coded using strategies from previously developed checklists to

Gender	Hirokawa, Kodama, & Harper, 1990; Lauterbach & Weiner, 1996; Yukl & Falbe, 1990; Yukl & Tracey, 1992
Influence objectives	Ansari & Kapoor, 1987; Erez et al., 1986; Harper & Hirokawa, 1988; Kipnis et al., 1980; Schmidt & Kipnis, 1984; Yukl & Falbe, 1990; Yukl et al., 1995; Yukl et al., 1999
Low vs. high power agents	Hirokawa et al., 1990; Mainiero, 1986; Schilit, 1987
Leader-member exchange	Deluga & Perry, 1991
Machiavellianism	Farmer et al., 1997; Vecchio & Sussman, 1991

Mediators and outcomes of tactic use
  Commitment, compliance, or
    resistance
	Falbe & Yukl, 1992; Tepper, 1993; Tepper, Eisenbach, Kirby, & Potter, 1998; Yukl et al., 1999

Constituent earnings	Kipnis & Schmidt, 1988
Constituent effectiveness	Case et al., 1988; Kipnis & Schmidt, 1988
Constituent perceived interpersonal skills	Wayne, Liden, Graf, & Ferris, 1997
Constituent promotability	Thacker & Wayne, 1995
Constituent stress	Kipnis & Schmidt, 1988
Justice perceptions	Dulebohn & Ferris, 1999; Tepper et al., 1998
Leader effectiveness	Deluga, 1991b; Dosier et al., 1988; Falbe & Yukl, 1992; Yukl & Tracey, 1992
Leader stress	Deluga, 1991b
Satisfaction	Deluga, 1991b
Task commitment	Yukl & Tracey, 1992

form a coding scheme (e.g., Falbe & Yukl, 1992; Hirokawa, Kodama, & Harper, 1990; Hirokawa & Miyahara, 1986) or based on emergent categories in the data (e.g., Case, Dosier, Murkison, & Keys, 1988; Dosier, Case, & Keys, 1988; Lauterbach & Weiner, 1996). Alternatively, other studies code for specific message features such as supportiveness, powerlessness, punitiveness, or threat (Mainiero, 1986; Tjosvold, 1985).

Factors Influencing Tactic Use

As Table 11.1 reveals, a wide range of studies have looked at the influences on tactic use including directional differences, influence objectives, agent versus target perspectives, and a host of other relationship and individual variables.

Among the more notable findings are the various directional differences (upward, downward, and lateral) in tactic use. Research consistently shows that exchange of benefits is used in downward and lateral as opposed to upward influence, while assertiveness is favored in downward more than lateral or upward influence. Findings related to the other tactics remain inconsistent (e.g., Erez, Rim, & Keider, 1986; Kipnis et al., 1980; Yukl & Falbe, 1990; Yukl & Tracey, 1992).

Individuals also select influence tactics based on their objectives and goals. For example, pressure is often used to change the behavior of constituents (Erez et al., 1986; Harper & Hirokawa, 1988; Kipnis et al., 1980; Schmidt & Kipnis, 1984; Xin & Tsui, 1996; Yukl & Falbe, 1990). Rational persuasion and coalition tactics are often used with peers and leaders to win support for major changes in policies and programs (Erez et al., 1986; Kipnis et al., 1980; Schmidt & Kipnis, 1984; Xin & Tsui, 1996). But more than one study has reached the conclusion of Yukl et al. (1995), "Even though some tactics are used more often for particular objectives, the relationship between tactics and objectives was not a strong one . . . most of the tactics could be used for any objective" (p. 294).

Finally, hard influence tactics (e.g., assertiveness) are reportedly chosen more frequently when expectations for success are low versus high (Kipnis, Schmidt, Swaffin-Smith, & Wilkinson, 1984) and with authoritarian versus participative leaders (Ansari & Kapoor, 1987), high- versus low-power agents (Hirokawa et al., 1990), high versus low levels of Machiavellianism and education in agents (Farmer et al., 1997), low versus high levels of consideration and initiating structure in leaders (Chacko, 1990; Cheng, 1983), American versus Japanese leaders (Hirokawa & Miyahara, 1986), low versus high LMX relationships (Deluga & Perry, 1991), and unattractive versus attractive constituents (Garko, 1992).

Outcomes of Tactic Use

A number of studies suggest that the use of hard influence tactics are associated with the most negative outcomes including constituent effectiveness ratings, leader stress levels, task commitment, and constituent promotability (Case et al., 1988; Deluga, 1991b; Kipnis & Schmidt, 1988; Thacker & Wayne, 1995; Yukl & Tracey, 1992). Studies also suggest that some form of rational persuasion yields the most positive outcomes (Case et al., 1988; Falbe & Yukl, 1992; Wayne, Liden, Graf, & Ferris, 1997; Yukl & Tracey, 1992).

Finally, there is a growing body of literature that focuses on constituents' use of influence tactics to influence the performance ratings they receive (e.g., Barry & Watson, 1996; Ferris, Judge, Rowland, & Fitzgibbons, 1994; Wayne & Ferris, 1990; Wayne et al., 1997). Soft supervisor-focused tactics have been associated with perceptions of procedural justice in this context (Dulebohn & Ferris, 1999). Also in this context, rational persuasion and hard tactics like assertiveness have been associated with leaders' perceptions of constituents' interpersonal skills (Wayne et al., 1997).

New Directions: Conversational Practices, the Recovery of Meaning, and Systems Concerns

While the social cognitive basis of this work contributes to our understanding of social action, the influence process is more complex and more interesting than current research allows. However, we can recover some of this complexity by focusing on the understudied areas in this work: conversational practices, a meaning-centered view of communication, and system concerns.

Conversational Practices

A focus on conversational practices should reveal more of the reciprocal nature of influence and the complexity of influence messages. A focus on the reciprocal nature of talk in the influence literature might call into question the usual emphasis on compliance gaining. Compliance resisting has not been explored in any systematic way in the organizational influence tactic literature, which may be more of a function of researchers' assumptions about its aberrance in reporting relationships. Empirical treatments of the subject, especially in organizations and/or relationships promoting empowerment, participation, and dialogue, will likely reveal that compliance resisting occurs with some frequency in both hierarchical and lateral relationships. Regardless of base rate, compliance resisting is worthy of study in the context of everyday influence. The study of empowerment with its emphasis on leader support for constituent autonomy may be the venue in which this emerges (e.g., Chiles & Zorn, 1995; Conger & Kanungo, 1988). The study of resistance is also prominent in critical theory approaches to organizations (e.g., Jermier, Knights, & Nord, 1994) because as Phillips (1997) observed, "upward influence is referred to as resistance and is understood to be a part of any asymmetrical power relation; where there is power, there is resistance, the two are mutually constituting and reinforcing" (p. 47).

A focus on conversational practices should also reveal more complexity in influence messages. In studying actual dialogue, as opposed to a self-reported strategy selection, specific message features that accompany a broad characterization of a strategy (e.g., "rationality," "exchange of benefits") are more difficult to ignore. For many organizational scientists who see communication only as a medium for the exercise of power, adding complexity to message schemes is not high yield (cf. Yukl et al., 1999). For example, variations on the tactic "exchange of benefits" may matter little if the comparison to other tactics is the primary concern.

Yet the introduction of status and power into interactional contexts frequently produces actors with multiple goals who want to pursue a task (task goal), usually without offending influential others (relationship goal), while promoting an image of competence (identity goal). In turn, multiple goals create multifunctional utterances. Typically, these utterances are marked by language that cloaks or moderates the influence attempt in order to address relational and identity aims while still achieving the task. Such language may include politeness strategies, semantic indirectness, language that triggers cognitive scripts, and the framing of intent (e.g., disclaimers, credentialling) (Brown & Levinson, 1978;

Drake & Moberg, 1986). All help the actor to position the self, assuage other's ego, reinforce relational ties, and/or trigger scripted behavior.

Despite promising recent efforts to examine episodic influence (Maslyn, Farmer, & Fedor, 1996), different versions of strategies (Yukl et al., 1999), and the combined use of tactics (Tepper, Eisenbach, Kirby, & Potter, 1998), survey studies tend to paint influence strategies in such broad strokes that the details of their instantiation are often lost. Yet the inconsistency across studies regarding tactic use and associated variables (e.g., directional differences, influence objectives) reminds us that the devil is in the details. To continue with my earlier "exchange of benefits" example, when this strategy is paired with linguistic palliatives or sedatives, it can suspend calculation of the exchange and win compliance in ways that "exchange of benefits" without these linguistic devices cannot. This is because the form of the influence attempt itself becomes an inducement (Drake & Moberg, 1986).

In a similar vein, Kellermann and Cole (1994) argue that we know very little about regularities in message behavior because most schemes neither cover an adequate range of influence strategies, nor do they identify theoretically relevant features of influence messages. Based on the notion that a strategy is conceived of a higher-order unit comprising other units, Kellermann and Cole state that the scheme advanced by Kipnis et al. (1980) contains strategies defined by form (e.g., sanctions), content (e.g., rationality), presentation (e.g., ingratiation, assertiveness), context (e.g., upward appeal, coalitions), and interactive use (e.g., exchange). From their perspective, the Kipnis scheme is a data-driven hodgepodge of elements that render nonsensical the study of "strategy use" as the variable of interest. As Kellermann and Cole (1994) observe, "The values 'strategy use' takes on are unknown (i.e., over what values does it vary?) and the one feature, quality, or characteristic of behavior that it tracks is not specified" (p. 45). They argue that the study of compliance-gaining message behavior requires a feature-based approach where researchers focus on theoretically driven and specific message features (i.e., the underlying dimensions of message variation such as target adaptiveness, prosocialness, politeness, threat, etc.) rather than on strategies (see also O'Keefe, 1994).

Kellermann and Cole's point is well taken. Most taxonomy approaches involve an overly general and simplistic characterization of the basic message strategy, thus would do well to incorporate more aspects of message features into their schemes. For example, Yukl and his colleagues increasingly use critical incident scenarios alongside checklist approaches and code for multiple strategy use (e.g., Falbe & Yukl, 1992). But if taxonomy approaches are lacking in depth (regarding the range of messages that forms dimensions of message behavior), their strength lies in their breadth. And if one's interest in communication is strictly as a medium for the self-conscious exercise of power, a taxonomy serves a useful role in setting forth a range of categorically distinct influence options available in typical organizational situations. However, the problem is that even with a sophisticated taxonomy, there is so much more to understanding power, influence, and communication between leaders and constituents.

The Recovery of Meaning

Frost (1987) reminded us that communication is not just a medium for the exercise of power as a result of some resource imbalance or dependency relationship. Communication also is intricately involved in the formation of meaning. Communication is used to develop social consensus around labels and definitions of decisions and actions (Pfeffer, 1981; Shotter, 1993). Thus, getting others to do things rests as much on the framing and sensemaking of everyday life, which define the bounds of what is logical and sensible in a context of action. "Our situation here and now," "the mistakes of the past," and "what we strive for" are just a few of the ongoing socially negotiated meanings that form the warrant for action including compliance gaining. When researchers are preoccupied with forcing influence forms into static typologies, meaning is taken for granted thereby stripping human communication of one of its most essential elements. In so doing, they artificially impose stability on power and influence processes obscuring both the complexity and fluidity of power dynamics as a result (Clegg, 1979; Conrad, 1983).

The recovery of meaning can begin by asking leaders and constituents not just to report their use of tactics, but by asking them to account for their strategy selection. When individuals are asked why they chose a particular tactic, social meanings emerge with respect to their own actions, the actions of others, or other aspects of the environment (Tompkins & Cheney, 1983).

Wider Systems Concerns and Deep Structure

The argument for a more complex understanding of power and influence in leader-constituent relationships is further buttressed by the fact that communication as medium (vis-à-vis tactic use) and communication as meaning (vis-à-vis sensemaking and labeling) are surface manifestations of power that influence and are influenced by systemwide deep structures of power (Clegg, 1979; Conrad, 1983; Frost, 1987; Phillips, 1997). In seeking or resisting compliance, Conrad (1983) notes, "Organizational members will observe, interpret, and remember their choices and their presumed relationship to the structure of power which exists in the organization" (p. 178). At deep-structure levels, all choices are political in that some interests are served over others. Surface-level choices create structures of power that act back upon the choice-making process in taken-for-granted assumptions about what is real, what is fair, and what is legitimate in ways actors are scarcely aware of (Deetz, 1985) simultaneously reproducing and adjusting the structure of organizational power (Giddens, 1979).

Deep-structure systems of meaning are operative at wider systems levels (e.g., culture). These systems are a preconscious foundation for interpretation and action that limit the perception of choice and available options (Deetz & Kersten, 1983). But underlying tensions between surface-level tactics, surface-level meaning making, and deep structure can be observed. Examples include a focus on language, especially stories, and the myths and metaphors used to describe power relationships; behavior during conflict situations in which organizational constraints are most likely to be consciously violated and questioned; and organizational game playing in which surface-level political activities become intertwined with deep-level meanings (Conrad, 1983; Clegg, 1975, 1979; Frost, 1987). Unfortunately, deep-structure influences on surface-level tactic use have rarely emerged in the literature.

In summary, the understudied areas of the influence literature suggest that a focus on conversational practices, the recovery of meaning, and wider systems concerns may reveal more complexity in influence processes between leaders and constituents. Some of these same recommendations surface for the study of feedback.

FEEDBACK

For most of this century, scholars have been interested in the link between feedback, motivation, and performance (Ammons, 1956; Kluger & DeNisi, 1996). Feedback research continues because of a possible performance-enhancing effect, although the literature increasingly suggests that the effects of feedback on performance and worker attitudes are quite variable and even damaging at times. Cybernetic theorist Wiener (1948) is credited with introducing the concept of feedback into general usage defining it as "a method of controlling a system" (Wiener, 1954, p. 61). However, the following discussion reveals very strong pulls toward the individual that has lessened only slightly in the past several years.

The Individual-System Dualism and Other Tensions

In his review of the feedback literature, Cusella (1987) correctly observed that despite the systemic origins of the feedback concept, almost all models of feedback and feedback research emphasized the internal psychological processes of feedback sending and receiving. Whether the emphasis was on feedback characteristics (goals, sources, types, functions) or its relationship to motivation and performance, the internal psychological state that formed the basis for feedback choices, rather than the actual feedback process, was the primary focus. Cusella's review was significant for communication scholars because his lone voice attempted to stem the tide of individualistic over systemic thinking: "From a communication perspective, feedback processes consist of an exchange of behaviors that emphasize the (1) symbolic; (2) relational; and (3) systemic aspects to feedback-motivation/ performance relationships" (Cusella, 1987, p. 625).

Cusella's arguments centered on two chief points. First, patterns of control in feedback systems, sometimes characterized as "feedback loops," are frequently spoken of, but rarely operationalized in research. In operationalizing feedback loops, Cusella argued against the standard checklist approaches to selecting feedback messages. Instead, he focused on the conversational practices of feedback, practices that are best studied as an interconnected series of double interacts (Weick, 1969). Feedback is a process that takes place in "a circular closed loop of interaction" (Fisher, 1978, p. 298). Yet too often it is conceptualized as a mere response that ne-

TABLE 11.2 Feedback Research

Feedback sending and receiving	
360-degree feedback	Albright & Levy, 1995; Antonioni, 1994; Atwater, Rousch, & Fischthal, 1995; Atwater & Waldman, 1998; Barclay & Harland, 1995; Bernardin, Dahmus, & Redmon, 1993; Church & Bracken, 1997; Facteau, Facteau, Schoel, Russell, & Poteet, 1998; Funderburg & Levy, 1997; Hazucha, Hezlett, & Schneider, 1993; London, Smither, & Adsit, 1997; Smither, London, Vasilopoulos, Reilly, Millsap, & Salvemini, 1995; Smither, Wohlers, & London, 1995
Feedback sign	Atwater et al., 1995; Fedor, 1991; Kluger & DeNisi, 1996; Louie, 1999; Martocchio & Webster, 1992; Podsakoff & Farh, 1989; Reilly, Smither, & Vasilopoulos, 1996
Feedback sources	Becker & Klimoski, 1989; Fedor, 1991; Herold, Liden, & Leatherwood, 1987; Northcraft & Earley, 1989
Feedback style	Korsgaard, Meglino, & Lester, 1997; Zhou, 1998
Goal-setting and self-regulatory mechanisms	Earley, Northcraft, Lee, & Lituchy, 1989; Locke, Frederick, Lee, & Bobko, 1984; Latham & Locke, 1991; Locke & Latham, 1990; Mento, Steel, & Karren, 1987; Wood & Bandura, 1989
Negative feedback effects	Baron, 1988, 1990; Geddes & Baron, 1997; Gioia & Longenecker, 1994; Kluger, Lewinsohn, & Aiello, 1994; Larson, 1989; Skarlicki & Folger, 1997
Feedback seeking	
Influences on feedback seeking Feedback context (public vs. private)	Ashford, 1986; Ashford & Northcraft, 1992; Levy, Albright, Cawley, & Williams, 1995; Northcraft & Ashford, 1990; Walsh, Ashford, & Hill, 1985; Williams, Miller, Steelman, & Levy, 1999

glects the unfolding context in which feedback is administered and received. Moreover, contiguous feedback messages need to be analyzed to explicate the relational meaning or control function of feedback (Deci, 1975; Watzlawick, Beavin, & Jackson, 1967).

The second argument involving the systemic aspects of feedback concerns the cultural manifestations of consistent patterns of feedback. These patterns create feedback environments where cultural norms and values emerge around the sources of feedback and the types of information conveyed. Cusella (1987) argued that when the study of feedback is conceptualized in terms of feedback loops and feedback environments, the internal psychological (individual) and the external com-

municative (system) are jointly operative. He noted "a communication perspective to feedback processes, while representing a clear separation from cognitive models of feedback is, nevertheless, interdependent with them" (Cusella, 1987, p. 625). As Table 11.2 reveals, recent feedback research may be classified in terms of four general trends, the first two adhering to the traditional view of the concept.

Feedback Sending and Receiving

The first trend reflects a strong interest in psychological views of sending and receiving feedback including the sources of feedback

Feedback seeking costs/risks	Ashford, 1986; Fedor, Rensvold, & Adams, 1992
Feedback source	Callister, Kramer, & Turban, 1999
Goal orientation	VandeWalle & Cummings, 1997
Performance	Ashford, 1986; Fedor et al., 1992; Northcraft & Ashford, 1990
Role clarity	Callister et al., 1999
Self-esteem	Ashford, 1986; Fedor et al., 1992; Northcraft & Ashford, 1990
Source credibility	Fedor et al., 1992
Tolerance for ambiguity	Bennett, Herold, & Ashford, 1990; Fedor, et al., 1992
Uncertainty	Ashford, 1986; Fedor et al., 1992; Northcraft & Ashford, 1990
Outcomes of feedback seeking Amount of negative feedback	Larson, 1989
Impression management	Ashford & Northcraft, 1992; Ashford & Tsui, 1991; Levy et al., 1995; Morrison & Bies, 1991
Performance	Fedor et al., 1992
Understanding	Ashford & Tsui, 1991
Feedback message analysis Attributional influences on feedback messages	Dugan, 1989; Gioia & Sims, 1986; Kim & Miller, 1990; Tjosvold, 1985
Dimensionality	Geddes, 1993; Geddes & Linnehan, 1998; Larson, Glynn, Fleenor, & Scontrino, 1987
Face support	Zorn & Leichty, 1991
Control chains	Fairhurst, Green & Snavely, 1984a, 1984b; Gavin, Green, & Fairhurst, 1995; Green, Fairhurst, & Snavely, 1986; Morris, Gaveras, Baker, & Coursey, 1990

and their credibility, goal-setting and self-regulatory mechanisms, and feedback sign.

Feedback sources. Previous research on feedback sources (Greller & Herold, 1975; Hanser & Muchinsky, 1978; Herold & Greller, 1977) established differences in the perceived informativeness of five sources of performance feedback. In rank order, they are (1) oneself, (2) the task, (3) supervisors, (4) coworkers, and (5) the organization. Herold, Liden, and Leatherwood (1987) and Northcraft and Earley (1989) present confirmatory results. However, this order has been disputed (Becker & Klimoski, 1989), and there is some controversy over whether the self and task are distinct sources of feedback.

In his review of the literature, Fedor (1991) examines this conflict and the mitigating role of source credibility and relative power on recipient responses to different sources.

Finally, 360-degree feedback has been one of the most popular management innovations of the 1990s. This involves the systematic collection of feedback from a wide range of sources even those thought to be nontraditional or taboo such as internal and external customers or higher levels of management (Atwater & Waldman, 1998). Much attention has been paid to what 360-degree feedback is, how to implement it, and to the psychometric properties of ratings from various sources (e.g., Church & Bracken, 1997; Greguras & Robie, 1998). While less attention has been paid to outcomes, a few studies support a generally positive relationship between 360-degree feedback and leader performance (Atwater, Rousch, & Fischthal, 1995; Smither, London, Vasilopoulos, Reilly, Millsap, & Salvemini, 1995), although there are moderating factors like obtaining input on development plans from coworkers (Hazucha, Hezlett, & Schneider, 1993). Other studies focus on the characteristics of the feedback system that may garner a positive response by leaders. These include rater anonymity (Antonioni, 1994), rater accountability (London, Smither, & Adsit, 1997), multiple versus single sources (Bernardin, Dahmus, & Redmon, 1993), individual and normative data versus normative data alone (Smither, Wohlers, & London, 1995), rater competence (Barclay & Harland, 1995), source credibility (Albright & Levy, 1995), perceptions of organizational support (Facteau, Facteau, Schoel, Russell, & Poteet, 1998), and perceived social costs (Funderburg & Levy, 1997). The combined written and verbal aspects of 360-degree feedback is an understudied area.

Self-regulatory mechanisms in goal setting. In terms of goal-setting and self-regulatory mechanisms, Latham and Locke (1991) continue to assert that the effects of feedback are greatly misunderstood without acknowledging the goal-related processes that mediate the impact of feedback on performance (cf. Becker & Klimoski, 1989; Florin-Thuma & Boudreau, 1987). Put simply, in the absence of goal setting, feedback has no necessary relationship to performance. In the absence of feedback, goal setting is less effective. Locke and Latham (1990) reviewed 33 studies that compared the effects of goals plus feedback versus either goals or feedback alone. The vast majority supported the combined hypothesis (see also Mento, Steel, & Karren, 1987).

Self-regulatory processes are implicit in goal-setting theories; however, most goal-setting experiments have not emphasized them in their research designs (Latham & Locke, 1991). (Goals are typically assigned in these studies in order to manipulate goal level and type adequately.) However, developments in social learning theory suggest the means whereby feedback and goals combine to influence performance (Bandura, 1986, 1991; Bandura & Cervone, 1983). According to social learning theory, there are two cognitive regulatory mechanisms affecting how an individual will respond to performance feedback. The first is a self-evaluative mechanism where feedback helps gauge the extent to which prior behavior meets an internal goal standard. Negative feedback usually indicates a failure to achieve the goal, and if self-efficacy beliefs remain high, individuals should be motivated to set higher goals and increase their effort to achieve them. In contrast, positive feedback indicates that the performance is "on target" with few changes in performance required (Atwater et al., 1995; Podsakoff & Farh, 1989; Reilly, Smither, & Vasilopoulos, 1996).

The second process concerns self-efficacy, or individuals' assessments of their capabilities to undertake one or more courses of action successfully to achieve designated types of performance (Bandura, 1986). Self-efficacy information may come from both direct and mediated experiences (Bandura, 1982) including that of performance feedback (Bandura, 1986, 1991). Research on self-efficacy has shown it to be a significant predictor of performance (Locke, Frederick, Lee, & Bobko, 1984; Wood & Bandura, 1989). Moreover, combining self-evaluation and efficacy influences can predict the level of performance motivation (Bandura & Cervone, 1983).

Feedback sign. Latham and Locke (1991) note that the key to understanding performance improvement and feedback sign depends on the degree of dissatisfaction individuals have with their present performance as well as the confidence they have that their performance can be improved (i.e., self-efficacy remains high). Recent findings offer support for this view (Fedor, 1991; Martocchio & Webster, 1992; Podsakoff & Farh, 1989).

However, Kluger and DeNisi (1996) critique the feedback-standard discrepancy argument on which Latham and Locke's argument rests. In addition, in Kluger and DeNisi's (1996) meta-analysis of feedback research feedback sign did not emerge as a significant moderator of the feedback-performance relationship. Kluger and DeNisi (1996) note that "at present, there is no FI [feedback intervention]-related theory that can predict a priori the effects of all the important moderators that determine how feedback sign affects performance" (p. 276). Those moderators likely include a number of personality, cognitive processing, and task variables that direct attention more or less to the task or oneself with varying effects on the effort expended to alter task performance. Feedback sign is just one of several moderators of the feedback-performance relationship that Kluger and DeNisi (1996) investigate. They conclude generally that feedback affects performance through changes in locus of attention. The more attention is directed away from the self and toward the task, the stronger the benefit of feedback on performance. In addition, feedback's effects are moderated by the nature of the task, although the exact task properties that moderate feedback's effects are still poorly understood.

Finally, recent feedback sign research has also focused on its joint impact with feedback style (Korsgaard, Meglino, & Lester, 1997; Zhou, 1998) as well as the detrimental effect of negative feedback. Feedback that is perceived as destructive versus constructive can serve as the source of ego threat, defensiveness, conflict, and even aggression among organizational participants (Baron, 1988, 1990; Fedor, 1991; Geddes & Baron, 1997; Gioia & Longenecker, 1994; Kluger, Lewinsohn, & Aiello, 1994; Larson, 1989; Skarlicki & Folger, 1997). While "going postal" or other forms of active retaliation are less common re-

sponses to negative feedback, Geddes and Baron's (1997) work suggests a clear need to prepare leaders for potentially aggressive constituent responses. Feedback interventions that are conciliatory and attribution-shifting versus cathartic may counter the effects of destructive criticism (Baron, 1990), a potential antidote to the increasing spillover of violence into the workplace.

Feedback Seeking

The second trend in feedback research involves a decided shift toward recasting workplaces as information environments (Ashford & Cummings, 1983). This recasting allows feedback recipients to become active monitors and information seekers rather than passive information receivers. The two primary strategies of seeking are monitoring and inquiry.

As Table 11.2 suggests, a number of individual and relational influences have been found either to thwart or encourage feedback inquiry. These influences include source of feedback and role clarity (Callister, Kramer, & Turban, 1999), supervisor unavailability (Walsh, Ashford, & Hill, 1985), goal orientation (VandeWalle & Cummings, 1997), self-esteem (Fedor, Rensvold, & Adams, 1992), uncertainty and fear of failure (Ashford, 1986), the presence of an audience or public context (Ashford & Northcraft, 1992; Northcraft & Ashford, 1990; Levy, Albright, Cawley, & Williams, 1995), and source supportiveness and peer reactions in a public context (Williams, Miller, Steelman, & Levy, 1999).

In terms of outcomes, Larson (1989) offered a theoretical account of the ways feedback seeking elicits less negative supervisory feedback than the unsolicited feedback a supervisor might otherwise give. Empirically, it has been shown that seeking positive feedback leads to more negative impressions by observers, while seeking negative feedback enhances impressions and produces more accurate understanding of the evaluations of others (Ashford & Northcraft, 1992; Ashford & Tsui,

1991). Finally, Fedor et al. (1992) found that performance was negatively related to feedback inquiry. This finding is important since this is one of the first studies to establish a link between feedback seeking and performance. However, they argue that different contextual conditions could also support a positive inquiry-performance relationship.

Feedback Message Analysis

A third general trend involves the increasing complexity recognized in the content of feedback messages. Larson, Glynn, Fleenor, and Scontrino (1987) raised concerns about treating the feedback message characteristics identified by Ilgen, Fisher, and Taylor (1979) (sign, timing, specificity, frequency, and sensitivity) as independent constructs. From feedback target and sender perspectives, Geddes (1993) analyzed the dimensionality of written feedback messages and found strong parallels with Larson et al. (1987). In Geddes's study, message valence (positive vs. negative) and message sensitivity were key dimensions. However, Geddes and Linnehan (1998) argue for the treatment of positive and negative feedback as distinct constructs each with its own dimensional structure.

Attributional influences on actual feedback message production have been studied by several scholars. Tjosvold (1985) coded the feedback messages of students role-playing supervisors of a low-performing worker. Messages were coded for supportiveness, assertions of power, and threat. Attributions associated with low effort elicited punitive and strong influence, while low-ability attributions generated attraction and a willingness to work together in the future. However, using a relational control coding scheme also in a laboratory simulation, Dugan (1989) found that a "tell and sell" approach was used to a greater degree when lack of ability was the attributed cause of poor performance and a more negotiative stance when lack of effort was the attributed cause.

Gioia and Sims (1986) studied attributional influences on the coded verbal behavior of both leaders and constituents. They discovered an attributional shift toward leniency as a result of constituents' ability to account for the leaders' behavior plausibly, a finding incorporated into Larson's (1989) arguments about the effects of feedback seeking. Gioia and Sims (1986) also found attribution-seeking "why" questions were asked of poor-performing constituents, while "what do you think" or "how" questions were asked of the more successful ones. Kim and Miller (1990) developed a coding scheme based on a combination of various influence tactic typologies to assess nurse managers' feedback messages. In contrast to Gioia and Sims (1986), attributions did not affect feedback message production. However, the research design appeared to preclude attributional effects.

Although Zorn and Leichty (1991) were not concerned with attributional effects, their study of face support in feedback messages revealed a positive relationship between leaders' use of autonomy and constituent job experience. As the following section reveals, the use of face support in feedback messages is also a concern in control chain studies.

Control Chains

A fourth and smaller trend is the study of poor performance as a chain of events and the impact of performance history on feedback message production. Fairhurst, Green, and Snavely (1984a, 1984b) argued that most research is based on single incidents of poor performance, but lacks veridicality because sequences of poor performance are more common than single incidents. While Gioia and Sims (1986) considered "effective" versus "ineffective" work history as a manipulated variable, Green, Fairhurst, and Snavely (1986) argued that the number, sequence, and relationship of a leader's actions to previous actions within a chain of poor-performance incidents has to be considered. Their study of bank branch managers showed that the use of formal disciplinary action was associated with less face support (positive face and autonomy) and greater escalation in harshness of actions within control chains.

Gavin, Green, and Fairhurst (1995) used a longitudinal lab design conducted in real time to simulate the dynamics of a chain phenomenon under more controlled conditions. They found evidence of both consistency and experimentation with leaders' punitive control strategies and verbal influence tactics over time. Constituents' perceptions of interactional justice were also related to the leaders' use of control tactics. Finally, Morris, Gaveras, Baker, and Coursey (1990) positioned their study of supervisory aligning actions at the problem-solving breakpoint in the model of supervisory control advanced by Fairhurst et al. (1984b). Aligning messages accompany messages of supervisory control, but are distinguished from them in that their goal is to enhance actor understanding of the situation. According to Morris et al. (1990), this could be done through explanation seeking, coorientation or alignment tests, accounts, or faultfinding.

New Directions: Feedback Loops, the Recovery of Meaning, and Message Analysis

I began this section by noting that Cusella's (1987) review of the feedback literature attempted to shift the focus of feedback research to include feedback environments and a focus on conversational practices. To accomplish this, he called for the study of interactional patterns that are embedded within feedback systems, the content and relational dimensions of feedback messages, contextual influences on message production, and the cultural embeddedness of feedback messages. Recent research is beginning to address several of his recommendations. However, the numbers are not large, thus the understudied areas direct us to reinforce Cusella's call for systemic message-based research. In addition, a meaning-centered versus transmission view of communication also appears necessary.

Systemic concerns are addressed most prominently in research that operationalizes feedback loops.

Feedback Loops

There are a few studies that have operationalized feedback loops (Dugan, 1989; Gavin et al., 1995; Gioia & Sims, 1986). Although these studies differ in their approaches, they capture the immediate feedback context by acknowledging the contested nature of constituents' performance. Previous feedback models and research capture several antecedent contextual influences or those influences that are present prior to a feedback encounter. However, they often fail to capture emergent influences including the discourse and the interaction between the discourse and perceptions of context (Haslett, 1987). Attributional shifts, leniency effects (Dugan, 1989; Gioia & Sims, 1986), and departures from progressive discipline policies (Gavin et al., 1995; Green et al., 1986) emerge because of discourse (most often, excuses and justifications) that triggers new attributions and behavioral responses.

Expanding the feedback process to include feedback seeking is important because of the potential to short-circuit the emotional build-up surrounding continued poor performance (Larson, 1989). This is clearly a different kind of feedback loop than when feedback is unsolicited and suggests a whole range of linguistic, emotional, cognitive, relational, and contextual processes that can be usefully contrasted with loops that begin with the leader. With its combined written and verbal components, the recent move to 360-degree feedback is also just beginning to be understood as a feedback mechanism of a different kind.

The Recovery of Meaning

The mitigating role of the immediate context is not just a function of feedback loops. It is the interaction between the discourse and the perceptions of context in the sensemaking and meaning attributed to the unfolding encounter. However, most research tends to employ a transmission model of communication where issues of meaning are rarely made problematic. In his review of the feedback literature, Fedor (1991) argues that perceptions of feedback messages have rarely been studied. Recipient expectations should have a significant impact on feedback perceptions, potentially changing even the sign of feedback. For example, praise may not be favorably evaluated if laudatory comments were anticipated. Given his earlier research on the multiple sources of uncertainty that accompany feedback messages (Fedor, 1990, cited in Fedor, 1991), Fedor's arguments suggest that the sensemaking and interpretive requirements of most feedback encounters are neglected topics.

To understand the shift that must be made from a transmission view to a meaning-centered view of communication in feedback encounters, consider the subject of performance history. In the performance history research of Fairhurst, Green, and colleagues (Fairhurst et al., 1984a, 1984b; Gavin et al., 1995; Green et al., 1986), memory is seen as an internal property of managers, the unreliability of which could lead to distorted self-reports (Nisbett & Wilson, 1977). This effect holds even if leaders are aided by memory prompts such as documentation.

Rather than focusing on the way mental processes like memory construct action, a meaning-centered approach focuses on the way actions construct mental processes (Weick & Roberts, 1993). Under this approach, remembering and forgetting are seen as social constructions. Middleton and Edwards (1990) explain:

The "truth" of the past is always, at least potentially, at issue. It is not to be found unambiguously deposited in some objective social record or archive, nor yet as infinitely malleable in the service of the present. It obtains neither as "fact" nor "invention," but an epistemological enterprise, created in dialectic and argument between those contrary positions. (p. 9)

Based on the social practice of commemoration, the act of leader and constituent remembering together opens up the potential for viewing history as problematic—not simply as an element of the interactional context, but as a ubiquitous, socially negotiated phenomena in its own right. History (like motives) is contestively established in talk each time feedback is given (Middleton & Edwards, 1990). The variation in the control chains reported by Green et al. (1986), which reflected a significant departure from progressive discipline policy, now makes a great deal more sense. It is not objective history that is considered when taking action. It is the intersubjective reconstruction of history within the moment that spurs action.

A potentially rich area of new research would ask about the functioning of conversational remembering as the basis for social action within the control chains. The work of Morris and Coursey (1989), although restricted to leaders' evaluations of poor performers' accounts, provides clues as to the nature of the inferences used to construct versions (real or imagined) of worker performance histories. The evaluations of accounts also draw on culture as a repository of acceptable and unacceptable explanations because, as Morris and Coursey (1989) suggest, accounts are never thrown into an explanatory vacuum. Thus, this approach also addresses Cusella's enjoinder to study the cultural embeddedness of feedback messages, an area that still remains largely unexplored.

Message Analysis

Understanding the idea that feedback messages go beyond simple correction and feedback seeking goes beyond simple inquiry (in addition to monitoring) is also critical. Gioia and Sims's (1986) discovery of attribution-seeking "why" questions, Kim and Miller's (1990) discovery of counseling messages, Morris et al.'s (1990) focus on aligning actions, and Ashford and Tsui's (1991) and Larson's (1989) focus on identity management within feedback inquiry all point to the multifunctionality of feedback messages and the simultaneous management of multiple communication goals. At this early stage of exploring message analysis, variations in the conceptualization of feedback and the resulting coding schemes need to be expected. Echoing Cusella's (1987) idea, greater standardization is necessary to facilitate comparisons across studies. For example, it is not clear that Kim and Miller's (1990) "counseling" and Morris et al.'s (1990) "alignment" are conceptually distinct constructs. Finally, research on message analysis reveals the value of studying actual behavior as it occurs, a clearly positive trend. Unfortunately, it will likely increase an already strong tendency to use student samples in laboratory simulations where experimental conditions guarantee the monitoring of real-time behavior. However, external validity issues continue to loom large (Martocchio & Webster, 1992).

To summarize, this review of the feedback literature strongly supports Cusella's (1987) arguments to supplement psychologically oriented feedback research with a systemic focus on feedback environments, feedback loops, and the conversational practices of feedback. In addition, a meaning-centered view of communication in feedback encounters will add insight into its socially constructed aspects. I turn now to charisma and visionary leadership.

CHARISMATIC AND VISIONARY LEADERSHIP

To understand the importance of charismatic and visionary leadership, one must under-stand the arguments of leadership's nay-sayers who, at various times, have either predicted its demise or weakened its utility as an explanatory construct (Hunt, 1999). For example, leadership purportedly makes little difference to the bottom line (Salancik & Pfeffer, 1977). There are substitutes that render leadership less necessary (Kerr & Jermier, 1978). Its impact gets overestimated, especially when cause-effect relationships are difficult to establish (Meindl et al., 1985). It puts too little emphasis on situational causes of behavior (Davis-Blake & Pfeffer, 1989). Finally, leaders may not affect culture in unique ways (Frost, Moore, Louis, Lundberg, & Martin, 1991; Martin, 1992). The most frequent response to these arguments is that leadership's true impact lies not in tangible outcomes, but in human sentiment and understanding: meaning, affect, belief, and commitment (Bennis & Nanus, 1985; Pondy, 1978; Pfeffer, 1981).

One of the cornerstones of charismatic and visionary leadership is symbolic leadership. Distinct from managership, symbolic leadership connotes (1) possession of a vision; (2) the ability to articulate it; and (3) a strategic use of slogans, symbols, rituals, ceremonies, and stories of success or heroism that amplify desirable values and promote identification with the organization (Bennis & Nanus, 1985; Conger, 1989, 1991; Gardner & Avolio, 1998; Rost, 1991; Shamir, House, & Arthur, 1993). Symbolic leaders' primary conversational goals are sensemaking and linking the conversation to organizational goal achievement (Barge, Downs, & Johnson, 1989).

Several recent reviews and critiques of this literature have appeared (Conger & Hunt, 1999; House & Aditya, 1997; Hunt & Conger, 1999; Jermier, 1993; Lowe, Kroeck, Sivasubramaniam, 1996).[10] This review focuses only on those aspects most relevant to communication. However, the individual-system dualism must first be explored because it occupies a central role in the literature on charisma and vision.

The Individual-System Dualism

One of the strongest oppositions in the charisma literature is that between the individual and the system. This opposition first surfaced in a nonantagonistic pull away from the individual toward the relational, only to be followed by an antagonistic reframing of the individual and the relational as too micro in favor of meso and macro social system concerns. All of this movement can be traced to the ambiguity in Weber's theory of charisma.

Swayed by Weber's view that charismatic leaders were extraordinary, prophetic, and heroic, leadership scholars quickly psychologized charisma as they wrote about it (Calás, 1993). House's (1977) theory of charismatic leadership and Bass's (1985) theory of transformational leadership both have decided individualistic leanings. House's work was billed as "personal celebrity charisma" because of his focus on leaders' personality characteristics (Graham, 1991). Bass's theory of transformational leadership, based on the writing of Burns (1978) sans a moral component, focused on three key leader activities: charisma that included vision, intellectual stimulation, and individualized consideration. These were distinct from more transactional (contract-based) leader activities such as contingent reward and management-by-exception. However, the most blatant of the individualist charisma approaches is in the popular business press, which lionizes a familiar choir of CEOs and entrepreneurs and minimizes alternative explanations for firm success (Meindl et al., 1985).

But Weber was also ambiguous and somewhat contradictory about the relative emphasis of the individual over the relational. While writing about the extraordinary qualities of charismatic leaders, he also repeatedly stressed that constituents' collective beliefs in the wisdom and knowledge of the charismatic was the crucial test of charisma (Dow, 1969). Weber's relational emphasis led to the "social psychologizing" of the business charisma model. House extended his early work to focus on constituent characteristics and the means by which charismatic leaders are able to strike a chord in constituents to act in accordance with the mission (House & Howell, 1992; House, Spangler, & Woycke, 1991; Klein & House, 1995; Shamir et al., 1993). Bass's theory of transformational leadership adopted a relational focus most explicitly with its individualized consideration component (emphasizing meeting the personal needs of constituents), but also a measurement emphasis on constituent attributions of charisma.

House, Bass, Conger, and their colleagues accounted for most of the individual and relational research on business charisma focusing on personality correlates (House et al., 1991), reported behavioral factors and associated judgments of charisma (Bass, 1985; Bradford & Cohen, 1984; Conger, 1989; Conger & Kanungo, 1988), perceived differences between charismatic and noncharismatic leaders (Bass, 1985; Ehrlich, Meindl, & Viellieu, 1990; House, 1977; Howell & Frost, 1989; Yammarino & Bass, 1990; Yammarino, Spangler, & Bass, 1993), and the outcomes of charismatic leadership in both constituents and leaders (Avolio, Waldman, & Einstein, 1988; Bass, 1985; Hater & Bass, 1988; House et al., 1991; Howell & Frost, 1989; Yammarino & Bass, 1990; Howell & Higgins, 1990a, 1990b; Yammarino et al., 1993).

In 1993, a special issue of *Leadership Quarterly* was premised on an antagonistic reframing of individual and relational charisma research as too micro (Jermier, 1993). Many contributors to that volume argued that Weber's sociological leanings needed to be reclaimed because he situated charisma in a sociohistorical context (Weber, 1925/1968; see also Beyer, 1999). Among Weber's arguments were the following:

1. Difficult times were fertile grounds for the emergence of charisma.
2. Charismatic authority was a potential revolutionary force and a bridge between traditional and rational-legal forms of authority.

3. Charismatic authority was naturally unstable, an instability that could produce one of two outcomes for charismatic social movements and the development of charisma (Weber, 1925/1968). Charisma either dies out in the departure of the leader from the social scene or becomes institutionalized and incorporated into the routines of everyday life.

A number of contributors to this issue argued for reclaiming the meso and macro features of charisma through a renewed focus on its routinization, the instability and potential loss of charisma, the context surrounding the emergence of charisma, and the way charisma resides not in persons, but in the group processes of the community (e.g., Bryman, 1993; Calás, 1993; Conger, 1993; DiTomaso, 1993).

More recently, House, Bass, and Conger have extended their respective models beyond the individual and dyad to group and organizational levels (Avolio & Bass, 1995; Conger & Kanungo, 1998; Klein & House, 1995). There has also been more attention to context (Conger, 1999; House & Aditya, 1997; Hunt, Boal, & Dodge, 1999; Pawar & Eastman, 1997; Shamir & Howell, 1999; Shea & Howell, 1999). Finally, using a dramaturgical and interactive perspective, Gardner and Avolio (1998) examine the roles that context, actor (leader) and audience (constituents) play in jointly constructing a "charismatic relationship." The 1993 debate in *Leadership Quarterly* notwithstanding, this most recent work suggests movement away from the individual toward the system although emphasis on the dyadic relationship appears dominant.

Charisma, Vision, and Communication

Communication and language have always been a concern of the charisma and vision literature (Awamleh & Gardner, 1999; Bass, 1988; Conger, 1991; Gardner & Avolio, 1998;

Howell & Frost, 1989; Kuhnert & Lewis, 1987; Riggio, 1987; Shamir et al., 1993; Zorn, 1991). As Table 11.3 reveals, studies generally fall into three categories. When reporting research testing Bass's (1985) model, the word *transformational* will be used instead of charisma to be consistent with his work.

Charismatic Communication

The first category contains case studies of charismatic leaders (e.g., Conger, 1989, 1991; Seeger, 1994; Shamir et al., 1994; Trice & Beyer, 1986; Wendt & Fairhurst, 1994). This body of work, including much that is found in the popular press, is more suggestive than definitive in its approach to charismatic communication in business settings. It focuses heavily on charismatic political leaders, their style and vision in public communication settings, and the largely unacknowledged role that the media play in enhancing a charismatic persona. Work by Trice and Beyer (1986), Beyer and Browning (1999), and Fairhurst, Cooren, and Cahill (2000) are notable exceptions.

The second category consists of more traditional social scientific research on charismatic communication focusing on influence tactics and the outcomes associated with the delivery aspects of a charismatic's style. This research emphasizes the individual, cognitive outcomes, and a transmission view of communication. For example, in two studies of informal emergent leaders championing technological innovations, Howell and Higgins (1990a, 1990b) found that in comparison to champions, nonchampions displayed many of the qualities of charismatic leadership. Using Kipnis and Schmidt's (1982) typology, champions initiated more influence attempts; used a greater variety of influence strategies; and relied on coalition, reason, higher authority, and assertiveness more than nonchampions.

Using Yukl and Tracey's (1992) scheme, Tepper (1993) found that in routine influence attempts transactional leaders reportedly used more exchange and pressure tactics over

TABLE 11.3   Charisma and Vision-Based Communication Research

Case studies of charismatic leaders	Beyer & Browning, 1999; Conger, 1989, 1991; Fairhurst, Cooren, & Cahill, 2000; Shamir, Arthur, & House, 1994; Trice & Beyer, 1986; Wendt & Fairhurst, 1994
Behavioral studies of charismatic leaders	
Delivery style	Awamleh & Gardner, 1999; Avolio, Howell, & Sosik, 1999; Holladay & Coombs, 1993, 1994; Howell & Frost, 1989; Kirkpatrick & Locke, 1996
Influence strategies	Howell & Higgins, 1990a, 1990b; Tepper, 1993; Zorn, 1991
Visionary leadership	
Cultural consequences of a vision	Martin, 1992; Nadler, 1988; Pettigrew, 1979; Siehl, 1985; Siehl & Martin, 1984; Swanson & Ramiller, 1999; Tichy & DeVanna, 1986
Vision articulation	Conger & Kanungo, 1998; Den Hartog & Verburg, 1997; Fiol, Harris, & House, 1999; Gardner & Avolio, 1998; Shamir et al., 1994; Shamir, House, & Arthur, 1993
Vision content	Baum, Locke, & Kirkpatrick, 1998; Bennis & Nanus, 1985; Connell & Galasinski, 1996; Kotter, 1990; Larwood, Falbe, Kriger, & Miesing, 1995; Larwood, Kriger, & Falbe, 1993; Rogers & Swales, 1990; Swales & Rogers, 1995; Westley & Mintzberg, 1989
Vision implementation/routinization	Beyer & Browning, 1999; Fairhurst, 1993b; Fairhurst, Jordan, & Neuwirth, 1997; Trice & Beyer, 1986; Weierter, 1997

transformational leaders, who used more legitimating tactics. Tepper also found that transformational leaders engendered higher levels of identification and internalization in constituents than did transactional leaders. Zorn's (1991) research suggests that cognitive complexity and person-centered message production may explain the success of transformational leaders.

Cognitive outcomes associated with the delivery aspects of a charismatic's style such as eye contact, fluid rate, gestures, facial expressiveness, energy, eloquence, and voice tone variety (Bass, 1988; Conger & Kanungo, 1987; Holladay & Coombs, 1993; Howell & Frost, 1989) have also been studied. Howell and Frost (1989) conducted a laboratory experiment in which leaders were cast as either charismatic, considerate, or structuring. In the charismatic condition, the leader's use of the delivery features to communicate a vision yielded higher task performance, greater task satisfaction, and lower role conflict than did leaders in the other two conditions.

Because content (in the form of a vision) and delivery were confounded in this study, Holladay and Coombs (1993) isolated the effects of delivery on the communication of an organizational vision. Using the same delivery aspects described above, subjects in the "strong" delivery condition made stronger leader attributions of charisma than subjects in the "weak" delivery condition. Unexpectedly, the dramatic and animated communicator style constructs were not among the best predictors of charisma. However, the constructs of friendly, attentive, dominant, and open were. Avolio, Howell, and Sosik's (1999) research on transformational leaders suggests the addition of humor to that list.

Two studies examined the differential effects of vision content and delivery on perceptions of charisma. Both Holladay and Coombs (1994) and Awamleh and Gardner (1999) found that delivery contributes more strongly to perceptions of charisma than vision content. However, Kirkpatrick and Locke (1996) found just the opposite. Vision content was more strongly related to perceptions of charisma than stylistic features.

Visionary Leadership

Very closely related to charisma, the third category of communication studies falls under the rubric of visionary leadership. The study of vision processes is an emerging area of research with a history in studies that focused on the consequences of senior leaders' visions on corporate cultures. Visions establish, maintain, or help cultures survive environmental fluctuations (Martin, 1992; Morgan, 1986; Nadler, 1988; Pettigrew, 1979; Schein, 1992; Siehl, 1985; Tichy & DeVanna, 1986; Trice & Beyer, 1991). They may also be the source of conflict and poor performance when discrepancies arise between the vision and some aspect of the environment (e.g., Beyer, 1999; Smircich, 1983; Smircich & Morgan, 1982).

Vision is central to the charisma literature. However, while charisma implies having a vision (Conger, 1999), the reverse is not necessarily true. Vision studies draw on the charisma and culture literatures quite often, but many neither explore the cultural consequences of a vision nor measure attributions of charisma. Instead, the focus is on actual vision content or its process aspects including development, articulation, and implementation (Larwood, Falbe, Kriger, & Miesing, 1995). For example, Swanson and Ramiller (1997) use the concept of an "organizing vision" to explain innovation surrounding new technologies. Such visions are thought to facilitate three important aspects of the information systems innovation process: interpretation, legitimation, and mobilization.

While vision is broadly defined as an envisioned future, this literature makes apparent several definitional issues related to visions (Bryman, 1992; Larwood et al., 1995; Larwood, Kriger, & Falbe, 1993). Of particular concern is a blurring of the lines between vision, mission, values, and the implementing programs. While conceptually distinct, they are often collectively referred to as "governing ideas" (Senge, 1990), a "corporate philosophy" (Ledford, Wendenhof, & Strahley, 1995), a "well-conceived vision" (Collins & Porras, 1996), or a "mission statement" (Rogers & Swales, 1990; Swales & Rogers, 1995). Despite confusing and unstable language, distinctions are typically drawn between a future direction (vision), a purpose (mission), a set of principles (values), and the initiatives intended to realize them (programs). However, a well-conceived future is almost always premised on a clear purpose and set of principles, and therein may lie the definitional confusion if writers fail to make this explicit. With these definitional caveats in mind, the reviewed literature focuses primarily on vision content and two aspects of vision process, articulation and implementation/routinization.

Vision content. Several studies on vision content may be found in case studies in the popular press (Bennis & Nanus, 1985; Doz & Prahalad, 1987; Conger, 1989; Fairhurst & Sarr, 1996; Kotter, 1990; Nanus, 1992; Nussbaum, Moskowitz, & Beam, 1985). However, empirical examples of vision content research are also beginning to surface. For example, Larwood et al. (1995; Larwood et al., 1993) studied a national sample of chief executives and business school deans to see how they defined their visions. Chief executives focused either on formulation, communication and implementation, or innovative realism. The group that was high on communication perceived more rapid changes in their organization, felt senior executives strongly accepted their vision, exercised a high degree of control over the business, and perceived that their visions extended farther into the future than did the other two groups. The analysis of business school deans was roughly comparable to that of the chief executives. In a longitudinal study, Baum, Locke, and Kirkpatrick (1998) examined the impact of vision content, vision attributes, and vision communication on venture growth in entrepreneurial firms. They found that both vision content (in the form of growth imagery) and vision attributes (such as quality or clarity) affected venture growth directly, but the indirect impact of these variables through vision communication was greater.

In contrast to the empirical methods of the previous studies, three studies used critical discourse analysis to study corporate philosophy statements (Connell & Galasinski, 1996; Rogers & Swales, 1990; Swales & Rogers, 1995). These studies examined recurring themes and tensions, differences in communicative purpose, authorial voice, and the rhetorical devices used to promote identification and affiliation (e.g., the assumed "we"). Corporate philosophy statements are significant for leadership communication study because their content predisposes leaders and constituents to communicate the vision/mission in particular ways. For example, work in the area of "soft missions" suggests that loosely formulated missions allow more flexibility in interpretation at local levels to capitalize on the opportunities of a turbulent environment (Bartlett & Ghoshal, 1994; Fairhurst, 1996).

Vision articulation. In vision articulation, Conger and Kanungo (1998) argue that the verbal aspects of a vision must focus on the negative aspects of the status quo and the positive aspects of the future path. Shamir et al. (1993) hold that charismatic leaders must target the self-concept of constituents in their communication. Leaders can promote frame breaking, frame alignment, and sensemaking for constituents by making references to (1) values and moral justifications, (2) the collective and its identity, (3) history, (4) constituents' positive worth and efficacy as individuals and a collective, (5) high expectations from collectives, and (6) distal over proximal goals. A rhetorical analysis of Jesse Jackson's 1988 speech to the Democratic convention supported several of their arguments (Shamir et al., 1994). Also drawing from Shamir et al. (1993), Fiol, Harris, and House (1999) conducted a semiotic analysis of 42 speeches from all 20th-century presidents. They examined the differential use of three communication techniques (negation, abstraction, and inclusion) over the time span of the presidencies. Their findings showed that all three techniques peaked during the middle phase of the presidents' tenure. They also found support for the charismatic leaders' frequent use of the word *not* as an unfreezing technique.

The speeches of international business leaders were analyzed by Den Hartog and Verburg (1997) for rhetorical content dealing with international business and rhetorical devices such as contrast, lists, puzzle-solution, position taking, pursuit, and alliteration. Finally, unlike previous research that focused heavily on the charismatic leader, Gardner and Avolio's (1998) interactive and dramaturgical model of charisma focuses on impression management by charismatic leaders thought to be desirable by constituents. These impression management behaviors are grouped into four categories (framing, scripting, staging, and performing), which purportedly shape the content of the articulated vision.

Vision implementation/routinization. Fairhurst (1993a) used discourse analysis to study vision implementation in routine leadership communication. She found five framing devices (i.e., consistent themes in framing) in the routine work conversations of an organization charged with implementing Deming's total quality management (TQM) to achieve their vision. Out of the five framing devices (jargon use, positive spin, agenda setting, experienced predicaments, and possible futures), two stood out. Experienced predicaments, originating out of a perceived mismatch between the vision (or its programs) and local conditions, exposed the choice points around what and what not to adopt (Hosking & Morley, 1988). Possible futures for the vision were realized when steps were taken to resolve the predicament. Fairhurst,

Jordan, and Neuwirth (1997) created a "management of meaning" scale based on these framing devices. They found that organizational role and organizational commitment best predicted whether individuals managed the meaning of a company mission statement.

Trice and Beyer (1986) studied the charismatic leaders of two social movement organizations. They observed that the routinization of the leader's vision was critical to the success of that organization. Echoing many of their findings, Beyer and Browning (1999) found five elements marked the routinization of a charismatic leader in the semiconductor industry. These included an administration structure, the transference of charisma to constituents through cultural forms, incorporation of the charismatic mission into organizational traditions, the selection of a successor who resembles the charismatic, and continuity of the charismatic mission and continued coherence of members around it.

In contrast to the second group of studies on influence tactics and outcomes associated with the delivery aspects of a charismatic leader's style, the emerging research on visionary leadership is more balanced in its emphasis on communicative practices and cognitive outcomes as well as a transmission and a meaning-centered view of communication.

New Directions: Conversational Practices, the Recovery of Meaning, and Wider Systems Concerns

The emerging vision communication research notwithstanding, an analysis of the charisma literature directs us to place additional emphasis on communicative practices, the recovery of meaning, and wider systems concerns. This focus should fill a great need to understand the dynamic nature of charisma and visionary leadership.

Conversational Practices

Beyer (1999) recently noted how much the extant research on charisma is tied to the traits and behaviors of leaders as measured by constituent self-reports. Indeed, in early charisma research much was made about "stripping the aura of mysticism" from charisma to deal with it only as a set of behaviors (Conger & Kanungo, 1987, p. 639, 1993). Yet we still know comparatively little about specific communication behaviors because of a propensity in the literature to measure metabehaviors and outcomes over behaviors. Riley (1988) described metabehaviors not as "descriptions of what these individuals actually do but categories and patterns of action that include evaluations of successful outcomes" (p. 81). Riley made this point of Sashkin and Fulmer's (1988) measure, but the same can be said of Conger and Kanungo's (1993) more popular behavioral attribute measure of charisma. Conger and Kanungo's scale includes items such as "exciting public speaker," "skillful performer when presenting to a group," "inspirational," and "able to motivate by articulating effectively the importance of what organizational members are doing." The specific behaviors or behavioral combinations under public speaking and inspirational deliveries are too numerous even to mention.

The charisma scale of Bass's (1985; Avolio & Bass, 1988) Multifacet Leadership Questionnaire (MLQ) is perhaps the most widely used measure of charisma. Lowe et al. (1996) report on some 75 studies using this scale. While the scale appears capable of measuring variance in charisma, it too does not measure specific charismatic leader behaviors (House & Aditya, 1997). Metabehaviors such as "provides a vision of what lies ahead" and "shows determination in pursuit of goals" and outcomes such as "makes others feel good," "generates respect," "instills confidence," and "transmits a sense of mission" typify this scale.

Although others would argue otherwise (Brown & Lord, 1999; Wofford, 1999), the variable analytic tradition may not be particularly well suited to the study of charisma and vision. Riley (1988) and other researchers (Westley & Mintzberg, 1989) offer a possible explanation:

The notions of charisma, vision, and culture all share a sense of the aesthetic—the art form of leadership (another Bennis term). This requires some forms of analysis that are sensitive to style, to the creation of meaning, and to the dramatic edge of leadership. Symbols like "leader" and "charismatic" have power in and of themselves because of their ability to evoke expressive and nonrational images and feelings. To use these terms as mere categories of behaviors runs the risk of stripping them of this power and moving them to the level of the mundane—plain-label symbols. (Riley, 1988, p. 82)

Riley's point is well taken. To anyone seeing a painting of Van Gogh, the labels "bold color" and "heavy brush stroke" do not even begin to capture the essence of his art. So, too, capturing the essence of charisma requires some attention to aesthetics, which variable analytic studies find difficult to capture. Apparently, Shamir et al. (1994) drew the same conclusion as they chose a rhetorical analysis for initial support of their theory.

The Recovery of Meaning

To see the shift toward discursive practices and a meaning-centered approach fully realized, as well as to continue to explore the individual-system tensions in charisma, organizational scholars could turn to the study of rhetoric (Conger, 1991). Symbolic leadership has an unacknowledged rich history in the study of rhetoric dating back to Vico in the 18th century; Nietzsche in the late 19th century; and Richards, Burke, Perelman, and Foucault, to name a few, in the 20th century. All of these writers focus on the relationship between discourse and knowledge, communication and its effects, language and experience (Bizzell & Herzberg, 1990). Moreover, in speech communication the rhetorical studies of leadership at Purdue in the 1960s and interpersonal theories such as coordinated management of meaning (Cronen, Pearce, & Harris, 1982) also supply a rich heritage for leadership as symbolic management.

Using a theatrical model by Brook (1968), Westley and Mintzberg (1989) propose a very useful framework for the rhetorical study of charisma and vision. They conceive of leadership as a drama with the interaction of three concepts: repetition, representation, and assistance. In Westley and Mintzberg's interpretation of Brook's "repetition" concept, visionaries "practice" for the moment of a vision through the development of their craft just as actors practice for a performance (Mintzberg, 1987). In representation, the craft is turned into art with a variety of rhetorical devices. Finally, the audience must play a very active role in the performance, hence, "vision comes alive only when it is shared" (Westley & Mintzberg, 1989, p. 21).

Westley and Mintzberg go on to identify different visionary styles: creators, proselytizers, idealists, bricoleurs, and diviners. Visionaries' styles are distinguished on the basis of the external context, the vision's mental origin and evolution, and its strategic content, which the authors explain in terms of core and circumference. A vision's core defines its central theme. For example, creators focus on products, proselytizers on markets, idealists on ideals, bricoleurs on organizations, and diviners on services. A vision's circumference is composed of its symbolic aspects such as its rhetorical and metaphorical devices. A vision's contribution can be at the core, the circumference, or both.

With a few enhancements, Westley and Mintzberg's (1989) model can make an even greater contribution to the study of vision and charisma. For example, although they interpret repetition as the development of a craft to arrive at a vision, repetition may also be seen from the perspective of leaders' communicating a vision. For example, charismatic leaders are widely regarded as verbally skilled and often eloquent. However, Bass (1985) appeared in the minority in stating that these verbal skills can be learned and earned. Other scholars see charisma as personality and/or circumstance driven.

What is not well recognized is that the eloquence of charismatic or visionary leaders may be the result of priming themselves for spontaneity (Fairhurst & Sarr, 1996). Priming is a process through which concepts or information become activated or made readily accessible for recall (Bargh, 1989; Wyer & Srull, 1980, 1986). Priming typically centers on unobtrusive exposure to a stimulus that is later recalled in a spontaneous fashion. However, intentional exposure such as by leaders to their visions before and/or during repeated communication with constituents may enable them to be spontaneous, yet give very strategic performances with respect to the vision. For example, Shamir et al. (1994) noted columnist William Safire's comment about Jesse Jackson's 1988 speech to the Democratic National Convention. It suggests that priming played a prominent role in Jackson's success:

> This was a speech whose main elements have been shaped and honed on the road; we were listening to Jesse's Greatest Hits, the passages and metaphors that proved effective for months and years. . . . The speech was not written but grown (William Safire, *New York Times,* July 21, 1988). (p. 37)

Priming can occur through imagining the vision's relevance in the recurring contexts in which leaders and constituents find themselves, reviewing of the vision's core concepts, and/or reviewing its imagery and other symbolic aspects—all of which contribute to a script for spontaneous communication at a later time. In addition, the more communication with followers, the more the vision is permanently primed (Fiske & Taylor, 1991). Efficient and effective articulation of a vision to constituents occurs as long as overscripting is avoided so that leaders remain vigilant to distinctions that require the mindful adaptation of a message to a particular audience (Fairhurst & Sarr, 1996). By priming for spontaneity, Westley and Mintzberg's notion of "repetition" has a broader application than their original interpretation.

Westley and Mintzberg's representational concepts of core and circumference resemble Kenneth Burke's (1954, 1957, 1962; Weaver, 1953) work on ultimate terms, which describes in somewhat greater detail the nature of the symbols that leaders may employ in an engaging vision (Fairhurst & Sarr, 1996). According to Burke, an ultimate term is little more than an extreme good or bad form of a concept or theme out of which another more derivative set of terms may coincide. For example, a "god" term introduces a concept and infuses it with maximum value. There is a clear idea of what is good, what should be pursued, and why sacrifice in a material sense is required. A "devil" term does just the opposite. The adoption of ultimate terms like god terms can transcend disagreement among people with opposite views by identifying values or principles that nearly all people can agree upon. This was what Burke termed *transcendence.*

Ultimate terms correspond to the core of the vision, while the circumference corresponds to their frequency of use, strength, and clarity of the imagery, and the manner in which they may be linked with other key terms. As research is beginning to suggest, frequency, imagery, opposition, and association should thus provide some very specific clues as to the way charismatic and visionary leaders manage meaning from a vision (Den Hartog & Verburg, 1997; Fiol et al., 1999). Fairhurst and Sarr (1996) argue that this was the case with Deming's (1982) vision of TQM, although not all visions will be the sweeping, transformative philosophies of Deming's TQM. Visions may have fewer ultimate terms. They may also be modest and evolutionary rather than revolutionary, yet transformative because of the chord they strike in constituents and their ability to affect incremental change (Jermier, 1993).

Audience "assistance," the third part of the Westley and Mintzberg theatrical model, raises questions about the way visions get shared. Here is where the literature on charisma and vision parts company. Charisma researchers are much more likely to assume a monologic stance where constituents are believed to assent to the meanings of the charismatic (Conger, 1999). For example,

Wasielewski (1985) argues that the genesis of charisma lies in emotional interaction in which the leader articulates the feelings of constituents in an emotionally charged situation, challenges their appropriateness, and then reframes constituents' interpretations of their world and their emotional responses. The distinguishing features of charismatic leaders rest with the leaders' exceptional role-taking ability and emotional sincerity.

Shamir et al. (1993) suggest that constituents play a role in the emergence of charisma, but it appears to be one of heightening or lessening the charismatic impact based on whether the leader appeals to existing values and social identities. This view is supported by the analysis of speeches by charismatic leaders (Fiol et al., 1999; Shamir et al., 1994). Similarly, Gardner and Avolio (1998) and Weierter (1997) argue that it is the orientation of constituents that establishes the type of charismatic relationship (which, in turn, establishes the role of the charismatic message and personal charisma associated with the leader). It is a view of charisma that is more relational, yet the leader is still the primary symbolizing agent. On the monologic stance of much of the charisma literature, Jermier (1993) stated that

> charisma is not a one way influence process, as often imagined. It is a reciprocal relationship that is reproduced through interactions in which each participant exercises power. Of course, the charismatic relationship is not constituted by an equal balance of power among participants. Especially with mature, well-developed charismatic relationships, asymmetrical power can emerge and rapidly turn into tyranny (Couch, 1989). (p. 222)

In contrast to the monologic stance of charisma research, the organizational vision literature is much more likely to assume a dialogic focus. For example, Westley and Mintzberg (1989) argued against a one-way, hypodermic needle model of the vision communication process. They wrote, "Stripped to its essence, this model takes on a mechanical

quality which surely robs the process of much of its evocative appeal" (p. 18). As argued at the start of the chapter, Senge (1990) suggests that the art of visionary leadership resides in shared visions constructed from personal visions and the creative tensions that arise from a lofty vision as it collides with local realities.

The more personal visions are encouraged in organizations, the more contested is the big picture. Recall contestation is not about something that already exists, but "what might be, what could be the case, or what something should be like" (Shotter, 1993, p. 154). "Our situation here and now," "our concept of purpose," and "our concept of the future" are all part of the *negotiated* politics of everyday life that may affect the ongoing frame alignment of visionary leaders as much as their constituents. Especially in more democratic and participative organizations, the role of the charismatic or visionary leader may be to initiate or trigger, rather than orchestrate, the symbolic management of the vision. This is not a subtle difference, but has major implications for vision content and process including implementation and routinization.

Wider Systems Concerns

Beyer (1999) uses the term *charisma* rather than *charismatic leadership* so as to define charisma as a social process and emergent social structure that encompasses more than what leaders do. Similarly, the concept of audience also suggests that we may go beyond immediate constituent reactions to the ripple of interactions that constituents carry forth to implement and routinize the vision. Although discussions of the routinization of charisma are instructive in a broad sense (Bryman, 1992; Trice & Beyer, 1986), scholars know very little about vertical chains of communication in organizations (McPhee, 1988). This is particularly important for the study of charismatic leaders who may be socially distant versus close in the organizational hierarchy (Yagil, 1998). Even though these chains play an acknowledged role in endorsing or discounting new initiatives, there is much to learn about the way dyads use information relayed from higher-ups to affect innovation and routine production. Fairhurst's (1993a) study of framing devices in vision implementation suggests there are innumerable sites of audience assistance (i.e., opportunities for local usage of the vision and credible endorsements) and why the death knell sounds gradually when a vision is rejected. Much can be learned about vision implementation and routinization from analysis of the discourse and its silences within these chains. The vision's negotiated meanings will feed into and be fed by a cultural repository of vision-based understandings.

In summary, the following arguments prevail. First, in characterizing communication research on charisma, the focus until recently has been on cognitive outcomes and a transmission view of communication. Research on the understudied areas directs us to the recovery of meaning and different individual-system foci. Second, a theatrical model of visionary leadership by Westley and Mintzberg (1989), along with some enhancements, is a way to effect this change. Among the enhancements are priming for spontaneity, clarifying the symbolic aspects of the vision, and the role of vertical dyads in vision implementation and routinization. In the next section, I turn to leader-member exchange, which began with a leader-centered focus that quickly assumed a relational orientation.

LEADER-MEMBER EXCHANGE

In the LMX model, leaders exchange their personal and positional resources for a member's performance (Graen & Scandura, 1987). The LMX model is based on Jacobs's (1971) distinction between leadership and authority. In this model, effective leadership is defined in terms of incremental influence, which is interpersonal influence earned beyond that which accompanies one's formal

position (Graen & Uhl-Bien, 1991; Katz & Kahn, 1978). In high-quality relationships (high LMXs) leader and member exert high levels of incremental influence. Mature "leadership" relationships develop because there is mutual trust, internalization of common goals, extra-contractual behavior and the exchange of social resources, support, and mutual influence. These relationships are also considered transformational in Bass's (1985) sense because members move beyond self-interests (Gerstner & Day, 1997; Graen & Uhl-Bien, 1995).

At the other extreme is "managership" where incremental influence is lacking and little more than the terms of the formal employment contract are fulfilled (Uhl-Bien & Graen, 1992). These low-quality relationships (low LMXs) are characterized by the use of formal authority, contractual behavior exchange, role-bound relations, low trust and support, and economic rewards.

Since its inception more than two decades ago, the research on LMX theory has been marked by four stages summarized in Table 11.4 (Graen & Uhl-Bien, 1995). However, Table 11.4 presents only those studies with an explicit communication focus. Gerstner and Day (1997), Graen and Uhl-Bien (1995), Liden, Sparrowe, and Wayne (1997), and Schriesheim, Castro, and Cogliser (1999) present more exhaustive reviews. As will become apparent, the interplay around the individual-system dualism defines the four stages.

LMX Stages and the Individual-System Dualism

In Stage 1, initial LMX research was known as vertical dyad linkage (VDL). VDL successfully refuted leaders' use of an average leadership style finding instead that leaders differentiate among members. The term *in-group* was commonly used to describe high-quality exchanges, and *out-group* described low-quality exchanges. VDL research assumed that differentiated relationships emerged because a leader's time and re-

TABLE 11.4 Stages of Leader-Member Exchange Research

Stage 1: Vertical dyad linkage
    Differentiated dyads vs. average leadership style   Cashman, Dansereau, Graen, & Haga, 1975; Graen & Cashman, 1975

Stage 2: Leader-member exchange (LMX)
    Influences on LMX
        Affect   Dockery & Steiner, 1990; Liden, Wayne, & Stilwell, 1993; Wayne & Ferris, 1990

        Gender   Duchon, Green, & Taber, 1986; Fairhurst, 1993a; Wayne, Liden, & Sparrowe, 1994

        High LMX member characteristics   Graen, 1989; Graen, Scandura, & Graen, 1986

        Performance   Deluga & Perry, 1991; Liden et al., 1993; Wayne & Ferris, 1990

        Similarity   Bauer & Green, 1996; Liden et al., 1993

    LMX communication and relationship maintenance
        Communication frequency   Baker & Ganster, 1985; Schiemann & Graen, 1984

        Control patterns in routine interaction   Borchgrevink & Donohue, 1991; Fairhurst, Rogers, & Sarr, 1987

        Coworker communication   Kramer, 1995; Sias, 1996; Sias & Jablin, 1995

        Impression management   Wayne & Ferris, 1990; Wayne & Green, 1993

        Influence   Deluga & Perry, 1991; Dockery & Steiner, 1990; Krone, 1991; Liden & Mitchell, 1989; Maslyn, Farmer, & Fedor, 1996; Wayne & Ferris, 1990

        Ingratiation   Deluga & Perry, 1994; Wayne et al., 1994

        Relationship maintenance   Lee & Jablin, 1995; Waldron, 1991; Waldron, Hunt, & Dsliva, 1993

        Social construction of LMX   Fairhurst, 1993a; Fairhurst & Chandler, 1989; Sias, 1996

        Cross-cultural LMXs   Graen & Wakabayashi, 1994; Graen, Wakabayashi, Graen, & Graen, 1990; Hui & Graen, 1997; Wakabayashi & Graen, 1984

    Outcomes of LMX
        Career progress   Graen & Wakabayashi, 1994

sources were limited, and social exchanges were needed to accomplish the unstructured tasks of the work unit. In the history of LMX research, Stage 1 was the only one to focus exclusively on leaders. However, significant variance in member responses to queries about leaders during this stage led to casting the dyad as the unit of analysis in subsequent stages (Graen & Uhl-Bien, 1995).

In Stage 2, the nomenclature changed from vertical dyad linkage to leader-member exchange and the abandonment of references to

Citizenship	Wayne & Green, 1993
Commitment	Duchon et al., 1986; Schriesheim, Neider, Scandura, & Tepper, 1992
Cooperative communication	Lee, 1997
Decision influence	Duchon et al., 1986; Scandura, Graen, & Novak, 1986; Schriesheim et al., 1992
Empowerment	Keller & Dansereau, 1995; Sparrowe, 1994
Equity/fairness	Scandura, 1995
Job enrichment	Duchon et al., 1986
Job problems	Keller & Dansereau, 1995
Performance	Graen et al., 1986; Keller & Dansereau, 1995; Schriesheim et al., 1992
Satisfaction	Duchon et al., 1986; Schriesheim et al., 1992; Seers, 1989; Sparrowe, 1994
Support	Keller & Dansereau, 1995
Teamwork	Seers, 1989; Uhl-Bien & Graen, 1992, 1993
Turnover	Kramer, 1995
Measurement	Barge & Schleuter, 1991; Borchgrevink & Boster, 1994; Dienesch & Liden, 1986; Liden & Maslyn, 1998; Schriesheim et al., 1992
Stage 3: Stages of LMX growth	
High LMX training for all members	Graen, Novak, & Sommerkamp, 1982; Graen et al., 1986; Scandura & Graen, 1984
Leadership making model	Graen & Uhl-Bien, 1991, 1995; Uhl-Bien & Graen, 1993
Relationship development	Bauer & Green, 1996; Boyd & Taylor, 1998; Dienesch & Liden, 1986; Liden et al., 1993; Liden, Sparrowe, and Wayne, 1997; Sparrowe & Liden, 1997; Wayne et al., 1994; Zorn, 1995
Stage 4: Group and network levels of LMXs	Graen & Uhl-Bien, 1995; Liden et al., 1997; Sparrowe & Liden, 1997; Uhl-Bien & Graen, 1992, 1993

"in-" and "out-groups" (Graen, Novak, & Sommerkamp, 1982). The research is voluminous and centers on the antecedents and determinants of LMX, communication and relationship maintenance, cross-cultural applicability, LMX outcomes, and measurement issues. In Stage 2, there is a greater recognition that both leaders and members influence the nature of the exchange and that the consequences of a high LMX could be significant.

Still focusing on the dyad, Stage 3 has the look of an emancipatory shift. In contrast to

VDL research that assumed a kind of natural selection model of high LMX members because of a leader's limited resources, Stage 3 drew on two longitudinal LMX studies that offered the promise of a high LMX relationship to any member who would take it (Graen et al., 1982; Scandura & Graen, 1984; Graen, Scandura, & Graen, 1986). Members who accepted the high LMX offer not only improved their performance, they enhanced overall unit functioning by increasing the percentage of high LMXs.

This work led to the development of the leadership making model, which describes the process through which relationships may become high quality. In this model, there are three proposed stages of LMX growth and development (Graen & Uhl-Bien, 1995; Uhl-Bien & Graen, 1992). The first stage, role finding, is an initial "stranger" phase in which members relate mostly on a formal basis with a "cash and carry" contractual economic exchange. If an offer for an improved working relationship is made (either implicitly or explicitly) and accepted, the dyads may mature into the second stage of relationship development, role making, also known as the "acquaintance" stage. This stage is marked by a testing period where both social and contractual exchanges are made. Not all dyads reach the final stage, role implementation, or the "mature partnership" stage. In this stage the exchange is highly developed; the exchanges made are "in kind" and marked by loyalty, support, and trust.

However, other researchers have contributed to our knowledge of LMX development. Bauer and Green (1996) recast role finding, role making, and role implementation in terms of trust development, arguing that high LMXs are the result of a successful series of member performance-leader delegation interacts. Liden and his colleagues (Dienesch & Liden, 1986; Liden, Wayne, & Stilwell, 1993) focused on leader-member expectancies and member performance as determining influences on relationship development. Sparrowe and Liden (1997) explored the effects of social networks on LMX development. Finally,

Boyd and Taylor (1998) and Zorn (1995) examined friendship development in the context of an LMX relationship.

Stage 4 expands the dyadic relationship to group and network levels. Higher-order system levels are cast in terms of "network assemblies" (Scandura, 1995) or systems of interdependent dyadic relationships (Liden et al., 1997; Sparrowe & Liden, 1997). Unlike the concept of charisma, which is held to change as one moves up system levels (e.g., Avolio & Bass, 1995), the basic nature of LMX does not change as one aggregates sets of dyadic relationships. LMX researchers have taken the network perspective in two directions.

First, Graen and Uhl-Bien's (1995) focus on network assemblies helps to explain the leadership structure of the organization. Using a network perspective, the leadership structure emerges both as a function of the task structure and the individual characteristics of leaders and members. The task structure is a particularly important moderating influence on the emergent structure of the organization. The primary research questions at the group level include examining the effects of mixed-quality relationships on unit functioning and task performance. Equity issues, peer influences, and optimum numbers of high, medium, low LMXs for different task structures also come into play. At organizational levels, questions include the dyadic enactment of critical task networks and the impact of relationships of varying quality on performance beyond the work unit both within the organization (e.g., with cross-functional work teams or hierarchically adjacent dyads) and with external stakeholders.

Second, Liden et al. (1997) use a network perspective to critique the emancipatory shift of Stage 3. Citing limitations on a leader's time and resources, they argue that a competitive advantage in information access will accrue only to those leaders who have nonredundant contacts in their networks. They write that "positive outcomes from differentiation may result when leaders invest time in nonredundant contacts with members who themselves are especially well connected with others beyond the boundaries of the work group" (Liden et al., 1997, p. 47). In contrast, social outcomes that are dependent on trust and cohesion will be enhanced by networks with strong ties (Sparrowe & Liden, 1997).

The primary research questions focus on (1) the sponsorship process through which newcomers are either assimilated into the leader's network or isolated from it; (2) the outcomes of differentiation on work group effectiveness especially when leader competence is taken into account; and (3) given the social networks of which leaders are a part, the likelihood that differentiation by them fosters homogeneity of high LMX constituent selection within social networks.

Communication-Based LMX Research

The study of communication in LMX weighs in most heavily in Stage 2. Even though communication frequency has been linked to LMX (Baker & Ganster, 1985; Schiemann & Graen, 1984), more recent studies examine the interactive means by which members manage and maintain the quality of the exchange. Those studies that look at upward influence and relationship maintenance tactics emphasize cognitive outcomes and a transmission view of communication.

For example, upward influence tactics have been studied as impression management strategies designed to ingratiate and promote liking within the LMX. Wayne and Ferris (1990) report two studies where supervisor-focused tactics (as opposed to self- or job-focused tactics) affected supervisor's liking for members that, in turn, affected the quality of the exchange. Dockery and Steiner (1990) found three upward influence tactics (ingratiation, assertiveness, and rationality) used by members affected their rating of the quality of the exchange. Deluga and Perry (1991) found member-perceived high LMXs were significantly and inversely related to the reported use of coalition, higher authority, and

assertiveness. They also confirmed that high-quality LMXs were significantly related to member upward influence success. Finally, revisiting Likert's (1961) Pelz effect, Lee (1997) extended work by Cashman, Graen, and associates (Cashman, Dansereau, Graen, & Haga, 1976; Graen, Cashman, Ginsburg, & Schiemann, 1977) by demonstrating that work group members engage in more cooperative communication when they perceive their leaders' have high upward LMXs and when their relationship with their leaders was also high.

In the area of relationship maintenance, Waldron (1991) investigated the communication strategies that members reportedly used in maintaining upward influence. High LMX members reportedly used more personal and informal tactics, but they also displayed more contractual upward influence tactics. Low LMX members tended to report more regulative tactics (e.g., message distortion and avoidance) that are designed to avoid relational difficulties and aggressively manage impressions. However, Waldron, Hunt, and Dsilva (1993) found that contextual factors influenced the nature and size of LMX effects on influence behavior. Lee and Jablin (1995), to be discussed later, consider three types of LMX relational maintenance contexts: escalating, deteriorating, and routine relationship maintenance conditions.

In contrast to the study of reported communication tactics, a few LMX studies focus on the conversational practices of power and control. Researchers investigating interactional measures of power distance (Borchgrevink & Donohue, 1991), powerless speech forms (Fairhurst, 1991), relational control analysis of routine interaction (Fairhurst, Rogers, & Sarr, 1987), and culturally based language patterns (Fairhurst, 1993a; Fairhurst & Chandler, 1989) have shown how powerful/powerless language can vary across LMXs.

A few studies focus on the social construction of meaning. Two studies treat high, medium, and low LMX relationship labeling (as determined by members) as problematic. Fairhurst and Chandler (1989) found that choice framing, disconfirmation, topic control, and sustained challenges distinguished between a high, medium, and low LMX. Focusing on female-led LMXs, Fairhurst (1993b) found combinations of aligning, accommodating, and polarizing moves successfully discriminated between high, medium, and low LMXs. Aligning moves minimized power differences by including member extensions of the leader's view and spiraling agreement reflective of convergent thinking. Power and control issues were still being negotiated with accommodating moves such as role negotiation, choice framing, and polite disagreement. Polarizing moves such as performance monitoring, competitive conflict, and power games maximized power differences. Finally, based on work suggesting that members' perceptions of differential LMX treatment may influence coworker communication and relationships (Kramer, 1995; Sias & Jablin, 1995), Sias (1996) found that the social construction of differential treatment hung on frequent references to equity standards.

New Directions: LMX Individual-Systems Concerns, Conversational Practices, and Relationship Dialectics

LMX Individual-Systems Concerns

Despite its popularity, LMX theory, research, and measurement have been widely criticized (Barge & Schleuter, 1991; Dienesch & Liden, 1986; Keller & Dansereau, 1995; Schriesheim et al., 1999; Schriesheim, Cogliser, & Neider, 1995; Yukl, 1994). In a special issue of *Leadership Quarterly* devoted to a multiple-levels approach, Dansereau, Yammarino, and Markham (1995) also took Graen and Uhl-Bien (1995) to task for marginalizing the role of the individual leader and member within current conceptualizations of

LMX. Similarly, House and Aditya (1997) call LMX a theory of dyadic relationships not leadership (in addition to suggesting that the empirical literature is less supportive of LMX theory than Graen and Uhl-Bien imply). However, Graen eschews an individualistic focus and calls the path of individualism a "failed paradigm" (personal communication, 1995) to draw attention to leadership as an inherently social phenomena. Nevertheless, a number of individual-level questions remain including the influence of communicative style, skills, and expectancies for the relationship on the negotiation of the exchange (Fairhurst & Chandler, 1989; Sparrowe & Liden, 1997).

If Graen and colleagues' stand against individualism is at least understandable given leadership's history, their stand on wider systems concerns is less so. Recall that group and organizational levels are reframed in dyadic terms as network assemblies. Dyadic functioning aside, organizations where high LMX opportunities are widely available would likely produce cultures of opportunity, while those that offered few such opportunities would produce cultures of difference. Cultures reflecting these themes would be apparent in the management systems, reward systems, value structures, cultural norms, and organizational identities, all forming intertwined systems of meaning quite apart from individual dyads. As cultural or subcultural understandings, they are part of the context for all dyadic interactions. They also provide the resources individuals draw on, but also occasionally reject, as they negotiate their individual relationships. Therefore, network assemblies are more than interconnected dyads; they also form cultures. The dyadic aspects of social networks emphasize leadership as a form of social influence; the cultural aspects emphasize leadership as a form of organizing.

As the following discussion suggests, there is also a corresponding need to understand the cultural and historical influences on LMX. This is done through a focus on conversational practices.

Conversational Practices

Like the previously reviewed literature in this chapter, LMX shares a dominant epistemology rooted in psychology that stresses the role of individual perceptions (cognitive outcomes) and little attention to cultural or historical processes. A social cognition perspective is assumed when an individual's perceptions of the relationship operate within an information-processing model. When the focus is on an individual's perception of the relationship, explanation shifts to the psychological constructs of intention and planning rather than social processes (Baxter, 1988, 1992). Similarly, when the focus is on individuals' perception of their communicative practices, it privileges the belief that individuals are freely in control of their experience and marginalizes how the practices themselves influence interpretation. Lannamann (1991) noted that "these practices are concrete; they are not determined solely by the subjective state of individuals but rather by the grounded practices of subjects in interaction with other subjects, symbol systems, and social objects" (p. 191).

Therefore, in the study of leader-member relationships one must also ask, "What are the communication practices that shape interpretation of the relationship?" This question is analogous to Sigman's (1992) "micro-macro" issue, which examines the microcommunication practices that make relationships possible. To address this issue, one must acknowledge that interactional patterns are produced within relationships not only by drawing on private and restricted knowledge but also on shared cultural knowledge (societal and organizational) including that of language. By acknowledging the culturally recognized functions of language, individuals become members of language communities rather than distinct cognitive players (Baxter & Goldsmith, 1990; Hewes & Planalp, 1987; Sigman, 1987).

Therefore, the study of relationships should proceed on at least two levels. One level of inquiry is to ask how leaders and members use the culturally recognized functions of language to enact a relationship that is culturally recognizable as a leader-member relationship (e.g., Fairhurst, 1991, 1993b; Fairhurst & Chandler, 1989). A second level of inquiry must proceed into how a unique relationship culture is simultaneously established through private message systems that may or may not adhere to public or cultural language rules (Baxter, 1992; Montgomery, 1992). Meanings are socially negotiated. Relationship partners may make use of standard meaning systems, but may also discard them as relationships accumulate history and uniqueness (Baxter, 1992; Montgomery, 1992; Watzlawick et al., 1967). As Montgomery (1992) puts it, the question is how can we study the interactive input of both culture and dyad?

Relationship Dialectics

More than most leadership theories, LMX has been very concerned with -relationship development (Stage 3). An examination of Graen and Uhl-Bien's (1995) leadership making model, Liden and colleagues' expectancies model (Liden et al., 1993), Bauer and Green's (1996) trust model, Sparrowe and Liden's (1997) social network model, and Boyd and Taylor's (1998) friendship model reveals two similarities. First, all of these models represent traditional psychological views that treat communication in LMX development as incidental, implicit, or intervening. It must be quickly acknowledged that these views of LMX development are not necessarily incorrect; external causal influences on LMX development, influences of which the actors themselves may be unaware, must be studied along with the retrospective judgments of the actors concerning each other, the relationship, expectations, outcomes, and the like.

However, marginalizing communication leaves researchers unable to explain the effects of social interaction fully. Coconstructed relational dynamics, especially those that produce relational bonding, transformation, or fusion, are not easily explained by the additive contributions of individuals and their perceptions. This is because the process of relationship development is glossed and reified. The many contexts through which relationships evolve are summed over, and an artificial stability and order are imposed on a process that can be simultaneously orderly and disorderly, stable and unstable. In short, marginalizing communication comes at the expense of a more complex view of the relationship's dynamics.

Second, even though caveats about continual relationship evolution and change are usually offered (e.g., Bauer & Green, 1996; Boyd & Taylor, 1998), the models themselves reflect an assumption that successful LMXs follow a unidirectional and cumulative path toward increasing levels of closeness or fusion, openness, relational stability, and transformation beyond self-interests. Jablin (1987) argued that a focus on the communicative practices of leader-member role negotiation may lead to questioning the usual assumption of relational stability. Recent work in dialectical approaches to relationship development similarly calls this thinking into question. Instead, these approaches argue that healthy relationships are marked by dialectical oppositions that create simultaneous pulls to fuse with and differentiate from the other (Altman, Vinsel, & Brown, 1981; Baxter, 1988, 1992; Baxter & Montgomery, 1996; Montgomery, 1992; Rawlins, 1992). Relationship bonding not only implies fusion, closeness, and interdependence but also separation, distance, and independence.

Dialectics is defined as the copresence of two relational forces that are interdependent, but mutually negating. But in this case, the oppositions specify the contradictory tensions that forge the relationship. Several different types of dialectical oppositions have been named in the relationships literature (Altman et al., 1981; Baxter, 1988; Rawlins, 1992). The connection/autonomy dialectic has been named as the principal contradiction because connection is as central to a relationship's

identity as autonomy is to an individual's identity. However, Baxter (1988) argued that openness/closedness and predictability/novelty form two secondary dialectical contradictions endemic to all interpersonal relationships. Openness is a prerequisite for bonding, yet creates vulnerability necessitating closedness. Relationships require predictability, but too much predictability leads to a rigidity that necessitates novelty or change (see also Altman et al., 1981).

However, it is the *strategic responses to contradiction* in message behavior that form the basis for understanding how relationships are forged. Baxter (1988, 1990) identified a number of communicative strategies through which the contradictions may be managed. These strategies include making one pole dominant (e.g., when closedness is consistently favored over openness); alternation of poles by time or by topic (e.g., when individuals choose to be open about some topics and closed about others); diluting or neutralizing the intensity of the poles (e.g., when ambiguity is favored over full disclosure or complete refusal to communicate); and reframing one pole as no longer the opposite of another.

Although Baxter was writing about social relationships in general, the three dialectics proposed and the strategies for managing them appear to have strong relevance for the leader-member relationship (Eisenberg, 1990; Zorn, 1995). Member latitude in decision making is a form of autonomy that has been reframed as connection in high LMX relationships (Graen & Scandura, 1987), but also in transformational relationships (Avolio & Bass, 1988) as well as within relationships with socialized as opposed to personalized charismatics (House & Howell, 1992). However, the management of the autonomy-connection dialectic over the life cycle of the leader-member relationship has rarely been viewed as an ever-evolving negotiated process between opposite poles. However, Phillips's (1996) study of LMX and friendship during "crunch times" in team functioning and Zorn's (1995) work on simultaneously hierarchical and friendship relationships offer a promising beginning.

Lee and Jablin's (1995) work provides strong evidence for the operation of the openness-closedness dialectic especially in the maintenance phase of the leader-member relationship. Arguing that the maintenance phase could be in flux (Jablin, 1987), they inductively derived a set of communication tactics for escalating, deteriorating, and routine relationship maintenance situations. In escalating situations where the relationship may be moving quickly to a higher level, high LMX members reportedly were less likely to avoid interaction or redirect the topic of conversation. In deteriorating situations where the relationship may be deteriorating to an unwanted level, low LMX members reported both more openness and deception and fewer attempts to create closeness. Finally, in routine situations where the parties are unconcerned about becoming more close or more distant, low LMX members reported using more avoidance and restrained expression and less supportiveness than high LMX members. Beginning with the premise of possible relational instability such as with Lee and Jablin's work is a novel approach that could greatly inform future work on LMX development.

Finally, leaders might manage the predictability-novelty dialectic for the low LMX member by selecting or favoring the predictability pole. This might be done through exaggerating knowledge of the member, reducing vigilance in keeping current with the member, and stereotyping the qualities of the member (Sillars & Scott, 1983). Although it may or may not seem scripted to members, leaders should initiate a much higher number of scripted episodes relative to unscripted episodes as a result (Fiske & Taylor, 1991). By contrast, leaders in high LMX relationships should initiate a larger number of unscripted episodes than in low LMX relationships because the former are expected to maintain a better balance in managing the predictability-novelty dialectic. Leaders would alternate scripted episodes with ones marked by information vigilance and perspective taking through active listening, more time spent with the other, and sharing information about one's work and personal activities (Waldron, 1991). Increased monitoring of other enhances the chances for introducing more novelty and change in the relationship.

Indirect, neutralizing strategies are likely in the testing stage of leader-member relationships where leaders typically try to manage the predictability-novelty dialectic through secret tests of members (Baxter, 1988; Baxter & Willmott, 1984; Graen & Uhl-Bien, 1995). For example, endurance tests may emerge by making the relationship costly in order to determine the upper limits of commitment. Phillips's (1996) study of crunch times and LMX team functioning nicely illustrates this point. Separation tests may emerge to see what happens when the leader is away from the office. Loyalty tests surface when allegiances get divided, while knowledge tests are introduced to determine competency levels. Integrity tests surface within the presentation of moral dilemmas to determine a member's ability to do the right thing. Although the LMX literature suggests this testing period is relatively brief, a dialectical focus on message strategies or a situational orientation to relationship maintenance may call this assumption into question. Loyalty, integrity, endurance, and other tests may span the life cycle of the leader-member relationship.

As can be seen from the above discussion, a dialectical perspective provides a theoretical base for a communication-based view of relational development. Its chief distinguishing feature is that each contradictory pole is equally important in understanding relationships over time. Additionally, the study of conversational practices would add specificity and nuance to the identification and description of the coping strategies used to reconcile dialectical oppositions over the life cycle of the relationship (Baxter, 1988). In keeping with earlier concerns about cultural contributions to relationships, longitudinal language-in-use data also permit the study of interactive input to the relationship of both the culture and the dyad. Language analysis also characterizes systems-interactional research, the last area to be reviewed.

SYSTEMS-INTERACTIONAL
LEADERSHIP RESEARCH

A systems-interactional perspective on leadership seeks to understand the patterned sequential communication of leaders and constituents as part of an interactional system. Consistent with general systems theory, sequences of behavior are thought to define the system and are more salient than any one particular message. The minimum unit of analysis is the interact, a sequence of two contiguous messages, or the double interact, a sequence of three contiguous messages. Analysis of the data is usually stochastic in that the analysis examines the probabilities of a given state from an antecedent state. Finally, phasic analyses or recurring cycles of interaction may also be a subject of interest.

The Individual-System
Dualism and Other Tensions

Although not without its own limitations, this program of research provides a contrast from the previously reviewed research in this chapter. As the "systems-interactional" name implies, systemic over individual concerns dominate. Measurement and analysis focus heavily on relational systems, although a few studies in the area of relational control address wider systems concerns. Conversational practices are emphasized over cognitive outcomes. Meaning is either transmissional or derives from the structure of messages in evolving conversations. For example, relational control research distinguishes between the content and relational aspects of a message to focus exclusively on a definition of the relationship at the relational level as control patterns form.

Relational Control Research

This line of research is based on the work of Edna Rogers and her colleagues (Courtright, Millar, & Rogers-Millar, 1979; Fairhurst et al., 1987; Rogers-Millar & Millar,

1979) and by Don Ellis (1979; Watson, 1982a, 1982b). This work is based on coding schemes that focus on control in relationships by assessing how people establish rights that define and direct relationships. Interactants reciprocally define their positions in terms of three specific types of control moves. "One-up" moves attempt to define a situation such as orders and instructions, while "one-down" moves accept or request another's definition of the situation. "One-across" moves are nondemanding, nonaccepting, leveling moves such as elaborations and extensions. Importantly, the Rogers and Farace (1975) and Ellis (1979) schemes differ in their treatment of the one-across category making comparisons across studies more difficult.

Using the Rogers and Farace (1975) relational control coding scheme, Fairhurst and colleagues have studied control patterns in routine work conversation in manufacturing settings. Fairhurst et al. (1987) found measures of leader dominance to be correlated with lower constituent performance ratings, leader understanding of constituents, and constituent desire for decision making as perceived by the leaders. Courtright et al. (1989) tested Burns and Stalker's (1961) theory of organic and mechanistic control. They compared the communication of leaders and constituents in a plant organized by an organic, self-managing team philosophy with a plant that had a mechanistic, authority-based philosophy. Consistent with Burns and Stalker's theory, they found that question-answer combinations initiated by the leader and conversational elaboration characterized the organic plant. The mechanistic plant was characterized by more hierarchical communication, nonsupport, and competitive interchanges.

A follow-up study conducted by Fairhurst et al. (1995) analyzed the potential effects of organizational inertia on the implementation of a sociotechnical systems (STS) philosophy in five manufacturing plants. Plant history (conversion from a hierarchical system, STS from start-up) and plant manager style (autocratic, participative) were posed as potential sources of inertia. When both counterproductive inertial forces were present (conversion plant, autocratic plant manager), participation between leaders and constituents as equals was less (e.g., fewer challenges by constituents, more leader-led discussion, and more constituent approval-seeking). When these inertial forces were absent (STS since start-up, participative plant manager), constituents assumed a more assertive and equal role in communication (e.g., more constituent-led discussion and challenges of leader assertions and fewer leader control attempts).

Using the Ellis (1979) coding scheme, Dugan (1989) used relational control analysis to study control patterns in performance feedback sessions. As indicated in the feedback section, she found that when attributions were based on a lack of constituent ability, leaders resisted and constituents complied with their partners' attempts to control. When attributions were based in constituents' lack of effort, leaders and constituents alternated in their attempts to control the relationship and were significantly more likely to comply with the other's structuring attempts. Attributional shifts, agreements about performance, and salary increases were associated with the more negotiated lack of effort condition.

Operant Models of Effective Supervision

A second line of interactional research is grounded in the theory of operant conditioning (Honig & Stadden, 1977; Skinner, 1974). Komaki and her colleagues have developed an operant model of effective supervision to explain what leaders do to motivate their constituents to perform consistently especially for tasks requiring coordination (Komaki, 1986, 1998; Komaki, Zlotnick, & Jensen, 1986). Komaki makes a tripartite distinction between three categories of supervisory communication. Performance antecedents occur before performance and involve the communication of expectations via instructions, rules, training, or goals. Performance monitoring occurs during or after performance and involves the

gathering of performance information through work sampling and inquiries. Performance consequences occur during or after performance and involve communicating knowledge about performance in the form of feedback, recognition, or corrections. Central to this model is the notion that effective leaders go beyond providing performance antecedents to both monitor and provide consequences in a timely fashion.

Komaki (1998) reviewed 18 studies conducted over the past several years that test various aspects of her model. This review reports on a triangulation between field and laboratory studies, intercultural studies, and field sites as diverse as sailboat competitions, police organizations, insurance firms, newspapers, construction sites, and government offices. Tests of the model reveal that effective leaders spend more time monitoring and providing consequences than their lackluster counterparts (Brewer, Wilson, & Beck, 1994; Komaki, 1986; Komaki, Desselles, & Bowman, 1989). Work sampling is the most frequent type of performance monitoring used, and a variety of reinforcers (positive, negative, and neutral) form the consequences. Moreover, it is monitoring combined with consequences that is crucial to effectiveness (Brewer, 1995; Larson & Callahan, 1990). Lackluster leaders not only spend less time monitoring and providing consequences, but they are more likely to spend time alone or be passive participants by failing to steer the conversation toward performance-related discussion (Komaki, 1998).

More recent tests of the model have focused on the timing of the antecedent-monitoring-consequence (AMC) sequence where effective leaders have been found to deliver the AMC sequence quickly (Komaki, 1998). In contrast, lackluster leaders belabor their instructions, become distracted by discussions of work minutia, fail to participate fully in work discussions, or leave the scene to do their own work. Addressing the issue of why performance monitoring and consequences are effective, Komaki and colleagues (Goltz, 1993; Komaki, 1998; Komaki & Citera, 1990) found that monitoring stimulated constituents to talk about their own performance. This prompted leaders to continue monitoring or provide consequences. In contrast to providing performance antecedents to constituents, performance monitoring increases the likelihood that discussions of the constituents' performance were specific and focused rather than vague and general.

New Directions: Individual Concerns and Cognitive Outcomes

Systems-interactional research is carefully designed and uses sophisticated methods to study communication (Schnell & Sims, 1993). However, relational control and performance-monitoring studies can be a narrow basis on which to understand leadership communication. With respect to Komaki's work, Schnell and Sims (1993) note some potential confusion between the three categories of supervisory communication (antecedents, monitors, and consequences). For example, asking questions about how work is done or why it was done in a particular way (performance monitor) could be perceived as an evaluation (consequence) especially if the work is highly autonomous and involves singular outcomes.

Similar validity questions have been raised about relational coding (Folger, Hewes, & Poole, 1984) where the issue boils down to a simple question: Would a participant in the interaction code an utterance the same way that an observer would? Research in this area distinguishes between construct validity based on the culturally recognized functions of language versus validity based on private and idiosyncratic meanings (Folger et al., 1984). Systems-interactional research employs the former since cultural meanings often prefigure private interpretations (Sigman, 1987, 1992), and queries are not made about individual interpretations (Folger, 1991; Newell & Stutman, 1991).

Nevertheless, systems-interactional research neglects the private experiential side of discourse and its threefold impact. First, personal and cultural interpretations of discourse may diverge. However, coding across numerous messages and attention to how the coding scheme might play out in specific organizational contexts could minimize this problem. For example, Fairhurst (1990) modified the "backchannel" code from Courtright et al. (1989) to Fairhurst et al. (1995) for precisely this reason. Komaki's (1998) attention to context is most apparent in the evolution of her coding of consequences, particularly those delivered directly versus indirectly and the range of effectiveness measures that she employs. Second is the even more damaging fact that a focus on individual interpretations will reveal some segments of discourse as more important than others. This runs counter to the systems-interactional assumption that every message is like every other message and given equal weight. Third, prospective and retrospective summaries and judgments of discourse are the self-conscious, social cognitive basis of action. As argued, much can be learned about why people act as they do based on how they interpret the behaviors of the interactional systems of which they are a part. Although systems-interactional coding schemes must continue their coding of language at a culturally recognizable level to retain a measure of efficiency in the coding process (thereby accepting the first two points as limitations), more research such as by Dugan (1989), Fairhurst et al. (1987), and Komaki (1998) would address the much needed focus on systems-interactional patterns and their cognitive outcomes.

CONCLUSION

This chapter is premised on a dualistic reframing of the leadership communication literature. Wherever possible, I have sought to represent the complexities of the dualisms and the nuanced positions that may reflect this. For example, multiple operationalizations of system characterize the individual-system dualism. A meaning-centered view of communication is represented as surface and deep-structure systems of meaning such as in the discussion of influence tactics. Early symbolic views of leadership (Bennis & Nanus, 1985; Pfeffer, 1981; Pondy, 1978) are characterized as both transmissional and meaning centered because managers are the primary symbolizing agents. These are just a few examples.

Because "either-or" thinking about key dualisms often surfaces in research, this style of thinking mitigates against adopting a "both-and" orientation.[11] However, both the individual and the system are constitutive elements of leadership. Both transmission and meaning are necessary elements of the communication process. Likewise, both cognitive outcomes and conversational practices must be studied to understand the communicative management of leadership fully.

Each of the five research programs reviewed tends to favor one side of the dualism; its counterpart was used to push the research agenda toward a more complex view of the subject. This analysis revealed that there is still much to learn about leader-constituent influence, feedback processes, charisma and vision, leader-member exchange, and systems-interactional functioning.

And it is here that this review of the leadership communication literature ends with a call not to abandon individualistic, psychological approaches in the study of influence tactics, feedback, or charisma, but to embrace more fully systemic approaches. Alternatively, leader-member exchange and systems-interactional leadership research should not be satisfied with its relational systems orientation, but should more fully embrace wider systems and individualistic concerns. When this is done, and when communication is conceived of more complexly (as both transmission and meaning) and studied more complexly (as both cognitive outcomes and conversational

practices), there will be even greater strides in our understanding of the communication between leaders and their constituents.

NOTES

1. The terms *dualism, duality, dialectic,* and *dichotomy* appear to be used differently by different scholars (e.g., Giddens, 1984; Werner & Baxter, 1994). My use of the term dualism is necessarily very broad to capture wide-ranging tensions within the literature (e.g., both epistemological and ontological). I use the term dualism to characterize two opposing influences making no generalizable assumptions about independence, simultaneity, or possible unification.

2. Jacques Derrida (1976) and other postmodernists offer several criticisms of oppositional or dualistic thinking. First, language creates meaning, and because interpretations of language are highly context sensitive, meaning should be endlessly deferred (hence Derrida's notion of *différance*). Second, positions that reflect mixed or compromise stances between opposites are often ignored, effectively removing the ambiguities and complexities that exist in the space between dichotomous ends. Third, dualistic thinking is inevitably hierarchical where one end is defined only in terms of the dimensions salient to the dominant end (Collins, 1986). However, postmodernists also use dualistic thinking as a heuristic—as a form of deconstruction rather than as presumed sedimented oppositional forms.

3. The work of Leslie Baxter and colleagues (Baxter & Montgomery, 1996; Werner & Baxter, 1994) was a significant influence in this regard.

4. Some programs of research are moving beyond the dyadic level of analysis to focus on group and organization levels (e.g., charisma, leader-member exchange).

5. See Barge (1994a), Rost (1991), and Smith and Peterson (1988) for discussions that analyze and critique these assumptions.

6. Other dualisms can certainly be named including the tension between theory and practice, a tension born of the view that much of what we know about leadership is not easily operationalized in practical settings (House & Aditya, 1997). There is also a tension between the study of leadership and management, and a tension that is based on the large number of studies (especially through the 1970s) that ignores senior-level leadership while focusing on lower- and middle-level managers whose only concern appears to be direct supervision of their immediate constituents (House & Aditya, 1997). While these and other dualisms can certainly be named, for purposes of this review (which is biased toward the dyadic) they play a less central role.

7. Bopp and Weeks (1984) made a related argument in family therapy.

8. As will become apparent, leader-member exchange is a notable exception. LMX takes a systems view, typically from a social cognitive perspective.

9. Though it may be argued that in the case of social desirability, the cultural is clearly at work. Unfortunately, there is often no way to know for sure because there is so little testing for social desirability.

10. Although I use the term *charismatic and visionary leadership,* Bryman (1993) refers to the charisma theories as "the new leadership theories," while House and Aditya (1997) use the term "neocharismatic theory." All generally refer to the same body of work beginning with House (1977) and Bass (1985).

11. Baxter and Montgomery (1996), among others, discuss a "both-and" orientation.

REFERENCES

Albright, M. D., & Levy, P. E. (1995). The effects of source credibility and performance rating discrepancy on reactions to multiple raters. *Journal of Applied Social Psychology, 25,* 577-600.

Altman, I., Vinsel, A., & Brown, B. B. (1981). Dialectic conceptions in social psychology: An application to social penetration and privacy regulation. In L. Berkowitz (Ed.), *Advances in experimental social psychology* (pp. 107-160). New York: Academic Press.

Ammons, R. B. (1956). Effects of knowledge of performance: A survey and tentative theoretical formulation. *Journal of General Psychology, 54,* 279-299.

Ansari, M. A., & Kapoor, A. (1987). Organizational context and upward influence tactics. *Organizational Behavior and Human Decision Processes, 40,* 39-49.

Antonioni, D. (1994). The effects of feedback accountability on upward appraisal ratings. *Personnel Psychology, 47,* 349-356.

Arkin, R. M., & Sheppard, J. A. (1990). Strategic self-presentation: An overview. In M. J. Cody & M. L. McLaughlin (Eds.), *The psychology of tactical communication* (pp. 175-193). Clevedon, UK: Multilingual Matters.

Ashford, S. J. (1986). Feedback-seeking in individual adaptation: A resource perspective. *Academy of Management Journal, 29,* 465-487.

Ashford, S. J., & Cummings. L. L. (1983). Feedback as an individual resource: Personal strategies of creating information. *Organizational Behavior and Human Performance, 32,* 370-398.

Ashford, S. J., & Northcraft, G. B. (1992). Conveying more (or less) than we realize: The role of impression-management in feedback seeking. *Organizational Behavior and Human Decision Processes, 53,* 310-334.

Ashford, S. J., & Tsui, A. S. (1991). Self-regulation for managerial effectiveness: The role of active feedback seeking. *Academy of Management Journal, 34,* 251-280.

Atwater, L. E., Roush, P., & Fischthal, A. (1995). The influence of upward feedback on self- and follower ratings of leadership. *Personnel Psychology, 48,* 35-59.

Atwater, L. E., & Waldman, D. A. (1998). Introduction: 360-degree feedback and leadership development. *Leadership Quarterly, 9,* 423-426.

Avolio, B. J., & Bass, B. M. (1988). Transformational leadership, charisma and beyond. In J. G. Hunt, B. R. Baglia, H. P. Dachler, & C. A. Schriesheim (Eds.), *Emerging leadership vistas* (pp. 29-50). Lexington, MA: Lexington Books.

Avolio, B. J., & Bass, B. M. (1995). Individual consideration viewed at multiple levels of analysis: A multi-level framework for examining the diffusion of transformational leadership. *Leadership Quarterly, 6,* 183-198.

Avolio, B. J., Howell, J. M., & Sosik, J. J. (1999). A funny thing happened on the way to the bottom line: Humor as a moderator of leadership style effects. *Academy of Management Journal, 42,* 219-227.

Avolio, B. J., Waldman, D. A., & Einstein, W. O. (1988). Transformational leadership in a management game simulation: Impacting the bottom line. *Group and Organization Studies, 13,* 59-80.

Awamleh, R., & Gardner, W. L. (1999). Perceptions of leader charisma and effectiveness: The effects of vision content, delivery, and organizational performance. *Leadership Quarterly, 10,* 345-374.

Baker, D. D., & Ganster, D. C. (1985). Leader communication style: A test of average versus vertical dyad linkage models. *Group and Organization Studies, 10,* 242-259.

Bandura, A. (1982). Self-efficacy: Mechanism in human agency. *American Psychologist, 37,* 122-147.

Bandura, A. (1986). *Social foundations of thought and action: A social cognitive theory.* Englewood Cliffs, NJ: Prentice Hall.

Bandura, A. (1991). Social cognitive theory of self-regulation. *Organizational Behavior and Human Decision Processes, 50,* 248-287.

Bandura, A., & Cervone, D. (1983). Self-evaluative and self-efficacy mechanisms governing the motivational effects of goal systems. *Journal of Personality and Social Psychology, 45,* 1017-1028.

Barclay, J. H., & Harland, L. K. (1995). Peer performance appraisals: The impact of rater competence, rater location, and rater correctability on fairness perceptions. *Group & Organization Management, 20,* 39-60.

Barge, J. K. (1994a). *Leadership: Communication skills for organizations and groups.* New York: St. Martin's.

Barge, J. K. (1994b). Putting leadership back to work. *Management Communication Quarterly, 8,* 95-109.

Barge, J. K., Downs, C. W., & Johnson, K. M. (1989). An analysis of effective and ineffective leader conversation. *Management Communication Quarterly, 2,* 357-386.

Barge, J. K., & Schleuter, D. W. (1991). Leadership as organizing: A critique of leadership instruments. *Management Communication Quarterly, 4,* 541-570.

Bargh, J. A. (1989). Conditional automaticity: Varieties of automatic influence in social perception and cognition. In J. S. Uleman & J. A. Bargh (Eds.), *Unintended thought* (pp. 3-51). New York: Guilford.

Baron, R. A. (1988). Negative effects of destructive criticism: Impact on conflict, self-efficacy, and task performance. *Journal of Applied Psychology, 73,* 199-207.

Baron, R. A. (1990). Countering the effects of destructive criticism: The relative efficacy of four interventions. *Journal of Applied Psychology, 75,* 235-245.

Barry, B., & Watson, M. R. (1996). Communication aspects of dyadic social influence: A review and integration of conceptual and empirical developments. In B. R. Burleson (Ed.), *Communication yearbook 19* (pp. 269-318). Thousand Oaks, CA: Sage.

Bartlett, C. A., & Ghoshal, S. (1994). Changing the role of top management: Beyond strategy to purpose. *Harvard Business Review, 72*(6), 79-88.

Bass, B. M. (1981). *Stogdill's handbook of leadership.* New York: Free Press.

Bass, B. M. (1985). *Leadership and performance: Beyond expectations.* New York: Free Press.

Bass, B. M. (1988). Evolving perspectives on charismatic leadership. In J. A. Conger & R. N. Kanungo (Eds.), *Charismatic leadership* (pp. 40-77). San Francisco: Jossey-Bass.

Bateson, G. (1972). *Steps to an ecology of the mind.* New York: Ballantine.

Bauer, T., & Green, S. G. (1996). The development of leader-member exchange: A longitudinal test. *Academy of Management Journal, 39,* 1538-1567.

Baum, J. R., Locke, E. A., & Kirkpatrick, S. A. (1998). A longitudinal study of the relation of vision and vision communication to venture growth in entrepreneurial firms. *Journal of Applied Psychology, 83,* 43-54.

Baxter, L. (1988). A dialectical perspective on communication strategies in relationship development. In S. Duck, D. Hay, S. Jobfoll, W. Ickes, & B. Montgomery (Eds.), *Handbook of personal relationships: Theory research, and interventions* (pp. 257-274). Chichester, UK: Wiley.

Baxter, L. (1990). Dialectical contradictions in relationship development. *Journal of Personal and Social Relationships, 7,* 69-88.

Baxter, L. (1992). Interpersonal communication as a dialogue: A response to the "social approaches" forum. *Communication Theory, 2,* 330-336.

Baxter, L. A., & Goldsmith, D. (1990). Cultural terms for communication events among some American high school adolescents. *Western Journal of Speech Communication, 54,* 377-394.

Baxter, L. A., & Montgomery, B. M. (1996). *Relating: Dialogue and dialectics.* New York: Guilford.

Baxter, L. A., & Willmott, W. (1984). Secret tests: Social strategies for acquiring information about the state of the relationship. *Human Communication Research, 11,* 171-201.

Becker, T. E., & Klimoski, R. J. (1989). A field study of the relationship between the organizational feedback environment and performance. *Personnel Psychology, 42,* 343-358.

Bennett, N., Herold, D. M., & Ashford, S. J. (1990). The effects of tolerance for ambiguity on feedback seeking behavior. *Journal of Occupational Psychology, 63,* 343-348.

Bennis, W. G., & Nanus, B. (1985). *Leaders: Strategies for taking charge.* New York: Harper & Row.

Benson, J. K. (1977). Organizations: A dialectical view. *Administrative Science Quarterly, 22,* 1-20.

Berger, P., & Luckmann, T. (1966). *The social construction of reality.* Garden City, NY: Anchor.

Bernardin, H. J., Dahmus, S. A., & Redmon, G. (1993). Attitudes of first-line supervisors toward subordinate appraisals. *Human Resource Management, 32,* 315-324.

Beyer, J. M. (1999). Taming and promoting charisma to change organizations. *Leadership Quarterly, 10,* 307-330.

Beyer, J. M., & Browning, L. D. (1999). Transforming an industry in crisis: Charisma, routinization, and supportive cultural leadership. *Leadership Quarterly, 10,* 483-520.

Bies, R. J., & Sitkin, S. B. (1992). Excuse-making in organizations: Explanation as legitimation. In M. L. McLaughlin, M. J. Cody, & S. Read (Eds.), *Explaining oneself to others: Reason giving in a social context* (pp. 183-198). Hillsdale, NJ: Lawrence Erlbaum.

Bizzell, P., & Herzberg, B. (Eds.). (1990). *The rhetorical tradition: Readings from classical times to the present.* Boston: Bedford/St. Martin's.

Bopp, M. J., & Weeks, G. R. (1984). Dialectical metatheory in family therapy. *Family Process, 23,* 49-61.

Borchgrevink, C. P., & Boster, F. J. (1994). Leader-member exchange: A test of the measurement model. *Hospitality Research Journal, 17,* 75-100.

Borchgrevink, C. P., & Donohue, W. A. (1991). *Leader-member exchange and power distance reduction theory.* Unpublished manuscript, Michigan State University.

Boyd, N. G., & Taylor, R. R. (1998). A developmental approach to the examination of friendship in leader-follower relationships. *Leadership Quarterly, 9,* 1-26.

Braaten, D. O., Cody, M. J., & DeTienne, K. B. (1993). Account episodes in organizations: Remedial work and impression management. *Management Communication Quarterly, 6,* 219-250.

Bradford, D. L., & Cohen, A. R. (1984). *Managing for excellence: The guide to developing high performance in contemporary organizations.* New York: John Wiley.

Brewer, N. (1995). The effects of monitoring individual and group performance on the distribution of effort across tasks. *Journal of Applied Social Psychology, 25,* 760-777.

Brewer, N., Wilson, C., & Beck, K. (1994). Supervisory behavior and team performance amongst police patrol sergeants. *Journal of Occupational and Organizational Psychology, 67,* 69-78.

Brook, P. (1968). *The empty space.* Markham, Ontario: Penguin.

Brown, D. J., & Lord, R. G. (1999). The utility of experimental research in the study of transformational/charismatic leadership. *Leadership Quarterly, 10,* 531-540.

Brown, P., & Levinson, S. (1978). Universals in language usage: Politeness phenomena. In E. N. Goody (Ed.), *Questions and politeness: Strategies in social interactions* (pp. 56-289). Cambridge, UK: Cambridge University Press.

Bryman, A. (1992). *Charisma and leadership in organizations.* London: Sage.

Bryman, A. (1993). Charismatic leadership in business organizations: Some neglected issues. *Leadership Quarterly, 4,* 289-304.

Burke, K. (1954). Fact, inference, and proof in the analysis of literary symbolism. In L. Bryson (Ed.), *Symbols and values: An initial study* (Thirteenth Symposium of the Conference on Science, Philosophy, and Religion, pp. 283-306). New York: Harper.

Burke, K. (1957). *The philosophy of literary form.* New York: Vintage.

Burke, K. (1962). *A rhetoric of motives.* Berkeley: University of California Press.

Burns, J. M. (1978). *Leadership.* New York: Harper & Row.

Burns, T., & Stalker, G. M. (1961). *The management of innovation.* London: Tavistock.

Calás, M. B. (1993). Deconstructing charismatic leadership: Re-reading Weber from the darker side. *Leadership Quarterly, 4,* 305-328.

Callister, R. R., Kramer, M. W., & Turban, D. B. (1999). Feedback seeking following career transitions. *Academy of Management Journal, 42,* 429-438.

Case, T., Dosier, L., Murkison, G., & Keys, B. (1988). How managers influence superiors: A study of upward influence tactics. *Leadership and Organizational Development Journal, 9,* 25-31.

Cashman, J., Dansereau, F., Graen, G., & Haga, W. (1976). Organizational understructure and leadership: A longitudinal investigation of the managerial role-making process. *Organizational Behavior and Human Performance, 15,* 278-296.

Chacko, H. E. (1990). Methods of upward influence, motivational needs, and administrators' perceptions of their supervisors' leadership styles. *Group and Organization Studies, 15,* 253-265.

Cheng, J. L. C. (1983). Organizational context and upward influence: An experimental study of the use of power tactics. *Group and Organization Studies, 8,* 337-355.

Chiles, A. M., & Zorn, T. E. (1995). Empowerment in organizations: Employees' perceptions of the influences of empowerment. *Journal of Applied Communication Research, 23,* 1-25.

Church, A. H., & Bracken, D. W. (1997). Advancing the state of the art of 360-degree feedback. *Group & Organization Management, 22,* 149-161.

Clegg, S. (1975). *Power, rule, and domination: A critical and empirical understanding of power in sociological theory and organizational life.* London: Routledge and Kegan Paul.

Clegg, S. (1979). *The theory of power and organization.* London: Routledge and Kegan Paul.

Collins, J. C., & Porras, J. I. (1996). Building your company's vision. *Harvard Business Review, 74,* 65-77.

Collins, P. (1986). Learning from the outsider within: The sociological significance of black feminist thought. *Social Problems, 33,* S14-S32.

Conger, J. A. (1989). *The charismatic leader.* San Francisco: Jossey-Bass.

Conger, J. A. (1991). Inspiring others: The language of leadership. *The Executive, 5,* 31-45.

Conger, J. A. (1993). Max Weber's conceptualization of charismatic authority: Its influence on organizational research. *Leadership Quarterly, 4,* 277-288.

Conger, J. A. (1999). Charismatic and transformational leadership in organizations: An insider's perspective on these developing streams of research. *Leadership Quarterly, 10,* 145-180.

Conger, J. A., & Hunt, J. G. (1999). Charismatic and transformational leadership: Taking stock of the present and future. *Leadership Quarterly, 10,* 121-128.

Conger, J. A., & Kanungo, R. N. (1987). Toward a behavioral theory of charismatic leadership in organizational settings. *Academy of Management Review, 12,* 637-647.

Conger, J. A., & Kanungo, R. N. (1988). The empowerment process: Integrating theory and practice. *Academy of Management Review, 13,* 471-482.

Conger, J. A., & Kanungo, R. N. (1993, August). *A behavioral attribute measure of charismatic leadership in organizations.* Paper presented at the annual meeting of the Academy of Management, Atlanta, GA.

Conger, J. A., & Kanungo, R. N. (1998). *Charismatic leadership in organizations.* Thousand Oaks, CA: Sage.

Connell, I., & Galasinski, D. (1996, May). *Missioning democracy.* Paper presented at the annual meeting of the International Communication Association, Chicago.

Conrad, C. (1983). Organizational power: Faces and symbolic forms. In L. L. Putnam & M. E. Pacanowsky (Eds.), *Communication and organizations: An interpretive approach* (pp. 173-194). Beverly Hills, CA: Sage.

Cooperrider, D., Barrett, F., & Srivastva, S. (1995). Social construction and appreciative inquiry: A journey in organizational theory. In D. Hosking, P. Dachler, & K. Gergen (Eds.), *Management and organization: Relational alternatives to individualism* (pp. 157-200). Aldershot, UK: Avebury.

Corman, S. R., & Krizek, R. L. (1993). Accounting resources for organizational communication and individual differences in their use. *Management Communication Quarterly, 7,* 5-35.

Couch, C. J. (1989). From hell to utopia and back to hell. *Symbolic Interaction, 12,* 265-279.

Courtright, J. A., Fairhurst, G. T., & Rogers, L. E. (1989). Interaction patterns in organic and mechanistic systems. *Academy of Management Journal, 32,* 773-802.

Courtright, J. A., Millar, F. E., & Rogers-Millar, L. E. (1979). Domineeringness and dominance: A replication and expansion. *Communication Monographs, 46,* 179-192.

Cronen, V. E., Pearce, W. B., & Harris, L. M. (1982). The coordinated management of meaning: A theory of communication. In F. E. X. Dance (Ed.), *Human communication theory* (pp. 61-89). New York: Harper & Row.

Cusella, L. P. (1987). Feedback, motivation, and performance. In F. M. Jablin, L. L. Putnam, K. H. Roberts, & L. W. Porter (Eds.), *Handbook of organizational communication: An interdisciplinary perspective* (pp. 624-678). Newbury Park, CA: Sage.

Dansereau, F. (1995a). Leadership: The multiple-level approaches, Part 1. *Leadership Quarterly, 6*(2), 97-247.

Dansereau, F. (1995b). Leadership: The multiple-level approaches, Part 2. *Leadership Quarterly, 6*(3), 249-450.

Dansereau, F., Graen, G., & Haga, W. (1975). A vertical dyad linkage approach to leadership in formal organizations. *Organizational Behavior and Human Performance, 13,* 380-397.

Dansereau, F., Yammarino, F. J., & Markham, S. E. (1995). Leadership: The multiple-level approaches. *Leadership Quarterly, 6,* 97-109.

Davis-Blake, A., & Pfeffer, J. (1989). Just a mirage: The search for dispositional effects in organizational research. *Academy of Management Review, 14,* 385-400.

Deci, E. L. (1975). *Intrinsic motivation.* New York: Plenum.

Deetz, S. A. (1985). Critical-cultural research: New sensibilities and old realities. *Journal of Management, 11,* 121-136.

Deetz, S. A., & Kersten, A. (1983). Critical models of interpretive research. In L. L. Putnam & M. E. Pacanowsky (Eds.), *Communication and organizations: An interpretive approach* (pp. 147-171). Beverly Hills, CA: Sage.

Deluga, R. J. (1991a). The relationship of subordinate upward influence behavior, health care manager interpersonal stress, and performance. *Journal of Applied Psychology, 21,* 78-88.

Deluga, R. J. (1991b). The relationship of upward-influencing behavior with subordinate-impression management characteristics. *Journal of Applied Social Psychology, 21,* 1145-1160.

Deluga, R. J., & Perry, J. T. (1991). The relationship of subordinate upward influencing behavior, satisfaction, and perceived superior effectiveness with leader-member exchanges. *Journal of Occupational Psychology, 64,* 239-252.

Deming, W. E. (1982). *Out of the crisis.* Cambridge, UK: Cambridge University Press.

Den Hartog, D. N., & Verburg, R. M. (1997). Charisma and rhetoric: Communicative techniques of international business leaders. *Leadership Quarterly, 8,* 355-392.

DePree, M. (1993). *Leadership jazz.* New York: Doubleday.

Derrida, J. (1976). *Grammatolgie* (G. C. Spivak, Trans.). Baltimore: Johns Hopkins University Press.

DiTomaso, N. (1993). Weber's social history and Etzioni's structural theory of charisma in organizations: Implications for thinking about charismatic leadership. *Leadership Quarterly, 4,* 257-276.

Dienesch, R. M., & Liden, R. C. (1986). Leader-member exchange model of leadership: A critique and further development. *Academy of Management Review, 11,* 618-634.

Dockery, T. M., & Steiner, D. D. (1990). The role of the initial interaction in leader-member exchange. *Group and Organization Studies, 15,* 395-413.

Dosier, L., Case, T., & Keys, B. (1988). How managers influence subordinates: An empirical study of downward influence tactics. *Leadership and Organizational Development Journal, 9,* 22-28.

Dow, T. E., Jr. (1969). The theory of charisma. *Sociological Quarterly, 10,* 306-318.

Doz, Y. L., & Prahalad, C. K. (1987). A process model of strategic redirection in large complex firms: The case of multinational corporations. In A. Pettigrew (Ed.), *The management of strategic change* (pp. 63-83). Oxford, UK: Basil Blackwell.

Drake, B. H., & Moberg, D. J. (1986). Communicating influence attempts in dyads: Linguistic sedatives and palliatives. *Academy of Management Review, 11,* 567-584.

Drecksel, G. L. (1991). Leadership research: Some issues. In J. A. Anderson (Ed.), *Communication yearbook 14* (pp. 535-546). Newbury Park, CA: Sage.

Duchon, D., Green, S., & Taber, T. (1986). Vertical dyad linkage: A longitudinal assessment of antecedents, measures, and consequences. *Journal of Applied Psychology, 71,* 56-60.

Dugan, K. W. (1989). Ability and effort attributions: Do they affect how managers communicate performance feedback information? *Academy of Management Journal, 32,* 87-114.

Dulebohn, J. H., & Ferris, G. R. (1999). The role of influence tactics in perceptions of performance evaluations' fairness. *Academy of Management Journal, 42,* 288-303.

Earley, P. C., Northcraft, G. B., Lee, C., & Lituchy, T. R. (1989). Impact of process and outcome feedback on the relation of goal-setting to task performance. *Academy of Management Journal, 33,* 87-105.

Ehrlich, S. B., Meindl, J. R., & Viellieu, B. (1990). The charismatic appeal of a transformational leader: An empirical case study of a small high-technology contractor. *Leadership Quarterly, 1,* 229-248.

Eisenberg, E. M. (1990). Jamming: Transcendence through organizing. *Communication Research, 17,* 139-164.

Ellis, D. (1979). Relational control in two group systems. *Communication Monographs, 46,* 245-267.

Erez, M., Rim, Y., & Keider, I. (1986). The two sides of the tactics of influence: Agent vs. target. *Journal of Occupational Psychology, 59,* 25-39.

Facteau, C. L., Facteau, J. D., Schoel, L. C., Russell, J. E. A., & Poteet, M. L. (1998). Reactions of leaders to 360-degree feedback from subordinates and peers. *Leadership Quarterly, 9,* 427-448.

Fairhurst, G. T. (1990). *Supplemental coding rules and modification of the relational control coding scheme.* Unpublished manuscript, University of Cincinnati, Cincinnati, OH.

Fairhurst, G. T. (1991). *The leader-member exchange patterns of women leaders in industry.* Paper presented at the Society for Organizational Behavior, Albany, NY.

Fairhurst, G. T. (1993a). Echoes of the vision: When the rest of the organization talks Total Quality. *Management Communication Quarterly, 6,* 331-371.

Fairhurst, G. T. (1993b). The leader-member exchange patterns of women leaders in industry: A discourse analysis. *Communication Monographs, 60,* 321-351.

Fairhurst, G. T. (1996, May). *"Governing ideas" that really govern.* Paper presented at the annual meeting of the International Communication Association, Chicago.

Fairhurst, G. T., & Chandler, T. A. (1989). Social structure in leader-member interaction. *Communication Monographs, 56,* 215-239.

Fairhurst, G. T., Cooren, F., & Cahill, D. (2000). *A structuration approach to management policy in suc-*

cessive downsizings. Paper presented at the National Communication Association Conference, Seattle, WA.

Fairhurst, G. T., Green, S. G., & Courtright, J. A. (1995). Inertial forces and the implementation of a sociotechnical systems approach: A communication study. *Organization Science, 6,* 168-185.

Fairhurst, G. T., Green, S. G., & Snavely, B. K. (1984a). Face support in controlling poor performance. *Human Communication Research, 11,* 272-295.

Fairhurst, G. T., Green, S. G., & Snavely, B. K. (1984b). Managerial control and discipline: Whips and chains. In R. Bostrom (Ed.), *Communication yearbook 8* (pp. 558-593). Beverly Hills, CA: Sage.

Fairhurst, G. T., Jordan, J. M., & Neuwirth, K. (1997). Why are we here? Managing the meaning of an organizational mission. *Journal of Applied Communication Research, 25,* 243-263.

Fairhurst, G. T., Rogers, L. E., & Sarr, R. A. (1987). Manager-subordinate control patterns and judgments about the relationship. In M. McLaughlin (Ed.), *Communication yearbook 10* (pp. 395-415). Newbury Park, CA: Sage.

Fairhurst, G. T., & Sarr, R. A. (1996). *The art of framing: Managing the language of leadership.* San Francisco: Jossey-Bass.

Falbe, C. M., & Yukl, G. (1992). Consequences for managers of using single influence tactics and combinations of tactics. *Academy of Management Journal, 35,* 638-652.

Farmer, S. M., Maslyn, J. M., Fedor, D. B., & Goodman, J. S. (1997). Putting upward influence strategies in context. *Journal of Organizational Behavior, 18,* 17-42.

Fedor, D. B. (1990). *Feedback recipients' responses to negative feedback: Investigating the role of uncertainty.* Paper presented at the fifth annual conference of the Society for Industrial and Organizational Psychology, Miami, FL.

Fedor, D. B. (1991). Recipient responses to performance feedback: A proposed model and its implications. In G. R. Ferris & K. M. Rowland (Eds.), *Research in personnel and human resources management* (Vol. 9, pp. 73-120). Greenwich, CT: JAI.

Fedor, D. B., Rensvold, R. G., & Adams, S. M. (1992). An investigation of factors expected to affect feedback seeking: A longitudinal field study. *Personnel Psychology, 45,* 779-805.

Ferris, G. R., Judge, T. A., Rowland, K. M., & Fitzgibbons, D. E. (1994). Subordinate influence and the performance evaluation process: Test of a model. *Organizational Behavior and Human Decision Processes, 58,* 101-135.

Fine, G. (1992). Agency, structure, and comparative contexts: Toward a synthetic interactionism. *Symbolic Interaction, 15,* 87-107.

Fiol, C. M., Harris, D., & House, R. (1999). Charismatic leadership: Strategies for effecting social change. *Leadership Quarterly, 10,* 449-482.

Fisher, B. A. (1978). *Perspectives on human communication.* New York: Macmillan.

Fisher, B. A. (1985). Leadership as medium: Treating complexity in group communication research. *Small Group Behavior, 16,* 167-196.

Fisher, B. A. (1986). Leadership: When does the difference make a difference? In R. Hirokawa & M. S. Poole (Eds.), *Communication and group decision-making* (pp. 197-215). Beverly Hills, CA: Sage.

Fiske, S. T., & Taylor, S. E. (1991). *Social cognition.* New York: McGraw-Hill.

Fleishman, E. A. (1953). The description of supervisory behavior. *Journal of Applied Psychology, 37,* 1-6.

Florin-Thuma, B. C., & Boudreau, J. W. (1987). Performance feedback utility in a small organization: Effects on organizational outcomes and managerial decision processes. *Personnel Psychology, 40,* 693-713.

Folger, J. P. (1991). Interpretive and structural claims about confrontations. In J. A. Anderson (Ed.), *Communication yearbook 14* (pp. 393-402). Newbury Park, CA: Sage.

Folger, J. P., Hewes, D., & Poole, M. S. (1984). Coding social interaction. In B. Dervin & M. J. Voight (Eds.), *Progress in communication sciences* (Vol. 4, pp. 115-161). Norwood, NJ: Ablex.

Frost, P. J. (1987). Power, politics, and influence. In F. M. Jablin, L. L. Putnam, K. H. Roberts, & L. W. Porter (Eds.), *Handbook of organizational communication: An interdisciplinary perspective* (pp. 503-548). Newbury Park, CA: Sage.

Frost, P. J., Moore, L. F., Louis, M. R., Lundberg, C. C., & Martin, J. (1991). *Reframing organizational culture.* Newbury Park, CA: Sage.

Funderburg, S. A., & Levy, P. E. (1997). The influence of individual and contextual variables on 360-degree feedback system attitudes. *Group & Organization Management, 22,* 210-235.

Gardner, W. L., & Avolio, B. J. (1998). The charismatic relationship: A dramaturgical perspective. *Academy of Management Review, 23,* 32-58.

Garko, M. G. (1992). Persuading subordinates who communicate in attractive and unattractive styles. *Management Communication Quarterly, 5,* 289-315.

Gavin, M. B., Green, S. G., & Fairhurst, G. T. (1995). Managerial control strategies for poor performance over time and the impact on subordinate and manager reactions. *Organizational Behavior and Human Decision Processes, 63,* 207-221.

Geddes, D. (1993). Examining the dimensionality of performance feedback messages: Source and recipient perceptions of influence attempts. *Communication Studies, 44,* 200-215.

Geddes, D., & Baron, R. A. (1997). Workplace aggression as a consequence of negative performance feedback. *Management Communication Quarterly, 10,* 433-454.

Geddes, D., & Linnehan, F. (1998). Exploring the dimensionality of positive and negative performance feedback. *Communication Quarterly, 44,* 326-344.

Gergen, K. J. (1985). The social constructionist movement in modern psychology. *American Psychologist, 40,* 266-275.

Gerstner, C. R., & Day, D. V. (1997). Meta-analytic review of leader-member exchange theory: Correlates and construct issues. *Journal of Applied Psychology, 82,* 827-844.

Giddens, A. (1979). *Central problems in social theory: Action, structure, and contradiction in social analysis.* London: Macmillan.

Giddens, A. (1984). *The constitution of society.* Berkeley: University of California Press.

Gioia, D. A., & Longenecker, C. O. (1994). Delving into the dark side: The politics of executive appraisal. *Organizational Dynamics, 22,* 47-58.

Gioia, D. A., & Sims, H. P., Jr. (1986). Cognition-behavior connections: Attribution and verbal behavior in leader-subordinate interactions. *Organizational Behavior and Human Decision Processes, 37,* 197-229.

Goltz, S. M. (1993). Dynamics of leaders' and subordinates' performance-related discussions following monitoring by leaders in group meetings. *Leadership Quarterly, 4,* 173-187.

Graen, G. B. (1989). *Unwritten rules for your career: 15 secrets for fast-track success.* New York: John Wiley.

Graen, G. B., & Cashman, J. (1975). A role-making model of leadership in formal organizations: A developmental approach. In J. G. Hunt & L. L. Larson (Eds.), *Leadership frontiers* (pp. 143-166). Kent, OH: Kent State University Press.

Graen, G., Cashman, J. F., Ginsburg, S., & Schiemann, W. (1977). Effects of linking-pin quality on the quality of working life of lower participants. *Administrative Science Quarterly, 22,* 491-504.

Graen, G. B., Novak, M., & Sommerkamp, P. (1982). The effects of leader-member exchange and job design on productivity and satisfaction: Testing a dual attachment model. *Organizational Behavior and Human Performance, 30,* 109-131.

Graen, G. B., & Scandura, T. (1987). Toward a psychology of dyadic organizing. In B. Staw & L. L. Cummings (Eds.), *Research in organizational behavior* (Vol. 9, pp. 175-208). Greenwich, CT: JAI.

Graen, G. B., Scandura, T. A., & Graen, M. R. (1986). A field experimental test of the moderating effects of growth need strength on productivity. *Journal of Applied Psychology, 71,* 484-491.

Graen, G. B., & Uhl-Bien, M. (1991). The transformation of professionals into self-managing and partially self-designing contributors: Towards a theory of leadership making. *Journal of Management Systems, 3,* 33-48.

Graen, G. B., & Uhl-Bien, M. (1995). Relationship-based approach to leadership: Development of a leader-member exchange (LMX) theory of leadership over 25 years—Applying a multi-level multi-domain perspective. *Leadership Quarterly, 6,* 219-247.

Graen, G. B., & Wakabayashi, M. (1994). Cross-cultural leadership-making: Bridging American and Japanese diversity for team advantage. In H. C. Triandis, M. D. Dunnette, & L. M. Hough (Eds.), *Handbook of industrial and organizational psychology* (Vol. 4, pp. 415-446). New York: Consulting Psychologists Press.

Graen, G. B., Wakabayashi, M., Graen, M. R., & Graen, M. G. (1990). International generalizability of American hypothesis about Japanese management progress: A strong inference investigation. *Leadership Quarterly, 1,* 1-11.

Graham, J. W. (1991). Servant-leadership in organizations: Inspirational and moral. *Leadership Quarterly, 2,* 105-119.

Green, S. G., Fairhurst, G. T., & Snavely, B. K. (1986). Chains of poor performance and supervisory control. *Organizational Behavior and Human Decision Processes, 38,* 7-27.

Greguras, G. J., & Robie, C. (1998). A new look at within-source interrater reliability of 360-degree feedback ratings. *Journal of Applied Psychology, 83,* 960-968.

Greller, M. M., & Herold, D. M. (1975). Sources of feedback: A preliminary investigation. *Organizational Behavior and Human Performance, 13,* 244-256.

Hanser, L. M., & Muchinsky, P. M. (1978). Work as an information environment. *Organizational Behavior and Human Performance, 21,* 47-60.

Harper, N. L., & Hirokawa, R. Y. (1988). A comparison of persuasive strategies used by female and male managers: An examination of downward influence. *Communication Quarterly, 36,* 157-168.

Haslett, B. J. (1987). *Communication: Strategic action in context.* Hillsdale, NJ: Lawrence Erlbaum.

Hater, J. J., & Bass, B. M. (1988). Superiors' evaluations and subordinates' perceptions of transformational and transactional leadership. *Journal of Applied Psychology, 73,* 695-702.

Hazucha, J. F., Hezlett, S. A., & Schneider, R. J. (1993). The impact of 360-degree feedback on management skills development. *Human Resource Management, 32,* 325-351.

Hemphill, J. K., & Coons, A. E. (1957). Development of the Leader Behavior Description Questionnaire. In R. M. Stogdill & A. E. Coons (Eds.), *Leader behavior: Its description and measurement.* Columbus: Ohio State University, Bureau of Business Research.

Herold, D. M., & Greller, M. M. (1977). Feedback: The development of a construct. *Academy of Management Journal, 20,* 142-147.

Herold, D. M., Liden, R. C., & Leatherwood, M. L. (1987). Using multiple attributes to assess source of performance feedback. *Academy of Management Journal, 30,* 826-835.

Hewes, D. E., & Planalp, S. (1987). The individual's place in communication science. In C. R. Berger & S. H. Chaffee (Eds.), *Handbook of communication science* (pp. 146-183). Newbury Park, CA: Sage.

Hirokawa, R. Y., Kodama, R. A., & Harper, N. L. (1990). Impact of managerial power on persuasive strategy selection by female and male managers. *Management Communication Quarterly, 4,* 30-50.

Hirokawa, R. Y., & Miyahara, A. (1986). A comparison of influence strategies utilized by managers in American and Japanese Organizations. *Communication Quarterly, 34,* 250-265.

Hofstede, G. (1981). *Culture's consequences: International differences in work-related values.* Beverly Hills, CA: Sage.

Holladay, S. J., & Coombs, W. T. (1993). Communicating visions: An exploration of the role of delivery in the creation of leader charisma. *Management Communication Quarterly, 6,* 405-427.

Holladay, S. J., & Coombs, W. T. (1994). Speaking of visions and visions being spoken: An exploration of the effects of content and delivery on perceptions of leader charisma. *Management Communication Quarterly, 8,* 165-189.

Honig, W. K., & Stadden, J. E. R. (1977). *Handbook of operant behavior.* Englewood Cliffs, NJ: Prentice Hall.

Hosking, D. M., & Morley, I. E. (1988). The skills of leadership. In J. G. Hunt, B. R. Baglia, H. P. Dachler, & C. A. Schriesheim (Eds.), *Emerging leadership vistas* (pp. 89-106). Lexington, MA: Lexington Books.

House, R. J. (1977). A 1976 theory of charismatic leadership. In J. G. Hunt & L. L. Larson (Eds.), *Leadership: The cutting edge* (pp. 189-207). Carbondale: Southern Illinois University Press.

House, R. J., & Aditya, R. (1997). The social scientific study of leadership: Quo vadis? *Journal of Management, 23,* 409-473.

House, R. J., & Howell, J. M. (1992). Personality and charismatic leadership. *Leadership Quarterly, 3,* 81-108.

House, R. J., Spangler, W. D., & Woycke, J. (1991). Personality and charisma in the U.S. presidency: A psychological theory of leader effectiveness. *Administrative Science Quarterly, 36,* 364-396.

Howell, J. M., & Frost, P. J. (1989). A laboratory study of charismatic leadership. *Organizational Behavior and Human Decision Processes, 43,* 243-269.

Howell, J. M., & Higgins, C. A. (1990a). Champions of technological innovation. *Administrative Science Quarterly, 35,* 317-341.

Howell, J. M., & Higgins, C. A. (1990b). Leadership behaviors, influence tactics, and career experiences of champions of technological innovation. *Leadership Quarterly, 1,* 249-264.

Hui, C., & Graen, G. (1997). Guanxi and professional leadership in contemporary Sino-American joint ventures in Mainland China. *Leadership Quarterly, 8,* 451-466.

Hunt, J. G. (1999). Transformational/charismatic leadership's transformation of the field: An historical essay. *Leadership Quarterly, 10,* 129-143.

Hunt, J. G., Boal, K. B., & Dodge, G. E. (1999). The effects of visionary and crisis-responsive charisma on followers: An experimental examination of two kinds of charismatic leadership. *Leadership Quarterly, 10,* 423-448.

Hunt, J. G., & Conger, J. A. (1999). From where we sit: An assessment of transformational and charismatic leadership research. *Leadership Quarterly, 10,* 335-344.

Huspek, M., & Kendall, K. E. (1991). On withholding political voice: An analysis of the political vocabulary of a "nonpolitical" speech community. *Quarterly Journal of Speech, 77,* 1-19.

Ilgen, D. R., Fisher, C. D., & Taylor, M. S. (1979). Consequences of individual feedback on behavior in organizations. *Journal of Applied Psychology, 64,* 359-371.

Isaacs, W. N. (1993). Taking flight: Dialogue, collective thinking, and organizational learning. *Organizational Dynamics, 22,* 24-39.

Isaacs, W. N. (1999). *Dialogue: The art of thinking together.* New York: Currency.

Jablin, F. M. (1987). Organizational entry, assimilation, and exit. In F. M. Jablin, L. L. Putnam, K. H. Roberts, & L. W. Porter (Eds.), *Handbook of organizational communication: An interdisciplinary perspective* (pp. 679-740). Newbury Park, CA: Sage.

Jacobs, T. (1971). *Leadership and exchange in formal organizations.* Alexandria, VA: Human Resources Research Organization.

Jermier, J. M. (1993). Charismatic leadership: Neo-Weberian perspectives. *Leadership Quarterly, 4,* 217-412.

Jermier, J. M., Knights, D., & Nord, W. R. (1994). *Resistance and power in organizations.* London: Routledge.

Katz, D., & Kahn, R. L. (1978). *The social psychology of organizations* (2nd ed.). New York: John Wiley.

Keller, T., & Dansereau, F. (1995). Leadership and empowerment: A social exchange perspective. *Human Relations, 48,* 127-145.

Kellermann, K., & Cole, T. (1994). Classifying compliance messages: Taxonomic disorder and strategic confusion. *Communication Theory, 4,* 3-60.

Kerr, S., & Jermier, J. M. (1978). Substitutes for leadership: Their meaning and measurement. *Organizational Behavior and Human Performance, 22,* 375-403.

Kim, Y. Y., & Miller, K. I. (1990). The effects of attributions and feedback goals on the generation of supervisory feedback message strategies. *Management Communication Quarterly, 4,* 6-29.

Kipnis, D., & Schmidt, S. M. (1982). *Profiles of organizational influence strategies.* Toronto, Canada: University Associates.

Kipnis, D., & Schmidt, S. M. (1985). The language of persuasion. *Psychology Today, 42,* 40-46.

Kipnis, D., & Schmidt, S. M. (1988). Upward-influence styles: Relationship with performance evaluations, salary, and stress. *Administrative Science Quarterly, 33,* 528-542.

Kipnis, D., Schmidt, S. M., Swaffin-Smith, C., & Wilkinson, L. (1984). Patterns of managerial influence strategies: Shotgun managers, tacticians, and bystanders. *Organizational Dynamics, 12,* 58-67.

Kipnis, D., Schmidt, S. M., & Wilkinson, I. (1980). Intra-organizational influence tactics: Explorations in getting one's way. *Journal of Applied Psychology, 65,* 440-452.

Kirkpatrick, S. A., & Locke, E. A. (1996). Direct and indirect effects of three core charismatic leadership components on performance and attitudes. *Journal of Applied Psychology, 81,* 36-51.

Klein, K. J., & House, R. J. (1995). On fire: Charismatic leadership and levels of analysis. *Leadership Quarterly, 6,* 183-198.

Kluger, A. N., & DeNisi, A. (1996). The effects of feedback interventions on performance: A historical review, a meta-analysis, and a preliminary feedback intervention theory. *Psychological Bulletin, 119,* 254-284.

Kluger, A. N., Lewinsohn, S., & Aiello, J. R. (1994). The influence of feedback on mood: Linear effects on pleasantness and curvilinear effects on arousal. *Organizational Behavior and Human Decision Processes, 60,* 276-299.

Knapp, M. L., Miller, G. R., & Fudge, K. (1994). Background and current trends in the study of interpersonal communication. In M. L. Knapp & G. R. Miller (Eds.), *Handbook of interpersonal communication* (2nd ed., pp. 3-20). Thousand Oaks, CA: Sage.

Kolb, D. M., & Putnam, L. L. (1992). The dialectics of disputing. In D. M. Kolb & J. M. Bartunek (Eds.), *Hidden conflicts in organizations* (pp. 1-31). Newbury Park, CA: Sage.

Komaki, J. L. (1986). Toward effective supervision: An operant analysis and comparison of managers at work. *Journal of Applied Psychology, 71,* 270-278.

Komaki, J. L. (1998). *Leadership from an operant perspective.* London: Routledge.

Komaki, J. L., & Citera, M. (1990). Beyond effective supervision: Identifying key interactions between superior and subordinate. *Leadership Quarterly, 1,* 91-106.

Komaki, J. L., Desselles, M. L., & Bowman, E. D. (1989). Definitely not a breeze: Extending an operant model of effective supervision to teams. *Journal of Applied Psychology, 74*, 522-529.

Komaki, J. L., Zlotnick, S., & Jensen, M. J. (1986). Development of an operant-based taxonomy and observational index. *Journal of Applied Psychology, 71*, 260-269.

Korsgaard, M. A., Meglino, B. M., & Lester, S. W. (1997). Beyond helping: Do other-oriented values have broader implications in organizations? *Journal of Applied Psychology, 82*, 160-177.

Kotter, J. P. (1990). *A force for change: How leadership differs from management.* New York: Free Press.

Kouzes, J. M., & Posner, B. Z. (1993). *Credibility: How leaders gain and lose it, why people demand it.* San Francisco: Jossey-Bass.

Kouzes, J. M., & Posner, B. Z. (1995). *The leadership challenge.* San Francisco: Jossey-Bass.

Kramer, M. W. (1995). A longitudinal study of superior-subordinate communication during job transfers. *Human Communication Research, 22*, 39-64.

Krone, K. J. (1991). Effects of leader-member exchange on subordinates' upward influence attempts. *Communication Research Reports, 8*, 9-18.

Kuhnert, K. W., & Lewis, P. (1987). Transactional and transformational leadership: A constructive/developmental analysis. *Academy of Management Review, 12*, 648-657.

Lannamann, J. W. (1991). Interpersonal communication research as ideological practice. *Communication Theory, 1*, 179-203.

Larson, J. R., Jr. (1989). The dynamic interplay between employees' feedback-seeking strategies and supervisors' delivery of performance feedback. *Academy of Management Review, 14*, 408-422.

Larson, J. R., Jr., & Callahan, C. (1990). Performance monitoring: How it affects work productivity. *Journal of Applied Psychology, 75*, 530-538.

Larson, J. R., Jr., Glynn, M. A., Fleenor, C. P., & Scontrino, M. P. (1987). Exploring the dimensionality of managers' performance feedback to subordinates. *Human Relations, 39*, 1083-1102.

Larwood, L., Falbe, C. M., Kriger, M. P., & Miesing, P. (1995). Structure and meaning of organizational vision. *Academy of Management Journal, 38*, 740-769.

Larwood, L., Kriger, M. P., & Falbe, C. M. (1993). Organizational vision: An investigation of the vision construct-in-use of AACSB Business School deans. *Group & Organization Management, 18*, 214-236.

Latham, G. P., & Locke, E. A. (1991). Self-regulation through goal-setting. *Organizational Behavior and Human Decision Processes, 50*, 212-247.

Lauterbach, K. E., & Weiner, B. J. (1996). Dynamics of upward influence: How male and female managers get their way. *Leadership Quarterly, 7*, 87-108.

Lee, J. (1997). Leader-member exchange, the "Pelz effect," and cooperative communication between group members. *Management Communication Quarterly, 11*, 266-287.

Lee, J., & Jablin, F. M. (1995). Maintenance communication in superior-subordinate work relationships. *Human Communication Research, 22*, 220-257.

Ledford, G. E., Jr., Wendenhof, J. R., & Strahley, J. T. (1995). Realizing a corporate philosophy. *Organizational Dynamics, 23*, 5-19.

Leont'ev, A. N. (1978). *Activity, consciousness and personality.* Englewood Cliffs, NJ: Prentice Hall.

Levine, S. (1949). An approach of constructive leadership. *Journal of Social Issues, 5*, 46-53.

Levy, P. E., Albright, M. D., Cawley, B. D., & Williams, J. R. (1995). Situational and individual determinants of feedback seeking: A closer look at the process. *Organizational Behavior and Human Decision Processes, 62*, 23-37.

Liden, R. C., & Maslyn, J. M. (1998). Multidimensionality of leader-member exchange: An empirical assessment through scale development. *Journal of Management, 24*, 43-72.

Liden, R. C., & Mitchell, T. R. (1989). Ingratiation in the development of leader-member exchanges. In R. A. Giacalone & P. Rosenfeld (Eds.), *Impression management in the organization* (pp. 343-361). Hillsdale, NJ: Lawrence Erlbaum.

Liden, R. C., Sparrowe, R. T., & Wayne, S. J. (1997). Leader-member exchange theory: The past and potential for the future. In G. R. Ferris (Ed.), *Research in personnel and human resources management* (Vol. 15, pp. 47-119). Greenwich, CT: JAI.

Liden, R. C., Wayne, S. J., & Stilwell, D. (1993). A longitudinal study on the early development of leader-member exchange. *Journal of Applied Psychology, 78*, 662-674.

Likert, R. (1961). *New patterns of management.* New York: McGraw-Hill.

Littlejohn, S. W. (1983). *Theories of human communication* (2nd ed.). Belmont, CA: Wadsworth.

Locke, E. A., Frederick, E., Lee, C., & Bobko, P. (1984). Effect of self-efficacy, goals, and task strategies on task performance. *Journal of Applied Psychology, 69*, 694-699.

Locke, E. A., & Latham, G. P. (1990). *A theory of goal-setting and task performance.* Englewood Cliffs, NJ: Prentice Hall.

London, M., Smither, J. W., & Adsit, D. J. (1997). Accountability: The Achilles' heel of multisource feedback. *Group & Organization Management, 22*, 162-184.

Louie, T. A. (1999). Decision makers' hindsight bias after receiving favorable and unfavorable feedback. *Journal of Applied Psychology, 84*, 29-41.

Lowe, K. B., Kroeck, K. G., & Sivasubramaniam, N. (1996). Effectiveness correlates of transformational and transactional leadership: A meta-analytic review of the MLQ. *Leadership Quarterly, 7*, 385-425.

Mainiero, L. A. (1986). Coping with powerlessness: The relationship of gender and job dependency to empowerment strategy usage. *Administrative Science Quarterly, 31,* 633-653.

Manz, C. C., & Sims, H. P. (1987). Leading workers to lead themselves: The external leadership of self-managing work teams. *Administrative Science Quarterly, 32,* 106-128.

Manz, C. C., & Sims, H. P. (1989). *Super-leadership: Leading others to lead themselves.* New York: Prentice Hall.

Martin, J. (1992). *Cultures in organizations: Three perspectives.* Oxford, UK: Oxford University Press.

Martocchio, J. J., & Webster, J. (1992). Effects of feedback and cognitive playfulness on performance in microcomputer software training. *Personnel Psychology, 45,* 553-578.

Maslyn, J. M., Farmer, S. M., & Fedor, D. B. (1996). Failed upward influence attempts: Predicting the nature of subordinate persistence in pursuit of organizational goals. *Group & Organization Management, 21,* 461-480.

McPhee, R. D. (1988). Vertical communication changes: Toward an integrated approach. *Management Communication Quarterly, 1,* 455-493.

Meindl, J. R. (1990). On leadership: An alternative to conventional wisdom. In B. M. Staw & L. L. Cummings (Eds.), *Research in organizational behavior* (Vol. 12, pp. 159-203). Greenwich, CT: JAI.

Meindl, J. R., Ehrlich, S. B., & Dukerich, J. M. (1985). The romance of leadership. *Administrative Science Quarterly, 30,* 78-102.

Mento, A. J., Steel, R. P., & Karren, R. J. (1987). A meta-analytic study of the effects of goal-setting on task performance: 1966-1984. *Organizational Behavior and Human Decision Processes, 39,* 52-83.

Middleton, D., & Edwards, D. (1990). Introduction. In D. Middleton & D. Edwards (Eds.), *Collective remembering* (pp. 1-22). Newbury Park, CA: Sage.

Mintzberg, H. (1987, July-August). Crafting strategy. *Harvard Business Review, 65,* 66-75.

Montgomery, B. M. (1992). Communication as the interface between couples and culture. In S. A. Deetz (Ed.), *Communication yearbook 15* (pp. 475-507). Newbury Park, CA: Sage.

Morgan, G. (1986). *Images of organization.* Beverly Hills, CA: Sage.

Morris, G. H., & Coursey, M. (1989). Negotiating the meaning of employees' conduct: How managers evaluate employees' accounts. *Southern Communication Journal, 54,* 185-205.

Morris, G. H., Gaveras, S. C., Baker, W. L., & Coursey, M. L. (1990). Aligning actions at work: How managers confront problems of employee performance. *Management Communication Quarterly, 3,* 303-333.

Morrison, E. W., & Bies, R. J. (1991). Impression management in the feedback-seeking process: A litera-

ture review and research agenda. *Academy of Management Review, 16,* 522-541.

Nadler, D. A. (1988). Organizational frame bending: Types of change in complex organizations. In R. Kilmann & T. Covin (Eds.), *Corporate transformation: Revitalizing organizations for a competitive world* (pp. 66-84). San Francisco: Jossey-Bass.

Nanus, B. (1992). *Visionary leadership.* San Francisco: Jossey-Bass.

Newell, S. E., & Stutman, R. K. (1991, May). *Stalking culturally shared interpretations and restricted meanings in conflict episodes.* Paper presented at the International Communication Association Convention, Chicago.

Niehoff, B. P., & Moorman, R. H. (1993). Justice as a mediator of the relationship between methods of monitoring and organizational citizenship behavior. *Academy of Management Journal, 63,* 527-556.

Nisbett, R. E., & Wilson, T. (1977). Telling more than we can know: Verbal reports on mental processes. *Psychological Review, 84,* 231-259.

Northcraft, G. B., & Ashford, S. J. (1990). The preservation of self in everyday life: The effects of performance expectations and feedback context on feedback inquiry. *Organizational Behavior and Human Decision Processes, 47,* 42-64.

Northcraft, G. B., & Earley, P. C. (1989). Technology, credibility, and feedback use. *Organizational Behavior and Human Decision Processes, 44,* 83-96.

Nussbaum, B., Moskowitz, D. B., & Beam, A. (1985, January 12). The new corporate elite. *Business Week,* pp. 62-81.

O'Keefe, D. J. (1994). From strategy-based to feature-based analyses of compliance gaining message classification and production. *Communication Theory, 4,* 61-68.

Pawar, B. S., & Eastman, K. K. (1997). The nature and implications of contextual influences on transformational leadership: A conceptual examination. *Academy of Management Review, 22,* 80-109.

Peterson, M. F., & Sorenson, R. L. (1991). Cognitive processes in leadership: Interpreting and handling events in an organizational context. In J. A. Anderson (Ed.), *Communication yearbook 14* (pp. 501-534). Newbury Park, CA: Sage.

Pettigrew, A. M. (1979). On studying organizational cultures. *Administrative Science Quarterly, 24,* 570-581.

Pfeffer, J. (1981). Management as symbolic action: The creation and maintenance of organizational paradigms. In L. L. Cummings & B. M. Staw (Eds.), *Research in organizational behavior* (Vol. 3, pp. 1-52). Greenwich, CT: JAI.

Phillips, E. T. (1996). *Life cycle of project team effectiveness, from creation to conclusion, as a function of dyadic team composition: A naturally occurring field simulation.* Unpublished doctoral dissertation, University of Cincinnati, Cincinnati, OH.

Phillips, N. (1997). Bringing the organization back in: A comment on conceptualizations of power in upward influence research. *Journal of Organizational Behavior, 18,* 43-47.

Podsakoff, P. M., & Farh, J. L. (1989). Effects of feedback sign and credibility on goal-setting and task performance. *Organizational Behavior and Human Decision Processes, 44,* 45-67.

Pondy, L. R. (1978). Leadership is a language game. In M. W. McCall, Jr. & M. M. Lombardo (Eds.), *Leadership: Where else can we go?* (pp. 88-99). Durham, NC: Duke University Press.

Prasad, P. (1993). Symbolic processes in the implementation of technological change: A symbolic interactionist study of work computerization. *Academy of Management Journal, 36,* 1400-1429.

Putnam, L. L. (1983). An interpretive perspective: An alternative to functionalism. In L. L. Putnam & M. E. Pacanowsky (Eds.), *Communication and organizations: An interpretive approach* (pp. 31-54). Beverly Hills, CA: Sage.

Putnam, L. L., Phillips, N., & Chapman, P. (1996). Metaphors of communication and organization. In S. R. Clegg, C. Hardy, & W. R. Nord (Eds.), *Handbook of organization studies* (pp. 375-408). London: Sage.

Rawlins, W. K. (1992). *Friendship matters: Communication, dialectics, and the life course.* New York: Aldine.

Reilly, K. R., Smither, J. W., & Vasilopoulos, N. C. (1996). A longitudinal study of upward feedback. *Personnel Psychology, 49,* 599-612.

Ricoeur, P. (1971). The model of the text: Meaningful action considered as text. *Social Research, 38,* 529-562.

Riggio, R. E. (1987). *The charisma quotient: What it is, how to get it, and how to use it.* New York: Dodd, Mead and Company.

Riley, P. (1988). Chapter 4 commentary: The merger of macro and micro levels of leadership. In J. G. Hunt, B. R. Baglia, H. P. Dachler, & C. A. Schriesheim (Eds.), *Emerging leadership vistas* (pp. 80-83). Lexington, MA: Lexington Books.

Rogers, L. E., & Farace, R. V. (1975). Relational communication analysis: New measurement procedures. *Human Communication Research, 1,* 222-239.

Rogers, L. E., & Millar, F. E., & Bavelas, J. B. (1985). Methods for analyzing marital conflict discourse: Implications of a systems approach. *Family Process, 24,* 175-187.

Rogers-Millar, L. E., & Millar, F. E. (1979). Domineeringness and dominance: A transactional view. *Human Communication Research, 5,* 238-246.

Rogers, P. S., & Swales, J. M. (1990). We the people? An analysis of the Dana Corporation policies document. *Journal of Business Communication, 27,* 293-314.

Rost, J. C. (1991). *Leadership for the twenty-first century.* New York: Praeger.

Rychlak, J. F. (1977). *The psychology of rigorous humanism.* New York: John Wiley.

Salancik, G. R., & Pfeffer, J. (1977). Constraints on administrative discretion: The limited influence of mayors on city budgets. *Urban Affairs Quarterly, 12,* 485-498.

Sashkin, M., & Fulmer, R. (1988). Toward an organizational leadership theory. In J. G. Hunt, B. R. Baglia, H. P. Dachler, & C. A. Schriesheim (Eds.), *Emerging leadership vistas* (pp. 51-60). Lexington, MA: Lexington Books.

Scandura, T. (1995). *Leader-member exchange model of leadership and fairness issues.* Unpublished manuscript, University of Miami, Miami, FL.

Scandura, T. A., & Graen, G. B. (1984). Moderating effects of initial leader-member exchange status on the effects of a leadership intervention. *Journal of Applied Psychology, 69,* 428-436.

Scandura, T. A., Graen, G. B., & Novak, M. (1986). When managers decide not to decide autocratically. *Journal of Applied Psychology, 69,* 428-436.

Scheflen, A. E. (1974). *How behavior means.* Garden City, NY: Anchor.

Schein, E. H. (1992). *Organizational culture and leadership* (2nd ed.). San Francisco: Jossey-Bass.

Schiemann, W. A., & Graen, G. B. (1984). *Structural and interpersonal effects in patterns of managerial communication.* Unpublished manuscript, University of Cincinnati, Cincinnati, OH.

Schilit, W. K. (1987). Upward influence activity in strategic decision-making. *Group and Organization Studies, 12,* 343-368.

Schlenker, B. R. (1980). *Impression management: The self-concept, social identity, and interpersonal relations.* New York: Brooks/Cole.

Schmidt, S. M., & Kipnis, D. (1984). Managers' pursuit of individual and organizational goals. *Human Relations, 37,* 781-794.

Schnell, E. R., & Sims, H. P., Jr. (1993, August). *The language of leadership: A review of observational studies of leader verbal behavior.* Paper presented at the annual meeting of the Academy of Management Association, Atlanta, GA.

Schonbach, P. (1990). *Account episodes: The management or escalation of conflict.* Cambridge, UK: Cambridge University Press.

Schriesheim, C. A., Castro, S. L., & Cogliser, C. C. (1999). Leader-member exchange (LMX) research: A comprehensive review of theory, measurement, and data-analytic practices. *Leadership Quarterly, 10,* 63-114.

Schriesheim, C. A., Cogliser, C. C., & Neider, L. L. (1995). "Is it trustworthy?" A multiple levels-of-analysis reexamination of an Ohio State leadership study with implications for future research. *Leadership Quarterly, 6,* 111-145.

Schriesheim, C. A., & Hinkin, T. R. (1990). Influence tactics used by subordinates: A theoretical and empirical analysis and refinement of the Kipnis, Schmidt, and Wilkinson subscales. *Journal of Applied Psychology, 75,* 246-257.

Schriesheim, C. A., Neider, L. L., Scandura, T. A., & Tepper, B. J. (1992). Development and preliminary validation of a new scale (LMX-6) to measure leader-member exchange in organizations. *Educational and Psychological Measurement, 52,* 135-147.

Seeger, M. W. (Ed.). (1994). *"I gotta tell you": Speeches of Lee Iacocca.* Detroit, MI: Wayne State University Press.

Seers, A. (1989). Team-member exchange quality: A new construct for role-making research. *Organizational Behavior and Human Decision Processes, 43,* 118-135.

Senge, P. (1990). *The fifth discipline.* New York: Doubleday.

Senge, P., Kleiner, A., Roberts, C., Ross, R., Roth, G., & Smith, B. (1999). *The dance of change: The challenge to sustaining momentum in learning organizations.* New York: Doubleday.

Shamir, B., Arthur, M. B., & House, R. J. (1994). The rhetoric of charismatic leadership: A theoretical extension, a case study, and implications for research. *Leadership Quarterly, 5,* 25-42.

Shamir, B., House, R. J., & Arthur, M. B. (1993). The motivational effects of charismatic leadership: A self-concept based theory. *Organization Science, 4,* 577-594.

Shamir, B., & Howell, J. M. (1999). Organizational and contextual influences on the emergence and effectiveness of charismatic leadership. *Leadership Quarterly, 10,* 257-284.

Shea, C. M., & Howell, J. M. (1999). Charismatic leadership and task feedback: A laboratory study of their effects on self-efficacy and task performance. *Leadership Quarterly, 10,* 375-396.

Shotter, J. (1993). *Conversational realities: Constructing life through language.* London: Sage.

Sias, P. M. (1996). Constructing perceptions of differential treatment: An analysis of coworker discourse. *Communication Monographs, 63,* 171-187.

Sias, P. M., & Jablin, F. M. (1995). Differential superior-subordinate relations, perceptions of fairness, and coworker communication. *Human Communication Research, 22,* 5-38.

Siehl, C. (1985). After the founder: An opportunity to manage culture. In P. Frost, L. Moore, M. Louis, C. Lundberg, & J. Martin (Eds.), *Organizational culture* (pp. 125-140). Beverly Hills, CA: Sage.

Siehl, C., & Martin, J. (1984). The role of symbolic management: How can managers effectively transmit organizational culture? In J. G. Hunt, D. M. Hosking, C. A. Schriesheim, & R. Stewart (Eds.), *Leaders and managers: International perspectives on managerial behavior and leadership* (pp. 227-239). Elmsford, NY: Pergamon.

Sigman, S. J. (1987). *A perspective on social communication.* Lexington, MA: Lexington Books.

Sigman, S. J. (1992, May). *A social communication contribution to the micro-macro question.* Paper presented at the International Communication Association Convention, Miami, Miami, FL.

Sillars, S., & Scott, M. (1983). Interpersonal perception between intimates: An integrative review. *Human Communication Research, 10,* 153-176.

Skarlicki, D. P., & Folger, R. (1997). Retaliation in the workplace: The roles of distributive, procedural, and interactional justice. *Journal of Applied Psychology, 82,* 434-443.

Skinner, B. F. (1974). *About behaviorism.* New York: Vintage.

Smirich, L. (1983). Organizations as shared meanings. In L. Pondy, P. Frost, G. Morgan, & T. Dandridge (Eds.), *Organizational symbolism* (pp. 55-65). Greenwich, CT: JAI.

Smirich, L., & Morgan, G. (1982). Leadership: The management of meaning. *Journal of Applied Behavioral Science, 18,* 257-273.

Smith, P. B., & Peterson, M. F. (1988). *Leadership, organizations, and culture.* London: Sage.

Smither, J. W., London, M., Vasilopoulos, N. L., Reilly, R. R., Millsap, R. E., & Salvemini, N. (1995). An examination of the effects of an upward feedback program over time. *Personnel Psychology, 48,* 1-34.

Smither, J. W., Wohlers, A. J., & London, M. (1995). A field study of reactions to normative versus individualized upward feedback. *Group & Organization Management, 20,* 61-89.

Sparrowe, R. T. (1994). Empowerment in the hospitality industry: An exploration of antecedents and outcomes. *Hospitality Research Journal, 17,* 51-73.

Sparrowe, R. T., & Liden, R. C. (1997). Process and structure in leader-member exchange. *Academy of Management Review, 22,* 522-564.

Sullivan, J., & Taylor, S. (1991). A cross-cultural test of compliance-gaining theory. *Management Communication Quarterly, 5,* 220-239.

Sullivan, J. J., Albrecht, T. L., & Taylor, S. (1990). Process, organizational, relational, and personal determinants of managerial compliance-gaining communication strategies. *Journal of Business Communication, 4,* 331-355.

Swales, J. M., & Rogers, P. S. (1995). Discourse and the projection of corporate culture: The mission statement. *Discourse & Society, 6,* 223-242.

Swanson, E. B., & Ramiller, N. C. (1997). The organizing vision in information systems innovation. *Organization Science, 8,* 458-474.

Sypher, B. D. (1991). A message-centered approach to leadership. In J. A. Anderson (Ed.), *Communication yearbook 14* (pp. 547-559). Newbury Park, CA: Sage.

Tannenbaum, R., & Schmidt, W. H. (1958). How to choose a leadership pattern. *Harvard Business Review, 36,* 95-101.

Tedeschi, J. (1990). Self-presentation and social influence: An interactionist perspective. In M. J. Cody & M. L. McLaughlin (Eds.), *The psychology of tactical communication* (pp. 299-323). Clevedon, UK: Multilingual Matters.

Tepper, B. J. (1993). Patterns of downward influence and follower conformity in transactional and transformational leadership. In D. P. Moore (Ed.), *Academy of Management best papers proceedings* (pp. 267-271). Madison, WI: Omni.

Tepper, B. J., Eisenbach, R. J., Kirby, S. L., & Potter, P. W. (1998). Test of a justice-based model of subordinates' resistance to downward influence attempts. *Group & Organization Management, 23,* 144-160.

Thacker, R. A., & Wayne, S. J. (1995). An examination of the relationship of upward influence tactics and assessments of promotability. *Journal of Management, 21,* 739-756.

Tichy, N., & DeVanna, M. (1986). *The transformational leader.* New York: John Wiley.

Tjosvold, D. (1985). The effects of attribution and social context on superiors' influence and interaction with low performing subordinates. *Personnel Psychology, 38,* 361-376.

Tompkins, P. K., & Cheney, G. (1983). Account analysis of organizations: Decision-making and identification. In L. L. Putnam & M. E. Pacanowsky (Eds.), *Communication and organizations: An interpretive approach* (pp. 123-146). Beverly Hills, CA: Sage.

Trice, H. M., & Beyer, J. M. (1986). Charisma and its routinization in two social movement organizations. In B. M. Staw & L. L. Cummings (Eds.), *Research in organizational behavior* (Vol. 8, pp. 113-164). Greenwich, CT: JAI.

Trice, H. M., & Beyer, J. M. (1991). Cultural leadership in organizations. *Organization Science, 2,* 149-169.

Uhl-Bien, M., & Graen, G. B. (1992). Self-management and team-making in cross-functional work teams: Discovering the keys to becoming an integrated team. *Journal of High Technology Management, 3,* 225-241.

Uhl-Bien, M., & Graen, G. B. (1993). Leadership-making in self-managing professional work teams: An empirical investigation. In K. E. Clark, M. B. Clark, & D. P. Campbell (Eds.), *The impact of leadership* (pp. 379-387). West Orange, NJ: Leadership Library of America.

VandeWalle, D., & Cummings, L. L. (1997). A test of the influence of goal orientation on the feedback seeking process. *Journal of Applied Psychology, 82,* 390-400.

Vecchio, R. P., & Sussman, M. (1991). Choice of influence tactics: Individual and organizational determinants. *Journal of Organizational Behavior, 12,* 73-80.

Wakabayashi, M., & Graen, G. B. (1984). The Japanese career progress study: A 7-year follow-up. *Journal of Applied Psychology, 69,* 603-614.

Waldron, V. R. (1991). Achieving communication goals in superior-subordinate relationships: The multi-functionality of upward maintenance tactics. *Communication Monographs, 58,* 289-306.

Waldron, V. R., Hunt, M. D., & Dsilva, M. (1993). Towards a threat management model of upward communication: A study of influence and maintenance tactics in the leader-member dyad. *Communication Studies, 44,* 254-272.

Walsh, J., Ashford, S., & Hill, T. (1985). Feedback obstruction: The influence of information environment on employee turnover intentions. *Human Relations, 38,* 23-46.

Wasielewski, P. L. (1985). The emotional basis of charisma. *Symbolic Interaction, 8,* 207-222.

Watson, K. M. (1982a). An analysis of communication patterns: A method for discriminating leader and subordinate roles. *Academy of Management Journal, 25,* 107-120.

Watson, K. M. (1982b). A methodology for the study of organizational behavior at the interpersonal level of analysis. *Academy of Management Review, 7,* 392-403.

Watzlawick, P., Beavin, J. H., & Jackson, D. D. (1967). *Pragmatics of human communication.* New York: Norton.

Wayne, S. J., & Ferris, G. R. (1990). Influence tactics, affect, and exchange quality in supervisor-subordinate interactions: A laboratory experiment and field study. *Journal of Applied Psychology, 75,* 487-499.

Wayne, S. J., & Green, S. A. (1993). The effects of leader-member exchange on employee citizenship and impression management behavior. *Human Relations, 46,* 1431-1440.

Wayne, S. J., Liden, R. C., Graf, I. K., & Ferris, G. R. (1997). The role of upward influence tactics in human resource decisions. *Personnel Psychology, 50,* 979-1006.

Wayne, S. J., Liden, R. C., & Sparrowe, R. T. (1994). Developing leader-member exchanges. *American Behavioral Scientist, 37,* 697-714.

Weaver, R. (1953). *The ethics of rhetoric.* South Bend, IN: Gateway Editions.

Weber, M. (1968). *Economy and society* (3 vols., G. Roth & C. Wittich, Eds.). New York: Bedminister. (Original work published 1925)

Weeks, G. R. (1986). Individual-system dialectic. *American Journal of Family Therapy, 14,* 5-12.

Weick, K. E. (1969). *The social psychology of organizing.* Reading, MA: Addison-Wesley.

Weick, K. E. (1987). Theorizing about organizational communication. In F. M. Jablin, L. L. Putnam, K. H. Roberts, & L. W. Porter (Eds.), *Handbook of organizational communication: An interdisciplinary perspective* (pp. 97-122). Newbury Park, CA: Sage.

Weick, K. E., & Roberts, K. H. (1993). Collective mind in organizations: Heedful interrelating on flight decks. *Administrative Science Quarterly, 38,* 357-381.

Weierter, S. J. M. (1997). Who wants to play "follow the leader"? A theory of charismatic relationships based on routinized charisma and follower characteristics. *Leadership Quarterly, 8,* 171-193.

Wendt, R., & Fairhurst, G. T. (1994). Looking for "the vision thing": The rhetoric of leadership in the 1992 presidential election. *Communication Quarterly, 42,* 180-195.

Werner, C. M., & Baxter, L. A. (1994). Temporal qualities of relationships: Organismic, transactional, and dialectical views. In M. L. Knapp & G. R. Miller (Eds.), *Handbook of interpersonal communication* (2nd ed., pp. 323-379). Thousand Oaks, CA: Sage.

Westley, F., & Mintzberg, H. (1989). Visionary leadership and strategic management. *Strategic Management Journal, 10,* 17-32.

Wheatley, M. J. (1992). *Leadership and the new science: Learning about organization from an orderly universe.* San Francisco: Berrett-Koehler.

Wiener, N. (1948). *Cybernetics: On control and communication in the animal and the machine.* New York: John Wiley.

Wiener, N. (1954). *The human use of human beings: Cybernetics and society.* Garden City, NY: Doubleday Anchor.

Williams, J. R., Miller, C. E., Steelman, L. A., & Levy, P. E. (1999). Increasing feedback seeking in public contexts: It takes two (or more) to tango. *Journal of Applied Psychology, 84,* 969-976.

Wofford, J. C. (1999). Laboratory research on charismatic leadership: Fruitful or futile? *Leadership Quarterly, 10,* 523-530.

Wood, R. E., & Bandura, A. (1989). Impact of conceptions of ability on self-regulatory mechanisms and complex decision-making. *Journal of Personality and Social Psychology, 56,* 407-415.

Wyer, R. S., Jr., & Srull, T. K. (1980). The processing of social stimulus information: A conceptual integration. In R. Hatie, T. M. Ostrom, E. B. Ebbesen, R. S. Wyer, Jr., D. L. Hamilton, & D. E. Carlston (Eds.), *Person memory: The cognitive basis of social perception* (pp. 227-300). Hillsdale, NJ: Lawrence Erlbaum.

Wyer, R. S., Jr., & Srull, T. K. (1986). Human cognition in its social context. *Psychological Review, 93,* 322-359.

Xin K. R., & Tsui, A. S. (1996). Different strokes for different folks? Influence tactics by Asian-American and Caucasian-American managers. *Leadership Quarterly, 7,* 109-132.

Yagil, D. (1998). Charismatic leadership and organizational hierarchy: Attributions of charisma to close and distant leaders. *Leadership Quarterly, 9,* 161-176.

Yammarino, F. J., & Bass, B. M. (1990). Long-term forecasting of transformational leadership and its effects among Naval officers. In K. E. Clark & M. B. Clark (Eds.), *Measures of leadership* (pp. 151-169). West Orange, NJ: Leadership Library of America.

Yammarino, F. J., Spangler, W. D., & Bass, B. M. (1993). Transformational leadership and performance: A longitudinal investigation. *Leadership Quarterly, 4,* 81-102.

Yukl, G. (1994). *Leadership in organizations* (3rd ed.). Englewood Cliffs, NJ: Prentice Hall.

Yukl, G., & Falbe, C. M. (1990). Influence tactics and objectives in upward, downward, and lateral influence attempts. *Journal of Applied Psychology, 75,* 132-140.

Yukl, G., Falbe, C. M., & Youn, J. Y. (1993). Patterns of influence behavior for managers. *Group & Organization Management, 18,* 5-28.

Yukl, G., Guinan, P. J., & Sottolano, D. (1995). Influence tactics used for different objectives with subordinates, peers, and superiors. *Group & Organization Management, 20,* 272-296.

Yukl, G., Kim, H., & Chavez, C. (1999). Task importance, feasibility, and agent influence behavior as determinants of target commitment. *Journal of Applied Psychology, 84,* 137-143.

Yukl, G., & Tracey, B. (1992). Consequences of influence tactics used with subordinates, peers, and the boss. *Journal of Applied Psychology, 77,* 525-535.

Zaleznik, A. (1977). Managers and leaders: Are they different? *Harvard Business Review, 55*(5), 67-78.

Zhou, J. (1998). Feedback valence, feedback style, task autonomy, and achievement orientation: Interactive effects on creative performance. *Journal of Applied Psychology, 83,* 261-176.

Zorn, T. E. (1991). Construct system development, transformational leadership, and leadership messages. *Southern Communication Journal, 56,* 178-193.

Zorn, T. E. (1995). Bosses and buddies: Constructing and performing simultaneously hierarchical and close friendship relationships. In J. T. Wood & S. Duck (Eds.), *Understudied relationships: Off the beaten path* (pp. 122-145). Thousand Oaks, CA: Sage.

Zorn, T. E., & Leichty, G. B. (1991). Leadership and identity: A reinterpretation of situational leadership theory. *Southern Communication Journal, 57,* 11-24.

12

Emergence of Communication Networks

PETER R. MONGE
University of Southern California

NOSHIR S. CONTRACTOR
University of Illinois

Communication networks are the patterns of contact between communication partners that are created by transmitting and exchanging messages through time and space. These networks take many forms in contemporary organizations, including personal contact networks, flows of information within and between groups, strategic alliances between firms, and global network organizations, to name but a few. This chapter examines the theoretical mechanisms that theorists and researchers have proposed to explain the creation, maintenance, and dissolution of these diverse and complex intra- and interorganizational networks. This focus provides an important complement to other reviews of the literature that have been organized on the basis of antecedents and outcomes (Monge & Eisenberg, 1987) or research themes within organizational behavior (Brass & Krackhardt, in press; Krackhardt & Brass, 1994).

AUTHORS' NOTE: National Science Foundation Grants ECS-94-27730, SBR-9602055, and IIS-9980109 supported preparation of this chapter. We wish to express our appreciation to George Barnett, Steve Corman, Marya Doerfel, Andrew Flanagin, Janet Fulk, Caroline Haythornthwaite, Maureen Heald, Fred Jablin, David Johnson, David Krackhardt, Leigh Moody, Linda Putnam, Heidi Saltenberger, Stan Wasserman, Rob Whitbred, and Evelien Zeggelink for helpful comments on earlier drafts of this chapter.

The chapter begins with a brief overview of network analysis, an examination of the relationship between formal and emergent networks, and a brief discussion of organizational forms. The core of the chapter focuses on ten families of theories and their respective theoretical mechanisms that have been used to explain the emergence, maintenance, and dissolution of communication networks in organizational research. These are (a) theories of self-interest (social capital theory and transaction cost economics), (b) theories of mutual self-interest and collective action, (c) exchange and dependency theories (social exchange, resource dependency, and network organizational forms), (d) contagion theories (social information processing, social cognitive theory, institutional theory, structural theory of action), (e) cognitive theories (semantic networks, knowledge structures, cognitive social structures, cognitive consistency), (f) theories of homophily (social comparison theory, social identity theory), (g) theories of proximity (physical and electronic propinquity), (h) uncertainty reduction and contingency theories, (i) social support theories, and (j) evolutionary theories. The chapter concludes with a discussion of an agenda for future research on the emergence and evolution of organizational communication networks.

NETWORK ANALYSIS

Network analysis consists of applying a set of relations to an identified set of entities. In the context of organizational communication, network analysts often identify the entities as people who belong to one or more organizations and to which are applied one or more communication relations, such as "provides information to," "gets information from," and "communicates with." It is also common to use work groups, divisions, and entire organizations as the set of entities and to explore a variety of relations such as "collaborates with," "subcontracts with," and "joint ventures with."

Relations in a World of Attributes

Relations are central to network analysis because they define the nature of the communication connections between people, groups, and organizations. This focus stands in sharp contrast to other areas of the social sciences, which have tended to study *attributes,* the characteristics of people, groups, and organizations rather than the relations between them. Relations possess a number of important properties, including the number of entities involved, strength, symmetry, transitivity, reciprocity, and multiplexity. A large literature exists that describes these properties and other fundamentals of network analysis, including network concepts, measures, methods, and applications (see, e.g., Haythornthwaite, 1996; Marsden, 1990; Monge, 1987; Monge & Contractor, 1988; Scott, 1988, 1992; Stohl, 1995; Wasserman & Faust, 1994; Wigand, 1988). Since the focus of this chapter is on theory and research results, it is not feasible to further explore the details of network analysis. However, in addition to the references cited above, Tables 12.1, 12.2, and 12.3 (from Brass, 1995b) summarize major network concepts. These tables describe measures of network ties, measures assigned to individuals, and measures used to describe entire networks.

Network linkages

Network linkages are created when one or more communication relations are applied to a set of people, groups, or organizations. For example, in organizational contexts Farace, Monge, and Russell (1977) identified three distinct important communication networks in terms of production, maintenance, and innovation linkages.

Other kinds of communication linkages are possible. For example, Badaracco (1991) distinguished two types of knowledge, which he called migratory and embedded, each associated with a different type of linkage. Migra-

TABLE 12.1 Typical Social Network Measures of Ties

Measure	Definition	Example
Indirect links	Path between two actors is mediated by one or the other	A is linked to B, B is linked to C; thus A is indirectly linked to C through B
Frequency	How many times, or how often the link occurs	A talks to B 10 times per week
Stability	Existence of link over time	A has been friends with B for 5 years
Multiplexity	Extent to which two actors are linked together by more than one relationship	A and B are friends, they seek out each other for advice, and work together
Strength	Amount of time, emotional intensity, intimacy, or reciprocal services (frequency or multiplexity often used as measure of strength of tie)	A and B are close friends, or spend much time together
Direction	Extent to which link is from one actor to another	Work flows from A to B, but not from B to A
Symmetry	Extent to which relationship is bi-directional	A asks B for advice, and B asks A for advice

SOURCE: Reprinted from D. J. Brass. "A Social Network Perspective on Human Resources Management," in G. R. Ferris (Ed.), *Research in Personnel and Human Resources Management*, Vol. 13. Copyright 1995, p. 44, with permission from Elsevier Science.

tory knowledge is that information that exists in forms that are easily moved from one location, person, group, or firm to another. Migratory knowledge tends to be contained in books, designs, machines, blueprints, computer programs, and individual minds, all of which encapsulate the knowledge that went into its creation. Embedded knowledge is more difficult to transfer. It "resides primarily in specialized relationships among individuals and groups and in the particular norms, attitudes, information flows, and ways of making decisions that shape their dealings with each other" (Badaracco, 1991, p. 79). Craftsmanship, unique talents and skills, accumulated know-how, and group expertise and synergy are all difficult to transfer from one place to another and particularly difficult to transfer across organizational or even divisional boundaries.

The two types of network linkages Badaracco (1991) identified were the product link, associated with migratory knowledge, and the knowledge link, associated with embedded knowledge. In the interfirm context, a product link is an arrangement whereby a company relies on "an outside ally to manufacture part of its product line or to build complex components that the company had previously made for itself" (p. 11). Knowledge links are alliances whereby companies seek "to learn or jointly create new knowledge and capabilities" (p. 12). These "alliances are organizational arrangements and operating poli-

TABLE 12.2   Typical Social Network Measures Assigned to Individual Actors

Measure	Definition
Degree	Number of direct links with other actors
In-degree	Number of directional links to the actor from other actors (in-coming links)
Out-degree	Number of directional links from the actor to other actors (out-coming links)
Range (diversity)	Number of links to different others (others are defined as different to the extent that they are not themselves linked to each other, or represent different groups or statuses)
Closeness	Extent to which an actor is close to, or can easily reach all the other actors in the network. Usually measured by averaging the path distances (direct and indirect links) to all others. A direct link is counted as 1, indirect links receive proportionately less weight
Betweenness	Extent to which an actor mediates, or falls between any other two actors on the shortest path between those actors. Usually averaged across all possible pairs in the network
Centrality	Extent to which an actor is central to a network. Various measures (including degree, closeness, and betweenness) have been used as indicators of centrality. Some measures of centrality weight an actor's links to others by centrality of those others
Prestige	Based on asymmetric relationships, prestigious actors are the object rather than the source of relations. Measures similar to centrality are calculated by accounting for the direction of the relationship (i.e., in-degree)
Role	
Star	An actor who is highly central to the network
Liaison	An actor who has links to two or more groups that would otherwise not be linked, but is not a member of either group
Bridge	An actor who is a member of two or more groups
Gatekeeper	An actor who mediates or controls the flow (is the single link) between one part of the network and another
Isolate	An actor who has no links, or relatively few links to others

SOURCE: Reprinted from D. J. Brass. "A Social Network Perspective on Human Resources Management," in G. R. Ferris (Ed.), *Research in Personnel and Human Resources Management*, Vol. 13. Copyright 1995, p. 45, with permission from Elsevier Science.

cies through which separate organizations share administrative authority, form social links, and accept joint ownership, and in which looser, more open-ended contractual arrangements replace highly specific, arm's length contracts" (Badaracco, 1991, p. 4).

Research on interorganizational linkages began almost 40 years ago with the work of Levine and White (1961) and Litwak and Hylton (1962), which spawned a quarter century's worth of interest on the exchange of goods and material resources (see, e.g.,

TABLE 12.3 Typical Social Network Measures Used to Describe Networks

Measure	Definition
Size	Number of actors in the network
Inclusiveness	Total number of actors in a network minus the number of isolated actors (not connected to any other actors). Also measured as the ratio of connected actors to the total number of actors
Component	Largest connected subset of network nodes and links. All nodes in the component are connected (either direct or indirect links) and no nodes have links to nodes outside the component
Connectivity (reachability)	Extent to which actors in the network are linked to one another by direct or indirect ties. Sometimes measured by the maximum, or average, path distance between any two actors in the network
Connectedness	Ratio of pairs of nodes that are mutually reachable to total number of pairs o nodes
Density	Ratio of the number of actual links to the number of possible links in the network
Centralization	Difference between the centrality scores of the most central actor and those of all other actors in a network is calculated, and used to form ratio of the actual sum of the differences to the maximum sum of the differences
Symmetry	Ratio of number of symmetric to asymmetric links (or to total number of links) in a network
Transitivity	Three actors (A, B, C) are transitive if whenever A is linked to B and B is linked to C, then C is linked to A. Transitivity is the number of transitive triples divided by the number of potential transitive triples (number of paths of length 2)

SOURCE: Reprinted from D. J. Brass. "A Social Network Perspective on Human Resources Management," in G. R. Ferris (Ed.), *Research in Personnel and Human Resources Management*, Vol. 13. Copyright 1995, p. 44, with permission from Elsevier Science.

Mitchell, 1973; Warren, 1967). More recent work has focused on communication, information, and knowledge linkages (Gulati, 1995). Eisenberg et al. (1985) developed a two-dimensional typology of interorganizational linkages based on linkage content and linkage level. The content dimension separated material content from symbolic or informational content. The level dimension distinguished three forms of exchange. Eisenberg et al. (1985) state:

An *institutional* linkage occurs when information or materials are exchanged between orga-

nizations without the involvement of specific organizational roles or personalities (e.g., routine data transfers between banks). A *representative* linkage occurs when a role occupant who officially represents an organization within the system has contact with a representative of another organization (e.g., an interagency committee to formulate joint policies). The emphasis here is on the official nature of the transaction and the representative capacities of the individuals. Finally, a *personal* linkage occurs when an individual from one organization exchanges information or material with an individual in another organization, but in a nonrepresentative or private capacity (i.e., via friendship or "old school" ties). (p. 237, emphasis in the original).

Formal Versus Emergent Networks

Historically, organizational communication scholars have made important theoretical and empirical distinctions between formal and emergent networks. Theoretically, the notion of "emergent network" was a designation that originally differentiated informal, naturally occurring networks from formal, imposed, or "mandated" networks (Aldrich, 1976), the latter of which represented the legitimate authority of the organization and were typically reflected by the organizational chart. The formal networks were presumed to also represent the channels of communication through which orders were transmitted downward and information was transmitted upward (Weber, 1947). Early organizational theorists were aware that the formal organizational structure failed to capture many of the important aspects of communication in organizations and discussed the importance of informal communication and the grapevine (Barnard, 1938; Follett, 1924). Several scholars developed ways to study the grapevine and informal networks such as Davis's (1953) episodic communication in channels of organizations (ECCO) analysis, a technique for tracing the person-to-person diffusion of rumors or other items of information in an organization.

Researchers have provided considerable evidence over the years for the coexistence of the two networks. For example, using a variant of ECCO analysis, Stevenson and Gilly (1991) found that managers tended to forward problems to personal contacts rather than to formally designated problem solvers, thus bypassing the formal network. Similarly, Albrecht and Ropp (1984) discovered that "workers were more likely to report talking about new ideas with those colleagues with whom they also discussed work and personal matters, rather than necessarily following prescribed channels based upon hierarchical role relationships" (p. 3). Stevenson (1990) argued

that the influence of formal organizational structure on the emergent structure could be best understood on the basis of a status differential model. In a study of a public transit agency, he found evidence that the social distance across the hierarchy reduced the level of communication between higher- and lower-level employees, with middle-level employees serving as a buffer.

An important rationale for studying emergent communication networks has evolved out of the inconclusive findings relating formal organizational structure to organizational behavior (Johnson, 1992, 1993; see also McPhee & Poole, Chapter 13, this volume). Jablin's (1987) review of the empirical research on formal organizational structures pointed to the inconclusive nature of studies involving structural variables such as hierarchy, size, differentiation, and formalization. More recently, a series of meta-analytic studies has concluded that the relationships between formal structure, organizational effectiveness (Doty, Glick, & Huber, 1993; Huber, Miller, & Glick, 1990), and technology (Miller, Glick, Wang, & Huber, 1991) are largely an artifact of methodological designs. The fact that formal structural variables have failed to provide much explanatory power has led several scholars to argue that emergent structures are more important to study than formal structures because they better contribute to our understanding of organizational behavior (Bacharach & Lawler, 1980; Krackhardt & Hanson, 1993; Krikorian, Seibold, & Goode, 1997; Roberts & O'Reilly, 1978; Roethlisberger & Dickson, 1939).

These problems with formal structures and the recent priority given to emergent structure have prompted scholars to develop network measures that capture in emergent networks the key concepts used to describe formal organizational structure. For example, Krackhardt (1994) has developed four measures of informal structure—connectedness, hierarchy, efficiency, and least-upper-boundedness (unity-of-command)—that map onto theories of an organization's formal organizational structure.

Further, the increased use of new computer-mediated communication systems has spawned research that uses formal organizational structure as a benchmark against which to compare communication networks that emerge in an electronic medium. Several interesting, though somewhat conflicting, findings have emerged. In a two-year study of over 800 members of an R&D organization, Eveland and Bikson (1987) found that electronic mail served to augment, and in some cases complement, formal structures. On the other hand, Bizot, Smith, and Hill (1991) found that electronic communication patterns corresponded closely to the formal organizational structures in a traditionally hierarchical R&D organization. Lievrouw and Carley (1991) argued that new communication technologies might usher in a new era of "telescience" by offering alternatives to the traditional organizational structures in universities and industry. However, Rice (1994b) found that the electronic communication structures initially mirrored formal organizational structures, but these similarities diminished over time. Hinds and Kiesler (1995) explored the relationship between formal and informal networks in a telecommunications company. They found that communication technologies were increasingly used as a tool for lateral communication across formal organizational boundaries; this finding was most pronounced for technical workers.

The literature comparing face-to-face or mediated emergent communication structures with formal structures generally demonstrates a "pro-emergent bias." That is, the theory and empirical evidence focus on the advantages of informal communication to individuals and organizations. However, Kadushin and Brimm (1990) challenged the assumption that three types of emergent networks, (a) the shadow networks (the "real" way things get done), (b) the social interaction networks, and (c) the career networks (the venue for so-called networking) always serve to augment the limitations of the organization's formal network. Instead, they argued that these three informal networks frequently work at

cross-purposes, thereby restricting rather than promoting the organization's interests. In a study of senior executives in a large, international high-technology company, they found that by saying, "Please network, but don't you dare bypass authority," organizations create what Bateson (1972) called a "double bind," a choice situation where each alternative conflicts with the others. They argued that "an important first step is to recognize the incompatibilities between emergent network structures and corporate authority structures and to move this inconsistency from the realm of double bind to the domain of paradox" (Kadushin & Brimm, 1990, p. 15).

Clearly, there is continuing scholarly interest in the study of the differences between formal and emergent networks in organizations. Ironically, however, the distinction between formal and informal structures in organizations has diminished significantly in recent years and may become increasingly irrelevant in the coming decade. Reasons for this center on shifts in organizational structure and management philosophy. Prominent among these are changes to more team-based forms of organizing, the adoption of matrix forms of organizational structure (Burns & Wholey, 1993), and shifts to network forms of organizing (Miles & Snow, 1986, 1992, 1995; Monge, 1995). At the core of these changes has been the explosion of lateral forms of communication (Galbraith, 1977, 1995) made possible by new information technologies that facilitate considerable point-to-point and broadcast communication without regard for traditional hierarchy.

These developments have eroded the distinction between prior structural categories used to characterize organizations, specifically, between formal and informal and/or between formal and emergent. Contrary to traditional views, contemporary organizations are increasingly constructed out of emergent communication linkages, linkages that are ephemeral in that they are formed, maintained, broken, and reformed with considerable ease (Palmer, Friedland, & Singh, 1986). As Krackhardt (1994) says,

An inherent principle of the interactive form is that networks of relations span across the entire organization, unimpeded by preordained formal structures and fluid enough to adapt to immediate technological demands. These relations can be multiple and complex. But one characteristic they share is that they *emerge* in the organization, they are not preplanned. (p. 218, emphasis in the original)

The networks that emerge by these processes and the organizations they create are called network and organizational forms. Both are reviewed in the following section.

Network and Organizational Forms

Communication network patterns that recur in multiple settings are called *network forms*. An early theoretical article by Bavelas (1948) based on Lewin's (1936) psychological field theory identified a number of small-group communication network forms in organizations, including the chain, circle, wheel, and comcon (*com*pletely *con*nected), and theorized about how the different forms processed information. These network forms varied in the degree to which they were centralized, with the wheel being the most centralized and the comcon the least centralized.

This theoretical article and an imaginative experimental design created by Leavitt (1951) generated hundreds of published articles over some 25 years. The primary focus of these efforts was the impact of information processing via the different network forms on productivity and satisfaction (see Shaw, 1964, for a review of this literature). Two prominent findings emerged from this research. First, centralized organizations were more efficient for routine tasks, while decentralized networks were more efficient for tasks that required creativity and collaborative problem solving. Second, people in decentralized organizations were more satisfied with the work processes than people in centralized organizations, with the exception in the latter case that the central

person in centralized networks was extremely satisfied. Unfortunately, little further theoretical development accompanied this plethora of empirical research. As a result, this line of inquiry has essentially died; almost no articles have been published on small-group network forms in organizations during the past 20 years.

Organizational structures, including communication networks, that share common features or patterns across a large number of organizations are called *organizational forms* (McKelvey, 1982). Weber (1947) argued that bureaucracy was the universal organizational form. Three principal theoretical mechanisms that created bureaucracy were rationalization, differentiation, and integration. Rationalization occurred by specifying legitimating instructions that produced standard operating procedures, thus leaving little opportunity for individual autonomy. Rationalizing the network meant specifying who could say what to whom, often summarized by the injunction that commands should flow downward and information upward in the bureaucracy. Differentiation was the process of breaking work up into its various components. This often led to job specialization particularly as production processes proliferated and increased in size and complexity. As work became differentiated, the various parts needed to be coordinated, and thus processes of integration came into operation. Weber argued that bureaucracy differentiated along vertical organizational lines and primarily integrated that way as well. Bureaucracy allowed little room for lateral, cross-level, or cross-boundary communication networks, that is, informal or emergent networks, a feature for which it has been frequently criticized (Heckscher, 1994).

Miles and Snow (1986, 1992) identified four major organizational forms that have developed over the past century: (a) the traditional functional form, which emerged during the early part of the century; (b) the divisional (or multidivisional) form, which was begun by Alfred P. Sloan at General Motors in the 1940s (see Chandler, 1977); (c) the matrix form, which evolved during the 1960s and

1970s; and (d) the network form, which has emerged over the past decade. Miles and Snow (1992) argue that each of these forms contains its own operating logic, or in terms of this chapter, theoretical mechanism. The functional form uses a logic of "centrally coordinated specialization" (p. 58), which enables it to efficiently produce a limited set of standardized goods or services for a stable, relatively unchanging market. The divisional form operates by a logic of "divisional autonomy with centrally controlled performance evaluation and resource allocation" (p. 60). Divisions produce separate products or focus on separate markets but are collectively accountable to centralized authority through their communication networks. The ability to develop new divisions enables the multidivisional form to pursue new opportunities in changing markets. The matrix form combines the operating logic of functional and multidivisional forms, using the functional form to produce standardized goods and services and the shared resources of the multidivisional form to explore new opportunities via project groups or teams. The network form uses flexible, dynamic communication linkages to connect multiple organizations into new entities that can create products or services.

THEORETICAL MECHANISMS TO EXPLAIN THE EMERGENCE OF NETWORKS

Communication network analysis falls within the intellectual lineage of structural analysis, which has had a long and distinguished history. In sociology, Herbert Spencer (1982) and Émile Durkheim (1895/1964) are often credited with introducing structural concepts into sociological thinking. In anthropology, Radcliffe-Brown (1952/1959) incorporated structural-functionalist ideas into his watershed analysis of cultures. And in linguistics, structural thinking can be traced to the pio-

neering work of de Saussure (1916/1966). Most structural analyses of organizations and communication can be located in one of three traditions: positional, relational, and cultural.

The *positional* tradition is rooted in the classical work of Max Weber (1947), Talcott Parsons (1951), and George Homans (1958). Organizational structure is viewed as a pattern of relations among positions. Sets of organizational roles are associated with positions and specify designated behaviors and obligatory relations incumbent on the people who assume the positions. The positions and attached roles constitute the relatively stable and enduring structure of the organization independent of the people who fulfill the roles. This tradition leads to the view that positions and roles determine who communicates with whom, and consequently, the communication structure of the organization. White, Boorman, and Breiger (1976) and Burt (1982) have developed the most significant recent positional theories applicable to organizational communication under the rubric of structural equivalence. This theory argues that people maintain attitudes, values, and beliefs consistent with their organizational positions irrespective of the amount of communication that they have with others in their organizational networks. The positional tradition has been criticized for its inability to take into account the active part individuals play in creating and shaping organizational structure (Coleman, 1973; Nadel, 1957; White et al., 1976).

The *relational* tradition focuses primarily on the direct communication that establishes and maintains communication linkages. Taken collectively, these linkages create an emergent communication structure that connects different people and groups in the organization irrespective of their formal positions or roles. Rooted in systems theory (Bateson, 1972; Buckley, 1967; Watzlawick, Beavin, & Jackson, 1967), the relational tradition emphasizes the dynamic, constantly changing, enacted nature of structure created by repetitive patterns of person-to-person message flow. Rogers and Kincaid (1981) claim that it is the dominant tradition in organizational communication.

The *cultural* tradition examines symbols, meanings, and interpretations of messages transmitted through communication networks. As part of the resurgence of interest in organizational culture (Frost, Moore, Louis, Lundberg, & Martin, 1985), much of the work has been based on Giddens's (1976, 1984) writings on structuration, which attempt to account for both the creative and constraining aspects of social structure. These studies are characterized by an explicit concern for the continual production and reproduction of meaning through communication, examining simultaneously how meanings emerge from interaction and how they act to constrain subsequent interaction. The cultural tradition has spawned recent work on semantic networks (Monge & Eisenberg, 1987) described later in this chapter. These three traditions are discussed in greater detail in Monge and Eisenberg (1987).

Although interesting and useful, these network traditions focus attention at a metatheoretical level and fail to specify the *theoretical mechanisms* that describe how people, groups, and organizations forge, maintain, and dissolve linkages. Further, while a number of scholars over the past decade have called for greater explication of network theory (e.g., Rogers, 1987; Salancik, 1995; Wellman, 1988), almost none have provided it. Finally, while several reviewers have identified theories that are applicable to network research within and between organizations (Brass & Krackhardt, in press; Galaskiewicz, 1985; Grandori & Soda, 1995; Mizruchi & Galaskiewicz, 1994; Smith, Carroll, & Ashford, 1995), none have systematically explored the theories and their theoretical mechanisms.

This chapter addresses these omissions in the organizational communication network literature by focusing on the role of theory and theoretical mechanisms in explaining the emergence of communication networks. More specifically, it examines the extant organiza-

tional literature using a network perspective with special attention to the mechanisms that help explain the *emergence* of networks. This review will demonstrate that a wide array of theories is amenable to network formulations. In some cases, different theories, some using similar theoretical mechanisms, offer similar explanations but at different levels of analysis. The review will also underscore the considerable variation in the depth of conceptual development and empirical research across the different theories and theoretical mechanisms. Since the chapter focuses on theoretical mechanisms, many other interesting network articles that have little or no bearing on these issues have not been included. The theories and their theoretical mechanisms are summarized in Table 12.4.

Theories of Self-Interest

Social theorists have long been fascinated by self-interest as a motivation for economic and other forms of social action (Coleman, 1986). Theories of self-interest postulate that people make what they believe to be rational choices in order to acquire personal benefits. The strong form of this theoretical mechanism stipulates that people attempt to maximize their gains (or minimize their losses). The weaker theoretical form says that people "satisfice" rather than maximize, which means that people choose the first good alternative they find rather than exploring all alternatives and selecting the best. Two theories of self-interest that have been used to explore communication network issues are examined in this section: the theory of social capital and transaction cost economics theory.

Theory of Social Capital

The deployment of social capital (Coleman, 1988) in networks is best represented in Burt's (1992) theory of structural holes. This theory argues that people accumulate social resources, or "social capital," which they in-

TABLE 12.4 Ten Families of Theories and Their Theoretical Mechanisms to Explain the Emergence of Networks

Theories	Theoretical Mechanisms	Relevant Organizational Variables

1. Theories of self-interest
   Theory of Social Capital
   Theory of Structural Holes
   Transaction Cost Economics Theory
	Investments in opportunities
	Control of information flow
	Cost minimization
		Employee autonomy, flexibility
		Employee effectiveness
		Employee efficiency
		Organizational innovation
		Coordination by markets and hierarchies

2. Theories of mutual self-interest and
   collective action
   Public Goods Theory
   Critical Mass Theory
	Joint value maximization
	Inducements to contribute
	Number of people with resources and interests
		Contributions to collective good
		Mobilization of resources
		Adoption of innovations

3. Exchange and dependency theories
   Social Exchange Theory
   Resource Dependency Theory
   Network Organizations
	Exchange of valued resources (material or information)	Power, leadership
		Trust and ethical behavior
		Interorganizational linkages
		Coordination by networks
		Virtual organizing

4. Contagion theories
   Social Information Processing Theory
   Social Learning Theory
   Institutional Theory
   Structural Theory of Action
	Exposure or contact leading to:
	   Social influence
	   Imitation, modeling
	   Mimetic behavior
	   Similar positions in structure and roles
		General workplace attitudes
		Attitudes toward technologies
		Behavior through contagion
		Interorganizational contagion

5. Cognitive theories
   Semetic and Knowledge Networks
   Cognitive Social Structures
   Cognitive Consistency theories
   Balance Theory
   Theory of Cognitive Dissonance
	Cognitive mechanisms leading to:
	   Shared interpretations
	   Similarity in perceptual structures
	   Drive to restore balance
	   Drive to reduce dissonance
		Shared interpretations on key organizational concepts
		Shared attributions of other individuals
		Shared perceptions of the social structure
		Workplace attitudes such as satisfaction
		Workplace behaviors such as turnover

6. Homophily theories Social Comparison Theory Social Identity Theory	Choose similar others as basis of comparison Choose categories to define one's own group identity	Demographic variables such as age, tenure, gender, and race
7. Theories of physical and electronic proximity Physical Proximity Electronic Proximity	Influence of distance Influence of accessibility	Workplace attitudes
8. Uncertainty reduction and contingency theories Uncertainty Reduction Theory Contingency Theory	Choose communication links to reduce uncertainty	Communication about innovation Organizational structural characteristics Introduction of new technologies Market exchanges Interorganizational conflict
9. Social support theories	Choose communication links to gain or mobilize social resources	Buffer social and psychological stress Coping with stress General workplace attitudes
10. Theories of network evolution Structuration Theory Computation and Mathematical Organizational Theory Organizational Life Cycle and Developmental Theories	Selection and retention Duality of structure Nomothetic non-linear generative mechanisms Evolution of structures as a function of life-cycle stages	Foundings and extinctions Change in network configurations, role configurations, appropriation of new structures and media

vest in social opportunities from which they expect to profit. These investments are largely motivated by self-interest, defined as the return people expect to get on the social capital they invest. Network "holes" are those places in a network where people are unconnected. Consequently, holes provide opportunities where people can invest their social capital. To invest in, fill, or exploit these holes, people link directly to two or more unconnected others, thus creating indirect ties between the people to whom they link. People who link others by filling structural holes also enhance their own structural autonomy because they can control the information that flows between others. Consequently, Burt (1992) argues that the diversity of individuals' networks is a better predictor of their social capital than network size. Researchers have examined the relationships between social capital and organizational effectiveness, efficiency, and innovation. Each area is reviewed below.

Social capital and effectiveness. Researchers (Benassi & Gargiulo, 1993; Burt, 1992) have argued that network linkages enable and constrain the flexibility, autonomy, and therefore, the effectiveness of organizational members. Consistent with Burt's (1992) argument, Papa (1990) found that organization members with diverse networks across departments and hierarchical levels were significantly more likely to both increase productivity and hasten the speed with which this change occurred. Similarly, Burt (1992) found that the occurrence of structural holes in managers' networks was positively correlated with managerial effectiveness. However, he notes that this finding was not supported among female managers and recent recruits, where effectiveness was correlated with strong ties to others. Ibarra and Andrews's (1993) research showed that individuals who were central in the advice and friendship networks were more likely to perceive autonomy in their work. Benassi and Gargiulo (1993) found that the flexibility of managers in an Italian subsidiary of a multi-

national computer manufacturer significantly affected their likelihood of success in coordinating critical interdependencies. Managers were rated as having high flexibility if (a) their communication networks were constrained by a low level of aggregate interdependencies and consultations with others in their network, and (b) their communication network had structural holes among the people imposing these constraints. More recently, Burt (1997) reports that social capital is especially valuable for managers with few peers because such managers do not have the guiding frame of reference provided by numerous competitors, or the legitimacy provided by numerous people doing the same kind of work (p. 356). In addition, Burt (1991) has developed computational measures of "structural autonomy" to assess the level and distribution of constraints affecting individuals in a network.

Walker, Kogut, and Shan (1997) tested Burt's theory of structural holes at the interorganizational level. Their research showed that developing and nurturing social capital in the biotechnology industry was a significant factor in "network formation and industry growth" (p. 109). In the development of enduring relationships, firms choose to increase social capital rather than exploit structural holes. However, they argue that "structural hole theory may apply more to networks of market transactions than to networks of cooperative relations" (p. 109). In the case of market transactions, firms are not bound by the structural constraint to cooperate over time and may therefore be more inclined to exploit structural holes.

In related research, Baker (1987) found that organizations with low levels of debt improved their autonomy in managing transactions by establishing communication relationships with many, rather than one or a few, investment banks. Kosnik (1987) found that companies who had more outside directors, especially directors from firms that had transactions with the focal firm, had less autonomy in engaging in "greenmail," the private repurchase of company stock. In contrast, the

CEOs of firms that had more outside directors had greater autonomy in negotiating "golden parachute" policies for the firms' top executives (Cochran, Wood, & Jones, 1985; Singh & Harianto, 1989; Wade, O'Reilly, & Chandratat, 1990).

Social capital and efficiency. Granovetter's (1982) theory of the "strength of weak ties" was also based on the premise that the people with whom a person has weak ties are less likely to be connected to one another; that is, the person is embedded in a structural hole. Consequently, the information obtained from these weak ties is less likely to be redundant and more likely to be unique, thereby making weak ties "information rich." Burt (1992) argued that being embedded in a structural hole allows actors to be more efficient in obtaining information. Using data from the 1985 and 1987 General Social Survey, Carroll and Teo (1996) found that the members of managers' core discussion networks were less likely to be connected to one another than members of nonmanagers' networks; consequently, nonmanagers' core discussion networks were less efficient in obtaining information. Contrary to conventional wisdom, Granovetter (1982) found that individuals were more likely to find jobs through their weak ties than through strong ties or formal listings. However, Lin, Ensel, and Vaughn's (1981) research showed that weak ties were effective only if they connected individuals to diverse others who could provide nonredundant information.

Social capital and innovation. The diversity of information obtained from ties has also been used to explain the introduction of innovations in organizations. Rogers (1971) noted that innovations were more likely to be introduced to an organization by cosmopolites, that is, people with diverse networks, including several external to the organization. In a study of the inventory and control systems of manufacturing industries, Newell and Clark (1990) reported that British firms were less innovative than their U.S. counterparts in part because they were less central in their interorganizational communication networks. More recently, Burns and Wholey (1993) found that hospitals that were centrally located in an interorganizational network were more likely to be early adopters of an innovation (the matrix form of management) than other hospitals in their network. Brass (1995a) suggested that being embedded in networks with structural holes can also enhance employees' ability to provide creative solutions to organizational problems.

Extensions to social capital. Since the introduction of the "social capital" concept in 1988 by Coleman, an impressive body of theoretical and empirical evidence has demonstrated its relevance. It was developed as a concept distinct from "human capital," which focuses on the attributes of individuals, such as seniority, intelligence, and education. Many of the informal means by which individuals accrue social capital rely on their knowledge of the existing communication networks. However, as the workforce moves from being physically co-located to "virtual environments," it is unclear whether electronic forms of communication such as email, which provide such things as distribution lists and records of messages, make it easier or more difficult for individuals to assess the existing social structure. Hence, as scholars examine the workforce of the 21st century, there is a pressing need for research that examines the distinctive strategies by which individuals can identify structural holes and thereby accumulate social capital in virtual organizations.

Transaction Cost Economics Theory

From the viewpoint of traditional economic theory, the market was the classical organizational form, where buyers and sellers communicated their intentions to each other, and where supply and demand were presumed to determine prices for goods. This is the purest form of self-interest theory. By contrast, neoclassical economics examined the development of hierarchical and vertically integrated forms as a more efficient alternative to markets (Coase, 1937), though one that is equally self-interested. However, over the past decade important changes in theories and views of organizational structuring have been occurring. A new organizational form, the network organization, is emerging as an alternative to both markets and vertically integrated organizations. This section examines these two traditional organizational forms, the market and hierarchies; the following section explores the development of the new alternative, the network form.

Williamson (1975, 1985) developed transaction cost economics to explain the organization of economic activity. All organizations require raw materials or components to manufacture their own goods or services. Thus, Williamson argued, organizations face a choice between buying resources from other firms or acquiring other firms in order to make the suppliers' goods or services at lower costs than what they could buy them, what is frequently called the buy-or-make decision. (It is also possible to develop internal capabilities, but this is generally seen as a more expensive option.) Williamson viewed the first alternative as governed by market mechanisms, where an organization hunts for the best prices among the alternative supplier firms. "Transaction costs" are the expenses associated with finding information about prices and quality from the available firms and negotiating contracts. He saw the second alternative, vertical integration, as governed by hierarchical forces, the administrative costs, including communication, associated with managing the internal production of acquired supplier firms. Economic organizations, Williamson argued, attempt to minimize transaction costs by making a choice between markets and hierarchies. Vertical integration, he said, is the efficient alternative when the transaction costs for markets are greater than the administrative costs of production through hierarchical ownership (Zajac & Olsen, 1993, p. 133). Clearly, the theoretical mechanism in Williamson's theory is efficient self-interest. Organizations make self-interested choices among alternative organizational forms by attempting to minimize the communication, information search, and decision-making costs associated with finding sellers in the market or acquiring suppliers. It should be clear that this mechanism is centered very much in the decision framework of individual firms. The alternative forms generated by this mechanism differ considerably in the nature of their communication networks.

Gupta and Govindarajan (1991) have extended Williamson's theory to the arena of multinational corporations. They argued that governance in multinational corporations can be viewed as a network of transaction cost exchanges. Home offices govern subsidiaries by regulating three critical transaction flows: capital, product, and knowledge. The fact that subsidiaries are located in different countries creates different strategic contexts and communication problems that determine the magnitude and direction of transaction flows.

A number of criticisms have been leveled against transaction cost economics. Granovetter (1985) observes that analyses of human and organizational economic behavior generally cluster at two ends of a continuum. Traditional neoeconomics treats human behavior and institutional action independent of social relations and interpersonal communication, a view that Granovetter calls an undersocialized viewpoint. More reformist economists and sociologists (e.g., Piore, 1975) tend to see economic action as severely constrained by social influences, a position he calls an oversocialized view. By contrast, Granovetter argues for a third alternative, that economic behavior of both individuals and organizations occurs within existing communication structures and ongoing social relations, a position he calls the embedded view. "The embeddedness argument," he says, "stresses instead the role of concrete personal relations and structures (or 'networks') of such relations" (p. 490). This view was supported by Uzzi's (1996) study of New York dress apparel firms, which showed that "embeddedness is an exchange system with unique opportunities relative to markets and that firms organized in networks have higher survival chances than do firms which maintain arm's-length market relationships" (p. 674).

Of course, there are drawbacks to embeddedness. Just as theory about the behavior of individual people or organizations can be over- or undersocialized, so can organizations be overembedded or underembedded. As Grabher (1993) says, "Too little embeddedness may expose networks to an erosion of their supportive tissue of social practices and institutions. Too much embeddedness, however, may promote a petrifaction of this supportive tissue and, hence, may pervert networks into cohesive coalitions against more radical innovations" (pp. 25-26). Similarly, Uzzi (1997), recognizing the paradox of embeddedness in the New York apparel economy, identified three conditions that turn embeddedness into a liability: "(1) There is an unforeseeable exit of a core network player, (2) institutional forces rationalize markets, or (3) overembeddedness characterizes the network" (p. 57).

Another criticism developed by Granovetter (1985) and Powell (1990) is that the dichotomy between markets and hierarchies does not exhaust all of the important organizational forms. Lazerson (1993) claims that "the false promises of vertical integration have stimulated interest in alternative organizational forms that are neither hierarchies nor markets" (p. 203). Williamson (1985, 1991) acknowledged this possibility in his discussion of alliances as hybrid forms. These, he said, exist between the other two and occur when the transaction costs associated with market exchange are too high but not high enough to justify vertical integration. However, a number of scholars, including Powell (1990), have argued that at least one alternative, the network organization, is neither market nor hierarchy in form. This issue is discussed in a later section of the chapter.

Zajac and Olsen (1993) critiqued Williamson's perspective on two accounts. First, they pointed out that Williamson's analysis fails to account for communication and other processes encountered in the transaction costs analysis. Instead, they proposed an alternative three-stage process that they argue enables firms to determine whether they should enter into the relation. These three are the initializing stage, the processing stage, and the reconfiguring stage. During the first stage each potential partner to the relation determines its own objectives, reviews exchange alternatives, and begins exploratory contacts to examine the feasibility of the relationships. Here, Zajac and Olsen (1993) contend, the first rounds of exchange "often take the form of preliminary communication and negotiation concerning mutual and individual firm interests, and/or feasibility studies and general information exchange" (p. 139). During the second stage firms engage in both serial and parallel information processing, "interfirm communications . . . occurring between individuals at multiple organizational levels and multiple functional areas" (p. 140). The third stage, reconfiguration, consists of evaluation of the relationship followed by a return to either of the previous two stages to (a) seek relational changes or (b) reaffirm the status quo. In essence, this stage affirms the information and communication network linkages on which the organizational relations can be established.

The second problem they identified is that Williamson's view of transaction cost minimization takes the perspective of only one organization. This is an error, they claimed, because a relationship has two sides, both of which should be included in any comprehensive account. Thus, they argued that transaction cost minimization from the perspective of one firm be replace by a "joint value maximization principle" that focuses on the benefits to both (or multiple) firms. More specifically, they propose that "value estimations of interorganizational strategies require that a focal firm consider the value sought by that firm's exchange partner. By taking the partner's perspective, the focal firm can better estimate the value and duration of the interorganizational strategy, given that value and duration are determined interdependently by other firms" (p. 137).

It is worth noting that Zajac and Olsen's critique transforms the self-interest theoretical mechanism for creating organizational communication networks into one that is jointly rather than individually self-interested. Further, it attempts to maximize collective value rather than minimize individual costs. This theoretical mechanism to account for the emergence of communication networks, mutual self-interest, is reviewed more fully in the following section.

Theories of Mutual Self-Interest and Collective Action

Collective action is a term that has been broadly applied to a wide range of phenomena in the social sciences, including organizational communication (Coleman, 1973). Its main focus is on "mutual interests and the possibility of benefits from coordinated action" (Marwell & Oliver, 1993, p. 2) rather than on individual self-interests. Samuelson (1954) first articulated public goods theory to explain how people could be induced to contribute to collective goods in the public domain such as bridges, parks, and libraries. Applications of this perspective to the interactive communication public goods of connectivity and communality have been made recently by Fulk, Flanagin, Kalman, Monge, and Ryan (1996).

The logic of collective action is based on the assumption that individuals motivated by self-interest will avoid investing resources in a joint endeavor whenever possible, leaving others to contribute their share even though all will benefit (Olson, 1965). This phenomenon is known as "free riding." Peer pressure is often applied to overcome this tendency to free ride and serves to make individuals comply with the need to contribute their fair share, thus facilitating collective action. Original formulations treated individuals as if they were isolated and independent of others making similar decisions. Oliver (1993), Markus (1990), and Marwell and Oliver (1993) have criticized this view and emphasized the importance of the network of relations in which people are embedded. Computer simulation experiments by Marwell and Oliver (1993) showed that the extent to which people are interconnected in communication networks increases their willingness to support the collective good. Using a similar research strategy, Marwell, Oliver, and Prahl (1988) showed that centralization and resource heterogeneity in the network influenced aggregate contributions to a collective good.

Empirical studies using collective action as an explanatory mechanism fall into two categories: the group's mobilization as indexed by its level of involvement, and the adoption of innovations. Research using a collective action mechanism has focused on the effect of the network on mobilization, as well as more specifically the adoption of innovations. Each of these two areas is discussed below.

Collective Action and Mobilization

In a retrospective study of the insurgency in the Paris Commune of 1871, Gould (1991) underscored the importance of examining multiple, partially overlapping networks in explaining the insurgents' solidarity and commitment. He found that the

> importance of neighborhood identity and the patterns of arrests showed that preexisting social ties among neighbors and organizational ties formed by the National Guard worked together to maintain solidarity in the insurgent ranks. . . . Cross-neighborhood solidarity could not have emerged in the absence of enlistment overlaps that linked each residential area with Guard units in other areas. (p. 727)

Applied to organizational contexts, Gould's findings suggest that collective action is less likely to succeed if the informal networks are structured so as to be either isomorphic with preexisting formal ties, or if they "completely cut across preexisting networks" (p. 728).

Knoke (1990, p. 5) examined the determinants of member participation and commitment among 8,746 respondents from 35 "collective action organizations," professional associations, recreational clubs, and women's associations. He discovered that "members' involvements in their collective action organizations are enhanced by extensive communication networks that plug them into the thick of policy discussions, apart from whatever degree of interest they may have in particular policy issues" (p. 185). At the interorganizational level, Laumann, Knoke, and Kim (1985) found that health organizations central in their industry's communication networks were more involved in mobilizing efforts on national policy issues affecting their domain. However, this relationship did not hold up among organizations in the energy industry. Laumann et al. (1985) concluded that centrality in a communication network was more important in predicting collective action in industries that were less institutionalized.

Collective Action and the Adoption of Innovations

Theories of collective action have also been used to examine the adoption of new interactive communication technologies (Markus, 1990; Rafaeli & LaRose, 1993). Valente (1995, 1996) has examined the effect of "threshold" (Granovetter, 1978) on adoption behavior. The *threshold* is defined as the number of other adopters that must be present in a person's network before the person decides to adopt. The threshold levels of individuals determine whether the group as a whole can achieve the critical mass necessary for rapid and widespread collective action. Rice, Grant, Schmitz, and Torobin (1990) examined the role of critical mass in predicting the adoption of an electronic mail system at a decentralized federal agency. They found that individuals' decisions to adopt the system were contingent on the decisions of others with whom they reported high levels of task interdependence.

Further, individuals' adoption decisions were influenced by the extent to which they valued the potential communication with others who were likely to be accessible via the new system. Gurbaxani (1990) used an adoption model based on critical mass theory to predict with considerable accuracy university adoption of the Bitnet computer network. At the interorganizational level, studies on governmental and nonprofit organizations have examined the role of network ties in overcoming obstacles to collective action (Mizruchi & Galaskiewicz, 1994; Rogers & Whetten, 1982; Turk, 1977).

Extensions to Collective Action Theory

The interest in examining the emergence of networks from a collective action perspective is relatively recent. It has been used persuasively to address issues of mobilization and the adoption of innovation. However, unlike some other mechanisms discussed in this chapter, the theoretical developments in this area have not been well complemented by empirical evidence. Scholars have proposed mathematical models, and some have carried out simulations. However, few of these efforts have been empirically validated.

In addition to the need for more empirical research, there are also some conceptual issues that continue to be advanced. First, the conceptualization of information technologies, such as discretionary databases, as "public goods" (Fulk et al., 1996), suggests that collective action theories can offer a more sophisticated explanation of the emergence of organizational networks, extending their present use to study the adoption of technologies in organizations. Discretionary databases are the message repositories that link knowledge suppliers and consumers, thereby creating connective and communal networks of individuals who share knowledge domains.

Second, there is potential for the application of network approaches to the conceptualization of free riding and its role in collective action. Collective action by groups is based on an underlying premise of social control. Homans's (1974) cohesion-compliance hypothesis predicts that group members are able to enforce social control on one another by exchanging peer approval for compliance with group obligations. Flache and Macy (1996) argue that under some circumstances members may choose to offer peer approval in exchange for peer approval rather than compliance from others. Using computer simulations of groups' networks, they observed that in these situations groups may reach a high level of cohesion that is not accompanied by a higher level of compliance or better group performance. Contrary to Homans's cohesion-compliance hypothesis, Flache and Macy (1996) concluded that "peer pressure can be an effective instrument for blocking compliance, especially in groups in which the cost of compliance is high relative to the value of approval" (p. 29). Oliver (1980) describes this phenomenon, where social control is directed toward the maintenance of interpersonal relationships at the expense of compliance with group obligations, as the "second-order free-rider problem."

Exchange and Dependency Theories

Extensive research has been conducted that seeks to explain the emergence of networks based on exchange and dependency mechanisms. Social exchange theory, originally developed by Homans (1950, 1974) and Blau (1964), seeks to explain human action by a calculus of exchange of material or information resources. In its original formulation, social exchange theory attempted to explain the likelihood of a dyadic relationship based on the supply and demand of resources that each member of the dyad had to offer. Emerson (1962, 1972a, 1972b) extended this original formulation beyond the dyad, arguing that to examine the potential of exchange and power-dependence relationships, it was critical to examine the larger network within

which the dyad was embedded. Since then, several scholars have developed this perspective into what is now commonly referred to as network exchange theory (Bienenstock & Bonacich, 1992, 1997; Cook, 1977, 1982; Cook & Whitmeyer, 1992; Cook & Yamagishi, 1992; Markovsky, Willer, & Patton, 1988; Skvoretz & Willer, 1993; Willer & Skvoretz, 1997; Yamagishi, Gillmore, & Cook, 1988).

Network exchange theory posits that individuals' power to bargain is a function of the extent to which they are vulnerable to exclusion from communication and other exchanges within the network. The argument is that individuals forge network links on the basis of their analysis of the relative costs and returns on investments. Likewise, individuals maintain links based on the frequency, the uncertainty, and the continuing investments to sustain the interaction. Location in the network may confer on some people an advantage over others in engaging in exchange relationships. Aldrich (1982) notes that this argument is at the core of several theories dealing with social exchange as well as resource dependency theories. Within organizations, network researchers have proposed a social exchange mechanism for the study of (a) power, (b) leadership, and (c) trust and ethical behavior. At the interorganizational level, researchers have (a) tested resource dependency theory, (b) examined the composition of corporate elites and interlocking board of directorates, and (c) sought to explain the creation, maintenance, and dissolution of interorganizational links. Each area is examined in greater detail below. The section concludes with proposed extensions to the study of organizational networks from a social exchange perspective.

Power

Social exchange theory has been used to examine the power that ensues from a structural position. In terms of exchange theory, power is defined as a function of dependence on others in the network. Location in the communication network is associated with greater power to the extent it offers greater access to valued material and informational resources. Specifically, people, groups, and organizations have power to the extent that they have access to alternate sources of a valued resource, and the extent to which they control resources valued by others in the network (Emerson, 1962). In a series of experimental and simulation studies, Cook and her colleagues (Cook & Emerson, 1978; Cook, Emerson, Gillmore, & Yamagishi, 1983) found evidence to support a power-dependence relationship. Carroll and Teo (1996) found that to increase their resources, organizational managers were more motivated than nonmanagers to have larger core discussion networks and to create more communication links outside the organization by memberships in clubs and societies. In her study of interorganizational social services, Alter (1990) found that the existence of a centralized, dominant core agency reduced the level of conflict and competition between service organizations and improved their level of cooperation. However, Hoffman, Stearns, and Shrader (1990) found that organizational centrality in four multiplex interorganizational networks depended on the nature of the network.

Several studies have equated network centrality with different sources of power. Brass (1984) suggested two measures of centrality that reflect different dimensions of power. Closeness, the extent to which people, groups, and organizations can reach all others in a network through a minimum of intermediaries, corresponds to the "access of resources" dimension of power (Sabidussi, 1966). Betweenness, the extent to which a network member lies between others not directly connected, corresponds to the "control of resources" dimension of power (Freeman, 1977, 1979). Brass (1984, 1985b) showed that both measures of centrality correlated with reputational measures of power. Further, Brass (1984, 1985b) found that employees with high scores on network indicators of power were

more likely to be promoted to supervisory positions, and Burkhardt and Brass (1990) discovered that early adopters of a new technology increased their power. Ibarra (1993a) found that centrality in the informal network was at least as important as the formal hierarchical network in predicting power; Krackhardt (1990) reported similar results for advice and friendship networks. Interestingly, Brass and Burkhardt's (1992) research revealed that measures of centrality at the departmental level were more strongly related to several indexes of power than measures at the subunit or the organizational levels.

Leadership

The success of network formulations to predict power has prompted some scholars to suggest its use in extending theories of leadership such as Graen's (1976) leader-member exchange theory (Krackhardt & Brass, 1994) and attribution theories of leadership (McElroy & Shrader, 1986). Fernandez (1991) found that the effects of informal communication networks on perceptions of leadership were different in three types of organizations. Specifically, he found that informal communication predicted perceptions of leadership most strongly in the participatory organization, a telephone-counseling center; only weakly in the professional organization, a public finance department of a large investment bank; and not at all in the hierarchical organization, a metallurgical firm.

Trust and Ethical Behavior

Researchers have also used social exchange theory to study the development and utility of trust in organizational and interorganizational networks. As Burt and Knez (1996) note, "Trust is committing to an exchange before you know how the other person will reciprocate" (p. 69). In a study of managers in a large high-technology firm, they found that the communication networks in which two individuals were embedded predicted the probability of a trust relationship between them. In particular, the trust between two individuals in close contact was high if other members in the organizations indirectly connected the two members to one another. Further, the *dis*trust between two individuals who were not in close contact was further attenuated if other members in the organization indirectly connected them to one another. This research indicates that indirect communication linkages reinforce trust and distrust relations between people. Labianca, Brass, and Gray (1998) also reported a similar amplification effect. They suggest that the amplification effect occurs because the secondhand information transmitted by indirect communication linkages "may be more polarized or exaggerated (either positively or negatively) than firsthand information" (p. 64), as grapevine (rumor) studies have found (e.g., DeFleur & Cronin, 1991; Schachter & Burdick, 1955).

In a study involving trust as measured via friendship networks, Krackhardt and Stern (1988) found that a relatively higher proportion of interunit (as compared to intraunit) friendship ties was particularly helpful to organizations coping with crisis conditions. In this case, the high level of trust was seen as a prerequisite for the increased interunit coordination required during a period of high uncertainty and the ensuing potential conflict. Larson's (1992) study of entrepreneurial firms indicated that trust as well as shared reciprocity norms, close personal relations, and reputation determined with whom and how exchanges occurred.

Researchers examining ethical behavior in organizations also deploy the exchange mechanism. Brass, Butterfield, and Skaggs (1995) suggest that networks could also offer an explanation for the likelihood of unethical behavior in a dyad since the connectedness of people is highly related to their observability. Brass et al. (1995) propose that "the strength of the relationship between two actors will be positively related to the opportunity to act in an unethical manner, but negatively related to the motivation to act unethically. Frequency and trust provide increased opportunity, but

intimacy and empathy decrease the motivation" (p. 6).

Resource Dependency Theory and Power in Interorganizational Networks

In his now classic article, Benson (1975) defined interorganizational networks as a political economy. By this he meant that interorganizational communication and exchange networks were the mechanisms by which organizations acquired and dispensed scarce resources, thus creating and perpetuating a system of power relations. Organizations were viewed as dependent on their positions in the network, which subsequently influenced their ability to control the flow of scarce resources.

Pfeffer and Salancik (1978) drew on Benson's work on political economy and social exchange mechanisms (Emerson, 1962, 1972a, 1972b) to formulate resource dependency theory. This theory argues that organizations structure their resource linkages to buffer themselves from the organization's environment (Pfeffer & Salancik, 1978). In particular, they identify two mechanisms that organizations can use toward this end. First, by network extension, organizations can seek to increase the number of exchange alternatives by creating new network links. Second, by network consolidation, they can decrease the number of exchange alternatives for others by forming a coalition with other resource providers. These counterbalancing mechanisms provide an explanation for the stability of exchange relationships and potential redistribution of power among the individuals. Burt (1991) developed a measure of equilibrium to assess the likelihood that network members have the resources to reconfigure their exchange networks and thereby the distribution of power.

A major tenet of resource dependency theory is that organizations tend to avoid interorganizational linkages that limit their decision making and other forms of autonomy. Oliver (1991; see also Oliver, 1990) tested this assumption across five relational types that ranged from highest to lowest levels of autonomy: personal meetings, resource transfers, board interlocks, joint programs, and written contracts. Surprisingly, she found no evidence that linkages that implied greater loss of autonomy led to lower likelihood of establishing the relationship.

A substantial body of empirical research draws on a resource dependency framework to study the pattern of interorganizational networks. These studies examine a wide variety of resource relationships, including money, material, information, and messages. However, the focus of these relationships is more concerned with the pattern of relationships than their content; thus, the majority of resource dependency research is conducted from a positional perspective. In some of the earlier studies in this area, Laumann and Pappi (1976) and Galaskiewicz (1979) reported that organizations that were more central in their networks had greater reputational influence. In a broad-based study assessing the power of the U.S. labor force, Wallace, Griffin, and Rubin (1989) discovered that the labor force in industries that were more central in the network of interindustry transactions were more likely to receive higher wages than the labor force in peripheral industries. Gerlach's (1992) study of the Japanese corporate network, including intercorporate *keiretsu* groupings, found strong evidence of the centrality of financial institutions in these networks and their resultant ability to control the capital allocation process (see also Lincoln, Gerlach, & Takahashi, 1992). However, in a study of health systems, Oliver and Montgomery (1996) observed that "the organization with greatest influence within the system (because of its ability to allocate funds) may not be the organization that takes the largest role in terms of coordinating routine contacts" (p. 771), such as client referrals.

Two studies show the impact of resource exchange on effectiveness. Miner, Amburgey, and Stearns's (1990) research on 1,011 newspaper publishers in Finland from 1771 to 1963

found that publishers with a greater number of interorganizational resource linkages, typically to political parties, had a higher overall success rate. Goes and Park (1997) found that "a greater volume of [resource] exchanges between hospitals increases the likelihood that innovation will spread between them" (p. 771).

Provan and Milward (1995) reported research designed to extend resource dependency theory by focusing on the effectiveness of the entire interorganizational network (see also Provan, 1983) rather than the antecedents and outcomes of individual organizations. Further, they pointed out that how well individual organizations perform is less important than how the interorganizational network as a whole performs. Studying the mental health care delivery system in four cities, they found that networks with a centralized decision-making agency were more effective than networks in which decision making was widely dispersed across agencies. Their data also suggested that the relationship between network structure and network effectiveness is influenced by the existence of a relatively munificent environment and the degree to which the overall network is stable.

Corporate Elites and Interlocking Boards of Directors

Corporate elites and networks created by linkages among people who serve on multiple corporate boards are areas that have received considerable research attention in interorganizational relations. As Knoke (1993) indicated, "A power elite is established at the intersection of three social formations: a class-conscious upper social class of wealth-holders, interlocked directors of major corporations, and a policy-planning network of foundations, research institutes, and nonpartisan organizations" (p. 26). Useem's (1984) classic study argued that these overlapping networks of friendship, ownership, membership, and directorship produced a core set of individuals, or "inner circle," which wields enormous power. Knoke (1993) explained that "because its members simultaneously hold multiple directorships, the core can act politically in the interests of the class, which transcend the parochial concerns of its individual firms" (p. 26). Consistent with this view, Romo and Anheier (1996) found evidence that a core group of elites explained the emergence and institutionalization of consortia for private development organizations in Nigeria and Senegal. Studies have also shown that individuals who were more centrally located in the interlocking board of directors were also more likely to play a leadership role in cultural, philanthropic, and policy-making organizations (Domhoff, 1983; Mizruchi & Galaskiewicz, 1994; Ogliastri & Davila, 1987; Ratcliff, Gallagher, & Ratcliff, 1979; Useem, 1980).

Historically, the focus of interlocking directorate research has been on corporate control. However, Minz and Schwartz (1985) argued that "the most compelling interpretation of the overall network created by the collection of individual reasons for and response to director recruitment is a general communication system" (p. 141). In fact, as Mizruchi (1996) contends, "the emphasis on interlocks has moved increasingly toward their value as a communication mechanism rather than as a mechanism of control" (p. 284).

Creation, Maintenance,
Dissolution, and Reconstitution
of Interfirm Links

Studies have also deployed a resource dependency framework to explain the creation of links in interorganizational networks. Mizruchi and Stearns (1988) found two general factors that explained the addition of new financial members to an organization's board of directors. Under favorable economic conditions, when capital demand and supply are increasing, organizations initiate links with financial institutions through their board of directors to co-opt these institutions' financial and informational resources. However, during unfavorable economic conditions, including contractions in the business cycle, lower solvency, and lower profitability, it is the financial institutions that infiltrate companies' boards of directors to protect their investments. This finding is qualified by Boyd's (1990) research that showed high-performing firms responded to resource scarcity and competitive uncertainty by decreasing the number of their directors but increasing the density of their linkages with other firms. Mizruchi (1996) argued that a number of other factors also affect the creation of interlocking directorates. These include creating legitimacy for the firm, advancing the careers of those who serve as directors, and fostering the social cohesion of the corporate upper class.

Palmer et al. (1986) used resource dependency theory to hypothesize the conditions under which a broken interlock tie between two organizations (due to death, retirement, etc.) would be reconstituted. They found that interlock ties were likely to be reconstituted if the departing member represented an organization with which the focal organization had (a) formal coordination, such as long-term contracts or joint ventures; (b) direct business ties; or (c) headquarters that were physically proximate.

Larson (1992) demonstrated that firms tend to enter repeated alliances with each other; thus, dependencies tend to generate further dependencies. Gulati's (1995) research showed that the information provided by both direct and indirect ties of prior alliances established the basis for the formation of additional alliances. However, his research also showed that as the benefits of linking with specific others declined over time organizations looked for new alliances. Of course, as Baum and Oliver (1992) noted, there is a carrying capacity to alliances in that most organizations can successfully support only a limited number of connections, and many firms fear the overdependence that too many ties might bring.

Seabright, Levinthal, and Fichman (1992) theorized that reductions in the resource fit between organizations would lead to pressures to dissolve interorganizational relations while increases in personal and structural attachments would counter those pressures and lead to continued relations. Their results supported the hypotheses but also showed that personal and structural attachments attenuated the firms' likelihood of dissolving ties under conditions of reduced fit. This finding underscores the importance of established communication and social attachments in maintaining interorganizational relations beyond the point where a strict exchange or resource dependency perspective would predict that they would dissolve, even at times when it might be disadvantageous to maintain them. Overall, however, Mizruchi's (1996) review of the research literature on corporate interlocks led him to conclude that "although the findings have been mixed, on balance they support the view that interlocks are associated with interfirm resource dependence" (p. 274).

The research on interlocking directorates assumes that each organization is a separate entity tied together at the top by corporate elites. While interest continues in interlocking directorates, a new field of research has developed over the past decade that focuses on an emergent organizational form, network organizations. This perspective relaxes these two assumptions of separate entities and executive ties only. We explore this new area in the next section.

Network Organizations

Network organizations are composed of a collection of organizations along with the linkages that tie them to each other, often organized around a focal organization. There are numerous variations on the network organizational form including joint partnerships, strategic alliances, cartels, R&D consortia, and a host of others.

The theoretical mechanisms that generate most network organizations are exchange and dependency relations. Rather than being organized around market or hierarchical principles, network organizations are created out of complex webs of exchange and dependency relations among multiple organizations. In a sense, the network organization becomes a supraorganization whose primary function is linking many organizations together and coordinating their activities. Unlike interlocking directorates, the network ties usually occur throughout the entire organization rather than only at the top, and the separate organizations often give up some or all of their individual autonomy to become a part of the new network organization.

Miles and Snow (1992) observe that network organizations differ from their predecessors (functional, multidivisional, and matrix forms) in four important ways. First, rather than subsume all aspects of production within a single hierarchical organization they attempt to create a set of relations and communication networks among several firms, each of which contributes to the value of the product or service. Second, networks are based on a combination of market mechanisms and informal communication relations. As they say, "The various components of the network recognize their interdependence and are willing to share information, cooperate with each other, and customize their product or service—all to maintain their position within the network" (p. 55). Third, members of networks are often assumed to take a proactive role in improving the final product or service, rather than merely fulfilling contractual obligations. Finally, a number of industries are beginning to form network organizations along the lines of the Japanese keiretsu, which links together producers, suppliers, and financial institutions into fairly stable patterns of relations.

Poole (in press) argues that new organizational forms, including network organizations, are constituted out of six essential qualities:

1. The use of information technology to integrate across organizational functions
2. Flexible, modular organizational structures that can be readily reconfigured as new projects, demands, or problems arise
3. Use of information technology to coordinate geographically dispersed units and members

4. Team-based work organization, which emphasizes autonomy and self-management
5. Relatively flat hierarchies and reliance on horizontal coordination among units and personnel
6. Use of intra- and interorganizational markets to mediate transactions such as the assignment and hiring of personnel for projects and the formation of interorganizational networks.

In today's world, nearly all organizations are embedded to some extent in an emergent interorganizational communication network. For example, most economic institutions are linked together in "value chains" (Porter, 1980) or "value constellations" (Norman & Ramirez, 1993) where each receives a partially finished product from an "upstream organization," adds its contribution, and then delivers it to the next "downstream organization" for its contribution. Similarly, educational institutions typically relate to other educational institutions in a chain from preschool to postgraduate education. And religious organizations are frequently affiliated with coalitions of other like-minded religious groups. Of course, all must deal with the taxation authorities of federal, state, and local governments.

In one sense, network organizations create what have come to be called "boundaryless organizations" (Nohria & Berkley, 1994). Where one organization begins and the other ends is no longer clear. Organizations come to share knowledge, goals, resources, personnel, and finances, usually with highly sophisticated communication technology (Monge & Fulk, 1999). To accomplish this they must establish collaborative work arrangements, since that is the only way to transfer embedded knowledge.

Ghoshal and Bartlett (1990) argued that multinational corporations (MNCs) have traditionally been viewed as an intraorganizational network, in many ways not different from traditional national companies. Each satellite, subsidiary, or foreign partner has been seen as directly connected to the home corporate office, thus tying the MNC into an integrated hub-and-spoke structural whole. However, they point out that this view of the MNC fails to take into account the extended networks in which each of the subsidiaries is embedded. These national, regional, and competing global networks require a reconceptualization of MNCs as network organizations.

Limitations of Network Organizations

Several authors have pointed out that network organizations have a number of limitations. Miles and Snow (1992) observe that network organizations contain the vestigial weaknesses of their predecessors, the functional, multidivisional, and matrix forms. To the extent that parts of these prior forms remain in the network organization, the new form retains their prior limitations. Krackhardt (1994) identifies four potential constraints on communication and other networks. The first he calls the "law of N-squared," which simply notes that the number of potential links in a network organization increases geometrically with the number of people. In fact, it grows so quickly that the number of people to which each person could be linked quickly exceeds everyone's communication capacity. The second constraint is the "law of propinquity," a rather consistent empirical finding that "the probability of two people communicating is inversely proportional to the distance between them" (p. 213). Though numerous communication technologies have been designed to overcome this phenomenon, Krackhardt argues that the tendency remains and is difficult for people to overcome. The third constraint he identifies is the "iron law of oligarchy," which is the tendency for groups and social systems, even fervently democratic ones, to end up under the control of a few people. Finally, Krackhardt (1994) notes the potential problem of overembeddedness. He observes that "people as a matter of habit and preference are likely to seek out their old standbys, the people they have grown to trust, the people they always go to and depend on, to deal with new problems, even though they may not be the ones best able to address these problems" (p. 220).

Poole (in press) also points to several human problems that stem from the tightly coupled technology but fluid management philosophies on which most network organizations are built. Foremost among these are maintaining a sense of mission, commitment, loyalty, and trust, and dealing with increased levels of work stress and burnout.

Extensions to Exchange and Dependency Theories

While some variation exists across different studies, the preponderance of evidence suggests that many inter- and intraorganizational communication networks are created and maintained on the basis of exchange mechanisms. Further, as people and organizations find their exchanges no longer rewarding or as new or competitive others offer better bargains in the exchange, linkages begin to dissolve.

Despite its intellectual roots in the study of interpersonal relationships, exchange and dependency theories have been more extensively deployed in the study of interorganizational networks, often within the context of resource dependency theory, rather than intraorganizational networks. Much of the intraorganizational research reviewed above, while premised in a social exchange perspective, does not invoke the theory explicitly. Further, in areas such as leadership, trust, and ethical behavior, the studies so far are more illustrative then programmatic attempts at applying social exchange theory. X-Net, a computer simulation tool developed by Markovsky (1995), should help researchers explore the emergence of networks in terms of different rules of exchange and varied resources. Researchers have also proposed integrating net-

work exchange theory with rational choice theory (Markovsky, 1997) and identity theory (Burke, 1997), and a general theoretical method called E-state structuralism (Skvoretz & Fararo, 1996; Skvoretz & Faust, 1996), which integrates research on expectation states theory (Berger, Cohen, & Zelditch, 1966) with network exchange theory. Expectation states theory argues that a person's "behavior towards social objects depends on postulated and unobservable states of relational orientations to objects, E-states for short" (Skvoretz & Fararo, 1996, p. 1370). The social objects toward which individuals orient are the networks of ties among the individuals. E-state models specify "how the state of this network, i.e., the number and nature of the ties linking actors, changes over time as individuals interact" (Skvoretz & Fararo, 1996, p. 1370).

Contagion Theories

Contagion theories are based on the assumption that communication networks in organizations serve as a mechanism that exposes people, groups, and organizations to information, attitudinal messages, and the behavior of others (Burt, 1980, 1987; Contractor & Eisenberg, 1990). This exposure increases the likelihood that network members will develop beliefs, assumptions, and attitudes that are similar to those of others in their network (Carley, 1991; Carley & Kaufer, 1993). The contagion approach seeks to explain organizational members' knowledge, attitudes, and behavior on the basis of information, attitudes, and behavior of others in the network to whom they are linked. Rogers and Kincaid (1981) refers to this as the *convergence* model of communication.

Theories that are premised on a contagion model, at least in part, include social information processing theory (Fulk, Steinfield, Schmitz, & Power, 1987; Salancik & Pfeffer, 1978), social influence theory (Fulk, Schmitz, & Steinfield, 1990; see also Marsden &

Friedkin, 1994), structural theory of action (Burt, 1982), symbolic interactionist perspectives (Trevino, Lengel, & Daft, 1987), mimetic processes exemplified by institutional theories (DiMaggio & Powell, 1983; Meyer & Rowan, 1977), and social cognitive theory (Bandura, 1986). Fulk (1993) notes that these constructivist perspectives "share the core proposition that social and symbolic processes produce patterns of shared cognitions and behaviors that arise from forces well beyond the demands of the straightforward task of information processing in organizations" (p. 924). She also points out that the mechanisms offered by these theories differ not so much because of conflicting premises as because the theories focus on different aspects of the social construction process.

The contagion mechanism has been used to explain network members' attitudes as well as behavior. Erickson (1988) offers a comprehensive overview of the various theories that address the "relational basis of attitudes" (p. 99). She describes how various network dyadic measures such as frequency, multiplexity, strength, and asymmetry can shape the extent to which others influence individuals in their networks. Moving beyond the dyadic level of network contagion, she also describes cohesion and structural equivalence models that offer alternative, and in some cases complementary, explanations of the contagion process. Contagion by cohesion implies that the attitudes and behaviors of the others with whom they are directly connected influence network members. Contagion by structural equivalence implies that others who have similar structural patterns of relationships within the network influence people.

An impressive body of empirical research at both the intraorganizational and interorganizational levels is based on the contagion mechanism. At the intraorganizational level, studies have proposed a contagion mechanism to explain (a) general workplace attitudes, (b) attitudes toward technologies, and (c) organizational behavior such as turnover and absenteeism. Researchers have also used contagion

to explain interorganizational behavior. Each of these topics is reviewed on the following pages. The section concludes with suggestions for extensions of organizational research based on a contagion mechanism.

General Workplace Attitudes

Several studies have examined the extent to which contagion explains individual attitudes in the workplace. Friedkin's (1984) early research showed that educational policy makers were more likely to perceive agreement with others who were either in the same cohesive social circle or were structurally equivalent. Walker (1985) discovered that members of a computer firm who were structurally equivalent were more likely to report similar cognitions about means-ends relationships of product development. And Rentsch (1990) found that members of an accounting firm who communicated with one another were more likely to share similar interpretations of organizational events.

Goodell, Brown, and Poole (1989) use a structurational argument (Poole & McPhee, 1983) to examine the relationship between communication network links and shared perceptions of organizational climate. Using four waves of observation over a ten-week period from an organizational simulation, they found that members' communication networks were significantly associated with shared perceptions of the organizational climate only at the early stages of organizing (weeks two and four). In another study comparing the cohesion and structural equivalence mechanisms of contagion, Hartman and Johnson (1989, 1990) found that members who were cohesively linked were more likely to have similar levels of commitment to the organization. However, those who were structurally equivalent were more likely to have similar perceptions of role ambiguity in the workplace. Pollock, Whitbred, and Contractor (1996) compared the relative efficacy of three models that seek to explain an individual's satisfaction in the workplace: the job characteristics model (Hackman & Oldham, 1976), the individual dispositions model (Staw & Ross, 1985), and the social information processing model (Salancik & Pfeffer, 1978). Using data from the public works division of a military installation, Pollock et al. (1996) found that employees' satisfaction was significantly predicted only by the social information processing model, that is, by the satisfaction of friends and communication partners in their social networks, but not by the characteristics of their jobs or their individual dispositions.

Attitudes Toward Technologies

Several researchers have examined the extent to which contagion explains organizational members' attitudes toward technologies. Drawing on social information processing theory (Salancik & Pfeffer, 1978) and social cognitive theory (Bandura, 1986), Fulk and her colleagues (Fulk, Schmitz, & Ryu, 1995; Schmitz & Fulk, 1991) found that organizational members' perceptions and use of an electronic mail system were significantly influenced by the attitudes and use of the members' supervisors and five closest coworkers. Further, Fulk (1993) found that social influence was even more pronounced in more cohesive groups. The attitudes and use of other members in their communication networks significantly influenced individuals' attitudes and use of an electronic mail system. This effect was attenuated, but persisted, even after she controlled for the effect of the work group's attitudes and use on each group member.

Rice and Aydin's (1991) research showed that hospital employees who communicated with one another or shared supervisory-subordinate relationships were more likely to share similar attitudes about a recently introduced information technology. Rice et al. (1990) found that individuals' use of email in a decentralized federal agency was predicted by the use of the technology by others in their communication network. Further, groups of individuals who communicated more strongly with one another were more likely to share similar distinct email usage patterns.

Using longitudinal data from a federal government agency, Burkhardt (1994) found that individuals' attitudes and use of a recently implemented distributed data-processing computer network were significantly influenced by the attitudes and use of others in their communication network. She found that individuals' perceptions of their self-efficacy with (or mastery of) the new technology were significantly influenced by those with whom they had direct communication, which is the theoretical mechanism of contagion by cohesion. However, individuals' general attitudes and use of the technology itself were more influenced by the attitudes and behaviors of those with whom they shared similar communication patterns, that is, contagion by structural equivalence. Burkhardt also found that the contagion effect was higher for individuals who scored higher on a self-monitoring scale.

Extending this line of longitudinal research on contagion effects, Contractor, Seibold, and Heller (1996) conducted a study comparing the evolution of the social influence process in face-to-face and computer-augmented groups. They found that group members initial influence on each others' perceptions of the structures-in-use (i.e., the interaction norms enacted during the meeting) was high in the face-to-face condition, while group members using group decision support systems (GDSSs) started out with low levels of social influence on one another. However, the difference between face-to-face and technologically augmented groups was only transient. By their third meeting, members in all groups heavily influenced each other's perceptions of the structures-in-use. While the preponderance of research has focused on similarity in attitudes based on contagion, Bovasso (1995) reports results from a process he calls "anticontagion." In a study of managers at a large, multinational high-tech firm, Bovasso found that "individuals who perceive themselves as strong leaders are influenced by peers who do not perceive themselves as strong leaders" (pp. 1430-1431) and vice versa.

Behavior Through Contagion

Several network studies have used a contagion explanation for organizational members' behaviors, including voluntary turnover, absenteeism, job-seeking, socialization, and unethical behavior. Krackhardt and Porter (1986) found that employees voluntarily quitting their jobs were more likely to be structurally equivalent to one another than those who remained. However, they found that employees who were absent were more likely to be cohesively connected with one another through friendship ties. They suggested that decisions about turnover were more closely related to individuals' roles in the organization and hence, members were more influenced by others in similar roles. On the other hand, decisions about absenteeism reflected norms in the organizations that were communicated through cohesive friendship ties. In a more recent study, Feeley and Barnett (1996) examined employee turnover at a supermarket and found that both social influence and structural equivalence networks predicted the likelihood of employees leaving the organization. Kilduff (1992) studied graduate business students' job-seeking behavior and found that students' decisions to interview with particular organizations were influenced by the opinions communicated to them by others in their friendship networks. The contagion effect was more pronounced for students who reported being high self-monitors. Zey-Ferrell and Ferrell (1982) reported that employees' self-reported unethical behavior was better predicted by their perceptions of their peer behavior than either their own beliefs or those of top management. Research on organizational socialization (Jablin & Krone, 1987; Sherman, Smith, & Mansfield, 1986) has also identified newcomers' positions in their new communication networks as a predictor of their assimilation into the organization.

Interorganizational Contagion

The contagion mechanism has also been used to explain behavior at the interorganizational level. Organizations can link to other organizations in many ways. Useem (1984) describes how organizations use director interlocks as a tool to scan their environment. These linkages are important because they provide the opportunity for communication and the exchange of ideas, practices, and values. Both the formal activities surrounding the board meetings and the informal activities and acquaintance ties that are created enable people to discover how things are done in other organizations. In these and similar interorganizational studies, the opportunity to communicate afforded by the existence of linkages is viewed as more important than specific message content.

Consistent with Useem's (1984) view, much of the more recent literature examines the mechanisms by which organizations use these linkages to transfer organizational practices and structural forms. Davis (1991) found that *Fortune* 500 corporations were more likely to adopt the "poison pill" strategy to defend against corporate takeovers if their boards had directors from organizations that had already adopted a similar strategy. Haunschild's (1993) research showed that the number and types of corporate acquisitions undertaken by their interlock partners significantly influenced the number and type of takeovers attempted by firms. Likewise, her 1994 research demonstrated that "acquisition premiums" (p. 406), the price that a firm pays to acquire another firm over the market value prior to the takeover announcement, are similar to those that their partner firms paid for their acquisitions. Other research by Palmer, Jennings, and Zhou (1993) has shown that firms are more likely to adopt a multidivisional form when they are linked to corporations that have already adopted that form. Similarly, Burns and Wholey (1993) found that a hospital's decision to adopt a matrix management program was significantly predicted by the adoption decision of other local hospitals with high prestige and visibility. Goes and Park (1997) found that hospitals that were structurally tied to other hospitals in a multihospital system were more likely to adopt innovations, and Westphal, Gulati, and Shortell (1997) found that contagion also explained the adoption of total quality management (TQM) practices in the organization. However, they observed that early adopters of TQM were more likely to use the other early adopters in their medical alliance network to clarify their functional understanding of TQM. The early adopters were therefore more likely to customize the program to their organizational needs. In contrast, late adopters were more likely to seek out other adopters in their alliance network to determine the legitimacy of using TQM. Hence, the late adopters were more likely to adopt the TQM program without any customization. Stearns and Mizruchi (1993) found that the type of financing used by a firm, short- versus long-term debt, was influenced by the types of financial institutions to which it was linked by its board of directors, commercial bankers versus representatives of insurance companies. However, the embeddedness of an organization's board of directors has a somewhat counterintuitive influence on the selection of its CEO. Khurana (1997) found that *Fortune* 500 companies whose boards of directors were well embedded into the system of interlocking directorates were *less* likely to choose an outsider as a CEO because "a high level of embeddedness is likely to constrain actions rather than facilitate them" (p. 17).

Interlocking directorates are only one of several possible mechanisms for linking organizations. Organizations are likely to be linked to bankers, attorneys, accountants, suppliers, and consultants, all of whom serve as conduits for the flow of information between organizations. Basing their arguments on the mimetic processes articulated by institutional theory (DiMaggio & Powell, 1983), Galaskiewicz and Burt (1991), and Galaskiewicz and Wasserman (1989) discovered that contribution officers who were structurally equivalent in an interorganizational corporate network were more likely to give charitable donations to the same nonprofit groups than those who were cohesively linked. Mizruchi (1989, 1992) found that organizations that were structurally equivalent in the interorganizational network were more likely to have similar patterns of political contributions. Baum and Oliver (1991) showed that increased ties to legitimating institutions significantly reduced the likelihood of failure among new organizations. And in a ten-year study, Goes and Park (1997) found that hospitals linked to their institutional environments through industry and trade associations were more likely to adopt innovations in an effort to gain legitimacy. This effect was even more pronounced when the hospital industry entered a turbulent phase after introduction of two regulatory events in 1983. Interestingly, these findings are similar to those obtained under predictions from exchange and resource dependency theories, though obviously generated by a different theoretical mechanism.

Extensions to Contagion Theories

Contagion theories offer by far the most common theoretical mechanisms for studying the emergence of networks. The notion of a network as labyrinth of conduits for information flow lends itself to theoretical mechanisms based on contagion. However, while network researchers frequently invoke contagion theories, they often fall short of articulating specific mechanisms and network models by which individuals, groups, and organizations influence each other's actions and behaviors (Contractor & Eisenberg, 1990; Marsden & Friedkin, 1994; Rice, 1993b). There are four recent attempts to articulate mechanisms that make the contagion process more theoretically specific and comprehensive for communication networks.

First, Krackhardt and Brass (1994) note that the contagion processes described by social information processing theory must over time lead to an equilibrium wherein everyone in the network will eventually converge in their attitudes or actions. They note that this conclusion undermines the very premise of social information processing theory, which seeks to explain the variation in people's attitudes based on their differential exposure to social information. Krackhardt and Brass (1994) suggest that the *principle of interaction* that is assumed by contagion theories needs to be augmented by a second contagion mechanism, the *principle of reflected exclusivity.* The principle of interaction states that greater interaction leads to greater similarity in attitudes. By contrast, the principle of reflected exclusivity states that "the degree of influence person j has on person i's evaluation . . . is inversely proportional to the amount of time person j spends with all others" (Krackhardt & Brass, 1994, p. 219).

Second, Krassa (1988) advocates the inclusion of members' threshold levels in a social influence model. In its simplest form, the threshold is the number of others that people must be influenced by before succumbing (Granovetter, 1978). Individuals' thresholds could be a function of the intensity of their opinion and their aversion to the risk of being socially isolated. Krassa (1988) uses computer simulations of a contagion model to demonstrate the effects of people's threshold distributions on their opinions.

Third, Rice (1993b) has argued that a network contagion model of social influence should also take into consideration the ambiguity of the situation. Drawing on research by Moscovici (1976), Rice (1993b) argues that people are more vulnerable to social influence by contagion when confronted with ambiguous, or novel, situations. Based on this argument, Contractor and Grant (1996) hypothesized that groups using new collaboration technologies (a novel situation) would be more likely to influence each other's perceptions of the medium than groups in a traditional face-to-face meeting. However, they found that social influence was actually greater in face-to-face groups, perhaps because the novelty in this case was associated with the very medium used to socially influence one another.

Finally, in an attempt to extend the current debate surrounding the relative efficacy of contagion via cohesion versus structural equivalence, Pattison (1994) argued for a closer examination of automorphic or regular equivalence in addition to mechanisms based on contagion by cohesion and structural equivalence. Unlike structural equivalence, which in its strict operationalization is defined as two individuals having identical network links to the same others, regular equivalence is defined as two people having similar patterns of relationships, but not necessarily with the same others (White & Reitz, 1989). Pattison (1994) argues that people who are regularly equivalent are more likely to have similar social cognitions because "cognitive processes may directly involve the individual's perceptions of his or her social locale" (p. 93). In a longitudinal study of students in an undergraduate class, Michaelson and Contractor (1992) found that students who were regularly equivalent were more likely to be perceived as similar by their classmates than those who were structurally equivalent.

Cognitive Theories

The contagion mechanisms discussed in the previous section focused on the extent to which others who were linked to individuals via cohesion or structural equivalence influenced their attitudes and actions. These studies explain attitudes and behavior based on individuals' actual interactions. Researchers have employed four concepts to gain insight into the structure of individuals' cognitions: semantic networks, knowledge structures, cognitive social structures, and cognitive consistency. These areas are discussed in greater detail below.

Semantic Networks

With an eye toward a more systematic treatment of message content, semantic networks were introduced into the organizational communication literature by Monge and Eisenberg (1987; see also Carley, 1986; Danowski's [1982] word network analysis; Dunn & Ginsberg, 1986; Fiol's [1989] semiotic analysis; Rogers & Kincaid's [1981] convergence theory of networks; Woelfel & Fink's [1980] Galileo system). The essential feature of this perspective was a focus on the shared meanings that people have for message content, particularly those messages that comprise important aspects of an organization's culture, such as corporate goals, slogans, myths, and stories. Monge and Eisenberg (1987) argued that asking people to provide their interpretations of one or more significant communication messages, events, or artifacts could create semantic networks. Content analysis of members' responses provides categories of interpretation. Linkages can then be created between people who share similar interpretations. The resultant network articulation provides a picture of the groups of people who share common understandings, those who have idiosyncratic meanings such as isolates, and those who serve as liaisons and boundary spanners between the various groups.

With respect to empirical studies of semantic networks Lievrouw, Rogers, Lowe, and Nadel (1987) used four methods to identify the invisible research colleges among biomedical scientists: (a) co-citation analysis, (b) coword occurrence, (c) interpretive thematic analysis, and (d) network analysis. They concluded that their focus on the content of the networks helped clarify the structure of the invisible colleges. On the basis of communication network patterns alone, all the scientists would have been clustered into one invisible college. However, a closer examination of content helped them identify several invisible colleges, "each of which represents a distinct and identifiable line of research" (p. 246).

In a study of a high-technology firm, a library, and a hospital, Contractor, Eisenberg, and Monge (1996) examined the semantic networks representing the extent to which employees shared interpretations of their organizations' missions. In addition to their actual agreement, employees were also asked to report their perceived agreement, that is, the extent to which they believed others shared their interpretations in the organization. They found that employees at higher levels in the hierarchy were more likely to perceive agreement, even in cases when there was no agreement. However, employees with more tenure in the organization were more likely to have actual agreement, even though they did not perceive that others shared their interpretations of the mission. Contrary to the accepted view that communication builds shared meaning, employees cohesively connected in the communication network were not more likely to agree with their colleagues' interpretations of the organizational mission, even though they perceived agreement. However, employees who were structurally equivalent were more likely to share actual agreement, even though they were not as likely to perceive agreement.

Krackhardt and Kilduff (1990) applied the notion of semantic networks to examine individuals' attributions about others in the network. They asked individuals in an organization to make cultural attributions on seven dimensions about the behaviors of each other member in the organization. They found that individuals who were friends were more likely than nonfriends to make similar attributions about other members in the organization. Rice and Danowski (1993) applied the notion of semantic networks to examine individuals' attributions of the appropriation of a voice mail system. They found that individuals who used the system for "voice processing" (i.e., routing and structuring the flow of messages among individuals) characterized their use of the technology in terms that were systematically distinct from those who used the voice mail technology as a substitute for traditional answering machines.

Two studies have used semantic networks to examine variations in national cultures. Jang and Barnett (1994) analyzed the chief operating officer's letter that 17 Japanese and 18 U.S. organizations published in the organization's annual report to stockholders. They found that the co-occurrence of words in these messages resulted in two distinct clusters for the Japanese and U.S. companies. Further, the words co-occurring in the Japanese annual reports focused on concepts related to organizational operations, while the U.S. documents focused on concepts related to organizational structure. In a study of 12 managers from five European countries, Stohl (1993) examined the cultural variations associated with managers' interpretation of a key communicative process, worker participation. She found that the semantic network based on shared interpretations of the concept reflected greater connectedness within countries than between countries. Further, similarities in interpretations about worker participation were systematically associated with three of Hofstede's (1984) dimensions of cultural variability across countries. These were (a) the power distance index, the extent to which less powerful people accept inequality in power; (b) the uncertainty avoidance index, the extent to which people avoid uncertainty by relying on strict codes of behavior; and (c) individualism, the extent to which citizens place primary importance on the needs of the individual rather than the collective.

Extensions to semantic networks. The theoretical mechanisms of contagion have also been used to explain the co-evolution of communication and semantic networks. Contractor and Grant (1996) developed a computer simulation of the effects of social contagion in communication and semantic networks that contained varying levels of initial network density and heterogeneity. They found that the time required for semantic convergence within groups was positively related to the density of the communication and semantic networks, inversely related to the heterogeneity of the communication network, and inversely related to the individual's inertia against being influenced socially. Significantly, the initial heterogeneity in the seman-

tic network, an indicator of initial variation in interpretations, was not a significant predictor of the time required for semantic convergence.

In a similar endeavor, Carley (1991) offered a "constructural" theory of group stability, modeling the parallel cultural and social evolution of a group. Social structure was defined as the distribution of interaction probabilities, and culture was defined as the distribution of distinct facts. Carley's (1991) model described a cycle of three events for each group member: "(1) action—exchange information with their partners; (2) adaptation—acquire the communicated information and update the probabilities of interaction; and then (3) motivation—choose new interaction partners on the basis of their new probabilities of interaction" (p. 336). Results of computer simulations showed that these groups did not evolve monotonically toward greater homogeneity. Instead they often oscillated through cycles of greater and lesser cohesiveness. Her simulations also indicated that groups with "simpler" cultures (i.e., fewer facts to be learned by group members) tended to stabilize more quickly. Further, those in less homogeneous groups (i.e., where facts were not equally distributed) were less likely to stabilize, since they could form enduring subcultures. One corollary of constructural theory is that the probabilities for two individuals to interact are not symmetric (Carley & Krackhardt, 1996).

Network Organizations as Knowledge Structures

A complementary view of semantic networks as meaning structures is provided by Kogut, Shan, and Walker (1993), who argued that it is interesting to view interorganizational networks as structures of knowledge. Organizations seek out other organizations because they want to establish some form of relationship. But to do so, they must first find at least some of the other organizations that are also interested in entering into the relationship with them and choose among the alternatives. This means they must acquire information about the other organization and compare it with information from other organizations. Often, in searching for partners, organizations begin close to home or on the basis of recommendations from others with whom they are already linked. Over time, this searching process builds up a knowledge base about the skills, competencies, trustworthiness, and other capabilities of the organizations.

Once organizations choose partners, however, they tend to spend less time seeking other partners. As Kogut et al. (1993) say, "Because information is determined by previous relations and in turn influences the subsequent propensity to do more relations, the structure of the network tends to replicate itself over time. The early history of cooperation tends to lock in subsequent cooperation" (p. 70). Further, they observe:

> The replication of the network is a statement of the tendency of learning to decline with time. The structure of the network is a limiting constraint on how much new learning can be achieved. . . . But when viewed from the perspective of the evolution of networks, there is a tendency for old lessons to be retaught. (p. 71)

Powell, Koput, and Smith-Doerr (1996) argue that learning networks are particularly important in industries where there is rapid technological development, knowledge is complex, and expertise is distributed around many organizations. Using data collected on 225 firms over four years, they found strong evidence for increasing levels of interorganizational communication and collaboration in the biotechnology industry, including increases in ties and network density. In a study of two new biotechnology firms (NBFs), Liebeskind, Oliver, Zucker, and Brewer (1996, p. 428) documented how they used social networks to "source their most critical input—scientific knowledge." They found that "almost none of the individual-level exchanges of knowledge through research collaboration involved organiza-

tions with which either NBF had a market agreement" (p. 439). The lack of market-based contractual arrangements increased their flexibility to create and dissolve networks as well as adapt strategically to evolving research interests.

Bovasso (1992) used four network measures of an organization's structure—density, range, prominence, and elitism—to examine the changes that resulted when three high-technology, knowledge-intensive firms on three continents were merged by the parent corporation to create a single networked organization. In the newly formed networked organization, Bovasso found support for the emergence of a structural convergence, with geographic divisions and hierarchical levels having a smaller impact on members' involvement in the influence of ideas and control of resources. More specifically, geographical and hierarchical differences in prominence, elitism, and density scores between middle and upper management in the three firms were reduced.

Cognitive Social Structures

Several researchers (Corman & Scott, 1994; Krackhardt, 1987) have sought to distinguish people's cognitions of social structures from their actual, observed communication networks. This line of research was precipitated by a series of studies in the early 1980s questioning the ability of informants to accurately report their own communication network patterns (Bernard, Killworth, & Sailer, 1980, 1982; Bernard, Killworth, & Cronenfeld, 1984; Freeman, Romney, & Freeman, 1987). Their results underscored the problematic nature of collecting self-report measures of communication network data if the underlying theory being tested was based on the assumption that individuals' attitudes and behavior were shaped by their actual communication networks. However, as Richards (1985) argued, the differences between self-reported and observed network data are problematic only if the underlying theoretical construct being measured was actual communication behavior (see also Marsden, 1990). In fact, Richards (1985) notes, many social and psychological theories are based on individuals' perceptions—an assertion well captured by W. I. Thomas's observation that "perceptions are real in their consequences even if they do not map one-to-one onto observed behaviors" (Krackhardt, 1987, p. 128; Pattison, 1994). For researchers drawing on such social and psychological theories, a discrepancy between observed and self-reported measures would suggest a measurement error in using data about observed communication.

Krackhardt (1987) developed the concept of cognitive social structures to characterize individuals' perceptions of the social networks. Cognitive social structures assume the status of socially shared, structural "taken-for-granted facts" (Barley, 1990, p. 67) by individuals about the predictable and recurrent interactions among individuals in the network, even if these cognitions are at variance with the actual communication. Krackhardt (1987) aggregated individuals' cognitive social structures to estimate a "consensual" cognitive social structure, in which a link existed between two individuals if others in the network perceived this tie, irrespective of whether it was acknowledged by either of the people in the dyad. As such, a link in the "consensual" cognitive social structure indexed a common adage: It is not who you know, but who others think you know.

Several empirical studies have demonstrated the explanatory power of the cognitive social structure concept. Krackhardt (1987) found that managers in a high-technology entrepreneurial firm who were deemed as highly central (betweenness) in the consensual cognitive social structure were significantly more likely to be able to reconstruct the "actual" advice network reported by the people involved. Krackhardt (1990) also found that the perceived influence of organizational members was significantly associated with their ability to accurately estimate the consensual cognitive social structure in terms of advice relationships. Krackhardt's (1992) research chronicled how a union's inability to accurately assess the organization's social structure led to its failure in organizing employees. Further, Kilduff and Krackhardt (1994) demonstrated that individuals' reputations in the organization were more closely associated with their centrality in the consensual cognitive structure than in the "actual" communication network based on the self-reports of the people involved. Finally, Heald, Contractor, Koehly, and Wasserman (1996) found that individuals of the same gender, in the same department, and in a supervisor-subordinate relationship were more likely to share similar cognitive social structures. Those individuals who were linked in acquaintance and communication networks were also more likely to share similar cognitive social structures.

Extensions to cognitive social structures. The conceptual and empirical work on cognitive social structures has moved the initial debate about differences between actual and perceived communication from the methodological and measurement domain to a substantive exploration of the ways in which actual and perceived communication enable and constrain each other. Corman and Scott (1994) deployed Giddens's (1984) structuration theory to argue that three modalities explain the recursive relationships between observable communication and cognitive social structures: reticulation, activation, and enactment. Reticulation denotes the duality in which perceived communication relationships are produced and reproduced in observable communication behavior. Activation represents the duality of activity foci in the structural domain with joint activity in the interaction domain. Enactment relates coding conventions in the structural domain to triggering events in the interaction domain (Corman, 1997, p. 69). They refer to this perspective as the latent network of perceived communication relationships.

Research on cognitive social structures has taken on additional currency with the advent of virtual organizations, supported by information and communication technologies. In traditional organizations, individuals who are physically co-located have several opportunities to observe face-to-face interactions, and thereby shape their perceptions and social cognitions (Brewer, 1995) of the organization's social structures. The pervasiveness of electronic communication media in virtual organizations makes it increasingly difficult for individuals to discern social structures. Consequently, organizational members have significant problems accurately determining "Who knows who?" and "Who knows who knows who?" Information technologies that are responsible for triggering this problem can also be used to overcome these obstacles. Because information transacted over electronic media such as the Web can be stored in digital form, a new generation of software called "collaborative filters" has emerged (Contractor, 1997; Contractor, O'Keefe, & Jones, 1997; Contractor, Zink, & Chan, 1998; Kautz, Selman, & Shah, 1997; Nishida, Takeda, Iwazume, Maeda, & Takaai, 1998). These filters can be used to make visible the organization's virtual social and knowledge structures. Collaborative filters process individuals' interests, relationships, and the structure and content of their electronically stored information (such as Web pages). They can assist individuals in searching the organization's databases to automatically answer questions about the organization's knowledge network, that is, "Who knows what?" as well as questions about the organization's cognitive knowledge networks, that is, "Who knows who knows what?" within the organization. The use of these kinds of tools is likely to have a leveling effect on the organization's cognitive social structure, because they can potentially undermine the perceived centrality of those individuals in the organization who are viewed as important resources about the organization's social and knowledge networks.

Cognitive Consistency

Like the semantic networks and cognitive social structures discussed above, consistency theories focus on members' cognitions. However, in this case the explanatory mechanism underscores individuals' aspirations for consistency in their cognitions. When applied to organizational communication networks, consistency theories seek to explain the extent to which a drive for consistency is manifest in people's networks and attitudes. That is, members' attitudes are viewed as a function of the balance in their networks rather than alternative mechanisms such as contagion. Heider's (1958) balance theory posited that if two individuals were friends, they should have similar evaluations of an object. This model was extended and mathematically formulated by Harary, Norman, and Cartwright (1965), and later by Davis and Leinhardt (1972), and Holland and Leinhardt (1975), who argued that the object could be a third person in a communication network. If the two individuals did not consistently evaluate the third person, they would experience a state of discomfort and would strive to reduce this cognitive inconsistency by altering their evaluations of either the third person or their own friendship. They extended this line of argument to all possible triads in a network. Researchers have examined the effects of cognitive consistency on both attitudes and behavior.

The effect of cognitive consistency on attitudes. Consistency theories have played an important role in clarifying an earlier debate about the relationship between involvement in communication networks and work attitudes such as job satisfaction and organizational commitment. Early studies (e.g., Brass, 1981; Eisenberg, Monge, & Miller, 1984; Roberts & O'Reilly, 1979) reported contradictory and inconsistent findings about the extent to which individuals who were well connected, integrated, or central in their communication networks were more likely to be satisfied and committed to their organizations. Consistency theories suggest that it is not the centrality or number of links in individuals' networks but the perceived balance within the network that influences level of satisfaction and commitment. Krackhardt and Kilduff (1990) found that individuals' job satisfaction scores were predicted by the extent to which they agreed with their friends on cultural attributions about other members in the network. Kilduff and Krackhardt (1993) found that individuals who were highly central in the friendship network were less satisfied than others who were less central; however, those who saw their friendship networks in balance (they call it "schema consistent") were more likely to be satisfied and committed. In a study of three organizations (described earlier in the Semantic Networks section), Contractor, Eisenberg, and Monge (1996) also found that the extent to which employees shared common interpretations of their organization's mission had no direct bearing on their level of satisfaction or organizational commitment. However, those who perceived greater agreement with others' interpretations were more likely to be satisfied and committed. Barnett and Jang (1994), while not explicitly invoking consistency theories, found that members of a police organization who were central and connected in their communication networks were more likely to perceive their views of salient organizational concepts as being consistent with those of others. Researchers have used network concepts of transitivity to operationalize the effect of balance in the network.

The effect of cognitive consistency on behavior. Consistency theories have also been related to the behavior of organizational members. Krackhardt and Porter (1985) found that friends of those who voluntarily left an organization were no longer exposed to their former coworkers' unhappiness and were therefore able to restore their previous perceived balance; as a result they reported greater levels of satisfaction following the departure of these friends from the organization. Brass et al. (1995) argued that the need for balance among three people can also influence the likelihood of unethical behavior. "The addition of the third party with strong ties to both other actors will act as a major constraint on unethical behavior when the two actors are only weakly connected" (p. 7). Further, they proposed that the likelihood of

unethical behavior is least likely to occur when all three people are connected by strong ties (i.e., a Simmelian triad; Krackhardt, 1992).

Extensions to cognitive consistency theories. The deployment of consistency theories to explain organizational phenomena is relatively recent. Conceptually and analytically, it challenges network researchers to move from the dyad to the triad as the smallest unit of analysis. As the examples above indicate, it has the potential of resolving many of the inconsistent results in network studies that use the dyad as the primary unit of analysis.

Like the other cognitive theories discussed in the previous section, consistency theories have also been used to address the ongoing debate about differences between actual and perceived communication. Freeman (1992) suggested that consistency theories offer a systematic explanation for differences between actual and self-report data on communication. He argued that individuals' needs to perceive balance in observed communication networks help explain some of the errors they make in recalling communication patterns. Using experimental data collected by De Soto (1960), Freeman found that a large proportion of the errors in subjects' recall of networks could be attributed to their propensity to "correct" intransitivity, a network indicator of imbalance, in the observed network.

Theories of Homophily

Several researchers have attempted to explain communication networks on the basis of homophily, that is, the selection of others who are similar. Brass (1995b) notes that "similarity is thought to ease communication, increase predictability of behavior, and foster trust and reciprocity" (p. 51). Homophily has been studied on the basis of similarity in age, gender, education, prestige, social class, tenure, and occupation (Carley, 1991; Coleman, 1957; Ibarra, 1993b, 1995; Laumann, 1966; Marsden, 1988; McPherson & Smith-Lovin, 1987).

Several lines of reasoning support the homophily hypothesis. These fall into two general categories: the similarity-attraction hypothesis (Byrne, 1971) and the theory of self-categorization (Turner, 1987). The similarity-attraction hypothesis is exemplified in the work of Heider (1958), who posited that homophily reduces the psychological discomfort that may arise from cognitive or emotional inconsistency. Similarly, Sherif (1958) suggested that individuals were more likely to select similar others because by doing so they reduce the potential areas of conflict in the relationship. The theory of self-categorization (Turner & Oakes, 1986) suggests that individuals define their social identity through a process of self-categorization during which they classify themselves and others using categories such as age, race, gender. Schachter (1959) argued that similarity provided individuals with a basis for legitimizing their own social identity. The manner in which individuals categorize themselves influences the extent to which they associate with others who are seen as falling into the same category.

A substantial body of organizational demography research is premised on a homophily mechanism. In addition, several studies have focused specifically on gender homophily. Each area is reviewed below.

General Demographic Homophily

The increased workforce diversity in contemporary organizations has seen a rise in the creation of heterogeneous work groups that complicate individuals' desires for homophily. Several studies have examined the extent to which individuals' predilection for homophily structures organizational networks. Zenger and Lawrence (1989) found that technical communication among researchers in a high-technology firm was related to their age and tenure distribution. Studies by O'Reilly and colleagues (Tsui, Egan, & O'Reilly, 1992; Tsui & O'Reilly, 1989; Wagner, Pfeffer, & O'Reilly, 1984) found that differences in age among employees hindered communication and social integration and resulted in lower

commitment and greater turnover among employees.

Basing their arguments on the principle of homophily, Liedka (1991) studied the age and education distribution of members recruited to join voluntary organizations such as youth groups, farm organizations, and sports clubs. Using data collected in the 1985 and 1986 General Social Survey, he found results at the aggregate level, suggesting that members of voluntary organizations were more likely to persuade others similar to their age and education to join the organization. He also found that when people in the same age groups were more densely connected, they were more likely to be represented in voluntary organizations. At the interorganizational level, Galaskiewicz (1979) and Schermerhorn (1977) found that interorganizational links were more likely to occur among individuals who perceived similarity in religion, age, ethnicity, and professional affiliations.

Gender Homophily

Considerable research has examined the effect of gender homophily on organizational networks. Lincoln and Miller (1979) found that similarities in sex and race of organizational employees were significant predictors of their ties in a friendship network. Brass's (1985a) research indicated that communication networks in an organization were largely clustered by gender.

Several studies have examined the effects of gender homophily on friendship. For instance, Leenders (1996) discovered that gender was a more influential predictor of enduring friendship ties than proximity. In a study of 36 female and 45 male senior managers in two New York state government bureaucracies, Moore (1992) found that "half of the advice cliques and nearly that proportion of cliques in the friendship network contain men only" (p. 53). Ibarra's (1992) research of an advertising agency revealed that even though women reported task-related, communication, advice influence ties with men, they were more likely to select other women in their social support and friendship networks. Men, on the other hand, were more likely to have instrumental as well as noninstrumental ties with other men. She pointed out that the constraints of social exchange (see earlier section) and the resulting need to be connected with the organization's predominantly male power base often force women to forgo their propensity for homophily in terms of their instrumental relationships.

Some aspects of culture bear on the preceding results. For example, contrary to other findings, research by Crombie and Birley (1992) showed that the network of contacts among female entrepreneurs in Ireland was not different from that of men in terms of size, diversity, density, and effectiveness. Perhaps the reason for this result is that the people in this study were entrepreneurs. However, the women tended to be younger, owners of smaller businesses that had been established for shorter periods of time, and less involved in traditional exterior activities such as belonging to civic organizations. Women also tended to rely on men and women for advice while men consulted largely with other men. In similar fashion, Ethington, Johnson, Marshall, Meyer, and Chang (1996) studied two organizations with different gender ratios. They found that men and women were equally integrated into and prominent in each other's networks in an organization that had an equal ratio of men and women and an equal gender distribution in the power hierarchy. However, in an organization that had a 75%–25% female-to-male ratio, the networks were more segregated and women were more prominent.

Extensions to Theories of Homophily

Communication scholars have maintained an enduring interest in the principle of homophily as a theoretical mechanism to explain the emergence of networks. In response to the ongoing focus on workforce diversity, they have invoked this mechanism in the study of gender and race issues. The principle of homophily has also been suggested as a network mechanism that is relevant to researchers interested in the social comparison processes used by individuals to make assessments, for instance, about their perceptions of equity in the workplace. According to equity theory (Adams, 1965), individuals' motivations are a direct function of the extent to which their input (i.e., efforts) to output (i.e., rewards) ratios are commensurate with those of "relevant" others. Social comparison theory (Festinger, 1954) suggests that these relevant others are selected on the basis of being similar, or homophilous, in salient respects. Likewise, social identity theory (Turner & Oakes, 1989) proposes that these relevant others are those who are seen as sharing the same "social identity" as the focal person. Krackhardt and Brass (1994) suggest that the selection of relevant others is constrained and enabled by the networks in which individuals are embedded. Individuals could select as relevant others those with whom they have close communication ties (i.e., a cohesion mechanism) or with others who they see as having similar roles (i.e., a structurally equivalent mechanism).

Several scholars have urged that similarity of personality characteristics be used to explain involvement in communication networks (Brass, 1995b; Tosi, 1992). McPhee and Corman (1995) adopted a similar perspective in an article that drew on Feld's (1981) focus theory to argue that interaction is more likely to occur among individuals who share similar foci, including being involved in the same activities. They found limited support for their hypotheses in a study of church members, suggesting the need for further research.

Theories of Physical and Electronic Proximity

A number of researchers have sought to explain communication networks on the basis of physical or electronic propinquity (Corman, 1990; Johnson, 1992; Rice, 1993a). Proximity facilitates the likelihood of communication by increasing the probability that individuals will meet and interact (Festinger, Schachter, & Back, 1950; Korzenny & Bauer, 1981; Monge, Rothman, Eisenberg, Miller, & Kirste, 1985). If these interactions were to occur, they would allow individuals the opportunity to explore the extent to which they have common interests and shared beliefs (Homans, 1950). Early research in organizational settings indicated that the frequency of face-to-face dyadic communication drops precipitously after the first 75-100 feet (Allen, 1970; Conrath, 1973). Zahn's (1991) more recent research also demonstrated that increased physical distance between offices, chain of command, and status led to decreased probability of communication. Likewise, Van den Bulte and Moenaert (1997) found that communication among R&D teams was enhanced after they were co-located. Therefore, individuals who are not proximate are deprived of the opportunity to explore these common interests and are hence less likely to initiate communication links. As such, physical or electronic proximity is a necessary but not sufficient condition for enabling network links. Dramatic evidence of the influence of physical proximity involves the physical dislocation of 817 employees of the Olivetti factory in Naples following the 1983-1984 earthquakes. Bland et al. (1997) report that employees who were permanently relocated rather than evacuated only temporarily reported the highest distress levels due to the disruption in their social networks. Rice (1993b) notes that physical proximity may also facilitate contagion (see section above) by exposing spatially co-located individuals to the same ambient stimuli. Rice and Aydin (1991) found modest evidence of the role played by physical proximity on employees' attitudes toward a new information system. At the interorganizational level, Palmer et al. (1986) found that interlock ties were more likely to be reconstituted if departing members represented organizations whose headquarters were physically proximate to that of focal organizations.

The effects of new communication technologies on the creation and modification of social networks are well documented (Barnett & Salisbury, in press; Rice, 1994a; Wellman et al., 1996). Less intuitive, but just as evident, are the effects of new technologies in preserving old communication structures. In a study of three sectors of the UK publishing industry (the book trade, magazine and newspaper trade, and the newsprint suppliers), Spinardi, Graham, and Williams (1996) found that the introduction of electronic data interchange consolidated and further embedded existing interorganizational relationships, thereby preventing business process reengineering.

Extensions to Theories of Proximity

The proliferation of information technologies in the workplace capable of transcending geographical obstacles has renewed interest in the effects of physical and electronic proximity and their interaction on communication patterns (Kraut, Egido, & Galegher, 1990; Steinfield & Fulk, 1990). Fulk and Boyd (1991) underscored the potential of network analysis "to test the situational moderating effect of geographic distance on media choice" (p. 433). Corman (1996) suggested that cellular automata models are particularly appropriate for studying the effects of physical proximity on communication networks. Cellular automata models can be used to study the collective and dynamic effects of proximity on the overall communication network when individuals in the network apply theoretically derived rules about creating, maintaining, or dissolving links with their "local," that is, proximate, network neighbors.

Uncertainty Reduction and Contingency Theories

Uncertainty about individual and organizational environments has played an important role in explaining organizational processes. Two theories have incorporated communication network concepts to explain how people reduce this uncertainty. Uncertainty reduction theory (URT) and contingency theory are reviewed in this section.

Uncertainty Reduction Theory

URT (Berger, 1987; Berger & Bradac, 1982) suggests that people communicate to reduce uncertainty thereby making their environments more predictable (Weick, 1979). Researchers have examined how communication networks help manage and reduce the organization's uncertainty (Leblebici & Salancik, 1981; Miller & Monge, 1985). However, as Albrecht and Hall (1991) note, "innovation, and especially *talk* about innovation, is inherently an uncertainty-*producing* process" (p. 537). As a result, Albrecht and Ropp (1984) found that communication about innovation is most likely to occur among individuals who have strong multiplex ties (i.e., both work and social ties) that guarantee them a level of relational certainty and thereby greater perceived control in a potentially uncertain situation. Albrecht and Hall (1991) found evidence that the need to reduce uncertainty also explained the creation of dominant elites and coalitions in innovation networks. Burkhardt and Brass (1990) chronicled the changes in the communication network following the introduction of a new technology. They found that the uncertainty resulting from the introduction of the technology motivated employees to seek out new contacts and hence change their communication networks. Kramer (1996) found that the employees who had experienced job transfers were more likely to have positive attitudes about the adjustment if their reconstituted network offered the quality of communication that reduced their uncertainty.

At the interorganizational level, Granovetter (1985) argued that organizational decision makers use social networks to reduce uncertainty associated with market exchanges, thereby reducing their transaction costs (see earlier discussion). Picot (1993) suggested that network organizations were superior to markets and hierarchies when task uncertainty was high and task specificity was low. In a study of relationships between firms and their investment banks, Baker (1987) reported that the firms' financial officers often drew on their informal networks to reduce uncertainty surrounding the creation of a market tie. The reduction of uncertainty due to strong ties was also useful to explain the reduction of interorganizational conflict. Using data from intergroup networks in 20 organizations, Nelson (1989) found that organizations with strong ties between their groups were less likely to report high levels of conflict than those organizations that had groups that were connected by weak ties.

Contingency Theory

In the early 1960s, organizational scholars began to focus their attention on the environment and ways to reduce the uncertainty it created. Emery and Trist (1960) developed sociotechnical systems theory in which they argued that the nature of an organization's environment significantly influences its structure and operations (Emery & Trist, 1965). A contingency theory approach to formal organizational structures is based on the premise that an organization should structure itself in a manner that maximizes its ability to reduce the uncertainty in its environment. For example, Burns and Stalker (1961) contrasted "organic" with bureaucratic organizations, which they labeled "mechanistic." The defining feature of organic organizations was that their structures were internally adaptable to changing features of the environment while mechanistic organizations were not. Lawrence and Lorsch's (1967) contingency theory formalized this view and argued that all internal relations and structures were contingent on external conditions. Galbraith (1977) argued that organizations needed to develop slack resources and flexible, internal lateral communication networks to cope with environmental uncertainty. Thus, the theoretical mechanism in contingency theory that accounted for the formation, maintenance, and eventual dissolution of communication networks was the level of uncertainty in the organization's environment. Stable environments led organizations to create long-standing, entrenched networks, while turbulent environments led organizations to create flexible, changing networks.

In an empirical study of Burns and Stalker's distinction between mechanistic and organic organizations, Tichy and Fombrun (1979) found that the differences between the formal and informal communication networks were more pronounced in mechanistic organizations than they were in organic organizations. Barney's (1985) inductive blockmodeling, clustering, and scaling techniques identified the dimensions of informal communication structure in interaction data collected by Coleman (1961) from the entire student population of ten Midwestern high schools. One dimension identified was "analogous to Burns and Stalker's (1961) organic-mechanistic dimension of formal structure" (Barney, 1985, p. 35), which proved to be consistent with contingency theory's proposed relationship between environmental diversity and formal organizational structure (Miles, 1980).

Shrader, Lincoln, and Hoffman (1989) tested Burns and Stalker's argument that organic forms of organizational structure would result in informal organizational communication networks that were denser, more highly connected, and more multiplex than those found in mechanistic organizations. They found that organic "smaller organizations made up of educated staff applying nonroutine technologies have denser, more cohesive, and less-segmented networks consisting largely of symmetric or reciprocated ties" (p. 63). By contrast, vertically and horizontally differentiated, as well as formalized, mechanistic organizations were less densely connected, more segmented, and less likely to have symmetric and reciprocated communication ties.

Contingency theory's proposed relationship between technology and the organization's structure was examined in a study by Brass (1985b). Using network techniques to measure pooled, sequential, and reciprocal interdependencies in an organization's workflow, Brass (1985b) found that the relationship between interpersonal communication and performance was contingent on the extent of horizontal differentiation in the organization's structure and the coordination requirements of the task.

Extensions to Uncertainty Reduction and Contingency Theories

The review above suggests that the deployment of uncertainty reduction theory was more prevalent in the 1980s and has been on the decline lately. This decline corresponds, not coincidentally, with the increasing critique of the scope and operationalization of the "uncertainty" concept (Huber & Daft, 1987). Future network research from an uncertainty reduction perspective should respond to calls for a conceptual delineation between uncertainty reduction and equivocality reduction (Weick, 1979). The relative efficacy of networks to help reduce uncertainty and equivocality is a potentially useful but as yet untapped area of inquiry. Further, past network research based on uncertainty reduction theory has not distinguished between uncertainty reduction and uncertainty avoidance (March & Weissinger-Baylon, 1986). The use of communication networks to reduce uncertainty implies the presence or creation of links, while the avoidance of uncertainty may imply the absence or dissolution of links.

Although the research literature testing the validity of the contingency mechanism is sparse, it tends to support the importance of internal adaptability to external constraints. In fact, most theorists today accept the contingency thesis without significant empirical support because the enormous increase in the rates of environmental change in the contemporary world makes it seem intuitively obvious. No subsequent theory has argued against the contingency mechanism, and Galbraith's

(1977) extensive analysis of the development of slack resources and deployment of lateral communication linkages remains the clearest statement of how to develop communication networks to cope with rapidly changing environmental uncertainty.

Social Support Theories

Interest in social support networks can be traced back to Durkheim's (1897/1977) groundbreaking work on the impact of solidarity and social integration on mental health. A social support explanation focuses on the ways in which communication networks help organizational members to cope with stress. Wellman (1992) and others have adopted this framework in their study of social support networks. Their research is largely based on the premise that social networks play a "buffering" role in the effects of stress on mental well-being (Berkman & Syme, 1979; Hall & Wellman, 1985).

Two general mechanisms exist by which social networks buffer the effects of stress. First, an individual in a dense social support network is offered increased social support in the form of resources and sociability. Lin and Ensel's (1989) research produced evidence that strong ties in the support network provided social resources that helped buffer both social and psychological stress. Second, Kadushin (1983) argued that social support can also be provided by less dense social circles. Social circles (Simmel, 1955) are networks in which membership is based on common characteristics or interests. Membership in a social circle can help provide social support "by (1) conveying immunity through leading the members to a better understanding of their problems, (2) being a resource for help, or (3) mobilizing resources" (Kadushin, 1983, p. 191).

A substantial amount of research exists on the role of networks in providing social support in varying organizational contexts, such as families, communities, and neighborhoods (for reviews, see O'Reilly, 1988; Walker, Wasserman, & Wellman, 1994). In a classic longitudinal study of residents in a northern California county, Berkman and Syme (1979) found that respondents "who lacked social and community ties were more likely to die in the follow-up period than those with more extensive contacts" (p. 186). Berkman (1985) found that individuals with fewer social support contacts via marriage, friends, relatives, church memberships, and associations had a higher mortality rate.

Researchers (Barrera & Ainlay, 1983; Cutrona & Russell, 1990; Wellman & Wortley, 1989, 1990) have identified four dimensions of social support, including emotional aid, material aid (goods, money, and services), information, and companionship. Considerable empirical evidence demonstrates that individuals cannot rely on a single network link, except to their parents or children, to provide all four dimensions of social support. Studies by Wellman and Wortley (1989, 1990) of a community in southern Ontario, Canada, found that individuals' specific network ties provided either emotional aid or material aid, but not both. Additionally, studies have found that women are more likely to offer emotional aid than men (Campbell & Lee, 1990).

Remarkably few studies have examined networks of social support in organizational contexts even though several scholars have underscored the need for research in this area (Bass & Stein, 1997). For example, Langford, Bowsher, Maloney, and Lillis (1997) propose the examination of networks to study social support in nursing environments such as hospitals and nursing homes. A comparison of six hospital units by Albrecht and Ropp (1982) found that the volume and tone of interaction in the medical surgical unit's communication network improved their ability to cope with chronic pressures and stress. In one of the few studies of social support networks in organizations, Cummings (1997) found that individuals who reported receiving greater social support from their network were more likely to generate radical (i.e., "frame-breaking") innovation.

Hurlbert (1991) used ego-centric network data for a sample of respondents from the 1985 General Social Survey (the first national sample containing network data) to examine the effect of kin and coworker networks on stress, as measured by individuals' job satisfaction. She argued that individuals' networks may (a) provide resources to decrease the level of stress created by job conditions, or (b) provide support thereby helping the individual cope with job stress. She found that membership in a coworker social circle was positively associated with job satisfaction, even after controlling for other social and demographic variables. The effect on job satisfaction was even higher if the coworkers were highly educated, suggesting that they were able to offer additional instrumental resources. However, Hurlbert (1991) also found that for individuals who were in blue-collar jobs or those with low security, "kin-centered networks may exacerbate, rather than ameliorate, negative job conditions" (p. 426). Consistent with this latter finding, Ray (1991) and Ray and Miller (1990) found that individuals who were highly involved in networks offering social support to friends and coworkers were more likely to report high levels of emotional exhaustion. The negative effects of the network on individuals were also reported in a longitudinal study of relatively well-functioning older men and women. Seeman, Bruce, and McAvay (1996) found that men who had larger instrumental support networks were more likely to report the onset of activities of daily living disability. They speculated that these results may reflect "the consequences of greater reliance on others, a behavior pattern which may, over time, erode the recipient's confidence in their [*sic*] ability to do things independently" (pp. S197-S198).

At the interorganizational level, Eisenberg and Swanson (1996) noted that Connecticut's Healthy Start program served an important social support role for pregnant women by serving as referral to hospitals and agencies. Zinger, Blanco, Zanibbi, and Mount (1996) reported that Canadian small businesses relied more heavily on an informal support network than government programs. Paterniti, Chellini, Sacchetti, and Tognelli (1996) described how an Italian rehabilitation center for schizophrenic patients successfully created network links with other organizations to reflect "the social network that surrounds the patient and from which he [*sic*] has come" (p. 86).

Extensions to Social Support Theories

The amount of research on social support networks has increased substantially in the past few years. Some of these changes are perhaps motivated by changes in the organizational landscape, such as the increase in outsourcing, telecommuting, job retraining for displaced workers (Davies, 1996), and small business start-ups (Zinger et al., 1996). All of these activities often serve to isolate the individual worker from the institutional support structures of traditional organizations. Hence, there is greater salience today for improving our understanding of the role of social support mechanisms in the emergence of networks.

Early research on the role of networks in providing social support focused on structural characteristics of the networks, such as tie strength, frequency, reciprocity of the links, the size, and the density of the networks. Walker et al. (1994) noted that recent network research has abandoned the notion of social support as a unitary construct as well as the assumption that the presence of a tie can be equated with the provision of social support. Instead, they model social support as "a complex flow of resources among a wide range of actors rather than as just a transaction between two individuals" (p. 54). Indeed, in a study of low-income, immigrant women Vega, Kolody, Valle, and Weir (1991) found that the women's overall frequency of interaction with friends and family was not correlated with levels of depression. However, the quality of social support, measured as the frequency of specific social support messages, was the best predictor of low depression scores among the women.

Theories of Network Evolution: Emergent Versus Emergence

In a special issue of the *Journal of Mathematical Sociology,* "The Evolution of Networks," Stokman and Doreian (1996) examined the distinction between the terms *network dynamics* and *network evolution.* They argued that the study of network dynamics provides a quantitative or qualitative temporal characterization of change, stability, simultaneity, sequentiality, synchronicity, cyclicality, or randomness in the phenomena being observed (Monge & Kalman, 1996). The focus is on providing sophisticated descriptions of the manifest change in networks. In contrast, Stokman and Doreian define the study of network evolution to contain an important additional goal: an explicit, theoretically derived understanding of the mechanisms that determine the temporal changes in the phenomena being observed. While most of the longitudinal network studies reviewed in this chapter contain theoretical mechanisms to explain changes over time, many of them could be more explicit about this connection and move more in the direction of fully developed theories of network evolution.

In an early example, Fombrun (1986) theorized about evolution in terms of infrastructures, sociostructures, and superstructures that interacted dynamically with each other across organizational, population, and community levels. He identified two dynamically opposing forces that led both to conflict and to eventual resolution: processes of convergence and processes of contradiction. In a more recent example, Salancik (1995) critiqued the intellectual contributions of Burt's (1992) structural theory of holes. He noted that it was important to acknowledge Burt's finding that a person occupying a structural hole will gain political advantage, but he also asserted that "a more telling analysis might explain why the hole exists or why it was not filled before" (Salancik, 1995, p. 349). Salancik challenged network researchers to invest efforts in creating a more specific network theory. Such a theory does not take a network as given. Instead, it seeks to uncover the mechanisms that create network evolution.

Two of the more comprehensive reviews of network studies have called for greater attention to the evolution of networks (Brass, 1995b; Monge & Eisenberg, 1987). While both were organized around antecedents and outcomes of networks, they acknowledged that such distinctions are often nonexistent and potentially misleading. Monge and Eisenberg (1987, p. 310) offered a hypothetical scenario to illustrate the ongoing evolution of a network, a concept they term *reorganizing.* Brass (1995b) underscored the importance of articulating the dynamic nature of the relationships between networks, their antecedents, and outcomes.

Four lines of research emphasize the importance of this perspective. The first articulated a recursive model of communication networks and media (Contractor & Eisenberg, 1990). Drawing on structuration theory (Giddens, 1984) and the theory of structural action (Burt, 1982), they proposed that while networks influence individuals' adoptions, perceptions, and use of new media, this use has the potential for altering the very networks that precipitated their use in the first place. In some instances, this altered network has the potential of subverting individuals' continued use of the media. Hence, the co-evolution of communication networks and the activities they shape are inextricably linked and must be examined as a duality.

Similarly, Barley (1990) and Haines (1988) have argued for the use of network analytic techniques to articulate and extend structuration theory. Barley (1990) used network analytic tools to describe the situated ways in which relatively small role differences in initial conditions reverberated through seemingly similar social systems, resulting over time in widely different social structures. Barley (1990) rejected contingency theories because they offer static predictions of a match between technologies and social structures. Instead, he argued for using networks as a way of making explicit the theory of negotiated order (Fine & Kleinman, 1983).

According to this theory, structures are by-products of a history of interactions and are subsequently perceived as fact by organizational members. However, he notes that theories such as structuration or negotiated order provide few analytic tools for explicating the links between the introduction of a technology, the interaction order, and the organization's structure. He offers network analytic tools as one way of explicating these links. Barley (1990) chronicled how the material attributes of a CT scanner recently adopted in two radiology departments affected the nonrelational elements of employees' work roles, including their skills and tasks; this, in turn, affected their immediate communication relationships and precipitated more widespread changes in the department's social network. Significantly, his analysis explains why the technology was appropriated differently in the two radiology departments. Barley's empirical work exemplifies several symbolic interactionists who argue for the importance of understanding the emergence of social order as a process of social construction (Berger & Luckmann, 1966; Giddens, 1976, 1984).

From Barley's (1990) standpoint, network techniques offer an opportunity to illustrate the ideographic and idiosyncratic nature of organizational phenomena. The ideographic assumption reflects an ontological viewpoint that rejects the nomothetic goal of seeking generalizable regularities in explaining organizational phenomena. Instead, the goal of the researcher with an ideographic viewpoint is to understand the processes that unfold in the particular organization being studied. Zack and McKenney (1995) offer a more recent example of work in this tradition. They examined the appropriation of the same group-authoring and -messaging computer system by the managing editorial groups of two morning newspapers owned by the same parent corporation. Drawing on Poole and DeSanctis' (1990) theory of adaptive structuration, they discovered that the two groups' appropriation of the technology, as indexed by their communication networks, differed in accordance with the different contexts at the two

locations. Further, they found evidence that the groups' performance outcomes for similar tasks were mediated by these interaction patterns.

A second line of research embraces the central precept of focusing attention on evolution of networks, but seeks nomothetic, that is, lawful and generalizable, underlying theoretical mechanisms to explain the appearance of seemingly ideographic, nongeneralizable, surface phenomena (Stokman & Doreian, 1996). These authors argue for the development of computational models that incorporate network mechanisms that both influence and are influenced by people in the social network. This line of research extends recent work in object-oriented modeling, cellular automata (CA), and neural networks to capture the ongoing, recursive, and nonlinear mechanisms by which organizational networks evolve over time (Abrahamson & Rosenkopf, 1997; Banks & Carley, 1996; Corman, 1996; McKelvey, 1997; Stokman & Zeggelink, 1996; Woelfel, 1993). Banks and Carley (1996) compared three mathematical models of network evolution based on social comparison theory (Heider, 1958), exchange theory (Blau, 1964), and constructuralism (Carley, 1990, 1991). They noted that the pattern of network evolution associated with the three models were not always distinct, thereby making it difficult to empirically validate one model over the other. They offer statistical tests that, at the very least, allow for the falsification of a particular model.

Corman (1996) suggested that multidimensional CA models offer insights into the unanticipated consequences of collective communication behavior. His computer simulations of a simplified CA model based, in part, on Giddens's structuration theory, suggested that integrationist strategies by individuals were, unintentionally and perversely, most responsible for segregation in communication structures.

Zeggelink, Stokman, and Van de Bunt (1996) modeled the likelihood of various configurations of friendship networks that may emerge among an initial set of mutual strangers. Their stochastic model deployed network mechanisms of selection and contagion to explain the creation, maintenance, and dissolution of friendship ties among the individuals. The complex specifications of such models make it impossible to mentally construe the long-term dynamics implied by the models. Further, given the nonlinearities implied by the mechanisms, these models are often analytically intractable. Hence, researchers use computer simulations to help assess the long-term evolutionary implications of the proposed network mechanisms. For instance, Stokman and Zeggelink (1996) developed simulations and then empirically tested the network configuration of policy makers charged with determining the fate of a large farming cooperative in the Netherlands. This research (see also Robinson, 1996) is based on the assumption that ideographic differences in the dynamics of friendship networks can be adequately explained and stochastically predicted by nomothetic underlying network mechanisms.

The use of computer simulations to study the evolution of networks requires considerable programming knowledge by researchers. To make these efforts more accessible to a larger community of researchers, Hyatt, Contractor, and Jones (1997) have developed an object-oriented simulation environment, called Blanche (available online at http://www.tec.spcomm.uiuc.edu/blanche.html). Blanche provides an easy user-interface to support the specification of mathematical models, execution simulations, and the dynamic analysis of the network evolution.

A third line of research examines the evolution of organizational networks as a function of the stage in an organization's life cycle. Monge and Eisenberg (1987) suggested that at early stages organizations are likely to have structures that are less stable and formal. Building on this suggestion, Brass (1995b) noted that structuration theory would suggest that these patterns would become more stable and formalized as organizations mature.

A fourth line of research focuses on the emergence of network organizations, such as strategic alliances, partnerships, and research consortia, in lieu of discrete market transactions or internal hierarchical arrangements. Ring and Van de Ven (1992, 1994) focused attention on the developmental processes of interorganizational relations: emergence, evolution, and dissolution. They proposed, as a framework for this process, "repetitive sequences of negotiation, commitment, and executions stages, each of which is assessed in terms of efficiency and equity" (p. 97). Drawing on much of the same literature, Larson and Starr (1993) proposed a model to explain the emergence of entrepreneurial organizations. Finally, Topper and Carley (1997) described the evolution of a multiorganization network organization in a hyperturbulent environment: the integrated crisis management unit network that responded to the Exxon *Valdez* disaster.

The four streams of research reviewed in this section share an intellectual commitment to a better understanding of the situational evolution of organizational networks. Future research that combines this commitment to situated evolution with the theoretical mechanisms reviewed in this chapter has the potential to significantly extend our knowledge of organizational communication networks and the explanatory power of our models and theories.

CONCLUSION

This chapter has focused on emergence of communication networks—their creation, maintenance, and dissolution—within and among organizations. Ten major families of theories were reviewed to explore the theoretical mechanisms that have been used by network scholars to examine these evolutionary processes in organizational communication networks. Six conclusions seem warranted from this review.

First, the literature reviewed in this chapter focuses much more on the creation of networks than their maintenance or dissolution. This imbalance reflects a serious shortcoming in current theoretical perspectives and empirical research. Theories that describe conditions under which the likelihood of creating network links is lower rather than higher must be examined more carefully to see if these conditions also predict the dissolution of network links. The Seabright et al. (1992) research, reviewed earlier, offers a notable example of such an attempt. Their study found evidence that reductions in the resource fit between organizations would lead to pressures to dissolve interorganizational network links.

Second, considerable additional work is required to reduce or eliminate the extensive redundancy that exists among the different theoretical perspectives. For example, as discussed earlier, the theoretical mechanisms in exchange theory and social support theory share a great deal in common with each other. Likewise, homophily, which is defined as similarity of individual characteristics, can be viewed as conceptually overlapping with proximity, which can be viewed as similarity of location. Other examples abound in this review. Some of this redundancy stems from conceptual vagueness, as was mentioned earlier with the notion of uncertainty. Other aspects of redundancy are attributable to the fact that the theories were developed in different contexts, as is the case for network organizational forms, which clearly use exchange mechanisms though they emerged out of interests in economic markets and transaction costs. Still another source of overlap is that different theories were developed in different disciplinary traditions, including communication, economics, political science, social work, and sociology, to name but a sample.

The third conclusion is that the time may have come to explore a more eclectic, multitheoretical approach to network theory in which several theories are used simultaneously to predict communication network behavior and outcomes. While elimination of conceptual and theoretical redundancy will be beneficial, it seems unlikely to produce a general, integrated theory (and there are those who argue in principle that such a feat is impossible). None of the theories reviewed in this chapter, by themselves, seem sufficiently powerful to explain large portions of the variance in network emergence. Nor do they individually seem capable of predicting the emergence, maintenance, and dissolution of communication networks with anything near a reasonable level of precision. Consequently, an integrative, multitheoretical alternative appears worth exploring. A multitheoretical approach would use different theories to account for different aspects of network phenomena or to account for the same aspects at different points in the evolutionary process. There is some precedence for this strategy in the public goods literature, which examines one set of mechanisms for the creation of public goods but an alternative set for their maintenance (Monge et al., 1998).

A fourth conclusion is that it is important to focus attention on uniquely network forms of communication network theory. This review has highlighted the fact that most theoretical explanations for communication networks, though not all, stem from nonnetwork theories applied to network phenomena. More theoretical effort is required like the work that helped to develop network exchange theories, structural holes theory, and network evolution theories. Wasserman and Pattison (1996) have recently made important contributions in this direction with the development of "p*" models, which explore how the various endogenous characteristics of a matrix of network relations, together with other exogenous explanatory variables, shape the outcomes of the network.

Fifth, much work needs to be done to develop network theories that bridge the expansive analytic levels covered by network analysis. In one sense, the fact that networks span such diverse phenomena and operate on so many levels underscores their importance in everyday life. On the other hand, these expansive and multilevel qualities make theoretical integration a very challenging task. Theories that range from internal cognitive social structures to global network organizations make formidable intellectual leaps that need careful examination and theoretical development.

Finding commonalities as well as disjunctures across levels will be an important part of building a more integrated theory of communication networks.

Finally, as the literature reviewed here demonstrates, the study of emergence in communication networks continues to be overwhelmingly influenced by structural perspectives. Of the three network traditions employed throughout this chapter, the positional and relational traditions continue to dominate, while the cultural tradition has struggled to bridge the gap between structure and the content of communication networks. The theoretical mechanisms used in network research invest greater currency in the structural relationships among people than on the types of network linkages (e.g., material vs. symbolic, product vs. knowledge; see the earlier discussion in this chapter) or the content of the messages within these networks. Wellman (1988) notes that the genesis for this bias goes back to Georg Simmel's influence on the pioneers of network research (e.g., Simmel, 1955). In fact, Wellman (1988) characterizes the early work of an influential minority of formalists (e.g., Fararo, 1973; Holland & Leinhardt, 1979; Lorrain & White, 1971) by asserting that in "concentrating on the form of network patterns rather than their content . . . they have shared a Simmelian sensibility that similar patterns of ties may have similar behavioral consequences no matter what the substantive context" (p. 25). Even the network studies based on the cultural tradition (e.g., semantic networks) are largely focused on structural explanations for the emergence of these networks, despite the fact that they are based on network linkages representing common interpretations. They seek to explain variation in the structure of the semantic networks rather than variation in the content (e.g., types of linkages or messages) within these networks. Missing from the network literature is any systematic theoretical or empirical work aimed at examining the relationship between the structure of networks and the content of messages, symbols, and interpreta-

tions that produce and reproduce them. Consequently, we know very little about the manner in which different network configurations (e.g., centralized networks, dense networks) are likely to facilitate the creation of certain types of messages (e.g., supportive, critical). Conversely, little is known about how the production and reproduction of certain types of messages or symbols are likely to influence the structural emergence of communication networks.

The field of organizational network analysis has grown exponentially since the original chapter on emergent communication networks was published in the *Handbook of Organizational Communication* more than a decade ago (Monge & Eisenberg, 1987). The diversity of scholars from various intellectual backgrounds who are currently developing theories of communication and other networks in organizations is truly impressive, as is the high quality of their work. Even more important, as this review has demonstrated, is the development and application of theories and theoretical mechanisms in what once was a very atheoretical field. There is, of course, a great deal remaining to be done. But continued work in these theoretical areas, with special attention to network evolution, promises to make the years ahead a very exciting time for organizational communication network scholars.

REFERENCES

Abrahamson, E., & Rosenkopf, L. (1997). Social network effects on the extent of innovation diffusion: A computer simulation. *Organization Science, 8,* 289-309.

Adams, J. S. (1965). Inequity in social exchange. In L. Berkowitz (Ed.), *Advances in experimental social psychology* (pp. 267-300). New York: Academic Press.

Albrecht, T., & Ropp, V. A. (1982). The study of network structuring in organizations through the use of method triangulation. *Western Journal of Speech Communication, 46,* 162-178.

Albrecht, T. L., & Hall, B. (1991). Relational and content differences between elites and outsiders in innovation networks. *Human Communication Research, 17,* 535-561.

Albrecht, T. L., & Ropp, V. A. (1984). Communicating about innovation in networks of three U.S. organizations. *Journal of Communication, 34,* 78-91.

Aldrich, H. (1976). Resource dependence and interorganizational relations: Relations between local employment service offices and social service sector organizations. *Administration & Society, 7,* 419-454.

Aldrich, H. (1982). The origins and persistence of social networks. In P. V. Marsden & N. Lin (Eds.), *Social structure and network analysis* (pp. 281-293): Beverly Hills, CA: Sage Press.

Allen, T. (1970). Communication networks in R&D laboratories. *R&D Management, 1,* 14-21.

Alter, C. (1990). An exploratory study of conflict and coordination in interorganizational service delivery systems. *Academy of Management Journal, 33,* 478-502.

Bacharach, S. B., & Lawler, E. J. (1980). *Power and politics in organizations.* San Francisco: Jossey-Bass.

Badaracco, J. L., Jr. (1991). *The knowledge link: How firms compete through strategic alliances.* Boston: Harvard Business School Press.

Baker, W. E. (1987). *Do corporations do business with the bankers on their boards? The consequences of investment bankers as directors.* Paper presented at the Nags Head Conference on Corporate Interlocks, Kill Devil Hills, NC.

Bandura, A. (1986). *Social foundations of thought and action.* Englewood Cliffs, NJ: Prentice Hall.

Banks, D. L., & Carley, K. M. (1996). Models for network evolution. *Journal of Mathematical Sociology, 21,* 173-196.

Barley, S. R. (1990). The alignment of technology and structure through roles and networks. *Administrative Science Quarterly, 35,* 61-103.

Barnard, C. I. (1938). *The functions of the executive.* Cambridge, MA: Harvard University Press.

Barnett, G. A., & Jang, H. (1994). *The relationship between network position and attitudes toward the job and organization in a police organization.* Paper presented at the annual meeting of the International Communication Association, Sydney, Australia.

Barnett, G. A., & Salisbury, J. G. T. (in press). Communication and globalization: A longitudinal analysis of the international telecommunication network. *Journal of World-Systems Research.*

Barney, J. B. (1985). Dimensions of informal social network structure: Toward a contingency theory of informal relations. *Social Networks, 7,* 1-46.

Barrera, M., Jr., & Ainlay, S. L., (1983). The structure of social support: A conceptual and empirical analysis. *Journal of Community Psychology, 11,* 133-143.

Bass, L. A., & Stein, C. H. (1997). Comparing the structure and stability of network ties using the social support questionnaire and the social network list. *Journal of Social and Personal Relationships, 14,* 123-132.

Bateson, G. (1972). Double bind, 1969. In G. Bateson (Ed.), *Steps to an ecology of mind* (pp. 271-278). New York: Ballantine.

Baum, J., & Oliver, C. (1991). Institutional linkages and organizational mortality. *Administrative Science Quarterly, 36,* 187-218.

Baum, J., & Oliver, C. (1992). Institutional embeddedness and the dynamics of organizational populations. *American Sociological Review, 57,* 540-559.

Bavelas, A. (1948). A mathematical model for group structure. *Applied Anthropology, 7,* 16-30.

Benassi, M., & Gargiulo, M. (1993, June). *Informal hierarchy and managerial flexibility in network organization.* Paper presented at the Third European Conference on Social Network Analysis, Munich, Germany.

Benson, J. K. (1975). The interorganizational network as a political economy. *Administrative Science Quarterly, 20,* 229-249.

Berger, C. R. (1987). Communicating under uncertainty. In M. E. Roloff & G. R. Miller (Eds.), *Interpersonal processes: New directions in communication research* (pp. 39-62). Newbury Park, CA: Sage.

Berger, C. R., & Bradac, J. J. (1982). *Language and social knowledge: Uncertainty in interpersonal relations.* London: Edward Arnold.

Berger, J., Cohen, B., & Zelditch, M., Jr. (1966). Status characteristics and expectation states. In J. Berger, M. Zelditch, Jr., & B. Anderson (Eds.), *Sociological theories in progress* (Vol. 1, pp. 29-46). Boston: Houghton Mifflin.

Berger, P., & Luckmann, T. (1966). *The social construction of reality.* Garden City, NY: Doubleday.

Berkman, L. (1985). The relationship of social networks and social support to morbidity and mortality. In S. Cohen & S. L. Syme (Eds.), *Social support and health* (pp. 241-262). Orlando, FL: Academic Press.

Berkman, L., & Syme, S. L. (1979). Social networks, host resistance, and mortality. *American Journal of Epidemiology, 109,* 186-204.

Bernard, H., Killworth, P., & Sailer, L. (1980). Informant accuracy in social network data IV: A comparison of clique-level structure in behavioral and cognitive network data. *Social Networks, 2,* 191-218.

Bernard, H., Killworth, P., & Sailer, L. (1982). Informant accuracy in social network data V. An experimental attempt to predict actual communication from recall data. *Social Science Research, 11,* 30-66.

Bernard, H. R., Killworth, P., & Cronenfeld, D. (1984). The problem of informant accuracy: The validity of retrospective data. *Annual Review of Anthropology, 13,* 495-517.

Bienenstock, E. J., & Bonacich, P. (1992). The core as solution to exclusionary networks. *Social Networks, 14,* 231-244.

Bienenstock, E. J., & Bonacich, P. (1997). Network exchange as a cooperative game. *Rationality and Society, 9*, 37-65.

Bizot, E., Smith, N., & Hill, T. (1991). Use of electronic mail in a research and development organization. In J. Morell & M. Fleischer (Eds.), *Advances in the implementation and impact of computer systems* (Vol. 1, pp. 65-92). Greenwich, CT: JAI.

Bland, S. H., O'Leary, E. S., Farinaro, E., Jossa, F., Krogh, V., Violanti, J. M., & Trevisan, M. (1997). Social network disturbances and psychological distress following earthquake evacuation. *Journal of Nervous and Mental Disease, 185*, 188-194.

Blau, P. M. (1964). *Exchange and power in social life.* New York: John Wiley.

Bovasso, G. (1992). A structural analysis of the formation of a network organization. *Group & Organization Management, 17*, 86-106.

Bovasso, G. (1995). A network analysis of social contagion processes in an organizational intervention. *Human Relations, 49*, 1419-1435.

Boyd, B. (1990). Corporate linkages and organizational environment: A test of the resource dependence model. *Strategic Management Journal, 11*, 419-430.

Brass. D. J. (1981). Structural relationships, job characteristics, and worker satisfaction and performance. *Administrative Science Quarterly, 26*, 331-348.

Brass, D. J. (1984). Being in the right place: A structural analysis of individual influence in an organization. *Administrative Science Quarterly, 29*, 518-539.

Brass, D. J. (1985a). Men's and women's networks: A study of interaction patterns and influence in organizations. *Academy of Management Journal, 28*, 327-343.

Brass, D. J. (1985b). Technology and the structuring of jobs: Employee satisfaction, performance, and influence. *Organizational Behavior and Human Decision Processes, 35*, 216-240.

Brass, D. J. (1995a). Creativity: It's all in your social network. In C. M. Ford & D. A. Gioia (Eds.), *Creative action in organizations* (pp. 94-99). London: Sage.

Brass, D. J. (1995b). A social network perspective on human resources management. *Research in Personnel and Human Resources Management, 13*, 39-79.

Brass, D. J., & Burkhardt, M. E. (1992). Centrality and power in organizations. In N. Nohria & R. G. Eccles (Eds.), *Networks and organizations: Structure, form, and action* (pp. 191-215). Boston: Harvard Business School Press.

Brass, D. J., Butterfield, K. D., & Skaggs, B. C. (1995, June). *The social network structure of unethical behavior.* Paper presented at the International Association of Business and Society, Vienna, Austria.

Brass, D. J., & Krackhardt, D. (in press). Communication networks and organizations: A meso approach. In H. L. Tosi (Ed.), *Extensions of the environment/or-ganization/person model* (Vol. 2). Greenwich, CT: JAI.

Brewer, D. D. (1995). The social structural basis of the organization of persons in memory. *Human Nature, 6*, 379-403.

Buckley, W. (1967). *Sociology and modern systems theory.* Englewood Cliffs, NJ: Prentice Hall.

Burke, P. J. (1997). An identity model for network exchange. *American Sociological Review, 62*, 134-150.

Burkhardt, M. R. (1994). Social interaction effects following a technological change: A longitudinal investigation. *Academy of Management Journal, 37*, 869-896.

Burkhardt, M. E., & Brass, D. J. (1990). Changing patterns of patterns of change: The effects of a change in technology on social network structure and power. *Administrative Science Quarterly, 35*, 104-127.

Burns, T., & Stalker, G. M. (1961). *The management of innovation.* London: Tavistock.

Burns, L., & Wholey, D. R. (1993). Adoption and abandonment of matrix management programs: Effects of organizational characteristics and interorganizational networks. *Academy of Management Review, 36*, 106-138.

Burt, R. S. (1980). Models of network structure. *Annual Review of Sociology, 6*, 79-141.

Burt, R. S. (1982). *Toward a structural theory of action: Network models of stratification, perception and action.* New York: Academic Press.

Burt, R. S. (1987). Social contagion and innovation: Cohesion versus structural equivalence. *American Journal of Sociology, 92*, 1287-1335.

Burt, R. S. (1991). Contagion. In R. S. Burt, *Structure: A computer program.* New York.

Burt, R. S. (1992). *Structural holes: The social structure of competition.* Cambridge, MA: Harvard University Press.

Burt, R. S. (1997). The contingent value of social capital. *Administrative Science Quarterly, 42*, 339-365.

Burt, R. S., & Knez, M. (1996). Trust and third-party gossip. In R. M. Kramer & T. R. Tyler (Eds.), *Trust in organizations: Frontiers of theory and research* (pp. 68-89). Thousand Oaks, CA: Sage.

Byrne, D. E. (1971). *The attraction paradigm.* New York: Academic Press.

Campbell, K. E., & Lee, B. A. (1990). Gender differences in urban neighboring. *Sociological Quarterly, 31*, 495-512.

Carley, K. (1986). An approach for relating social structure to cognitive structure. *Journal of Mathematical Sociology, 12*, 137-189.

Carley, K. (1990). Group stability: A socio-cognitive approach. In L. E. B. Markovsky, C. Ridgeway, & H. Walker (Eds.), *Advances in group processes: Theory and research* (Vol. 7, pp. 1-44). Greenwich, CT: JAI.

Carley, K. (1991). A theory of group stability. *American Sociological Review, 56*, 331-354.

Carley, K. M., & Kaufer, D. S. (1993). Semantic connectivity: An approach for analyzing symbols in semantic networks. *Communication Theory, 3,* 183-213.

Carley, K. M., & Krackhardt, D. (1996). Cognitive inconsistencies and non-symmetric friendship. *Social Networks, 18,* 1-27.

Carroll, G. R., & Teo, A. C. (1996). On the social networks of managers. *Academy of Management Journal, 39,* 421-440.

Chandler, A. D. (1977). *The visible hand: The managerial revolution in American business.* Cambridge, MA: Harvard University Press.

Coase, R. H. (1937). The nature of the firm. *Economica, 4,* 386-405.

Cochran, P. L., Wood, R. A., & Jones, T. B. (1985). The composition of boards of directors and incidence of golden parachutes. *Academy of Management Journal, 28,* 664-671.

Coleman, J. S. (1957). *Community conflict.* New York: Free Press.

Coleman, J. S. (1961). *The adolescent society: The social life of the teenager and its impact on education.* New York: Free Press.

Coleman, J. S. (1973). *The mathematics of collective action.* Chicago: Aldine.

Coleman, J. S. (1986). *Individual interests and collective action: Selected essays.* New York: Cambridge University Press.

Coleman, J. S. (1988). Social capital in the creation of human capital. *American Journal of Sociology, 94,* 95-120.

Conrath, D. (1973). Communication environment and its relationship to organizational structure. *Management Science, 4,* 586-603.

Contractor, N., Zink, D., & Chan, M. (1998). IKNOW: A tool to assist and study the creation, maintenance, and dissolution of knowledge networks. In *Proceedings of the Kyoto Meeting on Social Interaction and Communityware* [Lecture Notes in Computer Science]. Berlin: Springer-Verlag

Contractor, N. S. (1997). *Inquiring knowledge networks on the Web. Conceptual overview.* Available: http://www.tec.spcomm.uiuc.edu/nosh/IKNOW/sld001.htm.

Contractor, N. S., & Eisenberg, E. M. (1990). Communication networks and new media in organizations. In J. Fulk & C. Steinfield (Eds.), *Organizations and communication technology* (pp. 143-172). Newbury Park, CA: Sage.

Contractor, N. S., Eisenberg, E. M., & Monge, P. R. (1996). *Antecedents and outcomes of interpretative diversity.* Unpublished manuscript.

Contractor, N. S., & Grant, S. (1996). The emergence of shared interpretations in organizations: A self-organizing systems perspective. In J. Watt & A. VanLear (Eds.), *Cycles and dynamic processes in communication processes* (pp. 216-230). Thousand Oaks, CA: Sage.

Contractor, N. S., O'Keefe, B. J., & Jones, P. M. (1997). *IKNOW: Inquiring knowledge networks on the Web* [Computer software]. University of Illinois. (http://iknow.spcomm.uiuc.edu)

Contractor, N. S., Seibold, D. R., & Heller, M. A. (1996). Interactional influence in the structuring of media use in groups: Influence of members' perceptions of group decision support system use. *Human Communication Research, 22,* 451-481.

Cook, K. S. (1977). Exchange and power in networks of interorganizational relations. *Sociological Quarterly, 18,* 62-82.

Cook, K. S. (1982). Network structures from an exchange perspective. In P. V. Marsden & N. Lin (Eds.), *Social structure and network analysis* (pp. 177-218). Beverly Hills, CA: Sage.

Cook, K. S., & Emerson, R. M. (1978). Power, equity, and commitment in exchange networks. *American Sociological Review, 43,* 721-739.

Cook, K. S., Emerson, R. M., Gillmore, M. R., & Yamagishi, T. (1983). The distribution of power in exchange networks: Theory and experimental results. *American Journal of Sociology, 89,* 275-305.

Cook, K. S., & Whitmeyer, J. M. (1992) Two approaches to social structure: Exchange theory and network analysis. *Annual Review of Sociology, 18,* 109-127.

Cook, K. S., & Yamagishi, T. (1992). Power in exchange networks: A power-dependence formulation. *Social Networks, 14,* 245-265.

Corman, S. R. (1990). A mode of perceived communication in collective networks. *Human Communication Research, 16,* 582-602.

Corman, S. R. (1996). Cellular automata as models of unintended consequences of organizational communication. In J. H. Watt & C. A. Van Lear (Eds.), *Dynamic patterns in communication processes* (pp. 191-212). Thousand Oaks, CA: Sage.

Corman, S. R. (1997). The reticulation of quasi-agents in systems of organizational communication. In G. A. Barnett & L. Thayer (Eds.), *Organization communication emerging perspectives V: The renaissance in systems thinking* (pp. 65-81). Greenwich, CT: Ablex.

Corman, S. R., & Scott, C. R. (1994). Perceived networks, activity, foci, and observable communication in social collectives. *Communication Theory, 4,* 171-190.

Crombie, S., & Birley, S. (1992). Networking by female business owners in Northern Ireland. *Journal of Business Venturing, 7,* 237-251.

Cummings, A. (1997). *The radicalness of employee ideas: An interactive model of co-worker networks and problem-solving styles.* Unpublished doctoral dissertation, University of Illinois, Champaign.

Cutrona, C. E., & Russell, D. W. (1990). Type of social support and specific stress: Toward a theory of optimal matching. In B. R. Sarason, I. G. Sarason, & G. R. Pierce (Eds.), *Social support: An interactional view* (pp. 319-366). New York: John Wiley.

Danowski, J. A. (1982). Computer-mediated communication: A network-based content analysis using a CBBS conference. In M. Burgoon (Ed.), *Communication yearbook 6* (pp. 905-924). Beverly Hills, CA: Sage.

Davies, G. (1996). The employment support network—An intervention to assist displaced works. *Journal of Employment Counseling, 33,* 146-154.

Davis, G. F. (1991). Agents without principles? The spread of the poison pill through the intercorporate network. *Administrative Science Quarterly, 36,* 583-613.

Davis, J., & Leinhardt, S. (1972). The structure of positive interpersonal relations in small groups. In J. Berger (Ed.), *Sociological theories in progress* (Vol. 2, pp. 218-251). Boston: Houghton Mifflin.

Davis, K. (1953). A method of studying communication patterns in organizations. *Personnel Psychology, 6,* 301-312.

DeFleur, M. L., & Cronin, M. M. (1991). Completeness and accuracy of recall in the diffusion of the news from a newspaper versus a television source. *Sociological Inquiry, 61,* 148-166.

DiMaggio, P. J., & Powell, W. W. (1983). The iron cage revisited: Institutional isomorphism and collective rationality in organizational fields. *American Sociological Review, 48,* 147-160.

de Saussure, R. (1966). *Course in general linguistics.* New York: McGraw-Hill. (Original work published 1916)

De Soto, C. B. (1960). Learning a social structure. *Journal of Abnormal and Social Psychology, 60,* 417-421.

Domhoff, G. W. (1983). *Who rules America now? A view of the '80s.* Englewood Cliffs, NJ: Prentice Hall.

Doty, D. H., Glick, W. H., & Huber, G. P. (1993). Fit, equifinality, and organizational effectiveness: A test of two configurational theories. *Academy of Management Journal, 36,* 1196-1250.

Dunn, W. N., & Ginsberg, A. (1986). A sociocognitive network approach to organizational analysis. *Human Relations, 39,* 955-976.

Durkheim, É. (1964). *The rules of sociological method.* London: Free Press. (Original work published 1895)

Durkheim, É. (1977). *Suicide: A study in sociology* (J. A. Spaulding & G. Simpson, Trans.). New York: Free Press. (Original work published 1897)

Eisenberg, E. M., Farace, R. V., Monge, P. R., Bettinghaus, E. P., Kurchner-Hawkins, R., Miller, K., & Rothman, L. (1985). Communication linkages in interorganizational systems. In B. Dervin & M. Voight (Eds.), *Progress in communication sciences* (Vol. 6, pp. 210-266). Norwood, NJ: Ablex.

Eisenberg, E. M., Monge, P. R., & Miller, K. I. (1984). Involvement in communication networks as a predictor of organizational commitment. *Human Communication Research, 10,* 179-201.

Eisenberg, E. M., & Swanson, N. (1996). Organizational network analysis as a tool for program evaluation. *Evaluation and the Health Professions, 19,* 488-507.

Emerson, R. M. (1962). Power-dependence relations. *American Sociological Review, 27,* 31-41.

Emerson, R. M. (1972a). Exchange theory, Part I: A psychological basis for social exchange. In J. Berger, M. Zelditch, & B. Anderson (Eds.), *Sociological theories in progress* (Vol. 2, pp. 38-57). Boston: Houghton Mifflin.

Emerson, R. M. (1972b). Exchange theory, Part II: Exchange relations and networks. In J. Berger, M. Zelditch, & B. Anderson (Eds.), *Sociological theories in progress* (Vol. 2, pp. 58-87). Boston: Houghton Mifflin.

Emery, F. E., & Trist, E. L. (1960). Sociotechnical systems. In C. W. Churchman & M. Verhulst (Eds.), *Management science, models and techniques* (pp. 83-97). New York: Pergamon.

Emery, F. E., & Trist, E. L. (1965). The causal texture of organizational environment. *Human Relations, 18,* 21-32.

Erickson, B. (1988). The relational basis of attitudes. In B. Wellman & S. D. Berkowitz (Eds.), *Social structures: A network approach* (pp. 99-121). Cambridge, UK: Cambridge University Press.

Ethington, E. T., Johnson, J. D., Marshall, A., Meyer, M., & Chang, H. J. (1996, May). *Gender ratios in organizations: A comparative study of two organizations.* Paper presented at the annual conference of the International Communication Association, Chicago.

Eveland, J. D., & Bikson, T. K. (1987). Evolving electronic communication networks: An empirical assessment. *Office: Technology and People, 3,* 103-128.

Farace, R. V., Monge, P. R., & Russell, H. M. (1977). *Communicating and organizing.* Reading, MA: Addison-Wesley.

Fararo, T. J. (1973). *Mathematical sociology: An introduction to fundamentals.* New York: John Wiley.

Feeley, T. H., & Barnett, G. A. (1996). Predicting employee turnover from communication networks. *Human Communication Research, 23,* 370-387.

Feld, S. (1981). The focused organization of social ties. *American Journal of Sociology, 86,* 1015-1035.

Fernandez, R. M. (1991). Structural bases of leadership in intraorganizational networks. *Social Psychology Quarterly, 54,* 36-53.

Festinger, L. (1954). A theory of social comparison processes. *Human Relations, 7,* 114-140.

Festinger, L., Schachter, S., & Back, K. (1950). *Social pressures in informal groups: A study of human factors in housing.* Palo Alto, CA: Stanford University Press.

Fine, G. A., & Kleinman, S. (1983). Network and meaning: An interactionist approach to structure. *Symbolic Interaction, 6,* 97-110.

Fiol, C. M. (1989). A semantic analysis of corporate language: Organizational boundaries and joint venturing. *Administrative Science Quarterly, 34,* 277-303.

Flache, A., & Macy, M. W. (1996). The weakness of strong ties: Collective action failure in a highly cohesive group. *Journal of Mathematical Sociology, 21,* 3-28.

Follett, M. P. (1924). *Creative experience.* New York: Longmans, Green.

Fombrun, C. J. (1986). Structural dynamics within and between organizations. *Administrative Science Quarterly, 31,* 403-421.

Freeman, L. (1977). A set of measures of centrality based on betweenness. *Sociometry, 40,* 35-41.

Freeman, L. (1979). Centrality in social networks: I. Conceptual clarification. *Social Networks, 1,* 215-239.

Freeman, L. C. (1992). Filling in the blanks: A theory of cognitive categories and the structure of social affiliation. *Social Psychology Quarterly, 55,* 118-127.

Freeman, L. C., Romney, A. K., & Freeman, S. C. (1987). Cognitive structure and informant accuracy. *American Anthropologist, 89,* 31-325.

Friedkin, N. E. (1984). Structural cohesion and equivalence explanations of social homogeneity. *Sociological Methods & Research, 12,* 235-261.

Frost, P., Moore, L., Louis, M. R., Lundberg, C., & Martin, J. (1985). *Organizational culture.* Beverly Hills, CA: Sage.

Fulk, J. (1993). Social construction of communication technology. *Academy of Management Journal, 36,* 921-950.

Fulk, J., & Boyd, B. (1991). Emerging theories of communication in organizations. *Yearly Review of the Journal of Management, 17,* 407-446.

Fulk, J., Flanagin, A. J., Kalman, M. E., Monge, P. R., & Ryan, T. (1996). Connective and communal public goods in interactive communication systems. *Communication Theory, 6,* 60-87.

Fulk, J., Schmitz, J., & Ryu, D. (1995). Cognitive elements in the social construction of communication technology. *Management Communication Quarterly, 8,* 259-288.

Fulk, J., Schmitz, J., & Steinfield, C. W. (1990). A social influence model of technology use. In J. Fulk & C. Steinfield (Eds.), *Organizations and communication technology* (pp. 117-140). Newbury Park, CA: Sage.

Fulk, J., Steinfield, C. W., Schmitz, J., & Power, J. G. (1987). A social information processing model of media use in organizations. *Communication Research, 14,* 529-552.

Galaskiewicz, J. (1979). *Exchange networks and community politics.* Beverly Hills, CA: Sage.

Galaskiewicz, J. (1985). Interorganizational relations. *Annual Review of Sociology, 11,* 281-304.

Galaskiewicz, J., & Burt, R. S. (1991). Interorganizational contagion in corporate philanthropy. *Administrative Science Quarterly, 36,* 88-105.

Galaskiewicz, J., & Wasserman, S. (1989). Mimetic and normative processes within an interorganizational field: An empirical test. *Administrative Science Quarterly, 34,* 454-479.

Galbraith, J. R. (1977). *Organization design.* Reading, MA: Addison-Wesley.

Galbraith, J. R. (1995). *Designing organizations: An executive briefing on strategy, structure, and process.* San Francisco: Jossey-Bass.

Gerlach, M. (1992). *Alliance capitalism.* Berkeley: University of California Press.

Ghoshal, S., & Bartlett, C. A. (1990). The multinational corporation as an interorganizational network. *Academy of Management Review, 15,* 603-625.

Giddens, A. (1976). *New rules of sociological method.* London: Hutchinson.

Giddens, A. (1979). *Central problems in social theory.* Cambridge, UK: Cambridge University Press.

Giddens, A. (1984). *The constitution of society: Outline of the theory of structuration.* Cambridge, UK: Polity.

Goes, J. B., & Park, S. H. (1997). Interorganizational links and innovation: The case of hospital services. *Academy of Management Journal, 40,* 673-696.

Goodell, A., Brown, J., & Poole, M. S. (1989). *Organizational networks and climate perceptions: A longitudinal analysis.* Unpublished manuscript.

Gould, R. V. (1991). Multiple networks and mobilization in the Paris Commune, 1871. *American Sociological Review, 56,* 716-729.

Grabher, G. (1993). Rediscovering the social in the economics of interfirm relations. In G. Grabher (Ed.), *The embedded firm: On the socioeconomics of industrial networks* (pp. 1-31). New York: Routledge.

Graen, G. (1976). Role making processes within complex organizations. In M. D. Dunnette (Ed.), *Handbook of industrial and organizational psychology* (pp. 1201-1245). Chicago: Rand McNally.

Grandori, A., & Soda, G. (1995). Inter-firm networks: Antecedents, mechanisms, and forms. *Organization Studies, 16,* 183-214.

Granovetter, M. (1978). Threshold models of diffusion and collective behavior. *Journal of Mathematical Sociology, 9,* 165-179.

Granovetter, M. (1982). The strength of weak ties: A network theory revisited. In P. Marsden & N. Lin (Eds.), *Social structure and network analysis* (pp. 105-130). Beverly Hills, CA: Sage.

Granovetter, M. S. (1985). Economic action and social structure: The problem of embeddedness. *American Journal of Sociology, 91,* 481-510.

Gulati, R. (1995). Social structure and alliance formation patterns: A longitudinal analysis. *Administrative Science Quarterly, 40,* 619-652.

Gupta, A. K., & Govindarajan, V. (1991). Knowledge flows and the structure of control within multinational corporations. *Academy of Management Review, 16,* 768-792.

Gurbaxani, V. (1990). Diffusion in computing networks: The case of Bitnet. *Communications of the ACM, 33,* 65-75.

Hackman, J. R., & Oldham, G. (1976). Motivation through the design of work: Test of a theory. *Organizational Behavior and Human Performance, 16,* 250-279.

Haines, V. A. (1988). Social network analysis, structuration theory and the holism-individualism debate. *Social Networks, 10,* 157-182.

Hall, A., & Wellman, B. (1985). Social networks and social support. In S. Cohen & S. L. Syme (Eds.), *Social support and health* (pp. 23-41). Orlando, FL: Academic Press.

Harary, F., Norman, R. Z., & Cartwright, D. (1965). *Structural models: An introduction to the theory of directed graphs.* New York: John Wiley.

Hartman, R. L., & Johnson, J. D. (1989). Social contagion and multiplexity: Communication networks as predictors of commitment and role ambiguity. *Human Communication Research, 15,* 523-548.

Hartman, R. L., & Johnson, J. D. (1990). Formal and informal group structures: An examination of their relationship to role ambiguity. *Social Networks, 12,* 127-151.

Haythornthwaite, C. (1996). Social network analysis: An approach and technique for the study of information exchange. *Library & Information Science Research, 18,* 323-342.

Haunschild, P. R. (1993). Interorganizational imitation: The impact of interlocks on corporate acquisition activity. *Administrative Science Quarterly, 38,* 564-592.

Haunschild, P. R. (1994). How much is that company worth? Interorganizational relationships, uncertainty, and acquisition premiums. *Administrative Science Quarterly, 39,* 391-411.

Heald, M. R., Contractor, N. S., Koehly, L., & Wasserman, S. (1996). *Formal and emergent predictors of coworkers' perceptual congruence on an organization's social structure.* Unpublished manuscript.

Heckscher, C. (1994). Defining the post-bureaucratic type. In C. Heckscher & A. Donnellon (Eds.), *The post-bureaucratic organization: New perspectives on organizational change* (pp. 14-62). Thousand Oaks, CA: Sage.

Heider, F. (1958). *The psychology of interpersonal relations.* New York: John Wiley.

Hinds, P., & Kiesler, S. (1995). Communication across boundaries: Work, structure, and use of communication technologies in a large organization. *Organization Science, 6,* 373-393.

Hoffman, A. N., Stearns, T. M., & Shrader, C. B. (1990). Structure, context, and centrality in interorganizational networks. *Journal of Business Research, 20,* 333-347.

Hofstede, G. (1984). *Culture's consequences: International differences in work-related values.* Beverly Hills, CA: Sage.

Holland, P. W., & Leinhardt, S. (1975). The statistical analysis of local structure in social networks. In D. R. Heise (Ed.), *Sociological methodology, 1976* (pp. 1-45). San Francisco: Jossey-Bass.

Holland, P. W., & Leinhardt, S. (1979). *Perspectives on social network research.* New York: Academic Press.

Homans, G. C. (1950). *The human group.* New York: Harcourt Brace.

Homans, G. C. (1958). Social behavior as exchange. *American Journal of Sociology, 63,* 597-606.

Homans, G. C. (1974). *Social behavior: Its elementary forms* (Rev. ed.). New York: Harcourt Brace.

Huber, G. P., & Daft, R. L. (1987). The information environments of organizations. In F. M. Jablin, L. L. Putnam, K. H. Roberts, & L. W. Porter (Eds.), *Handbook of organizational communication: An interdisciplinary perspective* (pp. 130-164): Newbury Park, CA: Sage.

Huber, G. P., Miller, C. C., & Glick, W. H. (1990). Developing more encompassing theories about organizations: The centralization-effectiveness relationship as an example. *Organization Science, 1,* 11-40.

Hurlbert, J. S. (1991). Social networks, social circles, and job satisfaction. *Work and Occupations, 18,* 415-430.

Hyatt, A., Contractor, N., & Jones, P. M. (1997). Computational organizational network modeling: Strategies and an example. *Computational and Mathematical Organizational Theory, 4,* 285-300.

Ibarra, H. (1992). Homophily and differential returns: Sex differences in network structure and access in an advertising firm. *Administrative Science Quarterly, 37,* 422-447.

Ibarra, H. (1993a). Network centrality, power, and innovation involvement: Determinants of technical and administrative roles. *Administrative Science Quarterly, 36,* 471-501.

Ibarra, H. (1993b). Personal networks of women and minorities in management: A conceptual framework. *Academy of Management Review, 18,* 56-87.

Ibarra, H. (1995). Race, opportunity, and diversity of social circles in managerial networks. *Academy of Management Journal, 38,* 673-703.

Ibarra, H., & Andrews, S. B. (1993). Power, social influence, and sense making: Effects of network centrality and proximity on employee perceptions. *Administrative Science Quarterly, 38,* 277-303.

Jablin, F. M. (1987). Formal organization structure. In F. M. Jablin, L. L. Putnam, K. H. Roberts, & L. W. Porter (Eds.), *Handbook of organizational communication: An interdisciplinary perspective* (pp. 389-419). Newbury Park, CA: Sage.

Jablin, F., & Krone, K. J. (1987). Organizational assimilation. In C. Berger & S. H. Chaffee (Eds.), *Hand-*

book of communication science (pp. 711-746). Newbury Park, CA: Sage.

Jang, H., & Barnett, G. A. (1994). Cultural differences in organizational communication: A semantic network analysis. *Bulletin de Methodologie Sociologique, 44,* 31-59.

Johnson, J. D. (1992). Approaches to organizational communication structure. *Journal of Business Research, 25,* 99-113.

Johnson, J. D. (1993). *Organizational communication structure.* Norwood, NJ: Ablex.

Kadushin, C. (1983). Mental health and the interpersonal environment: A reexamination of some effects of social structure on mental health. *American Sociological Review, 48,* 188-198.

Kadushin, C., & Brimm, M. (1990). *Why networking fails: Double binds and the limitations of shadow networks.* Paper presented at the Tenth Annual International Social Networks Conference, San Diego, CA.

Kautz, H., Selman, B., & Shah, M. (1997). Combining social networks and collaborative filtering. *Communications of the ACM, 40,* 63-65.

Khurana, R. (1997). *Director interlocks and outsider CEO selection: A field and statistical examination of the Fortune 500 between 1990-1995.* Unpublished doctoral dissertation, Harvard University.

Kilduff, M. (1992). The friendship network as a decision-making resource: Disposition moderators of social influences on organizational choice. *Journal of Personality and Social Psychology, 62,* 168-180.

Kilduff, M., & Krackhardt, D. (1993). *Schemas at work: Making sense of organizational relationships.* Unpublished manuscript.

Kilduff, M., & Krackhardt, D. (1994). Bringing the individual back in: A structural analysis of the internal market for reputation in organizations. *Academy of Management Journal, 37,* 87-108.

Knoke, D. (1990). *Political networks: The structural perspective.* Cambridge, UK: Cambridge University Press.

Knoke, D. (1993). Networks of elite structure and decision making. *Sociological Methods & Research, 22,* 23-45.

Kogut, B., Shan, W., & Walker, G. (1993). Knowledge in the network and the network as knowledge: Structuring of new industries. In G. Grabher (Ed.), *The embedded firm: On the socioeconomics of industrial networks* (pp. 67-94). New York: Routledge.

Korzenny, F., & Bauer, C. (1981). Testing the theory of electronic propinquity: Organizational teleconferencing. *Communication Research, 8,* 479-498.

Kosnik, R. D. (1987). Greenmail: A study of board performance in corporate governance. *Administrative Science Quarterly, 32,* 163-185.

Krackhardt, D. (1987). Cognitive social structures. *Social Networks, 9,* 109-134.

Krackhardt, D. (1990). Assessing the political landscape: Structure, cognition, and power in organizations. *Administrative Science Quarterly, 35,* 342-369.

Krackhardt, D. (1992). The strength of strong ties: The importance of *philos* in organizations. In N. Nohria & R. Eccles (Eds.), *Networks and organizations: Structure, form and action* (pp. 216-239). Boston: Harvard Business School Press.

Krackhardt, D. (1994). Constraints on the interactive organization as an ideal type. In C. Heckscher & A. Donnellon (Eds.), *The post-bureaucratic organization: New perspectives on organizational change* (pp. 211-222). Thousand Oaks, CA: Sage.

Krackhardt, D., & Brass, D. J. (1994). Intra-organizational networks: The micro side. In S. Wasserman & J. Galaskiewicz (Eds.), *Advances in social network analysis: Research in the social and behavioral sciences* (pp. 207-229). Thousand Oaks, CA: Sage.

Krackhardt, D., & Hanson, J. R. (1993). Informal networks: The company behind the chart. *Harvard Business Review, 71,* 104-112.

Krackhardt, D., & Kilduff, M. (1990). Friendship patterns and culture: The control of organizational diversity. *American Anthropologist, 92,* 142-154.

Krackhardt, D., & Porter, L. (1985). When friends leave: A structural analysis of the relationship between turnover & stayers' attitudes. *Administrative Science Quarterly, 30,* 242-261.

Krackhardt, D., & Porter, L. (1986). The snowball effect: Turnover embedded in social networks. *Journal of Applied Psychology, 71,* 50-55.

Krackhardt, D., & Stern, R. N. (1988). Informal networks and organizational crises: An experimental situation. *Social Psychology Quarterly, 51,* 123-140.

Kramer, M. W. (1996). A longitudinal study of peer communication during job transfers: The impact of frequency, quality, and network multiplexity on adjustment. *Human Communication Research, 23,* 59-86.

Krassa, M. A. (1988). Social groups, selective perception, and behavioral contagion in public opinion. *Social Networks, 10,* 109-136.

Kraut, R. E., Egido, C., & Galegher, J. (1990). Patterns of contact and communication in scientific research collaboration. In J. Galegher, R. E. Kraut, & C. Egido (Eds.), *Intellectual teamwork: Social and technological foundations of cooperative work* (pp. 149-172). Hillsdale, NJ: Lawrence Erlbaum.

Krikorian, D. D., Seibold, D. R., & Goode, P. L. (1997). Reengineering at LAC: A case study of emergent network processes. In B. D. Sypher (Ed.), *Case studies in organizational communication: Vol. 2. Perspectives on contemporary work life* (pp. 129-144). New York: Guilford.

Labianca, G., Brass, D., & Gray, B. (1998). Social networks and the perceptions of intergroup conflict:

The role of negative relationships and third parties. *Academy of Management Journal, 41,* 55-67.

Langford, C. P. H., Bowsher, J., Maloney, J. P., & Lillis, P. P. (1997). Social support: A conceptual analysis. *Journal of Advanced Nursing, 25*(1), 95-100.

Larson, A. (1992). Network dyads in entrepreneurial settings: A study of the governance of exchange relations. *Administrative Science Quarterly, 37,* 76-104.

Larson, A., & Starr, J. A. (1993). A network model of organization formation. *Entrepreneurship: Theory and Practice, 17,* 5-15.

Laumann, E. O. (1966). *Prestige and association in an urban community.* Indianapolis, IN: Bobbs-Merrill.

Laumann, E. O., Knoke, D., & Kim, Y.-H. (1985). An organizational approach to state policymaking: A comparative study of energy and health domains. *American Sociological Review, 50,* 1-19.

Laumann, E. O., & Pappi, F. U. (1976). *Networks of collective action.* New York: Academic Press.

Lawrence, R. R., & Lorsch, J. W. (1967). *Organization and environment: Managing differentiation and integration.* Cambridge, MA: Harvard University Press.

Lazerson, M. (1993). Factory or putting out? Knitting networks in Modena. In G. Grabher (Ed.), *The embedded firm: On the socioeconomics of industrial networks* (pp. 203-226). New York: Routledge.

Leavitt, H. J. (1951). Some effects of certain communication patterns on group performance. *Journal of Abnormal and Social Psychology, 46,* 38-50.

Leblebici, H., & Salancik, G. R. (1981). Effects of environmental uncertainty on information and decision processes in banks. *Administrative Science Quarterly, 26,* 578-596.

Leenders, R. T. A. J. (1996). Evolution of friendship and best friendship choices. *Journal of Mathematical Sociology, 21,* 133-148.

Levine, J. H., & White, P. (1961). Exchange as a conceptual framework for the study of interorganizational relationships. *Administrative Science Quarterly, 5,* 583-601.

Lewin, K. (1936). *Principles of topological psychology* (F. Heider & G. Heider, Trans.). New York: McGraw-Hill.

Liebeskind, J. P., Oliver, A. L., Zucker, L., & Brewer, M. (1996). Social networks, learning, and flexibility: Sourcing scientific knowledge in new biotechnology firms. *Organization Science, 7,* 428-443.

Liedka, R. V. (1991). Who do you know in the group? Location of organizations in interpersonal networks. *Social Forces, 70,* 455-474.

Lievrouw, L. A., & Carley, K. (1991). Changing patterns of communication among scientists in an era of "telescience." *Technology in Society, 12,* 457-477.

Lievrouw, L. A., Rogers, E. M., Lowe, C. U., & Nadel, E. (1987). Triangulation as a research strategy for identifying invisible colleges among biomedical scientists. *Social Networks, 9,* 217-248.

Lin, N., & Ensel, W. M., (1989). Life stress and health: Stressors and resources. *American Sociological Review, 54,* 382-399.

Lin, N., Ensel, W. M., & Vaughn, J. C. (1981). Social resources and strength of ties: Structural factors in occupational status attainment. *American Sociological Review, 46,* 393-405.

Lincoln, J., & Miller, J. (1979). Work and friendship ties in organizations: A comparative analysis of relational networks. *Administrative Science Quarterly, 24,* 181-199.

Lincoln, J. R., Gerlach, M. L., & Takahashi, P. (1992). *Keiretsu* networks in the Japanese economy: A dyad analysis of intercorporate ties. *American Sociological Review, 57,* 561-585.

Litwak, E., & Hylton, L. F. (1962). Interorganizational analysis: A hypothesis on coordinating agencies. *Administrative Science Quarterly, 6,* 392-420.

Lorrain, F., & White, H. (1971). Structural equivalence of individuals in social networks. *Journal of Mathematical Sociology, 1,* 49-80.

March, J. G., & Weissinger-Baylon, R. (1986). *Ambiguity and command: Organizational perspectives on military decision making.* Marshfield, MA: Pitman.

Markovsky, B. (1995). Developing an exchange network simulator. *Sociological Perspectives, 38,* 519-545.

Markovsky, B. (1997). Network games. *Rationality and Society, 9,* 67-90.

Markovsky, B., Willer, D., & Patton, T. (1988). Power relations in exchange networks. *American Sociological Review, 53,* 220-236.

Markus, M. L. (1990). Toward a "critical mass" theory of interactive media. In J. Fulk & C. Steinfield (Eds.), *Organizations and communication technology* (pp. 194-218). Newbury Park, CA: Sage.

Marsden, P. V. (1988). Homogeneity in confiding relations. *Social Networks, 10,* 57-76.

Marsden, P. V. (1990). Network data and measurement. *Annual Review of Sociology, 16,* 435-463.

Marsden, P. V., & Friedkin, N. E. (1994). Network studies of social influence. In S. Wasserman & J. Galaskiewicz (Eds.), *Advances in social network analysis: Research in the social and behavioral sciences* (pp. 3-25). Thousand Oaks, CA: Sage.

Marwell, G., & Oliver, P. (1993). *The critical mass in collective action: A micro-social theory.* Cambridge, UK: Cambridge University Press.

Marwell, G., Oliver, P. E., & Prahl, R. (1988). Social networks and collective action: A theory of the critical mass, III. *American Journal of Sociology, 94,* 502-534.

McElroy, J. C., & Shrader, C. B. (1986). Attribution theories of leadership and network analysis. *Journal of Management, 12,* 351-362.

McKelvey, B. (1982). *Organizational systematics: Taxonomy, evolution, and classification.* Berkeley: University of California Press.

McKelvey, B. (1997). Quasi-natural organization science. *Organization Science, 8,* 352-380.

McPhee, R. D., & Corman, S. R. (1995). An activity-based theory of communication networks in organizations, applied to the case of a local church. *Communication Monographs, 62,* 132-151.

McPherson, J. M., & Smith-Lovin, L. (1987). Homophily in voluntary organizations: Status distance and the composition of face to face groups. *American Sociological Review, 52,* 370-379.

Meyer, J. W., & Rowan, B. (1977). Institutionalized organizations: Formal structure as myth and ceremony. *American Journal of Sociology, 83,* 340-363.

Michaelson, A., & Contractor, N. (1992). Comparison of relational and positional predictors of group members' perceptions. *Social Psychology Quarterly, 55,* 300-310.

Miles, R. E. (1980). *Macro organizational behavior.* Santa Monica, CA: Goodyear.

Miles, R. E., & Snow, C. C. (1986). Organizations: New concepts for new forms. *California Management Review, 28,* 62-73.

Miles, R. E., & Snow, C. C. (1992, Summer). Causes of failure in network organizations. *California Management Review, 11,* 53-72.

Miles, R. E., & Snow, C. C. (1995). The new network firm: A spherical structure built on a human investment philosophy. *Organizational Dynamics, 23,* 5-18.

Miller, C. C., Glick, W. H., Wang, Y. D., & Huber, G. P. (1991). Understanding technology-structure relationships: Theory development and meta-analytic theory testing. *Academy of Management Journal, 34,* 370-399.

Miller, K. I., & Monge, P. R. (1985). Social information and employee anxiety about organizational change. *Human Communication Research, 11,* 365-386.

Miner, A. S., Amburgey, T. L., & Stearns, T. M. (1990). Interorganizational linkages and population dynamics: Buffering and transformational shields. *Administrative Science Quarterly, 35,* 689-713.

Mintz, B., & Schwartz, M. (1985). *The power structure of American business.* Chicago: University of Chicago Press.

Mitchell, J. C. (1973). Networks, norms and institutions. In J. Boissevain & J. C. Mitchell (Eds.), *Network analysis* (pp. 15-35). The Hague, Netherlands: Mouton.

Mizruchi, M. S. (1989). Similarity of political behavior among large American corporations. *American Journal of Sociology, 95,* 401-424.

Mizruchi, M. S. (1992). *The structure of corporate political action.* Cambridge, MA: Harvard University Press.

Mizruchi, M. S. (1996). What do interlocks do? An analysis, critique, and assessment of research on interlocking directorates. *Annual Review of Sociology, 22,* 271-298.

Mizruchi, M. S., & Galaskiewicz, J. (1994). Networks of interorganizational relations. In S. Wasserman & J. Galaskiewicz (Eds.), *Advances in social network analysis: Research in the social and behavioral sciences* (pp. 230-253). Thousand Oaks, CA: Sage.

Mizruchi, M. S., & Stearns, L. B. (1988). A longitudinal study of the formation of interlocking directorates. *Administrative Science Quarterly, 33,* 194-210.

Monge, P. R. (1987). The network level of analysis. In C. R. Berger & S. H. Chaffee (Eds.), *Handbook of communication science* (pp. 239-270). Newbury Park, CA: Sage.

Monge, P. R. (1995). Global network organizations. In R. Cesaria & P. Shockley-Zalabak (Eds.), *Organization means communication* (pp. 135-151). Rome: Sipi Editore.

Monge, P. R., & Contractor, N. (1988). Communication networks: Measurement techniques. In C. H. Tardy (Ed.), *A handbook for the study of human communication* (pp. 107-138). Norwood, NJ: Ablex.

Monge, P. R., & Eisenberg, E. M. (1987). Emergent communication networks. In F. M. Jablin, L. L. Putnam, K. H. Roberts, & L. W. Porter (Eds.), *Handbook of organizational communication: An interdisciplinary perspective* (pp. 304-342). Newbury Park, CA: Sage.

Monge, P. R., & Fulk, J. (1999). Communication technology for global network organizations. In G. DeSanctis & J. Fulk (Eds.), *Shaping organizational form: Communication, connection, community* (pp. 71-100). Thousand Oaks, CA: Sage.

Monge, P. R., Fulk, J., Kalman, M., Flanagin, A. J., Parnassa, C., & Rumsey, S. (1998). Production of collective action in alliance-based interorganizational communication and information systems. *Organization Science, 9,* 411-433.

Monge, P. R., & Kalman, M. (1996). Sequentiality, simultaneity, and synchronicity in human communication. In J. Watt & A. Van Lear (Eds.), *Cycles and dynamic patterns in communication processes* (pp. 71-92). New York: Ablex.

Monge, P. R., Rothman, L. W., Eisenberg, E. M., Miller, K. I., & Kirste, K. K. (1985). The dynamics of organizational proximity. *Management Science, 31,* 1129-1141.

Moore, G. (1992). Gender and informal networks in state government. *Social Science Quarterly, 73,* 46-61.

Moscovici, S. (1976). *Social influence and social change.* London: Academic Press.

Nadel, S. F. (1957). *The theory of social structure.* New York: Free Press.

Nelson, R. E. (1989). The strength of strong ties: Social networks and intergroup conflict in organizations. *Academy of Management Journal, 32,* 377-401.

Newell, S., & Clark, P. (1990). The importance of extra-organizational networks in the diffusion and appropriation of new technologies. *Knowledge: Creation, Diffusion, Utilization, 12,* 199-212.

Nishida, T., Takeda, H., Iwazume, M., Maeda, H., & Takaai, M. (1998) The knowledge community: Facilitating human knowledge sharing. In T. Ishida (Ed.), *Community computing: Collaboration over global information networks* (pp. 127-164). Chichester, UK: Wiley.

Nohria, N., & Berkley, J. D. (1994). The virtual organization: Bureaucracy, technology, and the implosion of control. In C. Heckscher & A. Donnellon (Eds.), *The post-bureaucratic organization: New perspectives on organizational change* (pp. 108-128). Thousand Oaks, CA: Sage.

Norling, P. M. (1996). Network or not work: Harnessing technology networks in DuPont. *Research Technology Management, 39,* 42-48.

Norman, R., & Ramirez, R. (1993, July-August) From value chain to value constellation: Designing interactive strategy. *Harvard Business Review, 71,* 65-77.

Ogliastri, E., & Davila, C. (1987). The articulation of power and business structures: A study of Colombia. In M. Mizruchi & M. Schwartz (Eds.), *Intercorporate relations* (pp. 233-263). New York: Cambridge University Press.

Oliver, A. L., & Montgomery, K. (1996). A network approach to outpatient service delivery systems: Resources flow and system influence. *Health Services Research, 30,* 771-789.

Oliver, C. (1990). Determinants of interorganizational relationships: Integration and future directions. *Academy of Management Review, 15,* 241-265.

Oliver, C. (1991). Network relations and loss of organizational autonomy. *Human Relations, 44,* 943-961.

Oliver, P. E. (1980). Rewards and punishments as selective incentives for collective action: Theoretical investigations. *American Journal of Sociology, 8,* 1356-1375.

Oliver, P. E. (1993). Formal models of collective action. *Annual Review of Sociology, 19,* 271-300.

Olson, M., Jr. (1965). *The logic of collective action.* Cambridge, MA: Harvard University Press.

O'Reilly, P. (1988). Methodological issues in social support and social network research. *Social Science and Medicine, 26,* 863-873.

Palmer, D., Friedland, R., & Singh, J. V. (1986). The ties that bind: Organizational and class bases of stability in a corporate interlock network. *American Sociological Review, 51,* 781-796.

Palmer, D., Jennings, P. D., & Zhou, X. (1993). Late adoption of the multidivisional form by large U.S. corporations: Institutional, political and economic accounts. *Administrative Science Quarterly, 38,* 100-131.

Papa, M. J. (1990). Communication network patterns and employee performance with new technology. *Communication Research, 17,* 344-368.

Parsons, T. (1951). *The social system.* New York: Free Press.

Paterniti, R., Chellini, F., Sacchetti, & Tognelli, M. (1996). Psychiatric rehabilitation and its relation to the social network. *International Journal of Mental Health, 25,* 83-87.

Pattison, P. (1994). Social cognition in context: Some applications of social network analysis. In S. Wasserman & J. Galaskiewicz (Eds.), *Advances in social network analysis: Research in the social and behavioral sciences* (pp. 79-109). Thousand Oaks, CA: Sage.

Pfeffer, J., & Salancik, G. (1978). *The external control of organizations.* New York: Harper & Row.

Picot, A. (1993). Structures of industrial organization—Implications for information and communication technology. In W. Kaiser (Ed.), *Vision 2000: The evolution of information and communication technology for the information society* (pp. 278-293). Munich, Germany: Munchner Kreis.

Piore, M. J. (1975). Notes for a theory of labor market stratification. In R. Edwards, M. Reich, & D. Gordon (Eds.), *Labor market segmentation* (pp. 125-150). Lexington, MA: D. C. Heath.

Pollock, T., Whitbred, R., & Contractor, N. S. (1996, February). *Social information processing, job characteristics and disposition: A test and integration of competing theories of job satisfaction.* Paper presented at the Sunbelt XVI International Social Network Conference, Charleston, SC.

Poole, M. S. (in press). Organizational challenges for the new forms. In G. DeSanctis & J. Fulk (Eds.), *Shaping organization form: Communication, connection and community.* Thousand Oaks, CA: Sage.

Poole, M. S., & DeSanctis, G. (1990). Understanding the use of group decision support systems: The theory of adaptive structuration. In J. Fulk & C. Steinfield (Eds.), *Organizations and communication technology* (pp. 173-193). Newbury Park: Sage.

Poole, M. S., & McPhee, R. D. (1983). A structurational analysis of organizational climate. In L. L. Putnam & M. E. Pacanowsky (Eds.), *Communication and organizations: An interpretive approach* (pp. 195-220). Beverly Hills, CA: Sage.

Porter, M. E. (1980). *Competitive strategy: Techniques for analyzing industries and competitors.* New York: Free Press.

Powell, W. W. (1990). Neither market nor hierarchy: Network forms of organization. In L. L. Cummings & B. Staw (Eds.), *Research in organizational behavior* (Vol. 12, pp. 295-336). Greenwich, CT: JAI.

Powell, W. W., Koput, K. W., Smith-Doerr, L. (1996). Interorganizational collaboration and the locus of innovation: Networks of learning in biotechnology. *Administrative Science Quarterly, 41,* 116-145.

Provan, K. G. (1983). The federation as an interorganizational linkage network. *Academy of Management Review, 8,* 79-89.

Provan, K. G., & Milward, H. B. (1995). A preliminary theory of interorganizational network effectiveness: A comparative study of four community mental health systems. *Administrative Science Quarterly, 40*, 1-33.

Radcliffe-Brown, A. R. (1959). *Structure and function in primitive society.* New York: Free Press. (Original work published 1952)

Ratcliff, R. E., Gallagher, M. E., & Ratcliff, K. S. (1979). The civic involvement of bankers: An analysis of the influence of economic power and social prominence in the command of civic policy positions. *Social Problems, 26*, 298-313.

Rafaeli, S., & LaRose, R. J. (1993). Electronic bulletin boards and "public goods" explanations of collaborative mass media. *Communication Research, 20*, 277-297.

Ray, E. B. (1991). The relationship among communication network roles, job stress, and burnout in educational organizations. *Communication Quarterly, 39*, 91-102.

Ray, E. B., & Miller, K. I. (1990). Communication in health-care organizations. In E. B. Ray & L. Donohew (Eds.), *Communication and health: Systems and applications* (pp. 92-107). Hillsdale, NJ: Lawrence Erlbaum.

Rentsch, J. R. (1990). Climate and culture: Interaction and qualitative differences in organizational meanings. *Journal of Applied Psychology, 75*, 668-681.

Rice, R. E. (1993a). Media appropriateness: Using social presence theory to compare traditional and new organizational media. *Human Communication Research, 19*, 451-484.

Rice, R. E. (1993b). Using network concepts to clarify sources and mechanisms of social influence. In G. Barnett & W. Richards, Jr. (Eds.), *Advances in communication network analysis* (pp. 1-21). Norwood, NJ: Ablex.

Rice, R. E. (1994a). Network analysis and computer-mediated communication systems. In S. Wasserman & J. Galaskiewicz (Eds.), *Advances in social network analysis: Research in the social and behavioral sciences* (pp. 167-206). Thousand Oaks, CA: Sage.

Rice, R. E. (1994b). Relating electronic mail use and network structure to R&D work networks and performance. *Journal of Management Information Systems, 11*(1), 9-20.

Rice, R. E., & Aydin, C. (1991). Attitudes toward new organizational technology: Network proximity as a mechanism for social information processing. *Administrative Science Quarterly, 36*, 219-244.

Rice, R. E., & Danowski, J. (1993). Is it really just like a fancy answering machine? Comparing semantic networks of different types of voice mail users. *Journal of Business Communication, 30*, 369-397.

Rice, R. E., Grant, A., Schmitz, J., & Torobin, J. (1990). Individual and network influences on the adoption of perceived outcomes of electronic messaging. *Social Networks, 12*, 27-55.

Richards, W. D. (1985). Data, models, and assumptions in network analysis. In R. D. McPhee & P. K. Tompkins (Eds.), *Organizational communication: Traditional themes and new directions* (pp. 109-147). Newbury Park, CA: Sage.

Ring, P. S., & Van de Ven, A. H. (1992). Structuring cooperative relationships between organizations. *Strategic Management Journal, 13*, 48-498.

Ring, P. S., & Van de Ven, A. H. (1994). Developmental processes of cooperative interorganizational relationships. *Academy of Management Review, 19*, 90-118.

Roberts, K. H., & O'Reilly, C. A. (1978). Organizations as communication structures: An empirical approach. *Human Communication Research, 4*, 283-293.

Roberts, K. H., & O'Reilly, C. A. (1979). Some correlates of communication roles in organizations. *Academy of Management Journal, 22*, 42-57.

Robinson, D. T. (1996). Identity and friendship: Affective dynamics and network formation. *Advances in Group Processes, 13*, 91-111.

Roethlisberger, F., & Dickson, W. (1939). *Management and the worker.* New York: John Wiley.

Rogers, D. O., & Whetten, D. A. (1982). *Interorganizational coordination.* Ames: Iowa State University Press.

Rogers, E. M. (1971). *Communication of innovations.* New York: Free Press.

Rogers, E. M. (1987). Progress, problems, & prospects for network research. *Social Networks, 9*, 285-310.

Rogers, E. M., & Kincaid, D. L. (1981). *Communication networks: Toward a new paradigm for research.* New York: Free Press.

Romo, F. P., & Anheier, H. K. (1996). Success and failure in institutional development—A network approach. *American Behavioral Scientist, 39*, 1057-1079.

Sabidussi, G. (1966). The centrality index of a graph. *Psychometrika, 31*, 581-603.

Salancik, G. R. (1995). Wanted: A good network theory of organization. *Administrative Science Quarterly, 40*, 345-349.

Salancik, G. R., & Pfeffer, J. (1978). A social information processing approach to job attitudes and task design. *Administrative Science Quarterly, 23*, 224-253.

Samuelson, P. (1954). The pure theory of public expenditure. *Review of Economics and Statistics, 36*, 387-389.

Schachter, S. (1959). *The psychology of affiliation.* Stanford, CA: Stanford University Press.

Schachter, S., & Burdick, H. (1955). A field experiment on rumor transmission and distortion. *Journal of Abnormal and Social Psychology, 50*, 363-371.

Schermerhorn, J. R. (1977). Information sharing as an interorganizational activity. *Academy of Management Journal, 20,* 148-153.

Schmitz, J., & Fulk, J. (1991). Organizational colleagues, information richness, and electronic mail: A test of the social influence model of technology use. *Communication Research, 18,* 487-523.

Scott, J. (1988). Trend report: Social network analysis. *Sociology, 22,* 109-127.

Scott, J. (1992). *Social network analysis.* Newbury Park, CA: Sage.

Seabright, M. A., Levinthal, D. A., & Fichman, M. (1992). Role of individual attachments in the dissolution of interorganizational relationships. *Academy of Management Journal, 35,* 122-160.

Seeman, T. E., Bruce, M. L., McAvay, G. J. (1996). Social network characteristics and onset of ADL disability: MacArthur studies of successful aging. *Journal of Gerontology, 51B,* S191-S200.

Shaw, M. (1964). Communication networks. In L. Berkowitz (Ed.), *Advances in experimental psychology* (Vol. 1, pp. 111-147). New York: Academic Press.

Sherif, M. (1958). Superordinate goals in the reduction of intergroup conflicts. *American Journal of Sociology, 63,* 349-356.

Sherman, J. D., Smith, H., & Mansfield, E. R. (1986). The impact of emergent network structure on organizational socialization. *Journal of Applied Behavioral Science, 22,* 53-63.

Shrader, C. B., Lincoln, J. R., & Hoffman, A. N. (1989). The network structures of organizations: Effects of task contingencies and distributional form. *Human Relations, 42,* 43-66.

Simmel, G. (1955). *Conflict and the web of group affiliations.* Glencoe, IL: Free Press.

Singh, H., & Harianto, F. (1989). Management-board relationships, takeover risk, and the adoption of golden parachutes. *Academy of Management Journal, 32,* 7-24.

Skvoretz, J., & Fararo, T. J. (1996). Status and participation in task groups: A dynamic network model. *American Journal of Sociology, 101,* 1366-1414.

Skvoretz, J., & Faust, K. (1996). Social structure, networks, and E-state structuralism models. *Journal of Mathematical Sociology, 21,* 57-76.

Skvoretz, J., & Willer, D. (1993). Exclusion and power: A test of four theories of power in exchange networks. *American Sociological Review, 58,* 801-818.

Smith, K. G., Carroll, S. J., & Ashford, S. J. (1995). Intra- and interorganizational cooperation: Toward a research agenda. *Academy of Management Journal, 38,* 7-23.

Spencer, H. (1982). *Principles of sociology* (Vol. 2, Pt. 2). New York: Appleton-Century-Crofts.

Spinardi, G., Graham, I., & Williams, R. (1996). EDI and business network redesign: Why the two don't go together. *New Technology, Work and Employment, 11,* 16-27.

Staw, B., & Ross, J. (1985). Stability in the midst of change. *Journal of Applied Psychology, 70,* 469-480.

Stevenson, W. B. (1990). Formal structure and networks of interaction within organizations. *Social Science Research, 19,* 113-131.

Stearns, L. B., & Mizruchi, M. S. (1993). Board composition and corporate financing: The impact of financial institution representation on borrowing. *Academy of Management Journal, 36,* 603-618.

Steinfield, C. W., & Fulk, J. (1990). The theory imperative. In J. Fulk & C. Steinfield (Eds.), *Organizations and communication technology* (pp. 13-25). Newbury Park, CA: Sage.

Stevenson, W. B., & Gilly, M. C. (1991). Information processing and problem solving: The migration of problems through formal positions and networks of ties. *Academy of Management Journal, 34,* 918-928.

Stohl, C. (1993). European managers' interpretations of participation: A semantic network analysis. *Human Communication Research, 20,* 97-117.

Stohl, C. (1995). *Organizational communication: Connectedness in action.* Thousand Oaks, CA: Sage.

Stokman, F. N., & Doreian, P. (1996). Concluding remarks. *Journal of Mathematical Sociology, 21,* 197-199.

Stokman, F. N., & Zeggelink, E. P. H. (1996). Is politics power or policy oriented? A comparative analysis of dynamic access models in policy networks. *Journal of Mathematical Sociology, 21,* 77-111.

Tichy, N. M., & Fombrun, C. (1979). Network analysis in organizational settings. *Human Relations, 32,* 923-965.

Topper, C. M., & Carley, K. M. (1997, January). *A structural perspective on the emergence of network organizations.* Paper presented at the International Sunbelt Social Networks Conference, San Diego, CA.

Tosi, H. L. (1992). *The environment/organization/person contingency model: A meso approach to the study of organizations.* Greenwich, CT: JAI.

Trevino, L., Lengel, R., & Daft, R. (1987). Media symbolism, media richness and media choice in organizations: A symbolic interactionist perspective. *Communication Research, 14,* 553-575.

Tsui, A. S., Egan, T. D., & O'Reilly, C. A. (1992). Being different: Relational demography and organizational attachment. *Administrative Science Quarterly, 37,* 549-579.

Tsui, A. E., & O'Reilly, C. A., III. (1989). Beyond simple demographic effects: The importance of relational demography in superior-subordinate dyads. *Academy of Management Journal, 32,* 402-423.

Turk, H. (1977). Interorganizational networks in urban society: Initial perspectives and comparative research. *American Sociological Review, 35,* 1-20.

Turner, J. C. (1987). *Rediscovering the social group: A self-categorization theory*. Oxford, UK: Basil Blackwell.

Turner, J. C., & Oakes, P. J. (1986). The significance of the social identity concept for social psychology with reference to individualism, interactionism, and social influence. *British Journal of Social Psychology, 25,* 237-252.

Turner, J. C., & Oakes, P. J. (1989). Self-categorization theory and social influence. In P. B. Paulus (Ed.), *Psychology of group influence* (pp. 233-275). Hillsdale, NJ: Lawrence Erlbaum.

Useem, M. (1980). Corporations and the corporate elite. *Annual Review of Sociology, 6,* 41-77.

Useem, M. (1984). *The inner circle: Large corporations and business politics in the U.S. and UK*. New York: Oxford University Press.

Uzzi, B. (1996). The sources and consequences of embeddedness for the economic performance of organizations: The network effect. *American Sociological Review, 61,* 674-698.

Uzzi, B. (1997). Social structure and competition in interfirm networks: The paradox of embeddedness. *Administrative Science Quarterly, 42,* 35-67.

Valente, T. W. (1995). *Network models of the diffusion of innovations*. Cresskill, NJ: Hampton.

Valente, T. W. (1996). Social network thresholds in the diffusion of innovations. *Social Networks, 18,* 69-89.

Van den Bulte, C., & Moenaert, R. K. (1997). *The effects of R&D team co-location on communication patterns among R&D marketing, and manufacturing*. ISBM Report 7-1997. University Park: Pennsylvania State University, Institute for the Study of Business Markets.

Vega, W. A., Kolody, B., Valle, R., & Weir, J. (1991). Social networks, social support and their relationship to depression among immigrant Mexican women. *Human Organization, 50,* 154-162.

Wade, J., O'Reilly, C. A., III, & Chandratat, I. (1990). Golden parachutes: CEOs and the exercise of social influence. *Administrative Science Quarterly, 35,* 587-603.

Wagner, W. G., Pfeffer, J., & O'Reilly, C. A. (1984). Organizational demography and turnover in top management groups. *Administrative Science Quarterly, 29,* 74-92.

Walker, G. (1985). Network position and cognition in computer software firm. *Administrative Science Quarterly, 30,* 103-130.

Walker, G., Kogut, B., & Shan, W. (1997). Social capital, structural holes and the formation of an industry network. *Organization Science, 8,* 109-125.

Walker, M. E., Wasserman, S., & Wellman, B. (1994). Statistical models for social support networks. In S. Wasserman & J. Galaskiewicz (Eds.), *Advances in social network analysis: Research in the social and behavioral sciences* (pp. 53-78). Thousand Oaks, CA: Sage.

Wallace, M., Griffin, L. J., & Rubin, B. A. (1989). The positional power of American labor, 1963-1977. *American Sociological Review, 54,* 197-214.

Warren, R. (1967). The interorganizational field as a focus for investigation. *Administrative Science Quarterly, 12,* 396-419.

Wasserman, S., & Faust, K. (1994). *Social network analysis: Methods and applications*. New York: Cambridge University Press.

Wasserman, S., & Pattison, P. (1996). Logit models and logistic regressions for social networks: I. An introduction to Markov graphs and p*. *Psychometrika, 61,* 401-425.

Watzlawick, P., Beavin, J., & Jackson, D. (1967). *Pragmatics of human communication*. New York: Norton.

Weber, M. (1947). *The theory of social and economic organization* (A. H. Henderson & T. Parsons, Eds. & Trans.). Glencoe, IL: Free Press.

Weick, K. E. (1979). *The social psychology of organizing* (2nd ed.). Reading, MA: Addison-Wesley.

Wellman, B. (1988). Structural analysis: From method and metaphor to theory and substance. In B. Wellman & S. D. Berkowitz (Eds.), *Social structures: A network approach* (pp. 19-61). Cambridge, UK: Cambridge University Press.

Wellman, B. (1992). Which types of ties and networks provide what kinds of social support? In E. J. Lawler (Ed.), *Advances in group processes* (Vol. 9, pp. 207-235). Greenwich, CT: JAI.

Wellman, B., Salaff, J., Dimitrova, D., Garton, L., Gulia, M., & Haythornthwaite, C. (1996). Computer networks as social networks: Collaborative work, telework, and virtual community. *Annual Review of Sociology, 22,* 213-238.

Wellman, B., & Wortley, S. (1989). Brothers' keepers: Situating kinship relations in broader networks of social support. *Sociological Perspectives, 32,* 273-306.

Wellman, B., & Wortley, S. (1990). Different strokes from different folks: Community ties and social support. *American Journal of Sociology, 96,* 558-588.

Westphal, J. D., Gulati, R., & Shortell, S. M. (1997). Customization or conformity? An institutional and network perspective on the content and consequences of TQM adoption. *Administrative Science Quarterly, 42,* 366-394.

White, D. R., & Reitz, K. P. (1989). Rethinking the role concept: Homomorphisms on social networks. In L. C. Freeman, D. R. White, & A. K. Romney (Eds.), *Research methods in social network analysis* (pp. 429-488). Fairfax, VA: George Mason University Press.

White, H. C., Boorman, S. A., & Breiger, R. L. (1976). Social structure from multiple networks: I. Block-models of roles and positions. *American Journal of Sociology, 81,* 730-780.

Wigand, R. T. (1988). Communication network analysis: History and overview. In G. Goldhaber & G. Barnett

(Eds.), *Handbook of organizational communication* (pp. 319-359). Norwood, NJ: Ablex.

Willer, D., & Skvoretz, J. (1997). Network connection and exchange ratios: Theory, predictions, and experimental tests. In E. J. Lawler (Ed.), *Advances in group processes* (Vol. 14, pp. 199-234). Greenwich, CT: JAI.

Williamson, O. E. (1975). *Markets and hierarchies: Analysis and antitrust implications, a study of the economics of internal organization.* New York: Free Press.

Williamson, O. E. (1985). *The economic institutions of capitalism: Firms, markets, relational contracting.* New York: Free Press.

Williamson, O. E. (1991). Comparative economic organization: The analysis of discrete structural alternatives. *Administrative Science Quarterly, 36,* 269-296.

Woelfel, J. (1993). Artificial neural networks in policy research: A current assessment. *Journal of Communication, 43,* 62-80.

Woelfel, J., & Fink, E. L. (1980). *The Galileo system: A theory of social measurement and its application.* New York: Academic Press.

Yamagishi, T., Gillmore, M. R., & Cook, K. S. (1988). Network connections and the distribution of power in exchange networks. *American Journal of Sociology, 93,* 833-851.

Zack, M. H., & McKenney, J. L. (1995). Social context and interaction in ongoing computer-supported management groups. *Organization Science, 6,* 394-422.

Zahn, G. L. (1991). Face-to-face communication in an office setting: The effects of position, proximity, and exposure. *Communication Research, 18,* 737-754.

Zajac, E. J., & Olsen, C. P. (1993). From transaction cost to transactional value analysis: Implications for the study of interorganizational strategies. *Journal of Management Studies, 30,* 131-145.

Zeggelink, E. P. H., Stokman, F. N., & Van de Bunt, G. G. (1996). The emergence of groups in the evolution of friendship networks. *Journal of Mathematical Sociology, 21,* 29-55.

Zenger, T. R., & Lawrence, B. S. (1989). Organizational demography: The differential effects of age and tenure distributions on technical communication. *Academy of Management Journal, 32,* 353-376.

Zey-Ferrell, M., & Ferrell, O. C. (1982). Role set configuration and opportunity as predictors of unethical behavior in organizations. *Human Relations, 35,* 587-604.

Zinger, J. T., Blanco, H., Zanibbi, L., & Mount, J. (1996). An empirical study of the small business support network—The entrepreneur's perspective. *Canadian Journal of Administrative Sciences, 13,* 347-357.

13

Organizational Structures and Configurations

ROBERT D. McPHEE
Arizona State University

MARSHALL SCOTT POOLE
Texas A&M University

Most theory and research in organizational communication must navigate between Scylla and Charybdis. The Scylla is the temptation to construe the adjective *organizational* too broadly, to argue that any system or process of interaction has some sort of organization, so that all communication becomes organizational communication and we are carried off to study pick-up ball games rather than the major leagues, parties rather than political parties. In avoiding this Scylla, we risk sailing into danger from the Charybdis of the "container metaphor" (Axley, 1984; Smith, 1993), assuming that *organizational communication* is encapsulated within the confines of an ontologically prior entity, the organization. Communication so situated is of course influenced if not determined by its preestablished, well-known wrapper.

The channel of safety is difficult to perceive. At one level, we must pay systematic attention to the "embeddedness" of organizational communication processes. Their relation to an unusually explicit and important large-scale structure marks processes of interaction in the conduct of work operations, supervision and leadership, decision making, and large-scale coordination and control. Typically, most members of an organization know what their jobs are, how they are related to other jobs, who the boss is, who has what organizational powers. Their communication, in broad content and in fine-detailed organization, depends on knowledge of these facts.

503

Studying that dependence is one major task of organizational communication. But as we study the relation of communication to its structured context, we must remember that *organizational structure* is not a physical object or ontological constant. It is a social "reality" partly constituted—and sometimes transformed—in real-time interaction. But only partly. Organizational structure endures and alters the course of events because it is "inscribed" in the memory stocks and the material setting of the organization, and because it is responsive to and legitimized by institutionalized expectations in society at large. As organizational communication scholars, we must be concerned to fashion our theories so that they respond adequately both to our common knowledge of organizations in our cultural life and to the theoretical demands of "organization" as a problematic concept. Life today is shaped by complex organizational forces and products. What is it about organizational structure that gives it influence over organizational communication processes? How does that influence work and with what results? And how does communication in turn enact and shape organizational structures?

In this essay, we will survey some answers offered by recent research to these and related questions. This chapter is the successor to Jablin's chapter "Formal Organization Structure," in the 1987 *Handbook of Organizational Communication*. A relatively small amount of space will be devoted to reviewing new literature along the lines Jablin surveyed, because there have not been many significant new findings in these areas and most findings reinforce his earlier conclusions. Most significant advances since Jablin's (1987) review have focused on different questions and explanatory modes. The study of organizational structures has been decisively influenced by arguments for nontraditional analyses of organizational configuration, by perspectives such as structuration theory and postmodernism, and by issues such as the controversy about the relation between macro- and microlevel theories and the relevance of typological constructs.

This chapter will build from the old to the new, as follows: In the first section, we review literature, which takes the traditional approach of decomposing structure into a set of dimensions or variables. In this perspective, communication structure and processes are cast up as variables that are related to other (noncommunicational) structural variables. Inquiry guided by this approach results in lists of propositions and findings. Those aligned with this stream of research would view these findings as a treasure trove of specifics about the variables that determine communication patterns and effectiveness, integrated by the theoretic tradition that stems from Weber's. To skeptics, they represent a pile of atomistic and fragmented ideas in need of organization. In general, the studies reviewed in this section assume, more or less consistently, the "container" metaphor, treating structure as prior to and different in kind from communication process (Axley, 1984).

The second section reviews a stream of research designed to unify these clusters of atomistic findings by offering configurational views of structure. The configurational approach defines organizational types that are composed of specific combinations of structural features. These types are wholes, and communication structures and processes are an integral part of each configuration. As a result, the configurational approach clarifies the relationship of communication to the other structural features and accords communication a more important place in organizational structure than does the traditional approach. Indeed, some types may be distinguished primarily on the basis of the communication that occurs within them. Configurational approaches also typically are concerned with how organizations evolve over time and in response to changes in their environments, and with how they develop from one type into another. The configurational perspective offers, from one perspective, an integrated, often communication-centered account and explanation of organizations' structural features, processes, overall character, and evolution. A more skeptical audience would challenge the mix of metaphors used to achieve this integration, noting the frequency of references to reified structure.

The third section of this review concentrates on approaches, which attempt to redefine organizational structure and its constitution in communicative terms or to replace reified-structure terms with communicative ones. We review theories and research that either (a) construe traditional structural dimensions in less reified communicative terms, (b) examine how information technology functionally displaces traditional structural options, (c) relate microlevel analyses to macrolevel structural categories, or (d) reanalyze in communication terms the traditional concept of structure itself. From one perspective, these approaches have the advantage of putting communication in the forefront and of emphasizing communication as the foundation of organizational structure. Traditionalists might argue, however, that they overemphasize process and interaction, treating organizations as fleeting and insubstantial and denying the very real material and institutionally sedimented specificity of organizations—a problem which many of these approaches themselves recognize and try to cope with.

We mean to convey a sense of progression from the first to the third approach to organizational structure. However, it is important to note that no historical progression is implied. Research on all three approaches continues to the present, and findings from one stream of research can be applied in the others.

TRADITIONAL DIMENSIONS OF STRUCTURE

The idea of organizational structure has traditionally been elaborated using concepts articulated by early formal theorists of administration: the overall organizational pattern, including the differentiation of work into distinct assignments or specialties and functional subunits and the hierarchical embedding of managers and subunits; formalization; and centralization. These characteristics are usually interpreted as properties of the whole organizational system, though they may also be applied to distinct subunits. Jablin (1987) has reviewed the empirical literature exploring the relations of these properties to organizational communication processes in the first edition of this handbook, and we will supplement his chapter with a discussion of research since his review.

The majority of research on organizational structure follows a pattern traced in the work of Weber and Taylor, and crystallized by Burns and Stalker. It presents structural properties such as differentiation, centralization, and formalization as elements of a bureaucratic or mechanistic style of organizing, opposed to a contrary, organismic style (Burns & Stalker, 1961). In the welter of theoretical argument and research findings, the major theme is that mechanistic elements involve more control over worker behavior and less flexibility than do organic structures. These consequences result partly from restricting and channeling internal organizational communication. Indeed, formal structures serve as a substitute for communication in organizations by providing the coordination that is otherwise achieved through communicating (McPhee, 1985; Perrow, 1986).

Organizational Pattern

This section will review literature concerning a variety of properties, which Jablin (1987) previously reviewed under the headings of "Configuration" and "Complexity." However, we use the term *configuration* in a different way in the next main section, so we will use the term *pattern* in this section. The properties discussed in this section describe the material "shape" of the organization's mandated relations of people and practices. The various constructs have common roots in scientific management theories, but are independent enough to stimulate their own autonomous research traditions.

Horizontal differentiation. This facet of organization, often called "division of labor," not only describes the organization, it also creates the problem for which organizational structure is the answer. Increasing differentiation means that work is divided up into ever-smaller sets of operations/skills and that each set of skills—job or occupation, of individual or work group—is more clearly and rigidly distinguished from others. The push toward greater differentiation was justified by advocates of scientific management as rational and necessary to the growth of knowledge about and control over work. More recently, the communication, cooperation, and conflict resolution problems created by rigid differentiation have been emphasized, and the "segmental" ideal has lost favor (Kanter, 1983; Mintzberg, 1989). The emphasis on "integration" (Lawrence & Lorsch, 1967) has been supplanted by an emphasis on overall and shared responsibility, especially in the popular literature (Peters & Waterman, 1982). In contrast, the argument by Karl Weick for loose coupling (the property of having fairly autonomous parts) and requisite variety (the requirement of having parts varied enough to respond appropriately to different parts of the environment) (1979; cf. Orton & Weick, 1990) seems to indicate that differentiation may have positive effects and be necessary for organizational adaptability.

Some studies on differentiation and organizational communication have supported the view that differentiation produces problems. Smith, Grimm, Gannon, and Chen (1991) found that complexity (which they viewed as an information-processing variable) deterred responses to external strategic initiatives among interdependent units. Shrader, Lincoln, and Hoffman (1989) found that differentiation led to more clustering and less density and reciprocity in interorganizational networks, resulting in greater fragmentation into isolated cliques. Souder and Moenaert (1992) argued that interfunctional convergence (which indicates lower differentiation) aids in uncertainty reduction and information transfer during innovation. A common idea across these studies is that differentiation blocks proactive, innovative cooperation among distinct units.

Contrariwise, several authors found evidence for a less negative view of differentiation. Miller, Droje, and Toulouse (1988) found that differentiation of special control and liaison units increased the rationality of and interaction about strategy decisions. Alter (1990) found that functional differentiation among organizations in a network reduced conflict. Finally, Colling and Fermer (1992) uncovered several dramatically different models of decision making as differentiation among parties increased; these were not necessarily inferior to more integrative, rational models of decision making, and may be better adapted to the contingencies of highly differentiated organizations. The common benefit of differentiation in these studies seems to be coordinated action rooted in complementarity, the classic advantage touted for differentiation. The problem of optimizing the trade-off of differentiated diversity and unity seems to remain as pressing for organizations as for society.

Size. The presumption among theorists is that greater organizational size leads to more mechanistic organization, as the coordination burden overwhelms informal organizing processes. In his original review, Jablin (1987) focused on the question of whether size negatively affected organizational communication amount and quality. Succeeding research has also yielded mixed results, but has focused on breadth of participation and nature of decision making. On the one hand, increasing size has been found to result in greater and broader decision participation (Connor, 1992) and more comprehensiveness in decision making—more breadth in number of alternatives scanned, as well as more employees involved in the decision (Smith et al., 1991). On the other hand, Smeltzer and Fann (1989) found size leading to some restrictions on decision-making breadth. They found managers from large companies to be quite similar to ones from small companies in concern about communication. However, in comparison with small companies, large-company managers were more oriented to internal communication with subordinates and within the formal hierarchy, more concerned with such functions as monitoring and exchanging routine information, and less concerned with external communication and organizational politics. These studies point to mixed benefits of communication in larger organizations.

Vertical hierarchy. Jablin's (1987) review summarized two types of studies related to hierarchy: Some focused on the impacts of individual hierarchical level (e.g., superior-subordinate communication) while others concentrated on vertical complexity as a property of the organizational system as a whole. Since his review, nearly all the relevant literature falls in the first type.

Several studies have shown variations in communication behavior by hierarchical level. Level was positively related to time spent communicating (but not to reported autonomy) in research reported by Yammarino and Naughton (1988). MacLeod, Scriven, and Wayne (1992) similarly found that hierarchical level raised the frequency of oral communication episodes. Their research also revealed complex effects of level on the location where interaction occurred, the medium involved, and for external contacts, the functional category of the contact. They also found that level sometimes interacted with group size, with middle-level females involved especially often in small-group meetings and in formally scheduled meetings (perhaps to function as token members). In research with a result partially contrary to this pattern of level-interaction relationships, Zenger and Lawrence (1989) found that level was positively related to amount of technical communication outside, but not inside, an electronics firm. Rice and associates reported mixed results concerning the influence of level on

adoption (but not use) of computer-mediated communication, with Rice, Chang, and Torobin (1992) supporting a relationship, but not Rice and Shook (1990).

Level also influences problem-solving communication, with higher levels tending toward more ad hoc and innovative solution processes. Barnard (1991) found that higher-level employees exhibited greater reliance on peers for advice than did those at lower levels. Stevenson and Gilly (1991) also report that when managers (as opposed to nonmanagers) refer problem cases to other parts of an organizational network, they pass the problem case less often to the person formally assigned to deal with it, and more often to an acquaintance of theirs, perhaps because they see the problem as nonroutine and needing special attention.

Several studies were concerned with the effects of level on communicative influence. Brass and Burkhardt (1993) found that the higher the level, the greater the use of influence styles of assertiveness and exchange-offering, but not of ingratiation or rationality. In a study that limited communication to one-way choice proposals, Driskell and Salas (1991) found that status and stress level related to response to influence, with higher status leading to reduced openness to influence while higher stress increased influence acceptance. Ragins and Cotton (1991) found that higher level led to more influence in the special case of gaining a mentor. So as we would expect, level in the formal hierarchy does covary with various sorts of communicative influence.

Some research also suggests that differences in perspective about communication exist across hierarchical levels. For instance, Clampitt and Downs (1993) found that the perception that corporate information has an impact on productivity was widespread among managers, and especially executives, but not regular employees (but all levels agreed that feedback from one's boss affected productivity). In a study by Thomas, Shankster, and Mathieu (1994), rank affected the likelihood that one will view a problem as political, with higher ranks seeing things as less political. Finally, McCauley, Ruderman, Ohlcott, and Morrow (1994) found a relationship of rank to the challenges newcomers see in their jobs (including weak increases for such communication-related challenges as influencing without authority and proving oneself, and a moderate effect for developing new directions).

Overall, this research is compatible with a view of the upper strata of organizations as relatively organic. Insofar as high-level managers use face-to-face communication to solve nonroutine problems and make (verbally expressed) policies, their communication behaviors would exhibit the differences suggested by these studies.

Formalization

Formalization is typically defined as the extent to which rules and procedures mandated for work are explicitly stated, usually in writing and/or a ceremonial announcement. The construct obviously is linked to Weber's (1946) characterization of bureaucracy as involving processes including communication that proceed "according to calculable rules" (p. 215) One theoretical presumption is that inflexible rules can lead to ineffectiveness. Olson (1995) illustrates this effect in a study of a public clinic where record-keeping rules forced structured interviews that were very effective for collecting information, but too inflexible to optimally serve clients. Another theoretical presumption is that appropriate rules, systematically followed, can enhance the systematic rationality of decisions. This claim received some recent research support, as Miller (1987) and Miller et al. (1988) found that the perceived rationality of strategic decision making was associated with formal controls over the decision process. Miller (1987) advanced the construct of "formal integration," referring to specific provision for information-gathering specialists and liaisons, as a structural dimension with direct communicative implications that increased perceived rationality of decision making.

Souder and Moenaert (1992) argued that formalization is valuable in innovation if preceded by effective uncertainty-reducing procedures in planning. Gilsdorf (1992) showed a beneficial side of formalization in discussing evidence for the need for written corporate policies governing communication of sensitive information, crisis communication, and communication of corporate values, among other things.

As a defining property of bureaucracy, formalization is also theoretically opposed to organicity (ongoing dynamic adaptiveness through mutual adjustment). This negative relationship was supported by the research of Shrader et al. (1989), who found that formalization led to reduced interorganizational network organicity, especially for a network of social service client referrals. In contrast, Hoffman, Stearns, and Shrader (1990) found formalization leading to higher network centrality.

Finally, the use of formalization as a means for rational control is widely discussed in the literature. Its general development as a control instrumentality was clearly presented by Beniger (1986), who argued that formalization along with other means of control were invented to allow the growing complexity and the growing geographic spread of corporate operations. In another intensive historical survey, Yates (1989) concentrated on the development of early-19th-century communication technologies, media, and forms conducive to such a mode of control. Her detailed analyses displayed the concern for corporation-wide coordination and control that led corporate executives to fight for widespread use of general orders, procedure manuals, and performance graphs as formal communication vehicles. These justly praised books were major contributions to our understanding of evolving corporate communication modes.

Centralization

The interesting question about the centralization/decentralization dimension is not what communication variables it influences, but what it is itself and what its broader implications are for communication. What exactly is centralization? Mintzberg (1979) argues that complete centralization, which grants all decisions to the top decision maker, can be defined unambiguously. However, in cases where power is ceded to lower levels, many different types of decentralization are possible. Mintzberg distinguishes several different types of decentralization, including (1) vertical decentralization, dispersal of formal power down the chain of authority; (2) horizontal decentralization, dispersal of power to nonmanagers who are near the same level as the managers; and (3) geographical dispersion of the organization. Moreover, decentralization may be done selectively, to some parts of the organization rather than others, and some types of decisions can be centralized while others are decentralized.

Mintzberg defined five generic parts of the organization in which power may be vested: strategic apex, middle management, operating core, support staff, and technostructure. Which part or parts become more powerful and significant determines the nature of organizational structures with very different organizational consequences. Mintzberg's predictions regarding the outcomes of decentralization are not as straightforward as the studies summarized below imply. For example, the configuration that involves most power for the "ordinary worker," the *professional bureaucracy,* also leads to high worker autonomy and a consequent lack of cohesion, leading in turn to destructive mobilization of interest groups during political conflicts.

As for centralization's effects, recent research supports the pattern found by Jablin (1987): Decentralization is accompanied by increased communication on many dimensions. The first dimension is raw amount of communication; for instance, Miller (1987) found decentralization of strategic decision making to lead to more interaction (along with a greater tendency toward risk taking, and somewhat more future orientation, though not to greater rationality of decisions). Supporting

this relationship, Yammarino and Naughton (1988) reported that increased autonomy was accompanied by reports of more time spent communicating. In addition, according to Pearson (1992), decentralization through autonomous work groups led to growing feedback.

This finding touches on a second group of dimensions—communication effectiveness—that are enhanced by reduced centralization. For instance, Macey, Peterson, and Norton (1989) revealed that a participation program led to increased influence by members, group cohesiveness, organizational involvement, and clarity of decision making. Managerial consideration and role clarification covaried weakly with a second-order factor involving decentralized decision making and autonomy, in a study by Evans and Fischer (1992). Finally, Trombetta and Rogers (1988) found that participation led to communicative openness and adequacy (though not commitment).

Openness was explored in a series of publications by Krone (1992, 1994, cf. 1986), focused on the use of open versus manipulative upward persuasive strategies. Following the suggestion of Hage and Aiken (1967), Krone used two measures of (de)centralization, autonomous control over own work and participation in broader decisions. Participation led to choice of more open communication and empathic influence strategies, with the latter involving appeal to commonalities and values important to the manager. Both participation and autonomy predicted the likelihood of attempting upward influence, the perceived likelihood of success, and the level of upward trust. Higher values of both measures of centralization also led to higher perceived quality of leader-member exchange (LMX). Krone's use of two conceptually and empirically distinct indicators of centralization illustrates the problem of polysemy facing the concept.

To sum up, the literature on centralization suffers from two important problems. First, (de)centralization is used in many different ways, which apply to quite different organizational communication processes. Horizontal decentralization requires communication across professional boundaries, which presents one set of problems and requires specific types of communication devices, such as integrating managers and task forces. Vertical decentralization confronts the organization with the need to maintain communication through multiple layers, with the problems of distortion and control loss through vertical communication (e.g., Conrad & Poole, 1998), which require a different set of measures such as managerial communication programs and decision support systems. Second, different studies, which ostensibly focus on the same variable, (de)centralization, may apply to quite different organizational levels or subsystems and yield quite different effects. What seems to be a single variable is really a family of quite diverse concepts. When we take this into account, apparent inconsistencies in findings may evaporate, and apparent consistencies may prove puzzling.

In general, participation and decentralization as systemic organizational properties should be distinguished from the way organizational members perceive these properties. Measures such as perceived autonomy and decision participation do not tell us much about overall organizational structure, but rather tell us about immediate experiences of members. These experiences probably depend more on immediate supervisory and coworker behavior than anything else and have little reference to structural features in distant parts of the organization. Even high values of perceived participation may be invalid structural indicators, if the mass of workers is unaware of important decisions or if organizational structures and processes leave workers uninterested in issues that otherwise would draw their concern (Kanter, 1977).

Concluding Comments

One problem with breaking structure down into numerous dimensions is that possible structures increase exponentially with each new dimension considered. This proliferation makes predictions about communication problematic. Moreover, it runs counter to experience and research, which implies that there are a relatively small number of types of organizations, or at least not an infinitude of different varieties. To capture covariations among dimensions and to distill the unique character of organizations, researchers have attempted to define organizational types, reflected in structural configurations. As we will see, configurations are important because communication can be understood within an organized frame rather than within the relationship-by-relationship array resulting from the dimensional approach.

ORGANIZATIONAL CONFIGURATIONS

The configurational view of structure can be traced back to Weber's concept of bureaucracy, and perhaps even to Aristotle's analysis of types of government. A number of authors have recently revived configurational thinking with vigorous and intriguing arguments (McKelvey, 1982; Miller, 1990; Mintzberg, 1979, 1989). Some authors argue for systems of configurations, and such theories shall be our primary concern. Other scholars have advanced very interesting cases for new configurations, with such names as the "learning organization," the "postbureaucratic organization," or "excellent organizations." One advantage of the configurational approach for organizational communication research is that it offers a more holistic conception of structure that can highlight communicative implications better than reductionist arguments that dissolve the organization into a number of dimensions, most of which have limited relevance to communication per se. Communication is part and parcel of many configuration concepts and permeates the organization when it is considered as a whole. In this section, we review the nature of the configurational approach along with some key examples.

There is some disagreement about the nature of configurational constructs. Perhaps the most common view is that a configuration is a specific set of values on multiple dimensions that has special descriptive or other utility (Lammers, 1988; McKelvey, 1982; Stinchcombe, 1968). This nominalist view contrasts with two others: (1) the view of organizational types as generated and rendered consistent by an underlying (metaphorically genetic) determining characteristic or causal process, and (2) the view of organizational types as comprised by similarities in causes or effects. So one might call a cluster of organizations "adhocratic" because they happen to share certain features, or because they have features determined by the same underlying causes, or because they are similar in origin and the kind of "niche" they occupy in the organizational ecosystem.

A second difference in the literature concerns the treatment of types as "real" versus "ideal." On the one hand, types can be viewed as empirical existents, defined by a combination of values on empirically measurable dimensions. On the other hand, they can be viewed as ideal types, never realized in practice but representing idealizations that are useful for theoretical and prescriptive purposes. Finally, there is disagreement in the literature over the question of generality: Is a configuration always a description of units of only one sort (organizations, say, or work groups), or can the same typal description apply in numerous ways—to different levels of analysis, to parts of organizations rather than the whole, or as styles/features—clusters that can overlay or apply in combination to a single organization?

A resolution of the first issue has the potential to resolve the others: If a type or configuration has an underlying source or logic, that source or logic will determine whether the type should be treated as real or ideal, and whether it applies at multiple levels and in hybrids. The connection among these three aspects—the logic, the array of traits, and the range/realism of application—is reflected in the requirements for configurational theory.

Construction of Configurational Theories

Scholars often distinguish between typologies and taxonomies; the former begin with theoretical analysis to generate ideal configuration-descriptions, while the latter seek empirical clusters to infer types. Both approaches are used to construct configurational theories, with Mintzberg (1979) exemplifying the typological approach and McKelvey (1982) the taxonomical. Hence, there is no optimal sequence of steps for constructing typological theories; scholars can start with data that lead to theory or vice versa. Rather than itemize steps for the construction of configurational theories, we list some necessary tasks, as follows:

1. Identify structural (and other) variables, characteristics, or elements, which can be used to describe the surface structure of the configuration. These traits include communication features such as the properties of channels and networks, structurally sedimented dimensions of communication climate, and so on.

2. Determine the specific combinations of values on variables, characteristics, or elements belonging to each configuration.

3. Determine the situations or contexts in which the various configurations are possible, likely, or appropriate.

4. Determine the consequences of each configuration in the range of contexts in which it might appear. As contingency theorists would argue, such consequences often depend on the information-processing and decision-making constraints and supports involved in the configuration.

5. Discover or work out a logic underlying the configurations and distinguishing them—a dynamic, imperative, or process sufficient to unify various structural elements into coherent ensembles and to account for their differences. As in the first and fourth tasks above, this procedure typically shows how communication assumptions are intrinsic to organizational structural theory—the bind-

ing logic of a configuration is often a logic of information processing, coordination, control, or some other communication process (McPhee, 1985).

6. Determine the ways in which configurations might be combined or partially realized within a particular organization. Clear types may not always be apparent in specific cases.

7. Determine the principles of generation, deviation, and/or transformation of organizations from one configuration, perhaps to another. Again, communicative considerations may lead to such changes.

8. Find evidence of the consistency or mutual affinity of the combination of elements, the presence and operation of the underlying logic, and/or the evolution of one configuration into others.

Configurational approaches are not commonly employed in organizational communication research, in part because organizational communication researchers have focused mostly on dyadic or group communication and avoided considering larger units of analysis. As we will argue, we believe that the development of configurational typologies is a promising direction for understanding the relation of communication and structure. This contention can be illustrated by considering a prominent example of configurational theory.

Mintzberg's Configurational Array

Henry Mintzberg (1979, 1983a, 1983b, 1989) has developed an especially influential and appealing typological theory over the past 20 years. It has special relevance to organizational communication scholarship because of the ubiquity of communication processes and ideas in the theory.

Mintzberg's theory begins with the distinction among five coordination mechanisms —direct supervision, standardization of work processes, of outputs, and of skills, and mutual adjustment—to which standardization of

norms, plus politics (an anticoordination process) were later added. Such mechanisms are important because they fulfill a necessary and formative prerequisite for any organization, making the work of the various employees related and "organized."

Mintzberg also noted that various parts of the organization, empowered by specific coordination mechanisms, exerted pressure on or "pulled" the organization to emphasize those mechanisms. The mechanism plus the power wielded by one part of the organization provided the logic that Mintzberg used to deduce the characteristics of and contingencies that determined his seven fundamental configurations. In 1989, these types were labeled the *entrepreneurial, machine, professional, diversified, innovative, missionary,* and *political* forms. Many of Mintzberg's configurations are similar to those in earlier typologies: The machine form, for instance, is very similar to Burns and Stalker's mechanistic type and Perrow's engineering type (Lammers, 1988). One of the strengths of Mintzberg's theory is its extensive elaboration: He identifies nine structural dimensions (called "design parameters") and five contingency dimensions, which vary across the configurations, and he is able to display striking and insightful relations between ideas explicit or implicit in the literature about these dimensions and the distinctions on which his typology rests. Among the design parameters are several that reflect centralization and formalization. Mintzberg argues that these parameters, like the ones more obviously reflecting communication processes, are best explained either by the requirements of organizational work patterns and coordination (the coordination mechanisms) or by a process of overall adjustment consistent with one of his configurations. In short, his theory gives a deep account of, for example, why decentralization is related to increased vertical communication.

Communication figures prominently in Mintzberg's theory. It is the substance of two of his coordinating mechanisms, mutual adjustment and direct supervision, and it is implicitly required by the others as well. Two of his design parameters are liaison devices (ways to achieve coordination through direct or facilitated communication) and planning/control systems (featuring feedback and plan-implementation interactions); others involve training and indoctrination, decentralization through delegation and multilevel decision making, and other processes in which communication plays an important part. Formalization and other structural dimensions with communication significance (see the preceding and especially the next main sections) are also implicated in a number of design parameters. Even the "pulls" exerted by different parts of the organization surface as logics of organizational argument and decision making (McPhee, 1988)

In his 1989 book, Mintzberg gives explicit and innovative attention to the issue of overlapping configurations, as well as to change among configurations. He mentions a number of different ways configurations can overlap or be combined; he also mentions important issues that arise in these hybrid forms and notes that they are difficult to handle. For instance, "contradiction" is a mode of integration where two mechanisms are both needed in the organization, but they tend to develop a problematic dialectical opposition. He also introduces a "life-cycle model" of organizational transformation that indicates the most likely changes from one configuration to another, as well as forces leading to such changes.

Despite its influence, Mintzberg's theory has been directly tested only once, by Doty, Glick, and Huber (1993). Their test finds little support for the theory; only about 25% of their organizations fit Mintzberg's descriptions well (in his 1989 book, Mintzberg mentions that the student groups he assigns to study organizations find fit in about half the cases). Doty et al. mention several problems with the theoretical validity of their test, especially that it includes only five of Mintzberg's configurations; in addition, we note that they give no special weight to coordinating mechanisms, treat hybrids in ways not strictly compatible with Mintzberg's analysis, and rely

only on CEO perceptions as data. Despite these possible problems with the study, the lack of convincing support for the theory's central empirical claims is frustrating, given its interpretive appeal and ability to reconcile a large amount of prior research.

Advantages of Configurational Theories

Why is the configurational approach important? We can discern at least five reasons. First, configurational theories avoid the problems of ambiguity raised in the above discussion of centralization, since specific structural features are always embedded in a more multidimensional and holistic view of the organizational system. Configurations automatically supply a context for particular constructs.

Second, such theories simplify complex interrelations of multiple variables to a few clearer and more easily exemplified gestalts that are easy to remember and use in analysis. So configurational theories are valuable heuristically—especially compared to the buzzing, booming confusion of reality—even if they are not wholly consistent with empirical situations (Miller & Mintzberg, 1983; Mintzberg, 1979).

Third, communication is an integral part of configurational theories. The traditional dimensional approach defines communication in terms of separate constructs that may or may not be included in a given proposition or theory (e.g., the more levels in a hierarchy, the greater the distortion due to transmission). However, a configurational theory defines organizations as whole types, and communication is a critical aspect of each type, an inherent part of its description. So the organic organization not only implies decentralization but also dense, shifting communication networks and greater amounts of informal communication. Moreover, some types are defined primarily in terms of their communication structures and processes.

Fourth, theorizing about configurations tends to lead to integrative formulations. To develop a configurational theory, researchers must focus on issues such as the systematic interconnectedness of organizational parts or dimensions; the multiple causal directions linking structure, strategy, and environment (Child, 1972); or the multiple consequences of a single organizational determinant such as coordination mechanism (Mintzberg, 1979). Configurational thinking requires researchers to capture and summarize the insights of varied theories and research in a common frame that explains or interprets them in common terms. For example, Mintzberg's (1979) theory uses a highly systematic and insightful reading of a vast array of research literature to support his configurational theory, which offers an integrative explanation of how various configurations evolve into each other. His view is architectonic, in the sense used by Kant (1970)—it organizes the major ideas and issues of organizational theory.

Finally, configurational theories can be tested through the evaluation of three types of hypotheses. The first is a "consistency" hypothesis: that the system characteristics and values for each configuration, including communication characteristics, "belong together." This hypothesis often reduces to the claim that real organizations approximate the types or a space determined by them. For instance, as Doty and Glick (1994) argue, configurational theories may imply a clustering of organizations around specific (ideal-typic) profiles of values. Researchers can test whether the average observed distance from organizations to the closest configuration was significantly less than the average distance for randomly distributed organizations (though this is not a test employed by Doty et al., 1993). As another example, Burns and Stalker's (1961) claim that organizations are arrayed along a continuum between extremely bureaucratic and extremely organismic could be tested as the hypothesis that their structure of variables is unidimensional (cf. Hage, 1965; also Ostroff & Schmitt, 1993). This sort of hypothesis might be of special interest to communication researchers because communication either might exhibit ideal-typic consistency

with other traits (mechanistic communication for a mechanistic organization), or it might function as a supplement compensating for the weaknesses of the type (e.g., Barker, 1993, describes group discipline as compensating for a "loose" democratic structure).

The second type of hypothesis posited by contingency theory revolves around claims about the processes that generate certain configurations. For instance, DiMaggio and Powell (1983) discussed the pressures and advantages that motivate structural change to resemble dominant configurations within specific industries. Probably the most popular variant of configuration-explaining theory is a "fit" hypothesis: the claim that organizations facing specific environmental or other contingencies are likely to resemble a type that is especially called for by those contingencies. For instance, Doty et al. (1993) use an array of contingencies to predict which of Mintzberg's configurations their organizations would resemble, then assessed the correctness of these predictions. Since communication processes would be involved in strategic choice about the environment and the structure (Child, 1972), communication research would be vital to the establishment of such hypotheses.

The third type of hypothesis is the prediction of certain consequences such as effectiveness or survival as results of consistently resembling a configuration. For example, Doty and his colleagues tested relations between similarity to an ideal type and other variables such as effectiveness. Of course, to motivate acceptance of a configurational theory the hypotheses suggested above must accumulate enough support to be encouraging.

Problems With Configurational Theories

Configurational theorizing has a number of strengths, but these assets are complemented by some unique weaknesses. One problem stems from the lack of consensus on just what a configuration or type is. As a result there is no agreement on the necessary components of configurational theories. This issue makes it difficult for researchers to judge when a configurational theory is complete and satisfactory. Second, arriving at a typology may prematurely terminate efforts at explanation. Once researchers have a clear, concrete, well-labeled configuration, there is a temptation to assume that the task of theorizing is finished (Reynolds, 1971). Therefore researchers do not take things further to provide explanation of the origin of the configurational forms and the differences among them, or the whole range of processes producing consistency and fit. Configurational theories can deter the development of process theories, which might more fully reveal the determining or constitutive role of communication.

Third, most configurational theories are what Althusser (1972) called "expressive totalities"—they are supposed to be consistent because each part reflects the underlying logic of the whole. But a good theory would question: Isn't this total consistency too strong—if every quality of an organization was "bureaucratic," might that not result in excessive rigidity that counteracts the useful features of the type? A better configuration might balance off conflicting logics, or list the necessary conditions for success and make sure that the configuration meets them. A fourth problem is that configurations may be culture bound, even if they seem universal; Meyer (1995), for example, mentions how much better the concept of bureaucracy worked in Germany than in America. Finally, there is always the danger that theorists will react to deviations from a type by constantly adding new types. This multiplication may complicate the theory until it is unworkable.

New Organizational Configurations

In recent years, a number of new organizational forms have been identified, which nonetheless seem fundamentally different and important enough to avoid the dangers just mentioned. They have been given diverse names, such as the "dynamic network" (Miles & Snow, 1986), the "shamrock" (Handy, 1989), the "postbureaucratic organization" (Heckscher, 1994), and the "virtual organization" (Davidow & Malone, 1992; Lucas, 1996; Mowshowitz, 1994). They are described as configurations, but they seem irreducible to any of the standard configurations identified by Mintzberg or others. The argument is often made that new forms are motivated by a fundamental change in economics and society and that they are replacing "outmoded," older forms. However, some analyses have suggested that so-called new forms have actually been around for hundreds of years, but have only recently garnered the interest of a wide group of scholars and analysts (Lammers, 1988; Winter & Taylor, 1996). Several of these new forms may well be criticized on the grounds that they needlessly multiply the number of configurations, thus leading to unwieldy and unworkable theories.

These new configurations are particularly interesting because of their dependence on communication. Moreover, as we will note later, the increasing prominence of new (or previously marginalized) forms may signal a changing relationship between communication and organizational structure. We can review only a selection of forms and issues surrounding them here.

Drivers of New Organizational Forms

A common analysis is that new organizational forms have been evolving at an increasingly rapid rate due to several important changes in the organizational environment (see, e.g., Drucker, 1994; Huber, 1984). The trend toward global economic and social integration has engendered increased competition for both private and public organizations. Scholars have observed the emergence of "hypercompetition" in industry sectors such as health care and consumer products (Ilinitch, D'Aveni, & Lewin, 1996). Hypercompetition is characterized by increasingly fierce competition among organizations (even those allied in joint ventures and traditionally stable markets) and organizational strategies that attempt to redefine the "rules" of competition through the development of new products and delivery modes to gain advantage.

A second driver is the evolution of most economically advanced countries into "knowledge societies" (Drucker, 1994). In knowledge societies, the most important work involves the generation and application of abstract knowledge, such as scientific theory or law. Knowledge work organizes and reorganizes other types of work. It evolves as research and scholarship develop improved understanding of the natural and social worlds. And with over 90% of the scientists who have ever lived currently working, the rate of change in knowledge is increasing rapidly (Drucker, 1994).

The third driver is the emergence of information technology, the key enabler of new organizational forms. This communication-centered technology has enjoyed unprecedented growth, driven mostly by the rapid decrease in cost for functionality. Benjamin and Scott-Morton (1988) report that while traditional production technologies showed a 170% improvement in the ratio of capital to labor prices over the 30-year period 1950-1980, information technology had a 2500% improvement in the capital/labor price ratio over the same period. This cost advantage of technology over labor has resulted in rapid implementation of information technologies, resulting in organizational restructuring and displacement of workers.

These forces have created several new imperatives for organizations. First, the most important resource organizations now have is their members' knowledge and skills, and organizations must preserve this knowledge and develop it further. Member competence, more than any physical plant or information system, is the key to being able to adapt to changing circumstances and to take advantage of scientific and technological advances. These features place an imperative on the organization to structure itself so that it can harness member competencies, develop them further, and keep members with critical competencies committed. Traditional organizational structures, based on division of labor, have paid remarkably little attention to capturing and exploiting the organization's knowledge base. For both new and traditional forms, this imperative is now a critical issue.

Another imperative that guides the new forms is the need to satisfy conflicting demands imposed by the "new order." Organizations must simultaneously respond to the need for flexibility, to find ways to address mounting exigencies and the need for control, to implement effectively the measures devised and to maintain coordinated action. Closely related is the need to institutionalize change and the capacity for evolutionary reorientation, which requires the organization to find a way of balancing stability and change. Organizations must also emphasize speed of product development and time to market, while at the same time maintaining high quality. The need to cope with these and other conflicting demands forces organizations to adopt forms that appear to be unusual hybrids of more traditional structures or that resemble networks and markets more than hierarchies.

Characteristics of New Forms

New forms are constituted by one or more of the following characteristics (Poole, 1999):

1. Use of information technology to integrate across organizational functions, to reengineer production and service processes, and to create tighter interdependence among activities. These characteristics speed up production and response time and enable the organization to adapt to customer needs and environmental demands in highly specific ways.

2. Flexible, modular organizational structures that can be readily reconfigured as new

projects, demands, or problems arise. These structures may be composed of units of a single larger organization, or they may be different organizations joined by brokers or through various types of interorganizational alliances. The accounting and information systems play important roles in the creation and maintenance of flexible structures, substituting for traditional hierarchical control (Child, 1987).

3. Use of information technology to coordinate geographically dispersed units and members. In the extreme case, there may be a virtual organization, whose dispersed members are linked primarily through telecommunications and information technology.

4. Team-based work organization, which emphasizes autonomy and self-management. This system is generally combined with high emphasis on quality and continuous improvement.

5. Relatively flat hierarchies and reliance on horizontal coordination among units and personnel. Power may be much more dispersed in such organizational arrangements.

6. Use of intra- and interorganizational markets to mediate transactions such as the assignment and hiring of personnel for projects and the formation of interorganizational networks. The market mechanism is used as an alternative to hierarchy when many comparable individual units or actors are involved.

These features include the modal qualities found in a range of descriptions of new organizations (Child, 1987; Eccles & Crane, 1987; Hammer & Champy, 1993; Heckscher, 1994; Jarvenppa & Ives, 1994; Konsynski & Sviokla, 1994; Lucas & Baroudi, 1994; Nohria & Berkley, 1994; Powell, 1990; Scott-Morton, 1991), though not every new organization embodies all six. To illustrate how these characteristics fit together, we will now turn to descriptions of two of the most common new configurations, the network organization and the virtual organization.

Variants of New Forms

The *network organization* refers not to a single formal organization but to a more or less formal relationship among several different organizations (Powell, 1990; for reviews, see Grandori & Soda, 1995). Baker (1992) writes:

> A network organization is characterized by integration across formal boundaries of multiple types of socially important relations. Such "thick" network organizations are integrated over many types of communication and other relationships—strong and weak task-related communication, informal socializing, advice-giving and advice-getting, and so on. (p. 400)

The model for these organizations is drawn from social network theory (Monge & Contractor, Chapter 12, this volume; cf. Johnson, 1993). Several different types of network organizations can be distinguished. In some cases, a group of highly independent organizations takes on differentiated roles within an interdependent network organized by a broker (Miles & Snow, 1986). Miles and Snow referred to these organizations as "dynamic networks" because their component organizations were assembled and disassembled to meet specific needs for a limited period of time. Dynamic networks have long been used in industries such as construction, where contractors assemble various building functions from smaller, specialized firms. Most scholars considered such organizations marginal or unusual until recently, when this form spread through sectors traditionally dominated by integrated organizations. Network organizations may also be more permanently organized around one or more major firms, with the smaller organizations functioning as dependent satellites. One example of a satellite network is the agglomeration of large automobile manufacturers and their supplier networks. Another type of network organization evolves when firms enter into joint ventures or contract relationships (Ring & Van de Ven, 1994). The component organizations in such networks tend to have more equal power and status than those in dynamic networks or satellite networks.

Larson (1992) argues that network organizations are a distinctive configuration: "They are distinct from market or hierarchical arrangements in their heavy reliance on reciprocity, collaboration, complementary interdependence, a reputation and relationship basis for communication, and an informal climate oriented toward mutual gain" (p. 77). She joins a number of authors in pointing to trust and trust building as the fundamental necessity for network relationship growth and maintenance (Handy, 1989).

However, while trust is a foundation of some types of network organizations, it may also be supplemented by full disclosure information systems to sustain integration. A full disclosure information system includes an accounting information system and electronic communication systems (Child, 1987). The accounting information system is a set of open databases that shows participating units whether other units are meeting their responsibilities and contributing value to the organization, while the electronic communication system integrates workflow and coordinates activities.

A *virtual organization* is one that has no physical existence, but instead exists in whole or part across a computer network (Davidow & Malone, 1992; Lucas, 1996). What appears to be an integrated organization is in fact a virtual network comprised by a negotiated agreement among different organizations. Information technology and telecommunications enable these dispersed organizations to coordinate their activities and to maintain coherent work processes. Each part of the virtual organization is able to focus on its particular function. By staying small, the component organizations keep their costs for management and overhead down, enhancing efficiency. Smallness also makes communication easier within the components, opening them up for fast development and testing of new ideas.

Virtual organizations generally evolve gradually, as organizations move one function, such as order handling, to an outside source that manages it using information technology. Hence, many organizations are at least partly "virtual." However, most descriptions of virtual organizations go much further, and depict them as primarily linked by information technology and highly flexible in joining different units into the working whole. As we will see below, taken to its extreme, the virtual organization implies a whole new logic of organizational design.

Mowshowitz (1994, 1997) gives a thoroughgoing definition of the virtual organization as one in which there are (a) multiple possible goals and requirements, (b) multiple structures and processes for achieving these goals and requirements, (c) the capacity to switch between different structures and processes as goals shift, and (d) the capacity to switch between different structures and processes for the same goal, as costs and benefits of the structures and processes shift. This definition of virtual organization implies extreme flexibility, because the switching is assumed to occur relatively rapidly, as it does in memory allocation in computers. The virtual organization takes design one step past traditional contingency theories: It posits that organizational structures not only change in response to different goals and requirements, but that there are multiple structural features that can be switched as the need arises. Of course, communication here is not merely a structural feature, but is basic to the switching process. It is unclear how many actual organizations could achieve this extreme degree of flexibility in practice. Mowshowitz cites global production organizations such as Shell and IBM as examples. Whether it is real or an ideal type, the virtual organization defined by Mowshowitz suggests a new logic of organizational design.

Implications of New Organizational Configurations

While the configurational view in general gives a more complete treatment of the structure-communication relationship than dimensional views, new organizational forms emphasize it still further. One interesting implication is that the organizing principle of the new forms is not the chain of command, but the network. New forms still have authority distributions, but higher authority is not logically associated with the "top" of the organization. In some cases, the broker or hub organization holds primary authority. In others, authority and power are distributed, with different parts of the network predominating at different contexts or times. In such configurations, power is influenced by network dynamics as well. For example, a network with many structural holes would be expected to have more dispersed power than one with few (see Monge & Contractor, this volume).

Second, structure and communication are more obviously related in new and looser configurations than traditional views of organizational structure allow. Sometimes communication requirements are the drivers of organizational structure, as when organizations form integrated engineering-production-marketing teams to handle product design to reduce reworking and redesign. In other cases, communication is driven by structural forces, as the traditional theories reviewed at the beginning of this chapter suggest. In the new forms, communication comes into the foreground as a major facet of structure rather than as a secondary variable that "comes with" or "is influenced by" structure. Studies of the new forms may have emphasized the communicative and coordinating functions of structure almost totally—the financial and external functions have received much less attention.

When communication was considered in traditional theories of structure, it was usually construed as information transmission. Discussions of new forms suggest that structures serve other communication-related functions in addition to information transfer, such as fostering trust and the creation and retention of knowledge. When trust is recognized as an essential underpinning of structure in the new configurations (Handy, 1989), then the role of structure in promoting (or hindering) the interactions that facilitate trust becomes important. When "knowledge management" requires structures that identify important knowledge, provide means for linking forms of knowledge, generate new knowledge, and retain valuable knowledge, it becomes apparent that "organizational cognition and learning" are more than information processing. Communication fostering organization-level learning must foster productive interactions among members that create higher-order learning and insight. When the dynamism of temporary, flexible forms puts jobs at risk and brings new opportunities to the best, structural designers must consider how to nurture valued employees. So some companies develop novel methods of reputational rating that gives employees credentials to move through their fluid, shifting unit compositions (Heckscher, 1994), while others try to develop egalitarian structures that make work meaningful and create a sense of shared ownership among employees. Theories of human relations and organizational culture have long emphasized these aspects of communication, but structural theories have only recently come to see them as important.

The importance of information technology in many new organizational forms has made it easier for theorists to acknowledge the communication-structure relationship. In a sense, information technology provides a material embodiment of communication processes that may have seemed too transitory and ephemeral to consider as structural variables in earlier research. Information technology also makes communication a commodity that can be stored, operated on, manipulated, and transferred. Somewhat paradoxically, this works against viewing communication as more than information transfer. So there are trends in studies of new forms that both promote and inhibit moving beyond the informational view of communication.

A final important implication of new configurations is the high emphasis they place on integration. With such fluid, unmappable forms, it is critical to have strong integration mechanisms. So methods of integration ranging from linking roles to teams to advanced information technology are crucial in new organizations, as well as in older communication-intensive forms such as the matrix and the adhocracy (see Conrad & Poole, 1998, chap. 5, for a review of integration forms). Cushman and King (1993, 1995) have described *high-speed management* as one logic of organizing that amalgamates aspects of the technological basis for new forms mentioned above, with a variety of other communication and governance features. The unifying logic of high-speed management is the contribution of the various design choices to integrate the organization to achieve proactivity in innovation, speed of diagnosis and response, mutually beneficial cooperation with complementary organizations, and constant adaptation to excellent standards.

Conclusion

It is unclear at this point in time how many of the "new forms" will stand the test of time. On further analysis, some may be reducible to previously defined forms. Others may well be unstable transitional forms. However, the issues raised by the new forms promise to redefine how the structure-communication relationship is conceptualized.

In this section, we have reviewed some of the literature on organizational configurations and its relationship to organizational communication. We believe this second current of literature has some unique strengths that organizational communication theories can take advantage of; however, we also believe that a theoretically adequate account must go beyond current versions of "configurationism" to cope with some problems raised by the issues surveyed in the next section.

NEW VIEWS OF STRUCTURE AND COMMUNICATION

The preceding review illustrates the tendency of structural research in sociology and management to treat communication as a supporting actor rather than as featured star. Communication research has, for the most part, returned the favor by largely neglecting formal structural variables in favor of emergent structures such as networks. We believe that part of the reason for this neglect is the recognition by communication researchers that traditional conceptions of structure are too narrow relative to the communication phenomena they are intended to explain. In this section, we discuss several emerging perspectives that conceptualize traditional structural ideas in communicational and process-oriented terms. These perspectives reveal both new implications and theoretical problems for future research.

New Social Theories Applying to Traditional Structural Dimensions

As the social-theoretic paradigm culminating in structural-functionalism has been challenged and superseded (Gouldner, 1970), conceptions of formal structure linked to functionalism have been transformed. We review here a number of developments in social and communication theory that deal with, but alter our view of, structure and pattern. These developments highlight major conceptual problems and suggest transformations in concepts that have important implications for communication.

Organizational Pattern and Hierarchy: The Problem of Relational Context

Studies of the influence of vertical rank on communication, as well as of superior-subordinate communication in general, rarely examine the overall relational context in which the manager's communication is embedded. This problem plagues configurational as well as traditional studies. Two theoretical positions argue that the neglect of such contextual phenomena may block the growth of insights into managerial communication.

Dansereau, Yammarino, and their colleagues have developed a theoretical and methodological basis for the detailed examination of the context effects on superior-subordinate communication processes (Yammarino & Dubinsky, 1992). They argue that any communication behavior by a manager may reflect the influence of several units of analysis—the individual (manager), the work group he or she manages, and/or a larger unit that he or she is part of. Those larger units can have two kinds of effects: They can determine the average level of behavior by managers (a between-groups effect), or they can be the sites of differential behavior by the manager, say, toward a specific employee (a within-groups effect). This model allows the study of multiple levels both of behavior and of covariation. For instance, Yammarino and Dubinsky (1992) find differences between retail and insurance supervision in the extent to which superiors and subordinates in dyads are similar in the relations among their attitudes—for example, in the extent to which they reason similarly. They attribute this difference to a contrast in the interaction environments of dyads in the two industries. In general, they argue that studies ignoring the possible impacts of different units of analysis may be deficient.

Another argument, influenced by the structuration perspective, is posed by McPhee (1988). He emphasizes the flow of influence, information, and empowerment in the vertical chains connecting the top of any organizational pyramid with bottom-level employees. The analysis starts with the premise that every manager except the top one is not an autonomous controller, but instead a person maneuvering "in the middle" (Roethlisberger, 1941), under pressure from both sides. Studies by Pettigrew (1973, 1985) nicely illustrate how

managers in a hierarchy maneuver strategically, while dealing with the constraint posed by countervailing commitments elsewhere in the hierarchy, to influence decisions or implement programs. As a result, managerial communication is affected by the overall patterns of "flow" of resources and problems through the vertical chain. McPhee summarizes three theoretical positions that imply different communication patterns in the vertical chain. One pattern, the homogeneous model, portrays dyadic links in the vertical chain as basically similar in function and process. A second pattern, the multiple strata model, suggests that there are several qualitatively distinct strata in any reasonably long vertical chain, each of which represents a different social milieu and perspective in the organization. A manager and his or her subordinate within a stratum will communicate easily and from a similar perspective; communication in dyads where a manager on one level has a subordinate on a distinctly lower level is more incongruous and may therefore involve less mutual understanding and support. In the latter case, we could say that a "gap" between the strata existed, due perhaps to different fundamental task concerns (Parsons, 1960). A final pattern, the multiple clusters model, assumes that superior-subordinate communication is strong (frequent, consensual, and cooperative rather than controlling) mainly when it involves considerable coinvolvement in activities and/or alliances.

A cross-organizational interview study of organizational vertical chains revealed most support for the multiple strata model (McPhee, 1998). The study found that the hierarchy typically divides into three sections or strata, each composed of relatively strong and multiplex relationships, but with the sections separated by relatively weak links revealing mutual autonomy of the strata. If the multiple strata model holds more generally in organizations, it would change the way we view many of the phenomena of vertical communication. For instance, a famous and quite well-confirmed pattern exhibited in organizational hierarchies is the Pelz effect (Pelz,

1952): The impact of managerial behavior on a subordinate's job satisfaction depends on the manager's upward influence. However, the multiple strata model would lead us to predict three possible patterns: If there is no stratum gap separating the manager from the superior or subordinate, the manager will tend to share an outlook with those above and below him or her, and the manager should be able to get resources that the subordinate would value. However, if a stratum gap separates the manager from his or her boss, the manager will tend to have trouble eliciting resources from above. Finally, if the gap separates the manager from the subordinate, the manager often will not perceive the need to elicit resources, leading again to dissatisfaction from the subordinate.

This argument asserts the communicative consequences of level, not in general, but for interaction within versus across strata boundaries. To explore it, researchers would have to identify, first, markers of strata and gaps, then discover the typical and exceptional results of gaps. For instance, across the same type of gap one manager might avoid the troublesome attempt to communicate more than perfunctorily, another might enter into full conflict with the subordinate, while a third might attempt to change the subordinate's perspective enough to allow confirming communication. One of these reactions (or another) might be most frequent, but all three are interpretative responses to a common condition of action, responses that all would confirm the existence and importance of the gap.

Centralization: The Problem of Fields of Control

The key issue facing research on centralization is the question of the relation of centralization to control. High centralization of power over broad classes of decisions is one mode of control, but control becomes increasingly difficult with the growing complexity and dynamism of organizations and their environments. Moreover, the lines of scholarship reviewed below suggest that a distribution of decision power is not incompatible with a growth of overall control in line with the wishes and interests of a central authority.

One example of theory and research that separates centralization from control is Foucault's (1977). He is famous for reviving interest in Bentham's "Panopticon" and for suggesting that the design of modern office buildings often followed panoptic principles of allowing the constant observation of workers by superiors. But the main concept underlying Foucault's panoptic model is not provision for potentially constant visual observation, nor is it the idea that a central authority maintains surveillance, whether visually, through communication media, or through a pyramid of officials. "Although it is true that pyramidal organization gives it a 'head,' it is the apparatus as a whole that produces 'power' and distributes individuals in this permanent and continuous field" (Foucault, 1977, p. 177). It is the sense of being under scrutiny, inscribed into the very being of organization members, that changes them so as to give power to the center. One good example of this is Perin's (1991) study of telecommuting in the Internal Revenue Service (IRS). She found that her sample of professionals came into the office far more often than necessary, because they felt uncomfortable not being "provably working" in the way that on-site scrutiny guarantees. (For other discomforts of decentralization, see Colling & Ferner, 1992; for other analyses of centralized surveillance as embodied in organizational structure, see Dandeker, 1990.)

Two lines of work illustrate the implications of Foucault's ideas for the communicative study of organizational centralization and fields of control. One is Zuboff's (1988) application of Foucault's analysis to information technology, as described at some length below. Second is James Barker's (1993) work on concertive control, which explores decentralization from a different direction. His studies of self-managing work teams reveal not only the persuasive inculcation of decision premises from above but also the strikingly intense pressure exerted by teammates in the organization's interests. Such teams are commonly thought to be instruments of decentralization, but instead may bring increased control, through a process the workers themselves constitute.

The implication of this work is that decentralization is limited as a measure of worker autonomy and participation. Research is needed to clarify how communication interacts with structural moves to either increase or decrease power sharing in organizations.

Formalization: The Problem of Implications

Developing currents of scholarship are transforming the traditional literature on formalization by elaborating the nature and implications of the concept of formalization itself. Formalization certainly contributes to systematic rationality and to control (Dandeker, 1990), but perhaps more important is the sense of trust it fosters, since formalization clarifies commitments, gives a standard for procedural fairness, and provides recourse in case of violations (Breton & Wintrobe, 1982; Morand, 1995; Perrow, 1986). Moreover, since formalized rules or criteria promise systematic attention by the organization, they can be used to signal the interest of the organization. Peters (1980) notes the direct communicative functions of formalization. Meyer and Rowan (1977) began the analysis of the more covert use of formal organizational documents as signals to varied audiences that the organization is rational and conformable in other ways (cf. Jermier, Slocum, Fry, & Gaines, 1991). Langley (1990) notes four purposeful uses of formal analysis: for information, for communication, for direction/control, and for (political) symbolism. Her analysis indicates that the consequences of formalization vary with the combinations of these functions.

But the sense of formality as a resource for communication carries over into another important stream of ideas, focusing on formality as a quality of conduct or discourse. To act or

speak formally, argues Morand (1995), is to use a certain array of codes (often not formalized themselves) that mandate elaboration, finishing of acts, sobriety, consideration of others, and maintenance of attention (cf. Stohl & Redding, 1987). We might note that such codes include not only language, dress, and other surface attributes but also substantive codes of organizational evaluation, such as numerical systems for measuring productivity and cost. Behavior and talk that are formal, says Morand, have a variety of effects, including ratification of authority, routinization, a sense of detached impersonality, a sense of procedural fairness, and status differentiation. He argues that such codes are likely to arise in organizational structures that are bureaucratic, but this claim may be too limited. Formal codes of behavior, in more or less unrecognized organizational ceremonies, are part and parcel of the constitution of any formal order, as noted by Katovich (1985) and Golding (1991). Regular ceremonies, by marking the status claims of organizational authorities, dramatize the organization itself. As Baxter (1993) illustrates, "putting it in writing" can be a stylistic preference that reflects assumptions about personhood and social order that are quite different from those reflected in the stylistic preference for "talking things through" and relying on the word of all parties.

Recent scholarship on formalization also goes to a deeper level. Formalization is not simply a communication or control tool or ceremonial marker, it is a quality that helps constitute the subjectivity characteristic of the organizational domain. As Foucault (1977; cf. Fox, 1989) argues, the medium of information gathering, management, and use are correlated with a formalized type of knowledge that generates and represents disciplinary power. This power/knowledge complex cuts up and orders space and time to allow maximum regulation and creates a mode of subjectivity that makes us liable to such power. Giddens (1991) qualified this with the argument that capacities for surveillance, requiring formalization as a basis for recording information, are characteristic of modernity and are linked to the trust in abstract systems that we routinely grant to organizations today. Hassard (1991), like Giddens, notes how formalization recreates time as a medium of regulation vital to capitalism and implicit on the design of organizations (which are arranged to save time). Cooper (1992) distinguishes three aspects of formalized systems: their capacity as "communicable" to substitute for immediate presence and allow long-distance control; their capacity as representations to substitute for the thing itself in analysis and planning; and their capacity as symbolic representations to be abbreviated, compressed, and thereupon processed in ways impossible with the original referents. All these analyses place the tendency toward formality at the core of the phenomenon of organization, but we must also remember, as Cooper and Burrell (1988) argue, that formalization implies its opposite, the tendency toward informality (cf. Katz, 1965, for evidence that more formalized work leads organizations to grant a "sphere of informality" to workers). In all these ways "formalization" is conceptually close kin to "organization" itself and becomes a vehicle for understanding the influence of communication on organization.

The Challenge of the New Forms

Clearly, various features of organizational structure depended on communication. However, the advent of information technology as an important adjunct to traditional structural modes underscores the bond of structure and communication. Indeed, the improvements wrought by information technology suggest that insufficiency in communication and information processing is probably the critical factor that has kept structures from realizing their potential prior to the "information age." Information technology enables organizations to "perfect" classical structural parameters by providing rapid, accurate, and monitorable communication.

Centralization and "Informating"

We noted in the previous section how new research is transforming the concept of centralization into a broader sense of fields of control. As numerous commentators have noted, information technology seems foreordained to enable organization to realize Bentham's panoptic vision (see, e.g., Finlay, 1987; Garson, 1988; Mulgan, 1991; Poster, 1990; Zuboff, 1988). Information technology enables organizations to monitor the number of keystrokes per minute, time spent booking reservations, access to libraries, and adherence to budgets, all of which can be used to control members who know they are being watched. This situation changes the nature of work to make it more open to control than ever before. Yet by providing information at the points where work is done and decisions made, information technology can also enable lower members to enjoy a degree of flexibility and control. On one hand, information technology can reassure those in authority that they can always check on subordinates, and encourage them to delegate and empower. On the other hand, broader information access and power brings with it dangers of employee discretion that may tempt managers to exert control by limiting access to the system or by designing the information technology so that it allows only limited and prestructured sequences of operations.

As Zuboff (1988) has noted, firms that employ information technology to improve work processes may "informate" their work, allowing workers to use the information technology to study work processes and improve them even further. On the other side of the coin are those firms that use technology to further "post-Fordism," the tight control of management over work processes (Prechel, 1994). Somewhere in between are organizations that use information technology as a form of technical/bureaucratic control in which the technology is imbued with managerial values. Lower-echelon members are given apparent control over their jobs, while the main parameters are subtly set by managerial control over the design of the technology. Garson (1988), for example, discusses a case where investment advisers were given an expert system to help them in their decision making; they were given what appeared to be extensive control over investment decisions, subject to the parameters set by the expert system. In effect they were indirectly controlled by the system, while thinking they were making "their own" moves.

Zuboff (1988) also shows that information technology allows control of both ordinary employee work and the work of managers, even at fairly high levels, and also allows simultaneous control of work by prefabricated programs and multiple layers of managers. That information technology enables such different "flavors" of centralization to be enacted indicates the much finer degree of control over authority distributions possible when the communicative side of centralization is made more manageable.

Formalization and New Formal Parameters

Benjamin and Scott-Morton (1989) note several advances in integration that information technology makes possible, each of which is dependent on improvements in formalization:

1. Information technology makes it possible to integrate the forms and processes that govern several different transactions in one interface. This enables linkage of different formal processes, such as travel reservation services involving airline ticketing, car rental, and hotel reservations. Moreover, these forms can be linked so that information moves between them and the linkages and nature of the forms can be changed fairly easily and quickly.

2. Information technology also supports integration of multiple forms of representation into a single representation. For example, a design database might integrate and substitute for traditional engineering drawings, production specifications, bills of materials, and machine tool instructions. In this instance, four different representations of different aspects of a product are replaced by a single representation that translates them into common terms.

3. "The integration of expert knowledge to provide a standardized process for accomplishing or supporting tasks" (p. 94) is another advance in which knowledge as well as rules constitutes the formalizing mode.

These results of implementing information technology indicate a different side of organizational formalization, one highlighting positive empowerment rather than one relying on red tape and stultifying constraint. Information technology makes it easy to reconfigure formal structures, enabling the organization to be more flexible and responsive. Further, because it is an integral part of the work process, information technology makes formal structures much more "enforceable" than they are by human agents. Information technology also enables types of formalization that were not previously feasible, such as the incorporation of expert systems into organizational processes.

The potency of information technology in integrating the organization has been widely discussed. Integration of members through electronic mail, conferencing, and groupware systems enables geographically dispersed organizations to act and react as though they operated at a single site. But perhaps even more important is the growing use of information technology for knowledge integration. Information systems can be used to index important knowledge, create knowledge communities, and capture knowledge in the forms of expert systems and process analyses. What is easy to miss in the attention given to hardware and software is the critical role of communication and interaction in the creation and harnessing of knowledge in formal languages, databases, and other organization-constituting resources. While the technology makes knowledge communities possible, the interactions among the members of these communities are what actually create and apply knowledge.

A key dimension of information technology, *interactivity,* seems likely to become an increasingly important design parameter for organizations. Interactivity (Rice & Associates, 1984) refers to the extent to which a communication technology permits interaction between members that is similar to face-to-face communication in pacing and interchange. Information technologies permit transactions via forms and formal channels, which have traditionally been time-consuming and burdensome, to be conducted much more rapidly and interactively, often in real time. Information technology makes structured activities much more like interpersonal communication than routing through "channels." Traditionally, the reference points for structural design have been the flowchart and the rulebook; new configurations suggest that an additional reference point is the interpersonal interaction.

Theory and research on new configurations also suggest new structural models. Most models of organizational structure are premised on uncertainty reduction (e.g., Galbraith, 1973). Newer models are premised instead on the need to create uncertainty. Volberda (1996) develops a novel scheme for structuring organizations in hypercompetitive environments on the basis of their flexibility, which he defines as a function of the variety of capabilities they can employ and the speed with which they can employ them. Volberda defines four types of organizational structures based on their degree of flexibility: The rigid form has a few capabilities and can change them only slowly; the planned form has relatively more and more varied capabilities and can change them within the parameters of the plan, but is otherwise limited in what it can achieve; the flexible form has a large mix of

capabilities and can flexibly adapt them to exigencies; finally, the chaotic form has an extensive and varied mix of capabilities, but cannot control the application as well as the flexible form can. The strength of the chaotic form is that it proliferates new ideas and adaptations; its weakness is that it cannot easily capitalize on them due to its lack of organization.

In all four forms, communication plays a central role. However, rather than reducing uncertainty or providing information, the focus is on enacting ambiguity and problematizing current arrangements. The nature of the organization's communication system influences its ability to marshal ideas and organizational capabilities. And communication is critical in maintaining members' commitment, which affects the pool of knowledge that determines flexibility.

Multilevel Analysis

The substantive theoretical advances described in the preceding two sections have been accompanied, especially over the past decade, by progress at the metatheoretical level. A large and growing literature addresses the issue of the relationship among "system levels," also termed the "macro-micro" or "meso" relationship. Of course, many of the theoretic currents discussed above implicitly or explicitly involve cross-level concepts and claims. Various scholars who have addressed the macro-micro and levels problems have challenged the validity of traditional theoretical approaches and offer new resources for theory development in organizational communication.

The macro-micro problem has a long history in sociology. Since the writings of Durkheim (1938) and Weber (1949), sociologists have been divided between those emphasizing explanation based on large-scale societal characteristics and those emphasizing explanation based on the individual experience, interpretive schemes, and actions of individuals. The revolt against Talcott Parsons's

(1960) functionalism by symbolic interactionists and exchange theorists exhibited their commitment to explaining social patterns as the result of processes of social interaction among individuals. Today, it is generally accepted that the problem is not whether both levels of phenomena should be recognized, but rather how to give each level its due and how to spell out coherent relationships among levels. Theories that seem perfectly good at one level are often found to be "weak" at the other (Giddens, 1976), either because they incorrectly reduce one level to an adjunct of the other, because they oversimplify one level, because they neglect to theorize one level (treating that level as transparent or common sense), or because they neglect relationships between levels.

For most organizational communication scholars, the macro-micro problem is often a question of how to avoid the temptation to overemphasize the microlevel. The general tendency is to concentrate on microsituations such as influence, superior-subordinate communication, or group communication, with macrolevel or structural variables entering in as context. The unit of analysis in most quantitative communication studies is either the individual or the episode, and such units are analyzed as batches, without much concern for their interrelationships.

Opponents of the microlevel reductionism have developed new conceptualizations of the nature of levels and how they relate to each other that promise to uncover different avenues of thinking in communication research. First, several theorists have discussed what differentiates levels. The most popular basis for level distinction is spatial and temporal extension, but Wiley (1988; cf. Weick, 1995) has argued persuasively that levels can be distinguished on several other dimensions as well. McPhee (1998) has adapted Wiley's scheme to array five dimensions:

1. *Abstractness,* ranging from knowledge and norms related only to a specific group of people and situations to knowledge/norms that have meaning independent of the social

positions/roles of people involved (e.g., mathematics).

2. *Time-space,* with more macrophenomena involving interdependence across longer distances.

3. *Social differentiation,* in the straightforward sense of "differences." More macrophenomena involve people and mixed groups whose backgrounds, resource bases, and other characteristics are more diverse and varied, within the single unit involving them, than microphenomena.

4. *Reticular or network size/complexity,* ranging from one (or more) isolated individuals or relationships to increasing network extent and interconnectedness in macrolevel phenomena.

5. *Systemic/functional complexity,* with "macro" systems exhibiting more diverse tasks or operations that are more complexly interdependent with one another.

The first three dimensions are not essentially social—they can characterize sets of people who are almost completely oblivious of one another. In contrast, the fourth and especially the fifth dimensions imply social contact among parties. Each of these dimensions can underlie relations among smaller units that may constitute a larger unit, with emergent causal powers, at a higher level of analysis. Communication scholars can study the (often communicative) relations among smaller units, without assuming that the larger unit simply reduces to the smaller ones or that communication works the same way inside and outside such relational contexts.

The initial contribution of the macro-micro literature is that macro-micro axes can shed new light on traditional structural concepts. For instance, "formalization" can be a trait of a particular worker's job or of a corporate system. Formalization in the latter is more "macro" than the former because it describes (1) many different types of jobs, (2) of workers at different points geographically and perhaps historically, (3) probably involving a variety of individual-job formalization levels, (4) with formalization levels linked in various ways, and (5) with a variety of groups and practices involved in supporting formalization as a social enterprise. Such groups might include the consultants, governmental bodies, and professions that do so much to influence the level of formalization in American organizations. This example makes it evident that formalization is a complex phenomenon that cannot be satisfactorily characterized with a single variable. If formalization is characteristic of a society, the theoretical significance of individual-level formalization must be portrayed in the context of that social phenomenon, in relation to the distribution and connections of the social form, as supported by conformity or innovative resistance. This suggests that researchers must pay more attention to macro-oriented conceptual analysis.

The second contribution of this literature is its development of the idea of multiple "dynamics," "mechanisms," or "logics" that reproduce or condition the effects of social structure (Alexander, 1987; House, Rousseau, & Thomas-Hunt, 1995; Kontopoulos, 1993; Turner, 1988; cf. McPhee, 1985; Van de Ven & Poole, 1995). Some of these theories posit multiple, relatively simple processes that appear or combine only under partly specifiable conditions (including subjective choice). For the example of formalization, rather than assuming that rule writing/dissemination is a necessary managerial response to routine work, formalization could be a function of larger social imperatives that have been drilled into managers in business schools and exemplified in communicative genres such as policy-and-procedure manuals. Socialization and the influence of genre may well operate through different mechanisms, and the relationships among the two generative mechanisms must be specified to develop clear explanations. Other theories (such as the examples given in House et al., 1995) specify variables or situations that determine the causal power of a given level of analysis. For instance, House et al. note that the existence of "entrainment" (synchrony in the activity of subunits) implies an increase in the influence of other higher-level units. Thus, if subunits work at synchronous rates, they find it easier to cooperate in adapting to new situations.

The micro-macro literature thus registers two main critiques of standard theory and research about organizational structure and communication. First is the problem of conceptualization: Structural and communication phenomena that primarily characterize groups must not be studied at the individual or dyadic levels. Second is the problem of explanation: Explanations involving macrolevel phenomena may require a more complex pattern than do relatively simple phenomena. Developing more complex, layered, and nuanced explanations for communication and its relationship to other structural features will increase our appreciation of how communication enters into the constitution of organizational structure in the larger sense.

Communication Concepts of Structure

One move toward more nuanced explanation is to give primacy to the discursive and communicative dimensions of organizations. This view implies that structure is inherently a communicative phenomenon and suggests a fundamentally different understanding of structure. However, it is hard to theorize how communication could constitute formal structure. Often communication researchers have fallen back on several lines of argument. One argument is that communication networks are the essence of structure, which results in placing informal structure in the primary position and giving formal structure a subsidiary role as a resource for generating networks or as a variable that influences their emergence. However, the research summarized to this point shows the importance of maintaining formal structure as a key term in our theories. A second line of argument is that communicative process generates formal structure, which is important only because it in turn affects process (see McPhee, Habbel, & Fordham-Habbel, 1987, for a survey of the major theories that elaborate this argument). In this work, formal structure also occupies a peripheral and epiphenomenal role: It is the dead chitin left behind as the insect of interest (process) emerges to live. But just as the skin was vital to the pupa, formal structure is useful to and distinctive of the organization—it is not just reproduced, but is drawn on in and constrains organizational processes. Researchers must face the question: What is it about formal structure that makes it efficacious, yet is fundamentally communicative or discursive? In recent years, several lines of work have shed insight on this question.

Formal Structure as Product/Feature of Communication

McPhee (1985, 1989) has argued that the formal structure of organizations is communicative in nature, but is the result of an analytically distinct communicative system in any particular organization. He labeled communication taking place within this system as "structure-communication." To simplify matters, we will use the acronym FSC (formal structural communication) for communication processes that are part of this system.

This theory of organizational structure is oriented toward the self-consciously organized systems that dominate economic, political, and civic life. Authors as different as Perrow (1986) and Giddens (1991) stress that organizations multiply both human productive effectiveness and social capacities for domination. This theory is meant to illuminate the distinctive features of organizational communication that help explain the proliferation of the complex organization as a social form; the effectiveness of complex, formalized organizations in concentrating power and producing goods and services; and the importance and functions of references to formal structure in organizational communication.

FSC is really an aspect of most communication in formal organizations. It is the meaning or property of organizational communication that establishes, explains, enforces, obeys, resists, or assumes the existence, power, and authority of an organization's structure. Prototypical examples of such communication take many forms, from an organizational charter, to company newspaper articles about a structural change, to a manager's explanation of the structure, to coworkers' explanations of what the manager really meant and how far the structure can be stretched. Obviously, such communication differs in quantity and quality across and within organizations, times, and contexts.

Formal structure itself, then, is produced and reproduced by FSC. McPhee's theory of FSC argued that the system of FSC prototypically centers on written documents and, more generally, that the medium of writing is primal for constituting organizations. The term *written* is meant to include all symbolic inscriptions on relatively permanent media, certainly including drawn organizational charts, and could extend in principle to cover memory formulations. Written orders and organization charts have two important qualities: They are (1) *enduring,* and so able to be stored, copied, and liable to be treated as real even if not immediately present in a situation; and (2) *abstract,* and so especially able to be interpreted and obeyed consistently in multiple settings.

These foundational qualities lead easily to some other typical ones. For instance, written structural documents can *reify and characterize* acts, practices, and relations. Once a statement such as "Al will report to Betty" is authoritatively announced and inscribed in official records, the abstract relation of superior to subordinate defines and conditions the human communicative relationship between Al and Betty, leading both of them, and outsiders as well, to see Betty as more important and properly commanding. (Obviously, this relation is just one element in any concrete setting, and it is interpreted and transformed as discussed below.) The enduring and abstract character of written structure formulations also makes *technical elaboration and manipulation* of practices and relations easy. Few things come as easily to an experienced boss as redrawing an organization chart. Finally, their existence "in writing" allows formal structural inscriptions to be *powerful though absent,* in a way characterized by Smith's (1990) concept of textually mediated social interaction, discussed below. Even if no one has a copy of a set of rules around, they still often argue about the content of the rules, then may go and check them—they rarely argue that the rules *should* say *X,* so we should do *X.*

Structure-communication has three important properties: First, structure-communication is a substitute for direct communication. For instance, instead of endless disputes about what new products to produce, executives will usually stipulate a hierarchy of officials responsible for deciding about new products, plus a decision-making procedure. The organization typically announces the structure, managers explain and enforce the structure, adjusting problems, and that's it. This one-way process deprives lower-level participants of a voice in establishing and negotiating the structure. And of course, plenty of communication remains, including that involved in making decisions, along with informal "sensemaking" on the part of employees, as they deal with the structure day-to-day, puzzle it out, and talk about it with colleagues. Members construct a meaning for the structure based on their own interpretation of available cues. Organizational structure is valuable only if it eliminates enough communication to yield efficiency without lowering decision quality and legitimacy too much. This property implies that decision discussions in a formal organization should refer to formal structure rather than carry out some of the functions that would be found in totally informal groups, and the references to formal structure should lead group decisions to contribute to organizational power.

Second, FSC is authoritative metacommunication about members' relationship to the organization. For instance, Yates (1989) reported that the Scoville Manufacturing Company required orders by supervisors to be written, and approved from above, to control downward relations and the conduct of those supervisors. It is commonplace to acknowledge that formal position in an organization signals responsibilities, status level, and power (Peters, 1980). Members' histories of position moves indicate the development of their place in the firm and whether they are rising, as well as the development of their competency. But there is also other, more subtle authoritative communication concerning relationships. Structures symbolize what the organization values and what kinds of people it wants its members to become. The fact that formal structure is part of organizations as an institutionalized form, elaborating property or political rights protected in contract and law, gives authority to the formal structural presuppositions of FSC. "Authoritative metacommunication," though, is probably different from the tacit, analogic metacommunication of Watzlawick, Beavin, and Jackson (1967), and their different processes deserve study.

In addition, the structure of the organization is itself the topic of member metacommunication. An important aspect of the member's relation to the organization is the attitude he or she has toward structures themselves. Are rules, procedures, hierarchies to be taken strictly seriously or can they be circumvented? Are structures a public trust, not to be altered or violated, or are they the "property" of the user, to be used for whatever ends he or she deems suitable? Communication about structures from managers, colleagues, and others informs members' use of structures, and therefore how the structure is reproduced and whether it is maintained or changed.

Third, FSC is differentiated—it does not work the same way everywhere in the organization. This is crucial to the "systemness" of organizations—their economic or political unity is "carried" in the abstract authority of their structural documents (cf. Yates, 1989). Giddens's (1984) concept of "distantiation" is important here—it refers to the fact that interaction such as FSC produces and reproduces, enacts and binds human presence (and absence) in space and time. The geography of the organization is elaborated along an axis of structural power—who has what powers in what parts of the organization, who can change the structure and who cannot. For instance, two structurally distinct parts of complex organizations occupy the process of "conception" where executive goals and basic structuring decisions are made, and of the "reception" stage where formal structure is renegotiated in the course of work practices. As complex structures have evolved, between those stages a stage of implementation has become common, where middle managers and staff members (most commonly) elaborate and inscribe an elaborated structure in the organization's official memory stocks.

During the stage called "implementation" in FSC theory, there are certain key communicators, including organizational designers, consultants, top executives, middle managers, and experts in the use of particular structures. These experts include industrial engineers, organizational development specialists, accountants, strategic planners, and MIS specialists, who all have highly specialized vocabularies and approaches that others must learn and live with if they are to use their structures effectively. The hitch is that others are not as facile at using specialists' concepts as are the specialists. This gives specialists a great deal of power, not just because they control important processes but because they can impose their vocabulary and views on other members. Others must work on unfamiliar ground and in many respects must simply accept the definition of the situation imposed by the specialists, and those not facile with the vocabulary and style of structure-communication will have two strikes against them from the start.

This specialization has both advantages and disadvantages for the organization. One advantage is that having these professional specialties makes it fairly easy for organizations in the same sector of the economy to work with each other. If one company, for example, is entering a joint venture with another, their financial people can negotiate fairly easily, because they have similar views of the world and share a common profession. It is also advantageous, because specialists can use esoterica to protect the firm from outsiders or impress outsiders (Meyer & Rowan, 1977). The problems the IRS has in interpreting a firm's records during audits illustrate this point clearly.

But specialized structural vocabularies may be used to silence nonspecialists. They may also unnecessarily limit the structural options the firm considers. Nonspecialist members may have good ideas about problems and possible solutions to structural problems. But if these ideas don't fit in the conceptual scheme of the experts, they may be disregarded. The specialized vocabulary may be a trap that keeps the organization from seeing new structural options. For example, Kanter (1983) observes that overemphasis on formal structures by designers and top management has limited their ability to see the usefulness of less formal organization forms, such as quality circles. Ironically, Kanter gave these forms a technical name, "parallel organizations," to make them more acceptable to organizational designers. The power of the specialized vocabulary of implementers, combined with the inaccessibility of structural conception decisions, makes it very difficult for ordinary organizational member experience to affect fundamental organizational structural attributes.

The specialist's expertise and control over the terms of discourse is a powerful resource in the structuring of organizations. But like all resources, this is produced and reproduced as the expert works with others. As others become more knowledgeable about theories of structure and terminology, the expert's power wanes. And an expert who throws his or her weight around unadvisedly may undermine faith in expertise, thus hastening his or her own eclipse. But after we join the chorus of criticism of middle management and staff,

FSC theory forces us to confront a major premise: These specialists are the most persistent enunciators of the stream of discourse crucial to the constitution of organizations.

The impact of FSC is tempered by other structural elements—technology, other professions, market competition, national culture, constructions of gender and race, for example. The efficacy of formal structure will depend on the transformative action of organizational agents. One structural element deserves special mention, as has been indicated above: information technology. Research described above, and popular images of information technology, portray the mediated communication network as the new medium for fundamental organizational structuring. We must emphasize the importance of maintaining a critical perspective toward the new hucksterism of information technology, by keeping three possibilities in mind. First, the new media may simply be new, better media for conveying the same old control relationships, reflecting the formal structure. Second, formal structure may remain in hidden control, determining information access or becoming apparent only during resource allocation or conflict resolution. Finally, the popular image may be correct, and formal structure may be much less important in organizations of the future. Only time and future research will tell.

FSC is the vehicle through which abstract structures are enacted in organizations. But between the inscribed structure and the immediate, practical control relations that guide work processes is a gap. The existence of this gap has led many to argue that formal structure is often ignored, and thus unimportant, and that it has been superseded by informal processes. Such views fail to recognize that cases of apparent inaccuracy and irrelevance of formal structure can be interpreted as cases of miscommunication, or more likely resistance as a typical part of the process of reception. More explicit attention to structure-communication and its various modalities may help bridge the gap between abstract conception and execution of organizational structures.

Textually Mediated Social Relations

In her attempt to characterize patriarchal relations of ruling, the feminist sociologist Dorothy Smith (1990) introduces the term *textually mediated social relations*. This term has important theoretical implications for understanding the communicative underpinnings of structure, and further elaborates some aspects of FSC.

Smith notes that texts are not dead objects for study; their life is refractive and involves "organizing a course of concerted social action."

> The appearance of meaning in the permanent material form of a text detaches meaning from the lived processes of its making. The text's capacity to transcend the essentially transitory character of social processes and to remain uniform across separate and diverse local settings is key to the distinctive social organization and relations they [*sic*] make possible. (p. 168)

Texts operating this way ideologically conceal the relations involved in their production and use; they constitute subjective positions, possibilities, and facts. Smith continues:

> A job description, for example, is misread by the sociologist if she expects to be able to treat it as an account of an actual work process. In fact, its organizational force is in part achieved precisely because it does not describe any particular work process but can enter a variety of settings and order the relations among them. (p. 218)

Smith gives the example of a female secretary whose work overlaps that of her boss considerably, but who is not a candidate for advancement because she receives no credit for executive experience due to the "systems of representations ordering the internal labor market of the organization" (p. 219). Her relations with other people at work are organized by her job description, no matter how inaccurate it may be, because it is one of the documents that patterns the organization and holds it together.

Smith's work suggests that formal organizational structure can be reconceptualized as the textually mediated social relational pattern of the organization. This definition is useful because it avoids situational solipsism. The text is not part of most social episodes, though it organizes them and its effects can be found. As argued in the section about FSC, this text stands outside the typical organizational communication process, so that an organization is not a communicative act or process, but a reflexive relationship among communications on varied levels. Thus, formalization is not merely a set of mandated rules, but the restricted possibilities for control of their own work emerging in the discourse of coworkers.

Conversation analysts and postmodernists are endeavoring to turn our attention to the practices and mechanisms underlying the communicative production of meaning and order. A shortcoming of this work is that it is not usually linked to long-term control decisions about organizational design and strategy. The notion of textually mediated organization offers the possibility of making this connection. Texts such as job descriptions or strategic plans are typically produced in the context of major managerial initiatives such as long-term planning or job reorganizations. Hence, they serve as the link between global managerial and control moves and local enactments of them.

Taylor's Textual/Conversational Theory of Organizations

James Taylor and his colleagues have discussed the constitution of organizations as communication in an extensive body of work (Taylor, 1993; Taylor, Cooren, Giroux, & Robichaud, 1996; Taylor & Van Every, 1993).

Responding to their studies of computerization in organizations, as well as to Ruth Smith's (1993) challenging exploration of alternative assumptions about the organization-communication relationship, Taylor and his colleagues have devoted themselves to integrating and adapting a varied list of philosophical and linguistic concepts so as to analyze "organization" as "communication." Thus, Taylor and Van Every (1993) write, "An organization, as we visualize it, is nothing but a fabric of communication: a collection of people in a process of talking, writing, and transacting with each other" (p. xiii). But they try to avoid a simple reductionist stance by identifying the specific features of communication that lead to the phenomenon of organization.

The array of communication concepts they have analyzed and marshaled is daunting, but two themes seem to persist through their work. One is the shift from a linear to a transactional model of communication. Taylor and his colleagues argue that a transactional model correctly elaborated can improve our understandings of agency and the subject/object dichotomy, which in turn allows a better understanding of seemingly linear processes like supervision, computerized information transmission, and speech act articulation. They note that the grammar of transactional forms includes relationships involved in formal organizational structure. The other, and more relevant, thread is the argument that communication is a dialogue of two modalities, conversation and text (where, to foreshadow, text will include phenomena like an organization's formal structure). The argument here is that two simultaneous processes occur in all communication. First is the "translation of text into conversation," as the content of remarks is given illocutionary force through the communicative action of speaker and hearer (Taylor et al., 1996, pp. 8-12). This force, which is what makes a locution by a boss into an order, is "precisely what we usually mean by *organization*" (p. 12). But a second process is also always present: "textuallization of the conversation" (p. 14). At its most basic, this is the process wherein conversation is bracketed, interpreted, and retained, even in the course of later conversational narrative. Taylor and his colleagues emphasize the framing, objectifying power and note that to preserve that power in writing is a matter of artistry (Taylor, 1993, p. 218; Taylor & Van Every, 1993, pp. 119, 130). Texts can be authoritative, but that property requires a "master conversation," a process that has or appropriates the responsibility "to write the text for the organization as a whole" (Taylor & Van Every, 1993, p. 126). This authority is a result of networking and consensual validation (Taylor et al., 1996, p. 16). The result is a "authentic text," comprising "the official organization," fixing its "macrostruc- ture" in a way that "specifies the organizational agents and their duties, . . . describes the activities and their expected outcomes," and allowing bosses to marshal illocutionary force (and have their writings be authoritative in turn) (Taylor & Van Every, 1993, p. 126). This text is the organizational structure.

In its application to organizational structure, this view of organizations as communication is similar in many ways to the view of organizational structure stated by McPhee in 1985. Similarities between the two approaches include the view that organization as an enduring system is "generated" by production of a text (Taylor & Van Every, 1993, p. 107) and the idea that organizational structure is "a fabrication of language" (p. 115). McPhee's concept of sites or stages is parallel to the idea of the disjunction between textually articulated structure and practical interactive relationships (p. 120, 136) and the view that "authorities" are specially privileged as authors of organization-generating texts (though the idea that top managers alone are "writers" of structure seems too limiting) (p. 126). The properties of FSC presaged the idea of structural text as "meta" to more mundane communication, informing its interpretation (p. 126, 122, 127), as well as the idea that the

constitution of organization by text involves distantiation.

Of course, there are also two important differences. One is the nature of Taylor and colleagues' project: They intend to show how organizational process is explicable directly from the nature and resources of communication in general, while FSC theory concentrates on formal structure, portraying it as constituted by a unique configuration of communication systems. Second, Taylor and his colleagues draw on a broad range of ideas from philosophy, linguistics, and social psychology, while FSC theory has focused on the elaboration of structuration theory to handle a notion of formal structure that is more circumscribed.

One limitation of Taylor et al.'s approach is that it attempts to use communication concepts that apply to all interaction, perhaps influenced by the idea that if organization and communication are equivalent, all communication should be organizational. Since these concepts must of necessity apply to marriages, mobs, and communities that intercommunicate, they are hindered from finding crucial explanatory concepts for specifically organizational communication. Thus, one member of a mob can give another orders ("Go that way"), but there are crucial differences between such "orders" and those given by a boss, and that difference must be central to a theory of organizational communication. Taylor and his colleagues analyze necessary conditions for the possibility of organization, and they argue that such conditions are important in practice, especially in the case of information technology. But an important remaining task is the determination of sufficient conditions for the kinds of organizations so important in the modern world.

A second issue arises because this position is structured along dichotomous lines. Thus, in Taylor (1993, p. 222), a dichotomy between the governors and the governed is portrayed as parallel to two rival texts and two rival conversations. However, it is likely that explaining the possibility of organization inescapably requires a third standpoint or site (internal to the system, not an external one such as "beneficiary"; Taylor, 1993). Throughout history and before, there have been power differences, rulers and the ruled; organization appeared when that relationship became recognized, objectified, but above all, instrumentalized. Once reified, a leadership position can be used as a tool to motivate or to aid coordination. As orders, promises, and other speech acts gain the stability of text, they are no longer simply subject to the will of the boss—the boss is committed to a set of decisions once he or she makes them, and an independent authority (possibly external, such as the state, or internal, such as the specialists discussed by FSC) is needed to validate and implement them. In their most recent work, Taylor and colleagues seem to be moving closer to this view through such concepts as distantiation and mediation (Cooren & Taylor, 1997; Taylor et al., 1996).

Comments

The three perspectives discussed in this section all offer ways to "catch quicksilver." They try to capture the (perhaps) fleeting moments in which structures are produced and reproduced, enacted and carried forth through communication and interaction. Years ago, Herbert Simon (1976) argued that organizational structures were simply the sum total of relationships among organizational members. However, it is one thing to make this claim and another to theorize it in a way amenable to constructive research. One response to this challenge has been to emphasize the informal, emergent aspects of organizational structure, and in communication research this has produced an efflorescence of research on communication networks. However, it is important to complement this important research with analysis of how communication constitutes even the most permanent-seeming aspects of organizations, their formal structures.

Attacking this problem puts communication firmly on its feet as the major instrument of structure in organizations.

CONCLUSION

This review has presented multiple approaches to formal structure and communication. We highlight the differences and live issues involved in each major approach or perspective in Table 13.1.

The traditional reductive *dimensional* approach differentiates various structural properties of organizations, some of which pertain to or characterize communication. Structural features are then related to communication variables and to communication processes. This approach considers communication to be one variable among many and tends to relegate it to a secondary position, behind more substantial structural features as formalization or centralization. The dimensional approach illuminates structural causes and correlates of particular types of communication or communication structures. This approach yields a number of interesting and useful findings for practitioners. However, it suffers from the disadvantage of endless multiplication of relationships and inability to see "the bigger picture" of how structural dimensions fit together and how communication fits within the whole. Its definitions seem hard to link to powerful communication theories. And, since most structural variables are construed as noncommunicative, the dimensional view has paradoxically turned communication research away from most types of structure.

The *configurational* view is intriguing but inchoate. Most configurational theorizing explicitly considers communication as an important feature of organizational structure. Studies of new organizational forms especially have emphasized the importance of communication in organizational structuring. However, there is some debate as to whether

TABLE 13.1 Approaches to the Structure-Communication Relationship

Approach	View of Formal Structure	Relation to Communication	Key Research Issues
Dimensional	Set of variables	It serves as an independent variable; also serves as a container/channel for processes	Mediating processes leading to the effects of structure
Configurational	Set of internally related elements constituting the organization	Totality that includes communication in an encompassing system	Identifying an adequate set of configurations; integrating configurations with organizational process theories; communication-based configurations; processes involved in inconsistent configurations
New views of structural dimensions	Structured processes embedded in multiple systemic levels	Communication as a medium of structuring processes	Relationship of new to old conceptions of dimensions
Structure/communication	A product of communication	Communication mediates structure in dialogue; is a metacommunication; is a reification of communication processes	Effects of context and other factors on communication and enactment of structures; relation of structuring processes to other organizational processes

so-called new forms are actually qualitatively different types of organizations. Moreover, new technologies offer the opportunity to enhance the operation of older structural forms. Configurational thinking is holistic, where dimensional thinking is reductionistic. The former has the advantage of providing a more complex view of structure and how communication figures in it. Configurational theories embrace the complexity of organizations and highlight the interconnected nature of structures and design choices. This very complexity, however, makes configurational theories daunting to construct and elaborate. A promising research avenue is to concentrate first on identifying processes that have the power to generate configurations and then derive the configurations and their relationships, as Mintzberg has attempted to do. This would provide a positive basis for explaining conditions of, interruptions in, or blockages of this configuring power. Several of the new views of structure and communication presented in this chapter derive process-based views of structure, though they do not explicitly address configuration.

Many of the most interesting insights into the structure-communication relationship have resulted from deeper analysis of traditional structural dimensions. By considering the *social system that embeds hierarchies,* we can illuminate the uneven nature of superior-subordinate relationships in any given hierarchy. Processes that create different strata or social groups in organizations play an important role in determining how formal structure controls member behavior. Reconceptualizations of formalization subordinate its rationalizing, instrumental character and consider it instead as a stylistic element, which emerges in discourse. Studies of new organizational forms suggest how information technology enables centralization and formalization to be enacted more effectively. However, they also highlight multiple new and effective modes of organizing that may "dissolve" these traditional dimensions by enabling structures that are decentralized but offer the possibility of reasserting centralized control

rapidly when the power center deems it necessary and that rewrite formalizations rapidly (removing the rigidity of formalization), in response to organizational learning and discursive changes. Multilevel analyses highlight the complexity of structural effects and call into question the assumptions that structural effects emerge from "one way" causal relations in which structures determine microlevel behavior or in which microlevel processes enact structures. Instead, multilevel research suggests that there is great variety in the causal fields set up by structures. Multilevel studies highlight the need to identify factors that influence the nature and strength of relationships across different levels. For example, in a strongly litigious environment, formalization of organizational policies and procedures may have a much stronger effect on member behavior than in organizations in a more benign environment, where there is greater room for slippage and transactional mistakes.

In recent years, several theories have emerged that consider *structure primarily as a communicative phenomenon.* The thrust of these views is that structures are constituted by and operate through communication. The FSC and textual theories of organizations explore how more substantial features of organizations, such as hierarchies or rules, are produced and reproduced in communicative processes. FSC, grounded in the theory of structuration, emphasizes the actions of agents such as managers and design units in promulgating written or diagrammatic representations that project structures and how they should be taken. The textual theory of organization, grounded in theories of language and discourse, locates organization in the cycling between reified and interactive discourses. Both views encourage researchers to focus on the evanescent processes in which structures unfold and on the texts in which they are preserved to be drawn on at a later time to mobilize and to reproduce structural features in action. This is an intriguing move, which could uncover the processes by which structures influence activity, rather than simply reifying structure into variables whose mode of action is left unarticulated. A major disadvantage of these theories is that they create a tendency to see everything as fluid and continuously being reconstituted. However, language is a much more flexible medium than, for example, physical layout. While likening organizations to physical systems can overstate their stability, likening them to language can lead researchers to assume more fluidity and flexibility than is possible given the physical and economic constraints placed on organizations in actual contexts.

Directions for Future Research

Based on this review, we can make several suggestions for future research in organizational communication. We believe that it is counterproductive for organizational communication theory and research to reduce formal structure simply to a set of variables such as centralization. Exploring structural configurations or the communicative nature of formal structure offers much more promising routes of inquiry. The work reviewed in the third section represents an extensive effort to set a foundation for a theory of communication and organizational structure. However vague and sketchy it may seem, it explores fundamental issues and makes some initial choices that seem productive. The elusive nature of the communicative underpinnings of structure presents a continuing temptation to start over again and again, producing analyses that essentially repeat earlier efforts but use somewhat different terminology. We believe it is important for the next generation of scholarship to push past these initial efforts and to flesh out, evaluate, and revise our understanding of how communication constitutes, enacts, or enforces structure and of structure's discursive nature.

One way this might be done is to focus on some specific areas that have a high probability of exposing the dynamic influence of communication on structure: communication technology, the surveillance/control nexus, interorganizational and societal influences on organizational form (i.e., institutionalization and diffusion of "faddish" structural forms), the role of trust in the formation and maintenance of structures, and conflicts over structure. Other productive avenues for research might focus on processes of structural creation/change, the "expression" of structure in communication, and its interpretive application and effects in work practice and politics.

Most previous explanations of the communication-structure relationship have posited a single mechanism, however complex. It seems quite likely, however, that this relationship is multiply determined by several different mechanisms. Van de Ven and Poole (1995) argue that organizational patterns are often generated by more than one explanatory mechanism. They suggest several ways in which different types of generative mechanisms might interact to produce seemingly complex patterns. Different generative mechanisms may operate at different levels of abstraction or in different parts of a complex system, or they may operate on different temporal clocks or alternate in their influence on the system. Given the complexity of structure and communication, considering multiple generative mechanisms (each of which might be rather simple in its own right) offers a way to build a theory commensurate with the phenomenon. Of course, such theoretical systems must be elaborated with care to avoid loss of integrated explanatory power, parsimony, testability, and generality.

Finally, we believe there may be a tendency in organizational communication research to overemphasize socially created or symbolic features at the expense of material aspects of structure (cf. the similar argument by Tompkins, 1987). The material nature of organizations provides a matrix that preserves and provides resources for communication and interaction processes. It is important not to overemphasize communication to the point that we delude ourselves into thinking communication is really everything. An important issue for organizational communication theory is the relation of the material and symbolic/interactional aspects of structuring.

REFERENCES

Alexander, J. (Ed.). (1987). *The micro-macro link.* Berkeley: University of California Press.

Alter, C. (1990). An exploratory study of conflict and coordination in interorganizational service delivery systems. *Academy of Management Journal, 33,* 478-502.

Althusser, L. K. (1972). *For Marx.* London: NLB.

Axley, S. (1984). Managerial and organizational communication in terms of the container metaphor. *Academy of Management Review, 9,* 428-437.

Baker, W. (1992). An introduction to network analysis for managers. *Connections, 12,* 29-48.

Barker, J. (1993). Tightening the iron cage: Concertive control in self-managing teams. *Administrative Science Quarterly, 38,* 408-437.

Barnard, J. (1991). The information environment of new managers. *Journal of Business Communication, 28,* 312-325.

Baxter, L. A. (1993). "Talking things through" and "putting it in writing": Two codes of communication in an academic institution. *Journal of Applied Communication Research, 23,* 303-326.

Beniger, J. R. (1986). *The control revolution.* Cambridge, MA: Harvard University Press.

Benjamin R. I., & Scott-Morton, M. S. (1988). Information technology, integration, and organizational change. *Interfaces, 18,* 86-98.

Brass, D. J., & Burkhardt, M. E. (1993). Potential power and power use: An investigation of structure and behavior. *Academy of Management Journal, 36,* 441-470.

Breton, A., & Wintrobe, R. (1982). *The logic of bureaucratic conduct: An economic analysis of competition, exchange, and efficiency in private and public organizations.* New York: Cambridge University Press.

Burns, T., & Stalker, G. M. (1961). *The management of innovation.* London: Tavistock.

Child, J. (1972). Organizational structure, environment, and performance: The role of strategic choice. *Sociology, 6,* 1-32.

Child, J. (1987). Information technology, organization, and the response to strategic challenges. *California Management Review, 29,* 33-50.

Clampitt, P. G., & Downs, C. W. (1993). Employee perceptions of the relationship between communication and productivity: A field study. *Journal of Business Communication, 30,* 5-28.

Colling, T., & Ferner, A. (1992). The limits of autonomy: Devolution, line managers, and industrial relations in privatized companies. *Journal of Management Studies, 29,* 209-228.

Comer, D. R. (1991). Organizational newcomers' acquisition of information from peers. *Management Communication Quarterly, 5,* 64-89.

Connor, P. E. (1992). Decision making participation patterns: The role of organizational context. *Academy of Management Journal, 35,* 213-231.

Conrad, C., & Poole, M. S. (1998). *Strategic organizational communication: Into the twenty-first century.* Fort Worth, TX: Harcourt Brace.

Cooper, R. (1992). Formal organization as representation: Remote control, displacement, and abbreviation. In M. Reed & M. Hughes (Eds.), *Rethinking organization: New directions in organizational theory and analysis* (pp. 254-272). Newbury Park, CA: Sage.

Cooper, R., & Burrell, G. (1988). Modernism, postmodernism, and organizational analysis: An introduction. *Organization Studies, 9,* 96-112.

Cooren, F., & Taylor, J. R. (1997). Organization as an effect of mediation: Redefining the link between organization and communication. *Communication Theory, 7,* 219-261.

Cushman, D. P., & King, S. S. (1993). High-speed management: A revolution in organizational communication in the 1990s. In S. A. Deetz (Ed.), *Communication yearbook 16* (pp. 209-236). Newbury Park, CA: Sage.

Cushman, D. P., & King, S. S. (1995). *Communication and high-speed management.* Albany: State University of New York Press.

Dandeker, C. (1990). *Surveillance, power, and modernity: Bureaucracy and discipline from 1700 to the present day.* New York: Cambridge University Press.

Davidow, W., & Malone, M. (1992, December 7). Virtual corporation. *Forbes, 150*(13), 102-108.

DiMaggio, P. J., & Powell, W. W. (1983). The iron cage revisited: Institutional isomorphism and collective rationality in organizational fields. *American Sociological Review, 48,* 147-160.

Doty, D. H., & Glick, W. H. (1994). Typologies as a unique form of theory building: Toward improved understanding and modeling. *Academy of Management Review, 18,* 230-251.

Doty, D. H., Glick, W. H., & Huber, G. P. (1993). Fit, equifinality, and organizational effectiveness: A test of two configurational theories. *Academy of Management Journal, 36,* 1196-1250.

Driskell, L. P., & Salas, E. (1991). Group decision making under stress. *Journal of Applied Psychology, 76,* 473-478.

Drucker, P. (1994, September). The age of transformation. *Atlantic Monthly, 274*(5), 49-56.

Durkheim, É. (1938). *The rules of sociological method.* Chicago: Free Press.

Eccles, R. G., & Crane, D. B. (1987). Managing through networks in investment banking. *California Management Review, 30,* 176-195.

Evans, B. K., & Fischer, D. G. (1992). A hierarchical model of participative decision-making, job autonomy, and perceived control. *Human Relations, 45,* 1169-1189.

Finlay, M. (1987). *Powermatics: A discursive critique of new communications technology.* London: Routledge and Kegan Paul.

Foucault, M. (1977). *Discipline and punish: The birth of the prison.* New York: Vintage.

Fox, S. (1989). The panopticon: From Bentham's obsession to the revolution in management learning. *Human Relations, 42,* 717-739.

Galbraith, J. (1973). *Designing complex organizations.* Reading, MA: Addison-Wesley.

Garson, B. (1988). *The electronic sweatshop.* New York: Penguin.

Giddens, A. (1976). *New rules of sociological method: A positive critique of interpretative sociologies.* New York: Harper & Row.

Giddens, A. (1984). *The constitution of society.* Cambridge, UK: Polity.

Giddens, A. (1991). *Modernity and self-identity: Self and society in the late modern age.* Cambridge, UK: Polity.

Gilsdorf, J. W. (1992). Written corporate policy on communicating: A delphi survey. *Management Communication Quarterly, 5,* 316-347.

Golding, D. (1991). Some everyday rituals in management control. *Journal of Management Studies, 28,* 569-583.

Gouldner, A. (1970). *The coming crisis of Western sociology.* New York: Avon.

Grandori, A., & Soda, G. (1995). Interfirm networks: Antecedents, mechanisms and forms. *Organization Studies, 16,* 183-214.

Hage, J. (1965). An axiomatic theory of organizations. *Administrative Science Quarterly, 10,* 289-320.

Hage, J., & Aiken, M. (1967). Relationship of centralization to other structural properties. *Administrative Science Quarterly, 12,* 71-92.

Hammer, M., & Champy, J. (1993). *Reengineering the corporation.* New York: HarperCollins.

Handy, C. (1989). *The age of unreason.* Boston: Harvard Business School Press.

Hassard, J. (1991). Aspects of time in organization. *Human Relations, 44,* 105-126.

Heckscher, C. (1994). Defining the post-bureaucratic type. In C. Heckscher & A. Donnellon (Eds.), *The post-bureaucratic organization: New perspectives on organizational change* (pp. 14-62). Thousand Oaks, CA: Sage.

Hoffman, A. N., Stearns, T. M., & Shrader, C. B. (1990). Structure, context, and centrality in interorganizational networks. *Journal of Business Research, 20,* 333-347.

House, R., Rousseau, D., & Thomas-Hunt, M. (1995). The meso paradigm: A framework for integration of micro and macro organizational behavior. In L. Cummings & B. Staw (Eds.), *Research in organizational behavior* (Vol. 17, pp. 71-114). Greenwich, CT: JAI.

Huber, G. (1984). The nature and design of post-industrial organizations. *Management Science, 30,* 928-951.

Ilinitch, A., D'Aveni, R., & Lewin, A. Y. (1996). New organizational forms and strategies for managing in hypercompetitive environments. *Organization Science, 7,* 211-220.

Jablin, F. M. (1987). Formal organization structure. In F. M. Jablin, L. L. Putnam, K. H. Roberts, & L. W. Porter (Eds.), *Handbook of organizational communication: An interdisciplinary perspective* (pp. 389-419). Newbury Park, CA: Sage.

Jarvenppa, S. L., & Ives, B. (1994). The global network organization of the future: Information management opportunities and challenges. *Journal of Management Information Systems, 10,* 25-57.

Jermier, J. M., Slocum, J. W., Fry, L., & Gaines, J. (1991). Organizational substructures in a soft bureaucracy: Resistance behind the myth and facade of an official culture. *Organization Science, 2,* 170-194.

Johnson, J. D. (1993). *Organizational communication structure.* Norwood, NJ: Ablex.

Kant, I. (1970). *Critique of pure reason* (N. K. Smith, Trans.). London: Macmillan.

Kanter, R. M. (1977). *Men and women of the corporation.* New York: Basic Books.

Kanter, R. M. (1983). *The change masters: Innovations for productivity in the American corporation.* New York: Simon & Schuster.

Katovich, M. A. (1985). Ceremonial openings in bureaucratic encounters: From shuffling feet to shuffling papers. *Studies in Symbolic Interactionism, 6,* 307-333.

Katz, F. E. (1965). Explaining informal work groups in complex organizations: The case for autonomy in structure. *Administrative Science Quarterly, 10,* 204-223.

Konsynski, B. R., & Sviokla, J. J. (1994). Cognitive reapportionment: Rethinking the location of judgment in managerial decision-making. In C. Heckscher & A. Donnellon (Eds.), *The post-bureaucratic organization: New perspectives on organizational change* (pp. 91-107). Thousand Oaks, CA: Sage.

Kontopoulos, K. M. (1993). *The logics of social structure.* New York: Cambridge University Press.

Krone, K. J. (1986, May). *The effects of decision type, message initiation, and perceptions of centralization of authority on subordinates' use of upward influence message types.* Paper presented at the annual meeting of the International Communication Association, Chicago.

Krone, K. J. (1992). A comparison of organizational, structural, and relationship effects on subordinates' upward influence choices. *Communication Quarterly, 40,* 1-15.

Krone, K. J. (1994). Structuring constraints on perceptions of upward influence and supervisory relations. *Southern Communication Journal, 59,* 215-226.

Lammers, C. J. (1988). Transience and persistence of ideal types in organization theory. *Research in the Sociology of Organizations, 6,* 205-224.

Langley, A. (1990). Patterns in the use of formal analysis in strategic decisions. *Organization Studies, 11,* 17-45.

Larson, A. (1992). Network dyads in entrepreneurial settings: A study in the governance of exchange processes. *Administrative Science Quarterly, 37,* 76-104.

Lawrence, P., & Lorsch, J. (1967). *Organization and environment.* Cambridge, MA: Harvard Graduate School of Business Administration.

Lucas, H. C. (1996). *The T-form organization.* San Francisco: Jossey-Bass.

Lucas, H. C., & Baroudi, J. (1994). The role of information technology in organizational design. *Journal of Management Information Systems, 10,* 9-23.

Macey, B., Peterson, M. F., & Norton, L. W. (1989). A test of participation theory in a work redesign field setting: Degree of participation and comparison site contrasts. *Human Relations, 42,* 1095-1165.

MacLeod, L., Scriven, J., & Wayne, F. S. (1992). Gender and management level differences in the oral communication patterns of bank managers. *Journal of Business Communication, 29,* 343-365.

McCauley, C. D., Ruderman, M. N., Ohlcott, P. J., & Morrow, J. F. (1994). Assessing the developmental components of managerial jobs. *Journal of Applied Psychology, 79,* 544-560.

McKelvey, B. (1982). *Organizational systematics—Taxonomy, evolution, classification.* Berkeley: University of California Press.

McPhee, R. (1985). Formal structure and organizational communication. In R. D. McPhee & P. K. Tompkins (Eds.), *Organizational communication: Traditional themes and new directions* (pp. 149-177). Beverly Hills, CA: Sage.

McPhee, R. (1988). Vertical communication chains: Toward an integrated view. *Management Communication Quarterly, 1,* 455-493.

McPhee, R. (1989). Organizational communication: A structurational exemplar. In B. Dervin, L. Grossberg, B. O'Keefe, & E. Wartella (Eds.), *Rethinking communication: Vol. 2. Paradigm exemplars* (pp. 199-212). Newbury Park, CA: Sage.

McPhee, R. (1998). Giddens' conception of personal relationships and its relevance to communication theory. In R. Conville & E. Rogers (Eds.), *The meaning of "relationship" in interpersonal communication* (pp. 83-106). Westport, CT: Praeger.

McPhee, R., Habbel, D., & Fordham-Habbel, T. (1987, May). *Process theories of organizational structure.* Paper presented at the annual meeting of the International Communication Association Convention, Montreal.

Meyer, H. D. (1995). Organizational environments and organizational discourse: Bureaucracy between two worlds. *Organization Science, 6,* 32-43.

Meyer, J. W., & Rowan, B. (1977). Institutionalized organizations: Formal structure as myth and ceremony. *American Journal of Sociology, 83,* 340-363.

Miles, R. E., & Snow, C. C. (1986). Organizations: New concepts for new forms. *California Management Review, 28,* 62-73.

Miller, D. (1987). Strategy making and structure: Analysis and implications for performance. *Academy of Management Journal, 30,* 7-32.

Miller, D. (1990). Organizational configurations: Cohesion, change, and prediction. *Human Relations, 43,* 771-789.

Miller, D., Droje, C., & Toulouse, J.-M. (1988). Strategic process and content as mediators between organizational context and structure. *Academy of Management Journal, 31,* 544-569.

Miller, D., & Mintzberg, H. (1983). The case for configuration. In G. Morgan (Ed.), *Beyond method: Strategies for social research* (pp. 57-73). Beverly Hills, CA: Sage.

Mintzberg, H. (1979). *The structuring of organizations.* Englewood Cliffs, NJ: Prentice Hall.

Mintzberg, H. (1983a). *Power in and around organizations.* Englewood Cliffs, NJ: Prentice Hall.

Mintzberg, H. (1983b). *Structure in fives: Designing effective organizations.* Englewood Cliffs, NJ: Prentice Hall.

Mintzberg, H. (1989). *Mintzberg on management: Inside our strategic world of organizations.* New York: Free Press.

Morand, D. A. (1995). The role of behavioral formality and informality in the enactment of bureaucratic versus organic organizations. *Academy of Management Review, 20,* 831-872.

Mowshowitz, A. (1994). Virtual organization: A vision of management in the information age. *Information Society, 10,* 267-288.

Mowshowitz, A. (1997). Virtual organization: Introduction. *Communications of the ACM, 40,* 30-37.

Mulgan, G. J. (1991). *Communication and control: Networks and the new economies of communication.* New York: Guilford.

Nohria, N., & Berkley, J. D. (1994). The virtual organization: Bureaucracy, technology, and the implosion of control. In C. Heckscher & A. Donnellon (Eds.), *The post-bureaucratic organization: New perspectives on organizational change* (pp. 108-128). Thousand Oaks, CA: Sage.

Olson, L. M. (1995). Record keeping practices: Consequences of accounting demands in a public clinic. *Qualitative Sociology, 18,* 45-70.

Orton, J. D., & Weick, K. E. (1990). Loosely coupled systems: A reconceptualization. *Academy of Management Review, 15,* 203-223.

Ostroff, C., & Schmitt, N. (1993). Configurations of organizational effectiveness and efficiency. *Academy of Management Journal, 36,* 1345-1361.

Parsons, T. (1960). *Structure and process in modern societies.* New York: Free Press.

Pearson, C. A. L. (1992). Autonomous workgroups: An evaluation at an industrial site. *Human Relations, 45,* 905-936.

Pelz, D. (1952). Influence: A key to effective leadership in the first-line supervisor. *Personnel, 29,* 209-217.

Perin, C. (1991). The moral fabric of the office: Panopticon, discourse, and schedule flexibilities. *Research in the Sociology of Organizations, 8,* 241-268.

Perrow, C. (1986). *Complex organizations: A critical essay* (3rd ed.). Glenview, IL: Scott, Foresman.

Peters, T. (1980). Management systems: The language of organization character and competence. *Organizational Dynamics, 9,* 3-26.

Peters, T., & Waterman, R. (1982). *In search of excellence.* New York: Harper & Row.

Pettigrew, A. M. (1973). *The politics of organizational decision making.* London: Tavistock.

Pettigrew, A. M. (1985). *The awakening giant: Continuity and change in ICI.* Oxford, UK: Basil Blackwell.

Poole, M. S. (1999). Organizational challenges for the new forms. In G. DeSanctis & J. Fulk (Eds.), *Shaping organization form: Communication, connection, and community.* Thousand Oaks, CA: Sage.

Poster, M. (1990). *The mode of information: Poststructuralism and social context.* Chicago: University of Chicago Press.

Powell, W. W. (1990). Neither market nor hierarchy: Network forms or organization. In L. L. Cummings & B. M. Staw (Eds.), *Research in organizational behavior* (Vol. 12, pp. 295-336). Westport, CT: JAI.

Prechel, H. N. (1994). Economic crisis and the centralization of control over the managerial process: Corporate restructuring and neo-Fordist decision-making. *American Sociological Review, 59,* 723-745.

Ragins, B. R., & Cotton, J. L. (1991). Easier said than done: Gender differences in perceived barriers to gaining a mentor. *Academy of Management Journal, 34,* 939-951.

Reynolds, P. D. (1971). *A primer in theory construction.* Indianapolis, IN: Bobbs-Merrill.

Rice, R., & Associates. (1984). *The new media: Communication research and technology.* Beverly Hills, CA: Sage.

Rice, R., Chang, S.-J., & Torobin, J. (1992). Communicator style, media use, organizational level, and evaluation of electronic messaging. *Management Communication Quarterly, 4,* 3-33.

Rice, R., & Shook, D. E. (1990). Relationships of job categories and organizational levels to use of communication channels, including electronic mail: A meta-analysis and extension. *Journal of Management Studies, 27,* 375-399.

Ring, P., & Van de Ven, A. (1994). Developmental processes of cooperative interorganizational relationships. *Academy of Management Review, 19,* 90-118.

Roethlisberger, F. J. (1941). *Management and morale.* Cambridge, MA: Harvard University Press.

Scott-Morton, M. S. (Ed.). (1991). *The company of the 1990s: Information technology and organizational transformation.* New York: Oxford University Press.

Shrader, C. B., Lincoln, J. R., & Hoffman, A. N. (1989). The network structures of organizations: Effects of task contingencies and distributional form. *Human Relations, 42,* 43-66.

Simon, H. A. (1976). *Administrative behavior* (3rd ed.). New York: Free Press.

Smeltzer, L. R., & Fann, G. L. (1989). Comparison of manager communication patterns in small entrepreneurial organizations and large, mature organizations. *Group and Organization Studies, 14,* 198-215.

Smith, D. E. (1990). *Texts, facts, and femininity: Exploring the relations of ruling.* New York: Routledge.

Smith, K., Grimm, C., Gannon, M., & Chen, M.-J. (1991). Organizational information processing, competitive responses, and performance in the U.S. domestic airline industry. *Academy of Management Journal, 34,* 60-85.

Smith, R. (1993, May). *Images of organizational communication: Root-metaphors of the organization-communication relation.* Paper presented at annual meeting of the International Communication Association, Washington, D.C.

Souder, W. E., & Moenaert, R. K. (1992). Integrating marketing and RD project personnel within innovation projects: An information uncertainty model. *Journal of Management Studies, 29,* 485-512.

Stevenson, W. B., & Gilly, M. C. (1991). Information processing and problem solving: The migration of problems through formal positions and networks of ties. *Academy of Management Journal, 34,* 918-928.

Stinchcombe, A. (1968). *Constructing social theories.* New York: Harcourt, Brace, and World.

Stohl, C., & Redding, W. C. (1987). Messages and message exchange processes. In F. M. Jablin, L. L. Putnam, K. H. Roberts, & L. W. Porter (Eds.), *Handbook of organizational communication: An interdisciplinary perspective* (pp. 451-502). Newbury Park, CA: Sage.

Taylor, J. R. (1993). *Rethinking the theory of organizational communication: How to read an organization.* Norwood, NJ: Ablex.

Taylor, J. R., Cooren, R., Giroux, H., & Robichaud, D. (1996, February). *Are organization and communication equivalent?* Paper presented at the conference

Organizational Communication and Change: Challenges in the Next Century, Austin, TX.

Taylor, J. R., & Van Every, E. J. (1993). *The vulnerable fortress: Bureaucratic organization and management in the information age.* Toronto, Canada: University of Toronto Press.

Thomas, J. B., Shankster, L. J., & Mathieu, J. E. (1994). Antecedents to organizational issue interpretation: The roles of single-level, cross-level and content cues. *Academy of Management Journal, 37,* 1252-1284.

Tompkins, P. K. (1987). Translating organizational theory: Symbolism over substance. In F. M. Jablin, L. L. Putnam, K. H. Roberts, & L. W. Porter (Eds.), *Handbook of organizational communication: An interdisciplinary perspective* (pp. 70-96). Newbury Park, CA: Sage.

Trombetta, J. J., & Rogers, D. P. (1988). Communication climate, satisfaction, and organizational commitment: The effects of information adequacy, communication openness, and decision participation. *Management Communication Quarterly, 1,* 494-515.

Turner, J. (1988). *A theory of social interaction.* Stanford, CA: Stanford University Press.

Van de Ven, A. H., & Poole, M. S. (1995). Explaining development and change in organizations. *Academy of Management Review, 20,* 510-540.

Volberda, H. W. (1996). Toward the flexible form: How to remain vital in hypercompetitive environments. *Organization Science, 7,* 359-374.

Watzlawick, P., Beavin, J., & Jackson, D. D. (1967). *The pragmatics of human communication.* New York: Norton.

Weber, M. (1946). *Essays in sociology.* New York: Oxford University Press.

Weber, M. (1949). *Methodology of the social sciences* (E. Shils & H. Finch, Trans.). Chicago: Free Press.

Weick, K. E. (1979). *The social psychology of organizing* (2nd ed.). Reading, MA: Addison-Wesley.

Weick, K. E. (1995). *Sensemaking in organizations.* Thousand Oaks, CA: Sage.

Wiley, N. (1988). The micro-macro problem in social theory. *Sociological Theory, 6,* 254-261.

Winter, S. J., & Taylor, S. L. (1996). The role of IT in the transformation of work: A comparison of post-industrial, industrial, and proto-industrial organizations. *Information Systems Research, 7,* 5-21.

Witte, J. F. (1980). *Democracy, authority, and alienation in work: Workers' participation in an American corporation.* Chicago: University of Chicago Press.

Yammarino, F. J., & Dubinsky, A. J. (1992). Superior-subordinate relationships: A multiple levels of analysis approach. *Human Relations, 45,* 575-600.

Yammarino, F. J., & Naughton, T. N. (1988). Time spent communicating: A multiple levels of analysis approach. *Human Relations, 41,* 655-676.

Yates, J. (1989). *Control through communication: The rise of system in American management.* Baltimore: Johns Hopkins University Press.

Zenger, T. R., & Lawrence, B. S. (1989). Organizational demography: The differential effects of age and tenure distribution on technical communication. *Academy of Management Journal, 32,* 353-376.

Zuboff, S. (1988). *In the age of the smart machine: The future of work and power.* New York: Basic Books.

14

New Media and Organizational Structuring

RONALD E. RICE
Rutgers University

URS E. GATTIKER
Obel Family Foundation, Denmark

Try to imagine how a person in 1850 might explain organizational communication and organizational structures of the mid-20th century. That person would have no familiarity with telephones, telegraphs, vertical files, paper clips, photocopies, elevators, electricity, and a whole host of other communication and information technologies. Now, imagine explaining to someone in 1950—before personal computers, desktop publishing, multi-

AUTHORS' NOTE: We would like to thank editors Fred Jablin and Linda Putnam, anonymous reviewers, and Claire B. Johnson for their comments, and Michelle Seeman for her editorial assistance. Financial support for this research project was provided to the second author in part by the Social Sciences and Humanities Research Council of Canada, as well as the Burns and Cleo Mowers Endowment Fund, Faculty of Management, University of Lethbridge. Conclusions (if any) of this chapter represent those of the authors and do not necessarily reflect the views of the sponsoring agencies. Due to space limitations, we provide no methodological qualifications of reviewed studies. We do not mean this as a reflection on the importance of such considerations when assessing research and implications. Further, we could cover only a limited range of relevant issues. Again, this does not reflect on the significance of those other concerns. Indeed, the original manuscript bellied up at around 150 pages, indicating at least a slightly less biased and ideologically blind approach, research program, or worldview than does this short (*sic*) version.

media, the Internet and the World Wide Web, online databases, facsimiles, electronic mail, voice mail, videoconferencing, electronic funds transfer, data communication networks, cellular phones, and credit cards in most organizations—developments in organizational communication and structures at the beginning of this new millennium. Finally, imagine either explanation without referring to any extant communication and information systems or any extant theories of organizational communication and structure before either time period.

There are so many assumptions built into our notions and experiences of organizational communication and structure that are based on how people interact and communicate within and across organizations with these technologies that both of these explanations would be highly flawed, if not impossible. The implication is that our understandings of organizational communication, structure, and media are all influenced by preexisting media and structures, and in turn influence the development of new structures and media. We cannot know the future, but we can attempt to better understand the iterative and reciprocal influence of existing structures, underlying processes, and new media.

Thus, four propositions motivate this chapter. First, in addition to traditional concepts (such as centralization or formal communication flow), organizational structures include meanings (such as about the appropriate uses of familiar and new media) and relations (among members and units, within and across organizations). Second, these structures can constrain or facilitate the development and use of a computer-mediated communication and information system (CIS). Third, processes of transformation in organizational and CIS structures may range from subtle evolutions of usage norms to formal metastructuring activities. Fourth, CISs can constrain or facilitate changes within and across organizational structures.

The first section briefly introduces CISs and suggests some basic conceptual dimensions of organizational media in general. It ar-

gues that common conceptualizations of new media may be highly constrained (thus structured) by idealizations of familiar media that have become structured into media artifacts. The section outlines traditional approaches to studying organizational structure, then it presents a simple structurational approach as one way of organizing this diverse literature and research. The next section surveys concepts and results from selected research within three broad structurational processes (development, transformation, institutionalization). The last section provides a brief conclusion.

COMPUTER-MEDIATED COMMUNICATION AND INFORMATION SYSTEMS

Overview of CISs

CISs combine four major components. *Computing* allows processing of content and structuring of communication participation. *Telecommunication networks* allow access and connectivity to many others and to varieties of information across space and time. *Information or communication resources* range from databases to communities of potential participants. *Digitization of content* allows the integration and exchange of multiple communication modes—such as graphics, video, sound, text—across multiple media and distribution networks (Rice, 1987). This review emphasizes computer-mediated communication systems (CMC), but also refers to some research where information systems are associated with organizational communication.

Such systems include, for example, audiotex; automatic teller machines (ATMs) that are redesigned as information services terminals; cellular phones and pagers; collaborative systems such as screen-sharing and joint document preparation; computer bulletin boards; computer conferencing; conversational and workflow processors; cyberphones; decision support systems with communication components; desktop publishing and document distribution; multimedia desktop conferencing and screen-sharing; electronic document interchange (EDI); electronic mail; facsimile; gophers/World Wide Web; group support systems and other groupware; home shopping and banking; hypertext and hypermedia; intelligent telephone systems; Internet listservers; local area networks; mobile personal communication devices; multimedia computing; online and portable databases; optical media such as CD-ROM and lasercards; optically scanned and networked documents; personal information assistants; personal locator badges; presentation devices such as computer screen projectors; telephone services such as call forwarding, redial until delivery, or automatically transferring a pager message to one's voice messaging system; teletext; video teleconferencing; videotex; virtual reality and cyberspace; voice mail; wide area networks; and word processing.

All Media Are Multidimensional and Artifactual Structures

Such lists of example CISs are not, by themselves, particularly enduring or insightful. Further, they tend to conceptually structure the particular combination of components and uses into a singular system that appears stable and coherent. This institutionalization via labeling fosters both technological determinism (the "system" represents and imposes causal necessity) and critical determinism (any negative aspects associated with this system are due to the technology).

Thus, crucial to the general argument that meanings of CISs are a part of organizational structures is the awareness that both traditional and new media embed a wide, overlapping range of technical and social capabilities and constraints. Typically, researchers and ordinary folk alike tend to lump communication media into familiar, binary, and mutually exclusive categories. Examples include mass media/interpersonal, objective/socially constructed, information rich/lean, organic/technological, traditional/new, democratizing/he-

gemonic, same/different times/places, content sources/users are institutions/individuals/computer systems, and so forth (see the review of such typologies by Rice, 1992; see also Culnan & Markus, 1987; Soe & Markus, 1993).

Yet media in general and CISs in particular are inherently ambiguous (because they can be interpreted in multiple and possibly conflicting ways), can rarely be fully understood, and continue to be adapted, reinvented, and redesigned (Fulk, 1993; Johnson & Rice, 1987; Rice, 1992). So taking a multidimensional perspective toward conceptualizing media seems necessary and appropriate. Table 14.1 proposes four dimensions of a wide variety of capabilities and attributes of media: constraints, bandwidth, interactivity, and network flow (Rice, 1987; Rice & Steinfield, 1994). Table 14.1 also compares two very different communication channels—face-to-face and asynchronous computer conferencing—across these attributes as an example of how limited simple oppositions of "familiar" and "new" media are (see Rice, 1987, and Rice & Steinfield, 1994, for similar comparisons involving other media). An intriguing exercise would be to use this table to analyze one's own use of a variety of media (letters, telephone, meetings, e-mail, informal conversation, voice mail) in two very different social contexts (work, home).

This and other multidimensional typologies serve to emphasize that (a) all media may be perceived, constrained, adopted, used, and evaluated in different ways within social and technological constraints; and (b) overemphasis or idealization of some characteristics of one medium can de-emphasize and limit perceived as well as actual characteristics of other media.

Three main conclusions follow from such a multidimensional perspective. First, media may be compared in many ways, so no medium is absolutely preferable or inherently "better" or "worse." A multidimensional approach generates better understandings of how both familiar and new media are structured in particular organizations (Culnan &

TABLE 14.1 Dimensions and Attributes of Media, Comparing Use of Face-to-Face to Asynchronous Computer Conferencing

Dimensions and Attributes	Face-to-Face	Computer Conferencing
Constraints		
Receiver can identify sender	y at least appearance	n listservs, anonymous, aliases
Have to know receiver's account/name/ address/number	y to find	y if private message n if posting
Address where person receives message is fixed to physical location/terminal	y	n
Users have varying participation modes	y	y
Source or centrality of control	often one person	usually dispersed
Can overcome selectivity	easier	harder
Can maintain privacy	depends on trust	trust and/or features
Organizational norms for use	y institutionalized	n developing
Need temporal proximity	y	n
Need geographical proximity	y	n
Ease of access to physical location, physical device	y once in contact n if not	n improving y with wireless
Ease of access to and use of interface, commands	y for familiar n for novel	n improving
Access costs (time, money, energy, knowledge)	highly variable	variable
Diversity of content available	depends on person	extensive
Diversity of content sequencing	n	y
Can store content (short term, long term)	limited	extensive
Limits to message length	y	n
Use to transfer documents	y	y
Can indicate priority of message	y	y not as much
Can ensure levels of privacy	n usually	y
Can retrieve by indexes or browse in random or other order	n	y
Can use filtering or allocation processes	n once contacted	y developing
Message can initiate other processes directly	y depends	y developing
Receiver can reprocess, edit for further use	n not accurately	y
Users can structure flow and privileges	y if great power asymmetry	y developing
Can easily convert content to other medium	n	y developing
Bandwidth		
Analog/digital	analog	both
Color, images, sound, text, numbers, motion, other senses	most	developing
Physical distance	y	n
Gestures	y	n developing icons
Tone, emphasis	y	n paralinguistics

(continued)

TABLE 14.1   Continued

Dimensions and Attributes	Face-to-Face	Computer Conferencing
Connotation/denotation	y high level possible	n low level typically
Symbolic aspects or connotations of medium	y	y
Social presence/media richness	can be high	usually low
"Personalize" greeting	y	y
Interaction		
Synchronous or asynchronous	synchronous	both
Symmetry of initiation and response	usually asymmetric	symmetric
Type of feedback	multiple	limited
Quickness of response by intended receiver	can be simultaneous if person there but that takes time	quicker than face-to-face if count meeting scheduling time
Control receiving pace	n	y
Confirm correct receiver, receipt	y	n developing
Mutual discourse	possible	possible
Quick-reply feature	interrupting	y
Network		
Information flow (one-to-one, one-to-few, one-to-many, few-to-few, many-to-many—both of users and of content, such as multiple copies)	one-to-one, perhaps one-to-few	all flows, depending
Usage domain (human system, individual, dyadic, group, intraorganizational, community, interorganizational, transnational)	mostly dyadic group	most forms possible
Distortion through overload	y	y unless moderator
Distortion through forwarding edited message	y	y usually available record, though
Role effect (can flow be easily controlled)	y	n difficult in computer conferencing
Critical mass necessary	n	y

NOTE: y = yes; n = no. These allocations are highly subjective and contextual. Many situations might generate other evaluations. However, this shows the wide range of possible attributes within a medium as well as the wide range of comparisons across media.

Markus, 1987; Rice, 1993a). For instance, interpersonal communication may have many disadvantages with respect to constraints (everyone has to be in a particular place at a particular time) and network flow (in larger groups, a few talk and most listen, and everyone has to respond to topics immediately or not at all) for certain social contexts (such as organizational meetings) or participants (such as the physically disadvantaged or culturally discriminated).

Second, CISs have many more capabilities than just the by-now familiar "overcoming constraints of time and space." It may well be that the ability to reprocess, combine, and analyze information in many forms from multiple sources has far more profound implications for organizing than "fast" or "asynchronous" interaction. For example, the telegraph allowed people to communicate across time and space at a pace and amount never before experienced but also enabled railroad companies to collect, associate, and analyze information from stations about the dynamics of trains, shipments, and passengers. This transformed how organizations collected and processed information, and how they learned from that information to develop effective schedules, routing algorithms and billing procedures that changed the domains and design of railroads (Beniger, 1986; Yates & Benjamin, 1991).

A third, more subtle, conclusion is that much of what we feel is "natural" about traditional media is largely an "artifact" resulting from the confounding of particular characteristics (such as material production, forms of access, social conventions, etc.) with a particular communication medium (such as interpersonal "voice") (Rice, 1993a; Shudson, 1978). As a consequence, new media are often critiqued from the position of a privileged, artifactual, idealized notion of interpersonal communication and traditional media (Carey, 1990). This interpretative structuring of both familiar and new media leads to assessments of new media as a source of utopian benefits as well as a destroyer of traditional values and ideals (Jensen, 1990). Some historical analyses of how prior artifacts and interpretations constrained the development of new media have considered (a) how the memo evolved through intraorganizational battles from personal diaries and reports of branch managers or colonial administrators (Yates & Benjamin, 1991); (b) how the telephone and electricity were first embedded in prior social conventions and fears (Marvin, 1988); and how the typewriter, its supporting institutions, and even its technological design were developed, critiqued, and restructured through social practices (David, 1985; Walker, 1984).

Thus, we can conceptualize media artifacts as a particular kind of organizational "structure." Artifacts are the structuring of communication media through use and interpretation, until they become perceived as "familiar" or "natural" and thus "idealized" in ways that constrain possible interpretations of both those current as well as new media. A later section will identify some of the factors that generate as well as restructure such media artifacts.

Organizational Structure and Structuring

Organizational structure is generally conceived of as "constraints that organization members face in the communication process" (Jablin, 1987, p. 390). Stevenson (1993) provides a parsimonious review of major approaches to conceptualizing organizational structure, while Monge and Contractor (Chapter 12, this volume) look specifically at network aspects of structure. Johnson (1993) reviews five approaches toward organizational structure. Communication *relationships* (interactions, exchanges, and flow) are typically the surface manifestations of deeper relational structures, such as work dependencies, power, commitments, and obstructed or absent relations. *Entities* are the units or actors involved, such as dyads, groups, work units, and higher-order systems such as organizations; these represent different kinds and levels of structure. *Context* is the local and global environment of norms, tasks, rules, and prior relations that structure ongoing actions and interpretations. *Configuration* concerns recurrent and recognizable patterns. Formal approaches to structure often portray configuration in an organizational chart or through indexes such as formalization, centralization, size, complexity, and span of control. Finally, *temporal stability* is the extent of enduring or consistent organizational patterning, ranging from an enduring headquarter-branch organization to changing project groups. Johnson integrates these five forms of structure into a single definition (intentionally emphasizing intraorganizational and communication structures): "Organizational communication structure refers to the relatively stable configuration of communication relationships between entities within an organizational context" (p. 11).

Such reviews of prior approaches to organizational structure generate several implications relevant to our argument. First, structure is best conceptualized as a process. This process involves meaning (as reflected in norms, interpretations, and artifacts from individual interpretations to international regulatory environments) and relations (as reflected in formal and informal communication networks, within and across physical and regulated boundaries). Second, structure both constrains and facilitates human action in organizational contexts. Third, new structures can arise or be suppressed. Fourth, most approaches to structure reject strict determinism, whether of an optimistic or a critical sort (i.e., technological utopias or technophobias). So relations between structure and technology are contextual and dynamic, but (theoretically at least) understandably so, and involve both "positive" and "negative" aspects. Given these assumptions, a structuration perspective provides a general theoretical framework for organizing a review of relationships among organizational structures and CISs.

A structuration perspective allows us to generalize the domain of organizational structure well beyond limited concepts such as "formalization" or "complexity." It focuses on the ongoing reciprocal association among structures and technologies (Giddens, 1976, 1984). In this view, structure is manifested in properties of actual social systems. These properties include rules and resources that both mediate action and are institutionalized by human action. Social interaction involves meaning (structures of signification), power (structures of domination via authority and allocation), and norms (structures of legitimation). Interaction patterns (human agency) become institutionalized (as structural properties) through repeated, habitual action, which

are then referred to or applied through subsequent agency. Structural properties are therefore abstract properties of, and exhibited by, social systems. They are sustained only through contextualized human action and interpretation that are enabled by structural rules and resources in the form of objective conditions (Giddens, 1976; Orlikowski, 1992).

Systems have structures because they are conditioned by rules and resources. But these systems depend on routines being reproduced by (more or less) knowledgeable actors applying structural properties (intentionally and unintentionally) (Haines, 1988). However, actors are embedded in ongoing social and technical structures, which may both constrain and facilitate their knowledgeability and intentionality, as well as influence their access to those rules and resources. Thus, structure involves subjective and objective components, is manifested in social relations, and requires multiple levels of analysis.

We can see, then, that organizational media artifacts are a specific source as well as consequence of structuration. Attitudes toward and uses of current organizational media become institutionalized in the form of media artifacts. These structures of acceptable norms, evaluations, and resources of familiar media then constrain and facilitate the adoption and implementation of new media. Social actions, organizational policies, user attitudes, technology developments, and so on may interact in transformational processes that may or may not institutionalize new structures that themselves may well become artifacts over time.

Orlikowski refers to this as the *duality of technology* (1992; Orlikowski & Robey, 1991; see also Contractor & Eisenberg, 1990; Dutton & Danzinger, 1982; Kling & Jewett, 1994; Markus & Robey, 1988). Orlikowski's summary of this duality of technology involves four major propositions:

1. Technology is the product of human action.
2. Technology is the medium of human action (both constraining and facilitating action

through interpretations, capabilities, norms, use).

3. Institutional conditions provide the context for interaction with technology (such as professional standards, resources, implementation policies).

4. There are institutional consequences of interaction with technology (through structures of signification, domination, and legitimation).

Her model thus proposes two kinds of conditions for use (institutional and technological) and two kinds of consequences of use (technological and institutional), mediated through individuals' actions, specifically the use of technology (Orlikowski, Yates, Okamura, & Fujimoto, 1995).

Orlikowski et al. (1995) extend this model by identifying a metastructuring or transformational process: technology-use mediation. This explicit and ongoing adaptation of CISs in their changing use contexts, not just at formal implementation or maintenance periods, can facilitate ongoing changes in technology designs, social norms, and organizational forms. Technology-use mediation occurs through deliberate reinforcement and adjustment between institutional properties, with occasional periods of episodic change. Thus, metastructuration adds conditions for mediation and consequences for mediation to the model proposed by Orlikowski and colleagues. So institutions, technologies, and mediation present conditions as well as undergo consequences through the structuration process.

Thus, CISs—and the meanings and relations associated with them—are particular instances of some rules and resources representing organizational structure. The interpretations of new systems are constrained by earlier interpretations, perhaps by exaggeration or misunderstanding of its potential characteristics, comparisons to media artifacts, even by rationales for design choices that are now lost to the new users (such as reduced labor costs, a visionary supervisor, or strategic initiatives; see Johnson & Rice, 1987). Particular mani-

festations of CISs may be rejected or continually restructured through agency, or may remain stable through continued unreflective use, institutionalized procedures, or even considered choice. CISs may in turn be a catalyst or occasion for organizational restructuring. Thus, the structuring of CISs is manifested in widely diverse interpretations, uses, and outcomes (Dubinskas, 1993; Ehrlich, 1987; Johnson & Rice, 1987; Mackay, 1988; Markus, 1992).

Structuration of a CIS involves ongoing microprocesses, as individuals working together appropriate the technology in various ways, both consciously and unconsciously, intentionally and unintentionally, within organizational, social, and technological structures (Lea, O'Shea, & Fung, 1995; Poole & DeSanctis, 1990) such as preferences and abilities of users, design choices, and implementation and management strategies (Perio & Prieto, 1994). Lea et al. (1995) argue that "actors" may include both humans and other entities (such as technological infrastructure or industry regulations) that are co-constructed through interactions to constantly renegotiate both content and context. Taking a more macro view, Gattiker (1990) proposed that the forms and implications of technology in organizations are based on the mutual interaction among (a) internal labor markets (rules and regulations pertaining to human resources), (b) strategic choices by the firm (or how much planning may take advantage of environmental opportunities and constraints), and (c) the socially construed work environment.

We now turn to summarizing, within this structuration framework, some prior research on CISs and organizations.

REVIEWS WITHIN GENERAL STRUCTURATIONAL PHASES

The following sections generalize the structuration process somewhat by identifying three processes of CIS structuration: adoption/implementation, transformation, and institutionalization (Orlikowski, 1992; Rice, 1987). There is debate as to the temporal location of structuration processes. Lea et al. (1995), for instance, say that unpacking context and action into "temporal cycles of alternating cause and effect" somewhat weakens the power of structuration theory. Nonetheless, we agree with Haines's (1988) characterization of Giddens's position that actors are primarily motivated to integrate habitual practices across place and time, and thus do not perceive structuration as a constantly simultaneous process. So organizing our review by three general structurational processes is both parsimonious as well as general. Across these three processes, the following illustrative research identifies ways in which organizational structures (both meaning and relations) and CISs may constrain or facilitate each other. Of course, almost none of the CIS research traditions grouped within each of these three processes was developed and studied with structuration theory in mind. And many of them may well be implicated in one or more of the three processes. However, we propose that the various research traditions may be thought of as ways of framing different aspects and microprocesses of a general structuration process, and we summarize them within the process that best characterizes their underlying argument.

Structural Influences on Adoption/Implementation of CISs

The following subsections summarize several prominent research traditions that consider how organizational structures constrain or facilitate the adoption/implementation of CISs. To the extent that each of these processes reflects differential control over and access to material resources, influence, and forms of discourse, these also represent sites of organizational power. However, we defer discussion of power to the institutionalization section. The subsections are ordered, somewhat arbitrarily, from a greater emphasis on structuring through structures of meaning

(genres and norms, culture, and perceptions of CISs) to a greater emphasis on structuring through structures of relations (social influence through networks, critical mass, and physical location). More macrostructural relations such as environmental factors, unions, and regulatory policies—both domestic and international—also influence CIS use and related changes in organizations (Gattiker, 1990; Gattiker & Paulson, 1999). And new CISs generate occasions for restructuring such policies and organizational environments. But these topics are beyond the scope of this chapter.

Media Genres and Usage Norms

As one way of understanding the adoption and evolution of familiar and new media forms and uses, Yates and Orlikowski (1992) introduced the concept of *organizational communication genres*. Genres are specific variants of a general form of a medium, associated with identifiable formats, circumscribed content, established practices, and a specific community of users. One example is the moderated online listserv (with a boilerplate masthead, brief summary of entries, edited contributions by listserv members) as a genre from the general CIS medium of e-mail messages. These genres are invoked in response to commonly recognized recurrent situations, involving the "history and nature of established practices, social relations, and communication policies within organizations," as well as accepted rights and responsibilities of participants.

Examples of how meaning in the form of social conventions structures media genres include rules about appropriate communication behavior (when is a voice mail response "too late"?), taboos (you can't send an e-mail directly to the CEO), expectations (how much detail is required in e-mail responses?), and roles (how much message communication filtering should listserv moderators perform?) (Ehrlich, 1987). McKenney, Zack, and Doherty's (1992) study of a programming team's use of various media found that as people develop routines for solving initially new problems and organizational challenges, they also develop shared understandings and expectations for future interactions that include issues such as topics, timing, participants, and medium. Thus, they argue that face-to-face "effectively serves as a context-creating medium, while [e-mail] is a context-reliant medium" (p. 285). As CISs become more familiar and institutionalized, they too will be appropriated into new genres, and become context-creating media.

Orlikowski and Yates (1993) studied nearly 1,500 messages from an e-mail system used by 17 members of a distributed group in a three-year computer language design project, and followed up with personal interviews. The use of traditional genres (memo, proposal, and ballot) declined, while the use of a new genre ("dialogues"—chained conversations, identified by associated content in the subject line, and including portions of the message being referred to) increased. Influences on the development of the new genre included the group's social history, the project life cycle, and the capabilities of the system.

One implication of the genre approach is that how CISs are conceptualized strongly influences their adoption, application, and success/failure. For example, conceptualizing, implementing, and using voice mail as a single, fixed genre similar to a telephone with recording capabilities stifles the emergence of the possibly new organizational genre of voice messaging (Adams, Todd, & Nelson, 1993; Rice & Danowski, 1993; Rice & Tyler, 1995; Stewart, 1992). Bikson and Law (1993) described how technical constraints in the World Bank's e-mail system strongly limited its conceptualization and application (such as integrating several documents, preparing letters and envelopes, sharing of structured files, storing messages in different electronic file categories). Learning, experimentation, awareness of initial adoption rationales, expanded or new system capabilities, and sharing new ways of using systems with others all facili-

tate the development of new media genres (Johnson & Rice, 1987; Orlikowski, 1992).

Culture

Johnson (1993) argues that meanings and cultural elements are consequential organizational structures: "Communication rituals themselves, in addition to being reflections of culture, are also elements of communication structure, since they represent relatively stable configurations of communication relationships between entities within an organization" (p. 79). Configurational and cultural structures may well overlap, such as when a charismatic leader manages through bureaucratic forms. So both formal configuration and cultural meanings facilitate and constrain each other, promoting both temporal stability and change through different forms of structure.

The more traditional and formal aspects of organizational structures may initially look similar across national borders. However, different cultural myths, attitudes, and opinions will generate different interpretations, applications, social networks, and communication patterns within these structures (Gattiker & Willoughby, 1993). The enhanced ability of individuals using group support systems to offer comments that are anonymous and not necessarily embedded in ongoing group conversational threads are presumed by much of the CIS literature to be a positive capability. However, this interpretation is usually grounded in the context of "individualist" cultures. Such implementations may be not only counterproductive, but inherently distasteful, to more "collectivist" and "high power distance" cultures (Hofstede, 1993). Maurice, Sorge, and Warner (1980) showed that organization processes develop within an institutional logic that is unique to a society. For example, French manufacturing firms have a more hierarchical structure, whereby decisions are often made by technicians or engineers. Britain seems to be in the middle, while in Germany the decision about work-related matters is made whenever possible by the journeyperson at the bottom of the organizational hierarchy. So the range of adoption and implementation decisions about CISs is likely to be differentially constrained and interpreted in different organizational and national cultures (Gattiker & Kelley, 1999; Gattiker, Kelley, Paulson, & Bhatnagar, 1996; Gattiker & Nelligan, 1988).

As Acker (1990) argues, the typical implementation of CISs leaves technology in men's control because skilled work is defined as men's work, creating more negative outcomes for women (Gutek, 1994). Such relations may vary cross-nationally. Whereas women from the United States differed from men in how they assessed quality of work life, Canadian women differed from men in how they perceived communication and control by working with computers (Gattiker & Nelligan, 1988; Pazy, 1994). While more and more CISs are used by managers regardless of gender, male managers in today's Russia still refuse to take advantage of CISs since using a keyboard has the typing stigma attached to it; consequently, assistants (primarily female) use the manager's workstation. Firms and managers are less likely to support additional training required for skill upgrading for women than for men in Israel (Pazy, 1994) and New Zealand (Murray, 1994).

Media Richness and Social Presence

These two theoretical perspectives can be construed as identifying structures of meaning in which CIS adoption and implementation processes are embedded. Social presence (Short, Williams, & Christie, 1976) and media richness (Daft & Lengel, 1986) theories both emphasize how communication media differ in the extent to which (a) they can overcome various communication constraints of time, location, permanence, distribution, and distance; (b) transmit the social, symbolic, and nonverbal cues of human communication; and (c) convey equivocal information. The essential underlying principle in both theoretic traditions is contingency theory. A good match (generally, but not necessarily, implying con-

sciousness and intention) between the characteristics of a new medium (such as relatively high social presence in multimedia conferencing) and one's communication activities (such as equivocal tasks like strategic decision making) will lead to "better" (more effective, less time-consuming, satisfying, etc.) communication performance. The primary argument of media richness theory is that the relation between CIS use and performance is likely to be mediated by task equivocality and by users' "media awareness" of the suitability of new media to these tasks. Theoretically, CISs may not only be "too lean" for particular tasks, but also may be "too rich" (McGrath & Hollingshead, 1992). Proposed rankings of media on richness or social presence scales, and proposed associations of those perceptions with evaluations of new organizational media, are generally but weakly supported by study results (Rice, 1993b; Rice, with Hart et al., 1992; Rice, Hughes, & Love, 1989).

Critiques of this approach include: (a) the strength of the empirical support for media richness has usually been greatly exaggerated or nonexistent (especially concerning CISs), (b) media richness concepts have been well developed theoretically but poorly operationalized, (c) CISs can foster equivocal organizational innovations, (d) some higher-level managers seem to use e-mail contrary to media richness predictions, (e) CMC can support considerable socioemotional content, and (f) media use does not have to be nor is necessarily intentional (Lea, 1991; Rice, 1987, 1993b; Rice, Chang, & Torobin, 1992; Rice, with Hart et al., 1992; Rice & Love, 1987; Trevino, Lengel, & Daft, 1987). The negative effects associated with media low in information richness or social presence may be limited to a narrow set of situations including laboratory experiments, zero-history groups, and short initial usage periods (Walther, 1992).

The initial theories have spawned a variety of extensions. These include emphases on usage contexts (Moore & Jovanis, 1988), social influences (Fulk, 1993; Rice & Aydin, 1991; Rice, Grant, Schmitz, & Torobin, 1990; Rice,

Kraut, Cool, & Fish, 1994), symbolic aspects (Bozeman, 1993; Sitkin, Sutcliffe, & Barrios-Choplin, 1992; Trevino et al., 1987), time and knowledge specificity (Choudhury & Sampler, 1997), timeliness and sequential relations among different media (Valacich, Paranka, George, & Nunamaker, 1993), status differences across lines of authority and organizational boundaries (D'Ambra & Rice, 1995), expansion of perceptions of media richness with experience (Carlson & Zmud, 1994), distinctions between initiator and responder (Zmud, Lind, & Young, 1990), and the extent to which problem solving becomes routinized over time (Dawson, 1995; McKenney et al., 1992).

Both the original theoretical formulations and these extensions represent some ways in which the meanings (such as social presence or media richness) of CISs are structured in light of past meanings and uses of familiar media, potentially influencing if and how CISs are adopted and evaluated. For example, due to processes of "idealization" discussed in the beginning of this chapter, face-to-face interactions become social artifacts that seem necessarily and universally "rich." Conversely, due to the role of technology, especially the computer, voice mail becomes implicated as necessarily "lean." These two structurings of meaning are based on emphasizing one or two characteristics of each medium instead of the wide variety of capabilities and constraints of both. Thus, native theories of "media richness," forming preexisting interpretive structures, often stifle innovative and personal uses of voice mail (as Rice & Shook, 1990, and Rice & Danowski, 1993, found).

Communication Networks

Potential adopters of CISs are embedded in various formal and informal organizational networks (see Monge & Contractor, Chapter 12, this volume). These relational structures both limit and enable people's access to resources (such as potential communication partners on a new system, or expertise as to

how to use the system) and to rules (such as attitudes toward, and usage norms for, a new medium). These structures may indeed be aspects of the media artifacts themselves, such as a well-established voice mail distribution list that fosters a self-supporting decision-making elite.

For example, Papa and Papa (1992) reported that greater network diversity and size, but not sheer frequency of communication, influenced how and the rate at which employees learned to increase their performance using an insurance information query system. Pava (1983) described how informal communication coalitions dynamically develop around topics of contention such as new CIS development and influence subsequent decisions and support for different solutions. Adoption of e-mail by lower-level users is often stimulated by higher-level employees (who are sources of greater initial resources) adopting e-mail first (Kaye & Byrne, 1986; Rice & Case, 1983). Asynchronous media such as electronic mail compared to, say, the telephone may not be as useful for weak relations, because of the preexisting social as well as substantive content of these infrequent but important ties (Hinds & Kiesler, 1995). At the interorganizational level, Newell and Clark (1990) suggested that one of the reasons why British inventory and control system manufacturers were less innovative than comparable U.S. manufacturers was that they had less communication with external organizations, conferences, and associations.

Social Influence Networks

Social influence models are one conceptualization of the microprocesses whereby organizational communication networks play a role in the structuration of CIS interpretation, adoption, use, and evaluation. One's perceptions of ambiguous phenomena such as a new CIS are likely to be influenced by the opinions, information, uncertainty reduction, behaviors, and rewards or sanctions of others accessible through one's communication structures, such as work groups, supervisors, and informal relations (Albrecht & Hall, 1991; Fulk, 1993; Fulk, Steinfield, & Schmitz, 1990; Howell & Higgins, 1990; Rice, 1993c; Rice & Aydin, 1991; Salancik & Pfeffer, 1978).

There is some empirical evidence of a network-based social influence on CIS adoption and evaluation. Rice and Aydin (1991) found a weak positive influence on one's attitude toward a hospital information system only from those with whom one communicated directly, and a weak negative influence from those who shared one's organizational position. This second result implies that social influence from others with whom one occupies an organizational position but with whom one may have no communication may lead to discrepant, rather than converging, attitudes. Anderson, Jay, Schweer, and Anderson (1987) found a more pervasive effect of social influence, as measured by the "normative values" of other physicians with whom one communicated frequently. These values of salient others predicted adoption time of, use of, attitude toward, and time between when the organization adopted and the physician started using a hospital information system. Schmitz and Fulk (1991) showed that the attitudes of a respondent's supervisor and the five closest communication partners positively influenced the respondent's attitude toward an e-mail system. Self-reported usage of the system by these significant others predicted the respondent's self-reported usage.

Social influences on CIS use and evaluation may be heightened by how those very influences themselves are structured. Factors moderating structural influence include greater attraction to one's group (Fulk, 1993), lower self-monitoring (Burkhardt, 1994), negative word-of-mouth (Galletta, Ahuja, Hartman, Teo, & Peace, 1995), subordinates' task-related skills, and lower innovativeness (Leonard-Barton & Deschamps, 1988). In a longitudinal study of voice mail use (Rice & Shook, 1990), for those with more analyzable tasks, the number of voice mail messages sent by one's supervisor predicted the number of voice mail messages one received. However,

for those with less analyzable tasks, the number of voice mail messages sent by one's coworkers reciprocally predicted the number of voice messages one sent and received. These results implied a more iterative and collaborative use of voice mail for more ambiguous tasks, providing some support for media richness theory, but not in its treatment of voice mail as a necessarily lean medium.

However, Rice and Aydin (1991) did not find any influence of group integration on one's susceptibility to social influence on attitudes about a medical information system, and reviewed other studies that failed to find any evidence of direct or moderated social influence on attitudes toward, or use of, CISs. Finally, analyzing a variety of media in four organizations, Rice (1993b) found a small social information processing effect only for the newest medium (desktop videoconferencing), and then only for organizational newcomers who communicated with each other through the new medium itself.

Theoretically, then, social influence in general is one microprocess of organizational structuring of the adoption and implementation of CISs. However, such influence does not seem to be a strong factor, and seems highly contingent on other structural contexts. Research might do well to better specify which contingent conditions structure how, why, and whether social influence affects the adoption and implementation of CISs, rather than make sweeping assertions about the pervasive role of social influence.

Critical Mass

The value of a CIS rises, and the relative cost of each person's potential adoption of the CIS decreases, as a critical mass develops. A *critical mass* is enough initial users to stimulate rapid later adoption by others (Markus, 1990; Rice, 1982, 1990). The greater the structural heterogeneity of interests and resources (such as task interdependence, centralization of resources, group size, and geographic dispersion) among potential users, the more likely it is that there will be initial users for whom the system initially has sufficient worth, or who can afford the start-up costs. These initial adopters then decrease the costs and increase the value of adoption for later users (Markus, 1990). Local critical masses of other users are especially crucial to the successful diffusion of group CISs precisely because they are more likely to share similar benefits and costs (Rice, 1990). We distinguish critical mass from social influence as structural processes for two reasons, though some do not (Fulk et al., 1990). One is that critical mass theory does not usually posit a role for others' perceptions. The second is that it operates at a fundamentally different level of analysis: the network as a whole rather than individuals.

Rice et al. (1990) found that the best predictor of an individual's adoption of an e-mail system nine months after implementation was the extent to which that individual communicated with others in the office network before implementation. The best predictor of some communication-related outcomes after adoption was the extent to which individuals communicated with others who had also adopted the system. Comparing usage of two email systems in a multinational high-tech firm, Kaye and Byrne (1986) found that the benefits of an e-mail system were not realizable until almost all members within each user's local critical mass (about 15-30 others) used it as a normal mode of communication. Several studies of voice mail have emphasized the importance of implementation policies that foster a general overall critical mass of users or several local critical masses within relevant groupings (Ehrlich, 1987; Finn, 1986; Rice, 1990; Rice & Danowski, 1993; Trevino & Webster, 1992).

E-mail use at the World Bank was more strongly influenced by critical mass measures than by social pressure measures of e-mail use (Bikson & Law, 1993). Soe and Markus's (1993) study of the use of several new media in two organizations found that social utilities (especially critical mass) were better predictors of use of voice mail and facsimile, though not of e-mail, than were technological utilities (functionality, convenience, and appropriateness for one's tasks, barriers to use such as technological and physical accessibility, and substitutability with other media). These two analyses (and that by Rice et al., 1990) controlled for social influence, providing empirical grounds for distinguishing between these two processes, and for proposing that critical mass is a more influential structural factor than social influence in CIS adoption.

In a study of desktop videoconferencing among R&D workers, critical mass and task factors were initially strong influences on one's later usage, but habituation of one's own usage patterns over time removed those influences as predictors (Rice et al., 1994). This implies that some structurational microprocesses play a role primarily during the early stages of adoption, eventually becoming subsumed by and embedded in individuals' institutionalized behaviors and attitudes. The study also identified four forms of critical mass factors that do overlap with social influences: (a) local critical masses must involve relevant others, (b) a critical mass of others' experiences is necessary to institutionalize new norms and behaviors and leads to the development and subsequent awareness of new ways to use a CIS, (c) widespread usage may critically reduce system resources, and (d) widespread usage may also decrease trust among users because of lower personal familiarity among all the newer participants (Fish, Kraut, Root, & Rice, 1993; Johnson & Rice, 1987).

Macrolevel studies of large computer networks have also found support for critical mass propositions (Gurbaxani, 1990; Schaefermeyer & Sewell, 1988). New group media such as computer bulletin boards are classic public goods that represent problems for achieving critical mass and ongoing adoption. Rafaeli and LaRose (1993) reported that critical mass characteristics (such as diversity of content and symmetry of participation in 126 computer bulletin boards) of collaborative mass media were more important than management policies (such as access fees, time limits, etc.) in predicting patterns of use.

Interorganizational aspects of critical mass affecting CIS adoption include symmetric and asymmetric relations between and among vendors, users, and innovations. These forms of critical mass contribute to the development of media artifacts, such as the persistence of the originally intentionally inefficient typewriter keyboard layout known as the QWERTY system (David, 1985). National and cross-national programming and transmission compatibilities, and general communication infrastructure, are other forms of critical mass in telecommunications (Gattiker, in press; Gattiker, Kelley, & Janz, 1996).

Thus, critical mass seems a conceptually general, and empirically robust, aspect of CIS structuring. It embeds both social and technological factors, and it is both an influence on as well as an outcome of adoption and implementation processes.

Physical Location

Few researchers other than Allen (1977) have seriously considered the ways in which physical structures constrain or facilitate organizational communication. Physical environments within organizations represent material, though subtle, constraints on behavior, interaction, and possible interpretations. Influential aspects of physical environments include social density, proximity, access, exposure, privacy, mobility, time-space paths, physical structure (architectural and construction choices), physical stimuli (artwork, noise), and symbolic artifacts (office size and windows) (Archea, 1977; Davis, 1984; Johnson, 1993). Physical elements not only facilitate and constrain activities and relations but often represent particular resources and contexts (consider the familiar concept of the influence of "the water cooler" on emergent relations and communication climate). Physical and temporal distances constrain network relations, increasing the costs of signaling one's interests and of finding other people with similar interests (Feldman, 1987). Indeed, some researchers "view space as equivalent to context in providing the medium within which social interaction is embedded" (Johnson, 1993, p. 93).

Visual access to a terminal reduces some uncertainty associated with the costs of checking for e-mail messages and thus influences CISs' later use and evaluation (Rice & Shook, 1988). The fact that nearly half of the e-mail messages sent by employees of one R&D organization were exchanged among close coworkers was explained by factors such as cost, access, and task interdependencies (Eveland & Bikson, 1987; Markus, 1990). Thus, physical locations clearly structure access to, adoption of, use of, and outcomes associated with CISs. But as we shall see, CISs in turn have major consequences for those physical and temporal aspects of organizational structures. So adoption and use (as well as nonuse) of new media such as electronic mail may well be heavily constrained/ facilitated by prior physical structures (old buildings that cannot be easily networked, or small project groups who work together closely), and in turn, pervasively restructure access to others, potential interactions, and shared meanings.

Summary

This section has summarized some of the more frequent and influential microprocesses that structure how CISs are interpreted, adopted, and implemented. Previously institutionalized conceptions of media usage, such as traditional media genres or initial adoption rationales, can prevent CISs from fostering new ways of doing work. Organizational communication research should consider these preexisting yet difficult-to-identify factors in studies of CIS adoption and use. Organizational and cultural norms represent boundaries around acceptable ways of implementing CISs and communicating through CISs. They may well be deeply embedded in media artifacts, heavily structuring how CISs are conceptualized and implemented. Alternatively, many implementations of CISs are so decoupled from an understanding of cultural structures that they foster limited adoption and negative outcomes. Social presence, media richness, and social influence theories, while not strongly supported by the data, do emphasize how interpretations of old and new media are structured, and how social influence itself operates through communication structures in shaping attitudes about new media. Their strength may be largely as manifestations of media artifacts, where "richness" or "influence" derive mainly from what's "familiar" and "natural." Various forms of critical mass influence the adoption and diffusion of CISs. For example, national telecommunications regulatory policies affect and structure not only domestic but also cross-national uses, perhaps stifling the emergence of a critical mass of international users. While CISs can overcome physical constraints, sometimes these boundaries of time and space are characteristics of real task interdependencies that cannot be ignored. However, those task interdependencies may themselves be restructured to take advantage of the other positive characteristics of CISs.

Transformations of Structures and CISs

The following subsections review studies that discuss processes whereby CISs and organizational structures are used, converted, reinvented, or integrated through their interaction. These may involve more or less emphasis on CISs or organizational structure. Again, the subsections are ordered from more emphasis on structuring through meaning (changes in the nature, form, and temporal aspects of content, and group communication), and through relations (group communication and metastructuring).

Nature of Content

Because of the potential capabilities of CISs suggested earlier in this chapter, content is processible. This allows for diverse entry, storage, massaging, retrieval, and distribution strategies (Mackay, 1988; Malone, Grant,

Turbak, Brobst, & Cohen, 1987; Rice & Case, 1983). Digitization structures information in CISs into a universal format (bits) so that content may appear in any communication mode (text, sounds, video, numbers) through any digital medium. Digitization also separates content from the traditional associations with specific media and institutional structures (e.g., words with books, accurate images with photography, music with records) (Brand, 1987; Mulgan, 1991; Rice, 1987). This detachment removes control of the content from the author, producer, publisher, custodian, librarian, and so forth. But it also creates contradictions and problems in the traditional policies and assumptions associated with those physical and institutional structures. Typically, individuals initially enact familiar genres with a new medium (such as conceptualizing word processing as a fancy typewriter, Johnson & Rice, 1987; or voice mail as a fancy telephone answering machine, Rice & Danowski, 1993). But they may develop or choose an entirely new genre (virtual reality) or develop new subgenres within a new medium (electronic novels), which changes the nature, form, and temporal aspects of that mediated content.

The *nature* of message content in CISs can differ from that of traditional organizational media. For example, e-mail communication among seven ad hoc programming task groups involved more discussion of scheduling, task assignment, and socioemotional topics, while face-to-face communication involved more consensus building and problem solving (Finholt, Sproull, & Kiesler, 1990). CISs may allow individuals to exchange messages, vote, or express preferences anonymously, supposedly separating content from identity and its attendant attributions and biases (Hayne & Rice, 1997; Hiltz, Turoff, & Johnson, 1989; Jessup, Connolly, & Tansik, 1990; Nunamaker, Dennis, Valacich, Vogel, & George, 1991). Craipeau (1994) notes one study that found electronic mail messages, compared to memos, placed less or no importance on closing signatures. There was decreased emphasis on hierarchical status and symbolic value, and increased emphasis on the content. While this reduces the role of organizational hierarchy in communicative content, it may also reduce the role of the social, as indicated and symbolized through closings, signatures, and position titles.

But the nature of the CIS content may be so strongly structured by the organizational context that it mirrors traditional media content, reinforced by and reinforcing the "artifact" of "familiar" organizational communication. Both Bikson and Law (1993) and Bizot, Smith, and Hill (1991) reported that over 90% of a sample of e-mail messages sent in each study's organization were clearly related to business, reflecting the strong intentional administration policies at both sites against social uses of the system, rather than technological causation. Among World Bank e-mail users, higher-level staff reported more substantive e-mail, while lower-level staff reported more administrative messages (Bikson & Law, 1993). Sherblom's (1988) study of the 157 e-mail messages to and from one middle-level manager found that messages sent upward in the hierarchy were more restricted in function (mostly involving exchange of information), functional categories were more evenly distributed among peer messages, and subordinates were more likely to "sign" their mail than were superiors. These aspects of e-mail content indicated that "an electronic paralanguage reflects, reinforces, and recontextualizes the organizational structural hierarchy" (p. 50).

Form of Content

The form of CIS content and message flow may also be different. "Multiple threads of conversation" occur in bulletin boards, computer conferencing, and listservs. These occur when e-mail postings are responses to an item added several entries ago by one user but just recently read by another user, a response to multiple previous topics, or conditional comments embedded in a message that reduce the likelihood of another person having to wait for a response from the original sender to a particular question before being able to provide some information or make a decision (Black, Levin, Mehan, & Quinn, 1983; Kolb, 1996). One consequence of such multiple threads is that online discussions can suffer from tangential comments and loss of coherence (Bump, 1990). Even regular private and synchronous e-mail messages may arrive at different users' screens in different order, due to different log-on schedules and different routings of the messages' packets through packet-switched computer networks.

On the other hand, the multiple threads identified in transcripts of online discussions can provide a visual structure of portions of an emerging virtual organization (Dubinskas, 1993). As an example of such analysis, Berthold, Sudweeks, Newton, and Coyne (1996) coded 3,000 messages from 30 newsgroups on three information services (Bitnet, Compuserve, Internet) over one month. They used neural network analysis to group 51 coded categories (such as emotion, gender, message was referenced later on) that highly co-occurred across the messages. Among other results, they found that messages that were part of conversational threads tended to have medium length, include an appropriate subject line, contain statements of fact, and not introduce a new topic. Organizational members interested in fostering enduring communication relations across otherwise diverse and distant teams or virtual firms might intentionally develop message genres with these thread attributes (see the discussion on metastructuring, below).

Hypertext links will relax our familiar notions of a sequential textual structuring even more. Users may now move from any content node (such as a word, picture, or reference) in a (possibly multimedia) document directly to associated content nodes in other documents, both within and across documents. They may also restructure hypertext documents by adding their own associations for other users to explore. Thus, an annual report posted as part of an organization's World Wide Web home page could allow stockholders to click on summary figures to inspect or reanalyze the full auditor's report, follow links to an industry association's home page for market comparisons of the organization's products and services, or discuss upcoming policy decisions with watchdog agencies. The structure of an organization's identity could be transformed repeatedly through mediated forms created by internal and external publics, many unknown to the organization. Note that hypertext structures are currently being conceptualized as novel or unique because the linear structuring of traditional printed documents has become institutionalized into media artifacts. Actually, hypertext and online relational/keyword searches share some characteristics of preprint oral culture (Grande, 1980) and the ongoing commentaries and annotations of early religious texts such as the Bible.

Temporal Aspects of Content

Time is another intrinsic aspect of the structure of communication that may be transformed within CISs. As well, changes in the use and meaning of time in CISs are transforming how people conceptualize media in general: consider evaluations of the interactivity or social presence of the traditional telephone in light of voice mail, cellular telephones, and videophones. Hesse, Werner, and Altman (1988) discuss a range of temporal aspects in CISs. These include how much communication can occur in a given synchronous period, how to sequence asynchronous contributions by multiple users, mismatches between communication pace of different participants, and the ability to recall prior contributions by participants. Kolb (1996) suggests that the limited length but rapid feedback inherent in CMC likely will foster discourse that builds up arguments over "point-for-point statements and rebuttals" (p. 16) rather than by lengthy linear arguments, and allows clarification and inquiries rather than unchallengeable pronouncements. However, the prevalence of conversational threads may make it difficult to keep the focus on a specific line of discourse and even suppress

discourse that arises out of thoughts long incubating. Temporal aspects that may be explicitly structured into group communication system capabilities, according to Johnson-Lenz and Johnson-Lenz (1991), might include identifiable stages, orientations, transitions, beginnings and endings, and rhythms such as patterns of periodic contact and participation. Conscious understanding of and attention to social aspects of how systems are used—open space, timing, rhythms, boundaries, containers, and procedures—can lead to "purpose-centered groupware." They propose that emphasis on these social aspects would allow users and designers to iteratively and continuously use the current state of groupware to design and implement the next state. Highlighting the duality of structure and technology, they argue for "the emergence of background processes that inform the next generation of foreground forms" (p. 402). Thus, even traditional artifacts of a temporally sequential design-build-implement-use system process may be transformed.

Group Communication

Considerable research has looked at how groupware may be used to structure group communication, processes, and outcomes (such as decision quality or consensus) (Kraemer & Pinsonneault, 1990; Rice, 1984; Valacich, Paranka, George, & Nunamaker, 1993) and how, in turn, groupware is structured through use and interpretation. Poole and DeSanctis (1990; DeSanctis & Poole, 1994) have developed a theoretical framework called adaptive structuration theory, and refined it through empirical coding schemes. The use and outcomes associated with groupware are influenced by (a) social structures of group processes, tasks, and organization, (b) how groups produce and reproduce their structures through their use and adaptation of technologies, and (c) technical features, limitations, and spirit of CISs (such as interface design). Teleconferencing, and group communication, are discussed elsewhere in this volume (Chapter 16).

Metastructuring

We have seen that transformation involving CISs and organizational structuring may involve the adaptation of an innovation during and after its initial adoption, sometimes called *reinvention*. An early application of the concept to CISs was a cross-organizational study showing how different management and user practices (sometimes intentional, sometimes not) involving word processing fostered or constrained different levels of reinvention (Johnson & Rice, 1987). For example, some units were managed by the supervisor into organization-wide consulting groups that restructured word processing as a foundation for document and transaction processing. Other units were administered strictly as industrial typing pools without proactive management, and eventually were disbanded.

Orlikowski et al. (1995) generalize this concept, labeled *metastructuring,* as part of their model of the duality of technology. They studied how a newsgroup and e-mail system were initiated, used, and iteratively redesigned by a team of software engineers. A few individuals influenced others' use of the medium, changed the system's features, and changed the context of system use. This mediation helped to establish norms and expectations for subsequent use, sometimes through major changes in either the system or the organization of project teams. There were four types of mediating activities: (a) establishment (such as shifting official announcements from a traditional lunchtime meeting to a new newsgroup), (b) reinforcement (such as promoting effective use), (c) adjustment (such as providing online feedback to clarify rules and resources), and (d) episodic change (such as adding a moderator). Indeed, without such ongoing metastructuring and reinvention, a CIS is likely to be irrelevant, damaging, unsatisfying, or rejected. Sure enough, when the engineers' organization was restructured, there was no formal provision for technology-use mediation, and the newsgroups and other services fell into disuse.

Summary

There are many dimensions of transformations involving CISs and organizations. CISs may be used in ways that transform the nature, form, and temporal aspects of content. To the extent that these microprocesses of communication influence the structuring of meaning and relations in organizational settings, they may be one of the primary ways in which new media genres emerge. These may possibly transform our ways of conceptualizing what has been considered "natural" conversational relations and meanings. Group CIS systems have been adapted to facilitate better group interaction, idea generation, and decision making—but also may be used to reinforce familiar group communication processes and structures. They may also seriously challenge traditional notions of organizational structure that presume most interaction is within the functional work group, rather than across organizational units or even across organizations themselves. Metastructuring may be designed into the implementation process as an ongoing, intentional transformation of social and technical aspects of CISs.

Institutionalization: CIS Influences on Organizational Structures

CISs may expand or reduce characteristics associated with traditional media, and alter the mix of available media. Associated patterns of communication and transactional processes are likely to change as well. New communication systems shorten the time between events and their consequences, reduce internal and external organizational buffers, and increase but also allow the management of interdependence (Rockart & Short, 1991). These processes may generate new behavioral and conceptual spaces, changing both actions in, and thinking about, organizations (Taylor & Van Every, 1993). That is, CISs provide occasions for institutionalization of changes in power, participation in communication networks, and meanings and relations within and across organizations.

Power

Organizational power is associated with access to and control over informal and formal rules and resources, such as communication flow, interaction norms, and hierarchical position (Blair, Roberts, & McKechnie, 1985). But *any* organizational medium (from memos to meetings) structures access to resources (intentionally or not). Current organizational information is already prefiltered, but largely in ways that we do not perceive, cannot control, or generally idealize rather than recognize as artifacts of how communication is structured and constrained. Pettigrew (1972) provides a classic case study of how differential access to interaction (involving pre-CIS media of face-to-face meetings, reports, memos, telephone calls, etc.) among organizational members was used to control the flow of information and the range of interpretations during the process of deciding on a new CIS. Moreover, differential structuring of access (by any particular medium) is neither universally good nor bad for an organization (Choo & Auster, 1993). Organizational members have always had opportunities to use unmediated and mediated interaction as ways to structure power, and will continue to do so with CISs. As Markus (1984) and others show, whether and how power is reallocated cannot be easily predicted because that depends considerably on personalities, internal organizational changes, and preexisting access to resources. For example, women are more likely to experience negative changes in work structures and skills, primarily because they hold jobs that have less power and in which CISs can play a greater role, such as routine processing (Gattiker, Gutek, & Berger, 1988; Gattiker & Howg, 1990; Gutek, 1994).

To the extent that CISs can alter some constraints—say, by reducing hierarchy, providing the occasion for development of expertise,

increasing one's centrality in online space, and allowing greater interaction and thus visibility through the network—more organizational members may share power (Blair et al., 1985; Sproull & Kiesler, 1991). And such outcomes are quite salient to those members: Joshi (1992) concluded that inequity with regards to the allocation of resources (measured in terms of role ambiguity and role conflict) was the single strongest predictor of users' reported dissatisfaction with a CIS.

CISs have the potential for changing power through providing new sources of organizational socialization and informational resources, such as ad hoc groups, distribution lists, and informal social interest groups (Eveland & Bikson, 1988; Finholt & Sproull, 1990; Rice & Steinfield, 1994; Sproull & Kiesler, 1991). For instance, increased network density, increased ability to recognize other members of the organization, less centralization of interaction, more cross-group communication, and quicker emergence of expertise were found in a group that used e-mail, compared with a comparable group of nonusers (Bikson & Eveland, 1990; see also Sproull & Kiesler, 1991). Several studies have found that over time, users in general, but early adopters in particular, increase their power and relational network centrality as they use a new CIS (Burkhardt & Brass, 1990; Hesse, Sproull, Kiesler, & Walsh, 1993; Huff, Sproull, & Kiesler, 1989).

CISs may well contribute to the erosion of organizational and even national hierarchies (Cleveland, 1985; Taylor & Van Every, 1993). Information via CISs flows easily across boundaries (so that many instead of few can be informed and participate). A CIS does not necessarily require a small set of leaders to coordinate decision making. But it may require greater cooperation among leaders. CISs may attenuate the influence of organizational legitimization and managerial trust by increasing the social space in which organizational members participate, and by emphasizing principles of self-management and semiautonomy (Perin, 1991). Indeed, Mulgan

(1991) argues that greater use and scale of telecommunications networking increases the decentralization of usage, with a corresponding loss of control and a rise in the costs of control.

Paradoxically, CISs themselves might be particularly vulnerable to changes in policy or concerns about power loss because they are not as visible or institutionalized as more traditional media structures (Perin, 1991). Perin suggests that new CIS structures may also obscure important differences in power and interests, and are not themselves necessarily free of hierarchy or conflict. Indeed, the very nature of organizational CISs may foster "strategic information behaviors" such as manipulation or distortion (Zmud, 1990). This may happen in two primary ways (in the content of a message that a system transmits/stores/distributes, or in how a message directs operations of the system itself) at a variety of system nodes (sensor, filter, router, carrier, interpreter, learner, and modifier). Zmud describes how information overload fosters the delegation, summary, or dilution of initial e-mail messages, increasing users' reliance on symbols of expertise and authority, and creating opportunities for manipulation and susceptibility to misrepresentation.

Bloomfield and Coombs (1992) emphasize "the potential role of computer-based information systems in the renegotiation of professional knowledge, discourses, and practices within organizations" (p. 461). Thus, to the extent that organizational activities involve technological terminology and jargon, and to the extent that these terms are differentially understood and valued by different members, a CIS is necessarily discursively associated with power relations (p. 467). Bloomfield and Coombs note that this power disciplines actors via norms (such as users being judged as more or less "competent" depending on their usage of technical terms). A CIS may foster a loss of power that is based on technical expertise and a weakening of group boundaries because of changes to in-group terminology

(Nelson, 1990). But it also empowers members by providing access to bodies of knowledge or discourses, enabling different kinds of action (such as technical staff members becoming internal consultants to high-level managers). Even *perceptions* of power may be influenced: In 27 CIS groups, users of "powerful" language were perceived as more attractive, credible, and persuasive relative to users of "powerless" language (Adkins & Brashers, 1995).

The potential for interconnectedness across boundaries of time and space may encourage the development of virtual communities (Rheingold, 1993) that in the long run reduce the power of geopolitical identities in politics (what Cleveland, 1985, calls the "passing of remoteness"). However, the openness of networked, participatory communication can also hinder innovation and bold initiatives, because they are then subject much earlier on to public scrutiny, defensiveness, and suspicion (Cleveland, 1985; Dutton, 1996). Cultural differences and identities may become blurred, with subsequent loss of diversity.

Communication Structures and Participation

Many studies show that CISs can overcome physical and temporal structural constraints and thereby facilitate more diverse communication (see, e.g., the early reviews by Rice & Associates, 1984). CISs may help solve some of the problems of traditional bureaucracies by reducing organizational complexity, hierarchical structures, and procedures; facilitating a better sense of members' opinions; and increasing participation and democratic interaction (Keen, 1991; Sackman & Nie, 1970; Taylor & Van Every, 1993).

In some cases, the empirical changes are considerable, such as the ability of organizational members to participate in ongoing multiple, overlapping committees because physical and temporal constraints have been reduced (Eveland & Bikson, 1988). Bishop (1993) found nearly two thirds of 950 aerospace engineers who used a variety of network applications reported increases in the amount of information available, exchange of information across organizational boundaries, and communication with others outside their own organizations. Kaye and Byrne's (1986) study of an organizational e-mail system revealed that ideas were recorded and circulated that would otherwise have been lost, opinions and decisions were better considered, information flow between organizational levels and departments increased, and more communication could be managed in the same time.

Simple increased access ("overcoming time and space") is not the whole story behind such changes, though. Lind and Zmud (1995) studied the influence of voice mail on the communication and sales performance of a multinational truck manufacturing firm by comparing sales regions that had used voice mail for nearly a year to regions that had not. They found increased and improved communication relations between sales representatives and dealership managers, primarily through direct benefits from the store-and-forward capabilities of voice mail. But voice mail was also used to signal a need for communication episodes between dealers and sales representatives, or to asynchronously establish a context for subsequent written exchanges, both of which increased dealers' satisfaction with their interactions with sales representatives.

Participation is usually less unequal in CISs than in face-to-face groups (Hiltz & Turoff, 1993; Kraemer & Pinsonneault, 1990; Rice, 1984). But users can participate more across vertical and external boundaries, as well. Online courses can foster more equal discussion among students than do traditional classrooms (Harasim, 1990; Hartman et al., 1991; Hiltz, 1986). Users in one organizational study sent 78% of their (computer-monitored) messages to others outside of their own work group, indicating extensive cross-

ing of traditional work boundaries (Bizot et al., 1991). Eveland and Bikson's (1987) study of 800 users in an R&D organization found that three quarters of the messages crossed departmental boundaries, while 40% of the messages crossed specific research project boundaries, indicating high cooperation on projects among research disciplines within broad organizational functions.

Such changes seem more likely in novel situations or new groups, when groups are not embedded in organizational structures, when other communication channels are not constrained, and when jobs are more technical than administrative. For example, Markus (1992) analyzed four field study groups that had access to groupware systems as well as participated in weekly face-to-face meetings. The groups' social contexts helped explain system usage—including one group using the system primarily so that two antagonistic members would not have to meet face-to-face! Rice (1994) found that initially the network of e-mail communication among new interns and their mentors in an R&D organization was strongly correlated with work and social networks. Over time, though, it diverged from those traditional structures as well as from formal mentor-intern relations. Eveland and Bikson (1988; Bikson & Eveland, 1990) provided strong evidence that CISs can influence the development and maintenance of both task and social networks among groups that had not interacted before, including fluctuating leadership patterns over three time periods, greater communication in all channels, greater connectedness, less centralization over time, more multiplex subcommittee relations, continued online communication after the report was completed, and considerable messaging across the task subgroups. Feldman's (1987) study of messages exchanged among 96 users indicated that 60% of the messages would not have been sent without the system, but this was even higher for people who did not know one another, who did not communicate other than by the CIS, who were spatially or organizationally distant, and who used distribution lists. Other reviews (Hiltz & Turoff, 1993; Rice, 1980, 1987, 1992; Rice & Associates, 1984; Sproull & Kiesler, 1991) summarize similar results from many studies.

Increases in horizontal and collaborative communication also seem more likely among certain types of users. An analysis of dyadic communications among administrators and technical workers found increased horizontal relations among technical workers who used e-mail. This was partially explained by the flatter internal structures of their project teams, more frequent boundary crossing to avoid extreme specialization, less analyzable tasks, and their professional socialization to work on projects in teams, and of course, e-mail use (Hinds & Kiesler, 1995). Such changes are even more likely among members of professional, dispersed occupational communities, such as academic researchers, whose values and perspectives transcend the norms of their employing organizations (Pickering & King, 1995). So organizations may have good reasons to be cautious about personnel using the Internet. These increased external network relations may weaken managerial control, provide access to unmonitored values and norms, increase external job opportunities, and allow leakage of organizational information (Gattiker, Janz, Kelley, & Schollmeyer, 1996).

Potential changes in communication associated with CISs may institutionalize new traditional organizational structures of meaning and relations, but may reinforce old ones. In one traditionally hierarchical R&D organization, 83% of all messages collected from 188 users over a three-day period were sent within a division, and 93% of messages were sent to a recipient either one job type above or below the sender, indicating little circumventing of the traditional organizational structure (Bizot et al., 1991). Eveland and Bikson (1987) found little evidence of changes in departmental or project communication clusters during 18 months of e-mail use in an R&D firm, indicating that the electronic mail system supported the intraorganizational structure of the R&D organization.

Mantovani (1994) underscores the strong organizational structurings of culture, social actors' goals, and local situations on the extent to which any democratization of participation through CISs may actually occur. He argues that access (physical, cultural, technical, and economic) to CISs is inherently unequally distributed. Equal participation does not necessarily mean equal attention from others (especially in noncooperative social contexts) because it is far easier to be selectively attentive in CISs than in face-to-face communication. Symbolic group norms may be stronger in CISs than in face-to-face contexts, and certain phases of group decision making such as negotiation and means-ends debates tend to be minimized in online discussions (Mantovani, 1994; McGrath, 1990; Rice, 1987, 1990; Spears & Lea, 1992).

Dutton (1996) suggests the possibility that the absence of formal as well as social norms that otherwise regulate online discussions may actually "undermine the very existence of such forums by chasing key individuals, such as opinion leaders and public officials, off the system" (p. 284). However, Ess (1996) applied Habermas's theory of communicative action to show that CISs have the potential to "facilitate the unconstrained discourse of communicative reasons, a discourse that leads to consensus over important norms" (p. 215), as represented by the "diverse plurality of democratic communities" of listservs and newsgroups.

Relationships among gender and participation in CISs have received considerable attention (Ebben & Mastronardi, 1993; Gattiker, 1994; Hackett, Mirvis, & Sales, 1991; Perry & Greber, 1990; Zimmerman, 1983). Because of their supposed limited bandwidth and the use of pseudonyms or anonymous accounts, CISs should reduce the influence of social and other status cues. Thus, discussion via a CIS would be expected to include more diversity of viewpoints, egalitarian participation, interpretative risk taking, and challenges to textual authority than in traditional face-to-face settings. Also, Internet connectivity can foster new organizational forms of particular interest to women, such as discussion groups centered around a specific professional interest (such as women's career development, sexual harassment awareness, or organizational mentoring).

Some studies do find evidence for empowerment and nondiscriminatory participation in CISs. Adoption of Santa Monica's Public Electronic Network (PEN) by women was encouraged by the free system and public terminals, public norms supporting community participation, system administrators' support for reinvention in design and implementation, and women's greater involvement in community politics (Collins-Jarvis, 1993).

However, some argue that the use of CISs in traditional ways may just reinforce existing gender inequities (Frissen, 1992; Sparks & van Zoonen, 1992). For example, women constitute small percentages (from 10% to 40%) of users on the major online systems (Brail, 1996). Selfe and Meyer's (1991) study of 56 teachers using a computer conference reported that men and high-profile members initiated more communications (although used fewer words per message) and disagreed more, and these differences were unaffected by options for using pseudonyms during a second 20-day usage period.

Precisely because context may be depersonalized due to anonymity and weak social feedback, online communication may be more disinhibited and critical, and lessen public awareness of social sanctions (Collins-Jarvis, 1996). This may lead to more, rather than fewer, gender-based stereotypical comments, especially when online social cues make groups' unequal and unstable power relations salient (Collins-Jarvis, 1996). Such content leads some women to drop out of, or never join, online discussions (Brail, 1996; Ebben, 1993). On the PEN system, initially, female users experienced instances of discrimination and harassment, so a few of these female users restructured some aspects of the system by forming a women's user group (Rogers, Collins-Jarvis, & Schmitz, 1994). Several of Brail's women respondents noted, however, that unpleasant disturbances occur in all communication environments (another instance of demythologizing the artifact of idealized interpersonal communication), and they would not let that discourage them from taking advantage of the Internet.

Intraorganizational Structures

Early studies of CISs and organizational structure concluded that computerization increased organizational centralization (Mowshowitz, 1976; Mumford & Banks, 1967; Whisler, 1970), increased number of job titles (Gerwin, 1981), or deskilled work by extracting local control (Braverman, 1974). Caufield's (1989) meta-analysis of technology as industrial process concluded that technology does have a direct effect on hierarchical and administrative structures. Outcomes such as increased consolidation of departments and reduced span of control occur, however, mostly within general subunits and not across broad organizational units (Perio & Prieto, 1994).

Later research included more contextual measures, such as the particular function of the system and environmental stability. These studies concluded that computerization primarily reinforced the status quo, whether that was a trend toward centralization or decentralization (Blau, Falbe, McKinley, & Tracy, 1976; Robey, 1981). Others found evidence of increased horizontal differentiation, but argued that increased differentiation does not necessarily mean a bureaucratic hierarchy: It can also support matrix and lateral relations (Bjorn-Andersen, Eason, & Robey, 1986). Along with Child (1986), they conclude that the primary influence is not technology per se but implementation and operational strategies, which are, however, typically decided by power elites.

Some familiar organizational communication roles will likely be restructured with the diffusion of CISs. For example, top managers can handle more of their correspondence through e-mail, voice mail, and word processing. One subtle consequence of this shift is the removal of secretaries from their accustomed informal role as gatekeepers and liaisons. Note, however, that in some ways this represents a reinstitutionalization of office roles before the typewriter separated secretarial from managerial activities, creating the "idealized" artifact of the now threatened executive secretary position (Johnson & Rice, 1987).

But the opposite role transformation may also occur. The unnecessary monitoring and filtering represented by middle management is being excised from many organizational structures. This change leads to a flattening of organizations' hierarchies, and new forms such as orchestration, group management, and teamwork, involving greater trust, motivation by more than pay, a willingness to change, and collaboration (Davidow & Malone, 1992; Wigand, 1985). Using CISs to access updates or relevant service processes, "lower-level" personnel now can solve nonroutine problems and take on informal guru roles, thus altering decision roles throughout the organization (Quinn & Paquette, 1990). (However, these informal roles rarely have their authority or resources restructured; Bikson & Law, 1993; Johnson & Rice, 1987.) Thus, different authority structures are being institutionalized—from one of control to one of interpersonal boundary management and empowerment (Johnson & Rice, 1987). But Hirschhorn and Gilmore (1992) warn that the loss of familiar internal organizational boundaries must be managed through formerly transparent but now exposed boundaries of authority, task, political, and identity. Such ongoing restructuring requires iterative communication within and across organization boundaries.

The physical structures of one's work, office, and organization are also evolving into new forms through the use of CISs (Fulk & DeSanctis, 1995). The physical structures of buildings and offices create considerable constraints on communication, and thus quality of work life, performance, and innovation (Al-len, 1977; Johnson, 1993). Developments such as modular offices, shared drawing displays, wireless communication, and personal locator badges may overcome some of these constraints, while also generating others ("The New Workplace," 1996; Stone & Luchetti, 1985; Want, Hopper, Falcao, & Gibbons, 1992). Bikson and Eveland (1990) found that while there was a high negative association between the spatial distance network and the self-reported communication network for respondents of one ad hoc task force without an e-mail system, for the other task force that used the system there was little association. As many organizations are finding out, "the new work styles don't work in buildings designed for the old top-down corporation" ("The New Workplace," 1996, p. 108). Thus, traditional communication relations may, to some extent, be an artifact of "natural" physical structures, institutionalized into an "ideal" organizational communication context, which is being "threatened" by CISs. Consider, for example, how being in an elevator essentially silences all but the most ritualized interaction; compare that to anonymous brainstorming through group support systems. Integration of facsimile, mobile phone, voice messaging, rerouting of phone calls, and "smart buildings" may well foster changes in the familiar association of high organizational status with a large, remote office. Truly influential members may well become the most "virtual."

It is true, though, that the removal of these traditional aural and visual constraints can lead to a loss of sense of work privacy and an associated decline in job satisfaction (Sundstrom, Burt, & Kamp, 1980). But organizational norms of access and privacy have usually already been institutionalized for familiar media such as telephone, the office doorway, elevator interactions, and so on, creating "artifacts" that confound technological possibilities and limitations with social structuring. A case in point is a study of a networked desktop video conference system that showed that while it facilitated R&D workers' ability to make contacts and collaborate with others across offices, it still raised issues concerning norms of privacy, interruption, and access (Fish et al., 1993).

Certainly, telecommuting and telework are one form of restructuring organizations (Dürrenberger, Jaeger, Bieri, & Dahinden, 1995; Kraut, 1989; Nilles, Carlson, Gray, & Hanneman, 1976). New structures for telework range from prosaically working from home with visits to employer or client; to distance working enterprises, where enterprise workers provide information-based services to distant customers; to distributed business systems that are physically separated units (either part of same, or different enterprises) that are networked together to produce a final good or service (Dürrenberger et al., 1995; Holti, 1994, p. 263). Lower-level, female, and clerical workers, who might become even more disenfranchised through remote work (Calabrese, 1994; Soares, 1992), could decrease their isolation and simultaneously develop basic computer skills, through use of CISs (Matheson, 1992).

New organizational structures might include (a) answer networks, where networks of experts and databases can refer problems to the sufficient level of resolution; (b) overnight organizations, that assemble short-term project teams through a network, via a database of skills, evaluations, and availability; (c) internal labor markets, where services are allocated on the basis of project requirements, rather than by supervisory assignment; (d) computer-mediated decision networks that connect opinions and suggestions from multiple people at different decision phases; and (e) more effective and contextual information gatekeeping services (Malone & Rockart, 1993). Federal Express uses a CIS to avoid most middle organizational levels (an "infinitely flat" structure) and keep in constant communication with its vans and airplanes, leading to increased value-added services. This is an example of Mulgan's (1991) paradox that centralized CIS networks enable decentralized and customized decisions and service.

In the "spider's web" organization, relations among consultants and clients are supported by centralized CISs (such as expertise bulletin boards), allowing any participant to request information from, or make suggestions to, any other participant (Quinn & Paquette, 1990). As an example of "critical mass of expertise," this solution also reduces some of the potential loss to corporate memory that turnover by knowledge workers represents. Additionally, this increases switching costs for consultants considering jumping to firms that do not participate in the web, in turn allowing the more networked firms to invest more in specialized training.

Other new forms include "postmodern" (Bergquist, 1993) and "postbureaucratic" (Heydebrand, 1989) organizations. Such new organizational structures tend to involve fewer physical assets, customer information and communication as primary assets, increased informality, greater cross-organizational networking, and more permeable and transitory organizational boundaries. Crucial to their success is an increased dependence on strong cultures within, and trust and relationships across, organizations, implying increased interdependence. This in turn requires more mutual adjustment and cooperative mechanisms across suborganizations, such as cross-functional teams, ad hoc project teams, task rotation, overlapping electronic group memberships, and novel reward policies (Quinn & Paquette, 1990).

Interorganizational Structures

CISs can be used to restructure interorganizational boundaries, and these new structures also require and foster new forms of CISs. Such systems influence the transaction costs of acquiring knowledge, communicating, coordination, distribution, and producing and enforcing contracts, within and across organizations (Gurbaxani & Whang, 1991; Malone, Yates, & Benjamin, 1989; Monge & Contractor, Chapter 12, this volume).

The restructuring of organizations from clearly bounded, hierarchical structures to new forms has increased the possibilities for interorganizational relations. CISs can allow formerly separate and rival organizations to engage in new forms of cooperation, such as joint marketing partnerships (online services), intraindustry partnerships (electronic publishing ventures), customer-supplier partnerships (electronic document interchange), and CIS vendor-driven partnerships (using liaison CIS networks to enter new markets) as well as many other emerging structures (Cronin, 1994; Gale, 1994; Granstrand & Sjölander, 1990; Hart & Rice, 1988; Hepworth, 1989; Konsynski & McFarlan, 1990; Monge & Contractor, this volume).

Paradoxically, CISs may foster a return to small organizations, embedded in larger organizational networks involving long-term relationships with one or more suppliers (Ciborra, 1987; Davidow & Malone, 1992). These would be communication-rich environments where information flows blur traditional internal and external boundaries, perhaps leading to "boundaryless organizations" (Ashkenas, Ulrich, Jick, & Kerr, 1995; Rockart & Short, 1991). Other transformations include the creation of virtual electronic markets where customers, suppliers, and distributors interact in a largely seamless web (Dordick, Bradley, & Nanus, 1981). The Internet has ushered in the era of electronic commerce; online interactive sales are estimated to rise from the $350 million exchanged in 1995 to nearly $7 billion in 2000 (Kalakota & Whinston, 1996; Rupley, 1996). Another example is the French videotext network, where the national telephone system provides the transmission technology and the gateway software for information providers, individuals, or other businesses to exchange services and information (Steinfield, Caby, & Vialle, 1992).

Any discussion of the benefits or transcendence of the "network organization" should, however, consider the limitations and disadvantages of this new structure. These may include stifling of innovation, ambiguities in the nature of relationships, asymmetric commitment, conflict over control, personality and cultural differences, loss of autonomy and security, time lags, managing complexity, structural constraints, narrow managerial perspectives, manipulation and ulterior motives, mismatched or incomplete knowledge and competence, increased dependencies, and so on (Camagni, 1993; Nohria & Eccles, 1992).

Universities and academic professionals have always been a somewhat unique organizational form. They already incorporate various aspects of the "boundaryless organization" (conceptualized as "the invisible college"), but they, too, are undergoing transformations associated with CISs. The traditional cycle of scientific communication (conceptualization, documentation, and popularization, with some feedback loops) may change, by increased collaboration, diffusion, and feedback, through CISs, leading to an era of "telescience" (Lievrouw & Carley, 1990). CIS networks increase the intensity and diversity of communication and participants, the "stock" of ideas, and awareness of others' work (Hiltz, 1984; Hiltz & Turoff, 1993; Kerr & Hiltz, 1982).

The academic journal may evolve into new structures such as separate articles published and distributed on demand or retrieved by "intelligent agents," independently of other articles that have traditionally, but artifactually, been seen as constituting a regularly published "journal issue" (Kolb, 1996). Further, the content of the "article" may no longer be fixed, as readers and colleagues may provide ongoing feedback, evaluations, or addenda associated with the original material, through hypermedia linkages managed through World Wide Web interfaces. In the extreme, academic institutions may be restructured through direct distribution of materials from authors to readers via the Internet and personal or organizational Web pages. Readers may use on-demand publishing from optical archives, online databases, and Internet file transfer protocol (Gattiker, in press). Online courses, degrees, and educational organizations will not only challenge traditional organizational forms such as university campuses and classrooms but also redefine how learning itself is structured (Harasim, 1990; Harrison & Stephen, 1996). However, many boundaries in scholarly communication have been changing for some time, obscured by the "artifacts" of "familiar" academic media. For example, photocopying, microfilm, facsimile, and online databases have dramatically, but quietly, transformed relations among scholars, producers, publishers, vendors, libraries, and students (Schauder, 1994).

Summary

CISs can provide the occasion for the evolution of the fundamental basis of organizational power—the structuring of interaction—into new forms and locations. One way this may occur is through exposing hierarchy and authority as largely artifacts of traditional constraints on organizational structures. CISs have been associated with transformations in the communication flow within organizations when groups are less embedded in preexisting organizational structures (such as new or project-based groups, or cross-structural roles such as technical workers). A variety of social and organizational structures foster differences in men's and women's attitudes toward, and use of, CISs. To the extent that CISs, like other media, are malleable and socially adapted, they can be structured to foster positive or negative differences, or even mute differences, for good and ill.

CISs, by removing some structural constraints, will expose widely accepted communication norms as the artifacts they are, generating the need to develop and manage new norms. Unfortunately, limited conceptualizations of media will foster applying familiar norms to evaluating CISs, thus institutionalizing limited and constrained uses and interpretations of CISs. Managers may develop more integrated communication processing through CISs, and need to develop new ways of managing increasingly amorphous boundaries. At the same time, the role of "middle manager" may be largely deinstitutionalized from organizational structure. A wide diversity of orga-

nizational forms is emerging. New institutionalized structures associated with CIS networks are far more complex than the traditional opposition of "centralized or decentralized structures." This ongoing process probably best highlights the constant interactive and iterative relationships among CISs and organizational structuring. Academic institutions and communities, an early form of "virtual organization," are also undergoing structural changes associated with CISs.

CONCLUSION

This chapter has suggested both explicit and latent themes concerning theory and research on organizational structure and new communication and information systems.

Several explicit themes structured this review. Organizational structures include meanings and relations, within and across orga-n izations. Such structures can constrain or facilitate the development and use of CISs. Transformations of structures of organizational communication and CISs may involve intentional processes of metastructuring, or nearly invisible evolutions of the form, nature, and temporal orientation of communication content. And CISs can constrain or institutionalize changes within and across organizational structures.

Table 14.2 summarizes these arenas of interaction between CISs and structure. This is not intended to portray a comprehensive, fully specified, or causal theoretical model, but rather to suggest various strands of research that seem to focus on different microprocesses of these three generalized processes involving CISs and organizational structuring of relations and meaning.

This framework may help to identify arenas for future research that would illuminate how microprocesses co-occur or moderate each other within each generalized process, and how microprocesses influence each other across generalized processes. For example,

TABLE 14.2 Summary Model of Macro- and Microprocesses of CISs and Organizational Structuring of Meaning and Relations

Structural influences on adoption and implementation of CISs
    Media genres and usage norms
    Culture
    Media richness and social presence
    Communication networks
    Critical mass
    Physical location

            Transformations of organizational structures and CISs
                Nature of content
                Form of content
                Temporal aspects of content
                Group communication
                Metastructuring

                          CIS influences on organizational structures
                            Power
                            Communication networks and participation
                            Intraorganizational forms
                            Interorganizational forms

there has been increasing work on the contingent relations among media richness/social presence, communication networks, social influences, critical mass, and physical location in how they influence adoption, choice, and use of new media (Rice & Aydin, 1991; Rice et al., 1990). However, few of these and other prior structures have been considered in analyzing transformations of the nature, form, and temporal aspects of content, except perhaps in qualitative approaches to describing new media genres (Orlikowski et al., 1995). Only a few studies have considered how these transformations may be institutionalized into new intraorganizational forms, ranging from the role of signatures in e-mail messages (Sherblom, 1988) to forms of power embedded in participatory discourse enabled through organization-wide listservs (Sproull & Kiesler, 1991) and public computer conferences (Dutton, 1996).

This framework might be useful in developing implementation policies that emphasize metastructuring. For example, a better understanding of how new media can (though not necessarily) facilitate increased participation can be used to foster metastructuring discussion groups. These could then intentionally and consciously develop possible metastructuring procedures and roles to help shape transformations between prior structures and desired restructurings. This process itself, however, is a topic ripe for research. To what extent has the by-now familiar notion of "free agency" and "social construction of reality" become idealized into an invisible artifact of uninformed and unmanaged "social influences"? Once we have identified processes of adaptive structuration (Poole & DeSantis, 1990), should these microprocesses be managed by participants in any conscious way? Can they be? Is the process of sociotechnical design inherently flawed because it must be intentional and conscious?

One latent theme of this chapter is that research on organizational structure and CISs—both supportive and critical—tends to be structured by past conventions about and research traditions in communication processes, new media, and organizational structure (for a review of perspectives, see Rice, 1992). In particular, organizational researchers and ordinary folk alike tend to compare the constraints and advantages of new media not to those of older media at similar stages of development, implementation, and structuring, but to idealizations and consequent artifacts of familiar media. Thus, we argue, one goal of a structurational approach toward CISs and organizational communication should be to "uncover" asymmetric assumptions about "old" and "new" media in organizational settings. It should force us to identify factors and processes that are conceptually distinguishable, but artifactually confounded, in familiar media and research practices. It seems fairly obvious that neither the determinism of technological utopianism nor the determinism of critical pessimism is free from constraining assumptions that limit our understanding of how CISs are embedded in organizational structures and in restructurings of organizational meanings and relations.

A second latent theme of this chapter is that pluralistic, multimethod approaches that involve triangulation of both method and analysis are necessary to better identify and understand the microprocesses of (re)structuring. A more subtle aspect of this theme, however, is that specific theoretical approaches that appear to be opposed may, in fact, be complementary approaches that just focus on different components of one of the three generalized processes. For example, some have tried to artificially characterize media richness theory as a "rational choice theory," which then obviously suffers in comparison to social influence models that are "social construction of reality theory." But this confounds structural facilitation with "meaning" and structural constraints with "technology." It may well be more enlightening to show how both objective and subjective influences both constrain and facilitate, so that media richness theory and social influence theory can both contribute to understanding structural influence on the adoption and implementation of CISs.

REFERENCES

Acker, J. (1990). Hierarchies, jobs, bodies: A theory of gendered organizations. *Gender & Society, 4*(2), 139-158.

Adams, D., Todd, P., & Nelson, R. (1993). A comparative evaluation of the impact of electronic and voice mail on organizational communication. *Information & Management, 24*(1), 9-22.

Adkins, M., & Brashers, D. (1995). The power of language in computer-mediated groups. *Management Communication Quarterly, 8*(3), 289-322.

Albrecht, T., & Hall, B. (1991). Relational and content differences between elites and outsiders in innovation networks. *Human Communication Research, 17*(4), 535-561.

Allen, T. (1977). *Managing the flow of technology.* Cambridge, MA: MIT Press.

Anderson, J. G., Jay, S. J., Schweer, H. M., & Anderson, M. M. (1987). Physician communication networks and the adoption and utilization of computer applications in medicine. In J. G. Anderson & S. J. Jay (Eds.), *Use and impact of computers in clinical medicine* (pp. 185-199). New York: Springer-Verlag.

Archea, J. (1977). The place of architectural factors in behavioral theories of privacy. *Journal of Social Issues, 33*(3), 116-137.

Ashkenas, R., Ulrich, D., Jick, T., & Kerr. S. (1995). *The boundaryless organization: Breaking the chains of organizational structure.* San Francisco: Jossey-Bass.

Beniger, J. (1986). *The control revolution: Technological and economic origins of the information society.* Cambridge, MA: Harvard University Press.

Bergquist, W. (1993). *The postmodern organization: Mastering the art of irreversible change.* San Francisco: Jossey-Bass.

Berthold, M., Sudweeks, F., Newton, S., & Coyne, R. (1996). "It makes sense": Using an autoassociative neural network to explore typicality in computer mediated discussions. In S. Rafaeli, F. Sudweeks, & M. McLaughlin (Eds.), *Network and netplay: Virtual groups on the Internet* (pp. 191-220). Cambridge, MA: AAAI/MIT Press.

Bikson, T., & Eveland, J. D. (1990). The interplay of work group structures and computer support. In J. Galegher, R. Kraut, & C. Egido (Eds.), *Intellectual teamwork: Social and technological bases of cooperative work* (pp. 245-290). Hillsdale, NJ: Lawrence Erlbaum.

Bikson, T., & Law, S. (1993). Electronic mail use at the World Bank: Messages from users. *Information Society, 9(2),* 89-134.

Bishop, A. (1993). *The role of computer networks in aerospace engineering.* Urbana: University of Illinois, Graduate School of Library Science.

Bizot, E., Smith, N., & Hill, T. (1991). Use of electronic mail in a research and development organization. In J. Morell & M. Fleischer (Eds.), *Advances in the implementation and impact of computer systems* (Vol. 1, pp. 65-92). Greenwich, CT: JAI.

Bjorn-Andersen, N., Eason, K., & Robey, D. (1986). *Managing computer impact: An international study of management and organizations.* Norwood, NJ: Ablex.

Black, S., Levin, J., Mehan, H., & Quinn, C. (1983). Real and non-real time interaction: Unraveling multiple threads of discourse. *Discourse Processes, 6,* 59-75.

Blair, R., Roberts, K. H., & McKechnie, P. (1985). Vertical and network communication in organizations: The present and the future. In R. D. McPhee & P. K. Tompkins (Eds.), *Organizational communication: Traditional themes and new directions* (pp. 55-79). Beverly Hills, CA: Sage.

Blau, P., Falbe, C., McKinley, W., & Tracy, P. (1976). Technology and organization in manufacturing. *Administrative Science Quarterly, 21(1),* 20-40.

Bloomfield, B., & Coombs, R. (1992). Information technology, control and power: The centralization and decentralization debate revisited. *Journal of Management Studies, 29(4),* 459-484.

Bozeman, D. (1993). Toward a limited rationality perspective of managerial media selection in organizations. In D. Moore (Ed.), *Proceedings of the 1993 Academy of Management meeting* (pp. 278-282). Madison, WI: Omni.

Brail, S. (1996). The price of admission: Harassment and free speech in the wild, wild west. In L. Cherny & E. Weise (Eds.), *Wired-women: Gender and new realities in cyberspace* (pp. 157-182). Seattle, WA: Seal.

Brand, S. (1987). *The media lab: Reinventing the future at MIT.* New York: Viking.

Braverman, H. (1974). *Labor and monopoly capital: The degradation of work in the 20th century.* New York: Monthly Review Press.

Bump, J. (1990). Radical changes in class discussion using networked computers. *Computers and the Humanities, 24,* 49-65.

Burkhardt, M. (1994). Social interaction effects following a technological change: A longitudinal investigation. *Academy of Management Journal, 37(4),* 869-898.

Burkhardt, M., & Brass, D. (1990). Changing patterns or patterns of change: The effects of a change in technology on social network structure and power. *Administrative Science Quarterly, 35(1),* 104-127.

Camagni, R. (1993). Inter-firm industrial networks: The costs and benefits of cooperative behaviour. *Journal of Industry Studies, 1(1),* 1-15.

Calabrese, A. (1994). Home-based telework and the politics of private woman and public man: A critical appraisal. In U. E. Gattiker (Ed.), *Studies in technical innovation and human resources: Women and technology* (Vol. 4, pp. 161-199). Berlin and New York: Walter de Gruyter.

Carey, J. (1990). The language of technology: Talk, text, and template as metaphors for communication. In M. Medhurst, A. Gonzalez, & T. Peterson (Eds.), *Communication and the culture of technology* (pp. 19-39). Pullman: Washington State University Press.

Carlson, J., & Zmud, R. (1994). Channel expansion theory: A dynamic view of media and information richness perceptions. In D. Moore (Ed.), *Proceedings of the 1994 Academy of Management meeting* (pp. 280-284). Madison, WI: Omni.

Caufield, C. (1989). An integrative research review of the relationship between technology and structure: A meta-analytic synthesis (Ph.D. dissertation, University of Iowa, Ames). *Dissertation Abstracts International, 51,* 553A.

Child, J. (1986). New technology and developments in management organisation. In T. Lupton (Ed.), *Human factors: Man, machine and new technology* (pp. 137-156). Berlin: IFS Pub. Ltd., UK and Springer-Verlag.

Choo, C. W., & Auster, E. (1993). Environmental scanning: Acquisition and use of information by managers. In M. Williams (Ed.), *Annual review of information science and technology* (Vol. 28, pp. 279-314). Medford, NJ: Learned Information.

Choudhury, V., & Sampler, J. (1997). Information specificity and environmental scanning: An economic perspective. *MIS Quarterly, 21(1),* 25-54.

Ciborra, C. (1987). Reframing the role of computers in organizations—The transaction costs approach. *Office: Technology and People, 3,* 17-38.

Cleveland, H. (1985, January-February). The twilight of hierarchy: Speculations on the global information society. *Public Administration Review, 45,* 185-195.

Collins-Jarvis, L. (1993). Gender representation in an electronic city hall: Female adoption of Santa Monica's PEN system. *Journal of Broadcasting and Electronic Media, 37(1),* 49-65.

Collins-Jarvis, L. (1996, May). *Discriminatory messages in on-line discussion groups: The role of gender identity and social context.* Paper presented at International Communication Association, Chicago.

Contractor, N., & Eisenberg, E. (1990). Communication networks and new media in organizations. In J. Fulk & C. Steinfield (Eds.), *Organizations and communication technology* (pp. 143-172). Newbury Park, CA: Sage.

Craipeau, S. (1994). Telematics and corporate regulations. In J. E. Andriessen & R. Roe (Eds.), *Telematics and work* (pp. 289-311). Hillsdale, NJ: Lawrence Erlbaum.

Cronin, M. (1994). *Doing business on the Internet: How the electronic highway is transforming American companies.* New York: Van Nostrand Reinhold.

Culnan, M. J., & Markus, M. L. (1987). Information technologies. In F. M. Jablin, L. L. Putnam, K. H. Roberts, & L. W. Porter (Eds.), *Handbook of organizational communication: An interdisciplinary perspective* (pp. 420-443). Newbury Park, CA: Sage.

Daft, R. L., & Lengel, R. H. (1986). Organizational information requirements, media richness and structural design. *Management Science, 32,* 554-571.

D'Ambra, J., & Rice, R. E. (1994). The equivocality of media richness: A multi-method approach to analyzing selection of voice mail for equivocal tasks. *IEEE Transactions on Professional Communication, 37*(4), 231-239.

David, P. (1985). Clio and the economics of QWERTY. *American Economic Review, 75*(2), 332-337.

Davidow, W., & Malone, M. (1992). *The virtual corporation: Structuring and vitalizing the company for the 21st century.* New York: Burlingame/Harper.

Davis, T. R. (1984). The influence of the physical environment in offices. *Academy of Management Review, 9,* 271-283.

Dawson, K. (1995). Comments on "Read me what it says on your screen . . . " *Technology Studies, 2,* 80-85.

DeSanctis, G., & Poole, M. S. (1994). Capturing the complexity in advanced technology use: Adaptive structuration theory. *Organization Science, 5*(2), 121-147.

Dordick, H., Bradley, H., & Nanus, B. (1981). *The emerging network marketplace.* Norwood, NJ: Ablex.

Dubinskas, F. (1993). Virtual organizations: Computer conferencing and the technology-organization relationship. *Journal of Organizational Computing, 3*(4), 389-416.

Dürrenberger, G., Jaeger, C., Bieri, L., & Dahinden, U. (1995). Telework and vocational contact. *Technology Studies, 2,* 104-131.

Dutton, W. (1996). Network rules of order: Regulating speech in public electronic fora. *Media, Culture & Society, 18,* 269-290.

Dutton, W. H., & Danziger, J. N. (1982). Computers and politics. In J. N. Danziger, W. H. Dutton, R. Kling, & K. L. Kraemer (Eds.), *Computers and politics: High technology in American local governments* (pp. 1-21). New York: Columbia University Press.

Ebben, M. (1993, October). *Women on the net: An exploratory study of gender dynamics on the Soc.women computer network.* Paper presented at the 16th annual conference of the Organization for the Study of Communication, Language and Gender, Tempe, AZ.

Ebben, M., & Mastronardi, J. (1993). Women and information technology: An annotated bibliography. In J. Taylor, C. Kramarae, & M. Ebben (Eds.), *Women, information technology and scholarship* (pp. 78-121). Urbana-Champaign: University of Illinois, Center for Advanced Study.

Ehrlich, S. (1987). Strategies for encouraging successful adoption of office communication systems. *ACM Transactions on Office Information Systems, 5*(4), 340-357.

Ess, C. (1996). The political computer: Democracy, CMC, and Habermas. In C. Ess (Ed.), *Philosophical perspectives on computer-mediated communication* (pp. 197-230). Albany: State University of New York Press.

Eveland, J. D., & Bikson, T. E. (1987). Evolving electronic communication networks: An empirical assessment. *Office: Technology and People, 3,* 103-128.

Eveland, J. D., & Bikson, T. E. (1988). Workgroup structures and computer support: A field experiment. *ACM Transactions on Office Information Systems, 6*(4), 354-379.

Feldman, M. S. (1987). Electronic mail and weak ties in organizations. *Office: Technology and People, 3,* 83-101.

Finholt, T., & Sproull, L. (1990). Electronic groups at work. *Organization Science, 1*(1), 41-64.

Finholt, T., Sproull, L., & Kiesler, S. (1990). Communication and performance in ad hoc task groups. In J. Galegher, R. Kraut, & C. Egido (Eds.), *Intellectual teamwork: Social and technological bases of cooperative work* (pp. 291-325). Hillsdale, NJ: Lawrence Erlbaum.

Finn, T. A. (1986). An introduction to voice mail. In S. Guengerich (Ed.), *1986 office automation conference digest* (pp. 43-51). Washington, DC: American Federation of Information Processing Societies.

Fish, R., Kraut, R., Root, R., & Rice, R. E. (1993). Video as a technology for informal communication. *Communications of the ACM, 36*(1), 48-61.

Frissen, V. (1992). Trapped in electronic cages? Gender and new information technologies in the public and private domain: An overview of research. *Media, Culture & Society, 14,* 31-39.

Fulk, J. (1993). Social construction of communication technology. *Academy of Management Journal, 36*(5), 921-950.

Fulk, J., & DeSanctis, G. (1995). Electronic communication and changing organizational forms. *Organization Science, 6*(4), 337-349.

Fulk, J., Steinfield, C. W., & Schmitz, J. (1990). A social information processing model of media use in organizations. In J. Fulk & C. Steinfield (Eds.), *Organizations and communication technology* (pp. 117-140). Newbury Park, CA: Sage.

Gale, I. (1994). Price competition in noncooperative joint ventures. *International Journal of Industrial Organization, 12(1),* 53-70.

Galletta, D., Ahuja, M., Hartman, A., Teo, T., & Peace, A. (1995). Social influence and end-user training. *Communications of the ACM, 38*(7), 70-79.

Gattiker, U. E. (1990). *Technology management in organizations.* Newbury Park, CA: Sage.

Gattiker, U. E. (Ed.). (1994). *Studies in technical innovation and human resources: Women and technology* (Vol. 4). New York: Walter de Gruyter.

Gattiker, U. E. (in press). *Moral and economic issues on the information highway: Balancing interests.* Mahwah, NJ: Lawrence Erlbaum.

Gattiker, U. E., Gutek, B., & Berger, D. (1988). Office technology and employee attitudes. *Social Science Computer Review, 6,* 327-340.

Gattiker, U. E., & Howg, L. W. (1990). Information technology and quality of work life: Comparing users with non-users. *Journal of Business and Psychology, 5,* 237-260.

Gattiker, U. E., Janz, L., Kelley, H., & Schollmeyer, M. (1996). Information technology—The Internet and privacy: Do you know who's watching? *Business Quarterly, 60*(4), 79-85.

Gattiker, U. E., & Kelley, H. (1999). Morality and computers: Attitudes and differences in moral judgments across populations. *Information Systems Research, 10,* 223-254.

Gattiker, U. E., Kelley, H., & Janz, L. (1996). The information highway: Opportunities and challenges for organizations. In R. Berndt (Ed.), *Global management* (pp. 417-453). Berlin and New York: Springer-Verlag.

Gattiker, U. E., Kelley, H., Paulson, D., & Bhatnagar, D. (1996). User information satisfaction: A comparison of three countries. *Journal of Organizational Behavior.*

Gattiker, U. E., & Nelligan, T. (1988). Computerized offices in Canada and the United States: Investigating dispositional similarities and differences. *Journal of Organizational Behavior, 9*(1), 77-96.

Gattiker, U. E., & Paulson, D. (1999). Unions and new office technology. *Relations Industrielles, 54,* 245-276.

Gattiker, U. E., & Willoughby, K. (1993). Technological competence, ethics, and the global village: Cross-national comparisons for organization research. In R. Golembiewski (Ed.), *Handbook of organizational behavior* (pp. 457-485). New York: Marcel Dekker.

Gerwin, D. (1981). Relationships between structure and technology. In P. C. Nystrom & W. H. Starbuck (Eds.), *Handbook of organizational design: Vol. 2.*

Remodeling organizations and their environments (pp. 3-38). New York: Oxford University Press.

Giddens, A. (1976). *New rules of sociological method.* London: Hutchinson.

Giddens, A. (1984). *The constitution of society.* Berkeley: University of California Press.

Grande, S. (1980). Aspects of pre-literate culture shared by online searching and videotex. *Canadian Journal of Information Science, 5,* 125-131.

Granstrand, O., & Sjölander, S. (1990). The acquisition of technology and small firms by large firms. *Journal of Economic Behavior and Organization, 13,* 367-386.

Gurbaxani, V. (1990). Diffusion in computing networks: The case of Bitnet. *Communications of the ACM, 33*(12), 65-75.

Gurbaxani, V., & Whang, S. (1991). The impact of information systems on organizations and markets. *Communications of the ACM, 34*(1), 59-73.

Gutek, B. A. (1994). Clerical work and information technology: Implications of managerial assumptions. In U. E. Gattiker (Ed.), *Technological innovation and human resources: Women and technology* (Vol. 4, pp. 205-225). Berlin and New York: Walter de Gruyter.

Hackett, E., Mirvis, P., & Sales, A. (1991). Women's and men's expectations about the effects of new technology at work. *Group and Organization Studies, 16*(1), 60-85.

Haines, V. (1988). Social network analysis, structuration theory and the holism-individualism debate. *Social Networks, 10*(2), 157-182.

Harasim, L. (1990). *Online education: Perspectives on a new environment.* New York: Praeger.

Harrison, T., & Stephen, T. (Eds.). (1996). *Computer networking and scholarly communication in the twenty-first-century university.* Albany: State University of New York Press.

Hart, P., & Rice, R. E. (1988). Inter-industry relations in electronic news services. *Journal of the American Society for Information Science, 39*(4), 252-261.

Hartman, K., Neuwirth, C., Kiesler, S., Sproull, L., Cochran, C., Palmquist, M., & Zubrow, D. (1991). Patterns of social interaction and learning to write. *Written Communication, 8*(1), 79-113.

Hayne, S., & Rice, R. E. (1997). Accuracy of attribution in small groups using anonymity in group support systems. *International Journal of Human Computer Studies, 47,* 429-452.

Hepworth, M. (1989). *Geography of the information economy.* London: Belhaven.

Hesse, B., Sproull, L., Kiesler, S., & Walsh, J. (1993). Returns to science: Computer networks in oceanography. *Communications of the ACM, 36*(8),90-101.

Hesse, B., Werner, C., & Altman, I. (1988). Temporal aspects of computer-mediated communication. *Computers in Human Behavior, 4,* 147-165.

Heydebrand, W. (1989). New organizational forms. *Work and Occupations, 16*(3), 323-357.

Hiltz, S. R. (1984). *Online communities: A case study of the office of the future.* Norwood, NJ: Ablex.

Hiltz, S. R. (1986). The "virtual classroom": Using computer-mediated communication for university teaching. *Journal of Communication, 36*(2), 95-104.

Hiltz, S. R., & Turoff, M. (1993). *The network nation: Human communication via computer* (2nd ed.). Reading, MA: Addison-Wesley.

Hiltz, S. R., Turoff, M., & Johnson, K. (1989). Experiments in group decision making, 3: Dis-inhibition, de-individuation and group process in pen name and real name computer conferences. *Decision Support Systems, 5*(2), 217-232.

Hinds, P., & Kiesler, S. (1995). Communication across boundaries: Work, structure, and use of communication technologies in a large organization. *Organization Science, 6*(4), 373-393.

Hirschhorn, L., & Gilmore, T. (1992, May-June). The new boundaries of the "boundaryless" company. *Harvard Business Review, 70*(3), 104-116.

Hofstede, G. (1993). Cultural constraints in management theories. *Academy of Management Executive, 7*(1), 81-94.

Holti, R. (1994). Telematics, workplaces and homes: The evolving picture of teleworking. In J. E. Andriessen & R. Roe (Eds.), *Telematics and work* (pp. 261-288). Hillsdale, NJ: Lawrence Erlbaum.

Howell, J., & Higgins, C. (1990). Champions of technological innovation. *Administrative Science Quarterly, 35,* 317-341.

Huff, C., Sproull, L., & Kiesler, S. (1989). Computer communication and organizational commitment: Tracing the relationship in a city government. *Journal of Applied Social Psychology, 19,* 1371-1391.

Jablin, F. M. (1987). Formal organization structure. In F. M. Jablin, L. L. Putnam, K. H. Roberts, & L. W. Porter (Eds.), *Handbook of organizational communication: An interdisciplinary perspective* (pp. 389-419). Newbury Park, CA: Sage.

Jensen, J. (1990). *Redeeming modernity: Contradictions in media criticism.* Newbury Park, CA: Sage.

Jessup, L., Connolly, T., & Tansik, D. (1990). Toward a theory of automated group work: The deindividuating effects of anonymity. *Small Group Research, 21,* 333-348.

Johnson, B., & Rice, R. (1987). *Managing organizational innovation: The evolution from word processing to office information systems.* New York: Columbia University Press.

Johnson, J. D. (1993). *Organizational communication structure.* Norwood, NJ: Ablex.

Johnson-Lenz, P., & Johnson-Lenz, T. (1991). Post-mechanistic groupware primitives: Rhythms, boundaries and containers. *International Journal of Man-Machine Studies, 34,* 395-417.

Joshi, K. (1992). A causal path model of the overall user attitudes toward the MIS function: The case of user information satisfaction. *Information & Management, 22,* 77-88.

Kalakota, R., & Whinston, A. (1996). *Frontiers of electronic commerce.* Reading, MA: Addison-Wesley.

Kaye, A. R., & Byrne, K. E. (1986). Insights on the implementation of a computer-based message system. *Information & Management, 10,* 277-284.

Keen, P. (1991). *Shaping the future: Business design through information technology.* Boston: Harvard Business School Press.

Kerr, E., & Hiltz, S. R. (1982). *Computer-mediated communication systems.* New York: Academic Press.

Kling, R., & Jewett, T. (1994). The social design of worklife with computers and networks: An open natural systems perspective. *Advances in Computers, 39,* 239-293.

Kolb, D. (1996). Discourse across links. In C. Ess (Ed.), *Philosophical perspectives on computer-mediated communication* (pp. 15-41). Albany: State University of New York Press.

Konsynski, B., & McFarlan, W. (1990). Information partnerships—Shared data, shared scale. *Harvard Business Review, 68*(5), 114-120.

Kraemer, K., & Pinsonneault, A. (1990). Technology and groups: Assessments of the empirical research. In J. Galegher, R. Kraut, & C. Egido (Eds.), *Intellectual teamwork: Social and technological foundations of cooperative work* (pp. 373-404). Hillsdale, NJ: Lawrence Erlbaum.

Kraut, R. (1989). Telecommuting: The trade-offs of home work. *Journal of Communication, 39*(3), 19-47.

Lea, M. (1991). Rationalist assumptions in cross-media comparisons of computer-mediated communication. *Behaviour and Information Technology, 10*(2), 153-172.

Lea, M., O'Shea, T., & Fung, P. (1995). Constructing the networked organization: Content and context in the development of electronic communications. *Organization Science, 6*(4), 462-478.

Leonard-Barton, D., & Deschamps, I. (1988). Managerial influence in the implementation of new technology. *Management Science, 32*(10), 1252-1265.

Lievrouw, L., & Carley, K. (1990). Changing patterns of communication among scientists in an era of "telescience." *Technology in Society, 12,* 1-21.

Lind, M., & Zmud, R. (1995). Improving interorganizational effectiveness through voice mail facilitation of peer-to-peer relationships. *Organization Science, 6*(4), 445-461.

Mackay, W. (1988). Diversity in the use of electronic mail. *ACM Transactions on Office Information Systems, 6*(4), 380-397.

Malone, T., Grant, K., Turbak, F., Brobst, S., & Cohen, M. (1987). Intelligent information-sharing systems. *Communications of the ACM, 30*(5), 390-402.

Malone, T., & Rockart, J. (1993). How will information technology reshape organizations? Computers as coordination technology. In S. Bradley, J. Hausman, & R. Nolan (Eds.), *Globalization, technology, and competition: The fusion of computers and telecommunications in the 1990s* (pp. 37-56). Boston: Harvard Business School Press.

Malone, T., Yates, J., & Benjamin, R. (1989). The logic of electronic markets. *Harvard Business Review, 67*(3), 166-170.

Mantovani, G. (1994). Is computer-mediated communication intrinsically apt to enhance democracy in organizations? *Human Relations, 47*(1), 45-62.

Markus, M. L. (1984). *Systems in organizations: Bugs & features.* Boston: Pitman.

Markus, M. L. (1990). Toward a critical mass theory of interactive media: Universal access, interdependence and diffusion. In J. Fulk & C. Steinfield (Eds.), *Organizations and communication technology* (pp. 194-218). Newbury Park, CA: Sage.

Markus, M. L. (1992). Asynchronous technologies in small face-to-face groups. *Information Technology & People, 6*(1), 29-48.

Markus, M. L., & Robey, D. (1988). Information technology and organizational change: Causal structure in theory and research. *Management Science, 34*(5), 583-598.

Marvin, C. (1988). *When old technologies were new.* New York: Oxford University Press.

Matheson, K. (1992). Women and computer technology: Communicating for herself. In M. Lea (Ed.), *Contexts of computer-mediated communication* (pp. 66-88). New York: Harvester-Wheatsheaf.

Maurice, M., Sorge, A., & Warner, M. (1980). Societal differences in organizing manufacturing units: A comparison of France, West Germany, and Great Britain. *Organization Studies, 1,* 59-86.

McGrath, J. (1990). Time matters in groups. In J. Galegher, R. Kraut, & C. Egido (Eds.), *Intellectual teamwork: Social and technological foundations of cooperative work* (pp. 23-62). Hillsdale, NJ: Lawrence Erlbaum.

McGrath, J. E., & Hollingshead, A. B. (1992). Putting the "group" back in group support systems: Some theoretical issues about dynamic processes in groups with technological enhancements. In L. M. Jessup & J. S. Valacich (Eds.), *Group support systems: New perspectives* (pp. 78-96). New York: Macmillan.

McKenney, J., Zack, M., & Doherty, V. (1992). Complementary communication media: A comparison of electronic mail and face-to-face communication in a programming team. In N. Nohria & R. Eccles (Eds.), *Networks and organizations: Structure, form and action* (pp. 262-287). Boston: Harvard Business School Press.

Moore, A., & Jovanis, P. (1988). Modelling media choices in business organizations: Implications for analyzing telecommunications-transportation interactions. *Transportation Research, 22A,* 257-273.

Mowshowitz, A. (1976). *The conquest of will: Information processing in human affairs.* Menlo Park, CA: Addison-Wesley.

Mulgan, G. (1991). *Communication and control: Networks and the new economies of communication.* Oxford, UK: Polity.

Mumford, E., & Banks, O. (1967). *The computer and the clerk.* London: Routledge and Kegan Paul.

Murray, L. W. H. (1994). Women in science occupations: Some impacts of technological change. In U. E. Gattiker (Ed.), *Technological innovation and human resources: Women and technology* (Vol. 4, pp. 93-129). Berlin and New York: Walter de Gruyter.

Nelson, D. (1990, March). Individual adjustment to information-driven technologies. *MIS Quarterly, 14,* 79-98.

Newell, S., & Clark, P. (1990). The importance of extra-organizational networks in the diffusion and appropriation of new technologies. *Knowledge: Creation, Diffusion, Utilization, 12*(2), 199-212.

The new workplace. (1996, April 29). *Business Week,* pp. 106-117.

Nilles, J., Carlson, F., Gray, P., & Hanneman, G. (1976). *The telecommunication-transportation tradeoff: Options for tomorrow.* New York: Wiley Interscience.

Nohria, N., & Eccles, R. (1992). *Networks and organizations: Structure, form and action.* Boston: Harvard Business School Press.

Nunamaker, J., Dennis, A., Valacich, J., Vogel, D., & George, J. (1991). Electronic meeting systems to support group work. *Communications of the ACM, 34*(7), 40-61.

Orlikowski, W. (1992). The duality of technology: Rethinking the concept of technology in organizations. *Organization Science, 3*(3), 398-427.

Orlikowski, W., & Robey, D. (1991). Information technology and the structuring of organizations. *Information Systems Research, 2*(2), 143-169.

Orlikowski, W., & Yates, J. (1993, August). *From memo to dialogue: Enacting genres of communication in electronic media.* Paper presented at the annual meeting of the Academy of Management, Atlanta, GA.

Orlikowski, W., Yates, J., Okamura, K., & Fujimoto, M. (1995). Shaping electronic communication: The metastructuring of technology in the context of use. *Organization Science, 6*(4), 423-443.

Papa, W., & Papa, M. (1992). Communication network patterns and the re-invention of new technology. *Journal of Business Communication, 29*(1), 41-61.

Pava, C. (1983). *Managing new office technology.* New York: Free Press.

Pazy, A. (1994). Trying to combat professional obsolescence: The experience of women in technical careers. In U. E. Gattiker (Ed.), *Technological innovation and human resources: Women and technology*

(Vol. 4, pp. 65-91). Berlin and New York: Walter de Gruyter.

Perin, C. (1991). Electronic social fields in bureaucracies. *Communications of the ACM, 34*(12), 75-82.

Perio, J., & Prieto, F. (1994). Telematics and organizational structure and processes: An overview. In J. E. Andriessen & R. Roe (Eds.), *Telematics and work* (pp. 175-208). Hillsdale, NJ: Lawrence Erlbaum.

Perry, R., & Greber, L. (1990). Women and computers: An introduction. *Signs: Journal of Women in Culture and Society, 16*(1), 74-101.

Pettigrew, A. (1972). Information control as a power resource. *Sociology, 6*(2), 187-204.

Pickering, J., & King, J. L. (1995). Hardwiring weak ties: Interorganizational computer-mediated communication, occupational communities, and organizational change. *Organization Science, 6*(4), 479-486.

Poole, M. S., & DeSanctis, G. (1990). Understanding the use of group decision support systems: The theory of adaptive structuration. In J. Fulk & C. Steinfield (Eds.), *Organizations and communication technology* (pp. 173-193). Newbury Park, CA: Sage.

Quinn, J. B., & Paquette, P. (1990). Technology in services: Creating organizational revolutions. *Sloan Management Review, 31*(2), 67.

Rafaeli, S., & LaRose, R. (1993). Electronic bulletin boards and "public goods" explanations of collaborative mass media. *Communication Research, 20*(2), 277-297.

Rheingold, H. (1993). *The virtual community: Homesteading on the electronic frontier.* Reading, MA: Addison-Wesley.

Rice, R. E. (1980). Impacts of organizational and interpersonal computer-mediated communication. In M. Williams (Ed.), *Annual review of information science and technology* (Vol. 15, pp. 221-249). White Plains, NY: Knowledge Industry.

Rice, R. E. (1982). Communication networking in computer conferencing systems: A longitudinal study of group roles and system structure. In M. Burgoon (Ed.), *Communication yearbook* (Vol. 6, pp. 925-944). Beverly Hills, CA: Sage.

Rice, R. E. (1984). Mediated group communication. In R. E. Rice & Associates, *The new media: Communication, research and technology* (pp. 129-154). Beverly Hills, CA: Sage.

Rice, R. E. (1987). Computer-mediated communication systems and organizational innovation. *Journal of Communication, 37*(4), 65-94.

Rice, R. E. (1990). Computer-mediated communication system network data: Theoretical concerns and empirical examples. *International Journal of Man-Machine Studies, 30,* 1-21.

Rice, R. E. (1992). Contexts of research on organizational computer-mediated communication: A recursive review. In M. Lea (Ed.), *Contexts of computer-mediated communication* (pp. 113-144). London: Harvester-Wheatsheaf.

Rice, R. E. (1993a). Artifacts, freedoms, paradoxes and inquiries: Some ways new media challenge traditional mass media and interpersonal effects paradigms. *MultiMedia Review/Virtual Reality World, 4*(2), 30-35.

Rice, R. E. (1993b). Media appropriateness: Using social presence theory to compare traditional and new organizational media. *Human Communication Research, 19*(4), 451-484.

Rice, R. E. (1993c). Using network concepts to clarify sources and mechanisms of social influence. In W. Richards, Jr. & G. Barnett (Eds.), *Advances in communication network analysis* (pp. 43-52). Norwood, NJ: Ablex.

Rice, R. E. (1994). Relating electronic mail use and network structure to R&D work networks and performance. *Journal of Management Information Systems, 11*(1), 9-20.

Rice, R. E., & Associates. (1984). *The new media: Communication, research and technology.* Beverly Hills, CA: Sage.

Rice, R. E., & Aydin, C. (1991). Attitudes toward new organizational technology: Network proximity as a mechanism for social information processing. *Administrative Science Quarterly, 36,* 219-244.

Rice, R. E., & Case, D. (1983). Computer-based messaging in the university: A description of use and utility. *Journal of Communication, 33*(1), 131-152.

Rice, R. E., Chang, S., & Torobin, J. (1992). Communicator style, media use, organizational level, and use and evaluation of electronic messaging. *Management Communication Quarterly, 6*(1), 3-33.

Rice, R. E., & Danowski, J. (1993). Is it really just like a fancy answering machine? Comparing semantic networks of different types of voice mail users. *Journal of Business Communication, 30*(4), 369-397.

Rice, R. E., Grant, A., Schmitz, J., & Torobin, J. (1990). Individual and network influences on the adoption and perceived outcomes of electronic messaging. *Social Networks, 12*(1), 27-55.

Rice, R. E. (with Hart, P., Torobin, J., Shook, D., Tyler, J., Svenning, L., & Ruchinskas, J.). (1992). Task analyzability, use of new media, and effectiveness: A multi-site exploration of media richness. *Organization Science, 3*(4), 475-500.

Rice, R. E., Hughes, D., & Love, G. (1989). Usage and outcomes of electronic messaging at an R&D organization: Situational constraints, job level, and media awareness. *Office: Technology and People, 5*(2), 141-161.

Rice, R. E., Kraut, R., Cool, C., & Fish, R. (1994). Individual, structural and social influences on use of a new communication medium. In D. Moore (Ed.), *Proceedings of the 1994 Academy of Management meeting* (pp. 285-289). Madison, WI: Omni.

Rice, R. E., & Love, G. (1987). Electronic emotion: Socio-emotional content in a computer-mediated communication network. *Communication Research,* *14*(1), 85-108.

Rice, R. E., & Shook, D. (1988). Access to, usage of, and outcomes from an electronic message system. *ACM Transactions on Office Information Systems, 6*(3), 255-276.

Rice, R. E., & Shook, D. (1990). Voice messaging, coordination and communication. In J. Galegher, R. Kraut, & C. Egido (Eds.), *Intellectual teamwork: Social and technological bases of cooperative work* (pp. 327-350). Hillsdale, NJ: Lawrence Erlbaum.

Rice, R. E., & Steinfield, C. (1994). New forms of organizational communication via electronic mail and voice messaging. In J. E. Andriessen & R. Roe (Eds.), *Telematics and work* (pp. 109-137). Hillsdale, NJ: Lawrence Erlbaum.

Rice, R. E., & Tyler, J. (1995). Innovativeness, organizational context, and voice mail use and evaluation. *Behaviour and Information Technology, 14*(6), 329-341.

Robey, D. (1981). Computer information systems and organization structure. *Communications of the ACM, 24*(10), 679-687.

Rockart, J., & Short, J. (1991). The networked organization and the management of interdependence. In M. S. Scott Morton (Ed.), *The corporation of the 1990s: Information technology and organizational transformation* (pp. 189-219). New York: Oxford University Press.

Rogers, E. M., Collins-Jarvis, L., & Schmitz, J. (1994). The PEN project in Santa Monica: Interactive communication, equality, and political action. *Journal of the American Society for Information Science, 45,* 401.

Rupley, S. (1996). Digital bucks? Stop here. *PC Magazine, 15*(10), p. 54ff.

Sackman, H., & Nie, N. (Eds.). (1970). *The information utility and social choice.* Montvale, NJ: American Federation of Information Processing Societies.

Salancik, G. R., & Pfeffer, J. (1978). A social information approach to job attitudes and task design. *Administrative Science Quarterly, 23,* 224-252.

Schaefermeyer, M., & Sewell, E. (1988). Communicating by electronic mail. *American Behavioral Scientist, 32*(2), 112-123.

Schauder, D. (1994). Electronic publishing of professional articles: Attitudes of academics and implications for the scholarly communication industry. *Journal of the American Society for Information Science, 45*(2), 73-100.

Schmitz, J., & Fulk, J. (1991). Organizational colleagues, information richness and electronic mail: A test of the social influence model of technology use. *Communication Research, 18*(4), 487-523.

Selfe, C., & Meyer, P. (1991). Testing claims for on-line conferences. *Written Communication, 8*(2), 163-192.

Sherblom, J. (1988). Direction, function and signature in electronic mail. *Journal of Business Communication, 25,* 39-54.

Short, J., Williams, E., & Christie, B. (1976). *The social psychology of telecommunications.* New York: John Wiley.

Shudson, M. (1978). The ideal of conversation in the study of mass media. *Communication Research, 5*(3), 320-329.

Sitkin, S., Sutcliffe, K., & Barrios-Choplin, J. (1992). A dual-capacity model of communication media choice in organizations. *Human Communication Research, 18*(4), 563-598.

Soares, A. S. (1992). Telework and communication in data processing centres in Brazil. In U. E. Gattiker (Ed.), *Studies in technological innovation and human resources: Technology-mediated communication* (Vol. 3, pp. 117-145). Berlin and New York: Walter de Gruyter.

Soe, L., & Markus, M. L. (1993). Technological or social utility? Unraveling explanations of email, vmail, and fax use. *Information Society, 9,* 213-236.

Sparks, C., & van Zoonen, L. (1992). Gender and technology. *Media, Culture and Society, 14,* 5-7.

Spears, R., & Lea, M. (1992). Social influence and the influence of the "social" in computer-mediated communication. In M. Lea (Ed.), *Contexts of computer-mediated communication* (pp. 30-65). London: Harvester-Wheatsheaf.

Sproull, L., & Kiesler, S. (1991). *Connections: New ways of working in the networked organization.* Cambridge, MA: MIT Press.

Steinfield, C., Caby, L., & Vialle, P. (1992). Internationalization of the firm and impacts of videotex networks. *Journal of Information Technology, 7,* 213-222.

Stevenson, W. (1993). Organization design. In R. Golembiewski (Ed.), *Handbook of organizational behavior* (pp. 141-168). New York: Marcel Dekker.

Stewart, C. (1992). Innovation is in the mind of the user: A case study of voice mail. In U. E. Gattiker (Ed.), *Studies in technological innovation and human resources: Technology mediated communication* (Vol. 3, pp. 151-185). New York: Walter de Gruyter.

Stone, P. J., & Luchetti, R. (1985, March-April). Your office is where you are. *Harvard Business Review, 63,* 102-117.

Sundstrom, E., Burt, R., & Kamp, D. (1980). Privacy at work: Architectural correlates of job satisfaction and job performance. *Academy of Management Journal, 23*(1), 101-117.

Taylor, J., & Van Every, E. (1993). *The vulnerable fortress: Bureaucratic organizations and management in the information age.* Toronto, Canada: University of Toronto Press.

Trevino, L. K., Lengel, R. H., & Daft, R. L. (1987). Media symbolism, media richness and media choice in organizations: A symbolic interactionist perspective. *Communication Research, 14*(5), 553-575.

Trevino, L., & Webster, J. (1992). Flow in computer-mediated communication: Electronic mail and voice mail evaluation and impacts. *Communication Research, 19,* 539-573.

Valacich, J., Paranka, D., George, J., & Nunamaker, J. (1993). Communication concurrency and the new media. *Communication Research, 20*(2), 249-276.

Walker, S. (1984). How typewriters changed correspondence: An analysis of prescription and practice. *Visible Language, 28*(2), 102-117.

Walther, J. (1992). Interpersonal effects in computer-mediated interaction: A relational perspective. *Communication Research, 19*(1), 52-90.

Want, R., Hopper, A., Falcao, V., & Gibbons, J. (1992). The active badge location system. *ACM Transactions on Information Systems, 10*(1), 91-102.

Whisler, T. (1970). *The impact of computers on organizations.* New York: Praeger.

Wigand, R. T. (1985). Integrated communications and work efficiency: Impacts on organizational structure

and power. *Information Services and Use, 5,* 241-258.

Yates, J., & Benjamin, R. (1991). The past and present as a window on the future. In M. S. Scott Morton (Ed.), *The corporation of the 1990s: Information technology and organizational transformation* (pp. 61-92). New York: Oxford University Press.

Yates, J., & Orlikowski, W. (1992). Genres of organizational communication: A structurational approach to studying communication and media. *Academy of Management Review, 17,* 299-326.

Zimmerman, J. (Ed.). (1983). *The technological woman: Interfacing with tomorrow.* New York: Praeger.

Zmud, R. (1990). Opportunities for strategic information manipulation through new information technology. In J. Fulk & C. Steinfield (Eds.), *Organizations and communication technology* (pp. 95-116). Newbury Park, CA: Sage.

Zmud, R., Lind, M., & Young, F. (1990). An attribute space for organizational communication channels. *Information Systems Research, 1*(4), 440-457.

PART IV

Process: Communication Behavior in Organizations

15

Power and Politics

❖ DENNIS K. MUMBY
❖ *Purdue University*

This chapter focuses on the relationships among communication, power, and organization. Its central premise is that organizations are intersubjective structures of meaning that are produced, reproduced, and transformed through the ongoing communicative activities of its members. As a critical organization scholar, however, I will argue that this process is fundamentally mediated by power, which I see as a defining, ubiquitous feature of organizational life. At the same time, and to be appreciated in all its complexities, power itself must be made sense of through a communication lens. From this perspective, communication, power, and organization are interdependent and coconstructed phenomena. The primary goal of this chapter is to explore this tripartite relationship, and to show how, as a field, we can contribute to an understanding of organizational power that is distinct from that offered by such disciplines as management studies, sociology, and political science.

Because of this distinctly communication focus, a secondary goal will be to examine noncommunication views of organizational power, and to show how such work both provides insights into, and places limitations on, our understanding of power. Indeed, given

AUTHOR'S NOTE: I thank George Cheney, Bob Gephart, Fred Jablin, Linda Putnam, and Cynthia Stohl for their constructive and challenging critiques of various drafts of this chapter.

that power has been a focus of research in various disciplines for several decades, it makes sense that such work will have loci of inquiry other than communication processes. Individual, interpersonal, and structural theories of power are all common in this vast and complex literature. However, many of these approaches contain implicit notions of communication that often remain untheorized. A tertiary goal of this chapter, then, will be to tease out, where relevant and appropriate, implicit perspectives on communication that are built into theories of power developed in other disciplines.

Given the complex terrain of the power literature, Table 15.1 provides definitions of constructs that will be central to the argument I develop. Definitions of each concept are drawn not from specific theorists (although in many ways each definition is the distillation of the work of many authors), but from my own attempt to privilege a communication orientation toward the literature reviewed in this chapter. Thus, each term reflects a perspective—rooted in my own work—that views communication as creating the very possibility for organizing, exercising power, engaging in political activity, and so forth. This conception of communication as *constitutive* of both organizing and power therefore serves as the benchmark against which we can review and critique the theory and research on organizational power and politics.

The structure of this chapter will unfold in the following manner. First is a brief historical and theoretical context for the study of power, focusing on Weber, Marx, and the sociological study of power since the 1950s. Second, I pick up the point at which power became an object of study in the management literature, beginning with the structural-functional tradition. Third, I delineate interpretive approaches to power and, fourth, examine the emergence of the critical perspective on organizations and power. Fifth, I discuss the recent emergence of postmodern conceptions of organizational power. Finally, I situate feminist studies as the latest contribution to understanding the relations among communication, power, and organization.

POWER AND POLITICS: IN THE BEGINNING . . .

It is difficult to make sense out of organizational power without reference to the works of Marx (1967) and Weber (1978). Both were concerned—albeit in different ways—with explaining how power is exercised under conditions of the division of labor. Neither paid much attention to power as a communication phenomenon, although Marx's theory of ideology presumes a process by which the ideas of the capitalist class are widely disseminated, and Weber envisions a bureaucratic system of rules, the communication and internalization of which legitimate a rational system of authority. For Marx, the focus was on the means by which capitalist relations of production extracted surplus value from expropriated labor through various coercive techniques, including the lengthening of the working day and the intensification of the labor process. Marx provides us with a class analysis of the capitalist relations of production as a means of critiquing bourgeois economic models and exposing the contradictions inherent in capitalism.

Weber, on the other hand, was more concerned with analyzing the system of rationality manifest in Western industrial societies. Weber (1978) situates his discussion of bureaucracy within the larger context of a general model of authority. Situating rational, bureaucratic authority in relation to traditional and charismatic forms of authority, Weber conceives of the former as "modernist" in its rejection of forms of power characterized by nepotism, raw force, and arbitrary decision making. As Cheney (personal correspondence) has suggested, Weber shows "how the bureaucratic ethos narrows our vision" to rationally, systematically—and perhaps most important—exercise authority in a nonarb-

TABLE 15.1 Definitions of Central Concepts

Communication: The process of creating intersubjective meanings through ongoing, interactional symbolic—verbal and nonverbal—practices, including conversation, metaphors, rituals, stories, dress, space, and so forth.

Organizational communication: The process of creating collective, coordinated structures of meaning through symbolic practices oriented toward the achievement of organizational goals.

Power: The production and reproduction of, resistance to, or transformation of relatively fixed (sedimented) structures of communication and meaning that support the interests (symbolic, political, and economic) of some organization members or groups over others.

Politics: The articulation of various individual and group interests through the everyday enactment of communicative processes that produce, reproduce, resist, and transform collective (intersubjective) structures of meaning. Politics is power enacted and resisted.

Ideology: The process of symbolically creating systems of meaning through which social actors' identities are constructed and situated within relations of power. Ideological struggle entails the attempts of various groups to "fix" and "naturalize" their worldview over others (Althusser, 1971; Therborn, 1980).

Hegemony: The ability of one class or group to link the interests and worldviews of other groups with its own. Hegemony does not refer to simple domination, but rather involves attempts by various groups to articulate meaning systems that are actively taken up by other groups (Gramsci, 1971).

Reification: The process through which humanly created structures take on an objective, "natural" existence, independent from those who constructed them. Reification leads to a sense of alienation, which engenders the possibility for self-reflection and social change (Lukács, 1971).

itrary fashion. Weber thus left us with both a structural and ideological legacy: a bureaucratic system of rules and regulations constitutive of authority, along with an ideology of rationality that shapes and constrains the behavior of actors in organizational contexts.

Both Marx and Weber were concerned with the direction in which modernity was moving: Marx focused on the exploitative nature of capitalism, while Weber expressed reservations with bureaucratic rationality and its eclipsing of other forms of rationality, particularly the charismatic, which he saw as an essential, magical feature of human collective action. Thus, while Weber articulated an "ideal type" of rational legal authority—

rooted in technical criteria and expertise—that overcame the capriciousness of other authority systems, he was concerned with the reification of this ideal type and its manifestation as an "iron cage" that imprisoned those it was intended to empower.

How does this translate into contemporary accounts of organizational power? While Marx's legacy has been fairly diverse in its spawning of a variety of Marxisms (neo, structural, functional, etc.), some of which impinge on organization studies (see below), Weber tends to be rather narrowly appropriated as *the* "theorist of bureaucracy," rather than as a social theorist in the wider sense (for exceptions, see Barker, 1993, 1999; Barker &

Cheney, 1994; Clegg, 1975, 1994b; O'Neill, 1986). Thus, although radical readings of Weber exist, most of management and organization studies read his work as a simple affirmation of bureaucratic rationality. For example, his work on *Verstehen* (understanding) as an interpretive method for analyzing human behavior is almost completely ignored. As such, most of the work on organizational power in the 1960s and 1970s was conducted in the context of this rather narrow reading of Weber. Power, then, is conceptualized largely within a systems-rational model of organizational structure, which sees decision making and the concomitant exercising of power as the logical, optimal, and adaptive response to changes in an organization's environment.

A debate in the field of political science that slightly predates such work implicitly embodies the tension between the conservative and radical readings of Weber. The "community power debate," conducted during the 1950s, 1960s, and 1970s addressed the status of power as an empirical phenomenon. That is, what is the structure and distribution of power in contemporary society? Attempts to answer this question developed roughly into two camps: the pluralists (Dahl, 1957, 1958, 1961; Wolfinger, 1971), and the elitists (Bachrach & Baratz, 1962, 1963; Hunter, 1953; Mills, 1956). The pluralists argued that power was equitably distributed throughout society and that no particular group had undue influence over decision-making processes. The elitists, on the other hand, claimed that power was concentrated in the hands of a privileged few who controlled political agendas.

In some respects, the two groups represent conservative (pluralist) and radical (elitist) readings of modernity, the former claiming that modernity/capitalism/bureaucracy has largely realized democracy, while the latter argues that modernity has emancipated only a privileged few. Dahl (1957) reflects this conservative reading of modernity with a rational, causal, behavioral model of power conceived in terms of decision-making processes. Thus, "A has power over B to the extent that he [or she] can get B to do something that B would

not otherwise do" (Dahl, 1957, pp. 202-203). This often cited definition focuses on the manifest *exercise* of power, and not on power as a potential or dispositional quality of actors. Such exercising can be identified only in explicit decision-making situations where overt conflict between parties is present.

On the other hand, Bachrach and Baratz (1962) criticize Dahl's exclusive focus on concrete decision-making situations, arguing that power is also exercised in situations of "non-decision making." They suggest that in this context, power is exercised when A is able to create and reinforce situations in which the political process is limited to the consideration of issues that do not endanger A's power. "To the extent that A succeeds in doing this, B is prevented, for all practical purposes, from bringing to the fore any issues that might in their resolution be seriously detrimental to A's set of preferences" (Bachrach & Baratz, 1962, p. 948). Quoting Schattschneider (1960), Bachrach and Baratz refer to this process as the "mobilization of bias":

> All forms of political organization have a bias in favour of the exploitation of some kinds of conflict and the suppression of other because *organization is the mobilization of bias.* Some issues are organized into politics while others are organized out. (Schattschneider, 1960, p. 71, emphasis in original)

While there is no explicit model of organizational *communication* operating here, Bachrach and Baratz set the stage for a rhetorical approach to organizational power taken up by theorists such as Tompkins and Cheney (Bullis & Tompkins, 1989; Cheney, 1983; Tompkins & Cheney, 1985) in which they examine the processes through which organizational identification and control are rhetorically managed. Further, Clegg (1989a, p. 75) suggests that Bachrach and Baratz's "two faces of power" is an attempt to make explicit the link between agency and structure, demonstrating that power resides not simply in relations of cause and effect (as Dahl suggests), but in the structured relations of autonomy and dependence that are an endemic feature of organizational life. In many respects, communication is the mediating link between agency and structure, as the process that functions as the constitutive element in relations of autonomy and dependence.

The last move in the community power debate is provided by Lukes's (1974) "radical," three-dimensional view of power that criticizes both Dahl's "one-dimensional" model and Bachrach and Baratz's "two-dimensional" model. Lukes argues that both models are problematic because they reduce power to a focus on decision-making processes and actual, observable conflict (p. 22). In contrast, he argues that power may be exercised in the absence of any observable conflict, suggesting that A exercises power over B "by influencing, shaping or determining his [*sic*] very wants" (Lukes, 1974, p. 23). In addition, Lukes rejects Bachrach and Baratz's notion that non-decision-making power exists only where grievances are denied access to the political process. Lukes disputes the idea that if a group has no grievances, then there must be a genuine consensus, and no one's interests are being hurt. Sounding remarkably like Habermas, Lukes (1974) argues that "to assume that the absence of grievance equals genuine consensus is simply to rule out the possibility of false or manipulated consensus by definitional fiat" (p. 24). Gaventa's (1980) analysis of the effects of landlord absenteeism on the local population in Appalachia provides an insightful application of this model to a real-world context.

Again, Lukes has no explicit conception of communication in his framework, but there is an implicit one that expands our view of power and makes muted connections to organizational communication studies. For example, his model clearly suggests that processes of socialization and identification—central concerns in our field—are important contexts for the exercise of power (Cheney, 1983; Tompkins & Cheney, 1985). That is, he suggests that power is exercised most effectively when social actors internalize and identify

with the interests of dominant groups—a process that is accomplished rhetorically. Further, his tying of power to false or manipulated interests prefigures critical studies of organizational communication, in which connections are made among communication, ideology, and power (see below). As such, the community power debate represents an important attempt to come to grips with how power functions in institutional settings, providing organizational scholars with insight into how to move beyond individual and relationally focused conceptions of power.

Power, Systems Rationality, and Management Studies

While power has clearly been a central analytic construct in sociology and political science for decades, its emergence as a focal point of research among management researchers is more recent. This is perhaps partly explainable by the field of management's rather narrow appropriation of Weber, resulting in an almost exclusive focus on organizations as sites of rational decision making. In other words, organizational behavior is viewed as explicable through mathematical, economic models of decision making, hence making power irrelevant as an explanatory construct.

This "classic" model of organizational behavior is somewhat modified by the work of the Carnegie group and its development of a model of "administrative man" that focuses on the cognitive and contextual limitations placed on "pure" forms of decision making (Cyert & March, 1963; March & Simon, 1958; Simon, 1976). In Simon's (1976) terms, an individual "satisfices" (makes decisions based on limited information) rather than "optimizes" (makes decisions based on the assessment of all available information). As March and Simon (1958) state:

> This, then, is the general picture of the human organism that we will use to analyze organizational behavior. It is a picture of a choosing, decision-making, problem-solving, organism

that can do only one or a few things at a time, and that can only attend to a small part of the information recorded in its memory and presented by the environment. (p. 11)

Cyert and March (1963) extend this model by shifting focus away from individual levels of decision making, and instead develop a decision-making coalition model. In this context, decision making is seen as a political process, resulting from the conflicts of interest characteristic of subgoal differentiation within organizational life.

As Pettigrew (1973) points out, however, the Carnegie group has a consistent bias in favor of psychological explanations of behavior, drawing heavily on learning theory and individual psychology. Little attention is paid to the larger, structural mechanisms that organizations use in making decisions and forming coalitions. Pettigrew argues that "critical questions related to the generation of support and how the structure of the organization might limit such a process are ignored. . . . [Further] they ignore role and communication structures and how they are devised and changed" (p. 10). Thus, for our purposes, the Carnegie group has little to say about the communicative dimensions of power and decision making. Although Simon (1976) does address the role of decision premises in shaping organizational behavior and decision making, there is no attempt to explicitly articulate this process as communication based.

Thompson's (1967) study extends the work of the Carnegie group through an early appropriation of the newly emergent systems perspective (Von Bertalanffy, 1968). Thompson (1967) defines complex organizations as "open systems, hence indeterminate and faced with uncertainty, but at the same time as subject to criteria of rationality and hence needing determinateness and certainty" (p. 10). The central problem of organization thus involves coping with uncertainty and assessing the impact of technologies and environments on the process of uncertainty absorption. Thompson's work is important not only because he fleshes out and extends the work of the Carnegie group, but also because he situates power as a critical element in the process of problem solving and uncertainty absorption. He recognizes that the indeterminacy of organizational processes creates relations of dependence that shape organizational problem solving and task orientation. Bounded rationality cannot be explained through purely cognitive means, but must be understood as a fundamentally political phenomenon. Thompson's discussion of organizational systems, decision making, and power lays the groundwork for the emergence in the 1970s of two of the most widely adopted theories of organizational power: strategic contingencies theory (Hickson, Hinings, Lee, Schneck, & Pennings, 1971; Hinings, Hickson, Pennings, & Schneck, 1974) and resource dependency theory (Pfeffer, 1981; Pfeffer & Salancik, 1974, 1978; Salancik & Pfeffer, 1974, 1977).

The advent of these theories marks an intense period of study of organizational power in management studies proper, an intensity that has led some researchers to claim that "power is the cornerstone of both management theory and management practice . . . and . . . is a vital and ubiquitous reality in organizational life" (Cavanagh, Moberg, & Velasquez, 1981, p. 363). Some scholars claim that "power" is a better explanatory factor in organization studies than either "goals" or "rationality," given that organizations are not the paragons of logical decision making they were at one time conceived to be (Sunesson, 1985). This research marks a shift from a focus on individual power to departmental/structural power (Enz, 1988). Indeed, criticism of individual and interpersonal models of power is one of the most persistent features of the wave of research that began in the early 1970s:

The term [power] takes on different meanings when the unit, or power-holder, is a *formal group* in an *open system* with *multiple goals,* and the system is assumed to reflect a political-domination model of organization, rather than only a co-operative model. (Perrow, 1970, p. 84, emphasis in original)

Despite this shift in emphasis, much of the work carried out during this period still had little to do directly with communication (conceived as constitutive of the organizing process). Below I briefly adumbrate both strategic contingencies theory and resource dependency theory, suggesting why both have limited application to our understanding of the relationship between power and organizational *communication*.

Hickson et al. (1971; Hinings et al., 1974) pull together a number of different perspectives to create a theory that places power at the center of their definition of organization. Operating on the principle that organizations are fundamentally characterized by a division of labor, they argue that power must be examined as that which characterizes the relationships among functional subunits of organizations:

> Thus organizations are conceived of as interdepartmental systems in which a major task element is coping with uncertainty. . . . The essence of an organization is limitation of the autonomy of all its members or parts, since all are subject to power from the others; for subunits, unlike individuals, are not free to make a decision to participate, as March and Simon (1958) put it, nor to decide whether or not to come together in political relationships. They must. They exist to do so. (Hickson et al., 1971, p. 217)

Strategic contingencies theory is a structural theory of power, concerning itself not with the psychological attributes of individuals, but with the sources of power that result from the structural characteristics of collective, task-oriented behavior. For Hickson et al. (1971, p. 217), following Emerson (1962), the central question in the study of organizations is: What factors function to vary dependency, and thus to vary power? They identify uncertainty (and coping with uncertainty), substitutability, and centrality as the principal variables that determine the relations of power and dependence among organizational subunits. Hinings et al. (1974) provide a test of the initial formulation of this theory, concluding that coping with uncertainty does not in itself explain subunit power, but rather, as their initial theory suggests, such coping must be accompanied by workflow centrality (immediacy and pervasiveness) and low substitutability. Uncertainty is a theme common to the work of March and Simon (1958), Thompson, (1967), and Crozier (1964), the last theorist suggesting—in his study of maintenance engineers in French tobacco manufacturing plants—that power and uncertainty are closely interrelated. In Crozier's study, the maintenance engineers enjoyed a level of power out of all proportion with their positions in the bureaucratic hierarchy, due largely to the unpredictability of machine breakdowns. Crozier was able to assert that these engineers had "control over the last source of uncertainty remaining in a completely routinized organizational system" (p. 154).

The development of resource dependency theory is another important critique of the "rational choice" model of organizational behavior and, particularly, decision-making processes (Pfeffer, 1981; Pfeffer & Salancik, 1974, 1978; Salancik & Pfeffer, 1974, 1977). Drawing on the work of Cyert and March (1963), Pfeffer and Salancik develop a coalitional model of power, which argues that—especially with regard to resource allocation—organizational decision making is a political process that can be explained by considering the relative power of the various subunits within an organization. Resource dependency theory represents a variation of the strategic contingencies theory of power. As Pfeffer (1981) indicates, both perspectives "focus either on the dependence of the organization as a whole or of other subunits on the particular resources or certainty provided by other social actors within the organization" (p. 101). In addition, both theories view power as being derived from the ability of social actors or organizational subunits to address and to ameliorate objectively defined organizational exigencies.

Resource dependency theory studies power both within and between organizations (Pfeffer & Salancik, 1978). Organizations are viewed as open systems that are constantly in need of an ongoing supply of resources, and hence must engage in a continual series of transactions with their environments to secure these resources. Necessary organizational resources include money, prestige, legitimacy, rewards and sanctions, expertise, and the ability to deal with uncertainty. Two early studies by Pfeffer and Salancik (1974; Salancik & Pfeffer, 1974) examine the relative power of subunits (departments) within a university through an analysis of budget allocations. Both studies view organizational decision making as a political process that can be explained only through the analysis of relative subunit power. In addition, Pfeffer and Salancik adopt a coalitional view of organizations that emphasizes differences in the objectives and preferences of the various departments and attempts to demonstrate how conflict between competing preferences and beliefs are resolved. The political character of organization life is rooted in "nonbureaucratic decision mechanisms" (Salancik & Pfeffer, 1974, p. 454) that are used to resolve conflicts between subunits. For resource dependency theory, then, "power is first and foremost a structural phenomenon, and should be understood as such" (Pfeffer, 1981, p. x).

Both strategic contingencies theory and resource dependency theory have been heavily influential in the study of organizational power and politics. Recent literature in this area would suggest that, while modifications of the initial formulations of power have been fairly frequent, little related work has appeared that questions the fundamental assumptions of this early work. Rather, the tendency has been to build on and expand these perspectives (Astley & Sachdeva, 1984; Cobb, 1984; Enz, 1988; Lachman, 1989; Turow, 1984). For example, Astley and Sachdeva bemoan the theoretically fragmented character of work on power and suggest integration through a focus on the interdependent

relationships among three structural sources of power: hierarchical authority, resource control, and network centrality. However, the three sources of power are each borrowed from different theoretical perspectives, and the connections between them are emphasized (hierarchical authority from bureaucratic theory, resource control from resource dependency theory, and network centrality from strategic contingencies theory). As such, Astley and Sachdeva's intervention represents not so much a theoretical synthesis as a theoretical aggregation.

With few exceptions (Pettigrew, 1973; Pfeffer, 1981), little attention has been paid to the relationship between communication and power in this body of research. This stems from rather primitive conceptions of the communication-organization relationship. As Axley (1984) has demonstrated, most managerial conceptions of communication function according to a "conduit" model in which communication involves the relatively unproblematic transmission of ideas and information between senders and receivers. In research on organizational power, communication is largely taken for granted. While a subunit's power is measured in terms of its centrality, autonomy, and access to resources, little or no attention is paid to how this power is communicated to other subunits. The presumption is that such communication occurs mechanically and unproblematically, simply relaying or representing the power of a subunit.

Pfeffer (1981) provides the most sophisticated resource dependence model of communication, examining political language and symbols as a way to mobilize organizational support and reduce opposition. Using Edelman (1964) as a conceptual foundation, Pfeffer discusses the various linguistic and symbolic practices that organizational actors draw on to solidify or enhance their influence in organizations. However, Pfeffer (1981) places strict parameters on the role of communicative processes in relation to organizational power:

The view developed here . . . is that language and symbolism are important in the *exercise* of power. It is helpful for social actors with power to use appropriate political language and symbols to legitimate and develop support for the decisions that are reached on the basis of power. However, in this formulation, language and the ability to use political symbols contribute only marginally to the development of the power of various organizational participants; rather, power derives from the conditions of resource control and resource interdependence. (p. 184, emphasis in original)

This representational view positions communication as auxiliary to power relations, rather than constituting them. For Pfeffer, relations of power are established prior to the communication of relations of autonomy and dependence. Despite the careful consideration of communication as an important organizational phenomenon, Pfeffer ultimately relegates it to the role of reproducing and legitimating already existing relations within the organization. Pfeffer privileges resource control over communication, failing to recognize that the latter constitutes a resource that controls organizational goals. Pfeffer thus neglects communication as an intersubjective process in which what counts as power involves struggles over meaning.

In sum, while the systems-rational approach established power as a legitimate area of research, its narrow conceptions of communication and power limit the kind of insights that can be developed about the political character of organizing. Table 15.2 outlines the principal strengths and weaknesses of this early research on organizational power and summarizes the other approaches to communication, power, and organizing to be discussed in this chapter. Readers are encouraged to refer back to this table as my argument unfolds.

The next section examines interpretive approaches to organizational power, a development that occurred in the wake of the so-called linguistic turn in philosophy and social theory (Rorty, 1967).

INTERPRETIVE APPROACHES TO ORGANIZATIONAL POWER

Interpretive research on power represents an important paradigm shift in organizational communication research and signals the point at which communication becomes central to our understanding of organizing processes. While the work reviewed in the previous section either ignored communication entirely or positioned it as an unproblematic extension of cognitive or structural factors, research conducted from an interpretive perspective sees communication as constitutive of organizing (Pacanowsky & O'Donnell-Trujillo, 1982; Putnam, 1983; Smith & Eisenberg, 1987). In other words, organizations have ontological status only insofar as members communicatively and collectively construct a shared reality.

Much of this literature develops out of the phenomenological, ethnomethodological, and hermeneutic traditions, where the central concern is intersubjectivity. That is, how does one articulate an alternative to the Cartesian bifurcation of subject and object, which positions knowledge as the mind's discovery of a preexisting reality? The interpretive approach shows how subject and world (including other subjects) are mutually constituted. In this perspective, communication is the process of creating an intersubjectively meaningful reality (Gadamer, 1989; Mehan & Wood, 1975; Merleau-Ponty, 1960; Schutz, 1962). It is not possible to review the entire sociological tradition that has emerged out of this work, but its orientation is perhaps expressed most forcefully by Gadamer's (1989) notion of *Sprachlichkeit* (linguisticality) and Heidegger's (1977) conception of language as the "house of being." In both perspectives, language is not merely a vehicle for the expression of already formed thoughts and identities, but is that which creates self, meaning, and the world as we know it.

The elements of this intersubjective approach to meaning have existed in the field of communication for more than 25 years

TABLE 15.2 Perspectives on Communication and Organizational Power

Theoretical Perspective	Conception of Power	Conception of Communication	Strengths	Limitations
Systems-Rationality	◆ Decision making ◆ Behavior of actors ◆ Control of resources ◆ Ability to create dependencies	◆ Representational ◆ Expresses existing power relations ◆ Groups translate power bases into effective communication	◆ View of actor as boundedly rational ◆ Legitimates "political" view of organizations ◆ Shift from interpersonal to structural view of power	◆ Power limited to struggle for scarce resources ◆ Ignores power exercised through consensus ◆ Role of communication peripheral
Interpretivism	◆ Normative system of shared meanings and values internalized by organization members	◆ Constitutes intersubjective systems of meaning ◆ Focus on relation between sensemaking and symbolic forms	◆ Communication central ◆ Focus on relation of power and meaning ◆ Links culture and control ◆ Power as socially constructed	◆ Fails to situate power in larger political and economic context ◆ No theory of society ◆ Inadequate view of contradiction and power
Critical theory	◆ Deep-structure group interests ◆ Relations of hegemony ◆ Dialectic of control ◆ Sovereign model	◆ Political; creates reality through ideological meaning systems ◆ Communication systematically distorted	◆ Communication central ◆ Links power to consent ◆ Ideology central to power ◆ "Thick" model of organizational power	◆ Totalizing view of power ◆ Most work studies domination, little on resistance
Postmodernism	◆ Dispersed in multiple sites ◆ Constituted through games of truth ◆ Discursive and nondiscursive practices ◆ Disciplinary model ◆ Positive rather than negative	◆ Produces multiple, fragmented positions and identities ◆ Linked intrinsically to power and knowledge ◆ Focus on "discursive formations"	◆ Focus on relation of power and subjectivity ◆ Critique of modernist, totalizing view of power ◆ Deconstructs dominant power/knowledge regimes ◆ Focus on discursive micropractices	◆ Resistance located at level of individual ◆ Limited theory of collective action ◆ Few empirical studies ◆ Many studies text based ◆ Undertheorizes politics
Feminism	◆ Embodied in gendered systems of exploitation and resistance ◆ Patriarchy as locus of power	◆ Communication creates gendered systems of meaning and identity ◆ Social actors "do gender" through communication	◆ "Genders" the study of power and identity ◆ Focus on alternative organizations ◆ Politicizes knowledge generation ◆ Critiques binary views	◆ Much research text based; little study of communication processes ◆ Limited development in organizational communication studies

(Deetz, 1973a, 1973b, 1978; Hawes, 1977), but the impact on organizational communication studies is more recent. The "interpretive paradigm" thus centers on the process of organizing as emerging from the intersubjective act of communication (Bittner, 1974; Burrell & Morgan, 1979; Gephart, 1978; Putnam, 1983; Putnam & Pacanowsky, 1983).

In studying power, the interpretive approach focuses on the relationships among communication, power, and meaning (Fowler, Hodge, Kress, & Trew, 1979). Kunda (1992) provides an insightful account of these relationships in his ethnographic study of the culture at a high-tech engineering company. Examining culture as a form of normative control (i.e., the process of shaping organization members' underlying experiences, feelings, and values in an effort to guide behavior), Kunda shows that employees do not simply *behave* in the corporation's interests, but actually develop a sense of identity through commitment to the organization and its goals. Such a commitment is not realized unproblematically, but occurs through a "struggle over meaning" in which the corporation and its members compete over definitions of organizational reality. As Kunda states: "The struggle between organizations bent on normative control and individuals subjected to it is over the definition of reality, and it is a difficult one, for meanings both personal and collective have become part of the contested terrain" (p. 227).

Kunda's study focuses on the communicative practices in which organization members engage, showing how organizing is produced in the moment to moment, as members "do" meetings, engage in hallway talk, and tell stories (Boden, 1994; Taylor, 1995; Taylor, Cooren, Giroux, & Robichaud, 1996). At issue, then, are the sensemaking practices of social actors. That is, how do organization members construct meanings—both collective and individual—out of communication processes that are inherently ambiguous and open to multiple interpretations? As Eisenberg (1984) has shown, such ambiguity can be used strate-

gically by managers as forms of control. Sensemaking is not simply the product of mutually shared assumptions and interpretive procedures, but rather is shaped by the political context in which it occurs. Sensemaking and the creation of intersubjective structures of meaning exist in a dialectical relationship with organizational relations of power. Organizational power is defined in terms of the ability of individuals and groups to control and shape dominant interpretations of organizational events.

Although a ubiquitous feature of organizational life, control over meanings becomes particularly salient in organizational crises. At such times, dominant interpretations are challenged and taken-for-granted meanings are problematized. Gephart's (1988, 1992; Gephart, Steier, & Lawrence, 1990) study of inquiries into industrial accidents demonstrates this process at work, showing how various interest groups (the company, government investigators, families of employees) compete to shape interpretations of such events. For Gephart (1992), the key issue involves "determining how sensemaking practices are used to transform (varied) preliminary interpretations of disasters into culturally rational, sensible, and standardized interpretations assumedly shared by key inquiry participants" (p. 119). One of the most interesting features of this research is the extent to which dominant, institutionalized meanings appropriate and thus neutralize alternative, oppositional interpretations of events. For example, in his analysis of testimony at a public inquiry into a gas pipeline fire, Gephart (1992) shows how the official, "top-down," regulatory logic of the organization prevails over the "situated logic" (that developed on-site by workers) of work in action. The latter operates informally, makes sense to workers, and reflects an ad hoc, commonsense way of dealing with safety issues; however, it conflicts with the deductive, state-mandated logic employed by the company. In this context, the public inquiry is analyzed as a remedial process that attempts to relegitimate the state's role as the arbiter of "correct" organizational safety procedures, while simultaneously closing off alternative interpretations of events.

Gephart's work helps us to see the interconnections among communication, power, and meaning by showing how discourse can *construct* (as opposed to simply represent) meanings and sensemaking practices that legitimate certain interests over others. However, his studies focus on public discourse and its construction practices rather than the day-to-day communication in which organization members engage. In the latter case, focus is on the emergent, interactional, and often precarious character of organizing. In terms of power issues, the question is one of how organization members co-construct meanings that legitimate authority and control, moment to moment. Such research is relatively rare (given the difficulty of collecting interaction-based data), but the little that has been conducted provides insight into intersubjectivity as an ongoing process. For example, Boje's (1991) analysis of organizational storytelling—although not explicitly addressing power issues—shows that stories are co-constructed phenomena rather than symbolic artifacts produced by a single actor with a passive audience. This work contrasts with other research on organizational narrative that treats stories as self-contained events (e.g., J. Martin, 1990; Martin, Feldman, Hatch, & Sitkin, 1983; Mumby, 1987; Witten, 1993).

Fairhurst's (1993) discourse approach to the leader-member exchange (LMX) model of leadership is a further example of interpretive work that examines power and authority as an ongoing, situational accomplishment involving the management of meaning. Fairhurst operates from the premise that "as members of speech communities, leaders and members draw upon different strategies and use linguistic resources in particular ways because of the dilemmas they face at that moment and the meaningfulness of the social relation of which they are a part" (p. 322). Taking women leaders as the focus of her study, Fairhurst shows that in high LMX situations (characterized by mutual trust, internalization of common goals, and mutual influence and support), leaders successfully manage interactions through particular communication strategies that enhance and, indeed, constitute the ongoing character of the relationship. Thus, leadership is conceived as the product of the interaction between leader and member. Fairhurst's focus on gender issues also points to important ways in which women leaders "do gender" interactionally by negotiating issues of power, conflict, and participation.

In sum, interpretive studies of organizational power provide important insight into the constitutive character of communication and the relationship of communication to both organizing and power. By treating power as socially constructed, researchers show how organization members employ interpretive procedures that produce, reproduce, or resist dominant organizational realities. However, such work often fails to address adequately the larger political and economic contexts within which relations of power develop. Issues such as ideology, hegemony, and contradiction go largely untheorized in the interpretive literature. In the next section, therefore, I address critical studies of organizational power, which draw extensively on Marxist and neo-Marxist traditions.

CRITICAL THEORIES OF ORGANIZATIONAL POWER

This section focuses on the ways that critical studies have helped to reshape conceptions of organizational power. Again, this approach will be examined from a communication perspective, with a focus on the processes through which systems of organizational power are produced, reproduced, and resisted. An appreciation of the richness of this work requires that one understands three of its central concepts: ideology, hegemony (Gramsci, 1971), and reification (Lukács, 1971). Thus, prior to examining the critical literature I briefly discuss these concepts. Then, I contextualize critical organizational communication studies with an examination of work that emanates from the sociological tradition. Finally, I examine the emergence of the critical perspective in organizational communication studies proper.

Central Concepts in the Critical Tradition

The concept of ideology plays a central role in neo-Marxist critiques of capitalism and, by extension, organizations (Eagleton, 1991; Geuss, 1981; Larrain, 1979; McClellan, 1986; Therborn, 1980; Thompson, 1984). Despite its slippery and contentious status, we can operate from a number of premises regarding this concept:

1. Ideology is most usefully conceived not as beliefs that are epiphenomenal to social actors' identities, but as that which constitutes those identities, or subjectivities (Althusser, 1971).
2. Ideology creates complex systems and chains of signification and interpretive schemas (Hall, 1985) through which people experience intersubjectively their social relations.
3. Ideology provides the framework for the privileging of certain interpretive schemas and interests over others. Hence, ideology has a strong legitimation function in its production and reproduction of the dominant relations of power (Habermas, 1975).
4. Ideology does not simply reflect the dominant relations of power in a straightforward manner, but rather transforms and hence obscures these relations, hiding them from immediate experience (Deetz & Kersten, 1983; Mumby, 1989).
5. Ideology is not simply ideational; rather, it is material insofar as (a) it is expressed in the everyday communication and behavioral practices of social actors, and (b) it has direct consequences in the construction of the lived experience of those actors.
6. Ideology is not monolithic, simply reproducing a seamless and totalizing reality. Rather, "ideology . . . sets limits to the degree to which a society-in-dominance can easily, smoothly, and functionally reproduce itself" (Hall, 1985, p. 113).
7. Social actors are thus never completely determined by ideology but are, in Therborn's (1980) terms, constantly implicated in the process of "subjection-qualification" whereby they are both "subjects" of (in the dual sense) and "qualified" by (in the dual sense) ideology.

For organizational communication studies, ideology concerns the ways in which the identities of organization members are constructed through everyday communicative practices, such that particular relations of power are produced, reproduced, or transformed (Deetz, 1982; Deetz & Kersten, 1983; Mumby, 1987, 1988). In this context, Gramsci's (1971) concept of hegemony plays an important role in critical organization studies.

Much confusion exists regarding the relationship between ideology and hegemony. In Gramsci's (1971) terms, hegemony involves not simple domination of one group by another, but rather the development of a "collective will" through "intellectual and moral reform" (pp. 60-61). Thus, hegemony explains "the ability of one class to articulate the interests of other social groups to its own" (Mouffe, 1979, p. 183) and is achieved through "the colonization of popular consciousness" (Grossberg, 1984, p. 412). Hegemony therefore includes the ideological but cannot be reduced to it. For Gramsci, hegemony places focus on the dialectical relation of various class forces not only in the ideological and cultural realms but also in the economic and political realms. Eagleton (1991) provides a useful way of distinguishing ideology and hegemony when he states:

Ideology refers specifically to the way power-struggles are fought out at the level of signification; and though such signification is involved in all hegemonic processes, it is not in all cases the *dominant* level by which rule is sustained. Singing the National Anthem comes as close to a "purely" ideological activity as one could imagine. . . . Religion, similarly, is probably the most purely ideological of the various institutions of civil society. But hegemony is also carried in cultural, political, and economic forms—in non-discursive practices as well as in rhetorical utterances. (p. 113)

Gramsci's notion of hegemony is important insofar as it marks a shift from ideology viewed as a relatively fixed, static "system of ideas" imposed on subordinate groups, to a dynamic conception of the lived relations of social groups and the various struggles that constantly unfold between and among these groups. As such, hegemony can be viewed as a process that is communicative in character, involving attempts by various groups to articulate systems of meaning that are actively taken up by other groups. By focusing on "civil society"—the "ensemble of organisms called 'private,' " including the media, family, religion, education, and so forth—as the primary realm where hegemony is exercised, Gramsci is able to conceptualize power as a consensual, noncoercive, and contested process.

Finally, the concept of reification is central to critical models of organizational communication. Lukács's (1971) *History and Class Consciousness* represents a restoration of the Hegelian influence in Marxism. He develops a humanist position that conceives of Marxism as an articulation of working-class, revolutionary consciousness. Extending Marx's analysis of the commodity form, which focuses primarily on the economic dimensions of the process of reification, Lukács asks the question, "How far is commodity exchange together with its structural consequences able to influence the *total* outer and inner life of society?" (p. 84). For him, the commodity form pervades every dimension of social life, mechanizing and dehumanizing experience such that "man's activity becomes estranged

from himself" (Lukács, 1971, p. 87) and develops a "phantom objectivity." This alienated existence provides the catalyst for a self-recognition in which the working class transcends itself. The moment of revolutionary recognition occurs "when the working class acknowledges this alienated world as its own confiscated creation, reclaiming it through political praxis" (Eagleton, 1991, p. 98).

The concept of reification figures prominently in critical approaches to organizational communication. Ranson, Hinings, and Greenwood (1980) develop a structurational approach to power in arguing that "interested action is typically oriented toward the framework of an organization, with members striving to secure their sectional claims within its very structure, which then operates to mediate or reconstitute those interests" (p. 7). In other words, groups strive to reify organizational structures that serve their interests. Deetz (1992a) discusses the various discursive strategies employed in the systematic distortion of communication (Habermas, 1970, 1979), showing how discourse "naturalizes" socially constructed, human creations, providing them with objective qualities that appear to be independent from their creators.

Critical Studies and the Sociology of Organizations

The critical sociological tradition has long attempted to come to grips with, and explain, the exploitative character of capitalism. For Marx, the expropriation of labor and the securing of surplus value was largely a coercive process. The ongoing accumulation of capital meant wresting more and more work from the laborer, either through lengthening the working day or by speeding up the labor process. Braverman's (1974) famous analysis of deskilling shows how 20th-century monopoly capitalism secures surplus value by simplifying and cheapening the cost of labor, reducing workers to abstract and undifferentiated elements in the labor process. While these methods are still ubiquitous in corporate America (studies suggest that the average employee now works longer hours for the same or less pay), much of the critical sociological literature—particularly that associated with the cultural studies tradition (Grossberg, 1984; Hall, 1985)—addresses the cultural and symbolic processes through which capitalism is produced and reproduced. This marks a shift from studying power as principally located within the system of economic production to a focus on power as situated mainly within communication and discourse processes.

Two studies that reflect this shift toward cultural, ideological conceptions of power and organizing are Willis's (1977) study of British working-class school-leavers and Burawoy's (1979) analysis of a shop floor culture of "making out." In his analysis of a group of "lads" in their final school year before going into the workplace, Willis shows how they resist the dominant educational culture of good behavior and studiousness by creating their own counterculture founded on "having a laff" and fighting. The lads intersubjectively construct an alternative system of meaning that radically inverts the values of the dominant culture, thus creating a space of resistance. Willis argues that, ironically, such resistance ultimately functions to prepare the lads for working-class jobs—their rejection of education condemns them to a life of manual labor. In this sense, opposition to the dominant system of ideas functions to reproduce those ideas along with the capitalist relations of production that undergird them.

Burawoy's (1979) critical ethnography of the labor process critiques 20th-century Marxism for reducing wage laborers to objects of manipulation and coercion, creating what he calls a "subjectless subject" (p. 77). In redressing this limitation, Burawoy is interested in exploring the dynamics of Gramsci's (1971, p. 285) claim that "hegemony is born in the factory" (Burawoy, 1979, p. xi). Thus, he focuses on the organization of relations of domination through consent. Arguing that

"the defining essence of the capitalist labor process is the simultaneous securing and obscuring of surplus value" (p. 30), Burawoy shows how the game of "making out" (played by workers as a way of maximizing wages under a modified piece-rate system) organizes consent and maintains a culture of cooperation with management in the production of surplus value. In this sense, the game functions ideologically and dialectically, embodying worker autonomy and resistance to management control over the labor process, while simultaneously obscuring the relations of production in response to which the game was originally constructed.

Interestingly, Collinson (1988, 1992, 1994) critiques both Willis and Burawoy for their lack of an adequate theory of the subject and an overly structuralist conception of power:

> In the absence of any theorizing of subjectivity, Burawoy cannot fully explain workers' active involvement in the game of making out or the subjective conditions that shape how and why workers routinely reproduce the conditions of their own subordination. Hence, whilst Willis exaggerates working-class resistance and penetrations, Burawoy, conversely, overstates consent and conformity on the shop floor. What unites these authors, however, is their failure to theorize subjectivity and their dualistic analyses that focus upon structuralist theories of power on the one hand and working-class culture on the other. (1992, pp. 150-151)

In his own study of a British engineering plant, Collinson (1988, 1992) reveals a complex system of meaning and identity formation that revolves around the deployment of humor by the engineers. Collinson interrogates the ways in which a working-class masculine identity is symbolically constructed through humor and how, ultimately, the particular form that this identity takes serves to undermine the possibilities for genuine resistance to capitalist alienation and reification processes. He argues that resistance is undermined through a use of humor that constructs a form of masculine identity—rooted in aggressive sexuality, a careful separation of private and work lives, and competitive individualism—that limits the possibilities for solidarity and collective action.

From a communication perspective, Collinson's study advances beyond Willis's and Burawoy's insofar as it focuses on the communicative construction of identity, power, and resistance. While both Willis and Burawoy present undertheorized and essentialist conceptions of subjectivity tied to class (even though their aim is to show how these subjectivities are socially constructed), Collinson demonstrates how subjectivity is constructed through complex and often contradictory processes of communication and meaning formation; in this sense, subjectivity itself is contradictory and fragmented. Just as important, Collinson avoids the production of a dualism between agency and structure insofar as communication is situated as central to both, providing the possibility for agency and defining structure in terms of routinized patterns of communication. For example, Collinson (1988, 1992) identifies humor as performing the three functions of resisting managerial authority, controlling workers perceived as lazy, and promoting consent to the prevailing form of masculine identity. These three functions simultaneously produce routinized behavior (workers are expected to exhibit masculine bravado or risk ostracism) and create possibilities for agency (workers "see through" and resist management attempts to co-opt them into a more informal "Americanized" corporate culture).

In summarizing the critical sociological approach to organizational power, then, three themes can be identified. First, power is conceived in dialectical terms (Benson, 1977; Brown, 1978; Clegg, 1975, 1981, 1987; Clegg & Dunkerley, 1980; Edwards, 1979; Goldman & Van Houten, 1977; Hindess, 1982; Ranson et al., 1980). This move situates power not as a purely structural, coalitional phenomenon, but as rooted in the dialectical interplay between conscious, acting subjects and the insti-

tutionalized, sedimented structures that reflect the underlying relations of production in the workplace. In other words, the relationship between agency and structure, first hinted at by Bachrach and Baratz in their two-dimensional model, becomes a central issue in institutional studies of power.

Second, power is not framed simply as a struggle over resources (economic, political, informational, etc.) but rather as a struggle over *meaning* (Clegg, 1989a). Against Pfeffer's (1981) explicit separation of symbolic and material resources, neo-Marxism theorizes the dialectical interplay among the economic, political, and ideological dimensions of social relations (Benson, 1977). Interest lies in examining how social actors construct a meaning environment that functions ideologically, simultaneously securing and obscuring the power relations that undergird everyday practices.

Third, critical sociology of organizations is concerned with what might be termed a "hermeneutics of suspicion" (Ricoeur, 1970). This orientation eschews the notion that organizations can be read by examining the surface, relatively visible features of organizational life and argues for a distinction between "surface" and "deep structure" dimensions of organizations. The concept of ideology is central to this distinction insofar as it functions to obscure deep-structure power relations, articulating a relatively coherent and orderly surface structure of organizational life. It is only through "ideology critique" that the pathological, contradictory, and coercive features of capitalist institutional forms can be unmasked.

Despite this shift to a meaning-centered, dialectical approach to power and organizing, little of this work explicitly examines communication as a constitutive feature of this relationship. Thus, studies do not center on language, discourse, or symbolic processes per se. Despite the occasional exception (e.g., Clegg, 1975; Collinson, 1992), most studies presume that organizations are constituted through social actors' practices, but the communicative dimension of these practices is afforded little scrutiny. Ironically, as long ago as the 1920s, Volosinov (1973) was arguing for "the sign" as the primary arena of class struggle: "Everything ideological possesses meaning: it represents, depicts, or stands for something lying outside itself. In other words, it is a *sign. Without signs there is no ideology*" (p. 9, emphasis in original). Thus, the most important exercise of power is at the level of signification (i.e., communication); the group that is best able to get a certain meaning system to "stick" is the group that has the most power. It is the study of the communicative dimensions of this process that provides critical organizational communication studies with its distinctive character.

Critical Approaches to Communication, Power, and Organization

I divide critical studies of organizational communication into two areas. First, there is a large body of work that is theory oriented, simultaneously challenging the managerial assumptions that undergird most organization studies and developing alternative perspectives that focus heavily on issues of power and politics (Alvesson, 1985; Alvesson & Willmott, 1992a, 1992b; Deetz, 1982, 1985; Frost, 1980, 1987; Mumby, 1993a, 1997; Steffy & Grimes, 1986). In terms of the connections among power, hegemony, ideology, and reification, critical theorists show how management theory functions ideologically by reifying and naturalizing a particular way of knowing, thus excluding as illegitimate other forms of representing knowledge claims. Here, the concern is to make explicit the politics of knowledge representation, and to demonstrate how managerially defined theories of knowledge serve to sustain the hegemony of management interests.

Second, there is a growing body of research that examines empirically the relationships among communication, power, and organization, focusing on the ways in which power and resistance are manifested at the everyday level of organizing (Collinson, 1988, 1992; Graham, 1993; Huspek & Kendall, 1991; Markham, 1996; Murphy, 1998; Rosen, 1985, 1988; Scheibel, 1996; Witten, 1993; Young, 1989). This research takes seriously the notion that meaning, identity, and power relationships are produced, maintained, and reproduced through ongoing communicative practices. Researchers have examined specific forms of communication, including stories (Ehrenhaus, 1993; Helmer, 1993; Mumby, 1987, 1993b; Witten, 1993), rituals (Izraeli & Jick, 1986; Rosen, 1985, 1988), metaphors (Deetz & Mumby, 1985; McMillan & Cheney, 1996; Salvador & Markham, 1995; Wendt, 1994), corporate advertising (Fairclough, 1993), public announcements (Banks, 1994), conversational interaction (Clegg, 1975; Huspek & Kendall, 1991; Penkoff, 1995; van Dijk, 1993), work songs (Conrad, 1988), humor (Collinson, 1988, 1992), and organizational texts (Laird Brenton, 1993) as ways of getting at the complex dynamics that characterize the ideological structuring of organizations.

Given space limitations, I focus primarily on empirical work as a way of demonstrating the importance to critical studies of a communicative conception of organizational power. Here, power is conceptualized primarily as a struggle over meaning; the group that is best able to "fix" meaning and articulate it to its own interests is the one that will be best able to maintain and reproduce relations of power (Deetz, 1992a; Deetz & Mumby, 1990; Giddens, 1979; Gray, Bougon, & Donnellon, 1985; Hall, 1985; Mumby, 1987, 1988, 1989). As suggested above, issues of ideology, hegemony, and reification are central issues in this work, with critical researchers viewing language and communication as *constitutive* of organizational power relations.

The examination of this constitutive process has taken a number of different forms. Several critical scholars have used Giddens's (1976, 1979, 1984) structurational approach as a theoretical lens for explicating the relationship between agency (communication) and structure (rules and resources) (Banks & Riley, 1993; Mumby, 1987, 1988; Penkoff, 1995; Riley, 1983). Even though Giddens's work has been widely disseminated in our field, for the most part it has been appropriated in a rather conservative fashion, with emphasis on its compatibility with systems theory (e.g., Poole & DeSanctis, 1990). However, some organizational communication scholars have thematized the radical dimension of Giddens's work through a focus on the relationship between the notions of "duality of structure" and "dialectic of control." Giddens (1979, p. 69) argues that structure is both the medium and outcome of communicative practices. In this sense, structure is both enabling and constraining, simultaneously providing the possibility for agency and limiting its scope. Social actors draw on rules and resources to engage in communicative behavior and coordinated action, at the same time reproducing, resisting, or transforming that structure through social action. The dialectic of control thus addresses the extent to which a social actor could "act otherwise" (Giddens, 1979, pp. 145-150) as part of a structure of enablement and constraint.

Critical organization scholars have addressed the relationship between the structurational process and the communicative practices of organization members (Helmer, 1993; Howard & Geist, 1995; Mumby, 1987, 1988; Papa, Auwal, & Singhal, 1995; Ranson et al., 1980; Riley, 1983). Power, conceived as the ability to "act otherwise" in the context of the dialectic of control, is examined by focusing on how social actors draw on communication resources to privilege a structurational process that favors their interests. Researchers attempt to show the relationship between systems of signification and structures of domination. For example, Mumby (1987) provides an in-depth interpretation of an organizational story to demonstrate how it functions ideologically to maintain and reproduce relations of power. In analyzing the story, Mumby uses Giddens's (1979) three functions of ideology

and adds a fourth of his own. Thus, ideology functions to (1) transmute or deny contradictions, (2) naturalize the present through reification, (3) present sectional interests as universal, and (4) foster hegemonic forms of control.

While such an analysis is useful in drawing attention to the narrative-ideology-power constellation, it is limited insofar as (a) it is a secondary analysis (drawn from Martin et al., 1983); (b) the analysis is based on a single, fixed organizational story and must therefore make some large interpretive leaps (Boje, 1991); and (c) it lacks the context of naturally occurring storytelling events and is therefore limited in the kinds of conclusions it can draw. On the other hand, Helmer (1993) uses a structurational approach as the theoretical framework for his critical ethnography of a harness racing track. Through an analysis of the stories told by various groups (trainers, jockeys, etc.), he is able to provide insight into the system of legitimation and stratification that operates at the track, privileging some voices and marginalizing others. His analysis suggests that the discourse of the track is both characterized by, and understood through, three oppositional constructs: trainers versus administrators, "chemists" versus honest horsemen, and men versus women. Helmer shows how systems of signification (in this case, storytelling) connect to relations of domination by suggesting that these oppositional constructs function as sensemaking mechanisms, providing organization members with interpretive frames through which they produce, reproduce, or resist the dominant systems of meaning of the track as a capitalist site of profit making and labor exploitation.

While Giddens has provided critical scholars with a useful frame by which to examine organizational power, a number of researchers have taken up Habermas's (1979, 1984, 1987) critical theory of society as a way of critically exploring institutional power. The body of literature spawned by Habermas's work is voluminous, and it cannot be addressed fully here.

However, I will provide a sense of how it has been applied to organization studies.

Forester (1989, 1992, 1993) has applied Habermas's theory of communicative action to fieldwork settings, arguing that it "enables us to explore the continuing performance and practical accomplishment of relations of power. By refining Habermas's attention to a 'double structure of speech,' we come to examine specifically the micropolitics of speech and interaction" (1992, p. 62). Forester has used Habermas's "ideal speech situation" as a model for examining the ways in which discursive closure can occur in everyday organizational settings. Slightly reformulating Habermas's four claims to validity, he attempts to link them directly to issues of power and legitimation. Forester (1989) views organizations as structures of communicative interaction that reproduce particular social relations through relations of knowledge (truth), consent (rightness), trust (truthfulness), and comprehension (intelligibility). Placing these in a 3 by 4 matrix with three forms of power —decision making (Dahl, 1957), agenda setting (Bachrach & Baratz, 1962), and shaping felt needs (Lukes, 1974)—Forester (1989) comes up with 12 "forms of misinformation" that provide a map of the "micropolitics" of speech and interaction. Forester's work is unique in the extent to which it faithfully applies the principles of Habermas's work to ethnographies of organizational power.

Deetz (1992a, 1994, 1995) provides another important application of Habermas's work to the critical analysis of organizational power. Deetz's (1992a) work is particularly important in its development of a conception of power that is situated within a sociohistorical framework and that places issues of communication, identity, and meaning formation at its center. In brief, Deetz argues that the modern corporation has become the most important site of political decision making and, as such, plays a pivotal role in the development of our identities. Following Habermas (1984, 1987), Deetz argues that corporations have colonized the lifeworld (our sense of community) and the institutional forms associated with it (e.g., education, interpersonal relations, family), such that any productive conceptions of communication, identity, and democracy have been appropriated and reframed in terms of managerial interests and technical forms of rationality (e.g., the reduction of communication to efficient information transmission). Deetz focuses on the ways in which organizational practices produce discursive closure and constitute the corporate individual. As an alternative to this view of modern organizational life, Deetz (1992a, 1995) argues for a communication-based model in which democracy is the product of open communication among a variety of stakeholders in organizations, rather than being the unproblematic product of a supposedly already existing democratic society, as narrowly defined through the politics of individual expression and voting rights.

Other critical studies of organizational power, while not as well developed as Deetz's, focus similarly on the connections among communication, meaning, identity, and the ongoing dialectic of control in the workplace. Rosen's (1985, 1988) critical ethnography of an advertising agency is a good example of such work, placing emphasis on the role of ritualized corporate behavior in the production and reproduction of capitalist relations of domination. His analyses of a corporate breakfast (1985) and an annual Christmas party (1988) reveal the ways that such events simultaneously provide workers with an interpretive frame by which they can make sense of their corporate identities and ideologically obscure the deep-structure power relations that secure their subordination to managerial corporate interests.

While critical organizational communication studies have focused primarily on the relationships among communication, ideology, and relations of hegemony (defined in terms of domination through consent), recent work has examined processes of resistance, arguing that such resistance does not have to be framed as ultimately reproducing relations of domination (as in, e.g., Burawoy, 1979, and Willis, 1977). Such work takes up the possibilities for genuine challenges to the "dominant hegemony," and the creation of spaces of resistance that provide alternative worldviews. Scott (1990) adopts this approach in his analysis of the resistant practices of subordinate groups. He argues that the reason why most critical and Marxist studies of power have focused on issues of domination rather than resistance (i.e., "power over" rather than "power to") is because such studies focus almost exclusively on the *public* contexts for the exercise of power. Distinguishing between "public transcripts" and "hidden transcripts," Scott suggests that much of the creative resistance of subordinate groups takes place not in public, but rather in discourse and behaviors that occur "offstage" and beyond the direct surveillance of those in power. Arguing that "relations of domination are, at the same time, relations of resistance" (p. 45), Scott (1990) focuses his attention on the "infrapolitics of subordinate groups" (p. 19), that is, low-profile forms of resistance that create dissident subcultures beyond the purview of "official," dominant political structures and systems of meaning.

Scott's analysis is extremely useful in its demonstration that surface-level "quiescence" or silence may actually function as a cover for deeper-level challenges to the apparent seamlessness of the dominant power structure. In this sense, his study provides a provocative reversal of the thesis suggested by both Willis and Burawoy. That is, rather than arguing that apparent resistance obscures deeper-level reproduction of relations of domination, Scott argues that the "manufacture of consent" provides a convenient cover for subordinate groups to create a space for resistance and the articulation of politically alternative worldviews. From this perspective, Scott (1990) offers "a way of addressing the issue of hegemonic incorporation" (p. 19) without ignoring the fundamentally dialectical character of power. Such a thesis is important from a critical communication perspective because it suggests both that silence has important symbolic functions in terms of resistance and that public forms of communication may not provide researchers with a clear understanding of the dynamics of resistance and control.

In effect, critical studies have provided us with important insights into the relationships among identity, power, and everyday organizational practices. As mentioned earlier, critical studies attempt to explicate the agency-structure relationship, exploring the processes through which organizational actors both reproduce and resist the institutionalized meanings that are embedded in every act of communication. Importantly, critical studies have helped to contextualize discussions of ideology, hegemony, and reification and to situate organizing processes within larger social, political, and economic concerns. Critical studies have politicized organizational communication studies by exploring the intimate connections among communication, power, and identity formation and by suggesting possibilities for social change. However, the Marxist legacy of critical studies sometimes leads to rather totalizing, monolithic conceptions of power and resistance that overlook the multiple sites of struggle characteristic of modern social formations.

Partly in response to this limitation a development has occurred recently that has both enriched and complicated the terrain of critical studies, particularly in regards to our understanding of power as a pervasive, constitutive feature of organizational life. This development is the emergence of a postmodern perspective on organizations.

POWER, POSTMODERNISM, AND ORGANIZATIONAL COMMUNICATION

Postmodern analysis has emerged as an important and controversial mode of understanding and deconstructing contemporary human experience; it is the subject of a huge and ever-expanding body of literature in both the humanities and social sciences (Best & Kellner, 1991; Callinicos, 1989; Featherstone, 1988; Harvey, 1989; Rosenau & Bredemeier, 1993). A large corpus of literature has emerged in the past few years that directly addresses the impact of postmodern thought on organizational theory and research (Boje, Gephart, & Thatchenkery, 1996; Burrell, 1988; Cooper, 1989; Cooper & Burrell, 1988; Hassard, 1993a, 1993b; Hassard & Parker, 1993; Jeffcutt, 1994; Kilduff & Mehra, 1997; Parker, 1992a, 1992b; Tsoukas, 1992). My goal in this section is to map out the "basic contours" of postmodernism (recognizing that such a move is very unpostmodern!), articulating its relationship to organizational communication studies and the study of power. As in previous sections, I will examine the relationship between postmodernism and a conception of communication as constitutive of organizing.

Postmodernism is partly defined in terms of its relationship to modernism—it both comes after modernism and is a response to and critique of modernist sensibilities. In this sense, "the postmodern" characterizes both an epistemological break with "the modern" and a historical break with the epoch of modernity (Cooper & Burrell, 1988; Featherstone, 1988; Hassard, 1993a, 1993b). This distinction between an epistemological (modernism/postmodernism) and epochal (modernity/postmodernity) view of the modern-postmodern debate is also manifest in the literature of organization studies. Some scholars argue that the postmodern is a historical, ontological condition that demands new, postcapitalist, post-Fordist forms of organizing, characterized by small economies of scale, flexible production capabilities, and reintegration of the work process (e.g., Bergquist, 1993; Clegg, 1990; Harvey, 1989). On the other hand, a number of scholars pursue postmodern thought as a way to deconstruct the organization as a site of power that subjects members to various forms of disciplinary practice (Barker & Cheney, 1994; Burrell, 1992, 1993;

Daudi, 1986; Holmer-Nadesan, 1997, 1999: Jacques, 1996: Knights & Vurdubakis, 1994; Knights & Willmott, 1992; Linstead, 1993; Linstead & Grafton-Small, 1992). Given the focus of this chapter on the relationship between power and organizing, it is the latter perspective that will be explored here.

Postmodern thought has emerged in the context of a complex modernist landscape. Hassard (1993a, 1993b), for example, following Cooper and Burrell (1988), situates postmodernism in relation to two different and competing modernist orientations: systemic modernism and critical modernism. Systemic modernism represents the dominant orthodoxy in social thought today and, within organization studies, stands for progress in terms of the increasing rationalization of organizational life. From this perspective, "the main purposes of knowledge are to facilitate organizational control and to direct innovation and change" (Hassard, 1993a, p. 117). In most respects, the research discussed in this chapter under systems-rational perspectives falls under the rubric of systemic modernism.

Critical modernism, on the other hand, displays an ambiguous and ambivalent relationship with the Enlightenment project, simultaneously striving to maintain the emancipatory impulse of modernist thought and critiquing the direction that the Enlightenment has taken. It is the project of critical theory to oppose and deconstruct "traditional theory" (Horkheimer, 1986; Horkheimer & Adorno, 1988), and reappropriate self-consciousness and emancipation as the goals of knowledge. Critical modernism is thus both a deconstructive and reconstructive project, critiquing traditional science's lack of reflexivity and its connection to capitalist forms of power and domination, while at the same time developing a social theory that reclaims a sense of community and democracy (Habermas, 1979, 1984, 1987). The work discussed in the previous section falls under this domain.

Given this context, it is helpful to lay out some of the central issues that emerge across different postmodern writers:

1. Postmodernists challenge the very idea of rationality as it is developed in modernist thought. The idea of knowledge as progressive, cumulative, and continuous is rejected for a focus on discontinuity (Foucault, 1979).

2. Postmodernism rejects, or decenters, "the subject" as the origin of knowledge; instead, the subject is investigated as an effect of various power/knowledge regimes (Foucault, 1980b).

3. Following from this, language and discourse are conceived not as transparent, but rather as constitutive of knowledge and identity (Laclau, 1990; Laclau & Mouffe, 1985).

4. Postmodernism doesn't distinguish between truth and falsity, but rather attempts to understand how different kinds of power/knowledge relationships emerge at different historical conjunctures, thus laying out the rules for what counts as truth (Foucault, 1979, 1980b). Truth and power therefore implicate one another.

5. In contrast to the totalizing and universalizing tendencies of modernist thought, postmodern theorists view knowledge as ad hoc, local, and situational. Lyotard (1984) defines postmodernism as "incredulity toward metanarratives" (p. xxiv), arguing for paralogy, *petit récits* (little narratives), and "the search for instabilities" (p. 53) rather than for homology, grand narratives, and consensus.

6. The fomenting of a "crisis of representation" (Jameson, 1984) by postmodernism has translated into a concern with issues of marginality and otherness, and the articulation of worldviews that challenge the dominant orthodoxy (Clifford, 1988; Clifford & Marcus, 1986; Conquergood, 1991; West, 1993).

What impact have these developments had on our understanding of organizational power? While postmodern studies of organizations are still in a nascent state, there are some distinct trends. First, theorists such as Laclau and Mouffe (1985; Laclau, 1990), Foucault (1979, 1980a), and Derrida (1976) have provided radical organizational theorists and researchers with important understandings of organizations as sites of discursive power.

For example, Michel Foucault's (1975, 1979, 1980a, 1988) archaeological and genealogical studies of medicine, discipline, sexuality, and madness as well as his more philosophical writings on the status of knowledge (1973, 1980b) provide us with insight into the relationships among power, knowledge, subjectivity, and institutional forms and practices. Foucault's work has been adopted in organizational communication studies as a way of examining organizations as sites of disciplinary power (Barker, 1993, 1999; Clegg, 1989a, 1989b, 1994a, 1994b; Deetz, 1992a, 1992b; Holmer-Nadesan, 1997; Knights & Vurdubakis, 1994; Knights & Willmott, 1992; Marsden, 1993). In such a conception, power is not imposed from above (what Foucault critiques as a "sovereign" view of power), nor does it originate from a single source (e.g., as with Marxism's framing of all power relations within capitalist relations of domination—a position of which Foucault is highly critical); rather, power is widely dispersed, having multiple sites and modes of functioning. Social actors are "disciplined" to the extent that they become objects of knowledge of various discourses within these sites and thus come to know themselves (as subjects) in particular ways (e.g., as sexual, rule governed, normal). In Foucault's ("Florence," 1994) terms, "What are the processes of subjectivization and objectivization that allow the subject to become, as subject, an object of knowledge?" (p. 315). Discourses are thus texts and communicative practices that function within (and reproduce) certain "truth games" (rules for what counts as true or false), defining the subject and submitting him or her to processes of normalization.

For example, recent work on self-managing teams (Barker, 1993, 1999; Barker & Cheney, 1994; Mumby & Stohl, 1992) provides insight into how an ostensibly participative form of organizing has reconstituted the way power is exercised in "postbureaucratic" organizations. Barker (1993) shows how a shift from hierarchical, bureaucratic forms of control to "concertive control" (Tompkins & Cheney, 1985), in which locus of control shifts from managers to the workers themselves, is achieved through the establishment of work teams that engage in self-surveillance (what Foucault, 1979, calls "panopticism"). Power is produced from the bottom up through the everyday discursive practices that construct team members' identities. Similarly, Mumby and Stohl's (1992) analysis of work teams shows how absent members are labeled and identified as "deviant" by other team members and are required to provide an accounting of, or apology for, their deviant behavior. Both of these studies exemplify an important principle of Foucault's conception of power: it is positive rather than negative. Power does not forbid and negate, but rather produces identities, knowledge, and the possibilities for behavior. In this sense, power and knowledge are indissolubly linked, producing each other, and articulating what Foucault (1980a) calls "power/knowledge regimes."

Foucault's influence on the study of organizations as sites of disciplinary micropractices is complemented by work that evolves from Derrida's (1976, 1978) deconstructive approach to literary texts (Cooper, 1989). Derrida's deconstructive project is a critique of the "metaphysics of presence" as the privileged mode of rationality in Western thinking. This metaphysics is both logocentric and phonocentric, privileging the mind (logocentrism) and the speaking subject (phonocentrism) as that which validates human experience. Derrida (1976) deconstructs this metaphysics of presence by arguing that "there is nothing outside of the text" (p. 158); he shows how all attempts to impose meaning are rooted in hierarchically arranged binary oppositions, such that the stability and dominance of one term is dependent on a suppressed or marginalized opposite term (e.g., male/female, mind/body, public/private). De-

construction therefore involves a double movement of overturning these binary opposites (thus destabilizing the dominant term) and engaging in a process of "metaphorization," by which the opposing terms are shown to implicate and define one another in an endless play of signifiers (Cooper, 1989, p. 483). For example, Mumby and Putnam (1992) deconstruct the concept of "bounded rationality" by juxtaposing it with the notion of "bounded emotionality." However, rather than privileging the latter over the former as an alternate way of organizing, they metaphorically play the one against the other, speculating about "the rationality of emotions" and "the emotionality of the rational" as ways of thinking about organizing processes.

Derrida (1976) appropriates and transforms the Saussurian notion of *différence* (language as a system of difference) by coining the term *différance*. This term simultaneously conveys the ideas of deferring (or postponing) and differing. Meaning, then, involves a continuous play of différance, in which a text is never fully present to us, but derives its meaning from a system of signifiers that constantly defer to, and are different from, other absent signifiers. Meaning only appears fixed because of an apparently straightforward positive relationship between signifiers and signifieds. Derrida demonstrates that this positive relationship is chimerical by examining the play of presence and absence on which the meaning of a text depends. There is nothing outside of the text, then, in that there is no external referent to which a text refers, only other texts.

Derrida's work has been employed by a number of organization scholars to explore and critique the representational practices of canonical organizational texts (Calás & Smircich, 1991; Kilduff, 1993; Mumby & Putnam, 1992). Each of these researchers attempts to deconstruct the structures of presence and absence in such texts to expose the hierarchical oppositions that privilege certain meanings and forms of knowledge over others. Such deconstructive projects, like much of Foucault's work, draw attention to the relationships among representational practices, power, and institutionalized orthodoxies regarding what counts as "knowledge" in the field of organization studies. But deconstructionists have not focused purely on organization scholars. Deconstruction of the discursive practices of organizational life is also an emergent area of study. Linstead (1992), for example, argues for the development of a deconstructive ethnography by which to explore the tension between organization and disorganization. From this perspective, "organization . . . is continuously emergent, constituted and constituting, produced and consumed by subjects who, like organization, are themselves fields of the trace, sites of intertextuality" (Linstead, 1992, p. 60).

While it is hard to identify full-blown organizational ethnographies that take a deconstructive approach, several scholars have used deconstruction as a means to explore the tensions, absences, and contradictions that connect power and subjectivity (Burrell, 1993; Kondo, 1990; J. Martin, 1990). From this perspective, "organization always harbours within itself that which transgresses it, namely, disorganization" (Cooper, 1989, p. 480). One of the characteristics of such work is its tendency to engage in play, parody, and pastiche, undermining the reader's confidence in the authority of a conventional, linear, narrative style (Martin, 1992). For example, Burrell's (1993) whimsically titled "Eco and the Bunnymen" casts aside conventional academic form to question simultaneously the representational practices of academia and the structure of the modern university, and to provide a witty critique of the commodification of knowledge and bodies at the Academy of Management annual convention.

Finally, a considerable number of deconstructive and genealogical analyses of organizing practices are emerging from the field of accounting (Arrington & Francis, 1989; Hoskin & Macve, 1986, 1988; Miller & O'Leary, 1987; Power & Laughlin, 1992). This research provides an instance where the

work of Derrida and Foucault coincide. Given Derrida's concern with writing, and Foucault's concern with professional discourse and its relationship to disciplinary practices and power/knowledge regimes, the critical study of accounting practices is an important area through which to examine the relationships between discursive micropractices, on the one hand, and the macrostructures of organizational power, on the other. Thus, this work deconstructs the notion that accounting is "only a techné of progress" (Arrington & Francis, 1989, p. 22), and instead argues that it is "an important calculative practice which is part of a much wider modern apparatus of power which emerges conspicuously in the early years of this [20th] century" (Miller & O'Leary, 1987, p. 234). Similarly, Hoskin and Macve (1988) conceptualize accounting as "a mode of 'writing the world' which, like the modern examination, embodies the power relations and the knowledge relations of a disciplinary and self-disciplinary culture" (p. 68).

In sum, postmodern thought has had a growing influence on the field of organizational communication. Its focus on the relationships among power, knowledge, and discourse provides important insights into how modern organizations function as disciplinary sites that structure meanings and identities. Postmodernism situates communication as central to the creation of multiple, contested, and fragmented subjectivities and power relations. As such, communication is not simply the creation of consensual meanings and communities but is also integral to normalization processes, power/knowledge regimes, and disciplined subjectivities, as well as the means by which such processes are resisted.

It would be wrong, however, to claim a complete disjuncture between critical and postmodern conceptions of power and discourse. While it is true that the more "skeptical" postmodernists (Rosenau, 1992) are deeply suspicious of theorists who invoke notions of emancipation from systems of oppression, many theorists view the relationship between critical theory and postmodernism as productive and dialectical rather than adversarial. For example, Smart (1986) highlights important connections between Gramsci's (1971) conception of hegemony and Foucault's analysis of disciplinary micropractices, arguing that "Foucault's work has revealed the complex multiple processes from which the strategic combination of forms of hegemony may emerge" (p. 160). Similarly, Lentricchia (1988) suggests that "if Marx gives us the theory of pure capitalism, then Foucault, on discipline, gives us the theory of practical capitalism whose essential category is *detail*" (p. 60, emphasis in original).

Perhaps one of the tasks of radical organization theorists is not to articulate disjunctures and oppositions between critical theory and postmodernism, but rather to conceptualize ways in which the two function dialectically, hence providing new and insightful means of exploring the relationships among communication, meaning, and organizational power. Although some writers believe no such rapprochement is possible (Callinicos, 1989; Eagleton, 1995), theorists such as Agger (1991), Best and Kellner (1991), and Deetz (1992a) have all suggested ways in which we can overcome both the foundationalism and potential elitism of critical theory, on the one hand (Alvesson & Willmott, 1992b), and the nihilism and relativism of postmodern thought, on the other.

In the next section, I present feminist thought as one perspective through which the study of communication and power can retain the emancipatory potential of critical theory, while simultaneously adopting a multiperspectival approach to knowledge claims and the process of critique.

FEMINIST STUDIES OF POWER, POLITICS, AND ORGANIZATIONS

I turn to feminism as a way of examining organizational power for two reasons. First, this move partly reflects my own intellectual development, and my recognition that it is impossible to study and theorize adequately about organizational power without addressing its gendered character. Organizations are "gendered" in the sense that "advantage and disadvantage, exploitation and control, action and emotion, meaning and identity, are patterned through and in terms of a distinction between male and female, masculine and feminine" (Acker, 1990, p. 146). Second, while critical theory and postmodernism provide robust analytic frameworks for studying power, their link to everyday practices is sometimes tenuous. Feminism, on the other hand, emerges directly from recognizing the institutional character of women's economic, political, and ideological subordination. In this sense, feminism never loses sight of the relationship between theory and practice.

In comparison with other disciplines the field of organizational communication has been slow to take up feminist perspectives, but the past decade has seen a distinct upsurge in feminist-oriented theory and research (Allen, 1996, 1998; Ashcraft, 1998, 2000; Bullis, 1993; Buzzanell, 1994; Clair, 1998; Gregg, 1993; Holmer-Nadesan, 1996; Marshall, 1993; Mumby, 1996; Sotirin & Gottfried, 1999; Spradlin, 1998; Trethewey, 1997, 1999a, 1999b). Similarly, in the 1990s management studies began to develop an identifiable body of feminist-influenced research (e.g., Acker, 1990, 1992; Alvesson & Billing, 1992; Calás, 1992; Calás & Smircich, 1991, 1992a, 1992b; Ferguson, 1984; Gherardi, 1994, 1995; Mills, 1995; Mills & Tancred, 1992; Mumby & Putnam, 1992). However, the general neglect of a systematic gendered approach to organizations has led Rothschild and Davies (1994) to claim that "the assumption of gender neutrality may be one of the great blind spots, and errors, of twentieth-century organizational theory" (p. 583).

Feminist perspectives on organizational power examine and critique the ways in which binary thinking (male/female, culture/nature, rational/emotional, etc.) lies at the root of all attempts to make sense of and to construct institutional forms, social practices, and actors' identities and experiences. In this context, gender is a "site of difference" that constructs relations of domination, marginalization, and resistance (Barrett, 1995), defined within a system of hegemonic masculinity (Connell, 1985, 1987). Even though there are multiple feminist perspectives that analyze these issues (Tong, 1989), the focus here centers on three areas of theory and research that directly address the intersection of communication, gender, and power: (1) feminist rereading/rewriting of organizational theory and research, (2) organizations as gendered sites of domination and resistance, and (3) feminist alternatives to patriarchal forms of organizing. Each of these areas is briefly discussed below (see Mumby, 1996, for a more detailed discussion).

Feminist Rereading/Rewriting of Organizational Theory and Research

Research from this perspective draws on postmodern theory to deconstruct the assumptions that underlie mainstream organizational communication studies. Such work demonstrates how theory and knowledge are built on patriarchal models of scholarship and rationality that systematically exclude alternative ways of theorizing organizational structures and practices (Acker & Van Houten, 1974; Calás & Smircich, 1991, 1992a; Ferguson, 1994; Holvino, 1997; Jacques, 1992; Mumby & Putnam, 1992; Nkomo, 1992; Putnam & Mumby, 1993). As in postmodern studies, feminist studies problematize the notion of "representation" and show how it embodies and obscures numerous political, epistemological, and gender issues.

Feminists appropriate postmodern theory to address the gendered relationship between the representational practices of the scholarly enterprise and those of the corporate enterprise, and the ways in which this relationship reproduces power. For example, the work of Calás and Smircich (1991, 1992a, 1992b) explores "how the idea of 'gender' can be a strategy through which we can question what *has been represented* as organization theory"

(1992a, emphasis in original). Their analyses are deconstructive, exploring the ways in which gender is "normally" written into organizational theorizing. Their strategy is to problematize gender, demonstrating the various ways in which it is represented, suppressed, marginalized, and made absent in the process of theory and research. In their (1991) deconstruction of organizational leadership texts, they juxtapose against "leadership" the notion of "seduction" (drawing on Braudrillard, 1990). By providing "seductive" readings of leadership texts (through the use of a split page) they "analyze the dependency of supposedly opposite concepts on one another and [show] how rhetoric and cultural conditions work together to conceal this dependency" (p. 569). (See Schwartz, 1993, and Calás & Smircich, 1993, for the aftermath of this article.)

The body of deconstructive work that is developing within postmodern feminist thought exemplifies what Gergen (1992) refers to as the "replacement of the real by the representational" (p. 213). That is, once we undermine the idea that language and communication are merely tools for representing the real, then the positivist modernist attempt to determine organizational reality through various forms of empirical investigation becomes increasingly suspect. As beginning points for feminist theories of organization, these studies break the silence implied by the idea that objective truth is the only possibility, and they show how various truths are communicatively constructed. By interrogating the intersection of discourse, power, knowledge, gender, and organizational practice, this work opens spaces for rethinking organizational analysis. However, one of the limitations of such work is its privileging of formal—usually scholarly—texts and its general neglect of the mundane, quotidian, and communication dimensions of gendered forms of power and domination. Although there is clearly a connection between theorizing about organizing and organizational processes themselves, there is clearly a need to examine gendered organizational practices empirically and in situ.

Organizations as Gendered Sites of Domination and Resistance

This second position focuses on the systematic "engendering" of organizational practices that constitute men's and women's identities and access to power in differential ways. This research is theoretically eclectic, drawing on both neo-Marxist theory and the poststructuralist focus on discourse. Analyses examine the relationships among capitalism, patriarchy, organization, and gendered communicative practices (Clair, 1993b, 1994, 1998; Cockburn, 1984; Collinson, 1992; Ferguson, 1984; Kondo, 1990; J. Martin, 1990; Pringle, 1989). A characteristic of this literature is a dual focus on (1) power-as-domination, and (2) (em)power(ment)-as-resistance.

In the former category are studies that examine the communicative and material processes through which patriarchy is produced and reproduced. Such work ranges from the discursive construction of hegemonic gender identities (e.g., Angus, 1993; Collinson, 1988, 1992; Connell, 1985, 1987; J. Martin, 1990, 1994; Pringle, 1989) to the symbolic and material dimensions of sexual harassment in the workplace (Clair, 1993a, 1993b; MacKinnon, 1979; Strine, 1992; Taylor & Conrad, 1992; Townsley & Geist, in press; Wood, 1992). For example, J. Martin (1990) provides a deconstruction of an organizational story (told to demonstrate the company's pro-employee maternity policy) to show how it reaffirms dominant understandings of sexuality and gender in the workplace. Through textual strategies such as dismantling dichotomies, examining silences in the story, and attending to disruptions and contradictions, Martin shows how a story that—at least ostensibly—affirms the importance of women to an organization can be read as maintaining and reproducing patriarchal modes of reasoning, showing how both women and men are structured by, and are the effects of, institutionalized discursive practices that reproduce gendered power relations.

Similar themes are taken up in Pringle's (1989) study of secretaries, Ferguson's (1984) critique of bureaucracy, and recent work that examines the discursive construction of masculinity (Angus, 1993; Collinson, 1988, 1992; Hearn, 1992, 1994). In each, the central issue is the communicative processes through which certain forms of gendered identity are articulated and constructed, thus reproducing dominant relations of power. Hearn's (1994) development of a "violence" perspective on gender and organizations forcefully brings home the extreme consequences of hegemonic masculinity.

On the other hand, feminist studies also examine the possibilities for gendered forms of resistance to organizational power relations. Again, this work is eclectic in its theoretical orientation. Feminist neo-Marxist research focuses on the possibilities for collective resistance and change and examines the ways in which community and egalitarianism can emerge within hierarchical and patriarchal structures (Benson, 1992; Boyce, 1995; Gottfried, 1994; Gottfried & Weiss, 1994; Lamphere, 1985; Zavella, 1985). Gottfried and Weiss (1994), for example, develop the notion of feminist "compound organizations" to demonstrate how women faculty at a major research university created their own collective, nonhierarchical, compound decision-making system that operated within, yet transcended the usual constraints of bureaucratic university life. The authors propose "compound" as a metaphor that incorporates multiplicity, allowing women with different agendas and perspectives to come together as a community within a large, potentially hostile, community. Similarly, Boyce (1995) and Spradlin (1998) adopt critical feminist perspectives to show the links among gender, sexuality, and power, simultaneously critiquing the pervasive homophobia of organizations and pointing to a diverse and inclusive model of organizing.

Other feminist studies have adopted a postmodern orientation toward issues of gender, organizing, and resistance (Bell &

Forbes, 1994; Clair, 1998; Gregg, 1993; Holmer-Nadesan, 1996; Trethewey, 1997, 1999a, 1999b). For example, Gregg's (1993) analysis of two activist women's groups draws on poststructuralist theory to problematize the notion of collective action as rooted in shared and homogeneous identities. Developing a "politics of location," she shows how political action and agency involve a negotiation among various "subject positions." Thus, in her analysis of a union organizing campaign, Gregg shows how the women who were the targets of the campaign attempted to maintain coherent identities in the face of multiple, competing, and unstable subjectivities available through discourses of race, class, and political position. From a communication perspective, "identity is a matter of negotiating the inconsistencies and contradictions between subject positions and everyday realities . . . available in both discourse and practices" (Gregg, 1993, p. 25).

Feminist postmodern views of gender, organizing, and resistance, therefore, reject efforts to articulate universal principles of identity and collective action rooted in women's common experience of oppression. Instead, resistance is complex, local, and often contradictory. For example, Bell and Forbes's (1994) analysis of "office graffiti" illustrates secretarial resistance to bureaucratic discipline as an example of individual "tactics" (De Certeau, 1984) that parody and subvert dominant institutional meanings without any pretensions to collective action or an identity politics. Such politics are much more visible, however, in the third area of feminist research.

Feminist Alternatives to Patriarchal Forms of Organizing

The third broad area of concern in feminist approaches to organization studies examines women's alternative organizations. Such organizations are premised on the recognition that traditional bureaucratic structures are not gender neutral, but represent the institutionalization of patriarchy. Hence, egalitarian and participative organizational structures are realizable only in contexts where hierarchy and its attendant logics and forms of communication are transformed. Marshall (1989) uses the phrase "organizational heterarchy" to describe a structure that "has no one person or principle in command. Rather, temporary pyramids of authority form as and when appropriate in a system of mutual constraints and influences" (p. 289). While such an organizational structure rarely—if ever—sustains itself in pure form in the "real world," several scholars have studied attempts to enact this structure within the constraints of capitalist economic and political systems (Ferree & Martin, 1995; Hacker & Elcorobairutia, 1987; Lont, 1988; Maguire & Mohtar, 1994; P. Martin, 1990; Reinelt, 1994; Rodriguez, 1988; Rothschild-Whitt, 1979; Sealander & Smith, 1986).

Although collectivist and feminist organizations are not isomorphic, there appears to be considerable overlap in the values, structures, processes, goals, and outcomes of each. For example, Patricia Martin (1990) suggests that "feminist organizations are a unique species of the genus social movement organization [and are] pro-woman, political, and socially transformational" (pp. 183-184). Feminist values emphasize the importance of mutual caring, support, and empowerment, with work viewed as social rather than technical. Such values suggest a view of communication as focused on the construction of community rather than on the promotion of organizational efficiency. In addition, feminist outcomes revolve around both individual and societal transformation, aimed at the alleviation of women's oppression. Here, communication becomes a political act aimed at resisting patriarchy and articulating alternative, feminist realities.

For example, Maguire and Mohtar's (1994) study of a women's center shows how members discursively position themselves in opposition to state agencies and in solidarity with each other. However, Martin also notes the lack of consensus on the defining qualities of a feminist organization. For example, liberal feminists do not see hierarchy and bureaucracy as intrinsically patriarchal (Iannello, 1992), and many feminist organizations are for-profit rather than nonprofit, large/national rather than small/local, and dependent rather than autonomous. The National Organization for Women is the most visible example of an organization with a large membership (250,000) and extensive bureaucratic structure that works to improve the political and economic status of women.

In sum, feminist theory and research clearly provide important ways of understanding, critiquing, and transforming contemporary organizations. Feminist studies of organizational communication are critical to an appreciation of power as a central, constitutive feature of organizational life. To neglect feminism as a mode of analysis is to overlook the gendered character of organizational power and its relationship to "doing gender" (Gherardi, 1994; West & Zimmerman, 1987). However, the picture I have painted in this section contains its own elisions and aporia. For example, I have not addressed systematically the issue of race and its relationship to organizing processes. While black feminist theory has emerged as an important form of social critique (hooks, 1984, 1992; Wallace, 1992), little work of significance has emerged in organization communication studies that moves beyond the "race as variable" approach (see Allen, 1995, for an exception). Work by Calás (1992), Grimes (1994), and Nkomo (1992) begins to explore the representational practices through which race is constructed as a category in the organizational literature, but it is difficult to identify a distinct body of critical work in this area (although see Essed, 1991; van Dijk, 1993). One promising area of research involves "interrogating whiteness" (Frankenberg, 1993; hooks, 1992; Nakayama & Krizek, 1995). This work shows how "whiteness" as a racial and gendered category

is not neutral, but rather is socially constructed through various discursive practices.

Feminist studies thus examine organizational power in ways that are not easily reducible to other perspectives by virtue of their focus on gender as a constitutive feature of the power ↔ communication ↔ organization relationship. Its focus on praxis and the material implications of gender domination provides an important means of contextualizing critical and postmodern thought. At the same time, feminist studies must remain open to possibilities for transformation by previously marginalized voices. Feminism, by definition, avoids reification and the setting up of binary oppositions. Through the articulation of a multiplicity of voices, possibilities for critique and the development of inclusive communities are realized.

CONCLUSION AND FUTURE DIRECTIONS

Throughout this chapter, I have focused on the relationships among communication, power, and organization. Early models of organizational power focused largely on the cognitive, decision-making, and structural issues associated with the exercise of power. The most sophisticated of these perspectives elucidates a resource dependence approach in which power accrues to those groups that are able to position themselves as indispensable to the organization by virtue of resources held. In such models, communication plays a "handmaiden" role, functioning as the mechanism by which groups represent their power. This perspective, I have argued, neglects the extent to which power exists only as a product of the intersubjective systems of meaning that organization members create through their communication practices. The interpretive, critical, postmodern, and feminist perspectives on power represent varying attempts to explicate communication in its constitutive relationship to identity, power, and organizing. What, then, are the consequences of this work for the way we study organizational power?

First, it generates a much greater level of reflexivity in conceptualizing and researching organizational power. The metatheoretical issues addressed in this chapter make clear that we—as scholars of power—are never exempt from the processes that we analyze, but are always enmeshed in disciplinary practices that both enable and constrain our sensemaking attempts. We write about power, but we also are the "subject effects" of power/knowledge regimes. There is perhaps no clearer example of this process than Blair, Brown, and Baxter's (1994) stunning deconstruction of the blind review process in refereed journal publication. Their analysis exposes the fallacy of knowledge as somehow neutral, nonpolitical, and existing outside of the exercise of power. As scholars, we need to be aware of the extent to which we either produce or resist dominant discourses.

A second and related consequence of this view of power is that, in a basic sense, people are produced by power. Power is not something that can be taken up and used or discarded at will. This narrowly political sense of power overlooks the ways in which a subject's position exists through the intersection of discourses that "fix" meanings in certain ways. Power relations revolve around the production, maintenance, and transformation of those meanings. From a communication perspective, the study of organizational power requires theory and research that examine how communication practices construct identities, experiences, and ways of knowing that serve some interests over others. Part of our future agenda, then, is to engage in empirical analyses that explicate the ongoing, everyday character of this process. While Foucault, for example, has shown how this form of discipline has worked historically, we need to generate insight into its mundane (and perhaps most insidious) features.

Third, the shift to a focus on the relationships among communication, power, and organizing allows for a genuine move beyond the reification of organization-as-structure. If organizations are reconceptualized as discursive sites of identity formation and meaning creation, then the possibilities for what traditionally counts as "an organization" are greatly expanded. In such a move, organizations are viewed as communication communities in which the purpose of research is to understand how certain discourses get articulated to create systems of meaning and power. Organizations are reframed as constellations of intersubjective meaning and experience, that is, as "the sites where individuals 'inhabit' numerous discursive positions simultaneously, and those places in which established everyday discourses . . . give meaning to [inter]subjective experience by suggesting appropriate positions from which to make sense of one's life" (Gregg, 1993, p. 5).

Finally, we need to bring more theory, more voices, and more politics to the study of organization than most research addresses (Ferguson, 1994). This does not mean simply adding different voices and stirring, but rather developing alternative viewpoints and constructs as a way of fundamentally transforming our understanding of organizations and power. Opening the study of organizations to more voices is at one level concerned with addressing issues of race, class, gender, and sexuality as constitutive sites of organizational power, meaning, and identity formation. However, at another, related level, "other voices" highlight the study of noncorporate, nonbureaucratic organizational forms. For the most part, organizational research takes as its object of interest the business setting and industrial workplace. Given the connection of organizational scholars with managerial interests, this is hardly surprising. However, this chapter examines scholarship that questions extant organization theory and practice because it produces and reproduces systems of oppression that distort identity and meaning formation. In this context, future research needs to examine the ways in which social actors engage in identity formation through collective behavior that embodies alternative notions of community and that provides members with voices that make a difference in the ongoing life of the organization (Cheney, 1995, 1999; Rothschild-Whitt, 1979).

Given the amount of theory generated over the past few years in organizational communication studies, Ferguson's (1994) call for additional theory may seem strange. However, if we view theorizing not as a purely ideational, abstract process, but as ways of "thinking otherwise" and moving beyond common sense views of the world, then the ongoing theorizing of organizational life is indispensable. With the development of multiple perspectives on organizational power, it is important that we continue to explore their limitations and possibilities.

REFERENCES

Acker, J. (1990). Hierarchies, jobs, bodies: A theory of gendered organizations. *Gender & Society, 4,* 139-158.

Acker, J. (1992). Gendering organizational theory. In A. Mills & P. Tancred (Eds.), *Gendering organizational analysis.* Newbury Park, CA: Sage.

Acker, J., & Van Houten, D. (1974). Differential recruitment and control: The sex structuring of organizations. *Administrative Science Quarterly, 19,* 152-163.

Agger, B. (1991). *A critical theory of public life: Knowledge, discourse and politics in an age of decline.* London: Falmer.

Allen, B. J. (1995). "Diversity" and organizational communication. *Journal of Applied Communication Research, 23,* 143-155.

Allen, B. J. (1996). Feminist standpoint theory: A black woman's (re)view of organizational socialization. *Communication Studies, 47,* 257-271.

Allen, B. J. (1998). Black womanhood and feminist standpoints. *Management Communication Quarterly, 11,* 575-586.

Althusser, L. (1971). *Lenin and philosophy.* New York: Monthly Review Press.

Alvesson, M. (1985). A critical framework for organizational analysis. *Organization Studies, 6,* 117-138.

Alvesson, M., & Billing, Y. D. (1992). Gender and organizations. *Organization Studies, 13,* 73-102.

Alvesson, M., & Willmott, H. (Eds.). (1992a). *Critical management studies.* Newbury Park, CA: Sage.

Alvesson, M., & Willmott, H. (1992b). On the idea of emancipation in organization studies. *Academy of Management Review, 17,* 432-464.

Angus, L. B. (1993). Masculinity and women teachers at Christian Brothers College. *Organization Studies, 14,* 235-260.

Arrington, C. E., & Francis, J. E. (1989). Letting the chat out of the bag: Deconstruction, privilege and accounting research. *Accounting, Organizations and Society, 14,* 1-28.

Ashcraft, K. L. (1998). "I wouldn't say I'm a feminist, but . . . ": Organizational micropractice and gender identity. *Management Communication Quarterly, 11,* 587-597.

Ashcraft, K. L. (2000). Empowering "professional" relationships: Organizational communication meets feminist practice. *Management Communication Quarterly, 13,* 347-392.

Astley, W. G., & Sachdeva, P. S. (1984). Structural sources of intraorganizational power: A theoretical synthesis. *Academy of Management Review, 9,* 104-113.

Axley, S. (1984). Managerial and organizational communication in terms of the conduit metaphor. *Academy of Management Review, 9,* 428-437.

Bachrach, P., & Baratz, M. (1962). Two faces of power. *American Political Science Review, 56,* 947-952.

Bachrach, P., & Baratz, M. (1963). Decisions and nondecisions: An analytical framework. *American Political Science Review, 57,* 641-651.

Banks, S. (1994). Performing flight announcements: The case of flight attendants' work discourse. *Text and Performance Quarterly, 14,* 253-267.

Banks, S., & Riley, P. (1993). Structuration theory as an ontology for communication research. In S. A. Deetz (Ed.), *Communication yearbook 16* (pp. 167-196). Newbury Park, CA: Sage.

Barker, J. (1993). Tightening the iron cage: Concertive control in self-managing teams. *Administrative Science Quarterly, 38,* 408-437.

Barker, J. (1999). *The discipline of teamwork: Participation and concertive control.* Thousand Oaks, CA: Sage.

Barker, J., & Cheney, G. (1994). The concept and practices of discipline in contemporary organizational life. *Communication Monographs, 61,* 19-43.

Barrett, F. J. (1995). Finding voice within the gender order. *Journal of Organizational Change Management, 8*(6), 8-15.

Baudrillard, J. (1990). *Seduction.* New York: St. Martin's.

Bell, E. L., & Forbes, L. C. (1994). Office folklore in the academic paperwork empire: The interstitial space of gendered (con)texts. *Text and Performance Quarterly, 14,* 181-196.

Benson, J. K. (1977). Organizations: A dialectical view. *Administrative Science Quarterly, 22,* 1-21.

Benson, S. (1992). "The clerking sisterhood": Rationalization and the work culture of saleswomen in American department stores, 1890-1960. In A. J. Mills &

P. Tancred (Eds.), *Gendering organizational analysis* (pp. 222-234). Newbury Park, CA: Sage.

Bergquist, W. (1993). *The postmodern organization: Mastering the art of irreversible change.* San Francisco: Jossey-Bass.

Best, S., & Kellner, D. (1991). *Postmodern theory: Critical interrogations.* New York: Guilford.

Bittner, E. (1974). The concept of organization. In R. Turner (Ed.), *Ethnomethodology* (pp. 69-81). Harmondsworth, UK: Penguin.

Blair, C., Brown, J. R., & Baxter, L. A. (1994). Disciplining the feminine. *Quarterly Journal of Speech, 80,* 383-409.

Boden, D. (1994). *The business of talk.* Cambridge, UK: Polity.

Boje, D. M. (1991). The storytelling organization: A study of story performance in an office-supply firm. *Administrative Science Quarterly, 36,* 106-126.

Boje, D. M., Gephart, R. P., & Thatchenkery, T. J. (Eds.). (1996). *Postmodern management and organization theory.* Thousand Oaks, CA: Sage.

Boyce, M. E. (1995). Solidarity and praxis: Being a change agent in a university setting. *Journal of Organizational Change Management, 8*(6), 58-66.

Braverman, H. (1974). *Labor and monopoly capital: The degradation of work in the twentieth century.* New York: Monthly Review Press.

Brown, R. H. (1978). Bureaucracy as praxis: Toward a political phenomenology of formal organizations. *Administrative Science Quarterly, 23,* 365-382.

Bullis, C. (1993). At least it is a start. In S. A. Deetz (Ed.), *Communication yearbook 16* (pp. 144-154). Newbury Park, CA: Sage.

Bullis, C. A., & Tompkins, P. K. (1989). The forest ranger revisited: A study of control practices and identification. *Communication Monographs, 56,* 287-306.

Burawoy, M. (1979). *Manufacturing consent: Changes in the labor process under monopoly capitalism.* Chicago: University of Chicago Press.

Burrell, G. (1988). Modernism, postmodernism and organizational analysis 2: The contribution of Michel Foucault. *Organization Studies, 9,* 221-235.

Burrell, G. (1992). The organization of pleasure. In M. Alvesson & H. Willmott (Eds.), *Critical management studies* (pp. 66-89). Newbury Park, CA: Sage.

Burrell, G. (1993). Eco and the bunnymen. In J. Hassard & M. Parker (Eds.), *Postmodernism and organizations* (pp. 71-82). Newbury Park, CA: Sage.

Burrell, G., & Morgan, G. (1979). *Sociological paradigms and organisational analysis.* London: Heinemann.

Buzzanell, P. (1994). Gaining a voice: Feminist organizational communication theorizing. *Management Communication Quarterly, 7,* 339-383.

Calás, M. (1992). An/other silent voice? Representing "Hispanic woman" in organizational texts. In A. J. Mills & P. Tancred (Eds.), *Gendering organizational analysis* (pp. 201-221). Newbury Park, CA: Sage.

Calás, M., & Smircich, L. (1991). Voicing seduction to silence leadership. *Organization Studies, 12,* 567-601.

Calás, M., & Smircich, L. (1992a). Re-writing gender into organizational theorizing: Directions from feminist perspectives. In M. Reed & M. Hughes (Eds.), *Rethinking organization: New directions in organization theory and analysis* (pp. 227-253). Newbury Park, CA: Sage.

Calás, M., & Smircich, L. (1992b). Using the "F" word: Feminist theories and the social consequences of organizational research. In A. J. Mills & P. Tancred (Eds.), *Gendering organizational analysis* (pp. 222-234). Newbury Park, CA: Sage.

Calás, M., & Smircich, L. (1993). Desperately seeking—? Or who/what was Howard's car? *Organization Studies, 14,* 282.

Callinicos, A. (1989). *Against postmodernism.* Cambridge, UK: Polity.

Cavanagh, G. F., Moberg, D. J., & Velasquez, M. (1981). The ethics of organizational politics. *Academy of Management Review, 6,* 363-374.

Cheney, G. (1983). On the various and changing meanings of organizational membership: A field study of organizational identification. *Communication Monographs, 50,* 342-362.

Cheney, G. (1995). Democracy in the workplace: Theory and practice from the perspective of communication. *Journal of Applied Communication Research, 23,* 167-200.

Cheney, G. (1999). *Values at work: Employee participation meets market pressure at Mondragón.* Ithaca, NY: Cornell University Press.

Clair, R. P. (1993a). The bureaucratization, commodification, and privatization of sexual harassment through institutional discourse. *Management Communication Quarterly, 7,* 123-157.

Clair, R. P. (1993b). The use of framing devices to sequester organizational narratives: Hegemony and harassment. *Communication Monographs, 60,* 113-136.

Clair, R. P. (1994). Resistance and oppression as a self-contained opposite: An organizational communication analysis of one man's story of sexual harassment. *Western Journal of Communication, 58,* 235-262.

Clair, R. P. (1998). *Organizing silence: A world of possibilities.* Albany: State University of New York Press.

Clegg, S. (1975). *Power, rule, and domination.* New York: Routledge and Kegan Paul.

Clegg, S. (1981). Organization and control. *Administrative Science Quarterly, 26,* 545-562.

Clegg, S. (1987). The language of power and the power of language. *Organization Studies, 8,* 61-70.

Clegg, S. (1989a). *Frameworks of power.* Newbury Park, CA: Sage.

Clegg, S. (1989b). Radical revisions: Power, discipline and organizations. *Organization Studies, 10,* 97-115.

Clegg, S. (1990). *Modern organizations: Organization studies in a postmodern world.* Newbury Park, CA: Sage.

Clegg, S. (1994a). Power relations and the constitution of the resistant subject. In J. M. Jermier, D. Knights, & W. R. Nord (Eds.), *Resistance and power in organizations* (pp. 274-325). London: Routledge.

Clegg, S. (1994b). Weber and Foucault: Social theory for the study of organizations. *Organization, 1,* 149-178.

Clegg, S., & Dunkerley, D. (Eds.). (1980). *Organization, class and control.* London: Routledge and Kegan Paul.

Clifford, J. (1988). *The predicament of culture.* Cambridge, MA: Harvard University Press.

Clifford, J., & Marcus, G. (Eds.). (1986). *Writing culture: The poetics and politics of ethnography.* Berkeley: University of California Press.

Cobb, A. T. (1984). An episodic model of power: Toward an integration of theory and research. *Academy of Management Review, 9,* 482-493.

Cockburn, C. (1984). *Brothers.* London: Verso.

Collinson, D. (1988). "Engineering humor": Masculinity, joking and conflict in shop-floor relations. *Organization Studies, 9,* 181-199.

Collinson, D. (1992). *Managing the shop floor: Subjectivity, masculinity, and workplace culture.* New York: Aldine de Gruyter.

Collinson, D. (1994). Strategies of resistance: Power, knowledge and resistance in the workplace. In J. M. Jermier, D. Knights, & W. M. Nord (Eds.), *Resistance and power in organizations* (pp. 25-68). London: Routledge.

Connell, R. W. (1985). Theorising gender. *Sociology, 19,* 260-272.

Connell, R. W. (1987). *Gender and power: Society, the person and sexual politics.* Cambridge, UK: Polity.

Conquergood, D. (1991). Rethinking ethnography: Toward a critical cultural politics. *Communication Monographs, 58,* 179-194.

Conrad, C. (1988). Work songs, hegemony, and illusions of self. *Critical Studies in Mass Communication, 5,* 179-201.

Cooper, R. (1989). Modernism, postmodernism and organizational analysis 3: The contribution of Jacques Derrida. *Organization Studies, 10,* 479-502.

Cooper, R., & Burrell, G. (1988). Modernism, postmodernism and organizational analysis: An introduction. *Organization Studies, 9,* 91-112.

Crozier, M. (1964). *The bureaucratic phenomenon.* Chicago: University of Chicago Press.

Cyert, R. M., & March, J. G. (1963). *A behavioral theory of the firm.* Englewood Cliffs, NJ: Prentice Hall.

Dahl, R. (1957). The concept of power. *Behavioral Science, 2,* 201-215.

Dahl, R. (1958). A critique of the ruling elite model. *American Political Science Review, 52,* 463-469.

Dahl, R. (1961). *Who governs? Democracy and power in an American city.* New Haven, CT: Yale University Press.

Daudi, P. (1986). *Power in the organisation.* Oxford, UK: Basil Blackwell.

De Certeau, M. (1984). *The practice of everyday life* (S. Rendall, Trans.). Berkeley: University of California Press.

Deetz, S. (1973a). An understanding of science and a hermeneutic science of understanding. *Journal of Communication, 23,* 139-159.

Deetz, S. (1973b). Words without things: Toward a social phenomenology of language. *Quarterly Journal of Speech, 59,* 40-51.

Deetz, S. (1978). Conceptualizing human understanding: Gadamer's hermeneutics and American communication research. *Communication Quarterly, 26,* 12-23.

Deetz, S. (1982). Critical interpretive research in organizational communication. *Western Journal of Speech Communication, 46,* 131-149.

Deetz, S. (1985). Critical-cultural research: New sensibilities and old realities. *Journal of Management, 11*(2), 121-136.

Deetz, S. (1992a). *Democracy in an age of corporate colonization: Developments in communication and the politics of everyday life.* Albany: State University of New York Press.

Deetz, S. (1992b). Disciplinary power in the modern corporation. In M. Alvesson & H. Willmott (Eds.), *Critical management studies* (pp. 21-45). Newbury Park, CA: Sage.

Deetz, S. (1994). The new politics of the workplace: Ideology and other unobtrusive controls. In H. W. Simons & M. Billig (Eds.), *After postmodernism: Reconstructing ideology critique* (pp. 172-199). Thousand Oaks, CA: Sage.

Deetz, S. (1995). *Transforming communication, transforming business: Building responsive and responsible workplaces.* Cresskill, NJ: Hampton.

Deetz, S., & Kersten, A. (1983). Critical models of interpretive research. In L. L. Putnam & M. E. Pacanowsky (Eds.), *Communication and organizations: An interpretive approach* (pp. 147-171). Beverly Hills, CA: Sage.

Deetz, S., & Mumby, D. K. (1985). Metaphors, information, and power. In B. Ruben (Ed.), *Information and behavior* (Vol. 1, pp. 369-386). New Brunswick, NJ: Transaction.

Deetz, S., & Mumby, D. K. (1990). Power, discourse, and the workplace: Reclaiming the critical tradition. In J. A. Anderson (Ed.), *Communication yearbook 13* (pp. 18-47). Newbury Park, CA: Sage.

Derrida, J. (1976). *Of grammatology* (G. Spivak, Trans.). Baltimore: Johns Hopkins University Press.

Derrida, J. (1978). *Writing and difference*. London: Routledge and Kegan Paul.

Eagleton, T. (1991). *Ideology: An introduction*. London: Verso.

Eagleton, T. (1995). Where do postmodernists come from? *Monthly Review, 47*(3), 59-70.

Edelman, M. (1964). *The symbolic uses of politics*. Urbana: University of Illinois Press.

Edwards, R. (1979). *Contested terrain: The transformation of the workplace in the twentieth century*. New York: Basic Books.

Ehrenhaus, P. (1993). Cultural narratives and the therapeutic motif: The political containment of Vietnam veterans. In D. K. Mumby (Ed.), *Narrative and social control* (pp. 77-96). Newbury Park, CA: Sage.

Eisenberg, E. (1984). Ambiguity as strategy in organizational communication. *Communication Monographs, 51*, 227-242.

Emerson, R. M. (1962). Power-dependence relations. *American Sociological Review, 27*, 31-41.

Enz, C. (1988). The role of value incongruity in intraorganizational power. *Administrative Science Quarterly, 33*, 284-304.

Essed, P. (1991). *Understanding everyday racism*. Newbury Park, CA: Sage.

Fairclough, N. (1993). Critical discourse and the marketization of public discourse: The universities. *Discourse & Society, 4*, 133-168.

Fairhurst, G. (1993). The leader-member exchange patterns of women leaders in industry: A discourse analysis. *Communication Monographs, 60*, 321-351.

Featherstone, M. (1988). In pursuit of the postmodern. *Theory, Culture & Society, 5*, 195-215.

Ferguson, K. (1984). *The feminist case against bureaucracy*. Philadelphia: Temple University Press.

Ferguson, K. (1994). On bringing more theory, more voices and more politics to the study of organization. *Organization, 1*, 81-99.

Ferree, M. M., & Martin, P. (Eds.). (1995). *Feminist organizations: Harvest of the new women's movement*. Philadelphia: Temple University Press.

"Florence, M." [Michel Foucault]. (1994). Foucault, Michel, 1926-. In G. Gutting (Ed.), *The Cambridge companion to Foucault* (pp. 314-319). Cambridge, UK: Cambridge University Press.

Forester, J. (1989). *Planning in the face of power*. Berkeley: University of California Press.

Forester, J. (1992). Fieldwork in a Habermasian way. In M. Alvesson & H. Willmott (Eds.), *Critical management studies* (pp. 46-65). Newbury Park, CA: Sage.

Forester, J. (1993). *Critical theory, public policy and planning practice*. Albany: State University of New York Press.

Foucault, M. (1973). *The order of things: An archaeology of the human sciences*. New York: Vintage.

Foucault, M. (1975). *The birth of the clinic: An archaeology of medical perception* (A. Sheridan, Trans.). New York: Vintage.

Foucault, M. (1979). *Discipline and punish: The birth of the prison* (A. Sheridan, Trans.). New York: Vintage.

Foucault, M. (1980a). *The history of sexuality: An introduction* (Vol. 1, R. Hurley, Trans.). New York: Vintage.

Foucault, M. (1980b). *Power/knowledge: Selected interviews and other writings 1972-1977* (C. Gordon, L. Marshall, J. Mepham, & K. Soper, Trans.). New York: Pantheon.

Foucault, M. (1988). *Madness and civilization: A history of insanity in the age of reason* (R. Howard, Trans.). New York: Vintage.

Fowler, R., Hodge, B., Kress, G., & Trew, T. (1979). *Language and control*. London: Routledge and Kegan Paul.

Frankenberg, R. (1993). *White women, race matters: The social construction of whiteness*. Minneapolis: University of Minnesota Press.

Frost, P. (1980). Toward a radical framework for practicing organization science. *Academy of Management Review, 5*, 501-508.

Frost, P. J. (1987). Power, politics, and influence. In F. M. Jablin, L. L. Putnam, K. H. Roberts, & L. W. Porter (Eds.), *Handbook of organizational communication: An interdisciplinary perspective* (pp. 503-548). Newbury Park, CA: Sage.

Gadamer, H.-G. (1989). *Truth and method* (2nd ed., J. Weinsheimer & D. G. Marshall, Trans.). New York: Continuum.

Gaventa, J. (1980). *Power and powerlessness: Quiescence and rebellion in an Appalachian valley*. Urbana: University of Illinois Press.

Gephart, R. P. (1978). Status degradation and organizational succession: An ethnomethodological approach. *Administrative Science Quarterly, 23*, 553-581.

Gephart, R. P. (1988). Managing the meaning of a sour gas well blowout: The public culture of organizational disasters. *Industrial Crisis Quarterly, 2*(1), 17-32.

Gephart, R. P. (1992). Sensemaking, communicative distortion and the logic of public inquiry. *Industrial Crisis Quarterly, 6*(2), 115-135.

Gephart, R. P., Steier, L., & Lawrence, T. (1990). Cultural rationalities in crisis sense-making: A study of public inquiry into a major industrial accident. *Industrial Crisis Quarterly, 4*(1), 27-48.

Gergen, K. (1992). Organization theory in the postmodern era. In M. Reed & M. Hughes (Eds.), *Rethinking organization: New directions in organization theory and analysis* (pp. 207-226). London: Sage.

Geuss, R. (1981). *The idea of a critical theory: Habermas and the Frankfurt school*. Cambridge, UK: Cambridge University Press.

Gherardi, S. (1994). The gender we think, the gender we do in our everyday organizational lives. *Human Relations, 47*, 591-610.

Gherardi, S. (1995). *Gender, symbolism and organizational cultures.* London: Sage.

Giddens, A. (1976). *New rules of sociological method: A positive critique of interpretative sociologies.* London: Hutchinson.

Giddens, A. (1979). *Central problems in social theory: Action, structure and contradiction in social analysis.* Berkeley: University of California Press.

Giddens, A. (1984). *The constitution of society: Outline of the theory of structuration.* Berkeley: University of California Press.

Goldman, P., & Van Houten, D. R. (1977). Managerial strategies and the worker: A Marxist analysis of bureaucracy. In J. K. Benson (Ed.), *Organizational analysis: Critique and innovation.* Beverly Hills, CA: Sage.

Gottfried, H. (1994). Learning the score: The duality of control and everyday resistance in the temporary-help service industry. In J. M. Jermier, D. Knights, & W. R. Nord (Eds.), *Resistance and power in organizations* (pp. 102-127). London: Routledge.

Gottfried, H., & Weiss, P. (1994). A compound feminist organization: Purdue University's Council on the Status of Women. *Women and Politics, 14*(2), 23-44.

Graham, L. (1993). Inside a Japanese transplant: A critical perspective. *Work and Occupations, 20,* 147-173.

Gramsci, A. (1971). *Selections from the prison notebooks* (Q. Hoare & G. Nowell Smith, Trans.). New York: International Publishers.

Gray, B., Bougon, M., & Donnellon, A. (1985). Organizations as constructions and destructions of meaning. *Journal of Management, 11*(2), 83-98.

Gregg, N. (1993). Politics of identity/politics of location: Women workers organizing in a postmodern world. *Women's Studies in Communication, 16*(1), 1-33.

Grimes, D. (1994, November). *Building community: Race, resistance and dialogue.* Paper presented at annual conference of the Speech Communication Association, New Orleans, LA.

Grossberg, L. (1984). Strategies of Marxist cultural interpretation. *Critical Studies in Mass Communication, 1,* 392-421.

Habermas, J. (1970). On systematically distorted communication. *Inquiry, 13,* 205-218.

Habermas, J. (1975). *Legitimation crisis* (T. McCarthy, Trans.). Boston: Beacon.

Habermas, J. (1979). *Communication and the evolution of society* (T. McCarthy, Trans.). Boston: Beacon.

Habermas, J. (1984). *The theory of communicative action: Vol. 1. Reason and the rationalization of society* (T. McCarthy, Trans.). Boston: Beacon.

Habermas, J. (1987). *The theory of communicative action: Vol. 2. Lifeworld and system* (T. McCarthy, Trans.). Boston: Beacon.

Hacker, S. L., & Elcorobairutia, C. (1987). Women workers in the Mondragón system of industrial cooperatives. *Gender & Society, 1,* 358-379.

Hall, S. (1985). Signification, representation, ideology: Althusser and the poststructuralist debates. *Critical Studies in Mass Communication, 2,* 91-114.

Harvey, D. (1989). *The condition of postmodernity: An enquiry into the origins of cultural change.* Oxford, UK: Basil Blackwell.

Hassard, J. (1993a). Postmodernism and organizational analysis: An overview. In J. Hassard & M. Parker (Eds.), *Postmodernism and organizations* (pp. 1-24). Newbury Park, CA: Sage.

Hassard, J. (1993b). *Sociology and organization theory: Positivism, paradigms and postmodernity.* Cambridge, UK: Cambridge University Press.

Hassard, J., & Parker, M. (Eds.). (1993). *Postmodernism and organizations.* Newbury Park, CA: Sage.

Hawes, L. (1977). Toward a hermeneutic phenomenology of communication. *Communication Quarterly, 25*(3), 30-41.

Hearn, J. (1992). *Men in the public eye: The construction and deconstruction of public men and public patriarchies.* New York: Routledge.

Hearn, J. (1994). The organization(s) of violence: Men, gender relations, organizations, and violences. *Human Relations, 47,* 731-754.

Heidegger, M. (1977). *Basic writings.* New York: Harper & Row.

Helmer, J. (1993). Storytelling in the creation and maintenance of organizational tension and stratification. *Southern Communication Journal, 59,* 34-44.

Hickson, D. J., Hinings, C. R., Lee, C. A., Schneck, R. E., & Pennings, J. M. (1971). A strategic contingencies' theory of intraorganizational power. *Administrative Science Quarterly, 17,* 216-229.

Hindess, B. (1982). Power, interests and the outcomes of struggles. *Sociology, 16,* 498-511.

Hinings, C. R., Hickson, D. J., Pennings, J. M., & Schneck, R. E. (1974). Structural conditions of intraorganizational power. *Administrative Science Quarterly, 19,* 22-44.

Holmer-Nadesan, M. (1996). Organizational identity and space of action. *Organization Studies, 17,* 49-81.

Holmer-Nadesan, M. (1997). Constructing paper dolls: The discourse of personality testing in organizational practice. *Communication Theory, 7,* 189-218.

Holmer-Nadesan, M. (1999). The discourses of corporate spiritualism and evangelical capitalism. *Management Communication Quarterly, 13,* 3-42.

Holvino, E. (1997). Reading organizational development from the margins: Outsider within. *Organization, 3,* 520-533.

hooks, b. (1984). *Feminist theory: From margin to center.* Boston: South End.

hooks, b. (1992). *Black looks: Race and representation.* Boston: South End.

Horkheimer, M. (1986). *Critical theory* (M. O'Connell et al., Trans.). New York: Continuum.

Horkheimer, M., & Adorno, T. (1988). *Dialectic of enlightenment* (J. Cumming, Trans.). New York: Continuum.

Hoskin, K. W., & Macve, R. H. (1986). Accounting and the examination: A genealogy of disciplinary power. *Accounting, Organizations and Society, 11,* 105-136.

Hoskin, K. W., & Macve, R. H. (1988). The genesis of accountability: The West Point connections. *Accounting, Organizations and Society, 13,* 37-73.

Howard, L. A., & Geist, P. (1995). Ideological positioning in organizational change: The dialectic of control in a merging organization. *Communication Monographs, 62,* 110-131.

Hunter, F. (1953). *Community power structure.* Chapel Hill: University of North Carolina Press.

Huspek, M., & Kendall, K. (1991). On withholding political voice: An analysis of the political vocabulary of a "nonpolitical" speech community. *Quarterly Journal of Speech, 77,* 1-19.

Iannello, K. P. (1992). *Decisions without hierarchy: Feminist interventions in organizational theory and practice.* New York: Routledge.

Izraeli, D. M., & Jick, T. D. (1986). The art of saying no: Linking power to culture. *Organization Studies, 7,* 171-192.

Jacques, R. (1992). Critique and theory building: Producing knowledge "from the kitchen." *Academy of Management Review, 17,* 582-606.

Jacques, R. (1996). *Manufacturing the employee: Management knowledge from the 19th to 21st centuries.* London: Sage.

Jameson, F. (1984). Foreword. In J.-F. Lyotard, *The postmodern condition: A report on knowledge* (pp. vii-xi). Minneapolis: University of Minnesota Press.

Jeffcutt, P. (1994). The interpretation of organization: A contemporary analysis and critique. *Journal of Management Studies, 31,* 225-250.

Kilduff, M. (1993). Deconstructing organizations. *Academy of Management Review, 18,* 13-31.

Kilduff, M., & Mehra, A. (1997). Postmodernism and organizational research. *Academy of Management Review, 22,* 453-481.

Knights, D., & Vurdubakis, T. (1994). Foucault, power, resistance and all that. In J. M. Jermier, D. Knights, & W. R. Nord (Eds.), *Resistance and power in organizations* (pp. 167-198). London: Routledge.

Knights, D., & Willmott, H. (1992). Conceptualizing leadership processes: A study of senior managers in a financial services company. *Journal of Management Studies, 29,* 761-782.

Kondo, D. (1990). *Crafting selves: Power, discourse and identity in a Japanese factory.* Chicago: University of Chicago Press.

Kunda, G. (1992). *Engineering culture: Control and commitment in a high-tech corporation.* Philadelphia: Temple University Press.

Lachman, R. (1989). Power from what? A reexamination of its relationships with structural conditions. *Administrative Science Quarterly, 34,* 231-251.

Laclau, E. (1990). *New reflections on the revolution of our time.* London: Verso.

Laclau, E., & Mouffe, C. (1985). *Hegemony and socialist strategy: Towards a radical democratic politics.* London: Verso.

Laird Brenton, A. (1993). Demystifying the magic of language: A critical linguistic case analysis of legitimation of authority. *Journal of Applied Communication Research, 21,* 227-244.

Lamphere, L. (1985). Bringing the family to work: Women's culture on the shop floor. *Feminist Studies, 11,* 519-540.

Larrain, J. (1979). *The concept of ideology.* London: Hutchinson.

Lentricchia, F. (1988). *Ariel and the police: Michel Foucault, William James, Wallace Stevens.* Madison: University of Wisconsin Press.

Linstead, S. (1993). Deconstruction in the study of organizations. In J. Hassard & M. Parker (Eds.), *Postmodernism and organizations* (pp. 49-70). Newbury Park, CA: Sage.

Linstead, S., & Grafton-Small, R. (1992). On reading organizational culture. *Organization Studies, 13,* 331-355.

Lont, C. M. (1988). Redwood Records: Principles and profit in women's music. In B. Bate & A. Taylor (Eds.), *Women communicating: Studies of women's talk* (pp. 233-250). Norwood, NJ: Ablex.

Lukács, G. (1971). *History and class consciousness: Studies in Marxist dialectics* (R. Livingstone, Trans.). Boston: MIT Press.

Lukes, S. (1974). *Power: A radical view.* London: Macmillan.

Lyotard, J.-F. (1984). *The postmodern condition: A report on knowledge* (G. Bennington & B. Massumi, Trans.). Minneapolis: University of Minnesota Press.

MacKinnon, C. (1979). *Sexual harassment of working women.* New Haven, CT: Yale University Press.

Maguire, M., & Mohtar, L. F. (1994). Performance and the celebration of a subaltern counterpublic. *Text and Performance Quarterly, 14,* 238-252.

March, J. G., & Simon, H. (1958). *Organizations.* New York: John Wiley.

Markham, A. (1996). Designing discourse: A critical analysis of strategic ambiguity and workplace control. *Management Communication Quarterly, 9,* 389-421.

Marsden, R. (1993). The politics of organizational analysis. *Organization Studies, 14,* 93-124.

Marshall, J. (1989). Re-visioning career concepts: A feminist invitation. In M. B. Arthur, D. Hall, & B. Lawrence (Eds.), *Handbook of career theory* (pp. 275-291). Cambridge, UK: Cambridge University Press.

Marshall, J. (1993). Viewing organizational communication from a feminist perspective: A critique and some offerings. In S. A. Deetz (Ed.), *Communication yearbook 16* (pp. 122-141). Newbury Park, CA: Sage.

Martin, J. (1990). Deconstructing organizational taboos: The suppression of gender conflict in organizations. *Organization Science, 1,* 339-359.

Martin, J. (1992). *Cultures in organizations: Three perspectives.* New York: Oxford University Press.

Martin, J. (1994). The organization of exclusion: Institutionalization of sex inequality, gendered faculty jobs and gendered knowledge in organizational theory and research. *Organization, 1,* 401-432.

Martin, J., Feldman, M., Hatch, M. J., & Sitkin, S. J. (1983). The uniqueness paradox in organizational stories. *Administrative Science Quarterly, 28,* 438-453.

Martin, P. Y. (1990). Rethinking feminist organizations. *Gender & Society, 4,* 182-206.

Marx, K. (1967). *Capital* (S. Moore & E. Aveling, Trans.). New York: International Publishers.

McClellan, D. (1986). *Ideology.* Minneapolis: University of Minnesota Press.

McMillan, J. J., & Cheney, G. (1996). The student as consumer: The implications and limitations of a metaphor. *Communication Education, 45,* 1-15.

Mehan, H., & Wood, H. (1975). *The reality of ethnomethodology.* New York: John Wiley.

Merleau-Ponty, M. (1960). *Phenomenology of perception* (C. Smith, Trans.). London: Routledge and Kegan Paul.

Miller, P., & O'Leary, T. (1987). Accounting and the construction of the governable person. *Accounting, Organizations and Society, 12,* 235-265.

Mills, A. J. (1995). Man/aging subjectivity, silencing diversity: Organizational imagery in the airline industry: The case of British Airways. *Organization, 2,* 243-270.

Mills, A. L., & Tancred, P. (Eds.). (1992). *Gendering organizational analysis.* Newbury Park, CA: Sage.

Mills, C. W. (1956). *The power elite.* Oxford, UK: Oxford University Press.

Mouffe, C. (1979). Hegemony and ideology in Gramsci. In C. Mouffe (Ed.), *Gramsci and Marxist theory* (pp. 168-204). London: Routledge and Kegan Paul.

Mumby, D. K. (1987). The political function of narrative in organizations. *Communication Monographs, 54,* 113-127.

Mumby, D. K. (1988). *Communication and power in organizations: Discourse, ideology, and domination.* Norwood, NJ: Ablex.

Mumby, D. K. (1989). Ideology and the social construction of meaning: A communication perspective. *Communication Quarterly, 37,* 291-304.

Mumby, D. K. (1993a). Critical organizational communication studies: The next ten years. *Communication Monographs, 60,* 18-25.

Mumby, D. K. (Ed.). (1993b). *Narrative and social control: Critical perspectives.* Newbury Park, CA: Sage.

Mumby, D. K. (1996). Feminism, postmodernism, and organizational communication: A critical reading. *Management Communication Quarterly, 9,* 259-295.

Mumby, D. K. (1997). The problem of hegemony: Rereading Gramsci for organizational communication studies. *Western Journal of Communication, 61,* 343-375.

Mumby, D. K., & Putnam, L. L. (1992). The politics of emotion: A feminist reading of bounded rationality. *Academy of Management Review, 17,* 465-486.

Mumby, D. K., & Stohl, C. (1992). Power and discourse in organization studies: Absence and the dialectic of control. *Discourse & Society, 2,* 313-332.

Murphy, A. G. (1998). Hidden transcripts of flight attendant resistance. *Management Communication Quarterly, 11,* 499-535.

Nakayama, T., & Krizek, R. (1995). Whiteness: A strategic rhetoric. *Quarterly Journal of Speech, 81,* 291-309.

Nkomo, S. (1992). The emperor has no clothes: Rewriting "race in organizations." *Academy of Management Review, 17,* 487-513.

O'Neill, J. (1986). The disciplinary society: From Weber to Foucault. *British Journal of Sociology, 37,* 42-60.

Pacanowsky, M., & O'Donnell-Trujillo, N. (1982). Communication and organizational cultures. *Western Journal of Speech Communication, 46,* 115-130.

Papa, M. J., Auwal, M. A., & Singhal, A. (1995). Dialectic of control and emancipation in organizing for social change: A multitheoretic study of the Grameen Bank in Bangladesh. *Communication Theory, 5,* 189-223.

Parker, M. (1992a). Getting down from the fence: A reply to Haridimos Tsoukas. *Organization Studies, 13,* 651-653.

Parker, M. (1992b). Post-modern organizations or postmodern organization theory. *Organization Studies, 13,* 1-18.

Penkoff, D. (1995, May). *Communication and recovery: Structuration as an ontological approach to organizational culture.* Paper presented at the annual conference of the International Communication Association, Albuquerque, NM.

Perrow, C. (1970). Departmental power and perspective in industrial firms. In M. Zald (Ed.), *Power in organizations* (pp. 59-89). Nashville, TN: Vanderbilt University Press.

Pettigrew, A. (1973). *The politics of organizational decision-making.* London: Tavistock.

Pfeffer, J. (1981). *Power in organizations.* Marshfield, MA: Pitman.

Pfeffer, J., & Salancik, G. (1974). Organizational decision making as a political process: The case of a university budget. *Administrative Science Quarterly, 19,* 135-151.

Pfeffer, J., & Salancik, G. (1978). *The external control of organizations: A resource dependence perspective.* New York: Harper & Row.

Poole, M. S., & DeSanctis, G. (1990). Understanding the use of group decision support systems: The theory of adaptive structuration. In J. Fulk & C. Steinfield (Eds.), *Organizations and communication technology* (pp. 173-193). Newbury Park, CA: Sage.

Power, M., & Laughlin, R. (1992). Critical theory and accounting. In M. Alvesson & H. Willmott (Eds.), *Critical management studies* (pp. 113-135). Newbury Park, CA: Sage.

Pringle, R. (1989). *Secretaries talk: Sexuality, power and work.* London: Verso.

Putnam, L. L. (1983). The interpretive perspective: An alternative to functionalism. In L. L. Putnam & M. E. Pacanowsky (Eds.), *Communication and organizations: An interpretive approach* (pp. 31-54). Beverly Hills, CA: Sage.

Putnam, L. L., & Mumby, D. K. (1993). Organizations, emotion, and the myth of rationality. In S. Fineman (Ed.), *Emotion in organizations* (pp. 36-57). London: Sage.

Putnam, L. L., & Pacanowsky, M. E. (Eds.). (1983). *Communication and organizations: An interpretive approach.* Beverly Hills, CA: Sage.

Ranson, S., Hinings, B., & Greenwood, R. (1980). The structuring of organizational structures. *Administrative Science Quarterly, 25,* 1-17.

Reinelt, C. (1994). Fostering empowerment, building community: The challenge for state-funded feminist organizations. *Human Relations, 47,* 685-705.

Ricoeur, P. (1970). *Freud and philosophy: An essay on interpretation* (D. Savage, Trans.). New Haven, CT: Yale University Press.

Riley, P. (1983). A structurationist account of political culture. *Administrative Science Quarterly, 28,* 414-437.

Rodriguez, N. M. (1988). Transcending bureaucracy: Feminist politics at a shelter for battered women. *Gender & Society, 2,* 214-227.

Rorty, R. (Ed.). (1967). *The linguistic turn: Recent essays in philosophical method.* Chicago: University of Chicago Press.

Rosen, M. (1985). "Breakfast at Spiro's": Dramaturgy and dominance. *Journal of Management, 11*(2), 31-48.

Rosen, M. (1988). You asked for it: Christmas at the bosses' expense. *Journal of Management Studies, 25,* 463-480.

Rosenau, P. M. (1992). *Post-modernism and the social sciences.* Princeton, NJ: Princeton University Press.

Rosenau, P. V., & Bredemeier, H. C. (1993). Modern and postmodern conceptions of social order. *Social Research, 60,* 337-362.

Rothschild, J., & Davies, C. (1994). Organizations through the lens of gender. *Human Relations, 47,* 583-590.

Rothschild-Whitt, J. (1979). The collectivist organization: An alternative to rational bureaucratic models. *American Sociological Review, 44,* 509-527.

Salancik, G., & Pfeffer, J. (1974). The bases and uses of power in organizational decision making: The case of a university. *Administrative Science Quarterly, 19,* 453-473.

Salancik, G., & Pfeffer, J. (1977). Who gets power—and how they hold on to it: A strategic contingency model of power. *Organizational Dynamics, 5*(3), 3-21.

Salvador, M., & Markham, A. (1995). The rhetoric of self-directive management and the operation of organizational power. *Communication Reports, 8,* 45-53.

Schattschneider, E. E. (1960). *The semi-sovereign people: A realist's view of democracy in America.* New York: Holt, Rinehart & Winston.

Scheibel, D. (1996). Appropriating bodies: Organ(izing) ideology and cultural practice in medical school. *Journal of Applied Communication Research, 24,* 310-331.

Schutz, A. (1962). *Collected papers I: The problem of social reality.* The Hague, Netherlands: Martinus Nijhoff.

Schwartz, H. (1993). Deconstructing my car at the Detroit airport. *Organization Studies, 14,* 279-281.

Scott, J. C. (1990). *Domination and the arts of resistance: Hidden transcripts.* New Haven, CT: Yale University Press.

Sealander, J., & Smith, D. (1986). The rise and fall of feminist organizations in the 1970s: Dayton as a case study. *Feminist Studies, 12,* 321-341.

Simon, H. (1976). *Administrative behavior* (3rd ed.). Glencoe, IL: Free Press.

Smart, B. (1986). The politics of truth and the problem of hegemony. In D. C. Hoy (Ed.), *Foucault: A critical reader* (pp. 157-174). Oxford, UK: Basil Blackwell.

Smith, R., & Eisenberg, E. (1987). Conflict at Disneyland: A root metaphor analysis. *Communication Monographs, 54,* 367-380.

Sotirin, P., & Gottfried, H. (1999). The ambivalent dynamics of secretarial "bitching": Control, resistance, and the construction of identity. *Organization, 6,* 57-80.

Spradlin, A. L. (1998). The price of "passing": A lesbian perspective on authenticity in organizations. *Management Communication Quarterly, 11,* 598-605.

Steffy, B., & Grimes, A. J. (1986). A critical theory of organization science. *Academy of Management Review, 11,* 322-336.

Strine, M. (1992). Understanding "how things work": Sexual harassment and academic culture. *Journal of Applied Communication Research, 20,* 391-400.

Sunesson, S. (1985). Outside the goal paradigm: Power and the structured patterns of non-rationality. *Organization Studies, 6,* 229-246.

Taylor, B., & Conrad, C. (1992). Narratives of sexual harassment: Organizational dimensions. *Journal of Applied Communication Research, 20,* 401-418.

Taylor, J. R. (1995). Shifting from a heteronomous to an autonomous worldview of organizational communication: Communication theory on the cusp. *Communication Theory, 5,* 1-35.

Taylor, J. R., Cooren, F., Giroux, N., & Robichaud, D. (1996). The communicational basis of organization: Between the conversation and the text. *Communication Theory, 6,* 1-39.

Therborn, G. (1980). *The ideology of power and the power of ideology.* London: NLB.

Thompson, J. (1967). *Organizations in action.* New York: McGraw-Hill.

Thompson, J. B. (1984). *Studies in the theory of ideology.* Berkeley: University of California Press.

Tompkins, P. K., & Cheney, G. (1985). Communication and unobtrusive control in contemporary organizations. In R. D. McPhee & P. K. Tompkins (Eds.), *Organizational communication: Traditional themes and new directions* (pp. 179-210). Beverly Hills, CA: Sage.

Tong, R. (1989). *Feminist thought.* Boulder, CO: Westview.

Townsley, N. C., & Geist, P. (in press). The discursive enactment of hegemony: Sexual harassment in academic organizing. *Western Journal of Communication, 64.*

Trethewey, A. (1997). Resistance, identity, and empowerment: A postmodern feminist analysis of clients in a human service organization. *Communication Monographs, 64,* 281-301.

Trethewey, A. (1999a). Disciplined bodies. *Organization Studies, 20,* 423-450.

Trethewey, A. (1999b). Isn't it ironic: Using irony to explore the contradictions of organizational life. *Western Journal of Communication, 63,* 140-167.

Tsoukas, H. (1992). Postmodernism, reflexive rationalism and organizational studies: A reply to Martin Parker. *Organization Studies, 13,* 643-650.

Turow, J. (1984). *Media industries: The production of news and entertainment.* New York: Longman.

van Dijk, T. A. (1993). *Elite discourse and racism.* Newbury Park, CA: Sage.

Volosinov, V. N. (1973). *Marxism and the philosophy of language.* Cambridge, MA: Harvard University Press.

Von Bertalanffy, L. (1968). *General system theory.* New York: George Braziller.

Wallace, M. (1992). Negative images: Towards a black feminist cultural criticism. In L. Grossberg, C. Nelson, & P. Treichler (Eds.), *Cultural studies* (pp. 654-671). New York: Routledge.

Weber, M. (1978). *Economy and society* (G. Roth & C. Wittich, Trans.). Berkeley: University of California Press.

Wendt, R. (1994). Learning to "walk the talk": A critical tale of the micropolitics at a total quality university. *Management Communication Quarterly, 8,* 5-45.

West, C., & Zimmerman, D. (1987). Doing gender. *Gender & Society, 1,* 125-151.

West, J. (1993). Ethnography and ideology: The politics of cultural representation. *Western Journal of Communication, 57,* 209-220.

Willis, P. (1977). *Learning to labor: How working class kids get working class jobs.* New York: Columbia University Press.

Witten, M. (1993). Narrative and the culture of obedience at the workplace. In D. K. Mumby (Ed.), *Narrative and social control: Critical perspectives* (pp. 97-118). Newbury Park, CA: Sage.

Wolfinger, R. E. (1971). Nondecisions and the study of local politics. *American Political Science Review, 65,* 1063-1080.

Wood, J. (1992). Telling our stories: Narratives as a basis for theorizing sexual harassment. *Journal of Applied Communication Research, 20,* 349-362.

Young, E. (1989). On the naming of the rose: Interests and multiple meanings as elements of organizational culture. *Organization Studies, 10,* 187-206.

Zavella, P. (1985). "Abnormal intimacy": The varying networks of Chicana cannery workers. *Feminist Studies, 11,* 541-564.

16

Wired Meetings

Technological Mediation of Organizational Gatherings

JANET FULK
University of Southern California

LORI COLLINS-JARVIS
Lieberman Research Worldwide

I deal with people all the time who talk about how videoconferencing is going to save time. It's going to save time on travel. It will be more effective and efficient. Every single person I've talked with, every white-collar worker I've asked, "What's the biggest waste of your time?" has said, "Meetings." And then they talk about videoconferencing. Geez, why would we recreate in cyberspace the single biggest waste of time we have in the physical world?

—Schrage (1996, p. 57)

Meetings are very common organizational communication events. They involve fundamental communication processes including sensemaking, control, power relations, structuration, and decision making. Theory and research on mediated meetings

AUTHORS' NOTE: We thank Alan Dennis, Linda Putnam and Fred Jablin for valuable comments on an earlier draft of this chapter. We thank the 3M Meeting Management Institute for support of the research on which this chapter is based. This chapter was completed in September 1997.

are growing exponentially as communication technologies have become critical to new organizational forms (Fulk & DeSanctis, 1998; McPhee & Poole, Chapter 13, this volume). This chapter organizes this theory and research and suggests new directions for investigation. We describe three theoretical perspectives and overview research on three types of technological support: teleconferencing, computer conferencing, and group support systems. We organize the research by commonly studied communication-related issues in groups: (a) equality of participation, (b) socioemotional expression, (c) conflict and consensus, (d) efficiency (time to complete a task), (e) decision quality, and (f) satisfaction. Finally, we overview several new developments in mediated meeting technology and suggest how they are linked to significant changes in organizational forms.

SCOPE AND FRAMEWORK OF THE CHAPTER

The term *meeting* (e.g., *gemetan* in Old English) has been in the English language since before *Beowulf* was written (approximately the first quarter of the eighth century; R. Fulk, 1992). Over the millennium, the concept of "meeting" has held a variety of meanings in both academic and lay contexts. We use the term to mean the act of gathering together for a limited period of time for the purpose of communication. We use the criterion of synchroneity not as a convenience, but rather as an observable demarcation for initiation and conclusion of a communication episode. Some scholars apply the term to asynchronous communication, particularly when it is technology mediated. However, the asynchronous criterion makes it difficult for researchers (and for participants themselves) to demarcate the meeting itself from ongoing communications extending over periods of days, months, and even years. The

synchronous criterion links the meeting concept to its centuries-long history. The concept also implies that participants construe the communication episode as "meeting." Meeting typically excludes, for example, the "synchronous" open radio frequencies on police patrols, which officers do not consider to be a meeting in the sense that the preshift briefing is a meeting.

Managerial time allocation to meetings varies from about 25% (Monge, McSween, & Wyer, 1989; Mosvick & Nelson, 1987) to more than 60% (McCall, Morrison, & Hannan, 1978; Mintzberg, 1973; Uhlig, Farber, & Bair, 1979). For each meeting hour, managers spend up to an additional hour of time preparing (Monge et al., 1989). Meetings are implicated in many communication-related organizational processes. Historically, meetings were used during the industrial revolution to inform management about plant-level activity, facilitate coordination across superintendents, humanize the new work procedures, and reduce hostility in the ranks of superintendents (Yates, 1989). Meetings also have been found to control organizational work flow by focusing managerial attention, targeting some problems and decisions as more salient than others, and offering legitimate forums for political processes (Oppenheim, 1987). Kling (1991) and Fulk and Monge (1995) argue that technological mediation of group processes is as deeply implicated in control and coercion as in collaboration and cooperation. Yates and Orlikowski (1992, p. 301) describe the meeting as a *genre*, a "typified communicative action in response to a current situation" that guides communication behavior.

Meetings are also sensemaking forums (Weick & Meader, 1992) that define, represent, and reproduce social entities and relationships and "produce" organization. They are the organization or community "writ small," yet they also help to create community or organizational identity (Schwartzman, 1989). Meetings serve ceremonial and symbolic functions (Trice, 1985), and as locales and mechanisms for impression management (Clapper & Prasad, 1993).

New and highly sophisticated electronic meeting support is widely available to organizations and includes three generic categories of meeting technologies. *Teleconferencing* includes meetings held through audioconferencing and videoconferencing systems. *Computer conferencing* allows multiple participants to interact by contributing to an ongoing computer file accessible to all. *Group support systems* (GSSs) supplement computer conferencing with information management capabilities, decision support tools, graphics displays, and meeting process management software. Multimedia systems have become available recently, although there is little research on group processes in multimedia meetings.

Most reviews of mediated meeting research cumulate findings by type of technology, and some combine synchronous and asynchronous forms. Teleconferencing findings were reviewed by Johansen, Vallee, and Spangler (1979), Fowler and Wackerbarth (1980), Williams (1977), and Johansen (1984). Studies of computer-conferenced meetings were reviewed by Kerr and Hiltz (1982), Rice (1984), and Sproull and Kiesler (1991). Culnan and Markus (1987) focused on teleconferencing and computer conferencing. GSS research was reviewed by Dennis, Nunamaker, and Vogel (1991), Dennis and Gallupe (1992), Benbasat, DeSanctis, and Nault (1993), Jessup and Valacich (1992), Benbasat and Lim (1993), Dennis, Haley, and Vandenberg (1996), and Nunamaker, Briggs, Mittleman, Vogel, and Balthazard (1996). Computer conferencing and GSS research was reviewed by McGrath and Hollingshead (1994), Hollingshead and McGrath (1995), and Pinsonneault and Kraemer (1990). Seibold, Heller, and Contractor (1994) crafted a review of reviews on GSS meetings. DeSanctis (1992) and Poole and Jackson (1992) discuss assumptive foundations in GSS research.

Our purpose is to provide a historical perspective on the intellectual development of the field, one in which existing reviews may be situated. This approach chronicles how theory and research develop hand-in-hand and contextualizes theoretical developments to illustrate how new traditions are both constrained by and developed in opposition to existing thought. It illustrates Popper's (1962) contention that intellectual development proceeds as much through elimination of blind alleys as opening new doors. Due to space constraints, we limit our comparison to research that implicitly or explicitly contrasts mediated meetings with face-to-face. This delimitation may be unsatisfying to scholars interested in comparing the effects of different conditions in mediated meetings, such as group size (e.g., Valacich, Wheeler, Mennecke, & Wachter, 1995), anonymity (e.g., Connolly, Jessup, & Valacich, 1990; Hiltz, Turoff, & Johnson, 1989; Jessup, Connolly, & Tansik, 1990; Valacich, Dennis, & Nunamaker, 1992), interacting versus nominal groups (e.g., Dennis & Valacich, 1993, 1994; Valacich, Dennis, & Connolly, 1994), proximate versus distributed groups (e.g., Valacich, George, Nunamaker, & Vogel, 1994), facilitation and designated leadership effects (e.g., Gopal & Pollard, 1996; Hiltz, Johnson, & Turoff, 1991), and processes such as dialectical inquiry versus devil's advocate (e.g., Valacich & Schwenk, 1995). For reviews of research on different types of computer-based meeting support, see Dennis, George, Jessup, Nunamaker, and Vogel (1988), Easton, George, Nunamaker, and Pendergast (1990), and Kraemer and King (1988).

Comparison across technologies rather than specific features is a crude analysis, because features vary across implementations (Griffith & Northcraft, 1994). Seibold et al. (1994) argue that research should account not only for system features but also for use characteristics such as training and user characteristics, for example, computer expertise. Since prior research has not reported such variables, cumulating prior results on these bases is not possible.

Three main theoretical streams on mediated meetings developed over time: media capacity, input-process-output, and structuration. The next sections describe specific theories and research findings for each, and compare and critique underlying assumptions across the streams.

MEDIA CAPACITY THEORIES

The core premise is that media have different capacities to carry communicative cues. Simple cues can be communicated successfully using any medium, but complex interaction requires media with the capacity to transmit complex cues. This section (a) overviews two major theories, social presence and media richness; (b) discusses empirical research; and (c) critiques their assumptions.

Social Presence Theory

Statements on mediated meetings appeared in the 1970s, when audioconferencing was widely available and videoconferencing was in its early stages. An extensive series of experiments led to social presence theory (Short, Williams, & Christie, 1976). "Social presence" of a medium is linked to the nonverbal signals, including facial expression, direction of gaze, posture, dress, physical appearance, proximity, and orientation. Nonverbal cues relate to specific communication functions, including mutual attention and responsiveness, channel control, feedback, illustrations, emblems, and interpersonal attitudes.

A reasonable, but still naïve, hypothesis would thus be: we can predict the effects on interaction of varying medium of communication by listing the cues that are not transmitted via the different media, by discovering the functions of these cues by reference to research on face-to-face communication, and then deduc-

ing the way in which the outcome or processes of the conversation would be altered by the absence of these cues. (Short et al., p. 63)

Such an approach is inappropriate, they argued, for four reasons: (1) nonverbal cues occur in combination with verbal and with other nonverbal cues, which may compensate for or otherwise affect each other; (2) communicators may be aware of the reduced-cue situation and adjust by modifying behavior; (3) particular combinations of cues may mean different things in different contexts; and (4) we do not know enough about the tenuous relationship between visual cues and complex behavior.

The social presence concept responded to difficulties of developing predictions based on the presence or absence of single nonverbal cues in complex human interaction. Social presence is a single dimension that represents the *cognitive synthesis of combinations of cues* as attributed to the medium by the individual. Short et al. (1976) argue that social presence is a differential quality of each medium that describes "the degree of salience of the other person in the interaction and the consequent salience of the interpersonal relationships." Social presence is based on individual perceptions, and thus may vary somewhat across persons. On average across persons, however, the greatest social presence was found for face-to-face. Social presence decreased continuously as one moved to video, then audio forms of interaction.

Short et al. equivocate about medium effects in situations that require cooperation within a group, but they propose specific medium effects for negotiation and conflict situations. Drawing on a long history of the study of the bidimensional nature of group behavior (e.g., Argyle, 1957; Bales, 1955; Douglas, 1957), social presence theory proposes that interpersonal interactions involve both (1) acting out roles and (2) maintaining personal relationships. Depending on the nature of the interaction, the relationship maintenance dimension may be more or less important for the interaction compared with the role dimension.

> It is generally agreed that information transmission and cooperative problem-solving are activities in which interpersonal relationships are relatively unimportant; they are activities for which man-computer interaction is quite feasible. Since personal relationships are unimportant, it matters little whether interactors treat the other as a person or as an impersonal information source. (Short et al., 1976, p. 158)

By contrast, in conflict and negotiation situations each side's perception of the other's behavior is important to its own action choices: The relationship maintenance dimension is highly salient. Short et al. argue from existing research that removal of visual cues impairs the accuracy of person perception that is critical to development of trust. Where trust is impaired, there is more conflict. Specifically, the more types of cues the medium offers to person perception, the more cooperative the behaviors will be.

Thus, the theory proposed that mediated interaction would be less effective for highly interpersonally involving tasks, in proportion to the decreasing amount of social presence of the medium. Short et al.'s (1976) extensive research program investigated the hypothesized process changes in teleconferenced meetings, as well as the relative effectiveness of different levels of mediation (audio vs. video) for tasks that theoretically required high and low social presence media.

Social presence theory was explicitly a theory of interacting synchronous groups. Short et al. argued that the interactive factor was critical to limitations on their ability to generalize from social psychological research conducted in contexts that were not truly interactive. These include, for example, studies of anonymity effects in audio versus face-to-face where subjects only had knowledge of the judgment of others and were not permitted free verbal interaction. Nevertheless, the theory was applied by later researchers to asynchronous interaction, and came to be viewed simply as a theory of media effects.

Media Richness Theory

This theory draws on organizational information-processing premises. Theoretically, when tasks are simple and predictable (low uncertainty), preplanning is possible. Rules, standards, and procedures can achieve coordination without the need for direct communication among those whose activities need to be coordinated (Beniger, 1986; March & Simon, 1958). Under high task uncertainty, preplanning is not possible and direct communication is required for coordination, a process March and Simon called "coordination by feedback." A key premise is that the complexity of communication and information-processing mechanisms (e.g., rules vs. meetings) should match the uncertainty inherent in the task itself.

Later scholars proposed a distinction between uncertainty (lack of information) and equivocality (multiple possible meanings inherent in the information) (Daft & Lengel, 1984; Daft & Weick, 1984; Trevino, Daft, & Lengel, 1990; Weick, 1979). Uncertain situations can be made more certain through rationalization processes such as analysis routines (Perrow, 1970). Equivocal situations cannot be altered through rationalization, but must be managed by use of judgment strategies (Thompson & Tuden, 1959) or through "negotiation and construction of a mutually shared agreement" (Weick & Meader, 1992, p. 232).

Using this perspective, Daft and Lengel (1984) argued that media richness is the key to media capacity. A medium's richness is its information-carrying capacity, based on four criteria: (1) speed of feedback, (2) ability to communicate multiple cues such as body language and voice tone, (3) use of natural language rather than numbers, and (4) ability to readily convey feelings and emotions. Technological mediation restricts the capacity of meetings to handle tasks with the greatest complexity and equivocality (Daft & Lengel, 1984; McGrath & Hollingshead, 1992; Rice, 1984; Short et al., 1976). The fewer communication channels available (e.g., audio only vs. audio plus video) the more restricted is the medium's capacity, and the less uncertainty and equivocality it is able to manage. Media capacity decreases from face-to-face to teleconferencing, to computer-based systems.

Thus, the theory proposes that for equivocal communication tasks, face-to-face meetings are appropriate. And for unequivocal messages lean media such as written text should be used (Daft & Lengel, 1986, p. 560). The logic of "matching" media capabilities with task demands is similar to social presence theory, despite disparate theoretical underpinnings. Research testing media richness theory has focused heavily on asynchronous communication; research results are described in Rice and Gattiker (Chapter 14, this volume).

Empirical Evidence

Perceptions of social presence. Research indicates some perceived differences across media in salience of the other person and personal relationships. Short et al. (1976) report a series of studies in which the sense of social contact was greatest in face-to-face, less in video, and least in audio meetings. Reviews of teleconferencing research by Johansen et al. (1979) and Fowler and Wackerbarth (1980) and more recent studies (e.g., Dennis & Kinney, 1998; Dutton, Fulk, & Steinfield, 1982; Fulk & Dutton, 1984) generally support the conclusion that video dampens feelings of social contact and presence of the other party. This conclusion is reinforced by findings that coalitions tend to form within nodes (e.g., Weston, Kristen, & O'Connor, 1975; Williams, 1975). That is, people who are together face-to-face at one videoconferencing node develop a cohesion that does not extend to persons at the other node.

The strongest contrast in perceived social presence is for audio meetings, which are seen as less personal, less effective for getting to know someone, and communicate less affective content than face-to-face (Craig & Jull, 1974, cited in Johansen et al., 1979; Thomas & Williams, 1975; Williams, 1972). Yet the majority of studies suggest that audio is seen as no less effective than face-to-face in forming impressions of others (Johansen et al., 1979). One possible explanation for this apparent contradiction is that forming impressions may be less interactive than developing a personal relationship with someone. Whereas developing personal relationships may require the other party to be relatively salient in the interaction, impression formation can be more cognitive in focus (Fiske & Taylor, 1991).

Socioemotional content of teleconferenced meetings. The vast majority of studies found that compared to face-to-face meetings, both video and audio meetings were characterized by less emotional display (Champness, 1972; LaPlante, 1971; Weston et al., 1975; Williams, 1976). In addition, audio- and video-mediated meetings showed less conflict and unresolved disagreement (Barefoot & Strickland, 1982; Williams, 1976; Wilson, 1974). As discussed in the next section, subsequent research on computer conferencing produced a much more complicated set of findings, including some that show increased negative emotional display for that medium.

Participation. Johansen et al. (1979) argue that compared to mediated meetings, the personal nature of face-to-face meetings can inhibit broad participation across the participants. Face-to-face interaction conveys many visual status symbols that can cue deference behavior (Sproull & Kiesler, 1991), and it is easier for a single person to dominate. Research has consistently supported a finding of more equal participation in videoconferencing, with a single exception (Barefoot & Strickland, 1982). In videoconferenced meetings, participants are "more polite" and try to encourage participation among those who are reticent, leaders do not as readily emerge, and generally there is less developed hierarchy within the group (Dutton et al., 1982; Fulk & Dutton, 1984; George et al., 1975, cited in Johansen et al., 1979; Strickland, Guild, Barefoot, & Patterson, 1978). Equal participation has also been documented for audioconferencing (Champness, 1972), where participants were better able to exert control over domineering participants (Holloway & Hammond, 1976, and Short, 1973, cited in Johansen et al., 1979). The net effect is that audio meetings were more "orderly."

Conflict. Social presence theory predicts that when tasks are interpersonally involving, such as conflict and negotiation, more cooperation and agreement are likely with more communication channels. Short et al. (1976) report support for this prediction from four laboratory studies that involved two-person mixed-motive situations such as prisoner's dilemma; they also report one study that found no medium effects. Other studies have found mediated meetings to enhance agreement for audioconferencing (Williams, 1976; Wilson, 1974) and videoconferencing (Barefoot & Strickland, 1982). Rarely were *no* medium effects found in laboratory studies.

The central thesis of media capacity theories concerns how such process changes affect communication effectiveness and efficiency in mediated meetings. Theoretically, process changes have the greatest effect when tasks are complex, involving bargaining, negotiation, and personal relationships. The most thoroughly investigated effects are participant satisfaction, decision efficiency, and decision quality.

Satisfaction. Research has shown that participants are less satisfied in video- or audio-teleconferenced meetings (nine studies reported in Johansen et al., 1979; Korzenny & Bauer, 1979). Is satisfaction most affected when the tasks are more complex and personally involving? Field surveys and case research support this prediction for both audio (Albertson, 1977) and video (Albertson, 1977; Dutton et al., 1982; Fulk & Dutton,

1984; Noll, 1976) conditions. In direct contrast, laboratory studies found no differential effects on satisfaction by task complexity for either audio (Albertson, 1973; Champness & Davies, 1971; Korzenny & Bauer, 1979) or video (Dennis & Kinney, 1998; Korzenny & Bauer, 1979).

Efficiency. Many years of investigations in both lab and field have failed to demonstrate detrimental effects of teleconferencing versus face-to-face on efficiency in synchronous meetings. Indeed, the only efficiency effects have been in favor of teleconferenced meetings. In laboratory studies, no compromise in decision efficiency (time to complete the task) on high-complexity tasks has been found for video versus face-to-face meetings (Albertson, 1973; Barefoot & Strickland, 1982; Dennis & Kinney, 1998; Weeks & Chapanis, 1976). Valacich, Mennecke, Wachter, and Wheeler (1994) did find video meetings to be faster than face-to-face for a high-complexity task. Nor were differences in decision efficiency found for low-complexity tasks conducted via videoconferencing (Albertson, 1973; Dennis & Kinney, 1998; Ochsman & Chapanis, 1974; Valacich, Mennecke, et al., 1994; Weeks & Chapanis, 1976). Dennis and Kinney (1998) did find that video meetings were slower for both types of tasks when the meeting employed half-duplex technology (no feedback from the receiver was permitted during the sender's transmission, impeding true synchroneity). Dutton et al. (1982) and Johansen et al. (1979) also report results of three field surveys of managers in which video meetings were perceived to be shorter, although objective measures collected in one of the studies did not support the perceptions.

Similarly, no differences have been found for audioconferencing versus face-to-face for high-complexity tasks (Albertson, 1973; Weeks & Chapanis, 1976). For low-complexity tasks, although some research has shown no differences (Albertson, 1973; Ochsman & Chapanis, 1974; Weeks & Chapanis, 1976), most has shown greater decision efficiency for audio conditions (Davies, 1971: two experiments; Rawlins, 1989, and Johansen et al., 1979: six unpublished studies). One interpretation of these patterns is that the reduction in social presence achieved via mediation serves to limit the amount of distraction that "irrelevant" personal considerations inject into decision making for straightforward, low-complexity tasks. Without these distractions, groups may complete their work more quickly than if they needed to attend to and adjust to personal factors that are salient in each other's presence. Such an interpretation is consistent with Zajonc's (1965) "mere presence" hypothesis, on which social presence theory draws.

Quality. To recap, participants are less satisfied in teleconferenced meetings, especially in audio-only settings, and they participate more evenly. Further, teleconferenced meetings are at least as efficient and some save considerable time relative to face-to-face encounters. Assuming that participation and efficiency are generally valued in Western organizations, the findings for satisfaction appear somewhat curious. A partial explanation may relate to differences in perceived quality of decisions across media. Johansen et al. (1979) report ten studies in which respondents perceived teleconferencing as less effective for bargaining and negotiation (four video studies and six audio studies). These results suggest that despite some process-related benefits of mediation, the quality of work is perceived to suffer when complex interaction is required. Perceived quality decrements may counterbalance valuable process changes. An interesting aspect of the research on decision quality is that, in general, objective measures fail to support participant perceptions of reduced quality in teleconferenced meetings, even for complex tasks. With one exception for audioconferencing (Weston et al., 1975), no studies found a decrement in decision quality for complex tasks in a teleconferencing forum, although Lopez (1992) found lower-quality decisions in videoconferencing for a low-complexity

task. Most experiments found no differences in decision quality for face-to-face versus videoconferencing (Albertson, 1973; Dennis & Kinney, 1998) or audioconferencing (Albertson, 1973; Champness & Davies, 1971; Davies, 1971 [two studies], Harmon, Schneer, & Hoffman, 1995; Short, 1971; Williams, 1975). Rosetti and Surynt (1985) report higher quality under video than face-to-face for a complex task. Johansen et al. (1979) report empirical evidence from three experiments that showed no more breakdowns in audio negotiations than in face-to-face.

Divergences in perceptual versus objective measures of quality could result from researchers applying different criteria for decision quality than do meeting participants. Alternatively, meeting participants simply may prefer inclusion of those "irrelevant" personal considerations. Efficiency goals may be superseded by personal preferences for personalized contact and reinforcement of status cues. Participants may perceive a need for personal involvement in bargaining and negotiation situations to achieve a sense of personal satisfaction with the process.

Summary on Premises

A variety of critiques of the media capacity tradition have been published over the years. We review critiques of six types of premise; subsequent sections compare these media capacity premises to those from the other two dominant theoretical traditions that we review: input-process-output and structuration. The six areas are (1) group role in the meeting process, (2) task characteristics, (3) perspectives on processes in mediated meetings, (4) role of technology, (5) contextualization, and (6) nature of rationality. Table 16.1 summarizes the comparisons across the three theoretical traditions.

Group role in the meeting process. Media capacity theories offer little role for groups to actively manage the technology and context

TABLE 16.1 Evolution of Three Traditions

	Media Capacity	Input-Process-Output	Structuration
Intellectual heritage	Nonverbal communication Organizational information processing	Theories of groups Steiner's (1972) process losses	Structuration Self-organizing systems
Specific theories	Social presence Media richness	Input-Process-Output Time, interaction, and performance	Adaptive structuration Self-organizing systems
Premises			
Group role in the meeting process	Reacts passively to constraints	Responds to technological input factors	Proactively manages technology and group process
Task characteristics	Fixed	Partially altered by technology	Structured by groups in part via technology
Perspective on processes in mediated meetings	Process losses	Process gains and losses due to technological mediation	Articulation of group process with technology's structure and spirit
Role of technology	Connective	Constructive	Constructed and constructive
Contextualization	Minimal	Context as input factor	Context embedded in process through appropriation
Rationality	Objective	Objective	Subjective

of the meeting. Social presence theory, although built on theories of nonverbal communication and social psychology, portrays groups as responding relatively uncreatively to the situational constraints of mediation. Media richness theory follows its parent tradition in organizational information-processing theories in focusing on technology and tasks, largely devoid of human systems that interact through technology on specific tasks. An alternative assumption that situationally empowered groups actively manage task, technology, and context better fits findings that teleconferencing participants experienced process changes and lower satisfaction but no detrimental effects on performance. Groups may have actively altered their preferred processes to maintain performance under medium constraints, with the effect of depressing satisfaction with the experience.

Task characteristics. The media capacity perspective assumes that tasks are relatively unmalleable. Yet research on task design indicates that how tasks are interpreted varies considerably across individuals and groups and is subject to processes of social influence (Salancik & Pfeffer, 1978). Further, tasks that are uncertain but not equivocal may be modified and transformed by groups during the process of task accomplishment. One explanation for decision efficiency and effectiveness in teleconferenced groups with complex tasks is that the groups may have restructured and rationalized the tasks to a more manageable level. Such task rationalization to align task complexity with medium capacity could be incorporated within a revised social presence theory without violating the fundamental matching premise of the theory.

Perspective on processes. A central tenet of media capacity theories is that mediation involves losses in comparison to face-to-face interaction. The fewer the cues that are communicated through a medium, the less rich are the medium and the social presence involved in the interaction. Rice (1984) and

Culnan and Markus (1987) have criticized this perspective for assuming that face-to-face is the appropriate comparison and that mediated communication must involve losses. One could argue that channel capacity theorists of the 1970s could not have foreseen the future ability of computer support to provide improvements and as well decrements to interaction. However, even the established technology of speakerphone need not involve only losses in interactive capabilities. Culnan and Markus (1987, p. 433) point to mute buttons on speakerphones that allow unobtrusive private remarks that cannot be heard by listeners at another node—a capability not available in unmediated meetings. Fulk and Dutton (1984) also found that additional means of communication were available in teleconferenced meetings by people unobtrusively passing notes under the table outside the view of the camera.

Role of technology. Emphasis on process losses is linked to a 1970s perspective on communication processes as message transmission. Technology was seen to transmit cues to the maximum capacity of the pipe—if inflow exceeded a conduit's capacity, outflow would be reduced relative to inflow. As computing and telecommunications merged in the 1980s, researchers viewed media as capable of structuring interaction in ways other than simply filtering out cues. Culnan and Markus (1987) identify several factors available in computer-based meetings that make them substantively different from, rather than less capable than, face-to-face meetings. One feature is addressability, the ability to address communication selectively to some participants through distribution lists and private messaging features. A second is written memory, storage, and retrieval, which could inhibit opinion change or, as Fulk and Monge (1995) note, could exert control through collective sensemaking. A third is capabilities for controlling level of access and participation. Yet capabilities for structuring interaction need not rely on computing power. Fulk and Dutton (1984) found that voice-activated microphones structured interaction in a videoconference by eliminating talk-overs and favoring individuals with the stronger microphones. Virtually no theoretical development has been conducted to modify channel capacity theories to account for these capabilities of teleconference technologies to structure communication.

Contextualization. Media capacity theories largely seek explanations for meeting processes and effects within the mediated meeting itself. Little theoretical development focused on contextual factors beyond technology and task that could potentially affect meeting processes and effects. Short et al. (1976) briefly mention interpersonal attraction as potentially interacting with technology to affect meeting processes, indicating that evaluation of a medium may be "related to evaluation of people met via that medium" (p. 114). Yet they explain this contextual influence by reference to media factors: (1) people act more formally due to medium constraints and thus are viewed as displaying less warmth, and (2) people exhibit normal warmth cues but the reduced capacity of the medium inhibits transmission of such cues.

Social presence theory suggests several contextual factors that influence medium choice, including physical distance, status levels of participants, degree of acquaintance of participants, access to technology, and security needs. Media richness theory also proposes a list of factors, including physical distance, time pressures, and symbolic meanings of medium (e.g., use of written media symbolizes formality). Contextual effects on meeting processes per se are largely unexplicated in this tradition, however. This acontextual orientation is reflected in a body of research that is heavily based in controlled laboratory experiments, often with student subjects. Thus, one possible explanation for findings is that the artificial settings and contrived tasks may have produced atypical behavior. Culnan and Markus (1987, p. 430) argue that in most organizations people know each other, are familiar with and competent in using technologies they choose from a wide selection, and have a well-known and designated leader of higher status.

The consistent support in the few field studies contrasts markedly with the lack of support from many laboratory studies. Clearly, more investigations of channel capacity premises must be conducted in more naturally modeled contexts, whether these studies are laboratory experiments, field studies, or field experiments.

Rationality. Channel capacity models have been criticized for exhibiting a rationalist bias (Fulk, Schmitz, & Steinfield, 1990; Fulk, Steinfield, Schmitz, & Power, 1987; Lea, 1991). Scholars have argued that the efficiency and effectiveness purported to arise from properly matching task and medium are not the only or even the major goals of participants in interpersonal interaction. Participants have other goals, some of which may conflict with objectively rational choices toward efficiency and effectiveness. This criticism shares a conceptual heritage with Schwartzman's (1986) analysis of meetings as primary forums for playing out political processes and validating social relations rather than efficiently completing tasks.

A related issue is the theoretically ambiguous role of participant *perceptions* of media capabilities relative to "objective" features. Participants' perceptions of media limitations may not fit objective features as described by the theories. For example, pessimistic perceptions of medium constraints could serve as psychological barriers to creative solution seeking, whereas optimistic perceptions may guide a group to seek new and more successful approaches to their tasks. Conversely, optimistic perceptions by participants about the kinds of complex tasks that can be completed in a mediated meeting might produce unrealistic expectations and thus draw groups to attempt infeasible processes.

As documented in critiques, media richness theory is premised on objective media features. Social presence theory is more elusive. Short et al. (1976) stated, "We regard Social Presence as being a quality of the communications medium" (p. 65), which led some researchers to conclude that the concept is not based in perception (e.g., Walther, 1992, p. 55). Yet Short et al. also state, "Thus, when we said earlier that Social Presence is a quality of the medium we were not being strictly accurate. We conceive of Social Presence not as an objective quality of the medium, though it must surely be dependent upon the medium's objective qualities, but as a subjective quality of the medium . . . we believe that it is important to know how the user perceives the medium, what his [sic] feelings are and what his 'mental set' is" (pp. 65-66). The ambiguity of Short et al.'s statements is reflected in the differing measurement approaches across studies (some measured perceptions and some did not). The synthetic nature of the concept also poses challenges. It includes the capacity to transmit "facial expression, direction of looking, posture, dress, and nonverbal cues," and "the weights given to all these factors is determined by the individual" (p. 65). Rafaeli (1988) argues that because "there is no specification of how these qualities are achieved . . . it remains unclear whether social presence is a quality of the medium, channel, content, participants, or communication experience (Heeter, 1985; Rice, 1984). The multidimensional attraction of the 'social presence' construct is also its theoretical downfall" (p. 117).

INPUT-PROCESS-OUTPUT THEORIES

Computer-based meeting support was not widely available when social presence theory was originally formulated. Thus, social presence theorists had little to say about computer-based meeting support, arguing that "this medium is really too new to have been properly assessed" (Short et al., 1976, p. 8).

By the late 1970s, findings were beginning to accumulate on computer-conferencing systems, generally without the benefit of strong theoretical guidance (Johansen et al., 1979, provide a review). The availability of electronic text did not fit straightforwardly into social presence theory, due in part to potential improvements as well as decrements in nonverbal cues. Also, media richness theory originally focused on traditional written and telecommunication media and on computer-based reports, but not computer conferencing. With the increasing popularity of organizational computer-conferencing systems, researchers sought to develop theory that explained the ability of computer-based media not simply to transmit communicative cues but also to support and structure group interaction. Also, with the migration of social presence and media richness premises to asynchronous formats, it became evident that the interacting group had somehow been lost. In response, a new theoretical tradition that privileged the interacting, decision-making group was developed on a base of existing group communication theory.

The dominant model in this tradition is input-process-output (IPO) theory. Several variations of IPO theory exist, but all share several core premises that unite them in a theoretical tradition (e.g., Hiltz & Turoff, 1978; Kiesler, Siegel, & McGuire, 1984; Nunamaker, Dennis, Valacich, Vogel, & George, 1993; Rice, 1984). McGrath and Hollingshead's (1992, 1994) time, interaction, and performance theory integrates media richness theory into an IPO model, and thus is considered a separate IPO theory.

IPO Theory: Unified Formulation

Input-process-output theory proposes that the outcomes of a meeting depend on processes that occur in the meeting, which are significantly affected by input variables including contextual factors that frame the interaction. IPO research generally treats meeting technologies as an input factor (Hiltz & Turoff, 1978; McGrath & Hollingshead, 1992; Nunamaker, Dennis, George, Valacich, & Vogel, 1991), along with group characteristics, task characteristics, and broader contextual factors.

Drawing on Steiner (1972), IPO theory proposes that some aspects of the group's process improve outcomes (process gains) and some aspects impair outcomes (process losses) relative to individual decision makers. Achieving positive group outcomes depends on maximizing process gains while minimizing losses (Collins & Guetzkow, 1964; Hackman & Morris, 1975; Jarboe, 1988; Nunamaker et al., 1993). Process gains include such factors as more objective evaluation, synergy, more information availability, stimulation of individual performance, and learning effects across group members. Process losses occur due to "production blocking" because only one person can communicate at a time, and memory failures because when participants focus on their communication they may miss or forget others' contributions. Process losses include such factors as evaluation apprehension, domination of the group by a single member, coordination problems, information overload, conformance pressure, free riding, and incomplete task analysis (Nunamaker et al., 1993).

IPO and computer conferencing. IPO theory proposes that computer conferencing encourages certain process gains while avoiding other process losses. Because computer conferencing conveys information via written channels, it possesses limited ability to transmit cues about individual identities and relationships. By minimizing communication of non-task-related information, computer conferencing can reduce the importance of "unpredictable" interpersonal processes that often dominate face-to-face meetings (Hiltz & Turoff, 1978; Kiesler et al., 1984). For example, limiting information about individual identities could (1) encourage lower-status members to participate more fully without fear of social retribution, and (2) constrain participants to evaluate each other's arguments based on quality rather than status of source (Hiltz & Turoff, 1978; Kiesler et al., 1984).

Parallel communication in computer conferencing reduces participants' real-time information-processing needs because they can ignore other members' contributions while they input their own ideas. The collective memory feature creates an instantaneous permanent record of information exchanged, and thus reduces process losses related to the failure to attend to and remember information (Hiltz & Turoff, 1978; Kiesler et al., 1984). Collective memory rationalizes the group process by standardizing the idea store available to participants (Hoffer & Valacich, 1992; Nunamaker et al., 1993).

Theoretically, these unique features result in higher-quality and more efficient decisions. However, IPO theorists also recognized that the limited ability of computer conferencing to transmit interpersonal information could contribute to process losses that diminish productivity. Reduction of social context cues could force computer-conferencing groups to spend more time processing information to analyze their tasks and coordinate their efforts. Reduction of social cues could also reduce social inhibitions, resulting in more negative socioemotional behavior and less consensus among group members. Thus, computer-conferencing groups could actually take longer to agree on a decision than face-to-face groups (Hiltz & Turoff, 1978; Kiesler et al., 1984; Rice, 1984). Jessup and George (1997) also propose that anonymity can lead to social loafing (e.g., Williams, Harkins, & Latane, 1981), cognitive loafing (Weldon & Mustari, 1988), and frivolous remarks (Jessup & Connolly, 1991). Shepherd, Briggs, Yen, and Nunamaker (1995) demonstrated that invocation of social comparison processes can dramatically improve GSS group performance. The net effect on meeting outcomes will depend on the relative balance of gains and losses that the group is able to maintain.

IPO and group support systems. One solution to some of these process losses is to offer the group more sophisticated tools for monitoring and controlling their meeting processes so as to maximize gains while minimizing losses. Theoretically, GSSs affect the balance of gains and losses through four mechanisms (Nunamaker et al., 1993):

1. *Process support* includes three mechanisms also available through computer conferencing: anonymity, parallel communication, and group memory.
2. *Process structure* includes techniques and rules that direct communication patterns (e.g., Robert's Rules of Order), timing (e.g., talk queues that determine who communicates next), or content (e.g., support for agenda setting).
3. *Task structure* includes techniques, rules, and models for analyzing task-related information (e.g., Bayesian analysis).
4. *Task support* refers to the communication and information infrastructure that embeds the task, such as access to databases or prior meeting notes.

The basic premise is that group support systems encourage more orderly and rationalized processes by structuring the way that communication flows and information is processed. The rationalizing abilities of group support systems are posited to compensate for process losses experienced with computer-conferenced meetings by helping participants cope with information overload and compensate for losses due to reduced social context cues. Thus, although participation equality should remain high for GSS meetings, there should be less negative socioemotional expression and conflict compared to computer-conferenced meetings (DeSanctis & Gallupe, 1987). The advantages of structural support should be greatest for groups using more sophisticated GSS technologies that provide more assistance in organizing the decision process (Poole, Holmes, & DeSanctis, 1991; Sambamurthy, Poole, & Kelly, 1993).

Time, Interaction, and Performance Theory

The most developed model of input factors is McGrath and Hollingshead's (1992, 1994) time, interaction, and performance (TIP) theory. The theory proposes that communication tasks can be classified into one or more of four types, in increasing order of complexity, and hence information richness requirements.

1. Idea generation tasks involve simple information transmission (e.g., brainstorming). "Evaluative and emotional connotations about message and source are not required and are often considered to be a hindrance" (McGrath & Hollingshead, 1992, p. 92).
2. Intellective tasks require solving problems that have correct answers.
3. Judgment tasks involve no right answer but the group can potentially arrive at a consensual judgment (e.g., jury verdict).
4. Negotiation tasks require resolution of conflicts of interest and "may require the transmission of maximally rich information, including not only 'facts' but also values, attitudes, affective messages, expectations, commitments, and so on" (p. 92).

Drawing on media richness theory, McGrath and Hollingshead (1992, 1994) argue that the more complex the task is, the richer the meeting system employed should be. The model also proposes that matching media to task complexity depends on group development, in that groups need richer media to process the equivocal information that characterizes the early developmental stages. Most IPO theories recognize several phases of group problem solving that may require different support tools. Phase models typically propose a fixed series of phases in group development (e.g., Tuckman, 1965) that translates into fixed series of requirements for technological support (e.g., Kraut, Galegher, & Egido, 1990). TIP theory proposes that temporal aspects of groups are more complex. First, there is not a single series of phases, but rather several sets of phases each relating to one of three functions engaged in by groups: production, member support, and well-being. Second, groups do not necessarily pass through each phase for each function. Third, groups can engage in more than one task or project in a single meeting, and each project may progress at a different rate through each phase and function. Thus, although this perspective retains the linear model of input-process-output as its overall framework, it proposes that interactions among input factors are complex, interrelated, and dynamic.

Empirical Evidence

Socioemotional content of computer-supported meetings. A series of studies of student groups found more negative socioemotional expression within computer-conferencing groups for both low- and high-complexity tasks (Dubrovsky, Kiesler, & Sethna, 1991; Kiesler et al., 1984; Kiesler, Zubrow, Moses, & Geller, 1985; Siegel, Dubrovsky, Kiesler, & McGuire, 1986). This pattern was not consistently evoked, however. For example, Hiltz et al. (1978) found less negative emotion, Straus (1997) found higher rates of supportive communication and Walther (1995) found higher immediacy/affection, and other studies are divided between those showing more emotion of all types (e.g., Walther & Burgoon, 1992) and those showing less (e.g., Hiltz, Johnson, & Turoff, 1986), in no apparent relationship to task complexity. When groups used more structured GSSs rather than simple computer conferencing, the negative emotional effect was absent. Research has reported either no differences in negative affect exhibited (e.g., Poole et al., 1991) or less overall negative affect in GSS versus face-to-face meetings (e.g., Vician, DeSanctis, Poole, & Jackson, 1992).

If negative socioemotional behavior (also known as "flaming") results from limitations in interpersonal information exchange, why doesn't such behavior occur in teleconferencing meetings? Two explanations seem plausi-

ble. First, computer-conference participants may have difficulty monitoring socioemotional levels in the interaction. Audio cues are "leaky" (Ekman & Friesen, 1969), communicating a great deal about the mood and intention of the interaction partner. The loss of audio cues to regulate interaction may make it difficult to both encode and decode messages that transmit the emotional signals through subtle nonverbal behavior. Second, negative socioemotional behavior may be an artifact of the context in which computer-conferencing groups interacted. Theorists attribute flaming to reduced concerns regarding public self-presentation, which are most likely when participants are not identifiable to one another, do not maintain a preexisting relationship, and do not anticipate continuing their relationship with one another (Lea, O'Shea, Fung, & Spears, 1992; Olaniran, 1994; Walther, 1994; Walther, Anderson, & Park, 1994). Findings regarding flaming may be attributable to the fact that computer-conferencing experiments were mostly time limited and involved individuals who had no established (or anticipated) relational histories (Walther, 1992).

Walther (1992) posits two reasons why differential socioemotional expression was probably a coding artifact. First, studies did not code nonverbal behavior for face-to-face groups, where much socioemotional content lies. If nonverbal behavior were coded, "the overall ratio of socioemotional expressions to total messages may be no different in face-to-face than in CMC groups" (p. 63). Second, coding behavior as either task *or* socioemotional "is a notion contrary to axiomatic positions about the simultaneous content and relations functions of any message (Watzlawick, Beavin, & Jackson, 1967)" (p. 64). Walther argues that until both content and relational functions are adequately coded in all messages, one cannot draw conclusions about whether computer-supported meetings are more personal, less, or no different.

Participation. Participation patterns in computer-supported meetings have been heavily studied. Measures have focused primarily on leadership emergence, relative influence of each participant on the ultimate group decision, relative amounts of talk time, relative number of contributions by each participant, and participant perceptions of relative equity of participation. Groups have been studied in both identified and anonymous conditions, and in both field and laboratory. GSS research has studied both computerized support and equivalent paper-based support.

Field studies using either observation or self-report measures consistently document a participation equality effect for GSS groups relative to face-to-face (e.g., Tyran, Dennis, Vogel, & Nunamaker, 1992; Vician et al., 1992; Vogel & Nunamaker, 1989; Vogel, Nunamaker, Martz, Grohowski, & McGoff, 1989). Equality also was observed in some laboratory studies (Easton, 1988; Easton et al., 1990; George, Easton, Nunamaker, & Northcraft, 1990; Lewis, 1987; Nunamaker, Applegate, & Konsynski, 1987; Zigurs, Poole, & DeSanctis, 1988), but others found no differences in participation (Beauclair, 1987; Burke & Chidambaram, 1995; Gallupe, DeSanctis, & Dickson, 1988; McLeod & Liker, 1992; Poole et al., 1991; Poole et al., 1993; Walther, 1995; Watson, DeSanctis, & Poole, 1988). Findings on participation do not vary depending on task complexity. Finally, only one study found *greater* inequality in GSS groups, but this effect disappeared over time (Walther, 1995).

Virtually all computer-conferencing studies were conducted in controlled, laboratory contexts and show the same mixed trend as GSS laboratory studies. Regardless of task complexity, equalization was found in some studies (Dubrovsky et al., 1991; Hiltz, Johnson, & Agle, 1978; Hitz, Johnson, Aronovitch, & Turoff, 1980; Hitz et al., 1986 [high-complexity task only]; Johansen et al., 1979 [three studies]; Kiesler et al., 1984; McGuire, Kiesler, & Siegel, 1987; Siegel et al., 1986; Straus, 1996, 1997), but not in others (Hiltz et al., 1986 [low-complexity task only]; Jarvenpaa, Rao, & Huber, 1988; Walther & Burgoon, 1992; Weisband, Schneider, & Connolly, 1995 [three experiments]). No studies showed a reverse effect for computer support, and the pattern is unrelated to how participation was measured.

Mixed laboratory findings may reflect that status hierarchies emerge over time as groups develop norms and social structure. Laboratory groups may not exhibit a strongly differentiated social structure even face-to-face, for the reasons Culnan and Markus (1987) stated: lack of prior acquaintance, no shared history, no shared organizational context with its attendant status hierarchies, and no formally assigned leader. Lack of participation differences may reflect that face-to-face groups had no status hierarchies that could cue unequal participation. The results may say more about face-to-face laboratory groups as a comparison condition than about computer support. Walther and Burgoon (1992) argue that as groups continue to meet over time and their attention turns toward more interpersonal issues, status hierarchies and norms may become more evident, even in laboratory groups. This logic is consistent with a meta-analysis of 13 GSS and computer-conferencing studies that showed greater equalization for ad hoc than established groups, even for time-limited tasks in the laboratory (Benbasat & Lim, 1993).

Weisband et al. (1995) argue, alternatively, that the failure of many laboratory studies to find an equalization effect may result from the availability of some status cues even in the computer-mediated condition. Their conclusion is consistent with research that found status differentials to persist in computer-mediated meetings (Saunders, Robey, & Vaverek, 1994; Spears & Lea, 1994). It is also consistent with findings that individuals with no knowledge of another person use whatever minimal cue information is available in reaching judgments about others, even irrelevant information.

There is much to be learned about how social stratification develops over time in previously unacquainted laboratory groups participating in mediated meetings. Research should focus on temporal aspects, cue availability, how individuals and groups recognize and process status-related cues, and how this translates to specific group processes and overall participation. In-depth research that monitors key developmental processes for computer-supported groups in relation to their face-to-face counterparts is essential to any determination of medium effects on meeting participation.

Consensus and conflict. A series of time-limited laboratory studies found that computer-conferencing groups were less likely to reach consensus, regardless of task complexity (Hiltz et al., 1978; Hiltz et al., 1980; Hiltz et al., 1986). These results have been interpreted as supporting the IPO proposition that slower rates of information exchange in computer conferencing leaves groups with insufficient time to work through decision-making issues (Hiltz & Turoff, 1978; Rice, 1984). Lea and Spears (1991) found the effects to be stronger for anonymous than identified groups. The effect disappeared totally, for both anonymous and identified groups, when research was conducted in a field setting (Hiltz et al., 1989).

With the addition of GSS structural and process support, the consensus decrement was moderated. Although sometimes less consensus was found (Gallupe et al., 1988; George et al., 1990; Poole et al., 1991), other research found either no differences (Watson et al., 1988) or more consensus for supported groups (Sambamurthy & DeSanctis, 1990; Steeb & Johnston, 1981). Benbasat and Lim's (1993) meta-analysis of eight studies showed a positive moderating effect for level of support: Greater task and process structure was associated with greater consensus. Sambamurthy et al. (1993) reported that consensus was positively related to the extent that groups exhibited procedural insight, ideational connection, critical examination of ideas, and productive use of formal evaluation, each of which was more commonly found in groups with higher-level support tools. These results offer a rationale for the divergent findings on consensus, suggesting that the processes that

evolve in meetings are determinants of whether consensus is likely and that these processes themselves may be influenced by the type of technology.

Poole et al. (1991) found that GSS groups engaged in more open expressions of conflict than unsupported face-to-face groups, while Miranda and Bostrom (1994) found the opposite. A longitudinal study suggested that GSS groups eventually develop more conflict than face-to-face groups (Chidambaram, Bostrom, & Wynne, 1991). Increased conflict may result from the combined effect of a depersonalized communication medium and a structural process that surfaces differences of opinion between members. The ability of groups to reach consensus given these conditions may well depend on how the group chooses to employ its structural support in the service of reaching agreement.

Satisfaction. Early experiments found that mediated meetings were less satisfying for complex tasks such as bargaining, persuasion, and resolving conflicts (Vallee, Johansen, Lipinski, Spangler, & Wilson, 1978, cited in Johansen et al., 1979; Pye & Williams, 1977; Hiltz, Johnson, & Turoff, 1981, cited in Rice, 1984; Vallee, Johansen, Randolph, & Hastings, 1974) and less satisfying overall compared to face-to-face (Hiltz et al., 1980; Hiltz et al., 1986). Satisfaction in computer-conferenced meetings may be dampened by negative socioemotional expression, problems in reaching consensus, and difficulties in completing the task in a timely manner (Hiltz et al., 1989; Straus, 1996). Recent research compared groups on both task type and medium, with mixed results. For low task complexity, Valacich, Paranka, George, and Nunamaker (1993) found no satisfaction differential between face-to-face and computer conferencing, while Straus (1996) found mediated groups to be less satisfied. However, Straus and McGrath (1994) found this difference only for high-complexity tasks, and Dennis and Kinney (1998) found no effect of task complexity on satisfaction. Hollingshead, McGrath, and O'Connor's (1993) results suggest a possible explanation. They found that although in general groups were less satisfied in mediated conditions, the effect was dynamic. During the first week that a group changed from face-to-face to a mediated condition, satisfaction decreased, but for the next two weeks there were no differences in satisfaction across conditions. Since most computer-conferencing studies were conducted in time-limited laboratory contexts, it is not possible to draw conclusions regarding the persistence of any satisfaction differentials.

Theoretically, advanced GSS features help manage process difficulties, countering any satisfaction decrement. Although some experiments have found a satisfaction decrement in GSS meetings compared to face-to-face (Easton et al., 1990; Gallupe et al., 1988; George et al., 1990; Watson et al., 1988), the bulk of studies found no differences relative to face-to-face (Beauclair, 1987; Bui, Sivansankaran, Fijol, & Woodburg, 1987; Easton, 1988; Gallupe & McKeen, 1990; George et al., 1990; Lewis, 1987; Sharda, Barr, & McDonnell, 1988). Some experiments even produced greater satisfaction for GSS meetings (Jessup, Tansik, & Laase, 1988; Steeb & Johnston, 1981). The compensating effects for GSS process structure should also lead to more satisfied GSS groups relative to computer conferencing. Benbasat and Lim (1993) tested this hypothesis in a meta-analysis of 16 laboratory studies. They found that GSS groups with more sophisticated tools were more satisfied with meeting processes and outcomes compared to groups with less sophisticated support, such as computer-conference tools.

In the field, users generally reported high satisfaction with GSS meetings (Dennis, Heminger, Nunamaker, & Vogel, 1990; DeSanctis, Poole, Lewis, & Desharnais, 1992; Martz, Vogel, & Nunamaker, 1992; Nunamaker et al., 1987; Tyran et al., 1992; Vogel et al., 1989). However, these studies did not compare satisfaction in GSS versus the same type of meeting face-to-face, nor were control conditions included. Thus, field research results must be interpreted cautiously.

Efficiency. Computer-conferencing groups are less efficient than face-to face groups for high-complexity tasks (Dennis & Kinney, 1998; Hiltz et al., 1978; Kiesler et al., 1984; McGuire et al., 1987; Siegel et al., 1986; Straus & McGrath, 1994). For low-complexity tasks, most studies found that computer-conferencing groups are less efficient (Dennis & Kinney, 1998; Hightower & Sayeed, 1995; Hiltz et al., 1978; Olaniran, 1994; Straus, 1996), with few exceptions (Gallupe et al., 1992; Johansen et al., 1979 [two field surveys]; Straus & McGrath, 1994). Results support contentions that computer-conferencing groups process information more slowly and experience information overload, particularly for high-complexity tasks. Problems reaching consensus may also contribute to inefficiency.

Field studies typically reported superior performance for GSSs; laboratory results were less consistent. GSS meetings were more efficient in ongoing organizations (Dennis et al., 1990; Martz et al., 1992; Nunamaker et al., 1987; Tyran et al., 1992; Valacich et al., 1993; Vogel & Nunamaker 1989; Vogel et al., 1989) and a few experiments (Bui & Sivansankaran, 1990; Sharda et al., 1988; Steeb & Johnston, 1981). However, some GSS experiments found that decisions take more time (Gallupe & McKeen, 1990; George et al., 1990). Benbasat and Lim's (1993) meta-analysis of eight experiments found that more sophisticated support was associated with greater decision efficiency than less sophisticated support.

Quality. Does more equal participation influence decision quality? Some experiments found higher quality for computer-conferencing groups performing high-complexity tasks (Hiltz et al., 1980; Hiltz et al., 1986). For less-complex tasks, some studies found greater quality for computer-conferencing groups (Gallupe et al., 1992; Jarvenpaa et al., 1988), but others found no difference (Burke & Chidambaram, 1995; Olaniran, 1994; Valacich & Schwenk, 1995). Experiments by Dennis and Kinney (1998) and Straus and McGrath (1994) found no difference in decision quality by task type or medium. An over-time study (Hollingshead et al., 1993) found that decision quality was consistently lower for high-complexity tasks but that decision quality increased over time with low-complexity tasks.

GSSs have been linked to higher decision quality in both field studies (Dennis et al., 1990; Martz et al., 1992; Nunamaker et al., 1987; Tyran et al. 1992; Vogel et al., 1989) and experiments (Bui & Sivansankaran, 1990; Bui et al., 1987; Lam, 1997, for complex tasks; Sharda et al., 1988; Valacich et al., 1993), although some experiments found no differences (Dennis, 1996; Gallupe & McKeen, 1990; George et al., 1990; Lam, 1997, for simple tasks; Steeb & Johnston, 1981). Benbasat and Lim's (1993) meta-analysis of 22 experimental studies found greater decision quality for low-complexity tasks and for more sophisticated support tools. No analyses assessed potential interactions between support level and task complexity.

Summary and Comparison of Premises

Group role in the meeting process. IPO theories model group processes as critical to task accomplishment. First, group characteristics are inputs that contribute to decision processes. Research investigated inputs such as size (Valacich et al., 1995), anonymity (Valacich et al., 1992), and stage of group development (Chidambaram & Bostrom, 1997a, 1997b; Hollingshead et al., 1993). Second, because some group processes may interfere with efficient and effective decision making, systems are designed to guide group processes by reducing "irrelevant" socioemotional content, encouraging broad participa-

tion, supporting consensus building and conflict resolution, and assisting decision analysis.

How effective is computer support in achieving these goals?'

1. Research suggests that system support reduces socioemotional content but also has some unintended effects, such as reducing cues that regulate interaction in computer-conferenced meetings. GSS support tools may resolve this problem.

2. Both types of support may encourage broader participation for established groups. With unacquainted groups, equalization occurs in some supported groups and not in others, although system support does not make participation *more* unequal compared to face-to-face.

3. Consensus can be impaired in computer conferencing, although GSS support moderates this effect somewhat. Conflict has not been extensively studied, but some groups experience more conflict and some less in GSS conditions.

4. Decision efficiency is not improved in computer-conferenced meetings, and some groups take considerable time to reach a decision. GSS support moderated this problem in some experiments, but not in others. Field studies consistently report improved efficiency in GSS meetings.

5. Decision quality is higher for low-complexity tasks and for GSS versus computer-conferenced support, consistent with TIP theory.

IPO theories assume that meeting processes can be constrained via technological support that directs groups toward more productive interaction. Groups respond to inputs that include task, technology, and their own characteristics. The failure of some laboratory groups to behave as predicted suggests that they respond to other factors as well or may act in ways inconsistent with technological guides.

Task characteristics. Compared to media capacity premises, IPO theories assume that tasks are more malleable, in that technological support rationalizes tasks. Tasks are also input variables, and TIP theory specifically includes task complexity as a critical contextual factor. TIP theory borrows premises from media capacity theory that tasks have specific inherent richness requirements. Thus, TIP theory proposes an interesting juxtaposition of assumptions regarding task malleability. A valuable future area of research is to assess how task characteristics change over time in relation to both technology use and group processes. If groups are not only responsive but also proactive, they may influence task structure for uncertain but not equivocal tasks.

Perspective on processes. A centerpiece of IPO theory and research is significant process *gains* as well as losses in computer-supported groups, an outcome not envisioned by media capacity theories. Some features that support gains may also support losses. For example, reduced interpersonal cues in anonymous computer conferencing not only support more equal participation but also remove some cues used to regulate interaction, contributing to less orderly and sometimes more negative communication. By focusing on gains in conjunction with losses, IPO theories offer richer views of mediated meeting processes.

Role of technology. Compared to media capacity theories, IPO theories view meeting technologies as more than transmission devices. The role of technological support is to *influence* decision processes, not simply to *carry* them. The findings suggest that different decision processes are found in many computer-supported meetings versus face-to-face groups and that more sophisticated support produces differences even from less supported groups. The mixed findings in laboratory studies, however, pose an important puzzle which structuration theory, discussed next, attempts to resolve.

Contextualization. IPO theories model several types of contextual factors as inputs: technological support, group attributes, task characteristics, member characteristics, and larger context. Research has focused primarily on type of support, task complexity, group size, anonymity, and presence or absence of a facilitator. Less attention has been paid to characteristics of the larger institutional context. IPO research shares with media capacity findings: (1) the heavy basis in laboratory contexts, and (2) markedly greater support for the theories from the relatively few field investigations. Even field studies, however, have not systematically measured or accounted for the kinds of organizational context factors that Culnan and Markus (1987) claim are critical to understanding meeting processes in ongoing organizations. Jessup and George (1997) note that the difficulties in understanding subject motivation in the laboratory, which approximates some real settings, argues for much greater attention to context in uncontrolled field settings.

Rationality. IPO theories posit "objective" rationality (Simon, 1957). First, meeting tools rationalize decision processes. Second, rationalization is designed to improve objectively measured group efficiency and effectiveness, regardless of the subjective goals participants hold. Third, the tools are posited to exert consistent effects on groups that have the same input factors. TIP theory adds the rationalist assumption that there is an optimal "match" between objectively described task characteristics and type of group support required. By retaining the concept of richness from media capacity premises, TIP theory has distinguished itself from other IPO theories regarding the critical assumption of an ideal task-media fit. Clapper and Prasad (1993) argue that the overemphasis on rationality that permeates most GSS research in this tradition neglects important political, symbolic, and interpersonal aspects of communication in organizational meetings. They argue for multimethod research that marries study of the rational processes with attempts to assess other dimensions of real-life organizational meetings.

STRUCTURATION THEORIES

Structuration premises have been applied to organizational technologies, including communication media (e.g., Barley, 1986; Orlikowski, 1992; Orlikowski, Yates, Okamura, & Fujimoto, 1995). Two versions have been crafted for mediated meeting technologies: adaptive structuration theory (DeSanctis & Poole, 1994; Poole & DeSanctis, 1990) and self-organizing systems theory (Contractor & Seibold, 1993).

Adaptive Structuration Theory

Adaptive structuration theory (AST) is described as an IPO theory by it proponents (DeSanctis & Poole, 1994; DeSanctis, Poole, Dickson, & Jackson, 1993; Poole & Jackson, 1992), yet its premises are sufficiently different from other IPO models to form a distinct theory. AST "attempts to explain how communication processes mediate and moderate input-output relationships" (Poole & Jackson, 1992, p. 287). Inputs include structural properties of the group support system, tasks, leader direction, and decision techniques. Processes are appropriation of technology structures and decision processes. Outcomes include meeting efficiency, decision quality, group attitudes, and emergent social structures, which feed back to influence processes. Three key features distinguish this theory from traditional IPO theory. First, AST proposes that technologies do not directly affect processes, but rather that processes will vary across groups based on how technology is appropriated during interaction. Second, group structures are emergent outcomes of the process phase, as well as inputs. Third, the process-outcome relationship is mutually causal.

Drawing on structuration theory (Giddens, 1979), AST proposes that GSSs offer groups both structural features and spirit. *Structural features* are specific technical protocols such as anonymity and decision modeling. *Spirit* includes the design metaphor underlying the system (e.g., promotion of democratic decision making), user interface, and training and help functions provided for the system (DeSanctis & Poole, 1994). Groups draw on spirit and structural features to create social structures during interaction ("structures-in-use.") Other sources of social structure include task, organizational environment, and structures that emerge while groups use the technology. *Structuration* is "the process through which groups select, adapt, and develop their own working structures from among those on the GDSS [group decision support system]" (Poole, DeSanctis, Kirsch, & Jackson, 1995, p. 303). Appropriation occurs as groups produce and reproduce their own customized structures and validate them through use.

Groups select not only which technology features to use but also how to use them. "Ironic" rather than "faithful" appropriations occur when groups use them in ways that violate the spirit of the technology. Appropriations are related to groups' internal system, such as style of interaction, experience, and degree of consensus on appropriations. Appropriations, in turn, are influential in structuring decision processes. Thus, groups exert control over use of technology and the new structures that emerge from their use (DeSanctis & Poole, 1994, p. 131). Technological features provide the opportunity, if the group chooses, to rationalize both task and group processes through mechanisms embedded in the system. Alternatively, rationalization can be accomplished by social processes, by modifications to system support options, or not at all. Poole et al. (1995) provide the example of a group that interprets a GSS not as reinforcing rationality but rather as a way to speed up meetings. The participants use the private messaging feature not for offline information sharing but rather to pressure participants to conform to keep the meeting moving.

The move away from technological determinism leads to contingent predictions. When the group sticks to the spirit of the technology and appropriates faithfully, the proposed positive outcomes of traditional IPO theory will likely result (DeSanctis & Poole, 1994). As the studies of paper-based manual systems indicate, the theory also proposes that nontechnological structures of the same type may also produce the proposed effects (Poole, Holmes, Watson, & DeSanctis, 1993). The theory also suggests that although groups vary greatly in how they use GSS technologies, successful groups hold several characteristics in common (DeSanctis et al., 1993; DeSanctis et al., 1992; Poole et al., 1995). First, they understand GSS features deeply. More successful groups comprehend the underlying operations that features are designed to support, rather than just learn "how to use" those features. Thus, such groups take advantage of features that promote more sophisticated thought processes (i.e., problem solving). Second, successful groups interpret the spirit of GSSs as a way to explore meanings and emotions that underlie group processes, rather than simply as a way to organize and record group process. Thus, they take advantage of features that help manage conflict, examine emotions, or reflect on activities. Third, aided by deeper understandings and interpretations, successful groups select appropriate tools by matching GSS structures to structures and procedures in other aspects of the group's work. "Matching" goes beyond fitting technological features to tasks; it refers to the ability to simultaneously redefine tasks to fit technological capabilities, and technological capabilities to fit task requirements.

Self-Organizing Systems Theory

Contractor and Seibold (1993) propose a theory that draws from work by Prigogine (Glansdorff & Prigogine, 1971). Their self-organizing systems theory (SOST) proposes a recursive mathematical model that offers three extensions to AST. First, it proposes conditions for stable appropriation. Second, it specifies boundary conditions for appropriation of a set of norms. Third, it identifies proposed effects of initial conditions on appropriation. Based on results of a simulation, they propose six hypotheses that relate three input variables (prior GSS expertise, level of GSS training, and initial awareness of norms regarding use of GSSs for task communication) to both communication activity and awareness of norms regarding use of GSSs for task communication.

Research Findings for Structuration Theories

Very few empirical studies have tested AST. Instead, most research has examined how different technological structures influence group outcomes and has found that structural support has a more positive impact on group performance than computer-conferencing features (Poole et al., 1993; Watson et al., 1988; Zigurs et al., 1988).

Media perceptions and social processes. Gopal, Bostrom, and Chin (1992) found that attitudes toward GSSs formed before the meeting had significant effects on group process and performance. Contractor, Seibold, and Heller (1996) tested predictions from both media capacity and structuration perspectives. The media capacity hypothesis was that members' perceptions of structures-in-use would be influenced by communication and decision support tools (GSS vs. no support). Results did not support this hypothesis, but did show that use of GSSs initially reduced social influence effects on perceptions of structures-in-use. The results are consistent with Walther and Burgoon's (1992) proposition that media influences on social processes change over time. The structuration hypotheses proposed that (1) interactions among participants would affect participants' perceptions, and (2) the effect would diminish over time. Significant social influences were found with both types of technological support, but the effects tended to stabilize over time rather than decrease. Sambamurthy and Chin (1994) similarly found that group attitudes toward the GSS, which were developed through processes of social influence, influenced decision performance over and beyond the effects of GSS capabilities. Chidambaram (1996) found a similar effect but it appeared only over time, with group outcomes improving even more slowly than group attitudes. These results are consistent with AST and with the social influence perspective, which suggests that media-related perceptions are significantly influenced by one's social network (Fulk, 1993; Fulk et al., 1990; Schmitz & Fulk, 1991) or by the overall collective of users of a collaborative technology (Fulk, Flanagin, Kalman, Ryan, & Monge, 1996).

Appropriation and participation, quality, effectiveness, and satisfaction. Studies of how AST works in dynamic environments of real-life organizations reveal the limitations of generalizing about the ability of GSSs to guide "rational" appropriations in all organizational settings (DeSanctis et al., 1993; DeSanctis et al., 1992; Poole et al., 1995). An experiment by Poole and DeSanctis (1992) suggests that groups who appropriate a GSS in manners that are faithful with the technology's "spirit" achieve more efficient and consensual decisions than groups appropriating technologies in ways inconsistent with the intended spirit. However, one organizational case suggests something quite different (DeSanctis et al., 1993). In this setting, two group leaders consistently violated the democratic spirit of the GSS by strictly controlling members' use of participatory features. In one team, the leader's actions exerted a negative impact on the group's performance, as predicted. In the other team, however, the same actions coincided with a more efficient group decision-making process. The inconsistencies in these findings suggest that ap-

propriations of GSSs influence information processing in very complex ways (DeSanctis et al., 1993).

Wheeler and Valacich (1996) found that three appropriation mediators (facilitation, GSS configuration, and training) did increase faithful use of GSSs and ultimate decision quality. Wheeler, Mennecke, and Scudder's (1993) results were more complex. They proposed that (1) group interaction style moderates appropriation, and (2) when GSS technology restricts groups from "invoking group processes that violate the spirit" (p. 509), appropriation will be more faithful and decisions will be higher quality. Their laboratory research using a highly complex problem showed that groups with low preference for procedural order (LPO) produced better decision quality overall, and best quality but lower satisfaction in the nonrestrictive condition. For groups with high preferences for procedural order (HPO), decision quality and satisfaction did not vary by condition, but participation was greater in the restricted condition. They concluded that restrictiveness could promote more faithful appropriation and more satisfied groups, but lower-quality outcomes. Also, the relatively high restrictiveness in most current GSS technologies "favor HPO communication styles and may be inadequate to support LPO individuals effectively" (p. 520). This conclusion is consistent with George, Dennis, and Nunamaker's (1992) finding of no differences between unrestricted groups and groups whose transitions between meeting phases were controlled by a facilitator.

Summary and Comparison of Premises

Applications of structuration theory to mediated meeting systems developed in part in response to mixed findings on effects of GSSs (DeSanctis & Poole, 1994). At times, these systems produced the effects posited by IPO theories, but at times the opposite or no effects were found. Structuration premises were designed in part to identify the conditions under which positive effects would emerge.

Role of groups and technology. Structuration premises differ from IPO theories most fundamentally on questions of technological determinism and the role of groups (DeSanctis & Poole, 1994). In AST, these two premises are highly interrelated. First, AST proposes that technological effects on decision processes depend on how groups appropriate technology during interaction. Outcomes will vary across meetings to the extent that groups differ in appropriations of GSS features and spirit, as the findings by DeSanctis et al. (1993) illustrate. Second, group structure is not simply an input factor. Group structures-in-use are created and recreated during employment of the technology. Groups play active roles in enabling structures that guide and constrain decision processes. From a structuration perspective, IPO premises are a special case that arises under (a) faithful appropriation, and (b) reproduction of structures that match initial structures or consistent use of stable, institutionalized structures.

Structuration premises were developed specifically for GSSs. Other meeting technologies such as teleconferencing have not come under this theoretical lens, in part because teleconferencing support has typically been viewed as simply a conduit. There are examples, however, of teleconference participants employing features to structure group interaction, such as providing the group leader with a stronger microphone. Voice-activated microphones can be used to influence interaction: By speaking, a person can automatically turn off the microphone of another speaker. These potentially constructive uses of teleconferencing could be investigated from a structuration perspective.

Task characteristics. Structuration theories share two premises with IPO theories regarding task characteristics. First, tasks are input variables. Second, tasks can be rationalized

by use of meeting technology. Structuration premises depart from IPO in assumptions that (1) tasks can also be outputs, and (2) tasks can be altered in ways that do not rationalize them. For example, ironic appropriations of support tools may lead to tasks that are less rather than more structured. Even in successful cases based on faithful appropriations, technology and task are redefined in relation to each other.

Perspective on processes. Structuration premises concern how groups articulate their processes with the structural features and spirit of the technology. The key to such articulation is appropriation. Faithful appropriations are posited to increase process gains and reduce losses in ways predicted by IPO theories. Ironic appropriations are not expected to produce such results. The mixed results for IPO laboratory research could be explained by differences across groups in appropriation. Data about appropriations are not available for most prior GSS research. The contribution of structuration theories can be addressed by future research designed to investigate structuration and appropriations. DeSanctis and Poole (1994) describe the types of data and research designs needed. Appropriations are assessed by examining discourse; it is evident in "sentences, turns of speech, or other specific speech acts" (p. 133) at the microlevel, and should be studied over time. At the institutional level, appropriation is studied through longitudinal observation of organizational discourse about technology. Contractor and Seibold (1993, p. 536) also argue that AST research must be more precise regarding the *forms* and *dynamics* of production and reproduction related to faithful versus ironic appropriations and must "identify the boundary conditions under which these dynamics reflect gradual or major shifts in the structures." They also argue that although AST acknowledges the potential for ironic appropriations and unintended consequences, the main hypotheses focus on faithful appropriations and intended consequences.

Contractor and Seibold's (1993) formulation of SOST is designed, in part, to respond to this limitation in AST theory. George and Jessup (1997) also note that little research has been conducted on longer-term appropriation of meeting support tools into group processes, including which GSS tools are used for what purposes, and how appropriation of a tool emerges over time. If Chidambaram and Bostrom's (1997a) contention is correct that groups are more capable of effectively appropriating a GSS as they learn to use it and become more comfortable with it, over-time research to track processes is particularly critical. They suggest protocol analysis of audio- and videotapes, focusing on how naive versus experienced groups interact with technology and respond to alternative features.

Contextualization. Context is critical to the concept of appropriation, since it offers not only factors to appropriate but also influences on the appropriation process itself. Future research and conceptual development should target explanatory and predictive environmental variables for faithful versus ironic appropriations, such as group characteristics, level of training or experience, institutional environment, group history, time constraints, and decision type. Contextual influences on GSS success can be identified by research that attempts to explain how and when such attitudes are developed, and how they influence faithful versus ironic appropriation. AST's value will be enhanced when it offers testable contingent predictions about faithful appropriations.

An emerging area of context research focuses on group development. Chidambaram and Bostrom (1997b) argue that "the same group is capable of making high- or low-quality decisions, taking more or less time to reach consensus, and being satisfied or dissatisfied with its performance based on stage of development" (p. 250). They integrate the concept of entrainment from time-based theories (e.g., McGrath & Hollingshead, 1994) with AST to explain variations in group behavior. Based on an extensive review of group development

models (Chidambaram & Bostrom, 1997a), they present eight propositions on how GSS tools, if effectively appropriated, can assist group development. George and Jessup (1997) review results from 12 studies of computer-supported groups over time. They found that very few studies investigated appropriation, groups rarely had choices of which tools to employ, and groups worked primarily in the constraints of the laboratory. Further, what little attention was paid to group development focused on simple-stage models such as that of Tuckman (1965), rather than the more complex nonsequential models that dominate contemporary group development research (e.g., Gersick, 1989; Poole & Roth, 1989). They propose several research designs that overcome these limitations.

Rationality. Structuration premises retain two of the rationalizing assumptions of IPO theories. First, the structural features and spirit of the technology are designed as rationalizing mechanisms. Second, when appropriation is faithful, this rationalization should lead to greater efficiency and effectiveness. Structuration approaches depart from IPO in that (1) technology is not deterministic, (2) consistent efficiency effects are not expected unless groups employ the tools faithfully, and (3) compared to TIP theory, technologies and processes are not matched to unmalleable tasks. Rather, groups attempt to jointly optimize task, technology, and group structures through appropriation, production, and reproduction processes. Joint optimization is not designed to approach an objective standard for perfect match, but rather to meet each group's individual, subjective definitions of its goals. What is optimal for one group may not be for another, and in this sense rationality is subjective.

FUTURE RESEARCH CHALLENGES

As noted in the beginning of this chapter, meetings grew in importance as mechanisms for coordination and control with the growth of complex organizations in the late 1800s (Yates, 1989). Bureaucratic structures still dominated 25 years ago when research on mediated meetings began, although even then researchers predicted that mediated systems would stimulate new organizational configurations (Short et al., 1976). As the new millennium begins, these predictions are being realized through new technologies and new organizational forms (Fulk & DeSanctis, 1998; Rice & Gattiker, 1997). This section sketches some research issues linked to how meeting systems interact with trends in organizational form. Two technological trends include (1) advancements in integrated multimedia meeting technology, and (2) development of common communication infrastructures, primarily the Internet, that facilitate communication across globally dispersed organizational activities. Fulk and DeSanctis (1998) identify four changes in organizational form: (1) size, scope, and product domain; (2) vertical control; (3) horizontal coordination; and (4) forms of coupling.

Technological Developments in Mediated Meeting Systems

Integrated multimedia technology. Communication and computing continue to converge. Increasing integration of voice, video, and data into interactive systems offers significantly different capabilities than traditional media. First, multimedia systems are complex and multidimensional. Meeting support is increasingly ill fitted to unidimensional descriptions such as social presence or media richness. If voice, video, and data channels each has a different social presence, what social presence do we attribute to complex systems that integrate these features in nonadditive ways? Consider, for example, new systems for conferencing based on avatars (a graphic image designed to represent a person or object). Each user has a handheld "videophone" that displays the movements of the speaker's avatar, which is custom pro-

grammed to display specific behaviors associated with the speaker. How "rich" is avatar conferencing? Also, many other factors are relevant to how meetings are shaped, such as flow (Trevino & Webster, 1992) and reliability (Nass & Mason, 1990).

Second, newer meetings systems are flexible and readily customized to settings. Customization decreases comparability across implementations of a technology and poses important challenges for research design and causal inference regarding technological effects (Culnan & Markus, 1987). Comparability also is a problem with existing research, but it is exacerbated by dramatically increased system flexibility.

Third, systems are increasingly programmable and adaptable by users. System adaptability further reduces claims regarding unidimensional evaluations such as richness, which may vary depending on how systems are programmed and adapted by users. Adaptability to users limits comparability not only across implementations but also across uses of the "same" system over time and across meetings. Technological developments increasingly support assumptions that (1) group choices actively shape the technology as well as group process, and (2) meeting technologies not only construct group processes but also are constructed by them.

Public highways and global dispersion. Software developments support multimedia conferencing via local area networks or the Internet. For example, a program developed at the supercomputing center at the University of Illinois offers frameworks for sharing Java objects over the Internet (downloadable from http://www.ncsa.uiuc.edu/SDG/Software/Habanero). Such sophisticated tools support very complex interactions, such as real-time sharing of detailed 3D images of the human body among dispersed medical personnel, with each node using a low-power personal computer (*Wall Street Journal,* May 30, 1996, p. B-4). Downloadable Internet videoconferencing software such as Microsoft's Netmeeting™ (http://www.microsoft.

com) integrates voice, video, on-screen real-time graphics creation and data sharing. Users need only have an ordinary personal computer, Internet access, an inexpensive microphone ($10), and videocamera for the computer ($200). The availability of multimedia conferencing tools through public information highways has important implications for mediated meeting access, participation, and diffusion. In particular, this common infrastructure can facilitate meetings of multiple dispersed individuals rather than colocated participants situated in designated rooms. Although some research has focused on effects of co-located versus dispersed computer-supported meetings (e.g., Burke & Chidambaram, 1995; Jessup & Tansik, 1991), much more research is needed. Future research should assess how the new capabilities are linked to the conduct of mediated interorganizational meetings.

At this time, Internet conferencing (phone or video) has yet to achieve the critical mass (Markus, 1990) needed to initiate widespread adoption. The ability to connect to any other possible conference participant through a shared platform is a "public good" to which each individual can contribute by a modest investment in local hardware and expenditure of effort to develop the knowledge, skill, and motivation to employ conferencing software. When this public good is achieved in some reasonable measure, there will be increasing opportunities for (1) simultaneous inclusion of many widely dispersed participants through multipoint communication, (2) shared collaborative virtual environments (Schrage, 1989), and (3) increasing support for the emergent teams that characterize new organizational forms (DeSanctis & Poole, 1997).

Corporatewide conferencing tools on internal networks can contribute toward establishing widespread connectivity by permitting ready access to multimedia meetings by individuals at locations worldwide. The trend toward dispersed, global network forms of organization (e.g., Monge & Fulk, 1998; Nohria & Eccles, 1992; Powell, 1990) establishes conditions that require information sharing across far-flung organizational nodes. Much as the universal service aspect of the telephone has facilitated audio conferencing across organizations, Internet tools can facilitate multimedia conferencing with customers, suppliers, and alliance partners. "Virtual" corporations such as Verifone (http://www.verifone.com) already include customers in their internal electronic interactions (Tyabji, 1996). As technological solutions to security issues are developed further for the Internet, cross-organizational participation will be facilitated. The implications of cross-organizational participation in virtual meetings have not received either theoretical or empirical attention. (An exception is Dutton et al., 1982, who studied uses of a publicly available video-conferencing system, AT&T's now defunct Picturephone Meeting Service™, in which some meetings were cross-organizational.)

Existing research is of unknown generalizability to such new mediated meeting conditions. First, research to date lacks a cross-organizational component. Second, most GSS research lacks the dispersed component. Third, virtually all existing findings focus on predefined rather than emergent groups. Significant technological changes pose exciting new opportunities for theory and research on mediated meetings in organizations.

Mediated Meeting Systems and Changing Organizational Forms

Mediated meetings are intimately linked with changes in organizational forms, both as enablers and outcomes of form changes. Research on this linkage offers valuable new directions for organizational communication research.

Organizational size, scope, and product domain. Many researchers have observed the trend toward smaller, leaner, and more geographically dispersed organizational structures (Davidow & Malone, 1992; Heckscher, 1994; Heydebrand, 1989). Organizations redesign to create more integrated work processes and greater focus on the organization's core competencies, usually resulting in personnel reductions. Organizations can also reduce the scope of their production by changing their "value chain" or the integrated activities that produce a service or product (Fulk & DeSanctis, 1998).

Trends in meeting technologies accommodate the demands of smaller, more dispersed organizations. Desktop videoconferencing systems (DVSs) facilitate synchronous document and message sharing among multiple globally dispersed sites. Use of dispersed multimedia systems poses questions about how groups actively manage technology and group process to negotiate membership in meetings where perceptions of "who is participating" are variable. When meetings take place between fixed points such as two videoconferencing rooms, active participation in the meeting occurs between those members who are specifically invited, and who have a designated (and visible) "seat" equipped with support technology for communicating with all other participants. In contrast, dispersed systems such as DVSs can accommodate spontaneous meetings across multiple geographic sites (Alvear & Yaari, 1997, Brittan, 1995; Karpinski, 1997). For example, a study by Fish, Kraut, Root, and Rice (1993) examined how student interns and their engineering mentors used DVS technology to initiate spontaneous interactions. Although the technology was designed to support equal participation in spontaneous meetings, some individuals actively reduced participation by disconnecting from the system, while other individuals increased their participation by keeping their connections constantly open. Also, interns spontaneously contacted mentors more frequently than vice versa, suggesting that the organizational status structure was reproduced in the new technology (Fish et. al., 1993), rather than equalization.

In the area of product domain, movement to an information- and service-based economy is linked to a shift from creating products to manipulating information and symbols (Fulk & DeSanctis, 1998). An information product is difficult to distinguish from the process that created it (Heydebrand, 1989), especially when creation occurs online, rather than in physical space. The low cost and accessibility of the Internet overcome physical barriers to inclusion and thus allow for more diverse participation in virtual workspaces (Fulk & DeSanctis, 1998; Nohria & Berkley, 1994).

Virtual space may represent a "neutral" territory in which individuals from different organizational sites can meet with an equal degree of comfort. Yet ownership of the information product created within this neutral virtual space may not be clearly defined (Kumar & van Dissel, 1996). It could be jointly owned (Sudweeks & Rafaeli, 1996) or individual contributions and creations might be separately owned by their originators (Curtis, Dixon, Frederick, & Nichols, 1995; Curtis & Nichols, 1994). Ownership norms may depend on expectations that participants bring with them to virtual space, as well as the norms they produce and reproduce within the evolving culture of their online meetings.

Vertical control. New organizational forms are characterized by replacement of traditional vertical structures of control with flatter or more decentralized structures (Heckscher, 1994; Heydebrand, 1989). Organizations that redesign by reducing middle management and administrative support staff may decrease vertical control by delegating greater decision-making power to all members. For example, in a postbureaucratic structure (Heckscher, 1994) formal authority relationships are replaced with organization-wide dialogue and consensual decision making in which groups are guided by the organization's shared mission, as well as members' ability to personally influence one another. However, decentralization does not always reduce vertical control, since organizations can just as easily replace hierarchical control systems with information technology systems that perform the same functions (Zuboff, 1988), or can use technology to increase monitoring and control (Garson, 1988).

Future research should consider how technological features of mediated meetings are designed, implemented, and actively appropriated to enhance or resist the organization's structural control patterns. For example, Clement (1996) found that users of DVS in four research groups displayed relatively little concern that the technology would be employed as a centralized monitoring and control tool. Clement argued that this lack of resistance was attributable to users' control over the design of the technology, as well as the limited vertical control structures within the research-based organizations. Clement also proposed that as DVS use spreads to more hierarchical organizations, members will actively resist the technology as a perceived tool for centralized control (see also Dutton, 1998, for a discussion of the organizational control implications of new information and communication technologies in new organizational forms).

If new organizational forms rely on decision-making process based on personal influence, rather than formal authority (Heckscher, 1994), how do participants select particular features of multimedia systems to support these processes? TIP theory (McGrath & Hollingshead, 1994) proposes that in the early stages, decision-making groups should choose a richer channel (e.g., video) to undertake high-level information-processing tasks (such as judgment and negotiation tasks) that involve personal influence. How do groups make such choices when multiple channels are embedded in the technology in complex ways? Also, do participants follow media capacity premises to communicate more often through channels with the highest information-processing ability, or do they strategically appropriate channels to their personal influence goals (Markus, 1994)? For example, some participants could choose to use only audio-video channels to leverage their persuasive-speaking skills, whereas other members could use textual channels to support their persuasive-writing skills. How does the balance of channel use in multimedia systems change over time as groups develop norms and experience in meeting together? Future research should explore how meeting participants' personal influence goals affect the way that they use different media channels in multimedia meetings in new organizational forms.

Horizontal coordination. New organizational forms involve individuals from different expertise areas coordinating tasks, often in cross-functional teams (Fulk & DeSanctis, 1998). One example is concurrent engineering or parallel processing. Different stakeholders come together to work on different parts of a redesigned product simultaneously, instead of waiting for each functional unit (e.g., research and design) to finish its part and pass the design off to another unit (e.g., manufacturing) (Cushman & King, 1994; Davidow & Malone, 1992). Sometimes task coordination occurs between members who are geographically dispersed, such as in virtual organizations (Nohria & Berkley, 1994).

Horizontal coordination is supported by multimedia collaboration, particularly the ability for dispersed participants to manipulate shared documents, graphics, or simulated objects. Evidence suggests that work groups value information about their shared physical context (Brittan, 1995; Fish et al., 1993; Whittaker, 1995). In one study, individuals participating in cooperative design more frequently viewed images of the object being designed than images of their partner (Gaver, Sellen, Heath, & Luff, cited in Whittaker, 1995). However, researchers have yet to test how such channel choices affect the efficiency with which groups undertake tasks. Media richness theory (Daft & Lengel, 1984) would suggest that object sharing increases individuals' information-processing abilities, allowing them to undertake more uncertain work tasks. However, one interpretation of TIP theory (McGrath & Hollingshead, 1992) might be that focusing on object-sharing channels rather than channels that provide more interpersonal cues (e.g., voice and facial expressions) may delay the group development process. Future research based on the two perspectives should thus explore how multimedia choices such as object sharing influence the efficiency with which cross-functional teams complete their tasks.

Forms of connection. Changes in form occur with new types of connections or interorganizational couplings (Fulk & DeSanctis, 1998). One type involves organizations altering value chain connections by using information technology to support new forms of relationships with buyers and suppliers. Another type is the strategic alliance, whereby diverse firms form mutually beneficial associations, such as the complex interconnections between banking, travel, insurance, and telecommunications industries to offer such deals as frequent flier miles in exchange for other organizations' services (Ring & Van de Ven, 1994). Two other types are the federation, an organization that allows noncompetitive firms to pursue collective goals (Fulk, Flanagin, Kalman, Monge & Ryan, 1996), and the network organization (Monge & Fulk, 1998; Nohria & Eccles, 1992).

Kumar and van Dissel (1996) argue that dispersed multimedia systems are the appropriate mechanism for coordinating network organizations, because they allow members from globally dispersed organizations to meet frequently to exchange information and make decisions based on their evolving needs. However, they note that the task of electronically connecting different organizational sites is far simpler than the task of facilitating collaborative communication between members from vastly different organizational and national environments.

Future research from the IPO perspective should examine the impact of multimedia channel choices on the conflict management process in interorganizational meetings. For example, the task-media fit hypothesis proposes that conflict management tasks such as bargaining and negotiation will be performed more efficiently through richer communication channels, such as audio-/video-confer-

encing channels (Hollingshead & McGrath, 1995). However, some research suggests that even audio/video channels are insufficient to convey the subtle nonverbal cues and rapid conversational turn-taking that accompanies face-to-face negotiations (Dutton et al., 1982; Whittaker, 1995). Research from the IPO perspective suggests that GSS decision support tools can actually enhance conflict management in mediated meetings (Chidambaram et al., 1991; Miranda & Bostrom, 1994).

The choice of a particular mediated meeting system may itself become a source of sociopolitical conflict among participants of different national cultures, since Western assumptions about communication are embedded into the design of most mediated meeting systems. For example, the tendency for meeting systems to reduce contextual cues is more compatible with the American communication style, which relies relatively little on contextual cues, and therefore tends toward more direct (assertive, confrontational, explicit) conversation than many other cultures (Ma, 1996). The American value of individualism is also incorporated into GSS decision tools that rely on majority vote, rather than the consensual decision making practiced in more collectivist cultures (Ho, Raman, & Watson, 1989; Ishi, 1993). Serida-Nishimura (1994) adds that low power distance is implied by the focus on equal participation rather than status-based contributions, decision making is directed toward a rational rather than political process, and the focus on stages and sequences implies monochronic rather than polychronic approaches toward time. One consequence of these specific cultural assumptions embedded in meeting technologies may be that organizational members from other cultures will avoid communicating through mediated channels, particularly text-only channels. However, one study involving East Asian students suggests that participants from other cultures may adapt to computer-conferencing systems by adopting a more direct, self-disclosing style of communication than they normally adopt in face-to-face communication with Americans (Ma,

1996). Adaptiveness is also suggested by field research showing that Mexican users were more satisfied and produced more consensus and better-quality decisions in GSS meetings, whereas U.S. users reported no differences in any of these factors between manual and GSS meetings (Mejias, Shepherd, Vogel, & Lazeneo, 1996). Research should investigate how members from different cultural contexts actively structure both the technology and the group process to meet their particular needs.

CONCLUSION

As an embryonic field only a few decades old, the study of mediated meetings has made great strides. It has a solid base of strong theoretical perspectives that are integrated within a rich intellectual heritage of theory and research in organizations, technology, and social psychology. Each of the primary theories includes particular assumptions that shape advancements in theory and research on mediated meetings. These include assumptions about (1) the activeness of group role in the meeting process; (2) the degree to which group task characteristics are fixed or malleable; (3) the centrality of group processes; (4) the role of the technology as connective, constructive, and/or constructed; and (5) the influence of the environmental context. To advance the field, future research must take these differing assumptions into account when trying to synthesize theory and understand conflicting research findings.

Although meetings consume a large proportion of a manager's time (more than 60% by some estimates), mediated meetings are as yet a small proportion of all meetings conducted (as few as 13%; Volkema & Neederman, 1995). Nevertheless, there is every reason to believe that they will become much more prevalent. Advances in technology (e.g., multimedia capabilities and interconnected networks) are making such meeting support much more affordable and accessible at a time when it will be increasingly needed to facilitate the communication needs of new organizational forms (Fulk & DeSanctis, 1998). However, until the field of mediated meeting research can successfully investigate the complex world of real meetings within and between organizations, the potential of mediated meetings cannot be adequately assessed. Research on asynchronous meetings has a strong component of field studies, including studies of communication across organizations (see Rice & Gattiker, 1997). The challenge for synchronous meeting researchers is to expand the existing set of studies to these contexts. Even such field tests are limited, however, since it is difficult to assess how well results from firms that adopt mediated meetings early on will generalize to firms that adopt technologies once they become institutionalized. Leading firms often look quite different from firms later on the diffusion curve (Rogers, 1995). Nevertheless, with such a jump start on researching an innovation that is only beginning to take off, the field of mediated meetings is poised to provide even more valuable contributions to knowledge.

REFERENCES

Albertson, L. A. (1973). *The effectiveness of communication across media.* Melbourne: Telecom Australia Research Laboratories.

Albertson, L. A. (1977). Telecommunications as a travel substitute: Some psychological, organizational, and social aspects. *Journal of Communication, 27,* 32-43.

Alvear, J., & Yaari, R. (1997, February). You've got a video call . . . on your desktop. *Netguide,* pp. 149-150.

Argyle, M. (1957). Social pressure in public and private situations. *Journal of Abnormal Social Psychology, 54,* 172-175.

Badaracco, J. L., Jr. (1991). *The knowledge link: How firms compete through strategic alliances.* Boston: Harvard Business School Press.

Bales, R. F. (1955). How people interact in conferences. *Scientific American, 192*(3), 31-35.

Barefoot, J. C., & Strickland, L. H. (1982). Conflict and dominance in television-mediated interactions. *Human Relations, 35,* 559-566.

Barley, S. R. (1986). Technology as an occasion for structuring: Evidence from observations of CT scanners and the social ordering of radiology departments. *Administrative Science Quarterly, 31,* 78-108.

Beauclair, R. (1987). *An experimental study of the effects of group decision support system process support application on small group decision making.* Unpublished doctoral dissertation, University of Indiana, Bloomington.

Benbasat, I., DeSanctis, G., & Nault, B. (1993). Empirical research in managerial support systems: A review and assessment. In C. W. Holsapple & A. Whinston (Eds.), *Recent developments in decision support systems* (pp. 383-437). New York: Springer-Verlag.

Benbasat, I., & Lim, L. (1993). The effects of group, task, context, and technology variables on the usefulness of group support systems: A meta-analysis of experimental studies. *Small Group Research, 24,* 430-462.

Beniger, J. R. (1986). *The control revolution: Technological and economic origins of the information society.* Cambridge, MA: Harvard University Press.

Beniger, J. R. (1990). Conceptualizing information technology as organization, and vice versa. In J. Fulk & C. W. Steinfield (Eds.), *Organizations and communication technology* (pp. 29-45). Newbury Park, CA: Sage.

Biggart, N. W., & Hamilton, G. G. (1992). On the limits of a firm-based theory to explain business networks: The Western bias of neoclassical economics. In N. Nohria & R. Eccles (Eds.), *Networks and organizations: Structure, form and action* (pp. 471-490). Boston: Harvard Business School Press.

Brittan, D. (1995). Being there: The promise of multimedia communications. In R. M. Baecker (Ed.), *Groupware and computer-supported work* (pp. 57-65). San Mateo, CA: Morgan Kaufmann.

Bui, T., & Sivansankaran, T. R. (1990). Relation between GDSS use and group task complexity. In J. F. Nunamaker, Jr. (Ed.), *Proceedings of the Twenty-Third Hawaii International Conference on Systems Sciences* (Vol. 3, pp. 69-78). Los Alamitos, CA: IEEE Computer Society Press.

Bui, T., Sivansankaran, T., Fijol, Y., & Woodburg, M. (1987). Identifying organizational opportunities for GDSS use: Some experimental evidence. *Transactions of the Seventh Conference on Decision Support Systems* (pp. 68-75). San Francisco.

Burke, K., & Chidambaram, L. (1995). Developmental differences between distributed and face-to-face groups in electronically supported meeting environments: An exploratory investigation. *Group Decision and Negotiation, 4,* 213-233.

Champness, B. (1972). *The perceived adequacy of four communications systems for a variety of tasks* (Communication Studies Group Report No. E/72245/CH). London: University College.

Champness, B., & Davies, M. (1971). *The Maier pilot experiment* (Communication Studies Group Report No. E/71030/CH). London: University College.

Chidambaram, L. (1996). Relational development in computer-supported groups. *MIS Quarterly, 20,* 143-165.

Chidambaram, L., & Bostrom, R. P. (1997a). Group development I: A review and synthesis of development models. *Group Decision and Negotiation, 6,* 159-187.

Chidambaram, L., & Bostrom, R. P. (1997b). Group development II: Implications for GSS research and practice. *Group Decision and Negotiation, 6,* 231-254.

Chidambaram, L., Bostrom, R. P., & Wynne, B. E. (1991). The impact of GDSS on group development. *Journal of Management Information Systems, 7,* 325.

Clapper, D., & Prasad, P. (1993). The rationalization of the organizational meeting: Implications of group support systems for power, symbolism and face-work. *Proceedings of the Fourteenth International Conference on Information Systems* (pp. 321-329).

Clement, A. (1996). Considering privacy in the development of multi-media communications. In R. Kling (Ed.), *Computerization and controversy: Value conflicts & social choices* (2nd ed., pp. 907-931). San Diego, CA: Academic Press.

Collins, B. E., & Guetzkow, H. (1964). *A social psychology of group processes for decision-making.* New York: John Wiley.

Connolly, T., Jessup, L. M., & Valacich, J. S. (1990). Effects of anonymity and evaluative tone on idea generation in computer-mediated groups. *Management Science, 36,* 689-703.

Contractor, N. S., & Seibold, D. R. (1993). Theoretical frameworks for the study of structuring processes in group decision support systems: Adaptive structuration theory and self-organizing systems theory. *Human Communication Research, 19,* 528-563.

Contractor, N. S., Seibold, D. R., & Heller, M. A. (1996). Interactional influence in the structuring of media use in groups: Influence on members' perceptions of GDSS use. *Human Communication Research, 22,* 451-481.

Culnan, M. J., & Markus, M. L. (1987). Information technologies. In F. M. Jablin, L. L. Putnam, K. H. Roberts, & L. W. Porter (Eds.), *Handbook of organizational communication: An interdisciplinary perspective* (pp. 420-443). Newbury Park, CA: Sage.

Curtis, P., & Nichols, D. A. (1994, January). MUDs grow up: Social virtual reality in the real world. *Proceedings of the 1994 IEEE Computer Conference* [Online]. Available: ftp://parcftp.xerox.com/pub/MOO/papers/MUDsGrowUp.

Curtis, P., Dixon, M., Frederick, R., & Nichols, D. A. (1995). The Jupiter audio/video architecture: Secure multimedia in network places. *Proceedings of the*

1995 ACM International Conference on Multimedia [Online]. Available: ftp://parcftp.xerox.com/pub/MOO/papers/JupiterAV.ps.

Cushman, D. P., & King, S. S. (1994). High speed management: A revolution in organizational communication in the 1990's. In S. S. King & D. P. Cushman (Eds.), *High speed management and organizational communication in the 1990's: A reader* (pp. 5-41). Albany: State University of New York Press.

Daft, R. L., & Lengel, R. K. (1984). Information richness: A new approach to managerial information processing and organizational design. In L. L. Cummings & B. M. Staw (Eds.), *Research in organizational behavior* (Vol. 6, pp. 191-234). Greenwich, CT: JAI.

Daft, R. L., & Lengel, R. K. (1986). Organizational information requirements, media richness and structural design. *Management Science, 32*, 554-571.

Daft, R. L., & Weick, K. E. (1984). Toward a model of organizations as interpretation systems. *Academy of Management Review, 9*, 284-295.

Davidow, W. H., & Malone, M. S. (1992). *The virtual corporation: Structuring and revitalizing the corporation of the 21st century.* New York: HarperBusiness.

Davies, M. (1971). *Cooperative problem solving* (Communication Studies Group Report No. E/71159/DV). London: University College.

Dennis, A. R. (1996). Information exchange and use in small group decision-making. *Small Group Research, 27*, 532-550.

Dennis, A. R., & Gallupe, R. B. (1992). A history of group support systems empirical research: Lesson learned and future directions. In L. M. Jessup & J. S. Valacich (Eds.), *Group support systems: New perspectives* (pp. 59-77). New York: Macmillan.

Dennis, A. R., George, J. F., Jessup, L. M., Nunamaker, J. F., & Vogel, D. R. (1988). Information technology to support electronic meetings. *MIS Quarterly, 12*, 591-624.

Dennis, A. R., Haley, B. J., & Vandenberg, R. J. (1996). A meta-analysis of effectiveness, efficiency, and participant satisfaction in group support systems research. *Proceedings of the International Conference on Information Systems* (pp. 851-853). Cleveland, OH.

Dennis, A. R., Heminger, A. R., Nunamaker, J. F., & Vogel, D. R. (1990). Bringing automated support to large groups: The Burr-Brown experience. *Information & Management, 18*(3), 111-121.

Dennis, A. R., & Kinney, S. T. (1998). Testing media richness theory in the new media: The effects of cues, feedback, and task equivocality. *Information Systems Research, 9*(3), 256-274.

Dennis, A. R., Nunamaker, J. F., & Vogel, D. R. (1991). A comparison of laboratory and field research in the study of electronic meeting systems. *Journal of Management Information Systems, 7*, 107-135.

Dennis, A. R., & Valacich, J. S. (1993). Computer brainstorms: More heads are better than one. *Journal of Applied Psychology, 78*, 531-537.

Dennis, A. R., & Valacich, J. S. (1994). Group, subgroup, and nominal group idea generation: New rules for new media. *Journal of Management, 20*, 723-736.

DeSanctis, G. (1992). Shifting foundations in group support system research. In L. M. Jessup & J. S. Valacich (Eds.), *Group support systems: New perspectives* (pp. 97-111). New York: Macmillan.

DeSanctis, G., & Gallupe, R. B. (1987). A foundation for the study of group support systems. *Management Science, 33*, 589-609.

DeSanctis, G., & Poole, M. S. (1994). Capturing the complexity in advanced technology use: Adaptive structuration theory. *Organization Science, 5*, 121-147.

DeSanctis, G., & Poole, M. S. (1997). Transitions in teamwork in new organizational forms. *Advances in Group Processes, 14*, 157-176.

DeSanctis, G., Poole, M. S., Dickson, G. W., & Jackson, B. M. (1993). Interpretive analysis of team use of group technologies. *Journal of Organizational Computing, 3*, 1-29.

DeSanctis, G., Poole, M. S., Lewis, H., & Desharnais, G. (1992). Using computing in quality team meetings: Some initial observations from the IRS-Minnesota project. *Journal of Management Information Systems, 8*, 7-26.

Douglas, A. (1957). The peaceful settlement of industrial and intergroup disputes. *Journal of Conflict Resolution, 1*, 69-81.

Dutton, W. H. (1998). The virtual organization: Tele-access in business and industry. In G. DeSanctis & J. Fulk (Eds.), *Shaping organizational form: Communication, connection, community.* Thousand Oaks, CA: Sage.

Dutton, W. H., Fulk, J., & Steinfield, C. (1982, September). Utilization of video conferencing. *Telecommunications Policy, 6*, 164-178.

Dubrovsky, V. J., Kiesler, S., & Sethna, B. N. (1991). The equalization phenomenon: Status effects in computer-mediated and face-to-face decision-making groups. *Human-Computer Interaction, 6*, 119-146.

Easton, G. (1988). *An experimental investigation of automated versus manual support for stakeholder identification and assumption surfacing in small groups.* Unpublished doctoral dissertation, University of Arizona, Tucson.

Easton, G. K., George, J. F., Nunamaker, J. F., & Pendergast, M. F. (1990). Using two different electronic meeting system tools for the same task: An experimental comparison. *Journal of Management Information Systems, 7*, 85-100.

Ekman, P., & Friesen, W. V. (1969). Nonverbal leakage and clues to deception. *Psychiatry, 32*, 88-106.

Fish, R., Kraut, R., Root, R., & Rice, R. E. (1993). Video as a technology for informal communication. *Communications of the ACM, 36*(1), 48-61.

Fiske, S. T., & Taylor, S. E. (1991). *Social cognition*. New York: McGraw-Hill.

Fowler, G. D., & Wackerbarth, M. E. (1980). Audio teleconferencing versus face-to-face conferencing: A synthesis of the literature. *Western Journal of Speech Communication, 44*, 236-252.

Fulk, J. (1993). Social construction of communication technology. *Academy of Management Journal, 36*, 921-950.

Fulk, J., & DeSanctis, G. (1998). Articulation of communication technology and organizational form. In G. DeSanctis & J. Fulk (Eds.), *Shaping organizational form: Communication, connection, community*. Thousand Oaks, CA: Sage.

Fulk, J., & Dutton, W. (1984). Videoconferencing as an organizational information system: Assessing the role of electronic meetings. *Systems, Objectives, Solutions, 4*, 104-118.

Fulk, J., Flanagin, A., Kalman, M., Ryan, T., & Monge, P. (1996). Connective and communal public goods in interactive communication systems. *Communication Theory, 6*, 60-87.

Fulk, J., & Monge, P. R. (1995). *Control through computer-supported meetings*. Unpublished working paper, Annenberg School for Communication, University of Southern California, Los Angeles.

Fulk, J., Schmitz, J., & Steinfield, C. (1990). A social influence model for technology use. In J. Fulk & C. W. Steinfield (Eds.), *Organizations and communication technology* (pp. 117-140). Newbury Park, CA: Sage.

Fulk, J., Steinfield, C. W., Schmitz, J. A., & Power, J. G. (1987). A social information processing model of media use in organizations. *Communication Research, 14*, 529-552.

Fulk, R. D. (1992). *A history of Old English meter*. Philadelphia: University of Pennsylvania Press.

Gallupe, R. B., DeSanctis, G., & Dickson, G. W. (1988). Computer-based support for group problem-finding: An experimental investigation. *MIS Quarterly, 12*, 277-296.

Gallupe, R. B., Dennis, A. R., Cooper, W. H., Valacich, J. S., Bastianutti, L. M., & Nunamaker, J. F. (1992). Electronic brainstorming and group size. *Academy of Management Journal, 35*, 350-369.

Gallupe, R. B., & McKeen, J. D. (1990). Beyond computer-mediated communication: An experimental study into the use of a group decision support system for face-to-face versus remote meetings. *Information & Management, 18*, 113.

Garson, B. (1988). *The electronic sweatshop: How computers are transforming the office of the future into the factory of the past*. New York: Simon & Schuster.

George, J. F., Dennis, A. R., & Nunamaker, J. F. (1992). An experimental investigation of facilitation in an EMS decision room. *Group Decision and Negotiation, 1*(1), 57-70.

George, J. F., Easton, G. K., Nunamaker, J. F., & Northcraft, G. B. (1990). A study of collaborative group work with and without computer based support. *Information Systems Research, 1*, 394-415.

George, J. F., & Jessup, L. M. (1997). Groups over time: What are we really studying? *International Journal of Human Computer Studies, 47*(3), 497-511.

Gersick, C. (1989). Marking time: Predictable transitions in task groups. *Academy of Management Journal, 32*, 274-309.

Giddens, A. (1979). *Central problems in social theory*. Cambridge, UK: Cambridge University Press.

Glansdorff, P., & Prigogine, I. (1971). *Thermodynamic study of structure, stability and fluctuations*. New York: John Wiley.

Gopal, A., Bostrom, R. P., & Chin, W. W. (1992). Applying adaptive structuration theory to investigate the process of group support systems use. *Journal of Management and Information Systems, 9*, 45-69.

Gopal, A., & Pollard, C. E. (1996). Differences between workstation and keypad GSS facilitators. *Group Decision and Negotiation, 5*, 73-91.

Griffith, T. L., & Northcraft, G. B. (1994). Distinguishing between the forest and the trees: Media, features, and methodology in electronic communication research. *Organization Science, 5*, 272-285.

Hackman, J. R., & Morris, C. G. (1975). Group tasks, group interaction process, and group performance effectiveness: A review and proposed integration. In L. Berkowitz (Ed.), *Advances in experimental social psychology* (Vol. 8, pp. 47-99). New York: Academic Press.

Harmon, J., Schneer, J., & Hoffman, L. R. (1995). Electronic meetings and established decision groups: Audioconferencing effects on performance and structural stability. *Organizational Behavior and Human Decision Processes, 61*, 138-147.

Heckscher, C. (1994). Defining the postbureaucratic type. In C. Heckscher & A. Donnellon (Eds.), *The postbureaucratic organization: New perspectives on organizational change* (pp. 14-62). Thousand Oaks, CA: Sage.

Heeter, C. (1985). *Perspectives for the development of research on media systems*. Unpublished doctoral dissertation, Michigan State University.

Heydebrand, W. (1989). New organizational forms. *Work and Occupations, 16*, 323-357.

Hightower, R., & Sayeed, L. (1995). The impact of computer-mediated communication systems on biased group discussion. *Computers in Human Behavior, 11*(1), 33-44.

Hiltz, S. R., Johnson, K., & Agle, G. (1978). *Replicating Bales' problem-solving experiments on a computerized conferencing system* (Research Report No. 8). Newark: New Jersey Institute of Technology, Computerized Conferencing and Communications Center.

Hiltz, S. R., Johnson, K., Aronovitch, C., & Turoff, M. (1980). *Face-to-face vs. computerized conferences: A controlled experiment* (Research Report No. 12). Newark: New Jersey Institute of Technology, Computerized Conferencing and Communications Center.

Hiltz, S. R., Johnson, K., & Turoff, M. (1986). Experiments in group decision making: Communication process and outcome in face-to-face versus computerized conferences. *Human Communication Research, 13,* 225-252.

Hiltz, S. R., Johnson, K., & Turoff, M. (1991). Group decision support: The effects of designated human leaders and statistical feedback in computerized conferences. *Journal of Management Information Systems, 8,* 81-108.

Hiltz, S. R., & Turoff, M. (1978). *The network nation: Human communication via computer.* Reading, MA: Addison-Wesley.

Hiltz, S. R., Turoff, M., & Johnson, K. (1989). Experiments in group decision making, 3: Disinhibition, deindividuation, and group process in pen name and real name computer conferences. *Decision Support Systems, 5,* 217-232.

Ho, T. H., Raman, K. S., & Watson, R. T. (1989). Group decision support systems: The cultural factor. In J. I. Gross, J. C. Henderson, & B. R. Konsynski (Eds.), *Proceedings of the Tenth International Conference of Information Systems* (pp. 119-129). Baltimore: ACM.

Hoffer, J. A., & Valacich, J. S. (1992). Group memory in group support systems: A foundation for design. In L. M. Jessup & J. S. Valacich (Eds.), *Group support systems: New perspectives* (pp. 214-229). New York: Macmillan.

Hollingshead, A. B., & McGrath, J. E. (1995). The whole is less than the sum of its parts: A critical review of research on computer-assisted groups. In R. A. Guzzo & E. Salas (Eds.), *Team decision and team performance in organizations* (pp. 46-78). San Francisco: Jossey-Bass.

Hollingshead, A. B., McGrath, J. E., & O'Connor, K. M. (1993). Group task performance and communication technology: A longitudinal study of computer-mediated versus face-to-face work groups. *Small Group Research, 24,* 307-333.

Ishi, H. (1993). Cross-cultural communication and CSCW. In L. M. Harasim (Ed.), *Global networks: Computers and international communication* (pp. 143-151). Cambridge, MA: MIT Press.

Jarboe, S. (1988). A comparison of input-output, process-output, and input-process-output models of small group problem-solving effectiveness. *Communication Monographs, 55,* 121-142.

Jarvenpaa, S. L., Rao, V. S., & Huber, G. P. (1988). Computer support for meetings of groups working on un-structured problems: A field experiment. *MIS Quarterly, 12,* 645-668.

Jessup, L., & Connolly, T. (1991). *The effects of GSS interaction frequency on group process and outcome.* Working paper, California State University, San Marcos.

Jessup, L. M., Connolly, T., & Tansik, D. A. (1990). Toward a theory of automated group work: The deindividuating effects of anonymity. *Small Group Research, 21,* 333-348.

Jessup, L. M., & George, J. F. (1997). Theoretical and methodological issues in group support systems research: Learning from groups gone awry. *Small Group Research, 28,* 394-413.

Jessup, L. M., & Tansik, D. A. (1991). Decision making in an automated environment: The effects of anonymity and proximity with a group decision support system. *Decision Sciences, 22,* 266-279.

Jessup, L. M., Tansik, D. A., & Laase, T. L. (1988). Group problem solving in an automated environment: The effects of anonymity and proximity on group process and outcome with a group decision support system. *Proceedings of the Forty-Eighth Annual Meeting of the Academy of Management* (pp. 237-241).

Jessup, L. M., & Valacich, J. S. (1992). *Group support systems: New perspectives.* New York: Macmillan.

Johansen, R. (1984). *Teleconferencing and beyond.* New York: McGraw-Hill.

Johansen, R. (1988). *Computer support for business teams.* New York: Free Press.

Johansen, R., Vallee, J., & Spangler, K. (1979). *Electronic meetings: Technical alternatives and social choices.* Reading, MA: Addison-Wesley.

Karpinski, R. (1997, April). Net videoconferencing in the real world. *Netguide,* pp. 139-140.

Kerr, E., & Hiltz, S. R. (1982). *Computer-mediated communication systems: Status and evaluation.* New York: Academic Press.

Kiesler, S., Siegel, J., & McGuire, T. (1984). Social psychological aspects of computer-mediated communication. *American Psychologist, 39,* 1123-1134.

Kiesler, S., Zubrow, D., Moses, A. M., & Geller, V. (1985). Affect in computer-mediated communications: An experiment in synchronous terminal-to-terminal discussion. *Human-Computer Interaction, 1,* 77-104.

Kling, R. (1991). Cooperation, coordination and control in computer-supported work. *Communication of the ACM, 34,* 83-88.

Kraemer, K. L., & King, J. (1988). Computer-based systems for cooperative work and group decision-making. *Computing Surveys, 20,* 115-146.

Kraut, R., Galegher, J., & Egido, J. (1990). Patterns of contact and communication in scientific research collaboration. In J. Galegher, R. E. Kraut, & C. Egido (Eds.), *Intellectual teamwork: Social and* technological foundations of cooperative work (pp, 149-170). Hillsdale, NJ: Lawrence Erlbaum.

Korzenny, F., & Bauer, C. (1979, May). *A preliminary test of the theory of electronic propinquity: Organizational teleconferencing.* Paper presented at the annual meeting of the International Communication Association, Philadelphia.

Kumar, K., & van Dissel, H. G. (1996). Sustainable collaboration: Managing conflict and cooperation in interorganizational firms. *MIS Quarterly, 20,* 279-300.

Lam, S. S. K. (1997). The effects of group decision support systems and task structures on group communication and decision quality. *Journal of Management Information Systems, 13,* 193-215.

LaPlante, D. (1971). *Communication, friendliness, trust and the prisoner's dilemma.* Unpublished master's thesis, University of Windsor.

Lea, M. (1991). Rationalist assumptions in cross-media comparisons of computer-mediated communication. *Behavior & Information Technology, 10,* 153-172.

Lea, M., O'Shea, T., Fung, P., & Spears, R. (1992). "Flaming" in computer-mediated communication: Observations, explanations, implication. In M. Lea (Ed.), *Contexts of computer-mediated communication* (pp. 89-112). London: Harvester-Wheatsheaf.

Lea, M., & Spears, R. (1991). Computer-mediated communication, de-individuation and group decision-making. *International Journal of Man-Machine Studies, 34,* 283-301.

Lewis, L. F. (1987). A decision support system for face-to-face groups. *Journal of Information Science, 13,* 211-219.

Lopez, M. G. M. (1992). Is interaction the message? The effect of democratizing and nondemocratizing interaction in videoconferencing small groups on social presence and quality of outcome. In U. E. Gattiker (Ed.), *Technology-mediated communication* (pp. 187-223). New York: Walter de Gruyter.

Ma, R. (1996). Computer-mediated conversations as a new dimension of inter-cultural communication between East Asian and North American college students. In S. Herring (Ed.), *Computer-mediated communication: Linguistic, social and cross-cultural perspectives* (pp. 173-186). Philadelphia: John Benjamins.

March, J. G., & Simon, H. A. (1958). *Organizations.* New York: John Wiley.

Markus, M. L. (1990). Toward a critical mass theory of interactive media: Universal access, interdependence and diffusion. In J. Fulk & C. W. Steinfield (Eds.), *Organizations and communication technology* (pp. 194-218). Newbury Park, CA: Sage.

Markus, M. L. (1994). Finding a happy medium: Explaining the negative effects of electronic communication on social life at work. *ACM Transactions on Information Systems, 12,* 119-149.

Martz, W. B. J., Vogel, D. R., & Nunamaker, J. F. (1992). Electronic meeting systems: Results from the field. *Decision Support Systems, 8,* 141-158.

McCall, M., Morrison, A., & Hannan, R. (1978). *Studies of managerial work: Results and methods* (Technical Report No. 9). Greensboro, NC: Center for Creative Leadership.

McGrath, J. E., & Hollingshead, A. B. (1992). Putting the "group" back in group support systems: Some theoretical issues about dynamic processes in groups with technological advancements. In L. M. Jessup & J. S. Valacich (Eds.), *Group support systems: New perspectives* (pp. 78-96). New York: Macmillan.

McGrath, J. E., & Hollingshead, A. B. (1994). *Groups interacting with technology: Ideas, evidence, issues and an agenda.* Thousand Oaks, CA: Sage.

McGuire, T. W., Kiesler S., & Siegel J. (1987). Group and computer-mediated discussion effects in risk decision-making. *Journal of Personality and Social Psychology, 52,* 917-930.

McLeod, P. L., & Liker, J. K. (1992). Electronic meeting systems: Evidence from a low structure environment. *Information Systems Research, 3,* 195-223.

Mejias, R. J., Shepherd, M. M., Vogel, D. R., & Lazaneo, L. (1996). Consensus and perceived satisfaction levels: A cross-cultural comparison of GSS and non-GSS outcomes within and between the United States and Mexico. *Journal of Management Information Systems, 13,* 137-161.

Miller, K., & Stiff, J. (1993). *Deceptive communication.* Newbury Park, CA: Sage.

Mintzberg, H. (1973). *The nature of managerial work.* New York: Harper & Row.

Miranda, S. M., & Bostrom, R. P. (1994). The impact of group support systems on group conflict and conflict management. *Journal of Management Information Systems, 10,* 63-95.

Monge, P. R., & Fulk, J. (1998). Global network organizations. In G. DeSanctis & J. Fulk (Eds.), *Shaping organizational form: Communication, connection, community.* Thousand Oaks, CA: Sage.

Monge, P., McSween, C., & Wyer, J. (1989). *A profile of meetings in corporate America: Results of the 3M Meeting effectiveness study.* Unpublished manuscript, Annenberg School for Communication, University of Southern California, Los Angeles.

Mosvick, R., & Nelson, R. (1987). *We've got to start a meeting like this! A guide to successful business meeting management.* Glencoe, IL: Scott, Foresman.

Nass, C., & Mason, L. (1990). On the study of technology and task: A variable-based approach. In J. Fulk & C. W. Steinfield (Eds.), *Organizations and communication technology* (pp. 46-67). Newbury Park, CA: Sage.

Nohria, N., & Berkley, J. D. (1994). The virtual organization: Bureaucracy, technology, and the implosion of control. In C. Heckscher & A. Donnellon (Eds.), *The postbureaucratic organization: New perspec-*

tives on organizational change (pp. 108-128). Thousand Oaks, CA: Sage.

Nohria, N., & Eccles, R. (1992). Face-to-face: Making network organizations work. In N. Nohria & R. Eccles (Eds.), *Networks and organizations: Structure, form, and action* (pp. 288-308). Boston: Harvard Business School Press.

Noll, A. M. (1976). Teleconferencing communications activities. *Communications Society, 14*(6), 8-14.

Nunamaker, J. F., Applegate, L. M., & Konsynski, B. R. (1987). Facilitating group creativity: Experience with a group decision support system. *Journal of Management Information Systems, 3,* 5-19.

Nunamaker, J. F., Briggs, R. O., Mittleman, D. D., Vogel, D. R., & Balthazard, P. A. (1996). Lessons from a dozen years of group support systems research: A discussion of lab and field findings. *Journal of Management Information Systems, 13,* 163-207.

Nunamaker, J. F., Dennis, A. R., George, J. F., Valacich, J. S., & Vogel, D. R. (1991). Electronic meeting systems to support group work: Theory and practice at Arizona. *Communications of the ACM, 34*(7), 40-61.

Nunamaker, J. F., Dennis, A. R., Valacich, J. S., Vogel, D. R., & George, J. F. (1993). Issues in the design, development, use, and management of group support systems. In L. M. Jessup & J. S. Valacich (Eds.), *Group support systems: New perspectives* (pp. 123-145). New York: Macmillan.

Ochsman, R. B., & Chapanis, A. (1974). The effects of 10 communication modes on the behavior of teams during cooperative problem-solving. *International Journal of Man-Machine Studies, 6,* 579-619.

Olaniran, B. A. (1994). Group performance in computer-mediated and face-to-face communication media. *Management Communication Quarterly, 7,* 256-281.

Oppenheim, L. (1987). *Making meetings matter: A report to the 3M Corporation.* Unpublished manuscript, Wharton Center for Applied Research, Philadelphia.

Orlikowski, W. J. (1992). The duality of technology: Rethinking the concept of technology in organizations. *Organization Science, 3,* 398-427.

Orlikowski, W. J., Yates, J., Okamura, K., & Fujimoto, M. (1995). Shaping electronic communication: The metastructuring of technology in the context of use. *Organization Science, 6,* 423-444.

Perrow, C. (1970). *Organizational analysis: A sociological view.* London: Tavistock.

Pinsonneault, A., & Kraemer, K. L. (1990). The effects of electronic meetings on group processes and outcomes: An assessment of the empirical research. *Decision Support Systems, 5*(2), 197-216.

Poole, M. S., & DeSanctis, G. (1990). Understanding the use of group decision support systems. In J. Fulk & C. W. Steinfield (Eds.), *Organizations and communication technology* (pp. 173-193). Newbury Park, CA: Sage.

Poole, M. S., & DeSanctis, G. (1992). Microlevel structuration in computer-supported group decision-making. *Human Communication Research, 19,* 5-49.

Poole, M. S., DeSanctis, G., Kirsch, L., & Jackson, M. (1995). Group decision support systems as facilitators of quality team efforts. In L. Frey (Ed.), *Innovations in group facilitation techniques: Case studies of applications in naturalistic settings* (pp. 299-322). Creskill, NJ: Hampton.

Poole, M. S., Holmes, R., & DeSanctis, G. (1991). Conflict management in a computer-supported meeting environment. *Management Science, 37,* 926-953.

Poole, M. S., Holmes, M., Watson, R., & DeSanctis, G. (1993). Group decision support systems and group communication: A comparison of decision-making in computer-supported and nonsupported groups. *Communication Research, 20,* 176-213.

Poole, M. S., & Jackson, M. H. (1992). Communication theory and group support systems. In L. M. Jessup & J. S. Valacich (Eds.), *Group support systems: New perspectives* (pp. 282-293). New York: Macmillan.

Poole, M. S., & Roth, J. (1989). Decision development in small groups IV: A typology of group decision paths. *Human Communication Research, 15,* 323-356.

Popper, K. (1962). *Conjectures and refutations.* New York: Basic Books.

Powell, W. W. (1990). Neither network nor hierarchy: Network forms of organization. In B. M. Staw & L. L. Cummings (Eds.), *Research in organizational behavior* (Vol. 12, pp. 295-336.). Greenwich, CT: JAI.

Pye, L., & Williams, E. (1977). Teleconferencing: Is video valuable or is audio adequate. *Telecommunications Policy, 1,* 230-241.

Rawlins, C. (1989). The impact of teleconferencing on the leadership of small decision-making groups. *Journal of Organizational Behavior Management, 10,* 37-52.

Rafaeli, S. (1988). Interactivity: From new media to communication. In R. P. Hawkins, J. M. Wiemann, & S. Pingree (Eds.), *Advancing communication science: Merging mass and interpersonal processes* (pp. 110-134). Newbury Park, CA: Sage.

Rice, R. E. (1984). Mediated group communication. In R. Rice (Ed.), *The new media* (pp. 129-154). Beverly Hills, CA: Sage.

Rice, R., & Gattiker, U. (1997). *New media and organizational structuring of media and relations.* Unpublished manuscript, Rutgers University, New Brunswick, NJ.

Ring, P., & Van de Ven, A. (1994). Developmental processes of cooperative interorganizational relationships. *Academy of Management Journal, 19,* 90-118.

Rogers, E. M. (1995). *Diffusion of innovations* (4th ed.). New York: Free Press.

Rosetti, D. K., & Surynt, T. J. (1985). Video teleconferencing and performance. *Journal of Business Communication, 22,* 25-31.

Salancik, G. R., & Pfeffer, J. (1978). A social information processing approach to job attitudes and task design. *Administrative Science Quarterly, 23,* 224-253.

Sambamurthy, V., & Chin, W. W. (1994). The effects of group attitudes toward alternative GDSS designs on the decision-making performance of computer-supported groups. *Decision Sciences, 25,* 215-241.

Sambamurthy, V., & DeSanctis, G. (1990). An experimental evaluation of GDSS effects on group performance during stakeholder analysis. In J. F. Nunamaker, Jr. (Ed.), *Proceedings of the Twenty-Third Annual Hawaii International Conference on Systems Sciences* (Vol. 3, pp. 79-88). Los Alamitos, CA: IEEE Computer Society Press.

Sambamurthy, V., Poole, M. S., & Kelly, J. (1993). The effects of variations in GDSS capabilities on decision-making processes in groups. *Small Group Research, 24,* 523-546.

Saunders, C. S., Robey, D., & Vaverek, K. A. (1994). The persistence of status differentials in computer conferencing. *Human Communication Research, 20,* 443-472.

Schmitz, J., & Fulk, J. (1991). Organizational colleagues, information richness, and electronic mail: A test of the social influence model of technology use. *Communication Research, 18,* 487-523.

Schrage, M. (1989). *No more teams! Mastering the dynamics of creative collaboration.* New York: Doubleday.

Schrage, M. (1996). Design for facilitation, facilitation for design: Managing media to manage innovation. In J. Kao (Ed.), *The new business of design* (pp. 46-63). New York: Allworth.

Schwartzman, H. (1986). The meeting as a neglected social form in organizational studies. In B. M. Staw & L. L. Cummings (Eds.), *Research in organizational behavior* (Vol. 8, pp. 233-258). Greenwich, CT: JAI.

Schwartzman, H. (1989). *The meeting: Gatherings in organizations and communities.* New York: Plenum.

Seibold, D. R., Heller, M. A., & Contractor, N. S. (1994). Group decision support systems (GDSS): Review, taxonomy, and research agenda. In B. Kovacic (Ed.), *New approaches to organizational communication* (pp. 143-168). Albany: State University of New York Press.

Serida-Nishimura, J. F. (1994). An organizational culture perspective for the study of group support systems. *Proceedings of the Fifteenth International Conference on Information Systems* (pp. 201-211).

Sharda, R., Barr, S. H., & McDonnell, J. C. (1988). Decision support system effectiveness: A review and an empirical test. *Management Science, 34,* 139-159.

Shepherd, M. M., Briggs, R. O., Yen, J., & Nunamaker, J. (1995). Invoking social comparison to improve electronic brainstorming: Beyond anonymity. *Journal of Management Information Systems, 12,* 155-170.

Short, J., Williams, E., & Christie, B. (1976). *The social psychology of telecommunications.* New York: John Wiley.

Short, J. A. (1971). *Conflicts of interest and conflicts of opinion in an experimental bargaining game conducted over the media* (Communication Studies Group Report No. E/71065/SH). London: University College.

Siegel, J., Dubrovsky, V., Kiesler, S., & McGuire, T. W. (1986). Group processes in computer-mediated communication. *Organizational Behavior and Human Decision Processes, 37,* 157-187.

Simon, H. (1957). *Administrative behavior.* New York: Macmillan.

Spears, R., & Lea, M. (1994). Panacea or panopticon? The hidden power in computer-mediated communication. *Communication Research, 21,* 427-459.

Sproull, L., & Kiesler, S. (1991). *Connections: New ways of working in the networked organization.* Cambridge, MA: MIT Press.

Steeb, R., & Johnston, S. C. (1981). A computer-based interactive system for group decision-making. *IEEE Transactions on Systems, Man, and Cybernetics, SMCII, 8,* 544-552.

Steiner, I. D. (1972). *Group process and productivity.* New York: Academic Press.

Straus, S. (1996). Getting a clue: Communication media and information distribution effects on group process and performance. *Small Group Research, 27,* 115-142.

Straus, S. (1997). Technology, group process, and group outcomes: Testing the connections in computer-mediated and face-to-face groups. *Human Computer Interaction, 12,* 227-266.

Straus, S. G., & McGrath, J. E. (1994). Does the medium matter? The interaction of task type and technology on group performance and member reactions. *Journal of Applied Psychology, 79,* 87-97.

Strickland, L., Guild, P., Barefoot, J., & Patterson, S. (1978). Teleconferencing and leadership emergence. *Human Relations, 31,* 583-596.

Sudweeks, F., & Rafaeli, S. (1996). How do you get a hundred strangers to agree? Computer-mediated communication and collaboration. In T. M. Harrison & T. Stephen (Eds.), *Computer networking and scholarly communication in the twenty-first century university* (pp. 115-136). Albany: State University of New York Press.

Thomas, H. B., & Williams, E. (1975). *The University of Quebec audioconferencing system: An analysis of users' attitudes* (Communication Studies Group Report No. P/75190/TH). London: University College.

Thompson, J. D., & Tuden, A. (1959). Strategies, structures and processes of organizational decisions. In J. D. Thompson (Ed.), *Comparative studies in admin-*

istration (pp. 195-216). Pittsburgh, PA: University of Pittsburgh Press.

Trevino, L. K., Daft, R. L., & Lengel, R. H. (1990). Understanding managers' media choices: A symbolic interactionist perspective. In J. Fulk & C. W. Steinfield (Eds.), *Organizations and communication technology* (pp. 71-94). Newbury Park, CA: Sage.

Trevino, L. K., & Webster, J. (1992). Flow in computer-mediated communication. *Communication Research, 19,* 539-573.

Trice, H. (1985). Rites and ceremonials in organizational cultures. In S. B. Bacharach & S. M. Mitchell (Eds.), *Research in the sociology of organizations* (Vol. 4, pp. 221-270). Greenwich, CT: JAI.

Tuckman, B. W. (1965). Developmental sequence in small groups. *Psychological Bulletin, 64,* 384-399.

Tyabji, H. (1996). Managing the virtual company. In J. Kao (Ed.), *The new business of design* (pp. 64-79). New York: Allworth.

Tyran, C. K., Dennis, A. R., Vogel, D. R., & Nunamaker, J. F. (1992). The application of electronic meeting technology to support strategic management. *MIS Quarterly, 16,* 313-334.

Uhlig, R., Farber, D., & Bair, J. (1979). *The office of the future: Communication and computers.* New York: North Holland.

Valacich, J. S., Dennis, A. R., & Connolly, T. (1994). Idea generation in computer-based groups: A new ending to an old story. *Organizational Behavior and Human Decision Processes, 57,* 448-467.

Valacich, J. S., Dennis, A. R., & Nunamaker, J. F. (1992). Group size and anonymity effects on computer-mediated idea generation. *Small Group Research, 23,* 49-73.

Valacich, J. S., George, J. F., Nunamaker, J. F., & Vogel, D. R. (1994). Physical proximity effects on computer-mediated group idea generation. *Small Group Research, 25,* 83-104.

Valacich, J. S., Mennecke, B. E., Wachter, R., & Wheeler, B. C. (1994). Extensions to media richness theory: A test of the task-media fit hypothesis. *Proceedings of the Twenty-Third Hawaii International Conference on Systems Sciences* (Vol. 4, pp. 11-20). Los Alamitos, CA: IEEE Computer Society Press.

Valacich, J. S., Paranka, D., George, J. F., & Nunamaker, J. F. (1993). Communication concurrency and the new media: A new dimension for media richness. *Communication Research, 20,* 249-276.

Valacich, J. S., & Schwenk, C. (1995). Devil's advocacy and dialectical inquiry effects on face-to-face and computer-mediated group decision-making. *Organizational Behavior and Human Decision Processes, 63,* 158-173.

Valacich, J. S., Wheeler, B. C., Mennecke, B. E., & Wachter, R. (1995). The effects of numerical and logical group size on computer-mediated idea generation. *Organizational Behavior and Human Decision Processes, 62,* 318-329.

Vallee, J., Johansen, R., Randolph, R. H., & Hastings, A. C. (1974). *Group communication through computers, Vol. 2: A study of social effects.* Menlo Park: CA: Institute for the Future.

Vician, C., DeSanctis, G., Poole, M. S., & Jackson, B. M. (1992). Using group technologies to support the design of "lights out" computing systems: A case study. In K. E. Kendall, K. Lyytinen, & J. I. DeGross (Eds.), *The impact of computer supported technologies on information systems development* (pp. 151-178). New York: Elsevier Science.

Vogel, D. R., & Nunamaker, J. F. (1989, September). Automated planning support: Using computers to enhance group decision-making. *Administrative Radiology,* pp. 54-59.

Vogel, D. R., Nunamaker, J. F., Martz, W. B. J., Grohowski, R., & McGoff, C. (1989). Electronic meeting system experience at IBM. *Journal of Management Information Systems, 6,* 25-43.

Volkema, R. J., & Neederman, F. (1995). Organizational meetings: Formats and information requirements. *Small Group Research, 26,* 3-24.

Walther, J. B. (1992). Interpersonal effects in computer-mediated interaction: A relational perspective. *Communication Research, 19,* 52-90.

Walther, J. B. (1994). Anticipated ongoing interaction versus channel effects on relational communication in computer-mediated interaction. *Human Communication Research, 20,* 473-501.

Walther, J. B. (1995). Relational aspects of computer-mediated communication: Experimental observations over time. *Organization Science, 6,* 186-203.

Walther, J. B., Anderson, J. F., & Park, D. W. (1994). Interpersonal effects in computer-mediated interaction: A meta-analysis of social and antisocial communication. *Communication Research, 21,* 460-487.

Walther, J. B., & Burgoon, J. K. (1992). Relational communication in computer-mediated interaction. *Human Communication Research, 19,* 50-88.

Watson, R. T., DeSanctis, G., & Poole, M. S. (1988). Using a GDSS to facilitate group consensus: Some intended and unintended consequences. *MIS Quarterly, 12,* 463-477.

Watzlawick, P., Beavin, J. H., & Jackson, D. D. (1967). *Pragmatics of human communication: A study of interactional patterns, pathologies and paradoxes.* New York: Norton.

Weeks, G. D., & Chapanis, A. (1976). Cooperative versus conflictive problem solving in three telecommunication modes. *Perceptual and Motor Skills, 42,* 879-917.

Weick, K. E. (1979). *The social psychology of organizing* (2nd ed.). Reading, MA: Addison-Wesley.

Weick, K., & Meader, D. K. (1992). Sensemaking and group support systems. In L. M. Jessup & J. S. Valacich (Eds.), *Group support systems: New perspectives* (pp. 230-251). New York: Macmillan.

Weldon, E., & Mustari, E. L. (1988). Felt dispensability in groups of coactors: The effects of shared responsibility and explicit anonymity on cognitive effort. *Organizational Behavior and Human Decision Processes, 41,* 330-351.

Weisband, S., Schneider, S., & Connolly, T. (1995). Computer-mediated communication and social information: Status salience and status differences. *Academy of Management Journal, 38,* 1124-1151.

Weston, J. R., Kirsten, C., & O'Conner, S. (1975). *Teleconferencing: A comparison of group performance profiles in mediated and face-to-face interaction.* Ottawa, Ontario: University of Ottawa, Department of Communications.

Wheeler, B. C., Mennecke, B. E., & Scudder, J. N. (1993). Restrictive group support systems as a source of process structure for high and low procedural order groups. *Small Group Research, 24,* 504-522.

Wheeler, B. C., & Valacich, J. S. (1996). Facilitation, GSS, and training as sources of process restrictiveness and guidance for structured group decision-making: An empirical assessment. *Information Systems Research, 7,* 429-450.

Whittaker, S. (1995). Rethinking video as a technology for interpersonal communications: Theory and design implications. *International Journal of Human-Computer Studies, 42,* 501-529.

Williams, E. (1972). *Factors influencing the effect of medium of communication upon preferences for media, conversations and persons* (Communication Studies Group Report No. E/7227/WL). London: University College.

Williams, E. (1975). Coalition formation over telecommunications media. *European Journal of Social Psychology, 5,* 503-507.

Williams, E. (1976). *Chairmanships in audio-only teleconferencing* (Communication Studies Group Report No. E/76310/WL). London: University College.

Williams, E. (1977). Experimental comparisons of face-to-face and mediated communication: A review. *Psychological Bulletin, 84,* 963-976.

Williams, K., Harkins, S., & Latane, B. (1981). Identifiability as a deterrent to social loafing: Two cheering experiments. *Journal of Personality and Social Psychology, 40,* 303-311.

Wilson, C. (1974). *An experiment on the influence of the medium of communication on speech content* (Communication Studies Group Report No. E/74350/CW). London: University College.

Yates, J. (1989). *Control through communication: The rise of system in American management.* Baltimore: Johns Hopkins University Press.

Yates, J., & Orlikowski, W. (1992). Genres of organizational communication: An approach to studying communication and media. *Academy of Management Review, 17,* 299-326.

Zajonc, R. B. (1965). Social facilitation. *Science, 149,* 269-274.

Zigurs, I., Poole, M. S., & DeSanctis, G. (1988). A study of influence in computer-mediated group decision-making. *MIS Quarterly, 12,* 625-644.

Zuboff, S. (1988). *In the age of the smart machine: The future of work and power.* New York: Basic Books.

17

Participation and Decision Making

DAVID R. SEIBOLD

University of California, Santa Barbara

B. CHRISTINE SHEA

California Polytechnic State University

In most industrialized countries since World War II (Cole, 1985) and especially during the past five decades in America (Appelbaum & Batt, 1994; Mintzberg, 1991; Russell, 1988), traditional workplace designs and operations have been transformed to more "participative" work relationships and practices. Control by managers, pyramidal designs, stovepipe operational functions, vertical chain-of-command relationships, and rigid bureaucratic procedures have given way, increasingly, to workers' participation in managing, lattice organizations, cross-functional work arrangements, lateral collaborative relationships, and semiautonomous work teams (Fisher, 1993; Greenbaum & Query, 1999). Structurally, hierarchical organizations are be-

ing supplanted by "self-organizing," "shamrock," and "fishnet" organizations (DeSanctis & Poole, 1997; Seibold & Contractor, 1992). Many reasons have been offered for this change in organizations' structures and practices: the globalization of markets and resultant increases in international competition, economic turbulence, and pressures toward increased productivity; technological advances in the workplace, changes in workplace demographics, and the stance of organized labor toward these changes; and philosophical arguments and moral injunctions for workplace democracy, among other reasons (see Bachrach & Botwinick, 1992; Cheney, 1995, 1999; Cheney, Stohl, Dennis, & Harrison, 1998; Clegg, 1983; Fairhurst,

Green, & Courtright, 1995; Lawler, 1991; Stohl, 1995).

At root, this shift has entailed decreases in traditional forms of management and correlative increases in the extent and form of formal employee participation in organizational decision making and other organizational matters traditionally the province of managers (Seibold, 1995). Research reviews reveal equivocal findings with regard to the outcomes and effectiveness of various employee participation programs (Levine & Tyson, 1990; Locke & Schweiger, 1979; Miller & Monge, 1986; Schweiger & Leana, 1986; Wagner & Gooding, 1987b). As Cotton (1993) suggests, this may be because these reviews inappropriately combine several types of employee participation programs, since the type of involvement program and the level of participation it affords may determine its effectiveness (as well as other outcomes such as satisfaction). There is considerable controversy surrounding the claim that different involvement program outcomes are a function of the form(s) of employee participation organizations implemented (see Cotton, 1993; Cotton, Vollrath, Froggatt, Lengnick-Hall, & Jennings, 1988; Cotton, Vollrath, Lengnick-Hall, & Froggatt, 1990; Leana, Locke, & Schweiger, 1990; Wagner, 1994). The thesis undergirding this chapter is that the different effects are due, at least indirectly, to the *form* of employee participation implemented in the organization.

Further, since each type of program influences communication processes in the organization, this chapter focuses on the role of *communication* in mediating participation program outcomes and effectiveness as both an important theoretical and practical concern. "Communication is an integral part of participative processes in organizations" (Monge & Miller, 1988, p. 213), and evidence suggests that communication may moderate the effects of various types of participation or involvement programs (Marshall & Stohl, 1993; Stohl, 1989). Thus, it may be especially fruitful to examine the communication-related features of these programs, including their im-

pact on the communication processes in the organization, to determine how and why each program may have a different effect on relevant outcomes such as employee satisfaction and productivity.

Although space limitations preclude extensive discussion of a related argument entwined in this chapter, there also is evidence that the nature of communication within (and outside) the organization crucially affects the nature of the participation program implemented (Lawler, 1991; Margulies & Black, 1987; Pacanowsky, 1988; Stohl, 1987; Wagner & Gooding, 1987a). Of course, this is consistent with theoretical perspectives and research in other areas suggesting the *recursiveness* of communication and group/organizational structure (Barley, 1986; Contractor & Eisenberg, 1990; Contractor & Seibold, 1993; Pettigrew, 1990; Poole & DeSanctis, 1990; Poole, Seibold, & McPhee, 1996; Riley, 1983; Yates & Olikowski, 1992). Where evidence exists that communication processes and involvement program structures are recursively linked (each shaping the other), we shall integrate it into this review of five specific but pervasive organizational forms of employee participation in decision making: quality of work life, quality circles, self-directed work teams, gainsharing (and Scanlon plans in particular), and employee ownership programs (especially employee stock ownership plans).

It is difficult to do justice to the vast literature on political, economic, and social contexts for organizational change, including employee involvement (Deetz, 1994; Goll, 1991). Nor will we adequately address research findings concerning effects of employee participation programs that are government mandated or state sponsored, such as worker councils in European organizations (see Berggren, 1993; Clegg, 1983; Eijnatten, 1993; Kavcic & Tannenbaum, 1981; Koopman, Drenth, Bus, Kruyswijk, & Wierdsma, 1981; Stohl, 1993a, 1993b; Strauss, 1982), or other international and comparative national studies (e.g., Kavcic & Tannenbaum, 1981; Marsh, 1992; Veiga & Yanouzas, 1991). For the most part, the research we review is drawn from analyses of organizations "transitioning" (Lawler, 1990) to new or increased forms of participation, and we have not incorporated literature concerning organizations created around the principle of worker control and that define themselves in opposition to the "mainstream" (Ellerman, 1990; H. Glaser, 1994; Greenberg, 1980).

Finally, we will underscore in the final section of this chapter critical scholarship that focuses on workplace democracy, which has highlighted the possibilities for political "reordering" of the traditional workplace. Increasingly, communication scholars (e.g., Barker, 1993; Barker & Cheney, 1994; Cheney, 1995, in press; Cheney, Straub, et al., 1998; Deetz, 1992; Fairhurst, 1993; Fairhurst & Wendt, 1993; Frey, 1995; Harrison, 1994; Mumby & Putnam, 1992; Mumby & Stohl, 1992; Putnam, Phillips, & Chapman, 1996; Stohl, 1995) have critically addressed the values reflected in discourses and metaphors concerning the new workplace and, in doing so, have begun to balance the "people" inherent in participation programs with what has been a dominant focus on the "productivity" outcomes associated with them (e.g., Ahlbrandt, Leana, & Murrell, 1992; Blinder, 1990; Hoerr, 1989; Jones, Powell, & Roberts, 1990-1991; Lawler, 1995; Vandenberg, Richardson, & Eastman, 1999; Wellins, Byham, & Wilson, 1991). Before surveying the literature on five prevalent forms of employee involvement (quality circles, quality of work life, Scanlon plans, self-directed work teams, and employee stock ownership plans), we first examine the nature of participation in these programs, a matter that, in the research literature at least, has been inextricably tied to the effectiveness of these programs.

The preponderance of work on forms and effects of employee participation has been done by scholars outside of the communication discipline, especially organizational behavior, management, industrial and organizational psychology, and business administration researchers, who clearly endorse a managerial orientation. Thus, it is hardly surprising that the literature produced by these researchers primarily focuses on how effective these participation programs are in furthering management's goals. As Locke and Schweiger (1979) have stated flatly, "Business organizations [do not] exist for the purpose of satisfying their employees since employee feelings have no market price; the goal of such organizations is to satisfy their customers and stockholders" (p. 327). More generally, since many organizations view employee satisfaction as a means to an end, not an end itself, this orientation also has been reflected in participation research (see Wagner & Gooding, 1987a), especially in researchers' assumptions about the goals of these programs, their choices of dependent measures, and the values embedded in how they assay the outcomes of participation programs. Given this prevailing "managerial" orientation, communication researchers, as well as those outside of the discipline, have viewed communication within the context of employee participation from a "functionalist" perspective (see Putnam, 1982, 1983), which emphasizes directionality of information flow, information processing, amount and frequency of information, sources of information, and networks. In the final section of this chapter, we shall turn to critical scholars'—especially communication researchers such as those noted above—concerns about those aspects of the participation literature and other matters.

CONCEPTUALIZING EMPLOYEE PARTICIPATION

Locke and Schweiger (1979) point out that although *employee participation* is difficult to define, it is essentially joint decision making with managers on work activities and other aspects of organizational functioning traditionally considered to be the responsibility or prerogative of management. Cotton (1993) argues that employee participation is too limiting a concept, since it does not include the majority of programs operating in organizations today. He offers a more inclusive term, *employee involvement,* defined as "a participative process to use the entire capacity of workers, designed to encourage employee commitment to organizational success. This process typically comes about by giving employees some combination of information, influence, and/or incentives" (p. 3). Researchers have also noted the conceptual confusion surrounding the notion of participation:

> Some researchers equate participation with organizational practices, programs, or techniques, while others view participation as an overarching philosophy of management. . . . Still others view participation as a broader social issue with a variety of underlying implications, such as manipulation, oppression, and control. (Glew, O'Leary-Kelly, Griffin, & Van Fleet, 1995, p. 400)

Regardless of the definition employed, there is general agreement on the major dimensions along which employee participation or involvement programs may vary. Participation programs may be *forced* by government or law (legally mandated); *voluntary,* where the organization initiates the idea of participation; or *contractually based,* where programs evolve from collective bargaining agreements. Participation also may be *formal,* where officially recognized decision-making groups are created, or *informal,* where managers and employees work together to make decisions without an established program (Locke & Schweiger, 1979).

Participation programs also vary according to degree or level of influence, content, and social range. The *degree* of participation (level of influence) falls somewhere in these areas: (1) *no participation* by employees; (2) *consultation,* where managers receive input from employees but they make the decision themselves; and (3) *full participation,* where employees and management vote as equals on decisions. The *content* of participation refers to the types of decisions with which employ-

ees might be involved, including routine personnel functions, the work itself, working conditions, and company policies (Locke & Schweiger, 1979, p. 276). *Social range* is the range of people involved in a participation program. For instance, in some cases only certain individuals or groups may be involved in decision making, but under other circumstances, all members of the organizations may provide input into the process (Dachler & Wilpert, 1978). Program dynamics along any or all of these dimensions may affect the outcomes of a particular program.

The majority of studies have focused on two major outcome areas: employee *satisfaction* or morale and *productivity.* Research reviews indicate that employee participation has a positive but small effect on satisfaction and very little, if any, impact on productivity (Levine & Tyson, 1990; Locke & Schweiger, 1979; Miller & Monge, 1986; Schweiger & Leana, 1986; Wagner, 1994; Wagner & Gooding, 1987b). However, these equivocal and relatively weak results may be due to methodological deficiencies, unclear distinctions among the forms of employee participation, or differing outcome measures.

Moreover, there are a variety of variables that may mediate the relationship between employee participation and outcomes, and these factors may be cognitive or affective (motivational) in nature (Locke & Schweiger, 1979; Miller & Monge, 1986). *Cognitive models* of variables mediating participation-outcome relationships consider the fact that employee involvement programs affect the flow of information in the organization. They assume that since subordinates know more about their work than does management, worker participation in the decision-making process may be valuable to the organization. Participation in decision making also gives employees the opportunity to learn more about the organization and its policies, which may ultimately enhance decision quality and productivity. Finally, participation in decision making may help employees develop more accurate perceptions of reward contingencies in the organization (Miller & Monge, 1987;

Monge & Miller, 1988). However, Miller and Monge (1986) emphasize that cognitive explanations assume participation must be in areas where employees are interested and knowledgeable to have concrete effects on productivity and satisfaction.

Affective or motivational models, on the other hand, assume that "participation need not be centered on issues of which employees are particularly knowledgeable, for it is the act, not the informational content, of participation that is the crucial mechanism" (Miller & Monge, 1986, p. 731). Generally, affective explanations expect that participation fulfills some higher-order needs of employees, which is the key to their satisfaction. Specifically, employee participation fosters increased feelings of control, trust, and identification with the organization, which lead to less resistance to change and greater motivation (Locke & Schweiger, 1979; Monge & Miller, 1988). In turn, this directly enhances satisfaction, which may ultimately influence productivity.

As noted earlier, research reviews indicate some support for both cognitive and affective models. For instance, in a meta-analysis of participation studies, Miller and Monge (1986) found minimal support for cognitive models and stronger support for affective explanations. Research reviews conducted by Locke and Schweiger (1979) and Schweiger and Leana (1986) also reported greater support for affective explanations, since overall results were stronger and more consistent for satisfaction variables than performance factors. However, these reviews neglected to distinguish among different forms of employee participation, so it may be difficult to conclude whether cognitive or affective models are better predictors of effects.

Some researchers suggest that the *form of participation* may affect the outcomes of employee involvement programs (Cotton, 1993; Cotton et al., 1988; Cotton et al., 1990; Guzzo, Jette, & Katzell, 1985). In a major review of 91 empirical studies examining participation in decision making, Cotton et al. (1988) found that different forms of employee participation have different effects on satisfaction and productivity. Leana et al. (1990) criticized Cotton et al., claiming that their classification system was flawed, their reporting of the results of several studies was inaccurate, and they omitted relevant studies from their analysis. Leana et al. also noted that several of the studies analyzed by Cotton and colleagues confounded participative decision making (PDM) with quality circles or Scanlon plans.

In an attempt to help resolve some of the controversy surrounding the proposed effectiveness of employee participation, Wagner (1994) reanalyzed the results reported by Cotton et al. (1988) and examined other meta-analytic reviews of participation. He concluded that "research on participation has produced reliable evidence of statistically significant changes in performance and satisfaction that are positive in direction but limited in size" (p. 325). Although Wagner (1994) contends that his results do not support Cotton et al.'s claim about the differing effects of employee participation forms, he acknowledges that his own definition of participation is narrow and *excludes* the "concepts of delegation, consultation, and various multivariate interventions, many of which have been shown to have substantial effects on performance and satisfaction" (p. 326).

Scope of Review

Several reviews, even those that are critical of the research conducted by Cotton and colleagues, suggest that the form or type of employee participation may differentially affect outcomes, such as satisfaction and productivity (Beekun, 1989; Leana et al., 1990; Magjuka, 1989; Magjuka & Baldwin, 1991). Moreover, Leana et al. (1990) suggest there may be important intervening processes that influence how participation in decision making affects outcomes, and Cotton and colleagues (Cotton et al., 1988; Cotton et al., 1990) argue that researchers should consider contextual variables and the process through which the participation program operates.

Thus, to understand *why* certain forms of employee involvement may be more effective than others, we believe it is necessary to examine (a) the features of each program, (b) the contexts under which they are ordinarily implemented, and (c) the communication processes through which they function. Each of these foci will be addressed in our review of five types of employee involvement programs. Collectively, they provide a template for assessing the differential effectiveness of these programs, a template that will be summarized in the final section.

Cotton (1993) contends that the most effective forms of employee involvement are gainsharing plans (especially Scanlon plans) and self-directed work teams, while quality circles and representative participation are among the least effective. Quality of work life, job enrichment, and employee ownership programs have intermediate effects. The following sections examine five different types of employee involvement programs (Locke & Schweiger, 1979) that are *voluntarily* initiated by organizations and *formal* in status within the organization, yet have been found to vary in terms of effectiveness. The programs selected for analysis and comparison in this chapter are *quality circles* (QCs) (low effectiveness), *quality of work life* (QWL) programs and *employee stock ownership plans* (ESOPs) (moderate effectiveness), and both *self-directed work teams* (SDWTs) *in new-design plants* and *Scanlon gainsharing plans* (high effectiveness).

It also should be noted that the involvement programs to be reviewed differ in terms of the level of the organization at which they are introduced and their social range (Dachler & Wilpert, 1978) as defined previously. QCs are implemented at the group or department level. SDWTs may be implemented at the group or department level (especially when introduced on a pilot basis in "transitioning" organizations; Lawler, 1990), or they may be integral to "new plant" designs and thus employed throughout greenfield sites, which are new facilities specifically designed for SDWTs (Lawler, 1991). We shall emphasize the latter.

QWL programs, Scanlon plans, and ESOPs typically involve the entire organization.

Further, although the five types of involvement programs reviewed below are primarily "consultative" (Locke & Schweiger, 1979), they differ in terms of the degree of participation that they afford employees in (what is traditionally) managerial decision making, ranging from minimal participation (QC) to extensive participation (SDWT). As we shall see, degree of participation (or level of influence) is strongly related to program outcomes and effectiveness (see Table 17.1). Finally, as will be apparent, each type of program influences and is influenced by communication processes in the organization. In turn, this affords insights into the role of communication in mediating the effectiveness of involvement programs, an argument to which we return in the last section.

REVIEW OF EMPLOYEE INVOLVEMENT PROGRAMS

Quality Circles

Quality circles (QCs) have become the most popular employee involvement program in the world (Cotton, 1993), and hundreds of thousands of workers in the United States alone regularly participate in these programs (Lawler, 1986). The QC concept of using employee problem-solving groups to improve product quality originated in Japan in the late 1950s and early 1960s, and it spread in the early 1970s to the U.S. aerospace industry. As the QC movement grew in the United States, companies began viewing QCs not only as a way to improve product quality but also as a means of increasing employee participation, satisfaction, and productivity (Van Fleet & Griffin, 1989).

A QC is a small group of employees (generally 5-15 members) from the same work area who meet regularly to identify, discuss, and offer solutions to problems concerning product quality and productivity. QC mem-

TABLE 17.1 Form of Participation

	Quality Circles (QCs)	Quality of Work Life (QWL) Programs	Employee Stock Ownership Plans (ESOPs)	Scanlon Gainsharing Plans	Self-Directed Work Teams (SDWTs)/New Plant
Type of program	Voluntary Formal	Voluntary Formal	Voluntary Formal	Voluntary Formal	Voluntary Formal
Effectiveness	Low	Moderate	Moderate	High	High
Degree of participation	Low	Low	Low to moderate	Moderate to high	High
Type of influence	Consultative	Consultative	Varies with program	Consultative and full participation (can implement some decisions without management approval)	Consultative and full participation (can implement many decisions without management approval)
Content of decision making	Work itself Immediate work area	Work itself Working conditions Company policy (on occasion)	Varies (usually vote for representatives to sit on board of directors)	Work itself Working conditions Company policy Financial bonuses	Work itself Working conditions Schedules and budgets Hiring at team level Compensation
Social range of participation	Group/department (Employees from specific department or work area)	Group/organization (Employees, managers, union representatives across organization)	Individual/organization (Full-time employees, managers across organization)	Group/organization (Employees and managers work together across all levels)	Group/organization (Employees from specific areas across organization)
Financial component	No	No	Yes (indirect)	Yes (direct)	? (varies)

bers have volunteered to participate in the program and meet during regular working hours. Although QC members receive training in group process and problem-solving techniques, many companies appoint a group facilitator to meet with the group. After identifying and analyzing the problem, these groups prepare recommendations and present them to management, who may or may not implement the groups' suggestions. Lawler and Mohrman (1987) point out that QCs are "parallel" structures, separate from the organization's ongoing activities, and they have no formal authority in the organization (see also Herrick, 1985). Even if an organization saves money as a result of implementing the solutions proposed by the group, participants receive no direct financial rewards. Thus, using the dimensions outlined by Dachler and Wilpert (1978) and Locke and Schweiger (1979), QCs are voluntary, formal programs that are consultative in nature and have a limited social range (see Table 17.1). The types of decisions in which the members are involved deal primarily with the work itself (Bruning & Liverpool, 1993), where their creativity (DeToro, 1987) and problem-solving effectiveness (Greenbaum, Kaplan, & Metlay, 1988) have been foci of study.

Research findings on the outcomes and effectiveness of QC programs have been mixed; however, in general, studies indicate that most QCs eventually fail and the positive effects of successful QC programs are minimal (Cotton, 1993; Drago, 1988; Lawler, 1986; Lawler & Mohrman, 1987; Ledford, Lawler, & Mohrman, 1988; Steel & Lloyd, 1988; Van Fleet & Griffin, 1989). For instance, after reviewing numerous studies on QC outcomes, Cotton (1993) concluded that although participating in QC had a positive effect on program-specific attitudes, such as perceptions of influence and QC satisfaction, QC participation had little effect on general work attitudes, such as job satisfaction and organizational commitment. Additionally, researchers have found that QCs have had little impact on worker performance and productivity (Cotton, 1993; Steel, Jennings, & Lindsey, 1990; Steel

& Lloyd, 1988; Steel, Mento, Dilla, Ovalle, & Lloyd, 1985). However, Steel and Shane (1986) caution that in light of the methodological deficiencies in the QC research (e.g., lack of control groups, small sample sizes, few baseline measures, experimental mortality), it is difficult to conclude whether QCs are effective or ineffective.

Researchers have attempted to isolate the factors that may determine the effectiveness of QC programs. Lawler and Mohrman (1987) offer several reasons why QCs may be ineffective, including the in-group/out-group dynamics associated with implementing QCs only in some areas, which may cause negative backlash by nonparticipants; competition among circles for management attention; middle management's resistance to QC programs; upper management's failure to implement circle suggestions; and circles' limited range of decision-making tasks. Lawler and Mohrman contend that the primary barrier to QC program effectiveness is the fact that QCs are not well integrated into the organizational structure. Circle members often lack the information or knowledge needed to make viable suggestions. For instance, "circles often come up with good ideas that are not practical because of strategy changes or business decisions they don't know about" (Lawler & Mohrman, 1987, p. 52).

Other researchers have found empirical support for both the cognitive and attitudinal factors suggested by Lawler and Mohrman (1987). In a study of military and civilian employees at a U.S. Air Force base, Steel and Lloyd (1988) found that participating in a QC significantly affected cognitive factors, including perceptions of influence, competence, and interpersonal trust. However, QC participation did not lead to an increase in perceived participation. Steel and Lloyd found weak support for attitudinal outcomes, such as employee intention to remain with the organization. Also, Marks, Mirvis, Hackett, and Grady (1986) found that employees in a manufacturing firm who participated in a QC program did not experience a change in QWL variables (e.g., perceived opportunities to participate in decision making, quality of organizational and work group communication, feelings of accomplishment, and hopes for advancement), while employees who did not participate experienced a significant *decline* in these variables. Although QC participants experienced an increase in productivity, and both participants and nonparticipants had lower absenteeism rates after the program was implemented, this QC program resulted in some negative attitudinal and cognitive outcomes.

Other variables that may affect the survival rate and effectiveness of QCs include job insecurity, amount of participation in decision making, and presence of a union (Drago, 1988); self-esteem of QC members (Brockner & Hess, 1986); and willingness to participate in a QC program (Stohl & Jennings, 1988).

Although it appears as if participating in QCs may have inconsistent or little influence in overall work attitudes and productivity levels, research suggests that QC programs do affect the communication processes and patterns within the organization. For instance, Buch (1992) argues that QC programs can open once-closed or unidirectional boundaries between employees and management. She reports that QC members and management perceived that communication and teamwork improved after implementing a QC program. Stohl (1986) points out that "circle meetings introduce new communication links, and new channels of communication are opened. As workers remain in the circles and work on a variety of problems, they develop a richer, more diverse, and ever-expanding communication network" (p. 514).

In a study of manufacturing plants in New Zealand, Stohl (1986) found that once employees joined a QC, they talked to more people across hierarchical levels of the organization, which increased their knowledge of the organization. Compared to nonmembers and former circle members, currently active circle members also perceived a more positive communication climate. The positive effects of QC involvement were particularly strong for those members who were well integrated into the organizational network. Interestingly, former circle members reported the lowest level of organizational commitment and felt disillusioned about their input on job-related issues. Stohl points out that most of the circle dropouts were nonlinkers, which suggests that the members' communication patterns and level of integration into the organizational network affected whether or not they would remain in the QC program.

Moreover, the circle's level of connection with the rest of the organization may influence the effectiveness of the program. Stohl (1987) found that "circles that transcend their parallelism and cross over into the larger organization have more of their proposals accepted and implemented" (p. 426). Specifically, she found that solution effectiveness was strongly related to the number of different groups in the organization with which the circle was linked (network range) and that managers' perceptions of circle effectiveness were strongly correlated with the number of relationships that circle participants had with other organizational members (extended network). Despite the fact that communication networks seemed to influence solution effectiveness and managers' perceptions of program effectiveness, Stohl (1987) found that only group cohesion factors influenced the circle members' perceptions of program effectiveness. These findings are consistent with Lawler and Mohrman's (1987) points on the problems with parallel structures, as well as their suggestion that changes in the organization's information system may make QC programs more effective. Moreover, Buch's (1992) discussion of the boundary-tightening effects of QCs may shed some additional light on Stohl's (1987) findings on group cohesion. Buch contends that "the formation of circles introduces new boundaries around work groups, thereby increasing members' feelings of identity and inclusion and strengthening group cohesiveness" (p. 64). She suggests that these effects may be particularly strong in underbounded organizations, which have unclear boundaries between groups, lack clear communication channels, and have few mechanisms to bring people together. Buch's analysis is consistent with Putnam and Stohl's (1990) theoretical postulate that such effects are quite predictable given the embedded nature of bona fide groups (like QCs) but which vary in the degree to which their boundaries are permeable. Putnam and Stohl point out that individuals typically belong to several different groups within an organization, which may result in divided loyalties, or may facilitate information sharing among groups. QCs are indeed bona fide groups, since each QC member is also a member of some department, unit, or division within the organization and each individual holds a formal position other than "QC group member."

QC programs may have effects on microlevel communication variables as well. Berman and Hellweg (1989) found that compared to nonparticipants, participants in QCs that included their supervisor were more satisfied with their supervisor and perceived that he or she was more communicatively competent. Also, QC participants' perceptions of their supervisor's communication competence was strongly related to how satisfied they were with him or her. From this, Berman and Hellweg conclude that "quality circles provide opportunities for supervisors and subordinates to improve their communication relationship by joint participation in a decision-making process" (p. 114). Margulies and Black (1987) found similar results in a study of a QC program implemented at a large public transit agency, where management perceived that the program improved communication channels between supervisors and employees.

Thus, although a review of the research indicates that QCs may not be particularly effective in increasing productivity and satisfaction, a growing number of studies suggest that QC programs can influence and are influenced by communication processes and patterns within the organization. Moreover, research findings suggest that for QCs to be effective, circle members must be well inte-grated into the communication network, and organizations that have implemented these programs must make appropriate changes in their information system.

Quality of Work Life Programs

In the early 1970s, concerns for worker well-being expressed by researchers, labor unions, and the federal government sparked the quality of work life (QWL) movement in the United States. Two events encouraged the spread of QWL programs: an agreement between the United Automobile Workers of America (UAW) and General Motors to institute a cooperative quality-of-work-life program in that company (Lawler, 1986), and a major government-sponsored University of Michigan Quality of Work Life study (Nadler & Lawler, 1983). For a short time during the late 1970s, interest in QWL programs waned until international competition and a desire to increase productivity in U.S. companies renewed the concern with QWL issues.

QWL is a broad concept that has been used to describe a wide range of employee development approaches and methods (Cotton, 1993; Efraty & Sirgy, 1990; Mohrman, Ledford, Lawler, & Mohrman, 1986; Nadler & Lawler, 1983). QWL programs often include QCs and gainsharing plans as well as other organizational intervention methods that expand beyond the scope of employee participation, including job enrichment and plant redesign. However, to avoid conflating QWL with other employee involvement programs, this section will limit its discussion to QWL programs that are "joint labor-management cooperative projects, particularly those aimed at improving outcomes for both the individual and the organization" (Nadler & Lawler, 1983, p. 22).

Lawler (1986) points out that QWL programs have several participation-related features in common. First, all QWL programs rely on a joint committee structure, where committees consisting of both union and company officials oversee the program. Several "lower level" committees or groups, which resemble QCs, are formed to deal with improving work methods. Occasionally, these groups may choose to focus on organization-wide issues as well. Although the QWL committees have no official power to implement their ideas, Lawler contends that "if members are representatives of the key power groups of the organization, then it is highly probable that QWL committee recommendations will be implemented" (p. 129).

Next, there is usually a formal agreement between the union and management specifying that the QWL program will not deal with issues typically covered under the collective bargaining contract. This agreement also may include a list of union, management, and joint objectives to be achieved through the implementation of the program. The company usually shares information about the company with the union and the employees and, as with QC programs, participants receive training in problem solving. Often, a third-party consultant will assist the company and the union with setting up the QWL program and with training.

Thus, QWL programs are formal participation approaches that, although consultative in nature, give employees more influence through representation than QCs do. Since committees include members of union and management groups that represent different levels of the organization, the social range is wider than that of QCs. Finally, compared to QCs, QWL committees make decisions about a wider range of issues. Although these decisions usually concern working conditions and the work itself, sometimes QWL committees are involved in making decisions about company policies (see Table 17.1).

Research indicates generally positive results in the areas of labor-management relations, employee satisfaction, and product or service quality (Cotton, 1993; Lawler, 1986). However, their impact on productivity is less certain. A review of QWL studies suggests that factors relating to the levels of union involvement and employee participation as well as the employees' desire for participation seem to moderate the effects somewhat. For instance, Cooke (1989) found that compared to less active QWL teams, active teams who met regularly positively affected productivity and quality.

Other researchers have examined the effects of direct versus indirect participation in QWL programs. Nurick (1982) studied 380 utility company employees who either directly participated in a QWL program as a member of a QWL committee or a task force, or were indirect participants who merely received information about the program. Compared to indirect participants, direct participants perceived that they had more influence and that their suggestions were considered. They also indicated higher levels of job satisfaction, organizational involvement, and trust. Nurick also noted that some employees felt isolated from the change process, and the lack of communication between the direct and indirect participants fostered feelings of program mistrust among those who were not directly involved.

The type of employees who participate in a QWL program may differ from those who choose not to participate. Miller and Prichard (1992) compared a group of manufacturing plant employees who were interested in volunteering to serve on a QWL committee with those employees who were not interested. They found that those who were interested also were more satisfied with their jobs and the company, were younger and more educated, were more involved with the union and interested in advancement, and had higher expectations about the potential benefits of employee participation. However, these employees did not actually participate in a program but simply expressed an interest in doing so. Research indicates differences between those who volunteer to become involved and those who actually do participate.

For example, Leana, Ahlbrandt, and Murrell (1992) studied a medium-size steel manufacturing organization and found that employees who had indicated a desire to participate in a QWL program but had not yet done so (volunteers) were more satisfied with the union and had higher levels of job involvement and organizational commitment compared to nonparticipants. The employees in this group also were more satisfied with their supervisors than were the employees who actually participated in the program, and they "reported greater differences between the level of influence they would like to have in decision making and the level they perceived themselves to have" (Leana et al., 1992, p. 870). However, program participants did not perceive themselves to have greater influence in decision making, so Leana et al. concluded:

> The program may not be living up to its promise in the eyes of participants because it does not permit employees to exercise their enhanced desire for influence; in addition, it may arm them with information and knowledge that enable them to see how little influence they actually have. (pp. 870-871)

Organizational factors may also influence the effectiveness of QWL programs. In a study of five Canadian petrochemical plants, Ondrack and Evans (1987) found no differences between plants with QWL programs and those without these programs. However, compared to employees at redesign plants that had implemented QWL, those at greenfield sites with QWL programs perceived greater autonomy, feedback, work collaboration, and satisfaction with coworkers and supervisors. This suggests that it may be easier to introduce employee involvement programs in newer facilities, where employees and management may be less resistant to change. Goll (1991) also found that an organization's emphasis on participative decision making was positively related to amount of employee influence.

The union may be a key factor in the success of a QWL program. Cooke (1989) found that the intensity of collaboration between union and management affected productivity and quality. Compared to steering committees with less union leader participation, those with greater union involvement were associated with greater improvements in quality and productivity. Ellinger and Nissen (1987) studied an unsuccessful QWL program implemented in a large manufacturing facility. At first, people were convinced of the program's success:

> Representatives of the company and the union claimed that QWL had led to improved communications, more employee interest in the business, an end to adversarial relationships, better mutual respect and cooperation, greater efficiency, better product quality, lower absenteeism, improved morale, and the like. (p. 200)

Yet the QWL program was causing internal problems within the local union, including interference with collective bargaining and other union activities. Also, some members felt that employees were shifting their loyalties from the union to management.

As a result of these and similar findings, Ellinger and Nissen (1987) advise practitioners to be aware of the potential problems QWL programs can pose for unions. Many unions are already aware of these problems, and as a result, union attitudes toward QWL have been mixed. Some union officials may be uncomfortable with or even suspicious of QWL since many employee participation programs have been viewed as a threat to unionization or as a means to dilute union power (see Parker, 1985). Parker warns that companies may use QWL programs to increase employee commitment to management goals, and that "QWL is carefully designed so that any sense of power an individual gets from the experience is company power—not union power" (p. 44). On the other hand, in a major study assessing the effects of worker participation and QWL programs on trade unions and collective bargaining, Kochan, Katz, and Mower (1984) found that unions had a very positive attitude toward these programs, and a vast majority believed that "the union should support and actively participate in running the program with management" (p. 149).

Research on successful QWL programs suggests that in addition to guaranteeing union participation, QWL activities should involve all levels of the organization (Kanter, Stein, & Brinkerhoff, 1982; Nadler & Lawler, 1983). Nadler and Lawler argue, for example, that middle managers may block suggestions made by the involved groups if the managers feel excluded from the program. Also, as with QC programs, intergroup conflict and competition may occur when there are differences in the level of involvement among groups at the same level of the organization.

Although most of the studies on QWL do not elaborate on how these programs affect organizational communication patterns, Lawler (1986) asserts that QWL programs have a major effect on information sharing in the organization:

> The major impact of a QWL project is often in the area of information sharing. In many, but not all cases, the creation of committee structures and task forces causes an array of communication channels to open. As a result, people often come to understand the business better and to participate more effectively in problem-solving activities. (p. 130)

Further, the parallel structure that QWL programs may bring to the organization "cuts across the hierarchy and existing functional distinctions," which opens new communication channels (Kanter et al., 1982, p. 379). Since QWL programs have greater potential than do QCs to provide employees with the means to transcend hierarchical divisions within the organization, Stohl's (1986, 1987, 1989) findings on the positive relationship between QC participation and integration into the organizational network may apply to QWL projects as well. Moreover, since QWL programs involve virtually the entire organization and allow group and committee members to participate in decisions about broader company issues, macro-organizational communication variables such as those Stohl

studied (e.g., communication climate, communication problems, knowledge of the corporation, communication networks) may be even more salient. Additional research is needed to examine the relationship between employee participation in QWL programs and their integration into the communication network.

Scanlon Gainsharing Plans

Gainsharing has been used for more than 60 years and has expanded beyond manufacturing settings to service and nonprofit organizations (Miller & Schuster, 1987b). A "gainsharing plan is an organizational system of employee involvement with a financial formula for distributing organization-wide gains" (Bullock & Lawler, 1984, pp. 23-24). Lawler (1988) adds that some "gainsharing plans are as much an approach to participative management as they are a pay plan" (p. 324). Many gainsharing plans exist, including Scanlon, Rucker, Improshare, DARCOM, Group/Plant, and Productivity and Waste programs (e.g., see Kaufman, 1992; Welbourne & Gomez-Mejia, 1995). However, although "gainsharing always includes a financial system to reinforce gains in organizational performance . . . the inclusion of a participation system of employee committees to generate and evaluate cost-saving ideas has not been used by all programs" (Gowen, 1990, p. 79).

The Scanlon plan, in particular, is concerned with establishing a strong link between employee participation and financial rewards. Developed in 1938 by company accountant Joseph Scanlon "as a cost-saving employee suggestion system to turn around the nearly bankrupt Empire Steel" (Gowen, 1990, p. 79), the profit-sharing component of the plan was not added to the suggestion system until ten years later. Scanlon plans are based on the assumption that

> all people have needs of psychological growth and development and are capable of and willing to fulfill those needs in their employer's

service if they are allowed the opportunity to participate in organizational decision making and if they are equitably compensated for the participation. (Hammer, 1988, p. 337)

Compared with other gainsharing programs, especially the pervasive Improshare plan and other productivity gainsharing (PG) programs that have *excluded* a formal employee involvement system (Graham-Moore & Ross, 1983; Miller & Schuster, 1987b), Scanlon gainsharing provides for a relatively high level of employee participation and involvement. Given the results of Bullock and Tubbs's (1990) meta-analysis of 33 studies of gainsharing plans (i.e., that plans with formal involvement structures had more successful gainsharing overall, especially high employee innovativeness, and higher levels of employee satisfaction and labor-management cooperation), gainsharing programs that *include* employee participation (especially Scanlon plans) will be emphasized in this section.

Companies implementing Scanlon programs form production committees that meet regularly to review employee suggestions and to discuss ways to cut costs and improve productivity. Ordinarily, these production committees include supervisors and employees from all areas of the organization who are elected by their coworkers. These committees solicit, review, and implement employees' ideas concerning how to improve performance and productivity. Scanlon plan programs also include a screening committee consisting of members from many areas of the organization. This committee approves production committee suggestions that exceed cost guidelines or affect multiple departments, reviews appeals from employees whose suggestions were rejected by the production committees, and reviews the bonus formula (Miller & Schuster, 1987b). Bonus formulas vary across organizations, but generally the steering committee sets a standard based on past performance, and when the company exceeds this baseline and "gains" are realized, employees receive a financial bonus.

Typically, these bonuses are based on a percentage of the employees' wages and are paid monthly or quarterly. In some organizations, bonuses are distributed on a team basis to reward and encourage collective performance (DeBettengies, 1989).

Lawler (1986) points out that Scanlon plan committee structures are similar to the parallel structure approach used in QC and QWL programs but, unlike QCs and QWL groups, Scanlon committees have a small budget and can implement certain suggestions without management approval. Thus, Scanlon plans are formal participation programs that are basically consultative but, compared with QC and QWL programs, give employees more latitude in implementing some suggestions on their own. These programs have a more expansive social range since interaction among employees cuts across department lines, and all employees have the opportunity to make suggestions and receive financial bonuses. The content of participation is more comprehensive than that of QCs, because Scanlon plans allow employees to be involved in decisions about broader company policies as well as issues relating to their immediate work area (see Table 17.1).

Studies indicate that gainsharing plans produce generally positive results, including improvements in individual attitudes, labor-management relations, teamwork and decision making, work methods, service or product quality, and productivity, as well as increases in financial decision-making and group process skills (Bullock & Lawler, 1984; Bullock & Tubbs, 1990; Gowen, 1990; Hatcher, Ross, & Collins, 1991; Lawler, 1986; Welbourne & Gomez-Mejia, 1995). In a study of a large, unionized manufacturing firm, Miller and Schuster (1987a) found that implementation of a Scanlon plan resulted in long-term employment stability, increases in productivity, and significant improvements in the relationship between union and management. Doherty, Nord, and McAdams (1989) examined different gainsharing programs in manufacturing and nonmanufacturing environments and found that these programs improved productivity, safety, and attendance. These programs also improved communication between workers and management and increased employee understanding of operations.

Additional findings indicate that these positive effects may persist over time (Schuster, 1984). For example, Hatcher and Ross (1991) examined a U.S. manufacturing company two months prior to the implementation of a gainsharing plan and 15 months later. Results revealed significant increases in organizational members' concern for performance and in perceptions of teamwork (coordination, open communication, helpfulness, friendliness). Interrupted time series analyses of more than 4 years of objective data indicated a significant decrease in grievances and a significant increase in product quality.

Although the majority of published studies on gainsharing conclude that this type of employee involvement program is quite effective, some researchers have been critical of this body of research (see Cotton, 1993; Hanlon, Meyer, & Taylor, 1994; Hanlon & Taylor, 1991; Lawler, 1986, 1988). They point out the methodological limitations of research, including the lack of control groups and the less than rigorous statistical procedures used in most of the studies. In addition to criticizing the measures of effects of these programs, researchers have argued that studies are too limited in scope and should examine how and why gainsharing works (Bullock & Lawler, 1984; Cotton, 1993; Gowen, 1990; Hanlon et al., 1994; Hanlon & Taylor, 1991; Lawler, 1988; Welbourne & Gomez-Mejia, 1995). Moreover, there may be important intervening processes that mediate and explain the effectiveness of gainsharing programs. Hanlon and colleagues (Hanlon et al., 1994; Hanlon & Taylor, 1991) posit that communication is a key intervening variable in gainsharing plan outcomes:

> A major intervening effect of the implementation of gainsharing is a change in organizational communication content, quality, and climate. . . . [Specifically] changes in work group communication behaviors (the extent to which they talk about work and share job-related knowledge and ideas for performance improvement) increase group members' job knowledge or cognitions, which improves their ability to do their jobs and in turn partially accounts for improved job performance and economic gains for the employees and employer. (Hanlon & Taylor, 1991, pp. 242-243)

These researchers explain that since most members of organizations with gainsharing plans are economically motivated to improve their performance, they will increase the frequency and amount of interaction with one another to learn more about their job and the organization. This increase in job-related information leads to better job performance and organizational "gains," which are ultimately translated into financial bonuses in which employees "share." The relationship between performance and financial rewards increases the likelihood that employees will value their membership in the organization, which will lead to positive attitudinal outcomes as well.

Hanlon and Taylor (1991) found empirical support for this explanation of how gainsharing works. In a quasi-experimental field study of a modified Scanlon plan, they compared a regional facility of a priority package delivery company that had implemented a Scanlon plan with a primary facility of the same company that did not implement the program. Hanlon and Taylor found that compared to those employees at the nonparticipating facility, those at the Scanlon plan facility reported positive effects on communication. Specifically, "gainsharing participants perceived that they received useful and accurate information, had frank discussions about work situations, were encouraged to discuss problems, and talked about ideas for improving their work methods and environment more often than nonparticipants" (p. 258).

These findings are consistent with Lawler's (1986) suggestion that gainsharing influences the information flow in the organization, where information-seeking efforts are directed from employees to management, and financial information moves downward from management to the employees, resulting in increased knowledge about the economics of the business. Other studies suggest that gainsharing plans may improve communication and cooperation between supervisors and their employees as well (Bullock & Lawler, 1984; Bullock & Tubbs, 1990; Gowen, 1990).

Both cognitive and motivational models may explain these effects. For instance, Miller and Monge (1987) found a strong and direct link between employee cognitive factors and organizational commitment, and Hanlon and Taylor (1991) argued that cognitive models offered a useful explanation for their findings on gainsharing effects. This also is consistent with the claim that employee participation can help employees form more accurate perceptions of reward contingencies in the organization (Miller & Monge, 1987; Monge & Miller, 1988). Further, motivation is a factor, since the potential for financial gain may encourage employee interest in obtaining information.

In addition to affecting immediate changes in work group and organizational communication, gainsharing programs may have long-term attitudinal effects. A follow-up study conducted by Hanlon et al. (1994) found that even three months after the priority package delivery company eliminated the financial bonus component of the program, the facility that had participated in the plan exhibited higher levels of moral commitment and prosocial behavior and fewer turnover intentions than did the nonparticipating facility. Hanlon et al. assert that the bonus formula accounted for changes in communication behavior, and prosocial behavior became a group norm.

These findings are consistent with comments made by other researchers on the factors contributing to gainsharing program success. For instance, Lawler (1986, 1988) states that employee trust, understanding, acceptance, input, and cooperation are important to plan effectiveness. Other conditions that increase the likelihood of program success include an open communication policy, a management that is technically and communicatively competent and is able to deal with suggestions, a work force that is technically and financially knowledgeable and is interested in participation and higher pay (Lawler, 1988, p. 328), and involving members in the creation of a fair distribution rule (Cooper, Dyck, & Frohlich, 1992).

Thus, it is clear that managerial communication competence and willingness to share information are antecedents to effective Scanlon plan outcomes. Implementing these programs also may result in improved communication relationships between supervisors and employees, better information flow in the organization, and increased employee access to information about his or her job and the company. Further, gainsharing programs with higher levels of employee involvement (e.g., participation in the design of the plan and involvement in fair allocation rules) are associated with the most favorable outcomes in terms of innovativeness, performance, teamwork, climate and labor-management cooperation (Bullock & Tubbs, 1990; Hatcher & Ross, 1991).

Self-Directed Work Teams and New-Design Plants

Self-directed work teams (SDWTs) have their roots in human relations initiatives in the United States beginning in the 1930s, European coal mine and factory sociotechnical studies in the 1940s and 1950s, and Japanese quality circles following World War II. Beginning with their implementation in U.S. organizations in the 1960s and 1970s (Pasmore, Francis, Haldeman, & Shani, 1982; Walton, 1977), the discursive warrant for implementing "teams"—especially as they have been used in U.S. core manufacturing organizations—is organizational performance: improved quality, increased productivity, and decreased operating costs. Fisher (1993) reported that 7% of U.S. workers were organized in such teams, and more than 200 major corporations relied on them in at least one company location. In fact, the popularity of work teams continues to increase. As of 1999, 78% of U.S. corporations used self-managing teams (Lawler, 1999).

Typically, SDWTs are intact groups of employees who have collective responsibility for managing themselves and their work with minimal direct supervision. Usually, they plan and schedule work, order materials and handle budget expenditures, make production/service-related decisions, monitor productivity, and act on matters once reserved for management (Versteeg, 1990). Viewed in terms of Dachler and Wilpert's (1978) categories, SDWTs are voluntarily initiated by organizations, implemented at the group level and often throughout the entire organization, with direct and maximal participation by all employees involved in the SDWTs (see Table 17.1). Consider the SDWTs in a case study of a team-managed manufacturing plant (Seibold, 1995):

> Whereas production functions in traditional organizations are handled by some workers, and functions such as maintaining the equipment and assuring quality control and safety are handled by others, the organizational structure at BFSI cuts across those responsibilities. Multiskilled blue-collar workers (technicians), working in "area teams" of 4-5 persons, rotate jobs within and across areas to handle *all* aspects of the production process. There are also no foremen or supervisors at BFSI. The technicians, with two-year technical degrees and training in electronics and mechanics, are self-directed. They monitor and maintain the production process machinery with specialized support from a small team of certified engineers, who act more as consultants than quality control overseers. (pp. 288-289)

It is difficult to separate SDWTs from their organizational context, frequently "new-design plants" (Lawler, 1986). New-design plants and the SDWTs at their core are outgrowths of sociotechnical systems theory

(Emery & Trist, 1965). Patterned after self-regulating work teams in England and Norway (Burns & Stalker, 1968; Rice, 1958), as well as well-publicized participative management plants created in America during the 1970s by Procter & Gamble and by General Foods, U.S. corporations designed "new plants" in the 1980s that transferred to employees power, information, knowledge, and intrinsic rewards traditionally associated with management (Lawler, 1986). Walton (1985) noted that 200 new-design plants were in operation by the mid-1980s.

Characteristic of the participative practices common to new-design plants are coworker teams' selection of new employees, work team participation in the physical layout of the plant, design of jobs by employees, lack of much hierarchy in organizational structure, implementation of egalitarian pay and incentive systems, and the development of management philosophies that emphasize participation and shared decision making. In one study, the organization

> is designed to foster group participation in planning work, coordinating tasks, and solving problems. Each day, each shift begins with a meeting of everyone working in the plant during that rotation. Meetings of subunits or standing committees may follow or be held throughout the day. Standing committees, such as the Safety Committee, the Good Practices Committee, and the Design Committee, exist to address a variety of organization-wide issues. Personnel functions have been absorbed by other groups of employees, including preparation of an employee handbook, development of applicant screening/selection procedures, and monitoring compensation. Team members also administer most aspects of the reward system, including establishing skill-based pay levels, determining raises and bonuses, and monitoring a gainsharing program. All members are cross-trained in every aspect of the production process. Although there is a plant manager and an accountant, they primarily serve liaison roles in interfacing with the

parent companies. A strong egalitarian culture . . . is reflected in the absence of formal hierarchies (team members rotate as "area leaders") and the absence of status markers (e.g., there are no eating areas, restrooms, offices, recreational facilities, parking places, and the like that cannot be used by all members). Training is emphasized: on-the-job and paid off-site technical training is provided for everyone on a regular basis, as is training in interpersonal and group process skills, career planning, and other personal development. (Seibold, 1995, p. 289)

As Lawler (1986) summarized, "New-design plants are clearly different from traditional plants. . . . The reward system, the structure, the physical layout, the personnel management system, and the nature of jobs are all changed in significant ways. Because so many features are altered, in aggregate they amount to a new kind of organization" (p. 178).

The literature on SDWTs is replete with research on factors associated with degree of members' identification with the organization (Barker & Tompkins, 1994), external activity and performance in organizational teams (Ancona & Caldwell, 1992), job switching (Blumberg, 1980), work group characteristics and effectiveness (Campion, Medsker, & Higgs, 1993), the social structure of the organization (Carnall, 1982), teamwork and communication (S. Glaser, 1994), frontline members' views of SDWTs (Berggren, 1993; Katz, Laughlin, & Wilson, 1990), organizational factors that enable and constrain team effectiveness (Hackman, 1990), obstacles to team-based performance (Katzenbach & Smith, 1993), dysfunctional decision dynamics (Manz & Sims, 1982), leadership dynamics (Manz, 1986; 1992; Manz, Keating, & Donnellon, 1990; Manz & Sims, 1984, 1987), personal control (Manz & Angle, 1986), member selection (Neuman, 1991), design and activation (Pearce & Ravlin, 1987; Sundstrom, DeMeuse, & Futrell, 1990), evaluation (Pearson, 1992), restructuring (Poza & Markus, 1980), peer assessment (Saavedra &

Kwun, 1993), member requisites for teamwork (Stevens & Campion, 1994), and training (Swezey & Salas, 1992). In an often cited research program, Kemp, Wall, Clegg, and Cordery (1983) and Wall, Kemp, Jackson, and Clegg (1986) compared employees in SDWTs to employees in the same factory on another shift and at another of the company's plants. Members of the SDWTs had significantly higher satisfaction with factors intrinsic to the job (opportunities to use abilities, amount of responsibility and autonomy), an effect that endured over 30 months of the study. SDWT members also were more satisfied with extrinsic factors of the work (pay, work conditions), although this lessened over time. Neither work motivation nor performance was found to differ, although cost savings were highest in the SDWTs.

However, in new-design plants in particular, research has revealed a number of positive outcomes associated with SDWTs: improvements in work methods and procedures due to team problem solving, enhanced recruitment and retention of team members due to increased involvement and pay, high-quality work due to team motivation, fewer supervision requirements because teams are self-managing, improved decision making resulting from increased input, higher levels of skill development and staffing flexibility due to cross-training, and lower levels of grievances because teams resolve issues (Lawler, 1986, 1990). These effects may be due to the fact that the range of the SDWTs extends to the entire organization (Dachler & Wilpert, 1978). Seibold (1995) found that SDWT members perceived four advantages to working at their new design plant (compared with nonparticipative organizations in which some had been employed, and organizations in which SDWTs were on a "trial basis" and were restricted to one area of the plant): (1) greater opportunities to elicit input from all members of the organization, (2) better utilization of both human and technical resources, (3) freedom to express their opinions and ideas increased their morale and satisfaction with the organization, and (4) cross-training as a major opportunity and advantage. He also found the following performance outcomes: nearly on-time start up and at less than projected cost, output equivalent to comparable plants but with 60% less labor, 80% less rework, more frequent inventory turns, less production machinery downtime than normal, and near-zero turnover in personnel. Compared to a traditionally managed organization, SDWT members also felt that they had a greater sense of ownership, greater satisfaction and better decision making, greater autonomy and self-motivation, good communication and a high level of interaction among members, more opportunity to talk directly to managers, greater tolerance for individual differences, more flexibility in scheduling work hours, an increase in coworkers' helpfulness and honesty, and the acknowledgment of individual contributions by others in the organization. Cotter's (1983) review of organizations in seven countries that transitioned from traditional work systems to SDWTs revealed similar outcomes: 93% reported improved productivity, 86% reported decreased operating costs, 86% reported improved quality, and 70% reported improved employee attitudes.

However, as writers have reported about the "pitfalls" and "dilemmas" of employee involvement programs in general (Baloff & Doherty, 1989; Connors & Romberg, 1991; Kanter, 1982, 1986; Magjuka, 1991), SDWTs in new-design plants are prone to a variety of problems as well: member expectations can be too high because of the philosophy and selection process; surveillance by other areas of the organization (e.g., management in "parent" companies) can produce pressure and conflict; training costs are high due to the need for cross-training and team training; team meetings take more time and decision processes can be slow; establishing standards can be difficult in the absence of a "history" and meaningful benchmarks; and the timing of new decisions regarding compensation, schedule, and production changes is difficult (Lawler, 1986). Further, members may revert

to the practices of traditional workplaces and hierarchical management during times of information overload, environmental uncertainty, decision difficulty, work pressure, and interpersonal conflict (Barker, Melville, & Pacanowsky, 1993). Interpersonal and group-level difficulties have been observed in self-directed teams in general: conflict, decision making, efficiency, performance feedback, inter-area relationships, and the like. Too, many problems can be found in organizations making a transition to self-managing teams: first-line supervisors, middle managers, or union representatives who resist the teams; reductions in existing work force size; SDWTs may be limited to select units of the organization or introduced on an "experimental" basis; changes in preexisting organizational roles or patterns of communication that need to be facilitated; dysfunctional correlates to increased "permissiveness" within units suddenly given greater autonomy (for discussion of these problems, see Barker et al., 1993; Cordery, Mueller, & Smith, 1991; Cummings, 1978; Lawler, 1986). Further, when *self*-managed *teams* occur in the context of a *team*-managed *organization* (especially new-design plants), SDWT outcomes such as member satisfaction and team performance may interact with a number of other organizational contingencies including the timing of start-up decisions about shift work, bonuses, and production schedules; establishing plantwide standards; interfacing with parent companies; and negotiating the unique role of the plant manager.

Employee Stock Ownership Plans

Toscano (1983) distinguished among three types of employee ownership, which we can conceptualize as forming a continuum. At one end, *direct ownership* refers to the typical situation in which employees individually own stock in their company. At the other end are *worker cooperatives,* in which a group of individuals working in a company both own and personally operate the firm. Somewhere between these poles are *employee stock ownership plans,* formed when the company creates a plan in which all employees acquire stock as a part of their benefits. We shall emphasize this form of employee ownership for several reasons. First, although direct ownership can be important in smaller organizations (where percentage of stock owned may be sufficient to significantly involve employees and to influence the organization), this is not usually the case in large organizations. Further, as Cotton (1993) notes, research attention to direct ownership has been sparse, in part because it is operationally difficult "to draw a line between the employee-owned corporation and the publicly owned corporation where some of the stockholders are also employees" (p. 203). Second, although worker cooperatives are easy to identify, they represent the fewest in number of organizations with employee ownership. Drawing comparisons is difficult because the organizations tend to be concentrated in certain sectors and certain countries (for an excellent communication-based treatment of cooperatives, see Cheney, 1995).

Employee stock ownership plans (ESOPs) are the most prevalent and popular form of employee ownership, with more than 10,000 plans in existence in the United States involving more than 10 million employees (Pierce & Furo, 1990). In essence, an ESOP is a legal trust that must invest in the company's stock by contributing stock or cash to the trust and allocating stock to employees. It usually takes employees five to ten years to become vested, and they typically cannot take possession of their shares until they retire or otherwise leave the organization. ESOPs differ from direct ownership in important ways: employees need not invest their own funds since they automatically receive shares from the firm, and they have more limited voting rights than employees with direct ownership of stock.

Viewed from the standpoint of Dachler and Wilpert's (1978) typology, ESOPs are a *formal* method of employee participation involving members of the entire organization. Employees' potential for influence is high, although this can vary from plan to plan. Since they own a portion of the company, it is assumed that they will be more involved in it—leading to increased employee satisfaction and organizational performance (Buchko, 1992).

However, researchers have pointed out that only some ESOP firms have actually instituted formal participation mechanisms for their employees. In a review of several studies, Rosen (1991) found that between one third and one half of the ESOP firms provided opportunities for joint worker-management decision making on job-related issues. This may be due, in part, to the fact that in addition to serving as an employee benefit plan and as a way to increase employee participation, ESOPs traditionally have been used to save failing firms, reap tax advantages for companies, finance corporate growth, and prevent takeovers (Harrison, 1994; McWhirter, 1991; Rosen, Klein, & Young, 1986). However, more recent sources suggest that the *primary* motivations for forming ESOPs in larger firms have changed from preventing takeovers and reaping tax benefits in the 1980s to providing postretirement benefits to employees and increasing worker participation in the 1990s ("ESOPs, Employee Ownership Evolve," 1993). For example, according to E. W. Purcell, senior associate with a firm specializing in structuring and implementing ESOPs, "the basis of the ESOP concept . . . is to create more employee participation and empowerment [meaning that] employees are more involved in the department in which they work and in the day-to-day operations of the business" ("ESOPs, Employee Ownership Evolve," 1993, p. 30).

Although much of the evidence is anecdotal, introducing ESOPs may foster a change in the company's culture, where "there is more communication and more freedom for employees to make decisions" (Taplin, 1989, p. 53). "Along with the implementation of an employee stock ownership plan (ESOP) frequently comes a change in corporate culture that includes better management/employee communications and increased employee participation and involvement" ("ESOP Brings Change," 1992, p. 25). At the very least, ESOPs influence information flow in the organization. Most ESOP firms share with their employees via newsletters, reports, company-wide and department meetings, and one-on-one discussions, information about company finances, budget, and performance (Burzawa, 1992, 1993; Rosen et al., 1986; Taplin, 1989). Further, even without a formal participation program in place, research suggests that employees' increased financial stake may lead to informal interaction about managerial decisions (see Lewis & Seibold, 1993, 1996, for arguments and evidence on the positive relationship between the introduction of new programs and increased informal communication among coworkers).

Research results concerning the effectiveness of ESOPs have been positive but mixed. In terms of organizational performance, studies have found increased sales and growth in companies that have converted to ESOPs (e.g., Rosen & Quarrey, 1987). However, as Cotton (1993) has summarized, "although no studies found employee-owned companies to have lower performance than conventional firms, several studies found no differences" (p. 210). With regard to the effects of ESOPs and direct ownership on employees' attitudes and behaviors, Cotton (1993) also concluded a review of relevant studies with a "mixed" assessment:

> The studies of ESOPs and direct ownership found primarily positive, but also negative and null, results. To add to the confusion, most conversions to employee ownership are accompanied by a variety of other events (changes in worker population, financial rewards, sales and profits, etc.). Examples of positive changes in attitudes or the lack of changes can often be explained by these confounding effects. Overall, positive attitudes generally are found to be related to employee ownership. The attitude (sat-

isfaction, commitment, etc.) may vary, however, and in several cases the conversion to employee ownership produced more negative results. (p. 215)

Several explanations have been offered for why ownership influences employee attitudes and firm performance, controlling for factors such as those noted above. Proponents of a "financial investment" explanation (e.g., French, 1987; Sockell, 1985) contend that effects of this form of employee participation are a function of the financial rewards that members receive from their involvement. While considerable research has investigated the financial ownership hypothesis, according to Cotton (1993) results have been "extremely mixed": "Some research indicates that measures of financial stake (e.g., size of contribution by the company) are related to employee attitudes and/or organizational performance, yet the most obvious measure (amount of stock owned) shows few positive effects" (p. 233). Alternatively, some researchers (e.g., Buchko, 1992; Long, 1981; Paul, Ebadi, & Dilts, 1987; Pierce & Furo, 1990; Pierce, Rubenfeld, & Morgan, 1991) have proposed that the effects of employee ownership are moderated by the "psychological ownership" afforded by that form of participation in the organization. In an influential study of how employee attitudes are influenced by ESOPs, Klein (1987) used results from 2,804 employees in 37 ESOP firms to investigate organizational commitment, turnover intentions, satisfaction with the ESOP, ESOP philosophy, perception of work influence, and stock return performance. Findings revealed that employee satisfaction and commitment were positively related to strong contributions by the firm to the ESOP, a strong philosophy of employee ownership within management, and full and frequent communication by management. Cotton (1993) concluded that while there is less research concerning the psychological ownership hypothesis and ESOP effects, it has produced "more consistent evidence that perceptions of involvement or some type of employee participation program is related to more positive attitudes and/or organizational performance" (p. 222).

Other researchers also have concluded that ESOPs combined with employee participation in decision making are more effective in changing attitudes and performance than are ESOPs or participation alone (e.g., Blasi & Kruse, 1991; Burzawa, 1992, 1993; Long, 1982; Rosen, 1989; Rosen et al., 1986; Taplin, 1989; Turpin-Forster, 1989; Young, 1990, 1991). For instance, Young (1990) points out:

> Our research has very clearly shown that the most participative employee ownership companies have growth rates 11% to 17% per year higher than the least participative companies. Moreover, employees in the most participative companies were significantly more satisfied with their work and their ESOP, were more committed to their company, and were more likely to stay with their firm than workers in the less participative companies. (p. 177)

Some have even suggested that implementing ESOPs without encouraging employee participation in decision making may backfire (Blasi & Kruse, 1991; Turpin-Forster, 1989). For instance, ESOPs may make employees more responsible and committed to their jobs, but if they perceive that management is operating in a manner that is wasteful to the company and employees are not in a position to help change it, then frustrations may increase and employees may develop more negative attitudes (Turpin-Forster, 1989).

Unfortunately, as Cotton (1993) and others have noted, it is difficult to disentangle the participation effects from the financial ones. This is made even more difficult by the fact that the type of employee participation associated with ESOPs seems to vary somewhat among companies. The research reveals that the participation component of ESOPs may include one or more of the following techniques: suggestion boxes, employee commit-

tees, QCs, interdepartmental task forces, same-department work groups, joint problem-solving teams, and representative boards (Blasi & Kruse, 1991; Taplin, 1989; Young, 1990). Many of these programs differ in terms of how much influence employees are accorded, the types of decision making in which they are involved, and the social range required. This is perhaps why ESOPs have been found to be only moderately effective in changing employee attitudes and behaviors. More research certainly is needed in this area to separate the effects of participation and to distinguish the varying outcomes among the different types of participation programs associated with each ESOP. We now turn to a number of dynamics embedded in a "psychological" explanation for employee participation effects, and we explore their communication implications.

COMMUNICATION AND PARTICIPATION EFFECTS

Although some researchers have expressed a concern for understanding *why* different types of employee participation programs work (Leana & Florkowski, 1992), few have attempted to answer this question empirically. Leana and Florkowski argue, "The research based on intrinsic models of participative decision making has often been analyzed with little regard for differences among the types of participation programs and various aspects of its implementation" (p. 263). As noted earlier, methodological and conceptual problems make it difficult to isolate specific factors that account for each program's differing outcomes. However, reviews of numerous studies on QCs, QWL programs, gainsharing plans, SDWTs, ESOPs, and employee participation in general suggest that *communication* functions as an intervening variable in participation outcomes. Further, this chapter has maintained that the type of employee participation program influences the communication patterns and processes in the organization, which mediates the cognitive and affective (motivational) effects of participation. The following section briefly explains the relationship between information flow and the cognitive and motivational effects of participation.

Cognitive and Motivational Effects

Researchers have suggested that there is an important connection between message flow and decision making in the organization (O'Reilly, Chatman, & Anderson, 1987). Moreover, there is a strong link between employee participation and information-processing capabilities, and this significantly affects organizational effectiveness and quality of work life (Castrogiovanni & Macy, 1990, p. 314). These claims are consistent with the findings on the relationship between involvement in one of the employee participation programs outlined in this chapter and organizational communication patterns. Castrogiovanni and Macy (1990) found that the degree of employee participation positively affected information-processing capabilities. Specifically, compared to indirect participants, direct participants (members of QWL committees and task forces) perceived greater influence over work and integrating activities as well as increased improvements in coordination, external feedback, and organizational communication.

Researchers have attempted to explain how participation in decision making, and hence, involvement in organizational communication networks, influences outcomes. This participation often entails an increase in downward and upward information dissemination, which in turn provides employees at various organizational levels greater access to information. Monge and Miller (1988) explain:

> Participation in decision making will result in the individual employee having increased knowledge about the organization and his or her part in the organization. . . . Participative employees will have a greater understanding of the entire organization, its standing in the marketplace, and the part that individual employees play in the greater scheme of things. (p. 220)

Although these claims ordinarily are used to explain the cognitive influences of participation, they may offer insight into motivational and attitudinal forces as well. For instance, research suggests that employee participation in decision making and the corresponding involvement in communication networks may enhance employee feelings of empowerment and self-efficacy (Conger & Kanungo, 1988; Hammer, 1988; Jackson, 1983; Marshall & Stohl, 1993; Thomas & Griffin, 1989).

Within the vast literature on power sharing (Leana, 1987) and employee empowerment (Thomas & Velthouse, 1990), several researchers have elaborated on the relationship between access to other members of the organization, information, and empowerment. Conger and Kanungo (1988) define empowerment as a "process of enhancing feelings of self-efficacy among organizational members" (p. 474). Organizational conditions that may hamper empowerment or feelings of personal efficacy include poor network-forming and communications systems, lack of role clarity and network-forming opportunities, limited participation in decisions that have a direct impact on job performance, and limited contact with senior management (Conger & Kanungo, 1988, p. 477). Pacanowsky (1988) states that maintaining an open communication system and using integrative problem solving can empower employees. General adequacy of communication channels also enhances empowerment (Albrecht, 1988).

Marshall and Stohl (1993) expand the notion of empowerment to mean "the process of developing key relationships in the organization in order to gain greater control over one's own organizational life" (p. 141), and they found that empowerment was related to feelings of satisfaction. These findings are consistent with the suggestion made by Conger and Kanungo (1988) that increasing the number of communication opportunities and employee participation systems can be empowering; however, employees must also receive information that confirms their feelings of self-efficacy.

These points suggest that employee perceptions of control, personal influence, or self-efficacy may influence outcomes such as satisfaction. Based on a meta-analysis of studies examining the effects of perceived employee control, Spector (1986) concluded that employees who perceived high levels of control at work scored high on job satisfaction, organizational commitment, job involvement, and motivation.

This chapter has established that QCs, QWL programs, ESOP, SDWTs, and Scanlon plans differ somewhat in terms of the content and scope of decision making and the social range of participation, but they differ considerably in terms of the degree of participation and level of influence they afford members. As noted earlier, the differing dimensions of each employee involvement program influence the communication patterns within the organization, which subsequently affects organizational outcomes such as satisfaction and performance (Marshall & Stohl, 1993).

Participation Dimensions and Communication Patterns

Monge and Eisenberg (1987) argue that organizational change (i.e., implementing an employee participation program) may affect communication network participation, and the literature offers overwhelming support for this claim in general (Eisenberg, Monge, & Miller, 1983) and in the employee involvement area in particular (Buch, 1992; Hanlon et al., 1994; Hanlon & Taylor, 1991; Lawler, 1986, 1988; Marshall & Stohl, 1993; Stohl, 1986, 1987, 1989). However, no researchers have used this approach to explain the different effects of various employee involvement programs,

such as QCs, QWL programs, SDWTs, ESOPs, and Scanlon plans.

The level of program effects may depend on the degree to which it influences and is influenced by information use. As mentioned earlier, the conditions necessary for beneficial participation outcomes include a supportive and participative organizational climate, a management that is willing and able to share relevant information, and employees who are interested in participation (see also Shadur, Kienzle, & Rodwell, 1999; Tesluk, Vance, & Mathieu, 1999). Lawler (1986) points out that information is "a source of power and effectiveness in organizational coordination and cooperation. Without considerable information moving downward, employee participation and involvement become impractical and even dangerous" (p. 24). The literature suggests that QCs may be less effective in this area than are QWL programs, which in turn are less effective than SDWTs and Scanlon plan programs. Further, each type of employee participation program discussed in this chapter differs with regard to level of influence, decision content, and social range. These differences affect the communication patterns and relationships in the organization.

QCs may have weaker and less consistent effects due to the limitations on decision content, lower levels of influence, and limited social range. Since QC members deal primarily with issues concerning the work itself, they may have less of a need to communicate with many members outside of their work area or department. If the need arises, however, QC members may not have the ability or the connections to reach others in the organization. "Usually, the group is provided with no systematic information about company performance, costs, long-range plans, and other matters" (Ledford et al., 1988, p. 259). This lack of information may result in poor decisions or management unwillingness to implement circle suggestions, which could reduce members' feelings of empowerment or self-efficacy. That, in turn, may ultimately undermine satisfaction and performance.

This is not to suggest, however, that QC members are unable to communicate with others outside of their group. Rather, as Stohl (1986, 1987, 1989) points out, QC members' level of integration in the organizational network affects circle members' intention to withdraw and overall QC effectiveness. More specifically, Stohl (1989) states:

> The greater number of diverse groups from which a circle received relevant information, resources, and support, the more influential that group was in (a) convincing management that its proposal was sound and worthwhile, (b) gaining commitment of resources to carry out the solution, and (c) assuring implementation of the solution by those members of the organization who had to carry out the new plan. (p. 357)

Thus, the communication network perspective may explain the inconsistent findings with regard to QC program outcomes as well as predict why, as Cotton (1993) concludes, QCs are less effective than QWL programs and Scanlon plans.

QWL and Scanlon programs, on the other hand, include committees and groups that represent a wider range of employees. This makes it much easier for these groups to access the information they might need from other areas in the organization. Moreover, compared to QCs, these groups deal with broader organizational issues. This expanded scope of decision making requires that they communicate with employees across the entire organization.

Scanlon plans may have particularly strong effects because of the financial reward component. Leana and Florkowski (1992) state that "offering bonus payments may increase the perceived job outcomes flowing from greater inputs on the part of employees in ways that intrinsic benefits cannot" (p. 251). Moreover, since the monetary incentive may motivate employees to work harder and smarter, employees will have a greater desire to obtain and to share information. For in-

stance, "because employees receive financial information and their pay depends on effectiveness, they will challenge managers and demand change in ways that do not occur with QCs. For example, I have seen employees ask vice-presidents about accounts receivable and marketing issues" (Lawler, 1986, p. 166).

Hammer (1988) suggests that gainsharing facilitates employee empowerment by increasing access to management-level information. Additionally, "a sense of personal control develops among members of the organization when opportunities are afforded for the individual to attain rewards in sensible ways" (Albrecht, 1988, p. 385). As mentioned previously, participation gives employees information about which behaviors are likely to be rewarded, and the financial bonuses offered as part of the Scanlon plan certainly provide some tangible information about the results of the program.

As noted earlier, ESOPs may vary in their effectiveness because (1) although information flow (i.e., amount of financial information about the firm) is increased from management to employees, not all ESOPs include a formal employee participation component; and (2) even ESOP firms that do increase employee participation in decision making can differ with regard to both the type of participation program they implement and the type of formal involvement created. As with gainsharing, the financial incentive combined with participation may have powerful effects. However, some authors note that gainsharing plans may be more effective in increasing employee work effort than are ESOPs with a participation component, since ESOPs do not provide the same immediate financial rewards for employees as do annual gainsharing distributions (Rosen et al., 1986).

SDWTs may be most effective because the employees' level and scope of influence is high and the social range (Dachler & Wilpert, 1978) of the program extends to the entire organization in new-design plants. A parallel study of organizational work teams by Hirokawa and Keyton (1995) revealed that characteristics internal to the team (motivated members and competent group leadership) combined with organization-based factors (compatible work schedules, organizational assistance) and adequate informational resources best distinguished perceived volunteer-based work team effectiveness. It is precisely this combination of team, organizational, and informational factors that may inhere in the relative efficacy of SDWTs.

CRITICAL RESPONSES TO PARTICIPATION RESEARCH

As indicated earlier in this chapter, the five employee participation programs on which most previous research has focused are among the most popular choices of management (especially in North America) but are not necessarily the most "democratic." Among a variety of critical responses to these programs, critics have argued that managers' primary motivation is to increase profits rather than to relinquish control to workers. For instance, Rothschild-Whitt and Lindenfeld (1982) argue:

> What identifies such participative models is that the permissible level of workers' participation is strictly controlled and limited by management. Employees may be afforded some measure of decisional control over immediate work tasks and environments, but the primacy of managerial control is left intact. . . . In the end, it is top management that has the authority to order and to halt experiments in workers' participation and job enlargement. (p. 5)

Other critics, including communication scholars (e.g., Barker, 1997; Barker & Cheney, 1994; Barker & Tompkins, 1992, 1994; Cheney, 1995; Conrad & Ryan, 1985; Deetz, 1992; Deetz & Kersten, 1983; Harrison, 1994), have leveled similar criticisms. For instance, Deetz and Kersten (1983) point out:

First, organizational goals are commonly viewed in terms of economic growth, profit, or continued organizational survival. Other goals, such as welfare of organizational participants, are subordinate to these goals and have only instrumental importance. Humanistic and participatory programs, for example, are valued only for their ability to increase productivity. (p. 153)

To a great extent, this is indicative of what Alvesson and Deetz (1996) term the "universalization of managerial interests," or the tendency for the interests of organizational subpopulations to be rationalized and interpreted in terms of the interests of privileged managerial groups in organizations where those practices are located.

Critical theorists contend that the type of participation promoted by the programs so predominant in North American organizations and so prevalent in the participation literature cannot foster a truly democratic and humane workplace. Rather, these forms of employee participation are merely "a tool for handling dissatisfaction, absenteeism, and alienation, problems that are detrimental to the accomplishment of organizational objectives" (Deetz & Kersten, 1983, p. 169). The limited form of participation afforded organizational members by these programs differs markedly from "political participation" (Abrahamsson, 1977; Deetz & Kersten, 1983) or "democratic participation" (Rothschild-Whitt & Lindenfeld, 1982). Political participation is grounded in the value of equality (Deetz & Kersten, 1983) and thus involves meaningful employee participation in decision making across all levels of the organization (Bachrach & Botwinick, 1992; Cheney, 1995; Deetz & Kersten, 1983; Mason, 1982; Rothschild-Whitt & Lindenfeld, 1982). According to Bernstein (1982), there are five conditions that must be present for participation to be meaningful and maintained over a long period of time: (1) adequate employee access to management-level information, (2) employee protection from reprisals, (3) an independent adjudicator to resolve disputes, (4) a participatory-democratic consciousness, and (5) a share in the profits resulting from participation.

In addition to widespread, meaningful, and sustained employee participation in decision making, there are factors that distinguish the democratic workplace from the management-controlled one. Democratic workplaces do not maintain a traditional hierarchical structure of managers and workers; rather, "in one way or another, everyone manages and everyone works" (Rothschild-Whitt & Lindenfeld, 1982, p. 6). Harrison (1994) notes that democratic organizations provide members unhindered access to information and equal access to resources. Also, organization members' interaction is less restricted and is regulated more by knowledge and technical expertise than by formal position or status. Ultimately, as Cheney and Carroll (1996) observe, democratic organizations transcend necessary concerns with the *organization's* performance, productivity, efficiency, and the like with attention to *members'* happiness, fair treatment, and well-being, among other values.

It is clear that none of the programs reviewed in this chapter meet the conditions needed to achieve the "democratic" participation described by these scholars. With the exception of SDWTs in (greenfield site) new-design plants, the programs discussed herein do very little—if anything—to change the basic hierarchical structure of the organization in which the participatory program is introduced. Moreover, it appears as if these employee participation programs fail to meet the five conditions for sustained democratic participation that were outlined by Bernstein (1982). First, each program reviewed in this chapter appears to vary with regard to the amount of management-level information provided to employees, but probably none ensures employees adequate access to such information. QC members probably receive the least and SDWTs acquire the most, while Scanlon plan and QWL participants receive a

moderate amount. Although ESOP consultants recommend that managers in ESOP firms should provide their employees with financial and company performance information, there is no evidence suggesting that all firms follow this advice. Second, of the programs reviewed in this chapter, none appear to protect employees from reprisals, nor, third, do any of the five programs, about which so much research has been conducted, provide a neutral third-party to resolve disputes or even guarantee employee rights. Although the participation research reviewed here neglects to address the notion of employee rights, the organizational justice literature reflects a growing concern with fairness issues in the workplace (see Greenberg, 1990, 1996; Shea, 1995).

Fourth, there also is no clearly specified level of democratic consciousness associated with the employee participation programs reviewed here. As noted earlier, QC programs are often implemented by companies that are not necessarily concerned with worker fulfillment, except as a means to increase productivity. Indeed, Grenier (1988) has supplied compelling evidence of the way in which employee participation vis-à-vis quality circles has been a ruse for union-busting activities. New-design plants with SDWTs, and to some extent Scanlon plan companies, are far more likely to espouse a democratic philosophy. Even in these cases, as Cheney and Carroll (1996) note, the top-most level of such organizations are often filled with managers who situate themselves above the very team-based practices that they are promoting—including seeking to be free of bureaucratic (or team) constraints in exercising their latitude in decision making, while subordinates must work within team structures. This sort of rationalization by leaders (see Ritzer, 1993) is antithetical to the democratic consciousness necessary for meaningful and sustained workplace participation (Bernstein, 1982). Fifth, of the programs reviewed here, only Scanlon plans and SDWTs provide direct, financial rewards based on employee participation. Of course ESOPs are a financial plan, but the financial benefits are not tied directly to employee participation in decision making.

Some critical scholars even have suggested that most employee participation programs not only curtail employees' opportunity to exercise an equal voice in decision making, but these programs may be used to dominate and control workers (Fairhurst & Wendt, 1993; Mumby, 1988; Stohl, 1995; Stohl & Jennings, 1988). Cheney (1995) points out that participation programs may be used to pacify workers, diffuse resistance, and suppress potential opposition. Further, and this is most likely an unintended effect, some employee participation programs may actually increase concertive control over workers (Barker & Cheney, 1994; Tompkins & Cheney, 1985). Especially in SDWTs, concertive control "represents a key shift in the locus of control from management to the workers themselves, who collaborate to develop the means of their own control" (Barker, 1993, p. 411). In a study of self-managing teams, Barker (1993) examined how workers actually "developed a system of value-based normative rules that controlled their actions more powerfully and completely than the former system" (p. 408). Barker argued that concertive control, based on normative rules and peer pressure, paradoxically is far less apparent but much more powerful than are traditional forms of managerial control. Therefore, although SDWTs in new-design plants are probably the most democratic of all of the programs reviewed in this chapter, based on Barker's analysis, they may offer the greatest potential for worker control. To what degree are workers "controlling" other workers via mutually agreed-on norms, rules, and procedures antithetical to the notions of democracy advanced by the critical theorists? Although Barker and Tompkins (1992) acknowledge that a "communal-rational" system inheres in the transfer of authority from a hierarchical system to a team-based rules approach—which does not resemble the bureaucracy it has replaced—they concede

that the resulting concertive system fuses the peer pressure of team-based norms with the team's emergent rational rules to form a more powerful system of control (or what Barker, 1993, following Weber, termed a "tighter" iron cage). Given the pervasiveness of management approaches that propose to manage and control worker values, including the types of participation programs reviewed in this chapter, sustained critique may be needed to ensure that participants' dignity, happiness, sense of justice, and equality are maintained. As Cheney (1995) has summarized:

> The simple but profound question, "How do we implement democratic practices in work organizations?" leads us to think about the goals of organizations, the goals of the individuals who inhabit them, and the goals of the larger society, recognizing that those sets of aspirations can and perhaps should overlap even if not coincide perfectly. . . . Above all, I wish to promote the ideal of a humane workplace, a workplace not just for work but also for people, especially at a time when a simplistic form of the market principle and a crude impulse for greater productivity seem to preoccupy our factories, offices, schools, hospitals and universities. (p. 169)

RESEARCH AGENDA

As this review has emphasized, when the form of employee involvement studied is at the level of work *group* participation, there has been considerable imprecision and conflation of what are distinct forms of participation. For example, despite differences in the degree of participation, type of influence, and decision-making scope, semiautonomous and self-managing work teams have not only been treated as conceptually synonymous, but they often have been aggregated in empirical analyses of "teams." Careful taxonomic work is needed to provide precise conceptual and operational distinctions among these and related forms of group participation (e.g., self-directed teams, continuous process improvement teams, and the like). For example, Denison, Hart, and Kahn (1996) have distinguished cross-functional teams (CFTs) from other forms of organizational participation groups in terms of the greater role strain CFT members experience, greater expectations of CFTs than groups with longer-term goals, and the shorter life span of CFTs in which to accomplish those more immediate goals. In turn, Denison et al. demonstrate how these differences from other types of organizational teams will be associated with differences in interpersonal processes (development, collaboration, decision making, among others) these types of participation groups experience. Researchers also must be careful not to appropriate the label used by the host organization(s) for whatever involvement programs are studied. Instead, independent assessment of the form of work group should lead researchers to more accurately characterize their foci if comparison with other studies is sought.

A closely related concern should be the distinction between short-lived and long-term forms of employee participation. Continuous process improvement teams, cross-functional teams, and other teams created for the (brief) life of a project, for example, are likely to have communication-related processes and outcomes that are different from perennial agenda teams (e.g., ESOP and Scanlon oversight teams), SDWTs in a new-design plant, and so forth. Developmental changes in teams, to use but one area, underscore the potential import of this distinction. On one hand, research by Gersick (1988) with project teams, fund-raising committees, health care teams, and university groups has led to the repudiation of phasic models of group development—often borne of studies of short-lived laboratory groups—that emphasize a singular sequence of periods of defined group activity. Rather, Gersick found that the groups she studied experienced a "punctuated equilibrium" (periods of seeming inertia broken by burst of energy and transformation) and a "midpoint crisis" (a precipitating event at the midpoint of its life). However, it is important to note that even Gersick's foci were relatively short-lived teams, when compared with the long-term participative work arrangements noted above. Research on the developmental dynamics in those involvement structures could do much to confirm the applicability of the punctuated equilibrium model to participation forms with longer life spans, or to offer new understandings of the nature of group development in those arrangements.

Reviews of work group research repeatedly emphasize that work group performances are dependent on organizational contexts (Ancona & Caldwell, 1988; Denison et al., 1996; Guzzo & Dickson, 1996; Levine & Moreland, 1990; Shulman, 1996; Sundstrom et al., 1990). In the area of employee involvement programs, studies are needed that systematically relate the forms of individual and group participation to the culture of the organizations in which those involvement programs are embedded. Although case study research on workplace participation has underscored the inherent and recursive relationship between organizational culture and the processes and outcomes of their forms of participation, large-scale investigations have not studied this link explicitly (for a notable exception, see Lawler, Mohrman, & Ledford, 1992). Further, there has been a tendency by both individual researchers and reviewers to assume that the trans-bureaucratization of most forms of employee involvement somehow neutralizes or minimizes the effects of the organization's culture on those forms. There is evidence to the contrary. For example, Kornbluh (1984) chronicled the problems associated with the implementation of QCs and QWL programs in organizations that did not implement commensurate democratic forms of management. Research on employee participation could profit from efforts to link concerns with the dynamics and effects of involvement programs to theoretical perspectives on organizational culture and control. For instance, Walton and Hackman (1986) distinguished among control-strategy organizations (traditional, hierarchical, power-driven, controlling), commitment-strategy organizations (innovative, more flat, widely distributed power, participative), and mixed-strategy organizations (in transition from control- to commitment-strategy). We would expect not merely the range of employee participation to covary inversely with the degree of control inherent in these types of organizations, but important differences in the processes and success of the involvement programs to be determined by correlative dynamics in the degree of control in those cultures.

Also desperately needed are longitudinal studies of the over-time dynamics and outcomes of employee participation in organizations. As reviewed in this chapter, the overwhelming majority of studies on forms of employee involvement have been cross-sectional comparisons of organizations at single points in time. This is unfortunate when one considers studies that underscore the problems of such "snapshots" at specific points in time. For example, Hanlon et al. (1994) found that the positive effects of a Scanlon plan at a priority packaging company on employee participation endured even after a key financial component of the plan had been eliminated. Without that follow-up, the researchers, and readers, would have been led to inaccurate conclusions regarding the relative importance of the financial component. Similarly, a longitudinal field study of the impact of work teams on manufacturing performance (Banker, Field, Schroeder, & Sinha, 1996) demonstrated that quality and productivity improved over time after the introduction of teams. More studies of communication and various forms of employee participation, such as Monge, Cozzens, and Contractor's (1992) over-time analyses of Scanlon plans, are needed.

Indeed, as this review has demonstrated, broadly speaking, more research on the communication determinants, corollaries, and outcomes of organization participation programs is needed. For example, efforts at implementing various forms of organizational involve-

ment are often yoked communicatively to those organizations' mission statements. Ample research has underscored the problems surrounding communication of mission statements (e.g., Ackoff, 1987; Collins & Porras, 1991; Ledford, Wendenhof, & Strahley, 1995; Swales & Rogers, 1995), and Fairhurst, Jordan, and Neuwirth (1997) have offered preliminary evidence that communication about a company's mission statement is a function of an organizational member's information environment, level of work unit commitment, trust in management, and organizational role. To the degree that implementation of an organizational involvement program is yoked to the organization's mission statement, we hypothesize that the four variables identified by Fairhurst et al. also affect organizational members' communication surrounding involvement in participation programs.

More generally, and paralleling Lewis and Seibold's (1998) agenda for the study of communication and the implementation of planned organizational change, researchers interested in communication and organizational participation programs might profitably pursue answers to the following questions concerning (a) *formal* organizational communication efforts related to participation programs and (b) members' *informal* communication surrounding the programs. With regard to information dissemination, (a) how are these programs formally announced, and what channels are used to provide information about them? and (b) what meanings do members assign to these formal communications, with whom do they share these impressions informally, and what additional information is sought and from whom? In terms of persuasive communication, (a) what formal "campaign" tactics are used to engender involvement? and (b) are these messages met with informal support, neutrality, or resistance—and through what communicative means is collective response offered, if at all? Concerning social support, (a) what communicative efforts do organizations employ, if any, to monitor and to ease members' anxieties concerning new involvement programs? and (b) how are members' support and comforting informally communicated during the implementation of the programs? With regard to reward structures (whose effects on organizations, as we observed, need to be separated from the involvement programs with which they are combined—e.g., ESOPs), (a) what channels are most frequently used to communicate information concerning rewards? and (b) how do members' informal interactions concerning rewards affect involvement in, and outcomes of, organizational participation programs? Finally, in the area of roles and role relations, (a) what are the formal communication dynamics surrounding selection and socialization of involvement program members? and (b) through what informal processes do members adopt new roles associated with these programs, and what communicative influence is associated with their emergent status?

Scholarship on participation often has been concerned with *either* how its various forms are evidenced in practice *or* what it means as an ideal to be valued. As in notable exceptions (see Cheney, 1995, 1997; Stohl, 1993), more analyses are needed that examine how workplace participation is manifested in practice *and* discursively. To paraphrase a similar suggestion by Cheney, Straub, et al. (1998) with regard to research on democracy in the workplace, future empirical studies need to consider not only what practices *count* as participation but also what the *meanings* of participation are.

Scholars interested in participation and decision making must continue to examine the dialectical tension between participation and control identified by critical theorists (and apparent in their juxtaposition in preceding sections in this chapter). Alvesson (1993) has offered a cultural-ideological perspective for understanding labor processes through four frames: collective control, performance-related control, ideological control, and perceptual control. This approach compels analysis of the control of work in terms of the ideological framework in which work is achieved (i.e.,

respectively, these entail sense of community, norms for performance, values concerning importance, and perceptions of reality). Frameworks such as this encourage investigation of the ways in which communication functions in organizations, even in participatory forms, to provide, suppress, or distort members' voice (Putnam et al., 1996).

Finally, the reordering of the workplace, vis-à-vis downsizing, reengineering, and lean production, emphasizes not merely increased employee involvement but increased productivity, integrative coordination, and speed of performance (Rifkin, 1995). Communication researchers have formulated theoretical propositions concerning speed requirements, communication, and coordination in contemporary organizations—and their implications for employee participation (see Cushman & King, 1993), although considerable research is needed to test these claims. Perhaps more significant is the emphasis on advanced communication technology as an infrastructure for sustaining participation. Set against overarching debates concerning whether computer-mediated communication in the workplace will effect new democratic structures or more centralized control (e.g., Mantovani, 1994; Sclove, 1995; Sproull & Kiesler, 1991), the emerging realities are that network forms of organizing—involving high coordination among strong but ad hoc relationships—will become increasingly prevalent (Monge, 1995; Powell, 1990), that the communication media by which members participate in an organization can shape the nature and the extent of participation (Collins-Jarvis, 1997), and that one of the principal consequences of introducing new information technologies in organizations "has not been better communications, only faster misunderstandings" (Shulman, 1996, p. 367). Although there is a burgeoning literature linking organizational structures and new media (see Rice & Gattiker, Chapter 14, this volume) and mediated meetings in organizations (see Fulk & Collins-Jarvis, Chapter 16, this volume), considerably more research is required to understand the recursive relationships among communication technologies, organizational structuring, and specific forms of employee participation (Poole, Putnam, & Seibold, 1997; Seibold, 1998).

REFERENCES

Abrahamsson, B. (1977). *Bureaucracy or participation: The logic of organization.* Beverly Hills, CA: Sage.

Ackoff, R. L. (1987). Mission statements. *Planning Review, 15,* 30-31.

Ahlbrandt, R. S., Leana, C. R., & Murrell, A. J. (1992). Employee involvement programmes improve corporate performance. *Long Range Planning, 25*(5), 91-98.

Albrecht, T. L. (1988). Communication and personal control in empowering organizations. In J. A. Anderson (Ed.), *Communication yearbook 11* (pp. 380-390). Newbury Park, CA: Sage.

Alvesson, M. (1993). *Cultural perspectives on organizations.* Cambridge, UK: Cambridge University Press.

Alvesson, M., & Deetz, S. (1996). Critical theory and postmodern approaches to organizational studies. In S. R. Clegg, C. Hardy, & W. R. Nord (Eds.), *Handbook of organization studies* (pp. 191-217). London: Sage.

Ancona, D. G., & Caldwell, D. F. (1988). Beyond task and maintenance: Defining external functions in groups. *Group and Organization Studies, 13,* 468-494.

Ancona, D. G., & Caldwell, D. F. (1992). Bridging the boundary: External activity and performance in organizational teams. *Administrative Science Quarterly, 37,* 634-665.

Appelbaum, E., & Batt, R. (1994). *The new American workplace: Transforming work systems in the United States.* Ithaca, NY: Cornell University Press.

Bachrach, P., & Botwinick, A. (1992). *Power and empowerment: A radical theory of participatory democracy.* Philadelphia: Temple University Press.

Baloff, N., & Doherty, E. M. (1989). Potential pitfalls in employee participation. *Organizational Dynamics, 17*(3), 51-62.

Banker, R. D., Field, J. M., Schroeder, R. G., & Sinha, K. K. (1996). Impact of work teams on manufacturing performance: A longitudinal field study. *Academy of Management Journal, 39,* 867-890.

Barker, J. R. (1993). Tightening the iron cage: Concertive control in self-managing teams. *Administrative Science Quarterly, 38,* 408-437.

Barker, J. R. (1997). *The team makes the rules: Culture and control in self-managing teams.* Thousand Oaks, CA: Sage.

Barker, J. R., & Cheney, G. (1994). The concept and practices of discipline in contemporary organizational life. *Communication Monographs, 61,* 19-43.

Barker, J. R., Melville, C. W., & Pacanowsky, M. E. (1993). Self-directed teams at Xel: Changes in communication practices during a program of cultural transformation. *Journal of Applied Communication Research, 21,* 297-312.

Barker, J. R., & Tompkins, P. K. (1992, October). *Organizations, teams, control, and identification.* Paper presented at the University of Helsinki and the Helsinki University of Technology, Helsinki, Finland.

Barker, J. R., & Tompkins, P. K. (1994). Identification in the self-managing organization: Characteristics of target and tenure. *Human Communication Research, 21,* 223-240.

Barley, S. R. (1986). Technology as an occasion for structuring: Observations on CT scanners and the social order of radiology departments. *Administrative Science Quarterly, 31,* 78-108.

Beekun, R. I. (1989). Assessing the effectiveness of sociotechnical interventions: Antidote or fad? *Human Relations, 42,* 877-897.

Berggren, C. (1993). *Alternatives to lean production.* Ithaca, NY: Cornell University Press.

Berman, S. J., & Hellweg, S. A. (1989). Perceived supervisor communication competence and supervisor satisfaction as a function of quality circle participation. *Journal of Business Communication, 26,* 103-122.

Bernstein, P. (1982). Necessary elements for effective worker participation in decision-making. In F. Lindenfeld & J. Rothschild-Whitt (Eds.), *Workplace democracy and social change* (pp. 51-86). Boston: Porter Sargent.

Blasi, J. R., & Kruse, D. L. (1991). *The new owners: The mass emergence of employee ownership in public companies and what it means to American business.* New York: HarperCollins.

Blinder, A. S. (1990). Pay, participation, and productivity. *Brookings Review, 8*(1), 33-38.

Blumberg, M. (1980). Job switching in autonomous work groups: An exploratory study in a Pennsylvania coal mine. *Academy of Management Journal, 23,* 287-306.

Brockner, J., & Hess, T. (1986). Self-esteem and task performance in quality circles. *Academy of Management Journal, 29,* 617-623.

Bruning, N. S., & Liverpool, P. R. (1993). Membership in quality circles and participation in decision making. *Journal of Applied Behavioral Science, 29,* 76-95.

Buch, K. (1992). Quality circles and employee withdrawal behaviors: A cross-organizational study. *Journal of Applied Behavioral Science, 28,* 62-73.

Buchko, A. A. (1992). Employee ownership, attitudes, and turnover: An empirical assessment. *Human Relations, 45,* 711-733.

Bullock, R. J., & Lawler, E. E. (1984). Gainsharing: A few questions and fewer answers. *Human Resource Management, 23,* 23-40.

Bullock, R. J., & Tubbs, M. E. (1990). A case meta-analysis of gainsharing plans as organization development interventions. *Journal of Applied Behavioral Science, 26,* 383-404.

Burns, T., & Stalker, G. M. (1961). *The management of innovation* (2nd ed.). London: Tavistock.

Burzawa, S. (1992, July). Sharing financial info with employees: Three employee-owned firms tell how. *Employee Benefit Plan Review, 47*(1), 23-25.

Burzawa, S. (1993, August). Employee ownership = governance: Panel. *Employee Benefit Plan Review, 48*(2), 32-36.

Campion, M. A., Medsker, G. J., & Higgs, A. C. (1993). Relations between work group characteristics and effectiveness: Implications for designing effective work teams. *Personnel Psychology, 46,* 823-850.

Carnall, C. A. (1982). Semi-autonomous work groups and the social structure of the organization. *Journal of Management Studies, 19,* 277-294.

Castrogiovanni, G. J., & Macy, B. A. (1990). Organizational information-processing capabilities and degree of employee participation. *Group and Organization Studies, 15,* 313-336.

Cheney, G. (1995). Democracy in the workplace: Theory and practice from the perspective of communication. *Journal of Applied Communication Research, 23,* 167-200.

Cheney, G. (in press). Interpreting interpretive research: Toward perspectivism without relativism. In S. R. Corman & M. S. Poole (Eds.), *Paradigm dialogues in organizational communication.* New York: Guilford.

Cheney, G. (1997). The many meanings of "solidarity": The negotiation of values in the Mondragón worker-cooperative complex under pressure. In B. D. Sypher (Ed.), *Contemporary case studies in organizational communication* (2nd ed.). New York: Guilford.

Cheney, G. (1999). *Values at work: Employee participation meets market pressure at Mondragón.* Ithaca, NY: Cornell University Press.

Cheney, G., & Carroll, C. (1996, May). *Persons as objects in discourses in and about organizations.* Paper presented at the preconference The New Social Contract Between Individuals and Organizations, annual meeting of the International Communication Association, Chicago.

Cheney, G., Stohl, C., Dennis, M., & Harrison, T. M. (Eds.). (1998). Communication et democratic organisationnelle [Communication and organizational democracy]. *La revue Electronique de communication [The electronic journal of communication], 8*(1).

Cheney, G., Straub, J., Speirs-Glebe, L., Stohl, C., DeGooyer, D., Whalen, S., Garvin-Doxas, K., & Carlone, D. (1998). Democracy, participation, and

communication at work: A multi-disciplinary review. In M. E. Roloff (Ed.), *Communication yearbook 21* (pp. 35-91), Thousand Oaks, CA: Sage.

Clegg, S. (1983). Organizational democracy, power and participation. In C. Crouch & F. Heller (Eds.), *Organizational democracy and political processes* (pp. 3-34). New York: John Wiley.

Cole, R. E. (1985). The macropolitics of organizational change: A comparative analysis of the spread of small-group activities. *Administrative Science Quarterly, 30,* 560-585.

Collins, J. C., & Porras, J. I. (1991). Organizational vision and visionary organizations. *California Management Review, 34,* 30-52.

Collins-Jarvis, L. (1997). Participation and consensus in collective action organizations. *Journal of Applied Communication Research, 25,* 1-16.

Conger, J. A., & Kanungo, R. N. (1988). The empowerment process: Integrating theory and practice. *Academy of Management Review, 13,* 471-482.

Connors, J. L., & Romberg, T. A. (1991). Middle management and quality control: Strategies for obstructionism. *Human Organization, 50,* 61-65.

Conrad, C., & Ryan, M. (1985). Power, praxis, and self in organizational communication theory. In R. D. McPhee & P. K. Tompkins (Eds.), *Organizational communication: Traditional themes and new directions* (pp. 235-255). Beverly Hills, CA: Sage.

Contractor, N. S., & Eisenberg, E. M. (1990). Communication networks and new media in organizations. In C. Steinfield & J. Fulk (Eds.), *Organizations and communication technology* (pp. 145-174). Newbury Park, CA: Sage.

Contractor, N. S., & Seibold, D. R. (1993). Theoretical frameworks for the study of structuring processes in group decision support systems: Adaptive structuration theory and self-organizing systems theory. *Human Communication Research, 19,* 528-563.

Cooke, W. N. (1989). Improving productivity and quality through collaboration. *Industrial Relations, 28,* 299-319.

Cooper, C. L., Dyck, B., & Frohlich, N. (1992). Improving the effectiveness of gainsharing: The role of fairness and participation. *Administrative Science Quarterly, 37,* 471-490.

Cordery, J. L., Mueller, W. S., & Smith, L. M. (1991). Attitudinal and behavioral effects of autonomous group working: A longitudinal field study. *Academy of Management Journal, 34,* 464-476.

Cotter, J. J. (1983). *Designing organizations that work: An open sociotechnical systems approach.* Cambridge, MA: J. J. Cotter and Associates.

Cotton, J. L. (1993). *Employee involvement: Methods for improving performance and work attitudes.* Newbury Park, CA: Sage.

Cotton, J. L., Vollrath, D. A., Froggatt, K. L., Lengnick-Hall, M. L., & Jennings, K. R. (1988). Employee participation: Diverse forms and different outcomes. *Academy of Management Review, 13,* 8-22.

Cotton, J. L., Vollrath, D. A., Lengnick-Hall, M. L., & Froggatt, K. L. (1990). Fact: The form of participation does matter—A rebuttal to Leana, Locke, and Schweiger. *Academy of Management Review, 15,* 147-153.

Cummings, T. G. (1978). Self-regulating work groups: A socio-technical synthesis. *Academy of Management Review, 3,* 625-634.

Cushman, D. P., & King, S. S. (1993). High-speed management: A revolution in organizational communication in the 1990s. In S. A. Deetz (Ed.), *Communication yearbook 16* (pp. 209-236). Newbury Park, CA: Sage.

Dachler, H. P., & Wilpert, B. (1978). Conceptual dimensions and boundaries of participation in organizations: A critical evaluation. *Administrative Science Quarterly, 23,* 1-39.

Deetz, S. (1992). *Democracy in an age of corporate colonization.* Albany: State University of New York Press.

Deetz, S. (1994, November). *Economic and political contexts for organizational democracy.* Paper presented at the annual meeting of the Speech Communication Association, New Orleans, LA.

Deetz, S. A., & Kersten, A. (1983). Critical models of interpretive research. In L. L. Putnam & M. E. Pacanowsky (Eds.), *Communication and organizations: An interpretive approach* (pp. 147-171). Beverly Hills, CA: Sage.

DeBettignies, C. W. (1989). Improving organization-wide teamwork through gainsharing. *National Productivity Review, 8,* 287-294.

Denison, D. R., Hart, S. L., & Kahn, J. A. (1996). From chimneys to cross-functional teams: Developing and validating a diagnostic model. *Academy of Management Journal, 39,* 1005-1023.

DeSanctis, G., & Poole, M. S. (1997). Transitions in teamwork in new organizational forms. *Advances in Group Processes, 14,* 157-176.

DeToro, I. J. (1987). Quality circles and the techniques of creativity: A case history. *Journal of Creative Behavior, 21,* 137-140.

Doherty, E. M., Nord, W. R., & McAdams, J. L. (1989). Gainsharing and organization development: A productive synergy. *Journal of Applied Behavioral Science, 25,* 209-229.

Drago, R. (1988). Quality circle survival: An exploratory analysis. *Industrial Relations, 27,* 336-351.

Efraty, D., & Sirgy, M. J. (1990). The effects of quality of working life (QWL) on employee behavioral responses. *Social Indicators Research, 22,* 31-47.

Eijnatten, F. M. (1993). *The paradigm that changed the workplace.* Stockholm: Swedish Center for Working Life.

Eisenberg, E. M., Monge, P. R., & Miller, K. I. (1983). Involvement in communication networks as a predictor of organizational commitment. *Human Communication Research, 10,* 179-201.

Ellerman, D. (1990). *The democratic worker-owned firm: A new model for East and West.* Boston: Unwin Hyman.

Ellinger, C., & Nissen, B. (1987). A case study of a failed QWL program: Implications for labor education. *Labor Studies Journal, 11*(3), 195-219.

Emery, F. E., & Trist, E. L. (1965). The causal texture of organizational environments. *Human Relations, 18,* 21-32.

ESOP brings change in corporate culture. (1992, July). *Employee Benefit Plan Review, 47*(1), 25-26.

ESOPs, employee ownership evolve. (1993, August). *Employee Benefit Plan Review, 48*(2), 28-30.

Fairhurst, G. T. (1993). Echoes of the vision: When the rest of the organization talks total quality. *Management Communication Quarterly, 6,* 331-371.

Fairhurst, G. T., Green, S., & Courtright, J. (1995). Inertial forces and the implementation of a socio-technical systems approach: A communication study. *Organization Science, 6,* 168-185.

Fairhurst, G. T., Jordan, J. M., & Neuwirth, K. (1997). Why are we here? Managing the meaning of an organizational mission statement. *Journal of Applied Communication Research, 25,* 243-263.

Fairhurst, G. T., & Wendt, R. F. (1993). The gap in total quality: A commentary. *Management Communication Quarterly, 6,* 441-451.

Fisher, K. (1993). *Leading self-directed work teams.* New York: McGraw-Hill.

French, J. L. (1987). Perspectives on employee stock ownership: Financial investment of mechanism of control? *Academy of Management Review, 12,* 427-435.

Frey, L. R. (1995). Magical elixir or what the top tells the middle to do to the bottom? The promises and paradoxes of facilitating work teams for promoting organizational change and development. In R. Cesaria & P. Shockley-Zalabak (Eds.), *Organization means communication: Making the organizational communication concept relevant to practice* (pp. 199-215). Rome: Sipi Editore.

Gersick, C. J. G. (1988). Time and transition in work teams: Toward a new model of group development. *Academy of Management Journal, 31,* 9-41.

Glaser, H. (1994). *Structure and struggle in egalitarian groups: Reframing the problems of time emotion and inequality as defining characteristics.* Unpublished Ph.D. dissertation, University of Illinois at Urbana–Champaign.

Glaser, S. R. (1994). Teamwork and communication: A three-year case study of change. *Management Communication Quarterly, 7,* 282-296.

Glew, D. J., O'Leary-Kelly, A. M., Griffin, R. W., & Van Fleet, D. D. (1995). Participation in organizations: A preview of the issues and proposed framework for future analysis. *Journal of Management, 21,* 395-421.

Goll, I. (1991). Environment, corporate ideology, and employee involvement programs. *Industrial Relations, 30,* 138-149.

Gowen, C. R., III. (1990). Gainsharing programs: An overview of history and research. *Journal of Organizational Behavior Management, 11*(2), 77-99.

Graham-Moore, B. E., & Ross, T. L. (Eds.). (1983). *Productivity gainsharing.* Englewood Cliffs, NJ: Prentice Hall.

Greenbaum, H. H., Kaplan, I. T., & Metlay, W. (1988). Evaluation of problem-solving groups: The case of quality circle programs. *Group and Organization Studies, 13,* 133-147.

Greenbaum, H. H., & Query, J. L. (1999). Communication in organizational work groups: A review and synthesis of natural work group studies. In L. R. Frey, D. S. Gouran, & M. S. Poole (Eds.), *The handbook of group communication theory and research* (pp. 539-564). Thousand Oaks, CA: Sage.

Greenberg, E. S. (1980). Participation in industrial decision making and work satisfaction: The case of producer cooperatives. *Social Science Quarterly, 60,* 551-569.

Greenberg, J. (1990). Organizational justice: Yesterday, today, and tomorrow. *Journal of Management, 16,* 399-432.

Greenberg, J. (1996). *The quest for justice on the job: Essays and experiments.* Thousand Oaks, CA: Sage.

Grenier, G. J. (1988). *Inhuman relations: Quality circles and anti-unionism in American industry.* Philadelphia: Temple University Press.

Guzzo, R. A., & Dickson, M. W. (1996). Teams in organizations: Recent research on performance and effectiveness. *Annual Review of Psychology, 47,* 307-340.

Guzzo, R. A., Jette, R. D., & Katzell, R. A. (1985). The effects of psychologically based intervention programs on worker productivity: A meta-analysis. *Personnel Psychology, 38,* 275-291.

Hackman, J. R. (1990). *Groups that work (and those that don't): Creating conditions for effective teamwork.* San Francisco: Jossey-Bass.

Hammer, T. H. (1988). New developments in profit sharing, gainsharing, and employee ownership. In J. P. Campbell, R. J. Campbell, & Associates (Eds.), *Productivity in organizations: New perspectives from industrial and organizational psychology* (pp. 328-366). San Francisco: Jossey-Bass.

Hanlon, S. C., Meyer, D. G., & Taylor, R. R. (1994). Consequences of gainsharing: A field experiment revisited. *Group & Organization Management, 19,* 87-111.

Hanlon, S. C., & Taylor, R. R. (1991). An examination of changes in work group communication behaviors following installation of a gainsharing plan. *Group and Organization Studies, 16,* 238-267.

Harrison, T. M. (1994). Communication and interdependence in democratic organizations. In S. A. Deetz (Ed.), *Communication yearbook 17* (pp. 247-274). Thousand Oaks, CA: Sage.

Hatcher, L., & Ross, T. L. (1991). From individual incentives to an organization-wide gainsharing plan: Effects on teamwork and product quality. *Journal of Organizational Behavior, 12,* 169-183.

Hatcher, L., Ross, T. L., & Collins, D. (1991). Attributions for participation and nonparticipation in gainsharing-plan involvement systems. *Group and Organization Studies, 16,* 25-43.

Herrick, N. Q. (1985). Parallel organizations in unionized settings: Implications for organizational research. *Human Relations, 38,* 963-981.

Hirokawa, R. Y., & Keyton, J. (1995). Perceived facilitators and inhibitors of effectiveness in organizational work teams. *Management Communication Quarterly, 8,* 424-446.

Hoerr, J. (1989, July 10). The payoff from teamwork. *Business Week,* pp. 56-62.

Jackson, S. E. (1983). Participation in decision making as a strategy for reducing job-related strain. *Journal of Applied Psychology, 68,* 3-19.

Jones, S. D., Powell, R., & Roberts, S. (1990-1991). Comprehensive measurement to improve assembly-line work group effectiveness. *National Productivity Review, 10,* 45-55.

Kanter, R. M. (1982). Dilemmas of managing participation. *Organizational Dynamics, 11*(1), 5-27.

Kanter, R. M. (1986). The new workforce meets the changing workplace: Strains, dilemmas, and contradictions in attempts to implement participative and entrepreneurial management. *Human Resource Management, 25,* 515-537.

Kanter, R. M., Stein, B. A., & Brinkerhoff, D. W. (1982). Building participatory democracy within a conventional corporation. In F. Lindenfeld & J. Rothschild-Whitt (Eds.), *Workplace democracy and social change* (pp. 371-382). Boston: Porter Sargent.

Katz, A. J., Laughlin, P., & Wilson, J. (1990, December). Views on self-directed workteams from the line to the front office. *Journal for Quality and Participation,* pp. 48-51.

Katzenbach, J. R., & Smith, D. K. (1993). *The wisdom of teams.* Boston: Harvard Business School Press.

Kaufman, R. T. (1992). The effects of Improshare on productivity. *Industrial and Labor Relations Review, 45,* 311-322.

Kavcic, B., & Tannenbaum, A. S. (1981). A longitudinal study of the distribution of control in Yugoslav organizations. *Human Relations, 34,* 397-417.

Kemp, N. J., Wall, T. D., Clegg, C. W., & Cordery, J. L. (1983). Autonomous work groups in a greenfield site: A comparative study. *Journal of Occupational Psychology, 56,* 271-288.

Klein, K. J. (1987). Employee stock ownership and employee attitudes: A test of three models. *Journal of Applied Psychology, 72,* 319-332.

Kochan, T. A., Katz, H. C., & Mower, N. R. (1984). *Worker participation and American unions.* Kalamazoo, MI: W. E. Upjohn Institute for Employment Research.

Koopman, P. L., Drenth, P. J. D., Bus, F. B. M., Kruyswijk, A. J., & Wierdsma, A. F. M. (1981). Content, process, and effects of participative decision making on the shop floor: Three cases in the Netherlands. *Human Relations, 34,* 657-676.

Kornbluh, H. (1984). Workplace democracy and quality of worklife: Problems and prospects. *Annals of the American Academy of Political and Social Science, 473,* 88-95.

Lawler, E. E. (1986). *High-involvement management.* San Francisco: Jossey-Bass.

Lawler, E. E. (1988). Gainsharing theory and research: Findings and future directions. In W. A. Pasmore & R. W. Woodman (Eds.), *Research in organizational change and development* (Vol. 2, pp. 323-344). Greenwich, CT: JAI.

Lawler, E. E. (1990). The new plant revolution revisited. *Organizational Dynamics, 19*(2), 5-15.

Lawler, E. E. (1991). The new plant approach: A second generation approach. *Organizational Dynamics, 20*(1), 5-14.

Lawler, E. E. (1995). *Creating high-performance organizations.* San Francisco: Jossey-Bass.

Lawler, E. E. (1999). Employee involvement makes a difference. *Journal for Quality and Participation, 22*(5), 18-20.

Lawler, E. E., & Mohrman, S. A. (1987). Quality circles: After the honeymoon. *Organizational Dynamics, 15*(4), 42-54.

Lawler, E. E., Mohrman, S. A., & Ledford, G. E., Jr. (1992). *Employee involvement and total quality management: Practices and results in Fortune 1000 companies.* San Francisco: Jossey-Bass.

Leana, C. R. (1987). Power relinquishment versus power sharing: Theoretical clarification and empirical comparison of delegation and participation. *Journal of Applied Psychology, 72,* 228-233.

Leana, C. R., Ahlbrandt, R. S., & Murrell, A. J. (1992). The effects of employee involvement programs on unionized workers' attitudes, perceptions, and preferences in decision making. *Academy of Management Journal, 35,* 861-873.

Leana, C. R., & Florkowski, G. W. (1992). Employee involvement programs: Integrating psychological theory and management practice. In G. R. Ferris & K. M. Rowland (Eds.), *Research in personnel and human resources management* (Vol. 10, pp. 233-270). Greenwich, CT: JAI.

Leana, C. R., Locke, E. A., & Schweiger, D. M. (1990). Fact and fiction in analyzing research on participative decision making: A critique of Cotton, Voll-

rath, Froggatt, Lengnick-Hall, and Jennings. *Academy of Management Review, 15,* 137-146.

Ledford, G. E., Lawler, E. E., & Mohrman, S. A. (1988). The quality circle and its variations. In J. P. Campbell, R. J. Campbell, & Associates (Eds.), *Productivity in organizations: New perspectives from industrial and organizational psychology* (pp. 255-294). San Francisco: Jossey-Bass.

Ledford, G. E., Wendenhof, J. R., & Strahley, J. T. (1995). Realizing a corporate philosophy. *Organizational Dynamics, 23,* 5-19.

Levine, D. I., & Tyson, L. D. (1990). Participation, productivity, and the firm's environment. In A. S. Blinder (Ed.), *Paying for productivity: A look at the evidence* (pp. 183-243). Washington, DC: Brookings Institution.

Levine, J. M., & Moreland, R. L. (1990). Progress in small group research. *Annual Review of Psychology, 41,* 585-634.

Lewis, L. K., & Seibold, D. R. (1993). Innovation modification during intra-organizational adoption. *Academy of Management Review, 18,* 322-354.

Lewis, L. K., & Seibold, D. R. (1996). Communication during intraorganizational innovation adoption: Predicting users' behavioral coping responses to innovations in organizations. *Communication Monographs, 63,* 131-157.

Lewis, L. K., & Seibold, D. R. (1998). Reconceptualizing organizational change implementation as a communication problem: A review of literature and research agenda. In M. E. Roloff (Ed.), *Communication yearbook 21* (pp. 93-151). Thousand Oaks, CA: Sage.

Locke, E. A., & Schweiger, D. M. (1979). Participation in decision-making: One more look. In B. M. Staw (Ed.), *Research in organizational behavior* (Vol. 1, pp. 265-339). Greenwich, CT: JAI.

Long, R. J. (1981). The effects of formal employee participation in ownership and decision making on perceived and desired patterns of organizational influence: A longitudinal study. *Human Relations, 34,* 847-876.

Long, R. J. (1982). Worker ownership and job attitudes: A field study. *Industrial Relations, 21,* 196-215.

Magjuka, R. J. (1989). Participative systems: Toward a technology of design. *Research in the Sociology of Organizations, 7,* 79-115.

Magjuka, R. J. (1991). Examining barriers to integrating EIP into daily operations. *National Productivity Review, 10,* 327-337.

Magjuka, R. J., & Baldwin, T. T. (1991). Team-based employee involvement programs: Effects of design and administration. *Personnel Psychology, 44,* 793-812.

Mantovani, G. (1994). Is computer-mediated communication intrinsically apt to enhance democracy in organizations? *Human Relations, 47,* 45-62.

Manz, C. C. (1986). Self-leadership: Toward an expanded theory of self-influence process in organizations. *Academy of Management Review, 11,* 585-600.

Manz, C. C. (1992). Self-leading work teams: Moving beyond self-management myths. *Human Relations, 45,* 1119-1140.

Manz, C. C., & Angle, H. (1986). Can group self-management mean a loss of personal control: Triangulating a paradox. *Group and Organization Studies, 11,* 309-334.

Manz, C. C., Keating, D. E., & Donnellon, A. (1990). Preparing for an organizational change to employee self-management: The managerial transition. *Organizational Dynamics, 19*(2), 15-26.

Manz, C. C., & Sims, H. P. (1982). The potential for "groupthink" in autonomous work groups. *Human Relations, 35,* 773-784.

Manz, C. C., & Sims, H. P. (1984). Searching for the "unleader": Organizational member views on leading self-managed groups. *Human Relations, 37,* 409-424.

Manz, C. C., & Sims, H. P. (1987). Leading workers to lead themselves: The external leadership of self-managing work teams. *Administrative Science Quarterly, 32,* 106-128.

Margulies, N., & Black, S. (1987). Perspectives on the implementation of participative approaches. *Human Resource Management, 26,* 385-412.

Marks, M. L., Mirvis, P. H., Hackett, E. J., & Grady, J. F. (1986). Employee participation in a quality circle program: Impact on quality of work life, productivity, and absenteeism. *Journal of Applied Psychology, 71,* 61-69.

Marsh, R. M. (1992). The difference between participation and power in Japanese factories. *Industrial and Labor Relations Review, 45,* 250-257.

Marshall, A. A., & Stohl, C. (1993). Participating as participation: A network approach. *Communication Monographs, 60,* 137-157.

Mason, R. M. (1982). *Participatory and workplace democracy.* Carbondale: Southern Illinois University Press.

McWhirter, D. A. (1991). Employee stock ownership plans in the United States. In C. Rosen & K. M. Young (Eds.), *Understanding employee ownership* (pp. 43-73). Ithaca, NY: ILR.

Miller, C. S., & Schuster, M. (1987a). A decade's experience with the Scanlon plan: A case study. *Journal of Occupational Behavior, 8,* 167-173.

Miller, C. S., & Schuster, M. (1987b). Gainsharing plans: A comparative analysis. *Organizational Dynamics, 16*(1), 44-67.

Miller, K. I., & Monge, P. R. (1986). Participation, satisfaction, and productivity: A meta-analytic review. *Academy of Management Journal, 29,* 727-753.

Miller, K. I., & Monge, P. R. (1987). The development and test of a system of organizational participation and allocation. In M. L. McLaughlin (Ed.), *Commu-*

nication yearbook 10 (pp. 431-455). Newbury Park, CA: Sage.

Miller, R. W., & Prichard, F. N. (1992). Factors associated with workers' inclination to participate in an employee program. *Group & Organization Management, 17,* 414-430.

Mintzberg, H. (1991). The effective organization: Forces and forms. *Sloan Management Review, 32*(2), 54-67.

Mohrman, S. A., Ledford, G. E., Lawler, E. E., & Mohrman, A. M. (1986). Quality of worklife and employee involvement. In C. L. Cooper & I. Robertson (Eds.), *International review of industrial and organizational psychology* (pp. 189-216). New York: John Wiley.

Monge, P. R. (1995). Global network organizations. In R. Cesaria & P. Shockley-Zalabak (Eds.), *Organization means communication: Making the organizational communication concept relevant to practice* (pp. 131-151). Rome: Sipi Editore.

Monge, P. R., Cozzens, M. D., & Contractor, N. S. (1992). Communication and motivational predictors of the dynamics of organizational innovations. *Organization Science, 3,* 250-274.

Monge, P. R., & Eisenberg, E. M. (1987). Emergent communication networks. In F. M. Jablin, L. L. Putnam, K. H. Roberts, & L. W. Porter (Eds.), *Handbook of organizational communication: An interdisciplinary perspective* (pp. 304-342). Newbury Park, CA: Sage.

Monge, P. R., & Miller, K. I. (1988). Participative processes in organizations. In G. M. Goldhaber & G. A. Barnett (Eds.), *Handbook of organizational communication* (pp. 213-229). Norwood, NJ: Ablex.

Mumby, D. K. (1988). *Communication and power in organizations: Discourse ideology and domination.* Norwood, NJ: Ablex.

Mumby, D., & Putnam, L. (1992). The politics of emotion: A feminist reading of bounded rationality. *Academy of Management Review, 17,* 465-486.

Mumby, D., & Stohl, C. (1992). Power and discourse in organization studies: Absence and dialectic of control. *Discourse & Society, 2,* 313-332.

Nadler, D. A., & Lawler, E. E. (1983). Quality of work life: Perspectives and directions. *Organizational Dynamics, 11*(3), 20-30.

Neuman, G. A. (1991). Autonomous work group selection. *Journal of Business and Psychology, 6,* 283-291.

Nurick, A. J. (1982). Participation in organizational change: A longitudinal field study. *Human Relations, 35,* 413-430.

Ondrack, D. A., & Evans, M. G. (1987). Job enrichment and job satisfaction in greenfield and redesign QWL sites. *Group and Organization Studies, 12,* 5-22.

O'Reilly, C. A., Chatman, J. A., & Anderson, J. C. (1987). Message flow and decision making. In F. M. Jablin, L. L. Putnam, K. H. Roberts, & L. W. Porter (Eds.), *Handbook of organizational communication:*

An interdisciplinary perspective (pp. 600-623). Newbury Park, CA: Sage.

Pacanowsky, M. (1988). Communication in the empowering organization. In J. A. Anderson (Ed.), Communication yearbook 11 (pp. 356-379). Newbury Park, CA: Sage.

Parker, M. (1985). Inside the circle: A union guide to QWL. Boston: South End.

Pasmore, W., Francis, C., Haldeman, J., & Shani, A. (1982). Sociotechnical systems: A North American reflection on empirical studies of the seventies. Human Relations, 35, 1179-1204.

Paul, R. J., Ebadi, Y. M., & Dilts, D. A. (1987). Commitment in employee-owned firms: Involvement or entrapment? Quarterly Journal of Business and Economics, 26(4), 81-99.

Pearce, J. A., & Ravlin, E. C. (1987). The design and activation of self-regulating work groups. Human Relations, 40, 751-782.

Pearson, C. A. L. (1992). Autonomous workgroups: An evaluation at an industrial site. Human Relations, 45, 905-936.

Pierce, J. L., & Furo, C. A. (1990). Employee ownership: Implications for management. Organizational Dynamics, 18(3), 32-43.

Pierce, J. L., Rubenfeld, S. A., & Morgan, S. (1991). Employee ownership: A conceptual model of process and effects. Academy of Management Review, 16, 121-144.

Pettigrew, A. M. (1990). Longitudinal field research on change: Theory and practice. Organization Science, 1, 267-292.

Poole, M. S., & DeSanctis, G. (1990). Understanding the use of group decision support systems: The theory of adaptive structuration. In C. Steinfield & J. Fulk (Eds.), Organizations and communication technology (pp. 175-195). Newbury Park, CA: Sage.

Poole, M. S., Putnam, L. L., & Seibold, D. R. (1997). Organizational communication in the 21st century. Management Communication Quarterly, 11, 127-138.

Poole, M. S., Seibold, D. R., & McPhee, R. D. (1996). The structuration of group decisions. In R. Y. Hirokawa & M. S. Poole (Eds.), Communication and group decision making (pp. 114-146). Thousand Oaks, CA: Sage.

Powell, W. (1990). Neither market nor hierarchy: Network forms of organization. Research in Organizational Behavior, 12, 295-336.

Poza, E. J., & Markus, L. (1980). Success story: The team approach to work restructuring. Organizational Dynamics, 8(3), 3-25.

Putnam, L. L. (1982). Paradigms for organizational communication research: An overview and synthesis. Western Journal of Speech Communication, 46, 192-206.

Putnam, L. L. (1983). The interpretive perspective: An alternative to functionalism. In L. L. Putnam & M. E. Pacanowsky (Eds.), Communication and organizations: An interpretive approach (pp. 31-54). Beverly Hills, CA: Sage.

Putnam, L. L., Phillips, N., & Chapman, P. (1996). Metaphors of communication and organization. In S. R. Clegg, C. Hardy, & W. R. Nord (Eds.), Handbook of organization studies (pp. 375-408). London: Sage.

Putnam, L. L., & Stohl, C. (1990). Bona fide groups: A reconceptualization of groups in context. Communication Studies, 41, 248-265.

Rice, A. K. (1958). Productivity and social organization: The Ahmedabad experiments. London: Tavistock.

Rifkin, J. (1995). The end of work. Los Angeles: Jeremy Tarcher/Putnam.

Riley, P. (1983). A structurationist account of political culture. Administrative Science Quarterly, 28, 414-437.

Ritzer, G. (1993). The McDonaldization of society. Thousand Oaks, CA: Pine Forge.

Rosen, C. (1989). Ownership, motivation, and corporate performance: Putting ESOPs to work. In G. Kalish (Ed.), ESOPs: The handbook of employee stock ownership plans (pp. 271-289). Chicago: Probus.

Rosen, C. (1991). Employee ownership: Performance, prospects, and promise. In C. Rosen & K. M. Young (Eds.), Understanding employee ownership (pp. 1-42). Ithaca, NY: ILR.

Rosen, C. M., Klein, K. J., & Young, K. M. (1986). Employee ownership in America: The equity solution. Lexington, MA: Lexington Books.

Rosen, C. M., & Quarrey, M. (1987). How well is employee ownership working? Harvard Business Review, 65(5), 126-132.

Rothschild-Whitt, J., & Lindenfeld, F. (1982). Reshaping work: Prospects and problems of workplace democracy. In F. Lindenfeld & J. Rothschild-Whitt (Eds.), Workplace democracy and social change (pp. 1-18). Boston: Porter Sargent.

Russell, R. (1988). Forms and extent of employee participation in the contemporary United States. Work and Occupations, 15, 374-395.

Saavedra, R., & Kwun, S. (1993). Peer evaluation in self-managing work groups. Journal of Applied Psychology, 78, 450-462.

Schuster, M. (1984). The Scanlon plan: A longitudinal analysis. Journal of Applied Behavioral Science, 20, 23-38.

Schweiger, D. M., & Leana, C. R. (1986). Participation in decision making. In E. A. Locke (Ed.), Generalizing from laboratory to field settings (pp. 147-166). Lexington, MA: Lexington Books.

Sclove, R. E. (1995). Democracy and technology. New York: Guilford.

Seibold, D. R. (1995). Developing the "team" in a team managed organization: Group facilitation in a new-design plant. In L. Frey (Ed.), Innovations in *group facilitation: Applications in natural settings* (pp. 282-298). Cresskill, NJ: Hampton.

Seibold, D. R. (1998). Groups and organizations: Premises and perspectives. In J. S. Trent (Ed.), *Communication: View from the helm for the 21st century* (pp. 162-168). Needham Heights, MA: Allyn & Bacon.

Seibold, D. R., & Contractor, N. S. (1992). Issues for a theory of high-speed management. In S. A. Deetz (Ed.), *Communication yearbook 16* (pp. 237-246). Newbury Park, CA: Sage.

Shadur, M. A., Kienzle, R., & Rodwell, J. J. (1999). The relationship between organizational climate and employee perceptions of involvement. *Group & Organization Management, 24,* 479-503.

Shea, B. C. (1995). *Non-union grievance systems: The effects of procedural fairness, distributive fairness, outcome, and supervisor relationship on employee perceptions of organizational fairness and support.* Unpublished doctoral dissertation, University of California, Santa Barbara.

Shulman, A. D. (1996). Putting group information technology in its place: Communication and good work group performance. In S. R. Clegg, C. Hardy, & W. R. Nord (Eds.), *Handbook of organization studies* (pp. 357-374). London: Sage.

Sockell, D. (1985). Attitudes, behavior, and employee ownership: Some preliminary data. *Industrial Relations, 24,* 130-138.

Spector, P. E. (1986). Perceived control by employees: A meta-analysis of studies concerning autonomy and participation at work. *Human Relations, 39,* 1005-1016.

Sproull, L., & Kiesler, S. (1991). *Connections: New ways of working in the networked organization.* Cambridge, MA: MIT Press.

Steel, R. P., Jennings, K. R., & Lindsey, J. T. (1990). Quality circle problem solving and common cents: Evaluation study findings from a United States federal mint. *Journal of Applied Behavioral Science, 26,* 365-381.

Steel, R. P., & Lloyd, R. F. (1988). Cognitive, affective, and behavioral outcomes of participation in quality circles: Conceptual and empirical findings. *Journal of Applied Behavioral Science, 24,* 1-17.

Steel, R. P., Mento, A. J., Dilla, B. L., Ovalle, N. K., & Lloyd, R. F. (1985). Factors influencing the success and failure of two quality circle programs. *Journal of Management, 11,* 99-119.

Steel, R. P., & Shane, G. S. (1986). Evaluation research on quality circles: Technical and analytical implications. *Human Relations, 39,* 449-468.

Stevens, M. J., & Campion, M. A. (1994). The knowledge, skill, and ability requirements for teamwork: Implications for human resource management. *Journal of Management, 20,* 503-530.

Stohl, C. (1986). Quality circles and changing patterns of communication. In M. McLaughlin (Ed.), *Com-munication yearbook 9* (pp. 511-531). Beverly Hills, CA: Sage.

Stohl, C. (1987). Bridging the parallel organization: A study of quality circle effectiveness. In M. L. McLaughlin (Ed.), *Communication yearbook 10* (pp. 416-430). Newbury Park, CA: Sage.

Stohl, C. (1989). Understanding quality circles: A communication network perspective. In B. Dervin, L. Grossberg, B. O'Keefe, & E. Wartella (Eds.), *Rethinking communication: Vol. 2. Paradigm exemplars* (pp. 346-360). Newbury Park, CA: Sage.

Stohl, C. (1993a). European managers' interpretations of participation: A semantic network analysis. *Human Communication Research, 20,* 97-117.

Stohl, C. (1993b). International organizing and organizational communication. *Journal of Applied Communication Research, 21,* 377-384.

Stohl, C. (1995). Paradoxes of participation. In R. Cesaria & P. Shockley-Zalabak (Eds.), *Organization means communication: Making the organizational communication concept relevant to practice* (pp. 199-215). Rome: Sipi Editore.

Stohl, C., & Jennings, K. (1988). Volunteerism and voice in quality circles. *Western Journal of Speech Communication, 52,* 238-251.

Strauss, G. (1982). Workers' participation in management: An international perspective. In L. L. Cummings & B. Staw (Eds.), *Research in organizational behavior* (Vol. 4, pp. 173-265). Greenwich, CT: JAI.

Sundstrom, E., DeMeuse, K. P., & Futrell, D. (1990). Work teams: Applications and effectiveness. *American Psychologist, 45,* 120-133.

Swales, J. M., & Rogers, P. S. (1995). Discourse and the projection of corporate culture: The mission statement. *Discourse & Society, 6,* 223-242.

Swezey, R., & Salas, E. (1992). *Teams: Their training and performance.* Norwood, NJ: Ablex.

Taplin, P. T. (1989, August). Successful ESOPs include participatory management. *Employee Benefit Plan Review, 44*(2), 52-54.

Tesluk, P. E., Vance, R. J., & Mathieu, J. E. (1999). Examining employee involvement in the context of participative work environments. *Group & Organization Management, 24,* 271-299.

Thomas, J. G., & Griffin, R. W. (1989). The power of social information in the workplace. *Organizational Dynamics, 18*(2), 63-75.

Thomas, K. W., & Velthouse, B. A. (1990). Cognitive elements of empowerment: An "interpretive" model of intrinsic task motivation. *Academy of Management Review, 15,* 666-681.

Tompkins, P. K., & Cheney, G. (1985). Communication and unobtrusive control in contemporary organizations. In R. D. McPhee & P. K. Tompkins (Eds.), *Organizational communication: Traditional themes and new directions* (pp. 179-210). Beverly Hills, CA: Sage.

Toscano, D. J. (1983). Toward a typology of employee ownership. *Human Relations, 36,* 581-602.

Turpin-Forster, S. C. (1989). Communicating the message of employee stock ownership. In G. Kalish (Ed.), *ESOPs: The handbook of employee stock ownership plans* (pp. 253-269). Chicago: Probus.

Vandenberg, R. J., Richardson, H. A., & Eastman, L. J. (1999). The impact of high-involvement work processes on organizational effectiveness: A second-order latent variable approach. *Group & Organization Management, 24,* 300-339.

Van Fleet, D. D., & Griffin, R. W. (1989). Quality circles: A review and suggested further directions. In C. L. Cooper & I. Robertson (Eds.), *International review of industrial and organizational psychology* (pp. 213-233). New York: John Wiley.

Veiga, J. F., & Yanouzas, J. N. (1991). Differences between American and Greek managers in giving up control. *Organization Studies, 12,* 95-108.

Versteeg, A. (1990). Self-directed work teams yield long-term benefits. *Journal of Business Strategy, 11,* 9-12.

Wagner, J. A. (1994). Participation's effects on performance and satisfaction: A reconsideration of research evidence. *Academy of Management Review, 19,* 312-330.

Wagner, J. A., & Gooding, R. Z. (1987a). Effects of societal trends on participation research. *Administrative Science Quarterly, 32,* 241-262.

Wagner, J. A., & Gooding, R. Z. (1987b). Shared influence and organizational behavior: A meta-analysis of situational variables expected to moderate participation-outcome relationships. *Academy of Management Journal, 30,* 524-541.

Wall, T. D., Kemp, N. J., Jackson, P. R., & Clegg, C. W. (1986). Outcomes of autonomous workgroups: A long-term field experiment. *Academy of Management Journal, 29,* 280-304.

Walton, R. E. (1977). Work innovations at Topeka: After six years. *Journal of Applied Behavioral Science, 13,* 422-433.

Walton, R. E. (1985). From control to commitment: Transformation of workforce management strategies in the United States. In K. B. Clark, R. H. Hayes, & C. Lorez (Eds.), *The uneasy alliance: Managing the productivity-technology dilemma.* Boston: Harvard Business School Press.

Walton, R. E., & Hackman, J. R. (1986). Groups under contrasting management strategies. In P. S. Goodman et al. (Eds.), *Designing effective work groups* (pp. 168-201). San Francisco: Jossey-Bass.

Welbourne, T. M., & Gomez-Mejia, L. R. (1995). Gainsharing: A critical review and a future research agenda. *Journal of Management, 21,* 559-609.

Wellins, R. S., Byham, W. C., & Wilson, J. M. (1991). *Empowered teams: Creating self-directed work groups that improve quality, productivity, and participation.* San Francisco: Jossey-Bass.

Yates, J., & Orlikowski, W. J. (1992). Genres of organizational communication: An approach to studying communication and media. *Academy of Management Review, 17,* 299-326.

Young, K. M. (1990). Managing an employee ownership company. In K. M. Young (Ed.), *The expanding role of ESOPs in public companies* (pp. 159-188). Westport, CT: Quorum.

Young, K. M. (1991). Theory O: The ownership theory of management. In C. Rosen & K. M. Young (Eds.), *Understanding employee ownership* (pp. 108-135). Ithaca, NY: ILR.

18

Learning in Organizations

KARL E. WEICK

SUSAN J. ASHFORD
University of Michigan

Organizations often discover faulty learning when they experience failures on a large or small scale. Here are three examples of failure in communication that imply faulty prior learning and the necessity for further learning:

1. In response to a warning of enemy attack, which later proved to be false, a base commander is ordered to "be prepared for possible launch of your interceptors." The communiqué is heard as "launch interceptors!" The base commander does.

2. An aircraft is landing too low to make it to the runway, and the pilot asks the engineer for "takeoff power" so the plane can go around and try again. The engineer hears the request as "take off power" so he reduces power, and the aircraft crashes.

3. A ship commander facing a potentially hostile ship that is closing on his position says, "I'm not going to shoot first, but if he fires one then I'll fire one." "Fire One!" commands an ensign (examples are paraphrased from Sagan, 1993, pp. 241-242).

Each of these examples represents communication and interaction in an organizational context with unintended consequences and inadequate learning. Something needs to be understood more fully and corrected, which is not all that easy since communication and learning are intertwined. For example, these three misunderstandings could be seen as a problem of poor language use within a speech community. The specific problem common to these three examples is an inadequate differentiation between messages to prepare and messages to execute. The current language is poor because it is equivocal. The same word has more than one meaning. Time is used up trying to discover which meaning is intended, and different frames of reference generate different presumptions of intention.

Learning can occur in such systems, however. In the case of "takeoff power," for example, that phrase has now been dropped and the less equivocal phrase "maximum power" has been substituted. That substitution represents learning, but it also implies additional linkages between communication and learning. There are hints that richer language generates fewer problems, that languages create phenomena as well as represent them, that learning occurs when people change frames of reference as well as when they reaffirm them, that words and interactions can inhibit learning, and that words are central to the learning that occurs when people are socialized into an organizational culture.

Our goal in this chapter is to describe the nature of learning as it unfolds in organizational settings. We want to develop a picture of the individual and interpersonal processes inherent in organizational learning. Our intent is not to present a formal review of the literature on organizational learning (those interested in such reviews should see Cohen & Sproull, 1996; Huber, 1991; Levitt & March, 1988; Miller, 1996). Rather, we hope to highlight the essential elements of learning as it takes place in organizational settings that are sensitive to variations in communication.

This undertaking, it should be noted, is new to the handbook. The topic of organizational learning does not appear in the first edition of this handbook, there is no chapter by that name, and the phrase "organizational learning" is not in the index. The same thing might happen in the third edition. But for the moment, our purpose, in this second edition, is to explore whether scholars of organiza-

tional communication are better off with the concept "organizational learning" than they are without it. While this may be an open question, we believe that without doubt organizational learning scholars are better off considering communication issues. Indeed, we see communication as central to learning at the organizational level. This suggests an important role for communication research in the unfolding empirical effort to gain insights into organizational learning. One goal for this chapter is to highlight potential contributions in order to prompt research in this area.

There is no question that learning is a hot topic as of this edition. It is discussed in special issues of both practitioner (*Organizational Dynamics* in 1993) and researcher (*Organization Science* in 1991) journals, and the journal *Management Learning,* now in its 31st volume, continues to publish an increasing number of influential and significant contributions. Organizational learning is reviewed in the prestigious *Annual Review of Sociology* (Levitt & March, 1988), reviews of reviews are beginning to appear (e.g., Dodgson, 1993), proceedings of conferences devoted to learning have been published (Crossan, Lane, Rush, & White, 1993), and traditional concepts of organizational development and systems theory are being repackaged and sold as if they had been about learning all along (Senge, 1990).

To complement these existing resources, we intend to show how a communication perspective can deepen our understanding of the process of organizational learning. To do this we will develop the following argument. First, we define *organizational learning* by positioning it as an aspect of culture grounded in individual know-how. With that overview in place, we highlight selected properties of individual learning such as punctuation, reflection, action, categorization, and extrapolation. We then show how these properties are modified by organizational contexts and pay special attention to conflict, hierarchy, attribution, turnover, discontinuity, ambiguity, and speed. Next, we show how these organizational contexts are modified by language and communication processes. We conclude by examining a seemingly innocuous communication practice—NASA's use of "Monday Notes" as a communication system—and find that this practice has a powerful effect on learning through its effect on individuals and groups.

DEFINITIONS OF ORGANIZATIONAL LEARNING

Phenomena of organizational learning discussed could be subsumed under any one of the following three definitions. English and English (1958) argued that "the sign of learning is not a shift of response or performance as a consequence of a change in stimulus-situation or in motivation, but rather a shift in performance when the stimulus-situation and the motivation are essentially the same" (p. 289). This definition implies that learning occurs when an entity is able to respond differently to an identical stimulus over time. But as Weick (1991) demonstrated, these conditions rarely occur in organizations suggesting either that organizations don't learn or that their learning takes a different form. Furthermore, this definition seems to rule out strengthening of a response over time as an instance of learning (e.g., responding with more of the same to a constant stimulus). This definition also implies that learning should be difficult in ambiguous environments where stimuli are unclear and where action is necessary to create stimuli from which to learn. For these reasons, we see the English and English definition as problematic.

A second definition is offered by Weiss (1990): "Learning is a relatively permanent change in knowledge or skill produced by experience" (p. 172). However, the environments facing today's organization pose new challenges for this definition of learning. Specifically, in a rapidly changing world, how crucial is the permanent learning suggested by this definition? Are there instances where

such permanence might be a hindrance rather than an organizational benefit?

Finally Duncan and Weiss (1979), in a widely cited definition, proposed that learning is the "process within the organization by which knowledge about action-outcome relationships and the effect on the environment of these relationships is developed" (p. 84). This definition is attractive in that it highlights the theories of action and cause maps that are developed via a process of organizational learning. Knowledge, rather than any particular action pattern (same or new), is the outcome of learning. This suggests that inaction or continuing with the same action can be as much a reflection of learning as are new actions. Further, by giving action-outcome links center stage, this definition begins to point to organizational realities that should affect the learning process. In particular, Jaques (1989) has proposed that the link between actions and outcomes becomes more tenuous and more separated in time as one moves up the corporate hierarchy. Does this imply that learning will be more difficult at the upper levels of an organization? If action-outcome links become less directly observable as one moves up the organizational hierarchy, then do substitutes for direct observation and task feedback become more important to the learning process? What might those substitutes be?

While all three definitions are adequate, none of them portray learning in a way that incorporates communication as a core determinant. To do so, we can pursue Normann's (1985) intriguing suggestion that the flurry of interest in organizational culture was actually an interest in organizational learning. Normann (1985) states:

I would interpret the increasing interest in the concept of culture as really an increasing interest in organizational learning—in understanding and making conscious and effective as much as possible all the learning that has taken place in an organization. To be aware of culture is to come to know that which the organization has learned. Promoting awareness of culture within the organization increases the likelihood of subsequent learning. Thus, to be aware of culture is to increase the likelihood of learning. Only when the basic assumptions, beliefs, and success formulas are made conscious and visible do they become testable and open to reinforcement or modification. (p. 231)

The relevance of a culture perspective (e.g., Bantz, 1993) for communication scholars is that "culture has two absolutely crucial functions in any organization: It acts as a symbol and storage of past learning, and it works as an instrument to communicate this learning throughout the organization" (Normann, 1985, p. 23). While culture is changing continuously at the margin, at any point in time it represents the accepted ways of thinking and interpretations of reality. D'Andrade's description of culture underscores the importance of communication. Culture consists of "learned systems of meaning, communicated by means of natural language and other symbol systems, having representational, directive (task) and affective (socioemotional) function, and capable of creating cultural entities and particular senses of reality" (D'Andrade, 1984, p. 116, cited in Barnett, 1988, p. 104).

To bring these descriptions of culture back to the topic of learning, we need to emphasize that a culture perspective is less about what happens in people's heads (e.g., the organization is a brain) and more about what happens between people and among their actions, practices, and narrative interpretations of practice (e.g., the organization is a tribe). The importance of action for a cultural perspective was implied by Duncan and Weiss's definition and is made explicit by Eisenberg and Goodall (1993):

> An action is an interpretation of a situation and it sums up the actor's understanding of the culture as well as the actor's place in it. Everything an individual does and says is an action. An action is, therefore, a strategic performance within a culture that has called for or shaped that performance in some way. It is a strategy for dealing with news of the day by using the

interpretive tools the culture has provided, and it is a performance enacted within a particular situation or context that is constructed within that culture. (p. 136)

Actions reflect an individual's learning. Actions also serve as cues to others regarding appropriate responses. Thus, actions—like cultures—both embody learning and promote learning, as is evident in Sitkin, Sutcliffe, and Weick's (1999) definition of *learning* as "a change in an organization's response repertoire" (p. 7-70).

To highlight action and practice is to foreground know-how (knowledge-informed performance improvement, i.e., practices, skills, and routines) and "know-that" (knowledge acquisition) as central content for learning (Tetlock, 1991, p. 31). A focus on action and practice also legitimizes trial and error as a fundamental sequence in learning. Actions and practices are subject to the sequence, trial-failure-learning-revision-retrial (von Hippel & Tyre, 1993, p. 4). Such a focus on action also helps us clarify that organizational learning can be unsuccessful as well as successful. That is, organizations sometimes can learn the wrong lesson.

Culture, communication, learning, and organization are brought together informally if we treat organizational learning as the

> capacity of an organization to learn how to do what it does, where what it learns is possessed not only by individual members of the organization but by the aggregate itself. That is, when a group acquires the know-how associated with its ability to carry out its collective activities, that constitutes organizational learning. (Cook & Yanow, 1993, p. 378)

Stated more formally, organizational learning is the "acquiring, sustaining, or changing of intersubjective meanings through the artifactual vehicles of their expression and transmission and the collective actions of the group" (Cook & Yanow, 1993, p. 384).

The "artifactual vehicles" that carry the products of learning in the form of meanings are plentiful and diverse, as is evident in this description by Eisenberg and Goodall (1993):

> A culture is full of itself. That is, its values (always competing) are performed (Trujillo, 1985) and displayed (Goodall, 1990) *everywhere*—in symbols, language, stories, work routines, rituals, rites, advertisements, brochures, newsletters, parking lots, memos, cartoons, dress codes, office artifacts, and corporate histories. Thus, culture is not something an organization *has;* it is something an organization *is*. (p. 143)

Numbered among the key artifacts are the routines of a culture, which means that March's (1994) influential argument that rules and routines encode learning is included.

Three related definitional issues require attention before we explore individuals, contexts, and communication. The first deals with unlearning. There have been occasional efforts (e.g., Hedberg, 1981; Huber, 1991, pp. 104-105) to specify the dialectic of learning through conceptualization of its opposite, unlearning. Unlearning, indexed by the discarding of knowledge (Hedberg) or a decrease in the potential range of behaviors (Huber), has generated relatively little attention for reasons that seem fairly clear. Data suggest that there is some spontaneous loss of learning over time regardless of intervening activities (Estes, 1988, p. 383); rehearsal of any one behavior or routine necessarily reduces the time available to rehearse others' items, which means the unrehearsed tends to be unlearned. Data further suggest that the source of unlearning cannot unequivocally be pinned down to other learning that occurred before it and interfered proactively or occurred after it and interfered retroactively (Estes, 1988). If, to these relationships, we add the observation that most organizational learning is subject to intermittent reinforcement, which slows extinction; the observation that arousal tends to favor regression to and expression of older, more rehearsed actions; and finally the observation that there is continuous change, mean-

ing that antecedents are never literally the same, then we arrive at a composite picture in which newer learning overlays older learning, older learning is never fully forgotten, and learning is a perennial necessity since situations seldom repeat themselves. Hence, we concentrate on learning rather than unlearning in the belief that people in organizations distribute their attention in the same way.

The second definitional issue concerns the relationship between individual and organizational learning, an issue on which we find the thrust of Simon's (1991) argument to be persuasive. He proposed:

1. All learning takes place inside individual human heads.
2. An organization learns by the learning of its members or by the insertion of new members with new knowledge.
3. An important component of organizational learning is the transmission of information from one organizational member or group to another.
4. "Human learning in the context of an organization is very much influenced by the organization, has consequences for the organization, and produces phenomena at the organizational level that go beyond anything we could infer simply by observing learning processes in isolated individuals" (p. 126).

Of these four points, we feel the fourth is most useful and the first least useful. The first needlessly precludes the relational infrastructure of learning (e.g., Gergen, 1994; Wegner, 1987; Weick & Roberts, 1993). In the context of our definition here, individuals learn and they translate that learning into actions or routines. Their individual learning is influenced by others at the outset and is amended based on feedback from others. Individual learnings are also shared via verbal communication or by action patterns that send messages. They are shared in the new or altered cultural artifacts that manifest the new learning. Finally, individual learnings are collectively retained—in the memory of others and in the "organizational memory" (e.g., in files, standard operating procedures) (Walsh & Ungson, 1991). Thus, we believe that individual learning is both influenced by the collective (as represented by the culture, and the actions and communications of others), is transmitted to the collective, and is represented in the collective in the form of culture, action patterns (including coordinated actions), and standard operating procedures.

The third definitional issue concerns the relationship between learning and change. We want to make it clear that learning can be preservative as well as innovative. Cook and Yanow (1993, p. 384) show how people, in their case the craftsmen who make Powell flutes, learned to reaffirm existing patterns of coordination while experimenting with a new scale that threatened to undermine the distinctiveness of their product. The learning was subtle. Cook and Yanow (1993) describe it this way:

> The organization learns how to maintain the style and quality of its flutes through the particular skills, character, and quirks of a new individual. The organization engages in a dynamic process of maintaining the norms and practices that assure the constancy of its product. This is learning in a sense quite different from change-oriented learning: it is active reaffirmation or maintenance of the know-how that the organization already possesses. (pp. 381-382)

Notice two things. First, the organization is focused on what it does right, not on what it does wrong. This learning is not about the detection and correction of error but about things gone right and how to preserve them. Second, the organization learns to take on a new situation, not a new identity. People want to adopt a new innovation, in this case a new scale, yet remain who they are. It is not mandatory that both situations and identities change if learning is to occur. Observers who are mindful of culture and know-how as incentives for participation and as sources of competitive advantage are unlikely to equate

persistence with poor learning. Instead, they will entertain the hypothesis that persistent identity is a learned accomplishment in turbulent environments that lure firms toward entropy and the loss of distinctiveness.

To sum up this definitional overview, when people have experiences with the artifacts of an organization's culture or the artifacts of an organization's environment, they learn. They strengthen responses, they reaffirm the ways in which the artifacts fit together, they confront and temporarily resolve competing interpretations that arise from new coalitions or unsocialized newcomers, they wrestle with whether to exploit what they already know or to explore new possibilities. They undertake trials of new behaviors. These experiences are organized around know-how (practices, routines), which suggests that knowledge acquisition (know-that) operates in the service of these routines.

NATURE OF INDIVIDUAL LEARNING

Now that we have made culture central to our definition of learning, but also have argued that a learning analysis has its surest footing at the individual and small-group levels of analysis, we begin our elaboration of key learning dynamics with individual learning. In this section, we discuss a representative rather than exhaustive set of properties and look at those that seem to be especially susceptible to influence from organizational contexts and communication.

First, learning occurs within an ongoing stream that the individual can partition and label in a variety of ways. This is beautifully illustrated in Pye's (1994) elaboration of the insight that

> learning is a process by which we make a particular kind of sense of social life; that is, giving a particular significance to "an episode," by isolating a pattern or form and translation this

"duraction" into "an experience" from which one might conceive of lessons or learning and ultimately change one's behavior as a consequence. (p. 156)

Winograd and Flores (1986) provide a vivid account of just what it means to be thrown into ongoing situations that require structuring if any learning is to be extracted. When people are caught up in an ongoing situation, they cannot avoid acting, cannot step back and reflect on their actions, cannot predict accurately, cannot create stable representations, are at the mercy of interpretation, and resort to language as their primary resource for coping. Cohen, March, and Olsen (1972) preserve some of this ongoing character in their proposal that streams of problems, solutions, people, and choices flow through organizations and converge and diverge independent of human intention. What they overlook is that labels such as "problems" and "solutions" do not inhere in the streams but rather are differentially and opportunistically applied in response to such things as context, prevailing labels, social pressure, image concerns, and salience. The diversity of these influences can muddy appreciably action-outcome linkages that are actually learned.

Despite these challenges, people do continue to break ongoing streams into connected units that tell plausible stories within local subcultures. These punctuations are the raw material for learning.

A second property of individual learning is that it is primarily a controlled, mindful activity that is supplemented by tacit knowledge acquisition and operant conditioning. This mix of learning mechanisms was implied earlier in Normann's (1985) argument that an interest in culture is really an interest in learning. Recall that he refers to an interest in culture as "understanding and making conscious" learning that has taken place. He refers repeatedly to "awareness" of culture as a precursor to learning. And he concludes that only when assumptions "are made conscious and visible" can they be modified. While individuals are thought to do several things un-

consciously to adapt to their environments (Skinner, 1971), the essence of learning seems to be its conscious nature. Individuals monitor their environments, interpret what they see and formulate responses, all with some degree of consciousness regarding what they are doing. One implication of this observation is that to learn, individuals need to know that there is a need for learning. They also need to have a sense of what capabilities they have and what kind of environment they face. In other words, learners need to know who they are, what kind of situation they are in, and that there is a need for learning and possibly change (adaptation). This requirement holds whether the actor is attempting to learn something about his or her individual performance or about the organization and its situation. Recognizing the need for adaptation or learning is not always straightforward. Ashford and Taylor (1990), for example, cite the case of newcomers, who are often unaware of some of the dimensions along which they will be evaluated in a new setting. Given this awareness gap, they fail to see cues suggesting that some change in their personal style or behavior would make their contribution more acceptable and more effective. In a similar fashion, individuals charged with attending to an organization's performance might fail to account for all relevant aspects or performance demands. Because these executives fail to see the need to learn about, say, some emerging trend in their environment, the learning that they can do on behalf of the organization is limited.

Although considerable individual learning is primarily mindful, there is evidence that knowledge is also picked up tacitly, as a by-product of experience (Wagner & Sternberg, 1985). Tacit or implicit learning has several characteristics. Knowledge gained via implicit learning tends to be more complex; it is not fully accessible to consciousness; and the act of learning does not involve processes of conscious hypothesis testing (Seger, 1994). For example, Ashford and Black's (1996) work on organizational newcomers suggests that individuals learn in large part through conversations. Learning is often not the explicit goal of these interactions, but is an important by-product. Wagner and Sternberg (1985) place similar emphasis on the tacit learning that goes on during interactions between individuals in organizations. These examples suggest an important connection between learning and communication that involves the transmittal of tacit knowledge and the act of implicit learning. Indeed, scholars argue that implicit learning plays an important role in the development of procedural knowledge (Cohen & Bacdayan, 1994) of how complex, real-world systems function (Senge & Sterman, 1992), and in the development of skills, habits, and routines (Squire, Knowlton, & Musen, 1993). While scholars can attest to the existence and importance of implicit learning, just how implicit learning interacts with explicit learning and other cognitive processes is complex and less well studied (see Nonaka & Takeuchi, 1995, for a significant advance in explicating this relationship). For our purposes, it is sufficient to recognize that implicit or tacit learning occurs and that individuals may be unable to provide a full verbal account of what they have learned via this mechanism. This later recognition may make implicit learning more relevant for individual rather than organizational learning, given that an organization learns only when individual learnings are communicated and codified in some way.

A third observation is that in individual learning, activity often paves the way for thinking (e.g., Raelin, 1997). That is, one of the things that individual learners are conscious about is their own and others' activities. By seeing what I do, I learn. This observation suggests that contexts that offer individuals room to experiment, free from potential stigma, should promote learning. The idea that people learn by doing lies behind the long tradition of learning curve research in organizations (e.g., Arrow, 1962), which demonstrates that manufacturing performance improves with cumulative production experience. Pisano (1994) has recently suggested, using data from the pharmaceutical industry, that learning by doing may be more likely

"when organizations lack the underlying knowledge needed to simulate and predict effects 'off-line' " (p. 98). Firms with deep knowledge of cause-effect relationships tend to learn *before* doing.

Learning by doing does not require the presence of others nor does it require any abstract "environment." Individuals can learn by watching their own actions. This suggests that learning involves both a situational and a self-understanding. As such, learning may have the same preconditions that White (1974) associates with adaptability (the need to maintain adequate information about the environment, the need to maintain adequate internal conditions necessary to responding, and the need to maintain flexibility). The first two needs are often in tension. Thus, individuals learning about their own performance or that of their organization often make trade-offs between the desire for accurate information and the desire to defend the ego. Information often lowers self-esteem or threatens decision makers' sense of their good judgment, particularly if it is information that suggests that the organization's course of action or typical routines are incorrect. The manner in which individuals resolve these pressures will affect their level of learning and their ability to respond to changing environmental conditions. The third condition, flexibility, is crucial in fashioning a response to that which is detected. For example, in the Mann Gulch disaster (Weick, 1993) a group of young firefighters failed to maintain the internal condition necessary to respond (e.g., calmness, the internal organization of their group) and also lost flexibility as they engaged the explosive fire while remaining committed to their traditional ways of tackling small fires.

The need for accurate information noted in the last observation raises a further issue: Accuracy regarding what? Whether one finds learning to be a valuable concept or not may depend on one's belief in the existence of a reality and realism of some sort, and one's resourcefulness and creativity in selecting a reality in which one is willing to believe. Indeed, as we will see later, many observers treat organizational culture and environment as social facts (realities), which means that actions that accommodate more fully to them can be said to reflect learning (e.g., this is the central assertion in studies of socialization). Others argue that culture and environment are constituted by actions. They are not simply something out there to which actions accommodate. Instead, people create that to which they then respond. Different interests result in different communities of people who vouch for different creations. These multiple communities are clearly arenas for conflict, argument, and persuasion. But it is unclear what is learned other than rhetorical skill used to persuade others of the viability of one's view of the environment and skills at reaccomplishing structures that unravel.

We believe that both perspectives have merit. Organizational realities are socially constructed and some environmental imperatives do exist. Thus, if organizational learners socially construct an environment that is grossly out of tune with the actual demands imposed by powerful others, then performance should deteriorate. Within these limits, however, social construction does occur and is functional. That is, an organization that can socially construct an adequate reality and act on it ought to be better off than one that devotes an equivalent amount of time to developing an accurate sense of its environment and delays acting.

Individual learning is also dependent on cues, and it is this dependency that brings communication into discussions of learning. Individuals who are aware of the need for learning can learn by explicitly attending (to cues) offered by and punctuated from the environment regarding demands, requirements, and opportunities. Such attention gives the learner a sense of what ought to be done. To learn how adequate their (or their organization's) routines and practices are, individuals also need to attend to feedback cues offered by the environment. Such cues will suggest whether an individual performer or the organization is moving toward success or failure. Ashford's (1993) study of feedback cues suggests that these cues range from direct (someone provides the performer with an assessment) to indirect (actions occur that can be interpreted as performance feedback) and from positive to negative. For example, IBM lags Apple in a particular quarter. Is this feedback worth attending to by decision makers at either company, or is this quarter's performance due to some exogenous event? Cues are also provided by many sources, including one's relevant stakeholders and the task, and often are complex combinations of many of these (e.g., one's supervisor recognizes one's peers' performance on a similar but not exactly the same task in a public setting, but fails to recognize one's own performance—a feedback cue?). In reading the environment for cues regarding what the individual or the organization should be doing and how well it has been done, Ashford's (1989) research on self-assessments suggests that the individual learner needs to make three assessments about any available cue: Is this event, action, subtle gesture, and so forth a cue? Is this cue meant for me? What does this cue mean? For example, a firm loses market share. Is this a feedback cue from customers? If so, what does it mean (a lessening of desire for products of this type or for this firm's particular brand)?

Bandura (1986) suggested that individuals can use the actions of others as cues from which they learn vicariously. By watching what happens to individuals when they engage in different behavioral patterns, the learner comes to understand that a certain strategy leads to success while another leads to failure, without engaging in either strategy personally. Institutional theory suggests that a similar process occurs at the organizational level. Organizations learn what practices to adopt by watching successful firms in their industries (Zucker, 1987).

When neither environmental cues nor cues from models are available, learners can still resort to proactive action to obtain information and can create cues by trial and error. The individual or organization can try some action in an uncertain domain and monitor carefully the results.

Summary of Individual Learning

To sum up, organizational learning is grounded in several predispositions of humans including their tendency to break the ongoing stream of experience into meaningful units; their tendency to perceive and conduct learning as an explicit, controlled activity in which they engage intentionally; their tendency to overlook the reality that considerable learning also remains tacit and unexplicated; their tendency to learn by acting first in order to discover the consequences of that action; their tendency to use any occasion of learning as information about at least two things, the situation and the self; and their tendency to learn from cues that are treated as surrogates for more complex events. Organizational contexts and communication processes influence learning through their effect on these individual processes of punctuating, reflecting, acting, categorizing, and extrapolating. Variation in activities such as these, induced by variation in contexts and communication, should result in learning that is more or less adaptive, more or less permanent, and more or less positive to the learners themselves. To explore these variations in more detail, we turn next to the effects of organizational context on individual learning.

ORGANIZATIONAL CONTEXT

If organizational learning is about acquiring, sustaining, and revising action-outcome linkages that take the form of know-how embedded in culture, if that know-how is built up from interaction with artifacts and with other actors within and outside the organization, and if know-how is fleshed out when people learn new information (know-that) and beliefs (believe-that), then it is reasonable to view organizations as a context for learning (e.g., Tyre & von Hippel, 1997). What may be most characteristic of this context is its

multiple realities and combination of shared and unshared meanings. Eisenberg and Goodall (1997) quoting Conquergood (1991) put it this way:

> Cultures are composed of ongoing dialogues that are variously complicit or engaged. A dialogue is complicit when the individuals or groups participating in it go along with the dominant interpretation of meaning. It is engaged when the individuals and groups struggle against a dominant interpretation and try to motivate action based on an alternative explanation. In most organizations most of the time you can find both complicit and engaged resources for dialogues. For this reason, an organizational culture is necessarily a conflicted environment, a site of multiple meanings engaged in a constant struggle for interpretive control. (p. 142).

These notions prompt the idea of context as market.

Context: A Marketplace for Ideas

If people see things differently and learn different lessons from the "same" data, then persuasion and advocacy are critical to most organizational learning situations. In fact, it seems appropriate to think of an organization as a learning arena within which meanings compete in a marketplace of ideas. Like any marketplace, we believe that competition occurs for the time and attention of others, particularly for that of those in the top ranks of the organization. In organizations, there are multiple potential learners with multiple points of contact with the environment, the organization's task, or each other (i.e., multiple learning opportunities, and a high likelihood that learners will learn different things). Individuals also have a motivation to promote their particular "learning." For example, certain tangible rewards accrue to the sellers of particular issues (learnings/interpretations) (Dutton & Ashford, 1993; Kingdon, 1984).

These rewards may include a boost to the seller's image should the issue be looked on favorably by those at the top of the organization or a potential gain in tangible resources for the seller's department that may come with winning the competition for meaning in the organization. Given the potential rewards for those who can most influence the interpretation of or "lesson" drawn from the available data, we believe that a true marketplace exists in which sellers informally compete for the ability to define how the world is interpreted. Clearly, communication is critical to this process as individuals with more developed persuasion skills ought to be particularly adept at shaping the content of their organization's learning.

We also believe (as this last paragraph attests) that organizational learning is stratified. It takes place across the hierarchical and inclusionary boundaries defined by Van Maanen and Schein (1979). Whose meaning will be accepted will be partially a function of those boundaries: Old-timers' definitions of reality will be more influential than those offered by newcomers, and the power to define reality will be loosely correlated with one's place in the organization's hierarchy. This suggests that certain voices will be lost in the organizational learning process, and it allows us to specify the likely focus and direction of persuasion and influence attempts. Thus, newcomers will be particularly interested in influencing old-timers (and will need to in order to have their voices heard) and lower-level employees ought to be particularly interested in influencing higher-ups regarding how to interpret changing "realities."

This observation increases our confidence in the applicability of the marketplace metaphor and also suggests some likely dysfunctions in the organizational learning process. That is, it is difficult to get news across boundaries, especially hierarchical ones. Thus, it is hard to bring any news to the top of an organization. Individuals' concerns regarding their image (no one wants to look bad by bringing what might be bad news to the top) and the communication problems inherent in multiple layers (where each sender reinterprets the message slightly and delays its transmission somewhat) make communication upward difficult (e.g., the Hubble telescope failure). While the image concerns may be unique to the transmission of bad news, the problem of multiple layers mitigates against getting *any* news to the top. A quote attributed to Jack Welch, CEO of General Electric, exemplifies this problem: "Layers are like sweaters, you wear enough of them and you can't even tell what the weather is like outside."

In general, the communication literature has found that the more links in a communication chain, the more likely that information passed along the chain will be distorted (e.g., Fulk & Mani, 1986; O'Reilly & Roberts, 1974). One interesting question to pursue in the next several decades as organizations downsize and delayer is: What happens to difficulties of upward communication when organizational hierarchies flatten? Do they still exist but on a smaller scale? Do they disappear? Are they replaced by new, perhaps as yet unanticipated and perhaps more insidious, difficulties?

It is also worth noting that the marketplace for ideas, in which individual learning occurs and is communicated to others, takes place within a particular organizational culture. This culture affects preferred labels, interpretations, and attributions. These, in turn, affect learning. Not only do individual learners need to translate their findings into acceptable language (and by doing so, often shape and alter the learning slightly), but also the organization's culture affects the ability to learn. These comments suggest that the movement from individual to collective learning is by no means smooth and barrier free. In fact, we believe there are several predictable impediments to organizational learning. We now turn to an explicit discussion of these. Following this section, we will comment briefly on two other aspects of collective learning: the impact of movements of people in and out of the collective, and the dynamics of speedy learning in a collective context.

Context as Impediment to Learning

Sometimes the conflicts, alternative explanations, and subcultures in organizations operate at such cross-purposes that it is hard to believe that learning of any kind could occur. The impediments to organizational learning need to be kept in mind when assessing the potential value of a learning analysis. One impediment is the complexity of the environment. For example, in the domain of international politics, learning is slow because the environment is so causally complex. "Even when we sense that one factor or another contributed to outcomes, it is daunting to assign relative weights and to distinguish decisive from contributory-but-not-decisive causes, or to distinguish between necessary and sufficient conditions" (Breslauer & Tetlock, 1991, pp. 3-4). Compounding the difficulty of untangling causality is fact that people are unable to see what would have happened had they done something else (the problem of counterfactuals) and the fact that people are often motivated to misrepresent their intentions and capabilities. Add to that a labile environment capable of sudden qualitative discontinuities, field operators who give incomplete or inaccurate information, people concerned with protecting their own interests, and the temptation to "learn only the lessons that confirm their preconceptions, attribute success to their own actions and fit into their long-standing sense of mission" (Sagan, 1993, pp. 207-208), and it becomes clearer why the topic of organizational learning was not included in the first edition of this handbook. As Scott (1987) puts it, "We should not underestimate how difficult it is for organizational systems to learn anything useful, given a rapidly changing environment, selective attention and inattention processes, inertia, cognitive limits, and ambiguity of feedback" (p. 282).

Beyond ambiguity, contexts are also arenas of accountability in which people are, to a greater or lesser degree across contexts, held accountable for their actions (Tetlock, 1985). These variations should affect preoccupation with one's image, which in turn should affect learning. These dynamics are visible in Van de Ven and Polley's (1992) study of a new product team. The feedback and "experience" that the team had to learn from was largely a function of the team's own "impression management and 'sugar coated' administrative reviews" (p. 106). Van de Ven and Polley (1992, p. 107) concluded that in judging a new product, administrative reviews that are open to influence by the party being reviewed are a poor substitute for the "acid test of the market" in promoting learning. We believe that much of the "experience" from which individuals attempt to learn in organizations is similarly tainted by the learner's own and others' attempts to socially construct a positive image or scenario to help maximize their images. These realities make learning from experience difficult.

But image concerns as an impediment to learning go beyond simply looking good. Staw and Ross (1980, 1987) found, for example, that leaders who maintained a consistent course of action were seen as more effective than those who changed their course of action. This finding suggests some limitations on a learner's ability to try out various actions to see their effect. These self-imposed limits stem from the actors' needs to behave in self-consistent ways and their fears that inconsistency will tarnish their image with stakeholders. Staw and Ross (1980) interpreted their results as suggesting that experimentation would be problematic for those at the top of organizations. That is, experimentation may be a good way to gain information on how various strategies work (i.e., learn), but it may carry too high a price tag in terms of costs to the leader's image (unless you are Herb Kelleher of Southwest Airlines). These costs also may exist throughout the organization, where it may be more important to be right or predictable than to create opportunities for learning via experimenting with possible effective strategies. Indeed, our image of the good employee may be one who can foresee the results of various actions ahead of time and pick effective strategies consistently.

Thus, organizational norms regarding failure should affect organizational learning. The meaning of failure in a given organization affects the likelihood that people working within that organization will engage in trial-and-error learning. If failures are seen as catastrophic, then trial-and-error learning becomes less likely.

An additional complication associated with accountability occurs when people seek information and feedback in order to learn. Ashford and her colleagues (Ashford & Northcraft, 1992; Ashford & Tsui, 1991) have documented the pervasive fear that individuals seem to have about seeking feedback from others about the efficacy of their actions. That fear is based on concerns about how such seeking might be interpreted by others (i.e., as a sign of weakness). A key impediment to organizational learning, then, may be individuals' fears and concerns regarding how the primary activities involved in learning will "look" to others. These fears should reduce both information/feedback seeking on the part of organizational decision makers and constrain the variance in actions taken based on the information/feedback attained.

These impression-management or image concerns are different from the ego-defense concern mentioned earlier. Ego defense comes into play because some learning is unpleasant, as when one learns that a chosen course of action is failing. Given the need to maintain internal conditions adequate for response mentioned earlier, people exposed to failure information are likely to react in ways that undermine learning. People motivated by ego defense often restrict social comparisons (presumably in an attempt to avoid painful information) and to choose comparison referents with whom they would compare favorably (Festinger, 1954). Favorable comparison means that nothing much needs to be learned. In many organizational contexts, others may routinely aid and abet each other's ego defense. For example, Janis (1972) documented the tendency for subordinates of more senior managers to defend their managers' egos for them by preventing them from hearing disqui-

eting information. Not only do executives often prefer to hear good news but, in fact, subordinates often get promoted up the career ladder because they tell only good news. Thus, as managers move up in the organization, it becomes more difficult for them to get honest feedback on their efforts as their subordinates are busily portraying every effort as a success. These processes in which learners defend their own egos or their subordinates do it for them would seem to impede organizational learning since they create an impoverished and distorted information base from which to take action.

Thus, a context of accountability can undermine learning either through image concerns or ego concerns. Image concerns focus on how actions will be interpreted by others and ego concerns focus on how the lesson learned will feel to the learner. Either concern can filter out substantial information from which people might learn.

Organizational contexts also vary in the amount of ambiguity that is typical, the form this ambiguity takes, and the resources made available to reduce it. These too act as impediments to organizational learning. Consider an organization undergoing a culture shift from a warm but complacent company to an aggressive, "take no prisoners" type culture. The cues regarding the new behaviors required in the new environment are likely to be a mix of direct instructions, indirect hopes for new types of behavior, and lingering cues reinforcing the old way of doing things (given that these changes are profound and must stem from the value level). Individuals who try to learn how to act within the new aggressive culture are faced with a problem: What in the sometimes bewildering actions that I see around me should I take as a guide for my behavior, and what do these guides mean? What should I try to learn from? Answering these questions involves at least two types of interpretation problems. First, superstitious learning is possible. For example, learning during munificent periods is noisy since almost any cue and action is associated with success. In the munificent period following World War II, many companies "learned" that they needed large staffs and many organizational layers to survive when these factors may have been incidental (if not counterproductive) to their success (Peters & Waterman, 1982). Superstitious learning is especially troublesome when such learning creates schemes that are then used by organization members to screen further information.

Second, the environments that most organizations face today are characterized as much by equivocality (synonymous with ambiguity in this discussion) as by uncertainty. Uncertainty, or ignorance understood as the absence of information, can be resolved by acquiring and analyzing more data. Indeed, uncertainty is seen as the primary motivation for learning at the individual or organizational level. Equivocality, however, presents a different set of issues. Equivocality involves the existence of multiple and conflicting interpretations about an organizational situation. Equivocality is often characterized by confusion, disagreement, and lack of understanding. As Daft, Lengel, and Trevino (1987) put it: "Managers are not certain what questions to ask, and if questions are posed there is no store of objective data to provide the answer." Rather than search for more data, people manage equivocality by exchanging views in order to define adequately the situation they presume to face. Equivocality poses a much more difficult problem for organizations because there are fewer established routines to reduce it, which means organizations prefer to treat it as an issue of uncertainty. To deal with confusion requires extensive communication among key organizational participants to resolve disagreements, formulate a collective definition of the situation, and enact a response.

Ambiguity is also important for learning because newer inputs tend to be filtered through existing categories, which tend to favor constraint over creativity and to reduce learning. Henry Kissinger put it this way: "It is an illusion to believe that leaders gain in profundity while they gain in experience. . . . The convictions that leaders have formed be-

fore reaching high office are the intellectual capital they will consume as long as they continue in office" (quoted in Breslauer & Tetlock, 1991, p. 4). If current events fit a prior point of view, then there is nothing to learn. March, Sproull, and Tamuz (1991) provide a wonderful example of ambiguity, in the context of air safety and near misses between aircraft:

> Every time a pilot avoids a collision, the event provides evidence for the threat and for its relevance. It is not clear whether the learning should emphasize how close the organization came to disaster, thus the reality of danger in the guise of safety, or the fact that disaster was avoided, thus the reality of safety in the guise of danger. (p. 10)

A near miss is ambiguous and with ambiguity comes increased pressures to reduce it. As Kissinger hints, it is usually easier to resolve ambiguity by imposing old constraints rather than by creating new ones. If that happens, an opportunity for learning is lost. If people see a near miss as vindication of their past experience with accident avoidance (the reality of safety in the guise of danger), this interpretation will inhibit learning because it discourages "more thorough investigations, more accurate reporting, deeper imagination, and greater sharing of information" (Sagan, 1993, p. 247).

Given the tendency of interpretation under ambiguity to favor constraints rather than creativity and tactical changes rather than changes in strategy, communication can promote learning only if it openly encourages novel interpretations. Failure to do this can result in disaster, as in the case of the Mann Gulch disaster mentioned earlier. The wildland fire at Mann Gulch was ambiguous (it appeared to be both a major and minor fire) but communication was blocked (leader and co-leader gave contradictory messages, noise blocked vocal communication, communication language was inappropriate, firefighters were relative strangers), which led to an ineffective collective solution (individuals tried to outrun an exploding fire by going up a slippery 76% hill).

A final impediment to organizational learning is the organizational culture itself. For example, an organizational culture with a typical behavioral pattern that encourages external attributions for failure reduces the need for and ability to learn. If, as culture researchers contend, these typical behavioral patterns are tacit, accepted, and occur without notice (Schein, 1985), then learning opportunities (and the organization's failure to take advantage of them) may similarly be overlooked. Thus, in addition to the marketplace for ideas and the inclusionary and hierarchical stratification of organizations, it is important to recognize that strong cultural forces affect learning. As we will see in the next section, organizational culture sets a prescribed language for discussing learning that may or may not facilitate communication from some learners (their voices may not fit and may, therefore, be unattended to) on some topics. The culture also entails a set of tacit norms regarding how the environment is engaged. These norms, like the tendency toward external attribution of failure noted above, may both hinder or prevent organizational learning and go undetected by those who take culture for granted.

Despite these formidable impediments, it does remain true that there are pockets of people in organizations and moments in their everyday lives when know-how and artifacts shed some meanings and acquire new ones and when newer skills and understandings come to dominate older ones. These learnings are the result of change in features of organizational context such as patterns of competing ideas, stratification, attributional style, turnover, accountability, tolerance of ambiguity, and preoccupation with speed in decision making. Of these seven, two aspects have received recent research attention and may be fruitful avenues around which to design interventions to enhance learning. These two are the role that turnover and the rate of learning play in organizational learning. Before ex-

ploring each of these features, we want to emphasize that context is both something that people enact and something to which they react. They enact the marketplace of ideas that then constrains the options to which they react. They enact the levels of hierarchy that filter their communication, which filtering then rearranges the hierarchy, and so on. Learning is not simply a reactive event even though phrases such as "learnings are the result of changes" encourage just such an interpretation. Communication is just as important for its capability to enact a learnable environment as it is for its capability to mediate learning from something already enacted.

Context: The Impact of Personnel Movements

When we consider organizations as a collective context for learning, we also have to consider the effect of personnel movements in and out of that collective. Most treatments of organizational learning presume that organizations rely on experience and that experience is preserved in the memories of individuals (Johnson & Hasher, 1987; Steinbruner, 1974). Supporting these contentions is a simulation study conducted by Carley (1992). She found that organizations with a higher turnover rate learned less and learned more slowly. This effect was less pronounced, however, in larger organizations and organizations engaged in simpler tasks. According to Carley, this effect occurs because turnover removes part of the organization's memory and because with a high turnover rate, personnel leave before they are fully trained. Consequently, the organization's final level of learning is lower.

Of note, however, is one of the model limitations that Carley (1992) specifies. Her simulation assumes a relatively stable environment and, therefore, a stable task. She points out that turnover might be less costly in a less stable environment and that "in turbulent environments turnover even may be beneficial to the organization" (p. 41). Indeed Virany,

Tushman, and Romanelli (1992) make a similar argument with respect to executive turnover. These findings and theoretical statements raise several questions regarding the effect of personnel turnover on organizational learning. First, how can organizations maintain learning in a high turnover world (or does the high turnover help if the environment is turbulent)? Alternatively, does turnover help learning because the communication required in the continuous resocializing of newcomers reminds old-timers of what they once knew but have forgotten (Sutton & Louis, 1987)?

Some have argued that in situations of high turnover, organizations cope by institutionalizing memory (e.g., create handbooks, policies, and standard operating procedures; Bluedorn, 1982; McCain, O'Reilly, & Pfeffer, 1983; Walsh & Ungson, 1991). However, we feel that formalization is a poor substitute for individuals' memories and experiences especially when individual and collective know-how is salient. We suspect that managers rarely consult files and that standard operating procedures rarely are sufficiently nuanced to depict expert performance. In fact, the real compensation for the loss of "memory" represented by turnover lies in the newcomers brought in as replacements. Newcomers represent fresh views and insights that may be more important for an organization facing turbulence than long historical memories. Organizations interested in promoting learning, however, need to consider how they bring newcomers on board. In this regard, March (1991, p. 76) suggests that slower-learning newcomers may actually be better for the organization over the long run than fast learners. With slow learners, organizational codes (i.e., the languages, beliefs, and practices of an organization) are exposed longer to deviant behavior and, consequently, there are more opportunities to consider code changes. A crucial irony in a fast-changing world, then, is that slow individual learners accelerate organizational learning because organization-level codes remain exposed longer to new inputs. In a fast-changing world, organiza-

tions with many newcomers (higher turnover), slow-learning newcomers, and strong-minded newcomers (who are more willing to deviate from organizational codes in the first place) may be at an adaptive advantage as they are more likely to modify their codes. If such changes bring the codes more in line with environmental demands, effective collective learning has occurred. This finding also suggests the importance of communication. In fast-changing environments, organizations with cultures that promote expressions of deviance (disagreement, etc.) from slow learners should be better off than those without such cultures. However, recall from above that organizational contexts vary in the degree to which people are held accountable for their actions (Tetlock, 1985) and feel free to express divergent views.

Context: A Crucible for Speedy Learning?

The final property of organizational context that affects individual learning through its effect on communication is the emphasis on speed and high-velocity decision making (Cushman & King, 1994; Eisenhardt, 1989). Again, Henry Kissinger's experience frames the issue. Larson (1991) commented on Kissinger's inability and unwillingness to change his ideas about the Soviet Union while serving in the Nixon administration, with the following observation:

> Policy makers must make quick decisions without having time to think. As Kissinger recalled, "There is little time for leaders to reflect. They are locked in an endless battle in which the urgent constantly gains on the important." Policy makers assimilate what is new to what they already know. They act first, and rationalize later. (p. 388)

The consequences for learning of a culture that values speed can be inferred from Fiske's (1992, p. 885) comparison of information processing that is accuracy oriented and that which is decision oriented. A concern with accuracy is evidence driven and bottom-up, and closure is resisted in the interest of acquiring more information. A concern with speed is driven by expectancy confirmation rather than evidence, and is top-down with closure being sought in the interest of action. Fast learning that occurs in conjunction with decision-oriented goals should be mindless, single-loop, often superstitious, unreflective, tactical, superficial. It could also be adaptive if fast, small learnings match fast, small environmental changes. The problem is, fast learning is expectancy driven rather than evidence driven, which means that even small environmental changes may be missed if they are unexpected. In their place, expectancies may provide the map of what appears to be needed.

The potential differences in the kind of learning expected with a mindset favoring speed rather than accuracy shed new light on prescriptions for practice that emphasize the value of "fast failures" (Peters, 1987, p. 259), rapid prototyping (von Hippel & Tyre, 1993), and the value of learning quickly in ways that are hard to imitate. Each of these prescriptions for better adaptation should actually reinforce the presumptions people bring to a situation. Perceptions are filtered through those presumptions in ways that appear to confirm them. What is sacrificed is accuracy—and the very adaptation that was supposed to be facilitated.

Except that in a socially constructed world constituted and held together by communication, accuracy may be a moot issue. Accuracy is a vestige of the view that communication represents, whereas expectancy is a vestige of the view that communication constitutes. Of course, communication does both. But if the constraints to be represented are socially constituted, and if they are driven by expectancies as much as by perceptions, then what people really need to learn is more about the self and the group that generates the expectancies, how those expectancies are generated, and how to improve that process, rather than learning

about the environment on which those expectancies are imposed.

What managers need is confidence as much as accuracy (Steinbruner, 1974). They need confidence to create and impose expectations that produce a more preferred set of constraints. Viewed this way, communication enhances the conditions for learning when it involves rich disclosive discourse about the self and about the conditions under which stronger expectations and more confident action occur. To learn about self and confident action, rather than about the world, is to learn ways to alter that world so that it eventually imposes constraints that are more satisfying. An altered world is no less an outcome of learning than is an altered learner.

Summary

To sum up, we have argued that individuals tend to punctuate, reflect, act, categorize, and extrapolate in order to learn and that these tendencies unfold more or less successfully depending on the degree of ambiguity, conflict, hierarchy, accountability, external attribution, turnover, and preoccupation with speed found in the context where unfolding takes place. In a very crude sense, as these features of context increase in their frequency and intensity, individual learning decreases. The decrease in learning is brought about because these contextual changes tend to induce arbitrary punctuation, intermittent reflection, interrupted action, meaningless categorization, and faulty extrapolation, all of which preclude learning or encourage superstitious learning of that which is salient rather than that which is basic.

COMMUNICATION AND LEARNING

Up to this point, we have focused on organizational learning as figure and communication as ground. Now we intend to reverse that emphasis and bring communication to the forefront by asking what it adds to our understanding of learning. We attack this question in two ways. First, we suggest that an inadequate "communication language," in this case preoccupation with the language of finance, precludes learning. Second, we suggest that a communication process that does not adequately capture the complexities of the ongoing flow of events both internal and external to the organization also precludes learning. A remedy for both communication shortcomings is found in the communication practice adopted by NASA in the early 1960s —the Monday Notes—that created both a flexible communication language and an adaptive communication process.

Communication Language

To see the interdependence of communication and learning, we can look at poor communication language in an organizational setting. Normann (1985) observed that most organizations are dominated by

> a poor figure-oriented language, focusing on budgets, profits-and-loss performance, and procedures but not on the substance of the business. As one of the key officials of a large multinational company told me, suddenly getting a flash of insight: "We had this long and nice dinner with the managing directors of two of our largest subsidiaries, one corporate vice-president, and myself. And suddenly I realized that we had been together for three hours, talking about the company every minute, but not once had anybody used the words *clients, product,* or *people.* The only things we talked about were budgets, return on investment, and the company's long-range planning procedure. We do have profit problems—but *talking* about profits and procedures will not solve any of them!" (p. 229)

This executive's insight suggests that to learn better procedures for profit-maximization in competition, people need to commu-

nicate about something else. They need to talk about clients, what is delivered to them, and when, in the case of competition. When people are unable to shift their frames of reference or enrich the ones they have, they get caught in what Normann calls "a vicious learning circle maintained by poor communication language." Such a vicious circle is depicted in Figure 18.1.

This diagram illustrates several points that are crucial if we want to understand the joint effects of organization, communication, and learning. First, communication can conceal and silence and thereby inhibit learning, as is shown in variable B. That is, people use the company's philosophy to tell them what to bring up and what to keep silent about. If individuals keep silent, organizations cannot learn effectively (they may be able to interpret individuals' silence, but not usually with any degree of accuracy). Second, Figure 18.1 shows how communication about planning (as a function of the choices made in variable B) drive out communication about substance, which blocks attention to substance and learning more about it (variable C). Individual learning is thereby impaired. The figure also suggests that organizational learning is affected by the distribution of communication (variable D). Communication affects who knows what and how quickly they know it. If all we are talking about is planning and controls, then we aren't sharing learnings about business substance. Further learning is shaped by interpretations driven by particular frames of reference (described in variable H). These frames, in turn, can vary depending on the performance they need to explain (EH linkage) and on the firm's "philosophy" or culture embedded in frames and explanations (HA reciprocal linkage). For example, if a firm faces low and uneven performance, managers may interpret this as a need for formal and administrative solutions (such as incentive pay systems). Interpretations, culture, and learning tend to be self-perpetuating (HA reciprocal link). That is, once the incentive system in the above example is put into place, people talk more and more about the incentive system

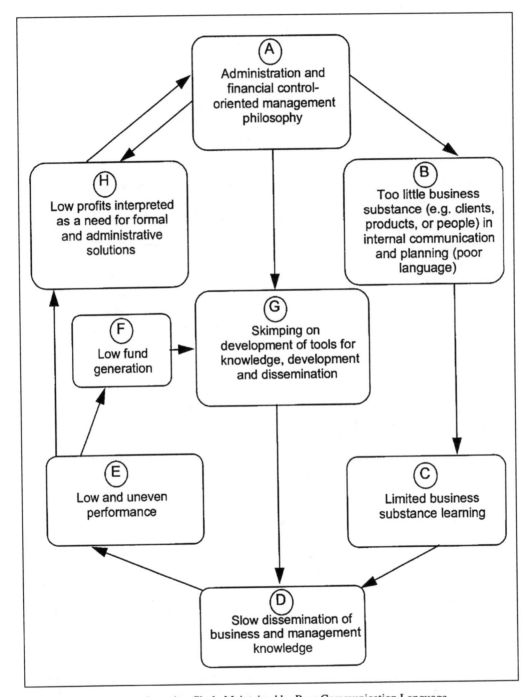

Figure 18.1. A Vicious Learning Circle Maintained by Poor Communication Language

SOURCE: Figure 1, p. 230, in Richard Normann, "Developing Capabilities for Organizational Learning," in J. M. Pennings & Associates, *Organizational Strategy and Change.* Copyright 1985 Jossey-Bass, Inc. Used with permission.

rather than about clients, products or people. Low performance is interpreted as a need for formal and administrative solutions, and this interpretation is reinforced by a philosophy that emphasized administration and financial controls in the first place and by continual talk and action involving controls.

The basic reason Normann calls this a "vicious" circle is because there is no way within this system to step outside, reexamine, and change its basic assumptions (the DEFGD loop is self-sealing). Said differently, this is what single-loop learning (Argyris & Schon, 1978) looks like. However, since this structure is a circle, it also means that if the direction in which any one of the variables is moving is reversed, for example, a retreat is convened to focus attention on business substance, which increases business substance learning thereby reversing the direction in which variable C (the amount of business substance learning) is moving, then each variable connected to C would also begin to move in the opposite direction. Thus, the circle is vicious only if control language is increased (as a manifestation of variable A), which then increases everything else. A movement of control language in the opposite direction (i.e., by its replacement with the rhetoric of self-regulation) has the opposite effect. Given the profit-oriented mindset of business practice, we expect that people will be preoccupied with financial controls and that this focus will be amplified. Nevertheless, theoretically this structure is capable of overriding this focus widely and swiftly, which makes it as much a volatile circle as one that is vicious.

There are two other ways this system could be changed and its language made more adequate. As depicted in Figure 18.1, the system is deviation-amplifying with an even number of inverse relationships (there are two, one between A and B, one between E and H). The system would become less dominated by the poor communication language of organizational control if one of these two inverse relationships were made direct (e.g., if lower performance led to less rather than more

interpretation of that lowered performance as demonstrating the need for even more formal solutions, the system would be stabilized), or if a third inverse relationship were created in the loop (e.g., if slower dissemination of knowledge [variable D] led to higher rather than lower performance [E], perhaps in a manner similar to March's slow-learning newcomers mentioned earlier, who accelerate adaptation).

Regardless of which form learning might take to increase the attention to substance and decrease the attention to financial controls, the learning will involve changes in communication at the relatively microlevel of words, conversation (Ford & Ford, 1995), and artifacts. Communication created the original blindspot toward business substance and it perpetuated this blindspot in ways that precluded learning. But communication also provides the means to dissolve the blindspot and the language to restructure the system and the medium for new learning.

Communication Process

Communication shapes learning through language as we have just seen, but also through process. While the role of process was implicit in the preceding discussion, here we make it more explicit. Freese's (1980) description, crafted in the context of a discussion of cumulative theorizing, provides the necessary tools. To describe the experiences that are the grist for learning, people have to use language:

> Constructing sentences to express statements about experience imposes discrete definitions on a subject matter that is continuous. One cannot report in a sentence an observation about experience without a concept that structures what one is observing. Observation statements describe not perceptions but planned perceptions. Data are not given by experience, but by the concept of the language used to interpret it.

Observational language imposes discrete boundaries on the continuity of the phenomenal world so as to define concrete, individual events in that world. Such events may be simple, solid objects like snowballs or complex, nontactile events like behavior sequences. Whether simple or complex, phenomenal events possess two properties whose significance for scientific inquiry cannot be overstated: They are unique and transitory. (Freese, 1980, p. 28)

Freese's description is a wonderful summary of the field for learning that is created by communication. It describes resources for learning when it refers to such things as sentences, discrete definitions, concepts, and interpretations that are imposed on observations, continuous subject matter, experiences, perception, and phenomenal events. It describes potential slippage between experience and the data that are available for learning when it suggests the kinds of simplifications produced by communication. Communication edits continuity into discrete categories, observations into interpretations, experience into bounded events, and perceptions into preexisting plans and frameworks. But most important, Freese's description pinpoints the difficulty that these simplifications create for learning. The clue to this difficulty is in the last sentence. If phenomenal events are unique, then how can knowledge of one unique event be used to deal with another unique event? If phenomenal events are transitory, why even bother with transfer of knowledge anyway?

Unique, transient phenomenal events are of no value for learning until they are made less unique and more enduring. These alternations are accomplished by discrete images and categories, imposed with some degree of consensus, as a result of coordinated communication practices and actions. To impose conversations on the world is to reconstitute that world in a form that is more learnable, because it has become more typical, more repetitive, more stable, and more enduring. However, the world of continuous flows to which that learning is directed has not itself become any less unique or transient simply because people choose to see it that way. Thus, there remains a chronic disjunction between the discrete products of communication and the continuous realities to which they refer, or in the language of learning, there is a disjunction between the reality an organization faces and the words used to represent that reality as organization members communicate with each other.

Learning has to bridge this disjunction. And its success in doing so is heavily dependent on the adequacy with which discrete communications approximate the continuity that ultimately validates or invalidates the learning. These approximates take at least three forms. First, successful learning depends on the adequacy with which the content of communication represents the flow and continuity in which learning is embedded. Content that is rich in dynamics, process imagery, verbs, possibilities, and unfolding narratives represents flows more accurately than does content that is dominated by statics, structures, nouns, the impractical, and arguments. Second, success also depends on the adequacy with which communication practices enact boundaries and categories into the world, thereby making its subject matter less continuous. Enacting boundaries into the world is what happens when discrete expectations trigger behavioral confirmation (e.g., Snyder, 1984, 1992). And third, success is also dependent on the adequacy with which communication practices themselves, not just their content, become isomorphic with the flows of which they are a part. Weick and Browning (1991, p. 7) describe an example of isomorphism when they discuss "pacing," a style of emotional contact among strangers consisting of precise and deliberate matching of micromovements in posture, gestures, language, voice pitch, and tempo, intended to accelerate familiarity, understanding, and deeper levels of rapport. Pacing appears to accelerate the evolution of cooperation.

Other efforts to bridge the disjunction between the continuous and the discrete in the service of learning are evident in work such as the dialogue project (Isaacs, 1993), which aims to create "a field of genuine meeting and inquiry." Isaacs (1993) defined dialogue as "a sustained collective inquiry into the processes, assumptions, and certainties that compose everyday experience" (p. 25). Conceivably, as dialogue develops, it will combine pacing, the imposition of learnable boundaries, and process imagery thereby improving the match between ongoing conversation and ongoing streams of events, and thereby improve learning. It is too early to tell. What interests us is the question of whether much of the recent repackaging of organizational development into the newer container of organizational learning may, either intentionally or unintentionally, create contexts in which communication matches referent events more closely and in doing so facilitates learning. For us the crucial issue is the degree to which that communication is compatible with reality both in form and content, the degree to which the communication is flexible and able to balance creativity and constraint (Eisenberg & Goodall, 1993), and the degree to which the communication replaces, at least temporarily, continuity and flow with bounded, self-contained, nameable, typical, recurrent events. Communication that can both represent flows by means of content and practice and create bounded events by means of self-fulfilling discrete definitions should be able to make the unique more typical and the transient more stable. Both of those changes promote learning. And both of these changes are the direct result of communication.

Learning, Communication, and the Monday Notes

The preceding theoretical answer to the question of what communication adds to our understanding of learning can be supple-mented with an example that covers the same ground. This example comes from Tompkins's (1977, 1993) experience as a faculty communication consultant to the Marshall Space Flight Center in 1967 at the time Wernher von Braun was its director. As part of his interviews with engineers at the center, Tompkins asked the question, "What works well?" With surprising regularity, the interviewees answered, "The Monday Notes" (Tompkins, 1977, pp. 8-10; 1993, pp. 62-66). Von Braun had asked approximately 24 key managers, spread across several units, who were at least one layer removed from him, to send him a one-page memo every Monday morning in which they described the preceding week's progress and problems. As von Braun read the notes, he initialed them and added marginalia in the form of questions, suggestions, and praise. "These collected and annotated notes, arranged in alphabetical order by the authors' surnames, were reproduced and returned as a package to all of the contributors" (p. 63). Tompkins then goes on to report an intriguing discovery:

> Curious about how the 24 contributors generated the content of their weekly notes, I systematically asked about their procedures. In most cases the lab director would ask his subordinates, the division chiefs, to provide him with a Friday Note about their activities. . . . Moreover, some of the directors and managers organized meetings to determine what should be put in next week's notes and to discuss von Braun's responses to the most recent packet of notes. Relevant portions of the notes were reproduced for distribution down the line. In short, von Braun's simple request for a weekly note had generated a *rigorous and regularly recurring discipline of communication within the organization.* (pp. 64-65)

As Tompkins noted, the practice of Monday Notes kept people informed; tied groups together laterally; provided feedback; created a personalized substitute for face-to-face communication; could be used as a quick, frank, and informal forum for conflicts and arguments; and provided redundant communication channels thereby improving reliability. Since the notes were written weekly, they are closely attuned to the flow of events that occur in a relatively short period and, therefore, accurately represent continuity. Since drafting the notes is done in part by people who are actually doing the work to be represented, the drafting is constitutive as well as representative. People do things they can talk about, which begins to enact discrete categories directly into the flow of phenomenal events. And since the content of the notes is about ongoing progress, process, and problems, the content itself is more about process than structure. In the Monday Notes, the flow of events through Marshall is mapped accurately by communication practices that mirror them. The result should be faster learning. Learning should slow down if the memos become less frequent, more detached from everyday action, drafted by fewer people, more filled with outcomes than process, less conversational, less crucial to the director, and if each memo is returned to its author and no one else.

There are other points worth noting about these notes. The notes came both from R&D Operations housed in 12 laboratories organized by science and engineering disciplines and from Industrial Operations, which had responsibility to direct and monitor prime contractors. Because the notes spanned units with quite different missions and know-how, their communication languages also differed. Therefore, when people read the notes they are reminded of several different ways to frame common problems. This guards against some of the traps mentioned earlier where groups get stuck in a narrow language, such as the language of profits, and are unable to see any other meanings that could help them dissolve or solve their problems. The Monday Notes also potentially enlarge the domain of what is discussible, and bring strategies and assumptions into play, as well as tactics. Thus, learning can engage more fundamental understandings.

The frequency with which the notes are written and the cascading process of drafting them also guards against distortions of hindsight. Hindsight bias, which involves the use of knowledge about outcomes to edit reconstructions of the antecedents of those outcomes, should lead people to learn the wrong things. Bukszar and Connolly (1988), for example, documented the tendency of those told that an organization's strategic outcomes were favorable to rate the initial decision on which those outcomes were based as less risky, and the decision process as more successful on a variety of dimensions, than did those told that the outcomes were unfavorable.

Hindsight bias should be reduced by the practice of Monday Notes for reasons outlined by Starbuck and Milliken (1988): "In the present people can distinguish their perceptions from the alternative actions they are considering, but in the past it is difficult to do so because people change their perceptions to fit what they did" (p. 44). As we move from the present to the past, options, possibilities, and alternatives are lost in the interest of justification. The action taken becomes reconstructed in hindsight as sensible, necessary, and fitting, in light of perceptions now edited to justify it. The fact that other perceptions present at the time of action might have supported other actions is lost. In hindsight, there appears to be one best way and nothing much to learn. This conclusion is troublesome because it was arrived at through severe editing out of complexity and ambiguity present at the time the action originally unfolded. Those complexities might suggest the wisdom of different choices in the future. Unfortunately, those complexities can't be retrieved once justification has masked them. However, frequent communicating, such as is represented by the Monday Notes, is one way to prevent such masking. Neither much history nor much justification are allowed to build up around a choice before it is subjected to weekly public scrutiny, criticism, praise, and alternative constructions by von Braun and his associates. It is easier to keep perceptions and actions separated when progress is reported frequently. If they are kept separate, this should make it easier to experiment with new perception-action linkages and improve performance.

CONCLUSIONS

This chapter's goal was to present a portrait of the individual and interpersonal processes inherent in organizational learning, to describe individual and organizational impediments to those processes and to specify the inherent link between communication and learning and how communication can help overcome some of the barriers described. We conclude by highlighting what we see as the key themes of this discussion and describing their implications for future research.

First, organizational learning is primarily about individuals learning within their organizations (about themselves and their performance or about how the collective does or should operate) and interacting and competing with others to get their learnings "heard" within the organization. If we take this perspective seriously, then literatures on individual learning, communication, and persuasion should all provide critical insights into organizational learning. This theme also suggests that we add to the literature a new focus. In addition to focusing on how managers process information in the learning process, we should also study the processes by which information is moved around within the organization and "reality" or "learnings" are created. We have described these processes as interpersonal ones involving competition among different definitions of reality. We believe that these processes are at least as important as those describing how the individual manager comes to know something in the first place.

Second, decision makers' natural tendencies in organizations (to move quickly, to judge learning in terms of current images and constraints, etc.) may be problematic. At various points in the chapter, we have offered case examples of how such tendencies have gotten decision makers in trouble (see Klein, 1998,

for a fuller set of examples and principles). Research that fully documents the natural tendencies of organizational learners and begins to specify the conditions under which those tendencies are problematic would be valuable.

Third, we have described several impediments to learning. This reflects our belief that the power to enhance learning in organizations stems from a good understanding of what blocks it (and the motivation to do something about those blocks). Thus, understanding that learning from continuous experience is problematic or that feedback regarding the efficacy of various organizational actions is not typically sought gives those in organizations with an interest in promoting learning some guidance as to where and how to intervene. Research that goes beyond simply documenting the various ways in which individuals have trouble learning and begins, instead, to describe the conditions necessary to maximize their learning effectiveness will be particularly important.

Fourth, a key to understanding an organization's learning potential and its limitations (biases, etc.) lies in a study of its culture. Culture is the embodiment of past learning and serves as a constraint for future learning. Culture (and therefore learnings and frameworks for future learnings) is conveyed in many ways, but of central importance for communication scholars is how culture is conveyed through the firm's formal and informal communication and through artifacts that embody messages. What norms are conveyed about the acceptability of experimentation or the seeking of feedback? How do cultural norms facilitate or inhibit communication, and how are those norms conveyed via communication within the organization? These and related questions might help ground the organizational learning research and to move it forward.

Finally, organizational learning appears to be enhanced in settings where conflicting forces are tolerated; where decision makers can live with tension and paradox. Throughout this chapter we have highlighted the tensions involved in organizational learning.

Whether the tension is between the need for certainty and the necessity of disorder in learning, between the desire for speed and the need for accuracy, or between the need to show a consistent pattern of behavior and the advantages of experimentation, settings that not only can live with the tension but can maximize both aspects should develop enhanced organizational learning capabilities. Research that sheds light on practices that enable organizations to do this will be particularly valuable. Our goal has been to point out the forces in tension and to specify the impediments that prevent one force or another from flourishing in organizational life.

REFERENCES

Argyris, C., & Schon, D. (1978). *Organizational learning: A theory of action perspective.* Reading, MA: Addison-Wesley.

Arrow, K. (1962, April). The economic implications of learning by doing. *Review of Economic Studies, 29,* 166-170.

Ashford, S. J. (1989). Self-assessments in organizations: A literature review and integrative model. In B. M. Staw & L. L. Cummings (Eds.), *Research in organizational behavior* (Vol. 11, pp. 133-174). Greenwich, CT: JAI.

Ashford, S. J. (1993). The feedback environment: An exploratory study of cue use. *Journal of Organizational Behavior, 14,* 143-157.

Ashford, S. J., & Black, J. S. (1996). Proactivity during organizational entry: Antecedents, tactics and outcomes. *Journal of Applied Psychology, 81*(2), 199-214.

Ashford, S. J., & Northcraft, G. B. (1992). Conveying more (or less) than we realize: The role of impression-management in feedback-seeking. *Organizational Behavior and Human Decision Processes, 53,* 310-334.

Ashford, S. J., & Taylor, M. S. (1990). Adaptation to work transition: An integrative approach. In G. R. Ferris & K. M. Rowland (Eds.), *Research in personnel and human resource management* (Vol. 10, pp. 1-41). Greenwich, CT: JAI.

Ashford, S. J., & Tsui, A. S. (1991). Self-regulation for managerial effectiveness: The role of active feedback seeking. *Academy of Management Journal, 34,* 251-280.

Bandura, A. (1986). *Social foundations of thought and action: A social cognitive theory.* Englewood Cliffs, NJ: Prentice Hall.

Bantz, C. R. (1993). *Understanding organizations: Interpreting organizational communication cultures.* Columbia: University of South Carolina Press.

Barnett, G. A. (1988). Communication and organizational culture. In G. M. Goldhaber & G. A. Barnett (Eds.), *Handbook of organizational communication* (pp. 101-103). Norwood, NJ: Ablex.

Bluedorn, A. C. (1982). A unified model of turnover from organizations. *Human Relations, 35*(2), 135-153.

Breslauer, G. W., & Tetlock, P. (1991). Introduction. In G. W. Breslauer & P. E. Tetlock (Eds.), *Learning in U.S. and Soviet foreign policy* (pp. 3-19). Boulder, CO: Westview.

Bukszar, E., & Connolly, T. (1988). Hindsight bias and strategic choice: Some problems in learning from experience. *Academy of Management Journal, 31,* 628-641.

Carley, K. (1992). Organizational learning and personnel turnover. *Organization Science, 3,* 20-46.

Cohen, M. D., & Bacdayan, P. (1994). Organizational routines are stored as procedural memory: Evidence from a laboratory. *Organization Science, 5,* 554-568.

Cohen, M. D., March, J. G., & Olsen, J. P. (1972). A garbage can model of organizational choice. *Administrative Science Quarterly, 17,* 1-25.

Cohen, M. D., & Sproull, L. S. (Eds.). (1996). *Organizational learning.* Thousand Oaks, CA: Sage.

Conquergood, D. (1991). Rethinking ethnography: Towards a critical cultural politics. *Communication Monographs, 58,* 179-194.

Cook, S. D. N., & Yanow, D. (1993). Culture and organizational learning. *Journal of Management Inquiry, 2,* 373-390.

Crossan, M. M., Lane, H. M., Rush, J. C., & White, R. E. (1993). *Learning in organizations.* London, Ontario: Western Business School.

Cushman, D. P., & King, S. S. (Eds.). (1994). *High-speed management and organizational communication in the 1990's: A reader.* Albany: State University of New York Press.

D'Andrade, R. G. (1984). Cultural meaning systems. In R. A. Shweder & R. A. LeVine (Eds.), *Cultural theory: Essays on mind, self, and emotion.* Cambridge, UK: Cambridge University Press.

Daft, R. L., Lengel, R. H., & Trevino, L. K. (1987). Message equivocality, media selection, and manager performance: Implications for information systems. *MIS Quarterly, 11,* 355-366.

Dodgson, M. (1993). Organizational learning: A review of some literature. *Organization Studies, 14,* 375-394.

Duncan, R., & Weiss, A. (1979). Organizational learning: Implications for organizational design. In B. M. Staw (Ed.), *Research in organizational behavior* (Vol. 1, pp. 75-123). Greenwich, CT: JAI.

Dutton, J. E., & Ashford, S. J. (1993). Selling issues to top management. *Academy of Management Review, 18,* 397-428.

Eisenberg, E. M., & Goodall, H. L., Jr. (1993). *Organizational communication: Balancing creativity and constraint.* New York: St. Martin's.

Eisenberg, E. M., & Goodall, H. L., Jr. (1997). *Organizational communication: Balancing creativity and constraint* (2nd ed.). New York: St. Martin's.

Eisenhardt, K. M. (1989). Making fast strategic decisions in high-velocity environments. *Academy of Management Journal, 32,* 543-576.

English, H. B., & English, A. C. (1958). *A comprehensive dictionary of psychological and psychoanalytical terms.* New York: Longmans, Green.

Estes, W. K. (1988). Human learning and memory. In R. C. Atkinson, R. J. Herrnstein, G. Lindzey, & R. D. Luce (Eds.), *Stevens handbook of experimental psychology* (Vol. 2, 2nd ed., pp. 351-415). New York: John Wiley.

Festinger, L. (1954). A theory of social comparison processes. *Human Relations, 7,* 117-140.

Fiske, S. T. (1992). Thinking is for doing: Portraits of social cognition from daguerreotype to laserphoto. *Journal of Personality and Social Psychology, 63,* 877-889.

Ford, J. D., & Ford, L. W. (1995). The role of conversations in producing intentional change in organizations. *Academy of Management Review, 20,* 541-570.

Freese, L. (1980). The problem of cumulative knowledge. In L. Freese (Ed.), *Theoretical methods in sociology: Seven essays* (pp. 13-69). Pittsburgh, PA: University of Pittsburgh.

Fulk, J., & Mani, S. (1986). Distortion of communication in hierarchical relationships. In M. L. McLaughlin (Ed.), *Communication yearbook 9* (pp. 483-510). Beverly Hills, CA: Sage.

Gergen, K. J. (1994). *Realities and relationships.* Cambridge, MA: Harvard University Press.

Goodall, H. L. (1990). Interpretive context for decision-making: Toward an understanding of the physical, economic, dramatic, and hierarchical interplays of language in groups. In G. M. Phillips (Ed.), *Teaching how to work in groups* (pp. 197-224). Norwood, NJ: Ablex.

Hedberg, B. (1981). How organizations learn and unlearn. In P. C. Nystrom & W. H. Starbuck (Eds.), *Handbook of organizational design* (Vol. 1, pp. 3-27). New York: Oxford University Press.

Huber, G. P. (1991). Organizational learning: The contributing processes and the literature. *Organization Science, 2,* 88-115.

Isaacs, W. N. (1993). Taking flight: Dialogue, collective thinking, and organizational learning. *Organizational Dynamics, 22*(2), 24-39.

Janis, I. (1972). *Victims of group think.* Boston: Houghton Mifflin.

Jaques, E. (1989). *Requisite organization: The CEO's guide to creative structure and leadership.* Arlington, VA: Cason Hall.

Johnson, M. K., & Hasher, L. (1987). Human learning and memory. *Annual Review of Psychology, 38,* 631-668.

Kingdon, J. W. (1984). *Agendas, alternatives, and public policies.* Boston: Little, Brown.

Klein, G. (1998). *Sources of power.* Cambridge, MA: MIT Press.

Larson, D. W. (1991). Learning in U.S.-Soviet relations: The Nixon-Kissinger structure of peace. In G. W. Breslauer & P. E. Tetlock (Eds.), *Learning in U.S. and Soviet foreign policy* (pp. 350-399). Boulder, CA: Westview.

Levitt, B., & March, J. G. (1988). Organizational learning. *Annual Review of Sociology, 14,* 319-340.

March, J. G. (1991). Exploration and exploitation in organizational learning. *Organization Science, 2,* 71-87.

March, J. G. (1994). *A primer on decision making.* New York: Free Press.

March, J. G., Sproull, L. S., & Tamuz, M. (1991). Learning from samples of one or fewer. *Organization Science, 2,* 1-13.

McCain, B. E., O'Reilly, C., & Pfeffer, J. (1983). The effects of departmental demography on turnover: The case of a university. *Academy of Management Journal, 26,* 626-641.

Miller, D. (1996). A preliminary typology of organizational learning: Synthesizing the literature. *Journal of Management, 22,* 485-505.

Nonaka, I., & Takeuchi, H. (1995). *The knowledge-creating company.* New York: Oxford University Press.

Normann, R. (1985). Developing capabilities for organizational learning. In J. M. Pennings & Associates (Eds.), *Organizational strategy and change* (pp. 217-248). San Francisco: Jossey-Bass.

O'Reilly, C. A., & Roberts, K. H. (1974). Information filtration in organizations: Three experiments. *Organizational Behavior and Human Performance, 11,* 253-265.

Peters, T. J. (1987). *Thriving on chaos: Handbook for a management revolution.* New York: Knopf, Random House.

Peters, T. J., & Waterman, R. H., Jr. (1982). *In search of excellence: Lessons from America's best-run companies.* New York: Harper & Row.

Pisano, G. P. (1994). Knowledge, integration, and the locus of learning: An empirical analysis of process development. *Strategic Management Journal, 15,* 85-100.

Pye, A. (1994). Past, present, and possibility: An integrative appreciation of learning from experience. *Management Learning, 25,* 155-173.

Raelin, J. A. (1997). A model of work-based learning. *Organization Science, 8,* 563-578.

Sagan, S. D. (1993). *The limits of safety.* Princeton, NJ: Princeton University Press.

Schein, E. H. (1985). *Organizational culture and leadership.* San Francisco: Jossey-Bass.

Scott, W. R. (1987). *Organizations: Rational, natural, and open systems*. Englewood Cliffs, NJ: Prentice Hall.

Seger, C. A. (1994). Implicit learning. *Psychological Bulletin, 115,* 163-196.

Senge, P. M. (1990). *The fifth discipline: The art and practice of the learning organization*. New York: Doubleday/Currency.

Senge, P. M., & Sterman, J. D. (1992). Systems thinking and organizational learning: Acting locally and thinking globally in the organization of the future. In T. Kochan & M. Useem (Eds.), *Transforming organizations* (pp. 353-371). New York: Oxford University Press.

Simon, H. A. (1991). Bounded rationality and organizational learning. *Organization Science, 2,* 125-134.

Sitkin, S. B., Sutcliffe, K. M., & Weick, K. E. (1999). Organizational learning. In R. C. Dorf (Ed.), *The technology management handbook* (pp. 7-70–7-76). Boca Raton, FL: CRC Press.

Skinner, B. F. (1971). *Beyond freedom and dignity*. New York: Knopf.

Snyder, M. (1984). When belief creates reality. In L. Berkowitz (Ed.), *Advances in experimental social psychology* (Vol. 18, pp. 248-305). Orlando, FL: Academic Press.

Snyder, M. (1992). Motivational foundation of behavioral confirmation. In M. Zanna (Ed.), *Advances in experimental social psychology* (Vol. 25, pp. 67-114). San Diego, CA: Academic Press.

Squire, L. R., Knowlton, B., & Musen, G. (1993). The structure and organization of memory. *Annual Review of Psychology, 44,* 453-495.

Starbuck, W. H., & Milliken, F. J. (1988). Executives' perceptual filters: What they notice and how they make sense. In D. C. Hambrick (Ed.), *The executive effect: Concepts and methods for studying top managers* (pp. 35-65). Greenwich, CT: JAI.

Staw, B. M., & Ross, J. (1980). Commitment of an experimenting society: An experiment on the attribution of leadership from administrative scenarios. *Journal of Applied Psychology, 65,* 249-260.

Staw, B. M., & Ross, J. (1987). Understanding escalation situations: Antecedents, prototypes, and solutions. In B. M. Staw & L. L. Cummings (Eds.), *Research in organizational behavior* (Vol. 9, pp. 39-78). Greenwich, CT: JAI.

Steinbruner, J. D. (1974). *A cybernetic theory of decision: New dimensions of political analysis*. Princeton, NJ: Princeton University Press.

Sutton, R. I., & Louis, M. R. (1987). How selecting and socializing newcomers influences insiders. *Human Resource Management, 26,* 347-361.

Tetlock, P. E. (1985). Accountability: The neglected social context of judgment and choice. In L. L. Cummings & B. M. Staw (Eds.), *Research in organizational behavior* (Vol. 7, pp. 297-332). Greenwich, CT: JAI.

Tetlock, P. E. (1991). Learning in U.S. and Soviet foreign policy: In search of an elusive concept. In G. W. Breslauer & P. E. Tetlock (Eds.), *Learning in U.S. and Soviet foreign policy* (pp. 20-61). Boulder, CO: Westview.

Tompkins, P. K. (1977). Management qua communication in rocket research and development. *Communication Monographs, 44,* 1-26.

Tompkins, P. K. (1993). *Organizational communication imperatives: Lessons of the space program*. Los Angeles: Roxbury.

Trujillo, N. (1985). Organizational communication as cultural performance: Some managerial considerations. *Southern Speech Communication Journal, 50,* 201-224.

Tyre, M. J., & von Hippel, E. (1997). The situated nature of adaptive learning in organizations. *Organization Science, 8,* 71-83.

Van de Ven, A. H., & Polley, D. (1992). Learning while innovating. *Organization Science, 3,* 92-116.

Van Maanen, J., & Schein, E. H. (1979). Toward a theory of organizational socialization. In B. M. Staw (Ed.), *Research in organizational behavior* (Vol. 1, pp. 209-269). Greenwich, CT: JAI.

Virany, B., Tushman, M. L., & Romanelli, E. (1992). Executive succession and organization outcomes in turbulent environments: An organization learning approach. *Organization Science, 3,* 72-91.

von Hippel, E., & Tyre, M. (1993, January). *How learning by doing is done: Problem identification in novel process equipment*. Working paper, Sloan School of Management, MIT. SSM WP BPS 3521-93.

Wagner, R. K., & Sternberg, R. J. (1985). Practical intelligence in real world pursuits, the role of tacit knowledge. *Journal of Personality and Social Psychology, 49,* 436-458.

Walsh, J. P., & Ungson, G. R. (1991). Organizational memory. *Academy of Management Review, 16,* 57-91.

Wegner, D. M. (1987). Transactive memory: A contemporary analysis of the group mind. In B. Mullen & G. R. Goethals (Eds.), *Theories of group behavior* (pp. 185-208). New York: Springer-Verlag.

Weick, K. E. (1991). The non-traditional quality of organizational learning. *Organization Science, 2,* 116-124.

Weick, K. E. (1993). The collapse of sense-making in organizations: The Mann-Gulch disaster. *Administrative Science Quarterly, 38,* 628-652.

Weick, K. E., & Browning, L. D. (1991). Fixing with the voice: A research agenda for applied communication. *Journal of Applied Communication Research, 19,* 1-19.

Weick, K. E., & Roberts, K. H. (1993). Collective mind in organizations: Heedful interrelating on flight decks. *Administrative Science Quarterly, 38,* 357-381.

Weiss, H. M. (1990). Learning theory and industrial and organizational psychology. In M. D. Dunnette & L. M. Hough (Eds.), *Handbook of industrial and organizational psychology* (Vol. 1, pp. 171-222). Palo Alto, CA: Consulting Psychologists Press.

White, R. E. (1974). Strategies for adaptation: An attempt at systematic description. In G. V. Coelho, D. A. Hamburg, & J. E. Adams (Eds.), *Coping and adaptation* (pp. 47-68). New York: Basic Books.

Winograd, T., & Flores, F. (1986). *Understanding computers and cognition: A new foundation for design.* Reading, MA: Addison-Wesley.

Zucker, L. G. (1987). Institutional theories of organization. *Annual Review of Sociology, 13,* 443-464.

19

Organizational Entry, Assimilation, and Disengagement/Exit

FREDRIC M. JABLIN
University of Richmond

Research exploring the nature of communication processes associated with organizational entry, assimilation, and exit has burgeoned over the past decade. Not only has empirical research become more extensive, but discussions of communication and assimilation processes have been integrated into many undergraduate textbooks (e.g., Conrad, 1994; Hickson, Stacks, & Padgett-Greely, 1998; Miller, 1995), and the literature and its various underlying foundations, models, and terminology have been the focus of critical scrutiny (e.g., B. Allen, 1996; Bullis, 1993, 1999; Clair, 1999; Kramer & Miller, 1999; Miller & Kramer, 1999; Smith & Turner, 1995; Turner, 1999).[1] Thus, if one judges the development of the area in terms of the typi-

cal, "normal" science indicators (Kuhn, 1970) its health appears quite robust. However, appearances can be deceiving and although certain systems of an entity may appear vigorous, their vigor may merely reflect the process of treading water versus progressing toward and achieving goals. In turn, the vigor of selective systems of an entity may also deflect attention away from other of its systems that may be struggling to perform their functions. To what extent do these conditions describe the state of research and theory exploring communication and the organizational entry, assimilation, and exit process? A major goal of this chapter is to address this question.

To assess the literature, this chapter will use the author's review and analysis of organizational entry, assimilation, and exit published in the earlier *Handbook of Organizational Communication* as a primary template for evaluating progress (Jablin, 1987). In that chapter, I described organizational entry/assimilation/exit as a life-span developmental process and thus began by "tracing" from childhood through employment in one's "chosen" vocation the development of an individual's work career. I will follow the same approach here. In addition, the focus of the present analysis, as was that of the earlier one, is on individuals' entry, assimilation, and exit into/from organizations in which they are paid for their labor. This focus is not intended to diminish the importance and legitimacy of nonpaid work in the family, assimilation into jobs in volunteer and nonprofit organizations (e.g., McComb, 1995), and the like, but merely reflects a means to limit the scope of the chapter. This approach also allows us to consider experiences prior to full-time, paid work as setting the stage for that experience. For some, this period may be quite traditional (paid work begins after formal education or training), while for others this period may be less conventional (e.g., paid work begins after a period of formal education, working to raise a family, and another period of formal training). In addition, and again for boundary-setting purposes, the discussion that follows will consider all experiences prior to one's first full-time employment in an organization (even if this first job is not exactly in one's preferred career area) as within the domain of vocational anticipatory socialization; subsequent experiences (including career changes) will be considered in terms of the more general, lifelong, vocational development/socialization process (for a discussion of the ideological implications of considering one period of socialization as anticipatory of another, see Clair, 1996).

Thus, the first section of this chapter examines how communication functions in the vocational and organizational entry processes. Generally, these processes serve as a form of "anticipatory socialization" for new organizational recruits, providing them with certain expectations (often of questionable accuracy) of the communication characteristics of their occupations and work environments. This discussion is followed by an examination of the organizational assimilation process, and in particular, how people become socialized into the communication cultures of organizations and concomitantly attempt to change these environments to better suit their needs and goals. Materials in this section are organized around basic communication-related processes associated with organizational assimilation—orienting, socialization, training, formal mentoring, informal mentoring, information seeking, information giving, relationships development, and role negotiation—rather than stages of the assimilation process. Subsequently, the role of communication in the organizational exit process is examined; however, unlike my 1987 discussion of research in this area, I do not focus on delineating communication antecedents of the voluntary turnover process but rather on "unpacking" communication processes and behaviors associated with disengaging from work environments in situations of voluntary organizational exit.

In assessing the status of research and theory, I attempt to discern what we know today that we didn't know in 1987, identifying specific areas in which we have achieved significant gains in understanding and those areas in which our knowledge remains limited. In addition, I suggest new or alternative directions for the study of communication in the organizational entry, assimilation, and disengagement/exit processes. The reader will note that in some sections of this chapter I have extrapolated material from my 1987 review and analysis; however, in these sections more recent research, if available, is cited to support conclusions and/or to develop ideas that were stated in the earlier chapter. Most sections of the chapter are new and reflect changes in my own thinking, recent developments in research and theory, and transformations in the nature of individual-organizational relationships that have occurred over the past decade (e.g., changes in the nature of the "psychological contract" between employer and employee, and growth in the size of the "contingent" workforce).

ANTICIPATORY SOCIALIZATION

Socialization to work and preparation to occupy paid organizational positions commences in early childhood (Crites, 1969). As part of this conditioning, most of us have developed, prior to entering any particular organization, a set of expectations and beliefs concerning how people communicate in particular occupations and in formal and informal work settings. Jablin (1985a) proposed that this anticipatory socialization contains two interrelated phases, one that encompasses the process of vocational choice/socialization and the second that involves the process of organizational choice/entry. Since vocational choice usually precedes organizational entry for those beginning their first full-time job (e.g., Wanous, 1977), research exploring the vocational anticipatory socialization process is considered here first, followed by a review and analysis of socialization processes that usually precede entry into paid organizational positions.

Vocational Anticipatory Socialization

The most widely accepted approaches to the vocational development process (e.g., Brown, Brooks, & Associates, 1996; Osipow, 1983; Walsh & Osipow, 1983) suggest that as individuals mature from childhood to young adulthood they intentionally and unintentionally are gathering occupational information from the environment, comparing this information against their self-concept, "weighing the factors and alternatives involved in choosing an occupation and finally making a series of conscious choices which determine the direction of [their] career" (Van Maanen, 1975,

p. 82). Individuals acquire vocational information during the occupational choice/socialization process through a variety of sources including (1) family members, (2) educational institutions, (3) part-time job experiences, (4) peers and friends (including nonfamilial adults), and (5) the media (Jablin, 1985b; Vangelisti, 1988). Each of these sources represents a "microsystem" (a direct context of influence) in the maturing person's career development environment/ecology (Bronfenbrenner, 1979; Moen, Elder, & Luscher, 1995). At the same time, however, these contexts are usually interconnected with one another (e.g., involvement in a part-time job may affect performance in school), as well as embedded within larger suprasystems (e.g., legal and social contexts) that indirectly affect a person's vocational development (Bronfenbrenner, 1986; Vonracek, Lerner, & Schulenberg, 1986). Unfortunately, most research has tended to treat each microsystem as an independent source of influence. As a consequence, research related to how each of the sources affects individuals' perceptions and behaviors with respect to communicating in work settings and different occupations is reviewed and interpreted below in relative isolation of the other sources.

Family

Family members, and in particular parents, are usually very influential in the career choices of children and adolescents (e.g., Bigelow, Tesson, & Lewko, 1996; Blyth, Hill, & Thiel, 1982; Sebald, 1986; Wilks, 1986; Young & Friesen, 1992). Thus, it is not surprising that adolescents and young adults frequently believe that their "parents were the primary determiners of their occupational choices" (Leifer & Lesser, 1976, p. 38).

Communication-related occupational and organizational information may be shared in families in a variety of ways. First, research findings indicate that in most families children participate in task-oriented organizing activity (e.g., Goldstein & Oldham, 1979; Larson, 1983; White & Brinkerhoff, 1981), typically in the form of performing household chores. Among others, Goodnow and her colleagues (Bowes & Goodnow, 1996; Goodnow, 1988; Goodnow, Bowes, Dawes, & Taylor, 1988; Goodnow, Bowes, Warton, Dawes, & Taylor, 1991; Goodnow & Delaney, 1989; Goodnow & Warton, 1991) have conceptualized the doing of household chores as involving the exchange of distinctive kinds of messages between parents and their children. Thus, for example, Ahlander and Bahr (1995) suggest that the manner in which family members, and especially parents, talk about household work can devalue it and make it drudgery or value it and use it to reinforce a sense of identification and community within the family. Thus, what household work *means* in any particular family is produced and reproduced in the everyday discourse of family members.

Findings from studies exploring children's household work suggest a number of interesting conclusions:

1. By the age of five, children know how to respond to requests for work and in particular know how to use justifications and accounts as excuses for refusing to perform a task (Dunn, 1988; Leonard, 1988).
2. Children learn early on how to solicit the help of others to perform tasks (e.g., remarking about the efficiency and expertise with which the other could perform the task; see Goodnow et al., 1988).
3. At a young age, children understand which chores they must do themselves and which tasks they can ask others to perform (Goodnow & Warton, 1991).
4. Many parents assign, label, and discuss tasks in terms of "boys'" or "girls'" work, thereby reinforcing traditional sex role stereotypes (e.g., boys perform outside chores and girls indoor ones; Peters, 1994). As Bowes and Goodnow (1996) note, children quickly learn a "set of criteria by which they can classify any activity as 'male' or 'female,' regardless of specific experience" (p. 306).
5. Fathers and mothers may differ in the manner in which they solicit their children to

perform tasks, with fathers more likely to tell their children to do something and mothers relying more on reminders and requests (Goodnow et al., 1988). Also, fathers tend to be more directive, interrupt more often, and experience more "communication breakdowns" than mothers (Bellinger & Gleason, 1982; Gleason, 1975; Malone & Guy, 1982; McLaughlin, White, McDevitt, & Raskin, 1983). At the same time, however, the difficulties that children may experience communicating with their fathers may be beneficial in that they encourage them to develop the sorts of communication skills required to be understood when interacting with persons in the "outside world" (Mannle & Tomasello, 1987).

6. Parents often communicate work principles to children through the use of metaphors (Goodnow & Warton, 1991).
7. A considerable amount of what children learn about work may focus on communication-related "procedures," including "the possibilities and the methods for raising questions or negotiating a change, the forms of talk or silence that are expected to accompany the work one does, and the extent to which people make decisions for themselves or need to follow orders" (Bowes & Goodnow, 1996, p. 308).
8. At least one study has found that while girls (14-18 years old) do not perceive differences in the procedures used to delegate a job (e.g., spelling out the details, the ways reminders are given) at home from in paid work, boys do perceive differences; boys believe that in paid work, "they just tell you" (Goodnow & Warton, 1991).

For a variety of reasons, caution is warranted in evaluating the above generalizations. In particular, the studies cited above tend to examine traditional, two-parent families (with neither party having been divorced) and may not generalize to single-parent households and families in which children live with a stepparent, which today is quite common (e.g., Barber & Eccles, 1992). Such variations in family structure create distinctive ambient and discretionary message environments for children (Jablin, 1987). For example, Asmussen and Larson (1991) report that in single-parent, mother-led families children's interactions with their mothers are more focused on household chores than in traditional, two-parent families. Relatedly, Barber and Eccles (1992) posit that "children in single-mother homes who participate in many required household tasks, and who have more household responsibility, may have more control in negotiations over rules" (p. 119).

Although children may implicitly learn about the communication characteristics of work relationships by participating in family-related organizing activity, discussions with their parents and other family members about work and careers provide such information in a more explicit fashion (e.g., Piotrkowski & Stark, 1987; Tucker, Barber, & Eccles, 1997; Young, Friesen, & Pearson, 1988). For example, in a study comparing the relative importance of work socialization agents in Colombia (in the city of Cali) and the United States, Laska and Micklin (1981) found that youths in both countries had fairly frequent discussions with their parents about the parents' jobs, though the frequency of such discussions was greater with mothers than with fathers. Similarly, in a study involving 82 children (ages 10-17) and their employed parents (fathers worked at an aerospace factory or for the postal service; mothers worked for a wide variety of employers), Piotrkowski and Stark (1987) found that 28% of the children reported their fathers spoke "often" to them about their jobs, while 53% reported their mothers "often" talked about work. This same pattern was also evident with respect to the children's reports of the frequency with which they visited their mothers and fathers at work. However, the children claimed to know similar amounts of information about their mothers' and fathers' jobs, and the more knowledge they claimed the more frequently they reported talking to their parents about work. It is also of interest to note that children's assessments of their

parents' job satisfaction were positively correlated with their parents' self-reports, suggesting that parents' general affective reactions to work were also being communicated fairly accurately to their children.

Parents' discussions about their jobs may be limited in scope, however, and in particular center on people and interpersonal relationships (Bowes & Goodnow, 1996; Crossen, 1985). Along these lines, Piotrkowski and Stark (1987), in the study noted above, compared children's descriptions of their parents' job conditions with their parents' self-reports. Results indicated that the children's descriptions were accurate only with respect to the physical work environment, fathers' relationships with supervisors, job effort required, and job insecurity (the researchers were not able to conduct similar analyses for mothers and their children). In addition, it is likely that from a very young age children may be cued to attend to and remember information about people and relationships in task settings, since these are frequent issues that parents ask them about with respect to their own daily activities (e.g., relationships with teachers and peers at preschool; see Flannagan & Hardee, 1994).

Discussions about work and careers may often occur in inveterate family interaction contexts such as dinner or in after-dinner conversations. Along these lines, a 1990 *New York Times*/CBS News poll showed that 80% of the respondents with children reported their family eating dinner together on most weeknights, with close to 60% reporting the main activity (besides eating) as conversation (Kleiman, 1990). In particular, dinnertime conversations between parents (in their children's presence but in which the children may not actively participate) frequently focus on the general day's events at work; company news; and relationships with supervisors, customers, and coworkers (Jablin, 1993). Children may also learn communication-related work principles from listening to their parents and other relatives telling family stories in which work is the central theme. In exploring the nature of family stories, Martin, Hagestad, and Diedrick (1988) found that 22% of family stories had work themes and in most of these stories (74%) a male family member was the hero. More generally, dinnertime talk represents a key source of children's socialization to how to tell stories and develop arguments (Blum-Kulka, 1997).

"Spillover" from parents' job settings to the family may occur in other ways as well. Greenberger, O'Neil, and Nagel (1994) report that parents whose jobs require "artfully persuading, reasoning, and explaining" may increase their use of these methods in managing their male but not necessarily their female children. Distressing interactions with supervisors and coworkers at work, as well as parental job insecurity, may also spill over to parents' after-work interactions with their children and affect their parenting behavior and their children's beliefs (Barling, Dupre, & Hepburn, 1998; Repetti, 1994; Repetti & Wood, 1997; Stewart & Barling, 1996). Other research suggests that the communication styles learned by parents at work as part of their involvement in participative management teams may influence their communication behavior in the family setting (Crouter, 1984).

In sum, it appears quite evident that children learn a considerable amount about communication at work in the family setting. As Stark (1992) observes, our homes may be one of the most important sources of on-the-job training (albeit we may be learning dysfunctional as well as functional ways of communicating and interacting that may carry over to our behavior in other task settings; e.g., Loraine, 1995; Oglensky, 1995).

Educational Institutions

As Jablin (1985a) suggests, schools and school-related activities are important sources of vocational information for children since (1) educational institutions have an explicit mandate to socialize people (e.g., Gecas, 1981); (2) school is typically the first socializing institution in a child's life that institutionalizes status differentiation and the hierarchical division of labor (e.g., Bowles & Gintis,

1976; Eccles, 1993); (3) for most individuals, school is a transitional institution between childhood and full-time work (e.g., Dreeban, 1968; Gecas, 1981); (4) school provides students with standards so that they can compare their competencies with others and develop realistic career aspirations; (5) school is probably the first formal context in which a child interacts in regular organizing activity (in the classroom as well as in extracurricular activities; e.g., Mihalka, 1974); and (6) the learning strategies developed in the classroom, and in particular the ways in which students learn to seek and interpret information in ambiguous situations, may be related to the strategies they later use to reduce uncertainty in the workplace (Hanson & Johnson, 1989).

Even in their earliest experiences in educational institutions (e.g., day care centers and preschools), children are learning about communicating with others in task settings. For instance, Meyer and Driskill (1997), in an observational study of children in a university child care center, found that the children were using a set of recurring communication strategies in developing and managing their relationships with others (strategies included appeal to rules, use of control, taking roles). Based on their findings, Meyer and Driskill (1997) suggest that "young children placed in day care centers are already developing and practicing the means for influencing and developing relationships" (p. 83), and in particular are experimenting with ways to balance their own needs with the needs of others in organizational environments. In like fashion, Corsaro (1990) discovered that children attending preschool know how to avoid "work" (e.g., cleaning up) by enacting a variety of communication strategies, including pretending not to hear the request, pleading a personal problem, or leaving the immediate area.

By the time students are in high school and college, they are acquiring distinctive forms of information about occupations in the specialized classes in which they are enrolled (Jablin, 1985a). For example, Cordes, Brown, and Olson (1991) collected data from university students enrolled in introductory accounting classes concerning their perceptions of the amount of social information conveyed in their classes (via teachers' comments, discussions with classmates, etc.) regarding the levels of autonomy, skill variety, and task significance in an accountant's job and the extent to which they expected these characteristics to typify an accountant's job. Results revealed the students perceived a moderate amount of classroom talk as focused on job characteristics, although those who intended to pursue accounting as a career perceived more sharing of information than those students who intended to enter other fields. Findings also showed a positive relationship between students' perceptions of the amount of information sharing about the job characteristics in their classes and their expectations that the characteristics would be present in an accountant's job. Similarly, Taylor (1985) found that college students' self-reports of the extent to which they talked to others (e.g., professors, peers) about careers to be predictive of their occupational knowledge.

Several studies have also shown that co-op experiences and internships help students clarify ideas about their fields, assess their competencies and interest in particular occupations, and develop basic protocols for interacting and communicating in the workplace (Feldman & Weitz, 1990; Gabriel, 1997; Moore, 1986; Staton-Spicer & Darling, 1986; Strom & Miller, 1993; Taylor, 1985, 1988). For example, in an enthnographic study, Moore (1986) found that internships can teach students "social procedures" (e.g., how to ask and answer questions) as well as expose them to different occupations.

In sum, as I concluded in 1987, it is likely that the information educational institutions (prior to professional or trade school) directly and indirectly disseminate to students focuses more on general job characteristics and the "ways" people communicate in different occupational/organizational roles, than with the specific content characteristics of such roles (e.g., DeFleur & Menke, 1975; Jablin, 1985a; Leifer & Lesser, 1976). However, it also seems clear that once a student has selected a vocation and receives specific education in that field, the manner in which he or she communicates with other members of the field, the public, clients, and so on is somewhat constrained by the "occupational rhetoric" (e.g., Nelson & Barley, 1997) and implicit interaction norms (including norms associated with the expression of emotion) learned during his or her occupational or professional education (e.g., Brown, 1991; Bucher & Stelling, 1977; Cahill, 1999; Enoch, 1989; Fine, 1996; Fisher & Todd, 1987; Fogarty, 1992; Hafferty, 1988; Kressin, 1996; Martin, Arnold, & Parker, 1988; Nicholson & Arnold, 1989; Oseroff-Varnell, 1998; Stradling, Crow, & Tuohy, 1993; Trice, 1993; Van Maanen, 1984). As Van Maanen and Barley (1984) observe, "Becoming a member of an occupation always entails learning a set of codes that can be used to construct meaningful interpretations of persons, events, and objects commonly encountered in the occupational world" (p. 300).

Part-Time Employment

Approximately one half of all persons of high school age are employed in part-time jobs, and about 80% of the nation's high school students will have been employed in part-time jobs prior to graduating from high school (Greenberger & Steinberg, 1986; Stern, McMillion, Hopkins, & Stone, 1990). Exactly what do adolescents learn about communication at work from these experiences, and how might these jobs affect their communication-related occupational expectations? Unfortunately, scant research exists directly exploring these issues. Moreover, few new studies have been completed in recent years that build on the seminal work of Greenberger and Steinberg and their colleagues discussed in this chapter in 1987 (Greenberger, Steinberg, & Ruggiero, 1982; Greenberger, Steinberg, Vaux, & McAuliffe, 1980; Ruggiero, Greenberger, & Steinberg, 1982; Ruggiero & Steinberg, 1981; Steinberg, Greenberger, Vaux, & Ruggiero, 1981). The results of the series of studies conducted by Greenberger, Steinberg et al. suggested that adolescent part-time workers do not have close communication relationships with others (especially their supervisors) at work, and often work unsupervised and in jobs that vary greatly with respect to the opportunities they provide young adults to interact with others and develop their communication skills. Thus, it seems clear that "all jobs do not provide young workers with identical experiences and as such are not likely to be equally facilitative of adolescents' development and socialization" (Greenberger et al., 1982, p. 93; see also Barling, Rogers, & Kelloway, 1995; Mortimer, Finch, Owens, & Shanahan, 1990; Stern & Nakata, 1989). At the same time, however, findings from various studies in this area also suggest that "adolescents who work are learning a good deal about relationships" (Greenberger et al., 1980, p. 200) and are often developing basic communication skills required in work settings (Charner & Fraser, 1988; Phillips & Sandstrom, 1990).

In summary, it seems apparent that certain types of part-time jobs (e.g., those that require workers to influence others) provide adolescents with opportunities to learn and apply relational communication skills that may generalize to other work contexts. However, the specific manner and extent to which these early job experiences may contribute to the relational communication styles individuals adopt when they eventually enter their chosen occupations remains to be explored.

Peers and Friends

Although most adolescents spend over 50% of their time during a typical week with their peers (Csikszentmihalyi & Larson, 1984), often talk with peers and friends about their educational and occupational plans and aspirations (e.g., Blyth et al., 1982; Montemayer & Van Komen, 1980), and consider peers "as significant others who confirm or disconfirm the desirability of occupations" (Peterson & Peters, 1983, p. 81), we know little of what adolescents and younger children learn from their conversations with their friends about the nature of communication in

work/organizational relationships and occupations. However, it is important to recognize that while children and adolescents may learn about work and occupations in their explicit conversations with friends, other characteristics of peer relationships may be equally important in helping them learn about communicating in organizational contexts. In particular, in comparison to other relationships adolescents are involved in, friendships with other adolescents are "coconstructed" and are not guided by outside rules or regulations (Bigelow et al., 1996; Lewko, 1996; Youniss & Smollar, 1985). Peer relationships are characterized by mutual trust, symmetricality, respect, and openness (Larson, 1983; Raffaelli & Duckett, 1989; Zarbatany, Hartmann, & Rankin, 1990). As Burleson, Delia, and Applegate (1995) observe, "Peers prefer to be treated in person-centered ways that acknowledge their points of view, take their goals and motivations into account, and display concern for interpersonal relationships as well as instrumental goals" (p. 66). Thus, for instance, since friends rarely go to higher authorities to resolve conflicts among themselves, it is likely that they learn a great deal about regulating the expression of emotions and negotiating solutions to problems and conflicts in the process of maintaining their relationships (Gecas, 1981; Hartup, 1996; Larson & Kleiber, 1993; Newcomb & Bagwell, 1995). In addition, since peers interact more with one another as equals than in other of their relationships (e.g., at home or in school), their roles tend to be more fluid and as a consequence they do more role making than role taking (Gecas, 1981; Hartup & Moore, 1990).

Children and adolescents may also learn a great deal about communicating in task settings from their participation in voluntary, organized, non-school-related activities (e.g., Eccles & Barber, 1999). For example, it is very common for preadolescents as well as adolescents to participate in youth organizations (e.g., Girl Scouts; Auster, 1985) and organized sports teams that represent combinations of work and play and allow peers to communicate with one another, as well as with non-familial adult leaders or coaches (Larson & Verma, 1999). Thus, for instance, in Little League baseball (even when competitiveness is not stressed), attributes not typically associated with "play" such as "hustle," mental concentration and attention, control and discipline, "taking the game seriously," and acceptance and respect for rules and authority are stressed (Fine, 1987). In other words, a major focus of these activities is teaching young people to behave and communicate "properly" in working with others (e.g., controlling emotions, displaying team spirit/unity, and managing impressions). The specific nature of the effects of such activities and other forms of peer interaction/socializing on adolescents' perceptions and expectations of communication at work and in occupations, however, awaits determination by future research.

Media

As Huston, Wright, Rice, Kerkman, and St. Peters (1990) observe, "By the time American children are 18 years old, they have spent more time watching television than in any other activity except sleep. Moreover, their experiences with television begin long before exposure to school or, in many cases, any socialization agent other than the family" (p. 409). Unfortunately, research also suggests that television programs (including network news shows and cartoons; e.g., Potts & Martinez, 1994; Ryan & Sim, 1990) often transmit distorted, stereotypic images of occupations and how people communicate in them and that children's beliefs about these images "may well persist into adulthood" (Christenson & Roberts, 1983, p. 88). Television has not only been criticized for representing people in sex-role-stereotyped occupations (e.g., Gunter & McAleer, 1990; Huston & Alvarez, 1990; Signorielli, 1991), although there is some evidence that this is improving (Atkin, Moorman, & Lin, 1991; Moore, 1992), and overrepresenting managerial and professional

occupations and underrepresenting jobs of lesser prestige (e.g., Greenberg, 1982; Katzman, 1972; Signorielli, 1993), but also for frequently portraying persons who are successful in their occupational roles as involved in exciting and glamorous activities (Signorielli, 1993; Steenland, 1990), spending the bulk of their conversational time giving orders and/or advice to others (e.g., Chesebro, 1991), and in general engaging in fairly aggressive communication behaviors (e.g., Turow, 1974, 1980). Results of studies also suggest that business characters in prime-time television shows are frequently (at least 60% of the time) portrayed negatively (e.g., antisocial, criminal, or greedy) when performing their occupational activities (Lichter, Lichter, & Amundson, 1997; Theberge, 1981). In fact, in their analysis of prime-time shows over a 30-year period, Lichter et al. (1997) found that "no other occupation or institution was criticized as heavily as business, in terms of either the frequency or proportion of negative thematic portrayals" (p. 79). In turn, findings from other investigations indicate that in television representations of the workplace, little of the content of conversations among role occupants concerns work-related issues; rather, discussions focus on such topics as romantic relationships, family and marriage problems, and similar forms of small talk (Katzman, 1972; Turow, 1974). In essence, "television's representation of occupational roles, as with other roles, is both a wider perspective than everyday experience and a caricature of the actual world of work" (Peterson & Peters, 1983, p. 81).

It is also of interest to note that prime-time television shows frequently focus on conflicts of authority in the workplace. In particular, since the mid-1960s programs have increasingly depicted bosses as less authoritative, and subordinates as more likely to ridicule their bosses and to prevail in conflicts (Lichter, Lichter, & Rothman, 1994). In brief, many contemporary television programs depict organizations as places "where workers tell off bosses and warm personal relationships are infinitely more important that economic productivity" (Lichter et al., 1994, p. 418; see also Taylor, 1989).

Though some studies suggest that frequent exposure to television may influence how children and adolescents view occupational roles, and in particular their beliefs about "actual" interpersonal and task behavior in the work setting (e.g., Signorielli & Lears, 1992; Wroblewski & Huston, 1987), the nature of these relationships is still somewhat unclear, and as a consequence additional study of these issues will be required before definitive conclusions about causality can be drawn (e.g., Christenson & Roberts, 1983; Kubey & Csikszentmihalyi, 1990; Wright, Huston, Reitz, & Piemyat, 1994). In particular, given research findings that suggest the influence of television representations of jobs on children's (and adults') beliefs may be most potent for jobs that are outside of their everyday contacts (e.g., Pfau, Mullen, Deidrich, & Garrow, 1995), the extent to which television characters provide children with "surrogate experience" to know how to behave and communicate in work situations before such situations have been encountered in real life still requires intensive investigation (e.g., Berg & Trujillo, 1989; Noble, 1983; Wroblewski & Huston, 1987).

Finally, it should be realized that in addition to television other of the mass media may also be providing distorted depictions of the occupational behavior/communication of persons in work settings. For example, studies suggest that even award-winning children's books contain distorted or out-of-date occupational, racial, and sexual stereotypes (e.g., Ingersoll & Adams, 1992, 1976; Purcell & Stewart, 1990). Similarly, in a content analysis of fiction stories in magazines primarily written for and marketed to adolescent girls (e.g., *Teen, Seventeen*), Pierce (1993) found that occupations were portrayed in a sex-role-stereotyped manner and that in more than half the stories "the main character did not actively solve her own problems but depended on someone else to do it for her" (p. 59).

In sum, the messages conveyed by the media, and especially television, with respect to communication in organizations and in various occupations do not appear to be random in nature; rather, these messages are frequently patterned and presented in persuasive ways. Thus, while television may be entertaining young people, it also "selectively reinforces certain types of communication" (Chesebro, 1991, p. 219). The specific nature and effects of this reinforcement on individuals' communication behavior once they enter the world of work remain unknown.

Summary

In 1987, I noted that research exploring the vocational organizational communication socialization (VOCS) process was still in its infancy. With notable exceptions (research exploring family and media influences), studies investigating the VOCS process are still few in number. Thus, we continue to be unable to (1) indicate the degree to which various VOCS sources reinforce or conflict with one another (i.e., their interactive effects), or (2) draw conclusions about long-term VOCS effects on organizational communication behavior and attitudes. Clearly, one major reason for the scarcity of VOCS research is that scholarship in this area often involves elaborate, multiyear, longitudinal studies, which are rare in the study of organizational communication generally. Further, disentangling the influences of the various VOCS sources on children's and adolescents' developing communication-related cognitions and behaviors represents a formidable challenge to those who conduct research in this area.

In light of the above noted challenges, perhaps future research should proceed in a somewhat different direction than extant efforts. More specifically, we might focus more attention on identifying consistencies across sources with respect to the basic foci and content of their explicit and implicit messages about communicating in task settings and occupations. For example, based on the research reviewed in the preceding pages, it seems reasonable to hypothesize that children and adolescents will be learning from the various sources ways of communicating in procedural communication "predicaments" that are common in task settings (e.g., Bowes & Goodnow, 1996), such as how to request information or help, how to decline others' requests, how to express emotions, and the like. If we focus on communication functions that permeate most task settings (e.g., Stohl & Redding, 1987), we could determine if commonalities exist across sources with respect to how they promote enactment of these functions. Alternatively, given that recent studies of the organizational selection process indicate that one of the best predictors of the success of newcomers is the "match" between their values and those of their organizations (e.g., Cable & Judge, 1997), we might examine the sorts of basic communicative values that are promoted by each source during the VOCS process. For instance, we might expect each of the sources to communicate about what honesty and credibility means in organizations and in different occupations. Is there consistency across sources with respect to these messages? Do the messages of each source about communicative values remain invariant as a person matures from childhood to young adulthood? Exploration of issues such as these can be pursued with longitudinal research designs and cross-sectional ones, in which messages associated with each source are examined in samples involving different age cohorts.

The research directions suggested here are not intended to oversimplify the VOCS process but rather to encourage research in the area, especially in relation to the study of VOCS and messages exchanged among peers and friends, coworkers and supervisors in part-time jobs, and students and teachers. Indeed, the VOCS process is quite complex and individuals actually experience the influence of the sources in combination with each other (Jablin & Krone, 1994). Moreover, children and adolescents should not be viewed as merely passive recipients of VOCS messages but rather as active agents who can seek out communication-related vocational information (e.g., individuals can obtain prevocational information and experience in particular fields by their involvement in volunteer and paid work; e.g., Birnbaum & Somers, 1991). Further, it is important to realize that they may acquire information directly in conversations with others or indirectly by listening to the talk of parents, siblings, and others (Jablin, 1987).

In closing this discussion, I would be remiss if I failed to address one other issue that future research should address: the impact that recent changes in the nature of work and organizations is having on VOCS. For example, how has organizational downsizing, the increasing use of "temporary" versus permanent employees in organizations, the phenomenal increase of individuals who work out of their homes versus the sites of their formal organizations, the aggregation of professionals who traditionally worked as sole proprietors or in partnerships into large corporate entities (e.g., medical doctors), and the increasing demands for self-management that organizations are asking of their employees affected what young people are learning about the nature of communication in organizations and occupations? How are these changes reflected in the messages communicated by different VOCS sources? Is the deception and meaninglessness of organizational life displayed in popular television shows such as *Friends* and *Seinfeld* (Zurawik, 1996) and in celebrated comic strips such as "Dilbert" and "Doonesbury" different from the VOCS messages communicated by the media in earlier eras? Do the "made up" games children play today such as "Outplacement Barbie" and "You're Fired" (Shellenbarger, 1995) reflect important changes in VOCS as compared to prior decades? Do the many children who today have parents who work at home experience a different kind of VOCS than children whose parents perform their job duties at the site of their employers? Clearly, questions such as these warrant consideration in our future research endeavors.

Organizational Anticipatory Socialization

Subsequent to deliberately or accidentally choosing a career direction and receiving the education and training required to competently perform tasks associated with the occupation, most individuals will attempt to find positions in which to perform the jobs for which they have been trained. In the process of seeking jobs, individuals will concomitantly develop expectations about the organizations and respective jobs for which they have applied for employment. Job seekers typically acquire information that may affect their job/organizational expectations from two basic sources: (1) organizational literature (e.g., job advertisements, annual reports, training brochures, job preview booklets), and (2) interpersonal interactions with other applicants, organizational interviewers, teachers, current employees, and other direct and indirect social network ties (e.g., Bian, 1997; Granovetter, 1995). Generally speaking, studies exploring each of these sources of information have focused on one of three broad areas of research: (1) the relative effectiveness of each of the information sources in recruiting/attracting newcomers, (2) the realism or accuracy of job/organizational expectations that result from individuals' contacts with each source, and (3) the role of the employment interview as a recruiting and selection device. Research findings relevant to each of these areas of study are briefly reviewed below.

Recruiting Source Effects

Although over 30 years have passed since researchers first started to explore the relative effectiveness of different recruiting sources in attracting and subsequently retaining new-

comers to organizations (Ullman, 1966), it is still very difficult to draw any firm conclusions from this corpus of study. Although some research (e.g., Conard & Ashworth, 1986; Decker & Cornelius, 1979; Gannon, 1971; Kirnan, Farley, & Geisinger, 1989; Reid, 1972; Saks, 1994; Taylor, 1994) suggests that newcomers recruited from informal (e.g., employee referrals, "walk ins") sources experience lower turnover than those recruited from more formal (e.g., newspaper ads, employment agencies) sources, the findings from other studies have brought this generalization into question. Not only have a number of investigations found minimal differences in the job survival and/or tenure of persons recruited via informal as compared to formal sources (Caldwell & Spivey, 1983; Griffeth, Hom, Fink, & Cohen, 1997; Swaroff, Barclay, & Bass, 1985; Werbel & Landau, 1996; Williams, Labig, & Stone, 1993), but the results from some recent studies suggest that in certain situations newcomers recruited through formal sources may have higher job survival rates than those recruited through informal sources (Rynes, Orlitzky, & Bretz, 1997; Saks & Ashforth, 1997). Further, with respect to recruiting source effects on newcomers' job performance, research results have been very inconsistent with some studies showing no differences among sources (e.g., Breaugh, 1981; Hill, 1970; Kirnan et al., 1989; Swaroff et al., 1985; Taylor, 1994; Williams et al., 1993), others indicating that personnel recruited via informal sources have higher performance than those recruited via formal sources (e.g., Blau, 1990; Breaugh, 1981; Breaugh & Mann, 1984), and still others suggesting that newcomers recruited via formal sources are the best performers (e.g., Caldwell & Spivey, 1983; Taylor & Schmidt, 1983; Werbel & Landau, 1996). Studies examining the impact of referral sources on job attitudes (such as job satisfaction and organizational commitment; e.g., Breaugh, 1981; Griffeth et al., 1997; Latham & Leddy, 1987; Saks, 1994; Saks & Ashforth, 1997; Taylor, 1994; Vecchio, 1995) and absenteeism (Breaugh, 1981; Griffeth et al., 1997; Taylor & Schmidt, 1983) have also produced equivocal results.

The generalizability of much of the research in this area is also clouded by evidence showing that many job applicants (upwards of 33%) rely on multiple versus singular sources for recruitment information (e.g., Vecchio, 1995; Williams et al., 1993), more prehire knowledge results from the use of multiple versus single sources, and combinations of sources may include mixes of formal and informal sources. Since the great majority of extant studies have asked respondents to identify only one recruitment source, their findings may not accurately reflect the manner in which recruitment sources affect potential job applicants. Moreover, if applicants obtain information from multiple sources, a variety of issues need to be explored including the manner in which they deal with inconsistencies in information obtained among sources and how variability across sources in the content, specificity, and amount of information they provide affects potential recruits.

Two basic explanations have been posited for the recruiting source effects described above. The "individual differences" hypothesis (Schwab, 1982) suggests differential source effectiveness is linked to individual differences in the applicant populations that are attracted to each communication/recruiting source. On the other hand, the "realistic information" hypothesis proposes that "individuals recruited via sources which provide more accurate information will be able to self-select out of jobs which do not meet their needs" (Breaugh & Mann, 1984, p. 261). In essence, this latter position suggests that recruiting sources vary with respect to the degree to which they provide "realistic job previews" (Wanous & Colella, 1989; see discussion below). Results from studies examining these explanations for recruiting source effects have not provided consistent support for either hypothesis and suggest that there may be other factors (for instance, applicants' perceptions of job fit; e.g., Saks &

Ashforth, 1997; Werbel & Landau, 1996) mediating the influence of recruiting sources on posthire outcomes (Blau, 1990; Griffeth et al., 1997; Vecchio, 1995; Werbel & Landau, 1996; Williams et al., 1993). In addition, studies in this area suffer from a variety of methodological problems (e.g., most studies have collected retrospective data and assume no within-source variation), and other potential confounds (e.g., one possible explanation for individual-differences effects may be differences in the realism of information provided by sources to different applicant populations [Wanous & Colella, 1989]; alternatively, several studies suggest that individual differences in race and self-esteem may moderate applicants' use of different recruiting sources [Blau, 1990; Caldwell & Spivey, 1983; Ellis & Taylor, 1983; Kirnan et al., 1989]).

In brief, research associated with recruiting source effects on job applicants appears ready for a shift in focus, and more specifically a shift that concentrates attention on message exchange processes associated with job candidates' contacts with recruiting sources. Basic descriptive research needs to be conducted to determine the content domains (e.g., information about organizational values and culture, supervision, company policies), specificity, consistency, valence, and so forth of messages provided by different sources (e.g., Saks, 1994). The likelihood that a source might be able to provide abundant, accurate information in some areas and not others needs to be considered (i.e., source credibility may vary with content domain). The extent to which a potential applicant may engage in one-way versus two-way communication with a source (for instance, newspaper ads can't answer questions) warrants study, since the latter (e.g., conversation with a current employee) allows an applicant to seek information about the job and/or organization that is most salient to him or her. At the same time, we need to recognize that face-to-face interaction between applicants and a recruiting source will result in considerable variability across applicants in the information they receive. If this is the case, then it may be important for us to also reconsider the relevance of the outcome variables that typify research in this area. Perhaps it makes more sense to evaluate the impact of recruiting sources in terms of their ability to generate pools of applicants who meet minimum job qualifications than to expect meaningful relationships between recruiting sources and criteria such as turnover and job performance, which may be more affected by organizational training and socialization practices (e.g., Werbel & Landau, 1996).

Finally, it seems apparent that changes in communication technology as well as in labor markets need greater consideration in future research. Potential job applicants can now obtain, 24 hours a day, information about job openings from an organization's homepage on the Internet and from participating in electronic chat groups and bulletin boards (forms of communication networks; e.g., Kilduff, 1990), or simply by contacting someone in the organization via electronic mail. Are these formal or informal recruiting sources, or a combination of the two? Also, we need to consider the extent to which "direct experience" may be replacing other recruiting sources in attracting applicants to organizations. For example, statistics suggest that 20% of the new jobs created between 1991 and 1993 were temporary ones and that 90% of companies use temporary employment agencies to meet some of their labor needs (Feldman, Doerpinghaus, & Turnley, 1994; Golden & Appelbaum, 1992). Given that most temporary employees consider their temporary jobs as temporary, it is of little surprise that about half report that they see these positions as a mechanism to find job leads and to examine companies without having to commit themselves (von Hippel, Mangnum, Greenberger, Heneman, & Skoglind, 1997). Does temporary employment represent a new, major recruiting source? To what extent are internships in which college students participate serving the same function (e.g., Taylor, 1988)? What, if anything, distinguishes the

nature of communication between job applicants and these recruiting sources in comparison to more traditional ones? Consideration of questions such as these represent exciting areas for future research.

Realism of Job/Organizational Expectations

Generally speaking, job applicants have unrealistic, typically positively "inflated" expectations about the organizations in which they are seeking employment (e.g., Jablin, 1984; Wanous, 1980). In part, it has been suggested that job candidates' expectations are unrealistic because organizations tend to follow traditional recruitment strategies in which they focus on primarily communicating the positive features of organizational membership to applicants (Wanous, 1977, 1980). Thus, the recruitment literature organizations provide students at college placement centers usually attempts to project companies as exciting and prestigious places to work (attraction) and typically focuses on extrinsic versus intrinsic job features (Herriot & Rothwell, 1981; "Recruiting Literature," 1981; Shyles & Ross, 1984). Given current and projected labor shortages in selective fields, evidence that qualified applicants respond most favorably to catchy employment advertisements that portray organizations in a positive manner and focus attention on extrinsic job characteristics (Barber & Roehling, 1993; Belt & Paolillo, 1982; Gatewood, Gowan, & Lautenschlager, 1993; Kaplan, Aamodt, & Wilk, 1991; Mason & Belt, 1986), and the increasing adoption by organizations of strategic marketing orientations to recruit and attract applicants (e.g., Martin & Franz, 1994; Maurer, Howe, & Lee, 1992; Palkowitz & Mueller, 1987), dramatic changes in contemporary (traditional) organizational recruitment strategies are probably unlikely in the immediate future.

As noted above, it also appears that applicants prefer traditional (positive focus) recruitment approaches (e.g., Saks, Wiesner, & Summers, 1994; Wiesner, Saks, & Summers,

1991), which may not present realistic views of jobs and organizations and inflate applicants' expectations. In theory, the desirability of recruits developing inflated job and organizational expectations, however, is problematic, since the more inflated the job candidates' preentry expectations are, the more difficult it usually is for them to meet these expectations once on the job. Along these lines, in a meta-analysis of 31 "met expectations" studies, Wanous, Poland, Premack, and Davis (1992) found fairly strong support for hypothesized relationships between unmet expectations and job satisfaction (mean $r = .39$) and organizational commitment (mean $r = .39$), but somewhat weaker relationships between unmet expectations and job survival (mean $r = .19$) and job performance (mean $r = .11$). As Wanous and his colleagues (Colella, 1989; Wanous & Colella, 1989; Wanous et al., 1992) have noted, however, an assumption underlying the met-expectations hypothesis, which remains to be tested, is that newcomers receive clear and consistent messages from insiders about the validity of their expectations. In other words, in work environments in which newcomers receive ambiguous or conflicting messages about job expectations from incumbents, it may not be possible for them to either confirm or disconfirm their expectations, and as a consequence the met-expectations hypothesis may not operate as predicted.

Although they have not been widely adopted by organizations, over the past several decades a considerable amount of research has been devoted to the study of realistic job previews (RJPs). Building on the met-expectations hypothesis, RJPs are intended to deflate applicants' expectations to more realistic levels (much like medical vaccinations) by providing them with a "dose of organizational reality" (Popovich & Wanous, 1982). Thus, it is believed that by presenting job applicants with RJP booklets, videotapes, films, work sample simulations, job visits, or oral presentations, job candidates' expectations will be deflated to more realistic levels, self-selection will occur among "marginal" applicants, and recruits will be better prepared

to cope with their jobs once they start work; because they are provided with accurate job/organizational information prior to making their employment decisions, newcomers are also expected to feel greater commitment to their jobs, exhibit higher levels of job satisfaction, and have lower rates of turnover.

Although over 40 studies have explored the reasons why RJPs should work and the relative effectiveness of RJPs in reducing turnover and enhancing recruits' job attitudes, their results have frequently been inconsistent (e.g., McEvoy & Cascio, 1985; Premack & Wanous, 1985; Rynes, 1991; Wanous, 1977, 1980; Wanous & Colella, 1989). In fact, one recent study suggests that newcomers' early work experiences may be more potent than their preentry expectations in predicting turnover, job satisfaction, and organizational commitment (Irving & Meyer, 1994). However, it does appear that RJPs can lower expectations and increase job survival (e.g., Buckley, Fedor, Veres, Wiese, & Carraher, 1998; Hom, Griffeth, Palich, & Bracker, 1998; Premack & Wanous, 1985; Wanous et al., 1992), although the decrease in turnover is typically small (yet even small decreases in turnover can produce big savings for organizations) and we still do not have an adequate understanding as to why RJPs have this effect (Saks et al., 1994; Wanous & Colella, 1989). A number of reasons have been posited for inconsistencies in research findings among RJP studies. Factors that have been suggested as "causes" of variant results include inconsistent operational definitions of *realism* across studies; disparities across studies with respect to the timing of RJP presentations (e.g., before or after an employment interview or job offer); inadequate sample sizes to afford sufficient statistical power in testing hypotheses; overreliance on laboratory versus field studies; variability among the organizational roles/positions in which RJPs have been tested; inconsistencies in the time periods at which turnover data have been collected by researchers; differences across studies in methods/modes of presenting RJP; and the general failure to adequately consider other source (e.g., credibility, trustworthiness), message (e.g., content, amount, specificity), and audience (receiver) characteristics in preparing RJPs (e.g., Breaugh, 1983; Jablin, 1987; Phillips, 1998; Popovich & Wanous, 1982; Reilly, Brown, Blood, & Malatesta, 1981).

To unravel some of the inconsistencies in research findings, recent studies have focused on identifying factors that might mediate the effects of RJPs on outcomes. In particular, it appears that the complexity of the job being previewed (Breaugh, 1983; McEvoy & Cascio, 1985; Reilly et al., 1981), applicants' self-efficacy (Pond & Hay, 1989; Saks et al., 1994), job alternatives available to applicants (Saks et al., 1994; Saks, Wiesner, & Summers, 1996; Wiesner et al., 1991), and communication characteristics of previews (e.g., Colarelli, 1984; Green, 1991; Saks & Cronshaw, 1990) mediate effects associated with RJPs. With respect to communication-related mediators, studies suggest that the adequacy (amount), descriptiveness, valence, and accuracy of information applicants receive from RJPs may influence their attraction to a firm and their knowledge about job and organizational characteristics, and as a result affect their ability to determine the extent to which a job and organization match their needs (Dilla, 1987; Phillips, 1998; Saks & Cronshaw, 1990; Saks et al., 1994; Vandenberg & Scarpello, 1990). In addition, at least one study has also shown that previews allowing for two-way communication (after initial interviews with recruiters) between job incumbents (high-credibility sources) and applicants may be more effective in reducing turnover than written previews (Colarelli, 1984).

In assessing the literature over a decade ago, I argued that the employment interview is probably the setting in which most job previews actually occur (Jablin, 1985b, 1987). I suggested this because of the frequent discussion of job/organizational topics in these interaction settings and the domination of "talk time" by recruiters (research has shown that applicants speak for only about 10 minutes in the average 30-minute interview and that recruiters spend considerable amounts of time

telling applicants about themselves, the job, and the organization and in answering applicants' questions, which typically focus on job/organizational topics; e.g., Babbitt & Jablin, 1985; Tengler & Jablin, 1983). Thus, I concluded that the "interview is important not only as an interpersonal communication event, but because of the role it plays in communicating job/organizational expectations to potential employees" (Jablin, 1985b, p. 621). While others have subsequently recognized that the interview is likely "the most popular means for RJPs in practice" (Wanous & Colella, 1989, p. 75) and may be "the method of choice for the future" (Wanous, 1989, p. 130), researchers have yet to adequately investigate the interview as a method to communicate RJPs. Rather, RJP researchers continue to focus on the preview as a formal, standardized, one-way form of communication in which applicants are viewed as "passive receptors of new information" (Wanous & Colella, 1989, p. 76).

However, two studies have explicitly considered the interview as a method of communicating RJPs. In the first study, Saks and Cronshaw (1990) examined RJPs in the laboratory using students participating in simulated, role-play employment interviews (applicants were applying for a summer job) in which the interviewer followed a script that included ten standard interview questions. In one condition, applicants received a written RJP before their interviews, in another condition RJPs were presented orally during the interviews, and in a control condition applicants received only general job information in their interviews. Findings indicated that both the written and oral RJPs lowered applicants' job expectations and increased role clarity, but did not affect commitment to job choice or job acceptance. In addition, those receiving the oral RJP had more positive perceptions of the honesty of their interviewers and their organizations than those in the other conditions. In the second study, Barber, Hollenbeck, Tower, and Phillips (1994) examined the interaction of interview focus (recruitment only, a combination of recruitment and selection) and interview content (traditional, realistic preview) on applicants' retention of information and desire to pursue an actual opening for a part-time, temporary office assistant position at a university research center. Two doctoral students conducted the interviews and "followed detailed scripts" (p. 890). The combined recruitment and selection interviews were highly structured and about 25 minutes in duration. Applicants in the recruitment condition were told that their interviews (which lasted about 15 minutes) were not part of the selection process but rather were for informative purposes only. Results revealed no significant effects for interview content (type of preview); however, the researchers suggest this may have been the result of a weak RJP manipulation (i.e., the negative attributes of the job may not have been sufficient to produce effects).

While the studies described above are laudable, the extent to which the previews employed in these investigations reflects the manner in which they occur in naturally occurring interviews is highly questionable. In light of current knowledge about communication in selection interviews (see next section), it is unlikely that job previews are as formal, standardized, and one way in communication as those incorporated in these studies. Rather, it is more likely that in naturally occurring interviews previews are less structured and are embedded into communication exchanges taking place throughout the duration of the interview (i.e., they are not just one-shot presentations). In other words, previews are coconstructed by interviewers and applicants as a by-product of discourse processes (e.g., question, answer, statements sequences) that evolve over the course of the interview (e.g., Jablin, Miller, & Sias, 1999). Assuming this is the case, then future research should focus on identifying how previews are constructed in actual interviews and then explore how variations in discourse processes and preview content affect applicants' subsequent attitudes and behaviors.

To review, several communication-related propositions appear tenable about RJPs and applicants' expectations. First, if RJPs are to have any effect then applicants need to obtain accurate, ample, and salient information about job and organizational characteristics. Second, it is possible that RJPs have a greater impact on applicants' assessment of the match between their needs and the ability of organizations to fulfill those needs, and on newcomers' initial job and organizational adjustment, than on long-term outcomes such as turnover and job satisfaction. Third, "in studying realistic recruitment as transmitted through booklets, films, or rehearsed recruiter presentations, we are studying a phenomenon that probably occurs in a very small percentage of recruitment efforts" (Rynes, 1991, p. 428; see also Phillips, 1998). Finally, although the employment interview is likely the most common context in which all forms of job previews are communicated, we know little of how this is accomplished in this interaction setting.

The Selection Interview

Although we may not know much about how job previews are jointly constructed by interviewers and applicants in selection interviews, a vast number of studies have been conducted exploring other communication-related characteristics and processes of the interview (see Eder & Ferris, 1989; Harris, 1989; Jablin & Krone, 1994; Jablin & McComb, 1984; Jablin & Miller, 1990; Jablin et al., 1999). Building on the generalizations that Jablin and Krone (1994, pp. 627-628) have suggested, as well as more recent research in the area, Table 19.1 summarizes major findings of studies exploring communication in the employment interview.

Caution should be exercised in generalizing the findings listed in Table 19.1 since a considerable number of methodological problems and conceptual biases have been associated with selection interview research (e.g., Eder & Ferris, 1989; Eder & Harris, 1999; Jablin & McComb, 1984; Ralston & Kirkwood, 1995). At the same time, the quality (and, it is hoped, the generalizability) of communication research in this area has improved

TABLE 19.1   Summary of Research Findings on Communication in the Selection Interview

1. Applicants' interview outcome expectations (including likelihood of accepting job offers) appear related to their perceptions of and affective reactions to their recruiters as trustworthy, competent, composed, empathic, enthusiastic, and well-organized communicators (see Alderfer & McCord, 1970; Fisher, Ilgen, & Hoyer, 1979; Jablin, Tengler, & Teigen, 1982; Liden & Parsons, 1986; Ralston, 1993; Ralston & Brady, 1994; Rynes & Miller, 1983; Schmitt & Coyle, 1976; Taylor & Bergmann, 1987; Teigen, 1983).

2. Recruiters and applicants tend to have differential expectations and perceptions of communication behaviors displayed in interviews, including levels of talkativeness, listening, questioning, and topics of discussion (see Cheatham & McLaughlin, 1976; Connerley, 1997; Connerley & Rynes, 1997; Engler-Parish & Millar, 1989; Herriot & Rothwell, 1981, 1983; Posner, 1981; Shaw, 1983; Taylor & Sniezek, 1984).

3. Applicants do not particularly like or trust interviewers and appear hesitant to accept job offers if their only sources of information are recruiters; however, interviewers who are job incumbents are perceived as presenting more realistic job and organizational information than are interviewers who are personnel representatives (see Downs, 1969; Fisher et al., 1979; Jablin, Tengler, & Teigen, 1985; Rynes, Bretz, & Gerhart, 1991; Taylor & Bergmann, 1987).

4. Interviewee satisfaction, attraction to an organization, and perceptions of recruiter effectiveness appear related to the quality and amount of organizational and job information the recruiter provides and the degree to which the recruiter asks the interviewee open-ended questions that are high in "face validity," allows him or her sufficient "talk time," and shows warmth toward and interest in the applicant (see DeBell, Montgomery, McCarthy, & Lanthier, 1998; Golitz & Giannantonio, 1995; Herriot & Rothwell, 1983; Jablin, Tengler, McClary, & Teigen, 1987; Karol, 1977; Powell, 1991; Tengler, 1982; Turban & Dougherty, 1992).

5. Interviewees who display high versus low levels of nonverbal immediacy (operationalized by eye contact, smiling, posture, interpersonal distance, and body orientation), who are high in vocal activity and engage their interviewers in more "response-response" than "question-response" interactions, tend to be favored by interviewers (see Anderson & Shackleton, 1990; Burnett & Motowidlo, 1998; Byrd, 1979; Einhorn, 1981; Forbes & Jackson, 1980; Imada & Hakel, 1977; Keenan, 1976; Keenan & Wedderburn, 1975; McGovern & Tinsley, 1978; Mino, 1996; Trent, 1978).

6. Recruiters find interviewees more acceptable if they receive favorable information about them prior to or during their interviews; while recruiters may adopt confirmatory questioning strategies to test positive preinterview impressions, they do not necessarily use confirmatory questioning to validate negative preinterview impressions (Binning, Goldstein, Garcia, & Scattaregia, 1988; Dougherty, Turban, & Callender, 1994; Herriot & Rothwell, 1983; Lindvall, Culberson, Binning, & Goldstein, 1986; Macan & Dipboye, 1990; McDonald & Hakel, 1985; Phillips & Dipboye, 1989; Sackett, 1982).

7. Interviewers may more positively evaluate applicants who display assertive, self-enhancing impression management techniques, including agreeing with the interviewer, emphasizing positive traits, self-promotion and the use of personal stories to support assertions, asking positive-closed questions, and claiming fit with the organization. In general, applicants try to convey that they are competent, hardworking, goal oriented, confident, adaptable and flexible, interpersonally skilled, and effective leaders (see Baron, 1989; Gilmore & Ferris, 1989; Kacmar, Delery, & Ferris, 1992; Stevens, 1997; Stevens & Kristof, 1995).

8. Spoken attributions (somewhat similar to "accounts"; see Morris, 1988) are fairly frequent elements of applicants' interview communication; applicants tend to offer unstable and universal attributions for negative events and internal and controllable attributions for positive events. In general, interviewers attribute applicant "social rule" breaking in interviews more to situational than personal causes (see Ramsey, Gallois, & Callan, 1997; Silvester, 1997; Struthers, Colwill, & Perry, 1992).

(continued)

TABLE 19.1 Continued

9. Most questions applicants ask their interviewers are closed-ended, singular in form, typically not phrased in the first person, asked after interviewers ask applicants for inquiries, and seek job-related information (Babbitt & Jablin, 1985; Einhorn, 1981).

10. Applicants' perceptions of their interviewers as empathic listeners appear to be negatively related to the degree to which interviewers interject "interruptive statements" while the interviewees are speaking (see McComb & Jablin, 1984).

11. Interviewers tend to rate more highly and be more satisfied with applicants who talk more of the time in their interviews (though this talk is not necessarily in response to interviewers' questions), who elaborate on answers, and whose discussion of topics more nearly matches interviewers' expectations (Einhorn, 1981; Herriot & Rothwell, 1983; Tengler & Jablin, 1983; Tullar, 1989; Ugbah & Majors, 1992).

12. Interviewers tend to employ inverted-funnel question sequences (they begin with closed questions and then progress to more open-ended questions), thus limiting applicant talk time during the opening minutes of interviews. Recruiters also tend to "hold the floor" more after answering questions (Axtmann & Jablin, 1986; Tengler & Jablin, 1983).

13. Relational control analyses of employment interviews suggest that applicants are "pushed" into dominance by interviewers' questions, while interviewers are "pulled" into giving information (dominance or one-across moves) by the support statements of applicants (see Engler-Parish & Millar, 1989; Kacmar & Hochwarter, 1995; Tullar, 1989).

14. Structured interview question formats (e.g., behavior description interviews, situational interviews, comprehensive structured interviews, and structured behavioral interviews) appear more valid than unstructured approaches (see Campion, Palmer, & Campion, 1997; Campion, Pursell, & Brown, 1988; Dipboye, 1994; Huffcutt & Roth, 1998; Janz, 1989; Janz, Hellervik, & Gilmore, 1986; Latham, 1989; Latham, Saari, Pursell, & Campion, 1980; Motowidlo et al., 1992; Pursell, Campion, & Gaylord, 1980; Williamson, Campion, Roehling, Malos, & Campion, 1997).

15. Applicants relatively high in communication apprehension prepare for and think about employment interviews differently than those low in apprehension; applicants high in communication apprehension also tend to be judged lower by interviewers than applicants relatively low in apprehension. It is possible, however, that interviewer behavior (e.g., displays of "warmth" vs. "coldness") may interact with applicants' level of anxiety to affect interviewers' ratings of applicants (see Ayres & Crosby, 1995; Ayres, Ayres, & Sharp, 1983; Ayres, Keereetaweep, Chen, & Edwards, 1998; Liden, Martin, & Parson, 1993).

16. Applicant communication ability/skill (e.g., fluency of speech, composure, appropriateness of content, ability to express ideas in an organized fashion) is frequently reported by interviewers to be a critical factor in their decisions (see Bretz, Rynes, & Gerhart, 1993; Graves & Karren, 1992; Hollandsworth, Kazelskis, Stevens, & Dressel, 1979; Kinicki & Lockwood, 1985; Kinicki, Lockwood, Hom, & Griffeth, 1990; Mino, 1996; Peterson, 1997; Posner, 1981; Riggio & Throckmorton, 1988; Spano & Zimmermann, 1995; Ugbah & Majors, 1992).

NOTE: Generalizations are extrapolated from Jablin and Krone (1994) and Jablin and Miller (1990), and from the findings of recent studies.

greatly in recent years. Thus, while most studies still focus on examining interviews of graduating students in university placement centers or the interviews of students involved in role-play situations, and rarely consider the effects of situational variables (e.g., labor market conditions) on results, an increasing number of studies have centered on collecting behavioral (as compared to perceptual) forms of communication data and have focused attention on investigating processual dimensions of interview communication (see Jablin et al., 1999). These studies usually involve audio- or videotaping interviews, coding behavior, and analyzing patterns of communicative acts (e.g., spoken attributions [Silvester, 1997], impression management tactics [Stevens & Kristof, 1995], and information-gathering tactics [Dougherty, Turban, & Callender, 1994]) and patterns of interacts, double interacts, and transition sequences (e.g., patterns of question, answer, and statement interacts [Axtmann & Jablin, 1986] and patterns of relational control and transaction structures [Engler-Parish, & Millar, 1989; Kacmer & Hochwarter, 1995; Tullar, 1989]). In turn, researchers studying nonverbal interview communication have asked judges to listen to audiotapes or view videotapes of actual interviews and rate the extent to which applicants have displayed such behaviors as smiling, eye contact, and upright body posture (Burnett & Motowidlo, 1998; Jablin, Hudson, & Sias, 1997; Liden, Martin, & Parsons, 1993; Riggio & Throckmorton, 1988). Moreover, researchers are increasingly combining the quantitative coding of interview communication behavior with qualitative analyses aimed at understanding how behaviors are enacted. Thus, for instance, Stevens and Kristof (1995) not only report the frequency with which applicants use self-promotion as an impression management tactic but also delineate the content themes applicants use to describe themselves and the discourse devices (e.g., elaborations, stories) they use to construct these images. In sum, the above trends represent important developments that portend significant advances in our understanding of communication in the selection interview.

Although nascent, a shift also appears to be occurring in what researchers consider to be the central goal of the selection interview. Traditionally, the selection interview has been considered a mechanism for determining person-job (P-J) fit (i.e., as a method of determining if an applicant has the requisite skills, knowledge, and abilities to perform a job; see Adkins, Russell, & Werbel, 1994; Jablin, 1975). This purpose is reflected in research exploring various forms of highly structured interviews; that is, regardless of specific format, highly structured interviews are job focused and are grounded in the assumption that by concentrating on such matters the validity of the interview as a selection device can be enhanced (e.g., Dipboye, 1994). An alternative perspective to the purpose of the selection interview has evolved from recent work exploring organizations as cultures (see Eisenberg & Riley, Chapter 9, this volume) and Schneider's (1987) attraction-selection-attrition (ASA) model of organizational behavior (which maintains that organizations and applicants are attracted to one another because of shared values, interests, and other attributes). These approaches propose that person-organization (P-O) fit may be more crucial than P-J fit for individual success in organizations, as well as long-term organizational effectiveness (e.g., Bowen, Ledford, & Nathan, 1991; Kristof, 1996; O'Reilly, Chatman, & Caldwell, 1991; Saks & Ashforth, 1997). In other words, these models are founded on the notion that people join and leave whole organizations/cultures, not just jobs, "whether they realize it or not" (Schneider, Goldstein, & Smith, 1995, p. 764), and as a consequence, selection processes should largely focus on assessing the fit between job seekers' values and those that characterize the organizations in which they are seeking employment. In light of the popularity of the employment interview as a selection device, it is not surprising that scholars have suggested that the interview may be a viable method for establishing P-O fit (e.g., Adkins et al., 1994; Bretz, Rynes, & Gerhart, 1993; Cable & Judge, 1997; Chatman, 1991; Judge & Ferris, 1992; Rynes & Gerhart, 1990).

To date, only a handful of studies has examined the potential of the interview for establishing P-O fit, and it is difficult to aggregate their findings into generalizable conclusions. Although some studies have shown that interviewers recognize and seek organization-specific values and qualities (e.g., leadership and warmth) in job candidates (Adkins et al., 1994; Rynes & Gerhart, 1990; Turban & Keon, 1993), other research suggests that recruiters are more interested in applicants with "universally" desirable values and traits than ones specific to organizations (Bretz et al., 1993). Evidence also indicates that interviewers' evaluations of P-O fit are based more on their *perceptions* of congruence between applicants' values and organizational values (typically assessed via responses to the Organizational Culture Profile; see O'Reilly et al., 1991) than on actual value congruence and that these perceptions influence interviewers' assessments of applicants and their hiring recommendations (Cable & Judge, 1997). In turn, research exploring *applicants' perceptions* has found that their perceptions of the congruence between their own values and those of the organizations in which they are seeking employment are related to their own P-O fit assessments and that their P-O fit assessments predict their job choice decisions and later levels of job satisfaction, organizational identification, and other outcomes (Cable & Judge, 1996; Moss & Frieze, 1993; Saks & Ashforth, 1997). With respect to how applicants develop their perceptions of P-O fit, job seekers report that their perceptions develop from their interviews with recruiters and informal contacts with other organizational members (Rynes, Bretz, & Gerhart, 1991) and that the more sources (especially formal ones) from whom applicants obtain information the greater their perceptions of P-J and P-O fit (Saks & Ashforth, 1997).

To review, employment interviews may be important settings in which recruiters and applicants exchange information that is relevant to their respective assessments of P-O fit, as well as P-J fit. However, at this juncture we do not know the kinds of messages that are exchanged in interviews that are interpreted by each party as value or culture related, the ex-

tent to which "accurate" information is shared (or even available), the sorts of value-related information recruiters and applicants would like to obtain from each other, or how each party's general verbal and nonverbal communicative performance, including their questioning and answering behavior, among other factors, affect their respective perceptions of P-O fit. In addition, it is important to note that a shift to using employment interviews to judge P-O fit brings into question the use by organizations of job-focused, highly structured interviews to assess applicants. As Cable and Judge (1997) observe, "Job-based structured interviews appear to be somewhat incompatible with assessing applicants' values and P-O fit, because these criteria extend well beyond immediate job-related factors. . . . In fact, subjective fit impressions typically are what structured interviews remove from interviewer decision making" (p. 558). This may explain, in part, interviewers' resistance to the use of structured interviews (e.g., Dipboye, 1994); they do not allow interviewers to obtain information related to the match between applicants' values and beliefs and the values and assumptions that are central to their organizations.

If the employment interview is more suited to assess P-O fit than P-J fit (e.g., Jablin, 1975; Cable & Judge, 1996), and P-O fit is predictive of positive outcomes for both applicants and organizations, then it is essential that applicants and recruiters share accurate information with one another in the interview. However, contemporary approaches to employment interviewing tend to emphasize competitive as compared to collaborative approaches to communication (e.g., Jablin & McComb, 1984; Ralston & Kirkwood, 1995), which do not necessarily encourage "dialogue" but rather "monologue," "parroting," and other forms of "distorted" communication (Cable & Judge, 1996; Ferris & Judge, 1991; Habermas, 1970; Kirkwood & Ralston, 1999; Ralston & Thomason, 1997). In part, the use of highly structured interviews attempts to limit these tendencies by focusing discussion on specific, job-focused behavior (including ethical work behavior; e.g., Hollwitz & Pawlowski, 1997) and by constraining the nature of the information exchange process. However, if, as Cable and Judge (1997) suggest, highly structured approaches to interview communication are not especially effective in generating information useful for assessing individual and organizational values and P-O fit, then we may need to consider alternative approaches to generating valid information in employment interviews. Research along these lines should consider relevant communication processes not only in screening interviews but in (1) second or on-site interviews as well, since these interactions are fairly distinct from screening interviews (e.g., in location of interview, length, number of interviewers, display of "scripted" behavior, and appropriate topics of discussion; see Fink, Bauer, & Campion, 1994; Miller & Buzzanell, 1996) yet appear central to applicants' and employers' assessments of P-O fit (e.g., Turban, Campion, & Eyring, 1995); and (2) explore how *both* interviewers and applicants use communication to coconstruct meanings/generate valid information, and produce and reproduce interview structure (e.g., Dipboye, 1994; Jablin et al., 1999).

Finally, we need to more extensively explore the nature of communication between organizations and applicants, as well as among applicants, subsequent to screening and on-site interviews, but prior to applicants' receiving and accepting job offers. Although at present we know that delays in an organization's postinterview communications with job candidates are perceived negatively by applicants and often "signal" to them that something is wrong with the organization (Rynes et al., 1991) and that after their interviews applicants talk to peers and others about their experiences and that these conversations may affect their own and other applicants' organizational attitudes (Miller, Susskind, & Levine, 1995), little is known about the characteristics and effects of the message strategies applicants and organizational representatives use to negotiate employment conditions associated with job offers (e.g., Powell & Goulet, 1996).

Preentry

Although the period of time between when a person is offered and accepts a position and actually begins working in a new organization (which for new college graduates may last several months) has been an infrequent object of investigation, it is one deserving of study and likely represents "a distinct and under-researched phase of newcomer socialization" (Barrios-Choplin, 1994, p. 265). Three issues in particular warrant examination: (1) the nature and effects of the messages newcomers receive from their new employers prior to their first day of work; (2) how newcomers manage their "reputations" (others' impressions of them) prior to beginning work in their organizations; and (3) how "insiders" converse about and make sense of new hires during this period, and in particular how they socially construct or create a reputation for newcomers in their everyday conversations.

With respect to the first issue, research should explore the kinds of messages that new hires receive from their prospective employers prior to beginning work and how these messages may affect their initial job/organization expectations and attitudes. Future studies might build on the work of Barrios-Choplin (1994), who, in exploring the nature of the "surprises" (Louis, 1980) organizational newcomers experience, found that of all the surprises individuals reported, about 11% occurred during the preentry period and that the nature of these surprises were distinct from those associated with postentry. In particular, his research showed that (1) the types of surprises new hires experienced in the preentry period tended to be more pleasant than those they experienced later in the assimilation process (see also Gundry & Rousseau, 1994), and (2) one of the most common types of pleasant surprises was the "expression of caring" by members of the organization. For example, new hires reported being pleasantly surprised to receive a personal note from the boss welcoming the person to the organization and offering assistance in the relocation process. Although not explored in this research, this kind of symbolic activity (which might be conceived of as a form of impression management) may set a trajectory for newcomers' communication relationships with managers and overall identification with the organization (e.g., Allen, 1995; Myers & Kassing, 1998), affect their images of and commitment to the organization (e.g. Treadwell & Harrison, 1994), and the manner in which they interpret other messages they receive from members of the organization prior to and after they begin work.

While organizational insiders may communicate with newcomers prior to the recruit's first day of work, it is not unusual for newcomers to communicate with selective members of the organization as well. Thus, for example, a newcomer might send an e-mail message to those the newcomer met during the on-site interview expressing appreciation of their confidence and support and expounding on how he or she is looking forward to working with them. This might be conceptualized as a form of "anticipatory" impression management (Elsbach, Sutton, & Principe, 1997) that is aimed at insiders and employs messages designed to project a positive image of the newcomer. At the same time, new hires may also engage in "self-handicapping" (e.g., Greenberg, 1996) in their communications with insiders by offering disclaimers to manage others' attributions and expectations of their skills and performance capabilities (e.g., "I've never really performed X before, so it will probably take me some time to do it well"), and thereby engage in an "anticipatory" form of role negotiation/accommodation (e.g., Moreland & Levine, in press). In sum, we should realize that "a newcomer might arrange for word of his or her reputation to be spread in advance, so that people are prepared for what is to come" (Bromley, 1993, p. 23).

Finally, it is important to recognize that organizational members converse about and make sense of new hires during the preentry period (Sutton & Louis, 1984). They engage in collective sensemaking to reduce uncertainty about the newcomer, to make him or her

"comprehensible and manageable" (Bromley, 1993). Thus, prior to their first day of work newcomers are preceded by one or more reputations that they may have had little or no role in creating. As Bromley (1993) has observed, in most cases "when we join a group or interact with someone for the first time, people will have heard something about us and will have formed attitudes and expectations on the basis of the information" (p. 23). In the organizational context, it is likely that those persons involved in the selection and recruitment process are key sources of information for others about the newcomer, since they have observed or interacted with the person and have firsthand information about him or her. However, their impressions will be affected by what others involved in the selection and recruitment process say about the person. In other words, others' impressions of the new person may unconsciously become assimilated into one's own beliefs and subsequently be communicated to other employees in everyday conversations about the new hire. As a consequence of this process of selecting, editing, and even inventing information about the newcomer, one or more newcomer reputations may be created. While what organizational insiders may communicate to others about the newcomer may be detailed, most of the time that will not be the case; rather, information that is shared will "take the form of simple stereotypes encapsulated in a few words or phrases; 'A hard-working, no-nonsense chap,' 'A real bitch,' 'Quiet and aloof' " (Bromley, 1993, p. 23). In brief, it is likely that insiders' preentry collective sensemaking about the newcomer will revolve around the expression of stereotypic categories and labels shared among employees through systems of social networks.

The social construction of newcomers' reputations by old-timers during the preentry period has its benefits in terms of reducing uncertainty about new hires, but it also may create difficulties for newcomers. "The effect of reputation is that our expectations about other people, based on hearsay, influence our behavior when we come into face-to-face contact with them . . . possibly in a way that makes our expectation a self-fulfilling prophecy" (Bromley, 1993, p. 23). In other words, consistent with social information processing theory (Salancik & Pfeffer, 1978), the general "character" of a person that has been created in socially constructing his or her reputation may serve as the "template" against which the person is viewed and judged when insiders first interact with the person. However, it is also possible that insiders' conversations about newcomers may result in the creation of a "prototypical" newcomer reputation (e.g., Niedenthal, Cantor, & Kihlstrom, 1985) that becomes a template against which *all* newcomers are viewed. Thus, even though newcomers may not have actively participated in the creation of their reputations, they may find it difficult to change the way others talk and think about them once they actually begin work in the organization.

To date, we know little of the communication and sociocognitive processes (e.g., Levine, Resnick, & Higgins, 1993; Resnick, Levine, & Teasely, 1991) insiders use in the social construction of newcomers' preentry organizational reputations. Seemingly, task interdependence and the extent to which insiders are motivated to achieve consensus and accuracy in their impressions about newcomers will affect the substance of the information they share in conversations about them, as well as the degree to which they question and explore one another's impressions and seek new or more complete information about the new hires (e.g., Fiske & Neuberg, 1990; Ruscher, Hammer, & Hammer, 1996).

Summary

The preceding discussion has provided an overview of communication processes relevant to anticipatory organizational socialization. The focus of this presentation was on how job seekers and employers acquire and use information that affects their respective application/recruitment and employment decisions and expectations about one another.

The specific topics discussed in this section —recruiting sources, realism of expectations, the selection interview, and the preentry period—were examined in relative isolation of one another. In reality, many of these activities and processes are more overlapping, seamless, and fluid. In addition, in considering the literature presented here it is important to recognize that our knowledge of anticipatory organizational socialization is based primarily on data gathered from new college graduates—entry-level employees—and not seasoned veterans (e.g., Rynes et al., 1997). Further, many problems and limitations were noted in the communication between job candidates and organizations during anticipatory organizational socialization. As a consequence, employment decisions made by applicants and organizations are often based on less-than-perfect information and may result in ill-formed beliefs and expectations of each party's employment duties, implicit obligations, and identities, among other things. Regardless of the sources of these inaccurate, often inflated beliefs and expectations, their effects seems very clear: Discrepancies between expectations and reality increase the surprises (Louis, 1980) newcomers *and* incumbents experience as the new recruits enter the organization and engage in the organizational assimilation process.

ORGANIZATIONAL ENTRY AND ASSIMILATION

Organizational assimilation concerns the processes by which individuals become integrated into the culture of an organization (Jablin, 1982). It is generally considered to be composed of two dynamic interrelated processes: (1) planned as well as unintentional efforts by the organization to "socialize" employees, and (2) the attempts of organizational members to "individualize" or change their roles and work environments to better satisfy their values, attitudes, and needs (Jablin, 1987). To a large extent, these two reciprocal processes are also central components of the organizational "role-making" process (Graen, 1976; Jablin, 1982), since it is "through the proactive and reactive communication of expectations to and from an individual by members of his or her 'role set' (Katz & Kahn, 1966) that organizational roles are negotiated and individuals share in the socially created 'reality' of organizations" (Jablin, 1987, p. 694).

For most newcomers, organizational entry is a time for learning "pivotal" behaviors, values, and beliefs associated with their job and organization (Schein, 1968). In other words, it is a time for learning what insiders consider to be "normal" patterns of thinking and behaving (Van Maanen, 1975), and in particular what things *mean* to members of the organization (including what the newcomer means to insiders). Much of what must be learned will eventually become mundane aspects of communication for newcomers, including such things as how to address others (e.g., Morand, 1996), how to dress (e.g., Pratt & Rafaeli, 1997; Rafaeli, Dutton, Harquail, & Mackie-Lewis, 1997; Rafaeli & Pratt, 1993), the uses and functions of humor (e.g., Meyer, 1997), norms associated with the communication of emotion (e.g., Conrad & Witte, 1994; Morris & Feldman, 1996; Waldron, 1994), formal and informal rules of communicating (e.g., Gilsdorf, 1998), and appropriate media to use in communicating with others (e.g., Donabedian, McKinnon, & Bruns, 1998), among other things. How does the newcomer acquire this knowledge? The recruit develops initial interpretation schemes and scripts for his or her new work environment primarily through formal and informal communication, in both ambient and discretionary forms, with others in the organization including message exchanges with supervisors, peers/coworkers, and management sources (e.g., Harris, 1994; Teboul, 1997).

To a substantial extent, newcomers learn what things mean in the organization by learning the labels that insiders apply to actions, objects, and people. As Ashforth and Humphrey (1997) suggest, labels are critical devices for "interpreting, organizing, and communicating experience within organizations, and, in turn, for guiding experience. . . . Thus, to the extent that specific labels and cognitions are shared, labels constitute a parsimonious means of understanding and communicating about an object" (p. 43). In brief, organizational members usually assign labels to people, objects, and activities to reduce uncertainty and make sense of their experiences. However, in most organizational environments it is unlikely that all insiders use identical labels to categorize and assign meaning to the same referents; rather, many different and often contradictory labels may be used by veterans to assign meaning to phenomena in any particular situation. Consequently, the labels that insiders use, and the labels that newcomers adopt, are not "neutral"; since they denote and connote distinct definitions of "reality" they represent forms of social control and power (Ashforth & Humphrey, 1995). Thus, to a considerable degree, recruits make sense of their new environments by observing and participating in the ongoing "labeling contest" (Ashforth & Humphrey, 1995) in which organizational members, in general, engage.

As noted in the discussion of the preentry period, newcomers enter into organizations with some sort of reputation, usually concisely packaged in the form of one or more labels. At a minimum, they will be labeled "new" by insiders, which has both advantages and disadvantages. Being labeled new may be advantageous in that oldtimers may not expect newcomers to perform well and perceive it to be "OK" for them to make numerous errors on the job (e.g., Greenberg, 1996); however, veterans' use and acceptance of this label may also lead them to view the new person as just a member of a category—newcomers—and as a result to deindividuate or reify the newcomer and set in motion a "Pygmalion effect" (e.g., Ashforth & Humphrey, 1997). Thus, it is likely newcomers are not passive recipients of all the labels others assign to them; rather, from their earliest days in the organization they may engage in self-labeling and other forms of sense/information giving directed at conveying preferred images about themselves that they wish others to accept.

To review, newcomers do not begin work in organizations *tabula rasa*; they not only have experienced some form of vocational and organizational anticipatory socialization that has affected their expectations, but they find themselves entering a discourse milieu in which the way others talk and think about them may already be somewhat established. At the same time, as noted several times in the preceding discussion, the process of entering into a new organization is usually one of surprise and uncertainty for both newcomers and incumbents (e.g., Falcione & Wilson, 1988; Louis, 1980).

Newcomers often experience surprises because of differences in their expectations and the reality they experience in their organizations (e.g., Danielson, 1995; Dean, Ferris, & Konstas, 1988; Feij, Whitely, Peiró, & Taris, 1995; Holton & Russell, 1997; Nelson, Quick, & Eakin, 1988; Nelson & Sutton, 1991; Nicholson & Arnold, 1989, 1991). For example, it is not uncommon for newcomers to report that they receive significantly less feedback from others in the organization then they had expected (Dean et al., 1988) or are surprised at the way "communications" are handled at higher levels of the organization (Nicholson & Arnold, 1989). Unfortunately, while research has identified the areas in which newcomers experience expectation-reality "gaps" and has shown that interactions with and social support from insiders help newcomers make sense of these experiences and reduce levels of distress (Fisher, 1986; Major, Kozlowski, Chao, & Gardner, 1995; Nelson & Quick, 1991; Reichers, 1987), we know little of how newcomers talk to others about these incongruencies in their efforts to resolve or manage them (with some notable exceptions as discussed below).

When one enters the organization, the initial "psychological contracts" between the organization and the newcomer also unfold and may be actively negotiated (Nelson, Quick, & Joplin, 1991; Robinson, 1996; Tsui, Pearce, Porter, & Hite, 1995). Rousseau and Parks

(1993) note that both contracts and expectations serve to reduce uncertainty, but that contracts are special forms of expectations: expectations or beliefs that include promises (the communication of a commitment to do something). Employees' expectations, if not fulfilled, tend to result in moderate levels of emotional arousal (e.g., disappointment; see Nelson et al., 1991) whereas perceived violations in psychological contracts often arouse more intense emotions such as anger, aggression, or hostility (e.g., Morrison & Robinson, 1997). To some degree, the terms established in the psychological contracts of newcomers affect veterans as well (Feldman, 1994), since new terms may create "drift" in "normative" elements (aspects shared among employees) of the contracts of incumbents (Rousseau & Parks, 1993). In particular, this may be true in situations where elements of the contract are communicated publicly or can be observed by veterans. Such drift may be considered as a breach of contract by incumbents and diminish their willingness to abide by the new contract's terms or it may result in their adopting new contract "scripts," among other alternatives. Thus, "it is quite common to find newcomers and veterans working side by side holding different psychological contracts" (Rousseau, 1996, p. 52).

Expectations and contracts lay the groundwork for the role negotiation process; in other words, these dynamic cognitions represent templates by which assimilation experiences are understood. Yet we still know little of the communication processes and activities associated with how newcomers and organizational agents construct psychological contracts. Moreover, we need to recognize that unrealistic and unmet expectations and promises are not just phenomena experienced by newcomers but by all organizational members as they are continuously negotiating the assimilation process (e.g., Lawson & Angle, 1998; Pearson, 1995). As Rousseau and Parks (1993) have suggested:

> Organizations and individuals create contracts through communications at critical junctures

or personnel actions in the employment relationship: recruitment, job change (including promotion and lateral moves), and organizational change and development (e.g., team building, restructuring). . . . Messages containing employer promises come from organizational history and reputation, formal commitments (Rousseau & Anton, 1988, 1991), the interpretations of procedures and policies (Parks & Schmedemann, 1992), and the experiences of fellow employees (Brockner, 1988). Contracts emerge from experience as well as observation and may in fact be continuously created and renegotiated. (p. 29)

In sum, organizational entry is typified by relatively high levels of uncertainty, surprise, discrepancies between expectations and reality, and related efforts to make sense of these experiences through reformulating cognitive schemas, scripts, and behavioral models; categorizing and labeling people, activities, and objects; and related methods of interpreting and constructing social reality. Traditionally, the entry period has been conceptualized as the "breaking-in" period or "encounter" stage of assimilation, at the end of which time newcomers are supposed to have a sufficient understanding of the organization, the job, and the people they work with so that they are capable of negotiating or individualizing their roles with members of their role set (e.g., Jablin, 1987; Schein, 1968; Van Maanen, 1975). In other words, the entry period is often viewed as a discrete stage or phase of the assimilation process.

Stage Models of Assimilation Reconsidered

In recent years, researchers have focused a considerable amount of attention on developing stage or phase models of the organizational assimilation process (e.g., Feldman, 1976; Jablin, 1987; Van Maanen, 1975). Most of these models include (1) an anticipatory socialization phase; (2) an entry or "encounter" stage; and (3) a long-term period of "meta-

morphosis" in which role conflicts are managed, and role negotiation and resocialization occur, among other activities. Although none of these models has been thoroughly tested, extant studies have produced mixed results with respect to the notion that most newcomers exhibit particular kinds of behaviors and develop specific kinds of attitudes at discrete stages of the assimilation process. There are a number of likely reasons for these results.

First, a common problem faced by researchers is determining when one stage of assimilation is ending and another beginning. Generally speaking, researchers have adopted a chronological approach to depicting when one stage of the process ends and another begins (e.g., Bauer, Morrison, & Callister, 1998). For example, it has become somewhat of a convention to assume that the organizational encounter or entry stage ends sometime between three and six months after a newcomer has been employed in an organization. However, just because an organization, for example, chooses to consider the first six months of employment a "probationary period" does not mean that the encounter stage of assimilation did not end months before this point or may end sometime later. Thus, while most stage models of the assimilation process posit certain kinds of behavioral and attitudinal "markers" as indicative of transitions from one phase to another, few studies have actually employed these criteria to determine shifts across stages. Rather, studies have been driven more by practical methodological issues; that is, one chooses particular points in time to collect data from *all* newcomers and then attempts to discern their attitudes and behaviors at those "stages" (vs. determining if there are any commonalities among newcomers with respect to the chronological points in time at which transitions occur based on shifts in their attitudes and behaviors).

A second problem associated with testing stages of the assimilation process is that few investigations have actually collected data from newcomers for more than two or three points in time (usually the first few days a person is on the job and then three to six months later). In other words, it is possible that studies have not been as longitudinal as required to adequately test stage models.

A final issue related to problems associated with stage models is conceptual in nature. Specifically, it is likely that stages of the assimilation process are not quite as discrete as some models posit (e.g., Bullis & Bach, 1989; Hess, 1993) and that newcomers' attitudes and behaviors differ more in degree than kind over time. In fact, research suggests that for many newcomers aspects of organizational assimilation happen very quickly and that within days of their initial employment some patterns of behavior and attitudes have already stabilized (e.g., Bauer & Green, 1994; Liden, Wayne, & Stilwell, 1993; Ostroff & Kozlowski, 1992; Teboul, 1997). It is even possible that newcomers may engage in role innovation as early as the first few days of work through their asking incumbents "dumb"/ naive questions that encourage oldtimers to reconsider their expectations about newcomers' roles.

To review, while it is apparent that newcomers are learning over time about the people, policies, language, history, and values of their organizations (Chao, O'Leary-Kelley, Wolf, Klein, & Gardner, 1994), among other things, whether or not discrete points exist at which newcomers move from the organizational encounter phase to the metamorphosis phase of assimilation remains debatable. Further, since it is unlikely that newcomers develop competence in and acquire knowledge of each of the various facets of their jobs/organizations at the same rate across time, it may be more useful to view the assimilation process as involving "layered" (Lois, 1999), intersecting stages of development. Along these lines, the following discussion of organizational assimilation is founded on the notion that assimilation involves a chain of events, activities, message exchanges, interpretations, and related processes—essentially "links"— in which individuals use what they have learned in the past (the extant chain of sensemaking moments) to understand new organizational situations and contexts, and as

appropriate realign, reshape, reorder, overlap, or fabricate new links so they can better adapt to their own and their organizations' requirements in the present and future (e.g., Van Maanen, 1984). Thus, in the discussion that follows I will not suggest that certain communication activities, processes, and outcomes are distinct to particular stages of assimilation; rather, I assume that these phenomena are ongoing in nature and to some degree are relevant to understanding the assimilation process from the time a newcomer enters an organization to the time she or he formally leaves the organization. However, as in other of my work, this presentation does focus on newcomers' communication relationships with essential sources of information during the assimilation processes, including the organization/management, supervisors, and coworkers (Jablin, 1982, 1987).

The sections that follow are organized in terms of communication-assimilation processes. The first set of processes—orienting, socialization, training, formal mentoring— tends to focus on newcomers' communication interactions with organization/management sources of information, and to some degree represents "planned" activities (although this varies widely from organization to organization and among the processes). The remainder of the processes focus on interpersonal communication interactions between newcomers and their supervisors and coworkers, and tend to be more discretionary in nature (i.e., not part of any formal, planned assimilation activities). Rather than discuss communication and noncommunication "outcomes" associated with assimilation, at the conclusion of the presentation of the communication-assimilation processes (as I did in my 1987 model), outcomes are discussed along with each of the processes to better reflect their dynamic nature. In addition, I have attempted wherever possible to reflect the processes in terms of dual perspectives and behaviors, that is, to consider the processes in terms of insiders/incumbents as well as newcomers. Finally, I would like to stress that the communication-assimilation processes developed in the following sections are not exhaustive of all relevant processes (and might not be grouped by others as I have done), but focus on what appear to be some of the most basic ones.

Communication-Assimilation Processes

Orienting

Almost all organizations provide newcomers with some sort of oral and written orientation to their jobs and companies (e.g., Arthur, 1991; Cook, 1992; Jerris, 1993). Many formal orientations are very brief, lasting no more than a day, and may merely involve the distribution of an employee handbook; discussion of organizational rules, policies, and the like; and the completion of paperwork related to employee benefits. In light of the brevity of most orientations programs, yet the tendency for these programs to offer new hires extensive amounts of information, it is of little surprise that the "how-to" literature frequently warns practitioners to avoid information overload in designing these activities (e.g., Jerris, 1993). However, some formal orientation programs may last weeks or months and are considered to be part of an ongoing process of assimilating newcomers into the organization. Departmental orientations are usually provided to newcomers as well and are typically the responsibility of the recruit's supervisor or senior coworkers with whom the new employee will work (e.g., Noe, 1999). Along these lines, practitioners often suggest that supervisors and line managers have the "ultimate responsibility for orienting new employees" (Jerris, 1993, p. 101).

Formal orientation programs may serve a variety of objectives, including welcoming the new employee and helping him or her feel comfortable; providing the person with information on organizational history, products and services, policies, rules, mission, and philosophy and the interpretation of these principles; introducing the recruit to key staff in other units and departments in the organiza-

tion; review of compensation and benefits plans and safety rules; orientation to the physical plant of the company; and in organizations that view orientation as an ongoing process, providing support for the newcomer beyond the first days on the job by assigning the person a "mentor" or "buddy" (e.g., Davis, 1994). Programs often use line employees to assist human resource professionals in teaching classes since these workers may be perceived of as high-credibility sources by newcomers and more easily "connect" with them (e.g., Kennedy & Berger, 1994). In general, orientation programs involve the presentation of many "checklists," which are completed by the newcomer to indicate that he or she understands the information provided (e.g., Arthur, 1991; Jerris, 1993). The use of checklists as part of orientation programs is sensible since as forms of communication lists legitimate particular beliefs and techniques, provide rules of thumb to guide and evaluate behavior, and order preferences of the organization (Browning, 1992).

Unfortunately, while an elaborate how-to literature exists pertaining to the planning, administration, and evaluating of new-employee orientation programs, little empirical research has explored the efficacy of these programs in achieving their goals. However, studies by Louis, Posner, and Powell (1983) and Nelson and Quick (1991) indicate that about two thirds of organizational newcomers (samples of MBAs and bachelor degree graduates) participate in formal orientations and view them as moderately helpful in learning about their organizations. At the same time, these investigations did not find any significant relationships between the availability of the orientation programs and newcomers' job attitudes and adjustment. In contrast, Gates and Hellweg (1989), in research examining employee orientation programs presented to newcomers during their first week of work ($n = 5$ organizations), found that those who participated in orientation programs reported higher levels of organizational identification but similar levels of job satisfaction in comparison to those who did not participate in programs ($n = 2$ organizations). Cawyer and Friedrich's (1998) research, however, showed that the number of hours new college faculty spent in institutional and department orientation sessions were predictive of their satisfaction with organizational entry/socialization.

Building on Gomersall and Myers (1966) often cited finding that informal, "anxiety-reduction" sessions following formal, conventional personnel department orientation briefings can dramatically shorten the length of time it takes for employees to obtain minimal job competency, several recent studies have explored the effects of orienting newcomers on ways of coping with their new jobs. Waung (1995), in a field experiment involving new hires ($n = 61$) to entry-level service jobs (in a fast-food chain and hospital), compared the effects of two orientation approaches on newcomers' adjustment and job survival. One group "received information warning of negative aspects of the job and about specific coping behaviors," and the other group received the same information plus self-regulatory training, that is, "training in cognitive restructuring, positive self-talk, and statements to bolster self-efficacy" (Waung, 1995, p. 633). Orientations were presented to newcomers in individual sessions. After four weeks of work, analyses showed the opposite of what was predicted: Those who received orientations that included training in self-regulatory coping behaviors exhibited more turnover than those who received just the "realistic" orientation. Other findings showed that newcomers in the self-regulatory training treatment also perceived they had received more negative information in their orientation sessions than those assigned to the "realistic" orientation condition, although they actually were presented with identical information concerning negative features of their jobs. Waung (1995, p. 645) speculated that the additional information and training provided to those in the self-regulatory condition may have increased their apprehension, reduced their self-efficacy, and caused them to rethink their job choices. Future research should explore this possibility and attempt to determine newcom-

ers' "threshold levels for negative information" in orientation sessions (Waung, 1995, p. 645).

Buckley et al. (1998) also explored how lowering job expectations in orientation sessions may influence job-related outcomes among newcomers. In this field experiment, new hires participated in one of four conditions: (1) control group (received no orientation program, just an employee handbook and a welcoming talk); (2) traditional group (received normal orientation program consisting of distribution of employee handbook and presentation of an organization film); (3) RJP group (received and discussed a written realistic job preview, watched organization film, and were given employee handbook); and (4) ELP group (participated in an expectation-lowering procedure [ELP], watched the organization film, and were given the employee handbook). In contrast to the RJP, the ELP included no specific *job* information; rather, in this seminar "discussion was focused on expectations and their effects on subsequent organizational outcomes: that expectations were set early, that they were usually inflated, and that violated expectations resulted in negative organizational outcomes" (Buckley et al., 1998, p. 455). Results showed the RJP and ELP to be more effective than the other conditions in lowering newcomers' initial job expectations; in addition, after six months employees in the RJP and ELP groups also had significantly lower turnover rates and higher levels of satisfaction than those in the other conditions. In sum, results from the above experiments suggest that what is talked about in orientation sessions can affect newcomers' job attitudes and turnover, and as a consequence represents an assimilation activity deserving of further study.

As noted above, most orientation programs involve the distribution and review of a wide variety of organizational publications, including official house organs, indoctrination and orientation booklets, and the employee handbook (Arthur, 1991; Jerris, 1993; Kennedy & Berger, 1994). With respect to this latter kind of publication (many of which are now online and electronic in form; e.g., Duff, 1989), Cohen (1991) suggests that a handbook should "educate, inform, and guide employees toward qualities of behavior and performance that will be beneficial both to themselves and the company" (p. 9). In terms of specific content, most handbooks appear to focus on three basic issues: (1) organizational history, mission, and policies; (2) work rules and related procedures and practices; and (3) employee benefits and services (Anson, 1988; Arthur, 1991). Given the problems most organizations experience in effectively communicating benefits-related information to new and continuing employees (e.g., Barocas, 1993; Driver, 1980; Huseman & Hatfield, 1978), it is not surprising that up to half the information in employee handbooks often focuses on communicating information related to compensation and benefits plans (Wolfe & Baskin, 1985).

Curiously, we know little of the relative effectiveness of company publications in orienting newcomers or whether or not they provide accurate depictions of their respective organizational environments. Thus, while printed orientation materials may be effective in informing newcomers of general organizational procedures and policies, they may be quite limited in their ability to inform them about an organization's culture (Briody, 1988). Moreover, while it is important for legal reasons that organizational members understand the content of the employee handbook (courts in over half the states have ruled that the contents of handbooks represent legally binding contracts), these documents have historically been plagued by readability problems (Davis, 1968). Yet it is not unusual for organizations to require all employees to sign a statement indicating that they "have received a copy of the company handbook, have read its contents, and understand them" (Arthur, 1991, p. 257).

Many large organizations also use expository videos as a key element in their orientation programs. For example, Berger and Huchendorf (1989) describe an orientation program at Metropolitan Life Insurance in which newcomers view a series of documentary style videotapes over the course of their first year of employment that are designed to introduce them to the traditions, customers, products, businesses, and future plans of the organization. Along these lines, Thralls (1992), in a qualitative analysis of organizational videos, concludes that orientation videos serve as rites of passage for new members by providing them with "visualized enactments" that socialize them to behaviors and attitudes compatible with key organizational identities and goals. Similarly, Pribble (1990), in a rhetorical case study of a medical technology firm's formal orientation program, found that a slide and audiotape presentation about the company, its products, and employees, followed by a speech by the firm's CEO, were strategically designed to foster shared values, organizational identification, and in the long run commitment to the company and its objectives.

To conclude, although it seems apparent that organizational members, not just newcomers, are continuously being oriented to organization-wide changes and initiatives, little attention has focused on "orientation" as an ongoing process (e.g., Jerris, 1993). For example, when an organization develops a new mission statement it is not unusual for employees to receive both written and oral orientations (often presented by organizational leaders) designed to unpack its meaning (e.g., Fairhurst, Jordan, & Neuwirth, 1997). Future research should explore potential linkages between newcomer orientation programs and communication processes associated with the ongoing efforts of organizations to orient their members to such things as new objectives, employment policies (e.g., layoffs, sexual harassment), and organizational citizenship behaviors (e.g., Allen, 1992; Organ, 1990).

Socialization Strategies

A substantial number of studies have been completed in recent years examining relationships between organizational socialization strategies and the adjustment of newcomers (typically assessed in terms of "adjustment" outcomes such as role ambiguity, role conflict, stress, intent to quit, organizational commitment, and job satisfaction). Most of this work has explored organizational socialization in terms of Van Maanen and Schein's (1979) "people processing strategies" and has used variations of Jones' (1986) self-report questionnaire of these strategies as a means to do so (e.g., Allen & Meyer, 1990; Ashforth & Saks, 1996; Ashforth, Saks, & Lee, 1998; Baker & Feldman, 1990, 1991; Black, 1992; Black & Ashford, 1995; Blau, 1988; Cooper, Graham, & Dyke, 1993; Fogarty, 1992; Fullagar, McCoy, & Shull, 1992). Results of these studies suggest that Van Maanen and Schein's typology of socialization strategies (formal-informal, individual-collective, sequential-nonsequential, fixed-variable, serial-disjunctive, investiture-divestiture) are interrelated with one another and tend to describe two basic ways of processing people into organizations: Batch/institutional/structured (formal, collective, sequential, fixed, serial) and unit/individualized/unstructured (informal, individual, nonsequential, variable, disjunctive). Research has also shown that investiture and divestiture socialization tactics are either not highly intercorrelated with the other tactics or they are not correlated with the same tactics in a consistent fashion (Allen & Meyer, 1990; Ashforth & Saks, 1996; Baker & Feldman, 1990; Black & Ashford, 1995; Jones, 1986). However, since most research in this area has relied on data gathered from new college graduates, who usually experience investiture rather than divestiture socialization tactics (e.g., Miller, 1996), the above results may be an artifact of the kinds of samples studied.

Several communication issues associated with socialization strategy/tactic research warrant discussion. First, the general adoption by researchers of the Van Maanen and Schein (1979) typology of socialization strategies implies the acceptance of a fairly one-way (organizations "process people") versus two-way or interactional view of socialization processes. Granted that organization agents may be highly proactive in their endeavors to socialize newcomers, the participation and engagement of newcomers is required for these tactics to be "successfully" enacted. Thus, while it is clear that socialization strategies and tactics are cocreated by organizational agents *and* newcomers, the typologies used to study socialization processes tend to be one-sided in nature (Bauer et al., 1998; Feldman, 1994; Saks & Ashforth, 1997).

Second, although a considerable amount of research has been directed at testing typologies of socialization strategies and tactics, few studies have explicitly focused on unpacking the communication attributes and the specific kinds of messages associated with the enactment of the strategies and tactics. Rather, most studies focus on identifying associations between the frequency of use of particular strategies and tactics and selective communication outcomes, including relationships between the use of socialization tactics and newcomers' levels of communication satisfaction (Mignerey, Rubin, & Gordon, 1995), organizational identification (Ashforth & Saks, 1996), and communication-related variables such as role clarity (Jones, 1986) and role innovation (Ashforth & Saks, 1996; Black & Ashford, 1995; West, Nicholson, & Rees, 1987). Although research along these lines is of value, it does not reveal much about communication processes associated with the enactment of organizational socialization strategies and tactics. Thus, while we may know that in certain contexts organizations tend to use institutionalized socialization, we know little of how such strategies are communicatively performed by organizational agents; "the content of socialization—the values, norms, beliefs, skills, and knowledge—that is communicated through the medium of the socialization tactics" (Ashforth et al., 1998, p. 921; see also Chao et al., 1994); the communication behaviors (with notable exceptions) of newcomers' coconstructing the socialization process with organizational agents; or if the messages communicated via the various strategies and tactics are done so in a consistent, persuasive manner such that they are believed by newcomers.

Third, as briefly noted above, we have little understanding of how the content of messages exchanged between organizational agents and newcomers varies among socialization strategies. Although Chao et al. (1994) recently developed and tested an instrument designed to measure socialization content (as compared to process), the instrument's focus is not on the content of messages exchanged in the socialization process but rather on what newcomers are supposed to learn as a result of socialization. In other words, this instrument measures outcomes of socialization, including newcomers' perceptions of their performance/task proficiency; understanding of organizational goals, values, and history; knowledge of organizational politics and power structures; the extent to which they feel like they fit in and have developed relationships with other people in the organization; and their comprehension of organizational jargon, acronyms, and professional terminology. Although this information is useful, it does not enunciate the types of messages and message exchange processes that typify learning socialization content, or how these processes might vary among socialization strategies. For example, studies suggest that stories are a frequent vehicle via which newcomers learn about their organizations (e.g., Brown, 1985). Are stories a more common means by which newcomers acquire information about certain of the Chao et al. (1994) socialization content areas than others? Are the kinds of stories that are shared with newcomers (including who or what they are about, how they are framed, and their morals), when they are told and by whom, and the involvement (passive/active) of newcomers in the storytelling process related to an organization's socialization strategy (or the interaction of an organization's socialization strategy and the extent to which it emphasizes particular socialization content areas)? Posing and answering these sorts of questions are central to furthering our understanding of how messages and message exchange processes are re-

lated to socialization strategies and newcomers' acquisition of socialization content.

Research along the above lines might benefit from findings of investigations that have explored the sorts of memorable messages (Stohl, 1986), turning points (Bullis & Bach, 1989), and critical incidents (Gundry & Rousseau, 1994) newcomers report during their socialization experiences. These studies have identified events, activities, and interactions —messages—that newcomers perceive had important effects on their understandings of "appropriate" organizational behavior and beliefs, the development of relationships, and the like (socialization content). To what extent do memorable messages/turning points/critical incidents vary across types of socialization strategies and areas of learning? Findings from Gundry and Rousseau's (1994) research suggest that variations are likely. Specifically, they found that newcomers entering into organizational cultures typified by high satisfaction norms (humanistic-helpful, affiliative, achievement oriented, emphasis on self-actualization) reported different types and interpretations of critical incidents than new hires working in task security-oriented (oppositional, competitive) and people security-oriented (approval oriented, conventional, dependent) organizational cultures. Although these cultures are not isomorphic with the organizational socialization strategies or socialization content areas discussed above, overlap among them is evident; thus, it is possible that recurrent patterns exist between the memorable messages/turning points/critical incidents newcomers experience and their organizations' formal and informal socialization efforts.

Training

Feldman (1989), among others, has suggested that organizational training programs have become one of the primary processes for socializing new employees. These programs are typically formal (occur away from the work setting and present newcomers with activities specifically designed for them), experienced collectively by newcomers as a group (Van Maanen & Schein, 1979), and vary in the extent to which they positively affect newcomers (e.g., Chatman, 1991; Nicholson & Arnold, 1989). More specifically, results of studies evaluating newcomer-training programs suggest that they are available to about one third of employees (Nelson & Quick, 1991); their effects can be enhanced by providing trainees with realistic information about the nature of the programs prior to their participation in them (Hicks & Klimoski, 1987); training may have its greatest effects on newcomers with low levels of initial work-related self-efficacy who may be experiencing difficulty coping and are in need of job and organizational information (Saks, 1995); pretraining motivation "may prepare participants to receive the maximum benefits from training" (Tannenbaum, Mathieu, Salas, & Cannon-Bowles, 1991, p. 765); training manuals and recruits' conversations about training programs may articulate and reinforce "root metaphors" that are central organizational guiding principles (Smith & Eisenberg, 1987; Suchan, 1995); newcomers' perceptions of the amount of training they have received are positively related to their perceptions of the helpfulness of that training and to their supervisors' ratings of their communicative performance (among other outcomes) once on the job (Saks, 1996); group training in comparison to individual training can enhance "transactive memory" (i.e., one's own knowledge and an awareness of what other specific members know) within a work group (Liang, Moreland, & Argote, 1995); and contradictions often exist between the messages newcomers receive in training about adhering to established rules and procedures and the application of these policies once they begin work (DiSanza, 1995; Fielding, 1986).

A rather rare field experiment exploring the differential effects of formal/collective as compared to informal/individual training warrants special attention. In this study, Zahrly and Tosi (1989) examined the early work adjustment of blue-collar workers in a startup manufacturing facility in which employees were assigned to semiautonomous work teams. All newcomers experienced the same selection process and then about one half of the employees ($n = 40$) experienced formal, collective training while the other half ($n = 40$) did not receive any systematic training or orientation. Each work team to which newcomers were assigned contained roughly an equal number of persons from each induction mode. Beta weights from regression analyses showed that after four months on the job, those employees who had experienced the collective training were higher in job satisfaction and lower in work-family and role conflict than those who were trained individually. While only approaching statistical significance ($p < .10$), employees who experienced collective training also reported lower levels of role ambiguity and higher levels of group cohesion than those who were trained on an individual basis. Although the organization, situation, and sample examined in this research are rather unique, results of the study suggest that in certain contexts the group interaction fostered by collective training may enhance newcomers' sensemaking abilities and early work role adjustment (see also Liang et al., 1995). Future studies of the communication characteristics and effects of newcomers' training experiences would profit from the use of research designs similar to the one used by Zahrly and Tosi (1989).

Finally, those studying communication and organizational assimilation would benefit from broadening their view of the functions and goals of training beyond the initial employment period. Formal (and informal) training has become a part of the "continuous learning" movement in organizations (e.g., Goldstein & Gilliam, 1990), and thus training is an ongoing experience for most employees. (In 1995, over $52 billion was budgeted for formal training in U.S. organizations with 100 or more employees; "1995 Industry Reports," 1995.) In fact, research suggests that "senior executives are now as likely to be the target of training initiatives as entry or technical employees" (Martocchio & Baldwin, 1997, p. 5).

Some organizations now even train their vendors and business partners to the organization's work methods, procedures, and culture; in part this is done to facilitate operations, but it also serves to encourage (socialize) stakeholders to share in the organization's vision, values, and strategy. In addition, as organizations pursue major changes, develop new strategies, and attempt to reinforce existing ones, training presents a venue for the corporation to persuade employees to accept and support these activities, as well as learn about new technical and nontechnical developments (Drobrynski, 1993, cited in Martocchio & Baldwin, 1997). Moreover, the availability, type, content, and extent of training made available to organizational members represent "messages" to them about their membership status and can affect their perceptions of organizational support (e.g., Shore & Shore, 1995; Wayne, Shore, & Liden, 1997). As Abelson (1993) observes, "Those who receive training to help them more effectively function in the organization most likely interpret that to mean the organization values their membership and wants to help them succeed. Those not receiving development opportunities, through training or other means, frequently perceive an opposite message" (p. 354). In brief, training represents a mode of cultural transmission (Harrison & Carroll, 1991) and "resocialization" (e.g., Bullis & Clark, 1993; Kossek, Roberts, Fisher, & DeMarr, 1998) and thus is deserving of study as a part of the assimilation process across the entirety of an individual's tenure in an organization.

Formal Mentoring

Since it is often suggested that "mentoring speeds up socialization into the work role, encourages social interaction, provides an opportunity for high-quality interpersonal interactions, and enhances identification with and commitment to the organization" (Wigand & Boster, 1991, p. 16), it is not surprising that organizations have tried to formalize the mentoring relationship to facilitate the assimilation of newcomers (e.g., Zey, 1991). A formal mentoring relationship is not a spontaneous relationship that naturally develops between an incumbent and a newcomer, but rather is a "deliberate pairing of a more skilled or experienced person with a lesser skilled or experienced one, with the agreed-upon goal of having the lesser skilled or experienced person grow and develop specific competencies" (Murray & Owen, 1991, p. xiv). Although formal, "assigned" mentoring relationships aim to fulfill a specific set of organizational functions and goals, formal mentors may also fulfill career-related (e.g., coaching, protection, exposure) and psychosocial (e.g., counseling, role-modeling, acceptance) functions for their protégés (similar to informal mentoring relationships; e.g., Kram, 1988; Noe, 1988). However, as Evans (1994) notes, formal mentoring relationships are distinct from informal ones in that "formal mentors are selected and trained by the organization while informal mentors are not likely to have had any mentoring training prior to the mentoring relationship" (p. 26).

Formal mentoring programs usually have one of two general goals: "grooming" experienced incumbents for advancement in the organization (e.g., Klauss, 1981; Noe, 1988; Ostroff & Kozlowski, 1993) or facilitating the adjustment of organizational newcomers (e.g., Chao, Walz, & Gardner, 1992; Wigand & Boster, 1991). In this section, our attention is focused on the latter goal.

Although many organizations have established formal mentorship programs for new employees, only a handful of empirical studies have explored the nature and effects of these programs on the assimilation of *newcomers* into organizations. The results of these studies provide mixed, but tentative support with respect to the benefits of these programs (e.g., Allen, McManus, & Russell, 1999; Seibert, 1999). For example, Chao et al. (1992), in a survey of college graduates, found no significant differences between newcomers involved in formal versus informal mentoring programs with respect to psychosocial benefits, and only a slight career-related benefit for those involved in informal mentoring relationships. In addition, results showed that while those involved in informal mentorships scored higher on all "outcome" measures (socialization, satisfaction, and salary) compared with nonmentored individuals, newcomers involved in formal mentorships scored higher than nonmentored individuals on only three socialization subscales: establishing satisfying work relationships with others, knowledge of organizational politics, and understanding of organizational goals and values.

More recently, Heimann and Pittenger (1996), in a study examining a formal mentorship program among new and senior faculty at a university ($n = 22$), found newcomers' perceptions of the "closeness" of their mentoring relationship (e.g., open, supportive, helpful) to be strongly associated with their self-reported levels of organizational socialization and organizational commitment, as well as their perceptions of the value of the mentoring program (see also Blau, 1988). Newcomers' perceptions of their opportunity to interact with their mentor were also positively related to their perceptions of each of the outcome measures. However, in a study of a formal peer mentoring program among MBA students (groups of second-year students served as mentors to teams of first-year students), Allen, Russell, and Maetzke (1997) found, after controlling for the extent of mentoring functions served, time spent interacting with mentors and protégés' satisfaction with their experiences were not significantly related. These findings led Allen et al. (1997) to conclude that "it is not so much the amount of time spent together as it is the quality of the mentor-protégé relationship that creates a satisfactory mentoring experience (at least from the perspective of the protégé)" (p. 500). Overall, their results led them to suggest, as have others (e.g., Seibert, 1999), that different mentoring functions may be more important at some stages of a protégé's career than other functions, and in particular that psychosocial

functions may be more important than career-related functions early in a worker's organization tenure.

In one of the only studies to date to specifically explore communication issues associated with formal mentoring programs, Evans (1994) collected communication network data from individuals participating in nursing "preceptor" programs at two large hospitals. Among other things, results of her research revealed that (1) protégés ($n = 23$) spent more time talking with their formal mentors than with coworkers (especially about organizational topics); (2) multiplexity of the protégé-mentor link was a predictor of newcomer organizational commitment; (3) protégés and formal mentors differed in many of their perceptions concerning communication with each other (including specific topics and functions of messages); (4) social support provided by the mentor was related to a number of protégé socialization outcomes (e.g., critical care and communication effectiveness); and (5) nonmentored newcomers ($n = 10$) were more connected in the communication networks of their groups while mentored newcomers evidenced higher levels of multiplexity in their network links.

In sum, the results of the studies discussed above provide tentative support for the notion that newcomers who participate in formal mentoring programs, in comparison to those who are not involved in any form of mentoring, experience a variety of benefits. In particular, involvement in a formal mentoring program can enhance a newcomer's understanding of organizational issues and potentially his or her level of satisfaction. However, given the paucity of research in this area, and differences in methods used across the few studies that have been conducted (e.g., variation in when data were collected in the assimilation process, differences in the operationalization of variables, variations in the occupations of those included in samples), it is difficult to determine if formal mentoring programs are more effective in facilitating newcomers' assimilation than informal mentoring processes. In particular, although "mentoring is essentially a communicative activity" (Evans, 1994, p. 2), we still know little of the communication characteristics and outcomes of formal mentoring processes in comparison to informal ones.

Informal Mentoring

Although conceptualizations vary across studies (e.g., Merriam, 1983; Noe, 1988), informal mentors are usually considered to be "experienced personnel who respect, guide, protect, sponsor, promote, and teach younger less experienced personnel—the protégés" (Pollock, 1995, p. 114). They are distinct from formal mentors in that they are not assigned to employees by the organization. Thus, informal mentoring relationships develop naturally at the discretion of the mentor and protégé and persist as long as the parties involved experience sufficient positive outcomes (e.g., career development and success).

Although informal mentoring is an interaction process, most of the research related to the dynamics of these relationships has *not directly* examined the nature of *communication* between mentor and protégé; rather, studies have focused on such issues as individuals' motivation and willingness to mentor others (e.g., Aryee, Chay, & Chew, 1996; Olian, Carroll, & Giannantonio, 1993), the organizational and personal characteristics of mentors and protégés (e.g., Eagen, 1996; Fagenson, 1992; Koberg, Boss, Chappel, & Ringer, 1994; Olian, Carroll, Giannantonio, & Feren, 1988), similarities and distinctions in the mentoring experiences of men and women (e.g., Dreher & Ash, 1990; Ragins & Cotton, 1999; Ragins & Scandura, 1997; Scandura & Ragins, 1993), and the experiences of those in diversified mentoring relationships (e.g., diverse in terms of race, ethnicity, and class; see Ibarra, 1993; Koberg, Boss, & Goodman, 1998; Ragins, 1997) and situations (Dreher & Cox, 1996; Kalbfleisch & Davies, 1991; Thomas, 1990). When communication processes and issues are considered, they are usu-

ally explored implicitly via respondents' retrospective reports of the frequency with which they have experienced mentoring "functions" (e.g., Noe, 1988; Riley & Wrench, 1985; Scandura & Katterberg, 1988), and in particular, psychosocial support (e.g., the extent to which a mentor offered coaching, acceptance, confirmation) and career-related guidance (e.g., the extent to which the mentor provided exposure and visibility, protection, sponsorship, and challenging assignments).

What do the few studies that have specifically focused on newcomers, and/or followed new organizational members over time, suggest about communication in informal mentoring relationships? First, it appears that mentors are most instrumental in providing newcomers with information about the organizational domain (for instance, information about organizational power and politics, history, culture) relative to the other content domains, such as information about job features and work groups (Dirsmith & Covaleski, 1985; Ostroff & Kozlowski, 1993). Second, protégés in informal mentoring relationships tend to receive more career-related support and at least equivalent amounts of psychosocial support when compared to those in formal mentoring relationships (Chao et al., 1992; Ragins & Cotton, 1999). Third, despite these benefits, informal mentors are not always available or easy for newcomers to establish relationships with (Nelson & Quick, 1991; Waldeck, Orrego, Plax, & Kearney, 1997). Fourth, it is likely that one of the best ways to initiate informal relationships with mentors is to ensure contact with the person, that is, be visible to the target and regularly meet and talk with him or her (Waldeck et al., 1997). Fifth, mentors do not necessarily provide the types of information and display the sorts of communication behaviors that are proposed by stages models (e.g., Kram, 1983; Missirian, 1982) of the mentoring process (e.g., Bullis & Bach, 1989; Green & Bauer, 1995; Pollock, 1995). For example, Pollock (1995) found that protégés report that their mentors provide the full range of mentoring functions (with at least moderate frequency) from early in their relationships and continue to do so as their relationships progress.

Recent studies that have not necessarily focused on organizational newcomers and mentor-protégé relationship development but have examined communication issues associated with informal mentoring also suggest several conclusions:

1. Generally speaking, protégés perceive that the more they communicate with their mentors, the more psychosocial benefits, career guidance, and role modeling they receive (Fagenson, 1992, 1994).
2. Protégés with higher levels of self-esteem and communication competence, and "who perceive less risk in intimacy, are more likely to participate in mentoring relationships than those with reduced communication competence and self-esteem, and perceptions of greater risk in intimacy" (Kalbfleisch & Davies, 1993, pp. 412-413).
3. Differences may exist in the communication patterns displayed by male and female protégés, and between protégés whose mentors are male as compared to female (Bahniuk, Dobos, & Hill, 1990; Bahniuk, Hill, & Darius, 1996; Burke, McKeen, & McKenna, 1990; Ragins & Scandura, 1997).
4. Those without mentors tend to rely more on coworkers for information (Ostroff & Kozlowski, 1993).
5. Protégés involved in informal supervisory mentorships (relationships in which the mentor is supervisor of the protégé) in comparison to those involved in formal supervisory mentorships, nonsupervisory mentorships, or nonmentoring supervisory relationships may differ in their communication behaviors, and in particular may use more direct and less regulative and contractual communication tactics to maintain relational stability (Burke, McKenna, & McKeen, 1991; Tepper, 1995).

In conclusion, from the perspective of understanding assimilation processes, extant research exploring informal mentoring pres-

ents several dilemmas. Most studies have not employed longitudinal research designs; in fact, few have even collected data from organizational newcomers. Rather, the typical research design is retrospective and cross-sectional in nature and includes a sample of persons who range from those with little career and organizational experience to those with decades of tenure in their organizations. In addition, most studies relying on self-reports of behavior have not distinguished among mentoring relationships at different phases of individuals' careers and in general have failed to explore relationship development issues. As a consequence, our understanding of the sorts of communication behaviors protégés and mentors display as their relationships develop, and the functions these behaviors serve, remain somewhat muddled. Even if research reveals there are no clear-cut, linear stages associated with the development of informal mentorships, there still may be foundational patterns of communication behavior that are requisite for the initiation and maintenance of these relationships. Along these lines, future research might elaborate on the results of Pollock's (1995, p. 159) study, in which she found that "challenging and respecting the subordinate seems to form the foundation of mentor-protégé relationships and this foundation is not subsequently taken for granted" as the relationship progresses.

Information Seeking

Founded on the notion that newcomers are active agents in their organizational assimilation, researchers have devoted a considerable amount of attention in the past decade to exploring new hires' proactive information-seeking tactics and behaviors. Much of this work has explored elements of Miller and Jablin's (1991) model of information seeking during organizational entry, which posits that newcomers' information seeking is influenced by their perceptions of uncertainty and the social costs involved in seeking information, the type/content of information sought (referent—information required to function/perform on the job; appraisal—feedback on the degree one is functioning successfully on the job; and relational—information on the nature of one's relationships with others), the source from whom the information is sought, and several individual difference (e.g., self-esteem, tolerance for ambiguity) and contextual (e.g., organizational socialization strategy) factors.

Expanding on research exploring feedback-seeking behavior in organizations (e.g., Ashford, 1986; Ashford & Cummings, 1985) and information seeking in interpersonal relationships generally (e.g., Berger & Bradac, 1982), Miller and Jablin (1991) argued that the factors noted above will influence newcomers to seek information via use of one or more of the following tactics:

Overt: Asking for information in a direct manner

Indirect: Getting others to give information by hinting and use of noninterrogative questions

Third party: Asking someone else rather than the primary information target

Testing: Breaking a rule, annoying the target, and so on and then observing the target's reaction

Disguising conversations: Use of jokes, verbal prompts, self-disclosure, and so on to ease information from the target without the person's awareness

Observing: Watching another's actions to model behavior or discern meanings associated with events

Surveillance: Indiscriminately monitoring conversations and activities to which meaning can retrospectively be attributed.

In subsequent empirical research, Miller (1996) found the "disguising conversations" and "indirect" information-seeking approaches to be closely associated and therefore grouped them together to represent one general "indirect" information-seeking tactic; for similar reasons, "observing" and "surveillance" were collapsed to form an index of "observing."

Other research has provided support for many of the propositions associated with the Miller and Jablin (1991) model. However, since researchers have not been consistent in the ways in which they have conceptualized and operationalized constructs, it is difficult to draw generalizations across studies. For example, whereas Miller and Jablin conceptualized technical and procedural information associated with role demands and task performance as elements of "referent" information, others have considered these to be unique content areas and have measured them as such (e.g., Comer, 1991; Morrison, 1993a, 1993b, 1995; Ostroff & Kozlowski, 1992). Albeit these distinctions, the results of studies suggest the following tentative conclusions:

1. As newcomers' perceptions of the social costs of seeking information increase, their use of overt/direct information seeking decreases and their use of "covert" tactics (e.g., indirect, observing) increases (e.g., Fedor, Rensvold, & Adams, 1992; Holder, 1996; Miller, 1996; Teboul, 1995).

2. The most frequent kinds of information sought by newcomers concern referent/task/technical issues (e.g., Morrison, 1993b, 1995; Ostroff & Kozlowski, 1992; Teboul, 1994), and they tend to seek such information through overt/direct information seeking (Comer, 1991; Morrison, 1995).

3. In general, the most frequent information-seeking tactics used by newcomers are overt/direct and observing, with some studies reporting overt/direct as the most frequent approach (Comer, 1991; Holder, 1996; Kramer, 1994; Kramer, Callister, & Turban, 1995; Miller, 1989, 1996; Myers, 1998; Teboul, 1994, 1995) and others monitoring (Morrison, 1993b; Ostroff & Kozlowski, 1992).

4. Supervisors and coworkers are the most common targets of newcomers' information seeking (as compared to subordinates,

friends, spouses, and impersonal organizational sources such as reports and training manuals; e.g., Morrison, 1993b; Teboul, 1994).

5. When seeking relational/social information newcomers most frequently employ observation and monitoring (Miller, 1996; Morrison, 1995), whereas when seeking appraisal information they most often use overt and monitoring tactics (Miller, 1996; Morrison, 1995).

6. The frequency and use by newcomers of particular information-seeking behaviors are associated with outcomes such as role ambiguity, role conflict, task mastery, role orientation, organizational commitment, job involvement, intent to leave, performance, and job satisfaction, although these relationships are not consistent across studies and rarely account for large amounts of variance (Ashford & Black, 1996; Holder, 1996; Kramer, 1994; Kramer et al., 1995; Mignerey et al., 1995; Miller, 1989; Morrison, 1993a; Ostroff & Kozlowski, 1992).

7. Newcomers' perceptions of target social support (Miller, 1996; Teboul, 1995), levels of self-esteem (Miller, 1989; Teboul, 1995), tolerance for ambiguity (Fedor et al., 1992; Teboul, 1995), value of feedback (Mignerey et al., 1995), and organizational domain/field of study (Comer, 1991; Miller, 1996) are related to their information-seeking behavior.

8. Newcomers' information-seeking behaviors vary with their experience of "institutional" as compared to "individualized" organizational socialization (Mignerey et al., 1995; Miller, 1996; Teboul, 1995).

In addition, initial evidence suggests that over time newcomers seek less normative (information about expected behaviors and attitudes in the organization) and social information and more referent and appraisal information (Morrison, 1993b) and that newcomers find the appraisal and referent/technical information they obtain as most useful and the organizational and social/relational information they acquire the least

useful (Morrison, 1995). Further, although researchers have experienced difficulty in gathering data reflective of the range of uncertainty newcomers experience on the job (e.g., Miller, 1996; Teboul, 1994), at least one investigation has reported correlational data showing that as uncertainty increases newcomers use observing, third-party, and indirect tactics more and overt/direct information seeking less (Holder, 1996).

Several studies of newcomers' information-seeking behavior have also explored the extent to which they passively obtain information. Passively acquired information is information that is not actively sought by newcomers but is voluntarily provided to them by others in the organization (either formally via organizational activities such as training programs or informally on the job). For example, Comer (1991) found that about one third of the technical and social information newcomers obtain from *peers* is acquired in a passive/explicit manner (explicit in the sense that the information is provided in verbal vs. nonverbal form). In contrast, Morrison's (1995) research showed that while newcomers obtain social, technical, political, referent, and appraisal information more actively, they acquire organizational information more passively, and normative information about equally through active and passive means. Ironically, she also discovered that newcomers rated the organizational information they received as the least useful of all information types, yet the kind of information they received more than any other type. In turn, in two different studies Kramer (1994; Kramer et al., 1995) discovered that newcomers' receipt of unsolicited feedback from peers and supervisors had a greater impact on their adjustment than information acquired through more active means (e.g., requests, monitoring). Unfortunately, the results of these studies do not provide much insight into the interrelationships between newcomers' active and passive information acquisition, although a theme underlying the research is the notion that if others in the organization volunteer useful information to newcomers then the new hires will feel more comfortable (perceive lower social costs) in actively seeking information from those sources. In brief, while research in this area appears promising, future studies should investigate sequential relationships that may exist between newcomers' passive information acquisition and their active information-seeking behavior.

As noted above, it is difficult to draw many firm conclusions from research exploring newcomers' information-seeking behavior. All extant studies have relied on self-report methods of data collection, including interviews, open-ended descriptions of information-seeking incidents, and questionnaires (the latter the most common data-gathering technique). While these methods have their advantages, their use assumes that people are highly conscious of their information-seeking behavior (e.g., Miller & Jablin, 1991) and can easily provide accurate self-reports of their use of all tactics. However, this assumption may be problematic and requires testing, especially with respect to implicit tactics (e.g., surveillance, indirect), which newcomers may be less conscious of using. Our choice of research methods has also hampered our ability to understand information-seeking behaviors and tactics as part of the ongoing stream of communication activity in which newcomers engage; in other words, we have yet to "examine the dialogue of newcomers seeking information" (Miller, 1996, p. 20), that is, how information seeking unfolds in discourse. In addition, with notable exceptions, research has tended to focus on the frequency with which newcomers report their use of information-seeking tactics, and not the value or usefulness of the information they acquire. In some situations, it may require only one information-seeking effort to acquire desired information while in others acquiring information may be a long-term endeavor. Along these lines, we also need to focus more attention on how newcomers' information seeking develops over time; to date, only a few studies have collected data over at least two points in time, and none beyond a period of six months.

Rather, most studies are cross-sectional in design and some even ask persons who have been working in their organizations for many years to provide retrospective accounts of their information seeking during their first few months on the job.

Also, given the inconsistent results evident across studies examining relationships between newcomers' information seeking and various outcomes (e.g., performance, role ambiguity), it might be useful to revisit some of our assumptions about relationships among these variables. In many cases, it might be possible to predict both positive as well as negative relationships between newcomers' information seeking and their adjustment to their jobs and organizations (e.g., Ashford & Black, 1996; Fedor et al., 1992). For example, we might predict a negative relationship between newcomers' information seeking and their performance, arguing that because they are performing well they will require less feedback, job instructions, and the like. However, it is also reasonable to predict that those who are high performers achieve that status because they seek information and feedback from those around them; consequently, we would predict a positive association between information seeking and performance. In sum, greater attention needs to be focused on studying the mutual influences of newcomers' information seeking on relevant outcomes and the effects of those outcomes on newcomers' information seeking.

Findings from the studies reviewed here also suggest several other areas that future research should explore including possible distinctions in newcomers' information seeking and their gender, race, and ethnicity (e.g., evidence indicates that in some organizations it is easier for white males to access information than other persons; see Holder, 1996; Lovelace & Rosen, 1996; Teboul, 1995); relationships that may exist between how newcomers are recruited and their information-seeking behavior (e.g., Saks, 1994, suggests that those who are recruited through informal means may already have "inside" contacts when they begin their jobs, thus facilitating their ability to acquire information); the extent to which newcomers' information-seeking behavior is stable over time (e.g., Morrison, 1993b; Ostroff & Kozlowski, 1992); and the information-seeking behavior of other career entrants besides new college graduates. Finally, although the preceding discussion has focused on how newcomers' information seeking may facilitate their adjustment, future studies need to consider what incumbents do with the information they acquire about new hires (and themselves) from the newcomers' information-seeking efforts. In other words, we should explore how newcomers' information-seeking behavior affects insiders' efforts to seek information from and make sense of newcomers.

In summary, it appears that newcomers are active agents in their assimilation in part due to their proactive information-seeking behaviors. Not surprisingly, we find that newcomers use monitoring-like tactics across almost all situations and that most of the variation in their behavior occurs in the use of more overt/direct information-seeking tactics. Further, it is also not surprising that newcomers tend to seek more information when the social costs of information seeking are low, and focus a considerable amount of attention on seeking referent and appraisal information, types of information that are crucial in their becoming competent in the performance of their jobs. The notion that the more information newcomers *seek* about their social and normative environments the more competent they will be in their jobs is not fully supported in the research. Does this imply that newcomers are not acquiring considerable amounts of information about these issues, or that acquisition of this information is not related to their development of job competence (or other outcomes)? Not necessarily; rather, it is possible that newcomers are obtaining social and normative information through other mechanisms, including formal and informal mentoring, and from incumbents who volunteer this information to them.

Information Giving

Although researchers have begun to explore newcomers' information-seeking behavior, scant research has focused on their information-giving behavior (i.e., utterances either initiated by newcomers or solicited of newcomers by another party) and its goals, functions, and effects in the assimilation process. There are several basic reasons for exploring newcomers' information giving. First, studying newcomers' information-giving behavior acknowledges that newcomers can and do play active communication roles (display "voice"; e.g., Gorden, Infante, & Graham, 1988) as they begin their new jobs (Reichers, 1987). While a portion of a newcomer's voice is evident in his or her information-seeking behavior, information seeking only addresses the manner in which a newcomer can proactively "receive" additional information about his or her new role. The newcomer can also be a source of information. Along these lines, Jablin (1984) found that even during the earliest days of newcomers' organizational tenure information giving comprised at least 25% of their total communication behavior. Second, a newcomer's information giving represents an important indicator of his or her sensemaking and ability to cope with the stress of the organizational entry process. In other words, the degree to which newcomers are making sense of and effectively coping with the new organizational environment will, to some extent, be reflected in the communication they initiate with others in the organization as well as the responses they give to others' questions. Moreover, a newcomer's information giving can provide others with signals as to how the newcomer's construction of self, role, and orientation to the new social and work environment may be changing (e.g., Arnold & Nicholson, 1991; Fournier, 1997; Fournier & Payne, 1994; Morrison, 1994).

Jablin's (1984) study of the assimilation of nursing assistants ($n = 44$) over the first 24 weeks of their employment was the first to detail both newcomers' information-giving and information-seeking behaviors. A portion of the data collected included communication logs completed by a third of the nursing assistants during their third and ninth weeks on the job (the first two weeks of employment involved a training program). Results showed that information giving comprised about a quarter of a newcomer's total communication during the initial weeks of work (Week 3 = 25.6%; Week 9 = 28.1%). Of their interactions with superiors, about 15% involved newcomers' giving information; of their interaction with peers, about one third involved newcomer information giving; of their interactions with patients, about 25% involved information giving. Findings also indicated that about one fourth of all newcomers' interactions were for the purpose of giving instructions. Not surprisingly, most of the instructions given by newcomers were to patients within the nursing homes. Unfortunately, this research did not attempt to identify the specific content areas associated with newcomers' information giving.

Building on Jablin's (1984) research, Hudson and Jablin (1992) proposed a descriptive model of the context and factors that influence newcomers' information-giving behavior and a scheme for categorizing these messages. They suggest that newcomers' information-giving behavior reflects the surprise or shock they are experiencing in relation to their expectations, the uncertainty and emotions they are experiencing in the new environment, the extent to which the newcomers are learning work group and organizational norms and values, and the level of development of their relationships with others in the work setting.

Accordingly, they developed the Information-Giving Message Categorization Scheme consistent with these four experiences, as well as with two basic dimensions in which "content" is frequently framed in organizational message typologies: work/nonwork and evaluative/nonevaluative (e.g., Gioia & Sims, 1986; Komaki, Zlotnick, & Jensen, 1986). Evaluative work information includes utterances expressing opinions or judgments related to discrepancies between expectations and experiences (overt surprises), job stress,

self-evaluation of performance, qualities and attributes of the work role, and evaluations of individuals affiliated with the organization and the organization itself. Evaluative nonwork information includes utterances that express opinions or judgments on such things as participation in nonwork activities and the pressures or conflicts experienced by the newcomer outside the organization. Descriptive work information includes nonevaluative utterances related to such matters as task understanding, causes for task performance, task goals, and task instructions. Descriptive nonwork information includes nonevaluative utterances focused on issues unrelated to the organization or task including information about one's interests, hobbies, family, and personal goals (e.g., I hope to run the marathon).

Although the Hudson and Jablin (1992) model and message categorization scheme has yet to be fully tested, two studies have explored issues related to it. In a survey study of the employment experiences of new college graduates, Ashford and Black (1992) asked newcomers to respond to a scale associated with providing others with task- or project-related information. Although this measure did not distinguish evaluative from nonevaluative information giving or determine if the information was solicited by others or volunteered by newcomers, results showed positive association between the extent to which newcomers provided others with information and their organizational commitment and organizational knowledge. More recently, Kramer et al. (1995) examined the information-receiving and information-giving behaviors of new hires and experienced employees (transfers) beginning work at a new location of a retail food store. Again information giving focused on task issues and did not distinguish evaluative from nonevaluative messages. Specifically, respondents indicated the extent to which they answered information requests from others concerning "tasks, making decisions, and improving the work setting," modeled appropriate actions and behaviors, and provided unrequested suggestions to peers and supervisors "for improving the work setting." Results showed modeling to be negatively associated with intent to quit; not surprisingly, veterans who transferred to the new store reported more information giving than newcomers. In addition, findings revealed that newcomers' answering of information requests from others and their providing unsolicited information to others were fairly strongly correlated ($r = .63$), suggesting that there may be some reciprocity between these two forms of information giving.

In brief, the above studies provide some support for the importance of newcomers' *task/work* information giving in the assimilation process. Unfortunately, neither of these investigations explored non-work-related information giving nor distinguished between evaluative and nonevaluative information giving and newcomers' adjustment. Future research should do so. In addition, we need to explore how the information-giving (and -seeking) behavior of incumbents is related to the information-giving (and -seeking) behavior of newcomers. Support for such a relationship is evident in the results of Kramer et al.'s (1995) research, in which they found a positive association ($r = .42$) between newcomers' receipt of unsolicited information from others and newcomers' providing unrequested information to others.

Studies should also consider information giving in terms of written and nonverbal as well as oral, verbal messages (the emphasis to date). For example, in the written reports and e-mail messages that newcomers send to others they are providing information that allows incumbents to make attributions about the newcomers' substantive, rhetorical, and social competence (e.g., Katz, 1998; Larson, 1996). Newcomers give information to others in the work setting via their nonverbal behavior as well. For instance, in light of the uncertainty they face when they begin their jobs, newcomers may act in awkward ways or make task-related and communication "mistakes" (e.g., Gilsdorf, 1998) that cause them to experience embarrassment (e.g., Keltner & Buswell, 1997; Miller, 1992). When a newcomer's face turns bright red with embarrassment, the newcomer may be sharing information about his or her affective state, what makes the person self-conscious, his or her cognitive limitations (e.g., forgetfulness, stupidity), and his or her understanding of scripts that guide interaction or task performance (e.g., the newcomer's understanding of forms of work group and organizational humor [e.g. Meyer, 1997; Vinton, 1989], appropriate forms of address [e.g., Morand, 1996], and norms for expressing emotions [e.g., Waldron, 1994] and telling stories [e.g., Stevenson & Bartunek, 1996]). Such forms of nonverbal information giving are important indicants of how newcomers are making sense of and adjusting to their new work environments and are deserving of study from both the perspectives of newcomers and insiders.

Situations in which newcomers experience embarrassment may also initiate other forms of information giving, including the presentation of excuses, justifications, and accounts as means of saving face/identity and managing impressions. Accordingly, some forms of newcomers' (and insiders') information giving may be conceptualized in terms of impression management, an "inherently communicative process" (Bozeman & Kacmar, 1997, p. 10) that is concerned with how individuals attempt to control the image they are projecting to others by manipulating information (Schlenker, 1980). Thus, for example, in conversations with other organizational members newcomers may blame their poor performance on external sources, or use apologies, deception, and the "relabeling" of their actions (for instance, as successful) to disguise their failures (e.g., Bozeman & Kacmar, 1997; Caldwell & O'Reilly, 1982; Fandt & Ferris, 1990; Greenberg, 1996). Moreover, since newcomers are often more conscious of their behavior than oldtimers, future research should also consider the extent to which newcomers' use of impression management tactics may be tied to particular message design logics (O'Keefe, 1988, 1990) and plans to promote desired identity goals (e.g., Bozeman & Kacmar, 1997). Investigations might also explore if a newcomer's frequent use of highly manipulative impression management tactics communicates to incumbents that the newcomer is manipulative (Snyder, 1985), and how this may affect the willingness of others to share information with the newcomer. However, since a newcomer's use of impression management tactics does not necessarily mean that the newcomer is trying to "score points" with others, it is important that we also consider how these forms of information giving may represent attempts at building positive relationships (e.g., Wayne & Kacmar, 1991). As Bozeman and Kacmar (1997) suggest, impression management tactics may serve a variety of identity functions (e.g., identity enhancement, protection, or adjustment) and may be content or relationship oriented.

To conclude, to date few studies have explored newcomers' information-giving behavior (and its interrelationship with the communication behavior of incumbents). If we are to more fully understand how and with what effects (positive and negative) newcomers and oldtimers share information, we need to supplement our studies of information-seeking behavior with research exploring information-giving behavior as well.

Relationship Development

As evident in the earlier discussion of formal and informal mentoring, it is usually vital for newcomers to develop relationships with others in the work setting, especially with leaders and peers (including other newcomers). Among other things, relationships with peers and leaders provide newcomers with support that facilitates the learning process and reduces stress associated with adjusting to the new work environment (e.g., Allen, McManus, & Russell, 1999; Cawyer & Friedrich, 1998; Comer, 1992; Feij et al., 1995; McCauley, Ruderman, Ohlott, & Morrow, 1994; Myers, 1998; Nicholson & Arnold, 1989; Oseroff-Varnell, 1998; Ostroff & Kozlowski, 1992). At the same time, however, our knowledge of the communication processes associated with the development and maintenance of newcomers' relationships

with others in the work setting is very limited. Thus, we are in the curious position of being able to identify the types and characteristics of interpersonal relationships in work settings (e.g., Boyd & Taylor, 1998; Bridge & Baxter, 1992; Graen & Uhl-Bien, 1995; Kram & Isabella, 1985; Myers, Knox, Pawlowski, & Ropog, 1999) but know relatively little about how these relationships form and are maintained. However, it is apparent that the communication-assimilation processes discussed in the preceding pages (e.g., information seeking and information giving) provide newcomers and incumbents with information that facilitates the process of building relationships with one another beyond the basic interdependencies associated with their work roles.

Peer relationships. Since most newcomers have numerous peers in their work groups but typically just one immediate supervisor, they tend to have more contact with coworkers and as a consequence more opportunities to share information with them and develop relationships (e.g., Comer, 1992; Teboul, 1994). However, it is important to recognize that most interpersonal relationships formed in organizations are not close but rather acquaintance type in nature (Fritz, 1997). The manner in which coworker relationships may develop from acquaintances to "best friends" has recently been explored by Sias and Cahill (1998). They proposed that a variety of contextual factors, including shared tasks and group cohesion (e.g., Fine, 1986), physical proximity (e.g., Griffin & Sparks, 1990), lack of supervisor consideration (Odden & Sias, 1997), and life events outside the workplace, as well as individual factors (e.g., perceived similarity in attitudes and beliefs as well as demographic similarity; Adkins, Ravlin, & Meglino, 1996; Duck, 1994; Glaman, Jones, & Rozelle, 1996; Kirchmeyer, 1995), may affect the development of relationships with peers. However, the influence of these factors was not explored in a longitudinal manner in the research. Rather, retrospective interviews were conducted between pairs of coworkers ($n = 19$ pairs) exploring their relationships with one another (average length of relationships = 4.7 years). Respondents were asked to identify points at which their relationships changed across time, factors that caused these developments, and communication changes that were associated with transitions in their relationships.

Respondents in the Sias and Cahill (1998) study reported that the move from acquaintance to friend averaged 12 months from initially meeting, the passage from friend to close friend averaged an additional 19 months, and the transition from close friend to best friend another 17 months (total of four years). Factors that were important in the transition from acquaintance to friend included proximity, shared tasks, socializing outside the work settings (e.g., having lunch together), and perceived similarity. This transition was accompanied by increased discussion of personal topics and non-work-related issues, some decrease in caution in sharing opinions and information, but not much intimacy.

> Relationships developed into close friendships usually because of important personal or work-related problems, although perceived similarity and extra-organizational socializing continued to impact relational development. At this point, the coworker became a trusted source of support with communication becoming increasingly more intimate and less cautious. (Sias & Cahill, 1998, p. 289)

The same factors were associated with the transition from close friend to best friend; that is, communication continued to decrease in caution and increase in intimacy and discussion of work- and non-work-related problems.

Several other findings from the Sias and Cahill (1998) research are of interest. In particular, results showed moderate levels of agreement between coworkers with respect to the factors affecting, and the communication changes that characterized, their relationship development. Further, their results suggest that relational development among coworkers

may be driven by frustrations and problems they experience with their supervisors (consistent with the research of Gundry & Rousseau, 1994, who found the most frequent "critical incident" that made an impression on newcomers was a conflict between the supervisor and subordinate). Finally, findings in the Sias and Cahill study also revealed that some employees were reluctant to leave what they considered to be less than desirable work environments because of close friendships with coworkers. These data reiterate the notion that the close relationships that newcomers develop with peers implicitly involve commitments that "pose constraints when the need to alter behavior becomes apparent" (Ashford & Taylor, 1990, p. 10).

Although newcomer-coworker relationships typically develop in the context of work groups, few studies have explored how group communication processes and norms affect the development of relationships between newcomers and particular group members. However, it does seem apparent that the more role and interpersonal conflict within work groups, the longer it takes for newcomers to develop friendships with members of their groups and role sets (Katz, 1985). It is also likely that communication processes associated with the development of relationships between newcomers and oldtimers in their work groups will be affected by other group characteristics, including level of group cohesiveness, characteristics of social networks, team member exchange quality, the length of time group members have been working together, stage of group development, group initiation activities, diversity in group membership, and the frequency with which new members enter the group (e.g., Arrow & McGrath, 1995; Gersick, 1988, 1989; Hautaluoma, Enge, Mitchell, & Rittwager, 1991; Jackson, Stone, & Alvarez, 1993; Katz, 1980; Larkey, 1996; Levine & Moreland, 1991; Seers, 1989; Shah, 1998; Ziller, Behringer, & Jansen, 1991). In addition, while we know that in many circumstances (e.g., collective, formal socialization) newcomers frequently develop relationships with one another and provide each other with support and assistance, little is known about communication processes associated with the development and maintenance of these relationships.

Supervisory relationships. Research has shown that a newcomer's communication relationship with his or her initial supervisor is a crucial factor in the newcomer's assimilation, since the supervisor frequently communicates with the newcomer, may serve as a role model (e.g., Ben-Yoav & Hartman, 1988; Javidan, Bemmels, Devine, & Dastmalchian, 1995; Weiss, 1977), filters and interprets formal downward-directed management messages, has positional power to administer rewards and punishments, is a central source of information related to job and organizational expectations as well as feedback on task performance, and is pivotal in the newcomer's ability to negotiate his or her role, among other things (e.g., Jablin, 1982, 1987). Given the importance of the newcomer-supervisor relationship in the assimilation process, several models have recently been proposed describing stages of the relationship development process. Generally speaking, these models represent variations of Altman and Taylor's (1973) social penetration theory of relationship development integrated with research related to leader-member exchange (LMX) theory (e.g., Graen & Scandura, 1987; Graen & Uhl-Bien, 1995).

Graen and Uhl-Bien (1995) proposed a three-stage leadership making model. In this model, the leader-newcomer relationship begins with a "stranger" phase, in which the leader and follower come together because of their task interdependence and display forms of exchange that are contractual in nature; in other words, "leaders provide followers only with what they need to perform, and followers behave only as required and do only their prescribed job" (p. 230). The second stage of relationship development is the "acquaintance" phase and is chiefly characterized by one of the parties making an "offer for an improved working relationship through career-oriented social exchange" (p. 230); at this point there is increased interaction, and although exchanges are still limited they are characterized by the "return of favors" and "testing" in the relationship. Graen and Uhl-Bien (1995) describe the third phase of the relationship development process as "maturity," or the establishment of mature partnerships. They suggest that these exchanges are highly developed and that the parties rely on each other for loyalty, mutual respect, and support. In brief, "they are exchanges 'in kind' and many have a long time span of reciprocation" (p. 230). Unfortunately, little empirical research has explored the leadership making model, nor does the model provide much detail with respect to the communication processes associated with transitions in the development of newcomer-leader relationships.

More recently, Boyd and Taylor (1998) presented a developmental four-stage model of friendships in leader-follower relationships in which they propose that the development of a high LMX "does not depend on the development of a close leader-follower friendship relationship" (p. 4). However, they do suggest that the "highest quality work experience for both leader and follower potentially occurs when both a close leader-follower friendship and a high LMX are present" (p. 4).

Somewhat similar to the coworker friendship development work of Sias and Cahill (1998), Boyd and Taylor (1998) propose that leaders and followers begin their relationships at a stage at which the parties explore the potential for friendship and that such factors as physical proximity and attitudinal and demographic similarity are important factors affecting relationship development at this point (e.g., Bauer & Green, 1996; Liden et al., 1993; Sparrowe & Liden, 1997). The second stage is concerned with exploration and orientation, and the leader and follower consider the costs and rewards of developing the relationship. According to Boyd and Taylor (1998), this stage is "characterized by caution and tentativeness. There is little open evaluation, criticism, or expression of conflict and information is exchanged only at a superficial level" (p. 10). However, they posit that during this period value congruence and perceived similarities between the parties become evident, along with displays of liking and positive affect (e.g., Dockery & Steiner, 1990; Meglino, Ravlin, & Adkins, 1989, 1991). During the third stage, the leader and follower become casual friends and test their relationship; relations are thought to be "superficial in nature, lacking the intimacy, sense of uniqueness, strength of affective bond, and reciprocal obligations of more personal friendship relations" (Boyd & Taylor, 1998, p. 12). This stage is characterized by medium LMX, role making versus role taking (Graen, 1976), and increased and more open communication and is similar to the acquaintance stage of Graen and Uhl-Bien's (1995) leadership making model. In the fourth and final stage, the leader and follower develop a stable exchange and become close friends. Boyd and Taylor (1998) suggest that this kind of relationship is characterized by mutual reciprocal influence, intimacy, support, frequent interaction across a variety of settings, high levels of understanding, and efficient communication. They believe these types of relationships are rare in organizations and that the communication patterns associated with high LMX relationships may facilitate the development of close friendships between leaders and followers.

Several other issues are noteworthy about the Boyd and Taylor (1998) model. First, to date, no empirical research has explored the validity of its assumptions and propositions. Second, the model focuses on the development of leader-newcomer relationships in isolation of the work group. Third, the model recognizes that relationship development processes are not necessarily linear. Thus, for example, Boyd and Taylor suggest that relationships escalate as well as deteriorate over time, and in most cases never advance beyond casual friendships (characterized by moderate to high levels of LMX).

Findings from two recent empirical studies associated with the development of leader-newcomer relationships are also of interest. In the first investigation, Bauer and Green

(1996) expanded on and tested a model of LMX originally developed by Graen and Scandura (1987). This model posits that leader-follower relationships involve three phases: (1) role taking, during which time the parties make cognitive evaluations of one another's trustworthiness; (2) role making (the acquaintance stage in Graen & Uhl-Bien's model), a period where behavioral trustworthiness is determined in large part through a leader's taking a risk in delegating work to the newcomer; and (3) role routinization, a phase in which the behaviors of each member of the dyad are fairly predictable and the leader and follower experience affective trust as an outcome of their high LMX relationship. In general, results of the study showed that variables that were expected to be associated with trust building were related to leader-member relationship development. However, the research did not directly measure trust building or its many communication correlates (e.g., Jablin, 1979). The second investigation explored superior-subordinate communication during job transfers over the course of one year. In this research, Kramer (1995) reported results that suggest that transferees were "reliant on supervisors' actions in defining the relationship rather than being proactive in their communication" (p. 58); in other words, their relationship resulted from the leader's "typical style." Further, findings revealed patterns between the types of supervisory relationships transferees developed and their communication relationships with peers (e.g., those who had "overseer" relationships with their supervisors tended to have more "informational" than "collegial" or "special" peer relationships). In brief, Kramer's (1995) work supports the notion that there are interdependencies between the quality of the developing communication relationships transferees experience with their supervisors and the quality of their developing communication relationships with peers.

Finally, it is important to note that scholars have also begun to explore how leader-follower relationships are maintained over time (Bridge & Baxter, 1992; Lee, 1997, 1998a, 1998b; Lee & Jablin, 1995; Tepper, 1995;

Waldron, 1991; Waldron & Hunt, 1992; Winstead, Derlega, Montgomery, & Pilkington, 1995). Unfortunately, none of this research traces the development of newcomer-leader relationships from their initiation, thereby exploring maintenance communication processes and relationship development over time. However, results of these studies do suggest that leader-follower relationships may alter trajectory (escalate or deteriorate) and that leaders and followers employ distinctive maintenance communication tactics to keep their relationships at a steady state or intact (e.g., avoidance of interaction, refocusing conversations, openness, procrastination, deception, self-promotion, circumspectiveness, small talk, and supportiveness). In addition, a variety of factors have been found to affect how the parties enact maintenance communication behaviors, including quality of LMX, interactional context and relationship state, hierarchical position, group social context (cooperative-competitive), and perceived effectiveness in relationship maintenance. The results of Lee's (1997, 1998a, 1998b) studies are of particular importance, in that they indicate that leader-follower communication maintenance processes are affected not only by the context of the work group but also by perceptions of the leader's relationship with his or her superiors (a variation of the Pelz effect; e.g., Jablin, 1980).

In summary, while a number of valuable models have been posited detailing relationship development processes during organizational assimilation, few empirical studies have been conducted exploring these models generally, and with respect to communication processes and issues in particular. Rather, the focus of most extant research has been on identifying the communication characteristics of various forms of posttransition relational states that may exist between newcomers and other organizational members. Clearly, more longitudinal research exploring how newcomers and their leaders and coworkers communicate in the process of developing relationship states is required. In addition, it also seems apparent that we should direct more of our efforts into exploring newcomer-leader, new-

comer-coworker, and if applicable, newcomer-subordinate (e.g., Kramer & Noland, 1999) communication and relationship development processes in combination with one another, rather than in isolation of each other. Within organizations, specific types of relationships develop and are embedded within networks of organizational relationships (e.g., McPhee, 1988; Sias & Jablin, 1995; Zorn, 1995). Further, since it is becoming increasingly common for organizational members to no longer work in the co-presence of their supervisors and coworkers, but rather communicate with each other via computer-mediated communication and information technologies from off-site locations (see Rice & Gattiker, Chapter 14, this volume), the manner in which newcomers develop relationships with others in their organizations may also be evolving (e.g., Sias & Cahill, 1998; Walther, 1992, 1996) and represents an important area for future research.

Role Negotiation

Role negotiation "occurs when two or more persons consciously interact with the express purpose of altering the others' expectations about how a role should be enacted and evaluated" (Miller, Jablin, Casey, Lamphear-Van Horn, & Ethington, 1996, p. 296). Most theories of organizational assimilation (e.g., Graen & Scandura, 1987) posit that during their early days in new jobs/organizations newcomers are more involved in "taking" (learning others' expectations of them) than in negotiating or generating coorientation about their roles (Jablin & Krone, 1987). In other words, although newcomers can actively attempt to "individualize" their roles to better satisfy their own needs, values, and beliefs at any time, for most this will not occur until they have reached a threshold level of adaptation to their new work environments. In addition, it is believed that the newcomer-leader role negotiation process is key to the newcomer's success in the role negotiation process generally; that is, if a newcomer is not successful in role negotiation with the immediate supervisor, the newcomer's chances of successfully individualizing his or her role in the organization become problematic (e.g., Jablin, 1987). As Graen (1976) has observed, "Although other members of the new person's role set can enter the negotiation of the definition of the new person's role . . . only the leader is granted the authority to impose formal sanctions to back up his [her] negotiations" (p. 1206).

Although newcomers' ability and success in negotiating their roles with leaders and coworkers appear central to the newcomers' success in satisfying their own needs and meeting organizational requirements, little research has focused on exploring the interaction that occurs among the relevant parties during the role negotiation process. Rather, most research that is typically associated with role negotiation focuses on subordinates' use of different kinds of upward influence tactics in various kinds of leader-member and peer relationships (e.g., Barry & Bateman, 1992; Deluga & Perry, 1994; Judge & Bretz, 1994; Krone, 1992; Maslyn, Farmer, & Fedor, 1996; Thacker & Wayne, 1995; Yukl, Guinan, & Sottolano, 1995); factors associated with employees' willingness to "voice" to their supervisors (e.g., Ashford & Taylor, 1990; Janssen, de Vries, & Cozijnsen, 1998; Saunders, Sheppard, Knight, & Roth, 1992); and newcomers' perceptions of their role innovation, role development, and personal/self change as they become assimilated into their organizations (e.g., Ashforth & Saks, 1996; Jones, 1986; Nicholson, 1984; Nicholson & West, 1988; Van Maanen & Schein, 1979; West, 1987). Thus, while it is evident that we need to conceptualize and study role negotiation in terms of the interdependent influence and negotiation strategies that newcomers and other organizational members use in the process of negotiating roles over time, research has not assumed that approach. Moreover, few studies have explored how the role negotiation strategies of newcomers and the sorts of issues or areas they attempt to negotiate change (if at all) as they progress from the initial stages of the formation of their roles to later periods in their organizational assimilation.

As noted above, only a few empirical studies have explored role negotiation processes and organizational assimilation. Dockery and Steiner (1990), in a laboratory study lasting only a few minutes in duration, assessed followers' use of upward influence tactics in their initial interactions with their leader. They found positive relationships between followers' use of ingratiation and rationality as strategies in their upward influence attempts and their perceptions of LMX; in addition, results showed a negative association between respondents' self-reports of assertiveness as an influence tactic and their perceptions of LMX. However, it is also important to observe that the researchers found assertiveness used so infrequently by followers that they suggest that newcomers may be reluctant to use this tactic in initial interactions with their leaders.

Jablin and Miller (1993) conducted a longitudinal study of newcomer-supervisor role negotiation processes, in which data ($n = 65$ across all time periods) were collected from newcomers (recent college graduates) at their 6th and 18th months of employment. Generally speaking, results did not show that newcomers were attempting to negotiate many role changes with their supervisors (an average of two attempts in the preceding 6 months), although they perceived themselves as very successful in these negotiations. Frequent topics newcomers attempted to negotiate with their supervisors concerned job responsibilities and duties, issues related to job procedures and scheduling tasks, and human resources/personnel matters. Other findings revealed that the more newcomers used a particular influence strategy (rationality, exchange, ingratiation, coalitions) in their negotiation efforts at 6 months of employment, the more they used it at 18 months of work; newcomers' use of ingratiation and to some degree rationality and coalitions as negotiation strategies decreased over time; and newcomers who perceived themselves as more communicatively competent or worked in groups high in cohesiveness increased their use of the exchange strategy in their role negotiations between their 6th and 18th months of employment. In addition, Jablin, Miller, and Keller (1999) found, in data collected from a sample of new college graduates (n = 24) employed for 6 months, no differences between newcomers' use of influence methods in their successful as compared to relatively unsuccessful role negotiations with their supervisors (and as in the Jablin & Miller, 1993, study, findings indicated that rationality was the most commonly reported influence tactic).

Using a sample of newly promoted (average time in position = 4.5 months) restaurant employees (not fast food), Kramer and Noland (1999) also provide data relevant to role negotiation processes subsequent to job transitions. Results derived from interviews with the new managers (n = 20) indicated that almost two thirds had attempted to negotiate changes in others' expectations of their roles. Negotiations usually occurred during informal discussions; involved a wide range of issues, including procedures, policies, and responsibilities related to their roles; and most frequently involved attempts to change the role expectations of subordinates (persons who had previously been the newly promoted employees' peers) and supervisors. In brief, these role negotiations usually involved people the newly promoted person already knew, and thus tended to focus on developing mutual understandings of the new leader-follower relationship and the person's role in social networks. Results also suggested that "testing" might have been used by subordinates and leaders in negotiating the newly promoted employee's role. In addition, Kramer and Noland found that only about half of the new managers explicitly negotiated role-related issues with their supervisors and that when such negotiations did occur, they were not always successful.

Another group of studies is also noteworthy, in that they suggest communication-related factors that may affect a newcomer's ability to negotiate his or her role with others in the organization. Exploring factors that increase the probability that workers will voice to their supervisors (e.g., offer suggestions,

discuss grievances and problems), Saunders et al. (1992) found that when workers changed supervisors they were less likely to exhibit voice with their new bosses and that employees' perceptions of their supervisors as "voice managers" (responsive and approachable communicators) affected their propensity to voice. In turn, Janssen et al. (1998) also found that employees are more likely to voice to their supervisors if they perceive them as effective voice managers, but in addition, they discovered that employees whose cognitive styles are more adaptive (oriented to work within established paradigms) than innovative (oriented to shifting paradigms) are more likely to voice ideas when they are dissatisfied, whereas innovators are more likely to voice ideas when they are satisfied with their jobs. In other words, it is possible that innovators tend to negotiate changes in their roles even when they are generally satisfied with them.

The notion that a supervisor's voice management skills are central to employee role negotiation is also evident in the results of a recent study by Miller, Johnson, Hart, and Peterson (1999). These researchers found that "open and facilitative supervisory relationships and the perception of the leader as facilitating work in the unit are central to employees' evaluation of their role negotiation ability" (p. 39). Although some research has found that an individual's need for feedback is associated with his or her self-change at work (Black & Ashford, 1995), Miller et al. did not find an employee's need for feedback or self-esteem related to perceptions of role negotiation ability. In elaborating on their results, Miller et al. also suggest that employees who work for supervisors who are open and responsive and facilitate work in their groups may actually experience less need to negotiate their roles, since their bosses tend to be more aware of problems and opportunities and therefore manage issues as they arise. Future research should explore this possibility.

To review, it is clear that our understanding of the manner in which newcomers negotiate their roles with their supervisors and others in organizations is rudimentary, at best. Although negotiation is an interactive process in which the parties involved usually make provisional offers and counteroffers and work together to generate compromises or alternative solutions to sources of dissatisfaction or conflict (Thompson, 1990), we have tended to study role negotiation during organizational assimilation from just the perspective of the newcomer and in terms of unidirectional influence attempts despite the fact that so much of the literature associated with work in this area is based on role negotiation as a social exchange process (e.g., Blau, 1964; Settoon, Bennett, & Liden, 1996). Future research should focus more on identifying the discourse patterns that emerge over time in the role negotiations between newcomers and other organizational members. Along these lines, Fairhurst's (1993) study of the discourse patterns of a small sample of women leaders and their followers in various LMX relationships is instructive. Through the application of discourse analysis methods (see Putnam and Fairhurst, Chapter 3, this volume) to audio-taped records of conversations, she was able to uncover subtleties in the communication behaviors and patterns of leaders and followers in informal, routine role negotiations. Among other things, she found that those in medium and high LMX relationships displayed a "pattern of politely acknowledging and responding to the other before revealing one's own expectations for the role" and this helped create "the give-and-take dynamic of a negotiation with multiple goals in the areas of task and relationship" (Fairhurst, 1993, p. 336).

Future research should also explore distinctions and commonalities that may exist in the formal versus informal, everyday role negotiations that occur between newcomers and other members of their role sets. Generally speaking, in research exploring role negotiation there has been insufficient integration of research and theory exploring negotiation and bargaining (e.g., Putnam & Roloff, 1992) with

studies of how individuals attempt to influence one another in organizations. In addition, since newcomers frequently experience unmet role expectations upon entering organizations (see earlier discussion in this chapter), researchers might begin to track over time how and under what conditions newcomers attempt to negotiate these discrepancies. Conversely, similar issues might be explored from the perspective of organizational insiders who also experience unmet and unexpected expectations about newcomers' roles. Finally, as inferred earlier, research is still required that (1) directly examines LMX and the influence/negotiation tactics that newcomers and leaders use in their role negotiations as their relationships develop over time, (2) the interaction patterns associated with the negotiations of those who enact distinctive types of organizational role orientations (e.g., custodial vs. innovative), and (3) the communication strategies that newcomers use to negotiate their roles with members of their work groups (e.g., Jablin, 1987).

Summary

The preceding discussion of role negotiation highlights one of the central issues that I have attempted to stress in this section: Assimilation-communication processes overlap and are linked to one another in an evolving, intersecting manner. Thus, as pertains to exploring communication processes associated with how newcomers and organizational incumbents negotiate their roles with one another, it is necessary to consider other of the assimilation-communication processes I have developed here, including relationship development, information-seeking and information-giving behaviors, mentoring activities, and organizational socialization. In addition, it is important to reiterate that I have not necessarily enunciated all of the relevant communication processes associated with organizational assimilation. In fact, most of the variables that I have previously identified as dynamic communication outcomes of the assimilation process—for example, involvement in communication networks, development of cultural knowledge and shared meaning, communication competence (e.g., Jablin, 1987; Jablin & Krone, 1994)—could easily be conceptualized as links in the unfolding and mutating chain of assimilation-communication processes.

ORGANIZATIONAL DISENGAGEMENT/EXIT[2]

In light of the centrality of work in our lives, and the important functions that relationships in the work setting play in the development and maintenance of our self-identities, it is clear that organizational disengagement, regardless of its form, is a stressful experience for most of us (e.g., Latack, Kinicki, & Prussia, 1997). Certainly, it is as difficult to become an "ex" as it is to become a part of a social group. Organizational disengagement is not only a challenge for the leaver, but also for those who remain in the old work environment. The exit of a coworker induces uncertainty (usually at multiple levels of analysis, such as dyadic, group, organizational, extraorganizational; e.g., Shaw & Barrett-Power, 1997) into the social fabric of the organization. It brings the temporal nature of almost all facets of our lives into the forefront of consciousness.

In 1987, I offered a preliminary model of the communication antecedents of the voluntary turnover process, along with a number of propositions about the communication correlates of withdrawal and the communication consequences of voluntary turnover in organizations (Jablin, 1987). Since that time, relatively little research has been conducted exploring communication issues associated with the voluntary turnover process generally, although two empirical studies have explored selected relationships suggested in the model (M. Allen, 1996; Scott et al., 1999). Results

from these investigations supported predicted indirect (as well as direct) relationships between coworker communication, supervisory communication, and organization-wide/top management communication and turnover intentions (see also Johnson, Bernhagen, Miller, & Allen, 1996). Further, findings in the Scott et al. (1999) study showed complex relationships between targets of identification in organizations (e.g., Scott, Corman, & Cheney, 1998) and intent to leave. In related research, and consistent with the general predictions of the Jablin (1987) model, Feeley and Barnett (1997) found that those highly connected in communication networks or more central to networks were less likely to leave their jobs than individuals less connected/central in their networks (unfortunately, this study did not clearly distinguish voluntary from involuntary turnover). More recently, Cox (1999) reported that the most common strategy coworkers use to encourage voluntary turnover among peers is to avoid communication with them, which he suggests should cause those peers to become more decentralized in communication networks, consistent with Feeley and Barnett's (1997) research and the Jablin (1987) model.

Given the limited amount of research that has explored the 1987 model, and the focus of these few studies on just one part of the model—relationships between communication antecedents and turnover—my purpose here is to develop those aspects of the model that have received little research attention (withdrawal and communication consequences of turnover) and to develop a general perspective about the roles and functions of communication in situations involving *voluntary* disengagement/exit (i.e., voluntary turnover, transfers, retirement). However, the ideas presented here are based on a broad examination of previous research exploring communication and organizational disengagement in a variety of contexts (e.g., Jablin & Krone, 1994), not just voluntary turnover. In particular, I reviewed recent research exploring communication and organizational disengagement in *retirement* (e.g., Avery & Jablin, 1988; Beehr & Nelson, 1995; Cude & Jablin, 1992; Shultz, Morton, & Weckerle, 1998; Sonnenfeld, 1988; van Tilburg, 1992), *transfers* (e.g., Briody & Chrisman, 1991; Campion, Cheraskin, & Stevens, 1994; Jablin & Kramer, 1998; Kramer, 1989, 1993a, 1993b; Toliver, 1993), *promotions* (e.g., Cooper et al., 1993; Kilduff & Day, 1994; Kramer & Noland, 1999; Rudin & Boudreau, 1996), *job changes resulting from mergers and acquisitions* (e.g., Bastien, 1987, 1992; Cornett-DeVito & Friedman, 1995; Haunschild, Moreland, & Murrell, 1994; Howard & Geist, 1995; Schweiger & DeNisi, 1991), *layoffs as a result of downsizing* (e.g., Folger & Skarlicki, 1998; Johnson et al., 1996; Mishra & Spreitzer, 1998; O'Neill & Lenn, 1995; Skarlicki, Ellard, & Kelln, 1998), and the *dismissal* of individual employees (e.g., Cox & Kramer, 1995; Klaas & Dell'omo, 1997).

In sum, my goal is to use the results of a fairly broad analysis of the literature to build a perspective about communication phenomena/processes that are associated with voluntary organizational disengagement/exit. In particular, my focus is on this process as the communication antecedents of turnover reach a threshold point, that is, when employees begin to have sufficient negative affective responses to their jobs and organizations to consider turnover (see Jablin, 1987). Accordingly, this section unfolds as follows. First, I offer a brief conceptualization of the notion of organizational disengagement/exit. Second, I develop a general perspective about the roles and functions of communication during the voluntary disengagement/exit process. Given that empirical research is quite limited with respect to communication phenomena in many of the areas in which I offer propositions, much of the discussion that follows is highly speculative; in other words, the material presented here is intended to stimulate research exploring communication and organizational disengagement/exit processes and not to present a series of well-supported research generalizations.

Conceptualizing Organizational Disengagement/Exit

Organizational disengagement is a process, not an event. What we might normally associate with exit—the public, physical activity of leaving a particular job and organization—is something that happens midway through the process. The processual nature of exit is noted by Ebaugh (1984, p. 10), who offers a general model of the disengagement process based on Cumming and Henry's (1961) conception of disengagement as "mutual withdrawal": "[Disengagement] . . . involves both the individual's decreased association with a group and, simultaneously, the group's decreased demands on and involvement with the individual. As a group expects less from an individual, the rewards of belonging also decrease, such that withdrawal from the group becomes a viable option."

Given that work roles are embedded within role sets, work groups, departments, and divisions, disengagement at one level of analysis (e.g., the work group) will affect the individual's relationships and functions at other levels of analysis (e.g., at the organizational level). One does not necessarily disengage from all levels of analysis at once. Thus, one may seek a lateral transfer to a new work group to leave a dissatisfying work situation, yet remain a part of the organization and perform more or less the same tasks. In addition, as Ebaugh (1984) observes, it is essential to realize that disengagement is a mutual process—to fully understand the roles and functions of communication in the disengagement process we must study both those who leave and those who stay. Relatedly, although disengagement may be a mutual process between leavers and stayers, this does not imply that the disengagement process occurs at the same pace or manner for each party. Disengagement processes between leavers and stayers are interdependent, not equivalent. In brief, since organizations are "open systems" (Katz & Kahn, 1966), the exit of an organizational member, for whatever reasons, requires the organization to achieve a revised state of homeostasis among its various sub- and supra-systems.

Disengagement/Exit Process

Since it is not my purpose to explore the antecedents of voluntary organizational exit, but rather to explore the roles and functions of communication in the process of disengagement/exit, my approach includes unpacking three basic phases that appear indigenous to all forms of voluntary disengagement/exit: (1) preannouncement, (2) announcement and actual exit, and (3) postexit. Depending on the phase of the disengagement process, this discussion incorporates distinctive theoretical perspectives, such as open systems theory (e.g., Katz & Kahn, 1966), uncertainty reduction theory (e.g., Berger, 1979), attribution theory (e.g., Kelley, 1971), balance theory (Heider, 1958), cognitive dissonance theory (e.g., Festinger, 1957), social information processing theory (e.g., Salancik & Pfeffer, 1978), and theory and research related to social justice and the use of accounts and justifications in organizations (e.g., Bies, 1987; Scott & Lyman, 1968).

In considering each of the phases, I attempt to develop the process in communicative terms from both the vantages of leavers and stayers. However, I have minimized discussion of communication phenomena that tend to be unique to specific forms of voluntary disengagement; rather, I focus on communication issues common to multiple forms of disengagement. At the same time, even though this integrative approach is designed to be applicable to most forms of voluntary disengagement, it will be evident to the reader that depending on the form of disengagement, some elements of the model may be more or less relevant.

Preannouncement

All forms of voluntary organizational disengagement are preceded by cues, signals, or even "shocks" (e.g., Lee, Mitchell, Wise, & Fireman, 1996) that are evident in the form of discretionary and ambient messages in the work setting. The specific kinds and timing of cues may vary according to the form of disengagement. For example, specific cues may be shared with coworkers and supervisors for many months before the announcement of the employee's departure from the organization (for instance, in the leaver's messages suggesting an unwillingness to perform organizational citizenship behaviors [see Chen, Hui, & Sego, 1998] or in coworkers' messages to motivate a peer to exit [Cox, 1999]). Some of the leaver's cues may be communicated in an active, intentional manner (e.g., Hirschman's [1970] notion of "voice"), whereas other cues may be passive and unintentional in nature (e.g., Ferris & Mitchell, 1987). Certain cues may be readily available to most members of the work group (poor performance, lateness, or absenteeism of a coworker), while others may be communicated to specific targets (for instance, discretionary messages to supervisors and/or coworkers; e.g., Cox, 1999; Jablin, 1987). Some cues are communicated to third parties or organizational outsiders (customers, members of competing organizations), who may be more receptive to them than other targets (e.g., Cox, 1999; Kydd, Ogilvie, & Slade, 1990). Cues may convey explicit dissatisfaction or disidentification with particular people, the work group, and organization, or they may focus on more indirect, mundane matters, for example, the quality of supplies the organization provides to employees; concern about the quality of the firm's products or services; distinctions between one's attitudes about particular issues and those of other members of the organization (Wilson, 1983). Depending on the nature of the cue, it may be directed at just one target or a variety of targets (e.g., coworkers, bosses, clients, family members, the community). Cues may be noticed by significant others (including peers and customers) and acted on, noticed by significant others but ignored or given low priority as action items, or never noticed by members of target audiences (e.g., Cox & Kramer, 1995; Withey & Cooper, 1989). In turn, cues may be noticed and acted on by some targets sooner (e.g., family members may recognize cues of burnout before work associates) and with greater intensity than other targets.

Who attends to and responds to an individual's disengagement cues may be extremely important (e.g., Feeley & Barnett, 1997). In many respects, it is likely that "weak ties" (Granovetter, 1973, 1995), or ties embedded in networks with "structural holes" (Burt, 1992), who recognize and respond to cues may have a greater impact on the potential leaver than will his or her strong communication ties (Podolny & Baron, 1997). By definition, it would seem likely that the source of disengagement cues already knows the attitudes and feelings of strong ties because of his or her frequent interaction with them. However, the beliefs of weak ties (especially those high in credibility) concerning the person's disengagement are probably less well understood. Hence, communication with weak ties, especially with those who are not relied on for organizational identity information/support or role expectations (e.g., Podolny & Baron, 1997), may be very useful for the potential leaver in reducing uncertainty related to disengagement.

As suggested above, the manner in which feedback targets respond to disengagement cues will vary considerably across targets. Targets may respond with feedback that varies in sign (positive, negative, equivocal), intensity, choice of media, consistency, explicitness, and so on. In addition, responses may be made in public or private. For example, if a manager recognizes cues that one of her employees feels taken for granted, expressing appreciation for the worker's efforts in a public meeting may be more meaningful to the employee and have greater impact on his attitudes than expression of these sentiments in a private conversation.

Responses to disengagement cues may be "scripted" or created in a conscious, mindful manner (mindful responses are especially likely in situations where individuals are try-

ing to motivate another person to exit; e.g., Cox, 1999). The extent to which targets respond to disengagement cues with "socially acceptable" scripts may be problematic. In particular, it is quite possible that socially acceptable responses to disengagement cues may often be counterproductive in situations involving undesired (from the perspective of the organization) voluntary turnover. For example, in such contexts targets of disengagement cues may frequently respond to the feedback seeker in very neutral, sometimes equivocal ways. In other words, targets are cautious in expressing their feelings because they do not want to stand in the way of another person's opportunity to advance his or her career, achieve a higher standard of living, and so on. For instance, the target may not specifically state an opinion (stay, leave) but reverts the issue back to the person seeking feedback (e.g., the respondent might say, "It's difficult to know what to do," "I'm glad you have choices," "Have you considered all the possibilities?"). Although these responses are socially acceptable, they also can be conceived of as disconfirming forms of response (Watzlawick, Beavin, & Jackson, 1967), in that they provide equivocal content and relational feedback. Given the generally negative consequences of disconfirmation on the maintenance of organizational relationships (e.g., Jablin, 1978), such forms of response to disengagement cues may decrease the feedback seeker's attraction to the organization. Equally important, by its very nature equivocal feedback from targets does not provide the potential leavers with specific enough information to help them reduce the uncertainty they may be experiencing with respect to voluntarily exiting the organization.

Although an equivocal response by a target to the voluntary disengagement cues of another organizational member may have a negative impact on the feedback seeker's attitudes, such a response may help the target cope with the cognitive imbalance he or she may experience as a consequence of the cues. An equivocal response does not commit the target to any position concerning the other's potential exit from the organization. In contrast, a statement of support for leaving the organization may cause the target to question his or her own employment in the organization (create dissonance; e.g., Steers & Mowday, 1981); in turn, a statement encouraging the other party to remain in the organization may cause the target to feel somewhat responsible if the other party remains in the job and experiences increased levels of discontent (or diminished employment opportunities in the future).

The disengagement cues/feedback-seeking efforts of potential job changers, regardless of how (or if) they are responded to by targets, serve other functions for targets. In particular, they may allow targets to make attributions about the disengagement behavior of their colleague (e.g., Judge & Martocchio, 1996). In many situations, it likely that work group members will share with one another the disengagement cues they have detected in their interactions with a peer (i.e., they will engage in collective sensemaking; e.g., Isabella, 1990). Subsequently, group members may develop similar attributions to explain the peer's actions and comments (for instance, attributions about why person X is going on job interviews). Depending on the circumstances, group members may also develop accounts to share with "outsiders." These collectively constructed preexit accounts or disclaimers (e.g., Bennett, 1990) may provide the group/organization with an opportunity to "test the waters" or rehearse accounts that allow the group/organization to save face in light of its losing a member (e.g., Goffman, 1971; Scheff, 1988).

Clearly, the nature of disengagement cues will vary in terms of their substance and enactment as the individual moves closer to (or away from) exiting the organization. For example, we might hypothesize that as one enters into advanced stages of disengagement cues will be constructed and performed in ways that validate the accounts and justifications that the leavers and stayers have formed to support organizational exit (e.g., Eden, 1984). Thus, for instance, in the context of voluntary turnover, cues may contain more negative affect toward those with whom one works, thereby eliciting more negative affect in the responses of targets toward the source of the cues.

Certainly, there are other ways in which targets of cues could respond in the sample situations described above; the point, however, is that as individuals move closer to exiting an organization, there will be distinctive changes in the conscious and unconscious exit cues that they emit and concomitant changes in the ways they process any feedback that is received from targets. The nature of how a potential leaver's exit cues change over time, how targets' responses vary over time, and how both the source and receivers of cues alter the manner in which they process disengagement messages over time warrants attention in our research.

Studies exploring issues such as those described above will not be easy since it is likely that the preannouncement stage of disengagement cannot be characterized in simple, linear terms (for either potential leavers or stayers) but involves numerous reverse-causality cycles (e.g., Jablin, 1987), which may or may not result in sufficient arousal levels (threshold points) to consciously or unconsciously push or pull those involved to advance in the exit process (e.g., Somers, 1999). In addition, if we accept the notion that all members of organizations are to some degree experiencing organizational disengagement (e.g., Kahn, 1990), identification of "normal" kinds and levels of disengagement cues is a necessary prerequisite for recognizing patterns of cue enactment that are suggestive of movement along the disengagement continuum. Along these lines, it seems essential that we explore the cue patterns of work groups (and in some cases even organizations) as well as individuals, since in accordance with social information processing theory, it may be the collective pattern of disengagement cues and responses that pushes and pulls individuals along the disengagement continuum (e.g., Abelson, 1993; Blau, 1995; Cox, 1999; Harrison & Shaffer, 1994; Markham & McKee, 1995).

Finally, it is important to stress that disengagement cues are not direct causes of organizational exit; rather, these cues are signals (often progressive in nature; e.g., Cox & Kramer, 1995; Rosse, 1988) that can help all parties involved better understand the status of their respective states of organizational disengagement (obviously, in some cases such knowledge may also facilitate interventions designed to deal with the underlying factors associated with disengagement; e.g., Chen et al., 1998).

Announcement of Exit and Actual Exit

The announcement and exit stage is quite distinct from the preannouncement period. In particular, the announcement and exit stage focuses (relatively speaking) on public versus private events (though it is important to recognize that private announcements may occur weeks before public announcements, which is often the case in job transfers); announcements are often accompanied by written statements (which can be subjected to rhetorical and textual analysis; e.g., Allen & Tompkins, 1996); to some degree there are always some groups (internal and/or external to the organization) who are "surprised" by the announcement; it is socially acceptable to "publicly" talk about those who are leaving and why they are leaving once their exit has been announced; and as those involved move toward actually exiting the organization their impending boundary passage is often associated with numerous rites and rituals, such as office parties, gift giving, and speeches (e.g., Kramer, 1989, 1993a).

Curiously, other than in the context of major job layoffs, few studies have examined the content of announcements of organizational exit. It seems clear, however, based on research concerned with job layoffs that formal layoff announcements are communicated to employees and other stakeholders in impersonal, written documents, which may include many details but minimal amounts of information justifying or accounting for the layoffs

(e.g., Brockner, 1994; Folger & Skarlicki, 1998; Jablin & Krone, 1994; Skarlicki et al., 1998). In addition, research in this area indicates that the announcement of a layoff (or merger; e.g., Cornett-DeVito & Friedman, 1995) is often anticlimactic, since rumors are usually widespread prior to formal announcements (e.g., Smelzter & Zener, 1992). To what degree are these characteristics typical of formal announcements of forms of voluntary exit? Formal announcements that individuals are quitting their jobs, retiring, or transferring to another site of the organization are, in most circumstances, variations of "bad news" messages (e.g., Tesser & Rosen, 1975). Such messages are most frequently constructed to convey their respective content in "polite," diplomatic ways (e.g., Lee, 1993); thus, these missives may not always be frank and explanatory. At the same time, however, it is important to recognize that distinctions in the cultures of organizations, the extent to which managers are perceived as trustworthy and credible, and norms associated with legitimate accounts may moderate this generalization (e.g., Bies, 1987; Brockner, Siegel, Daly, Tyler, & Martin, 1997; Rousseau & Tijoriwala, 1999). In addition, as stressed in the discussion of the preannouncement period, disengagement cues are inherent in all forms of organizational exit. Thus, for most (but not all) internal and external constituents the formal announcement that a particular individual or group of workers is leaving an organization is often anticlimactic.

Like the preannouncement stage, the communication activities associated with the announcement and exit phase function, in part, to reduce uncertainty for leavers and stayers. However, as argued above, the formal announcement itself does not necessarily function in that manner. Rather, uncertainty is reduced by interpersonal communication between those who are leaving and staying (e.g., Kramer, 1993b). In particular, these individuals will share job-related information with one another and generate accounts and justifications to explain the exit of the employee. In line with Nicholson and West's (1988) research on the motives individuals report for job changes, it is likely that exit accounts will fall into one of four broad categories: (1) exit will facilitate the person's achieving long-term goals (future orientation), (2) exit allows one to avoid a bad situation/problems at work, (3) exit is due to unique circumstances (e.g., organizational restructuring, spouses' job, unique opportunity), or (4) some mixture of the above kinds of accounts.

Stayers can accept the account offered by the leaver, incorporate the leaver's account into the preannouncement account that may have been generated by the group, totally reject the validity of the leaver's account, construct a new account that is different from but compatible with the account of the person who is leaving, or negotiate a new common account that allows both the leaver and stayers to maintain face (essentially a form of impression/image management; e.g., Schlenker & Weigold, 1992). Even in the situation where an employee quits his or her job in a spontaneous, emotional fit of anger, it is very rare for an individual to "burn the bridges" behind him or her; rather, the parties involved usually negotiate an acceptable common account that allows all those involved to maintain an adequate amount of face (e.g., Theus, 1995).

The manner in which stayers and leavers communicate with each other during the period between the announcement of the exit and actual exit will vary considerably depending on the form of exit. In particular, the amount of time available for interaction will be highly dependent on the kind of exit. In addition, interactions between the parties will be tempered by the group's experience with turnover and the frequency with which it has occurred (e.g., Abelson, 1993; Arrow & McGrath, 1995). Groups that are fairly "open" (periodic turnover) will likely have established scripts for interacting with the leaver during his or her tenure as a "lame duck"; on the other hand, fairly "closed" groups will not have established norms or scripts to guide their communication behavior and may experience more awkwardness in their interactions with the leaver (Ziller, 1965).

In the latter case, it is possible that uncertainty will not be measurably reduced for the leaver or stayers during this stage of the disengagement process; rather, it is possible uncertainty will remain the same or even increase since those involved may avoid each other because they don't have established scripts to guide their behavior. In such cases, postexit dissonance may be high for stayers and the leaver since they may not have said to each other "what they needed to say." In like fashion, even activities (e.g., parties) designed to celebrate and acknowledge the leaver's contributions to the organization and wish the person bon voyage may fail to perform those functions if the parties involved don't possess appropriate scripts to guide their communicative behavior. Maladroit enactment of exit ceremonies may be especially problematic for stayers, since these rites of passage often function more to help them bring closure to the leaver's departure than to facilitate the leaver's disengagement from the organization.

While stayers and leavers may initially adopt a common account for the leaver's exit, it is important to recognize that the ways in which the two parties communicate the accounts to others may be quite distinct. Moreover, each time someone presents the account it will be somewhat different from the last time he or she discussed the situation. The person will actively reinterpret what happened and incorporate these insights as revisions to the account the next time it is told (e.g., Boje, 1991; Brown, 1990). In addition, when leavers present their accounts for exiting the organization it will usually be in narrative form, in comparison to a list of reasons for their actions (Riessman, 1990). Leavers might tell stories that include information that extends back to why they joined the organization in the first place, the feelings of what the organization was like back then, events that made the workplace change, and "what could have been" if things had worked out differently (e.g., Beach & Japp, 1983; Folger, 1986). In brief, leavers usually face a rhetorical situation, which requires them to draw the listener into their world so that the moral of the tale (the need to leave) goes without saying (though it is likely that the teller will help the listener reach this point by providing commentary about specific aspects of the narrative as it unfolds; e.g., Boje, 1991). In contrast, those who remain in the organization are unlikely to account for a coworker's exit by presenting the reasons in the form of a narrative. Rather, they may rationalize the situation by delineating in listlike fashion the reasons someone is leaving (e.g., Browning, 1992; Sheehan, 1991, 1995). This rational approach allows stayers to limit their emotional involvement in the situation, tends to cap the level of dissonance they may experience about remaining in the organization, and reduces the likelihood that they will question the values that form the foundation of the organization's ongoing story/culture.

Finally, it is possible that in some organizations the interval of time between the formal announcement of an individual's departure from an organization and the actual exit provides those involved (especially stayers) with an opportunity to discuss numerous topics that are usually taboo to openly talk about (e.g., Roth, 1991), such as problems with the firm's products or services, management's lack of understanding of what is "really" going on in the organization, examples of bad decision making by the boss, fairness and equity in salaries, and so forth (e.g., Abelson, 1993). While these conversations may help stayers make sense of what is happening, they may also have a hidden implication: the notion that if things had been different, person X would not be leaving to go to work at another company, or person Y would not be taking early retirement or be seeking a job transfer. Even as leavers and stayers reminisce about the past, they cannot escape the question of whether the future will be as good as the past. In brief, the impending exit of a colleague provides members of his or her role set with an ephemeral window in time to publicly vent their frustrations about their jobs, work groups, and organization. At the same time, however, these discussions also represent op-

portunities for those who remain in the organization to consider ways to improve their work environments and promote their own careers (e.g., Dalton & Tudor, 1979; Ford & Ford, 1995). Thus, in many work environments lamenting and overt displays of frustration among stayers will be brief in nature, followed by increased levels of social support among those involved as they prepare to cope with the loss of one of their associates and the concomitant changes that will occur in the social dynamics and communication patterns of their group/organization.

Postexit

Once an employee has left the organization, his or her "physical" and "symbolic" absence is experienced by those who remain. Similarly, assuming the leaver enters into a new organizational milieu, he or she will experience the contrast of being a relatively isolated node in a world of established communication networks. In brief, both the person exiting the organization and those remaining usually experience uncertainty as a consequence of the changes in their work environments. Thus, the postexit phase is usually a fairly stressful one for all those involved. For stayers, stress can be reduced as they acquire information that allows them to assess the actual absence of the leaver on the group/organization, and if necessary, locate a replacement for the leaver; for the leaver, stress can be reduced by clarifying/seeking information from the new colleagues about their expectations of the newcomer's role in the group/organization (e.g., Miller & Jablin, 1991). In addition, social support from significant others will also play a role in reducing stress for the leaver and stayers (e.g., Lim, 1996). At the same time, however, it is important to recognize that different kinds of social support may be required from different sources and the failure of the "right" sources to provide appropriate kinds of support for the target will yield problematic results. For example, a spouse who provides skill-based social support (endorsement of an individual's skills/abilities to perform a task) to his or her partner may have little impact on the level of skill-related stress experienced by the other party; rather, skills-based social support from a worker's boss is more likely to reduce a worker's concerns about job-related self-efficacy (Brett, 1984).

Once the leaver has exited the organization, his or her physical absence will serve as a stimuli for stayers to again converse about the causes of the person's departure from the organization (collective sensemaking), as well as to reminisce about their former coworker (e.g., Moreland & Levine, 1982). The period of remembrance may focus on retrospective evaluation of the leaver to arrive at a consensus about what the leaver contributed to the group while he or she was a member (Moreland & Levine, 1982). Depending on the nature of the disengagement, stayers may experience "counterfactual thinking" (Roese & Olson, 1995), betrayal (e.g., Moreland & McMinn, 1999; Morrison & Robinson, 1997), envy (e.g., Bedeian, 1995; Vecchio, 1995), guilt, insecurity, and other emotions as they engage in remembrance. The leaver is also likely to reminisce about and evaluate his former colleagues and the old work setting. For the leaver, reminiscence (and concomitant affective cognitive responses such as regret; e.g., Lawson & Angle, 1998) may be intrapersonal in nature or it may involve communication with others who are familiar with the old setting (e.g., others who once worked in the organization or one's spouse).

In situations where the leaver will be replaced in the old work group, a considerable amount of the stayers' time will be focused on finding a replacement for the leaver. In other words, stayers will center their energy on the recruitment and selection of a new worker (e.g., assessing resumes, interviewing prospective employees). During the process of selecting an individual to replace the leaver, it is likely that stayers will discover they possess many unconscious expectations of the leaver's role (e.g., questions asked by job applicants in the interviewing process will make incum-

bents aware of taken-for-granted assumptions about the role). In addition, in some cases stayers will be faced with the difficult rhetorical problem of explaining to potential recruits the reasons the leaver exited the organization. Along these lines, it would be interesting to assess the degree to which internal accounts for the leaver's exit are similar to the ones recruiters offer to job applicants. Once a replacement is hired, stayers will engage in information-giving (Hudson & Jablin, 1992) and information-seeking behaviors to make sense of the newcomer (figure out the newcomer's "story," reduce uncertainty). At the same time, stayers will adapt to the loss of a node in their communication networks by developing linkages with the newcomer (though these may not be the same as existed with the leaver).

The leaver will also be entering into some form of new role upon exit from former employer. As Jablin and Krone (1994) suggest, the realism of communication expectations "that individuals hold prior to their disengagement from work/organizational relationships appears to affect their ability to adapt successfully to the environments they are entering" (p. 656). The more realistic the expectations formed during anticipatory socialization, the easier the role adjustment upon entry into the new setting. At the same time, however, the leaver will experience some form of "encounter" upon organizational entry, during which time he or she must learn about the requirements of the new role (e.g., Jablin & Kramer, 1998). In addition, it is important to stress that significant variations in some types of newcomers' communication behavior may exist depending on the form of disengagement/entry considered (for instance, the reasons retirees offer to members of their new role set to account for leaving their organizations [e.g., Hanisch, 1994] may be quite distinct from those generated by individuals who voluntarily leave their old employers to take a job in a different organization). Communication may continue between the leaver and stayers at the old organization after the individual's departure from the firm. It is likely that initial communication will focus on work-related matters, but over time interactions will likely become focused only on personal issues and the maintenance of personal friendships/links (e.g., Kramer, 1989). In most situations, communication contact will greatly diminish over a period of time, as those involved become focused on maintaining the new organizational relationships they have formed. Thus, to some extent, many communication relationships that once were characterized as strong ties become weak ones. Also, different forms of disengagement/entry have distinctive effects on the extraorganizational communication networks of both stayers and leavers, as well as their families. For instance, disengagement that also involves geographic relocation (e.g., international transfers; see Arthur & Bennett, 1995; Black, Gregersen, & Mendenhall, 1992; Caligiuri, Hyland, Joshi, & Bross, 1998) will have a greater impact on stayers, leavers, and their respective families than disengagements in which individuals remain in the same community.

Finally, it is likely that a significant turning point signaling the consummation of the postexit phase for the leaver and stayers is when individuals internal and external to their respective organizations no longer show surprise (e.g., "I didn't know you [he/she] left X organization!") as to the leaver's change in employment status. In other words, when network links (especially weak ties) cease asking why the leaver no longer works at his or her former employer, ensuing conversations will no longer be framed by the past, but by the present and future. Thus, for example, stayers would no longer be offering accounts for why the leaver exited the organization (focus on the past), but would converse about the new person who was hired, future opportunities, and the like. In turn, leavers would no longer be telling the story of their departure from their former employer, but would talk about new colleagues, challenges associated with the new job, how they like the boss, and similar present- and future-oriented topics. In

sum, it is quite likely that the leaver and stayers have some control over the duration of the postexit period; however, the persistence of this stage is also partially determined by the speed with which "the word" of the leaver's exit from the organization is diffused through relevant communication networks and the frequency with which the leaver and stayers have contact with nodes in these networks.

Conclusion

In the preceding pages, I have attempted to build an integrative perspective about the roles and functions of communication in the voluntary organizational disengagement/exit process. As with most initial efforts I have likely failed to recognize or even excluded certain communication phenomena that should have been included here. At the same time, I may have included certain communication activities and processes that future research will show are not relevant across disengagement contexts. Despite these limitations, I hope the perspective presented here serves to stimulate future research in this area. As noted in the opening of this section, the corpus of existing research exploring communication and voluntary organizational disengagement remains rudimentary in nature. In conclusion, it is important to recognize that regardless of the form of organizational disengagement, the process of exiting an organization presents numerous communication dilemmas for all those involved. For both leavers and stayers as they progress through the process, they face "teller's problems" (Riessman, 1990), as well as listener's/receiver's problems. How they choose to manage (not necessarily solve) these problems will likely influence the stress they experience in adapting to the many changes that often are associated with the disengagement process. In fact, effective management of the communication dynamics of the process can just as easily result in "eustress" (positive stress that enriches us; see Selye, 1956) as it does problematic forms of stress that are often associated with organizational disengagement. Organizational disengagement is an opportunity for both stayers and leavers to reconstruct the "stories" they have constructed to explain the dynamics of their organizations, as well as numerous dimensions of their careers and identities.

CONCLUDING STATEMENT

As noted in the opening of this chapter, a major goal of the preceding review and analysis was to discern our progress since 1987 in developing our understanding of communication processes and phenomena associated with organizational entry, assimilation, and disengagement/exit. In the process of exploring this issue, a number of areas have been identified where we have achieved significant gains in understanding; at the same time, other areas have been identified where progress in building knowledge has been more limited or where alternative research strategies for generating knowledge may be useful. New directions for communication research have also been suggested with respect to each of the major foci of this chapter: anticipatory vocational and organizational socialization, organizational entry and assimilation, and voluntary organizational disengagement/exit.

It is hoped that these suggestions will be helpful in guiding future studies in these areas, and thereby further our understanding of communication processes and behaviors associated with organizational entry, assimilation, and disengagement/exit. As I concluded in 1987, the perspective presented in this chapter reiterates the notion that one of the keys to understanding human communication in organizations is to recognize its developmental nature.

NOTES

1. A useful discussion of the underlying foundations, models, and terminology used in communica-

tion-related organizational assimilation research was developed in a series of articles published in late 1999, subsequent to the preparation of this chapter. These essays explore a variety of issues central to the study of organizational assimilation, and I urge those interested in this area to read the original article by Kramer and Miller (1999) and the responses that it generated.

2. Some of the ideas presented here were originally outlined in an earlier paper by Jablin, Grady, and Parker (1994).

REFERENCES

Abelson, M. A. (1993). Turnover cultures. In G. R. Ferris (Ed.), *Research in personnel and human resources management* (Vol. 11, pp. 339-376). Greenwich, CT: JAI.

Adkins, C. L., Ravlin, E. C., & Meglino, B. M. (1996). Value congruence between co-workers and its relationship to work outcomes. *Group & Organization Management, 21,* 439-460.

Adkins, C. L., Russell, C. J., & Werbel, J. D. (1994). Judgments of fit in the selection process: The role of work value congruence. *Personnel Psychology, 47,* 605-623.

Ahlander, N. R., & Bahr, K. S. (1995). Beyond drudgery, power and equity: Toward an expanded discourse on the moral dimensions of housework in families. *Journal of Marriage and the Family, 57,* 54-68.

Alderfer, C. P., & McCord, C. G. (1970). Personal and situational factors in the recruitment interview. *Journal of Applied Psychology, 54,* 377-385.

Allen, B. J. (1996). Feminist standpoint theory: A black woman's (re)view of organizational socialization. *Communication Studies, 47,* 257-271.

Allen, B. J., & Tompkins, P. K. (1996). Vocabularies of motives in a crisis of academic leadership. *Southern Communication Journal, 61,* 321-322.

Allen, M. W. (1992). Communication and organizational commitment: Perceived organizational support as a mediating factor. *Communication Quarterly, 40,* 357-367.

Allen, M. W. (1995). How employees see the boss: Communication concepts related to perceived organizational support. *Western Journal of Communication, 59,* 326-346.

Allen, M. W. (1996). The relationship between communication, affect, job alternatives, and voluntary turnover intentions. *Southern Communication Journal, 61,* 198-209.

Allen, N. J., & Meyer, J. P. (1990). Organizational socialization tactics: A longitudinal analysis of links to newcomers' commitment and role orientation. *Academy of Management Journal, 33,* 847-858.

Allen, T. D., McManus, S. E., & Russell, J. E. A. (1999). Newcomer socialization and stress: Formal peer relationships as a source of support. *Journal of Vocational Behavior, 54,* 453-470.

Allen, T. D., Russell, J. E. A., & Maetzke, S. B. (1997). Formal peer mentoring: Factors related to protégés' satisfaction and willingness to mentor others. *Group & Organization Management, 22,* 488-507.

Altman, I., & Taylor, D. (1973). *Social penetration: The development of interpersonal relationships.* New York: Rinehart & Winston.

Anderson, N., & Shackleton, V. (1990). Decision making in the graduate selection interview: A field study. *Journal of Occupational Psychology, 63,* 63-76.

Anson, E. M. (1988). *How to prepare and write your employee handbook* (2nd ed.). New York: AMACOM.

Arnold, J., & Nicholson, N. (1991). Construing of self and others and work in the early years of corporate careers. *Journal of Organizational Behavior, 12,* 621-639.

Arrow, H., & McGrath, J. E. (1995). Membership dynamics in groups at work: A theoretical framework. In L. L. Cummings & B. M. Staw (Eds.), *Research in organizational behavior* (Vol. 17, pp. 373-411). Greenwich, CT: JAI.

Arthur, D. (1991). *Recruiting, interviewing and orienting new employees* (2nd ed.). New York: American Management Association.

Arthur, W., Jr., & Bennett, W., Jr. (1995). The international assignee: The relative importance of factors perceived to contribute to success. *Personnel Psychology, 48,* 99-114.

Aryee, S., Chay, Y. W., & Chew, J. (1996). The motivation to mentor among managerial employees. *Group & Organization Management, 21,* 261-277.

Ashford, S. J. (1986). The role of feedback seeking in individual adaptation: A resource perspective. *Academy of Management Journal, 29,* 465-487.

Ashford, S. J., & Black, J. S. (1992). *Self-socialization: Individual tactics to facilitate entry.* Paper presented at the annual meeting of the Academy of Management, Las Vegas, NV.

Ashford, S. J., & Black, J. S. (1996). Proactivity during organizational entry: The role of desire for control. *Journal of Applied Psychology, 81,* 199-214.

Ashford, S. J., & Cummings, L. L. (1985). Proactive feedback seeking: The instrumental use of the information environment. *Journal of Occupational Psychology, 58,* 67-79.

Ashford, S. J., & Taylor, M. S. (1990). Adaptations to work transitions: An integrative approach. In G. R. Ferris & K. M. Rowland (Eds.), *Research in personnel and human resources management* (Vol. 8, pp. 1-39). Greenwich, CT: JAI.

Ashforth, B. E., & Humphrey. (1995). Labeling processes in the organization: Constructing the individual. In L. L. Cummings & B. M. Staw (Eds.), *Re-search in organizational behavior* (Vol. 17, pp. 413-461). Greenwich, CT: JAI Press.

Ashforth, B. E., & Humphrey. (1997). The ubiquity and potency of labeling in organizations. *Organizational Science, 8,* 43-58.

Ashforth, B. E., & Saks, A. M. (1996). Socialization tactics: Longitudinal effects of newcomer adjustment. *Academy of Management Journal, 39,* 149-178.

Ashforth, B. E., Saks, A. M., & Lee, R. T. (1998). Socialization and newcomer adjustment: The role of organizational context. *Human Relations, 51,* 897-926.

Asmussen, L., & Larson, R. (1991). The quality of family time among young adolescents in single-parent and married-parent families. *Journal of Marriage and the Family, 53,* 1021-1030.

Atkin, D. J., Moorman, J., & Lin, C. A. (1991). Ready for prime time: Network series devoted to working women in the 1980s. *Sex Roles, 25,* 677-685.

Auster, C. J. (1985). Manuals for socialization: Examples from Girl Scout handbooks 1913-1984. *Qualitative Sociology, 8,* 359-367.

Avery, C. M., & Jablin, F. M. (1988). Retirement preparation programs and organizational communication. *Communication Education, 37,* 68-80.

Axtmann, L., & Jablin, F. M. (1986, May). *Distributional and sequential interaction structure in the employment screening interview.* Paper presented at the annual meeting of the International Communication Association, Chicago.

Ayres, J., Ayres, D. M., & Sharp, D. (1993). A progress report on the development of an instrument to measure communication apprehension in employment interviews. *Communication Research Reports, 10,* 87-94.

Ayres, J., & Crosby, S. (1995). Two studies concerning the predictive validity of the Personal Report of Communication Apprehension in Employment Interviews. *Communication Research Reports, 12,* 145-151.

Ayres, J., Keereetaweep, T., Chen, P., & Edwards, P. A. (1998). Communication apprehension and employment interviews. *Communication Education, 47,* 1-17.

Babbitt, L. V., & Jablin, F. M. (1985). Characteristics of applicants' questions and employment screening interview outcomes. *Human Communication Research, 11,* 507-535.

Bahniuk, M. H., Dobos, J., & Hill, S. E. K. (1990). The impact of mentoring, collegial support, and information adequacy on career success: A replication. *Journal of Social Behavior and Personality, 5,* 431-451. (Special issue, J. W. Neuliep, Ed., *Handbook of replication research in the behavioral and social sciences*)

Bahniuk, M. H., Hill, S. E. K., & Darius, H. J. (1996). The relationship of power-gaining communication strategies to career success. *Western Journal of Communication, 60,* 358-378.

Baker, H. E., & Feldman, D. C. (1990). Strategies of organizational socialization and their impact on newcomer adjustment. *Journal of Managerial Issues, 2,* 198-212.

Baker, H. E., & Feldman, D. C. (1991). Linking organizational socialization tactics with corporate human resource management strategies. *Human Resource Management Review, 1,* 193-202.

Barber, A. E., Hollenbeck, J. R., Tower, S. L., & Phillips, J. (1994). The effects of interview focus on recruitment effectiveness: A field experiment. *Journal of Applied Psychology, 79,* 886-896.

Barber, A. E., & Roehling, M. V. (1993). Job postings and the decision to interview: A verbal protocol analysis. *Journal of Applied Psychology, 78,* 845-856.

Barber, B. L., & Eccles, J. S. (1992). Long-term influence of divorce and single parenting on adolescent family- and work-related values, behaviors, and aspiration. *Psychological Bulletin, 111,* 108-126.

Barling, J., Dupre, K. E., & Hepburn, C. G. (1998). Effects of parents' job insecurity on children's work beliefs and attitudes. *Journal of Applied Psychology, 83,* 112-118.

Barling, J., Rogers, K., & Kelloway, E. K. (1995). Some effects of teenagers' part-time employment: The quantity and quality of work make the difference. *Journal of Organizational Behavior, 16,* 143-154.

Barocas, V. S. (1993). *Benefit communications: Enhancing the employer's investment.* New York: Conference Board.

Baron, R. A. (1989). Impression management by applicants during employment interviews: The "too much of a good thing" effect. In R. W. Eder & G. R. Ferris (Eds.), *The employment interview: Theory, research and practice* (pp. 204-215). Newbury Park, CA: Sage.

Barrios-Choplin, J. R. (1994). *Newcomers' surprise: An extension and exploratory study of Louis' conceptualization.* Unpublished doctoral dissertation, University of Texas at Austin.

Barry, B., & Bateman, T. S. (1992). Perceptions of influence in managerial dyads: The role of hierarchy, media, and tactics. *Human Relations, 45,* 555-574.

Bastien, D. T. (1987). Common patterns of behavior and communication in corporate mergers and acquisitions. *Human Resource Management, 26,* 17-23.

Bastien, D. T. (1992). Change in organizational culture: The use of linguistic methods in a corporate acquisition. *Management Communication Quarterly, 5,* 403-442.

Bauer, T. N., & Green, S. G. (1994). Effect of newcomer involvement in work-related activities: A longitudinal study of socialization. *Journal of Applied Psychology, 79,* 211-223.

Bauer, T. N., & Green, S. G. (1996). Development of leader-member exchange: A longitudinal test. *Academy of Management Journal, 39,* 1538-1567.

Bauer, T. N., Morrison, E. W., & Callister, R. R. (1998). Organizational socialization: A review and directions for future research. In G. R. Ferris & K. M. Rowland (Eds.), *Research in personnel and human resources management* (Vol. 16, pp. 149-214). Greenwich, CT: JAI.

Beach, W. A., & Japp, P. (1983). Storifying as time-traveling: The knowledgeable use of temporally structured discourse. In R. Bostrom (Ed.), *Communication yearbook 7* (pp. 867-888). Beverly Hills, CA: Sage.

Bedeian, A. G. (1995). Workplace envy. *Organizational Dynamics, 23*(4), 49-56.

Beehr, T. A., & Nelson, N. L. (1995). Descriptions of job characteristics and retirement activities during the transition to retirement. *Journal of Organizational Behavior, 16,* 681-690.

Bellinger, D. C., & Gleason, J. B. (1982). Sex differences in parental directives to young children. *Sex Roles, 8,* 1123-1139.

Belt, J. A., & Paolillo, J. G. (1982). The influence of corporate image and specificity of candidate qualifications on response to recruitment advertisements. *Journal of Management, 8,* 105-112.

Bennett, M. (1990). Children's understanding of the mitigating function of disclaimers. *Journal of Social Psychology, 130,* 29-47.

Ben-Yoav, O., & Hartman, K. (1988). Supervisors' competence and learning of work values and behaviors during organizational entry. *Journal of Social Behavior and Personality, 13,* 23-36.

Berg, L. V., & Trujillo, N. (1989). *Organizational life on television.* Norwood, NJ: Ablex.

Berger, C. R. (1979). Beyond initial understandings: Uncertainty, understanding, and the development of interpersonal relationships. In H. Giles & R. N. St. Clair (Eds.), *Language and social psychology* (pp. 122-144). Oxford, UK: Basil Blackwell.

Berger, C. R., & Bradac, J. J. (1982). *Language and social knowledge: Uncertainty in interpersonal relations.* London: Edward Arnold.

Berger, S., & Huchendorf, K. (1989, December). Ongoing orientation at Metropolitan Life. *Personnel Journal,* pp. 28, 30, 32, 34-35.

Bian, Y. (1997). Bringing strong ties back in: Indirect ties, network bridges, and job searches in China. *American Sociological Review, 62,* 366-385.

Bies, R. B. (1987). The predicament of injustice: The management of moral outrage. In L. L. Cummings & B. M. Staw (Eds.), *Research in organizational behavior* (Vol. 9, pp. 289-319). Greenwich, CT: JAI.

Bigelow, B. J., Tesson, G., & Lewko, J. H. (1996). *Learning the rules: The anatomy of children's relationships.* New York: Guilford.

Binning, J. F., Goldstein, M. A., Garcia, M. F., & Scattaregia, J. H. (1988). Effects of preinterview impressions on questioning strategies in same- and opposite-sex employment interviews. *Journal of Applied Psychology, 73,* 30-37.

Birnbaum, D., & Somers, M. J. (1991). Prevocational experience and post-entry behavior: Occupational influences on job attitudes and turnover. *Journal of Applied Social Psychology, 21,* 508-523.

Black, J. S. (1992). Socializing American expatriate managers overseas. *Group & Organization Management, 17,* 171-192.

Black, J. S., & Ashford, S. J. (1995). Fitting in or making jobs fit: Factors affecting mode of adjustment for new hires. *Human Relations, 48,* 421-437.

Black, J. S., Gregersen, H. B., & Mendenhall, M. E. (1992). *Global assignments: Successfully expatriating and repatriating international managers.* San Francisco: Jossey-Bass.

Blau, G. (1988). An investigation of the apprenticeship organizational socialization strategy. *Journal of Vocational Behavior, 32,* 176-195.

Blau, G. (1995). Influence of group lateness on individual lateness: A cross-level examination. *Academy of Management Journal, 38,* 1483-1496.

Blau, G. J. (1990). Exploring the mediating mechanisms affecting the relationship of recruitment source to employee performance. *Journal of Vocational Behavior, 37,* 303-320.

Blau, P. (1964). *Exchange and power in social life.* New York: John Wiley.

Blum-Kulka, S. (1997). *Dinner talk: Cultural patterns of sociability and socialization in family discourse.* Mahwah, NJ: Lawrence Erlbaum.

Blyth, D. A., Hill, J. P., & Thiel, K. S. (1982). Early adolescents' significant others: Grade and gender differences in perceived relationships with familial and nonfamilial adults and young people. *Journal of Youth and Adolescence, 11,* 425-450.

Boje, D. M. (1991). The storytelling organization: A study of story performance in an office-supply firm. *Administrative Science Quarterly, 36,* 106-126.

Bowen, D. E., Ledford, G. E., & Nathan, B. R. (1991). Hiring for the organization, not the job. *Academy of Management Executive, 5,* 35-51.

Bowes, J. M., & Goodnow, J. J. (1996). Work for home, school, or labor force: The nature and sources of changes in understanding. *Psychological Bulletin, 119,* 300-321.

Bowles, S., & Gintis, H. (1976). *Schooling in capitalist America: Educational reforms and the contradictions of economic life.* New York: Basic Books.

Boyd, N. G., & Taylor, R. R. (1998). A developmental approach to the examination of friendship in leader-follower relationships. *Leadership Quarterly, 9,* 1-25.

Bozeman, D. P., & Kacmar, K. M. (1997). A cybernetic model of impression management processes in organizations. *Organizational Behavior and Human Decision Processes, 69,* 9-30.

Breaugh, J. A. (1981). Relationship between recruiting sources and employee performance, absenteeism, and work attitudes. *Academy of Management Journal, 24,* 142-147.

Breaugh, J. A. (1983). Realistic job previews: A critical appraisal and future research directions. *Academy of Management Review, 8,* 612-619.

Breaugh, J. A., & Mann, R. B. (1984). Recruiting source effects: A test of two alternative explanations. *Journal of Occupational Psychology, 57,* 261-267.

Brett, J. M. (1984). Job transitions and personal development. In K. M. Rowland & G. R. Ferris (Eds.), *Research in personnel and human resources management* (Vol. 2, pp. 155-185). Greenwich, CT: JAI.

Bretz, R. D., Rynes, S. L., & Gerhart, B. (1993). Recruiter perceptions of applicant fit: Implications for individual career preparation and job search behavior. *Journal of Vocational Behavior, 43,* 310-327.

Bridge, K., & Baxter, L. A. (1992). Blended relationships: Friends as work associates. *Western Journal of Communication, 56,* 200-225.

Briody, E. K. (1988). Fitting in: Newcomer adaptation in a corporate research setting. *Central Issues in Anthropology, 7*(2), 19-38.

Briody, E. K., & Chrisman, J. B. (1991). Cultural adaptation on overseas assignments. *Human Organization, 50,* 264-282.

Brockner, J. (1988). The effect of work layoffs on survivors. In B. M. Staw & L. L. Cummings (Eds.), *Research in organizational behavior* (Vol. 10, pp. 213-255). Greenwich, CT: JAI.

Brockner, J. (1994). Perceived fairness and survivors' reactions to layoffs, or how downsizing organizations can do well by doing good. *Social Justice Research, 7,* 345-371.

Brockner, J., Siegel, P. A., Daly, J. P., Tyler, T., & Martin, C. (1987). When trust matters: The moderating effect of outcome favorability. *Administrative Science Quarterly, 42,* 558-583.

Bromley, D. B. (1993). *Reputation, image and impression management.* Chichester, UK: Wiley.

Bronfenbrenner, U. (1979). *The ecology of human development: Experiments by nature and design.* Cambridge, MA: Harvard University Press.

Bronfenbrenner, U. (1986). Ecology of the family as a context for human development: Research perspectives. *Developmental Psychology, 22,* 723-742.

Brown, D., Brooks, L., & Associates. (1996). *Career choice and development* (3rd ed.). San Francisco: Jossey-Bass.

Brown, J. D. (1991). Preprofessional socialization and identity transformation: The case of the professional ex-. *Journal of Contemporary Ethnography, 20,* 157-178.

Brown, M. H. (1985). That reminds me of a story: Speech action in organizational socialization. *Western Journal of Speech Communication, 49,* 27-42.

Brown, M. H. (1990). Defining stories in organizations: Characteristics and functions. In J. A. Anderson (Ed.), *Communication yearbook 13* (pp. 162-190). Newbury Park, CA: Sage.

Browning, L. D. (1992). Lists and stories as organizational communication. *Communication Theory, 2,* 281-302.

Bucher, R., & Stelling, J. G. (1977). *Becoming professional.* Beverly Hills, CA: Sage.

Buckley, M. R., Fedor, D. B., Veres, J. G., Wiese, D. S., & Carraher, S. M. (1998). Investigating newcomer expectations and job-related outcomes. *Journal of Applied Psychology, 83,* 452-461.

Bullis, C. (1993). Organizational socialization research: Enabling, constraining, and shifting perspectives. *Communication Monographs, 60,* 10-17.

Bullis, C. (1999). Mad or bad: A response to Kramer and Miller. *Communication Monographs, 66,* 368-373.

Bullis, C., & Bach, B. W. (1989). Are mentor relationships helping organizations? An exploration of developing mentee-mentor-organizational identifications using turning point analysis. *Communication Quarterly, 37,* 199-213.

Bullis, C., & Clark, C. L. (1993, November). *A longitudinal study of employee resocialization.* Paper presented at the annual meeting of the Speech Communication Association, Miami Beach, FL.

Burke, R. J., McKeen, C. A., & McKenna, C. S. (1990). Sex differences and cross-sex effects on mentoring: Some preliminary data. *Psychological Reports, 67,* 1011-1023,

Burke, R. J., McKenna, C. S., & McKeen, C. A. (1991). How do mentorships differ from typical supervisory relationships? *Psychological Reports, 68,* 459-466.

Burleson, B. R., Delia, J. G., & Applegate, J. L. (1995). The socialization of person-centered communication. In M. A. Fitzpatrick & A. L. Vangelisti (Eds.), *Explaining family interactions* (pp. 34-76). Thousand Oaks, CA: Sage.

Burnett, J. R., & Motowidlo, S. J. (1998). Relations between different sources of information in the structured selection interview. *Personnel Psychology, 51,* 963-983.

Burt, R. S. (1992). *Structural holes: The social structure of competition.* Cambridge, MA: Harvard University Press.

Byrd, M. L. V. (1979). *The effects of vocal activity and race of applicant on the job selection interview decision.* Unpublished doctoral dissertation, University of Missouri, Columbia.

Cable, D. M., & Judge, T. A. (1996). Person-organization fit, job choice decisions, and organizational entry. *Organizational Behavior and Human Decision Processes, 67,* 294-311.

Cable, D. M., & Judge, T. A. (1997). Interviewers' perceptions of person-organization fit and organizational selection decisions. *Journal of Applied Psychology, 82,* 546-561.

Cahill, S. E. (1999). Emotional capital and professional socialization: The case of mortuary science students (and me). *Social Psychology Quarterly, 62,* 101-116.

Caldwell, D., & O'Reilly, C. (1982). Responses to failure: The effects of choice and responsibility on impression management. *Academy of Management Journal, 25,* 121-136.

Caldwell, D. F., & Spivey, W. A. (1983). The relationship between recruiting source and employee success: An analysis by race. *Personnel Psychology, 36,* 67-72.

Caligiuri, P. M., Hyland, M. M., Joshi, A., & Bross, A. S. (1998). Testing a theoretical model for examining the relationship between family adjustment and expatriates' work adjustment. *Journal of Applied Psychology, 83,* 598-614.

Campion, M. A., Cheraskin, L., & Stevens, M. J. (1994). Career-related antecedents and outcomes of job rotation. *Academy of Management Journal, 37,* 1518-1542.

Campion, M. A., Palmer, D. K., & Campion, J. E. (1997). A review of structure in the selection interview. *Personnel Psychology, 50,* 655-702.

Campion, M. A., Pursell, E. D., & Brown, B. K. (1988). Structured interviewing: Raising the psychometric properties of the employment interview. *Personnel Psychology, 41,* 25-42.

Cawyer, C. S., & Friedrich, G. W. (1998). Organizational socialization: Processes for new communication faculty. *Communication Education, 47,* 234-245.

Chao, G. T., Walz, P. M., & Gardner, P. D. (1992). Formal and informal mentorships: A comparison on mentoring functions and contrast with nonmentored counterparts. *Personnel Psychology, 45,* 619-636.

Chao, G. T., O'Leary-Kelly, A. M., Wolf, S., Klein, H. J., & Gardner, P. D. (1994). Organizational socialization: Its content and consequences. *Journal of Applied Psychology, 79,* 730-743.

Charner, I., & Fraser, B. S. (1988). *Youth and work: What we know, what we don't know, what we need to know.* Washington, DC: W. T. Grant Foundation Commission on Youth and America's Future.

Chatman, J. (1991). Matching people and organizations: Selection and socialization in public accounting firms. *Administrative Science Quarterly, 36,* 459-484.

Cheatham, T. R., & McLaughlin, M. L. (1976). A comparison of co-participant perceptions of self and others in placement center interviews. *Communication Quarterly, 24,* 9-13.

Chen, X.-P., Hui, C., & Sego, D. J. (1998). The role of organizational citizenship behavior in turnover: Conceptualization and preliminary tests of key hypotheses. *Journal of Applied Psychology, 83,* 922-931.

Chesebro, J. W. (1991). Communication, values, and popular television series—A seventeen-year assessment. *Communication Quarterly, 39,* 197-225.

Christenson, P. G., & Roberts, D. F. (1983). The role of television in the formation of children's social attitudes. In M. J. A. Howe (Ed.), *Learning from television: Psychological and educational research* (pp. 79-99). New York: Academic Press.

Clair, R. P. (1996). The political nature of the colloquialism, "a real job": Implications for organizational socialization. *Communication Monographs, 63,* 249-267.

Clair, R. P. (1999). A review of Kramer and Miller's manuscript. *Communication Monographs, 66,* 374-381.

Cohen, P. (1991, May 9-10). Confessions of a handbook writer. *Personnel, 68*(5), 9.

Colarelli, S. M. (1984). Methods of communication and mediating processes in realistic job previews. *Journal of Applied Psychology, 69,* 633-642.

Colella, A. (1989). *A new role for newcomer pre-entry expectations during organizational entry: Expectation effects on job perceptions.* Unpublished doctoral dissertation, Ohio State University, Columbus.

Comer, D. R. (1991). Organizational newcomers' acquisition of information from peers. *Management Communication Quarterly, 5,* 64-89.

Comer, D. R. (1992). Factors that make peers effective information agents for organizational newcomers. *Journal of Management Systems, 4,* 13-27.

Conard, M. A., & Ashforth, S. D. (1986). *Recruiting source effectiveness: A meta-analysis and reexamination of two rival hypotheses.* Paper presented at the first annual meeting of the Society of Industrial/Organizational Psychology, Chicago.

Connerley, M. L. (1997). The influence of training on perceptions of recruiters' interpersonal skills and effectiveness. *Journal of Occupational and Organizational Psychology, 70,* 259-272.

Connerley, M. L., & Rynes, S. L. (1997). The influence of recruiter characteristics and organizational recruitment support on perceived recruiter effectiveness: Views from applicants and recruiters. *Human Relations, 50,* 1563-1586.

Conrad, C. (1994). *Strategic organizational communication: Toward the twenty-first century* (3rd ed.). Fort Worth, TX: Harcourt Brace.

Conrad, C., & Witte, K. (1994). Is emotional expression repression oppression? Myths of organizational affective regulation. In S. A. Deetz (Ed.), *Communication yearbook 17* (pp. 417-428). Thousand Oaks, CA: Sage.

Cook, M. F. (1992). *The AMA handbook for employee recruitment and retention.* New York: American Management Association.

Cooper, W. H., Graham, W. J., & Dyke, L. S. (1993). Tournament players. In G. Ferris (Ed.), *Research in personnel and human resources management* (Vol. 11, pp. 83-132). Greenwich, CT: JAI.

Cordes, C., Brown, J., & Olson, D. E. (1991). The role of social information processing in the career selection process. *Akron Business and Economic Review, 22,* 7-19.

Cornett-DeVito, M. M., & Friedman, P. G. (1995). Communication processes and merger success: An exploratory study of four financial institution mergers. *Management Communication Quarterly, 9,* 46-77.

Corsaro, W. A. (1990). The underlife of the nursery school: Young children's social representations of adult rules. In G. Duveen & B. Lloyd (Eds.), *Social representations and the development of knowledge* (pp. 11-26). Cambridge, UK: Cambridge University Press.

Cox, S. A. (1998, April). *A social exchange model of employee satisfaction, voice and exit.* Paper presented at the annual convention of the Southern Communication Association, San Antonio, TX.

Cox, S. A. (1999). Group communication and employee turnover: How coworkers encourage peers to voluntarily exit. *Southern Communication Journal, 64,* 181-192.

Cox, S. A., & Kramer, M. W. (1995). Communication during employee dismissals: Social exchange principles and group influences on employee. *Management Communication Quarterly, 9,* 156-190.

Crites, J. O. (1969). *Vocational psychology.* New York: McGraw-Hill.

Crossen, C. (1985, March 19). Kids of top executives are crazy about dad–especially his money. *Wall Street Journal,* Sec. 2, p. 33.

Crouter, A. C. (1984). Spillover from family to work: The neglected side of the work-family interface. *Human Relations, 37,* 425-442.

Cude, R. L., & Jablin, F. M. (1992). Retiring from work: The paradoxical impact of organizational commitment. *Journal of Managerial Issues, 4,* 31-45.

Cumming, E., & Henry, W. E. (1961). *Growing old: The process of disengagement.* New York: Basic Books.

Csikszentmihalyi, M., & Larson, R. (1984). *Being adolescent: Conflict and growth in the teenage years.* New York: Basic Books.

Dalton, D. R., & Tudor, W. D. (1979). Turnover turned over: An expanded and positive perspective. *Academy of Management Review, 4,* 225-235.

Danielson, M. A. (1995). *A taxonomy of newcomer university professors' expectancy violations during organizational assimilation.* Paper presented at the annual meeting of the Speech Communication Association, San Antonio, TX.

Davis, H. S. (1994). *New employee orientation.* New York: Neal-Schuman.

Davis, K. (1968). Readability changes in employee handbooks of identical companies during a fifteen-year period. *Personnel Psychology, 21,* 413-420.

Dean, R. A., Ferris, K. R., & Konstas, C. (1988). Occupational reality shock and organizational commitment: Evidence from the accounting profession. *Accounting, Organizations and Society, 13,* 235-250.

DeBell, C. S., Montgomery, M. J., McCarthy, P. R., & Lanthier, R. P. (1998). The critical contact: A study of recruiter verbal behavior during campus interviews. *Journal of Business Communication, 35,* 202-223.

Decker, P. J., & Cornelius, E. T., III. (1979). A note on recruiting sources and job survival rates. *Journal of Applied Psychology, 64,* 463-464.

DeFleur, L. B., & Menke, B. A. (1975). Learning about the labor force: Occupational knowledge among high school males. *Sociology of Education, 48,* 324-345.

Deluga, R. J., & Perry, J. T. (1994). The role of subordinate performance and ingratiation in leader-member exchanges. *Group & Organization Management, 19,* 67-86.

Dilla, B. L. (1987). Descriptive versus prescriptive information in a realistic job preview. *Journal of Vocational Behavior, 30,* 33-48.

Dipboye, R. L. (1994). Structured and unstructured selection interviews: Beyond the job-fit model. In G. R. Ferris (Ed.), *Research in personnel and human resources management* (Vol. 12, pp. 79-123). Greenwich, CT: JAI.

Dirsmith, M. W., & Covaleski, M. A. (1985). Informal communications, nonformal communications and mentoring in public accounting firms. *Accounting, Organizations and Society, 10,* 149-169.

DiSanza, J. R. (1995). Bank teller organizational assimilation in a system of contradictory practices. *Management Communication Quarterly, 9,* 191-218.

Dockery, T. M., & Steiner, D. D. (1990). The role of the initial interaction in leader-member exchange. *Group and Organization Studies, 15,* 395-413.

Donabedian, B., McKinnon, S. M., & Bruns, W. J. (1998). Task characteristics, managerial socialization, and media selection. *Management Communication Quarterly, 11,* 372-400.

Dougherty, T. W., Turban, D. B., & Callender, J. C. (1994). Confirming impressions in the employment interview: A field study of interviewer behavior. *Journal of Applied Psychology, 79,* 659-665.

Downs, C. W. (1969). Perceptions of the selection interview. *Personnel Administration, 32,* 8-23.

Dreeban, R. (1968). *What is learned in school.* Reading, MA: Addison-Wesley.

Dreher, G. F., & Ash, R. A. (1990). A comparative study of mentoring among men and women in managerial, professional and technical positions. *Journal of Applied Psychology, 75,* 539-546.

Dreher, G. F., & Cox, T. H. (1996). Race, gender, and opportunity: A study of compensation attainment and the establishment of mentoring relationships. *Journal of Applied Psychology, 81,* 297-308.

Driver, R. W. (1980). A determination of the relative efficacy of different techniques for employee benefit communication. *Journal of Business Communication, 17,* 23-37.

Duck, S. (1994). *Meaningful relationships: Talking, sense, and relating.* Thousand Oaks, CA: Sage.

Duff, K. (1989, February). An electronic employee handbook. *Personnel,* pp. 12-14, 17.

Dunn, J. (1988). *The beginnings of social understanding.* Cambridge, MA: Harvard University Press.

Eagen, K. S. (1996). Flexible mentoring: Adaptations in style for women's ways of knowing. *Journal of Business Communication, 33,* 401-425.

Ebaugh, H. R. F. (1984). *Becoming an ex: The process of role exit.* Chicago: University of Chicago Press.

Eccles, J. S. (1993). School and family effects on the ontogeny of children's interests, self-perceptions, and activity choices. *Nebraska Symposium on Motivation: Developmental Perspectives on Motivation, 40,* 145-208.

Eccles, J. S., & Barber, B. L. (1999). Student council, volunteering, basketball, or marching band: What kind of extracurricular involvement matters? *Journal of Adolescent Research, 14,* 10-43.

Eden, D. (1984). Self-fulfilling prophesy as a management tool: Harnessing Pygmalion. *Academy of Management Review, 9,* 64-73.

Eder, R. W., & Ferris, G. R. (Eds.). (1989). *The employment interview: Theory, research and practice.* Newbury Park, CA: Sage.

Eder, R. W., & Harris, M. M. (1999). *The employment interview handbook.* Thousand Oaks, CA: Sage.

Einhorn, L. J. (1981). An inner view of the job interview: An investigation of successful interview behaviors. *Communication Education, 30,* 217-228.

Ellis, R. A., & Taylor, M. S. (1983). Role of self-esteem within the job search process. *Journal of Applied Psychology, 68,* 632-640.

Elsbach, K. D., Sutton, R. I., & Principe, K. E. (1997). Averting expected challenges through anticipatory impression management: A study of hospital billing. *Organization Science, 9,* 68-86.

Engler-Parish, P. G., & Millar, F. E. (1989). An exploratory relational control analysis of the employment screening interview. *Western Journal of Speech Communication, 53,* 30-51.

Enoch, Y. (1989). Change of values during socialization for a profession: An application to the marginal man theory. *Human Relations, 42,* 219-239.

Evans, C. P. (1994). *Analysis of formal mentoring communication and subsequent socialization of newcomers into work groups.* Unpublished master's thesis, University of Texas at Austin.

Fagenson, E. A. (1992). Mentoring—Who needs it? A comparison of proteges' and nonproteges' needs for power, achievement, affiliation, and autonomy. *Journal of Vocational Behavior, 41,* 48-60.

Fagenson, E. A. (1994). Perceptions of proteges' vs. nonproteges' relationships with their peers, superiors, and departments. *Journal of Vocational Behavior, 45,* 55-78.

Fairhurst, G. T. (1993). The leader-member exchange patterns of women leaders in industry: A discourse analysis. *Communication Monographs, 60,* 321-351.

Fairhurst, G. T., Jordan, J. M., & Neuwirth, K. (1997). Why are we here? Managing the meaning of an organizational mission statement. *Journal of Applied Communication Research, 25,* 243-263.

Falcione, R. L., & Wilson, C. E. (1988). Socialization processes in organizations. In G. M. Goldhaber & G. A. Barnett (Eds.), *Handbook of organizational communication* (pp. 151-169). Norwood, NJ: Ablex.

Fandt, P. M., & Ferris, G. R. (1990). The management of information and impressions: When employees behave opportunistically. *Organizational Behavior and Human Decision Processes, 45,* 140-158.

Fedor, D. B., Rensvold, R. B., & Adams, S. M. (1992). An investigation of factors expected to affect feedback seeking: A longitudinal field study. *Personnel Psychology, 45,* 779-803.

Feeley, T. H., & Barnett, G. A. (1997). Predicting employee turnover from communication networks. *Human Communication Research, 23,* 370-387.

Feij, J. A., Whitely, W. T., Peiró, J. M., & Taris, T. W. (1995). The development of career-enhancing strategies and content innovation: A longitudinal study of new workers. *Journal of Vocational Behavior, 46,* 231-256.

Feldman, D. C. (1976). A practical program for employee socialization. *Organizational Dynamics, 5,* 64-80.

Feldman, D. C. (1989). Socialization, resocialization, and training: Reframing the research agenda. In I. L. Goldstein (Ed.), *Training and development in organizations* (pp. 376-416). San Francisco: Jossey-Bass.

Feldman, D. C. (1994). Who's socializing whom? The impact of socializing newcomers on insiders, workgroups, and organizations. *Human Resource Management Review, 4,* 213-233.

Feldman, D. C., Doerpinghaus, H. I., & Turnley, W. H. (1994, Fall). Managing temporary workers: A permanent HRM challenge. *Organizational Dynamics, 23,* 49-63.

Feldman, D. C., & Weitz, B. A. (1990). Summer interns: Factors contributing to positive development experiences. *Journal of Vocational Behavior, 37,* 267-284.

Ferris, G. R., & Judge, T. A. (1991). Personnel/human resource management: A political influence perspective. *Journal of Management, 17,* 447-488.

Ferris, G. R., & Mitchell, T. R. (1987). The components of social influence and their importance for human resources research. In K. M. Rowland & G. R. Ferris (Eds.), *Research in personnel and human resources management* (Vol. 5, pp. 103-128). Greenwich, CT: JAI.

Festinger, L. (1957). *A theory of cognitive dissonance.* Stanford, CA: Stanford University Press.

Fielding, N. G. (1986). Evaluating the role of training in police socialization: A British example. *Journal of Community Psychology, 14,* 319-330.

Fine, G. A. (1986). Friendships in the work place. In V. J. Derlega & B. A. Winstead (Eds.), *Friendship and social interaction* (pp. 185-206). New York: St. Martin's.

Fine, G. A. (1987). *With the boys: Little League baseball and preadolescent culture.* Chicago: University of Chicago Press.

Fine, G. A. (1996). Justifying work: Occupational rhetorics as resources in restaurant kitchens. *Administrative Science Quarterly, 41,* 90-115.

Fink, L. S., Bauer, T. N., & Campion, M. A. (1994, Spring). Job candidates' views of site interviews. *Journal of Career Planing and Development,* pp. 32-38.

Fisher, C. D. (1986). Organizational socialization: An integrative review. In B. Rowland & G. Ferris (Eds.), *Research in personnel and human resources management* (Vol. 4, pp. 101-145). Greenwich, CT: JAI.

Fisher, C. D., Ilgen, D. R., & Hoyer, W. D. (1979). Source of credibility, information favorability, and job offer acceptance. *Academy of Management Journal, 22,* 94-103.

Fisher, S., & Todd, A. D. (1987). *Discourse in institutional authority: Medicine, education and law.* Norwood, NJ: Ablex.

Fiske, S. T., & Neuberg, S. L. (1990). A continuum model of impression formation from category-based to individuating processes: Influence of information and motivation on attention and interpretation. In M. P. Zanna (Ed.), *Advances in experimental and social psychology* (pp. 1-74). New York: Academic Press.

Flannagan, D., & Hardee, S. D. (1994). Talk about preschoolers' interpersonal relationships: Patterns related to culture, SES, and gender of child. *Merrill-Palmer Quarterly, 40,* 523-537.

Fogarty, T. J. (1992). Organizational socialization in accounting firms: A theoretical framework and agenda for future research. *Accounting, Organizations and Society, 17,* 129-149.

Folger, R. (1986). Rethinking equity theory: A referent cognitions model. In H. W. Bierhoff, R. L. Cohen, & J. Greenberg (Eds.), *Justice in social relations* (pp. 145-162). New York: Plenum.

Folger, R., & Skarlicki, D. P. (1998). When tough times make tough bosses: Managerial distancing as a function of layoff blame. *Academy of Management Journal, 41,* 79-87.

Forbes, R. J., & Jackson, P. R. (1980). Non-verbal behavior and the outcome of selection interviews. *Journal of Occupational Psychology, 53,* 65-72.

Ford, J. D., & Ford, L. W. (1995). The role of conversations in producing intentional change in organizations. *Academy of Management Review, 20,* 541-570.

Fournier, V. (1997). Graduates' construction systems and career development. *Human Relations, 50,* 363-391.

Fournier, V., & Payne, R. (1994). Changes in self construction during the transition from university to employment: A personal construct psychology approach. *Journal of Occupational and Organizational Psychology, 67,* 297-314.

Fritz, J. H. (1997). Men's and women's organizational peer relationships: A comparison. *Journal of Business Communication, 34,* 27-46.

Fullagar, C., McCoy, D., & Shull, C. (1992). The socialization of union loyalty. *Journal of Organizational Behavior, 13,* 13-26.

Gabriel, Y. (1997). Meeting God: When organizational members come face-to-face with the supreme leader. *Human Relations, 50,* 315-342.

Gannon, M. J. (1971). Sources of referral and employee turnover. *Journal of Applied Psychology, 55,* 226-228.

Gates, L. R., & Hellweg, S. A. (1989, February). *The socializing function of new employee orientation programs: A study of organizational identification and job satisfaction.* Paper presented at the annual meeting of the Western Speech Communication Association, Spokane, WA.

Gatewood, R. D., Gowan, M. A., & Lautenschlager, G. J. (1993). Corporate image, recruitment image, and initial job choice decisions. *Academy of Management Journal, 36,* 414-427.

Gecas, V. (1981). Contexts of socialization. In R. Rosenberg & R. H. Turner (Eds.), *Social psychology: Sociological perspectives* (pp. 165-199). New York: Basic Books.

Gersick, C. J. G. (1988). Time and transition in work teams: Toward a new model of group development. *Academy of Management Journal, 31,* 9-41.

Gersick, C. J. G. (1989). Marking time: Predictable transitions in task groups. *Academy of Management Journal, 32,* 274-309.

Gilsdorf, J. W. (1998). Organizational rules on communicating: How employees are and are not learning the ropes. *Journal of Business Communication, 35,* 173-201.

Gilmore, D. C., & Ferris, G. R. (1989). The effects of applicant impression management tactics on interviewer judgments. *Journal of Management, 15,* 557-564.

Gioia, D. A., & Sims, H. P., Jr. (1986). Cognition-behavior connections: Attribution and verbal behavior in leader-subordinate interactions. *Organizational Behavior and Human Decision Processes, 37,* 197-229.

Glaman, J. M., Jones, A. P., & Rozelle, R. M. (1996). The effects of co-worker similarity on the emergence of affect in work teams. *Group & Organization Management, 21,* 192-215.

Gleason, J. B. (1975). Fathers and other strangers: Men's speech to young children. In D. P. Dato (Ed.), *Developmental psycholinguistics: Theory and application* (pp. 289-297). Washington, DC: Georgetown University Press.

Goffman, E. (1971). *Relations in public.* New York: Basic Books.

Golden, L., & Appelbaum, E. (1992). What was driving the 1982-88 boom in temporary employment? Preference of workers or decisions and power of employers. *American Journal of Economics and Sociology, 51,* 473-493.

Goldstein, B., & Oldham, J. (1979). *Children and work: A study of socialization.* New Brunswick, NJ: Transaction Books.

Goldstein, I. L., & Gilliam, P. (1990). Training systems in the year 2000. *American Psychologist, 45,* 134-143.

Golitz, S. M., & Giannantonio, C. M. (1995). Recruiter friendliness and attraction to the job: The mediating role of inferences about the organization. *Journal of Vocational Behavior, 46,* 109-118.

Gomersall, E. R., & Myers, M. S. (1966). Breakthrough in on-the-job training. *Harvard Business Review, 44*(4), 62-72.

Goodnow, J. J. (1988). Children's household work: Its nature and functions. *Psychological Bulletin, 103,* 5-26.

Goodnow, J. J., Bowes, J. M., Dawes, L. J., & Taylor, A. J. (1988, August). *The flow of work in families.* Paper presented at the fifth Australian Developmental Conference, Sydney.

Goodnow, J. J., Bowes, J. M., Warton, P. M., Dawes, L. J., & Taylor, A. J. (1991). Would you ask someone else to do this task? Parents' and children's ideas about household work requests. *Developmental Psychology, 27,* 817-828.

Goodnow, J. J., & Delaney, S. (1989). Children's household work: Task differences, styles of assignment, and links to family relationships. *Journal of Applied Developmental Psychology, 10,* 209-226.

Goodnow, J. J., & Warton, P. M. (1991). The social bases of social cognition: Interactions about work and their implications. *Merrill-Palmer Quarterly, 37,* 27-58.

Gorden, W. I., Infante, D. A., & Graham, E. E. (1988). Corporate conditions conducive to employee voice: A subordinate perspective. *Employee Responsibilities and Rights Journal, 1,* 101-111.

Graen, G. B. (1976). Role-making processes within complex organizations. In M. D. Dunnette (Ed.), *Handbook of industrial and organizational psychology* (pp. 1201-1245). Chicago: Rand McNally.

Graen, G. B., & Scandura, T. A. (1987). Toward a psychology of dyadic organizing. In L. L. Cummings & B. M. Staw (Eds.), *Research in organizational behavior* (Vol. 9, pp. 175-208). Greenwich, CT: JAI.

Graen, G. B., & Uhl-Bien, M. (1995). Development of leader-member exchange (LMX) theory of leadership over 25 years: Applying a multi-level multi-domain perspective. *Leadership Quarterly, 62,* 219-247.

Granovetter, M. (1973). The strength of weak ties. *American Journal of Sociology, 78,* 1360-1380.

Granovetter, M. (1995). *Getting a job: A study of contacts and careers* (2nd ed.). Chicago: University of Chicago Press.

Graves, L. M., & Karren, R. J. (1992). Interviewer decision processes and effectiveness: An experimental policy-capturing investigation. *Personnel Psychology, 45,* 313-340.

Green, S. G. (1991). Professional entry and the adviser relationship: Socialization, commitment, and productivity. *Group and Organization Studies, 16,* 387-407.

Green, S. G., & Bauer, T. N. (1995). Supervisory mentoring by advisers: Relationships with doctoral student potential, productivity, and commitment. *Personnel Psychology, 48,* 537-561.

Greenberg, B. S. (1982). Television and role socialization. In D. Pearl, L. Bouthilet, & J. Lazar (Eds.), *Television and behavior: Ten years of scientific progress and implications for the eighties* (Vol. 2, pp. 179-190). Rockville, MD: U.S. Department of Health and Human Services.

Greenberg, J. (1996). "Forgive me, I'm new": Three experimental demonstrations of the effects of attempts to excuse poor performance. *Organizational Behavior and Human Decision Processes, 66,* 165-178.

Greenberger, E., O'Neil, R., & Nagel, S. K. (1994). Linking workplace and homeplace: Relations between the nature of adults' work and their parenting behaviors. *Developmental Psychology, 30,* 990-1002.

Greenberger, E., & Steinberg, L. D. (1986). *When teenagers work: The psychological and social costs of adolescent employment.* New York: Basic Books.

Greenberger, E., Steinberg, L. D., & Ruggiero, M. (1982). A job is a job is a job . . . or is it? *Work and Occupations, 9,* 79-96.

Greenberger, E., Steinberg, L. D., Vaux, A., & McAuliffe, S. (1980). Adolescents who work: Effects of part-time employment on family and peer relations. *Journal of Youth and Adolescence, 9,* 189-202.

Griffeth, R. W., Hom, P. W., Fink, L. S., & Cohen, D. J. (1997). Comparative tests of multivariate models of recruiting source effects. *Journal of Management, 23,* 19-36.

Griffin, E., & Sparks, G. G. (1990). Friends forever: A longitudinal exploration of intimacy in same-sex pairs and platonic pairs. *Journal of Social and Personal Relationships, 7,* 29-46.

Gundry, L. K., & Rousseau, D. M. (1994). Critical incidents in communicating culture to newcomers: The meaning is the message. *Human Relations, 47,* 1063-1088.

Gunter, B., & McAleer, J. L. (1990). *Children and television: The one eyed monster?* London: Routledge.

Habermas, J. (1970). Towards a theory of communicative competence. In H. P. Dreitzel (Ed.), *Recent Sociology, 2,* 115-148.

Hafferty, F. W. (1988). Cadaver stories and the emotional socialization of medical students. *Journal of Health and Social Behavior, 29,* 344-356.

Hanisch, K. A. (1994). Reasons people retire and their relations to attitudinal and behavioral correlates in retirement. *Journal of Vocational Behavior, 45,* 1-16.

Hanson, D. A., & Johnson, V. A. (1989). Classroom lesson strategies and orientations toward work. In D. Stern & D. Eichorn (Eds.), *Adolescence and work: Influences of social structure, labor markets, and culture* (pp. 75-99). Hillsdale, NJ: Lawrence Erlbaum.

Harris, M. M. (1989). Reconsidering the employment interview: A review of recent literature and suggestions for future research. *Personnel Psychology, 42,* 691-726.

Harris, S. G. (1994). Organizational culture and individual sensemaking: A schema-based perspective. *Organization Science, 5,* 309-321.

Harrison, D., & Schaffer, M. (1994). Comparative examination of self-reports and perceived absenteeism norms: Wading through Lake Wobegon. *Journal of Applied Psychology, 79,* 240-251.

Harrison, J. R., & Carroll, G. R. (1991). Keeping the faith: A model of cultural transmission in formal organizations. *Administrative Science Quarterly, 36,* 552-582.

Hartup, W. W. (1996). The company they keep: Friendships and their developmental significance. *Child Development, 67,* 1-13.

Hartup, W. W., & Moore, S. G. (1990). Early peer relations: Developmental significance and prognostic implications. *Early Childhood Research Quarterly, 5,* 1-17.

Haunschild, P. R., Moreland, R. L., & Murrell, A. J. (1994). Sources of resistance to mergers between groups. *Journal of Applied Social Psychology, 24,* 1150-1178.

Hautaluoma, J. E., Enge, R. S., Mitchell, T. M., & Rittwager, F. J. (1991). Early socialization into a work group: Severity of initiations revisited. *Journal of Social Behavior and Personality, 6,* 725-748.

Heider, F. (1958). *The psychology of interpersonal relationships.* New York: John Wiley.

Heimann, B., & Pittenger, K. K. S. (1996). The impact of formal mentorship on socialization and commitment of newcomers. *Journal of Managerial Issues, 8,* 108-117.

Herriot, R., & Rothwell, C. (1981). Organizational choice and decision theory: Effects of employers' literature and selection interview. *Journal of Occupational Psychology, 54,* 17-31.

Herriot, R., & Rothwell, C. (1983). Expectations and impressions in the graduate selection interview. *Journal of Occupational Psychology, 56,* 303-314.

Hess, J. A. (1993). Assimilating newcomers into an organization: A cultural perspective. *Journal of Applied Communication Research, 12,* 189-210.

Hicks, W. D., & Klimoski, R. J. (1987). Entry into training programs and its effects on training outcomes: A field experiment. *Academy of Management Journal, 30,* 542-552.

Hickson, M., III, Stacks, D. W., & Padgett-Greely, M. (1998). *Organizational communication in the personal context: From interview to retirement.* Boston: Allyn & Bacon.

Hill, R. E. (1970). New look at employee referrals as a recruitment channel. *Personnel Journal, 49,* 144-148.

Hirschman, A. O. (1970). *Exit, voice, and loyalty: Responses to decline in firms, organizations, and the state.* Cambridge, MA: Harvard University Press.

Holder, T. (1996). Women in nontraditional organizations: Information-seeking during organizational entry. *Journal of Business Communication, 33,* 9-26.

Hollandsworth, J. G., Kazelskis, R., Stevens, J., & Dressel, M. E. (1979). Relative contributions of verbal, articulative and nonverbal communication to employment interview decisions in the job interview setting. *Personnel Psychology, 32,* 359-367.

Hollwitz, J. C., & Pawlowski, D. R. (1997). The development of a structured ethical integrity interview for pre-employment screening. *Journal of Business Communication, 34,* 203-219.

Holton, E. F., & Russell, C. J. (1997). The relationship of anticipation to newcomer socialization processes and outcomes: A pilot study. *Journal of Occupational and Organizational Psychology, 70,* 163-172.

Hom, P. W., Griffeth, R. W., Palich, L. E., & Bracker, J. S. (1998). An exploratory investigation into theoretical mechanisms underlying realistic job previews. *Personnel Psychology, 51,* 421-451.

Howard, L. A., & Geist, P. (1995). Ideological positioning in organizational change: The dialectic of control in a merging organization. *Communication Monographs, 62,* 110-131.

Hudson, D. C., & Jablin, F. M. (1992, May). *Newcomer information-giving during organizational entry: Conceptualization and the development of a message categorization scheme.* Paper presented at the annual meeting of the International Communication Association, Miami, FL.

Huffcutt, A. I., & Roth, P. L. (1998). Racial group differences in employment interview evaluations. *Journal of Applied Psychology, 83,* 179-189.

Huseman, R. C., & Hatfield, J. D. (1978). Communicating employee benefits: Directions for future research. *Journal of Business Communication, 15,* 3-17.

Huston, A. C., & Alvarez, M. M. (1990). The socialization context of gender role development in early adolescence. In R. Montemayor, G. Adams, & T. Gullotta (Eds.), *From childhood to adolescence: A transitional period?* Newbury Park, CA: Sage.

Huston, A. C., Wright, J. C., Rice, M. L. Kerkman, D., & St. Peters, M. (1990). Development of television viewing patterns in early childhood: A longitudinal investigation. *Developmental Psychology, 26,* 409-420.

Ibarra, H. (1993). Personal networks of women and minorities in management: A conceptual framework. *Academy of Management Review, 18,* 56-87.

Imada, A. S., & Hakel, M. D. (1977). Influence of nonverbal communication and rater proximity on impressions and decisions in simulated employment interviews. *Journal of Applied Psychology, 62,* 295-300.

Ingersoll, V. H., & Adams, G. B. (1992). The child is "father" to the manager: Images of organizations in U.S. children's literature. *Organization Studies, 13,* 497-519.

Irving, P. G., & Meyer, J. P. (1994). Reexamination of the met-expectations hypothesis: A longitudinal analysis. *Journal of Applied Psychology, 79,* 937-949.

Isabella, L. A. (1990). Evolving interpretations as a change unfolds: How managers construe key organizational events. *Academy of Management Journal, 33,* 7-41.

Jablin, F. M. (1975). The selection interview: Contingency theory and beyond. *Human Resource Management, 14,* 2-9.

Jablin, F. M. (1978). Message-response and "openness" in superior-subordinate communication. In B. D. Ruben (Ed.), *Communication yearbook 2* (pp. 293-309). New Brunswick, NJ: Transaction.

Jablin, F. M. (1979). Superior-subordinate communication: The state of the art. *Psychological Bulletin, 86,* 1201-1222.

Jablin, F. M. (1980). Superior's upward influence, satisfaction, and openness in superior-subordinate communication: A re-examination of the "Pelz effect." *Human Communication Research, 6,* 210-220.

Jablin, F. M. (1982). Organizational communication: An assimilation approach. In M. E. Roloff & C. R. Berger (Eds.), *Social cognition and communication* (pp. 255-286). Beverly Hills, CA: Sage.

Jablin, F. M. (1984). Assimilating new members into organizations. In R. N. Bostrom (Ed.), *Communication yearbook 8* (pp. 594-626). Beverly Hills, CA: Sage.

Jablin, F. M. (1985a). An exploratory study of vocational organizational communication socialization. *Southern Speech Communication Journal, 50,* 261-282.

Jablin, F. M. (1985b). Task/work relationships: A life-span perspective. In M. L. Knapp & G. R. Miller (Eds.), *Handbook of interpersonal communication* (pp. 615-654). Beverly Hills, CA: Sage.

Jablin, F. M. (1987). Organizational entry, assimilation, and exit. In F. M. Jablin, L. L. Putnam, K. H. Roberts, & L. W. Porter (Eds.), *Handbook of organizational communication: An interdisciplinary perspective* (pp. 679-740). Newbury Park, CA: Sage.

Jablin, F. M. (1993). *Dinner-time talk: Ambient messages from parents to children about work.* Unpublished manuscript, University of Texas at Austin.

Jablin, F. M., Grady, D. P., & Parker, P. S. (1984). *Organizational disengagement: A review and integration of the literature.* Paper presented at the annual meeting of the Speech Communication Association, New Orleans, LA.

Jablin, F. M., Hudson, D., & Sias, P. (1997). *Verbal and nonverbal correlates of communication satisfaction in employment screening interviews.* Unpublished manuscript, University of Richmond, Richmond, VA.

Jablin, F. M., & Kramer, M. W. (1998). Communication-related sense-making and adjustment during job transfers. *Management Communication Quarterly, 12,* 155-182.

Jablin, F. M., & Krone, K. J. (1987). Organizational assimilation. In C. R. Berger & S. H. Chaffee (Eds.), *Handbook of communication science* (pp. 711-746). Newbury Park, CA: Sage.

Jablin, F. M., & Krone, K. J. (1994). Task/work relationships: A life-span perspective. In M. L. Knapp & G. R. Miller (Eds.), *Handbook of interpersonal communication* (2nd ed., pp. 621-675). Thousand Oaks, CA: Sage.

Jablin, F. M., & McComb, K. B. (1984). The employment screening interview: An organizational assimilation and communication perspective. In R. N. Bostrom (Ed.), *Communication yearbook 8* (pp. 137-163). Beverly Hills, CA: Sage.

Jablin, F. M., & Miller, V. D. (1990). Interviewer and applicant questioning behavior in employment interviews. *Management Communication Quarterly, 4,* 51-86.

Jablin, F. M., & Miller, V. D. (1993). *Newcomer-supervisor role negotiation processes: A preliminary report of a longitudinal investigation.* Paper presented at the annul convention of the Speech Communication Association, Miami, FL.

Jablin, F. M., Miller, V. D., & Keller, T. (1999). *Newcomer-leader role negotiations: Negotiation topics/issues, tactics, and outcomes.* Paper presented at the annual conference the International Leadership Association, Atlanta, GA.

Jablin, F. M., Miller, V. D., & Sias, P. M. (1999). Communication and interaction processes. In R. W. Eder & M. H. Harris (Eds.), *The employment interview handbook* (pp. 297-320). Thousand Oaks, CA: Sage.

Jablin, F. M., Tengler, C. D., McClary, K. B., & Teigen, C. W. (1987, May). *Behavioral and perceptual correlates of applicants' communication satisfaction in employment screening interviews.* Paper presented at the annual convention of the International Communication Association, Montreal, Canada.

Jablin, F. M., Tengler, C. D., & Teigen, C. W. (1982, May). *Interviewee perceptions of employment screening interviews: Relationships among perceptions of communication satisfaction, interviewer credibility and trust, interviewing experience, and interview outcomes.* Paper presented at the annual meeting of the International Communication Association, Boston.

Jablin, F. M., Tengler, C. D., & Teigen, C. W. (1985, August). *Applicant perceptions of job incumbents and personnel representatives as communication sources in screening interviews.* Paper presented at the annual meeting of the Academy of Management, San Diego, CA.

Jackson, S. E., Stone, V. K., & Alvarez, E. B. (1993). Socialization amidst diversity: The impact of demographics on work team old-timers and newcomers. In L. L. Cummings & B. S. Staw (Eds.), *Research in organizational behavior* (Vol. 15, pp. 45-109). Greenwich, CT: JAI.

Janssen, O., de Vries, T., & Cozijnsen, A. J. (1998). Voicing by adapting and innovating employees: An empirical study on how personality and environment interact to affect voice behavior. *Human Relations, 51,* 945-967.

Janz, T. (1989). The patterned behavior description interview: The best prophet of the future is the past. In R. W. Eder & G. R. Ferris (Eds.), *The employment interview: Theory, research, and practice* (pp. 158-168). Newbury Park, CA: Sage.

Janz, T., Hellervik, L., & Gilmore, D. C. (1986). *Behavior description interviewing.* Boston: Allyn & Bacon.

Javidan, M., Bemmels, B., Devine, K. S., & Dastmalchian, A. (1995). Superior and subordinate gender and acceptance of superiors as role models. *Human Relations, 48,* 1271-1284.

Jerris, L. A. (1993). *Effective employee orientation.* New York: American Management Association.

Johnson, J. R., Bernhagen, M. J., Miller, V., & Allen, M. (1996). The role of communication in managing reductions in work force. *Journal of Applied Communication Research, 24,* 139-164.

Jones, G. R. (1986). Socialization tactics, self-efficacy, and newcomers' adjustments to organizations. *Academy of Management Journal, 29,* 262-279.

Judge, T. A., & Bretz, R. D. (1994). Political influence behavior and career success. *Journal of Management, 20,* 43-65.

Judge, T. A., & Ferris, G. R. (1992). The elusive criterion of fit in human resource staffing decisions. *Human Resource Planning, 15*(4), 47-67.

Judge, T. A., & Martocchio, J. J. (1996). Dispositional influences on attributions concerning absenteeism. *Journal of Management, 22,* 837-861.

Kacmar, K. M., Delery, J. E., & Ferris, G. R. (1992). Differential effectiveness of applicant impression management tactics on employment interview decisions. *Journal of Applied Social Psychology, 22,* 1250-1272.

Kacmar, K. M., & Hochwarter, W. A. (1995). The interview as a communication event: A field examination of demographic effects on interview outcomes. *Journal of Business Communication, 32,* 207-232.

Kahn, W. A. (1990). Psychological conditions of personal engagement and disengagement at work. *Academy of Management Journal, 33,* 692-724.

Kalbfleisch, P. J., & Davies, A. B. (1991). Minorities and mentoring: Managing the multicultural institution. *Communication Education, 40,* 266-271.

Kalbfleisch, P. J., & Davies, A. B. (1993). An interpersonal model for participation in mentoring relationships. *Western Journal of Communication, 57,* 399-415.

Kaplan, A. B., Aamodt, M. G., & Wilk, D. (1991). The relationship between advertisement variables and applicant responses to newspaper recruitment advertisements. *Journal of Business and Psychology, 5,* 383-395.

Karol, B. L. (1977). *Relationship of recruiter behavior, perceived similarity, and prior information to applicants' assessments of the campus recruitment interview.* Unpublished doctoral dissertation, Ohio State University.

Katz, D., & Kahn, R. L. (1966). *The social psychology of organizations.* New York: John Wiley.

Katz, R. (1980). Time and work: Toward an integrative perspective. In B. M. Staw & L. L. Cummings (Eds.), *Research in organizational behavior* (Vol. 2, pp. 81-128). Greenwich, CT: JAI.

Katz, R. (1985). Organizational stress and early socialization experiences. In T. Beehr & R. Bhagat (Eds.), *Human stress and cognition in organization: An integrative perspective* (pp. 117-139). New York: John Wiley.

Katz, S. M. (1998). A newcomer gains power: An analysis of the role of rhetorical expertise. *Journal of Business Communication, 35,* 419-441.

Katzman, N. (1972). Television soap operas: What's been going on anyway? *Public Opinion Quarterly, 36,* 200-212.

Keenan, A. (1976). Effects of non-verbal behaviour on candidates' performance. *Journal of Occupational Psychology, 49,* 171-176.

Keenan, A., & Wedderburn, A. A. I. (1975). Effects of non-verbal behaviour on candidates' impressions. *Journal of Occupational Psychology, 48,* 129-132.

Kelley, H. (1971). *Attribution in social interaction.* Morristown, NJ: General Learning Press.

Keltner, D., & Buswell, B. N. (1997). Embarrassment: Its distinct form and appeasement functions. *Psychological Bulletin, 122,* 250-270.

Kennedy, D. J., & Berger, F. (1994). Newcomer socialization: Oriented to facts or feelings. *Cornell Hotel and Restaurant Administration Quarterly, 35*(6), 58-71.

Kilduff, M. (1990). The interpersonal structure of decision making: A social comparison approach to organizational choice. *Organizational Behavior and Human Decision Processes, 47,* 270-288.

Kilduff, M., & Day, D. V. (1994). Do chameleons get ahead? The effects of self-monitoring on managerial careers. *Academy of Management Journal, 37,* 1047-1060.

Kinicki, A. J., & Lockwood, C. A. (1985). The interview process: An examination of factors recruiters use in evaluating job applicants. *Journal of Vocational Behavior, 26,* 117-125.

Kinicki, A. J., Lockwood, C. A., Hom, P. W., & Griffeth, R. W. (1990). Interviewer predictions of applicant qualifications and interviewer validity: Aggregate and individual analyses. *Journal of Applied Psychology, 75,* 477-486.

Kirchmeyer, C. (1995). Demographic similarity to the work group: A longitudinal study of managers at the early career stage. *Journal of Organizational Behavior, 16,* 67-83.

Kirkwood, W. G., & Ralston, S. M. (1999). Inviting meaningful applicant performances in employment interviews. *Journal of Business Communication, 36,* 55-76.

Kirnan, J. P., Farley, J. A., & Geisinger, K. F. (1989). The relationship between recruiting source, applicants' quality, and hire performance: An analysis by sex, ethnicity, and age. *Personnel Psychology, 42,* 293-308.

Klaas, B. S., & Dell'Omo, G. G. (1997). Managerial use of dismissal: Organizational-level determinants. *Personnel Psychology, 50,* 927-953.

Klauss, R. (1981). Formalized mentor relationships for management and executive development programs in the federal government. *Public Administration Review, 41,* 489-496.

Kleiman, D. (1990, December 6). Dinner still family time. *Austin-American Statesman,* Sec. A, p. 6.

Koberg, C. S., Boss, R. W., Chappel, D., & Ringer, R. C. (1994). Correlates and consequences of protégé mentoring in a large hospital. *Group & Organization Management, 19,* 219-239.

Koberg, C. S., Boss, R. W., & Goodman, E. (1998). Factors and outcomes associated with mentoring among health-care professionals. *Journal of Vocational Behavior, 53,* 58-72.

Komaki, J. L., Zlotnick, S., & Jensen, M. (1986). Development of an operant-based taxonomy and observational index of supervisory behavior. *Journal of Applied Psychology, 71,* 260-269.

Kossek, E. E., Roberts, K., Fisher, S., & DeMarr, B. (1998). Career self-management: A quasi-experimental assessment of the effects of a training intervention. *Personnel Psychology, 51,* 935-962.

Kram, K. E. (1983). Phases of the mentor relationship. *Academy of Management Journal, 26,* 608-625.

Kram, K. E. (1988). *Mentoring at work: Developmental relationships in organizational life.* New York: University Press of America.

Kram, K. E., & Isabella, L. A. (1985). Mentoring alternatives: The role of peer relationships in career development. *Academy of Management Journal, 28,* 110-132.

Kramer, M. W. (1989). Communication during intraorganizational transfers. *Management Communication Quarterly, 3,* 213-248.

Kramer, M. W. (1993a). Communication after job transfers: Social exchange processes in learning new roles. *Human Communication Research, 20,* 147-174.

Kramer, M. W. (1993b). Communication and uncertainty reduction during job transfers: Leaving and joining processes. *Communication Monographs, 60,* 178-198.

Kramer, M. W. (1994). Uncertainty reduction during job transitions: An exploratory study of the communication experiences of newcomers and transferees. *Management Communication Quarterly, 7,* 384-412.

Kramer, M. W. (1995). A longitudinal study of superior-subordinate communication during job transfers. *Human Communication Research, 22,* 39-46.

Kramer, M. W., Callister, R. R., & Turban, D. B. (1995). Information-receiving and information-giving during job transitions. *Western Journal of Communication, 59,* 151-170.

Kramer, M. W., & Miller, V. D. (1999). A response to criticisms of organizational socialization research: In support of contemporary conceptualizations of organizational assimilation. *Communication Monographs, 66,* 358-367.

Kramer, M. W., & Noland, T. L. (1999). Communication during job promotions: A case of ongoing assimilation. *Journal of Applied Communication Research, 27,* 335-355.

Kressin, N. R. (1996). The effect of medical socialization on medical students' need for power. *Personality and Social Psychology Bulletin, 22,* 91-98.

Kristof, A. L. (1996). Person-organization fit: An integrative review of its conceptualizations, measurement, and implications. *Personnel Psychology, 49,* 1-49.

Krone, K. J. (1992). A comparison of organizational, structural, and relationship effects on subordinates' upward influence choices. *Communication Quarterly, 40,* 1-15.

Kubey, R., & Csikszentmihalyi, M. (1990). *Television and the quality of life: How viewing shapes everyday experiences.* Hillsdale, NJ: Lawrence Erlbaum.

Kuhn, T. (1970). *The structure of scientific revolutions* (2nd ed.). Chicago: University of Chicago Press.

Kydd, C. T., Ogilvie, J. R., & Slade, L. A. (1990). "I don't care what they say, as long as they spell my name right": Publicity, reputation and turnover. *Group and Organization Studies, 15,* 53-43.

Larkey, L. K. (1996). Toward a theory of communicative interactions in culturally diverse workgroups. *Academy of Management Review, 21,* 463-491.

Larson, M. H. (1996). Patterns in transition: A writing teacher's survey of organizational socialization. *Journal of Business and Technical Communication, 10,* 352-368.

Larson, R. W. (1983). Adolescents' daily experience with family and friends: Contrasting opportunity systems. *Journal of Marriage and the Family, 45,* 739-750.

Larson, R. W., & Kleiber, D. (1993). Daily experience of adolescents. In P. Tolan & B. Cohler (Eds.), *Handbook of clinical research and practice with adolescents* (pp. 125-145). New York: John Wiley.

Larson, R. W., & Verma, S. (1999). How children and adolescents spend time across the world: Work, play and developmental opportunities. *Psychological Bulletin, 125,* 701-736.

Laska, S. B., & Micklin, M. (1981). Modernization, the family and work socialization: A comparative study of U.S. and Columbian youth. *Journal of Comparative Family Studies, 12,* 187-203.

Latack, J. C., Kinicki, A. J., & Prussia, G. E. (1995). An integrative process model of coping with job loss. *Academy of Management Review, 20,* 311-342.

Latham, G. P. (1989). The reliability, validity and practicality of the situational interview. In R. W. Eder & G. R. Ferris (Eds.), *The employment interview: Theory, research and practice* (pp. 169-182). Newbury Park, CA: Sage.

Latham, G. P., Saari, L. M., Pursell, E. D., & Campion, M. A. (1980). The situational interview. *Journal of Applied Psychology, 65,* 422-427.

Latham, V. M., & Leddy, P. M. (1987). Source of recruitment and employee attitudes: An analysis of job involvement, organizational commitment, and job satisfaction. *Journal of Business and Psychology, 1,* 230-235.

Lawson, M. B., & Angle, H. L. (1998). Upon reflection: Commitment, satisfaction, and regret after a corporate relocation. *Group & Organization Management, 23,* 289-317.

Lee, F. (1993). Being polite and keeping mum: How bad news is communicated in organizational hierarchies. *Journal of Applied Social Psychology, 23,* 1124-1149.

Lee, J. (1997). Leader-member exchange, the "Pelz effect," and cooperative communication between group members. *Management Communication Quarterly, 11,* 266-287.

Lee, J. (1998a). Effective maintenance communication in superior-subordinate relationships. *Western Journal of Communication, 62,* 181-208.

Lee, J. (1998b). Maintenance communication in superior-subordinate relationships: An exploratory investigation of group social context and the "Pelz effect." *Southern Communication Journal, 63,* 144-157.

Lee, J., & Jablin, F. M. (1995). Maintenance communication in superior-subordinate work relationships. *Human Communication Research, 22,* 220-257.

Lee, T. S., Mitchell, T. R., Wise, L., & Fireman, S. (1996). An unfolding model of voluntary employee turnover. *Academy of Management Journal, 39,* 5-36.

Leifer, A. D., & Lesser, G. S. (1976). *The development of career awareness in young children.* Washington, DC: National Institute of Education.

Leonard, R. (1988, August). *Ways of studying early negotiations between children and parents.* Paper presented at the fifth Australian Developmental Conference, Sydney.

Levine, J. M., & Moreland, R. L. (1991). Culture and socialization in work groups. In L. B. Resnick, J. M. Levine, & S. D. Teasley (Eds.), *Perspectives on socially shared cognition* (pp. 257-279). Washington, DC: American Psychological Association.

Levine, J. M., Resnick, L. B., & Higgins, E. T. (1993). Social foundations of cognition. *Annual Review of Psychology, 44,* 585-612.

Liang, D. W., Moreland, R., & Argote, L. (1995). Group versus individual training and group performance: The mediating role of transactive memory. *Personality and Social Psychology Bulletin, 21,* 384-393.

Lichter, S. R., Lichter, L. S., & Amundson, D. (1997). Does Hollywood hate business or money? *Journal of Communication, 47,* 68-84.

Lichter, S. R., Lichter, L. S., & Rothman, S. (1994). *Prime time: How TV portrays American culture.* Washington, DC: Regnery.

Liden, R. C., Martin, C. L., & Parsons, C. K. (1993). Interviewer and applicant behaviors in employment interviews. *Academy of Management Journal, 36,* 372-386.

Liden, R. C., & Parsons, C. K. (1986). A field study of job applicant interview perceptions, alternative opportunities, and demographic characteristics. *Personnel Psychology, 39,* 109-122.

Liden, R. C., Wayne, S. J., & Stilwell, D. (1993). A longitudinal study on the early development of leader-member exchanges. *Journal of Applied Psychology, 78,* 662-674.

Lim, V. K. G. (1996). Job insecurity and its outcomes: Moderating effects of work-based and nonwork-based social support. *Human Relations, 49,* 171-194.

Lindvall, D. C., Culberson, D. K., Binning, J. F., & Goldstein, M. A. (1986, April). *The effects of perceived labor market condition and interviewer sex on hypothesis testing in the employment interview.* Paper presented at the annual meeting of the Midwest Academy of Management.

Lois, J. (1999). Socialization to heroism: Individualism and collectivism in a voluntary search and rescue group. *Social Psychology Quarterly, 62,* 117-135.

Loraine, K. (1995). Leadership—Where does it come from? *Supervision, 56,* 14-16.

Louis, M. R. (1980). Surprise and sense making: What newcomers experience in entering unfamiliar organizational settings. *Administrative Science Quarterly, 25,* 226-251.

Louis, M. R. (1990). Acculturation in the workplace: Newcomers as lay ethnographers. In B. Schneider (Ed.), *Organizational culture and climate* (pp. 85-129). San Francisco: Jossey-Bass.

Louis, M. R., Posner, B. Z., & Powell, G. N. (1983). The availability and helpfulness of socialization practices. *Personnel Psychology, 36,* 857-866.

Lovelace, K., & Rosen, B. (1996). Differences in achieving person-organization fit among diverse groups of managers. *Journal of Management, 22,* 703-722.

Macon, T. H., & Dipboye, R. L. (1990). The relationship of interviewers' preinterview impressions to selection and recruitment outcomes. *Personnel Psychology, 43,* 745-768.

Major, D. A., Kozlowski, S. W. J., Chao, G. T., & Gardner, P. D. (1995). A longitudinal investigation of newcomers' expectations, early socialization outcomes, and the moderating effects of role development factors. *Journal of Applied Psychology, 80,* 418-431.

Malone, M. J., & Guy, R. (1982). A comparison of mothers' and fathers' speech to their 3-year-old sons. *Journal of Psycholinguistic Research, 11,* 599-608.

Mannle, S., & Tomasello, M. (1987). Fathers, siblings, and the bridge hypothesis. In K. E. Nelson & A. Van Kleek (Eds.), *Children's language* (Vol. 6, pp. 23-42). Hillsdale, NJ: Lawrence Erlbaum.

Markham, S. E., & McKee, G. H. (1995). Group absence behavior and standards: A multilevel analysis. *Academy of Management Journal, 38,* 1174-1190.

Martin, J. H., & Franz, E. B. (1994). Attracting applicants from a changing labor market: A strategic marketing framework. *Journal of Managerial Issues, 6,* 33-53.

Martin, P., Hagestad, G. O., & Diedrick, P. (1988). Family stories: Events (temporarily) remembered. *Journal of Marriage and the Family, 50,* 533-541.

Martin, S. C., Arnold, R. M., & Parker, R. M. (1988). Gender and medical socialization. *Journal of Health and Social Behavior, 29,* 333-343.

Martocchio, J. J., & Baldwin, T. B. (1997). The evolution of strategic organizational training: New objectives and research agenda. In G. R. Ferris (Ed.), *Research in personnel and human resources management* (Vol. 15, pp. 1-46). Greenwich, CT: JAI.

Maslyn, J. M., Farmer, S. M., & Fedor, D. B. (1996). Failed upward influence attempts: Predicting the nature of subordinate persistence in pursuit of organizational goals. *Group & Organization Management, 21,* 461-480.

Mason, N. A., & Belt, J. A. (1986). Effectiveness of specificity in recruitment advertising. *Journal of Management, 12,* 425-432.

Maurer, S. D., Howe, V., & Lee, T. W. (1992). Organizational recruiting as marketing management: An interdisciplinary study of engineering graduates. *Personnel Psychology, 45,* 807-833.

McCauley, C. D. Ruderman, M. N., Ohlott, P. J., & Morrow, J. E. (1994). Assessing the developmental components of managerial jobs. *Journal of Applied Psychology, 79,* 544-560.

McComb, K. B., & Jablin, F. M. (1984). Verbal correlates of interviewer empathic listening and employment interview outcomes. *Communication Monographs, 51,* 353-371.

McComb, M. (1995). Becoming a Travelers Aid volunteer: Communication in socialization and training. *Communication Studies, 46,* 297-316.

McDonald, T., & Hakel, M. D. (1985). Effects of applicant race, sex, suitability, and answers on interviewer's questioning strategy and rating. *Personnel Psychology, 38,* 321-334.

McEvoy, G. M., & Cascio, W. F. (1985). Strategies for reducing turnover: A meta-analysis. *Journal of Applied Psychology, 70,* 342-353.

McGovern, T. V., & Tinsley, H. E. A. (1978). Interviewers' evaluations of interviewee nonverbal behavior. *Journal of Vocational Behavior, 13,* 163-171.

McLaughlin, B., White, D., McDevitt, T., & Raskin, R. (1983). Mothers' and fathers' speech to their young children: Similar or different. *Journal of Child Language, 10,* 245-252.

McPhee, R. D. (1988). Vertical communication chains: Toward an integrated approach. *Management Communication Quarterly, 1,* 455-493.

Meglino, B. M., Ravlin, E. C., & Adkins, C. L. (1989). A work values approach to corporate culture: A field test of the value congruence process and its relationship to individual outcomes. *Journal of Applied Psychology, 74,* 424-432.

Meglino, B. M., Ravlin, E. C., & Adkins, C. L. (1991). Value congruence and satisfaction with a leader: An examination of the role of interaction. *Human Relations, 22,* 481-495.

Merriam, S. (1983). Mentors and protégés: A critical review of the literature. *Adult Education Quarterly, 33*(3), 161-173.

Meyer, D. C. (1997). Humor in member narratives: Uniting and dividing at work. *Western Journal of Communication, 61,* 188-208.

Meyer, J., & Driskill, G. (1997). Children and relationship development: Communication strategies in a day care center. *Communication Reports, 10,* 75-85.

Mignerey, J. T., Rubin, R. R., & Gordon, W. I. (1995). Organizational entry: An investigation of newcomer communication behavior and uncertainty. *Communication Research, 22,* 54-85.

Mihalka, J. A. (1974). *Youth and work.* Columbus, OH: Charles E. Merrill.

Miller, K. (1995). *Organizational communication: Approaches and processes.* Belmont, CA: Wadsworth.

Miller, R. S. (1992). The nature and severity of self-reported embarrassing circumstances. *Personality and Social Psychology Bulletin, 18,* 190-198.

Miller, V. D. (1989, May). *A quasi-experimental study of newcomers' information seeking behaviors during organizational entry.* Paper presented at the annual convention of the International Communication Association, San Francisco.

Miller, V. D. (1996). An experimental study of newcomers' information seeking behaviors during organizational entry. *Communication Studies, 47,* 1-24.

Miller, V. D., & Buzzanell, O. M. (1996). Toward a research agenda for the second employment interview. *Journal of Applied Communication Research, 24,* 165-180.

Miller, V. D., & Jablin, F. M. (1991). Information seeking during organizational entry: Influences, tactics, and a model of the process. *Academy of Management Review, 16,* 92-120.

Miller, V. D., Jablin, F. M., Casey, M. K., Lamphear-Van Horn, M., & Ethington, C. (1996). The maternity leave as a role negotiation process. *Journal of Managerial Issues, 8,* 286-309.

Miller, V. D., Johnson, J. R., Hart, Z., & Peterson, D. L. (1999). A test of antecedents and outcomes of employee role negotiation ability. *Journal of Applied Communication Research, 27,* 24-48.

Miller, V. D., & Kramer, M. K. (1999). A reply to Bullis, Turner, and Clair. *Communication Monographs, 66,* 390-392.

Miller, V. D., Susskind, A., & Levine, K. (1995). *The impact of interviewer behavior and reputation on job candidates.* Unpublished manuscript, Michigan State University.

Mino, M. (1996). The relative effects of content and vocal delivery during a simulated employment interview. *Communication Research Reports, 13,* 225-238.

Mishra, A. K., & Spreitzer, G. M. (1998). Explaining how survivors respond to downsizing: The roles of trust, empowerment, justice and work redesign. *Academy of Management Review, 23,* 567-588.

Missirian, A. K. (1982). *The corporate connection: Why executive women need mentors to reach the top.* Englewood Cliffs, NJ: Prentice Hall.

Moen, P., Edler, G. H., & Luscher, K. (Eds.). (1995). *Examining lives in context: Perspectives on the ecology of human development.* Washington, DC: American Psychological Association.

Montemayer, R., & Van Komen, R. (1980). Age segregation of adolescents in and out of school. *Journal of Youth and Adolescence, 9,* 371-381.

Moore, D. T. (1986). Knowledge at work: An approach to learning by interns. In K. M. Borman & J. Reisman (Eds.), *Becoming a worker* (pp. 116-139). Norwood, NJ: Ablex.

Moore, M. L. (1992). The family as portrayed on prime-time television, 1947-1990: Structure and characteristics. *Sex Roles, 26,* 41-61.

Morand, D. A. (1996). What's in a name? An exploration of the social dynamics of forms of address in organizations. *Management Communication Quarterly, 9,* 422-451.

Moreland, R. L., & Levine, J. M. (1982). Socialization in small groups: Temporal changes in individual-group relations. In L. Berkowitz (Ed.), *Advances in experimental social psychology* (Vol. 15, pp. 137-191). New York: Academic Press.

Moreland, R. L., & Levine, J. M. (in press). Socialization in organizations and work groups. In M. Turner (Ed.), *Groups at work: Advances in theory and research.* Hillsdale, NJ: Lawrence Erlbaum.

Moreland, R. L., & McMinn, J. G. (1999). Gone but not forgotten: Loyalty and betrayal among ex-members of small groups. *Personality and Social Psychology Bulletin, 25,* 1476-1486.

Morris, G. H. (1988). Accounts in selection interviews. *Journal of Applied Communication Research, 16,* 82-98.

Morris, J. A., & Feldman, D. C. (1996). The dimensions, antecedents, and consequences of emotional labor. *Academy of Management Review, 21,* 986-1010.

Morrison, E. W. (1993a). Longitudinal study of the effects of information seeking on newcomer socialization. *Journal of Applied Psychology, 78,* 173-183.

Morrison, E. W. (1993b). Newcomer information seeking: Exploring types, modes, sources, and outcomes. *Academy of Management Journal, 36,* 557-589.

Morrison, E. W. (1994). Role definitions and organizational citizenship behavior: The importance of the employee's perspective. *Academy of Management Journal, 37,* 1543-1567.

Morrison, E. W. (1995). Information usefulness and acquisition during organizational encounter. *Management Communication Quarterly, 9,* 131-155.

Morrison, E. W., & Robinson, S. L. (1997). When employees feel betrayed: A model of how psychological contract violations develop. *Academy of Management Review, 22,* 226-256.

Mortimer, J. T., Finch, M. D., Owens, T. J., & Shanahan, M. (1990). Gender and work in adolescence. *Youth & Society, 22,* 201-224.

Moss, M. K., & Frieze, I. H. (1993). Job preferences in the anticipatory socialization phase: A comparison of two matching models. *Journal of Vocational Behavior, 42,* 282-297.

Motowidlo, S. J., Carter, G. W., Dunnette, M. D., Tippins, N., Werner, S., Burnett, J. R., & Vaugh, M. (1992). Studies of the structured behavioral interview. *Journal of Applied Psychology, 77,* 571-587.

Murray, M., & Owen, M. (1991). *Beyond the myths and magic of mentoring: How to facilitate an effective mentoring program.* San Francisco: Jossey-Bass.

Myers, S. A. (1998). GTAs as organizational newcomers: The association between supportive communication relationships and information seeking. *Western Journal of Communication, 60,* 54-73.

Myers, S. A., & Kassing, J. W. (1998). The relationship between perceived supervisory communication behaviors and subordinate organizational identification. *Communication Research Reports, 15,* 81-82.

Myers, S. A., Knox, R. L., Pawlowski, D. R., & Ropog, B. L. (1999). Perceived communication openness and functional communication skills among organizational peers. *Communication Reports, 12,* 71-83.

Nelson, B. J., & Barley, S. R. (1997). For love or money? Commodification and the construction of an occupational mandate. *Administrative Science Quarterly, 42,* 619-653.

Nelson, D. L., & Quick, J. C. (1991). Social support and newcomer adjustment in organizations: Attachment theory at work? *Journal of Organizational Behavior, 12,* 543-554.

Nelson, D. L., Quick, J. C., & Eakin, M. E. (1988). A longitudinal study of newcomer role adjustment in US organizations. *Work and Stress, 2,* 239-253.

Nelson, D. L., Quick, J. C., & Joplin, J. R. (1991). Psychological contracting and newcomer socialization: An attachment theory foundation. *Journal of Social Behavior and Personality, 6*(7), 55-72.

Nelson, D. L., & Sutton, C. D. (1991). The relationship between newcomer expectations of job stressors and adjustment to the new job. *Work and Stress, 5,* 241-251.

Newcomb, A. F., & Bagwell, C. L. (1995). Children's friendship relations: A meta-analytic review. *Psychological Bulletin, 117,* 306-347.

Nicholson, N. (1984). A theory of work role transitions. *Administrative Science Quarterly, 29,* 172-191.

Nicholson, N., & Arnold, J. (1989). Graduate entry and adjustment to corporate life. *Personnel Review, 18*(3), 23-35.

Nicholson, N., & Arnold, J. (1991). From expectation to experience: Graduates entering a large corporation. *Journal of Organizational Behavior, 12,* 413-429.

Nicholson, N., & West, M. A. (1988). *Managerial job change: Men and women in transition.* Cambridge, UK: Cambridge University Press.

Niedenthal, P. M., Cantor, N., & Kihlstrom, J. F. (1985). Prototype-matching: A strategy for social decision-making. *Journal of Personality and Social Psychology, 48,* 575-584.

1995 industry reports: Training budgets. (1995, October). *Training, 21*(10), 42.

Noble, G. (1983). Social learning from everyday television. In M. J. A. Howe (Ed.), *Learning from television: Psychological and education research* (pp. 101-124). New York: Academic Press.

Noe, R. A. (1988). An investigation of the determinants of successful assigned mentoring relationships. *Personnel Psychology, 41,* 457-479.

Noe, R. A. (1999). *Employee training and development.* New York: Irwin McGraw-Hill.

Odden, C. M., & Sias, P. M. (1997). Peer communication relationships and psychological climate. *Communication Quarterly, 45,* 153-166.

Oglensky, B. D. (1995). Socio-psychoanalytic perspectives on the subordinate. *Human Relations, 48,* 1029-1054.

O'Keefe, B. J. (1988). The logic of message design: Individual differences in reasoning about communication. *Communication Monographs, 55,* 80-103.

O'Keefe, B. J. (1990). The logic of regulative communication: Understanding the rationality of message designs. In J. P. Dillard (Ed.), *Seeking compliance: The production of interpersonal influence messages* (pp. 87-105). Scottsdale, AZ: Gorsuch Scarisbrick.

Olian, J. D., Carroll, S. J., & Giannantonio, C. M. (1993). Mentor reactions to proteges: An experiment with managers. *Journal of Vocational Behavior, 43,* 266-278.

Olian, J. D., Carroll, S. J., Giannantonio, C. M., & Feren, D. B. (1988). What do proteges look for in a mentor? Results of three experimental studies. *Journal of Vocational Behavior, 33,* 15-37.

O'Neill, H. M., & Lenn, D. J. (1995). Voices of survivors: Words that downsizing CEOs should hear. *Academy of Management Executive, 9,* 23-33.

O'Reilly, C., Chatman, J., & Caldwell, D. F. (1991). People and organizational culture: A profile comparison approach to assessing person-organization fit. *Academy of Management Journal, 34,* 487-516.

Organ, D. W. (1990). The motivational basis of organizational citizenship behavior. In B. M. Staw & L. L. Cummings (Eds.), *Research in organizational behavior* (Vol. 12, pp. 43-72). Greenwich, CT: JAI.

Oseroff-Varnell, D. (1998). Communication and the socialization of dance students: An analysis of the hidden curriculum in a residential arts school. *Communication Education, 47,* 101-119.

Osipow, S. H. (1983). *Theories of career development* (3rd ed.). Englewood Cliffs, NJ: Prentice Hall.

Ostroff, C., & Kozlowski, S. W. J. (1992). Organizational socialization as a learning process: The role of information acquisition. *Personnel Psychology, 45,* 849-874.

Ostroff, C., & Kozlowski, S. W. J. (1993). The role of mentoring in the information gathering processes of newcomers during early organizational socialization. *Journal of Vocational Behavior, 42,* 170-183.

Palkowitz, E., & Mueller, M. (1987). Agencies foresee change in advertising's future. *Personnel Journal, 66,* 124-128.

Parks, J. M., & Schmedemann, D. (1992). *Pine River promises: A policy-capturing analysis of the legal and organizational properties of employee handbook provisions on job security.* Paper presented at the annual meeting of the Academy of Management, Las Vegas, NV.

Pearson, C. A. L. (1995). The turnover process in organizations: An exploration of the role of met-unmet expectations. *Human Relations, 48,* 405-420.

Peters, J. F. (1994). Gender socialization of adolescents in the home: Research and discussion. *Adolescence, 29,* 914-934.

Peterson, G. W., & Peters, D. F. (1983). Adolescents' construction of social reality: The impact of television and peers. *Youth & Society, 15,* 67-85.

Peterson, M. S. (1997). Personnel interviewers' perceptions of the importance and adequacy of applicants' communication skills. *Communication Education, 46,* 287-291.

Pfau, M., Mullen, L. J., Deidrich, T., & Garrow, K. (1995). Television viewing and public perceptions of attorneys. *Human Communication Research, 21,* 307-330.

Phillips, A. P., & Dipboye, R. L. (1989). Correlational tests of predictions from a process model of the interview. *Journal of Applied Psychology, 74,* 41-52.

Phillips, J. M. (1998). Effects of realistic job previews on multiple organizational outcomes: A meta-analysis. *Academy of Management Journal, 41,* 673-690.

Phillips, S., & Sandstrom, K. L. (1990). Parental attitudes toward youth work. *Youth & Society, 22,* 160-183.

Pierce, K. (1993). Socialization of teenage girls through teen-magazine fiction: The making of a new woman or an old lady? *Sex Roles, 29,* 59-68.

Piotrkowski, C. S., & Stark, E. (1987). Children and adolescents look at their parents' jobs. In J. H. Lewko (Ed.), *How children and adolescents view the world of work* (pp. 3-20). San Francisco: Jossey-Bass.

Podolny, J. M., & Baron, J. S. (1997). Resources and relationships: Social networks and mobility in the workplace. *American Sociological Review, 62,* 673-693.

Pollock, R. (1995). A test of conceptual models depicting the developmental course of informal mentor-protégé relationships in the work place. *Journal of Vocational Behavior, 46,* 144-162.

Pond, S. B., & Hay, M. S. (1989). The impact of task preview information as a function of recipient self-efficacy. *Journal of Vocational Behavior, 35,* 17-29.

Popovich, P., & Wanous, J. P. (1982). The realistic job preview as a persuasive communication. *Academy of Management Review, 7,* 570-578.

Posner, B. Z. (1981). Comparing recruiter, student and faculty perceptions of important applicant job characteristics. *Personnel Psychology, 34,* 329-339.

Potts, R., & Martinez, I. (1994). Television viewing and children's beliefs about scientists. *Journal of Applied Developmental Psychology, 15,* 287-300.

Powell, G. N. (1991). Applicant reactions to the initial employment interview: Exploring theoretical and methodological issues. *Personnel Psychology, 44,* 67-83.

Powell, G. N., & Goulet, L. R. (1996). Recruiters' and applicants' reactions to campus interviews and employment decisions. *Academy of Management Journal, 39,* 1619-1640.

Pratt, M. G., & Rafaeli, A. (1997). Organizational dress as a symbol of multilayered social identities. *Academy of Management Journal, 40,* 862-898.

Premack, S. L., & Wanous, J. P. (1985). A meta-analysis of realistic job preview experiments. *Journal of Applied Psychology, 70,* 706-719.

Pribble, P. T. (1990). Making an ethical commitment: A rhetorical case study of organizational socialization. *Communication Quarterly, 38,* 255-267.

Purcell, P., & Stewart, L. (1990). Dick and Jane in 1989. *Sex Roles, 22,* 177-185.

Pursell, E. D., Campion, M. A., & Gaylord, S. R. (1980). Structured interviewing: Avoiding selection problems. *Personnel Journal, 59,* 907-912.

Putnam, L. L., & Roloff, M. E. (Eds.). (1992). *Communication and negotiation.* Newbury Park, CA: Sage.

Rafaeli, A., Dutton, J., Harquail, C. V., & Mackie-Lewis, S. (1997). Navigating by attire: The use of dress by female administrative employees. *Academy of Management Journal, 40,* 9-45.

Rafaeli, A., & Pratt, M. G. (1993). Tailored meanings: On the meaning and impact of organizational dress. *Academy of Management Review, 18,* 32-55.

Raffaelli, M., & Duckett, E. (1989). "We were just talking . . . ": Conversations in early adolescence. *Journal of Youth and Adolescence, 18,* 567-582.

Ragins, B. R. (1997). Diversified mentoring relationships in organizations: A power perspective. *Academy of Management Review, 22,* 482-521.

Ragins, B. R., & Cotton, J. L. (1999). Mentor functions and outcomes: A comparison of men and women in formal and informal mentoring relationships. *Journal of Applied Psychology, 84,* 529-550.

Ragins, B. R., & Scandura, T. A. (1997). The way we were: Gender and the termination of mentoring relationships. *Journal of Applied Psychology, 82,* 945-953.

Ralston, S. M. (1993). Applicant communication satisfaction, intent to accept second interview offers, and recruiter communication style. *Journal of Applied Communication Research, 21,* 53-65.

Ralston, S. M., & Brady, R. (1994). The relative influence of interview communication satisfaction on applicants' recruitment interview decisions. *Journal of Business Communication, 31,* 61-77.

Ralston, S. M., & Kirkwood, W. G. (1995). Overcoming managerial bias in employment interviewing. *Journal of Applied Communication Research, 23,* 75-92.

Ralston, S. M., & Thomason, W. R. (1997). Employment interviewing and postbureaucracy. *Journal of Business and Technical Communication, 11,* 83-94.

Ramsay, S., Gallois, C., & Callan, V. J. (1997). Social rules and attributions in the personnel selection interview. *Journal of Occupational and Organizational Psychology, 70,* 189-203.

Recruiting literature: Is it accurate? (1981). *Journal of College Placement, 42,* 56-59.

Reichers, A. E. (1987). An interactionist perspective on newcomer socialization rates. *Academy of Management Review, 12,* 278-287.

Reid, G. L. (1972). Job search and the effectiveness of job-finding methods. *Industrial and Labor Relations Review, 25,* 479-495.

Reilly, R. R., Brown, R., Blood, M. R., & Malatesta, C. Z. (1981). The effects of realistic previews: A study and discussion of the literature. *Personnel Psychology, 34,* 823-834.

Repetti, R. L. (1994). Short-term and long-term processes linking job stressors to father-child interaction. *Social Development, 3,* 1-15.

Repetti, R. L., & Wood, J. (1997). Effects of daily stress at work on mothers' interactions with preschoolers. *Journal of Family Psychology, 11,* 90-108.

Resnick, L. B., Levine, J. M., & Teasley, S. D. (Eds.). (1991). *Perspectives on social shared cognition.* Washington, DC: American Psychological Association.

Riessman, C. K. (1990). *Divorce talk: Women and men make sense of personal relationships.* New Brunswick, NJ: Rutgers University Press.

Riggio, R. E., & Throckmorton, B. (1988). The relative effects of verbal and nonverbal behavior, appearance, and social skills on evaluations made in hiring interviews. *Journal of Applied Social Psychology, 18,* 331-348.

Riley, S., & Wrench, D. (1985). Mentoring among female lawyers. *Journal of Applied Social Psychology, 15,* 374-386.

Robinson, S. L. (1996). Trust and breach of the psychological contract. *Administrative Science Quarterly, 41,* 574-599.

Roese, R. J., & Olson, J. M. (1995). Counterfactual thinking: A critical overview. In N. J. Roese & J. M. Olson (Eds.), *What might have been: The social psychology of counterfactual thinking* (pp. 1-55). Mahwah, NJ: Lawrence Erlbaum.

Rosse, J. G. (1988). Relations among lateness, absence and turnover: Is there a progression of withdrawal? *Human Relations, 41,* 517-531.

Roth, N. L. (1991, February). *Secrets in organizations: Addressing taboo topics at work.* Paper presented at the annual meeting of the Western Speech Communication Association, Phoenix, AZ.

Rousseau, D. M. (1996). Changing the deal while keeping the people. *Academy of Management Executive, 10*(1), 50-61.

Rousseau, D. M., & Anton, R. J. (1988). Fairness and implied contract obligations in job terminations: A policy-capturing study. *Human Performance, 1,* 273-289.

Rousseau, D. M., & Anton, R. J. (1991). Fairness and implied contract obligations in job terminations: The role of contributions, promises, and performance. *Journal of Organizational Behavior, 12,* 287-299.

Rousseau, D. M., & Parks, J. M. (1993). The contracts of individuals and organizations. In L. L. Cummings & B. M. Staw (Eds.), *Research in organizational behavior* (Vol. 15, pp. 1-43). Greenwich, CT: JAI.

Rousseau, D. M., & Tijoriwala, S. A. (1999). What's a good reason to change? Motivated reasoning and social accounts in promoting organizational change. *Journal of Applied Psychology, 84,* 514-528.

Rudin, J. P., & Boudreau, J. W. (1996). Information acquisition in promotion decisions. *Human Relations, 49,* 313-325.

Ruggiero, M., Greenberger, E., & Steinberg, L. D. (1982). Occupational deviance among adolescent workers. *Youth & Society, 13,* 423-448.

Ruggiero, M., & Steinberg, L. D. (1981). The empirical study of teenage work: A behavioral code for the assessment of adolescent job environments. *Journal of Vocational Behavior, 19,* 163-174.

Ruscher, J. B., Hammer, E. Y., & Hammer, E. D. (1996). Forming shared impressions through conversation: An adaptation of the continuum model. *Personality and Social Psychology Bulletin, 22,* 705-720.

Ryan, J., & Sim, D. H. (1990). When art becomes news: Portrayals of art and artists on network television news. *Social Forces, 68,* 869-889.

Rynes, S. L. (1991). Recruitment, job choice, and post-hire consequences: A call for new research directions. In M. D. Dunnette & L. M. Hough (Eds.), *Handbook of industrial and organizational psychology* (2nd ed., Vol. 2, pp. 399-444). Palo Alto, CA: Consulting Psychologists.

Rynes, S. L., Bretz, R. D., & Gerhart, B. (1991). The importance of recruitment in job choice: A different way of looking. *Personnel Psychology, 44,* 487-521.

Rynes, S. L., & Gerhart, B. (1990). Interviewer assessments of applicant "fit": An exploratory investigation. *Personnel Psychology, 43,* 13-35.

Rynes, S. L., & Miller, H. E. (1983). Recruiter and job influences on candidates for employment. *Journal of Applied Psychology, 68,* 147-154.

Rynes, S. L., Orlitzky, M. O., & Bretz, R. D. (1997). Experienced hiring versus college recruiting: Practices and emerging trends. *Personnel Psychology, 50,* 309-339.

Sackett, P. R. (1982). The interviewer as hypothesis tester: The effects of impressions of an applicant on interviewer questioning strategy. *Personnel Psychology, 35,* 789-804.

Saks, A. M. (1994). A psychological process investigation for the effects of recruitment source and organization information on job survival. *Journal of Organizational Behavior, 15,* 225-244.

Saks, A. M. (1995). Longitudinal field investigation of the moderating and mediating effects of self-efficacy on the relationship between training and newcomer adjustment. *Journal of Applied Psychology, 80,* 211-225.

Saks, A. (1996). The relationship between the amount and helpfulness of entry training and work outcomes. *Human Relations, 49,* 429-451.

Saks, A. M., & Ashforth, B. E. (1997). A longitudinal investigation of the relationships between job information sources, applicant perceptions of fit, and work outcomes. *Personnel Psychology, 50,* 395-426.

Saks, A. M., & Cronshaw, S. F. (1990). A process investigation of realistic job previews: Mediating variables and channels of communication. *Journal of Organizational Behavior, 11,* 221-236.

Saks, A. M., Wiesner, W. H., & Summers, R. J. (1994). Effects of job previews on self-selection and job choice. *Journal of Vocational Behavior, 44,* 297-316.

Saks, A. M., Wiesner, W. H., & Summers, R. J. (1996). Effects of job previews and compensation policy on applicant attraction and job choice. *Journal of Vocational Behavior, 49,* 68-85.

Salancik, G., & Pfeffer, J. (1978). A social information processing approach to job attitudes and task design. *Administrative Science Quarterly, 23,* 224-253.

Saunders, D. M., Sheppard, B. H., Knight, V., & Roth, J. (1992). Employee voice to supervisors. *Employee Responsibilities and Rights Journal, 5,* 241-259.

Scandura, T. A., & Katterberg, R. J. (1988). *Much ado about mentors and little ado about measurement: Development of an instrument.* Paper presented at the annual meeting of the Academy of Management, Anaheim, CA.

Scandura, T. A., & Ragins, B. R. (1993). The effects of sex and gender role orientation on mentorship in male-dominated occupations. *Journal of Vocational Behavior, 43,* 251-265.

Scheff, T. J. (1988). Shame and conformity: The deference-emotion system. *American Sociological Review, 53,* 395-406.

Schein, E. H. (1968). Organizational socialization and the profession of management. *Industrial Management Review, 9,* 1-16.

Schlenker, B. R. (1980). *Impression management: The self-concept, social identity, and interpersonal relations.* Belmont, CA: Brooks/Cole.

Schlenker, B. R., & Weigold, M. F. (1992). Interpersonal processes involving impression regulation and management. *Annual Review of Psychology, 43,* 133-168.

Schmitt, N., & Coyle, B. W. (1976). Applicant decisions in the employment interview. *Journal of Applied Psychology, 61,* 184-192.

Schneider, B. (1987). The people make the place. *Personnel Psychology, 40,* 437-453.

Schneider, B., Goldstein, H. W., & Smith, D. B. (1995). The ASA framework: An update. *Personnel Psychology, 48,* 747-773.

Schwab, D. P. (1982). Recruiting and organizational participation. In K. Rowland & G. Ferris (Eds.), *Personnel management: New perspectives* (pp. 103-128). Boston: Allyn & Bacon.

Schweiger, D. M., & DeNisi, A. S. (1991). Communication with employees following a merger: A longitudinal field experiment. *Academy of Management Journal, 34,* 110-135.

Scott, C. R., Connaughton, S. L., Diaz-Saenz, H. R., Maguire, K., Ramirez, R., Richardson, B., Shaw, S. P., & Morgan, D. (1999). The impacts of communication and multiple identifications on intent to leave. *Management Communication Quarterly, 12,* 400-435.

Scott, C. R., Corman, S. R., & Cheney, G. (1998). Development of a structurational model of identifications in organizations. *Communication Theory, 8,* 298-336.

Scott, M. B., & Lyman, S. M. (1968). Accounts. *American Sociological Review, 33,* 46-62.

Sebald, H. (1986). Adolescents' shifting orientation toward parents and peers: A curvilinear trend over recent decades. *Journal of Marriage and the Family, 48,* 5-13.

Seers, A. (1989). Team-member exchange quality: A new construct for role-making research. *Organizational Behavior and Human Decision Processes, 43,* 118-135.

Seibert, S. (1999). The effectiveness of facilitated mentoring: A longitudinal quasi-experiment. *Journal of Vocational Behavior, 54,* 483-502.

Selye, H. (1956). *The stress of life.* New York: McGraw-Hill.

Settoon, R. P., Bennett, N., & Liden, R. C. (1996). Social exchange in organizations: Perceived organizational support, leader-member exchange, and employee reciprocity. *Journal of Applied Psychology, 81,* 219-227.

Shah, P. P. (1998). Who are employees' social referents? Using a network perspective to determine referent others. *Academy of Management Journal, 41,* 249-268.

Shaw, J. B., & Barrett-Power, E. (1997). A conceptual framework for assessing organization, work group, and individual effectiveness during and after downsizing. *Human Relations, 50,* 109-127.

Shaw, M. R. (1983). Taken-for-granted assumptions of applicants in simulated selection interviews. *Western Journal of Speech Communication, 47,* 138-156.

Sheehan, E. P. (1991). Reasons for quitting: Their effects on those who stay. *Journal of Social Behavior and Personality, 6,* 343-354.

Sheehan, E. P. (1995). Affective responses to employee turnover. *Journal of Social Psychology, 135,* 63-69.

Shellenbarger, S. (1995, November 15). Work and family. *Wall Street Journal,* Sec. B, p. 1.

Shore, L. M., & Shore, T. H. (1995). Perceived organizational support and organizational justice. In R. Cropanzano & K. M. Kacmar (Eds.), *Organizational politics, justice and support: Managing social climate at work* (pp. 149-164). Westport, CT: Quorum.

Shultz, K. S., Morton, K. R., & Weckerle, J. R. (1998). The influence of push and pull factors on voluntary and involuntary early retirees' retirement decision and adjustment. *Journal of Vocational Behavior, 53,* 45-58.

Shyles, L., & Ross, M. (1984). Recruitment rhetoric in brochures advertising the all volunteer force. *Journal of Applied Communication Research, 12,* 34-49.

Sias, P. M., & Cahill, D. J. (1998). From coworkers to friends: The development of peer friendships in the workplace. *Western Journal of Communication, 62,* 273-299.

Sias, P. M., & Jablin, F. M. (1995). Differential superior-subordinate relations, perceptions of fairness, and coworker communication. *Human Communication Research, 22,* 5-38.

Signorielli, N. (1991). *A sourcebook on children and television.* New York: Greenwood.

Signorielli, N. (1993). Television and adolescents' perceptions about work. *Youth & Society, 24,* 314-341.

Signorielli, N., & Lears, M. (1992). Children, television, and conceptions about chores: Attitudes and behaviors. *Sex Roles, 27,* 157-170.

Silvester, J. (1997). Spoken attributions and candidate success in graduate recruitment interviews. *Journal of Occupational and Organizational Psychology, 70,* 61-73.

Skarlicki, D. P., Ellard, J. H., & Kelln, B. R. C. (1998). Third-party perceptions of a layoff: Procedural, derogation, and retributive aspects of justice. *Journal of Applied Psychology, 83,* 119-127.

Smeltzer, L. R., & Zener, M. F. (1992). Development of a model for announcing major layoffs. *Group & Organization Management, 17,* 446-472.

Smith, R. C., & Eisenberg, E. M. (1987). Conflict at Disneyland: A root metaphor analysis. *Communication Monographs, 54,* 367-380.

Smith, R. C., & Turner, P. K. (1995). A social constructionist reconfiguration of metaphor analysis: An application of "SCMA" to organizational socialization theorizing. *Communication Monographs, 62,* 152-181.

Snyder, C. R. (1985). The excuse: An amazing grace? In B. R. Schlenker (Ed.), *The self and social life* (pp. 235-289). New York: McGraw-Hill.

Somers, M. J. (1999). Application of two neural network paradigms to the study of voluntary employee turnover. *Journal of Applied Psychology, 84,* 177-185.

Sonnenfeld, J. (1988). *The hero's farewell: What happens when CEOs retire.* New York: Oxford University Press.

Spano, S., & Zimmermann, S. (1995). Interpersonal communication competence in context: Assessing performance in the selection interview. *Communication Reports, 8*, 18-26.

Sparrowe, R. T., & Liden, R. C. (1997). Process and structure in leader-member exchange. *Academy of Management Review, 22*, 522-552.

Stark, A. (1992). *Because I said so.* New York: Pharos.

Staton-Spicer, A. Q., & Darling, A. L. (1986). Communication in the socialization of preservice teachers. *Communication Education, 35*, 215-230.

Steenland, S. (1990). *What's wrong with this picture? The status of women on screen and behind the camera in entertainment TV.* Washington, DC: National Commission on Working Women and of Wider Opportunities for Women.

Steers, R. M., & Mowday, R. T. (1981). Employee turnover and post-decision accommodation processes. In L. L. Cummings & B. M. Staw (Eds.), *Research in organizational behavior* (Vol. 3, pp. 235-281). Greenwich, CT: JAI.

Steinberg, L. D., Greenberger, E., Vaux, A., & Ruggiero, M. (1981). Early work experience: Effects on adolescent occupational socialization. *Youth & Society, 12*, 403-422.

Stern, D., McMillion, M., Hopkins, C., & Stone, J. (1990). Work experience for students in high school and college. *Youth & Society, 21*, 355-389.

Stern, D., & Nakata, Y. (1989). Characteristics of high school students' paid jobs, and employment experience after graduation. In D. Stern & D. Eichorn (Eds.), *Adolescence and work: Influences of social structure, labor markets, and culture.* Hillsdale, NJ: Lawrence Erlbaum.

Stevens, C. K. (1997). Effects of preinterview beliefs on applicants' reactions to campus interviews. *Academy of Management Journal, 40*, 947-966.

Stevens, C. K., & Kristof, A. L. (1995). Making the right impression: A field study of applicant impression management during job interviews. *Journal of Applied Psychology, 80*, 587-606.

Stevenson, W. B., & Bartunek, J. M. (1996). Power, interaction, position and the generation of cultural agreement in organizations. *Human Relations, 49*, 75-104.

Stewart, W., & Barling, J. (1996). Fathers' work experiences affect children's behaviors via job-related effect and parenting behaviors. *Journal of Organizational Behavior, 17*, 221-232.

Stohl, C. (1986). The role of memorable messages in the process of organizational socialization. *Communication Quarterly, 34*, 231-249.

Stohl, C., & Redding, W. C. (1987). Messages and message exchange processes. In F. M. Jablin, L. L. Putnam, K. H. Roberts, & L. W. Porter (Eds.), *Handbook of organizational communication: An interdisciplinary perspective* (pp. 451-502). Newbury Park, CA: Sage.

Stradling, S. G., Crowe, G., & Tuohy, A. P. (1993). Changes in self-concept during occupational socialization of new recruits to the police. *Journal of Community and Social Psychology, 3*, 131-147.

Strom, S. A., & Miller, V. (1993, November). *Socialization experiences of college co-ops and interns.* Paper presented at the annual meeting of the Speech Communication Association, Miami, FL.

Struthers, C. W., Colwill, N. L., & Perry, R. P. (1992). An attributional analysis of decision making in a personnel selection interview. *Journal of Applied Social Psychology, 22*, 801-818.

Suchan, J. (1995). The influence of organizational metaphors on writers' communication roles and stylistic choices. *Journal of Business Communication, 32*, 7-29.

Sutton, R. I., & Louis, M. R. (1984). *The influence of selection and socialization on insider sense-making.* Paper presented at the annual meeting of the Academy of Management, Boston.

Swaroff, P. G., Barclay, L. A., & Bass, A. R. (1985). Recruiting sources: Another look. *Journal of Applied Psychology, 70*, 720-728.

Tannenbaum, S. I., Mathieu, J. E., Salas, E., & Cannon-Bowles, J. A. (1991). Meeting trainees' expectations: The influence of training fulfillment on the development of commitment, self-efficacy, and motivation. *Journal of Applied Psychology, 76*, 759-769.

Taylor, E. (1989). *Prime-time families: Television culture in postwar America.* Berkeley: University of California Press.

Taylor, G. S. (1994). The relationship between sources of new employees and attitudes toward the job. *Journal of Social Psychology, 134*, 99-110.

Taylor, M. S. (1985). The roles of occupational knowledge and vocational self-concept crystallization in students' school-to-work transition. *Journal of Counseling Psychology, 32*, 539-550.

Taylor, M. S. (1988). Effects of college internships on individual participants. *Journal of Applied Psychology, 73*, 393-401.

Taylor, M. S., & Bergmann, T. J. (1987). Organizational recruitment activities and applicants' reactions at different stages of the recruitment process. *Personnel Psychology, 40*, 261-285.

Taylor, M. S., & Schmidt, D. W. (1983). A process-oriented investigation of recruitment source effectiveness. *Personnel Psychology, 36*, 343-354.

Taylor, M. S., & Sniezek, J. A. (1984). The college recruitment interview: Topical content and applicant reactions. *Journal of Occupational Psychology, 57*, 157-168.

Teboul, J. C. B. (1994). Facing and coping with uncertainty during organizational encounter. *Management Communication Quarterly, 8*, 190-224.

Teboul, J. C. B. (1995). Determinants of new hire information-seeking during organizational encounter. *Western Journal of Communication, 59*, 305-325.

Teboul, J. C. B. (1997). "Scripting" the organization: New hire learning during organizational encounter. *Communication Research Reports, 14*, 33-47.

Teigen, C. W. (1983). *Communication of organizational climate during job screening interviews: A field study of interviewee perceptions, "actual" communication behavior and interview outcomes.* Unpublished doctoral dissertation, University of Texas at Austin.

Tengler, C. D. (1982). *Effects of question type and question orientation on interview outcomes in naturally occurring employment interviews.* Unpublished master's thesis, University of Texas at Austin.

Tengler, C. D., & Jablin, F. M. (1983). Effects of question type, orientation, and sequencing in the employment screening interview. *Communication Monographs, 50*, 245-263.

Tepper, B. J. (1995). Upward maintenance tactics in supervisory mentoring and nonmentoring relationships. *Academy of Management Journal, 38*, 1191-1205.

Tesser, A., & Rosen, S. (1975). The reluctance to transmit bad news. In L. Berkowitz (Ed.), *Advances in experimental social psychology* (Vol. 8, pp. 193-232). New York: Academic Press.

Thacker, R. A., & Wayne, S. J. (1995). An examination of the relationship between upward influence tactics and assessments of promotability. *Journal of Management, 21*, 739-756.

Theberge, L. (1981). *Crooks, conmen and clowns: Businessmen in TV entertainment.* Washington, DC: Media Institute.

Theus, K. T. (1995). Communication in a power vacuum: Sense-making and enactment during crisis-induced departures. *Human Resource Management, 34*, 27-49.

Thomas, D. A. (1990). The impact of race on managers' experiences of developmental relationships (mentoring and sponsorship): An intra-organizational study. *Journal of Organizational Behavior, 11*, 479-492.

Thompson, L. (1990). Negotiation behavior and outcomes: Empirical evidence and theoretical issues. *Psychological Bulletin, 108*, 515-532.

Thralls, C. (1992). Rites and ceremonials: Corporate video and the construction of social realities in modern organizations. *Journal of Business and Technical Communication, 6*, 381-402.

Toliver, S. D. (1993). Movers and shakers: Black families and corporate relocation. *Marriage and Family Review, 19*, 113-130.

Treadwell, D. F., & Harrison, T. M. (1994). Conceptualizing and assessing organizational image: Model images, commitment and communication. *Communication Monographs, 61*, 63-85.

Trent, L. W. (1978). *The effects of varying levels of interviewee nonverbal behavior in the employment interview.* Unpublished doctoral dissertation, Southern Illinois University.

Trice, H. M. (1993). *Occupational subcultures in the workplace.* Ithaca, NY: ILR.

Tsui, A. S., Pearce, J. L., Porter, L. W., & Hite, J. P. (1995). Choice of employee-organization relationship: Influence of external and internal organizational factors. In G. R. Ferris (Ed.), *Research in personnel and human resources management* (Vol. 13, pp. 117-151). Greenwich, CT: JAI.

Tucker, C. J., Barber, B. L., & Eccles, J. S. (1997). Advice about life plans and personal problems in late adolescent sibling relationships. *Journal of Youth and Adolescence, 26*, 63-76.

Tullar, W. L. (1989). Relational control in the employment interview. *Journal of Applied Psychology, 74*, 971-977.

Turban, D. B., Campion, J. E., & Eyring, A. R. (1995). Factors related to job acceptance decisions of college recruits. *Journal of Vocational Behavior, 47*, 193-213.

Turban, D. B., & Dougherty, T. W. (1992). Influence of campus recruiting on applicant attraction to firms. *Academy of Management Journal, 35*, 739-765.

Turban, D. B., & Keon, T. L. (1993). Organizational attractiveness: An interactionist perspective. *Journal of Applied Psychology, 78*, 184-193.

Turner, P. K. (1999). What if you don't? A response to Kramer and Miller. *Communication Monographs, 66*, 382-389.

Turow, J. (1974). Advising and ordering in daytime, primetime. *Journal of Communication, 24*, 138-141.

Turow, J. (1980). Occupation and personality in television dramas: An industry view. *Communication Research, 7*, 295-318.

Ugbah, S. D., & Majors, R. E. (1992). Influential communication factors in employment screening interviews. *Journal of Business Communication, 29*, 145-159.

Ullman, J. C. (1966). Employee referrals: Prime tools for recruiting workers. *Personnel, 43*, 30-45.

Van Maanen, J. (1975). Breaking in: Socialization to work. In R. Dubin (Ed.), *Handbook of work, organization and society* (pp. 67-120). Chicago: Rand McNally.

Van Maanen, J. (1984). Doing new things in old ways: The chains of socialization. In J. L. Bass (Ed.), *College and university organization: Insights from the behavioral sciences* (pp. 211-247). New York: New York University Press.

Van Maanen, J., & Barley, S. R. (1984). Occupational communities: Culture and control in organizations. In B. M. Staw & L. L. Cummings (Eds.), *Research in organizational behavior* (Vol. 6, pp. 287-365). Greenwich, CT: JAI.

Van Maanen, J., & Schein, E. H. (1979). Toward a theory of organizational socialization. In B. M. Staw & L. L. Cummings (Eds.), *Research in organizational behavior* (Vol. 1, pp. 209-264). Greenwich, CT: JAI.

van Tilburg, T. (1992). Support networks before and after retirement. *Journal of Social and Personal Relationships, 9*, 433-455.

Vandenberg, R. J., & Scarpello, V. (1990). The matching model: An examination of the processes underlying realistic job previews. *Journal of Applied Psychology, 75*, 60-67.

Vangelisti, A. L. (1988). Adolescent socialization into the workplace: A synthesis and critique of current literature. *Youth & Society, 19*, 460-484.

Vecchio, R. P. (1995). The impact of referral sources on employee attitudes: Evidence from a national sample. *Journal of Management, 21*, 953-965.

Vinton, K. L. (1989). Humor in the workplace: It is more than telling jokes. *Small Group Behavior, 20*, 151-166.

von Hippel, C., Mangnum, S. L., Greenberger, D. B., Heneman, R. L., & Skoglind, J. D. (1997). Temporary employment: Can organizations and employees both win? *Academy of Management Executive, 11*, 93-104.

Vonracek, F. W., Lerner, R. M., & Schulenberg, J. E. (1986). *Career development: A life-span developmental approach.* Hillsdale, NJ: Lawrence Erlbaum.

Waldeck, J. H., Orrego, V. O., Plax, T. G., & Kearney, P. (1997). Graduate student/faculty mentoring relationships: Who gets mentored, how it happens, and to what end. *Communication Quarterly, 45*, 93-109.

Waldron, V. R. (1991). Achieving communication goals in superior-subordinate relationships: The multifunctionality of upward maintenance tactics. *Communication Monographs, 58*, 289-306.

Waldron, V. R. (1994). Once more, with feeling: Reconsidering the role of emotion in work. In S. A. Deetz (Ed.), *Communication yearbook 17* (pp. 388-416). Thousand Oaks, CA: Sage.

Waldron, V. R., & Hunt, M. D. (1992). Hierarchical level, length, and quality of supervisory relationship as predictors of subordinates' use of maintenance tactics. *Communication Reports, 5*, 82-89.

Walsh, W. B., & Osipow, S. H. (Eds.). (1983). *Handbook of vocational psychology: Foundations* (Vol. 1). Hillsdale, NJ: Lawrence Erlbaum.

Walther, J. B. (1992). Interpersonal effects in computer-mediated communication: A relational perspective. *Communication Research, 19*, 52-90.

Walther, J. B. (1996). Computer-mediated communication: Impersonal, interpersonal and hyperpersonal interaction. *Communication Research, 23*, 3-43.

Wanous, J. P. (1977). Organizational entry: Newcomers moving from outside to inside. *Psychological Bulletin, 84*, 601-618.

Wanous, J. P. (1980). *Organizational entry: Recruitment, selection and socialization of newcomers.* Reading, MA: Addison-Wesley.

Wanous, J. P. (1989). Installing a realistic job preview: Ten tough choices. *Personnel Psychology, 42*, 117-133.

Wanous, J. P., & Colella, A. (1989). Organizational entry research: Current status and future directions. In G. R. Ferris & K. M. Rowland (Eds.), *Research in personnel and human resources management* (Vol. 7, pp. 59-120). Greenwich, CT: JAI.

Wanous, J. P., Poland, T. D., Premack, S. L., & Davis, K. S. (1992). The effects of met expectations on newcomer attitudes and behaviors: A review and meta-analysis. *Journal of Applied Psychology, 77*, 288-297.

Watzlawick, P., Beavin, J., & Jackson, D. (1967). *The pragmatics of human communication.* New York: Norton.

Waung, M. (1995). The effects of self-regulatory coping orientation on newcomer adjustment and job survival. *Personnel Psychology, 48*, 633-650.

Wayne, S. J., & Kacmar, K. M. (1991). The effects of impression management on the performance appraisal process. *Organizational Behavior and Human Decision Processes, 48*, 70-88.

Wayne, S. J., Shore, L. M., & Liden, R. C. (1997). Perceived organizational support and leader-member exchange: A social exchange perspective. *Academy of Management Journal, 40*, 82-111.

Weiss, H. M. (1977). Subordinate imitation of supervisor behavior: The role of modeling in organizational socialization. *Organizational Behavior and Human Performance, 19*, 89-105.

Werbel, J. D., & Landau, J. (1996). The effectiveness of different recruitment sources: A mediating variable analysis. *Journal of Applied Social Psychology, 26*, 1337-1350.

West, M. A. (1987). Role innovation in the world of work. *British Journal of Social Psychology, 26*, 304-315.

West, M. A., Nicholson, N., & Rees, A. (1987). Transitions into newly created jobs. *Journal of Occupational Psychology, 60*, 97-113.

White, L. K., & Brinkerhoff, D. B. (1981). Children's work in the family: Its significance and meaning. *Journal of Marriage and the Family, 43*, 789-798.

Wiesner, W. H., Saks, A. M., & Summers, R. J. (1991). Job alternatives and job choice. *Journal of Vocational Behavior, 38*, 198-207.

Wigand, R. T., & Boster, F. S. (1991). Mentoring, social interaction, and commitment: An empirical analysis of a mentoring program. *Communications, 16*, 15-31.

Wilks, J. (1986). The relative importance of parents and friends in adolescent decision making. *Journal of Youth and Adolescence, 15*, 323-334.

Williams, C. R., Labig, C. E., & Stone, R. H. (1993). Recruitment sources and posthire outcomes for job applicants and new hires: A test of two hypotheses. *Journal of Applied Psychology, 78*, 163-172.

Williamson, L. G., Campion, J. E., Roehling, M. V., Malos, S. B., & Campion, M. A. (1997). Employment interview on trial: Linking interview structure with litigation outcomes. *Journal of Applied Psychology, 82,* 900-912.

Wilson, C. E. (1983). *Toward understanding the process of organizational leave-taking.* Paper presented at the annual meeting of the Speech Communication Association, Washington, DC.

Winstead, B. A., Derlega, V. J., Montgomery, M. J., & Pilkington, C. (1995). The quality of friendships and work and job satisfaction. *Journal of Social and Personal Relationships, 12,* 199-215.

Withey, M. J., & Cooper, W. H. (1989). Predicting exit, voice, loyalty, and neglect. *Administrative Science Quarterly, 34,* 521-539.

Wolfe, M. N., & Baskin, O. W. (1985, August). *The communication of corporate culture in employee indoctrination literature: An empirical analysis using content analysis.* Paper presented at the annual meeting of the Academy of Management, San Diego, CA.

Wright, J. C., Huston, A. C., Reitz, A. L., & Piemyat, S. (1994). Young children's perceptions of television reality: Determinants and developmental differences. *Developmental Psychology, 30,* 229-239.

Wroblewski, R., & Huston, A. C. (1987). Televised occupational stereotypes and their effects on early adolescents: Are they changing? *Journal of Early Adolescence, 7,* 283-297.

Young, R. A., & Friesen, J. D. (1992). The intentions of parents in influencing the career development of their children. *Career Development Quarterly, 40,* 198-207.

Young, R. A., Friesen, J. D., & Pearson, H. M. (1988). Activities and interpersonal relations as dimensions of parental behavior in the career development of adolescents. *Youth & Society, 20,* 29-45.

Youniss, J., & Smollar, J. (1985). *Adolescent relations with mothers, fathers, and friends.* Chicago: University of Chicago Press.

Yukl, G., Guinan, P. J., & Sottolano, D. (1995). Influence tactics used for different objectives with subordinates, peers, and superiors. *Group & Organization Management, 20,* 272-296.

Zahrly, J., & Tosi, H. (1989). The differential effect of organizational induction process on early work adjustment. *Journal of Organizational Behavior, 10,* 59-74.

Zarbatany, L., Hartmann, D. P., & Rankin, D. B. (1990). The psychological functions of pre-adolescent peer activities. *Child Development, 61,* 1067-1080.

Zey, M. (1991). *The mentor connection.* Homewood, IL: Dow Jones-Irwin.

Ziller, R. C. (1965). Toward a theory of open and closed groups. *Psychological Bulletin, 64,* 164-182.

Ziller, R. C., Behringer, R. D., & Jansen, M. J. (1961). The minority member in open and closed groups. *Journal of Applied Psychology, 45,* 55-58.

Zorn, T. E. (1995). Bosses and buddies: Constructing and performing simultaneously hierarchical and close friendship relationships. In J. T. Woods & S. Duck (Eds.), *Under-studied relationships: Off the beaten track* (pp. 122-147). Thousand Oaks, CA: Sage.

Zurawik, D. (1996, March 6). What we watch may reflect our attitudes about work. *Richmond Times-Dispatch,* Sec. D, pp. 1, 3.

20

Communication Competence

FREDRIC M. JABLIN
University of Richmond

PATRICIA M. SIAS
Washington State University

As Spitzberg and Cupach (1984), among others, have observed, "Competence is an issue both perennial and fundamental to the study of communication" (p. 11). However, although communication competence has been an object of study in Western cultures since the time of the ancient Greeks (Fisher, 1978), it remains a "fuzzy" concept that both scholars and practitioners have struggled to conceptualize and operationalize (e.g., Bochner & Kelley, 1974; Bostrom, 1984; Habermas, 1970; Hart, Olsen, Robinson, & Mandleco, 1997; Hymes, 1972; Parks, 1994; Rubin, 1990; Wiemann, 1977). Not surpris-

ingly, difficulties associated with the study of communication competence generally, including its tendency to be viewed as a "hybrid" concept (part social science/part art), are reflected in research focused on exploring organizational communication competence, in particular (e.g., Jablin, Cude, House, Lee, & Roth, 1994).

Our goal in this chapter is not to resolve all the controversies associated with the conceptualization of organizational communication competence. Nor is our goal to provide a complete review of empirical research focused on organizational communication competence,

AUTHORS' NOTE: We would like to thank Dave Seibold and Ted Zorn for their helpful comments on an earlier draft of this chapter.

since this literature has been the subject of recent review (see Jablin et al., 1994). Rather, our purpose here is to (1) describe the ways organizational communication competence has been viewed by those who have studied it, (2) discuss a series of assumptions and premises associated with extant conceptualizations and investigations of organizational competence that we believe have hampered research in the area, and (3) propose a developmental-ecological framework for organizing and critiquing existing competence research and suggest how this framework might help guide future investigation of the fuzzy concept we have come to call organizational communication competence.

CONCEPTUALIZATIONS OF ORGANIZATIONAL COMMUNICATION COMPETENCE

Communication competence has been conceptualized in a variety of ways. In fact, there are almost as many definitions of communication competence as there are researchers interested in the construct. One frequent approach to conceptualizing competence has been to focus on *goal achievement.* Monge, Bachman, Dillard, and Eisenberg (1981), for example, equate competence with effectiveness and argue that "competent communicators are those who are effective at achieving their goals" (p. 506). Parks (1994) is more specific in his goal/control-oriented conceptualization of communication competence:

> Communication competence represents the degree to which individuals satisfy and perceive that they have satisfied their goals within the limits of a given social situation without jeopardizing their ability or opportunity to pursue other subjectively more important goals. (p. 595)

Other conceptualizations of communication competence concentrate on the ability to display *appropriate communication behaviors* in given situations (without direct consideration of whether or not one obtains one's objectives). Along these lines, one of the most popular conceptualizations of competence is that of Spitzberg and Cupach (1984), who state that "communication competence refers to the ability to demonstrate appropriate communication in a given context" (p. 66). Obviously, the nature of "appropriate" communication behavior needs to be identified if one uses this approach. As applied to the organizational context, this requires at least an elemental analysis of how tasks, situations, and person(s) interact to affect what is considered to be appropriate communication behavior.

In contrast to the above conceptualizations, McCroskey (1984), among others, views communication competence as distinct from behavior/performance. In particular, he distinguishes among "understanding," "ability," and "doing" (performance) and points out that "communication competence requires not only the ability to perform adequately certain communication behaviors, it also requires an understanding of those behaviors and the cognitive ability to make choices among behaviors" (p. 264). For McCroskey, however, competence does not require the actual performance of adequate behaviors, just the knowledge and ability to do so.

Jablin et al. (1994) build on these perspectives in developing a *resource-oriented* view of competence that reflects the linkages of competence with the related concepts of behavior/performance and effectiveness/goal achievement. Accordingly, they define competence as "the set of abilities, henceforth, termed *resources,* which a communicator has available for use in the communication process" (p. 125, emphasis in original). These resources include strategic communication knowledge (e.g., knowledge of appropriate communication rules and norms) and communication capacities (e.g., traits and abilities such as cognitive differentiation, perspective taking, and general encoding and decoding skills). In turn, they conceptualize "communication *performance* as the display of communication behaviors, upon which attributions of competence are based" (Jablin et al., 1994, p. 125). Thus, they stress the necessity of recognizing the fundamental interrelationship between communicative performance and communication competence, but also suggest the importance of distinguishing between the two in our research. In addition, Jablin et al. do not consider effectiveness/goal achievement as necessary or sufficient conditions for one to be perceived of as a relatively competent communicator. Rather, they support McCroskey's (1982, p. 3) position that "one may be effective without being competent and one may be competent without being effective," a notion that is unfortunately a truism in many organizations (see, e.g., Luthans, 1988).[1]

Another rather unique feature of the Jablin et al. (1994) approach to competence is their proposition that organizational communication competence should be analyzed at multiple levels of analysis, rather than at just the individual level, which typifies extant research in the area. They suggest that groups and organizations can be characterized with respect to unique group and organizational forms of communication knowledge and capacities and that these resources are not necessarily a mere aggregate of the competencies of their respective constituent parts (consistent with the systems notion that the whole is greater than the sum of its parts). Further, by conceptualizing communication competence at multiple levels of analysis Jablin et al. focus attention on the dynamic interdependence among the various levels of analysis. Curiously, while communication research exploring higher-order forms of competence is still scarce, the notion that groups and organizations possess "core competencies" has become popular in other areas of organizational studies (e.g., the study of strategic management; see Lei, Hitt, & Bettis, 1996; Marino, 1996; Nadler & Tushman, 1999; Prahalad & Hamel, 1990; Ulrich & Lake, 1990). To conclude, our purpose in this section is not to argue that one approach to conceptualizing communication competence is superior to another; rather, we suggest that

each approach emphasizes a different sort of dynamic relative to understanding competence.

In general, however, when one examines the conceptualizations of communication competence discussed above, two primary dimensions of the construct are reflected: behavior and cognition. Behavioral studies seek to identify the specific communication behaviors and skills that organizational members associate with competence. Research conceptualizing competence as "appropriate behavior" or "goal achievement" often falls into this category (e.g., Hirokawa, 1988; Snavely & Walters, 1983; Wheeless & Berryman-Fink, 1985). Cognitive research examines the various types of social knowledge and cognitive abilities associated with communication competence. Many of these studies conceptualize (though often implicitly) competence as represented by cognitive "resources" (e.g., Harris & Cronen, 1979; Sypher & Sypher, 1981). Within each of these two general categories of research, we find some studies that seek to identify behaviors or cognitive factors, respectively, associated with "effective" communication. As might be expected, few cognition-oriented studies directly explore relationships between cognition and communicative performance. However, this is also true for most behaviorally oriented studies as well—the focus of investigation is individuals' *perceptions* of competent communication behaviors.

EMPIRICAL COMPETENCE RESEARCH: THE STATE OF THE ART

To orient the reader to empirical organizational communication competence research, as well as the strengths and weaknesses of research in the area, this section presents a brief but representative literature review. We summarize major findings from previous reviews of the literature, and we survey results from studies reported in the 1990s according to (1) basic conceptual orientation (i.e., behavioral or cognitive), and (2) level of analysis examined (i.e., individual, group, or organization). Before proceeding further, it is important to stress that although we discuss behavioral and cognitive approaches to communication competence in relative isolation of each other, we do so only to highlight salient features of the literature. As noted above, there are often close interrelations between cognitive and behavioral approaches to the study of competence, and the literature is not always as neatly divided as we present it here. For example, one might easily argue that implicitly embedded within all communication skills are elements of communication knowledge and that the two are in a constant state of development. Unfortunately, most studies do not reflect this mutuality between skills/behavior and knowledge/cognition. Our review of the literature is followed by a critique organized in terms of a series of problematic assumptions that we believe have characterized organizational communication competence research.

Individual-Level Competence

Behavioral/skill studies. The bulk of existing research at the individual level of analysis has examined competence from a behavioral orientation. A great deal of attention, for example, has been directed toward developing inventories of what organizational members (very frequently managers) or students perceive to be communication behaviors indicative of a competent organizational communicator (e.g., Cooper, 1997; DiSalvo, 1980; DiSalvo & Larsen, 1987; Maes, Weldy, & Icenogle, 1997; Morse & Piland, 1981; Rader & Wunsch, 1980; Wheeless & Berryman-Fink, 1985). Skills frequently reported in such inventories include behaviors such as listening, giving feedback, advising, persuading, instructing, interviewing, and motivating (Jablin et al., 1994). More recent studies report findings in line with earlier research (Maes et al., 1997). For example,

Reinsch and Shelby (1996, 1997) found that MBA students perceived their most pressing work-related communication needs to include enhanced self-confidence, persuasiveness, ability to clearly express ideas, and control of communication anxiety. Research in this area reflects a common problem evident in studies that attempt to develop inventories of communication competencies: It is often quite difficult for respondents to describe the specific *communication* skills they require on the job. For example, the most frequent communication need identified by Reinsch and Shelby (1996) was labeled "enhanced self-confidence," a notion that could have innumerable possibilities with respect to specific communication skills, affective and motivational states, and the like.

Researchers have not only sought to identify specific communication behaviors associated with competence but also to ascertain the basic dimensions or "simple structure" of the competence construct. Along these lines, Wheeless and Berryman-Fink (1985) found individual-level communication competence in organizations to be reflected by two behavioral dimensions: altercentrism (empathy, listening, supportiveness, other-orientation) and interaction management (including appropriate turn taking and episode punctuation). Others, such as Snavely and Walters (1983), have identified a larger number of basic behavioral dimensions of competence (Snavely and Walters's research resulted in five dimensions: empathy, listening, self-disclosure, social anxiety, and versatility). More recently, Scudder and Guinan (1989) proposed a four-factor model of supervisor communication competence. The first two factors were extrapolated from the work of Monge et al. (1981) and included encoding abilities (e.g., getting to the point, writing ability, clarity of expression) and decoding abilities (e.g., listening, attentiveness, sensitivity). Their third and fourth factors were related to special characteristics associated with their sample of systems developers and included "maintaining communication" with others generally and "maintaining user relationships" specifically (e.g., keeping users updated on project status, soliciting user input).

Other scholars have examined relationships between individuals' perceptions of the communicative behaviors of supervisors, coworkers, and others in the workplace and their attributions about the communication competence of those persons. Berman and Hellweg (1989), for instance, found that supervisor participation in quality circles enhanced subordinates' perceptions of their supervisor's communicative competence, as well as the supervisor's perceptions of his or her own communication competence. Also investigating subordinates' perceptions of their supervisors' communication competence, Johnson (1992) determined that subordinates' perceptions were significantly influenced by the compliance-gaining strategies used by the supervisor. In particular, supervisors using "prosocial" compliance-gaining tactics were perceived as more communicatively competent than those who used "antisocial" tactics (negative altercasting). In a study focused on peer competence, Haas and Arnold (1995) discovered that perceptions of listening-related behaviors accounted for about 32% of the attributes associated with judgments of communication competence in coworkers.

Finally, consistent with a long tradition of pedagogically oriented studies of competence, recent research has also assessed the effectiveness of a variety of training methods and programs in enhancing individuals' development of organizational communication skills (e.g., public speaking, listening, giving presentations, and interviewing; see Cooper & Husband, 1993; Ford & Wolvin, 1993; Goodall, 1982; Seibold, Kudsi, & Rude, 1993). Questioning the degree to which workers really benefit from such training, and assuming a more "critical" stance to competence research generally, other scholars have begun to debate the extent to which oral and written communication skills training in organizations is inherently manipulative and thereby another form of "unobtrusive" managerial control (e.g., Elmes & Costello, 1992; Hargie & Tourish, 1994; Thompson, 1996).

Cognitive studies. Research examining individual-level competence as a cognitive construct assumes that to be a competent communicator an individual must possess certain traits, knowledge, and cognitive abilities. Beverly Sypher, Ted Zorn, and their colleagues, for instance, have investigated a variety of cognitive traits and abilities associated with communication competence, including cognitive differentiation (Sypher, 1981; Sypher & Sypher, 1981; Sypher, Sypher, & Leichty, 1983; Sypher & Zorn, 1986; Zorn, 1991; Zorn & Violanti, 1996), perspective taking (Sypher, 1981), and self-monitoring (Sypher & Sypher, 1983). Overall, results of this program of research suggest that the more developed a person's social-cognitive abilities are, the more successful he or she is in organizations (success operationalized as frequency of promotion and level in the organizational hierarchy; see Sypher & Zorn, 1986; Zorn & Violanti, 1996).

Others have employed tenets of symbolic interactionism as a basis for exploring communication competence, and in particular have focused on exploring how individuals develop the communicative knowledge that allows them to negotiate meaning with others in the organization (Harris & Cronen, 1979; Wellmon, 1988). Based on rules theory (e.g., Cushman & Whiting, 1972; Shimanoff, 1980), this line of research considers communication competence to be "a by-product of an individual's understanding of the organization's 'master contract' [shared beliefs or culture that define the organization], as well as the constitutive rules [that allow members to assign meaning to communicative acts] and regulative rules [standards for 'appropriate' action to bring about outcomes] which guide interaction" (Jablin et al., 1994, p. 118).

Although it has not yet been tested in the organizational context and is still in its early stages of development, Duran and Spitzberg's (1995) work on a measure of cognitive communicative competence warrants discussion, since it integrates several approaches to the study of competence. More specifically, initial results of their studies (exploring interpersonal communication generally) support the position that "cognitive communication competence entails anticipating potentially influential contextual variables, monitoring the manner in which a conversation transpires, and reflecting upon one's performance for the purpose of eliminating unsuccessful communication tacts" (Duran & Spitzberg, 1995, p. 270). In brief, their work suggests that cognitive communication competence should be viewed as a "cyclical process that leads to the continual refinement of one's social communication repertoire" (p. 270). This refinement process may lead communicators to develop particular "message design logics" (O'Keefe, 1988), which influence the ways they create messages. O'Keefe (1988), for instance, suggests that "the level of message design logic a person has achieved reflects the acquisition and integration of knowledge about communication processes" (p. 97). Thus, cognitive communication competence may enable communicators to develop the complex cognitive resources (e.g., higher-order message design logics) necessary for designing situationally appropriate and effective messages.

To summarize, cognitive studies of individual-level communication competence indicate that competent communicators possess traits such as cognitive differentiation, perspective taking, and self-monitoring. They also are knowledgeable about communication rules and norms, and they have the ability to anticipate and reflect on the interaction of situational factors and their own communicative behavior.

Group-Level Competence

As noted earlier, to date few studies have explicitly explored communication competence at the group and organizational levels of analysis. Rather, we find studies framed in terms of communication skills/behaviors associated with "effectiveness." Since the skills/behaviors and forms of communication knowledge that groups and organizations use

in the pursuit of their goals also can be conceptualized as communication capacities or resources, in the sections that follow we extricate relevant competence findings from the results of effectiveness studies.

Behavioral studies. Among other processes, Jablin et al. (1994) suggest that behavioral studies of group communication competence frequently focus on a group's internal and external ability to gather, transmit, and interpret information. Hence, they suggest that many of the variables traditionally associated with the study of communication and group process can be recast "in terms of the functions they serve in providing groups with the capability of responding to the information requirements of their information environments" (p. 130). Thus, for example, a group's internal feedback structures, intergroup communication networks, and the communication practices and structures that help it maintain successful collaboration (e.g., Health & Sias, 1999) can be considered elements of the group's communication resources. Along these lines, the program of research of Randy Hirokawa and his colleagues investigating communication behaviors associated with "competent" group decision making and effective work teams is germane. For instance, Hirokawa (1988) found that effective decision-making groups display a variety of "vigilant" communication behaviors including capabilities associated with problem analysis, assessment of decision criteria, and critical evaluation of alternative courses of action. In subsequent research, Hirokawa and Rost's (1992) data showed that effective decision-making groups pay more attention to the procedures they use to solve problems (the "process") than do ineffective groups.

Finally, in a recent test of the ecological validity of Gouran and Hirokawa's (1983) "functional" theory of effective decision making, Propp and Nelson (1996) found that members' "analysis of the problem," "orientation/establishment of operating procedures," and "evaluation of the positive consequences of alternatives" each had independent effects on the level of decision utility (effectiveness) of 29 work groups in a midwestern manufacturing firm. In brief, such processes and functions represent group-level communication resources that may aid a group in the pursuit of its goals.

Similarly, recent research investigating the extent to which the use of computer-mediated group communication systems, such as group support systems (GSSs), can augment a group's capabilities can be considered in terms of communication competence. GSSs were designed to facilitate group communication and, thus, a group's communication capabilities, by allowing parallel communication, enhancing "group memory" (i.e., most systems record electronically all comments and ideas that are generated), and providing structure to enable a group to remain focused on the task at hand (Andrews & Herschel, 1996, pp. 120-121). In particular, several studies that have examined the extent to which the use of a GSS helps groups manage conflict (e.g., Nunamaker, Dennis, Valacich, Vogel, & George, 1991; Poole, Holmes, & DeSanctis, 1991; Sambamurthy & Poole, 1992) are of interest, since their findings suggest that GSSs can hinder group communication competence by slowing down the communication process (typing words on a computer terminal is slower than speaking) and by reducing the availability of nonverbal cues (Nunamaker et al., 1991). At the same time, however, results from these studies also generally indicate that GSSs can facilitate conflict management by helping members identify and resolve differences (including conflicts of interest).

Cognitive studies. As at the individual level of analysis, cognitive studies of group-level competence tend to employ resource-based conceptualizations of communication competence. In particular, group-level competence is often viewed as residing in cognitive resources associated with group rules, structures, culture, history, and the like (Jablin et al., 1994). Thus, phenomena such as group

"synergy" and "mentality" (Bion, 1959), history, rituals and culture, value structures, languages/codes, fantasy themes (e.g., Bormann, Pratt, & Putnam, 1978), distributed cognition (e.g., Cole & Engeström, 1993; Hinz, Tindale, & Vollrath, 1997), "group knowledge structures" (Walsh, 1995), "transactive memory" (Liang, Moreland, & Argote, 1995), and the like all have embedded within them forms of group-level communication knowledge/competence. As Schein (1985, p. 149) observed with respect to group culture, culture implies "shared solutions, shared understandings, and consensus," all of which are inherently associated with knowledge of a group's communication "rules" (e.g., Schall, 1983). However, as Jablin et al. (1994, p. 129) note, it does not necessarily follow that groups with "stronger" cultures are more communicatively competent than groups with "weaker" cultures, since groups with very strong cultures may fall into a "competency trap often experienced in the form of 'groupthink' [Janis, 1972]."

The notion that group-level communication knowledge may be embedded in the fantasy themes that "spin out" in groups has been investigated in a recent study by Baron and Clair (1996). A fantasy theme is "the creative interpretation of events that fulfills a group's psychological or rhetorical need" (Baron & Clair, 1996, p. 17) and serves to help members make sense of the realities of their groups and organizations. Accordingly, fantasy themes become interpretive resources for groups, which frame knowledge structures regarding effective communication. Through inspection of archival records, direct observation, and interviews with organizational members, Baron and Clair were able to identify four fantasy themes associated with communication competence in a small, primarily female staffed, not-for-profit organization. Among the themes that were identified across groups, one suggested that stereotypical forms of male communication (e.g., communication should be efficient, objective, clear, and task oriented) versus female communication (which organizational members tended to define in opposite terms) were "conceived as being the most effective way to communicate" (Baron & Clair, 1996, p. 21).

Group-level cognitive resources such as knowledge structures and shared understandings have also been shown to influence the degree to which GSS technology (mentioned above as a group competence resource) is appropriated and used effectively by groups. Poole and DeSanctis (1992), for example, examined the structurational processes associated with the use of a group decision support system and found that effective appropriation of the technology by the group was influenced by the group's interpretations of the "spirit" and the features of the technology. Specifically, groups whose interpretations were consistent with (i.e., "faithful to") the spirit and features of the technology tended to be more effective than those whose interpretations were inconsistent ("unfaithful"). Accordingly, a group's ability to use technological resources depends on the quality of the group's cognitive resources such as group interpretations, knowledge, and understanding of the technology.

In summary, the fantasy themes, rules, language attributes, cultures, and structuration processes of groups guide their communication activity (e.g., Poole, Seibold, & McPhee, 1996), and thus can be analyzed and deconstructed to reveal the knowledge dimension of group-level communication competence.

Organizational Level of Analysis

Behavioral studies. Behaviorally oriented studies of communication competence at the organizational level of analysis focus "on the communication structures and programs which allow for the production, reception, and basic interpretation of messages exchanged with external and internal audiences" (Jablin et al., 1994, p. 133). Although rarely framed in terms of competence, orga-

nizational public relations and advertising activities and programs; participation in interorganizational communication networks; organizational recruiting methods; information data storage, retrieval, and processing systems (from the simplest filing system to elaborate computerized expert systems); and organizational house organs/ publications and other forms of corporate communication all represent mechanisms that allow organizations to communicate with their internal and external environments. Hence, these activities, programs, and media all represent resources that organizations as entities can use in the communication process. For example, the intra- and interorganizational networks and media available to an organization to use in communicating with its environment during times of crisis reflect a distinct set of organizational communication capacities (e.g., Krackhardt & Stern, 1988). Thus, it would seem that the more behavioral choices available to an organization (or the size of its communication "genre repertoire"; Orlikowski & Yates, 1994), the more competent the organization (assuming related forms of knowledge to guide behavior and sufficient motivation to initiate and sustain communicative actions). In addition, an organization's behavioral competence may be reflected in the extent to which messages communicated via various media and representatives are consistent across one another (especially in times of crisis).

Cognitive studies. Jablin et al. (1994) suggest that communication knowledge at the organizational level of analysis is evident in resources such as organizational "knowledge bases" (Johnston & Carrico, 1988), "knowledge structures" (Walsh, 1995), organizational culture (e.g., Friedman, 1989; Sackmann, 1991), and mental maps and memories (Walsh & Ungson, 1991) and reflects "both the collective knowledge of groups and individuals within an organization and the strategies which guide the interpretation of situational and environmental cues" (p. 132). Moreover, Jablin et al. propose that it is these memories, embedded within communication processes such as an organization's "semantic networks" (Hutchins, 1991; Monge & Eisenberg, 1987), that allow an organization to "interpret as a system" (Daft & Weick, 1984, p. 285). Not surprisingly, there is a close overlap between the development of organization-level communication knowledge and organizational learning processes (see Miller, 1996; Raelin, 1997; Weick & Ashford, Chapter 18, this volume).

Organization-level communication knowledge also can be embedded within organizational routines, which represent ways of doing things (Winter, 1986) but do not necessarily represent activity that is performed in a mindless fashion; rather, organizational routines are continuously "worked at" in day-to-day conduct (Cohen & Bacdayan, 1994; Giddens, 1984). Along these lines, for example, Pentland and Rueter (1994) studied characteristics of supposedly nonroutine service interactions and discovered these interactions were "highly regular" in nature (when analyzed in terms of grammars of action—the normative rules and processes that set the possibilities for acting in the organization; see Pentland, 1995). More specifically, their research showed that organizational routines do not represent single patterns of action but "rather a set of possible patterns—enabled and constrained by a variety of organizational, social, physical, and cognitive structures—from which organizational members enact particular performances" (Pentland & Rueter, 1994, p. 491). In other words, similar to the ways in which knowledge of the grammar associated with a particular language allows one to construct innumerable sentences, organizational routines can be analyzed in terms of how they enable organizational members to enact a wide variety of communicative performances (and to improvise; e.g., Moorman & Miner, 1998).

To summarize, organization-level communication knowledge is embedded within organizational routines, procedures, policies, and values and in the collective knowledge of organizational members. Research exploring organization-level communication knowledge is still in its infancy, and we are just beginning to understand how organizations create and recreate their meaning systems so as to maximize their ability to interpret internal and external information, the consequences of their actions, and the like.

Underlying Assumptions in the Literature

Extant research reflects several underlying assumptions and problematic premises about organizational communication competence that we believe have hindered progress with respect to research in this area. This section provides a discussion of these issues, including some noted by Jablin et al. (1994), as well as others not considered in that review.

Discrete View of Competence

Although it is unlikely that most researchers believe communication competence is a dichotomous variable (i.e., that individuals can be classified as either competent or incompetent), with little variation between the two extremes, discussions of competence frequently present the construct in such terms. The heavy emphasis in the research literature on identifying communication skills associated with competent communicators, in part, accounts for the tendency to view competence as a discrete variable. More specifically, because researchers interested in developing skill inventories typically ask respondents to identify communication abilities associated with persons they perceive to be "competent" communicators, the issue of the "degree" to which one must evidence these qualities to be considered competent is not addressed; rather, it is assumed, by default, that if one does not possess the various skills, one is "incompetent." Relatedly, researchers often treat the various skills they associate with competence as if they are mutually exclusive of one another, whereas they may share considerable amounts of variance or be embedded within one another.

As evident from the above discussion, competence may be more fruitfully considered a continuous construct. Communicators should be viewed along a continuum as relatively more or less competent. Jablin et al. (1994) move toward this type of conceptualization with their distinctions between "threshold" and "proficient" levels of competence. Threshold competencies are "generic capabilities which are essential to performing jobs, but which are not sufficient to cause superior levels of effectiveness in communication" (Jablin et al., 1994, p. 120); they represent minimally required, role-related encoding and decoding capacities. Jablin et al. (1994, p. 120) argue that as a consequence of organizational selection, socialization, and training processes, most organizational newcomers are communicatively competent at the threshold level (although it must be recognized that what is considered threshold competence in one organization may be considered less than or more than the threshold level in another organization). Accordingly, although organizational newcomers may be considered competent, they are likely to be less competent communicators than veteran employees with several years tenure, who have developed proficient or above-threshold communication competencies (e.g., Jablin, 1994). Typically, those who are proficient communicators possess a "deep" versus "surface" level set of communication capabilities (e.g., they recognize messages that contain double meanings or require "reading between the lines" to understand), as well as a broader repertoire of communication resources to draw on in any given communication situation (e.g., they are capable of appropriately communicating a message via many available organizational media vs. a select few).

It is also important to recognize that it may not be appropriate to categorize a communicator as "incompetent" (relatively speaking) simply because she or he has not yet developed the capacities necessary to communicate competently in a particular environment. The absence of competence does not necessarily imply incompetence. Rather, it is possible for a communicator to be in a state of "precompetence," a notion that recognizes the person's potential for becoming competent (Langer & Parks, 1990). In other words, precompetence represents a temporary learning state in which the communicator is in the process of learning and developing the abilities necessary for competent organizational communication.

Competence as Static

In light of the preceding commentary, it is not surprising to discover that descriptions of organizational communication competence often fail to develop the dynamic, developmental nature of the construct; rather, competence is viewed in fairly static terms. On the whole, competence researchers have not adequately addressed the notion that levels of communication competence may change over time. For example, a newcomer who enters an organization with a threshold level of competence is likely to become increasingly more competent (or proficient) over time as he or she obtains more knowledge and skills (e.g., Jablin, 1994). However, competence levels also may *decrease* as communicators enter new situations (e.g., transfer jobs or move to different organizations) or experience the effects of broader societal developments (e.g., the proliferation of new computer-mediated communication technologies). Not only may a communicator's overall level of competence vary over time, but also the ways or strategies that she or he employs to achieve particular communicative goals. Consistent with the open-systems principle of equifinality (e.g., Katz & Kahn, 1978), communicators are capable of learning new ways to display their competence and perform their duties. Thus, a proficient communicator may not focus his or her efforts on determining the best communication strategy for any particular situation (a static orientation to competence), but rather focus on developing the capacity and knowledge to "enact several alternative strategies that might be equally appropriate for the situation" (Jablin et al. 1994, p. 124).

Extant research also tends to assume that once one learns a particular set of skills and abilities, one's level of competence with respect to those capabilities will remain constant over time. Although this may be true for some capabilities, especially those at the threshold level, it may not be true for other, more sophisticated forms of competence. In brief, research has focused on ways to develop communication competence (especially via skills training) and has neglected to consider how communicators can maintain their levels of competence over time. Clearly, the dynamic, processual nature of communication competence requires more attention in future research.

Assumption of Rationality

Consistent with most traditional approaches to organizational studies, research exploring organizational communication competence has tended to assume that organizational members think and behave rationally. However, as Jablin et al. (1994) caution, "in our conceptualizations of competence we need to recognize that people don't always use their communication capabilities in logical ways and that relationship history factors, motives, emotions, etc. can affect competence levels" (p. 123). For example, even though most managers are aware that punishment in the form of an angry reprimand of a subordinate in the presence of his or her coworkers is inappropriate (e.g., Cusella, 1987) and rarely solves any problems (if anything, it creates new problems), are there many managers who have not at one time or another acted in this manner?

It is also important to consider the notion of *mindless* versus mindful behavior when considering issues of competence (e.g.,

Langer, 1978). Research suggests that much behavior in organizations is guided by cognitive "scripts" (e.g., Gioia, 1986). These scripts are unconsciously triggered by situational cues that cause individuals to act automatically and without conscious thought ("mindlessly") in particular ways. These scripts are learned and developed over time, and their overuse may be an indication of "over-competence." That is, an individual who finds herself frequently engaging mindlessly in behaviors may have surpassed the proficient level of competency and become overcompetent. At this point, such an individual is likely to have fallen into the "competency trap" (March, 1988) where overlearning undermines the potential for new learning. Although it may seem somewhat counter-rational, it may be necessary for communicators to periodically experience overcompetence to maintain, over the long run, consistently high levels of competence. In other words, occasional minor falls into the competency trap may jar communicators to reconsider how they are communicatively responding to what appear to be routine situations, thereby facilitating the development of new communication knowledge and abilities, and diminishing the likelihood of falling into a competency trap from which one cannot escape. Ultimately, as Jablin et al. (1994) have observed, the more proficient communicator "not only possesses a repertoire of scripted communication knowledge, but is also capable of knowing when to shift from mindless (script-guided) to mindful behavior (active consideration of multiple interpretations/meanings of the situation)" (p. 124).

Invariance in Motivation

"Applied to communication, motivation is what sets in motion our communicative efforts, directs us toward specific strategies, and impels us to continue" (Zorn, 1993, p. 517). On the whole, researchers have tended to assume that organizational members maintain fairly constant levels of motivation with respect to their desire to communicate and be perceived of as competent communicators. In other words, the assumption is that if someone has the ability to communicate competently, that person will want to do so in most situations. It is likely, however, that people differ in the extent to which they are motivated to display the communication behaviors they are able to perform (between-person variation). In addition, it is likely that across time and situations, any particular individual's motivation to communicate in a competent fashion may vary (within-person variation).

Although motivation is generally recognized as an important antecedent to performance, it has received little attention among scholars exploring organizational communication competence. In particular, Zorn (1993) points out that "the construct of motivation has largely been overshadowed by constructs such as ability, skill, and knowledge in the communication competence literature" (p. 517). Consistent with principles associated with goal-setting theory (e.g., Locke & Henne, 1986), Zorn (1993) maintains that goals have the greatest impact on motivation. Specifically, he proposes that the more difficult, specific, and highly valued the goal, the more motivated an individual will be to communicate. Thus, for a competent person to be motivated to communicate, he or she must be motivated to do so in pursuit of a desired goal. Zorn (1993) recognizes that while some communicative goals are often below the conscious awareness level of interactants, given the purposive nature of organizations, "individuals are consciously aware of at least *some* of their communicative goals" (p. 541). In addition, he also supports O'Keefe's (1988, p. 82) argument that while communicative goals are not necessarily as clear and consciously recognized as other kinds of goals (e.g., performance goals), they often "are socially constituted objectives that are implicit in the predefined activities of human cultures." Similarly, Kellermann, Reynolds, and Chen (1991) emphasize the importance of "metagoals" in motivation to communicate. According to metagoal theory, an individual may have a va-

riety of goals motivating him or her to communicate (e.g., information seeking, comforting). The goals, however, are constrained by metagoals such as efficiency and appropriateness. Thus, for instance, one may be motivated to perform particular communication behaviors to comfort another person *if* the behavior can be performed in an appropriate (i.e., polite) and efficient (i.e., "without expending unnecessary time, energy, or resources"; Kellermann et al., 1991, p. 364) manner.

The notion of self-efficacy is also important to consider when assessing an individual's motivation to communicate. Self-efficacy is "concerned with people's beliefs in their capabilities to mobilize the motivation, cognitive resources, and courses of action needed to exercise control over task demands" (Bandura, 1990, p. 316). We already have noted that communication competence primarily has been studied as a cognitive and/or behavioral construct. The notions of motivation and self-efficacy provide an important link between the two. That is, when individuals know what to do, whether or not they enact a communicative behavior depends in large part on their belief that they are able to enact the behavior successfully (Spitzberg & Cupach, 1984, p. 158). Thus, a person may possess the knowledge and skills necessary to communicate competently, yet because of a low level of self-efficacy in a particular task setting, he or she may not be motivated to enact the behaviors (or persevere with the behaviors in the face of obstacles that arise as a consequence of the initial display of the behaviors). In other words, the less individuals perceive they are able to communicate competently with respect to a particular task (i.e., "felt" competence), the less they are motivated to communicate (Zorn, 1993, p. 542).

In sum, rather than assuming within-individual and between-individuals levels of motivation to communicate are relatively constant, we need to recognize that motivation fluctuates and may differentially affect individuals' levels of organizational communication competence. In addition, we need to consider the extent to which conscious and unconscious communicative goals (and metagoals; see Kellermann et al., 1991), as well as individuals' beliefs of self-efficacy with respect to communicative tasks (regardless of the accuracy of those beliefs), are associated with displays and perceptions of organizational communication competence. Also, research should explore how the labels that coworkers and others in the task setting use to describe a person's ability (such as classifying a person as "incompetent" with respect to a particular communicative task) may affect the individual's self-efficacy, motivation to communicate, access to important forms of organizational discourse and knowledge, and quality of communicative performance. As Bandura (1990) noted in discussing the notion of competence in general, "Research shows that when people are cast in subordinate roles or assigned inferior labels, implying limited competence, they perform activities at which they are highly skilled less well than when they do not bear the negative labels" (p. 324).

Assumption of Objectivity

Many, although certainly not all, discussions of organizational communication competence treat competence as though it was an "objective" construct. This is unfortunate, because

> competence and incompetence represent labeling phenomena. They cannot be understood as entities in themselves, apart from the people who ascribe them. Although certain kinds of performance can be measured objectively, competence cannot be, because competence is not itself an objective phenomenon. What is competence in one culture may be incompetence in another, and not only levels but even dimensions of performance may differ across cultures in terms of the extent to which they are viewed as relevant for judging competence. (Sternberg, 1990, p. 144)

Thus, it is essential that research exploring competence recognizes it as an attributional

rather than objective phenomenon. That is, we make attributions regarding an individual's level of competence by comparing him or her (generally and with respect to particular communicative performances) to others, and the standards by which we make such comparisons vary across individuals, groups, organizations, and cultures.

Along these lines, Jablin et al. (1994) point out that values play an important role in perceptions of communication competence, and such values differ across organizations. As they explain, "The deep-structure values of the organization inform members of the capabilities they need to possess, beyond the threshold level, in order to be optimal communicators in the organization" (p. 121). Because value structures differ across organizations, what is perceived as competent communication (especially above the threshold level) may differ across organizations and should be explicitly considered in studies exploring competence (e.g., Zorn & Violanti, 1996).

Ideological Assumptions Ignored

Although rarely discussed, conceptualizations of organizational communication competence reflect varying underlying organizational and disciplinary ideologies. As Spitzberg and Duran (1993) observe, "The criteria and content of competence theories have consistently reflected ideological undercurrents, which reveal themselves in terms of cultural, cocultural, and contextual variations" (p. 1). In other words, theories of organizational communication competence are not "neutral" in nature, but privilege certain qualities of communication over others (Baron & Clair, 1996). For example, in many organizations "masculine" approaches and models of communication (e.g., a competent communicator controls the expression of emotions) are privileged over more "feminine" ones (e.g., in which the expression of emotions is considered appropriate). Thus, "the socio-historical context in which competence research has been conducted has determined the specific constituents of competence. These constituents often reflect ideological preferences" (Spitzberg & Duran, 1993, p. 7).

In addition, the fact that most theories of competence assume that competent communicators not only have the requisite skills to communicate but must also possess knowledge of appropriate ways of communicating to achieve goals suggests a connection between understanding the discursive practices of organizations and of obtaining power in organizations. Moreover, the notion that there are "appropriate" versus "inappropriate" ways of communicating in organizations may stifle the creativity of organizational members and serve to reinforce "the status quo, conformity, and the maintenance of the extant social order" (Spitzberg & Duran, 1993, p. 11).

Finally, it is also important for us to recognize the ideological baggage we have assumed by borrowing competence concepts and related research methodologies from other fields such as psychology, sociology, and management. Even notions associated with communication competence extrapolated from the study of interpersonal communication competence in nonorganizational settings may be problematic when applied to the organizational setting (e.g., the extent to which openness in communication should be valued; see Eisenberg & Witten, 1987). In brief, as Redding (1979, p. 321) cautioned, organizational communication scholars need to be aware that when we "import" concepts from other disciplines, we also import ideologies that may constrain our understanding of various communication phenomena, including the notion of communication competence.

Ethical Issues Overlooked

Generally speaking, competence research has failed to consider the relationship between communication competence and standards of ethical communication. For example, while researchers often conceptualize communication competence as the successful attainment of communicative goals (e.g., Monge et al., 1981; Parks, 1994), they less frequently con-

sider the questions: Do the ends justify the means? Should "truth" be the central criterion for determining standards of ethical communication (e.g., Habermas, 1970)? It is not difficult, for instance, to imagine a situation in which lying enhances one's ability to successfully achieve a goal, perhaps the goal of presenting a particular image (i.e., impression management; see Giacalone & Rosenfeld, 1991; Wexley, 1986). Thus, although goal attainment may indicate communication competence, as Jablin et al. (1994) argue, "as scholars we are obligated to consider the issue of whether or not a competent communicator is an ethical communicator" (p. 122).

Ethical issues are not only relevant considerations at the individual level of analysis but are also important at higher-order levels of analysis. For example, organizations that are highly institutionalized in nature often seek to communicate to their relevant external audiences/stakeholders that they use "legitimate" practices (e.g., Meyer & Rowan, 1977). However, the practices perceived as legitimate by an organization's external audiences may not always be the most practical or efficient for the organization. Accordingly, in communicating with their environments, "competent" organizations may "decouple" their internal practices from what they present to their external audiences (e.g., in information provided in annual reports and in related financial and accounting reports). Are such practices deceptive or merely signs of competent organizational communication? How important should honesty and ethics be in classifying an organization as (relatively speaking) communicatively competent?

Focus on the Individual Level of Analysis

To date, most research exploring organizational communication competence has focused on competence at the individual/person level of analysis. However, as Jablin et al. (1994) explain, "workgroups and organizations as entities can be described in terms of their communication competence" (p. 119). Importantly, they also suggest that group and organizational competence each represents more than the aggregate competence of its constituent parts (i.e., individuals and groups). Thus, as reviewed earlier in this chapter, group competence may be evident in the mechanisms the group uses for processing information, the specialized languages and codes used for encoding and decoding messages, rituals for assimilating newcomers into communication networks, and so forth. At the same time, however, it is important to recognize that communication competence at any particular level of analysis influences, and is influenced by, competence at the other levels of analysis. In studying organizational communication competence, we need to explore the embeddedness of the various levels of competence within and between one another, and the degree to which the various levels mutually influence each other.

Perceptions of *individual* communication competence, for instance, are influenced by the behaviors valued and rewarded by the *organization*. At the same time, the types of behaviors valued by the organization are likely to be influenced by the communicative behavior of individuals. Similarly, *group* effectiveness is influenced by the knowledge and abilities of *individual* group members, as well as *organizational* factors such as reward and support systems (Hirokawa & Keyton, 1995). Concomitantly, group effectiveness exerts influence on attributes of individual and organizational communication competence. For example, being a member of a successful work group may influence the self-efficacy of an individual group member, providing that individual with more motivation to communicate in a competent manner.

In sum, we believe researchers studying organizational communication competence need to consider competence as a multiple-level construct, recognize that the various levels of competence are embedded within one another, and as a consequence, examine how the levels mutually influence each other with respect to what competence means.

AN ECOLOGICAL MODEL OF ORGANIZATIONAL COMMUNICATION COMPETENCE

In light of the limitations we have highlighted with respect to research exploring competence, we present an alternative model of organizational communication competence in this section. This model, which incorporates an ecological perspective (e.g., Bronfenbrenner, 1979; Johnson, Staton, & Jorgensen-Earp, 1995; Magnusson, 1995), proposes that human/group/organization development is best viewed as a product of the dynamic interaction of the environment and developing person/group/organization. That is, the development of communication competence (at the individual, group, or organizational level of analysis) is influenced by, and influences, the environment (and the various ecological systems that make up the environment) in which the process occurs. Accordingly, organizational communication competence may be profitably investigated by considering the influences of the environment or ecological systems in which the individual, group, or organization is embedded.

In particular, the model presented in Figure 20.1 conceptualizes organizational communication competence along three dimensions: competence assessment criteria, competence levels, and ecological systems. Such a conceptualization acknowledges the cognitive and behavioral components of communication competence, the developmental nature of communication competence, and the embeddedness of communication competence at various levels of analysis.

Communication Competence Indicators and Assessment Criteria

As suggested in the preceding sections, communication competence is generally conceptualized in terms of cognition (knowledge of communication rules, symbols, cognitive

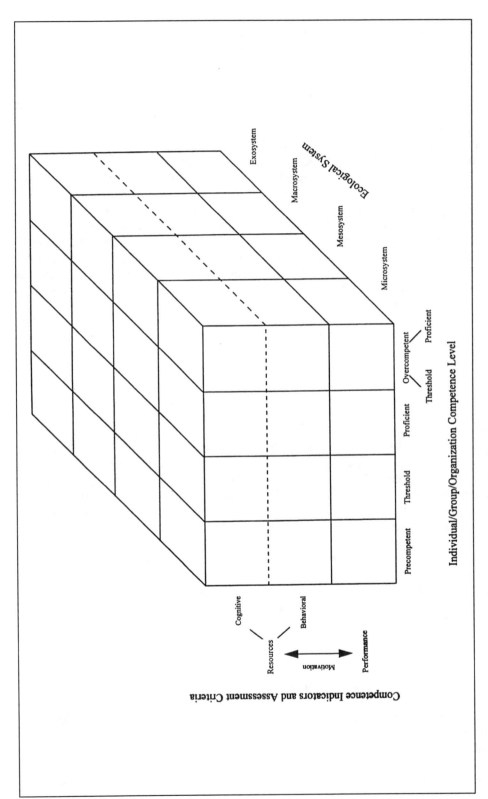

Figure 20.1. Ecological Model of Organizational Communication Competence

complexity, etc.), behavior/skill repertoire, and performance (actual display of communicative behavior upon which attributions of an entity's communication knowledge and skills are primarily based). In essence, the former two competence elements (which when considered together comprise the communication resources available to a communicator; see Jablin et al., 1994) represent the criteria used to evaluate communicative performance. As a consequence, one dimension of our model (the vertical dimension in Figure 20.1) focuses on organizational communication competence assessment criteria. Although these components can be conceptualized as representing distinct criteria, they are not necessarily mutually exclusive of one another; for example, judgments of a person's communication skills may be interrelated with judgments of the person's communicative knowledge.

In addition to communication resources, we include motivation to communicate as an assessment criterion, because it serves as a force linking the use of communicative resources with the actual performance of communicative behavior. In other words, the model reflects the possibility that communicators may have the necessary knowledge and skills to communicate competently, but may not always be motivated to do so. Thus, it is possible that even though a person may have performed inadequately, she or he may not be judged by others as communicatively incompetent (relatively speaking) unless the person is also judged to have expended a reasonable amount of effort in the communication process. The inclusion of motivation in our model also takes into consideration the possibility that a communicator may be perceived as possessing the necessary communication resources to perform competently, but does not do so because of low self-confidence/self-efficacy with respect to his or her capabilities (i.e., low "felt" competence). Finally, the reciprocal arrow linking resources and performance also recognizes that performance can affect resources; that is, how individuals perform certain communicative behaviors affects their motivation to enact the behaviors in the future and their willingness to learn new behaviors, thus increasing their resources.

Levels of Competence

As noted in the preceding section, communication competence is best represented as a continuum where communicators are relatively more or less competent. The horizontal dimension of our model presents varying levels of communication competence. As discussed earlier, in a move toward such a conceptualization, Jablin et al. (1994) offered the notions of *threshold* competence (e.g., "generic capabilities which are essential to performing jobs, but which are not sufficient to cause superior levels of effectiveness in communication"; p. 120) and *proficiency* (e.g., above-average or above-threshold communication knowledge and abilities). To these levels of competence, our model adds two additional levels: (1) precompetence and (2) overcompetence. *Precompetence* represents a temporary learning state where an individual obtains knowledge and develops the capabilities necessary to be a competent communicator. *Overcompetence* represents the state where an individual's communicative behavior in the organization is guided largely by cognitive scripts; that is, the person engages in communicative behavior in a largely "mindless," unconscious manner such that the individual is unable to recognize and process unique cues available in the task setting that should be considered in directing his or her communicative behavior. We further distinguish between threshold and proficient levels of overcompetence. Thus, just as an entity at the threshold level can engage in (essential) communicative behavior in a scripted, relatively mindless fashion, a communicator who is proficient and overcompetent can mindlessly perform communication behaviors, although these behaviors will be associated with superior as compared to essential communication effectiveness.

We therefore conceptualize communication competence as a continuum ranging from precompetence to overcompetence. Two issues are important to consider, however. First, we reemphasize here the notion that attributions or perceptions of competence are *relative,* not objective. That is, a communicator in a particular organization is perceived as relatively more or less competent compared to salient others (e.g., other employees in the same organization or work group), not compared to some objective "ideal" communicator (although attributions may, in part, be based on perceptions of prototypic or "average" communication competence in particular settings; e.g., Pavitt & Haight, 1986). Second, competence is a *local,* rather than global phenomenon; that is, one's level of communication competence likely varies across domains. For example, one may perform some communicative behaviors with little thought (e.g., is overcompetent when communicating with a customer), yet engage in other behaviors in a very *mindful* and proficient fashion (e.g., communicating with a supervisor about a work-related problem).

A developmental conceptualization of communication competence highlights the importance of two concepts: change and time (e.g., Magnusson, 1995). As mentioned earlier, levels of communication competence change as individuals (or groups or organizations) obtain knowledge and develop new abilities. Further, such change can be progressive or regressive. That is, competence does not always increase, but can decrease for a variety of reasons. Such change is also not likely to be a linear developmental process. One does not necessarily go from precompetence to threshold, proficient, and overcompetent levels in that order. Some communicators, for example, may never reach a proficient level of competence; rather, they vacillate between precompetent and threshold levels. On the other hand, one may be a proficient communicator and regress toward threshold or even precompetent levels.

As Magnusson (1995) notes, "Development always has a temporal dimension" (p. 20). Accordingly, the notion of time is important to consider. For instance, it is likely that changes in communication competency levels occur at different rates for different individuals, groups, and organizations. While some entities develop proficient communication competencies quickly, others may develop their competencies at a slower pace. Consistent with this notion, Alwin (1995) argues that an ecological perspective recognizes that "each individual is unique and that one aspect of this uniqueness is the heterogeneity of experience with the environment" (p. 220). Thus, individuals (and groups and organizations) in similar ecological systems are likely to be affected by those systems in unique ways, resulting in developmental variation between individuals (or groups or organizations).

Ecological Systems

The ecological perspective emphasizes the notion that "both individuals and environments change and interact as totalities [and] . . . changes do not take place in single aspects isolated from the totality" (Magnusson, 1995, p. 39). Consistent with this view, we suggest that the development of communication competence (progressive, maintenance, or regressive trajectories) and the rate at which such development occurs over time are likely to be influenced by individual, group, organizational, and sociocultural factors. In particular, our ecological model of organizational communication competence revolves around four systems represented along the depth dimension (z-axis) of Figure 20.1: (1) the microsystem, which contains the developing organizational member and other persons in the immediate work environment (e.g., supervisors, coworkers, and clients); (2) the mesosystem, which represents the interrelations among various microsystems (e.g., what individuals learn in their project teams may affect their competence in the functional work groups in which they are members); (3) the macrosystem, which does not represent the immediate context in which an individual works, but does impinge on him or her (i.e., major divisions of the organization and the organization itself as a whole); and (4) the exosystem, which represents the overarching cultural belief system, forms of knowledge, social, technological, and political ideologies, and so forth that manifest themselves in the form and content of the other subsystems (e.g., sex role stereotypes that are derived from societal beliefs but may be reflected in the other systems).[2]

In brief, an ecological perspective emphasizes system embeddedness. That is, the actions of one element of the system affect the other elements. Such impact is not unidirectional, however. Rather, our model highlights the notion of reciprocal influence (e.g., Bronfenbrenner, 1979). This notion acknowledges that each element in the total system is an active, not passive, participant in the overall functioning of that system. Accordingly, the various system levels influence, and at the same time are influenced by, each other (Friedman & Wachs, 1999; Moen, Elder, & Luscher, 1995).

In the following sections, we discuss characteristics of each ecological system and consider the potential influence of these systems on communication competence at individual, group, and organizational levels of analysis. In the interests of clarity, each section considers the influence of each ecological system on communication competence in relative isolation of the other systems. An example is then provided at the end of each section to illustrate the notions of mutual influence and the embeddedness of the levels of analysis discussed above. Many of our examples are speculative in nature and are designed merely to elucidate our developmental-ecological approach, and the ways in which the approach can be used to study communication competence. We begin by discussing the highest-order ecological system, the exosystem. We do this not to demonstrate higher-order determinism, but because it enables us to more clearly explain the characteristics of the model.

The Exosystem

The exosystem represents the overarching belief systems; forms of knowledge; and social, technological, and economic systems and trends as well as political ideologies of the larger society in which individuals, groups, and organizations exist. For the sake of brevity in discussing the exosystem, we consider only two recent trends in society that have important implications for communication competence in organizations. These trends, which have been highlighted throughout this volume, are the move toward a global economy and the rapid growth of information/communication technology.

Globalization

Industry is becoming increasingly global with more organizations doing business in other countries. As Eisenberg and Goodall (1993) point out, "About one-third of the profits of U.S. companies, as well as one-sixth of the nation's jobs, come from international business [Cascio, 1986; Offerman & Gowing, 1990]" (p. 9).

The move toward globalization carries a variety of expectations regarding what constitutes competent communication at the individual, group, and organizational levels of analysis. In general, a communicator "becomes interculturally competent when messages may be encoded and directed as if from within the new culture and when messages from the new culture may be decoded and responded to successfully" (Beamer, 1992). More specifically, to communicate competently in a global marketplace, individuals typically need adequate knowledge regarding the values, symbol systems, beliefs, and communication norms of cultures other than one's dominant culture, as well as knowledge about the economic situations of other countries (e.g., Adler & Bartholomew, 1992; Collier, 1994; Hogan & Goodson, 1990; Stohl, Chapter 10, this volume; Triandis, 1973; Triandis & Albert, 1987). Communication competence may also be enhanced if an individual is relatively high in tolerance for ambiguity, appreciates diversity, is capable of establishing relationships with those from other cultures, and has the ability to speak languages other than his or her native one (e.g., Barna, 1991; Hammer, 1987; Nishida, 1985; Ruben, 1977; Zimmermann, 1995). Other individual abilities often associated with intercultural communication competence include knowledge of ways to display respect in different cultures, empathy, flexibility, willingness to suspend judgment of others, and culture-specific knowledge of problem-solving methods and ways of managing interactions (e.g., Dinges & Lieberman, 1989; Koester, 1985; Koester & Olebe, 1988; Ruben & Kealey, 1979; Sell, 1983; Sriussadaporn-Charoenngam & Jablin, 1999).

Individuals who have never worked in a global context are likely to enter a new position in a precompetent state. This is often the case, for example, with newly expatriated employees in multinational organizations (e.g., Black, Gregersen, & Mendenhall, 1992; Wiseman & Shuter, 1994). Prior to leaving for an overseas assignment, these individuals are often provided with training covering topics such as language skills and overviews of cultural norms in the country to which they are dispatched. Presumably, once trained (though language skills may still require development), the expatriate employees are able to begin their new assignments with a threshold level of competence (e.g., basic encoding and decoding abilities appropriate to the new culture). Successful expatriate employees develop proficient levels of communication competence over time. Ratiu (1983), for instance, indicates that the most effective expatriate managers, whom he labels "internationals," demonstrate cognitive traits that go beyond the broad-based concepts of tolerance for ambiguity, flexibility, empathy, and knowledge of overall cultural communication norms. Rather, in communicating with others, internationals do not rely on overall cultural stereotypes but attempt to approach others as individuals and adjust to them accordingly.

The move toward globalization also has important implications for communication competence at the group level. Groups and teams in organizations are becoming more culturally diverse (e.g., Stohl, Chapter 10, this volume; Wiseman & Shuter, 1994). In light of the fact that national cultures vary among one another with respect to which they value "groupness" (as reflected in the cultural value of individualism-collectivism; see Hofstede, 1981), at a very basic level the move toward globalization and more culturally heterogeneous work groups creates new challenges for group process. For example, Americans, who tend to be individualistic, logical, and technical in decision making, and the Japanese, who tend to be more social/group oriented in decision making (Stewart, 1985), may experience difficulties when working together in teams. Other problems culturally diverse groups/ teams face include differential conversational norms, expectations about work, face-saving practices, meanings associated with the physical workspace the group occupies, ways of managing conflict, language capabilities, and the like (e.g., Bantz, 1993; Stohl, this volume). Under these conditions, one path to competence may be reflected in the notions of "third culture" or "culturally synergistic" groups (Adler, 1980; Casmir, 1993; Moran & Harris, 1981; Stohl, this volume), in which group members enact communication systems that transcend the characteristics of any particular culture.

Levels of communication competence in culturally diverse work groups also may change over time. Milliken and Martins (1996), for instance, note that cultural diversity tends to decrease group effectiveness at the early stages of the group's life. As they explain, this is "presumably because it takes some time for group members to get over their interpersonal differences on observable dimensions that tend to be associated with lower levels of initial attraction and social integration [O'Reilly, Caldwell, & Barnett, 1989]" (Milliken & Martins, 1996, p. 407). Research indicates that after this early stage group performance can be enhanced by diversity, particularly in terms of the group's ability to generate a variety of perspectives and ideas (Milliken & Martins, 1996). The development of group-level *communication* competence may parallel that of overall group competence. That is, group communication competence may lie at a fairly low, perhaps precompetent, level early on. As group members gain knowledge, particularly knowledge regarding how to communicate with the other members (which should develop as a by-product of working together), group-level communication competence is likely to increase to threshold or proficient levels.

Competence at the organizational level also is influenced by globalization. To succeed in a global marketplace, organizations must display a variety of capabilities. An organization must have knowledge about the global aspects of its particular industry, as well as knowledge of the cultures and communication norms and practices of the host countries in which it operates. An organization may also need to understand the communication implications of related issues, such as each country's political and ideological system, labor regulations, tax policies, and energy and safety regulations, to communicate in a competent manner (Teboul, Chen, & Fritz, 1994). Globalization and increased diversity also require that organizations prepare their employees for communication in a global world. Accordingly, competent organizations might include a commitment to diversity in their mission statements and provide instructional seminars for members on topics such as intercultural communication, diversity, and the global marketplace (Cox & Blake, 1991).

In addition, competent organizations need the resources to communicate on a global scale with their various constituents. Accordingly, competent organizations must have access to and the ability to use a wide variety of communication media and telecommunication systems, fax systems, the Internet and electronic mail, formal and informal interorganizational communication networks, and

the like (e.g., Kovacic, 1994, p. 11). Such systems can serve as mechanisms through which global organizations can communicate messages to foster a common identity and vision (which when internalized can unobtrusively guide communication behavior) among its geographically disparate members (see Cheney & Christensen, Chapter 7, this volume). These resources also provide organizations with a skill identified by King and Cushman (1994) as vital for organization-level communication competence in today's global society: high-speed management. In particular, King and Cushman suggest that for organizations to communicate effectively in a global economic environment, they must not only communicate appropriately but also quickly. These communication methods and media can also help the multinational organization manage one of its greatest challenges: coordination and control (e.g., Adler, 1980). Along these lines, a wide variety of organizational structures and forms have been developed to allow global organizations to coordinate their efforts. Because each organizational structure has rather unique communication values, patterns, policies, and properties associated with it, each structure fosters the development of distinctive kinds of organization-level communication knowledge and capability (e.g., Triandis & Albert, 1987).

While many organizations now operate facilities or conduct business across the globe, in recent years some firms have taken globalization one step further: They have established partnerships with organizations in other countries for the purpose of working together to found and operate new organizations (see McPhee & Poole, Chapter 13, this volume). Such arrangements (e.g., a multi-billion-dollar partnership between a German manufacturer and an American manufacturer of semiconductors) represent enormous challenges, since communication competence criteria associated with distinctive national as well as organizational cultures may clash and require reconciliation. In brief, it is apparent that the move toward globalization has important implications for the nature of communication competence at the individual, group, and organizational levels of analysis.

Technology

Another societal trend relevant to organizational communication competence, and related to the move toward a global economy, is a greater reliance on computer-mediated communication technology. By all accounts, we currently are living in the information age (see Fulk & Collins-Jarvis, Chapter 17, and Rice & Gattiker, Chapter 14, this volume). Recent technological advances such as the Internet and the World Wide Web provide access to more information than ever before.

Cetron, Rocha, and Luchins (1988) predicted that by the year 2000 approximately one half of all service jobs will involve collecting, analyzing, synthesizing, structuring, or retrieving information; five of the ten fastest-growing careers will be computer-related; and the typical large business will be "information-based" (Andrews & Herschel, 1996). In short, communication competence in the information age requires an understanding of and ability to use computer-mediated communication systems to send and receive messages and to obtain, process, and interpret information at all levels in an organization.

In the information age, individual communication competence requires that individuals possess a variety of relevant capabilities. Szajna (1994), for instance, suggests that "computer aptitude" (defined as the aptitude for accomplishing computer-related tasks other than programming, such as word processing, spreadsheets, and data tasks) consists of the following abilities: (1) logical reasoning, (2) alphabetic and numeric sequencing, (3) alphanumeric translation, (4) general quantitative abilities, and (5) visiospatial abilities (p. 928). Certain affective-cognitive characteristics also may enhance an individual's communication competence in the computer age. For example, individuals who report high levels of "computer anxiety" (generally defined as a fear of using computers) tend to avoid using computer-mediated communication systems. Thus, high levels of computer anxiety are likely to diminish individual communication competence. In particular, computer anxiety may affect an individual's motivation to communicate. Individuals high in computer anxiety tend to perceive themselves as being unable to use computers (i.e., low self-efficacy) (Kernan & Howard, 1990). Computer anxiety, therefore, may reduce motivation to communicate via computer, thus moderating the relationship between communication capabilities and actual performance.

Previous research also indicates that competence in computer-mediated communication is something that one develops over time. Results from studies consistently demonstrate, for instance, that computer anxiety decreases significantly as one gains experience using computers (e.g., Kernan & Howard, 1990; Szajna, 1994). Individuals high in computer anxiety, therefore, are likely to be precompetent (rather than incompetent) with respect to using computer-mediated communication technology. With more experience with the technology, they may increase their computer aptitude to threshold or proficient levels of competence. If most urban Americans are computer literate within the next decade, then within a few years employees are likely to enter organizations with at least threshold levels of computer-related communication competence. Thus, those who are considered proficient communicators will most likely have the ability to effectively use a variety of communication media and communication-related computer software and have the ability to choose the media and/or software appropriate to any particular situation.

Information technology also has important implications for group-level communication competence. As mentioned earlier, many groups are able to improve their overall performance by using group communication technology such as GSSs. Accordingly, group-level competence in today's business climate may be increased by having access to various forms of "groupware" (group communication software that allows for multiple users to simultaneously access and work in the same database; e.g., Wohlert, 1995). In addition, group-level communication competence may be enhanced if members understand how these systems affect group processes, and in particular, structuring and decision-making activities (e.g., Poole & DeSanctis, 1990), and develop ways to access group knowledge stored within the system itself.

As organizations increase their global operations, many of their constituent work groups and teams will be composed of members who rarely communicate in a face-to-face manner. For example, among software engineers and programmers it is not uncommon today for group members to be located in different countries around the world, for work to be conducted on a project 24 hours a day (one advantage of the use of global work groups), and for participants to communicate with one another via modem using asynchronous computer-mediated message systems. While these systems present challenges to work group effectiveness (e.g., Walther, 1995), related group processes, structures, practices, rules, and so forth that allow such groups to achieve their goals represent communication-related resources associated with competence.

At both the group and organizational levels of analysis the use of the new media can also facilitate the development of a wide array of unique group and organizational communication networks (Finholt & Sproull, 1990). These networks are important in that they not only allow for messages to be exchanged among network participants but also because each network represents a distinctive semantic knowledge structure that may augment a group's and/or organization's communication competence and power (e.g., Monge & Eisenberg, 1987).

Group and organizational communication competence may also be affected by the extent to which a "critical mass" of members use available communication technologies (Markus, 1987). Extrapolating from "critical mass theory," it is likely that groups using particular communication technologies such as groupware cannot exceed the threshold level of competence until a sufficient number (a critical mass) of members have access to and use the system. In turn, it is possible that a group's communication competence may be negatively affected by overuse/saturation of its mediated communication systems, since overuse may result in a state of overload, thereby inhibiting the group's ability to process information (Wohlert, 1995).

To be competent in the information age, organizations also must have knowledge regarding communication technology relevant to their particular industry. Because information technology changes at a very fast rate, organizations must be able to keep up with technological innovations and understand their organizational and human resources consequences (e.g., Beer, Spector, Lawrence, Mills, & Walton, 1985). It may be the ability to constantly update or reinvent these knowledge bases (and the interpretive systems associated with them; e.g., Griffith, 1999) that increases an organization's competence level from threshold to proficient. An organization's communication competence is also associated with its use of various kinds of computerized internal and external communication systems including Internet access, Web pages, electronic bulletin boards, and mail systems. Large organizations may even create departments ("information technology" or "network support") and positions ("chief information officer") to organize, implement, and maintain the organization's computer-mediated communication and information systems. While the creation of such units and positions centralizes knowledge and capabilities with respect to the use of organizational computer-mediated communication systems, centralization of these resources may also affect the "balance of power" among departments, and as a consequence the character of their communication relationships (e.g., Frost, 1987; Hickson, Hinings, Lee, Schneck, & Pennings, 1971).

Level Embeddedness

Individuals, groups, and organizations do not exist in isolation of each other. Rather, they affect one another in a variety of ways; hence, communication competence at any one level of analysis has an impact on communication competence at the other levels. We mentioned above, for example, that organization-level communication competence in a global economy requires the ability to develop global communication networks. One way to develop such networks is by assigning employees to overseas organizational branches (e.g., expatriate managers). Accordingly, to increase its level of communication competence, a multinational organization may dispatch an employee to an overseas branch in an attempt to enhance the quality of its global communication networks (e.g., Black et al., 1992). The expatriate employee may have problems adjusting to the new culture, however. In fact, adjustment problems are fairly common. Research indicates that approximately 40% of expatriate managers return to the United States before completing their overseas assignment (Hogan & Goodson, 1990). A common reason for the failure of expatriates to successfully adjust to overseas assignments is the failure of the employee and his or her family members to positively adjust to the new culture (e.g., Hogan & Goodson, 1990; Thornburg, 1990). Many organizations (approximately 65%) do not provide any predeparture cultural training for their expatriate employees (Hogan & Goodson, 1990; Tung, 1988). Moreover, most organizations do not help prepare the expatriate's family members for the new culture (Stohl, 1995). Simply put, the employee and his or her family members may lack the threshold communication competencies (e.g., knowledge about the other culture, ability to speak the language of the host culture) necessary for successful adjustment to the new culture. Consequently, the employee fails to complete the assignment, decreasing the organization's overall level of communication competence. This example highlights the role of the individual as an active participant in the functioning of the overall organizational system (i.e., the reciprocal influence of the individual and the organization). In particular, this example demonstrates how communication competence at the organizational level may be impaired by the communication competence of an individual employee and the employee's immediate family members.

An example also helps illustrate the notion of embeddedness with respect to the societal trend toward reliance on communication technology. In the preceding section, we suggested that a group's level of communication competence may be closely associated with its use of various forms of group communication technology, such as group decision support systems. We also noted that some individuals experience high levels of computer anxiety. The successful implementation of group communication technology requires, at a minimum, that most group members use the technology. If several group members experience computer anxiety, they are less likely to use the technology, hampering the ability of the group to use the software effectively (insufficient critical mass). Consequently, it is evident that low levels of communication competence at the individual level can impair the development of threshold communication competence at the group level.

The Macrosystem

Included in the macrosystem are elements of the overall system that do not directly contain the individual or immediate work group but that impinge on those entities. Thus, the macrosystem includes major divisions of the organization and the organization as a whole. Consistent with this conceptualization, our discussion below considers the potential impact of a variety of organizational forms and their related managerial philosophies (especially their beliefs and assumptions about people) on communication competence at the individual, group, and organizational levels of analysis.

Organizational Forms and Managerial Philosophies

Organizations, and major organizational divisions, often differ significantly among one another with respect to their forms and managerial philosophies. Although a number of schemes have been proposed to classify organization forms (see McPhee & Poole, this volume) and managerial philosophies (e.g., Barley & Kunda, 1992), these classification systems tend to examine issues related to organizational forms and managerial philosophies in relative isolation of one another. Miles and Creed (1995), in contrast, have developed a configurational approach to organizational analysis that classifies organizations in terms of both form and managerial philosophy (in part based on the argument that certain philosophies are more supportive of particular organizational forms than other ones). In the discussion that follows, we have adopted their model and classification scheme since "it creates bridges across traditional micro and macro concepts and theories" (p. 133), consistent with our orientation to the study of communication competence. Below we consider relationships between communication competence at various levels of analysis and in terms of three of the four organizational form/managerial philosophy configurations identified by Miles and Creed (1995): (1) the centralized/traditional organization, (2) the functional/human relations organization, and (3) the divisional (and matrix)/human resources organization. Due to space limitations and its still evolving character, we do not discuss the fourth configuration proposed by Miles and Creed, the network/human investment organization (e.g., Powell, 1990; Snow, Miles, & Coleman, 1992; see also McPhee & Poole, Chapter 13, and Monge & Contractor, Chapter 12, this volume). Finally, we wish to emphasize that our focus on these particular form/philosophy configurations does not reflect a belief that other configurations do not exist (there are many hybrid configurations). Rather, our concern is with suggesting possible relationships between characteristics of

communication competence and organizational forms/philosophies; as a consequence, the particular configurations we discuss and the hypothetical examples we offer should be viewed as only a means to achieve that end.

Centralized/traditional. The centralized/traditional organization is one in which control is centralized at the top of the hierarchy, employees are expected to adhere to formal rules and regulations, and close supervision of employees is the norm. Large and well-established organizations in stable environments typify the centralized form (Andrews & Herschel, 1996; Miles & Creed, 1995). According to Miles and Creed (1995), centralized organizations are usually managed according to traditional philosophies and, in particular, are guided by variations of the principles of bureaucracy (e.g., Weber, 1947) and scientific management (e.g., Taylor, 1911), which emphasize order and authority. As Miles and Creed (1995) observe, the traditional philosophy assumes that "managers and workers [are] cut from a different cloth" (p. 338). In particular, workers are seen to have limited capability (thus the need for close supervision) and to be motivated primarily by extrinsic rewards. Because of the assumed stability of the external environment, adaptability to external environmental turbulence or change is not emphasized. Communication in centralized/traditional organizations tends to be downward, formal, and written, mainly used for the dissemination of policies, rules, and instructions. Given the above characteristics, the types of resources required for communication competence in a centralized/traditional organization are likely somewhat distinct from those required in other organizational forms.

At the individual level of analysis, communication competence resources include knowledge of the organization's rules and regulations governing communication. Managers in centralized organizations must be aware of the requirements of their own tasks, as well as the requirements of their subordinates' tasks. Individual skills required for managerial competence revolve around the ability to give instructions and orders, and monitor compliance to communication policies. On the other hand, workers need knowledge of the requirements of their jobs and of appropriate (usually formal) ways of communicating in the organization (Morand, 1995). Because individual staff members are typically supervised closely and upward communication is not encouraged, in this configuration the primary abilities necessary for communication competence are related to the decoding of messages, and in particular "discriminative" listening (listening to acquire information for future use) and "evaluative" listening (listening to assess arguments and evidence; e.g., Wolff, Marsnik, Tacey, & Nichols, 1983). We hypothesize that because of the routineness of their communication environments and the limited use of their overall competencies, individuals in centralized/traditional organizations may easily become overcompetent with respect to their threshold communication capabilities.

In general, the communication competencies required at the group level in centralized/traditional organizations will be fairly restricted as well. At most, employees belong to functional groups and departments, whose efforts are coordinated through scheduled (planned) forms of communication (e.g., Hage, Aiken, & Marrett, 1971). Informal communication among department members is typically not strongly encouraged, and in some cases may even be discouraged. During group meetings, fairly formal means will be employed to guide interaction and discussion (e.g., agendas, parliamentary procedures). Hence, communication knowledge at the group level will be embedded within a group's rules, policies, and procedures and readily available to all group members. In brief, in comparison to the other organizational configurations discussed below, group communication competence in centralized/traditional firms may be reflected in relatively fewer, and more basic, resources. At the same time, however, it is important to note that because of the bureaucratic character of centralized/traditional organizations, groups and their members may develop informal/emergent communication networks and cliques to accomplish their tasks and to meet members' needs (e.g., Schein, 1980); although not officially sanctioned, such informal cliques and networks can be considered communication resources available for use in the communication process.

Given the fairly predictable and stable environments in which centralized/traditional organizations operate, organization-level competence will rest in well-defined structures such as the chain-of-command/hierarchy and in standard operating procedures for communication. As a consequence, communication competence will be centered on capabilities associated with use of "lean" media (Daft & Lengel, 1986) and knowledge of correct protocol for organization-wide communication. Thus, internal (mostly downward, one-way) communication mechanisms such as house organs, employee manuals, and internal memoranda represent key communication resources associated with organization-level communication competence in centralized/traditional organizations. In addition, because of the accuracy and relatively fast speed in which they disseminate information, organizational grapevines (although not "official" communication resources) may constitute an important part of a centralized/traditional organization's communication capabilities (e.g., Hellweg, 1987).

Functional/human relations. In functional organizations, control is delegated from top management to managers of various functional departments such as sales, finance, and production. According to Miles and Creed (1995), functional organizations work best with a human relations management philosophy. This philosophy assumes that workers are "motivated by social as well as economic factors" (Miles & Creed, 1995) and emphasizes the importance of informal interaction and working in groups. Managers focus attention on the satisfaction of individual employees, since the human relations perspective assumes (somewhat problematically) that, by satisfying the needs of individual workers, productivity will increase. Although control is not delegated to lower-level employees, managers seek input from staff, mainly as a way to satisfy the members' intrinsic involvement and personal growth needs.

Communication competence resources in functional organizations will likely differ significantly from those found in centralized/traditional organizations, primarily due to different assumptions about people. Because of the human relations emphasis on individual satisfaction, managers in functional organizations will need knowledge regarding not only the formal communication-related rules and regulations of the organization and their respective departments but also knowledge regarding informal group communication norms and of the character of emergent group communication networks. In addition, the human relations model recommends that managers be cognizant of individual staff members' personalities, and information and motivational needs (e.g., feedback needs). Consistent with this form of organization, competent managers will also likely be skilled in empathic as well as discriminative and evaluative listening, the use of feedback to motivate employees (e.g., Cusella, 1987), the use of persuasion (vs. authority) as a means of compliance-gaining, and supportive communication practices (e.g., Euske & Roberts, 1987). In sum, in the functional/human relations organization the hallmark of managerial communication competence will be a robust repertoire of communication knowledge and skills (thus allowing managers to be flexible and adaptive in their communication behavior).

In this type of organization, competent communicators will also be highly aware of the substantive and relational dimensions of their interactions with others (e.g., Watzlawick, Beavin, & Jackson, 1967; Zorn & Violanti, 1996). In addition, given that functional/human relations organizations stress the importance of work groups and informal

communication, those who are considered competent communicators will be capable of sharing information and opinions, managing conflict, involving others in decision making, and tolerating disagreement, and in general, will be highly skilled in face-to-face communication (e.g., Euske & Roberts, 1987).

In contrast to groups in centralized/traditional organizations, group competence in functional/human relations organizations will be reflected more in the emergent norms, languages, codes, informal role expectations, stories, rituals, symbols, and other cultural artifacts of the ongoing process of group development. A considerable amount of group communicative knowledge will be generated through everyday communication and collective sensemaking and feedback processes and will be shared among members via informal, emergent communication networks. Group (vs. individual) goals and rewards, shared sentiments, and feelings of potency (e.g., Homans, 1950; Shea & Guzzo, 1987; Zander, 1980) will serve as important sources of motivation to communicate in a competent manner, and groups will possess informal mechanisms to hold members accountable for undesirable communicative behavior (e.g., social loafing; see Latane, Williams, & Harkins, 1979). However, group communication norms and related pressures to conform may be quite strong and lead to overcompetence, similar in form to what Janis (1972) describes as "groupthink."

Capabilities associated with organization-level competence will include those characteristic of centralized/functional organizations, but will also involve numerous upward communication mechanisms (e.g., electronic mail, suggestion boxes, "open door" policies, employee attitude surveys). Organization-wide communication (e.g., house organs, company meetings) will emphasize identification with the organization's mission and goals and seek to encourage employees to internalize decision premises and attitudes conducive to the organization's objectives; hence, the ability of an organization to "unobtrusively control" (Barker & Tompkins, 1994; Cheney, 1983; Tompkins & Cheney, 1985) its members might be conceptualized as an element of communication competence. Formal "linking pin" roles and units (e.g., Likert, 1967) will often be used to build efficient communication networks among groups and departments, and training programs might be offered to help organizational members develop their communication skills, thus enhancing the organization's overall communication competence. To some extent, organizations operate under a "norm of reciprocity" assumption; that is, if they develop the communication abilities of their members, their members will be motivated to reciprocate by using their new competencies in the best interest of the organization.

Divisional (and matrix)/human resources. Divisional organizations tend to be larger and more decentralized than functional firms. The divisional organization is "essentially a collection of similar, special purpose machines, each independently serving its respective markets" (Miles & Creed, 1995, p. 337). These divisions enjoy a great deal of autonomy. According to Miles and Creed (1995), the divisional form is most consistent with the human resources management philosophy (they suggest this is also true for matrix organizations, which meld characteristics of both the functional and divisional forms). The human resources perspective is similar to human relations in its emphasis on the primacy of individual development and satisfaction and acknowledgment of the importance of informal communication. The main difference between the two is that while the human relations perspective stresses the importance of making employees feel important and providing them with ways to express their views, the human resources perspective views workers as not only wanting to share their views but also possessing untapped capabilities that can enhance organizational performance (Kreps, 1990). Accordingly, in organizations adhering to the human re-

sources perspective members are not just consulted when management makes decisions, but they are encouraged to actively participate in making decisions that affect their tasks and organizations. In this type of environment, management supports employees' efforts to broaden their self-direction, influence, and self-control (Miles, 1975); management's role is "one of facilitating employees' performance rather than controlling their behaviors" (Miles & Creed, 1995, p. 341).

Knowledge and skill requirements for communication competence at the organizational, group, and individual levels in a divisional organization are similar to the requirements in a functional organization. However, additional capabilities will likely be required. As mentioned earlier, managers adhering to the human resources philosophy listen to their employees not only to make them feel cared for and appreciated (as with the human relations perspective), but because they believe their employees' contributions can best be maximized if they are in control of their own decisions, behavior, and so on. Thus, for example, if a subordinate were to come to a supervisor with a work-related problem, a communicatively competent supervisor would not tell the worker how to solve the dilemma but rather ask the individual a series of questions that might help him or her frame the problem, develop criteria to assess solutions, and the like. Through the use of inquiry the supervisor would not only help the follower discover for himself or herself a viable solution to the problem, but would also model ways of approaching problem solving in general (the process), thereby facilitating the follower's ability to engage in self-directed problem-solving behavior in the future (e.g., Manz & Sims, 1989; Sims & Lorenzi, 1992). Competent leaders would also be capable of facilitating group discussions in a similar manner (e.g., they would be skilled at seeking information and opinions, providing meta-informational cues, and fostering meeting environments in which participants feel supported, included, and empowered; McGee, 1994).

Since organizational members are highly involved in decision-making processes, conflict within and between groups is quite common in divisional/human resources organizations. Thus, the ability to effectively manage conflict is an indicator of group-level communication competence in divisional (and matrix) organizations. Further, competent groups likely pay close attention to the decision-making process. According to "vigilant interaction theory," effective decision-making groups are skilled at analyzing their task, assessing the criteria used for evaluation, and distinguishing alternative choices in terms of their good and bad qualities (Hirokawa & Rost, 1992, p. 284).

Because of the emphasis on participative management (e.g., Follett, 1940; Likert, 1961), competent divisional (and matrix) organizations require mechanisms that enable communication among various organizational members for the purpose of problem solving, information sharing, and decision making. Mechanisms that might be used to solve problems and coordinate activities include quality circles, task forces, and self-managed teams (see Seibold & Shea, this volume). In a divisional/human resources organization, information about decisions and policies would not just be open and readily available (as it might in a functional/human relations organization), but also include explanations as to why particular decisions were made, the implications of decisions, and so on. Moreover, communication mechanisms would be available for those who disagree to voice their concerns with respect to particular actions and decisions. In sum, a communicatively competent divisional (or matrix)/human resources organization will have the capability of building and maintaining trust and confidence with its various stakeholders.

Level Embeddedness

The discussion above suggests that communication competence at the individual, group, and organizational levels is influenced, to some degree, by the overarching form and managerial philosophy of the organization itself. Consistent with the notion of embeddedness incorporated in our model of communication competence, we illustrate here how competence at one level is embedded in competence at other levels of analysis. To do so, we elaborate further on the notion of communication competence in a human resources/participatory organization or unit.

In participatory organizations, individual-, group-, and organization-level communication competence is tightly intertwined. We suggested above, for instance, that organization-level competence is indicated by the use of problem-solving groups such as quality circles. The communication competence of such groups is highly dependent on the ability (competence) and willingness (motivation) of individual group members to participate (Glew, O'Leary-Kelly, Griffin, & Van Fleet, 1995). Thus, a quality circle composed of many individuals who lack competencies related to group communication and decision-making processes is likely to experience numerous problems (e.g., Cotton, 1993). Similarly, if the individual members of a quality circle have the capabilities (e.g., knowledge and skills) necessary for competent communication, but are not sufficiently motivated to perform, group-level competence will be impaired. Employees invited to participate in quality circles often harbor doubts regarding the amount of influence the quality circle will actually have, for example (see Stohl & Jennings, 1988). Such doubts may result from having previously worked in an environment where employee opinions were sought but never considered for implementation (e.g., Cotton, 1993). Regardless of the source of the skepticism, however, the skepticism is likely to decrease a competent individual's motivation to be an active (rather than passive) quality circle participant. Accordingly, low levels of individual communication competence decrease group-level communication competence, leading to decreased organization-level communication competence.

The Mesosystem

Because of the multiple roles an individual occupies both in and out of the workplace (e.g., an employee may simultaneously be a subordinate, a supervisor, a functional group member, a work team member, a spouse, and a parent), that employee participates in multiple microsystems (e.g., the supervisor-subordinate microsystem, the work group microsystem, the work team microsystem, the marriage microsystem, and the family microsystem). The mesosystem represents the interrelations among these various microsystems. As will become evident in our later discussion of microsystems, the "primary building blocks of the mesosystem are the same as those for the microsystem: molar activities, interpersonal relations, and role transactions" (Vondracek, Lerner, & Schulenberg, 1986, p. 57). However, the mesosystem is distinct from the microsystem in that activities associated with the mesosystem occur across rather than within particular microsystem settings. Although individual organizational members typically serve as the linking pins between microsystems, what is learned as a consequence of these linkages may affect communication competence at the individual, group, and organizational levels of analysis.

Individual Microsystem Linkages

Individuals in organizations occupy a variety of roles both in and out of the workplace. In these roles, the individual often becomes a "linking pin" (a means for intersetting communication and knowledge sharing) among various microsystems. Many individuals, for instance, occupy both a supervisor and a subordinate role in their organization. Thus, they "link" the vertical relationship in which they are the subordinate to the vertical relationship in which they are the supervisor. Some research suggests the possibility that the communication resources developed as part of

one's experiences in one of these dyadic relationships (or microsystems) can influence the development of communication competencies in the other relationship/microsystem. Weiss (1977), for example, found that subordinates often imitate or model the communication behavior of their supervisor (assuming that the supervisor is perceived of as a credible and expert source of information and behavior). Thus, in some cases communication resources learned in an upper-level leader-follower relationship may be transferred to a lower-level leader-follower relationship. Similarly, a lower-level supervisor may learn the sorts of communication behaviors that are inappropriate to enact with his or her own followers (what not to do), by observing the boss' problematic display of those behaviors. In addition, it is possible that upper-level leaders may develop their own communication competence by modeling the behaviors of lower-level leaders who are (formally speaking) their followers.

The roles an individual holds outside the workplace can also affect that person's communication competence in workplace microsystems (e.g., Crouter, 1984; Jones & Fletcher, 1996). The notion of "sex role spillover" (Gutek & Morasch, 1982) provides an excellent illustration. Sex role spillover refers to the ways gender-based behavioral expectations developed outside the organizational sphere carry over into the workplace. For instance, a man may become accustomed to communicating with women outside the workplace (e.g., his spouse) in a particular way. He may find his communication knowledge, skills, and behavior to be appropriate and effective within those extraorganizational microsystems. In other words, he is a fairly competent communicator when interacting in extraorganizational microsystems. In a similar vein, Metts and Spitzberg (1996) argue that individuals' sexual communicative behavior is guided largely by scripts—the traditional sexual script being "one in which males play the role of initiator and females the role of regulator" (p. 73). Communicating with a female colleague at work the same scripted way you communicate with your spouse, however, is likely to be inappropriate. In fact, sex role spillover has been linked to sexual harassment (Gutek, 1985; Gutek & Morasch, 1982). Accordingly, sex role spillover can lead to reduced levels of communication competence in the workplace. That is, expectations regarding competent communication developed in one microsystem can affect (in this case, decrease) one's level of communication competence in another microsystem.

Group Microsystem Linkages

Organizations can be composed of many types of groups, ranging from functional work groups (e.g., a group of employees who work in a particular department or unit of an organization, but whose level of interdependence may be quite low) to work teams. In contrast to functional work groups, teams represent "an intact group of employees who are responsible for a 'whole' work process or segment that delivers a product or service to an internal or external customer" (Wellins, Byham, & Wilson, 1991, p. 3). An individual can be simultaneously a member of a functional work group and a team. Matrix organizations, for instance, often create multifunctional teams (MFTs) composed of employees from a variety of functional work groups (e.g., engineering, manufacturing, and sales departments) who work together on particular projects. Thus, an employee may link a functional work group with a project work team.

Recent research indicates that teams often develop shared cognitive knowledge structures. Klimoski and Mohammed (1994), for instance, discuss "team mental models," which represent emergent, shared, organized knowledge reflecting beliefs, assumptions, and perceptions. As Klimoski and Mohammed (1994) explain, these models reflect "how the group members *as a collectivity* think or characterize phenomena" (p. 426, emphasis added). Mental models also include the ways group members collectively think

about or characterize *communication* phenomena. Accordingly, teams likely develop shared beliefs, assumptions, and perceptions regarding the requirements for communication competence. Individual team members may carry these beliefs, assumptions, and perceptions back to their functional work groups, thus affecting the functional group's knowledge/mental models regarding the characteristics of competent communication.

At the same time, an individual may bring to a project team the shared/collective knowledge of his or her functional work group regarding communication, thereby influencing the team's mental models with respect to communication competence. As suggested earlier, the transfer of communication resources across intersetting linkages is often reciprocal in nature.

Organizational Microsystem Linkages

A variety of microsystem linkages exist at the organizational level of analysis (e.g., Eisenberg et al., 1985). Organizations participate in many types of interorganizational relationships, for example, including interlocking directorates, trade associations, joint ventures, and research and development partnerships. Powell, Koput, and Smith-Doerr (1996) suggest that "what is learned is profoundly linked to the conditions under which it is learned" (p. 118). They further argue that sources of learning and innovation typically reside outside, rather than inside, the organization. As they explain, these sources "are commonly found in the interstices between firms, universities, research laboratories, suppliers, and customers" (p. 118). Consequently, the sources of learning and innovation reside in interorganizational networks or relationships. We suggested earlier in this chapter that a sign of organization-level communication competence is the ability to keep up with rapidly changing innovations in communication technology. Along these lines, Powell et al. (1996) maintain that participation in external networks or alliances is vital for staying current in a rapidly changing field because "external collaboration provides access to news and resources that cannot be generated internally" (p. 119). This suggests that organizations can increase their communication competence by selectively transferring into their own systems communication-related knowledge and skills they learn about from their interorganizational relationships (e.g., Powell, 1990). For example, an organizational member who participates in a multiorganizational research and development consortium formed to develop new communication technologies will obtain competence resources (in this case, knowledge regarding communication technologies as well as knowledge about communicating in a consortium), which can be transferred back to his or her company for use, thus enhancing the organization's overall level of communication competence.

Level Embeddedness

Within the mesosystem, communication competence at the individual, group, and organizational levels is embedded within and mutually influences each other. For example, if an individual is a member of both a functional work group and a cross-functional project team (as one might find in a matrix organization), he or she is likely to develop communication relationships with some of the members of the project group that persist even after the team has completed its project and disbanded. These continuing relationships/ linkages, many of which might be characterized as "weak ties" (Granovetter, 1973), represent organization-level communication resources since they allow for the exchange (albeit infrequently) of messages across diverse parts/networks of the organization. In particular, they represent important communication resources since innovations, which might affect the communication capabilities of numerous groups and individuals in an organization, are often first learned about through interactions with weak ties (e.g.,

Monge & Eisenberg, 1987). Hence, individual-level competence in developing and maintaining communication relationships with persons met through mesosystem activities can affect organizational as well as group-level competence.

The Microsystem

The microsystem includes the organizational member and most directly considers his or her communication with others in the immediate work environment. More specifically, a microsystem is "a pattern of activities, roles, and interpersonal relations experienced by the developing person in a given setting with particular physical and material characteristics" (Bronfenbrenner, 1979, p. 22). Below we discuss two elements of the microsystem we believe have important implications for communication competence at the individual, group, and organizational levels of analysis: (1) gender expectations and related gender-related patterns of behavior, and (2) the employment status—permanent or contingent—of microsystem members and the impact of this status on interpersonal relationships. Clearly, there are numerous microsystem characteristics that we might have discussed in this section (e.g., differences among microsystem members in terms of race, occupation, education, and tenure; characteristics of leader-follower exchanges; interdependence among workers with respect to task performance; and emergent work group cliques and network roles). However, we chose the above noted characteristics to discuss because one represents a traditional focus of microlevel competence research (gender), whereas the latter issue (employment status) represents an area of growing interest among those studying organizations. Hence, the following discussion shows how a traditional microsystem element might be recast in terms of our model, while also demonstrating how the model might be used to study an emerging microsystem factor.

Gender

Communication competence is often conceptualized as the use of appropriate communication behaviors (e.g., Spitzberg & Cupach, 1984). Although recent research indicates that actual differences in the communication behavior of men and women are minimal (e.g., Wilkins & Andersen, 1991), the literature also indicates that others' perceptions of an individual's communication competence can be influenced by his or her gender. As Hearn (1993) points out, " 'Men at work' are generally not expected to display certain categories of emotion, especially those associated with women or those that are conventionally assumed to be 'what women show' " (p. 143). A man, therefore, who expresses his emotions (other than anger; see Hearn, 1993, p. 143) may be perceived by others to be incompetent because he communicates inappropriately.

Gender expectations can be particularly problematic for women. Organizations tend to be portrayed as rational, unemotional arenas where individuals are expected to behave in a rational, unemotional manner. As Putnam and Mumby (1993) explain, "In organizations, rationality is revered while emotions are illegitimate or inappropriate" (p. 40). Women, in general, however, are expected by society to be emotional beings. As a consequence, women are often faced with a double-bind with respect to being perceived as competent communicators. Communicating without emotion violates society's expectations of competent female behavior. Communicating with emotion, however, violates society's expectations of competent organizational behavior. Along these lines, research indicates that women who attempt to communicate "like men" (e.g., unemotional, competitive) are often perceived as hard-edged, aggressive, and shrill. At the same time, communication behaviors perceived as "feminine" are often perceived as "too soft," particularly for managers and higher-level organizational members (Mize, 1992). Accordingly, communicating in a "feminine" manner can lead to perceptions that women are unable to succeed in management positions.

Consistent with the notion of embeddedness, however, it is important to note that expectations regarding competent male and female communication may be affected by the organizational role of the individual and the managerial philosophy of the organization or department in which the individual works. Women in "caretaking" roles, for example, are expected to communicate in an emotional, supportive manner (see Burleson, Albrecht, & Sarason, 1994). Accordingly, emotional, supportive communication abilities would enhance a woman's communication competence in those roles. The same skills would likely lead to perceptions of a woman manager as having a low level of competence. Rosener (1990), however, indicates that many women have been very successful using these types of communication behaviors in organizations or units guided by "participatory" or human resources management philosophies. Thus, it is likely that women who are proficient communicators have a large repertoire of communication skills and abilities and keen insight into how gender expectations, organizational role, managerial philosophy, and related situational factors interact to affect what others in the microsystem consider to be appropriate communication behavior.

The issue of sexual harassment is also pertinent to any discussion of employee gender and communication competence. In particular, it is noteworthy that the U.S. Equal Employment Opportunity Commission (EEOC) considers sexual harassment that occurs in any organizational microsystem to be illegal (among other actions, sexual harassment includes conduct that interferes with an employee's work or creates an intimidating, hostile, or offensive work environment; see Sheffey & Tindale, 1992). Though sexual harassment has likely occurred since the first time men and women worked together in organizations, it has received increasing attention over the past two decades. Some estimate that as many as 40% of women in organizations experience some form of sexual harassment (Bingham & Burleson, 1989). Men also experience sexual harassment, though to a far lesser extent (estimates suggest that approximately 5%-15% of men encounter sexual harassment in the workplace; see Clair, 1993). Because it is also inappropriate (as well as illegal), an individual who communicates with another employee in a sexually harassing manner displays a precompetent level of communication competence. To communicate competently, individuals must be knowledgeable about sexual harassment law and policies. In particular, employees must have an understanding of what constitutes sexually harassing communication behavior and be motivated to communicate in ways consistent with the law. As mentioned earlier, Gutek and Morasch (1982) suggest that sex role spillover can cause confusion when men perceive their female coworkers as women rather than coworkers. In addition, because some men have developed rigid ways of interacting with women outside the workplace (e.g., with their spouses, partners), it may be difficult for them to develop appropriate ways of communicating with women in the workplace. However, it is apparent that such capabilities are required if one is to display situationally appropriate (i.e., competent) ways of communicating with both male and female coworkers.

Work group communication competence may also be affected by the development of informal communication networks and cliques that exclude males or females, respectively, from membership (e.g., Kanter, 1977). Although the members of these cliques and networks may not realize that during their informal interactions (e.g., during lunch), important information is often exchanged about issues related to appropriate and effective communication behavior, intra- and extraorganizational links that might be valuable sources of information, and the like, such activities do occur during their meetings (e.g.,

Brass, 1985; Moore, 1992), and if not shared with all members of the group diminishes the group's overall communication competence. Similarly, beliefs that develop at the group level that support the notion that female coworkers who become pregnant will not return to their jobs after their maternity leaves, and/or show bias against working mothers generally (e.g., Gueutal & Taylor, 1992; Miller, Jablin, Casey, Lamphear-Van Horn, & Ethington, 1996), can negatively affect group communication competence by treating women as "temporary" team members, who are not committed to the group and thus are excluded from participation in selective communication networks, not provided with helpful "insider" knowledge about ways of communicating in the organization, and so on.

Organization-level communication competence can also be negatively affected by the organization's unwillingness to recognize the existence of gender-related stereotypes and bias. For example, organizations that implicitly permit sexual harassment to occur or sanction retaliation of employees who voice charges of harassment may not only lose credibility with many employees, but they may also demotivate workers generally from voicing issues of concern, thereby diminishing the organization's overall communication competence. In addition, failure to respond to gender bias may lessen the organization's credibility and legitimacy with respect to its external stakeholders, and as a consequence limit the organization's access to information from key sources in its environment(s).

In brief, competent organizations will develop and communicate to their constituents policy statements outlining definitions of sexual harassment and the organizational consequences facing harassers, create mentoring programs that allow women as well as men access to the informal "ins and outs" of communication in the organization (e.g., Noe, 1988), offer workshops or seminars designed to help employees understand the nature and definition of sexual harassment, and in general, learn to communicate in a manner free of gender bias (Hulin, Fitzgerald, & Drasgow, 1996). As Hulin et al. (1996) explain,

> Establishing and communicating contingencies between sexually harassing behaviors and negative outcomes for harassers, establishing procedures that minimize the risk of reporting sexual harassment (i.e., retaliation), and establishing procedures that ensure complainants, or grievants, will be taken seriously can do a great deal to improve the climate for sexual harassment in an organization. (p. 148)

Permanent Versus Contingent Employment Status

Business has seen a fundamental change over the past ten years in the relationship between individuals and their jobs (e.g., Chilton & Weidenbaum, 1994; Rousseau & Parks, 1993). Traditionally, workers entered organizations with the assumption that they would remain with the organization for the duration of their career. This was particularly true until the 1970s and early 1980s. In other words, permanent employment was the norm. The mid-1980s and the 1990s saw a dramatic change with a considerable portion of the workforce becoming what has been labeled "contingent," that is, "workers who do not have a long-term attachment to their employers (for example, temporary, part-time, and subcontracted workers)" (Belous, 1989, p. 7).

The growth of the contingent workforce has, indeed, been dramatic. Experts estimate that approximately one fourth of the American workforce now consists of contingent workers (Fierman, 1994, p. 30). The number of temporary workers, in particular, has almost tripled since 1980 (Rogers, 1995). In essence, the United States and selective other countries may be moving toward a "two-tier" workforce "in which a core of essential full-time employees is supplemented by contingent workers" ("Economic Factors," 1995).

In other words, a relatively new type of "individual difference" has emerged as a factor distinguishing among workers: status as a permanent or contingent/temporary employee.

This difference among workers implies some equally fundamental changes in the nature of role expectations and interpersonal relationships in organizations (e.g., Tsui, Pearce, Porter, & Hite, 1995), and concomitantly the knowledge and skills required for organizational communication competence (at all levels). Competent contingent workers, for instance, may require knowledge regarding a variety of organizational/management styles and the ability to communicate effectively in various environments (e.g., the ability to listen critically in a traditional organization, the ability to be assertive and engage in "dialogue" in functional/human relations or divisional/human resources organizations). To be competent communicators, contingent workers also need to be highly flexible (Tsui et al., 1995) and, given the ever-changing demands of their work, have a high tolerance for ambiguity and uncertainty (Rogers, 1995). In addition, because of the brief length of their time in any particular job or organization, they may need to be proficient in skills associated with seeking information and developing communication relationships/linkages quickly and efficiently.

The growth of the contingent workforce may also have profound implications for the use of groups and teams in organizations (see Seibold & Shea, this volume). Because effective groups tend to have a history and share a "group mentality," growing reliance on contingent workers may result in fundamental changes in the substance of group-level communication competence, a decreased use of teams, or the use of teams with only permanent employees performing highly complex and interdependent tasks in which the maintenance of knowledge structures is essential for effectiveness (e.g., Davis-Blake & Uzzi, 1993; Thompson, 1967). On the other hand, we may see organizations hiring "temporary teams"—teams composed of individuals who have worked together before in a team capacity, but are not permanent members of the organization (in line with Toffler's [1970] notion of groups in "adhocracies").

However, the two-tier employee system can, at times, create a type of "caste" system within groups in which core (permanent) workers resent and look down on contingent workers who are hired to work on "temporary" projects (it is important to recognize that in some situations temporary may mean a few months, while in other cases it may mean a year or more; Belous, 1989). Accordingly, groups must either develop capabilities that allow for effective communication relationships between "in-group" and "out-group" members or act to prevent the development of caste systems. With respect to this latter point, permanent group members may need to be educated about the benefits of a contingent workforce, and in particular, how contingent workers benefit core employees in the long run (in theory, contingent workers help the overall health of the group and organization, making core workers' jobs more secure; Belous, 1989). In addition, some groups (and organizations) may use mentor or coaching programs to encourage the development of communication relationships between permanent and contingent workers (Belous, 1989).

At the organizational level, the use of both permanent and temporary employees provides the organization with the flexibility to produce a mix of labor that has the skills and knowledge (including communication resources) to meet needs associated with shifting workloads and special projects (e.g., Davis-Blake & Uzzi, 1993). At the same time, however, the use of temporary workers means that the quality and extent of the organization's communication competence may be highly variable, and to some degree unpredictable. Special mechanisms may be required to enable the organization to maintain communication ties with contingent workers external to the company. In essence, organizations must be able to establish long-term relationships with either individual contingent workers (perhaps through the maintenance of weak ties with them; e.g., Granovetter, 1973) or the providers of contingent workers including temporary agencies and professional associations (Belous, 1989).

In addition, competent organizations may need to develop distinctive internal systems of communication with permanent and contingent workers. In particular, it is likely that the sorts of organizational messages that might serve to motivate permanent employees will be irrelevant to temporary employees, who have contracts that clearly spell out their duties and responsibilities.

Many organizations provide formal socialization/orientation programs for newly hired permanent employees in which the employees receive information regarding the organization, their tasks, employee benefits, and so forth. Little is known, however, about the ways in which contingent workers are socialized into their temporary positions. It seems likely that communicatively competent organizations would have knowledge regarding the sorts of information contingent workers actually need to accomplish their tasks effectively and have the capacities to provide them with that information. Along these lines, Feldman, Doerpinghaus, and Turnley (1994, p. 60) suggest that organizations can more effectively employ contingent workers if they provide them with extensive training and orientation. Moreover, Feldman et al.'s research indicates that organizations should communicate with temporary employees before their assignments begin so as to provide clear expectations regarding the length of the assignment (p. 58).

Finally, because they have experience working in a variety of positions and organizations, contingent workers are likely to have a large array of skills and abilities with respect to task performance. Consequently, contingent workers may be a source of innovative ideas. Thus, a possible indicator of organization-level communication competence may be the development of ways to use contingent workers as a resource for innovation. This may require major "attitude" changes on the part of companies, since research suggests that organizations rarely seek information from temporary employees (Sias, Kramer, & Jenkins, 1997). However, organizations that nurture cultures that encourage permanent members to communicate with and learn from contingent workers may be more communicatively competent (perhaps proficient) than organizations that do not adopt this approach, since they will be reinforcing the process of continuous learning, which is central to organizational survival.

Level Embeddedness

In the preceding sections, we have implicitly highlighted the embeddedness of the effects of gender and employment status on communication competence within each of our three levels of analysis. Thus, for instance, we suggested that for an individual to be a competent communicator, he or she must understand the behaviors that constitute sexually harassing communication. However, if an organization does not have the threshold communication resources or motivation (e.g., to develop and disseminate policy statements and training programs to provide employees with such information, as well as develop methods to ensure compliance and to fairly process complaints), the ability of individual employees to communicate in a nonharassing manner may be impaired (primarily out of ignorance). In other words, if sexual harassment is tolerated at the organizational level (a sign of a low level of organizational communication competence), individual employees are more likely to engage in sexually harassing behavior (Hulin et al., 1996).

CONCLUDING STATEMENT

Although the discussion and examples we have offered to explicate our model of orga-

nizational communication competence highlighted the importance of considering how the characteristics of the various ecological systems may affect the nature of communication competence at the individual, group, and organizational levels, to conserve space we did not explicitly discuss how the interaction of the ecological systems affects the character of competence. This is an important issue, and we hope that some of the examples we have presented in the preceding pages have indirectly demonstrated that the ecological systems are in continuous, mutual interaction with one another. As a final, explicit example, we note that gender stereotypes and expectations that influence communication competence in various kinds of microsystems are derived, in part, from larger societal biases and socialization processes in the exosystem (e.g., Wood, 1994). At the same time, the increased number of women in leadership positions in organizations over recent decades has affected managerial philosophies, and consequently, communication expectations within macrosystems. Rosener (1990), for example, argues that "feminine" communication styles are at the core of transformational and interactive managerial philosophies. Thus, although not emphasized in detail in this chapter, we hope that the reciprocal influence of the various ecological systems and their possible effects on organizational communication competence are plainly evident and become more of a focus of study in future research.

In conclusion, we wish to emphasize that the model we have developed to consider extant research, as well as guide the future study of communication competence in organizations, does not frame the study of competence from any particular philosophical or methodological perspective. Rather, the developmental-ecological approach serves as framework that facilitates the process of "owning up" to underlying, value-laden, ideological assumptions about competence. Thus, for example, in the process of speculating about the nature of competence in functional/traditional organizations, we suggested that a hallmark of competence (at least from one viewpoint) might be the organization's capabilities to "unobtrusively control" its members through its use of organization-level communication resources. Is this desirable? Is this ethical? Our purpose here was not to answer those questions, but rather to provide a framework that inherently mandates that such issues be addressed in our research. We stated in the opening of this chapter that communication competence might be described as a hybrid construct (part social science, part art). Its elusive, fuzzy nature does not make it easy to study, but if competence is as fundamental to the study of organizational communication as many scholars claim, then we need to keep our eyes, ears, and minds open when pursuing research in this area.

NOTES

1. This is not to say that goal achievement is irrelevant to communication competence. Having a large repertoire of competence resources, for instance, may increase the likelihood that one will achieve one's goals. Similarly, consistent goal achievement is likely to enhance self-efficacy and, consequently, increase one's motivation to communicate, thereby increasing the likelihood of subsequent goal achievement.

2. For purposes of clarity, we have adapted Bronfenbrenner's (1979) labels with respect to the macrosystem and exosystem. Specifically, whereas Bronfenbrenner refers to the organizational level as the exosystem, we refer to it as macrosystem (which is more consistent with the use of the term *macro* in organizational studies), and whereas he labels the broader overarching environment (cultural and societal beliefs systems, political ideologies, etc.) the macrosystem we label it the exosystem.

REFERENCES

Adler, N. J. (1980). *Cultural synergy: The management of cross-cultural organizations.* San Diego, CA: University Associates.

Adler, N. J., & Bartholomew, S. (1992). Managing globally competent people. *Academy of Management Executive, 6,* 52-65.

Alwin, D. F. (1995). Taking time seriously: Social change, social structure and human lives. In P. Moen, G. H. Elder, Jr., & K. Luscher (Eds.), *Examining lives in context: Perspectives on the ecology of human development* (pp. 211-264). Washington, DC: American Psychological Association.

Andrews, P. H., & Herschel, R. T. (1996). *Organizational communication: Empowerment in a technological society.* Boston: Houghton Mifflin.

Bandura, A. (1990). Conclusion: Reflections on nonability determinants of competence. In R. J. Sternberg & J. Kolligian, Jr. (Eds.), *Competence considered* (pp. 315-362). New Haven, CT: Yale University Press.

Bantz, C. (1993). Cultural diversity and group cross-cultural team research. *Journal of Applied Communication Research, 20,* 1-19.

Barker, J. R., & Tompkins, P. K. (1994). Identification in the self-managing organization: Characteristics of target and tenure. *Human Communication Research, 21,* 223-240.

Barley, S. R., & Kunda, G. (1992). Design and devotion: Surges of rational and normative ideologies of control in managerial discourse. *Administrative Science Quarterly, 37,* 363-399.

Barna, L. M. (1991). Stumbling blocks in intercultural communication. In L. A. Samovar & R. E. Porter (Eds.), *Intercultural communication: A reader* (6th ed., p. 345-352). Belmont, CA: Wadsworth.

Baron, S., & Clair, R. P. (1996, May). *From coercion to manipulation: Communication competence as disciplinary discourse in the organization.* Paper presented at the annual meeting of the International Communication Association, Chicago.

Beamer, L. (1992). Learning intercultural communication competence. *Journal of Business Communication, 29,* 285-303.

Beer, M., Spector, B., Lawrence, P. R., Mills, D. Q., & Walton, R. E. (1985). *Human resource management: A general manager's perspective.* New York: Free Press.

Belous, R. S. (1989). *The contingent economy: The growth of the temporary, part-time, and subcontracted workforce.* Washington, DC: National Planning Association.

Berman, S. J., & Hellweg, S. A. (1989). Perceived supervisor communication competence and supervisor satisfaction as a function of quality circle participation. *Journal of Business Communication, 26,* 103-122.

Bingham, S. G., & Burleson, B. R. (1989). Multiple effects of messages with multiple goals: Some perceived outcomes of responses to sexual harassment. *Human Communication Research, 16,* 184-216.

Bion, W. R. (1959). *Experiences in groups.* London: Tavistock.

Black, J. S., Gregersen, H. B., & Mendenhall, M. E. (1992). *Global assignments: Successfully expatriating and repatriating international managers.* San Francisco: Jossey-Bass.

Bochner, A., & Kelly, C. (1974). Interpersonal communication competency: Rationale, philosophy and implementation of a conceptual framework. *Speech Teacher, 23,* 279-301.

Bormann, E. G., Pratt, J., & Putnam, L. (1978). Power, authority, and sex: Male response to female leadership. *Communication Monographs, 45,* 119-155.

Bostrom, R. N. (Ed.). (1984). *Competence in communication: A multidisciplinary approach.* Beverly Hills, CA: Sage.

Brass, D. (1985). Men's and women's networks: A study of interaction patterns and influence in an organization. *Academy of Management Journal, 28,* 327-343.

Bronfenbrenner, U. (1979). *The ecology of human development: Experiments by nature and design.* Cambridge, MA: Harvard University Press.

Burleson, B. R., Albrecht, T. L., & Sarason, I. G. (Eds.). (1994). *Communication of social support: Messages, interactions, relationships and community.* Thousand Oaks, CA: Sage.

Cascio, W. (1986). *Managing human resources.* New York: McGraw-Hill.

Casmir, F. (1993). Third-culture building: A paradigm shift for international intercultural communication. In S. A. Deetz (Ed.), *Communication yearbook 16* (pp. 407-428). Newbury Park, CA: Sage.

Cetron, M. J., Rocha, W., & Luchins, R. (1988). Into the 21st century: Long-term trends affecting the United States. *The Futurist, 22*(5), 29-40.

Cheney, G. (1983). The rhetoric of identification and the study of organizational communication. *Quarterly Journal of Speech, 69,* 143-158.

Chilton, K., & Weidenbaum, M. (1994). *A new social contract for the American workplace: From paternalism to partnering* (Policy Study No. 123). St. Louis, MO: Washington University, Center for the Study of American Business.

Clair, R. P. (1993). The use of framing devices to sequester organizational narratives: Hegemony and harassment. *Communication Monographs, 60,* 113-136.

Cohen, M. D., & Bacdayan, P. (1994). Organizational routines are stored as procedural memory: Evidence from a laboratory study. *Organization Science, 5,* 554-568.

Cole, M., & Engeström, Y. (1993). A cultural-historical approach to distributed cognition. In G. Salomon (Ed.), *Distributed cognitions: Psychological and education considerations* (pp. 1-46). Cambridge, UK: Cambridge University Press.

Collier, M. J. (1994). Cultural identity and intercultural communication. In L. A. Samovar & R. E. Porter (Eds.), *Intercultural communication: A reader* (7th ed., pp. 36-44). Belmont, CA: Wadsworth.

Cooper, L. O. (1997). Listening competency in the workplace: A model for training. *Business Communication Quarterly, 60*(4), 75-84.

Cooper, L. O., & Husband, R. (1993). Developing a model of organizational listening competency. *Journal of the International Listening Association, 7,* 6-34.

Cotton, J. L. (1993). *Employee involvement: Methods for improving performance and work attitudes.* Newbury Park, CA: Sage.

Cox, T. H., & Blake, S. (1991). Managing cultural diversity: Implications for organizational competitiveness. *Academy of Management Executive, 5,* 45-56.

Crouter, A. C. (1984). Spillover from family to work: The neglected side of the work-family interface. *Human Relations, 37,* 425-442.

Cushman, D., & Whiting, G. C. (1972). An approach to communication theory: Toward a consensus on rules. *Journal of Communication, 22,* 217-238.

Cusella, L. P. (1987). Feedback, motivation, and performance. In F. M. Jablin, L. L. Putnam, K. H. Roberts, & L. W. Porter (Eds.), *Handbook of organizational communication: An interdisciplinary perspective* (pp. 624-678). Newbury Park, CA: Sage.

Daft, R. L., & Lengel, R. H. (1986). Organizational information requirements, media richness and structural design. *Management Science, 32,* 554-571.

Daft, R. L., & Weick, K. E. (1984). Toward a model of organizations as interpretation systems. *Academy of Management Review, 9,* 284-295.

Davis-Blake, A., & Uzzi, B. (1993). Determinants of employment externalization: A study of temporary workers and independent contractors. *Administrative Science Quarterly, 38,* 195-223.

Dinges, N. G., & Lieberman, D. A. (1989). Intercultural communication competence: Coping with stressful work situations. *International Journal of Intercultural Relations, 13,* 371-385.

DiSalvo, V. S. (1980). A summary of current research identifying communication skills in various organizational contexts. *Communication Education, 29,* 283-290.

DiSalvo, V. S., & Larsen, J. K. (1987). A contingency approach to communication skill importance: The impact of occupation, direction, and position. *Journal of Business Communication, 24,* 3-22.

Duran, R. L., & Spitzberg, B. H. (1995). Toward the development and validation of a measure of cognitive communication competence. *Communication Quarterly, 43,* 259-275.

Economic factors fuel growth of two-tier workforce in U.S. (1995, April 17). *Spokane Spokesman-Review,* pp. E1, E3.

Eisenberg, E. M., Farace, R. V., Monge, P. R., Bettinghaus, E. P., Kurchner-Hawkins, R., Miller, K., & Rothman, L. (1985). Communication linkages in interorganizational systems. In B. Dervin & M. Voight (Eds.), *Progress in the communication sciences* (Vol. 6, pp. 231-261). New York: Ablex.

Eisenberg, E. M., & Goodall, H. L. (1993). *Organizational communication: Balancing creativity and constraint.* New York: St. Martin's.

Eisenberg, E. M., & Witten, M. (1987). Reconsidering openness in organizational communication. *Academy of Management Review, 12,* 418-426.

Elmes, M., & Costello, M. (1992). Mystification and social drama: The hidden side of communication skills training. *Human Relations, 45,* 427-445.

Euske, N. A., & Roberts, K. H. (1987). Evolving perspectives in organization theory: Communication implications. In F. M. Jablin, L. L. Putnam, K. H. Roberts, & L. W. Porter (Eds.), *Handbook of organizational communication: An interdisciplinary perspective* (pp. 41-69). Newbury Park, CA: Sage.

Feldman, D. C., Doerpinghaus, H. I., & Turnley, W. H. (1994). Managing temporary workers: A permanent HRM challenge. *Organizational Dynamics, 23,* 49-63.

Fierman, J. (1994, January 4). The contingency work force. *Fortune, 129*(2), 30-36.

Finholt, T., & Sproull, L. (1990). Electronic groups at work. *Organization Science, 1*(1), 41-64.

Fisher, B. A. (1978). *Perspectives on human communication.* New York: Macmillan.

Follett, M. P. (1940). The giving of orders. In H. C. Metcalf & L. Urwick (Eds.), *Dynamic administration: The collected papers of Mary Parker Follett* (pp. 50-70). New York: Harper.

Ford, W. S. Z., & Wolvin, A. D. (1993). The differential impact of a basic communication course on perceived communication competencies in class, work and social contexts. *Communication Education, 42,* 215-223.

Friedman, R. A. (1989). Interaction norms as carriers of organizational culture: A study of labor negotiations at International Harvester. *Journal of Contemporary Ethnography, 18,* 3-29.

Friedman, S. L., & Wachs, T. D. (Eds.). (1999). *Measuring environment across the life span: Emerging methods and concepts.* Washington, DC: American Psychological Association.

Frost, P. J. (1987). Power, politics, and influence. In F. M. Jablin, L. L. Putnam, K. H. Roberts, & L. W. Porter (Eds.), *Handbook of organizational communication: An interdisciplinary perspective* (pp. 503-548). Newbury Park, CA: Sage.

Giacalone, R. A., & Rosenfeld, P. (Eds.). (1991). *Impression management in organizations.* Hillsdale, NJ: Lawrence Erlbaum.

Giddens, A. (1984). *The constitution of society: Outline of a theory of structuration.* Berkeley: University of California Press.

Gioia, D. A. (1986). Symbols, scripts, and sensemaking: Creating meaning in the organizational experience. In H. Sims, D. Gioia, & Associates (Eds.), *The thinking organization: Dynamics of organizational social cognition* (pp. 49-74). San Francisco: Jossey-Bass.

Glew, D. J., O'Leary-Kelly, A. M., Griffin, R. W., & Van Fleet, D. D. (1995). Participation in organizations: A preview of the issues and proposed framework for future analysis. *Journal of Management, 21,* 395-421.

Goodall, J. L., Jr. (1982). Organizational communication competence: The development of an industrial simulation to teach adaptive skills. *Communication Quarterly, 30,* 282-295.

Gouran, D. S., & Hirokawa, R. Y. (1983). The role of communication in decision-making groups. In M. S. Mander (Ed.), *Communication in transition* (pp. 168-185). New York Praeger.

Granovetter, M. (1973). The strength of weak ties. *American Journal of Sociology, 78,* 1360-1380.

Griffith, T. L. (1999). Technology features as triggers for sensemaking. *Academy of Management Review, 24,* 472-488.

Gueutal, H. G., & Taylor, E. M. (1992). Employee pregnancy: The impact on organizations, pregnant employees and co-workers. *Journal of Business and Psychology, 5,* 59-476.

Gutek, B. A. (1985). *Sex and the workplace.* San Francisco: Jossey-Bass.

Gutek, B. A., & Morasch, B. (1982). Sex ratios, sex role spillover, and sexual harassment of women at work. *Journal of Social Issues, 38,* 55-74.

Haas, J. W., & Arnold, C. L. (1995). An examination of the role of listening in judgments of communication competence in co-workers. *Journal of Business Communication, 32,* 123-140.

Habermas, J. (1970). Toward a theory of communicative competence. In H. P. Dreitzel (Ed.), *Recent Sociology, 2,* 115-148.

Hage, J., Aiken, M., & Marrett, C. B. (1971). Organizational structure and communications. *American Sociological Review, 36,* 860-871.

Hammer, M. (1987). Behavioral dimensions of intercultural effectiveness: A replication and extension. *International Journal of Intercultural Relations, 11,* 65-88.

Hargie, O., & Tourish, D. (1994). Communication skills training: Management manipulation or personal development. *Human Relations, 47,* 1377-1389.

Harris, L., & Cronen, V. E. (1979). A rules-based model for the analysis and evaluation of organizational communication. *Communication Quarterly, 27,* 12-28.

Hart, C. H., Olsen, S. F., Robinson, C. C., & Mandleco, B. L. (1997). The development of social and communicative competence in childhood: Review and model of personal, familial, and extrafamilial processes. In B. R. Burleson (Ed.), *Communication yearbook 20* (pp. 305-373). Thousand Oaks, CA: Sage.

Hearn, J. (1993). Emotive subjects: Organizational men, organizational masculinities and the (de)construction of "emotions." In S. Fineman (Ed.), *Emotion in organizations* (pp. 142-166). London: Sage.

Health, R. G., & Sias, P. M. (1999). Communicating spirit in a collaborative alliance. *Journal of Applied Communication Research, 27,* 356-376.

Hellweg, S. (1987). Organizational grapevines: A state of the art review. In B. Dervin & M. Voight (Eds.), *Progress in communication sciences* (Vol. 8, pp. 213-230). Norwood, NJ: Ablex.

Hickson, D. J., Hinings, C. R., Lee, C. A., Schneck, R. J., & Pennings, J. M. (1971). A strategic contingencies theory of intraorganizational power. *Administrative Science Quarterly, 16,* 216-229.

Hinz, V. B., Tindale, R. S., & Vollrath, D. A. (1997). The emerging conceptualization of groups as information processors. *Psychological Bulletin, 121,* 43-64.

Hirokawa, R. Y. (1988). Group communication and decision-making performance: A test of a functional perspective. *Human Communication Research, 14,* 487-515.

Hirokawa, R. Y., & Keyton, J. (1995). Perceived facilitators and inhibitors of effectiveness in organizational work teams. *Management Communication Quarterly, 8,* 424-446.

Hirokawa, R. Y., & Rost, K. M. (1992). Effective group decision making in organizations: Field test of the vigilant interaction theory. *Management Communication Quarterly, 5,* 267-288.

Hofstede, G. (1981). *Culture's consequences: International differences in work-related values.* Beverly Hills, CA: Sage.

Hogan, G. W., & Goodson, J. R. (1990). The key to expatriate success. *Training and Development Journal, 44,* 50-52.

Homans, G. C. (1950). *The human group.* New York: Harcourt, Brace.

Hulin, C. L., Fitzgerald, L. F., & Drasgow, F. (1996). Organizational influences on sexual harassment. In M. S. Stockdale (Ed.), *Sexual harassment in the workplace: Perspectives, frontiers, and response strategies: Vol. 5. Women and work* (pp. 127-150). Thousand Oaks, CA: Sage.

Hutchins, E. (1991). The social organization of distributed cognition. In L. B. Resnick, J. M. Levine, & S. D. Teasley (Eds.), *Perspectives on socially shared cognition* (pp. 283-307). Washington, DC: American Psychological Association.

Hymes, D. (1972). *On communication competence.* In J. B. Pride & J. Holmes (Eds.), *Sociolinguistics: Selected readings* (pp. 269-293). Baltimore: Penguin.

Jablin, F. M. (1994). Communication competence: An organizational assimilation perspective. In L. van Waes, E. Woudstra, & P. van den Hoven (Eds.), *Functional communication quality* (pp. 28-41). Amsterdam: Rodopi.

Jablin, F. M., Cude, R. L., House, A., Lee, J., & Roth, N. L. (1994). Communication competence in organizations: Conceptualization and comparison across multiple levels of analysis. In L. Thayer & G. Barnett (Eds.), *Organization-communication: Emerging perspectives* (Vol. 4, pp. 114-140). Norwood, NJ: Ablex.

Janis, I. L. (1972). *Victims of group think.* Boston: Houghton Mifflin.

Johnson, G. M. (1992). Subordinate perceptions of superior's communication competence and task attraction related to superior's use of compliance-gaining tactics. *Western Journal of Communication, 56,* 54-57.

Johnson, G. M., Staton, A. Q., & Jorgensen-Earp, C. R. (1995). An ecological perspective on the transition of new university freshmen. *Communication Education, 44,* 336-352.

Johnston, H. R., & Carrico, S. R. (1988). Developing capabilities to use information strategically. *MIS Quarterly, 12,* 37-48.

Jones, F., & Fletcher, B. (1996). Taking work home: A study of daily fluctuations in work stressors, effects on moods and impacts on marital partners. *Journal of Occupational and Organizational Psychology, 69,* 89-106.

Kanter, R. M. (1977). *Men and women of the corporation.* New York: Basic Books.

Katz, D., & Kahn, R. (1978). *The social psychology of organizations* (2nd ed.). New York: John Wiley.

Kellermann, K., Reynolds, R., & Chen, J. B. (1991). Strategies of conversational retreat: When parting is not sweet sorrow. *Communication Monographs, 58,* 362-383.

Kernan, M. C., & Howard, G. S. (1990). Computer anxiety and computer attitudes: An investigation of construct and predictive validity. *Educational and Psychological Measurement, 50,* 681-690.

King, S. S., & Cushman, D. P. (1994). High speed management as a theoretic principle for yielding significant organizational communication behaviors. In B. Kovacic (Ed.), *New approaches to organizational communication* (pp. 87-116). Albany: State University of New York Press.

Klimoski, R., & Mohammed, S. (1994). Team mental model: Construct or metaphor? *Journal of Management, 20,* 403-437.

Koester, J. (1985). *A profile of the U.S. student abroad.* New York: Council on International Educational Exchange.

Koester, J., & Olebe, M. (1988). The Behavioral Assessment Scale for Intercultural Communication Effectiveness. *International Journal of Intercultural Relations, 12,* 233-246.

Kovacic, B. (1994). New perspectives on organizational communication. In B. Kovacic (Ed.). *New approaches to organizational communication* (pp. 1-37). Albany: State University of New York Press.

Krackhardt, D., & Stern, R. N. (1988). Structuring of information organizations and the management of crises. *Social Psychological Quarterly, 51,* 123-140.

Kreps, G. L. (1990). *Organizational communication* (2nd ed.). New York: Longman.

Langer, E. J. (1978). Rethinking the role of thought in social interaction. In J. H. Harvey, W. J. Ickes, & R. F. Kidd (Eds.), *New directions in attribution research* (Vol. 2, pp. 35-58). Hillsdale, NJ: Lawrence Erlbaum.

Langer, E. J., & Parks, K. (1990). Incompetence: A conceptual reconsideration. In R. J. Sternberg & J. Kolligian, Jr. (Eds.), *Competence considered* (pp. 149-166). New Haven, CT: Yale University Press.

Latane, B., Williams, K., & Harkins, S. (1979). Many hands make light the work: The causes and consequences of social loafing. *Journal of Personality and Social Psychology, 12,* 144-150.

Lei, D., Hitt, M. A., & Bettis, R. (1996). Dynamic core competencies through meta-learning and strategic context. *Journal of Management, 22,* 549-569.

Liang, D., Moreland, R., & Argote, L. (1995). Group versus individual training and group performance: The mediating role of transactive memory. *Personality and Social Psychology Bulletin, 21,* 384-393.

Likert, R. (1961). *New patterns of management.* New York: McGraw-Hill.

Likert, R. (1967). *The human organization.* New York: McGraw-Hill.

Locke, E. A., & Henne, D. (1986). Work motivation theories. In C. L. Cooper & I. Robertson (Eds.), *International review of industrial and organizational psychology* (Vol. 1, pp. 1-35). Chichester, UK: Wiley.

Luthans, F. (1988). Successful vs. effective real managers. *Academy of Management Executive, 11,* 127-132.

Maes, J. D., Weldy, T. G., & Icenogle, M. L. (1997). A managerial perspective: Oral communication competency is most important for business students in the workplace. *Journal of Business Communication, 34*(1), 67-80.

Magnusson, D. (1995). Individual development: A holistic, integrated model. In P. Moen, G. H. Elder, Jr., & K. Luscher (Eds.), *Examining lives in context: Perspectives on the ecology of human development* (pp. 19-60). Washington, DC: American Psychological Association.

Manz, C. C., & Sims, H. P., Jr. (1989). *Super-leadership: Leading others to lead themselves.* New York: Berkley.

March, J. G. (1988, April). *Learning and taking risks.* Keynote address at the annual Texas Conference on Organizations, Lago Vista.

Marino, K. E. (1996). Developing consensus on firm competencies and capabilities. *Academy of Management Executive, 10*(3), 40-51.

Markus, M. L. (1987). Toward a "critical mass" theory of interactive media: Universal access, interdependence and diffusion. *Communication Research, 14,* 491-511.

McCroskey, J. C. (1982). Communication competence and performance: A pedagogical perspective. *Communication Education, 31,* 1-8.

McCroskey, J. C. (1984). Communication competence: The elusive construct. In R. N. Bostrom (Ed.), *Competence in communication* (pp. 259-268). Beverly Hills, CA: Sage.

McGee, D. S. (1994, November). *Classroom discussion competence: A preliminary model.* Paper presented at the annual meeting of the Speech Communication Association, New Orleans, LA.

Metts, S., & Spitzberg, B. H. (1996). Sexual communication in interpersonal contexts: A script-based approach. In B. R. Burleson (Ed.), *Communication yearbook 19* (pp. 49-92). Thousand Oaks, CA: Sage.

Meyer, J., & Rowan, B. (1977). Institutionalized organizations: Formal structure as myth and ceremony. *American Journal of Sociology, 83,* 340-363.

Miles, R. E. (1975). *Theories of management: Implications for organizational behavior and development.* New York: McGraw-Hill.

Miles, R. E., & Creed, W. E. D. (1995). Organizational forms and managerial philosophies: A descriptive and analytical review. In L. Cummings & B. Staw (Eds.), *Research in organizational behavior* (Vol. 17, pp. 333-372). Greenwich, CT: JAI.

Miller, D. (1996). A preliminary typology of organizational learning: Synthesizing the literature. *Journal of Management, 22,* 485-505.

Miller, V. D., Jablin, F. M., Casey, M. K., Lamphear-Van Horn, M., & Ethington, C. (1996). The maternity leave as a role negotiation process. *Journal of Managerial Issues, 8,* 286-309.

Milliken, F. J., & Martins, L. I. (1996). Searching for common threads: Understanding the multiple effects of diversity in organizational groups. *Academy of Management Review, 21,* 402-433.

Mize, S. (1992). Shattering the glass ceiling. *Training and Development Journal, 46,* 60-62.

Moen, P., Elder, G. H., Jr., & Luscher, K. (Ed.). (1995). *Examining lives in context: Perspectives on the ecology of human development.* Washington, DC: American Psychological Association.

Monge, P. R., Bachman, S. G., Dillard, J. P., & Eisenberg, E. M. (1981). Communicator competence in the workplace: Model testing and scale development. In M. Burgoon (Ed.), *Communication yearbook 5* (pp. 505-527). Beverly Hills, CA: Sage.

Monge, P. R., & Eisenberg, E. M. (1987). Emergent communication networks. In F. M. Jablin, L. L. Putnam, K. H. Roberts, & L. W. Porter (Eds.), *Handbook of organizational communication: An interdisciplinary perspective* (pp. 304-342). Newbury Park, CA: Sage.

Moore, G. (1992). Gender and informal networks in state government. *Social Science Quarterly, 73,* 46-61.

Moorman, C., & Miner, A. S. (1998). Organizational improvisation and organizational memory. *Academy of Management Review, 23,* 698-723.

Moran, R., & Harris, P. (1981). *Managing cultural synergy.* Houston, TX: Gulf.

Morand, D. A. (1995). The role of behavioral formality and informality in the enactment of bureaucratic versus organic organizations. *Academy of Management Review, 20,* 831-872.

Morse, B. W., & Piland, R. N. (1981). An assessment of communication competencies needed by intermediate-level health care providers: A study of nurse-patient, nurse-doctor, nurse-nurse communication relationships. *Journal of Applied Communication Research, 9,* 30-41.

Nadler, D. A., & Tushman, M. L. (1999). The organization of the future: Strategic imperatives and core competencies for the 21st century. *Organizational Dynamics, 28*(1), 45-60.

Nishida, H. (1985). Japanese intercultural communication competence and cross-cultural adjustment. *International Journal of Intercultural Relations, 9,* 247-269.

Nunamaker, J., Dennis, A., Valacich, J., Vogel, D., & George, J. (1991). Group support systems research: Experience from the lab and field. In L. M. Jessup & J. S. Valacich (Eds.), *Group support systems: New perspectives* (pp. 78-96). New York: Macmillan.

Noe, R. A. (1988). Women and mentoring: A review and research agenda. *Academy of Management Review, 13,* 65-78.

Offerman, L., & Gowing, M. (1990). Organizations of the future: Changes and challenges. *American Psychologist, 45,* 95-108.

O'Keefe, B. J. (1988). The logic of message design: Individual differences in reasoning about communication. *Communication Monographs, 55,* 80-103.

O'Reilly, C. A., Caldwell, D. F., & Barnett, W. P. (1989). Work group demography, social integration, and turnover. *Administrative Science Quarterly, 34,* 21-37.

Orlikowski, W. J., & Yates, J. (1994). Genre repertoire: The structuring of communicative practices in organizations. *Administrative Science Quarterly, 39,* 541-574.

Parks, M. R. (1994). Communicative competence and interpersonal control. In M. L. Knapp & G. R. Miller (Eds.), *Handbook of interpersonal communication* (2nd ed., pp. 589-620). Thousand Oaks, CA: Sage.

Pavitt, C., & Haight, L. (1986). Implicit theories of communicative competence: Situational and competence level differences in judgments of prototype and target. *Communication Monographs, 53,* 221-235.

Pentland, B. T. (1995). Grammatical models of organizational processes. *Organization Science, 6,* 541-556.

Pentland, B. T., & Rueter, H. H. (1994). Organizational routines as grammars of action. *Administrative Science Quarterly, 39,* 484-510.

Poole, M. S., & DeSanctis, G. (1990). Understanding the use of group decision support systems. In J. Fulk & C. Steinfield (Eds.), *Organizations and communication technology* (pp. 173-193). Newbury Park, CA: Sage.

Poole, M. S., & DeSanctis, G. (1992). Microlevel structuration in computer-supported group decision making. *Human Communication Research, 19,* 5-49.

Poole, M. S., Holmes, M., & DeSanctis, G. (1991). Conflict management in a computer-supported meeting environment. *Management Science, 8,* 926-953.

Poole, M. S., Seibold, D. R., & McPhee, R. D. (1996). The structuration of group decisions. In R. Hirokawa & M. S. Poole (Eds.), *Communication and group decision making* (2nd ed., pp. 114-146). Thousand Oaks, CA: Sage.

Powell, W. W. (1990). Neither market nor hierarchy: Network forms of organization. In B. Staw & L. Cummings (Eds.), *Research in organizational behavior* (Vol. 12, pp. 295-336). Greenwich, CT: JAI.

Powell, W. W., Koput, K. W., & Smith-Doerr, L. (1996). Interorganizational collaboration and the locus of innovation: Networks of learning in biotechnology. *Administrative Science Quarterly, 41,* 116-145.

Prahalad, C. K., & Hamel, G. (1990, May-June). The core competence of the organization. *Harvard Business Review, 68,* 79-91.

Propp, K. M., & Nelson, D. (1986). Problem-solving performance in naturalistic groups: The ecological validity of the functional perspective. *Communication Studies, 47,* 35-45.

Putnam, L. L., & Mumby, D. K. (1993). Organizations, emotion and the myth of rationality. In S. Fineman (Ed.), *Emotion in organizations* (pp. 36-57). London: Sage.

Rader, M., & Wunsch, A. (1980). A survey of communication practices of business school graduates by job category and undergraduate major. *Journal of Business Communication, 17*(4), 33-41.

Raelin, J. A. (1997). A model of work-based learning. *Organization Science, 8,* 563-578.

Ratiu, I. (1983). Thinking internationally: A comparison of how international executives learn. *International Studies of Management and Organization, 8,* 139-150.

Redding, W. C. (1979). Organizational communication theory and ideology: An overview. In D. Nimmo (Ed.), *Communication yearbook 3* (pp. 309-341). New Brunswick, NJ: Transaction.

Reinsch, L., & Shelby, A. N. (1996). Communication challenges and needs: Perceptions of MBA students. *Business Communication Quarterly, 59,* 36-53.

Reinsch, L., & Shelby, A. N. (1997). What communication abilities do practitioners need? Evidence from MBA students. *Business Communication Quarterly, 60*(4), 7-29.

Rogers, J. K. (1995). Just a temp: Experience and structure of alienation in temporary clerical employment. *Work and Occupations, 22,* 137-166.

Rosener, J. B. (1990, November-December). Ways women lead. *Harvard Business Review, 68,* 119-125.

Rousseau, D. M., & Parks, J. M. (1993). The contracts of individuals and organizations. In L. Cummings & B. Staw (Eds.), *Research in organizational behavior* (Vol. 14, pp. 1-43). Greenwich, CT: JAI.

Ruben, B. D. (1977). Human communication and cross-cultural effectiveness. *International Journal of Intercultural Relations, 4,* 95-105.

Ruben, B. D., & Kealey, D. H. (1979). Behavioral assessment of communication competency and the prediction of cross-cultural adaptation. *International Journal of Intercultural Relations, 3,* 15-48.

Rubin, R. B. (1990). Communication competence. In G. M. Phillips & J. T. Wood (Eds.), *Speech communication: Essays to commemorate the 75th anniversary of the Speech Communication Association* (pp. 94-129). Carbondale: Southern Illinois University.

Sackmann, S. A. (1991). *Cultural knowledge in organizations: Exploring the collective mind.* Newbury Park, CA: Sage.

Sambamurthy, V., & Poole, M. S. (1992). The effects of variations in capabilities of GDSS designs on management conflict in groups. *Information Systems Research, 3,* 224-251.

Schall, M. S. (1983). A communication-rules approach to organizational culture. *Administrative Science Quarterly, 28,* 557-581.

Schein, E. H. (1980). *Organizational psychology* (3rd ed.). Englewood Cliffs, NJ: Prentice Hall.

Schein, E. H. (1985). *Organizational culture and leadership.* San Francisco: Jossey-Bass.

Scudder, J. N., Guinan, P. J. (1989). Communication competencies as discriminators of superiors' ratings of employee performance. *Journal of Business Communication, 26,* 217-229.

Seibold, D. R., Kudsi, S., & Rude, M. (1993). Does communication training make a difference? Evidence for the effectiveness of a presentation skills program. *Journal of Applied Communication Research, 21,* 111-131.

Sell, D. K. (1983). Research on attitude change in U.S. students who participate in foreign study experience: Past findings and suggestions for future research. *International Journal of Intercultural Relations, 7,* 131-138.

Shea, G. P., & Guzzo, R. A. (1987). Group effectiveness: What really matters? *Sloan Management Review, 28,* 25-31.

Sheffey, S., & Tindale, R. S. (1992). Perceptions of sexual harassment in the workplace. *Journal of Applied Psychology, 22,* 1502-1520.

Shimanoff, S. B. (1980). *Communication rules: Theory and research.* Beverly Hills, CA: Sage.

Sias, P. M., Kramer, M. W., & Jenkins, E. (1997). A comparison of the communication behavior of temporary employees and new hires. *Communication Research, 24,* 731-754.

Sims, H. P., Jr., & Lorenzi, P. (1992). *The new leadership paradigm: Social learning and cognition in organizations.* Newbury Park, CA: Sage.

Snavely, W. B., & Walters, E. V. (1983). Differences in the communication competence among administrator social styles. *Journal of Applied Communication Research, 11*(2), 120-135.

Snow, C. C., Miles, R. E., & Coleman, H. J. (1992). Managing 21st century network organizations. *Organizational Dynamics, 20*(3), 5-20.

Spitzberg, B. H., & Cupach, W. R. (1984). *Interpersonal communication competence.* Beverly Hills, CA: Sage.

Spitzberg, B. H., & Duran, R. L. (1993, July). *Toward an ideological deconstruction of competence.* Paper presented at the annual meeting of the International Communication Association, Sydney, Australia.

Sriussadaporn-Charoenngam, N., & Jablin, F. M. (1999). An exploratory study of communication competence in Thai organizations. *Journal of Business Communication, 36,* 382-412.

Sternberg, R. J. (1990). Prototypes of competence and incompetence. In R. J. Sternberg & J. Kolligian, Jr. (Eds.), *Competence considered* (pp. 117-145). New Haven, CT: Yale University Press.

Stewart, E. (1985). Culture and decision making. In W. Gudykunst, L. Stewart, & S. Ting-Toomey (Eds.), *Communication, culture and organizational processes* (pp. 177-211). Beverly Hills, CA: Sage.

Stohl, C. (1995). *Organizational communication: Connectedness in action.* Thousand Oaks, CA: Sage.

Stohl, C., & Jennings, K. (1988). Volunteerism and voice in quality circles. *Western Journal of Speech Communication, 52,* 238-251.

Sypher, B. D. (1981). *A multimethod investigation of employee communication abilities, communication satisfaction and job satisfaction.* Doctoral dissertation, University of Michigan.

Sypher, B. D., & Sypher, H. E. (1981, May). *Individual differences and perceived communication abilities in an organizational setting.* Paper presented at the annual meeting of the International Communication Association, Minneapolis, MN.

Sypher, B. D., & Sypher, H. E. (1983). Perceptions of communication ability: Self-monitoring in an organizational setting. *Personality and Social Psychology Bulletin, 9,* 297-304.

Sypher, B. D., Sypher, H. E., & Leichty, G. B. (1983). *Cognitive differentiation, self-monitoring and indi-*

vidual success in organizations. Paper presented at the Fifth International Congress on Personal Construct Psychology, Boston.

Sypher, B. D., & Zorn, T. (1986). Communication-related abilities and upward mobility: A longitudinal investigation. *Human Communication Research, 12,* 420-431.

Szajna, B. (1994). An investigation of the predictive validity of computer anxiety and computer aptitude. *Educational and Psychological Measurement, 54,* 926-934.

Taylor, F. W. (1911). *The principles of scientific management.* New York: Harper.

Teboul, J., Chen, L., & Fritz, L. (1994). Communication in multinational organizations in the United States and Western Europe. In R. Wiseman & R. Shuter (Eds.), *Communicating in multinational organizations* (pp. 12-29). Thousand Oaks, CA: Sage.

Thompson, I. (1996). Competence and critique in technical communication: A qualitative content analysis of journal articles. *Journal of Business and Technical Communication, 16,* 48-80.

Thompson, J. D. (1967). *Organizations in action.* New York: McGraw-Hill.

Thornburg, L. (1990, September). Transfers need not mean dislocation. *Human Resources Magazine,* pp. 46-48.

Toffler, A. (1970). *Future shock.* New York: Bantam.

Tompkins, P. K., & Cheney, G. (1985). Communication and unobtrusive control in contemporary organizations. In R. D. McPhee & P. K. Tompkins (Eds.), *Organizational communication: Traditional themes and new directions* (pp. 179-210). Beverly Hills, CA: Sage.

Triandis, H. (1973). Dimensions of cultural variation as parameters of organizational theories. *International Studies of Management and Organization, 12,* 139-169.

Triandis, H. C., & Albert, R. D. (1987). Cross-cultural perspectives. In F. M. Jablin, L. L. Putnam, K. H. Roberts, & L. W. Porter (Eds.), *Handbook of organizational communication: An interdisciplinary perspective* (pp. 264-296). Newbury Park, CA: Sage.

Tsui, A. S., Pearce, J. L., Porter, L. W., & Hite, J. P. (1995). Choice of employee-organization relationship: Influence of external and internal organizational factors. In G. Ferris (Ed.), *Research in personnel and human resources management* (Vol. 13, pp. 117-151). Greenwich, CT: JAI.

Tung, R. (1988). *The new expatriates: Managing human resources abroad.* New York: Ballinger.

Ulrich, D., & Lake, D. (1990). *Organizational capability.* New York: John Wiley.

Vondracek, F. W., Lerner, R. M., & Schulenberg, J. E. (1986). *Career development: A life-span developmental approach.* Hillsdale, NJ: Lawrence Erlbaum.

Walsh, J. P. (1995). Managerial and organizational cognition: Notes from a trip down memory lane. *Organization Science, 6,* 280-321.

Walsh, J. P., & Ungson, G. R. (1991). Organizational memory. *Academy of Management Review, 16,* 57-91.

Walther, J. B. (1995). Relational aspects of computer-mediated communication: Experimental observations over time. *Organization Science, 6,* 186-203.

Watzlawick, P., Beavin, J., & Jackson, D. (1967). *The pragmatics of human communication.* New York: Norton.

Weber, M. (1947). *The theory of social and economic organizations* (A. A. M. Henderson & T. Parsons, Trans.). New York: Oxford University Press.

Weiss, H. M. (1977). Subordinate imitation of supervisor behavior: The role of modeling in organizational socialization. *Organizational Behavior and Human Performance, 19,* 89-105.

Wellins, R., Byham, W., & Wilson, J. (1991). *Empowered teams.* San Francisco: Jossey-Bass.

Wellmon, T. (1988). Conceptualizing organizational communication competence: A rules-based perspective. *Management Communication Quarterly, 1,* 515-534.

Wexley, M. N. (1986). Impression management and the new competence: Conjecture for seekers. *Et cetera, 43,* 247-258.

Wheeless, V. E., & Berryman-Fink, C. (1985). Perceptions of women managers and their communicator competencies. *Communication Quarterly, 33,* 137-148.

Wiemann, J. A. (1977). Explication and test of a model of communication competence. *Human Communication Research, 3,* 195-213.

Wilkins, B. M., & Andersen, P. A. (1991). Gender differences and similarities in management communication: A meta-analysis. *Management Communication Quarterly, 5,* 6-35.

Winter, S. G. (1986). The research program of the behavioral theory of the firm: Orthodox critique and evolutionary perspective. In B. Gilad & S. Kaish (Eds.), *Handbook of behavioral economics* (Vol. A, pp. 151-188). Greenwich, CT: JAI.

Wiseman, R., & Shuter, R. (Eds.). (1994). *Communicating in multinational organizations.* Thousand Oaks, CA: Sage.

Wohlert, K. L. (1995). *A longitudinal, multilevel analysis of the implementation and non-mandated use of a group communication technology: The case of Lotus Notes.* Unpublished doctoral dissertation, University of Texas at Austin.

Wolff, F. I., Marsnik, N. C., Tacey, W. S., & Nichols, R. G. (1983). *Perceptive listening.* New York: Holt, Rinehart & Winston.

Wood, J. T. (1994). *Gendered lives: Communication, gender, and culture.* Belmont, CA: Wadsworth.

Zander, A. W. (1980). The origins and consequences of group goals. In L. Festinger (Ed.), *Retrospections on social psychology.* New York: Oxford University Press.

Zimmermann, S. (1995). Perceptions of intercultural communication competence and international student adaptation to an American campus. *Communication Education, 44,* 321-335.

Zorn, T. E. (1991). Construct system development, transformational leadership and leadership messages. *Southern Communication Journal, 56,* 178-193.

Zorn, T. E. (1993). Motivation to communicate: A critical review with suggested alternatives. In S. A. Deetz (Ed.), *Communication yearbook 16* (pp. 515-549). Newbury Park, CA: Sage.

Zorn, T. E., & Violanti, M. T. (1996). Communication abilities and individual achievement in organizations. *Management Communication Quarterly, 10,* 139-167.

Name Index

Subject Index

About the Editors

Fredric M. Jablin (Ph.D., Purdue University) is the E. Claiborne Robins Chaired Professor of Leadership Studies in the Jepson School of Leadership Studies at the University of Richmond. He joined the faculty in the Jepson School in 1994, after having served for many years as a Professor of Speech Communication and Management (in the Graduate School of Business) at the University of Texas at Austin. His research, which has been published in a wide variety of communication, psychology, personnel and management journals, and scholarly books, has examined various facets of leader-member communication in organizations, group problem-solving, communication competence, and communication processes associated with organizational entry, assimilation and exit. He has been a member of the editorial boards of over a dozen different professional journals, the recipient of numerous awards for his research and teaching, and has served as a researcher and/or consultant to organizations in both the public and private sectors. He is currently working on a research symposium and book project related to communication processes and paradoxes associated with leadership/followership in organizations.

Linda L. Putnam (Ph.D., University of Minnesota) is Professor of Organizational Communication in the Department of Speech Communication at Texas A&M University. Her current research interests include negotiation and organizational conflict, metaphors of organizational communication, and language analysis in organizations. She is coeditor of *Communication and Negotiation* (1992), *Handbook of Organizational Communication* (1987), and *Communication and Organizations: An Interpretive Approach* (1983). She has published over 80 articles and book chapters in the areas of organizational communication, conflict management, negotiation, and organizational studies. She is the 1993 recipient of the Charles H. Woolbert Research Award for innovative research in communication, the 1999 recipient of the Distinguished Scholar Award from the National Communication Association, and a Fellow and Past President of the International Communication Association and the International Association for Conflict Management.

About the Contributors

Susan J. Ashford (M.S. and Ph.D. in organizational behavior, Northwestern University) is currently the Michael and Susan Jandernoa Professor of Organizational Behavior at the University of Michigan Business School. She joined the Michigan faculty in 1991 after spending eight years at Dartmouth College's Amos Tuck School of Business Administration. Her research focuses on the ways that individuals are proactive in their organizational lives. Her work has been published in *Administrative Science Quarterly, Academy of Management Review, Academy of Management Journal, Journal of Applied Psychology, Organizational Behavior and Human Decision Processes, Research in Organizational Behavior,* and *Strategic Management Journal,* among others. Professor Ashford was the consulting editor for the *Academy of Management Journal,* 1990-1993, has served on the editorial board since 1984 and is currently a board member for *Organizational Behavior and Human Decision Processes.*

George Cheney (Ph.D., Purdue University, 1985) is Professor and Director of Graduate Studies in Communication at the University of Montana–Missoula. Also, he is Adjunct Professor of Management Communication at the University of Waikato, Hamilton, New Zealand. He specializes in the study of contemporary organizational life, focusing on such issues as human identity, the exercise of power, democracy at work, business and organizational ethics, the analysis of corporate public discourse, and quality of worklife. He has developed courses on, and has published in, nearly all these topics. He has published over 50 journal articles, book chapters, and reviews. He is author of two books: *Rhetoric in an Organizational Society: Managing Multiple Identities* (1991) and *Values at Work: Employee Participation Meets Market Pressure at Mondragón* (1999). Recognized for both teaching and research, he has lectured and consulted in the United States, Europe, Latin America, and Australasia.

Lars Thøger Christensen (Pd.D., Odense University) is Research Professor of Corporate Communication at the Department of Intercultural Communication and Management, The Copenhagen Business School, Denmark. Previously, he has held positions at The Southern Denmark Business School and at Odense University where he was department chair at the Department of Marketing. He specializes in the study of market-related communications—in the broadest sense of the term—issued and organized by corporate bodies. His theoretical perspective is meaning based and rooted in the socio-anthropological tradition. His primary research and teaching interests are in public discourse, corporate communications, advertising, semiotics, image/identity formation, strategy, and issue management. He is author of *Markedskommunikation som organiseringsmåde: En kulturteoretisk analyse* (Market Communication as a Way of Organizing: A Cultural Analysis). His current work continues to integrate "internal" and "external" dimensions of organizational communication. His research is published in *Organization Studies, European Journal of Marketing, Consumption, Markets and Culture,* and elsewhere.

Lori Collins-Jarvis (Ph.D., University of Southern California) currently works as a Senior Project Director in the Entertainment Division of Lieberman Research Worldwide (Los Angeles, CA), specializing in new media market research. Her early work focused on social and equity issues in implementation of the Public Electronic Network in Santa Monica, California and communication issues in nonprofit organizations. She has published articles in the *Journal of Broadcasting and Electronic Media* and *The Journal of the American Society for Information Science.* As Assistant Professor at Rutgers University, she advised a local consortium of libraries, public schools, and colleges in the development of a public computer-conferencing network.

Charles Conrad (Ph.D., Kansas University, 1980) is Professor of Speech Communication at Texas A&M University. His research focuses on the relationship between communi-

cation and social/organizational power and on organizational rhetoric. He is author or editor of five books, and his research has appeared in the *Quarterly Journal of Speech, Communication Monographs, Journal of Applied Communication Research,* and elsewhere.

Noshir S. Contractor (http://www.spcomm. uiuc.edu/contractor) is Associate Professor of Speech Communication and Psychology at the University of Illinois at Urbana-Champaign. His research interests include applications of complex adaptive systems theory to communication, the role of emergent communication and knowledge networks in organizations, and collaboration technologies in the workplace. He is currently investigating factors that lead to the formation, maintenance, and dissolution of dynamically linked knowledge networks in work communities. He is the principal investigator on a major three-year grant from the National Science Foundation's Knowledge and Distributed Intelligence Initiative to study the coevolution of knowledge networks and 21st-century organizational forms. He and Peter Monge have written a book, *Theories of Communication Networks and Flows,* which will be published next year.

Stanley Deetz, Ph.D., is Professor of Communication at the University of Colorado, Boulder, where he teaches courses in organizational theory, organizational communication, and communication theory. He is coauthor of *Leading Organizations Through Transition: Communication and Cultural Change* and *Doing Critical Management Research* and author of *Transforming Communication, Transforming Business: Building Responsive and Responsible Workplaces* and *Democracy in an Age of Corporate Colonization: Developments in Communication and the Politics of Everyday Life,* as well as editor or author of 8 other books. He has published nearly 100 essays in scholarly journals and books regarding stakeholder representation, culture, and communication in corporate organizations. He has served as a consultant on culture, diversity, and participatory decision making for several major corporations. He is a Fellow of the International Communication Association and served as its President, 1996-1997.

Eric M. Eisenberg is Professor and Chair of the Department of Communication at the University of South Florida. He received his doctorate in organizational communication from Michigan State University in 1982. After leaving MSU, he directed the master's program in applied communication at Temple University before moving to the University of Southern California. Over a ten-year period at USC, he twice received the Speech Communication Association award for outstanding publication in organizational communication, as well as the Burlington Foundation award for excellence in teaching. In 1994, his textbook *Organizational Communication: Balancing Creativity and Constraint* (with H. L. Goodall, Jr.) won the Academic Textbook Author award for best textbook of the year. This past year, he received the Florida State Legislature Teaching Incentive Award for Excellence in Teaching. He is an internationally recognized researcher, teacher, and consultant specializing in the strategic use of communication to promote organizational change.

Gail T. Fairhurst (Ph.D., University of Oregon) is Professor in the Department of Communication at the University of Cincinnati. Her research interests focus primarily on leadership communication and language analysis in organizational contexts. She has published in several communication and organizational science journals including *Hu-*

man Communication Research, Communication Monographs, Organization Science, Academy of Management Journal, Academy of Management Review, and *Organizational Behavior and Human Decision Processes,* as well as in *Communication Yearbooks* (8, 9, and 10). She is coauthor (with Bob Sarr) of *The Art of Framing: Managing the Language of Leadership,* which received the 1996-97 National Communication Association award for outstanding book in organizational communication. She has received an NCA Best Article Award for organizational communication as well as numerous top paper honors at the annual conferences of the International Communication Association. In addition to serving on a number of editorial boards, she has served as a consultant on leadership and organizational communication for several major corporations.

Dayna Finet (Ph.D., University of Southern California) taught at the University of Texas, Austin, and State University of New York, Albany, where she specialized on topics of social issues in organizational communication and organizational communication ethics. Now a writer based in Austin, Texas, she concentrates on biography, autobiography, and memoir. Her book, *With Courage and Common Sense,* a collection of memoirs from Texas women of the Depression/World War II generation, is scheduled for 2001 publication by the University of Texas Press. With grant support from the Texas Commission on the Arts, she is currently writing *Age and Youth in Action: An Oral History of the Gray Panthers.* She also writes biographical literature for children.

Janet Fulk is Professor of Communications in the Annenberg School for Communication and Professor of Management & Organization in the Marshall School of Business at the University of Southern California. She holds

M.B.A. and Ph.D. degrees in administrative sciences from The Ohio State University. A series of recent projects sponsored by the National Science Foundation examines how communication and information systems are employed to foster collaboration and knowledge distribution within and between organizations. A recently completed research project sponsored by the Annenberg Center for Communication examines the development of new virtual" organizational forms for global competition. Recent publications include *Shaping Organizational Form: Communication Connection and Community* (1999, with Gerardine DeSanctis), and *Organizations and Communication Technology* (1990, with Charles Steinfield), which won an award from the National Communication Association. Recent articles on organizations and communication technology have appeared in *Human Relations, Communication Theory,* and *Organization Science,* and an award-winning article appeared in *Academy of Management Journal.* She serves on several editorial boards and has completed a term on the Board of Governors of Academy of Management, where she was also elected Fellow in 1997.

Urs E. Gattiker (Ph.D., Management and Organization, Claremont Graduate School) is Professor of Technology and Innovation Management, Department of Production, at the Obel Family Foundation in Denmark. Formerly, he was Associate Professor of Organizational Behaviour and Technology Management at the University of Lethbridge, Alberta, Canada. He has edited the book series *Technological Innovation and Human Resources* and the journal *Technological Studies,* and he authored *Technology Management in Organization* (1990) and *Moral and Economic Issues on the Information Highway: Balancing Interests* (1996). He has published widely in management, technology, and information systems journals and

books. His research interests include skill acquisition and human capital theory, technological change, career development, quality-of-work-life issues, and privacy and ethical issues on the Internet. He has been an officer of two divisions in the Academy of Management.

Julie Haynes received her master's degree in speech communication from Texas A&M University under the direction of Charles Conrad. She is a doctoral candidate in speech communication at Penn State University and teaches in the Department of Communication Studies at Rowan University.

Robert D. McPhee (Ph.D., Michigan State University, 1978) is Herberger Professor in the Hugh Downs School of Human Communication at Arizona State University. Specializing in organizational communication and communication theory, he has served as the Chair of the Organizational Communication Division of the National Communication Association and as Associate Editor for *Human Communication Research.* His special interests are formal/hierarchical communication and structuration theory.

Katherine Miller (Ph.D., University of Southern California) is Professor of Speech Communication at Texas A&M University. Her research interests center on communication within human service organizations. In particular, her work has considered the effects of participation in human service agencies, the role of emotional communication in service provision, interorganizational coordination for service provision, and the development of stress and burnout among human service workers. She is author of *Organizational Communication: Approaches and Processes,* and her research has been published in such journals as *Human Communication Research, Journal of Applied Communication*

Research, Communication Monographs, Communication Research, Academy of Management Journal, and *Management Communication Quarterly.*

Peter R. Monge is Professor of Communication at the Annenberg School for Communication, University of Southern California. He has published *Communicating and Organizing* (with Vince Farace and Hamish Russell), *Multivariate Techniques in Human Communication Research* (with Joe Cappella), *Policing Hawthorne* (with Janet Fulk and Gregory Patton), and *Reasoning With Statistics* (5th ed., with Fred Williams). His research interests include organizational communication and knowledge networks, coevolutionary communication systems, globalization and communication processes, and research methods. He served as editor of *Communication Research* from 1986 to 1993 and as president of the International Communication Association, 1997-1998. He and Noshir Contractor have written a book, *Theories of Communication Networks and Flows,* which will be published next year.

Dennis K. Mumby (Ph.D., Southern Illinois University—Carbondale) is Professor of Communication at Purdue University. He has published in journals such as *Communication Monographs, Communication Theory, Academy of Management Review, Discourse & Society,* and *Management Communication Quarterly.* He is author of *Communication and Power in Organizations* and editor of *Narrative and Social Control.* His research focuses on the relationships among communication, organizing, identity, and power and their intersection in the dialectics of domination and resistance. His current research interests include an examination of the relationship between feminism and postmodernism, and its application for the development of dialectical conceptions of organizational power. He is currently working on a book for Sage titled *Organizing Gender: Feminism, Postmodernism, and Organization Studies.*

Marshall Scott Poole (Ph.D., University of Wisconsin, 1980) is Professor of Speech-Communication at Texas A&M University. He has conducted research and published extensively on the topics of group and organizational communication, computer-mediated communication systems, conflict management, and organizational innovation. He has coauthored or edited four books, including *Communication and Group Decision-Making, Working Through Conflict,* and *Research on the Management of Innovation.* He has published in a number of journals, including *Management Science, MIS Quarterly, Human Communication Research, Academy of Management Journal,* and *Communication Monographs.* He is currently a senior editor of *Information Systems Research and Organizational Science.*

Ronald E. Rice (M.A., Ph.D., Stanford University) is Professor in the School of Communication, Information & Library Studies, Rutgers University. He has coauthored or coedited *The Internet and Health Communication; Public Communication Campaigns; The New Media: Communication, Research and Technology; Managing Organizational Innovation;* and *Research Methods and the New Media.* He has conducted research and published widely in communication science, public communication campaigns, computer-mediated communication systems, methodology, organizational and management theory, information systems, information science and bibliometrics, and social networks. His publications have won awards as best dissertation from the American Society for Information Science, half a dozen times as best paper from International Communication Association divisions, and twice as best paper from Academy of Management divisions. He has been elected a divisional officer in both the International Communication Association and the Academy of Management and is currently on the ICA Publications Board. He has served as associate editor for *Human Communication Research* and *MIS Quarterly*.

Patricia Riley (Ph.D., University of Nebraska) is Associate Professor of Organizational Communication and Director of the School of Communication in the Annenberg School for Communication at the University of Southern California. Her work focuses on communication and institutional politics, organizational culture change, business process reengineering and organizational transformation. Her research has appeared in such books as *Organizational Culture Advances in Leadership Research*, and in *Communication Quarterly, Journal of Management, Argument and Advocacy, New Management,* and *Communication Reports*. She is presently working on a grant to study the role of communication and information systems in reengineering projects and a book with Warren Bennis called *Organizational Redevelopment*. An experienced organizational consultant, she conducts workshops and seminars for top executives in areas such as reengineering, leadership, advocacy, strategic communication, and managing cultural change.

David R. Seibold (Ph.D., Michigan State University) is Professor and Chair, Department of Communication, University of California, Santa Barbara. He is author of 100 publications on organizational communication, group dynamics, and interpersonal influence and has received numerous research and teaching awards. He is recent editor of the

Journal of Applied Communication Research and serves on the boards of many other journals. Former Chair of the Interpersonal Communication Division of both the National Communication Association and the International Communication Association, he currently is Chair of the Organizational Communication Division of the International Communication Association. He also works closely with many business, government, and health organizations.

B. Christine Shea (Ph.D., University of California, Santa Barbara) is Lecturer in Speech Communication at California Polytechnic State University, San Luis Obispo. She is author of more than 30 papers, articles, and book chapters on organizational communication, interpersonal relationships, and argumentation. She has served as a reviewer for several journals, including *Management Communication Quarterly* and *Journal of Applied Communication Research*. Her current research interests include organizational justice and fairness, non-union due process systems, and sex and gender issues in organizations.

Patricia M. Sias is Associate Professor of Communication in the Edward R. Murrow School of Communication at Washington State University. Her research centers primarily on workplace relationships. In particular, her work focuses on the development of peer relationships and workplace friendships and the ways such relationships influence, and are influenced by, the organizational context. She has published articles in a variety of journals including *Communication Monographs, Human Communication Research, Communication Research, Western Journal of Communication, Communication Quarterly,* and *Journal of Applied Communication Research*. She received the W. Charles Redding

Award for outstanding dissertation in organizational communication in 1993.

Cynthia Stohl (Ph.D., Purdue, 1982) is the Margaret Church Distinguished Professor of Communication and Head of the Department of Communication at Purdue University. She teaches a variety of courses at both the graduate and undergraduate levels in organizational, global, and group communication and has published widely in these areas. She is author of more than 45 articles in management, communication, and sociology journals and handbooks. Her book *Organizational Communication: Connectedness in Action* received the National Communication Association Award (1995) for the best book in organizational communication, and her article (coauthored with George Cheney, Joe Straub, Laura Speirs, Dan DeGooyer, Susan Whalen, Kathy Garvin-Doxas, and David Carlone) "Democracy, Participation, and Communication at Work" (1997) received the 1998 NCA Award for best article. She has also been the recipient of several departmental, school, and university teaching awards.

Kathleen M. Sutcliffe (Ph.D. in management, University of Texas–Austin) is a member of the Organizational Behavior and Human Resources Management faculty at the University of Michigan Business School. Her current research is focused both on understanding top management team perception and learning processes and how management teams can be designed to better sense and cope with changing contextual requirements, and on understanding how organizations remain reliable under uncertain and changing conditions. Her work has appeared in many journals including the *Academy of Management Journal, Academy of Management Review, Organization Science, Research in Organizational Behavior, Research in the Sociology of Organizations,* and *Strategic Management Journal.*

Bryan C. Taylor (Ph.D., Utah, 1991) is Associate Professor in the Department of Communication at the University of Colorado at Boulder. His interests include critical theory and interpretive methods associated with the study of organizational culture and symbolism. He is particularly interested in the culture of nuclear weapons production, and in developing potential relationships between the fields of organizational communication and cultural studies.

Phillip K. Tompkins is Professor Emeritus of Communication, University of Colorado at Boulder. For the past 18 months, he has worked as a volunteer at the St. Francis Center, a shelter for the homeless in Denver, Colorado. He is now doing research on poverty and homelessness and is the co-leader of the Affordable Housing Study Group within St. John's Episcopal Cathedral in Denver. He is at work on a book about these subjects with a working title of *Down, Out, and Up Again in Denver: A Theological Ethnography of Homelessness and Housing.*

Nick Trujillo (Ph.D., University of Utah, 1983) is Professor of Communication Studies at California State University, Sacramento. He is author of two books (*Organizational Life on Television,* with Leah Vande Berg, and *The Meaning of Nolan Ryan*) and of over 40 scholarly and popular articles. He conducts research on organizational communication, ethnography, and media sports, and he is currently finishing a book about the life and death of his grandmother. He can be contacted at nickt@csus.edu.

Maryanne Wanca-Thibault is Assistant Professor of Communication at the University of Colorado at Colorado Springs. Her teaching and research interests include changing organizational forms, women in organizations, and domestic violence.

Karl E. Weick (Ph.D., Ohio State University) is Rensis Likert Collegiate Professor of Organizational Behavior and Psychology at the University of Michigan. He has been associated with the faculties at Purdue University, the University of Minnesota, Cornell University, and the University of Texas at Austin. He is a former editor of *Administrative Science Quarterly* and author of a number of books including *The Social Psychology of Organizing* and *Sensemaking in Organizations*. He has also written numerous journal articles, book chapters, and book reviews and has received a variety of awards for his scholarship. He studies such topics as how people make sense of confusing events, the social psychology of improvisation, high-reliability systems, the effects of stress on thinking and imagination, indeterminacy in social systems, social commitment, small wins as the embodiment of wisdom, and linkages between theory and practice.